Metro

on the Styx

METROPOLIS ON THE STYX

The Underworlds of Modern Urban Culture, 1800–2001

DAVID L. PIKE

CORNELL UNIVERSITY PRESS

ITHACA AND LONDON

First published 2007 by Cornell University Press

First printing, Cornell Paperbacks, 2007

Printed in the United States of America

Library of Congress Cataloging-in-Publication Data

Pike, David L. (David Lawrence), 1963–
Metropolis on the Styx: the underworlds of modern urban culture, 1800-2001 / David L. Pike.
p. cm.
Includes bibliographical references and index.
ISBN 978-0-8014-4490-6 (cloth : alk. paper)
ISBN 978-0-8014-7304-3 (pbk. : alk. paper)
1. Underground areas—Social aspects. 2. Underground areas in literature. 3. Civilization, Subterranean. 4. Sociology, Urban. I. Title.
TA712.P55 2007
307.76—dc22
2007018953

Cornell University Press strives to use environmentally responsible suppliers and materials to the fullest extent possible in the publishing of its books. Such materials include vegetable-based, low-VOC inks and acid-free papers that are recycled, totally chlorine-free, or partly composed of nonwood fibers. For further information, visit our website at www.cornellpress.cornell.edu.

Cloth printing 10 9 8 7 6 5 4 3 2 1

Paperback printing 10 9 8 7 6 5 4 3 2 1

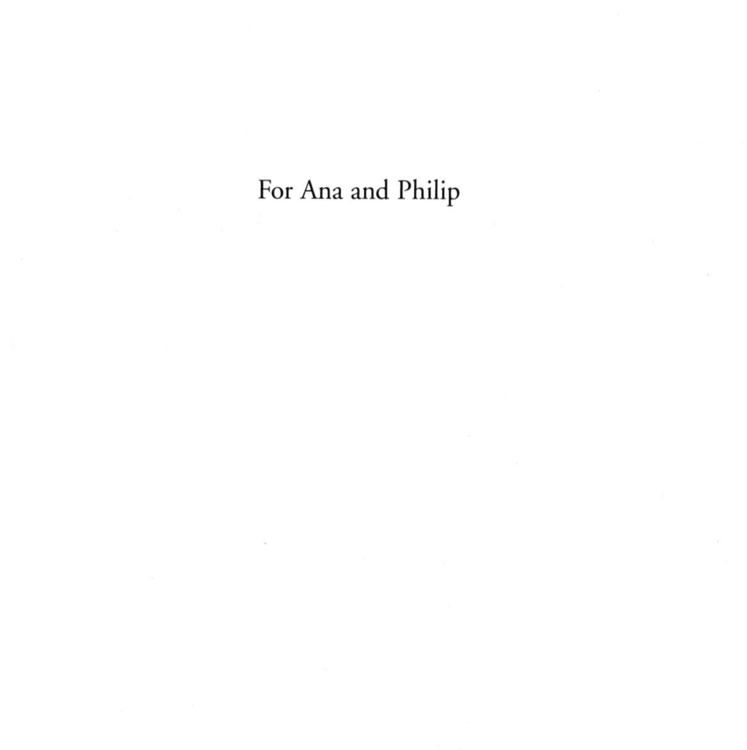

For Ana and Philip

Der Teufel steckt im Detail—
The Devil is hiding in the details
GERMAN PROVERB

Contents

List of Illustrations

Preface and Acknowledgments

I spent most of my childhood in a three-story Victorian-style house, built back in 1879, in what used to be the village of Anchorage, Kentucky, and is now a suburb of Louisville. My family lived in three stories in one half of the house, my grandfather waited out the last years of his life on the ground floor of the other side, and a succession of renters occupied the apartment above him. The basement, which belonged to us, extended beneath the entire house, divided into rooms that reflected the layout of the floors above. The stairs of the indoors entrance led through a closeted landing down to a long hallway where my father had set up a work area, full of tools, car parts, and household odds and ends. Beneath the stairs was a large room filled floor to ceiling with bound stacks of old magazines, decades of *Time* and *Life* along with my grandfather's collection of *Playboy*; it also served once or twice as a tornado shelter. At the base of the stairs on the left was another large room that my sisters and I once tried to convert into a play space. We cleaned it out, lugged down a couple of spare bookcases, some old mattresses, pillows, rugs, and our second-choice toys and games, but never used it much after that. It smelled musty, it was crawling with daddy longlegs and other less readily identifiable fauna, and no matter how many lights we put up, it always felt too much like a dark basement—the high-set and narrow windows made matters worse rather than better. Past the magazine room in the other direction was a door leading to the outer basement hallway, which had a ground level entrance to the back driveway; here we kept things that were used outside: lawnmowers and tools for gardening and yard work, bicycles, sleds, and a toboggan. Here there was a bright, windowed room full of big metal sinks that must once have been the servants' laundry room (they would have lived in the crumbling little three-room house out back) but which we used for washing the dogs and cleaning up when we were too messy to go directly upstairs. Just before the doorway to the outer basement, if you turned left, you entered the unfinished part, with a floor of dirt rather than concrete and exposed stone blocks rather than plastered and once-whitewashed walls. The furnace was there, along with an old coal chute and firewood and lumber for building and repairs. Off this dark room (it wasn't wired for electricity like the rest of the basement) was an opening that led to an even darker room (once probably used for coal storage) that I can't recall ever exploring except in nightmares. It shared a wall with my father's work area, but it inhabited a netherworld of its own. It terrifies me to this day, and its baleful influence lent a tinge of apprehension to every other part of the basement except perhaps the sunlit outer washroom.

We moved when I was fifteen, and I have not seen the inside of the house since; my early childhood memories of its spaces remain basically uncontaminated by later visits at a more rational and better socialized age. And in the multiplicity of its uses, spaces, and associations, and in the way it overlapped with the house above while never seeming part of it, that basement epitomizes for me the complexity of the modern experience of subterranean space. It was useful, although primarily for purposes deemed too dirty, too unwieldy, or too untidy for the house above. It was my father's space more than my mother's (she remembers almost nothing about it except for the outer rooms, while the work area is the only part he recalls clearly), and he spent much of his free time there, tinkering with car engines or, once, helping me to make a wooden sword with which to defend myself from the bullying of my elder sisters. It was an alternative, flexible space for us children as well as for him, as our attempt at a playroom conversion suggests. We even fantasized about sleeping down there, a kid's version of camping out. I don't think my father ever felt it to be haunted or frighteningly dark, but that otherworldly sensation remains my overriding feeling about the basement, as it does of subterranean space for most children, paired nearly always with fascination about and desire for all of the mysterious activities and possibilities it contains, so different from the regimented life upstairs.

Basements are not designed that way anymore, but my family's appropriation of a nineteenth-century space for its late twentieth-century needs, and my childhood reaction to it, suggest how powerfully present older conceptions and uses of space remain for us, how fragments of Victorian notions combine with newer ideas about space, even in the outskirts of a Kentucky metropolis. This book is devoted to these and others of the myriad and overlapping ways in which the nineteenth century used, conceived, and imagined its underground spaces, and to the myriad and overlapping ways in which those uses, conceptions, and imaginings remain with us today, influencing the very different spaces that characterize the twenty-first century.

While freestanding in its structure and argumentation, *Metropolis on the Styx* also fleshes out the theoretical and conceptual underpinnings of my previous book, *Subterranean Cities*, whose introduction constitutes a digest of the topics developed at length in chapter 1 here. In *Subterranean Cities*, I undertook a cultural history of three types of underground space that played a formative role in the imagination of the nineteenth-century city: the subway, the cemetery, and the sewer. As the title metaphor indicates, in *Metropolis on the Styx* I study the spatial framework within which that imagery arose and out of which my analysis of it developed: what I call the vertical city, its twin modes of perception—the view from above, the view from below—and the unstable thresholds between them. Chapter 1, "The Devil, the Underground, and the Vertical City," provides a theoretical and methodological introduction to the aspects of an analysis of underground space in the modern metropolis, establishing its role in modernity and the changing aspects of its representation and use over the past two centuries. The following two chapters, "The Devil Comes to Town" and "Mysteries of the Underground," set out in greater detail the workings of the view from above and the view from below through an analysis of the signature mode of each approach. Chapter 2 documents the relocation of the Devil from folklore and theology to the confines of the nineteenth-century metropolis, arguing that his overarching figure was employed to negotiate an ambivalent relationship to the new technology that marked the century, a novelty that was simultaneously terrifying and seductive. In Chapter 3, I argue that the fictions of urban mysteries that developed in the 1840s and the cultural representations thereafter associated with them developed a new image of the city rooted in its subterranean spaces and the truths they were thought to hide. Chapter 4, "Through the Looking Glass," studies the instability of the conceptual divisions between above- and underground in London and Paris through a history of their threshold spaces: the arcades, arches, and other public spaces that brought classes, sexes, and races together in new and unforeseen ways, culminating in the horror of trench warfare in the First World War and palliated through the fantastic space of the movie palaces of the 1920s and '30s. I conclude the book by addressing the persistence of the vertical city and the views from above and below as modes of conceptualizing urban environments that have, in fact, changed almost beyond recognition from those in which these modes came into being.

Because of its multifarious and contradictory character, the underground is best apprehended through a range of vantage points and a variety of theoretical, critical, literary, and historical sources. My goal has been threefold: to synthesize the standard analyses of the various aspects of the underground, to historicize the modern forms taken by the material and metaphorical undergrounds, and to construct a working theory of underground space. To organize a book around a particular category of space has necessitated different criteria of organization and presentation than are required by more conventional objects of study such as a specific period, genre, oeuvre, historical figure, or event. Not only did the spatial focus entail a comparative study of London and Paris but the need to account for subterranean space in the twentieth century expanded the scope beyond this cross-Channel center of gravity both spatially and temporally. Moreover, because the subject is vast, I have had to be selective, and because the subject is interdisciplinary and eclectic, so also my methodology has been interdisciplinary and eclectic. While attentive to chronology, I do not provide a linear history of underground space. While attentive to differences of genre and media, I do not treat them individually, but comparatively, in terms of their relation to and representation of the underground. While informed throughout by critical theory and by issues of race, class, gender, and sexuality, my argument has addressed these concerns only insomuch as they impinge upon my subject, signaling moments of intersection and of conflict rather than attempting to deal with them in any comprehensive manner. Scholarly discourse has had an enduring interest in the underground, but in the eminently respectable, aboveground approach it takes to the subject, its version of the underground is of necessity partial and distorted. To be sure, there is much about the underground that can be addressed directly and in the language and argumentation of everyday academic discourse, and when this has been the case, I have done so. But there is also much about the underground that the direct approach distorts and misrepresents, and when this has been the case, I have had recourse to indirection, to nonlinear forms of argumentation such as dialectics, and to connections and juxtapositions that may at first glance appear haphazard or counterintuitive. Throughout, I have done my best to steer my way safely between the Scylla of an overzealous structure and argument and the Charybdis of submersion in the details and digressions that are, in the end, the enduring pleasure of the subterranean world.

Published and unpublished material was made readily available to me in New York by the Billy Rose Theater Collection; in Paris, by the Bibliothèque historique de la ville de Paris, the Bibliothèque Nationale, and the Bibliothèque de l'Arsenal; in London, by the Bancroft Library, the Bermondsey Local Studies Library, the British Library, the Guildhall Library, the Imperial War Museum, the Institute for Historical Research, the Mander and Mitchenson Theatre Collection, the Minet Library, the Museum of London, the Theatre Museum Picture Library, and the Westminster Archives Centre. The Interlibrary Loan Office at American University's Bender Library made a wealth of essential materials readily available to me.

Although I cannot hope to name all of those who assisted me with their passing comments and hints, I do want especially to thank the following people whose help went much further, with the inevitable apology for whatever I may have done to distort their suggestions and advice: Michelle Allen, Antoinette Burton, Antoine Compagnon, David N. Damrosch, Rachel Falconer, Peter Fitting, Pamela Gilbert, Christina Glengary, Heidi Holder, Andreas Huyssen, Michael Levenson, Jonathan Loesberg, Steven Marcus, Joseph McLaughlin, Carol Jones Neuman, Karen Newman, Deborah Epstein Nord, Stephanie O'Hara, Nicole Pohl, Michael Riffaterre (in memoriam), Vanessa R. Schwartz, Richard Sha, Myra Sklarew, Scott Manning Stevens, Michael Taussig, David Trotter, and Graham Willcox. My students at Columbia and at American University contributed immeasurably to the writing of this book. My research assistant, Emily Davis, was invaluable in helping me obtain and organize images. I want to thank Bernhard Kendler and John Ackerman at Cornell University Press for their longtime support of my work. The Press's anonymous reader provided ample encouragement and expert advice for revision. Lou Robinson's long-suffering guidance last time around made preparation of images relatively pain-free for both of us this time around; I am grateful to her for the end results yet again. I am also grateful once again for John Raymond's expert copyediting, Karen Laun's efficient work as production editor, and Jessica Frazier's elegant index. Mary Allen de Acosta supported the writing of the book in many ways; I am especially grateful for her generosity in providing me with an ideal place for research in London, and another for writing in Suba. Finally, I want to thank my parents, Lucy Gould and Tom Pike, even if they are unable to remember our basement quite the way that I did.

Many of my textual debts should be apparent in the notes, and I have tried to be as clear about theoretical influence as possible; however, due to my combination of broad scope and idiosyncratic focus, I have tended to pillage historical sources, phrases, and images from wherever I could find them. I have tried to document such pillaging as much as possible; however, especially with older sources, I have not always done so if the reference or quote had nothing whatsoever to do with the source's argument. As in *Subterranean Cities*, I do want to single out my particular debt to Rosalind Williams's extraordinary book, *Notes on the Underground*, which (as will be evident to anyone who has had the pleasure of reading it) I have argued with, rifled through, and revisited time and again since the earliest stages of the project.

I was able to begin the book thanks to a Mellon postdoctoral fellowship at the Society of Fellows of Columbia University. My work gained enormously from my participation in Michael Levenson's National Endowment for the Humanities Seminar in London, 1995; my thanks to all involved, especially Michael. Further research was made possible by generous grants from American University, the National Endowment for the Humanities, the American Council of Learned Societies, and the Folger Library. The illustration costs were underwritten by a Mellon Grant from the College of Arts and Sciences and by the Department of Literature at American University. I benefited from the presentation of work in progress at American University, Columbia University, the British Comparative Literature Association (1995), the American Comparative Literature Association (1997), the Mid-Atlantic British Studies Association (1998), the Modern Language Association (1996 and 1999), the "New Modernisms" conference at Pennsylvania State University (1999), the University of London (2000), the Society for Utopian Studies (2001), the Folger Seminar on Early Modern Paris (2002), and the annual Monuments and Dust Conference. Scattered portions of the book have been adapted from "Underground Theater: Subterranean Spaces on the London Stage," *Nineteenth Century Studies* 13 (1999); portions of chapter 4 have been adapted from " 'Down by the Dark Arches': A Cultural History of the Adelphi," *London Journal* 27, no. 1 (2002): 19–41, and " 'The Greatest Wonder of the World': Brunel's Tunnel and the Meanings of Underground London," *Victorian Literature and Culture* 33, no. 2 (Sept. 2005): 341–67.

Unless otherwise noted, all translations are my own, rendered as literally as possible within the bounds of standard English. All emphases are the original author's unless otherwise noted.

Metropolis
on the Styx

1

THE DEVIL, THE UNDERGROUND, AND THE VERTICAL CITY

We must meantime occupy ourselves with a less resplendent, but still meritorious, task, namely, to level the ground and to render it sufficiently secure for moral edifices of these majestic dimensions. For this ground has been honeycombed by mole tunnels which reason, in its confident but fruitless search for hidden treasures, has carried out in all directions, and which threaten the security of its superstructures.

Immanuel Kant, *The Critique of Pure Reason* (1781)

Oh, I wish I was a mole in the ground
Yes, I wish I was a mole in the ground
Like a mole in the ground I would root that mountain down
And I wish I was a mole in the ground.

Bascom Lamar Lunsford,
"I Wish I Was a Mole in the Ground" (1928)

The underground has been a dominant image of modernity since the late eighteenth century: a site of crisis, of fascination, and of hidden truth, a space somehow more real but also more threatening and otherworldly than the ordinary world above. Whether imagined or real, subterranean spaces present a unique combination of the utterly alien with the completely familiar, of mythic timelessness with the lived experience of the present. As kingdom of death, realm of dust and decomposition, and site of the afterlife, the space beneath the earth has long possessed an unsurpassed power to evoke the negation of whatever has been defined as normal and belonging to the world above. At the same time, as the most heavily exploited and technologically developed space of the past few centuries, the material underground has dominated modern life as few other experiences have. Contrary to popular and scholarly opinion, however, it is not a simple place, and can more readily be defined negatively than positively. It is neither the polar opposite of the world above nor its unmediated and dominated reflection; it is neither wholly another world nor does it belong wholly to our own. On the one hand, while ostensibly depicting a space apart, the power of underworld imagery never lets us ignore its symbolic propinquity. Yet that same symbolism relies on the issues it addresses continuing to inhabit a space disconnected from our own, even while it cannot deny the existence of the myriad physical passages that link one world to the other. The underground is in no way a unified space: not only does it confuse the physical and the metaphorical to a dizzying degree, but even its symbolism is constituted of conflicting and conflicted concepts, images, figures and objects. Still, this confusion is by no means incoherent: in the overarching familiarity of its principal forms—the afterlife and under the earth—the underground is, paradoxically, simpler and more legible than the multifarious world above.

The key to getting at the meaning of the modern underground is to grasp it in its relationship with its open-air counterpart. First and foremost, it is the trash heap of the world above, the place to which everyone, everything, and every place posing a problem or no longer useful to it is relegated. Consequently, the underground is neither the source of any problem nor the site of its possible solution; instead, I will argue, it presents those problems in their true identity as problems, and in a form in which their actual causes may eventually be located. When interpreting the underground, we must remember that, whatever the form it takes, it always includes a displaced vision of something that poses a crisis of representation in the world above. Whatever, if anything, will in the end be authentically other or oppositional about the underground will not be whatever aspect of it is readily legible or most coherent. The meaning of the underground must be disentangled from the lingering threads of the aboveground identity and codes of representation that defined it as something subterranean in the first place. Now, it is a standard tenet of critical theory that any aspect of discourse can be cracked or deconstructed in this fashion; the underground is unique in two ways: there has always been a broad consensus that within it the cracks in society remain visible, and, over the last couple of centuries, those cracks have taken material form primarily within a single physical space: that of the modern city.

This chapter introduces the cluster of concepts, topics, and historical threads necessary to delineate the various aspects of the modern urban underground and to define their interrelationship. I begin by summarizing the changes the imagination of underground space has undergone over the past couple of centuries as it became closely identified with the modern city: the complex dialectic of old and new that characterized the nineteenth century, and the unrecognized shifts in that dialectic during the twentieth. Henri Lefebvre's spatial triad provides a theoretical armature that is able to analyze underground space as a historical category and consequently to develop a working definition of the term "underground." Lewis Mumford's derivation of a modernist theory of the city from the technology of mining suggests a material genealogy leading through the trench and deep into the twentieth century. From the material underground, I pass to the metaphorical underground and the two modes of representing the city over which the devil presided in the nineteenth century: the view from above and the view from below. I trace the afterlife of the views from above and from below in the twentieth century and lay out the relationship between popular culture, the underground, and the crisis of representation that the devil continues to personify today. The chapter concludes by engaging with two key legacies of modernist conceptions of the underground: first, in relation to changes in material conditions that dictated the change in attitude toward subterranean space, and, second, in the context of the newly interiorized models of vertical space devoted to memory and the past, which gave a novel resonance to the underground while making its relationship to the actual experience of the city all the more difficult to apprehend.

The Underground Metropolis

> Why the modernization of Russia began with the hanging of chandeliers beneath the earth I didn't know.
>
> ALEXANDER KALETSKI, *Metro* (1985)

From the industrialization of mining to the construction of underground railways all over the world, the underground from the late eighteenth century through the early twentieth century was more novel, more explored and exploited as a physical space, and more explicitly on the surface of Western culture than at any time before or since. This was the period when capital first extended large-scale exploitation beneath the surface of the earth; it was also when the technology of construction and heavy industry appeared both as a productive novelty and as an object of consumption (figures 1.1 and 1.2). Complex drainage systems, underground railways, utility tunnels, and storage vaults created a novel experience of urban space, while factories and slums took on the metaphorical attributes of the rural mines and caves that had previously dominated underground imagery. London and Paris were the avant-garde of this transformation, and they made a complementary pair of subterranean imagery. The most populous city in the West and the nerve center of technological revolutions in mechanization and transportation, London was, literally, the underground city. The capital of luxury goods and conspicuous consumption as well as the infernal locus of violent revolution and subversion, Paris was an underworld by turns magical and rebellious, ruled by the devil.

The history of the words themselves in English and in French—*subterranean, underground, underworld, hell; souterrain, bas-fond, enfers, enfer*—plots the convergence of the material and the metaphysical underground in the space of the nineteenth-century city.[1] The French terms and usages generally preceded and often generated those in English; this is consistent with a heightened awareness of the range of available meanings characteristic of the Parisian discourse of the underground by contrast to the more polarized discourse of London. In 1786,

1.1 The age of heroic engineering transforms the imagination of the space beneath the earth. *Entrance to the Thames Tunnel from the South Side.* Lithograph on paper by B. Dixie, 1836. Reproduced by permission of the London Borough of Southwark Local History Library.

1.2 *Under the Cascade of the Trocadero*, in imitation of the Falls of the Giesbach: "Art can make the stones overhead watertight, but cannot keep out the spray." "All the World at Paris, III." *Graphic*, 17 August 1878, 156.

Louis-Sebastien Mercier dubbed Paris "la ville souterraine" in order to describe the "shadowy ways" (*routes ténébreuses*) and "torturous paths" (*chemins tortueux*) of the duplicity and vice of its inhabitants;[2] following the Revolution, the figurative sense would be conflated with the material substrata of the city. By the nineteenth century, not only had the figurative meanings begun to proliferate but the words were also used for the first time to describe those who lived underground and their subterranean dwellings. The literal sense of bas-fond dates to 1798 ("terrain bas et enfoncé"), with the figurative meaning first used by Honoré de Balzac to refer to "the poorest layers of society" (*les couches misérables de la société*); the English term gambling "hell" was first borrowed in 1794 from the French of Mercier's *Tableau de Paris* (1783); the secular meaning of *underworld* was in use loosely by the 1860s, and to refer to crime in particular by the turn of the twentieth century. Even more confusingly, the single word *underground* was pressed into duty during the nineteenth century not only to describe clandestine or hidden activity but to denominate the new railways and the ever-more subterranean quality of the dwellings and workplaces of the urban poor. The language with which the underground is represented in discourse was influenced by and helped to produce the confusion between the moral and the physical, the imaginary and the material; it also indicates the very real but distorted relations between the terms it confuses.

Combining moral satire, mythic imagery, social critique, and visions of revolution and utopia, underground Paris and London were at the center of a complex if often less than coherent cultural discourse of modernity: from the poetry of William Blake, Percy Bysshe Shelley, and Charles Baudelaire to the realist and naturalist novels of Charles Dickens, Victor Hugo, Émile Zola, and George Gissing; from the popular theater of urban spectacle to serial fictions of urban "mysteries"; from the public tours of the Paris sewers and Catacombes and the Thames Tunnel in London, to the equally popular explorations of the London slums and the bas-fonds of Paris as foreign, underworld regions of the city (figures 1.3 and 1.4). Nineteenth-century imagery of the underground can be grouped into two distinct categories: a discourse of segregation and elimination, and a discourse of incorporation and recycling. The first of these was conventionally identified with London, the second with Paris; as we shall see, neither discourse fully accounts for the space of either city, nor can the two models be fully understood separately one from the other.[3] Unlike representations of the city in terms of the world above, those of the world below never appeared without manifestly displaying at least some of the underlying contradictions of modern society. The insufficiency of either of these discourses fully to account for its own underground is one example of such contradictions.

By the beginning of the twentieth century, the convergence of the metaphorical and literal spaces beneath the earth was no longer so novel; consequently we find it presented unconsciously, manifesting itself as second nature,

1.3 Shining a light on underground London. *Interior of a London lodging-house.* Engraving by Ebenezer Landells. *Illustrated London News,* 22 October 1853, 352.

and expressed more directly as ideology. The medieval and early modern imagination of the underground had been dominated by the vertical cosmos of Christianity. To be sure, many conflicting images made their way into the capacious receptacle labeled Hell, but, at the same time, the relationship between above and below was rigidly fixed and predominately metaphysical. As it became detached from the strongly localized subterranean phenomena of nineteenth-century London and Paris and the generally physical experience of their own subterranea by inhabitants of other cities, the metaphysical framework came again to dominate. Ostensibly secularized now as an abstract conception of the metropolis, the modernist city was pan-European and typical. Not only had the First World War reduced much of the population and landscape of Europe to an unrecognizable quagmire, but political instability, increasingly efficient transportation, and a heightened rate of modernization made the first half of the twentieth century a period of great popular as well as intellectual migration. A push toward economic and industrial standardization and rationalization was matched by the internationalization of political movements both Left and Right.

No longer a dialogue between cities, but a discourse of the city in general, urban culture became similarly internationalized. Where popular culture had offered a wide variety of urban expeditions in the previous century, the underground tourist between the two wars had to choose between, on the one hand,

ANNO MDCCCLX
LES DESSOUS
DE PARIS
PAR
LES DESSOUS DE PARIS
PAR
ALFRED DELVAU

extraurban excursions to the subterranean battlegrounds in the ravaged countryside of France and Belgium, and, on the other, weekly visits to the fabulous "underworld" of the huge movie palaces that sprang up in cities around the globe to showcase the dream products of a Hollywood that had emerged from the Great War with a new cultural hegemony. Now positioned in opposition to such popular manifestations, high culture between the wars presented itself as a sequence of distinct and conflicting schools and movements that were disseminated and debated across the West. The divergent meanings of subterranean space that had been so tightly interwoven and physically grounded in specific nineteenth-century cityscapes splintered off into distinct fragments, their interconnections no longer visible. Positive connotations of the underground were dissociated from representations of the city as well as from the material and social underground of poverty and exploitation. High modernist writers such as Virginia Woolf, T. S. Eliot, Ezra Pound, Franz Kafka, Thomas Mann, Rainer Maria Rilke, André Gide, Louis-Ferdinand Céline, and Marcel Proust dealt with the city as a place of mythic alienation. Although these writers all started from specific cityscapes and experiences, they generally extrapolated an allegorical type of the City from a now concealed material substratum. Avant-garde movements such as futurism in Italy, constructivism in revolutionary Russia, Dada in Berlin, Zurich, and Paris, and surrealism in Paris aimed to dissolve representation altogether into the crucible of everyday urban life. Influential antiurban historians and philosophers such as Lewis Mumford, Oswald Spengler, and Martin Heidegger presented the modern city as irredeemable and pernicious; the international style spearheaded by the architectural theories of Le Corbusier, Walter Gropius, and Ludwig Mies van der Rohe called for a hypermodern city materially and culturally purged of any identifiable underground whatsoever.

At the same time that twentieth-century representations of modernity had splintered off into different factions arguing over what to make of the urban monolith, other cultural critics were finding new ways to interpret the tightly constellated and contradictory images of urban life characteristic of the previous century. Paradoxically, the loss of novelty and the change in urban conditions—the fact that the underground was no longer at the cutting edge of urban discourse—made it newly available as a category for philosophical and theoretical analysis. In the writings of Mikhail Bakhtin, Walter Benjamin, Humphrey Jennings, Mumford, and others, the nineteenth-century underground was first theorized as the fundamental component of a unitary theory of modern culture; drawing primarily on the pathologies of late-nineteenth-century city dwellers,

Facing page

1.4 Journey into the lower depths of Paris. Frontispiece to *Les Dessous de Paris* by Alfred Delvau (Paris: Poulet-Malassis et De Broise, 1860).

Sigmund Freud produced a topographical model of the individual and society based on a new form of underground, the unconscious. Just as modernist theories of art have continued to dominate contemporary culture in unacknowledged ways, so have these theories of culture based on the detritus of the nineteenth-century continued to inform critical discourse.[4] The modernist re-imagination of the nineteenth century underground remains an essential critical tool for understanding that past, but it was able to make that past newly available to us only by casting it as a universalized space. In doing so it unknowingly revealed a fundamental truth about the shift of the subterranean away from material technology and back into its primary role as being the realm of myth, while also demonstrating the degree to which the Western city had taken over from Christian Hell as the space inhabited by that myth. As dumping ground of the West, the metaphorical confines of today's underground contain the tangled remains of Hell, of nineteenth-century Paris and London, of the modernist city, and of the two world wars. What has remained current is the vertical division of space common to all of these metaphors of the underground, even though it no longer in any way accurately represents either the metaphysical or the physical reality of a globalized, virtual economy. Still, through a detailed process of sifting through the discarded fragments of these past cultures of the underground, we can reconnect them with those other fragments that have been successfully integrated into today's picture of the world above, reconstructing a unitary vision of a present world that would include some way of dealing conceptually with everything that our present world's vision of global unity so successfully hides in plain sight all around us.[5]

The first step in this process is to develop a critical language able to represent both the unity and the fragmentation of images of subterranean space in the modern world. Given the general currency possessed by the lexicon of hell and the underground in literary criticism and cultural theory—not to mention in broader public discourse—it is all the more important to understand both the ways in which underground spaces generate meaning and the ways in which those meanings help to produce underground spaces. There have been numerous studies of the myriad aspects of the underground, all of them valuable for information about the single aspect they explore. Most common are surveys of various material subterranea: histories of the subways, the sewers, the mine, the tunnel. These tend to assume a single and fairly unproblematic relation between the material space and the meanings attributed to it, as, for example, Benson Bobrick's *Labyrinths of Iron: Subways in History, Myth, Art, Technology, and War* and Donald Reid's *Paris Sewers and Sewermen: Realities and Representations*.[6] When they are more comprehensive in scope, these surveys tend toward the popular history of the coffee-table book.[7] Studies of the underworld have long been dominated by the archetypal approach of Joseph Campbell, assuming the timelessness and immutability of the category of the afterlife.[8] Recent work informed by critical theory, such as my own *Passage through Hell* and Rachel Falconer's *Hell in Contemporary Literature*, has sharpened our sense of the complex uses to which the twentieth-century put the vast armature of underworld topoi, but without attending to the important role of the built environment and material space in the process of making meaning out of hell.[9] With the notable exception of Michael Taussig's important monograph on *The Devil and Commodity Fetishism in South America*, the vast field of devil studies has generally had as little to say about the material underground as studies of the latter have had to say about the figure that was long considered to reign over it.[10] Finally, those studies that address both the material and the metaphorical underground—I am thinking here especially of Rosalind Williams's *Notes on the Underground* and Wendy Lesser's *Life below the Ground*—nevertheless fail to historicize their subject beyond taking note of the sea change brought about by the Industrial Revolution.[11] Consequently, although they document changes in the response to technology and underground space during the nineteenth century, Williams and Lesser do not similarly historicize the imagery related to those spaces—in particular, the figure of the devil. A comprehensive cultural history of the underground over the past two centuries must account not only for the new relationship that developed between subterranean image and subterranean reality but also for the ways in which the old relationship continued to inform the new one, and for the ways in which that relationship has continued to develop since it first took form in the industrializing cityscapes of nineteenth-century Paris and London.

Modernist Space and Underground Theory

> If we are possessed by the devil, it cannot be by one, for then we should live, at least here on earth, quietly, as with God, in unity, without contradiction, without reflection, always sure of the man behind us. . . . Only a crowd of devils could account for our earthly misfortunes.
>
> Franz Kafka, "The Invention of the Devil" (1912)

The closest we possess to a unitary theory of modernism is the oeuvre of the French urban sociologist and Marxist philosopher Henri Lefebvre, who came of age between the wars, and whose work on space and what he called the *quotidien*, or everyday life, spanned the second half of the twentieth century from 1945 to his death in 1991.[12] Lefebvre's original insight was that, as a primary sector into which capitalism was expanding after the Second World War, the newly visible category of everyday life was in pressing need of renewed analytical attention. His second insight was that the category of space provided a means to theorize everyday life as simultaneously abstract and material in the same way as Marx had analyzed the commodity for the previous century: "The social relations of production," he wrote in his 1974 book *The Production of Space*, "have a social existence to the extent that they have a spatial existence; they project themselves into a space, becoming inscribed there, and in the process producing the space itself."[13] For Lefebvre, this meant first of all that space, rather than an inert category in which people lived, things existed, and events took place, had always been an integral part of any social process. Quite simply, as Edward Soja has summarized it, "there is no unspatialized social reality."[14]

Lefebvre identified three types of space produced through social existence: perceived, conceived, and lived. The earliest spatial practice, he argued, was identical to the "intelligence of the body," the gestures, traces, and marks by which the body in action distinguishes between right and left, high and low, central and peripheral, or by which a spider orientates itself in a web that is produced by and is part of its body while simultaneously marking its place in the space around it. Long before abstraction, "lived experience already possessed its internal rationality; this experience was *producing* long before *thought* space, and spatial thought, began *reproducing* the projection, explosion, image and orientation of the body."[15] As the historian Emmanuel Le Roy Ladurie established in his study of a population of medieval shepherds in the Pyrenees mountains, "Space, whether immediate, geographical, sociological or cultural, was basically linked to physical perception, especially that of the hand and arm."[16] Whereas perceived space is first and foremost a product of the individual body, representations of space arise out of the "order" imposed by social relations, including knowledge, signs, codes, and, especially, language.[17] This is a visible, ideal, and abstract space; it is represented in topographical terms primarily as aboveground space, in contradistinction to lived, or "representational spaces, embodying complex symbolisms, sometimes coded, sometimes not, linked to the clandestine or underground side of social life, as also to art."[18] Although conceived space is subordinated to the logic and ideology of the dominant social order, lived space need obey no rules of consistency or cohesiveness; rather, it is characterized by the confused traces of the ongoing conflict between childhood and society out of which it has been produced, "a conflict between an inevitable, if long and difficult maturation process and a failure to mature that leaves particular original resources and reserves untouched."[19] Rather than a coherent space of otherness or opposition, representational space and the underground qualities with which it has been associated for several centuries describes the embattled emergence of the "clandestine" in an uneasy compromise between the codes of representation and behavior and the exigencies and desires forbidden or distorted by those codes.

The originality of Lefebvre's spatial triad lies not so much in its individual components, the contours of which are indebted explicitly to Marx and implicitly to Freud, but in the way in which he showed them to be dialectically intertwined within a space itself produced by that dialectic. Once grasped as something that is produced rather than static, space becomes a rigorous category through which to incorporate into critical analysis those aspects of social life traditionally conceptualized only in such ghettoized, romanticized, and reductive Western categories of otherness as myth, folklore, popular culture, Oriental, primitive, and childhood. Our current critical idioms are well suited for the analysis of the dominant discourse of a field or culture, its conception of space; they also allow us to analyze categories of otherness in terms of those same conceptions, or as primary evidence of individual experience. But only with great difficulty will they help us either to analyze the interrelationship between these categories except in terms of a dominant discourse or to grasp what we conceive as otherness in anything approaching its complex and contradictory combinations of individual experience and fragmentary past or alien representations of space. The spatial triad may not give the direct access to the margins so keenly desired by so much contemporary theory and art, but it does at least promise a conceptual space for those margins that does not immediately contain them or repress them all over again.

Let us take as an example a contemporary underground space, the Paris Métro. Although classically vertical in its conception, as a social space it exhibits a much less easily mappable network of practices and experiences. Its tunnels, stations, and trains are dominated by the mechanisms of the state: the planned, abstract conceptual framework and pragmatic activities that construct, operate, and maintain the infrastructure of trains and tunnels, conductors, ticket sellers, and maintenance crews as well as the security system of transit police and surveillance equipment. Overlapping and interacting with this conceived space are the rhythms of commuting that constitute everyday life in the modern city and the unforeseen, underground rhythms of that city, from clochards, panhandlers, and subway musicians to pickpockets and muggers to systemic breakdowns and malfunctions to the overlapping personal and social histories imbricated throughout the system. As the anthropologist Marc Augé has formulated this last element:

> Riding the Métro indeed confronts us with our history, and in more than one sense. Today's routes intersect yesterday's, bits of life of which the métro map in the diary we carry in our hearts lets us glimpse only the piece that is simultaneously the most spatial and the most regular, but which we know fair well that just about everything depended on or was working toward, no airtight barrier separating—sometimes to our great discomfort—one individual from those who surround him or her, our private life from our public life, our history from that of others.[20]

Although Augé limits the space of the métro to the single interpretation of the individual's "sense of her relation to others,"[21] Lefebvre's spatial triad makes it possible to incorporate this meaning within a larger totality.

The single space of the métro is not reducible to the abstract conception of its map, to the particular itinerary followed each day, to the different social and individual memories encountered at every turn of that same itinerary, or even to the incomprehensible, sometimes threatening "others" invariably encountered within its confines. Augé reminds us of the unusual density of the métro's constellation of meanings; Lefebvre provides an interpretative model for untangling the threads of that constellation without losing sight of their interrelationships, without dissociating them from the space they share and which, together, they produce qua space. Even though his theory created a framework with which to do so, Lefebvre was less successful in conceptualizing such relationships of space outside of the vertical framework that dominates Western representation. His conception of the underground reductively identified it almost wholly with lived, or representational, space, dominated by the conceived space above, with perceived space occupying the threshold in between. This accounts well for the general, mythic qualities of the underground characteristic of preindustrial society that were resurrected by modernism, but hardly at all for the material character so crucial to the specificity of its role in the nineteenth-century city. Although Lefebvre implies that such a perceptual aspect would be an important factor in any given spatial interpretation, his lack of concern with the physically underground character of a given space is an unacknowledged modernist trace in his theory.

A rigorous definition of the underground should thus begin with the fact of its physical location: any space that exists beneath the surface of the earth. The perceived underground begins with the natural spaces of caves that would have produced images of shelter and protection long before the concepts themselves would have been formulated.[22] Seldom if ever does such a space remain for very long free of the associations of the dominant representation of space that defines what is unproblematically desirable in any society in contradistinction to what lies buried beneath it. As far back as the twenty-sixth century BCE, natural underground spaces were already overlapping with manmade spaces excavated beneath the earth by criminals or slaves: tunnels, sewers, catacombs, mines.[23] Only during the time of their construction were such spaces generally distinguished qualitatively from the natural underground; once built (or, in the case of the mine, once exhausted of valuable ore), they tended to be subsumed by the natural environment, for better or for worse, their technological origins either wholly forgotten or incorporated as natural features in ruins (figures 1.5 and 1.6).

While aboveground space may be defined positively by the aspiration toward homogeneity, the underground is defined negatively by its failure to be or to remain homogeneous according to the same model. Whenever any space ceases to be adequate to the constraints of its conceived role in a particular discourse, it reverts to the world below as represented by that discourse in the same way that a once desirable neighborhood becomes a slum or an exhausted mine engenders a ghost town. The Industrial Revolution, the vogue of the gothic, and the new genre of the picturesque in the visual arts brought renewed attention during the late

1.5 Folk art in a "natural" space: *In the World-Famous Rock-Salt City Captured by Russia: "Bethelehem" Cut in the Side of the Queen's Chapel of the Wieliczka Mines.* Photograph in *Illustrated London News*, 12 December 1914, 808.

eighteenth and early nineteenth centuries to natural and naturalized undergrounds, as well as to the wide variety of spaces, especially in the city, that could easily be perceived as such: the arches beneath a bridge, railway embankment, or viaduct; a railway cutting, a partially exposed quarry; a covered arcade, a dark alley, a labyrinthine pocket of medieval streets (figure 1.7). Truly subterranean space has been less predominant in the representation of the modern world than the spectrum of threshold spaces assimilated metaphorically to that underground. Combining attributes of above and below, threshold spaces introduce further complications to the definition of the underground. The closer to the open air, the more likely is it that a subterranean space will be appropriated for lodging or shelter in addition to its instrumental use, and the more likely it is to become a lived space as well as a conceived and perceived one. At the same time, to the degree that an everyday space such as a basement flat or the back room of a tenement takes on the attributes of enclosure, darkness, and dampness generally associated with the subterranean, it will also be assimilated to the conceived underground (figure 1.8). Moreover, even a conceived underground space such as a tunnel or sewer usually assumes at least a modicum of the mythical attributes of its physical situation. The more metaphorical the terms of definition, the further the conceptual underground can be extended: it is common enough to place an entire quarter or an entire city below the metaphorical surface; one finds examples, especially in the

1.6 Chislehurst Caves today: excavated at an unknown date, reverted to a "natural" site, reclaimed by shelterers during the Battle of Britain, and now a local tourist attraction. Courtesy of Chislehurst Caves.

metaphysical discourses of religion and philosophy and the speculative genres of literature, in which entire nations, continents, even worlds find themselves wholly submerged (figure 1.9).[24]

Like all spaces, but in an instructively self-evident way, an underground space is filled with conflicting definitions, and even when the majority may be in agreement as to the underground status of a particular space, individual valuations of that space are likely to differ widely. For example, although there were few celebratory readers of underground space in London before the Second World War, the mythology of underground Paris was nearly always ambivalent, when not resolutely positive, about the value of what was hidden from sight. Especially in fiction, but also in purportedly objective studies such as Henry Mayhew's landmark mid-nineteenth-century survey of *London Labour and the London Poor,* such a valuation can reverse itself within the space of a paragraph: the freedom of living outside the bounds of middle-class morality suddenly gives way to the moral

1.7 The arch as subterranean space: "*Where Adam delved": Sketches in the Adelphi Arches before they were restored.* Illustration in "Where Adam Delved: A Tour through the Adelphi Arches," by Percy Fitzgerald, *Daily Graphic*, 16 December 1896.

degeneracy of religious ignorance; in fiction, the marvelous catacomb becomes a death trap when the candle is extinguished; in war tales, the inhuman trench of warfare is transformed later in the same tale into the tunnel that leads the prisoner of war to freedom. These tropes of reversal are not simply doing the ideological work of containing the force of forbidden feelings and desires within a narrative framework; they also inform us that the ambivalent feelings mobilized by the powerful imagery of the world below have not been fully laid to rest by the framing constraints.

A similar ambivalence surfaces in the frequent battles over the underground character of a given place, generally determined by an allegiance either to conceived or to lived space: one person's subterranean hole is another one's home; one person's lucrative and productive factory is another one's living hell. A key to charting this ambivalence lies in determining whether the space is perceived as transient—a workplace one is able to leave, a train from which one will soon disembark, a catacomb or sewer to which one is paying a visit, a lower class or hidden space to which a lost heir is temporarily confined—or as a permanent situation, a

1.8 Spaces of the poor assimilated to the underground: "gloomy, murky . . . yet, how picturesque!" *A Rag-Warehouse in the Quartier Mouffetard, at Paris*, in *Illustrated London News*, 8 June 1861, 542.

perception that almost invariably consigns the space to the symbolic status of a tomb or of a hell. For the permanent habitation of a manmade underground space to be depicted positively and realistically at one and the same time is as nearly inconceivable as a truly utopian glimpse of the modern city, or a genuine representation of working-class life, although all three are eminently possible, at least momentarily, as lived experiences.[25] When it does appear, the desire to overcome the conceptual limits of city space is more characteristic of underground Paris than of underground London; as George Orwell commented in an essay on Charles Dickens, playing on the evocative connotations of another item in the underground lexicon, "If you look for the working-classes in fiction and especially English fiction, all you find is a hole."[26] You may find them in the mines, in the "nether world" of urban poverty, and in the dark recesses of low lodging houses, but what you find there, Orwell implied, is a hole, a lack of anything resembling a realistic representation.

While the nineteenth century that Orwell referred to here was dominated by the representation of aboveground space as if it were subterranean, and by the increasingly predominant experience of underground space in the everyday life of the lower classes, the twentieth century was characterized by the

1.9 The late Victorian world verticalized by the Salvation Army. Foldout frontispiece to *In Darkest England and the Way Out*, by William Booth (New York: Funk and Wagnalls, 1890).

representation of subterranean space as aboveground, and by the increasing predominance of underground space in the everyday life of the middle classes. The apparent fragmentation of physical and cultural space witnessed in the first half of the twentieth century was paralleled by a rationalization of the urban underground. As we saw with the example of the métro above, this rationalization in no way eliminated the affective, representational images associated with the underground. But it did introduce a novel category of space that has continued to expand in scope while its challenge to the traditionally vertical conception of space has remained unremarked. It is a space that is wholly aboveground but covered, windowless, or otherwise able to give the impression of being subterranean: the iron-and-glass arcade, the mausoleum, the factory, the prison cell, the interrogation room, the bunker, and the artificial environment of the office block, shopping mall, and climate-controlled apartment. This new set of spatial relationships, first intimated by the opening of the underground railway in London in 1863, requires a new formulation of Lefebvre's triads in order to pose any significance to contemporary culture beyond its outmoded role within early twentieth-century capitalism.

The systematic construction and expansion of underground railways during the early 1900s in world cities from London (1863; deep-level "Tube" tunnels from 1890) and Paris (1900) to New York (1904) and Buenos Aires (1913) marked a new wave of economic development that resulted in the concentration of business activities in urban centers and the dispersal of residential populations into suburbs.[27] Although its effects were registered in the consolidation of capital, the inexorable migration of workers to the capital cities, the growing spatial segregation of the classes within those cities, and the ensuing social and political upheavals, from suffrage movements to full-scale revolution, this transformed sense of space was most graphically expressed and has been most powerfully remembered through the trauma of the two world wars. Underground space played a fundamental role in each of them, for both conflicts depended materially and psychologically on the model of rationalized mechanization developed in the mines during the first Industrial Revolution. In the First World War, it was the material experience of the trenches; in the Second, the realization of hell on earth in the rationalized slaughter of the Holocaust and the manmade apocalypse of the atomic bomb. In an analogous manner to cultural responses during the nineteenth century to new forms of production and consumption, those persons caught between the wars seized on the only familiar imagery that was in any way adequate to the terrible novelty of these experiences: the underground. Twentieth-century technology was far less evidently Janus-faced than that of the past century; consequently, responses to such explicitly rationalized destruction were polarized to the extreme.

The new phenomenon of a fragmentary response to a global rationalization accurately reflects the effect of the newly rationalized production of the assembly line; both contradictions found expression in the changing representation, physical character, and use of underground space. The second half of the twentieth century saw an economic shift toward the United States as the center of automobile and television technology and toward the transportation infrastructure most suited to them. London and Paris ceased to be generative centers of underground metaphors as they ceased to be centers of world power; the postwar underground shifted to the bicoastal poles of the American cities of New York and Los Angeles, and the second global pole of Tokyo and, later, China and the rest of east Asia. Meanwhile, on the southern peripheries, the material experience of the third-world city, closer to the novelty of nineteenth-century London and Paris but without the imperial concentration of economic, military, and cultural power that had given rise to so many new forms of representation, became a second center for recycled images of the underground of poverty and crime in a global framework that coded developed nations as aboveground and all others as below, conveniently duplicating the north-south, up-down orientation of the conventional world map.

At the same time, a new form of underground has flourished in the twentieth century alongside and often intermingled with the nineteenth-century forms. This is the subterranean space as a reproduction of the world above in all but the exposure to the open air; its most representative contemporary spaces are the bunkerlike defense complexes scattered around the developed world, and the subterranean shopping mall—the underground cities, for example, of downtown Houston, Tokyo, Montreal and Toronto (figure 1.10). It is an underground space represented as if it had none of the qualities normally attributed to such a space; it is conceived to be light, antiseptic, modern, well-policed, segregated, and problem free. It is an image we find in science fiction at the end of the nineteenth century, in architectural modernism between the wars, and in the contemporary architectural forms of the suburban shopping mall and the subterranean downtown city.[28] Rather than based on difference, this underground form assures us that the world below is identical with the world above, or at least with what the world above ought to be. It is the urban reflection of the self-enclosed space promised by the personal computer, the laptop, the PDA (personal digital assistant), the iPod, the cellular phone, and their perpetually evolving progeny—a perfectly isolated monad wherever one may be. More disturbingly, the inorganic underground is less and less frequently represented: it took over half a century for the bombproof "citadel" constructed as a last resort by Winston Churchill's government during the Battle of Britain beneath the streets of the North London suburb of Dollis Hill to come to light; only after September 11 forced his hand did President George W. Bush reveal the existence of similar facilities (no doubt more luxurious) in an undisclosed location outside Washington; their predecessor, the governmental facilities beneath the Greenbrier Resort, are now open to public tours after their secrecy was compromised by a

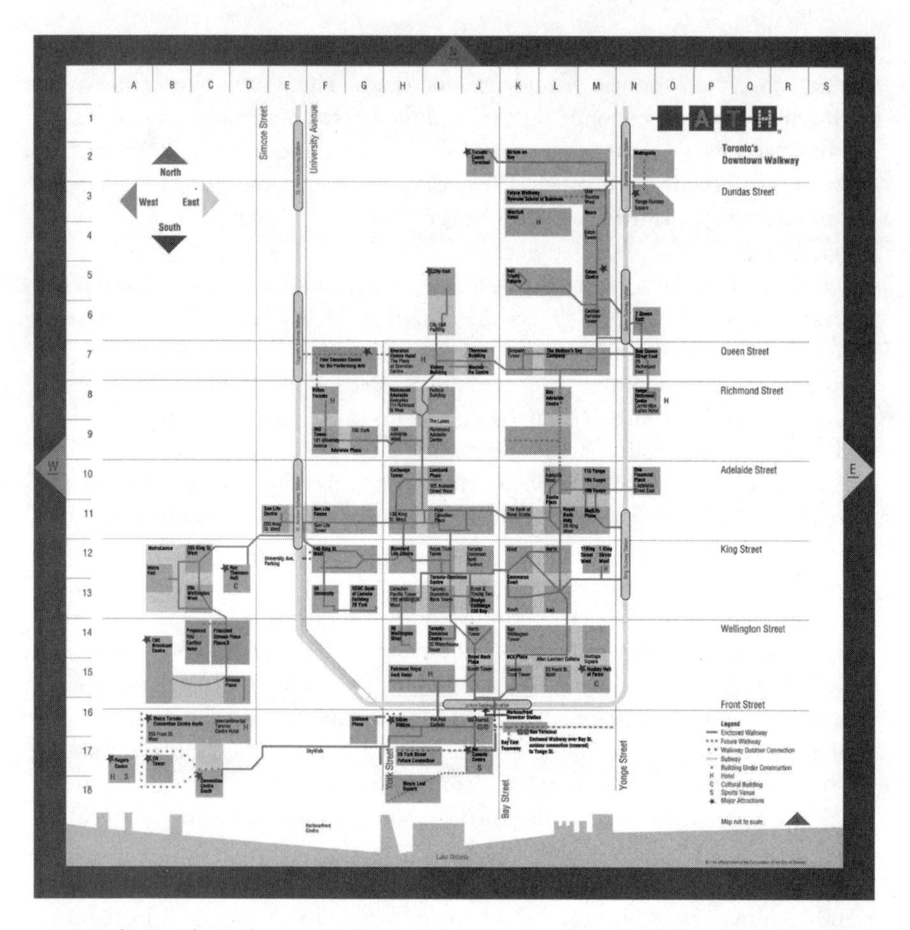

1.10 Pocket guide to the new underground. Diagram of the PATH underground shopping complex in downtown Toronto, 2005. PATH map provided by the City of Toronto Economic Development, Culture and Tourism Division—Small Business and Local Partnership Office.

reporter in 1993; the artist Andreas Magdanz was only with the greatest difficulty able to obtain permission to photograph the eighty-three thousand square meter Dienststelle Marienthal, built in an abandoned railway tunnel between 1960 and 1972 to house the government of the Federal Republic of Germany in the event of a nuclear war.[29] Whether used for the disposal of nuclear waste, for the concealment of weapons of mass destruction, or for the protection of human and other assets, the existence, not to mention the physical location and technical details, of these spaces is among the most closely kept secrets of the contemporary world. No less invisible is the multitude of what photographer Wayne Barrar terms a "commodified subterra," former mines and other sites of underground exploitation refurbished for alternate uses, from industrial parks to storage facilities to a distance learning center in Parkville, Pennsylvania (figures 1.11 and 1.12).[30] The reused mine, Barrar explains, is inexpensive, climate-controlled, and offers heightened security in the form of the limited access of (usually) a single entrance.

A further reason for the relative lack of cultural presence possessed by these spaces is the way in which their different nature has been masked by assimilation into conventional underground metaphorics. The Western public learned far more, for example, about the subterranean networks of al-Qaida in the mountains of Afghanistan—even if their familiar underground "vernacular" in the oldest troglodyte style happened to house the best Western technology money could buy—or about the primitive hole in which Saddam Hussein was finally run to ground in Iraq than it ever has about those of the government and multinational installations hidden beneath them somewhere much closer to home. Popular culture reinforces the message: at the end of the twentieth century, as at the end of the nineteenth, we find waves of apocalyptic imagery that show us the civilized world above remade as the atavistic world below. Although the spaces of the city and the spaces of capitalism are increasingly regimented and segregated, the ways in which they are conceived and represented continue

1.11 Mysteries of the new underground. *Machine floor, Poatina underground power station, Tasmania, 2005*. Photograph by Wayne Barrar. Courtesy of the photographer.

1.12 The commodification of the underground: *Film and tape storage, Underground Vaults and Storage, Inc., Hutchinson, Kansas, 2004*. Photograph by Wayne Barrar. Courtesy of the photographer.

to be governed by the underground imagery generated in the nineteenth century. Here, too, it is no accident that terrorists chose two of the highest buildings in the world as the most potent symbols for their attack on the American devil. Neither is it an accident, however, that, in contrast to earlier attacks both imagined and real, they chose to ignore the traditional vertical hierarchy that would have had them subvert from below, and instead to fly in from above, with devastating effect, in an unforeseen appropriation of space that symbolically inaugurated a new era of global relations.[31] Christine Boyer has argued that the current nostalgic form of urban development has leapfrogged the excesses of modern architecture to return to the Victorian;[32] I propose that criticism and theory, in their historicist desire for the plenitudes and certainties of the nineteenth century, have done the same thing. In both cases, what must be interrogated are the unresolved inheritances from modernism that unconsciously motivate and significantly modify the terms and results of each leap. The means for interpreting the space of the present are to be found not in a modernist reading of the Victorians but in a dialectical reading of the relationship between the present, the modernist era, and the nineteenth century. We begin in the mine, symbolically as well as economically the source of the underground domination of the nineteenth century.

From the Mine to the Trench

> Beneath the social structure, that marvellously complicated ruin of a building, there are tunnellings of every kind. There is the mine of religion, the mine of philosophy, the mine of economics, the mine of revolution. One digs with theories, one with numbers, one with anger. Voices call and respond from one catacomb to another. Utopias make their way through these conduits beneath the earth. They branch out in every direction. When, from time to time, they run into each other, they fraternize.
>
> VICTOR HUGO, *Les Misérables* (1862)

It is a testimony to its domination that a study of the term "underground" in the nineteenth century risks uncovering nothing but a truism: if everything is underground then the underground must be the source of all meaning. Perhaps the most compelling demonstration of this effect was made by Thomas Wallace Knox, an American world traveler and author primarily of armchair tour guides and exotic stories for young boys, who in 1873 published a thousand-page compendium entitled *Underground; or, Life below the Surface*, which he revised, expanded, and reprinted in several editions under several titles in several countries over a number of years, and who appears to have settled on this metaphor as the only possible rubric to unite the extraordinary range of places, experiences, and people he wished to relate (figure 1.13). In the various editions—for it was a popular book—there are anything from sixty-six to seventy-one chapters, each with around twenty subheadings, united only by some aspect of the unforeseen, the unusual, the devilish. The full subtitle imparts something of the flavor of this extraordinary work: "Incidents and Accidents beyond the Light of Day, Startling Adventures in All Parts of the World; Mines and the Mode of Mining Them; Under-Currents of Society; Gambling and Its Horrors; Caverns and Their Mysteries; The Dark Ways of Wickedness; Prisons and Their Secrets; Down in the Depths of the Sea; Strange Stories of the Detection of Crime."[33] Natural wonders follow on moral iniquity; industrial enterprise sits next to the lifestyles of the rich and famous; romantic adventure narrative joins stories of wild capitalist speculation. They share only a mythic location, and the act of convocation under one title serves only to underline the expansiveness of the myth.

If there is a single activity, a single method to moderate this apparent madness, it is the specific reality and metaphor of mining. In his preface, while acknowledging that he has borrowed liberally from countless texts, Knox singles out by name Louis Simonin's 1867 study of mining, *La Vie souterraine*.[34] In his opening chapter, Knox identifies coal as the most valuable of the many precious minerals to be found beneath the earth, and describes the "mysterious" life of the

JOHN ANDREW-SON
R.T. Sperry. fecit

miner, "so necessary for the functioning of modern society, and essential to the economies, among others, of Britain and the United States."[35] He uses mining as the vehicle of the shift away from "honest labor" into the realm of metaphor and speculation:

> Men devote time, and patience, and study to the acquisition of wealth by measures that are as far removed from the light of honesty as the tunnel the miner drives beneath the mountain is removed from the light of the sun. . . . Dishonest men hope for wealth, they care not how obtained, and in its pursuit they frequently imitate the labors of the miner. Shafts are sunk and tunnels are driven; the pick, the drill, and the powder-blast perform their work; operations are silently and secretly conducted, and all unknown to the outer world; dangers of falls of earth, of floods of water, of choke-damp, and fire-damp, are unheeded, and by and by the prize may be obtained. A great city, in its moral or immoral life, is cut and seamed with subterranean excavations more extensive than those of the richest coal-fields of England or Belgium. Wall Street is a mining centre far greater than the whole of Pennsylvania, and to one who knows it intimately it reveals daily more shafts and tunnels than can be found in Nevada or Colorado.[36]

There are several issues involved in the shift from the material realm of exploited laborers to the metaphorical underground of capitalism. For one thing, notwithstanding a straightforwardly bourgeois attitude toward the necessity of extracting riches from the depths of the earth and of mobilizing a force to perform this labor with which one will have nothing in common, and notwithstanding the "wonderful" appearance of this subterranean world when visited as an outsider from above, Knox is perfectly straightforward also about its dangers and hardships, and about the fact that "with all these perils there is no lack of men ready to meet them, as there is no lack of men ready to meet the perils and dangers of all branches of industry."[37] Just as the only and inevitable subterranean experience each of us must have is our death and burial in the ground, he suggests, so are the simple truths of supply and demand and of exploitation in order to gain wealth exposed in their baldest forms when we look underground. Granted, Knox thereby naturalizes the need for exploitation (not to mention sepulture), but the assumption that it is natural at least allows it to be presented in all its darkness, the representational choice I discuss later in the chapter as the view from below.

The shift to the realm of metaphor also involves a shift out of the black-and-white realm of class relations and into the world of the capitalist per se. Knox does at moments deal with the sphere of lower-class crime, but his stress is on the

Facing page

1.13 Life as a subterranean activity. R. T. Sperry, frontispiece to *Underground; or, Life below the Surface*, by Thomas Wallace Knox (London: Sampson, Low and Co., 1873).

high end, on politicians, speculators, and gamblers in the upper echelons of big-city finance. This is what I term the view from above, the world of appearances, a world apparently without boundaries; for unlike the mines and the working-class life represented by it, from which the bourgeois observer or armchair traveler can easily return to the upper air, the "Underground Life in its metaphoric . . . Sense" presents "the devious and hidden ways in which many of our fellow-men pass the greater part of their existence."[38] The metaphorical equation of one life with the other serves to naturalize the urban underworld nearly as much as it does the miner's tunnels; the difference is that the claim to metaphor lessens the sense of necessity while also precluding the need for a material solution to the evils of urban capitalism. Instead, as nearly always in the view from above, the metaphorical underground is figured as a moral problem, to be resolved either in the next life or by changes in the external behavior solely of the subterranean figure at fault.

In many ways, Knox's approach anticipated that of the cultural critic and urban historian Lewis Mumford half a century later, for whom the mine was both materially and metaphorically the image of capitalist exploitation. That the underground metaphor could be expanded to encompass all of life on earth, Mumford would have argued, simply reflects the equivalent dominance of capitalism, which places the infinite variety of life on earth under the single interchangeable rubric of exchange value. By recourse to the material reality of mining, Mumford sought to reveal the mechanism of the process that was eliminating any sense of what he still saw as the good life to be led aboveground. Mumford shared Knox's understanding of the city as underworld, although without sharing Knox's characteristically nineteenth-century enchantment with its subterranean marvels; he also followed Marx in linking the metaphorical reading directly to the material phenomenon of mining. If for Knox the mine had provided a convenient image for the practices of capitalism, for Mumford the practices of capitalism mirrored those of mining because the demands of mining had led to the development of the technology that was powering the modern world, and because the inhabitants of the modern world were unknowingly adapting ever more closely to the life of the miner.

First of all, mining as an early form of speculation, random effort resulting in failure or sudden rewards and leaving behind a trail of waste, "set the pattern for capitalist exploitation":

> For mining is a robber industry: the mine owner . . . is constantly consuming his capital, and as the surface measures are depleted the cost per unit of extracting minerals and ores becomes greater. The mine is the worst possible base for a permanent civilization: for when the seams are exhausted, the individual mine must be closed down, leaving behind its debris and its deserted sheds and houses. . . . The sudden accession of capital in the form of these vast coal fields put mankind in a fever of exploitation. . . .

> The animus of mining affected the entire economic and social organism: this dominant mode of exploitation became the pattern for subordinate forms of industry. The reckless, get-rich-quick, devil-take-the-hindmost attitude of the mining rushes spread everywhere: the bonanza farms of the Middle West were exploited as if they were mines, and the forests were gutted out and mined in the same fashion as the minerals that lay in their hills. Mankind behaved like a drunken heir on a spree.[39]

Mumford's final simile reminds the reader that the urban center was the final destination and full flowering of the mine, both materially as the center of accumulation and consumption and theoretically as the ultimate realization of the technology of capitalist exploitation. The mine was a particularly frightening metaphor of urban modernity for Mumford because it so vividly expressed what he viewed as the fundamental problem of modern life: the domination of and alienation from the natural world.

Life underground, life as a miner, meant both alienation from oneself, the discomfort and meaninglessness of life led in an artificial environment, and alienation from one's surroundings, the incorporation of a mind-set that caused one to treat the world around one as if one were a miner, rather than a traditional farmer:

> From the mine came the escalator, the elevator, which was first utilized elsewhere in the cotton factory, and the subway for urban transportation. . . . The combination of the railroad, the train of cars, and the locomotive, first used in the mines at the beginning of the nineteenth century, was applied to passenger transportation a generation later. Wherever the iron rails and wooden ties of this new system of locomotion went, the mine and the products of the mine went with it: indeed the principal product carried by railroads is coal. The nineteenth century town became in effect—and indeed in appearance—an extension of the coal mine.[40]

Mumford eloquently and persuasively detailed the ways, both materially and psychologically, in which the horror, the drudgery, the lack of natural rhythm, and the "social degradation" of the mining life were duplicated in the life of the city; how, in other words, a proper analysis of life underground could provide a correct diagnosis of the problems of modernity, and how, consequently, the solution would emerge of a return somehow to a life in the upper air.

In her summary of Mumford's various drafts on the mine as a model for the modern environment, Rosalind Williams has argued that the result of the process is a "complete detachment from the organic habitat": "It is the combination of enclosure and verticality—a combination not found either in cities or in spaceships—that gives the image of an underworld its unique power as a model of a technological environment."[41] Williams's analysis introduces a discussion of "imaginary underworlds," primarily of the future, underworlds that posit in various ways the material completion of the process described by Mumford. *Notes on the Underground* provides an eloquent and much-needed critical reading of nineteenth-century narratives of technological environments, but Williams's analytical stance remains within the totalizing framework of the fin-de-siècle novels and the modernist urban theory she is studying, including Mumford, whose antiurban animus precluded any stance but the most totalizing negation of the modern city.

On the one hand, although conceding that "environment and technology form not a dichotomy but a continuum," she continues to propose a historically bound conception of physical nature ("seeing the starry sky, picking berries, and walking by an unlittered brook") as an absolute and potentially subversive contrast to the "psychic and social consequences of human life in a predominantly self-constructed environment."[42] It is important to distinguish between the liberatory potentialities bound within representations of both ancient, pristine nature and new, inorganic technology, and the current reality that there cannot exist anything such as a wholly "natural" or a wholly "artificial" environment either within or outside the city as long as social relations inhere in either one. In other words, no environment, once it is known to human consciousness, can be considered wholly "natural"; nor can any environment produced, however indirectly, by human labor be considered wholly "artificial." This false dichotomy is a legacy of Cartesian space as filtered through modernism; the actual contradictions of capitalist, abstract space mean that, however much it may appear to the contrary, nature continues to exist everywhere generally construed as being within capitalism, and social relations have always existed everywhere generally construed as being outside of capitalism.

On the other hand, the leap made by Williams from the image of the mine as a model for thinking to the vision of a fully achieved inorganic environment elides the difference between a space where the material conditions of an artificial life do already for the most part apply—the mine—and a space where they apply primarily in a metaphorical manner, where they constitute, to paraphrase Mumford, a social and psychological condition rather than a material reality. Even the miner's environment remains materially different when he or she is below ground than when he or she is above it, when he or she is working and when he or she is not, even if, as Mumford so well demonstrated, the few moments of escape may be lived wholly under the terms of the conditions below, or even when, as also occurred, all aspects of life were conducted wholly below ground. This is not meant to belie the terrible reality of these conditions, but to maintain that the difference between thing and word, place and idea, however slim, can and must never wholly be eliminated, because in individual lives it never is, except by death (at least in the modern West). That human beings manage to remain recognizably human under inhumane conditions is, as Williams sees it, a frighteningly plausible image of the future, but it is also an essential reminder that lived space, the human fabric of everyday experience, is as stubbornly, startlingly, and sometimes even tragically enduring as the dehumanizing exploitation surrounding and impinging on it.

Williams's account of Mumford brings out another crucial factor of his work; her choice not to historicize its consequences is closely linked to her general neglect of the quotidian underground. As was the case with so much of modernist theory and art, the historical vision of the rise of mining technology as model of capitalism was clearly propelled by the immediate historical experience of the trenches of the First World War. Mixed in with, and not wholly distinguished from, Mumford's account of the mine as the model of capitalist exploitation is an argument for warfare as "the chief propagator of the machine" and for the army as "*the ideal form toward which a purely mechanical system of industry must tend.*"[43] To a certain degree, there was no need for him to resolve the confusion: he had already described mining as if it were a war against nature; actual warfare as another version of capitalism qua mining was a logical extension of this argument. Hence, the period between the wars—and Mumford during the early '30s was writing in the conviction that another, worse conflict was inevitable—was simply an extension of the Great War by peacetime means: "The ultimate outcome over this overstressed power ideology and this constant struggle was the World War—that period of senseless strife which came to a head in 1914 and is still being fought out by the frustrated populations that have come under the machine system."[44] It is equally clear, though never quite explicitly stated, that Mumford regarded the trenches as the culmination of the mines, and as the contemporary paradigm of the underground existence. This is evident, for example, in the captions to a pair of photographs (figure 1.14) included in *Technics and Civilization*:

> 3: Protection against poison gas in the mines: a necessary safety device for rescue work in the perpetually dangerous environment of the mine. Not merely the products but the tactics of the mine have been steadily introduced into modern warfare from Vauban onward, thus repaying the miner's earlier debt to gunpowder. 4: Protection against the deliberate use of poison gas in warfare: both the weapon and the defense against it derive from the mine.[45]

If the mine provided the basis for metaphors of the underground and the interpretation of modernity from the seventeenth century through to 1914, the traumatic experience of the Great War, on a level of mechanized inhumanity never before witnessed, was epitomized and worked through culturally by means of the underground space of the trench.

Consequently, the mine as nineteenth-century city was transformed into a different image of subterranean dread. In Paul Fussell's classic survey of trench mythology, we read:

> The rumor was that somewhere between the lines a battalion-sized (some said regiment-sized) group of half-crazed deserters from all the armies, friend and

1.14 Trench warfare as the culmination of mining technology. Photographs and captions in *Technics and Civilization*, by Lewis Mumford (New York: Harcourt, Brace, 1934), 84.

enemy alike, harbored underground in abandoned trenches and dugouts and caves, living in amity and emerging at night to pillage corpses and gather food and drink. This horde of wild men lived underground for years and finally grew so large and rapacious and unredeemable that it had to be exterminated. Osbert Sitwell was well acquainted with the story. He says that the deserters included French, Italians, Germans, Austrians, Australians, Englishmen, and Canadians; they lived . . . "in caves and grottoes under certain parts of the front line. . . . They would issue forth,

> it was said, from their secret lairs, after each of the interminable checkmate battles, to rob the dying of their few possessions. . . ." Ardern Beaman tells of meeting a salvage company at work on the battlefields of the Somme, where the "warren of trenches and dugouts extends for untold miles. They warned us, if we insisted on going further in, not to let any man go singly, but only in strong parties, as the Golgotha was peopled with wild men . . . deserters, who lived there underground, like ghouls among the mouldering dead, and who came out at nights to plunder and kill."[46]

The immediate response to the inhumanity of the trenches was not only Mumford's historical analysis but a new mythology that updated traditional imagery of the underworld and the afterlife—cannibalism, robbery, the undead, and the Christian locus of redemptive suffering, Golgotha—for a new underground context.[47]

The myth drew fine distinctions between different trench spaces and between different times of day in those spaces. There were the (relatively speaking) safe spaces of the trenches behind the lines, characterized by sameness and the fact that they were inhabited by the living, as opposed to the mixed nationality and allegiance of the spaces ruled by the undead wild men. There was the assertion that the trenches were, contrary to appearances, a natural environment, safer by day than by night. And, I would argue, there was an implicit division by class as well, and most likely by the East End and the West End, as this was a specifically English myth: the wild men not only broke down conceptions of nationality but also the fundamental (and fundamentally abstract) division of warfare, living in amity although originating from different sides of the struggle. Class warfare united all the workers of the world; the slums of London were frightening to West Enders and middle-class suburbanites not least for their commingling of Jews, Italians, Chinese, Irish, and, later, among others, Africans, Afro-Caribbeans, and Asians, living commonly, at least in the eyes of the outside viewer, and yet retaining many of their own customs and languages, to the perceived detriment of the properly English way of life, and always threatening to break out into disorder, anarchy, or something worse.

The simple truth, able to be represented only as the greatest cliché, that was expressed through and contained by this myth was that death was the greatest leveler, eliminating all distinctions, especially those of nation and social allegiance. The only escape conceivable was to distance it by asserting that the space one inhabited was not an infernal space, that one was not marked for death but had preserved a scrap of agency, some chance of survival. The only way to express this distinction under the circumstances was by asserting the most ordered aspects of everyday space and displacing disorder into another, this time truly infernal space. Contradictions inevitably emerged, for the image of demons has its own submerged utopian vitality as well: not only did the ever-growing troop of deserters purportedly coexist peacefully and possess the means to gather copious food and drink, but it lived on "for years," far longer than most of the nondeserting soldiers in the trenches could have hoped to do. Needless to say, the deep-seated desire to live outside the absolute space of discipline, of national ties, of duty, and of the need to labor and work in the brutal trenches for the rest of one's life could not be expressed positively in such a context; we find it only in the brutal language of the devil, the view from below, capped off with an image of sweeping denial—"it had to be exterminated." But the crude power of this expression of despair and desire becomes all the clearer if we compare it with the meager needs—so meager they were able to find direct rather than coded expression—that were manifested in the other view of the underground world of the trenches, the view from above that made them over in the more familiar image of central London.

If beyond the front lines lay a no-man's-land populated with the nightmares of horrible death and the dreams of another life, the British soldiers tried by contrast to make their own trenches familiar by mapping them onto the mental image of the representational spaces of the capital: "Piccadilly was a favorite; popular also were Regent Street and Strand; junctions were Hyde Park Corner and Marble Arch. . . . Directional and traffic control signs were everywhere in the trenches."[48] The enemy trenches, too, were familiarized, although here the naming was broadly allegorical as opposed to the topographic specificity proper to the city one knew as one's own. An account of the September 1916 British attack at Delville Wood recalls, "Our objective was Pint Trench, taking Bitter and Beer and clearing Ale and Vat, and also Pilsen Lane."[49] To the Christian temperance movements that set up aid huts behind the lines in competition with local prostitutes and cafés, such dissolute naming may have appeared as a sign of the infernal iniquity of the big city; to the soldiers it was a simple, darkly humorous assertion of knowledge and control over an otherwise ungraspable space, using the spatial conceptions of London to map the trenches (figure 1.15).

Following the war, the process would be repeated by travelers seeking some manner of understanding as to what had happened, so near in distance to London and Paris, but so far in terms of graspable experience. French, English, German, and American guidebooks to Paris began including information on the nearby battlefields, which became popular tourist attractions, a requisite excursion during the tour of the French capital. Along with its traditional cultural handbooks to the cities and countries of the world, Michelin published a series of guides to the most celebrated battlefields. One can readily

1.15 Representational space in the trenches: a German "street" designation replaced by the name of an infamous London rookery after the British captured the area. Archival photo. IWM negative no. Q. 1929. Reproduced by permission of the Imperial War Museum, London.

imagine Lewis Mumford joining one of these tours during the four-month visit to Europe in 1932 that a Guggenheim Fellowship funded to help him research *Technics and Civilization.* In the event, the only underground site we know for certain that he visited was the Deutsches Museum in Munich, where he was "captivated by the realistic life-size reproductions of ore, salt, and coal-mines."[50] While the material world beneath the surface provided a suitably modern metaphor for thinking about the world, its moral signposts derived from the philosophical aspect of the underworld as an age-old topic for rumination on the city. Mumford's theory of modernity syncopated the material descent to the underworld of labor and the metaphorical overview of the city as hell into a vision of total alienation. Both modes of apprehending the modern city had long been dominated by a specific manifestation of the diabolical, but to disentangle the threads of the modernist synthesis we must return to their nineteenth-century origins.

The Devil above and the Devil below

It is nothing like a moment one can pinpoint in space and time, but once it has become impossible to grasp a certain city in an instant, once a single person can no longer summon up its entirety in a single mental image, once, to borrow Jorge Luis Borges's metaphor, the map of the city is no longer commensurate point for point with the city itself, we can say that it has become a modern city, and that new vantage points are needed from which to begin to understand it. Two primary ways of approaching the modern city were codified in the nineteenth century, the view from above and the view from below; it is a token of their reliance on a metaphorics of the underground that both were formulated under the sign of Satan. The devil's association with the space of the nineteenth-century city in its aerial and its subterranean manifestations is both a symptom and a cause of modern ambivalence toward the urban. His presence also emblematizes the impossibility of uniting the two extremes of the modern underground within the orderly sphere of the middle ground; the devil's place is always on the godforsaken peripheries, never in the godliness of the center.

Emblematic of the first of these vantage points is the motif of the devil on crutches, which originated in the late seventeenth-century Madrid of Luis Vélez de Guevara's *El diablo cojuelo*, and was disseminated across Europe by Alain-René Le Sage's liberal translation of it in 1726 as *Le Diable boiteux* (figure 1.16).[51] The two versions share the defining moment where the eponymous devil takes the young student Don Cleofas above the city, peels back the rooftops with a sweep of his cloak, and proceeds to unfold the mysteries now revealed to their eyes. This mildly satirical conceit was enormously popular, imitated in and adapted to cities everywhere; the "Asmodeus flight" had become a commonplace of urban literature in general by the early decades of the nineteenth century.[52]

Le Sage's Asmodeus, two-and-a-half-feet tall and crippled, is a well-bred fiend who claims to have introduced the world to many of its vices, including "luxury, debauchery, games of chance and chemistry . . . the carousel, dance, music, comedy and all the new fashions in France."[53] This is the modern city as hell, and in its various versions it runs the gamut from metaphysical speculation to biting moral satire to humorous verbal anecdote and visual tableaux.

The devil assumes the all-seeing viewpoint no longer available to the mere mortal inhabitant of or visitor to the city; the gaze from above implies a need for supernatural power in order to continue to make sense of the metropolis. This need was represented in secular terms as the distanced, detached, often dispassionate, and initially upper-class perspective of the enlightened observer, yet it never quite shed the aura of sorcery and illicit power it had inherited from the discredited discourse of religion. Doubts regarding the demise of the traditional devil were expressed less within the discourse of enlightenment itself, however, than they were in art and literature and in the writings of those who clung stubbornly to former belief systems. As the authorizing figure in the emblem of the halting devil that frames popular nineteenth-century genres from the panorama to the realist novel, the satanic presence intimated that the entire city was an underworld, his proper demesne. As such, it remained a slightly unreal city; for the devil's province is the realm of surface appearances and the vanity of worldly things; once tempted, one is damned to be ruled by them eternally. There was seldom an alternative presented, for the hallmark of modernity is that it presents no alternative to itself; when the satirical impulse peels away false appearances along with the rooftops, it is only to show that nothing material inheres behind them either: there is an endless variety to the novelty of modernity, but there is also only ever a single meaning, endlessly repeated. This is the capitalist city in the traditional guise of the Catholic theater of the world, of the play of vices and virtues, a place of shifting roles, masks, and identities, where everyone, whether well- or ill-seeming, is already damned, no matter if the particular devil presiding be foul-tempered, or bent on frivolity, or just feeling gay.

The other approach was emblematized by the literal descent into the bas-fonds, the lower depths of the city, rather than the metonymic abstraction of its rooftops. This is the view from below, or at least from street level, and it promises a face-to-face meeting with Satan himself, not just the rather unimposing Asmodeus leaning on his crutches. Like the moral overview, the material descent has its antecedents. In the underground lore of Paris, for example, we find the story of a "charlatan," known only as César, said to have been strangled by the devil on the eleventh of March, 1615, in a cell in the Bastille where he had been incarcerated because of the "magic tours" he would give to view the devil in the *carrières*, the subterranean quarries in the southern suburbs of Paris near the aptly named rue d'Enfer.[54] Just as César was a man of many disreputable trades, an

1.16 The devil on crutches takes Don Cleophas on a tour of Madrid "un-roofed." Engraving by Dubercelle, in Alain-René Le Sage, *Le Diable boiteux*, 2 vols. (Paris: Veuve Pierre Ribou, 1726), 1:25. Reproduced by permission from Bibliothèque Nationale de France.

"astrologer, necromancer, chiromancer, physician, seer," so were his accomplices most likely moonlighting from the hard labor of mining the quarries, as well as from the more lucrative profession of underground smuggling (passages of the southern quarries ran underneath the various tollgates that restricted entrance to the city) and the criminal activity aboveground for which the Paris quarries both north and south were notorious as safe havens. Characteristic of the view from below, César's tours bring together the urban thrill seeker and the mythology of the otherworld in a convincingly material form.

Tours to see the devil were apparently common practice during the reigns of Louis XIV and his son, in the south of Paris as well in the Right Bank quarries of Montmartre in the north and the Buttes-Chaumont in the northeast. Having found someone who wished to meet the devil, the prisoner recounts, he would exact a hefty sum of money, an oath of silence, a promise of fortitude, and an assurance that during the tour the visitor would neither invoke any god nor pronounce any sacred phrases. If the first impression of the deep cavern under the streets, the many magic words and gestures he performed, and the infernal sounds emanating from below were sufficient to deter the visitor, César would let him escape at the point of entry, retaining his money as the price of idle curiosity. If the tourist proved intrepid enough to cross the threshold into the devil's realm, he would be presented with a spectacle of fire, rattling chains, and the devil, played in the dark by a tormented bull—a spectacle real enough, César claimed, to frighten even himself. The naive soul would then be beaten half-unconscious by a band of accomplices armed with sandbags and dressed as furies, beaten to such a degree that the loyal guide was often compelled to carry the victim back out to the open air. The parting words of this tour guide from hell would be piously to admonish his mark for the "dangerous and useless curiosity of wanting to see the devil."[55] We can safely assume the official version given by César to have been the best-case scenario; it is just as probable that the intrepid tourist would indeed be sent to the devil, and that the initial fee of fifty pistoles would be augmented by whatever else of value was to be found on his lifeless body.

The view from below involves descent rather than ascent, it proffers knowledge and power at the cost of danger and ordeal, and, rather than reducing the variety of the world to a play of appearances, it deals in contrasts, for the identity of the material underground and the activities consigned to it are always predicated on their opposition to the world above. While the view from above maintains what it regards as underground at a safe distance far below, hierarchized and conceptualized, the view from below revels in the sensations of its proximity to chaos. Like César's tour, it is a trip into the devil's own realm, and it leaves no doubt that the primary allure of the underground in the modern city is the cluster of illicit activities that have been at one time or another associated with various departments of Satan's realm. The list constitutes a rather comprehensive account of the topics that have preoccupied much of the "respectable" world, especially in the West, for the past several centuries: smuggling, counterfeiting, swindling, murder, kidnapping, blackmail, and the many varieties of petty and not-so-petty larceny; mining, scavenging, dredging, rag picking, interment and disinterment; prostitution, homosexuality, illicit trysts, and all manners of sexual perversion; child prostitution, juvenile delinquency, flower girls, telegraph boys, street arabs; degeneracy, paranoia, schizophrenia, shell shock, insanity; gin palaces, absinthe bars, opium dens, shooting galleries, crack houses; the Dark Continent, the jungle, the land Down Under, the exotic Orient; Irish, Italians, blacks, Arabs, Asians, Latinos; gambling, slumming, clubbing, raving; Freemasons, Knights Templar, Rosicrucians, and other secret societies; criminal organizations from the Great Family of Paul Féval's *Les Mystères de Londres* to the Cosa Nostra and the Kray brothers; pornography, pamphleteering, cartoons and caricatures; underground literature, art, cinema, theater and music; fortune-telling, table-turning, mesmerism, occultism, religious dissidence, black masses, witchcraft, satanism; slavery, nomadism, vagrancy, bohemianism, poverty, starvation; surveillance, spies, moles and informers; incarceration, persecution, torture, execution; radicalism, revolution, insurrection, treason, terrorism; waste, sewage, floodwaters, offal, bones; death, ruin, apocalypse. The relative value associated with many of these categories is easily revised when based on a perspective not dominated by a verticalized social structure and whenever one representation of space replaces another; nevertheless, once anything has been associated with the underground, the identity tends to stick, if in unpredictable and often fragmentary ways.

The definition of the object of opposition may change, but the location does not, for the view from below is an emblem that trades on its authenticity. Two recent books have studied the full range of these underworld phenomena, which they group under the general metaphorical rubric of "night." In *Nights in the Big City*, Joachim Schlör persuasively argues that modernity has been characterized by a battle over definition and control of the urban night, drawing attention to "the unfinished, not quite perfect modernization of our society, our cities."[56] For Schlör, night in the city offers (and therewith threatens the daytime world) images of freedom, of the fulfillment of desires not otherwise offered by the modern world. In *Cultures of Darkness*, Bryan Palmer uses a broader historical canvas to sketch out a more explicitly materialist thesis, reading "night" as a heuristic for "cultures of transgression, marginality, and alternative" which emerge in contrast to or rebellion against "capitalism's daytime power."[57] Both authors impart a keen sense of the complex exchanges involved in participating in "night" activities or choosing nocturnal identities, in what I term here the view from below; for night contains simultaneously zones of repression by the powers of day and rare glimpses of freedom and opportunities for resistance against those powers. My reading of underground space differs from these studies of night in two ways: first, I analyze the metaphorical registers of night and darkness in relation to the material spaces with which they were symbolically associated and in which their activities occurred with increasing frequency in the modern city; second, I factor in the positive attributes of the pagan underworld that have been confusedly interwoven with the transgressive imagery ever since the rise of Christianity—including subterranean space as shelter, a usage accepted even by the forces of daylight.

As the city changed, and the second industrial revolution introduced an ever more complex and varied underground infrastructure beside the more mythic or metaphorically underground spaces of poverty and crime, the satanic emblem became less predictable and more confused. The actual spaces of sewers, tunnels, underground railways, arches and viaducts, storage vaults, subterranean parking, and covered passageways become intertwined, sometimes materially, as when prostitutes plied London's Burlington and Lowther Arcades and the covered *passages* of central Paris, and far more often imaginatively, as when the quarters of poverty became spatially cut off from those of wealth. But the devil was still in it, although the genres availing themselves of this emblem—the realist and the naturalist novel, the urban mystery, the sensation scene, the pamphlet, the travel narrative, the sociological study, the religious tract—would often clothe their reigning evil genius in a less metaphysical garb, be it moral, genetic, social, spatial, or what have you.

What remains consistently diabolical whatever the discourse of evil invoked is the note of excess that haunts the view from below just as a superhuman power marks the view from above. And, indeed, one could not hazard a better general definition for any devil than to call it the embodiment of unpredictable power. The impulses of the night are dangerous to the order of the world because there is no place for them in it. The most persuasive of the modernist theories of the underground called this force the id, and spoke of the return of the repressed, but it became ever clearer during the second half of the twentieth century that this resolutely social and spatial phenomenon exceeded the individual mind within which Freud's theories had contained it, and the devil has demonstrated a persistence long outliving his putative role in Christian theology and has continued to embody that excess.

Catholicism has always attempted to codify and contain that power and excess in the category of sin, but the Christian Devil exceeded that rationality in various ways. Through his command of trickery and falsehood, he could make any appearance deceptive, any apparent good could turn out in fact to have been sinful, and so one could never be safe from his power. Moreover, corrupted through folklore, through the influence of prior belief systems, and through syncretism with non–Judeo-Christian religions, the Devil by no means remained a coherent conception even within Catholicism. Just as the coherence of the world above depends on everything incoherent being placed underground, so the unity of Christ and the god he incarnated required a devil for whatever that theology could not contain—most especially, the concept of evil. For Lefebvre, the only coherence to the conception of the devil was that

> the devil is always in the wrong; that is what he was invented for. . . . Right up to the present day, every era, every people, every class—and every group, every political party—has had its devil, has seen it, conjured it up, made it, lived it, pursued it, and

> immolated it, only to resuscitate it in order to kill it again. And as people are always *against* before being *for* anything (and to a greater and more effective extent more *against* than *for*), this pursuit of the real and imaginary monster has always been of the utmost importance.[58]

The singularity of the devil, Lefebvre continued, derives from the paradoxical fact that "myths speak of power, and justify it. Only with the myth of the devil is power challenged."[59] Negation is important not so much in itself as for the social insights expressed through it more than anywhere else.

Although he did concede that "there can be no devil without a false devil amalgamated with the (supposedly) real one,"[60] Lefebvre never really came to grips with the unpredictable power embodied in the devil's contradictory nature as simultaneously ideological and subversive, as a myth of power that also challenges its mythic status. His conception of the devil remains very much a descendant of the Miltonic Satan as embraced by the Romantics, a sublime figure of opposition and rebellion. This is a crucial conception for materializing the mythical imagination of the modern city, but it is only part of the representational armature with which the devil has been involved. Like the underground space with which he has been most consistently associated, the devil is an assemblage of contradictory ideas and beliefs, none of which supersedes the others. As the art historian Luther Link has noted of the iconography of the medieval devil, because amalgamated from different sources—early interpretations of the New Testament, the rebellious figure of the battle in heaven, the popular tradition of cults and the black Sabbath—it never cohered into a single unified image.[61] In medieval popular religion, there was, according to historian Aron Gurevich,

> an intricate interaction with Christian beliefs and ideas that had been assimilated, one way or another, by the common people. Traditional magic and Christianity did not form distinct layers or separate compartments in the medieval mind. A unity arose from their encounter—a unity surely not devoid of contradiction and ambivalence, but one in which the old magical beliefs and Christian teachings found meaning and function precisely in their mutual correlation.[62]

Because Paradise was highly structured and restricted to the Lord God and his court, it was Hell, realm of chaos, that was the prime location for this syncretism. Because so much of non-Christian tradition and magic was identified within Christian doctrine with the Devil, the Satan of popular religion was a highly ambivalent figure, powerfully evil but also powerful in other less sanctioned ways. The nineteenth century found two ways to give coherence to this inherited material, but neither mode of representation was able to express its full range of meanings. The devil's revolutionary potential was expressed positively only within a comic and fabulous framework—framed and contained by the view from above. When treated in a realistic discourse—demonized through the view from below—such potential was manifested only as a destructive threat. The full power embodied by the devil can be expressed only through a comparative reading of the different contradictions arising from the impossible roles he plays in each mode of representation.

Why is it so difficult to combine these two points of view, to match the synthetic vision from above with the material specificity of below? One answer is that it is not difficult at all; the dominant literary genre of the modern West, the narrative of the middle-classes from the courtship novel through the bildungsroman to the realist novel has always aspired to God's point of view on society and—especially in England—safely contained anything underground within its developmental frame. In Lefebvre's terms, it is a myth of power, describing through its plotting and narration how to become an acceptable individual within an acceptable society, how to avoid the devil's extremes at all costs. To be sure, these are highly conflicted narratives in their own right, but I would argue that to the extent that any of these texts does at moments challenge a ruling ideology, it does so by slipping into one of the two perspectives described above. It momentarily adopts, in other words, a diabolical point of view: the moments of pure darkness that punctuate Dickens's novels, the specter of calamity that stalks Jane Austen's comic plots before the fortuitously happy resolution. In this way, the attempt to draw on the insights of the abstract view from above and the specific view from below without incorporating the negativity intrinsic to each inevitably reveals the contradictions in their ideological middle.[63] In philosophical terms, such narratives represent what Fredric Jameson has termed the "category mistake," the "fundamental incommensurability between the individual and the collective," the impossible Cartesian desire "to deduce the larger social forms from the smaller ones and to build up notions and models of the collective from out of primary accounts of individual actions and immediate face-to-face encounters."[64] The middle ground is occupied by false resolutions of the contradictions of capitalism; the two extremes cannot be bridged differently in any other manner without presenting the appearance of paradox, incoherence, or brutality.

This gap is especially evident in the visual arts, where the convention of the picture frame makes visible the gesture of containment being enacted by the representation within. As Lynda Nead has shown in her work on representations of prostitution and of urban change in mid-Victorian London, when respectable painting came to address topics appertaining to the world below, it did so perforce in a set of conventions and codes that would render their subjects suitable to the exhibition hall and the drawing room.[65] In the case of the prostitute, for example, this iconography graphically severed any possible connection between the fallen middle-class woman as social victim and the debased prostitute as social threat, creature of the world below, even within a single sequence of linked paintings such as Leopold Egg's triptych, *Past and Present*.[66] One visual narrative staged the view from above, with the discovered woman throwing herself at the feet of her deceived husband; another staged the view from below, the woman with her lover's child abandoned beneath an arch opening onto the bank of the Thames (see figure 4.4). In a very different sort of study of a very different sort of city during the same time period, T. J. Clark has demonstrated the contradictory results that occurred when the impressionist painters tried to capture the very essence of changing space in Second Empire Paris through a set of visual codes that would be legible and marketable to their middle-class patrons.[67] Although the representational conventions of the Paris discourse permitted a greater focus on threshold figures than on those belonging to either side of the vertical divide, Clark's reading of the furor surrounding Édouard Manet's *Olympia* and the possibility of representing prostitution suggests a similar resistance to such simultaneous depictions of under- and aboveground space in Paris.[68] Although their analyses brilliantly dissect the boundaries of respectable art of the modern metropolis, neither Nead nor Clark pays much critical attention to the quite different codes offered by the ephemeral and disreputable images that appeared in newspapers, broadsheets, playbills, stage plays, and serialized fictions. Here, we find the view from below at its most formulaic but also at its rawest and most uncompromisingly diabolic. While the accompanying texts offered a fair amount of play in spatial meaning, the often crude and frequently recycled images went straight for the jugular, even if the popular sentiments of despair and desire they expressed came forth only in the base stereotypes of the view from below in its most concentrated and accessible form.

At their most radical, such extremes of negation escape representation altogether; once removed from the tolerated containers of vice and crime, they can be expressed coherently only by being placed back within such conveniently disposable conceptual containers as Romantic or adolescent—the Miltonic Satan. Confronted with Lefebvre's negative formulation "revolutionary-romantic" to refer to the cultural tendency founded on the specifically modern disaccord between the progressivist individual and the world, situationist theorist Guy Debord responded, "We will be 'revolutionary-romantics' precisely to the degree that we fail."[69] As long as social space continues to be conceived as a division between high and low, any radical desire, to be represented at all, will inevitably be tagged as underground, individual, and either naive or inhuman. When extended beyond the individual, it most commonly loses any remaining idealism and utopianism, either because it is further co-opted into acceptable modes of representation or because it is represented in the view from below as material, brutal, and atavistic.

In *Lipstick Traces*, his "secret history" of a series of events on the threshold between art and everyday life, the cultural critic Greil Marcus has analyzed the impossibility of representing radical culture as simultaneously radical and cultural. Marcus argues that something more than what persists in the official record must account for the extremes of emotion, action, and commitment exhibited fleetingly and almost imperceptibly during such now wholly romanticized or fully deadened historical episodes of modernity as the Paris Commune, Dada, the Situationist International, and the punk movement of the late 1970s: "Unfulfilled desires transmit themselves across the years in unfathomable ways, and all that remains on the surface are bits of symbolic distortion, deaf to their sources and blind to their objects—but these fragments of language, hidden in the oaths and blasphemy of songs like 'Anarchy in the U.K.' or 'God Save the Queen' . . . are a last link to notions that have gone under the ground. . . . All that remains are wishes without language."[70] Referring primarily to Eastern Europe, Neal Ascherson writes in similarly verticalized terms of the "authentic space . . . that human beings begin to excavate . . . in order to survive morally" under authoritarian regimes as "a cave which can be enlarged until it has hollowed out the foundations of the ruling order. Authenticity is like a termite or a death-watch beetle, gnawing away expanding spaces within apparently solid structures."[71] As Ascherson himself implies, however, such authenticity is severely limited in space and time, and its representational forms, like those Marcus discusses, are co-opted at nearly the same moment that they become perceptible, represented in terms of the world above.

For several centuries now, the vertical framework has provided a means both for those it imagines underground to give expression to their own unfulfilled desires and for sense to be made of those desires outside of their immediate context. Yet it is important to keep in mind that the devil and his underground demesne are not privileged concepts residing outside of capitalism and modern culture; they are figures for the most available and identifiable of the unfulfilled desires that are seamed through every aspect of society. Nietzsche formulated this social coherence in a counterintuitive image that emphasizes the way the status quo was being expressed as natural: "The world . . . lives on itself: its excrements are its nourishment."[72] Notwithstanding its often eerie correlation to actual conditions, the vertical conception of space would have us believe that there is a space to which such desires and vices are restricted, and in which they take a predictable range of forms. Nevertheless, it is merely a representation, if a powerfully enduring one, of a social space the complexity of which belies representation as such. The rare moments when we see the abstract negation united with close observation of social reality, the moments when the insights of the underground are combined with the analytic armature of the view from above are always expressed in art as moments of paradox or aporia and in criticism and philosophy as some form of dialectic—expressions that now find themselves, like the historical moments described above, enshrouded in romance and embedded in deadening layers of critical discourse: Marx and Baudelaire in the nineteenth century; Samuel Beckett, Kafka, Walter Benjamin, and Theodor Adorno in the twentieth. As Jameson observes of the category mistake, "the dialectic already knew . . . that there was a gap and a leap between the two."[73] But where Jameson's analysis, like those of the modernist theorists and artists just mentioned, remains content to use dialectics or aporia to observe the "gap and a leap," I propose to take the devil's role seriously as a figure for the requisite escape from the geometric order of Cartesian space. This is not simply because in Western myth Lucifer is the first creature to have been expelled from the perfectly ordered space of heaven, and not simply because that same Miltonic Lucifer was established as a fundamental figure of Romantic resistance through modernity, refusing to be contained even in Hell. It is because the devil is an indicator not only of negation but of contradiction; the greater the power he exudes, the greater the contradiction he reveals, and the greater the ambivalence expressed toward him, for contradiction has been a prodigious vehicle for fear in the modern world. As William Blake, the most innovative and eccentric of the Romantic satanists, wrote of his understanding of Satan and Hell, "Without Contraries is no progression . . . From these contraries spring what the religious call Good & Evil. Good is the passive that obeys Reason Evil is the active springing from Energy Good is Heaven. Evil is Hell."[74] Banished like Satan from the heaven of modern capitalism, the contraries fell with him down into hell, and followed him out again and as he made his way into the modern underground.

The Devil and the Rhythms of Modern Life

> The bourgeoisie resembles the sorcerer, who is no longer able to control the powers of the netherworld whom he has called up by his spells.
>
> KARL MARX AND FRIEDRICH ENGELS, *Manifesto of the Communist Party* (1848)

The twin modes of representation personified by the devil offered a potent force to give form to the dizzying experience of modernity. The combination of mythic endurance with a liberally employed and constantly shifting corpus of underground imagery was uniquely suited for expressing the contradictions inherent to the ever more refined and ever more baldly exposed mechanisms of capitalist—which is to say modern—society. Capitalism invents, uses, and discards; to succeed, each new technology, each new invention must present itself as both familiar enough not to frighten and new enough not to be familiar. The underground presents the opposite combination: it is familiar enough to be recognized and unfamiliar enough to be frightening, or at least enticing. Although always present, waves of underground imagery have tended to peak during the periods of especially rapid and difficult change that punctuate the "discontinuous but expansive" movement characteristic of capitalism.[75] To produce, capital needs ever new land to exploit and ever new labor with which to exploit it, ever new markets in which to expand and ever new products to be consumed by those markets. Expansion is not a uniform and continuous process; it takes time to find the most efficient form of each technology, and time to find the most attractive wrapper for each commodity. Nor is it an enduring process; the constant movement of capital makes technologies and products outmoded as quickly as it invents and packages new ones. The advance of capitalism leaves behind a trail of obsolescence: overexploited land, superfluous labor, and outmoded commodities. These ruins of things, places, people, techniques, and ideas end up both literally and figuratively underground, in the garbage dumps and landfills of the world.

Now, it is not axiomatic that what is no longer useful for capital is no longer useful for anything or anybody else; hence, the underground is equally the repository for possibilities of invention, innovation, and labor that were not exhausted in the production of surplus value. Because the underground has been frequently, although not exclusively, popular in origin and has been closely associated with traditional stereotypes, folklore, and the armature of popular culture, such possibilities are more often than not expressed in whatever unacceptable forms were repressed in the process of creating a respectable and cohesive discourse aboveground. Because only the negative extremes of the underground can be made directly visible in the world above, the contradictions they express manifest themselves instead as simple negation. Even at its most demonic and apocalyptic extremes of reductiveness, however, the view from below expresses critical truths about modern life unavailable as such through any other mode of representation.

The devil exists neither wholly within nor wholly outside of the system of capital; like the underground, he is a myth of opposition, as ideological as he is subversive. Michael Taussig has rigorously analyzed the quality of this ambivalence in his work on what he calls "devil-beliefs" in the folklore of peasant workers on sugar cane plantations in Colombia and in the tin mines of Bolivia. According to Taussig, the devil is incorporated into indigenous myths to provide an uneasy mediation between the traditional, peasant mode of production and the proletarianized mode of their new labor:

> Thus, the devil-beliefs . . . can be interpreted as the indigenous reaction to the supplanting of this traditional fetishism by the new. As understood within the old use-value system, the devil is the mediator of the clash between these two very different systems of production and exchange. This is so not only because the devil is an apt symbol of the pain and havoc that the plantations and mines are causing, but also because the victims of the expansion of the market economy view that economy in personal and not in commodity terms and see in it the most horrendous distortion of the principle of reciprocity, a principle that in all precapitalist societies is supported by mystical sanctions and enforced by supernatural penalties. The devil in the mines and cane fields reflects an adherence by the workers' culture to the principles that underlie the peasant mode of production, even as these principles are being progressively undermined by the everyday experience of wage labor under capitalist conditions. But until the capitalist institutions have permeated all aspects of economic life and the revolution

> in the mode of production is complete, the lower classes will persist in viewing the bonds between persons in their modern economic activities for what they really are—asymmetrical, non-reciprocal, exploitative, and destructive of relationships between persons—and not as natural relations between forces supposedly inherent in potent things.[76]

As a symbol, the devil incorporates the promise of power held out by capital—unforeseen riches—together with its destructive effects on any other mode of production.

Moreover, as Taussig demonstrates in the case of the tin miners, who incorporated the devil as spirit-owner of their mines in an ambivalent updating of their traditional animism, the devil is the only category within Western culture in which a place can be found for pagan—and I use the word to signify both non-Christian and noncapitalistic—beliefs. Far from being a unified and ahistorical category of Roman Catholic doctrine, the devil has tended to manifest himself most powerfully at the peripheries of capitalism, in the spaces and times in which the commodity principle is in direct conflict with other principles of social organization. Hence, as Jules Michelet argued in his nineteenth-century study of witchcraft in Europe, "the European devil of the early modern period was a figure emerging from popular paganism who was seen as an ally of the poor in their struggle against landlord and Church."[77] Hence, Claude Seignolle could still travel through rural France in the middle of the twentieth century, collecting folklore of the devil mixed with pre-Christian legend from peasants existing on the margins of twentieth-century society.[78] The devil is not a figure external to capitalist ideology and modern society any more than pristine nature or lost native tribes are; like the underground space he inhabits and controls, he is the most available symbol within that ideology for expressing the contradictions capitalism raises wherever it is extending itself into a realm that had been at least in some manner external to it.

An excellent record of the process whereby beliefs marginal or alien to Western, Christian, and capitalistic modes of thinking are gradually incorporated into those modes as pure myth through the figure of the devil can be found in historian Carlo Ginzburg's meticulous reconstruction of the Friulian figure of the *benandanti*.[79] What began as a vital pre-Christian fertility ritual was first transformed by contact with Christianity into the figures of the *benandante*, benign witches who did battle with malevolent forces over the fate of the harvest. This is the moment of contradiction in the process of appropriation: novel beliefs, beliefs alien to the dominant discourse, can find a place in that discourse only through the conception of the underground. Hence, the benandante become agents of the devil while clinging just as strongly to the positive connotations of that agency in the traces of their own beliefs. Witness the confusion to which Maria Panzona's beliefs gave rise: "Although she admitted having paid homage to the devil, she did not renounce her own powers as a benandante. It had been the devil himself, in fact, who had suggested to her the means of curing the victims of the witches."[80] As the popular practice came into conflict with the judicial and theological apparatus of the Inquisition, which could conceptualize the behavior of the benandante only in terms of witchcraft, the practice soon lost its potency as a ritual, devolved into a purely formal activity, and eventually vanished as a practice as well, leaving traces only in oral legend and in the records of prosecution. The process of assimilation from margin to center was limited in time; in the phenomenon studied by Ginzburg, about forty years passed between the first inquisitors' records of the practice in 1575–80 and its eradication by 1620.[81] The broad outlines of the devil figure and the myths and spaces surrounding him do not change, but they do accumulate an ever-greater range of alien forces that, although soon incorporated and emptied, stubbornly persist in the realm of language, discourse, and representation. It is only in the threshold moment of contact, however, that marginal practices can be made visible to the world while also retaining traces of their past vitality.

By the nineteenth century, the same process of syncretism that had occurred between folk belief, heresy, and Christianity in medieval Europe had come to pass between the villain of the now passé drama of Christianity and the culture of industry and the Enlightenment. Adopted wholeheartedly by a new urban popular culture, the devil served to contain the fears and express the hopes invoked by the rapidity and magnitude of social change, in particular the astonishing transformations being wrought by industrial technology on the urban space and those who dwelt within it. As the architectural historian Siegfried Giedion argued of the more general principle in his classic 1928 book, *Building in France*, "In every field the nineteenth century cloaked each new invention with historicizing masks. . . . New constructional possibilities were created, but at the same time they were feared; each was senselessly buried beneath stone age sets."[82] Giedion wrote *Building in France* as a manifesto for the "new way of living" that would "put aside the past" by careful study of "the expressions anticipated by, and latent within, the constructions of the nineteenth century."[83] In his millenarian enthusiasm, he failed to interrogate what new forms of "historicizing masks" were then cloaking which "new possibilities" of the 1920s, but Giedion's insight that the crucial element in the previous century had been iron-and-glass construction was sound, as was his insistence that such expressions were simultaneously backward- and forward-looking, and that their final form within capitalism might not be the only potential value they could offer.

Giedion's analysis of nineteenth-century technology added an important spatial component to the axiom of the *Communist Manifesto* that "within the old society, the elements of a new one have been created."[84] One of Lefebvre's most significant insights was to identify a similar dialectic in the prime area for capitalist expansion during the twentieth century: everyday life. As he wrote in 1957,

"The remarkable penetration of modern technics into everyday life has thus introduced into this backward sector the *uneven development* characteristic of our epoch from every point of view."[85] By 1981, Lefebvre had conceded that the further analogy he had made of the quotidian with the third world was "perhaps excessive" insofar as a prediction of simultaneous revolution, but nevertheless remained "not devoid of significance" as a basis for analysis.[86] Excessive because it was unsuccessful; significant because it pinpointed the new underground spaces in which contradiction became for a time represented. Everyday life and the developing world were both characterized by the phenomenon of uneven development: with London and Paris leading the way, the West had settled on the most efficient forms of industrial, productive technology by the beginning of the twentieth century; as it exported that technology to the developing world, this same form no longer worked in the same ways, just as the consequences of its application beyond the traditional marketplace and into everyday life in the West could not be perfectly predicted based on prior performance in the workplace.

Where Lefebvre's practice lagged behind his theory was precisely where life in the developing world differed from everyday life in the West: the behavior of the former was closer in character to that of the nineteenth-century urban underworld, if on a vastly larger scale and in a far more occulted manner, the ramifications of which are only now becoming comprehensible. Here, Lefebvre's cherished ideal of the "organicism and good life" of the southern French villages of his youth, and the medieval and Renaissance social structures underlying them, was perhaps more applicable;[87] as for everyday life in the postwar West, he was never quite able to embrace the new developments sufficiently in order to analyze them dialectically. This was the task taken up by the Situationist International, whose members longed only for some possible life in the future, the form of which, they argued, could be discovered in the cultural traces of the past as well as in the present. "Propaganda for the future" was to be fashioned from any and every aspect of contemporary society, as the situationists, like the surrealists before them, devised complex schemes for discovering the hidden potential, the cracks in the façade, of what they termed the society of the spectacle. As the lead editorial in *internationale situationniste* 5 stated, "The S.I. does not want to keep its place in the current artistic edifice, but is digging it out subterraneously [*le sape souterrainement*]. The situationists are in the catacombs of known culture."[88]

The principal theoretical weakness of the Situationist International was its excessive reliance on the sphere of culture to effect revolutionary transformation, on the assumption, to borrow their terminology, that one catacomb was the same as any other. It was a scheme that could have succeeded only if their theories had been universally applicable, if underground space were always identical. As we shall see, however, even Paris and London produced significantly different underground spaces in the nineteenth century. By definition, any "situation" was finite in time and space, just as the particular moment of capital to which it directly responded inhered only, at best, in the West; in the third world, for example, or in Latin America, the conflict remained primarily in the economic and political sectors. Because capital advanced unevenly, it could never fall or be toppled everywhere in one fell swoop. Fortunately, the converse equally applies: because it always does advance unevenly, capital can never wholly replace the "real world" either. The miscalculation of the situationists has been repeated by much of contemporary work on space within capitalism by cultural geographers, architects, and art historians. Such recent writing, as for example, Boyer's *City of Collective Memory* or Rosalind Deutsche's *Evictions*, transforms Lefebvre's influential definition of "abstract space" as the form of conceived space proper to modern capitalism into a universal model of contemporary society: "Henri Lefebvre has taught that city space is a product, marked, measured, marketed, and transacted; like any capitalist tool the efficiency and functionality of its performance is studied and perfected, and as a commodity its representational form is restylized and reformed."[89] The replacement of "abstract space" by "city space" in Boyer's otherwise accurate summary is symptomatic of her hypostasization of Lefebvre's dialectical triad of perceived, conceived, and lived space into "the homogenization of space at the global level."[90] The ruins of the nineteenth century continue to be read dialectically, plundered for their hidden traces of alternative possibilities while critiqued for their dominant phenomena, while the new developments of capitalism in the West—Boyer's "historical districts," Deutsche's gentrification, Williams's artificial environments—are analyzed for their (admittedly frightening) intentions rather than for their contradictory meanings as spatial practice.

The essential lesson shared by Lefebvre and the situationists was to apply Marxism rigorously rather than halfheartedly to such meanings, the way they put "continual pressure . . . on the question of representational forms in politics and everyday life, and the refusal to foreclose on the issue of representation versus agency."[91] If, as Marx wrote, capitalism by definition creates contradictions in whatever it produces, then by definition contradictions continue to be created. Where Lefebvre and the situationists would agree with the apocalyptic anticapitalist rhetoric of Boyer, Deutsche, Williams, and others is in the recognition that abstract space is rapidly gaining ground on any other type of space. The suitable image for this progression is not the modernist attitude of apocalypse or dystopia, however, but Zeno's second paradox, the race between Achilles and the tortoise: given a head start, the tortoise, moving one-tenth the speed of the swift-footed Achilles, will never be overtaken, for each time Achilles traverses half of the space between himself and the tortoise, half of the space will always remain to be traversed. Zeno's paradox long ago defined the "artificial infinity," a man-made infinity of logic; modern technology made it a material reality. Rosalind Williams has described the artificial infinity as a key feature of the industrial sublime of the early nineteenth century,[92] one of the ways in which the alien character of underground space was incorporated within acceptable modes of representation. In

1939, Borges reformulated Zeno's proof that "movement is impossible" as a parable of modernity: if William James could use the same procedure to deny that fourteen minutes can elapse, then, "the vertiginous *regressus in infinitum* can perhaps be applied to all subjects. . . . We . . . have dreamed the world. We have dreamed it strong, mysterious, visible, ubiquitous in space and secure in time; but we have allowed tenuous, eternal interstices of injustice in its structure so that we may know that it is false."[93] As Borges posited through the language of modernist paradox, the artificial infinity is the hallmark of any aspect of second nature. The infinitesimal space between Achilles and the tortoise, which one knows might not work in practice but which remains irrefutable in theory, is the proper province of capitalism; true infinities and true apocalypses may perhaps exist, but in first nature, not made by us.

In a fascinating demonstration of the devil's capacity for adaptation to new forms of contradiction in the representation of space, the Icelandic mathematician Ivar Ekeland recently employed an updated version of Maxwell's demon, an intelligent being invented in 1871 by the physicist James Clerk Maxwell to personify, within a rigorously logical argument, the possibility of contradiction within the second law of thermodynamics. Ekeland invokes the demon to illustrate not only the unavoidable introduction of chance into any deterministic (traditionally, God-created) system, but also the supernatural element necessary to measure and fully appreciate his own disruptive impact on that system. "Let us now imagine," he begins, a "demon [that] receives only the information that arrives by the sensory channel, each instance adding a new bit (that is, a O or a I) to the string. Since he's a demon, he lives for ever. So at the end of time he has accumulated an infinite series of Os and Is, and we ask him if the world makes sense."[94] Unable to conceptualize contingency within the rationalistic constraints of our current spatial practices, we must have recourse to a demon that can observe the system from without. Like the city that is its microcosm (as Ekeland observes, "There exist very simple systems whose behavior is just as unpredictable")[95], the universe is a nonintegrable system: it cannot be reduced to a linear series of cause and effect. We may either attribute causality to a cohesive aboveground force—God, science—or represent the impossibility of causality within an otherwise rational system through a personification of the underground within it:

> Yet there is not, and there cannot be, independent causal sequences in the universe. . . . To talk about independence is only a convenient approximation, a myopic view of events which we are forced to abandon if we are looking for more refined analyses or more distant horizons. A demon displaces an electron on Sirius, way below the range of our perception. In so doing, he modifies all the forces of attraction that this electron exerted on the other particles in the universe, notably the gaseous molecules that constitute the earth's atmosphere. In just a few seconds, this minute jolt, propagated and amplified by the collisions between molecules, translates into perceptible modifications.[96]

The supernatural being that observes from above and is actually able to grasp the full chain of effects of his actions in all their ramifications is the same being responsible for introducing the effect of contingency that makes it impossible for the human observer to do the same. He is a force of chaos but also the standpoint from which to begin to grasp chaos as an integral part of our social space, to grasp aboveground and underground within a single, nonverticalized system.[97]

In the last of his sixty-nine published books, *Éléments de rythmanalyse*, written just before his death at age ninety, Lefebvre formulated the inevitability of contradiction as a mathematical rule of nature. "Absolute repetition is nothing but a fiction," he declared, for, even according to logic, in a sequence of identical terms, each term is distinguished from the other by virtue of its unique place in relation to the other terms in the sequence.[98] Removing the essential insights of deconstruction from the domain of language and grounding them within the natural world, Lefebvre claimed that, just as social relations produce the space in which they exist, the very fact of repetition produces difference: "While there may be difference and distinction, there is neither separation nor abyss between so-called material bodies, living bodies, social bodies, and representations, ideologies, traditions, projects, and utopias. Everything is made up of interacting (and reciprocally influencing) rhythms. These rhythms can be analyzed, but the analyses will never reach an endpoint."[99] "Rhythmanalysis" would be the temporal analogue of the assertion that social realities exist only in space; existing only in space, social realities can be analyzed only in time, and the means of that analysis is through their rhythms.

It is important to stress the historicity that remains for the most part implicit in Lefebvre's theory of rhythmanalysis: it is because the reality of the everyday and its rhythms has not yet wholly been dominated by capitalist space and its rhythms that it remains more readily accessible to the senses, and hence to analysis: "The gaze and the intellect are still able directly to grasp certain aspects, rich in meaning, of our reality: notably, the quotidian and rhythms. Wherever there is an interaction of a place, a time, and an expenditure of energy, there is *rhythm*."[100] Nature has its rhythms of cyclical repetition, the alternation of night and day, always the same but unique each morning; second nature has its rhythms of linear repetition, the abstract, man-made repetition of mechanical reproduction. Both are subject to the same rule of difference, in both the *imprévu*, or unforeseen, will always arrive, but those of nature are easier to observe, and hence to analyze, especially as one of the properties of capitalist repetition is to simulate a temporal inertness, a presence, just as it simulates a spatial inertness.

Because it is a spatial metaphor as well as a material space of difference, the underground is used in both conceptual space and representational space to represent ways in which the everyday is inscribed in social space. "The film lover travels by Underground" reads a London Transport poster of the 1930s; "Métro boulot métro dodo" and "Tube work tube bed" run the postwar mantras of urban anomie in

Paris and London. Whether selling a dream-world spectacle or epitomizing a dreary existence, the trope of being hidden underground actually bestows conceptual visibility onto what would otherwise be obscured in the uniformity of the aboveground world. We represent the everyday as underground in order to be able to recognize it, but what we recognize is a differently coded version of its relation to the world above. In the vertical framework that continues to dominate the conception of modern space, the key component is the threshold, which figures the moments that link aboveground and underground, where what is hidden emerges into visibility, where all three types of space are figured simultaneously, in the closest we find in representation to an image of the spatial triad. In the nineteenth century, the underground was the locus of modernity because it was the material sector in the midst of being developed by capitalism. In the twentieth century, it remained the locus of modernity because of its traditional link to the new sector under development, everyday life, and because, as opposed to the previous century, so much of contemporary everyday life was in fact being conducted in underground conditions.

Seasons in Twentieth-Century Hell

> The ground, the ground beneath our feet. My father the mole could have told Lady Spenta a thing or two about the unsolidity of the ground. The tunnels of pipe and cable, the sunken graveyards, the layered uncertainty of the past. The gaps in the earth through which our history seeps and is at once lost, and retained in metamorphosed form. The underworlds at which we do not dare guess.
>
> SALMAN RUSHDIE, *The Ground beneath Her Feet* (1999)

If the coal mine opened up the city to a broad range of underground metaphors, dominating representations of London and Paris through the nineteenth century, the freewheeling mobilization of language such as we saw in Knox's *Underground* changed fairly rapidly in the early decades of the twentieth century under pressure from the experience of war. Simultaneously, as we saw with Mumford, the underground became newly available as a finely tuned philosophical and sociological category just as it was being transformed into something else in the popular imagination. Now, this is not to say simply that the war rigidified oppression by rigidifying the metaphorics in which it had been expressed. But what I do want to suggest is that by traumatizing such a dominant network of the cultural imagination, the trenches and the greater historical cataclysm embodied by them fixed into place a conception of social stratification that had been materially hastened by wartime changes anyway.

Lefebvre's combination of cyclical and linear repetition suggests an account of historical and cultural change as a dialectic of outmoded and novel forms rather than a modernist supplanting of one product by the next. A metaphor such as George Steiner's characterization of the *entre-deux-guerres* as "a season in hell" from the trenches to Auschwitz, for example, captures in a poetic register the double character of modern culture, caught between the traditional cycle of nature and the unvarying rhythms of modernity.[101] A stress on the second term of "a season in hell" invokes the natural passage of the seasons sardonically, since there *are* no seasons in hell, only an eternity of pain, an endless repetition of punishment for one's sins. At the same time, a stress on the first term recalls the sinful life before conversion, the life cycle of Christianity whereby the pilgrim descends into iniquity before rising into blessedness. Given the oppositional relationship between Christian and Jew during this period, we can assume Steiner employs this second sense ironically as well; indeed, the *katabasis*, or descent to the underworld, was more often invoked ironically than otherwise in modernist literature and art.[102] The broader periodization introduced by the allusion to Arthur Rimbaud's 1873 prose poem, *Une Saison en Enfer*, establishes the diachronic moment of descent into the hell of the twentieth century and implies that some hint of redemption lies in the season that followed 1945, in what Steiner terms "post-culture."

Steiner's argument, as Rosalind Williams has observed, was grounded in a Freudian cultural pessimism wherein repression leads to the resurgence of violent drives. In Steiner's words:

> By ca. 1900 there was a terrible readiness, indeed a thirst for what Yeats was to call the 'blood-dimmed tide.' Outwardly brilliant and serene, *la belle époque* was menacingly overripe. Anarchic compulsions were coming to a critical pitch beneath the garden surface. Note the prophetic images of subterranean danger, of destructive agencies ready to rise from sewerage and cellar, that obsess the literary imagination from the time of Poe and *Les Misérables* to Henry James's *Princess Casamassima*.[103]

With his careful attention to the "images of the past" that "rule us" in the present,[104] Steiner restored a broad metaphorical context to the vertical topography of Freud's theory of the unconscious. For Steiner, the eschatological outlook characteristic of Western culture from 1848 until 1945 was grounded not in the "disappearance of Heaven from active belief" but in the loss of Hell: "It may be that the mutation of Hell into metaphor left a formidable gap in the coordinates of location, of psychological recognition in the Western mind. . . . Of the two, Hell proved the easier to re-create. (The pictures had always been more detailed.)"[105] The "season in hell" was characterized, from the trenches to the concentration camps, by "Hell made immanent . . . the transference of Hell from below the earth to its surface."[106]

If we combine the imaginative leap of Steiner's historical metaphor with the foregoing analysis of space, it emerges that the apparent splintering of underground space and the development of everyday life during the *entre-deux-guerres* constituted in fact a new apprehension of the collapse between underground and aboveground space. During the same decades in which aboveground society had revealed itself in its most explicitly infernal mode yet, underground space was in the process of being rationalized for the aboveground commuter. The world above was being received as if it were an underworld; the world below was being developed as if it were the world above. Steiner powerfully analyzes the apogee of the transformation of the world above in terms of what he calls *l'univers concentrationnaire*,[107] but he duplicates the splinterings of modernism by ignoring its dialectical counterpart in the world below. Moreover, the dialectic cannot be completed without reintroducing a third term, the persistence of earlier, peripheral forms taken by both phenomena long before their manifestation in the cultural center of the middle class analyzed by Steiner.

Already in the sixteenth century we find a Friulian miller known as Menocchio asserting a doctrine with a long prior history in Gnosticism: "The hereafter doesn't exist, future punishment and rewards don't exist, heaven and hell are on earth, the soul is mortal."[108] Beyond the metaphysical refusal of the hereafter, the transference of Hell from the center of the earth had long been an everyday reality for miners and factory workers of the industrialized West. Nothing substantive changed about that reality during the first half of the twentieth century, nor did the conventional identification of the laboring and the criminal classes with the underground disappear. What did change was the introduction of a material underground for the first time into the everyday life of the entire urban population. As opposed to the mines, slums, and factories, the subterranean journey by tube train and métro was not bound to a single class. It simultaneously separated the classes spatially around a central metropolis devoted primarily to business and brought them in much closer contact with each other during the transient space and time of the journey.[109] By the end of the First World War, the experience of the metro was not only an integral part of the transportation infrastructure of nearly every major city, it was a central emblem of its identity, and one could not pretend to be a world city without one: the London Tube, the Paris Métro, the New York Subway all saw the parameters of their mythic images established between the wars.[110] It was not just a joke but a sign of its centrality to Argentinean modernism that Borges once described himself as "librarian, commuter on an urban tramway, and editor of 'A pseudo-scientific magazine called *Urbe*, which was really a promotional organ of a privately owned Buenos Aires subway system.' "[111]

The new urban conditions that had been metaphorically worked through and fought over during the nineteenth century were far more of a fait accompli by the end of the First World War; spatial practice had changed radically, but living conditions for most city dwellers had not. As the historian Paul Thompson has observed, "With the apparent contrast between the prosperity of its new suburbs and the apparently insoluble decay of its inner slums, London around 1900 had already become one of the socially segregated conurbations which were to be characteristic of the mid twentieth-century world."[112] One-sixth of London's population still lived in housing with more than two persons per room; conditions in turn-of-the-century Paris were even more extreme: at thirty-seven thousand persons per square kilometer it was twice as crowded as London, and probably the most densely populated city in the world.[113] The simultaneous rise in the visibility and the segregation of the underclasses and underworld was paralleled by the rise in power of women economically and politically, at least in England, by the rise of a new class, the petite bourgeoisie, somewhere between the working class and the middle class, and by the Russian Revolution and the peaking influence of socialist movements around the world—all phenomena that were readily conceptualized as fears of the underground. As the situation was described in 1909 from the point of view of the middle-class suburban commuter, "Every day, swung high upon embankments or buried deep in tubes underground, he hurries through the region where the creature lives. He gazes darkly from his pleasant hill villa upon the huge and smoky area of tumbled tenements which stretches at his feet. He is dimly distrustful of the forces fermenting in this uncouth laboratory."[114] C. F. G. Masterman portrayed the London Tube as an extension of the view from the hill villa above the infernal city. It was unfortunately an unstable and dangerous extension, and in the "hurry" and "dim distrust" felt by the hill dweller we can catch an anxious response to the new proximity of the "creature," a proximity that was displaced by Masterman onto the familiar verticality of nineteenth-century representations of space.

In its syncopation of natural ("where the creature lives") and technological ("tubes underground") space, Masterman's language retained the characteristic nineteenth-century confusion between natural and man-made undergrounds, as between first and second nature. The intersection of the physical space of sewers and slums by the new technological underworld of roads, tunnels and railways had been a primary preoccupation of representational space in the nineteenth century. Deriving their argument from Bakhtin's structural model of high and low, Peter Stallybrass and Allon White have written a persuasive synchronic analysis of the vertical character of this space: "The vertical axis of the body's top and bottom [was] transcoded through the vertical axis of the city and the sewer and through the horizontal axis of the suburb and the slum or of East End and West End."[115] The analogy between body and city is a crucial component of the expression of natural and man-made space; without a diachronic component, however, there is no way to comprehend its supersession by the images of the mechanized city and body that became central to the representation of modernist space in the twentieth century.

Steiner argued that modern capitalism had found new functions for the metaphysical spaces of Christianity; Bakhtin's theory suggests the Christian body was a similarly charged space in modernity. For Bakhtin, the "material bodily lower stratum" was as much a part of the underworld as Dante's realm of divine punishment. The locus of the discarded past and the unforeseen future, the space of Christian dogma and of everything forbidden by that dogma, from pagan monsters to Roman saturnalia to everyday obscenity, the underworld was the site where contradiction could be expressed rather than repressed, a dynamic force rather than the static bottom of the vertical world. For Bakhtin, it was most important in its identity as threshold, "the junction where the main lines of this system cross each other: carnivals, banquets, fights, beatings, abuses, and curses."[116] The human subject was the "profoundly historical" agent of this subterranean force, through which the highly charged matter of everyday life threatened to burst the constraints of the vertical hierarchy within which representation had contained them. "The images and ideas that fill this vertical world," Bakhtin wrote, "are in their turn filled with a powerful desire to escape this world, to set out along the historically productive horizontal, to be distributed not upward but forward."[117] Bakhtin's model, derived from Dante, is well applied to the newly verticalized hierarchies of the nineteenth-century city. Nevertheless, its overly schematic application of the principle of *le monde à l'envers* has often led (as in the case of Stallybrass and White above) to a simple inversion of surface dogma into underground transgression, echoing the occult maxim that "Diabolus est Deus inversus." "Containment" models, which champion horizontality, inversion, or a ground-level view to counter the top-down representation of space, tend to naturalize verticalized space as a monolithic force rather than to analyze it in conjunction with the view from below as dual components of a representation of space through which cracks are visible throughout, even if those cracks find expression solely as if they were confined to the world below.[118]

The vertical division of the body was a primary point of reference for the verticalization of urban space in the nineteenth century that underlies Bakhtin's theory of the chronotope, but it was, in fact, its wholesale fragmentation that was predominant in the modernist space in which he formulated that theory. The *locus communis* for this fragmentation was the mode of death in the trenches; in them, the body blown to bits became for the first time a routine experience. The factory and the city had already paved the way for this experience, however, through the new kinds of accident caused by mechanization and mechanized traffic, just as gaslight had introduced the nineteenth-century city to the novel possibility of sudden mass death by explosion along with the novel experience of an illuminated night.[119] There are many glimpses of the emergence of this experience in the nineteenth century, but only with modernist topography did the tendency crystallize into imagery either of total fragmentation or of mythic unity: the view from below expanded into the global overview of the view from above or the view from above laid claim to the *katabatic* truth of the view from below. Imagery of mythic unity abstracted the fractured inner and outer space of the trenches into an alienated modernist city, while imagery of fragmentation extrapolated a ruined world out of the material experience of war. We find the former, for example, in the infernal city of Charles Williams's novel, *Descent into Hell* (1937), where the military historian Wentworth flees the ghosts haunting his house in suburban Battle Hill only to find damnation on the Marylebone Road in London: "He was standing on the bottom of the abyss; there remained but a short distance in any method of mortal reckoning for him to take before he came to a more secret pit where there is no measurement because there is no floor. He turned towards the opening and began his last journey."[120] The material counterpart to the metaphysical hell of Williams's "infinite crowd" of London ghosts is evident in the English painter Paul Nash's apocalyptic vision of a wasted battlefield (see figure 4.32):

> Evil and the incarnate fiend alone can be master of this war. . . . Sunset and sunrise are blasphemous, they are mockeries to man, only the black rain out of the bruised and swollen clouds all through the bitter black of night is fit atmosphere in such a land. The rain drives on, the stinking mud becomes more evilly yellow, the shell holes fill up with green-white water, the roads and tracks are covered in inches of slime, the black dying trees ooze and sweat and the shells never cease. They alone plunge overhead, tearing away the rotting tree stumps, striking down horses and mules, annihilating, maiming, maddening, they plunge into the grave which is this land; one huge grave.[121]

This is the nihilistic sliver of the modernist splintering of the multisided nineteenth-century constellation of underground imagery: neither natural nor man made, no space, time, or rhythm, simply "one huge grave." As we will see in chapter 4, this visceral nihilism was readily taken up by the modernist novels of writers such as Céline and Ford Madox Ford, for it incorporated the experience of the trenches into its analysis of the fragmentation of modern life. But the rarified formalism as which high modernism has so long been received remained in fact strongly grounded in an underground metaphorics based in the city, drawn from the trenches and lived through the body.

Modernism, Memory, and Urban Space

> He could reconstruct all his dreams, all his half-dreams. Two or three times he had reconstructed a whole day; he never hesitated but each reconstruction had required a whole day. He told me "I alone have more memories than all mankind has probably had since the world has been the world." And again: "My dreams are like you people's waking hours." And again, toward dawn: "My memory, sir, is like a garbage heap."
>
> JORGE LUIS BORGES, *"Funes the Memorious"* (1944)

The concept of memory was a key source for modernist analogies between the city and the body, a privileged site of philosophical and literary activity, and an important social phenomenon in the years following the First World War. In

Freudian psychoanalysis, in the philosophy of Henri Bergson, in the fiction of Proust, and in the criticism of Benjamin, a sharp vertical distinction was drawn between deep and surface memory, what they respectively termed unconscious and conscious, *temps* and *durée*, involuntary and voluntary memory, and *Erfahrung* and *Erlebnis*. The second term of each pair refers to volitional, everyday memory, what in Lefebvre's language one could relate to linear rhythms and second nature; the first term refers to a deeper, more genuine and affective memory, what one could relate to cyclical rhythms and first nature. These paired definitions of memory were not new, however; what was new was the categorical separation and different valuation of each, the vertical division between an available superficies and a buried, precious core. Volitional memory was first codified as the practice of mnemonics by Cicero in ancient Rome. Its purpose was memorization of the facts of court cases, of poetry for performance, and of other data necessary for professional participation in public life. In other words, it was based on representation, and the public city was the preferred site of memorization, for artificial memory was founded on the mental fixation of images to loci in fixed patterns. Remembering would then take the form of a walk through the city, stopping at each familiar site along the way to retrieve the mnemonic image stored there.

Christine Boyer has suggestively linked the ancient and medieval art of memory to the monumental architecture of the nineteenth-century city epitomized by Napoleon III. His urbanism detached existent landmarks from the cityscape of Paris with which they had previously been intertwined and set new monuments within spacious, geometrically regular squares and places in order to subordinate individual and oppositional memory to official ideology. It thus acted "as a memory walk through the historic monuments and grandiose architectural facades that represented the heroic accomplishments and communal responsibilities of his directorship."[122] Boyer uses the modernist theory of Bergson's student Maurice Halbwachs to distinguish between a conception of memory as programmatic history, and a genuine, "not localizable" memory, which also "unfolds in a spatial framework" but "responds more than it records . . . [and] bursts upon the scene in an unexpected manner, demanding an alteration of established traditions."[123] Boyer is correct to stress Halbwachs's insistence on the rootedness of memory in "concrete social experiences" and its "association with temporal and spatial frameworks . . . linking an individual to family traditions, customs of class, religious beliefs, or specific places."[124] Just as in the Freud-Bergson-Proust-Benjamin model, a distinction was drawn between a degraded, volitional, surface memory and a genuine, involuntary, deep memory; Halbwachs additionally brought out the spatiotemporal dimension and the necessarily social aspect of every memory.[125]

Where Halbwachs remained fundamentally modernist, and where Boyer, in following him, also remains so, to the detriment of her theory, is in the reduction of instrumental memory, what Halbwachs dismissively labeled "history," to "abstract or intellectualized reconstructions, debased or faked recollections."[126] Boyer's distinction provides a nuanced critique of the mythic use of architecture, especially in its older forms, for the purpose of "inventing tradition" through the powerful spatial means of the modern city. Nevertheless, in its historicism, its implication that there is a single specific moment and use for any architectural or other form, that in its original manifestation it is pure, adequate, and new, and that only something equally pure, adequate, and new will answer the exigencies of the current moment, her distinction fails to deal adequately with the complexities of urban space.[127] Boyer's stance is a direct inheritance of modernist polarities: that to each historical moment there must correspond a single, unified artistic school and a particular theoretical program that must be supplanted by something wholly new in the next moment. The investment in the past and in memory as a pristine but endangered locus of buried truth and identity precisely mirrors the modernist investment in nature; both are indelibly rooted in a bourgeois ideology of progressive change and a now outmoded division between high and low culture. Both ignore the fact of uneven development in any given sector of society, the fact that gradual improvement or deterioration is something that affects only a limited class in a limited amount of places. For most people over most of history very little of any significance has changed either for better or for worse. As the historical conditions of modernity that gave rise to this particular ideology of memory recede ever further into the past, it applies to fewer and fewer actual situations.

Just as the capitalist appropriation of everyday life can never be absolute, so the distinction between two types of memory, between life within and life outside of capitalism, between above- and underground, can remain a useful distinction only if it remains dialectical. Something was clearly changing between the wars, and memory was an important site for articulating that change. One especially evocative example of a more dialectical understanding of memory within modernism has been gleaned by the French mathematician and poet Jacques Roubaud from two case studies made between the wars by the Soviet neurologist Alexander Romanovitch Luria. Between the mid-1920s and 1943, Luria encountered two extraordinary extremes of human memory: Shereshevsky, a newspaper reporter who possessed astonishing, apparently limitless, powers of memorization and recall, and Zazetsky, a young soldier whose head wound in the Second World War had left him incapable of apprehending the world around him except by random comparison to a store of memories over which he had no direct access.[128] The two cases present a factual analogue to modernist theories of memory, and an object lesson on the consequences of extricating one from the other.

The technique by which Shereshevsky was able to memorize long sequences of numbers or words and to recall them perfectly even decades later exactly duplicated the ancient and medieval art of memory, except that Shereshevsky developed it sui generis. What is particularly significant about his technique, which becomes evident in his explanation for a rare mistake, is its reliance on a mnemonic city, in this case Moscow, a city in which he can allow no temporal or spatial change: "I had placed the image of this pencil [the word he had forgotten in a sequence] near a fence—you remember, the one that was at the bottom of Gorky Street, where they were doing some repairs. But it was a bit in the shadows and got mixed up with one of the posts, and when I went past it again I didn't see it."[129] Like the plans of a modernist architect or urbanist, Shereshevsky's memory relied on the existence of a Cartesian city; the moment a shadow, a construction site, a threshold to the underground intruded on that space, he would founder. Now, it is instructive to recall that if Shereshevsky's mental city did contain such contradictions, they were infrequent. The cost of such perfection of representation, however, as Roubaud points out, is the poverty of a life in which one cannot forget all of the extraneous nonsense that constitutes everyday life; he was trapped, like Borges's miserable wartime creation Funes the Memorious, in an artificial infinity of second nature, unable to process its patterns in any meaningful way. When one day Luria presented his subject with a list of numbers in standard sequence, Shereshevsky took exactly the same amount of time to memorize them and recall them as if they had been a random selection. So with Funes: "I suspect, however, that he was not very capable of thought. To think is to forget differences, generalize, make abstractions. In the teeming world of Funes, there were only details, almost immediate in their presence."[130] Analogous to the fears of Bergson, Proust, Benjamin, or Halbwachs, and identical to the contemporary city as described by Boyer and Deutsche, his mind was so dominated by instrumental, volitional memory that he was unable to order it in any meaningful or affective way in space or time.

To consider life without the crutch of such an instrumental memory, however, turns out to be equally untenable, as we can witness in the results of the injury to Luria's other subject, Zazetsky. Each time the under-lieutenant left his house, he could never be sure of recognizing even the nearest and most familiar streets. He evidently had a complete store of memories lodged somewhere in his mind, but had not the slightest ability to recall them volitionally or to link them abstractly. Without the art of memory, the memory walk, the *Erlebnis*, all of his deep experience remained inaccessible to him in any systematic, and thus usable, manner. We must conclude, in agreement with the modernists, that there are two types of memory, but, unlike the modernists' assumption, that there are two types of memory without any intrinsic opposition between artifice and nature, between what was superficial and what was genuine, between what would be fixed aboveground and what would be fixed below. Instead, as Roubaud hypothesizes, there exists a natural and necessary complementarity between

> the memory of immediate impressions [*souvenirs*], of the incessant apprehension of the world . . . and the memory that controls impressions, makes connections between

> them and gives them meaning. Without this second memory there can exist no thought, no recognition of memories [*souvenirs*], no strategy for their use in reasoning, no reflective thought. It is true that neither of these two forms of memory can exist entirely without the other, but Shereshevsky and Zazetsky occupy the opposite extremes of the spectrum of their activity.[131]

If in the nineteenth century, as Boyer's analysis of monumental space suggests, capitalism remade the city primarily on the model of volitional, instrumental memory, the modernists' obsessive protection of involuntary memory suggests that its mechanisms were at that point also beginning to be mimicked by capitalism as it expanded the scope of its exploitation of everyday life. The historical necessity behind that assumption is clear in the poignant urgency of so much of modernist writing against alienation and historical amnesia; however, as a particular site of contention, that moment has long since passed. By the last decades of the twentieth century, both top and bottom of the vertical city had been incorporated into the spatial logic of capitalism.

The absolute vision of capital that has emerged from its domination of the underground is a world with no forgetting, no past, only an eternal present of novelty; nevertheless, contradiction enters the moment that change must be factored into the equation, for new thresholds appear more quickly than the old ones can be sealed up. As with Shereshevsky's construction site, forgetting is motivated as well as represented by a passing shadow and a moment of transition: the unforeseen moments in the rhythm of time and space. The modernists made the underground into the privileged site of genuine memory, but it has always also been identified with the necessity of forgetting, of change. This is the half of the dialectic that the situationists, following Marx, identified as the standpoint of the working class, claiming that they would place themselves, "in the service of the necessity of *forgetting*. The only power from which they can expect anything is this proletariat, theoretically without a past, obliged permanently to reinvent everything."[132] These are equally the terms in which Roubaud retells an ancient myth of the classical underworld: "Drinking the waters of the river Lethe in the Underworld, the dead would lose the memory of their terrestrial life, and, according to Plato, before returning to life, the souls, in their turn, would forget everything they had known and seen of the subterranean world."[133] The city streets above may be the locus for the art of memory, but the underworld is the locus for the memory of the soul. To communicate between one and the other, at the threshold, it becomes necessary to forget the soul and to remember the world above. The spatial separation of aboveground and underground is a topographical mnemonic like any other aspect of the art of memory, and a highly effective one, but its divisions should not blind us to the fact that it is a mnemonic based on the symbolic topography of a single social space. Both extremes of the vertical city produce and exist within a triad of perceived, conceived, and lived space;

both are subject to the spatial order of capitalism. The key to the topography is the third space in the triad, the threshold between them, for it figures the ways in which the two spaces overlap and the ways in which they remain fundamentally different. The polarized ways in which modernist culture formulated those differences expressed a new point of conflict in capitalism; present-day society must rediscover within modernism other ways of expression besides those which have persisted as dominant modes within capitalism. The modern underground has undergone a remarkable variety of inflections of what is in fact a quite limited set of narrative and spatial choices, a set of choices governed by the definition of its threshold spaces and divided between variations on a view from above and a view from below. It is the task of an analysis of these spaces and modes of representation neither to lose sight of the strict limitations of the vertical model, nor to ignore the creative ways in which they have nevertheless been appropriated and the brief glimpses of alternate modes of experience that periodically have emerged from them.

2

THE DEVIL COMES TO TOWN

Let this confession serve as a warning to all those who would prefer not to believe how much Satan continues to reign over the pavements of Paris. But I am neither the first to lose myself there, nor the last.

This devil haunts me, citizen-devil with whom I have never signed any sort of pact, but who serves me as if I were going to pay him.

He never ceases to weigh upon me, but I must grant him that, as generous as I could desire, he adroitly guides my curiosity, he raises certain heavy ramparts, he breathes upon the stuffing of Time, abolishes the distance between us, and, with one eye for himself and the other for me, he shows me the proper underside of things: reality.

CLAUDE SEIGNOLLE, *La nuit des Halles* (1930–60)

Since at least the early modern era, Paris has held a particular attraction for the devil. In Jacques Cazotte's novella *Le Diable amoureux* (1772), the eponymous lover, disguised as the beautiful page Biondetta, dreams of taking her beloved Don Alvaro to the center of the world: "It is in Paris, at court, that I should like to see you established. Resources of all kinds will be at your disposal; you will be able to cut whatever figure you choose, and I have unfailing means of ensuring that you would triumph."[1] When we meet Asmodeus, the title character of Le Sage's *Le Diable boiteux*, he has been crippled through a fight with Pillardoc, the demon of compound interest, over the right to corrupt a young man of La Mancha newly arrived in Paris. When Johann Faustus, Johannes Gutenberg's assistant, brought samples of newly printed books to Paris, they were seized and destroyed by the Parlement de Paris, which believed the technology of printing so far beyond human capabilities as to be the work of the Devil. Legend quickly assimilated this Faustus with his alchemist namesake, and told of how the imprisoned printer-sorcerer summoned the devil in order to escape his confinement. Industrial London epitomized the city as modern inferno, but Paris was the devil's chosen seat on this earth. A closer look at the multifaceted nature of the devil's attraction to nineteenth-century Paris elucidates the peculiar changes undergone by both Satan and the city under the pressures of modernity; at the same time, a glance across the Channel at the closely related but fundamentally different ways in which the devil was represented within discourses on London demonstrates why spatiotemporal precision is so essential in literary and cultural studies. A comparative reading of the two discourses uncovers the hidden lineaments of the key role of the devil and his subterranean realm in making sense of the experience of urban modernity.

There are two aspects to the identification of the devil with the City of Light; together, they define what I call the phantasmagoric aspect of the modern devil, the dazzling array of temptations he has to offer. First, there was the widespread belief, as a bored Satan is told at the start of Pierre-Jules Hetzel's compendium, *Le Diable à Paris,* that "il y a de tout à Paris"; that, as Thomas Wallace Knox wrote, it is "the gayest and brightest city in the world" while also possessing "an underground life surpassing that of any other metropolis"; that, in other words, it is the prime location for both satirizing and partaking of the variety of vice and virtue in the modern world.[2] Second, and certainly related to the first aspect, Paris was the seat of novelty and technological innovation, the capital of commodity culture. In the words of one of the contributors to *Le Diable à Paris,* "Nothing new under the sun if not under the sun of Paris."[3] For what other reason did Faustus bring his books first to the court of Louis XI? London and its northern neighbors were the locus for industrial technology and its dark products—coal, gas, iron and steel, printing—and for the dirtier aspects of the money economy (Satan's ambassador in London, the *Dictionnaire Infernal* informs us, was none other than Mammon);[4] Paris was the place to go to enjoy the fruits of that technology, the frivolous results rather than the infernal processes. When the devil goes to London, he is outmatched, fleeced by all and sundry; when he goes to Paris, he becomes a dandy, falls in love, and never leaves.

The devil's dominance of modes of representing both the infernal and the phantasmagoric sides of modernity signifies a subterranean inseparability denied in the world above, for both modes represent the city as if all of it were an underworld, the devil's realm. It is symptomatic of their ostensible separation in the upper world that London and the empire it stood for were conventionally identified with infernal commerce and industry and bereft of any sort of diabolic agency, while Paris emblematized the unbelievable riches produced by that industry and disseminated by Satan and his minions, just as today the glamorous one-world ideology of the global market continues to belie the ever more deeply rooted divisions between wealth and poverty fomented by that very market. Tracing the devil's activity in the urban underground requires working across a greater number of distinct spheres of language and representation than in the case of the more material spatial referents I address in chapters 3 and 4. Consequently, although I do historicize the changing role and status of the devil throughout the century, I have organized the chapter synchronically, rather than diachronically, to emphasize the divergent meanings of the different aspects of the devil's identity and the interplay between the London and Paris versions of those aspects. I begin by defining the infernal and phantasmagoric modes of representing the city as hell, and their relation to Paris, London, and the experience of the nineteenth-century city. I then examine the origins of this imagery in Milton's Pandaemonium and Dante's Dis, the reliance of infernal imagery on the latter and phantasmagoric on the former, and the rooting of both in the changing metropolis. The study of the heyday of satanism in the first half of the nineteenth century has generally focused on literary Romanticism; I address the canonical works in their relation to the much larger corpus of popular and nonliterary manifestations of the phenomenon. The devil and hell were a prominent presence in popular theater and art of the first half of the century in both cities, with the devil's subversive power constrained only by the comic framework in which he customarily appeared. By contrast, there was no comedy in talk of the devil in Paris when it was a question of revolution or of his metaphysical role in modern society; both topics testify instead to an undiminished belief in the supreme power of the archfiend. At the origin of the view from above were panoramic collections such as the *Diable à Paris* and the related genre of the devil in town, where the devil on crutches and his various avatars provide a frame for a portrait of the modern city. The counterpart of the popular culture devil can be found in Baudelaire's midcentury satanism, which provides a retrospective poetic summa of what Max Milner has termed the "golden age of Satanism" and the most sustained meditation in the nineteenth century on the relationship between the material and the metaphorical underground, Paris as simultaneously infernal and phantasmagoric. A proper account of the complexities of Baudelaire's satanism also entails a reckoning with the limitations of Walter Benjamin's influential reading of Paris in his *Arcades Project*, the most sustained meditation to date on the devil (inter alia) in the nineteenth-century metropolis.[5] Even after their initial star faded, the devil vogues persisted in popular culture in London and Paris through the latter half of the century, their meaning changing as the society they depicted was transformed and their currency receded. This process continued during the twentieth century, when the rags and tatters of the devil's days at the height of fashion persisted even as the phenomena addressed through his figure had been rationalized as far as possible and the identity of center and margin had shifted definitively away from the European centers of Paris and London.

The Devil in Paris and London

> Much has been written, from Julius Caesar to our own day, about *la douce France* but no one, I believe, has made the strange discovery about that country which I herewith reveal: France is the promised land of Satan.
>
> GIOVANNI PAPINI, *The Devil: Notes for a Future Diabology* (1955)

While most histories regard the devil as by all rights that most useless and obsolete of past things—an outmoded concept—the obsolescence to which the

Enlightenment hoped to condemn him in fact granted this protean figure a new, highly idiosyncratic and contradictory life. The range of the devil's influence in nineteenth-century French culture, from philosophy to theater, from epic poetry to fashion, from theology to politics, is astonishing, and has been comprehensively documented by Max Milner in his two-volume, thousand-page study, *Le Diable dans la littérature française de Cazotte à Baudelaire 1772–1861*: "Without doubt no figure imposed itself in a more consistent manner on the attention of French writers in the last quarter of the eighteenth and the first half of the nineteenth century than that of Satan."[6] Milner's central, and quite reductive, argument about this influence plots the disappearance of Satan from the realm of religious faith, and his new availability as a metaphysical figure of evil within Romanticism. The reductionism is typical of much scholarship on the Devil, but also of much work on modernity, plotting a unilateral trajectory that is valid as far as it goes, but it does not go far enough, and only ever in a single direction. In particular, what Milner does not discuss—although the sources painstakingly assembled by him can also be made to demonstrate it—is that the devil relocated to Paris as his theological existence began to be contested, and that when he did so he diversified his portfolio in dazzling fashion. The variety of the Devil's manifestations in the nineteenth century was actually greater than anything that had been seen up to that point, and the lion's share of his success came not in metaphysics, but in light drama and in comedy, from razor-sharp satire to broad farce, and in the iconography of capitalism, in advertisement, labeling, and style (figure 2.1). God, only ever susceptible to a single meaning, may have been out of fashion in the new metropolis—Christ, complained Baudelaire, had no tolerance for ambiguity and no appreciation of comedy; he would become angry or tearful, but would never laugh[7]—but the polysemous and ironic devil was the essence of modishness in a secular world.

The Devil's syncretic ability has been with him since his Christian identity was first formulated during the Middle Ages. As I argued in chapter 1, this quality has allowed him to function since medieval times as the locus within capitalist space where belief systems and modes of representation alien or marginal to that space come to be appropriated by it, and through whom the difficult negotiations of that process of appropriation can be seen to be expressed. During the late Middle Ages, the margins were constituted primarily by precapitalist agrarian communities and their pre-Christian beliefs and rituals, assimilated as heresy. The early modern fulcrum of this process was witchcraft; this conflict faded in the eighteenth century along with the dominance of the Church (the last witch was burned in 1782), and the animus her figure had attracted migrated with the devil to the city where it settled onto that new urban pariah, the prostitute. An analogous conflict at the margins was well documented in primarily Roman Catholic regions of the developing world during the twentieth century until at least the 1980s, where the presence of the devil delineated the growing global hold of late-capitalist modes of production.[8]

2.1 The devil in modern capitalism: multifarious, spectacular, and rootless. *John's Marvels* (n.d.).

The dominance by the devil of the modernizing cities of Europe between these two periods followed a similar pattern, but it differed in several ways. First, the marginalized belief system in question was the devil's own: the now outmoded doctrines and rituals of Christianity provided a discourse emptied of fixed meaning but full of cultural and moral resonance that was newly available for negotiating the punishing and unfamiliar spaces of industrialization and for representing the ambivalent pacts required for survival within those spaces. Second, the marginalized groups were those that had been drawn to the cities by the reorganization of labor and manufacturing processes rather than those to whose agrarian communities capitalism had extended its drive to rationalize production. Urban hell, with Satan the evil genius at its center, crystallized in its combination of moral condemnation and dark authority the sublime qualities of an experience that, in fact, had effectively disorientated not only the new proletariat but all save the most sheltered of the ruling classes. To borrow Lefebvre's language: during the nineteenth century, "the devil becomes lord of a demesne: the slums [*bas-fonds*] of the city, the underbelly of society, the underworld of crime."[9] The more material the spaces and experiences were shown to be, however, the more the negative power mobilized by them was diffused out of a proactive Satan into an omnipresent but inchoate force of evil, generally employed as a figure of rhetoric rather than as a character with agency in some manner of narrative. We witness this satanic discourse especially in the marginalized but ongoing theological tradition, in the discourse of revolution and political invective, and in novels of urban crime from Balzac to Hugo to Zola; it is here that we intersect with the perspective of the fiction of urban mysteries and the view from below explored in chapter 3.

Satan's new role was not limited to the personification of a new set of class relations forming out of the ancien régime and the new spaces produced by those relations. He was equally fundamental to the growing awareness of a new form of economic production, the commodity, a new ideology, democracy, and a new form of leisure, the spectacle, all of which rejected the ideological separations of class and the moral dichotomies of religion in favor of an ostensibly universal appeal. In addition to his metaphysical role, then, the devil frequently functioned positively, as a highly visible, fantastic, and slightly sinister but also comic figure under which to group an urban panorama (see figure 1.16). In the view from above, he retained individuality and character but was bereft of his social power as leader of the rebel angels, reduced at best to the seduction and damnation of the odd individual. He was often a court figure in a complex hierarchy of demons, as in the case of Le Sage's *diable boiteux*, associated with a baroque and somewhat antiquated but still dominant system of power. We observe him and his various minions in court intrigues, in upper-class farces (revealed in the end to have been a nonsupernatural masquerade), in the *féeries* and harlequinades of working-class culture, and in urban panoramas, portraits, and physiognomies of the city. Rather than the infernal metropolis of the urban mysteries or of industry, his realm in this manifestation was the glamorous underworld of gambling hells, courtesans, nightlife, and luxury goods. It is here that the visual iconography proliferated, even as the devil also lent an ambivalent undertone to remind the city's inhabitants that all that variety and cornucopia was really nothing more than the old-fashioned vanity of appearances (figure 2.2).

Rather than fixed poles of representation, these two categories frequently overlapped in practice over a broad variety of permutations on the ambivalent figure of the devil. The panoramic overview could range in tone from vicious satire to wholesale affirmation of the ruling classes; the glamorous devil could embody the magical progress of technology or its role in tempting the citizens to damnation; the material tradition might attack oppositional forces as satanic, as when Joseph de Maistre described the National Convention in terms of Milton's

2.2 The phantasmagoric devil. *Théâtre de Satan*. Magic lantern slide, nineteenth century. Collection of the Cinémathèque de France.

Pandaemonium, or, less frequently, embrace them, as when Paul Proudhon asserted to the bishop of Besançon that "liberty, for you, is the devil. . . . Come, Satan, calumnied by priests and kings, come, let me embrace you, let me hold you to my breast!"[10] In a London where potential Catholic dominance had for over a century been more of a political than a religious issue, and where there had been no overturning of the ruling class, the material devil was associated with the corruption and dissolution of the wealthy and the powerful and with a vocabulary that literalized these qualities.[11] Although coined to describe low gambling houses in seventeenth-century Paris, the term was epitomized by the gambling "hells" that dominated the cultural landscape of Regency London.[12] Metaphorical rather than metaphysical, the infernal vocabulary of London was literal and transparent in its usage, just as it was down-to-earth in its application to the technology of printing during the same period. Hells may have been the playground of the wealthy, but devils by the same token were servants rather than tormenters. A "printer's devil" was an errand boy in a printer's office, the lowest in the pecking order.[13] In Regency London, "a *devil* is a small gin-stunted sewing-boy, in frock-coat and top-boots—a lad of *any*-work,—, in olden time called 'a foot-page' . . . and latterly, by the special exclusives, denominated . . . 'a devil.' 'have any of you d—d fellows seen my *devil*?' lisps my Lord."[14] Glamorous dissolution would later be displaced to Paris as London vice was rendered unpronounceable under Victoria, but the division of power was starkly rendered in both cases. In the pandaemonic hells, the "exclusives" played, gently "d—d" by their life of dissolution; in the urban inferno, the poor devils were more literally damned by a life of enslavement to industry, service, the blue ruin of gin, and, more than likely, suffering from the "blue devils," or low spirits, as well.

The ostensibly jocular attitude of Regency writers toward both aspects of the urban underworld is characteristic of the general rule that the closer the devil approached to a truthful representation of the costs of capitalism and a negation of the powers that be, to a material force for change, the more he became either a wholly comic figure or a wholly demonic and barely sentient one, figurehead for the space of hell. Similarly, the devil as character and the materially urban underground seldom came together in nineteenth-century representations; even in Regency guides to London, geographical detail dominated the high life, and less specific comic satire the low. Where they did come together, as in certain manifestations of popular culture and certain works of art, we find ourselves close to the fault lines of modern urban space. Unlike the fictions of urban mysteries and other examples of the view from below, which ground their claims to authenticity directly in the bowels of the urban environment, those texts and images that invoke the devil directly, whether in jest or in all seriousness, generally take the milieu of the social elite, the entire city, or the whole world as their subject and setting. Because the primary myth of the Devil was his role as defined within Catholic Christianity, his presence continued to signify that we inhabit a fallen world (however the term "fallen" might be defined or valued in any particular instance) and thus metaphysically or metaphorically below the level of God and the ideal world, if not physically beneath the earth. That role could be twisted to the perspective of the view from below, but only at the cost of the viewer's soul, that is, of his or her God-given right to be treated as a human being.

Although both the view from above and the view from below foster holistic representations of the city, the latter depicted an opaque city seamed with mysteries and the former a transparently diabolical city. The underground city can at any moment anywhere spill over into the familiar world above; the infernal city is identical to whatever illusory form one might have of anything else, just as Satan occupies the spotlight as the genius at its center. The view from below stresses the representational city of everyday life, fundamentally unreadable and incoherent, the diachronic metropolis of specific crimes, laws, neighborhoods, and events; conversely, the view from above privileges the all-too-readable city of representation, placing its types and its myths within a distancing framework of abstraction or metaphysics rather than employing the emotive devices of the mysteries and other views from below. Just as the urban mysteries combined archaic plotting, morality, and themes with contemporary settings and urban problems, so was the devil, an outmoded figure of myth, appropriated to address a range of current crises rooted in the city, and so did his iconography come to brand the technology and spectacle of capitalism as novel and enticing while warning that in the end it offered nothing more than the same old story of damnation.

The Devil in Urban Hell

From the ball of Saint Paul's he had a full view
Of Commerce, and Industry's sway;
"Oh, would from this point I could act anew,
The scene of my Fortieth day."
The Real Devil's Walk. Not by Professor Porson (1831)

Just as it gave rise to the first unified theories of urban culture and the urban underground, so the period between the wars gave rise to the first theories about the modern devil. The antiurban theorists of the first half of the twentieth century self-consciously carried on the previous century's tradition of demonizing the modern city. For Lewis Mumford, as for Oswald Spengler, Martin Heidegger, and others, "Every man was for himself; and the Devil, if he did not take the hindmost, at least reserved for himself the privilege of building the cities."[15] Alongside this now familiar rhetoric, other (at the time) more marginal figures such as Benjamin, Bakhtin, and the English filmmaker and painter Humphrey

Jennings were invoking the phantasmagoric Satan as a crucial figure of modernity, explicitly making the connection between the Romantic rebel and the comic trickster of popular culture, and seeking to understand the unusual staying power of the imagery of urban hell. For Jennings, the germ of the shift was Milton's depiction of Satan as an infernal industrialist *avant la lettre*:

> The building of Pandaemonium is equated with the industrial revolution and the coming of the machine. . . . Pandaemonium is the Palace of All the Devils. Its building began c.1660. It will never be finished—it has to be transformed into Jerusalem. The building of Pandaemonium is the real history of Britain for the last three hundred years. . . . The first image, and in some sense the origin of all that follow, is the passage toward the end of Book 1 . . . describing the fallen angels setting work to mine, smelt, forge and mould the metals in the soil of hell:
>
> nor aught avail'd him now
> To have built in Heav'n high Towrs; nor did he scape
> By all his Engins, but was headlong sent
> With his industrious crew to build in hell.
> . . . Soon had his crew
> Op'nd into the Hill a spacious wound
> And dig'd out ribs of Gold. Let none admire
> that riches grow in Hell; that soyle may best
> Deserve the pretious bane. And here let those
> Who boast in mortal things, and wondring tel
> of Babel, and the works of Memphian Kings,
> Learn how thir greatest Monuments of Fame,
> And Strength and Art are easily outdone
> By Spirits reprobate, and in an hour. . . . (1.688–97)[16]

Newly contextualized by Jennings, Milton's account of the fall of the rebel angels revealed itself as a richly paradoxical image of the new metropolis (figure 2.3): a place of banishment, but also one where "riches grow," "the pretious bane"; a place of beauty to rival the best achievements of the ancients, but constituted out of suffering, industry, and exile. It would much later be called the industrial sublime, but Jennings was more interested, like Blake and Proudhon before him and like Lefebvre a few decades later, in the working-class identification buried within that language. Satan and his "industrious crew" are miners, artisans, and workmen, failed revolutionaries banished from the face of the earth who nevertheless have succeeded in creating things of beauty in the hell to which they have been consigned.

"Let none admire that riches grow in Hell" is a richly ambivalent imperative. Viewed from above, it warns us not to be deceived by this achievement, but the very admonition informs us that an achievement it remains nonetheless. It was as a portrait of the modern city that Milton's Pandaemonium inspired so many later imaginations, and as an unrepentant rebel that Satan was embraced by the

2.3 *Pandaemonium*: Hell as the modern city. Engraving by John Martin. *The Paradise Lost of Milton* (London: Septimus Prowett, 1827), Book 1, line 110. Georgetown University Libraries, Special Collections.

Romantics. In its ambivalence, the image is distinct from that of Dante's Lucifer, an impotent, three-headed monster frozen into the pit of Cocytus at the bottom of the city of Dis (figure 2.4). Evocations of the Dantesque inferno focus less on the corrupting and creative agency of the Dark Lord than on the fallen nature of the sinners who find themselves within his realm. Dis, with its flaming plains and tortured souls, was commonly used as a metaphor to evoke a nightmare vision of early nineteenth-century industrial England for whom apparently no one was responsible (figure 2.5). In its starkest forms, it was especially suited to the new cities of the north, rising as if ex nihilo and with none of the history or variety that could at times make London phantasmagoric as well—Dickens chose the northern "Coketown" rather than London for *Hard Times,* his most direct condemnation of underground industry, reserving the capital for his intricate and more ambiguous portraits of the city high and low.[17] Robert Napier described Manchester as "the chimney of the world. Rich rascals, poor rogues, drunken ragamuffins and prostitutes form the moral; soot made into paste by rain the physique, and the only view is a long chimney: what a place! The entrance to hell realized."[18] Friedrich von Raumer wrote of Birmingham that "as far as the eye can reach all is black, with coal mines and iron works; and from this gloomy desert rise countless slender pyramidal chimneys, whose flames illumine the earth, while their smoke darkens the heavens"; Alexis de Tocqueville saw in Manchester's river Mersey "the Styx of this new Hades."[19] As with Dante's *Inferno,* the syncretic combination of classical and Christian otherworld imagery is less significant than the overall perspective: this new English cityscape was an irredeemable place to which souls were damned to a life of pain.

Although equally condemnatory in their view from above, infernal visions of Paris were more likely to cut their Dantesque imagery with the local vocabulary of Paris filth. In Auguste Barbier's 1831 poem, "La Cuve" ("The Vat"), this filth and the natural eruption it was used to evoke were simultaneously universal and traceable back to the experience of the city. The echo of Dante's Hell in the "triple circles" of filthy water that enclose the city and the lyric enumeration of versions of natural filth created a powerful image of moral corruption freed of human or supernatural agency and without a trace of the material backdrop of industrialism so evident in the above depictions of Manchester:

> There is, there is on earth an infernal vat:
> It is called Paris; it's a great oven,
> A stone pit of immense dimensions
> That yellow dirty water encloses in triple circles,
> A smoky volcano that never stops respiring,
> And stirs up long waves of human matter;
> A precipice opened onto corruption,
> Into which the muck [*fange*] of every nation descends,
> And which, from time to time, full of a filthy slime [*vase immonde*],
> Bubbling over, flows out over the world.[20]

To be sure, Barbier almost certainly considered the Revolution of 1830 as the historical reference of the vague "from time to time" during which the city poured out its effluvia into the world. The metonymic assumption of the revolutionary crowd into the undifferentiated liquid mass of the *fange* filling up and flowing out of the subterranean recesses of the city is indicative of the poet's claim to distance from the space and events he was describing; conversely, the vitriol of the rhetoric suggests he remained in fact quite close to them.

Such metaphorical condensation would not emerge in the novel until naturalism later in the century, but it was evident earlier on in verse and in such paratextual writing as Balzac's celebrated preface to *La Fille aux yeux d'or* (1833–35): "Few words are needed to assign a physiological cause to the almost infernal tones of Parisian complexions, for it is not only in jest that Paris has been called an inferno [*un enfer*]."[21] Expanding the metaphor into a verticalized panorama, Balzac went on to catalog the "social spheres" of the city by analogy with the circles of Dante's equally verticalized hell.[22] As he concluded his taxonomy of the city's types, Balzac was careful to assert once more that the analogy was no mere conceit, but was based in the physical reality of the city itself:

2.4 Dante's impotent Lucifer, frozen amid damned souls at the bottom of the city of Dis. William Blake, *Lucifer (Inferno, Canto XXXIV)*. National Gallery of Victoria.

> If the air of the houses in which the majority of the middle-class citizens live is foul [*infect*], if the atmosphere of the streets spews out noxious vapours into practically airless back premises, realize that, apart from this pestilence, the forty thousand houses of this great city have their foundations plunged in filth [*baignent leurs pieds en des immondices*] which the authorities have not yet seriously thought of confining within concrete walls capable of preventing the most fetid mire [*la plus fétide boue*] from percolating through the soil, poisoning the wells and making the famous name Lutetia still appropriate, at least underground [*souterrainement*]. Half of Paris sleeps nightly in the putrid exhalations from streets, back-yards and privies.[23]

The nearer Balzac's vantage point took him to the literally lower depths of the city and to the laboring and the criminal poor, the closer his prose approached the fiction of urban mysteries, and its linking of metropolitan improvement with urban crime. Insofar as he remained in the homes of the bourgeoisie, and asserted that their infection emanated from the literal and figurative subsoil of the city as a whole, however, he remained within the register of the infernal panorama, combining topographical precision with a total lack of agency.

There is quite a different underworld evoked when the view, rather than being abstracted on moral and apocalyptic terms, is abstracted as an aesthetic spectacle. A more ambivalent reaction of awe replaces the condemnatory power of sheer vitriol. Writing in the devil's voice, Robert Montgomery could sing the lures of the city even as the framework of his epic poem *Satan* (1830) condemned them:

> Yet well for me, that Town's eventful sphere
> Enchants the many, more than nature can.
> No sound melodious as the roar of streets,
> No sky delightful as the smoky mass
> Above them, like a misty ocean hung.[24]

Although certainly possible in the face of the industrial north of England, such reactions were more amenable, as here, to the hybrid cityscape of modernizing London. Faced with the smog of the capital, the painter Benjamin Haydon received it enthusiastically as a visually evocative subject: "So far from the smoke of London being offensive to me, it has always been to my imagination the sublime canopy that shrouds the City of the World. Drifted by the wind or hanging in gloomy grandeur over the vastness of our Babylon, the sight of it always fills my mind with feelings of energy such as no other spectacle could inspire."[25] On a visit to the excavation works of the Thames Tunnel in London in 1827, the actress Fanny Kemble saw "the most striking picture you can conceive . . . with the red, murky light of links and lanterns flashing and flickering about. . . . As we returned I remained at the bottom of the stairs last of all, to look back on the beautiful road to Hades."[26] Kemble's perceptions were most likely colored by John Martin's famous 1825 mezzotint of the Bridge over Chaos at the entrance to

2.5 *Lambeth Gas Works*: the iconography of urban hell. Illustration by Gustave Doré, in *London: A Pilgrimage*, by Doré and Blanchard Jerrold (London: Grace and Co., 1872), 40/41.

Pandaemonium, which incorporated an image of the Thames Tunnel into its conception (figure 2.6).[27] Imagery of Dis conjured up a damned city without a head in which no sane person would possibly live; Pandaemonium is an infernal place that nevertheless remains inhabitable, its genius loci a proactive force, whether for good or for ill.

2.6 *The Bridge over Chaos*: Miltonic myth meets contemporary engineering. Engraving by John Martin. *The Paradise Lost of Milton* (London: Septimus Prowett, 1827), Book 10, lines 312–47. Georgetown University Libraries, Special Collections.

The ambivalence of the recourse to the sublime is the surface manifestation of the contradiction embodied in these new spaces. The basis of this contradiction is evident earlier on, in William Beckford's twin reactions to modernity: the subterranean hell of his Oriental tale *Vathek* (1782), and the fantastic spectacle staged for him at his estate. In *Vathek*, the eponymous caliph and his consort Nouronihar are trapped deep underground in the labyrinthine prison-palace of Eblis (a Muslim devil), surrounded by the riches they longed to possess, but doomed for eternity to wander the endless corridors, forever passing by the myriad other tortured souls, each one wholly consumed by an eternal flame of perdition burning in its heart: "A vast multitude was incessantly passing . . . they had all the livid paleness of death. Their eyes, deep sunk in their sockets, resembled those phosphoric meteors that glimmer by night in places of interment. . . . They all avoided each other; and, though surrounded by a multitude that no one could number, each wandered at random unheedful of the rest, as if alone on a desert where no foot had trodden."[28] Yet this dark image of damnation to an infernal and Piranesian dungeon was inspired by a phantasmagoric lighting display staged by the London-based artist, scenographer, and painter of "moving pictures" Philippe Jacques de Loutherbourg at Beckford's estate Fonthill for a select and libertine assembly of Christmas guests in 1781:

> I still feel warmed and irradiated by the recollections of that strange, necromantic light which Loutherbourg had thrown over what absolutely appeared a realm of Fairy, or rather, perhaps, a Demon Temple deep beneath the earth set apart for tremendous mysteries—and yet how soft, how genial was this quiet light. . . . The glowing haze investing every object, the mystic look, the vastness, the intricacy of this vaulted labyrinth occasioned so bewildering an effect that it became impossible for any one to define—at the moment—where he stood, where he had been, or to whither he was wandering—such was the confusion—the perplexity so many illuminated storys of infinitely varied apartments gave rise to. It was, in short, the realization of romance in its most extravagant intensity. No wonder such scenery inspired the description of the Halls of Eblis. I composed *Vathek* immediately upon my return to town thoroughly embued with all that passed at Fonthill during this voluptuous festival.[29]

As Rosalind Williams has astutely observed, the space in which the despotic and decadent Vathek is damned and the space in which Beckford and his companions celebrated his twenty-first birthday are closely related in every way except for the diametrically opposed reaction. The creation of a paradise by artificial means gave way to the vision of an inorganic environment of hell.[30]

It seems equally significant that the spectacular party was staged at Beckford's Wiltshire estate, while the infernal story was composed in London, just as it is significant that the country-house party with a select company became transmuted into an anonymous and damned urban crowd. There is no perfect separation between the two types of space, however. The palace of Eblis retains all the trappings of the Fonthill feast: vast numbers of tables covered with choice viands and sparkling crystal, magical and lascivious dancing by beautiful djinns and other "gay spirits," all the treasures of the pre-Adamite kings, and even a devil, Eblis, with the noble traits of a handsome man of twenty. Yet, all is changed by the urban consciousness of the damnation that is the price of possession of these wonders: Eblis's features appear as if "tarnished by malignant vapours" and his eyes are haunted by despair and pride;[31] once they know that they are to share the fate of the suffering hordes around them, Vathek and Nouronihar are unable to avert their eyes any longer. The mystery of the artificial wonders of Fonthill was revealed not in the secrets of Loutherbourg's magical techniques but in the bad conscience of the social cost of those techniques. The transformation of the Fonthill *féerie* into the infernal, alienated city is wrought by a devil whose powers of damnation were equally a force of social justice. The gothic genre proper in its country-house setting was primarily concerned with the "rationalized supernatural," apparently devilish occurrences caused in fact by human villainy. By contrast, *Vathek*'s subterranean vision of the urban crowd answered the same question not rationally but by transporting the isolated supernatural to its proper social sphere in the infernal city. Parodies of the gothic genre on the stage in Paris and London during this period followed a similar strategy, using the techniques and trickery of artist-technicians such as Loutherbourg to restore the devil to his proper seat in the city as a properly supernatural figure.[32] The two reactions show all the traces of Pandaemonium and Dis, respectively: a phantasmagoria masterfully created by a technological genius, supernatural yet harmless if not actively benevolent; and an inferno presided over by a devil so remote and so modern in temperament he does not even participate in the punishment of the damned.

The aestheticizing gaze that permitted later artist-spectators such as Haydon and Kemble to find beauty in the modernizing city without being crippled by guilt demonstrates the palliative effect of the infernal trope. Still, although it softens the outright horror of the place, it also combines the shock of an underworld vision with an attempt to represent it on its own terms rather than purely on those of a view from without. It suggested one way, at least, to reconcile the compelling promise of technology with the appalling human cost of its fulfillment. The light from coal gas, for example, wrought a transformation both on the bourgeois interior, "a light hauled up from caverns bored into the bowels of the earth, even if mineral coal did not shine with a crystal shimmer like that fairy diamond but had to be combusted to release the luminous gas . . . light from darkness, wrested from the night by a different magic, namely chemistry," and on the urban exterior, where gas lighting began to be installed during the first decades of the century.[33] While gaslight produced a magical effect, "enrich[ing] our festivities (aside from its infinite importance for the needs of life)," it was equally a further source of class exploitation and separation: "Nothing . . . can make an area, a locale poorer and the sight of it more dreadful than the absence of the transfiguring element; and nothing provoked the bitterness of the poor so sharply as the nimbuses of bouquets and sun-burners, the glitter of 'diamonds' at a nocturnal festivity in the halls of the rich."[34] Not only were the laboring classes forced to work deep in the earth to provide heating and lighting for the cities above, but their living quarters began to seem more and more literally subterranean by contrast with the increasingly luminous quarters of the wealthy. While producing spectacular visual (and aural) effects, artificial lighting also helped illuminate the distinction between classes. As Bob Logic put it to the naïve country visitor Jerry in one of the many theatrical adaptations of *Life in London*, "There's no occasion for candles, the gas throws such a light upon every subject, that many are enlightened subjects who are dark as Erebus."[35] It is a rule of modernity that the more sophisticated technology becomes, the more sharply its absence is felt. The popular spectacle and the figure of the devil within it offered a properly lower-class appropriation of the technology otherwise claimed solely for the world above. Paris and London not only provided the most striking examples of social extremes in close proximity, of the most primitive with the most advanced, they combined the most horrible with the most alluring aspects of the new technology in the spectacles they created for all classes both on their streets and in their shops and theaters.

Gaslight was introduced earlier to London, which had twenty-six miles of gas mains by 1815, than to Paris, but there too the technology was rapidly accepted:

from 203 street lamps in 1835 to 12,866 just four years later. It seems likely that the various devil vogues, as in the case of other changes in underground metaphorics, were related to this technological lag—darkness and fire were after all Satan's natural environment. As Joachim Schlör has observed, the development of street lighting was essential to the development of the nightlife of urban spectacle made possible by artificial illumination, as well as to the development of a genuine conception of night as such.[36] And indeed, the first street in the world to be lit by gas was Pall Mall (in 1807), the center of the clubs and hells of swell London. As Lord Byron wrote in *Don Juan* (1819–24), a key work of Romantic satanism, describing his hero's first impression of London:

> The line of lights, too, up to Charing Cross,
> Pall Mall, and so forth, have a coruscation
> Like gold as in comparison to dross,
> Match'd with the Continent's illumination,
> Whose cities Night by no means deigns to gloss.
> The French were not yet a lamp-lighting nation,
> And when they grew so—on their new-found lantern,
> Instead of wicks, they made a wicked man turn.[37]

Don Juan goes on to add that if Diogenes were unable to find an honest man in London, " 'Twere not for want of lamps," as he rattles up Pall Mall past "St. James's Palace and St. James's 'Hells.' "[38] Although the technology was resolutely English, the imagery with which to make sense of that technology was being imported from the Continent.

The novelty of gaslight and the new visibility it gave to London high life produced a dizzying effect far different from the shock elicited by the appalling conditions to the north. Herman Melville's Redburn thinks Liverpool a "coal-hole" when set beside an "unreal" London: "Whirled along through boundless landscapes of villages, and meadows, and parks: and over arching viaducts, and through wonderful tunnels; till, half delirious with excitement, I found myself dropped down in the evening among the gas-lights, under a great roof in Euston Square. London at last, and in the West-End!"[39] At the heart of this delirium of modernity—viaducts, tunnels, stations—lies one of Saint James's hells, "some semi-public place of opulent entertainment," that gives the lie to the "metropolitan magnificence," with a marble floor that "echoed to the tread, as if all the Paris Catacombes were underneath. I started with misgivings at that hollow, boding sound, which seemed sighing with a subterraneous despair, through all the magnificent spectacle around me; mocking it, where most it glared. . . . and I thought to myself, that though gilded and golden, the serpent of vice is a serpent still."[40] By the time of this whirlwind one-night visit in 1839, however, the high and low of the nocturnal underground had in fact been strictly delineated; that same year, the Metropolitan Police Act had forbidden prostitutes to loiter in public places. Meanwhile, the material sites of production of

2.7 The devil of commerce. *The Stockmarket in the Underworld.* Magic lantern slide, nineteenth century. Collection of the Cinémathèque de France.

gaslight had replaced the metaphorical underworld of Regency high life as the primary counterpoint for its nighttime dazzle. As Lynda Nead has argued, by 1840 the gasworks formed "a new sublime landscape within the metropolis"; there were twenty-three manufacturing works and six gasholder stations within the metropolis by the 1860s.[41] To be sure, London was no less infernal than it had been, but the heady first decades of rampant possibility had settled into a new consensus of representation in which morality dictated the expulsion of Satan from the confines of the metropolis. Victorian hell was Dantesque, its view from above stressed realism and authority, and its devils spoke French, performed few tricks, and seldom strayed from the boards of the theater and the pages of the serial novels.

As the predominant figure of power relegated to the world below, Satan's retention of agency emblematized the distinction between the Dantean and the Miltonic models of urban hell. In a note to his *Arcades Project*, Benjamin observed that the relation between art and technics underwent a significant change in Europe during the nineteenth century, as art was no longer able to keep up with technology, no longer able to "take its time" to assess and incorporate the new possibilities of new material, in both senses of the word. While the twentieth century raised the possibility "that art could no longer find the time to insert itself somehow in the technological process," in the nineteenth century art could still be found "breathlessly" trying to keep up.[42] The popular spectacle at the center of which the devil found himself, the frantic assimilation of diabolical motifs into every medium and genre of urban life, and, indeed, the devil's reputation as a soul doomed to wander endlessly the trackless earth: all of these can be seen to appropriate the devil as a figure of this new need for hurry, the stopgap measure in the face of an inability to process so much new information (figure 2.7). As Hans Christian Andersen wrote in his diary in 1840 on the experience of railway travel, "Mephistopheles could not fly more quickly with Faust in his cloak. By natural means we are, in our day, as powerful as in the Middle Ages man thought only the devil could be."[43] Within the commodity culture of nineteenth-century Paris and the representation of that culture across the Channel in London, the old proverb "Idle hands are the devil's playground" took on a renewed meaning for the modern world.

Spectacles of the Metropolitan Devil

Orphée: I've heard, you know, Offenbach's blare
And I'm fluent in Meilhac's French.
I've kept up to date, and the sign
Of my modernity is that Eurydice,
When newer charms are offered me,
Seems, by Pluto! fine down in hell.

MARCEL BELIARD, *Orphée et Pierrot, fantaisie en un acte* (1902)

At a cusp between universal acceptance of their existence and a loosening of the traditional confines of their identities, Satan and his subterranean capital offered the nineteenth century a powerful combination of the concrete with the fantastic. The infernal allure of novelty was manifested in the scenic representation of the underworld as well as in the personification of the devil as a monarch who came to the city in search of new sensations. The lingering metaphysical associations lent an added frisson to whatever new form the set designers, special-effects technicians, writers, and players presented to their public each season. Several prerevolutionary Parisian plays had staged *Paradise Lost* as a mechanical pantomime, one recounting the entire epic, another limiting itself to three acts: the fall of the rebel angels, the building of Pandaemonium and the infernal council, concluding with the departure for the assault on Heaven.[44] In London, Pandaemonium was one of a very few noncontemporary, real-life topographical subjects depicted in panoramas. The tableau of "Satan arraying his Troops on the Banks of the Fiery Lake, with the Raising of Pandemonium, from Milton" was given especial praise in reviews of Loutherbourg's *Eidosphusikon*, a late eighteenth-century combination of clockwork moving pictures, transparencies, concentrated light, sound, and color. Another view of Pandaemonium, in Burford's panorama of 1827, was singled out for criticism by the *Athenaeum*, which regarded its "picture of the capital of Satan, somewhat in the style of Martin," as overly "historical," the actions of the figures overwhelming "the view of the infernal abyss" which should take precedence in the pictorial genre of the panorama.[45] Its popularity is testified by a satirical poem of the time, in which, on a visit to London, the devil took in the sights:

> He then went to see Pandemonium,
> As BURFORD portrays it on earth;
> And it pleas'd him to see the thousands come,
> As packet passengers are known to run,
> To examine, before-hand, their berth.[46]

In both the Dantean and the Miltonic discourses, the devil is equated to technology and invention; what distinguishes the vision of Pandaemonium from the vision of Dis is that, paradoxically enough, it portrays a technology in the service of man, if at an eventually eternal cost, rather than as his oppressor. The fallen Lucifer is frozen into immobility at the center of Dante's Hell, his wings providing a preindustrial mechanism to freeze the lake surrounding him; Satan and his minions in Pandaemonium are industrious and full of productive energy, providing wonders and entertainment along with the requisite temptations (see figures 2.3 and 2.4).

The devil, modern stagecraft, and the underground have been intertwined since their inception.[47] The English pantomime is said to have developed out of the "ho ho ho" of the medieval mystery-play devil and the elaborate spectacle centered around Hellmouth, the entrance to his realm:

> What is now called the stage did then consist of three several platforms or stages, raised one above the other. . . . On one side of this lowest platform was the resemblance of a dark pitchy cavern, from whence issued appearance of fire and flames. . . . From this yawning cave the devils themselves constantly ascended, to delight and instruct the spectators. . . . Hell was imitated by a whale's open jaws, behind which a fire was lighted, in such a way, however, so as not to injure the 'damned,' who had to pass into its gaping mouth.[48]

Often the production's most expensive prop, the Hellmouth could be as much as nine feet wide, sometimes remained present as a visual symbol during the entire history of the world from Creation to the Last Judgment, and was usually introduced with an irreverent burst of diableries, or antics, counter to the more serious depictions seen in other forms of the hellmouth (figure 2.8).[49] Harlequin began life as a German demon, brought into the puppet theater of the commedia dell'arte that developed when "religious" devils were banned from the Italian stage.[50] Several of the first London pantomimes were based on explicitly infernal themes: John Weaver's *Orpheus and Eurydice* (1718), and John Rich's *The Necromancer, or Harlequin Dr. Faustus* (1723) and *Harlequin Sorcerer* (1724–25). The nineteenth-century pantomime blended otherworldly spaces, loosely derived from the infernal models, with recognizable elements of the contemporary cityscape. It was divided into two parts: a fantastic story, very loosely based on fairy tale or legend, and frequently set in a magical subterranean or subaqueous kingdom (figure 2.9), concluding in a spectacular scene in which the main characters were transformed into the stock figures of Harlequin, Columbine, Clown, and Pantaloon, leading to the harlequinade, a series of brief comic sketches frequently set in contemporary London locales. In schematic form, we find in the first part the underground realm of the devil providing the setting for plot difficulties, wild variations on familiar melodramatic or comedic situations; once posed, these difficulties are resolved with the wave of a fairy wand, as the scene is transferred to the London streets, and then played out in the pure comic mayhem of the harlequinade (figure 2.10).

In the puppet London of the early nineteenth-century Punch-and-Judy shows, Punch reveled in an anarchic power that bedevils even Satan:

> Punch . . . throws the baby from the window, and kills in turn his wife Judy, the dog Toby, and frequently a servant. Jack Ketch (sometimes called Mr. Graball) takes Punch to Newgate, sets up the gallows, and calls him to come out and be hanged. But the indestructible Punch is too wily for that. He must be shown what to do; and when Jack Ketch sticks his own head in the noose, Punch hangs the hangman. He completes his triumph by killing the Devil, who has come to claim him.[51]

Baudelaire recounts a similar episode in a London pantomime on tour in Paris. In the concluding scene, modified from the usual death by hanging for the benefit of the French audience, Pierrot (Punch) is to be guillotined: "After struggling and bellowing like an ox that smells the slaughterhouse, Pierrot finally suffers his fate. His head came away from his neck, a big white and red head, rolling down with a thump in front of the prompter's box and exposing the bleeding neck, split vertebrae and all the details of a piece of butcher's meat, just cut up for the shop window."[52] Out of a scene of brutal and visceral realism emerges the moment of comic triumph over death: "And then suddenly the truncated torso, driven by the irresistible monomania of thieving, got up, triumphantly filched its

2.8 A medieval hellmouth in the lower right-hand side of a Last Judgment. Detail of the portal of the church of Conques (Averyon). In *L'Art religieux du XIIe siècle en France*, by Emile Mâle (Paris: Armand Colin, 1922). Fig. 235.

own head, like a ham or a bottle of wine, and, being shrewder than the great St Denis, rammed it into his pocket!"[53] This is pure satanic humor, a celebration of rebellion that resolves itself into an affirmation of the right to one's own life, Pierrot reclaiming his head. Baudelaire's concluding simile elaborated that affirmation into an assertion of the requirements of a tolerable life: not just one's head, but also a joint of ham and a bottle of wine.

Such a rendering of lower-class chaos in the city streets could be represented only in the codified, unreal form of popular comedy. The popular devil traded on the purported harmlessness of humor. As one of the songs put it in rhyming quatrains in a summary of some of the many "devil" vogues up to 1844 in *Le Diable à Paris*, a boudoir comedy of the lower classes staged at the Théâtre de Beaumarchais on the boulevard of the same name:

> CHORUS: Long live the Devil! that sharp and lively spirit,
> How he knows how to please and imp about!
> In the studio, the salon, and on the stage,
> At this moment Lucifer is everywhere.
>
> MOUFFLOT: But perhaps it is wrong to accuse us
> Of celebrating him more than ever,
> He has always had, if I am not wrong,
> His greatest successes here in Paris:
> You remember, I hope, the *Diable à quatre*,
> A female demon who pinched snuff,
> Lord have mercy, all day long,

2.9 *The Gnome King and the Fairy of the Silver Mine," at the Queen's Theatre*: a typical pantomime plot and setting. Engraving by C. R. in *Illustrated London News*, 2 January 1869, 5.

And did it just to upset her husband.
At the Cirque we took *Les Pilules du Diable*;
Then from LeSage, author of *Turcaret*,
The Opera performed without scruples
A ballet of *Le Diable boiteux*.
Robert le Diable,
La Part du Diable,
And *Le Diable Amoureux*; and then
They did *Les Mémoires du Diable*;
And finally *Le Diable à Paris*.
(to the audience)
But would that from the charming *Devil in Paris*
When we offer its title here to you
Oh! Would that, by the power of the Devil
We can have a hell of a success![54]

The often execrable puns and fake-naughty innuendo (a running joke of London's *Orpheus in the Haymarket* was that the words "Hell" and "Devil" could not be pronounced in front of the polite company at the theater) played in mild fashion on the ambiguity of the Devil and the equally ambivalent demimonde of theater itself.

2.10 The conventions of pantomime applied to the boarding school: Harlequin consigning academic monsters to the world below. F. Elder, *The Schoolboy's Notion of What a Christmas Pantomime Ought to Be*, in *Illustrated London News*, 21 December 1867, 692.

The players might be damned, but they would obtain their "succès d'enfer" come hell or high water.

Still, as Baudelaire put it, the comic per se "is a damnable element of diabolical origin."[55] When the same humor wandered beyond its proper context, it continued to generate fear as well as laughter. During an eighteenth-century performance of *Harlequin Sorcerer*, a practical joke was played on the Christian credulity of the players. An extra actor appeared in the middle of "a dance of infernals," and was mistaken for "the principal fiend":

> A general panic ensued, and the whole group fled different ways; some to their dressing-rooms, and others, through the streets, to their own homes, in order to avoid the destruction which they believed to be coming upon them, for the profane mockery they had been guilty of. The odd devil was *non inventus*. He took himself invisibly away, through fears of another kind. He was, however, seen by many, in imagination, to fly through the roof of the house, and they fancied themselves almost suffocated by the stench he had left behind. . . . So thoroughly was its reality believed that every official assurance which could be made the following day did not entirely counteract the idea.[56]

Whether in truth or in jest, the fantasy and the reality of the underworld are easily manipulated. A review of an 1869 production of *Orphée aux enfers* at the St. James's Theatre in London reported an analogous incident in which the material danger of the stage flames of hell still seemed to hold a superstitious hint of extra peril, especially when originating from the Continent: "A certain fiery misfortune seems to attach itself to the French plays. A gas explosion took place the other day, and frightened poor Mdlle. Schneider and the ladies of the ballet out of their wits. . . . Those who have witnessed the *grand finale* of the bacchanalian scene which concludes the *Orphée aux enfers* will readily understand that Mdlle Schneider nightly runs a great risk of being roasted."[57] The gas jets, a "fitting and proper . . . representation of the lower regions," surrounded the diva and nearly set her costume alight. Just as acting the role of the devil bore a fear of punishment for "profane mockery" distinct from standard risks of playacting, so would the later descents of sensation drama into the lower depths of society provide an especially potent combination of the shock of the other and the thrill of the familiar.

The Parisian *féeries* and diableries were similarly dependent on trick effects and set design to depict the effect of a reliable world and physical laws gone haywire. An eminently popular genre, the *féerie* clearly positioned the audience on the side of the devil rather than the customarily middle-class victim, even if the devil here was present only in his titular responsibility for the mayhem and in his metaphorical association with the wizardry of the stagecraft that brought the mayhem to life. Who else but the devil could have been responsible for the sadistic torture inflicted on the hapless bourgeois protagonists of these spectacles? Here, for example, is John McCormick's account of *Les Pilules du diable* (1839), one of the most popular *féeries* of the century, where we find:

> a dazzling array of tricks, of which the central character, Seringuinos, was generally the victim. When he wished to go to sleep, chairs collapsed under him, or turned into ladders, hoisting him aloft, beds became baths or wells, and even the walls retreated as he leant on them. Portraits stole drinks. A railway carriage exploded, scattering Seringuinos into many pieces (which were subsequently brought together—allowing for a comic scene involving an arm that had been forgotten). When Seringuinos retired to a sanitorium for a rest, immediately all the windows flew open, and at every one somebody was seen carrying out an exceptionally noisy trade. A ride in a carriage resulted in the horses driving off with the front portion, the back wheels removing themselves and the part where Seringuinos was seated turning into a well. Another house in which he seeks peace turned out to be upside down, and he ended up having to walk on his hands. The frequent scene changes also made their contribution to the hectic pace of *Les Pilules* and created a sense of a world in which nothing is stable.[58]

The pleasure was derived from the combination of a skilled manipulation of novel technology and the unchanging familiarity of characters, situations, and jokes to create an atmosphere of fantastic mayhem realistically rendered.

While the diablerie, the *féerie*, the pantomime, and the Punch-and-Judy show celebrated the anarchic magic of the Devil, most satires and plays with Parisian settings treated of what Milner terms "le surnaturel appliqué" ("the rationalized supernatural"). Here, Satan framed a satirical view from above, with the pretense to supernatural power permitting a panorama of Parisian society. There was some justification, then, for the claim made by the editor of the most influential of the urban panoramas, *Le Diable à Paris*, that the current vogue had been prompted by its success in serial publication, and that each play had been written by one of the many demons sent by Satan to find the wayward Flammèche, his undermotivated Parisian correspondent: "Some of them found a home at the vaudeville, where they tried to do Flammèche a bad turn by stealing the title of his book; others, under various names, scattered through the diverse theaters of Paris, which were inundated in the blink of an eye with a flood of masterpieces where the devil naturally had the best part.—The count rose to seventeen of them."[59] Contrary to this assertion, however, the only supernatural elements in most of these plays and panoramas were reflections of modern technology: Frédéric Soulié's *Les Mémoires du Diable* used a magic lantern to expose the foibles of modern society, a motif copied in a series of *Lettres Infernales* (1843); the eponymous hero of Alfred Le Poittevin's *Une Promenade de Bélial* (ca. 1849) used a magic mirror to uncover the secrets of Parisian society. By the end, the authorizing figure was usually revealed to be a mere mortal, as in Antoine-Jean-Baptiste Simonnin and François Llaunet's *Le Diable à Paris* (1844), Louis François Clairville and É. Damarin's *Satan, ou Le Diable à Paris* (1844), adapted to the London stage by Charles Selby in the same year as *The Mysterious Stranger*, and Roger de Beauvoir and Lambert Thiboust's *Les Enfers de Paris* (1853). Although the motive for disguise was generally to reform a wayward soul, it also granted an unwonted freedom to the protagonist, especially when she was female. In *Les Enfers de Paris*, for example, Geneviève's Devil garb allows her entry into a wild party at the celebrated Café Anglais: "Here I am in Paris," she says, "where I have my little devils (*looking at the women*), female devils who work for me."[60] S/he takes a box at the Opéra, goes to see the cancan, visits the Musard and La Maison d'Or, and, in a demonstration of her tenet that "one damns oneself there so gently," breaks into a song about Paris as hell and the hells of Paris:

> Paris! you alone rule,
>   Lucifer!
> Paris!—the premier grotto
>   Of Hell! . . .
> This boudoir, where the gold of these ladies
>   Awaits you! . . .
> This palace of silk and flames . . .
>   It's Satan! . . .
> And there they are, my friends,
>   The Hells of Paris![61]

The pretend Satan provided a link between the dual theatrical necessities of plot and spectacle, between the love story and the tour of the city—the Asmodeus flight on the boards of the theater.

The frequency with which virtuous women played the devil role is striking. Like the moralization, however, the character's force in this genre was extremely diffused, and tightly interwoven with the traditional misogynistic trope that "the Lady and the Devil are very old acquaintances! . . . The Devil is not only the '*father of lies*,' but of a large family; his progeny being principally in petticoats"[62] (figure 2.11). Unlike supernatural temptresses in the late eighteenth century such as Cazotte's eponymous *Diable amoureux* or Mathilda in Matthew Lewis's gothic novel, *The Monk* (1796), these mid-nineteenth-century bourgeoises in disguise were neither immoral nor perilous beyond the narrow confines of the drawing room. The devil's guise was assumed only long enough to set the wandering men back on the proper path; seldom do we glimpse either a temptation to abuse the power of the disguise or any difficulty arising from its identity.

The London stage tended toward more realistic and businesslike inventions and settings. In the 1866 pantomime *The Devil on Two Sticks; or, Harlequin the Golden Tree Bird & Apple*, very loosely based on Le Sage, Asmodeus pleads for his freedom in quintessentially modern terms, concluding with a punning equation of his Luciferian identity with the vagaries of the stock market:

> I'm an exhibition of industry
> In the Crystal Palace—isn't it a lark. . . .
> Ah! a change all my frame comes over

I'm a railway share—London Chatham & Dover
I'm down to 95 below par—
Who'll take me up—for I'm a fallen star.[63]

One of the key technologies with which the Devil was connected is printing (figure 2.12). In *The Devil and Doctor Faustus*, an 1841 version of the Faust-as-printer myth, the satanic pact takes the form of a journey through time to present-day London to observe the progress of the printing press.[64] Because of its toleration of a radical press, London was frequently identified with the more infernal products of print culture. In *The Printer's Devil; or, A Type of the Old One* (1832), a supernatural adaptation of William Hogarth's engraving *The Idle Apprentice*, Old Nick finds that his disguise as an errand boy in a printer's office—and by extension as printed matter—gives him unquestioned access to households all over the city: "I lurk upon a lady's couch in the light form of a voluptuous novel, get under the patriot's pillow as a violent pamphlet against all order. Entertain a politician at his breakfast as a newspaper, & mislead the people as an inflammatory placard or a puffing playbill. Of all the Devil's machines, the printing press is the most useful."[65] James Robinson Planché's *The Printer's Devil* (1838) made the political connection even more explicit, setting its action in Versailles the years before the Revolution of 1789.[66] The farce revolves around the hiring of a Paris printer's devil from the unruly Faubourg Saint-Antoine by the Royal Printing Office at Versailles. This step up the ladder endangers the supposedly royalist Count de Maurepas, who had used the low-market devil to print inflammatory pamphlets under a pseudonym. The comic equation of Satan with the printing press again updates an antiquated figure through modern technology. The juxtaposition is humorous, of course, but significant nonetheless, as the devil figure continues to assert both moral truths—the idle apprentice eventually resists his temptations—and political power. Nor in the comic format is one ever able to take him seriously enough to be persuaded that he is entirely evil.

It is instructive to compare these comic variations on the topos of London as the home of the devil of dirt, business, and industry with William Blake's radical appropriation of the same topos by taking its components literally. Himself no stranger to the radical publishing world through his friendship with Joseph Johnson and his circle, Blake had a very special printer's devil through whose eyes the world was made legible in its "infernal or diabolical sense."[67] "I was in a Printing House in Hell," Blake wrote of his "Memorable Fancy," "& saw the method in which knowledge is transmitted from generation to generation."[68] An engraver by trade printing his own books in Lambeth in southern London, Blake

Facing page

2.11 Satan in the drawing room: *Une Jolie Diablesse*. Nineteenth-century illustration.

2.12 The devil as printer: *Blue Stocking Hall.* Robert Cruikshank, *The Devil's Visit: a Poem from the Original Manuscript, with notes by a barrister* (London: William Kidd, 1830), 25.

contrasted his materialist visions of an other world with the pernicious abstractions of Heaven, which were "to be expunged; this I shall do by printing in the infernal method by corrosives, which in Hell are salutary and medicinal, melting apparent surfaces away and displaying the infinite which was hid."[69] Blake's infernal theology aimed to revitalize the mystery of the incarnation; his word made flesh was the "Bible of Hell" with the Devil, the "active principle," having become the Messiah to awaken mankind from its stupor.[70] In its visionary realization of the potential of printing to render the paradoxes of modern technology both symbolically and materially, Blake cut to the heart of the Devil's paradoxical fascination as a figure of modernity; however, in his reliance on an artisanal mode of production and an idiosyncratic cosmology he remained severed from the mass audience he craved. The revolutionary and redemptive figure for which Blake yearned could only be realized through a hybrid and eccentric genre of poetry, theology, and art, simultaneously fantastic and mundane. The main devil genres of the eighteenth century had been theology and invective; the main genres of the next century were all imagination but no seriousness. At the cusp of this shift, Blake's work managed to unite them, but without finding any contemporary audience to speak of.

There was no place for such an artisanal endeavor in the burgeoning mass culture of the nineteenth century. By contrast with the moralism that the rationalized supernatural had adapted from the high seriousness of early modern rhetoric, directly fantastical plays and comic tableaux set their action in an underworld that was Paris or London in all but name, starring whichever comic figure was in vogue. In 1809, it was *Jocrisse aux enfers*, where the eponymous soul is tormented by a series of devils, including Paris's own *diable vert*, until Proserpine and Pluto have him saved in order to keep the dead laughing.[71] Other celebrated visitors included *Rocambule aux enfers* (1872) and *Elbeuf aux enfers* (1884). Perhaps most artistically successful was Grandville's *Un Autre Monde* (1844), with text by Taxile Delord. Rather than the mythico-Christian framework of its contemporary, *Le Diable à Paris* (to which Grandville also contributed), the artist proposed a "neo-paganist" phantasmagoria that burlesqued the view from above, the view from below, and all of society in between (figure 2.13).[72] Three scientists, Hahblle, Krackq, and Dr. Puff, following the lead of the Olympian gods, divide the endeavor between them, taking air, land, and sea respectively. The underworld combination of antiquity and modernity is a central motif throughout: traveling through space, Hahblle comes across a bridge linking two planets, "leading from one world to the other along a perfectly polished asphalt walk." The ferryman Charon accosts him in the manner of an unemployed city dweller who has been made obsolete, complaining that a similar walkway over the Styx has robbed him of his livelihood. Benjamin saw in Grandville's poetically satirical exaggerations an emblem of the not-yet assimilated technology of iron and the cornucopia of commodities that the world exhibitions would soon repackage as the universe.[73] Yet although putatively harmless in its comic tone and refusing the agency of either the Devil or his limping assistant Asmodeus, Grandville's combination of image and text not only perfectly captured early industrial capitalism's blend of wild imagination and eccentric execution, it also prefigured with a deft touch many of the primary concerns of twentieth-century cultural theory, including the loss of nature, commodification, and the rise of the spectacle.

2.13 A "neo-paganist" phantasmagoria. Frontispiece to Grandville, *Un Autre Monde* (Paris: H. Fournier, 1844).

Not surprisingly, Grandville was particularly insightful regarding the various facets of the devil craze. A vision of "Gods, Angels, Devils" in a "Celestial Macedoine" (mixed fruit salad) depicted a vertical division, angels above and devils below; of the latter, one is reading the *Mémoires du Diable*, while the others are performing a litany of devil-related jokes spanning the senses: "That one drank it, that one is singing, one is whistling, the other reading his memoirs, another has taken up residence in the font" (figure 2.14).[74] Krackq's dream of the Champs-Elysées managed simultaneously to extend the already familiar topos linking its namesake in the classical underworld, to play on the syncretic quality of nineteenth-century myth (combining ancient and modern, classical and biblical figures à la Dante), to document the variety of leisure activity in the Parisian locale, and to deflate the pomposity of Academy hero-worship with his depiction of the icons of French letters, Voltaire and Jean-Jacques Rousseau, playing fairground games (figure 2.15).[75] As the dream turns to nightmare, Grandville segued into "Krackq's Inferno as a Sequel to Dante's Inferno," with the epigraph quoted from "*Inferno*, canto primo": "O you who enter, leave your cane and your umbrella."[76] Virgil appears as "tour guide," speaking to Krackq in Latin hexameter, which the latter cannot understand.

As in all underworld travesties, the visual, linguistic, and topographical puns run hot and heavy, following the principle of deflation and localization by assimilation to the customs, topics, and hobbyhorses of the writers and bourgeois of Paris. Rather than taking the stock emblems of popular visual iconography at face value, Grandville twisted them around by mixing different registers of imagery into instantly recognizable but unexpected combinations. The result was to expand the scope of Paris to encompass the universe and to reduce the universe to the petty world of Paris. The effect could be vertiginous. "Charon's Bark" (figure 2.16), for example, did not simply contain Parisian notables; it anatomized recent Parisian visitors to the underworld, beginning with a Romantic poet and a Raphaelesque painter in the background who, "for the lack of an obole will wander these banks for a hundred years, where the air is far from good"[77]—hell was also the *îlots insalubres*, the *dessous* of Paris. In good Dantesque fashion, Virgil then enumerates the rest of the passengers, including comics, many of whom have already made the journey below in the theater (although in good katabasis fashion Grandville pretended to be unaware of these prior descents), and whose characters are of course associated with the demonic to start with: Jocrisse, Falstaff, Arlequin, Sganarelle, Crispin, Jean-Jean, Giles, Paillasse, and the Postillion of Lonjumeau.[78] Hell has been modernized just like Paris: a tunnel leads from the landing to Minos's courtroom at the Palais de Justice where the rogues Robert Macaire, Don Juan, Bluebeard, and Marty are condemned, the sentence to be posted in "l'Autre Monde."[79] The dream vision of the underworld not only wrapped up the satirical threads of the entire conceit of the "Other World," it served as the book's climax, a fitting monument to the wildly intertextual and

2.14 The gamut of devil jokes: Grandville, *Anges et Démons*, in *Un Autre Monde*, 196–97.

2.15 Playing on the afterlife: nineteenth-century syncretism. Frederick the Great and Voltaire weigh themselves while Galileo and Newton toss a globe. Grandville, *Les Champs-Elysées*, in *Un Autre Monde*, 214.

polysemous imagination of Grandville and to the complex interplay between text, image, and spectacle that was so integral to the culture of early mass publishing.[80]

The closest London equivalent to Grandville's underworld Paris was George Cruikshank's satanic London of the previous decade. With a comparable range of reference and flair for iconic caricature, Cruikshank's satirical discourse was nevertheless quite distinct from Grandville's embrace of spectacle. "The fiends frying pan or Annual Festival of Tom Foolery & Vice" (figure 2.17) syncretized the various stage devils with a condemnation of moral vice and accusations of government corruption to depict his metropolis as a dissipated inferno addicted to spectacle. Cruikshank's vision differed from those of Victorian London only in the energy with which he tackled the phantasmagoric scene and the fact that he based it on a traditional Christian metaphor of *theatrum mundi*, the world as a fair, rather than the vertically segregated representation that would soon dominate. Variety, detail, and enumeration rather than starkly defined high and low classes marked the satire, just as they did in the 1835 engravings that used devils to personify various ailments. In the foreground of "The Fiends Frying Pan," one grinning demon holds a list of "Popular Entertainments" and "Popular Works"

2.16 Ship of fools. Grandville, *Charon's Bark*, in *Un Autre Monde*, 224–25.

of the devil craze of the 1820s and early '30s, another a list of vices entitled "Amusements of the People." A larger devil, equally amused, stokes the fires of the frying pan that contains the background fair, and its popular spectacles of wild beasts, theater, and Punch and Judy. Although equally versed in the fads and novelties of his day, Cruikshank, like most Regency explorers of the underworld, continued to represent them in a theatrical iconography and moral Manichaeism dating back to Ben Jonson's Elizabethan London, and preferred an episodic structure to the narrative intertextuality of Grandville or the framing tale of the *Diable à Paris*. The different traditions in Paris regarding infernal technology and popular spectacle, and the temporal and spatial differences in the ways in which they were appropriated by modern industry, produced a dialectic between old and new in 1840s Paris quite distinct from what was generated in Regency London out of similar devilry.

2.17 *The fiends frying pan or Annual Festival of Tom Foolery & Vice*: the corrupt metropolis addicted to spectacle. Etching with hand coloring by George Cruikshank. 1832.

Few of the underworld burlesques in the theater proper possessed the range or subtlety of Grandville's or Cruikshank's collections, although it is perhaps unfair to judge them solely from their texts rather than in performance. Where they did excel was in the same wild interplay between a syncretic lexicon of Hell, the devil, and the classical underworld and a keen awareness of the urban setting and its newest fads and inventions. In London as well as in Paris (which was often blamed by the former for this inspiration), the discourse was playful rather than condemnatory. As Rachel Falconer has observed in a different context, while the Aenean descent was epic, sublime and public, that of Orpheus was based in romance, comic and individual.[81] Although Falconer does not account for the early synthesis of these mythic strands in Dante's *Commedia*, nor his combination of what had become the comic and debased classical tradition with the tragic and sublime Christian hell, her distinction does suggest why the classical underworld and the figure of Orpheus dominated burlesque depictions of the underworld in the nineteenth century, especially in high-brow theater and in operetta. Less politically and socially charged than the anarchic lower-class diableries or the tragic Romantic Satan, the Orpheus myth proved a popular vehicle for incorporating bits of both forms into a framework that rendered them inoffensive even in the face of contemporary material and locations. From Jacques Offenbach and Hector Crémieux's famous operetta at the

Bouffes Parisiens to Henry Byron's and James Robinson Planché's versions in London, the Orpheus plays specialized in quick shifts between hell and the contemporary comic scene, wildly mixing classical antiquity with technological novelty, spectacular verisimilitude with sheer fantasy.

Planché's *Olympic Devils; or, Orpheus and Eurydice* was self-consciously up front about its place in 1831 London. As Orpheus sings in the final scene, before being torn to bits for refusing to cease playing an irresistible waltz:

> O no, we never mention it,
> At least to ears polite;
> 'Twould give St. James's Square a fit,
> And shock Pall Mall outright;
> And yet in said St. James's Square
> And also in Pall Mall,
> There are some places, I declare
> Would very well it spell. . . .
> So, know when down stairs you go,
> High life above is like high life below![82]

The inability to pronounce the identity of this place in polite company functions as a trope for the related series of gibes about the social topography of London. Where Orpheus is burlesqued for his artistic pretensions and middle-class suburban identity, the Olympic gods consistently figure as members of high society whose slumming takes them to the gambling hells and pleasure rooms of urban Hades. The vertical cosmos of classical myth is joined to a vertical conception of class division. But the underlying thrust of the humor resides in the fiction of that separation; for in the reality of late Regency London, the high spaces and the low were shown readily to overlap: "And yet in said St. James's Square / And also in Pall Mall, / There are some places, I declare / Would very well it spell."

The West End continued to stand in for the underworld when Planché, in good Victorian fashion, renamed his popular adaptation of Offenbach and Crémieux's Parisian operetta, *Orphée aux enfers* (1858), according to the site in which it was to be performed: *Orpheus in the Haymarket* (1865). Planché made minor but telling changes to Crémieux's libretto, reproducing scenically the oft-repeated commonplace of the time that, in comparison to Paris, London was all business. Orpheus is no longer director of the Orphéon de Thèbes, but "Doctor of Music, Professor of Poetry & Eloquence, and Director of the Grecian Philharmonic Society," among other more menial services advertised by a large board over his front door. Planché's Pluto makes use of modern technology: departing with Eurydice, he calls for "my train!—/ The down express!"[83] Where his Parisian counterpart had left a note for Orpheus in letters of magic fire, this one writes a message using "electro-biology."[84] Along with the technological advances,

Planché's characters are far more aware of morality, not as a matter of opinion but as a matter of law. The note in Crémieux's libretto reads: "Je quitte la maison / Parce que je suis morte / Aristée est Pluton / Et le diable m'emporte" ("I'm leaving home / Because I am dead / Aristeus is Pluto / And the devil's taking me away").[85] Planché renders it as "I'm dead: but my loss you will scarce think an evil / Aristeus was Pluto—I'm going to the—" as Public Opinion breaks in with, "Stop! The word's neither classic nor correct, / And there's the Licenser, who might object."[86] It was a constant theme of the burlesques that the words "devil" and "Hades" and "hell" were unsayable in London; Planché pokes further fun at the means of his own production, the licenser, or censor, who had to pass the play before it could be performed. The Parisian underworld is imagined as a place of sport; the London version as a place of illegality. Public Opinion is burlesqued not as a comic actor but as a potential threat.

It may not be surprising, then, that for the actual descent, Planché had recourse not to London but to Paris *as* hell: Pluto says to Eurydice: "Now for the realms below. / The short cut there / is *vîa* Paris! *Barrière D'Enfer*!"[87] London had the industry, the technology, and the business, but Paris had the legendary past of its vast Catacombes, a popular, if perilous, tourist attraction during the first half of the century, the entrance to which was located at the Barrière d'Enfer. We find the same Parisian theme in a roughly contemporary chapter from "Punch's Heathen Mythology," where we read above the gate to Pluto's Premises not the Dantean "Lasciate ogni speranza" but "Ici on parle français." There is more than a straightforward link of moral satire between Hell and Paris for the London cultural scene, especially after 1830, however; with the exception of the "Satanic School" of Byron and Shelley, and the case of Blake discussed above, urban satanism was dominated by Paris-based artists and writers. If Paris was the capital of the Devil in popular culture, it was also the only place where Satan and underground culture received extensive consideration from canonical figures. From French Romantics such as Gérard de Nerval and Théophile Gautier, through Balzac and George Sand, and especially with Victor Hugo and Baudelaire, the figure of Satan played a central role. To treat Paris as Hell had literary as well as material, metaphysical, moral, and modish referents. Underpinning them all in the figure of the modern Satan, and also at the origin of Romantic satanism and the Regency devil in England, was the discourse of radical politics.

His Satanic Majesty's Court

> You are not unaware that it is the meeting place of all there has been of the most illustrious and virtuous on this earth: it is the homeland of the Socrateses, the Livys, the Platos, the Senecas, the Voltaires, the Rousseaus, the Diderots. All of them *unfortunates who died unconfessed*. . . . Young man, if you seek genius and virtue, do not be frightened

by words, descend to the underworld [*aux enfers*] like the heroes of antiquity. It is there that you shall find them.

ASMODEUS, in Pierre-Jean-Baptiste Chaussard, *Le Nouveau Diable Boiteux* (1798)

Unlike the specific links between the devil, the city, capitalism, and commodity culture that emerged during the first half of the nineteenth century, the use of the devil in political and religious invective was as old as the Old One himself. To invoke the devil as a term of abuse was particularly prominent in the movements of reformation beginning with the Cathars—during the period coinciding, that is, with the creation of the devil as he is most commonly known. "'Go to the Devil; be off with you, Devil . . . Sancta Maria, I can see the Devil!'—such were the mildest exclamations of Cathar peasants at the sight of a Catholic priest, or of orthodox Catholics at the sight of a goodman."[88] While such invective carried the threat of the Inquisition only for the heretical "goodmen," the efficacy with which it could be appropriated as a weapon of subversion was established beyond question by Luther's campaign against the Satan-possessed see of Rome. But it was the Revolution of 1789 that wholly transformed this lexicon, the final and traumatic step in the replacement of heresy by atheism as its primary target. "The sublimest ruse of the devil," as Baudelaire later wrote, "is to persuade you that he doesn't exist!"[89] The Jesuits had already revised the doctrinal hell into a picture of urban squalor, all flames and no monsters; now there was a material image of Satan himself sitting in the National Assembly, plotting the downfall of church and state, and eventually indulging in a bloodbath that even its most partisan supporters would not deny was infernal—it was, once again, only a question of whether you considered it the righteous punishment of damnable transgression or the evil work of a Satan broken loose from the divine tether to roam the streets of the capital. There was evidently no longer a coherent theology behind this invective any more than there was a dominant Catholic Church, but the powerful fragments of that discourse would be invoked out of the representational space of Paris long into the nineteenth century. Moreover, the concrete experience of cataclysmic social change gave a fresh new context to the imagery of the devil and hell that helped them assume a force of reality independent of the prior context of Catholicism and readily adaptable even by atheists.

The lexicon of satanism had (and still has today) a wide range of meanings. Characteristic of all of these meanings is the presumption of uniqueness: nothing comparable ever has happened before or ever could again, for in this discourse there is only one Satan, only one Hell, and both are irrevocable and unmatchable in their evil. Hence, Joseph de Maistre asserted that the revolution had "a *satanic* character which distinguished it from anything else one could see," arguing that the Terror was a punishment divinely ordained and merited by the abuses of the ancien régime.[90] Abbé Fiard took a shorter view, maintaining beyond dispute "that the Devil in person caused the revolution, that he inspired the philosophes, that he is the supernatural agent of all the evil committed in France, and finally that he was the master in impiety of Voltaire and Diderot, if in fact those philosophes were not themselves devils in disguise."[91] In François-René de Chateaubriand's more sympathetic but equally credulous characterization in *Les Martyrs* (1809), by contrast, Satan was employed as a literary metaphor for lost glory as well as for the fall, the first time that we find a "representation of the devil in which the traits of the revolutionary tribunal are blended with the traditional image of the fallen angel."[92] In addition to the ultimate rhetorical intensifier and a topos of religious invective, the Devil in his role within the divine narrative offered a chance for finding historical meaning in a sequence of events apparently bereft of it (at least until Napoleon Bonaparte hit the scene).[93]

As the immediate historical shock receded, other writers registered the eerie way in which the infernal metaphors leading up to the events had suddenly been realized in the actual spaces of France, and particularly in its capital. Aimé Martin related the infernal aspects of the Terror to the rapid growth simultaneously of the popular spectacle, the *féerie*, the pantomime, and especially the gothic melodrama:

> Is it not true, at the moment when in France there was nothing but executioners and victims, when hell seemed to have vomited up its inhabitants among us that those unhappy fictions with no other goal than inspiring terror came over from England? They were welcomed with a revolutionary enthusiasm; they released horrible specters; palaces and chateaus were abandoned, and became the asylum of the most infamous brigands. The very aspect of devils should not have surprised us, for there was not a single misdeed that could have been passed off as a fiction.[94]

It was considered no wonder that, having brought down the gods, the revolutionaries were now pleased to see themselves mirrored in the devils. Especially evocative was the reminder of demographic and topographic change on a grand scale. The stock settings and situations of the gothic that had been little but spatial metaphor in late eighteenth-century England—the deserted château, the abandoned palace, the noble hero and heroine in peril—were suddenly reality all over the French countryside and in the streets of Paris. The only difference, and this was what caused the shock of disdain registered by Aimé Martin, was that the ending had changed and the sympathy had shifted; the gothic devil haunting sublime ruins had a wholly different meaning in postrevolutionary France than it had in England.

Across the Channel, there was still perspective to be found, perspective that worked hard to vitiate the awesome spectacle of a satanic mob freed from the fetters of divine rule. In John Galt's novel *The Annals of the Parish* (written in 1813 and published in 1821), the Reverend Micah Balwhidder has a dream-vision of the Revolution cast as a battle between factions of the risen dead. Standing "on the tower of an old popish kirk," the clergyman beholds the dead rise up from their coffins: a multitude, "from the common graves," who stand off to the side as onlookers, and a host of kings, "from the old and grand monuments," who give battle to an invading army. The kings are defeated, and the scene shifts to a metropolis: "I then beheld a wide and dreary waste, and afar off the steeples of a great city, and a tower in the midst, like the tower of Babel, and on it I could discern written in characters of fire, 'Public Opinion.' "[95] The host reappears, and makes its way toward the city, where a hand comes out of a "tower of fire" and sweeps it away "like dust," leaving in its wake the same churchyard, with sealed graves and ancient tombs. The Reverend Balwhidder's vision is soon confirmed by news of the beheading of the king of France, whereupon he preaches one of his "greatest and soundest sermons" ever on the subject of the Revolution. Only within the confines of the metropolis, ancient as Babylon and modern as Paris, do the "common people" take shape in the vision, embodied in the writing on the wall, "Public Opinion," the *mene tekel* of Louis XVI. The view from above that opened Balwhidder's vision all the way across the Channel to the revolutionary metropolis equally worked to consign the inhabitants to the wholly underground space of an ancient necropolis.

The best-known English fictionalization of the Revolution, Dickens's *A Tale of Two Cities* (1859), portrayed the Paris of the Terror in many ways as an extension of London. The key metaphorical space of the novel is Tellson's bank, of which the narrator is a lifelong employee. The subterranean vaults of this establishment, first introduced in the City of London, safely contain the necessary ground for the proper functioning of the modern world of capital: gold, private documents, jewelry, and heirlooms—everything on which the symbolic and real power of the ruling class rested. It is Tellson's branch in the aristocratic Faubourg Saint-Germain that manages to counteract the revolutionary bloodlust centered in the working-class Faubourg Saint-Antoine and the Lafarge Café owner's wife's knitted list of guilty parties. One of the rare subterranean spaces in Dickens's novels, the staid, solid foundation of the underground strong rooms in London, is contrasted with the revolutionary zeal overflowing out of the depths of Paris. Dickens studiously avoided all demonization, however; his Revolution was one of justifiable motives gone terribly wrong.

If the Revolution established once and for all the satanic, underworld identity of Paris, grafting a serious political quality on to its reputation for technology, luxury commodities and fashion, the same imagery returned with each subsequent wave of uprising.[96] Victor Hugo would channel 1830 into the nocturnal march of the beggars of the cour des Miracles onto the cathedral of Notre Dame de Paris before eventually associating it indelibly with the sewers of Jean Valjean's flight from the barricades. 1848 saw the birth of a rash of revolutionary and satirical newspapers inspired by Le Sage—*Le Diable boiteux, Le Diable boiteux à l'Assemblée Nationale* (figure 2.18), *Le Diable rose* (see figure 2.22)—and the constant invocation of Dante as a model.[97] The year 1871 saw the communards taking refuge in the *carrières* and besieged Paris fearing invasion by the same route.[98] The Revolution was the last time, however, that, as in the report of the commissaire Sénart accusing Robespierre of "frequenting the cave of the Sibyl," the revolutionaries were directly associated with the devil; from that point on the association was incorporated on a metaphorical and topographical level within the subterranean city itself.[99]

As Jean Cayla would argue in 1864, the very atheism that was partly responsible for the earlier accusations of satanism had led to the loss of power for the religious conception of the same figure: "What religious critique on one side and the encyclopedists on the other had been unable to do was accomplished by free discussion and the loss of fear of intolerance. The Devil and Hell, his somber habitation, were both felled by the same blow, the pressure of 1789."[100] For Ernest Renan, however, the Revolution had merely freed Satan from his traditional bonds, enabling much evildoing in the world: "Of all the once accursed beings whom the toleration of our century has raised out of anathema, Satan is doubtless the one who has gained the most from the progress of the Enlightenment and universal civilization."[101] Just as the Revolution had shaken up the accepted vertical hierarchy, so had it disrupted the vertical cosmos. Not only was Satan now at large in the world but his scope was paradoxically widened as he became available as a potent symbol in no matter what medium. One need no longer be a Catholic to make use of the Devil; nor need a Catholic fear any longer to treat with the Devil in jest.

Satan's final refuge as a traditional force of evil, reported Cayla, was the realm of mysticism and spiritism, which had made their return under the Terror, and of which Paris was a hotbed.[102] The famous cartomancer, Marie-Anne Lenormand, who plied her trade at no. 5, rue de Tournon, from 1804 to 1830, was patronized by

Mardi 13 juin 1848. N° 4.

LE DIABLE BOITEUX

A L'ASSEMBLÉE NATIONALE.

	Un an.	6 mois.	3 mois.
Paris	6	3	2
Départements	12	7	4
Étranger	15	8	»

On s'abonne à Paris, rue des Grands-Augustins, 27.

Tous les Articles doivent être signés et adressés *franco* au Rédacteur en chef, Ch. Tondeur.

Paraissant les Mardi, Vendredi et Dimanche.

2.18 *Le Diable boiteux à l'Assemblée Nationale*: Asmodeus as revolutionary journalist. Newspaper masthead, 13 June 1848. Permission of the British Library.

the Empress Josephine, and was said to have made a pact with the Devil; the baroness de Krudner, who had emigrated to Paris from Riga in 1814–15, would go into "voluptuous ecstasies" under the influence of the spirits.[103] Collin de Plancy included an entry on "Sibylles Modernes" in the *Dictionnaire infernal*, mentioning Madame Lenormand along with several other fortune-tellers, including one so contemporary that she could not be named, but whose lengthy horoscopes were still selling well in 1829.[104] Alongside the high-society satanists there were apparently also survivors of the low-life devil worshippers of Paris of old, pushed along with the rest of the poor ever further from the center of the city:

> There still remained in Brie, on the outskirts of Paris, a cabal of shepherds who could cause beasts to die, made attempts on the lives of men, committed several other crimes, and had become a force to be reckoned with in the area. Arrests were eventually made; the judge in Pacy presided over the trial, and was able to establish with conclusive evidence that all these misdeeds had been committed by malefices and curses. . . . A singular circumstance in the trial led to the belief that they had made an actual pact with the Devil to commit these misdeeds.[105]

There were, needless to say, humorous repercussions to the residual beliefs as well. One anecdote reported that a concierge had denounced one of his tenants to the police in the belief that he was preparing to make a pact with Satan, only to discover that it was in fact Giacomo Meyerbeer and Labasse Levasseur rehearsing their 1831 opera *Robert le Diable*.[106] But while there remained a hard core of Catholic writers who saw the hand of the Devil in all aspects of spiritism and its associated activities, the Church authorities appeared less concerned about the ancient enemy: an ordinance of 1682 had already legally defined such practices as charlatanry, and even the Vatican had by 1840 pronounced hypnotism to be free of satanic imputations, if used responsibly.[107] Whether taken seriously as civil and political threat or alternatives to the church, or whether dismissed as a cynical con game, such marginal activities were invariably associated with the Devil just as revolutionary activity was ever more troped as underground by both practitioners and opponents.

What the vogue for occultism in the early nineteenth century demonstrates is that the liberation of the Devil from his doctrinal identity within Christian dualism had released into the mainstream all of the contradictions that had previously been explored only on the margins of orthodoxy. The suppressed traditions of esotericism, occultism, and Gnosticism had always distinguished between figures of varying degrees of evil and those playing various cosmic roles, especially Satan and Lucifer. Modern occultists such as Collin de Plancy (1794–1881) and Eliphas Levi (1810–75) popularized and bowdlerized these traditions; late nineteenth-century and early twentieth-century esotericists such as the New York-based Helena Blavatsky (1831–91), the Berlin- and then Switzerland-based Rudolph Steiner (1861–1925), and the Paris-based George Ivanovitch Gurdjieff

(1877–1949) synthesized earlier sources into demonologies for what they saw as a modern, post-Christian world. They recuperated theologies in which the Devil and the evil he embodied were integral to the function of the universe in an at least partly positive way. Steiner, in particular, distinguished between the satanic "Ahriman," "the prince of lies who seeks to bind man so closely to the earth that he forgets his spiritual heritage," and Lucifer, "the being of light, who seeks to seduce man from responsibility to the earth."[108] Rather than disappearing from a society no longer governed by religious doctrine, the many figures previously unified as the Devil fragmented into myriad overlapping and competing images. As late as 1953, the Italian philosopher and former futurist Giovanni Papini (1881–1956) published what he called a collection of "notes and notions for that future *Summa Diabologica* which a new St. Thomas may yet write," where he argued that "the people remember him unfailingly; the invocation of his name is part of their vocabulary, even if they are not aware that they live under his dominion."[109]

It is possible to continue to regard these images as unified only to the degree that they remain underground, oppositional to some manner of status quo, be it political, literary, artistic, philosophical, or spiritual. Milner is correct in continuing to group these diverse images under the rubric of the Christian Devil, but only because few who invoked them bothered to make fine distinctions between the Devil, Satan, Lucifer, and Asmodeus, to name the most common appellations; instead, they simply mixed and matched depending on generic constraints, fashion, and sympathy in the same way that they did not distinguish between the classical underworld and the Christian hell. It is important to keep sight of the consequences of the various choices and mixtures, but their significance resides not so much in the esoteric history of each demonic figure as in the particular social, historical, and spatial context within which it was deployed. Even those artists and writers who did delve deeply into the subtleties of demonology, such as William Blake and Gérard de Nerval, did so in order to formulate a personal mythology that, even if it was internally coherent, was disseminated with all manner of added confusion. It is as difficult to distinguish clearly between Satan and Lucifer in their works, between a sublime and rebellious dark lord and an earthly and mischievous demon, as it is to determine the degree of seriousness or of posing in the satanic stance of so many nineteenth-century writers.

What is certain is that the material underground was more closely related to the satanic in Paris than in London or any other city, and that it received a much broader range of treatment and perspective. Paris possessed not only a material history of revolt that was firmly rooted in the subterranean legends of Marat's shroud in the sewers and revolutionaries hiding out in the carrières but a metaphysics of rebellion and a positive image of the corrupted city. In the nineteenth-century novel, these traditions emerged primarily in the realism of the urban mysteries of Balzac, Eugène Sue, Hugo, and Alexandre Dumas; later, Zola brought a colder London attitude to underworld Paris. The specifically satanic was the province of the Parisian poets, from the Romantics through the symbolists to the surrealists, self-proclaimed explorers of the bas-fonds of the city and the hidden reaches of the human psyche; it reached its apogee in Baudelaire.

The Devil on Crutches

> He hasn't always simply gone by the name Asmodeus, but by turns he has been known as Aristophanes, Theophrastus, Terence, La Bruyère, and especially Molière; he has been called Voltaire, Rabelais, and Beaumarchais; he has borne the greatest names of the world of poetry and satire. . . . Asmodeus is philosophy through the centuries, summed up in a caricature.
>
> JULES JANIN, "ASMODÉE," *Le Livre des cent-et-un* (1831)

From 1830 to 1845, what Milner has termed "l'âge d'or du satanisme," the devil was everywhere in Paris:

> Applauded at the Opéra in one of the greatest successes of the century, invoked by the poets, invisible and present—sometimes visible—in the novel, treated with regard in the epic, he figures prominently in salons of painting and sculpture, abounds in sketches, frontispieces, and *culs-de-lampe*, grimaces in the illustrated papers, dictates his laws to dandies unafraid of ridicule and to young men who want to appear in style.[110]

Gautier introduced the figure of "Beelzebub dandy" in one of his poems; the frock coat with straight skirts ("frac à pans droits") was christened the "habit à pandemonium" because of its distinction from the bourgeois dress coat ("habit bourgeois").[111] There was even a prominent luxury goods shop called Le Diable Boiteux; it later merged with another shop to become Samaritaine, one of the principal grand department stores that transformed Parisian retail commerce during the Second Empire.[112] In a marvelous paradox, the unchanging ruler of the realm of eternal damnation was crowned king of that most transient world, fashion, to be subtly recut and reshaped for each successive mode of the century. Under the aegis of the *diable boiteux* (the "halting devil" or the "devil on crutches"), the panoramic view from above introduced an influential mode of representation able, in Paris at least, to encompass the phantasmagoria of capitalism from high to low.

The operative trope of the devil on crutches was litotes, or understatement; it was emblematized by the crippled legs that undercut any pretensions he may have had to satanic power, and was eminently suited to the superficial pleasures he ostensibly surveyed. In *Le Diable à Paris* (1844–45), one of the most accomplished and influential, although by no means the first, of the urban panoramas united by the framing device of a devil's view from above, the minor devil Flammèche ("little flame") is sent by his bored master Satan to relay weekly dispatches on the wonders of the City of Light. Evidently uninterested in the rooftop shenanigans of his Asmodean predecessors, however, Satan's new emissary is more concerned with being chic. The moment he arrives, Flammèche is noticed "smoking a cigarette with a melancholy air, on that part of the boulevard des Italiens that is the premier spot in the world, and that extends from the rue du Mont-Blanc to the rue Lepelletier. . . . He had felt a sort of pleasure in changing his otherworld figure for a human face, and hidden beneath his varnished boots—his cleft feet."[113] The Beelzebub dandy, unable to make any sense at all of the city on his own, commissions contributions from its many writers and artists, orders his faithful servant to send them off to his master with the talismanic order "Go to the devil!" and proceeds to fall in love and disappear from sight. Contributors to the weekly numbers included George Sand; Honoré de Balzac; Alfred de Musset; Alexandre Dumas, père; Eugène Sue; and Charles Nodier; the principal illustrations were by Bertall and Gavarni. The publisher Hetzel, writing under the pseudonym P. J. Stahl, was responsible for the framing story of Flammèche, whose traits were supposedly modeled on his own; the restless monarch Satan was received as a portrait of Louis-Philippe, the "Citizen King."[114] *Le Diable à Paris* was not radical in any way, but, as so often with the devil, it was resolutely contemporary and modish, even hip.

In the panoramic literature, the framing conceit of the halting devil was crucial, a fanciful but not negligible prosopopeia that motivated the pretense to a realistic representation of the spaces it framed.[115] Although, like Pierce Egan's influential *Life in London* before it (see figure 3.8), *Le Diable à Paris* depicted society on a vertical plane, it took a far more integrated view of that society, as in the well-known "Cross-Section of a Parisian House, 1 January 1845—Five Levels of Parisian Life" (figure 2.19).[116] By contrast with Egan's (and London's) simpler division between high life and low life, this drawing, like Eugène Sue's verbal depiction of the house at the top of which the family of the doomed lapidary Morel lived in *Les Mystères de Paris* (1842–43), peeled back the façade to reveal the microcosm of social class within a typically Parisian five-story building: from the servants and the concierge on the ground floor; to the well-to-do couple (or perhaps the second ménage of a wealthy Parisian and his mistress) on the first; the somewhat cramped middle-class family on the second, with four children and a grandmother; the bachelor being evicted from a small third-floor room, while next door an older couple offer food to their pet dog; and atop, in the garret's three rooms, a carousing pair of painters, a starving writer holding an umbrella against a rooftop leak, and a very hungry-looking family of the working poor. Where London life tended more and more toward horizontal segregation expressed metaphorically as a vertical division, the characteristic five- or six-story

Parisian building afforded both a more concrete image of vertical stratification and a greater material reality of class mingling.[117] It is significant, for example, that the only figures portrayed with the ability to see outside are the painters in their garret, with the skylight open over the (implied) rooftops, and the black cat perched on the roof itself. As Baudelaire would document in his poetry, the social space of Paris made possible, if not readily analyzable, a nonsupernatural view from above unavailable to the cellar- and rookery-bound lower classes in London.

There is much significant detail, and many analogies are drawn between rooms: the jolly painters above are balanced at the bottom corner by the dancing concierge; the wealthy couple sit stretched out over the expanse of their richly decorated room, the man raising his arms over his head in a gesture that simultaneously betokens ennui and effortless possession of his space, while the other two family men are occupied by their children—the middle-class father holding his youngest up to gaze in its eyes as his wife looks on, a disorderly but homely space around them, full of playthings, chairs, and signs of life and activity; and the impoverished father, standing arms crossed, staring despondently at his four children as they cling in desperation to their mother. A sense of interconnection is heightened by the figures on the staircase that appears on each floor but the top, with visitors on the staircase at every level, although fewer the higher up one goes, and only an energetic cat, tail held high, making the journey to the top, perhaps to comfort the lonely writer, the only solitary figure in the picture, or perhaps to join the other cat sitting on the rooftop beside the smoking chimney. One glimpses poverty, middle-class comfort, and wealth, although the extremes so dear to the urban mysteries are not in evidence, and neither is there any sense of division between above- or underground. The diabolic conceit of its frame in fact permitted *Le Diable à Paris* to appear eminently enlightened and level-headed in its portrayal of the city and its inhabitants, concerned to cover everything and to privilege nothing.

The same type of building could take quite a different form when viewed from below. Although Alfred Delvau's later guide to *Les Dessous de Paris* (1860; see figure 1.4) took the eminently ambivalent Parisian attitude that "the underneath is charming: the underneath is horrible," his perspective was delimited by the lower depths of the city.[118] Consequently, Delvau's version of the Parisian apartment building was topographically precise rather than paradigmatic, fantastic rather than a caricature, and hellish rather than lightly diabolical, partaking of the "true" urban mysteries genre's view from below rather than the panorama's view from above. The description leads the reader to the establishment in the passage Radzivil near the Palais-Royal of an *implanteur*, a man who "sows" the hair sold to him by impoverished young women. A topographical description of painstaking and verifiable detail concludes with the anticipated Dantesque metaphor of infernal space:

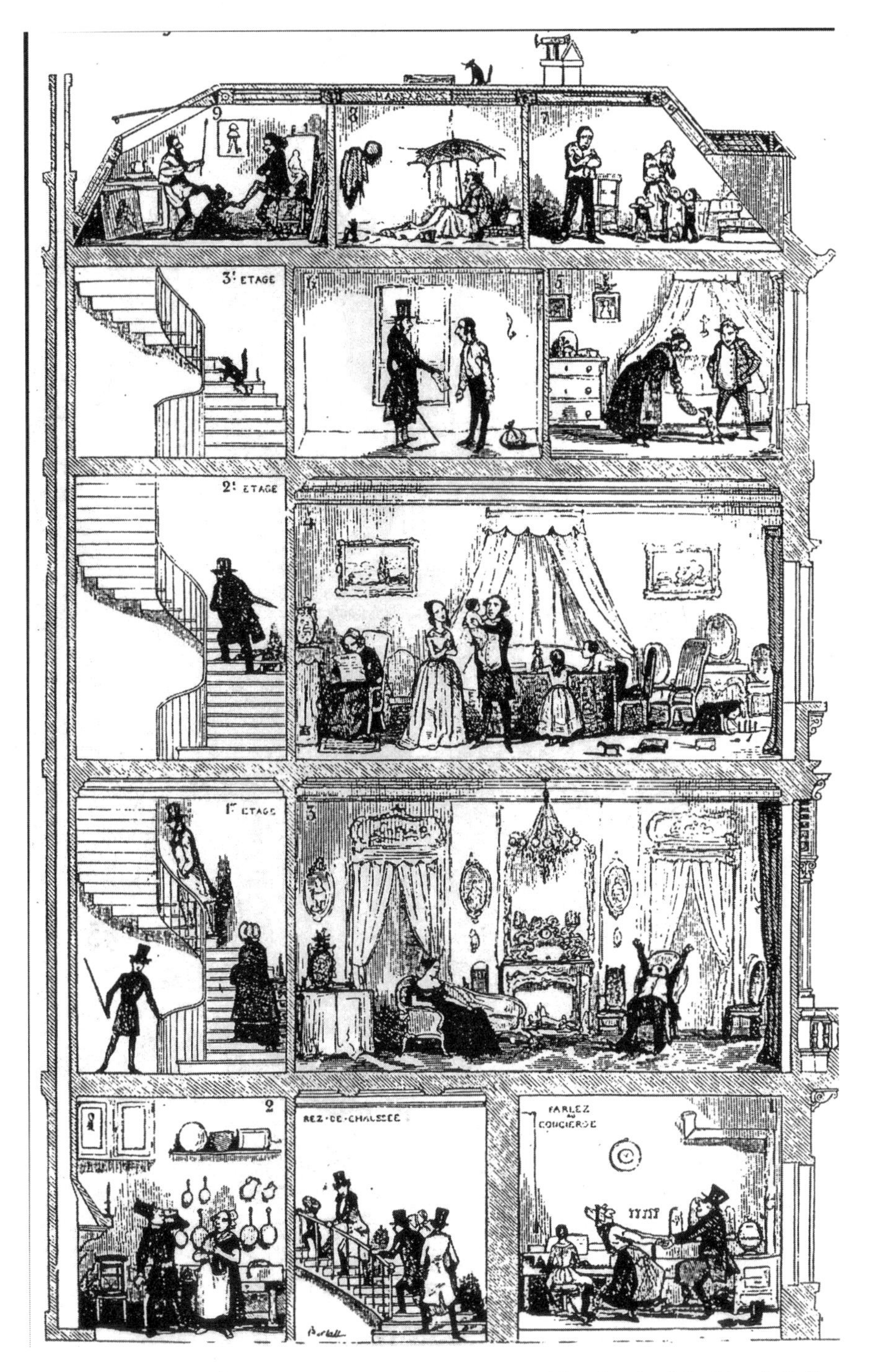

2.19 *Cross-Section of a Parisian House, 1 January 1845—Five Levels of Parisian Life*. Engraving by Gavarni, in *Le Diable à Paris*, ed. Hetzel (Paris: Hetzel, 1845–46).

> Two parallel alleyways, narrow, muddy [*fangeuses*], and dark, extend from the rue de Valois and come together again at the other end in an equally dark, muddy, and narrow corridor; in the middle of the corridor, which borders the sewer of the rue Neuve-des-Bons-Enfants, a stairway ascends to the right, ending as well in the middle of a higher corridor, from the two ends of which extend two other alleyways as narrow, as muddy, and as dark as the lower ones; these lead back to the aforementioned rue Neuve-des-Bons-Enfants. At the center of these two superimposed parallelograms rises an immense, shadowy, and infinite spiral staircase which, its feet in the mud [*la boue*], stops only where misery itself can climb no higher. Many times while contemplating this fantastic construction, I have imagined that the hand of some all-powerful magician had plunged into Dante's hell, which descends through nine circles all the way to the entrails of the earth, and, inverting it from bottom to top, as you would do with a cotton bonnet, had raised above the ground this filthy [*immonde*] monument and its nine levels.[119]

Unlike Balzac's comparison of Paris to the circles of Dante's hell, Delvau never actually universalized the image into a representation of the city as a whole; his "imagination" lent a sublime wonder to the sordid but geographically precise locale of the visit (figure 2.20).[120] The final, apparently inappropriate comparison of the cosmic inversion of hell to a "cotton bonnet" recalls the reader to the mundane context at hand, and places the *implanteur* directly into the place of Satan, now perched under the freezing rooftops of a Parisian tenement. Delvau pinpointed the urban mystery in time and space, but displaced the responsibility; this hell had indeed been created by human agency, but certainly not by the hand of any all-powerful magician.

In its refusal of any sensationalism within the confines of its framing conceit, *Le Diable à Paris* was at the opposite end of the spectrum from the fiction of urban mysteries to which it was exactly contemporary. In addition to the essays on diverse topics and of varying quality, but primarily focused on the people and their occupations and activities, Hetzel also chose to preface the first of the bound volumes with a thirty-page "History of Paris," and the second with an eighty-page "Geography of Paris," both by Théophile Lavallée, and to conclude the second volume with seventeen pages of "Statistics of the City of Paris": "It was decided also . . . to satisfy the ideas of order he knew Satan to possess—scientific and other sort of notes would be joined to the last article with an analytical table of contents, so as to satisfy the serious minds [*esprits*] of hell, in case there were any serious minds in hell."[121] The matter-of-fact, diffuse approach had interesting consequences for the comprehensive representation of the city that (in addition to financial gain) was apparently its goal.

Because Lavallée was wholly lacking in the sharp humor of his editor, he made no attempt to connect the underground spaces in his history and geography to the diabolic theme of the volumes. So, for example, when he detailed the history of the rue d'Enfer, related to an ancient and celebrated legend of the Diable Vauvert, he unimaginatively chose to give the linguistic derivation of the name, from its

2.20 *Coin de la rue Ratziwill et des Petits-Champs au 35 la maison à 9 étages de la rue de Valois.* Photograph by Eugène Atget. 1906. Permission of the Bibliothèque Nationale de France.

original designation as *via inferior*, rather than the more resonant folkloric choice. Lavallée's two versions of the carrières beneath the city were similarly bereft of diabolic references, although equally fanciful in their argumentation. In the section on geography entitled "Paris before the Flood," he took the long view on the city, regarding the mineral wealth beneath its soil as a sign of manifest destiny, lauding the judicious ruling of 1785 to remove "the entire population of Paris since Clovis" to the Catacombes, and condemning the vogue for visiting them as decadence of the imperial and royal years before 1830.[122] Lavallée's scientific rationalism led him into even wilder speculation, as he used paleontology to deduce national character from the remains of peaceable creatures found in Paris versus the "ferocious beasts" discovered beneath London.

Although capable of wild speculation on underground evidence, Lavallée was evidently free of more conventional prejudice. Writing about the Faubourg Saint-Jacques, he shows himself perfectly aware that to live around the carrières was a miserable experience rather than a criminal choice:

> In that so nobly Christian language of the seventeenth century, they named Thébaïde de Paris this neighborhood covered with great enclosures, lost in the middle of numerous carrières, situated above the catacombs, inhabited solely by a poor, pious, and peaceable population of quarriers and plasterers. . . . The venerable Cochin, curate of Saint-Jacques-du-Haut-Pas . . . founded [the hospice Cochin] with a modest patrimony for the workers of the carrières: the first stone was laid, not by a prince, nor by a magistrate, but by two poor men, selected by the entire quarter for this touching ceremony.[123]

Although the "poor, pious, and peaceable" qualities of Lavallée's neighborhood of quarriers were according to most other sources no less speculative than his paleontology, he certainly avoided the equation of physical location with social as well as moral pathology so common both in the urban mysteries' view from below and in the social documentation that shared his approach to the city from above.

Le Diable à Paris chose, instead of the claim to specificity and individual experience of the fiction of urban mysteries, the physionomical and typological view. Rather than assert the actual descent into the depths of the city, it approached from the categorizations of the scientist and the rationalist as well as those of the aphoristic writer and the journalist. The distancing humor of the frame in fact went hand in hand with the realist approach of the contributors. Gavarni's well-known interior frontispiece perfectly encapsulated this perspective (figure 2.21). It shows Flammèche, the devil, already attired à la mode of the Parisian dandy, down to the polished boots that disguise his cloven hoofs. Strapped to his back is a large wicker ragpicker's basket overflowing with paper, each sheet filled with handwriting: the many contributions he has assembled to send to his master below. He is standing in the countryside with windmills in the background and a map of Paris larger than himself spread out on the ground. He stands on the eastern end, legs straddling the river Seine upstream of the city's two main islands. In his left hand he holds a garbage picker's stick and a bull's-eye lantern; with his right hand, he holds a small loupe to his eye as he squints down at the map. It is a marvelous combination of precious satanic dandyism, nineteenth-century rationality—the enormous map, the illuminating lantern, the magnifying glass—and the mythology of the *chiffonnier*, of the simultaneously backward and forward-looking quality of the devil.[124]

2.21 Asmodeus dandy: Gavarni's frontispiece to *Le Diable à Paris*, ed. Hetzel (Paris: Hetzel, 1845–46).

There is a clear reference to the by then well-established tradition of the *diable boiteux*, to the Spanish landscape of Don Quixote to which the windmills may also broadly allude. The Parisian devil Asmodeus had introduced the view from above, the magical gesture of removing the rooftops to examine the behavior beneath, "to uncover the motives for their actions and reveal them to you down to their innermost thoughts,"[125] the spirit of satire, as it was often termed (figure 2.22; see also figures 1.16 and 2.18). *Le Diable à Paris* was squarely in the tradition of the "Asmodeus flight" that was a ubiquitous feature of the urban panorama in the first half of the nineteenth century, the inevitable point of comparison for whatever new twist one might propose. The term was Thomas Carlyle's, and fittingly enough occurred in *The French Revolution*: "Could the reader take an Asmodeus-flight, and, waving open all roofs and privacies, look down from the roof of Notre Dame, what a Paris were it!"[126] Jonathan Arac, discussing the use of this motif by English and American writers, has stressed the "ghostly uneasiness" resulting from the "narrative overview" provided by the "ambition to gain usable power for observation."[127] And yet such a rigidly satanic perspective was undercut as well in a panoramic work such as *Le Diable à Paris*. While within the cohesive realism of the midcentury novel the perspective could take on disturbingly authoritarian overtones and shades of Foucauldian panopticism, the dandyism of Flammèche and the diffused, ragpicker's

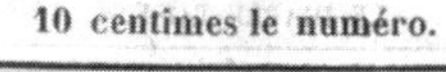

10 centimes le numéro.

Le *Diable Rose* paraît le dimanche et le jeudi de chaque semaine, depuis le 15 juin 1848.

ON S'ABONNE A PARIS
Rue Coquillière, 22.
Au bureau du Journal.

EN PROVINCE
Chez tous les libraires, dans tous les bureaux de poste et des messageries.

PRIX DE L'ABONNEMENT :

PARIS :		DÉPARTEMENTS :	
Six mois.....	6 f.	Six mois...	7 f.
Un an........	10	Un an......	12

NUMÉRO 3.

Adresser toutes demandes ou communications au Directeur du *Diable rose*, rue Coquillière, 22.

INSERTIONS.

Sur trois colonnes..... 75 c. la ligne.
Sur quatre colonnes... 50 c.

LES ABONNEMENTS
Datent du 1er ou du 16 de chaque mois.

ON NE REÇOIT QUE LES LETTRES AFFRANCHIES.

LE DIABLE ROSE.

2.22 *Le Diable rose*: the devil on sticks as the all-seeing voice of satire. Masthead of newspaper authored by Emile de La Bédollière. 1848. Reproduced by permission of the British Library.

perspective of the articles encompassed by the Asmodean framework mitigated the negative, metaphysical satanism analyzed by Arac, opting instead for the pandaemoniac approach.

There are thus two satanic points of view to be derived from the bird's-eye vantage point: the controlling all-powerful deity of the temptation on the mount, lord of all he surveys, the all-seeing, all-knowing Satan of Christian doctrine, urban authoritarianism, and also political invective; and the aestheticizing, fallen, ironic approach of the bohemian, the dandy, the flâneur, able to embrace the demonic city while at the same time keeping it at arm's length. Both versions of this point of view shared an approach that physiognomized and atomized its subjects rather than uncovering their social interrelations. Thus Benjamin could too easily dismiss the feuilleton "physiologies" of 1830s and '40s Paris as a petit-bourgeois and socially reactionary genre, and Louis James could characterize the closest London equivalent, the satirical papers of the 1830s such as *The Devil in London*, *Asmodeus in London*, and Edward George Bulwer-Lytton's *Asmodeus at Large*, as tending toward "the spirit of knowing intimacy, the clever wag in the public house," providing an overview of the city, but "out of no moral purpose."[128] In the words of Pierce Egan, the flight over the houses risked a crippling fall; he preferred the "safe" and "snug" view of the "*Camera Obscura*," which also offered the "invaluable advantages of seeing and not being *seen*."[129] Like Flammèche, Egan proposed a more passive approach to the urban panorama, a spectacle to observe rather than a space to explore. As Jules Janin wrote of the halting devil, eager evidently to put the upheavals of 1830 behind him, he was much happier as Rabelais than as Juvenal or Voltaire, for the latter were altogether too "sober and mean."[130]

In Victorian London, however, that satirical distance was being rejected as unsuitable for hard new times. The encyclopedic compendia about London produced after the 1830s eschewed the supernatural frame in favor of a rationalistic, investigative one. Henry Mayhew's mix of reportage and fiction may have leaned more toward the former than that of his Paris contemporaries, but his rhetorical approach could not have been more different: moral concern, pretense toward objectivity, and even, for pretty much the first time, the actual words of his subjects. A similar rhetoric adorned overtly sensational works such as Watts Phillips's guide to "the other half . . . the districts inhabited by those strange and neglected races designated as the Wild Tribes of London":

> Doubtless when the halting devil of Le Sage undertook to show the wonders of Madrid to his new acquaintance, it was from no higher purpose than might arise from a feeling of vanity on his part, and of gratitude to his deliverer; his comments, too, upon the houses and their inmates were generally of the scoffing and Mephistophelean sort, such as might have been expected from the somewhat jocular and exceedingly cynical friend of the respectable Don Cleophas; but it is with a far different aim

> that we prepare for our wanderings among the dwellings of the poor, for our journey among the savage districts of that vast tract that encircles our civilisation like a belt; prepare to seek out and enter those miserable homes where "Fear and Indignation sit by fireless hearths."[131]

As Arac has established, Anglophone realist novelists equally used the Asmodeus image as a counterpoint to their own representational endeavors: Nathaniel Hawthorne "worries over the power of a 'spiritualized Paul Pry' . . . 'the limping devil of Le Sage' "; Dickens associated omniscient narration to irresponsible journalism that "deal[s] in round abuse and blackguard names; pulling off the roofs of private houses, such as the Halting Devil did in Spain; pimping and pandering for all degrees of vicious taste."[132] Where these respectable fiction writers seem primarily to have been concerned with how best to maintain a properly middle-class conception of privacy in a voyeuristic world and through a voyeuristic form of fictional narration, others saw that same gesture in more directly political terms, testifying that a sense of agency from below had diminished as power from above had become material rather than magical. The *Examiner* of 14 July 1849 reported that when "crow's nests" were erected on top of Westminster and St. Paul's for the purpose of sanitary survey, "there was 'consternation' among the 'Chartist agitators' who saw a 'gigantic machinery of espionage.' "[133] Although the Asmodeus flight was an outmoded metaphor for the middle-class novelist, it was a lost vantage point of representational space for the inhabitant of an insalubrious neighborhood or the political agitator, targets of the increasingly sophisticated mechanisms of surveillance, and objects of study for the newly emerging figure of the detective, whose name, as Arac reminds us, derived etymologically from the same image, "an active 'uncoverer,' a 'lifter-off of roofs.' "[134] By the middle of the century, the Asmodeus flight was not the static image of sweeping power that Arac reads it to have been, but the figure of a space visibly fraught with contradictions of attitude, position, ideology, and change rapidly losing ground to a vertical separation whose contradictions were not so readily personified by the devil.

While the London discourse tended to keep separate as much as possible what it defined as the extremes of society, the Paris discourse tended to relate them, and this distinction holds for Asmodeus as for other aspects of the trope of verticality. A standard motif of the Parisian *diable boiteux* was a range that encompassed not merely the rooftops but the entire city, from the sewers to the stars. One author described the bottle in which the devil had been trapped by an enchanter as filled with "that excremental filth [*boue*] in which partisan journalists dip their pens."[135] Once released by the Madrid bachelor, however, the pair jump into a balloon and head for Paris, where they admire its clocks, its towers, and its newest wonders: the "majestic dome" of the Panthéon and the "golden ball of the Invalides, shining like a star through the clouds."[136] Thus they approach the city "of gold and of filth [*boue*]."[137] Janin too referred to this revolutionary devil, the genius of Juvenal and Voltaire, exchanging his walking stick for "a rag-picker's pannier. He sought out mores and histories in all the sewers of Paris."[138] In lieu of this muckraking devil, and in lieu of the all-powerful authority as which he had developed in England, Janin proposed a collective Asmodeus, the result of a "revolution in the study of mores." Playing on the diabolical identification of revolution, but shrugging off the traumas of 1789 and 1830, Janin instead asserted that "Asmodeus is everywhere; Asmodeus is no longer someone, Asmodeus is everyone [*tout le monde*]"; and only by this collective body was it possible adequately to describe "modern civilization, so jarring, so varied, so indecisive, whose most innocent caprice has been a revolution."[139] Once the phantasmagoric devil vogue of the 1830s and '40s, where the *boue* was primarily restricted to the urban mysteries, was over, the link between material and supernatural, high and low, was more often than not observed. In 1855, a "brother of Asmodeus" began his nocturnal journey with a writer by observing a cart laden with stinking filth on its way toward Montfaucon; he concluded with the vision of a future where night has been banished by the "mastery of electricity," and Paris has become the literal as well as the figurative capital of the world.[140]

The relation between the material and the figurative underground, the antiquity of the devil and his close ties to the technological cutting edge, his allegiance to authority and morality on the one hand and to rebellion and vice on the other: these are what link the various permutations of the *diable boiteux* just as they link up the various facets of the devil: the terrifying Satan figures of the omnipotent dictator, the despotic ruler, or the robber baron; the ambivalent gaze of the bohemian; the play Satan of popular culture. Technology develops as a rule with the funding of capital and under the auspices of exploitation—mining and warfare—and so has the literally panoramic viewpoint been a privilege and an accessory of power, a key component of the dominant conception of modern space. But the halting devil introduced a figure out of representational space, the chaotic space of everyday life, an image born of syncretic myth and commonplaces. Although potentially a satanic figure of panoptic control and a containing frame for the disorder of the quotidian, the halting devil was readily susceptible to appropriation by the disempowered, for being turned top to bottom, to adapt Bakhtin's formulation. Here, Satan no longer laughs scornfully from above but from below, and he uses the technology with which he is invariably associated to disrupt the structures of domination from beneath rather than rule them from above. The inversion is never so neatly accomplished as the cotton bonnet of Delvau's upside-down apartment building on the passage Radzivil. Rather, the oppressive and the subversive, the represented and the representational Satan shift rapidly from one to the other within the space of a single text and within the domain of spatial practice.

Satanic Verses

Within the bowels of these elements,
Where we are tortured and remain forever.
Hell hath no limits, nor is circumscribed
In one self place, but where we are is Hell,
And where Hell is there must we ever be.
And to be short, when all the world dissolves,
And every creature shall be purified,
All places shall be Hell that is not Heaven.

MEPHISTOPHILIS, IN CHRISTOPHER MARLOWE,
Doctor Faustus (end of the sixteenth century)

Bran de damnés abominable,
Noire fécale de l'enfer
Noire guingenarde du diable.

ANONYMOUS POET on the *boue de Paris*

Urban panoramas such as *Le Diable à Paris* had united the view from above and the view from below by vitiating any pretense to seriousness in the dandyish understatement of the halting frame and the diffuse points of view of their many contributors. It was the great enigma of Baudelaire to have succeeded in knotting together the myriad faces of the devil amid the rising flood of the new underground and the new morality, when no one before him had ever taken them seriously enough to consider them even to be connected or worth salvaging. And, indeed, Benjamin cautioned back in the 1930s that Baudelaire's satanism is not to be taken any more seriously than any other nineteenth-century devilry, its sole significance coming from its being the only nonconformist position he sustained for any period of time.[141] Many critics before Benjamin had regarded Baudelaire as simply passing through a series of dandyish poses: "Everywhere in his . . . poems is a backdrop of Parisian vice, as well as a backdrop of Catholic ritual"; "The liturgical language, the angels, the Satans . . . are merely a *mise en scène* for the artist who deems that the picturesque is well worth a Mass."[142] Nevertheless, there was in fact a more significant but equally simple explanation for calling Baudelaire a poseur, and Benjamin's failure to address it is the greatest limitation of his seminal reading of the poet, and, indeed, of his influential vision of nineteenth-century Paris in terms of hell. Contrary to the critics' tendency to collapse the Devil into a unified figure and space, there was no more a single satanism in Baudelaire's work than there was a single underworld in the nineteenth-century imagination, but a series of many, often contradictory satanisms, ranging from the most facile and clichéd to the most sublime and idiosyncratic. There was the theory of irony based in the double vision of the fallen Lucifer, caught between debased man and unblemished paradise, for whom all of nature was viewed through the corrupt rubric of the modern city. There were the good daemons and evil specters that haunted the poet's dreams and hallucinations, including the allegorical personifications that recur in the poetry under such names as "Death" and "Debauchery." There was the Satan whose proper domain was the literally infernal city of Paris, full of sewage and offal, roamed by beggars, ragpickers, and streetwalkers; and the Satan who reigned over the nocturnal city of endless temptation, of gambling hells, bars, Gomorrahs, and brothels. And, finally, there was the repeated comparison of the poet to Dante, superficial to be sure, but equally surely containing a kernel of insight about Baudelaire's literary relation to the Devil in nineteenth-century Paris.

Part of the reason for the Dante comparisons, Benjamin argued, was the sheer idiosyncrasy of the form of Baudelaire's verse. How could such an outdated poetic mode as allegory have played such a fundamental role in such an influential nineteenth-century book? How could such an isolated figure himself have played such a key role in the cultural history of modernity?[143] One clue is to be found in the above evaluations of the poetry as theater and as role-playing. Baudelaire treated religion and satanism as integral elements of modern Paris, which for him meant that they were interchangeable commodities just like all the rest; however, they were no less serious for being so. This is consistent with Baudelaire's social identification: his was a shopkeeper's satanism. As the literary critic Brunetière dismissively but tellingly phrased it, "He's just a Satan with a furnished apartment, a Beelzebub of the table d'hôte."[144] These are further clichés about the poet that must be reconciled with the quite different rhetoric of the Dante comparisons. Baudelaire's poses were transparent, his views riddled with petit-bourgeois prejudices and class resentment, his subject matter mundane and sordid. Even his verse could appear clumsy. Jules Laforgue commented on "these rough similes that suddenly, in the midst of a harmonious period, cause him to put his foot in his plate. . . . This is Americanisms superimposed on the metaphorical language of the 'Song of Songs.' "[145] Still, Laforgue went on to say that this combination of harmony and crassness was also the source of Baudelaire's force and originality, echoing Charles-Augustin Saint-Beuve's dictum that all the great topics of poetry had been covered already by Alphonse Lamartine, Hugo, and Musset. Posed with the problem of artistic novelty while at the same time being restricted to traditional themes and forms, Baudelaire resolved the dilemma by taking the big city itself for the first time as a subject for lyric poetry.[146] He was the first, Laforgue wrote,

> to speak of Paris from the point of view of one of her daily damned (the lighted gas jets tormented by the wind of Prostitution, the restaurants and their air vents, the hospitals, the gambling, the logs resounding as they are sawn and then dropped on the paved courtyard, and the chimney corner, and the cats, beds, stockings, drunkards, and modern perfumes—all in a noble, remote, and superior fashion.[147]

Allegory allowed Baudelaire to combine in his verse the haughty satanism of the view from above with the crude materiality of the view from below.

The expression of what was most novel through archaic modes of representation was a hallmark of the nineteenth century, but rarely, as Dolf Sternberger observed in a different context, was such an expression explicitly allegorical. Discussing an 1875 speech commemorating James Watts's invention of the steam engine as the matrimonial copulation between the "hot-headed and ill-mannered" husband, steam, and his wife, the engine, Sternberger noted that "the humor masks the sinister and enigmatic face of technology—or nature—which serves for a long time and then, unexpectedly and unforeseeably, flies into a destructive passion. . . . Far from belittling the enigma of that double face, Dr. Engel's allegory . . . reveals the underlying demonic nature all the more frighteningly."[148] In other words, the pedantic attempt at humor by the director of the Prussian Statistics Office exhibited unconsciously the same satanic view of nature that Baudelaire made explicit when he consciously adopted it to write about the "double face" of the city of Paris.

It is instructive to compare Baudelaire's satanism to the hermetic urban symbolism of Blake and Nerval, on the one hand, and to the translucent allegory of Shelley's hell on the other. Rather than Baudelaire's identification with the masses, his contemporary Nerval had pretensions to noble descent. Nerval's world was firmly rooted in Paris, but it was an interior Paris, a psychogeographical city that opened up beneath his feet at hallowed sites such as Montmartre and Les Halles. For Nerval, walking through the nighttime city was a "series of trials which . . . for the ancients, represented the idea of a descent to the underworld [*une descente aux enfers*]."[149] Like Baudelaire, Nerval's vision was wrought into a record of the material changes undergone by his city, but primarily because those very changes unlocked "the mysteries of my soul . . . a hazy underground [*souterrain*] which is illuminated little by little, and where out of the shadow of the night emerge the gravely immobile and pale figures that inhabit the abode of limbo. Then . . . the world of the Spirits opens for us."[150] Nerval's Satan, his "Diable rouge," was a figure of hidden, perhaps forbidden knowledge. He was an urban Satan simply because Paris was the landscape of Nerval's lived experience; his was an underground city simply because that experience could be unlocked through the nightscape, a world of shadows and of margins. The same Paris that Baudelaire would detail in its most sordid aspects became for Nerval a key to his dreams. One night at midnight, in the quarter where he lives, he happens to notice a house's numbered address; it is the number of his own years, and he sees in it an announcement of his own death. Certainly, Nerval's superstition is inextricable from the modernizing city: he was able to notice the number only because the house was caught in the glare of a streetlight; the number was there only as a result of the systematic numbering of houses undertaken in 1805. His beloved *noctambulage* could have taken place only in a newly gaslit city, but that dependence remained incidental to the personal meaning Nerval drew from Paris.

At the opposite extreme of the Nervalian imagination of an infernal city is Shelley's long satirical poem, *Peter Bell the Third* (1819).[151] Allegorical like Baudelaire's city poems, Shelley's depiction of Hell as "a city much like London" is, as Benjamin observed, crystal clear in its conception as well as its meaning. Shelley's Devil "Has neither hoof, nor tail, nor sting" (77); he takes the form of a city dweller:

> He is—what we are; for sometimes
> The Devil is a gentleman;
> At others a bard bartering rhymes
> For sack; a statesman spinning crimes,
> A swindler living as he can;
> A thief, who cometh in the night. (81–86)

The Devil takes Peter to "the world of fashion" (139), "Hell's Grosvenor Square" (264) to be exact. The sting of Shelley's poem was to update hell for the inhabitants of Regency London; he gleefully detailed the mistaking of vice for virtue throughout the city:

> Though to be sure this place was Hell;
> He was the Devil—and all they—
> What though the claret circled well,
> And Wit like ocean, rose and fell?—
> Were damned eternally. (368–72)

Shelley used the extended metaphorical comparison as a slightly archaic rhetorical figure for the slightly musty character of traditional Hell. The reader easily sees through the allegory; everyone knows what Hell is: the slight distancing allows the moral satire the possibility of persuasion and of change. If Hell was a city much like Regency London, then London itself could be altered, even if Hell might not be. On the other hand, the very lightness of the conceit belies the seriousness of intent; even with its moments of outrage, it remains a clever allegory rather than an angry tract. Shelley stands resolutely outside and above the space of his poem.

Blake's illuminations were much closer to Baudelaire in capturing the dialectical nature of modern urban satanism. What Blake gained in the revolutionary immediacy of the social milieu in which he was writing and the materiality of the printing and engraving he was performing, however, he lost in their metaphysical application. Blake's theology of the 1790s was one of fervent belief rather than blasé modernity or hard-hitting rationalism; his "Proverbs of Hell," he wrote, would "shew the nature of Infernal wisdom better than any description of buildings or garments."[152] Like most prophets, Blake would bridge the gap between abstract negation and material reality by pushing each of them to its extreme until they touched through dint of will and the power of the imagination: "Everything possible to be believed is an image of truth," reads one of the "Proverbs of Hell."[153] The pact of Blake's poetry was to exchange currency in the everyday world for the visionary Romanticism of the underground; that of Baudelaire's was to exchange any reach whatsoever beyond his Paris for the perfect representation of its particular time and place.

Baudelaire's Paris, then, is a city much like Hell, and the poet resolutely inhabited it as the only world available to him. Benjamin's analysis suggests the class basis to this sense of confinement: "Baudelaire's satanism—of which so much has been made—is nothing other than his way of taking up the challenge which bourgeois society flings at the idle poet. This satanism is only a reasoned reprise of the cynical and destructive velleities—delusions, in the main—that emanate from the lower depths of society."[154] Nerval identified himself with the aristocrat who chose the *vie de bohème*, and discovered a transfiguratively infernal dreamscape in the space of Paris; Shelley stepped magisterially outside the city, to view hell from above; Blake was an artisan striving to transform the city in which he labored. Baudelaire—and it matters not whether he was driven to or chose this strategy—grounded every aspect of his poetic vision within the givens of the "bas-fonds sociaux." The glimpses he provides of the longed-for *idéal* arise only out of such a ground, as Laforgue noted with reference to the poetic diction, by the combination of the traditionally beautiful with the "flat" and ugly sounds of modernity, "that strange mania," as Leconte de Lisle complained, "for dressing up the discoveries of modern industry in bad verse."[155] It was not solely a rhetorical move to assert, as Barbey d'Aurevilly did, that "Dante's Muse saw Hell as if in a dream; that of the *Fleurs du mal* breathes it in through inflamed nostrils, as a horse breathes in shrapnel!"[156] Only with the concluding word did d'Aurevilly slip out of the urban milieu, but he was right that Baudelaire's Paris was indeed composed out of the olfactory. What stinks is not the destruction of war, however; it is the organic and the cadaverous, the pollution and rubbish that, both materially and metaphorically, filled the streets of the city and the head of the poet, and made his stance far more than the flâneur's protest seen by Benjamin; for Baudelaire, the bas-fonds were literal as well as figurative. Baudelaire's satanism was limited neither to the lighter than air phantasmagoria of the play devils nor to the sublime tempter of the metaphysicians. Refusing to elevate his mind beyond the everyday, finding his analogies in the dirty and confined world around him, he equally refused to give up the traditional matter of lyric poetry.

The essence of modernity was to remake nature in the image of capitalism; Baudelaire reversed the message of Marxism that man makes history by asserting that nothing in nature was sheltered from the fallen nature of man. In a letter to Toussenel, author of a book comparing animal physiognomies to human types, Baudelaire wondered if "noxious, disgusting animals were, perhaps, merely the coming to life in bodily form, of man's *evil thoughts*. . . . Thus, the whole of *nature* participates in original sin."[157] Modern Paris was awash in fallen nature. The sheer bulk of manure and dead flesh produced by the city's carriage horses blanketed the city. Cholera epidemics raged through the so-called *îlots insalubres* of the oldest quarters. The cemetery question haunted the city during the end of the eighteenth and the first half of the nineteenth century, including the emptying of the pestiferous churchyards into the Catacombes, that modern necropolis famously recorded by Baudelaire's friend Félix Nadar. The necropolis in particular was a crucial contemporary image of both London and Paris as an infernal city.[158] Nerval's nighttime landscape was a graveyard of memories: following a funeral procession to the Cimetière de Montmartre atop the butte's ancient carrières, he found himself searching for the tomb of his lost Aurelia. Shelley, too, imagined all of London allegorically as a cemetery:

> All are damned—they breathe an air,
> Thick, infected, joy-dispelling:
> Each pursues what seems most fair,
> Mining like moles, through mind, and there
> Scoop palace-caverns vast, where Care
> In throned state is ever dwelling.[159]

There is doubtless a contemporary resonance to Nerval's personal obsession and Shelley's morality play, but each poet subordinates that resonance to the subject of his poetry. For Baudelaire, by contrast, the city itself was the subject, and his very mind was a necropolis, full of dead memories consumed by his verse (*vers*) and devoured by worms (*vers*); that necropolis existed in the midst of his waking life just as the cemetery entombed the rotting corpses of the city's dead in the midst of its bustling streets. This is the topic of "Spleen II," where Baudelaire equates his brain to

. . . une pyramide, un immense caveau, Qui contient plus de morts que la fosse commune. —Je suis un cimetière abhorré de la lune, Où comme des remords se trainent de longs vers Qui s'acharnent toujours sur mes morts les plus chers.[160]	this branching catacombs, this pyramid contains more corpses than the potter's field: I am a graveyard that the moon abhors, where long worms like regrets come out to feed most ravenously on my dearest dead.[161]

A similar synthesis of pathology and poetry occurs in "Au Lecteur" ("To the Reader") where the poet likens the brains of his readers to cadavers, and the daemons of vice that fill those brains to scavengers, parasites feeding on dead flesh:

Serré, fourmillant, comme un million d'helminthes,	Wriggling in our brains like a million worms,
Dans nos cerveaux ribote un peuple de Démons,	a demon demos holds its revels there,
Et, quand nous respirons, la Mort dans nos poumons	and when we breathe, the Lethe in our lungs
Descend, fleuve invisible, avec de sourdes plaintes.[162]	trickles sighing on its secret course.[163]

The poet describes life as a movement toward death ("Chaque jour vers l'Enfer nous descendons d'un pas") by an image of physical disease—the medical term "helminthes," or "intestinal worms"—that matches the mental and moral disorder of his verse.

The disorder was social as well. The most common sights the poet encounters in his wanderings are the detritus of modern society—beggars, prostitutes, ragpickers, and drunkards—and its organic waste, and he makes both of them representative of the world as a whole. We find the comparison in the opening poem of *Les Fleurs du mal*, "Au Lecteur":

Et nous alimentons nos aimables remords,	and we sustain our affable remorse
Comme les mendiants nourissent leur vermine. . . .	the way a beggar nourishes his lice. . . .
Aux objets répugnants nous trouvons des appas;	the things we loathed become the things we love;
Chaque jour vers l'Enfer nous descendons d'un pas,	day by day we drop through stinking shades
Sans horreur, à travers des ténèbres qui puent.[164]	quite undeterred on our descent to Hell.[165]

The physical details—the beggar's *vermine* (lice), the stink of hell that concludes the stanza like a lead weight ("qui puent")—anchor the metaphor in the proverbially sticky and stinking *boue de Paris.* The most frequent natural language we find is the lexicon of the sewer—*boue*, *fange*, *bouge*, *bourbe*, *voirie*—and the language of decomposition, especially in the double-edged *vers* ("verse" / "worms").

The image of poetic and physical decomposition occurs in the context of the love lyric in "La Charogne" ("Carrion") where the poet and his lover encounter the rotting corpse of a dog while on a quiet stroll, and he envisions his "amour décomposé," her body eaten by the kisses of carrion worms. We find a similar image in "Remords Posthume" ("Posthumous Remorse") where the poet fantasizes a revenge on a faithless lover:

Lorsque tu dormiras, ma belle ténébreuse,	The time will come when your dark loveliness
Au fond d'un monument construit en marbre noir,	must sleep alone beneath a marble slab
Et lorsque tu n'auras pour alcôve et manoir	and keep no couch or canopy but this:
Qu'un caveau pluvieux et qu'une fosse creuse	a rainy graveyard and a seeping pit.
. . .	. . .
le ver rongera ta peau comme un remords.[166]	And worms will gnaw your flesh, like a regret.[167]

The second verse provides the concrete urban detail of the funereal monument; the third and fourth equate it figuratively with a fall into poverty, from "manoir" to the lower depths of the "caveau pluvieux" and "fosse creuse"; the conclusion characteristically collapses the material and the metaphorical. When she is dead in her grave: this is the traditional message of *vanitas* embodied by the angel of death. When she loses her beauty, she will be reduced from luxurious chambers to the hovel of the aged courtesan. In either case, she remains an inhabitant of Paris and a dweller in hell, and in either case, she will be eaten by *vers*, whether her corpse by the worms or her reputation by the remorse of poverty and the venom of Baudelaire's verse.

There is a satanic laughter laced through these poems, an intentionally sick and sophomoric humor, not only in the overwrought misogyny but also in the gleeful attention to the disgusting details of decomposition; there is equally a sublime and subtle jest. The humor only works because it is cast within the high style of poetry: the favored sonnet form, the perfect rhyme and meter, the careful observation of the rules of prosody. Laughter is satanic, according to Baudelaire, because it is always double, sign of "infinite greatness and of infinite wretchedness [*misère*]. . . . It is from the constant clash of these two infinities that laughter flows."[168] This was the nineteenth-century devil, hovering between his ancient metaphysical sublimity and his modern fall into useless misery; this was modern Paris, the old become sublime with age and nostalgia, but also poor, decrepit, and verminous, and the new, a glittering, alluring promise of happiness, but also a stinking, noisy, ignorant crowd. Baudelaire looked at modern Paris and saw all this at once, employing the same gaze that saw in his lovers timeless beauty and organic decay. As we read in "Le Cygne" ("The Swan") the city broken into pieces by Baron Georges-Eugène Haussmann coexisted with the old city of his memory:

Paris change! mais rien dans ma mélancolie N'a bougé! palais neufs, échafaudages, blocs, Vieux faubourgs, tout pour moi devient allégorie,	Paris changes . . . But in sadness like mine nothing stirs—new buildings, old neighborhoods turn to allegory,
Et mes chers souvenirs sont plus lourds que des rocs.[169]	and memories weigh more than stone.[170]

This is not merely the sublime fall of Milton's Satan into hell; it is a ridiculous and pitiful fall as well, a wild swan bathing its wings in the filthy dust of a dry stream, a "negress" dreaming of Africa as she walks through the muck. It is an exile of time as well as of space. Nerval wrote of the days of his bohemian youth in the rue du Doyenné, the site of "Le Cygne" that was replaced by the Place du Carrousel in 1852, that he once had had enough money to buy two lots of wood paneling from the rooms painted by members of his coterie: "Where did you lose so many beautiful things? Balzac asked me one day.—In misfortune! I answered him with one of my favorite sayings."[171] In Nerval's private madness, he carried with him pieces torn from his past dwelling place, losing them nevertheless like so many memories. Baudelaire strove in his poetry to give memories the weight "des rocs." Doré's contemporary illustration to *Inferno* 34 of the brooding Satan, elbows leaning on the frozen ice of Cocytus, contemplated by a miniscule Dante and Virgil up on an ice ledge, captures the nineteenth-century figure of the Devil as melancholic, fallen from "grandeur infinie" to "misère infinie" (figure 2.23). Baudelaire's satanic gaze was equally melancholic, but

2.23 The brooding nineteenth-century version of Dante's Satan, sublimely frozen at the core of Hell. Illustration by Gustave Doré, in *Inferno,* by Dante Alighieri (Paris: L. Hachette et cie), 1865.

distinguished from Doré's because he remained in the same place from which he had fallen, and was forced to watch its loss occurring around him at every moment.

This is an important sense in which Baudelaire genuinely resembles Dante; for his Paris, like the latter's Inferno, superimposed past and present. For Dante, all of the damned souls have been caught in the moment that reveals the essence of their lives on earth, but which is also the identity they must endure for all eternity. As they were in life, so they remain in death: Dante's allegorical journey places the two moments in constant juxtaposition in order to strip bare for his readers the illusions of life that continue to obsess damned souls after their death. The essence of their punishment is not the worms that eat them—the specific torments of each circle—but the exculpatory stories each tells the pilgrim as he stops in his journey to speak with them. Satan's is the simplest of all: if you were as beautiful then as you are ugly now, how beautiful you must once have been! Baudelaire's Paris was a city whose beauty could be deciphered only through the ugliness of its current form, and whenever the poet glimpsed anything that appeared to be beautiful, he applied the same cipher to it, and conjured up the worms in its flesh. Whenever he forgot where he was, Baudelaire's devil turned his gaze to the gutter, and the decomposing worm returned.

This principle is well illustrated by the prose poem "Le Joueur Généreux," which proposes, rather than the philosophical and poetical satanism of *Les Fleurs du mal*, an encounter with the Old Man himself, and a glamorous vision of the phantasmagoric underworld enjoyed by the upper classes. Strolling with the crowd on the boulevard, a stranger brushes against him; the poet follows him into a sumptuous gambling hell, "a subterranean habitation, dazzling, where sparkled a luxury that none of the superior establishments of Paris could possibly approach."[172] Once inside, the poet loses everything at the gaming table, including his soul. Following the gaming, he sits and smokes with "His Highness," who discourses on his bad reputation, and claims only once to have been frightened over his power: when he heard a preacher shout to his audience to remember that "when you hear boasting of the progress of enlightenment, that the sublimest ruse of the devil is to persuade you that he doesn't exist!"[173] In conclusion, the poet's host, wishing to prove that the one "of whom one speaks so much evil" is "sometimes a *bon diable*," promises his victim in recompense for his lost soul the possibility of assuaging and vanquishing "l'Ennui," be his desire riches, travel, or voluptuousness.[174] After parting, the poet cannot believe in such happiness, and finds himself falling back on his old habits of prayer: "Dear God! Lord, my God! Grant that the devil keep his word!"[175] Everything about this prose poem is illusory: after all, the underworld of Paris is gutters and beggars, not glittering gambling parlors; Satan urges evildoing rather than promising happiness; praying to God that the promises of the city's shopwindows, streetwalkers, and poets actually be granted is to misunderstand the nature of both faith and atheism. The subtlest ruse of God (or of happiness) is to convince us that it exists; there is no such thing as a *bon diable* in this sense.

Still, out of the wide range he depicted, the Satan most fully embraced by Baudelaire was neither the suave Mephistophelean tempter of "Le Joueur Généreux" nor the brooding melancholic of "Le Cygne," but the "Demon of Action" in "Assommons les pauvres!" ("Let's Beat Up the Poor!"), the devil who pokes his fingers into the wounds of the city and its inhabitants, who whispers in the poet's ear that the only alms worthy of an urban beggar is to beat him until he has no choice but to return that beating blow for blow with pure hatred: "By my energetic medication, I had thus restored pride and life to him."[176] The Satan that counsels such actions is a hooligan philosopher, a low-life bigot who beats the beggar's head against a nearby wall only after having "verified that in that deserted banlieue I found myself safely beyond the grasp of any police officer."[177] It is a behavior so antisocial as only to be blamed on "those malicious Demons who slip inside us and make us perform, without our knowledge, their most absurd wishes," demons such as the one that on peering out a garret window over the city in "Le Mauvais Vitrier" ("The Bad Glazier") would pick out the titular glazier on the street, force him to lug his wares to the top of the building, send him away because he has no colored windows, and then drop a stone from the window onto his back when he has finally struggled back downstairs onto the street, shattering his wares to bits.[178] Only a maladjusted adolescent could consider such cruelty to be a poetic gesture; but the symbolic armature of the piece puts it beyond the life experience of any such adolescent. This is the paradox of Baudelaire's poetry, the paradox of his Satan, and the paradox of his Paris. It is presented in schematic, parable form in the prose poems, through cultural and philosophical clichés rather than through the stereotypes of poetry characteristic of *Les Fleurs du mal.* It is the paradox of the underground as well: composed of the dreck of society but the only remaining repository of its dreams, even if those dreams can be expressed only as they are coded under the auspices of the devil. Baudelaire is the nineteenth-century writer that attempted most rigorously to represent the workings of this paradox. To be effective, his writings argued, the paradox could be expressed only in subterranean Paris, in the recesses of his mind, and through the destructive armature of his language.

Baudelaire claimed to have chosen to seek beauty in evil because it was the only location in which beauty had not yet been celebrated in verse. It is easy to underestimate the range encompassed by the term *mal* in this pronouncement. Most readers and many critics still assume it to be simply a question of metaphysics and morals: the evil of sin. But it includes also the underground topics of the modern city, from the evil of urban poverty, disease, and pollution to the evil of metropolitan improvements; it includes the evils of bigotry, misogyny, prejudice, and political reaction; it includes the evils of language, the clichés, *idées reçues*, and overused topoi of poetry and urban writing. As Benjamin rightly observed, it was a wholly destructive, well-nigh anarchistic endeavor, for every moment of purported beauty or idealism only existed under the threat of being undercut at any time by ironic laughter. It is the voice of urban capitalism at its most seductive; its enduring contemporaneousness—another commonplace of Baudelaire studies is that his poetry has not aged—mirrors that of the underground, which, while reveling in the *mal* of the city, never ceases also to entice through the currency of that same *mal*.

The achievement of Baudelaire is to have laid bare the place of the devil in the modern city, to have demonstrated the inextricability of the view from above and the view from below, the incisive analysis and the material descent. To borrow Lefebvre's terminology, he categorically refused to employ the represented space of the city, restricting himself wholly to the representational, lived space generally imagined topographically as the bas-fonds, even when viewing the city from the traditional vantage points of the space of representation. Certainly, this could only have been accomplished in Paris in the middle of the nineteenth century. Unlike the impressionist painters analyzed by T. J. Clark in *The Painting of Modern Life*, the myth of modernity created in Baudelaire's poetry did not argue through its aesthetics that the city lacked intelligible form, celebrating a middle-class modernity of free-floating spectacle.[179] Instead, his resolutely petit-bourgeois viewpoint exposed the raw wounds of the changing social order just as it traced the changes in the social space of Paris that were eliminating the satanic world he clung to with a death grip. In this, the furor surrounding the purported obscenity of *Les Fleurs du mal* was analogous to that elicited by the nudity of Manet's *Olympia*, responding in both cases to an overly direct assertion of class.[180] What the medium of words allowed Baudelaire to accomplish that the iconicity and immediacy of Manet's visual image did not was to combine the emblematic assertion of the material body in the city with the metaphysical and epistemological history of the devil. He condensed a long subterranean history into the claustrophobic framework of the new petit-bourgeois perspective, neither a view from above nor a view from below but a view from within.

What especially distinguishes this poetry from other portraits of the devil and the underground city is that there was no time lapse in the relation of representation to history. The urban cruces of *Les Fleurs du mal* and *Le Spleen de Paris* were not displaced in either space or time, as they are in the fiction of urban mysteries and other views from below, nor, following the view from above, were they rendered as comic fantasies in the manner of the diableries and the framing conceits of the panoramas, nor did they dissolve the city into a psychological space as later portraits of urban alienation tended to do. They allegorized the city, allowing all these elements to be represented simultaneously, just as they exist in the complex space-time of the cityscape. And yet, just as each mode of representing the urban is faithful to one aspect while necessarily falsifying the others, so Baudelaire's oeuvre also entails a choice: he gained a holistic representation of the city as-is, including the manifold traces of the city as-was within the present, but at the cost of any sense of the future. This representational space is analogous to the sense of time Piero Camporesi has identified, "which in a world of destitution" never leads into the future (inheritance of the rich), unless ironically, but is consumed in the present, or in the obsessive repetition of an ever-identical past, recurring immutably, on a fixed date, like a constant nightmare."[181] Baudelaire's Satan has not a trace remaining of the utopian impulse that can be glimpsed in every other manifestation of the devil, however clichéd and hackneyed that impulse may appear. The very skill with which Baudelaire manipulated the linguistic and material commonplaces of nineteenth-century Paris exposed their complex social meaning while emptying them of the possibility of materializing somewhere in the future their diluted dreams of better things.

Baudelaire's ability to derive a comprehensive representational system out of the manifold and contradictory meanings of the devil and his underground demesne offers both a tool for uncovering the partial meanings in other versions and a dead end for a theory of the urban underground. He stands outside the waves of devil vogues that swept the modern West in the first half of the nineteenth century and were revived at later moments of crisis: the 1870s and '80s; the turn of the century; the postwar; the post–cold war. Baudelaire's use of the satanic serves to explain the contradictions in every other representation of the modern city, the allure and repulsion of urban modernity; he shows us how to read through the clichés and poses of other portrayals. What he did not provide was a solution; he evidently did not consider it possible to conceive of one, and eschewed the option of offering a partial one. Yet it is to partial formulations and partial solutions that this book is otherwise devoted. Baudelaire's poetry is a perfect analysis of the modern city, but we accept that perfection only at the cost of permanently inhabiting the modern city as manifested in Second Empire Paris and as experienced by Baudelaire. It is this specificity that gives his poetry such power and conviction; it is also paradoxically what limits it. Baudelaire's blindness makes his model applicable everywhere—but only in the place where he wrote—and always—but only in the moments when he wrote. The blindness of every other representation of the urban underground makes a different process necessary: the precise where and when must be restored in each case; but there also results a mythic imprecision that escapes that situation, the moments when the devil manages to point at something else surviving somewhere beyond the putative eternity of his fallen state.

The Devil Take the Hindmost

We're going to—H'm—Yes, we're going to—H'm—
We are going to town we will say
For it's still to be found
On the dark Underground—
That City that's dark all day!
The place where gold buys everything
All's marked with a price somehow,
From an M. P.'s seat to a wedding ring—
But they don't call it Hades now!
It's called L—It's called O—It's called N,D,O—
It's called L,O,N,D,O,N—London!
It was—Well! It was—oh! It was—
Oh dear no!
We'd much better call it London!

EDWARD ROSE AND "CAPTAIN COE," *Orpheus and Eurydice* (1891)

Baudelaire's isolated synthesis came at a crux in the formation of the modern city as the decades of ferment settled into the fixed coordinates of Victorian London and Second Empire Paris and the second industrial revolution, "the age of steam and steel," took over from the first.[182] Where earlier industry had been concerned with mechanizing familiar and timeworn activities such as mining and weaving, the transportation and building technologies that emerged during the middle of the century seemed by comparison sui generis, and the old modes of representation that had easily been adapted to mining and gaslight were harder pressed to make sense of subways and steamships. Milner's "golden age of Satanism" had been very much a phenomenon of the first industrial revolution. In Paris, it corresponded roughly with the July Monarchy; the height of the devil vogue in London had been even earlier, corresponding with the Regency and the years preceding the coronation of Victoria. In London, the vogue had coincided with the rise of gas lighting, but it predated much of the key phenomena of urban modernity, including the innovations in printing technology of the 1840s, and was primarily backward-looking in its infernal imagery. The representation of the devil in London's popular theater reflected these changes, even as the satirical moral remained the same: the city was too corrupt for him. The soon obsolete forms of the 1820s and '30s did not vanish later in the century, but without the legitimizing backdrop of Romanticism and the nurturing environment of Regency culture, they became fairly empty vessels for Victorian spectacle, or were alluded to as counterpoints for more current representations of space, as with

Dickens's hands-off attitude toward the Asmodeus flight, and the new stance of rationalism that characterized the later city panoramas, guides, and cyclopedias. In Paris, the *féerie* continued to wrap up the newest fads and fashions in a pandaemoniac framework for the consumption of the masses. Still, just as the new solidity of Victoria's regime put paid to the devil's dominion, so did the coup d'état of Louis Napoleon, as Baudelaire's bitterly nostalgic satanism bewailed, signal an end to an era in Paris—the diablerie would not regain its cultural capital until revitalized by motion picture technology at the turn of the century.

Where the Orpheus plays stressed the seductive if not downright pleasurable aspects of corruption consistent with their Parisian pedigree, the London devil redounded more and more to his morality play origins as the century wore on. The tradition of the devil in town dates back at least to Ben Jonson's *The Devil is an Ass* (1616), which unfairly matched an apprentice devil against the corruption of Jacobean London. Early on, translations of Luis Vélez de Guevara's novel to the stage had made their own local additions, as in Asmodeus's description of a London theater circa 1708, "the Master of which is so near a Relation of mine, that I may call it my own House upon that Foundation."[183] Combining the topos of the *theatrum mundi*, or theater of the world, with the newer topoi of urban hell, the theater exploited, often to excess, the humor inherent in the vertiginous spectacle available by re-creating on its boards the infernal sites outside its doors. Regency plays such as W. T. Moncrieff's operatic extravaganza, *Don Giovanni in London!* (Olympic, 1817), were based on the image of high and low life most familiar from Tom and Jerry, the famous swells of Egan's panoramic *Life in London* (1821), itself adapted for the stage many times during the period. *Giovanni*'s playbill promised "The River Styx, by Twilight," followed by "Charing Cross, by Bluelight" and "St. Giles's, by Gaslight" (figure 2.24); the text imagined the libertine, thrown out of Hell for seducing Pluto's wife, Proserpine, stealing Charon's bark, and heading straight for London, "dear emporium of pleasure," on the stolen wings of Mercury.[184] *The Devil's Walk! or, Pluto in London* (Surrey, 1830), adapted by Moncrieff from the much-imitated satirical poem by Samuel Taylor Coleridge and Robert Southey, took a more negative view toward Regency dissipation, as Satan concluded that he had much to learn from it about conducting his business down below.[185] In *The Devil in London* (Adelphi, 1840), we find Satan come to the capital on a bet with Mephistopheles: "I'll go with empty pockets, and prove to you that with common care, common sense, and the smallest possible grain of honesty, the devil himself may become respectable and well-to-do."[186] The satire was sprinkled with countless puns on the name of the devil, who loses his bet, finding that he can only survive in London through trickery and magic. Disconsolately seating himself on the steps of a house door in Jermyn Street, St. James's, he exclaims: "The world has excelled me in all the qualities for which I was once remarkable."[187]

Midcentury versions of the devil in London exhibit a growing tendency to portray a city obsessed with business rather than pleasure, and plagued by poverty; when dissipation is portrayed, as in the gambling "hells" of St. James's, it is now marked as something alien, often Parisian, rather than characteristic of the British capital. In *The Devil on Town* (Surrey, 1863), Sir Dugald is sent to London, to be granted an extra five years of life if he can find victims for the Devil. He appears as one "Dark Star" in Leicester Square, encounters the inevitable watercress girl, and pronounces of the gambling and dissolution he goes on to encounter in the neighborhood that "you might call this part Paris for there's more French than English about it."[188] What remains wholly Victorian about the play is that Dark Star's satanic mission is a simple twist on the melodramatic staple of the evil lord, foiled in his efforts to corrupt a country innocent.

The Regency devil had been an abstract moralizer or a pleasure-seeking swell; the infernal Victorian city and its inhabitants were depicted as if surrounded and possessed by their own individual devils. In *The Terror of London* (Marylebone, 1868), adapted from the popular serial *Spring-Heel'd Jack*, the protagonist is taken for the Devil because of his uncanny leaping ability (springs in his boots). He turns out instead to be an embittered nobleman, bent on vengeance toward the world for unjustly depriving him of his inheritance (figure 2.25). In *The Sorrows of Satan* (Shakespeare, 1897), adapted from Marie Corelli's bestselling novel of

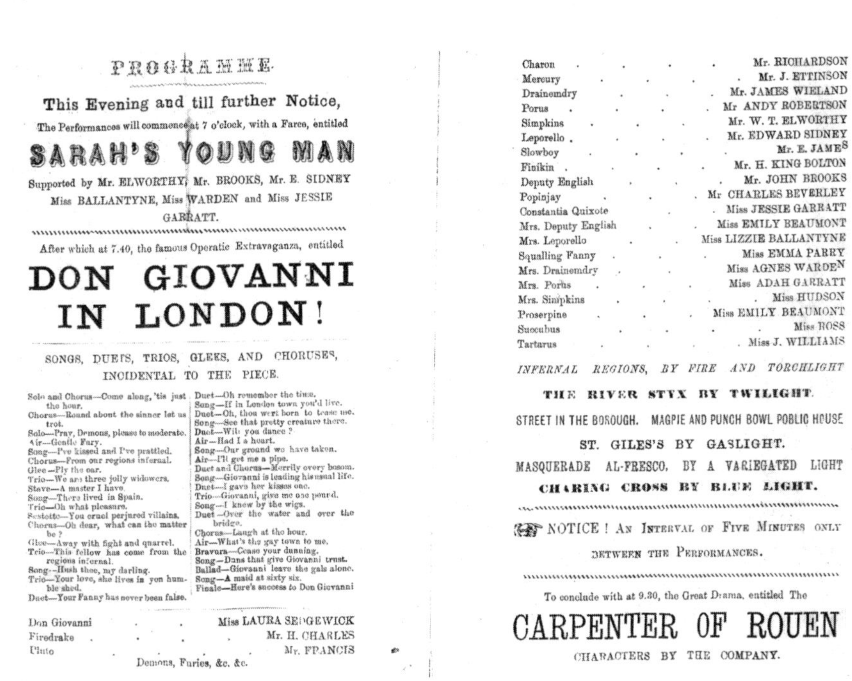
PROGRAMME.

This Evening and till further Notice,

The Performances will commence at 7 o'clock, with a Farce, entitled

SARAH'S YOUNG MAN

Supported by Mr. ELWORTHY, Mr. BROOKS, Mr. E. SIDNEY Miss BALLANTYNE, Miss WARDEN and Miss JESSIE GARRATT.

After which at 7.40, the famous Operatic Extravaganza, entitled

DON GIOVANNI IN LONDON!

SONGS, DUETS, TRIOS, GLEES, AND CHORUSES, INCIDENTAL TO THE PIECE.

Solo and Chorus—Come along, 'tis just the hour.
Chorus—Round about the sinner let us trot.
Solo—Pray, Demons, please to moderate.
Air—Gentle Fury.
Song—I've kissed and I've prattled.
Chorus—From our regions infernal.
Glee—Ply the oar.
Trio—We are three jolly widowers.
Stave—A master I have.
Song—There lived in Spain.
Trio—Oh what pleasure.
Sestetto—You cruel perjured villains.
Chorus—Oh dear, what can the matter be?
Glee—Away with fight and quarrel.
Trio—This fellow has come from the regions infernal.
Song—Hush thee, my darling.
Trio—Your love, she lives in yon humble shed.
Duet—Your Fanny has never been false.
Duet—Oh remember the time.
Song—If in London town you'd live.
Duet—Oh, thou wert born to tease me.
Song—See that pretty creature there.
Duet—Wilt you dance?
Air—Had I a heart.
Song—Our ground we have taken.
Air—I'll get me a pipe.
Duet and Chorus—Merrily every bosom.
Song—Giovanni is leading his usual life.
Duet—I gave her kisses one.
Trio—Giovanni, give me one pound.
Song—I knew by the wigs.
Duet—Over the water and over the bridge.
Chorus—Laugh at the hour.
Air—What's the gay town to me.
Bravura—Cease your dunning.
Song—Duns that give Giovanni trust.
Ballad—Giovanni leave the gals alone.
Song—A maid at sixty six.
Finale—Here's success to Don Giovanni

Don Giovanni	Miss LAURA SEDGEWICK
Firedrake	Mr. H. CHARLES
Pluto	Mr. FRANCIS

Demons, Furies, &c. &c.

Charon	Mr. RICHARDSON
Mercury	Mr. J. ETTINSON
Drainemdry	Mr. JAMES WIELAND
Porus	Mr ANDY ROBERTSON
Simpkins	Mr. W. T. ELWORTHY
Leporello	Mr. EDWARD SIDNEY
Slowboy	Mr. E. JAMES
Finikin	Mr. H. KING BOLTON
Deputy English	Mr. JOHN BROOKS
Popinjay	Mr CHARLES BEVERLEY
Constantia Quixote	Miss JESSIE GARRATT
Mrs. Deputy English	Miss EMILY BEAUMONT
Mrs. Leporello	Miss LIZZIE BALLANTYNE
Squalling Fanny	Miss EMMA PARRY
Mrs. Drainemdry	Miss AGNES WARDEN
Mrs. Porus	Miss ADAH GARRATT
Mrs. Simpkins	Miss HUDSON
Proserpine	Miss EMILY BEAUMONT
Succubus	Miss ROSS
Tartarus	Miss J. WILLIAMS

INFERNAL REGIONS, BY FIRE AND TORCHLIGHT

THE RIVER STYX BY TWILIGHT.

STREET IN THE BOROUGH. MAGPIE AND PUNCH BOWL PUBLIC HOUSE

ST. GILES'S BY GASLIGHT.

MASQUERADE AL-FRESCO. BY A VARIEGATED LIGHT

CHARING CROSS BY BLUE LIGHT.

NOTICE! AN INTERVAL OF FIVE MINUTES ONLY BETWEEN THE PERFORMANCES.

To conclude with at 9.30, the Great Drama, entitled The

CARPENTER OF ROUEN

CHARACTERS BY THE COMPANY.

2.24 Regency London as underworld. Programme for *Don Giovanni in London!* by W. T. Moncrieff, Olympic, 26 December 1817. Collection of author.

1895, the mysterious Prince Lucio Rimânez is a Romantic figure torn between his duty as a corruptor and his desire to be redeemed by failing to seduce. The humorless conflict is wholly internal, played out within a series of London and country-house interiors, and within the souls of an unsympathetic couple: the struggling writer, Geoffrey Tempest, desperate for money and fame, and the young Lady Sybil Elton, led astray by reading too much "New Woman" fiction. Just as the focus on poverty as the new urban underworld naturalized the city's social divisions, so did the internalization of the devil militate against any social basis for the ills attributed to him.

Whether depicted as a tyrant or a trickster, the power of the devil was imaginary, based on faith, deception, or delusion rather than fact. Whether a trick of lighting effects and staging or an imagined character, it is significant that the devil from above was a patently immaterial figure in the nineteenth century. What is important is the way he remained linked with the heights of fashion, with advanced technology, and with the complex mechanisms of capitalism into which so much of the faith of modern man has been relocated. From the balloons and lofty edifices that made Asmodeus's feat of magic a commonplace event to the technology of information, surveillance, and illumination on the one hand, and from the innovations in printing that gave rise to the panoramic literature of the 1830s and '40s, to the myriad moving pictures, sound and light shows, and to spectacles of visual effects that parade through the century from the theater at one end to the cinema at the other, the devil was associated both with the terrible ends to which technology is put and with the magnificent images that it makes possible. As Foucault observed, Jeremy Bentham's Panopticon was eagerly embraced by the Revolutionary government as a utopian scheme for eliminating the "darkened spaces . . . the pall of gloom which prevents the full visibility of things, men and truths" which it identified with the oppression of the ancien régime.[189] The equation is simple: the closer one gets to material use, the more wholly this laughing devil becomes an instrument of oppression pure and simple.

Although culture has always been able to serve as a direct vehicle for such expressions of power, the utopian impulse within Satan, threatening as it is, and well-nigh unimaginable within capitalistic systems of representation, whether spatially or otherwise, always manifests itself, however indirectly, within comedy, fairy tales, phantasmagorias, and other putatively unserious forms. Conversely, we find explicit empowerment from below not so much in the spectacle of the diablerie as in the crude potency of the criminal class in the fiction of urban mysteries, with its utter disdain for the codes, morals, and rules of the world above. As one of the victims of Anthony Tidkin, the bodysnatching "Resurrection Man" in G. W. M. Reynolds's *The Mysteries of London* (1844–48), exclaims, "Surely this man must be Satan himself, who comes at intervals to goad the wicked to desperation for their sins!"[190] Within the material and pathological underground of the urban mysteries it is impossible to gain the breadth and

2.25 Late Victorian satanic rationality: Playbill for Spring-Heel'd Jack in *The Terror of London*. Britannia Theatre, Hoxton, 1868. Collection of author.

perspective of a detached Asmodeus. Here, too, it is inextricably paired with an image from above, for the mystery of the pathological degree of Tidkin's villainy is that he was a displaced image of the ruling class. And it is this insight—the connection between Tidkin's crimes and the interrelated power structure of urban capital—that is precluded from the subterranean view; conversely, it is readily accessible to the view from above, but without the material context, the seriousness of intent and political will to put it into play. Although the threat was displaced within them, serials such as Reynolds's still posed directly its effect and power. No one ever saw fit to protest against or to directly censor the *féerie*, the pantomime, or the devil in town plays, granted of course that they did not touch directly on the privacy of a powerful individual; it was far easier simply to dismiss them as infantilism, as the morally and religiously serious concept of the devil in "danger of deteriorating into mere buffoonery," as one modern survey of the devil in literature has it.[191]

The threat of the mysteries was akin to the threat that during the second half of the century was the constant target of Christian invective and the lexicon of Satan and hell from above, and which for the most part replaced the mysteries as the primary topos of the view from below: the ever more polarized topography of the modern city. Late-century London fictional devils such as Robert Louis Stevenson's Mr. Hyde (1887), Bram Stoker's Dracula (1897), and Richard Marsh's diabolical Egyptian scarab in his bestselling novel *The Beetle* (1897), reflected this new topography; for they are resolutely individualized demons based on myths with resonance in a modernizing and secular city. Marsh's and Stoker's creations are alien invaders, vehicles of xenophobia related to the massive influx of immigrants to turn-of-the-century London; Stevenson's Hyde has internalized the alienation around him, his split personality echoing the segregation of classes. Although the fictional framework around them conjured up the specter of the far-reaching villainy of the earlier Resurrection Man, in the event these new devils managed to lead to their destruction only a handful of victims whose moral flaws had already marked them for lost anyway. There was no longer anything metaphysical about these characters; consequently, they could no longer stand in for the interconnectedness of society in the way that the Catholic Devil had long been able to do.

When the conditions of the urban poor provided prurient sensationalism to the fiction of urban mysteries in the 1840s, there had always been a sense of responsibility for the slumming reader, as if this were still somehow part of his or her own world. As the undeniably worsening conditions of the poor became the target of equally prurient descents to what was ever more represented as the alien underworld of the poor and the vicious, the creatures of Satan, there was no sense any longer of a political solution. As one appalled observer wrote in the *Edinburgh Medical Journal* in 1859, "Let anyone walk the streets of London, Glasgow, or Edinburgh, of a night, and, without troubling his head with statistics, his eyes and ears will tell him what a multitudinous army the devil keeps in his field service for advancing his own ends. The stones seem alive with lust, and the very atmosphere is tainted."[192] To be sure, the religious discourse of antiurbanism had always been fairly sweeping in its target. From the late eighteenth century to the mid-nineteenth century, however, even the most condemnatory view from above was dominated by the site-specific representational spaces of Paris and London. As the polarized metaphors of the Christian cosmos returned to predominance in the discourse of urban crisis, the specificity of particular cities tended to vanish under the weight of general damnation. As the Liberal politician C. F. G. Masterman wrote in 1909 against the religious optimism of G. K. Chesterton, who was "convinced that the Devil is dead. A Children's epileptic hospital, a City dinner, a political 'at Home,' a South African charnel camp, or other similar examples of cosmic ruin fail to shake this blasphemous optimism."[193] The devil had become the loosest of metaphors for social evil, just as his sites had become more and more generalized in an all too familiar litany of "cosmic ruin."

The effect would not prove overwhelming until the First World War provided a new metaphor for expressing the universality of damnation in concrete spatial terms, and the theories of modernism had provided a sophisticated new vocabulary for eliminating the old ambiguity that clung so tenaciously to the figure of the devil and his underground demesne. The sheer proliferation of the language of the underworld in the second half of the nineteenth century was matched in its ability to reiterate the tired tropes of filth and vice only by the tireless energy with which the new discourses of technological control of urban space could assert their total mastery of it. One of the main things to be learned by the unreflective repetition evident in the majority of examples of both discourses was the degree to which neither the claim to urban hell nor the claim to urban heaven could possibly be true.

The devil did not totally disappear from the urban panorama, but the dominant forms were doubtless the investigative journalism pioneered by Mayhew at the end of the 1840s and during the 1850s, and later more sensationalistic works such as William Stead's exposé of child prostitution in London, *The Maiden Tribute of Modern Babylon* (1885); and surveys and guidebooks such as Edouard Texier's vast *Tableau de Paris* (1853), Adolphe Joanne's capacious *Guides*, and Maxime Du Camp's encyclopedic *Paris: Ses organes, ses functions et sa vie jusqu'en 1870*. Regardless of the author's attitude to his or her material—Stead's outraged muckraking was characteristic of the London discourse just as Du Camp's nodding approval well reflects much of the Parisian discourse under Napoleon III—the rational approach self-consciously eschewed the urban supernatural, arguing that the technological city was far more mysterious and fantastic than the satanic one, but full of mysteries that could be explained according to the laws of nature and society. This was especially true of the Paris underground, now the trophy space of the Second Empire, which, as Texier assured his readers, provided not a walk through "the other world . . . in the realm of gnomes and hobgoblins" but a subterranean city bereft of even the few remaining traces of the diabolic to be witnessed aboveground.[194] Aboveground, too, the suspiciously satanic "devil-doctor" of old became in the new order a falsely accused moralist and rationalist whose only fault had been to be so good an individual and so advanced a physician as to be mistaken for a devil by the ignorant populace he was trying to assist. "A rare genius evoked the *diable boiteux*," wrote Eugène Sue in *Le Diable médecin* (1855–57), one of his unsuccessful efforts to duplicate the earlier success of *Les Mystères de Paris* and *Le Juif errant*, referring to the panorama vogue of the previous decades. "Our devil by contrast has nothing fantastic about him, but we knew him, we loved and honored him, because in spite of his eccentricities he was a great and good man."[195]

More common than Sue's characteristically populist attempt to appropriate the satanic power of the working classes for the forces of good was the demonized view of the underclass as demoralized by poverty, degraded by drink, and degenerated by several generations of urban slums indistinguishable one from the other, "dens of superfluous mankind" which preferred this life because it gave them "the liberty to be as vile as they pleased."[196] In the naturalized hell of Stead's journalism, Gissing's nether world, Arthur Morrison's Jago, Jack London's abyss, or Zola's *assommoir*, there was no escape, there was only the atavistic life force of the troglodyte. And the keenest indigenous insight into the cause of these conditions was to be had from the desperate rantings of a character like Gissing's Mad Jack: "This life you are now leading is that of the damned; this place to which you are confined is Hell! There is no escape for you. From poor you shall become poorer; the older you grow the lower shall you sink in want and misery; at the end there is waiting for you, one and all, a death in abandonment and despair. This is Hell—Hell—Hell!"[197] In their clinical descent into the inferno of urban suffering, such naturalist fictions reproduced the viewpoint of the Salvation Army and the many other crusading philanthropic societies and individuals that aimed, like the angels in Sodom, to separate the worthy poor from the deservedly damned (see figure 1.9). As Joachim Schlör has aptly phrased it, "The missionaries created a city after their own image, and they played the role of minor deities who—as representatives—pronounced judgement on the big city."[198] Whatever its religious or political sympathies, such a discourse painted an unflinching portrait of the costs of modernity, but with a lexicon of hell that permitted of no agency either individual or collective, no spatial intersection between high and low, as if the Last Judgment was upon them and Christ had come to separate the wheat from the chaff. Granted, the chaff were bestowed a great deal of satanic power, but the only souls they were allowed to punish were their own. Certainly they were preferable to their fellow crusaders who chose to rant from above and beyond on the iniquities of a world in which they would have no part at all, but as the individual cities and individual sufferers sank into the mire of the modern Babylon, the devil became once more a unified figure, only he had lost all relevance in the new urban hell.

In the harsh electric light of the late nineteenth century, darkness had lost all its charms. In a tired last gasp of the "devil in town" genre, George Sims, editor of the encyclopedic turn-of-the-century collection *Living London* and a veteran of the rationalistic city guides, brought back the "Prince of Darkness" for a tour of his "Agencies," the now rationalized competition of the urban missionaries (figure 2.26).[199] After a survey of turn-of-the-century dangers centered on Soho—alcoholism, the Devil's Acre training ground for boy and girl thieves, the white slave trade—his summoner, Alan Fairfax, decides that "he would need the fiend as a companion no more. He had found an angel—an angel with a woman's heart—to take the Devil's place and to be his companion

"I am the Devil," replied the stranger.
"What can I do for you?"

2.26 The Prince of Darkness in an Edwardian drawing room. Frontispiece to *The Devil in London*, by Geo. R. Sims (New York: Dodge Publishing, 1909).

through life."[200] Fairfax lives happily ever after with the former Sister Angela, courted out of St. Ethelbert's Mission in a rehearsal of New York's *Guys and Dolls* a half century later, and the Devil makes his way into oblivion.

The Modern Devil

> Very quickly, because nothing takes a long time any more, the image of the dream-devil started catching on. . . . While non-tint neo-Georgians dreamed of a sulphurous enemy crushing their perfectly restored residences beneath his smoking heel, nocturnal brown-and-blacks found themselves cheering, in their sleep, this what-else-after-all-but-blackman, maybe a little twisted up by fate class race history, all that, but getting off his behind, bad and mad, to kick a little ass. . . . Everyone, black brown white, had started thinking of the dream-figure as *real*, as a being who had crossed the frontier, evaded the normal controls, and was now roaming loose about the city.
>
> SALMAN RUSHDIE, *THE SATANIC VERSES* (1988)

In a peculiar little book published in 1933, Barbara Wingfield-Stratford imagined a sequel to the bestseller of a century before, *Life in London*, updating it over the ensuing years. In 1876, Jerry is visited from Hell by Corinthian Tom, who informs him that "we live just as we used to do. And, oh Jerry, the boredom of it!"[201] The Orpheus travesty was not much fun anymore either: in a 1911 adaptation, the bluestocking Mrs. Grundy was there in the underworld to spoil the fun (figure 2.27). The end-of-the-century devil was too bored to bother much with punishment; the sheer repetition of the life of leisure by then was enough. The two-act "satire" *L'Enfer! Tout le monde descend* (1904) gives a good sense of how even in Paris this new consciousness of boredom could generate not the resentment of Baudelaire's backward-looking satanism, but merely a revival of the devil as "modern' style." The (undoubtedly underground) train for "Enfer-ville" is the latest novelty:

C'est banal et pas difficile	It's banal, it's not at all hard
De voir Pékin, Vénise ou Meaux	To see Meaux, Venice or Peking
Mais voir l'Enfer, c'est modern' style,	But going to Hell, that's "modern style"
Et c'est vraiment dernier bâteau.[202]	And it's really the latest thing going.

The jaded travelers put up in the Hotel of the Deadly Sins, in a setting that bears more than a passing resemblance to Montmartre, where in the same decades were to be found, among others, the Cabaret du Ciel, the Cabaret du Néant, and the Cabaret de l'Enfer (figures 2.28 and 2.29). On the boulevard Clichy near the

2.27 The modern underworld without the fun: Edwardian Orpheus. *Mrs. Grundy Goes Below: "Orpheus in the Underground," at His Majesty's*. Photographs by F. W. Burford and Illustrations Bureau. *Sketch*, 3 January 1912, 399.

IN THE CABARET OF DEATH

There seemed to be no mechanical imperfection in the illusion of a charnel-house; we imagined that even chemistry had contributed its resources, for there seemed distinctly to be the odor appropriate to such a place We found a vacant coffin in the vault, seated ourselves at it on place Pigalle, the Cabaret du Néant, according to an Englishman's guide to "Bohemian Paris of To-day," was a "grisly caricature of eternal nothingness," decorated like a Paris mortuary, with coffins for tables, and even a suitable odor of decay, chemically produced.[203] A lugubrious young man would give a discourse on the horrors of death, illustrated by magic lantern slides, and then take visitors to see the "chambre de la mort," a special effects show of a "pretty young woman" slowly decomposing into a "semi-liquid mass of corruption."[204] The tour continues from death to the Cabaret de l'Enfer, adjoining the Cabaret du Ciel, its entrance a hellmouth out of medieval iconography, guarded by "a little red imp." Inside, male and female devil musicians, prodded by more imps, would play music from *Faust*, flames darted from the walls, and Satan wandered the cavern before consigning the clientele to the "hot room," where, as convention dictated, there were "many notables" and "charming society," but no "pickpockets and thieves, nor any others of the weak, stunted, crippled, and halting."[205] The tour of the other world is followed by a visit to the *pègre*, the criminal underworld. For longer than most cities, Paris retained a sense of the intertwinement of technology and outdated myth, just as the contemporaneous *édicules* of Guimard's métro entrances promised far more than just a mundane subway ride (see figure 3.12). But the devil and the underworld had come so close to the surface that they could scarcely any longer be considered to have anything of the underground about them.

What was still underground and still reeked convincingly of the devil's fire and brimstone was the cinema; when the same facades appeared on screen, they still had a kick to them, if not much artistic currency. The Cabaret de l'Enfer made its screen debut only in the 1920s, as the model for the Phantom of the Opera's luxurious abode in the subterranean lake beneath the Paris Opéra. The moving pictures and their prototypes had been keeping company with the devil since the days of Loutherbourg's eidophusikon and Etienne Robertson's phantasmagoria. The pioneer Parisian filmmaker Georges Méliès made his career through the inspiration of Satan. Having inherited a share of his father's shoe factory in 1888, Méliès promptly rented the Théâtre Robert-Houdin on the boulevard des Italiens and began staging "illusions," employing the full gamut of stage tricks and sleight of hand to thrill the boulevardiers with ghosts, devils, and conjuring. He was quick to embrace the new technology of the motion picture in 1895, updating the timeworn theatrical diableries into cutting-edge novelties, and quickly becoming one of the cinema's most successful practitioners, not least by

Facing page

2.28 *In the Cabaret of Death*. Drawing of the Café du Néant, Boulevard de Clichy, by Edouard Cucuel. *Bohemian Paris of To-day*, by W. C. Morrow from notes by Edouard Cucuel (London: Chatto and Windus, 1899), 266.

2.29 *The Cabaret of Hell.* Drawing of the Cabaret de l'Enfer, Boulevard de Clichy, by Edouard Cucuel. *Bohemian Paris of To-day,* by W. C. Morrow from notes by Edouard Cucuel (London: Chatto and Windus, 1899), 283.

exploiting its unsurpassed potential for tricks. Méliès made 520 films between 1896 and 1912; he acted in 300 of them, frequently playing a devil (figure 2.30).

By contrast to his competitor Louis Lumière, who was not only, as the clichéd distinction goes, the realistic counterpart to Méliès's fantasist, but also a portraitist of the bourgeoisie and its rituals, exploiting the potential of cinema for taking the ideology of realism to new heights, the latter filmmaker generally ridiculed the class with which his competitor identified. In the short film *Le Diable noir,* for example, Méliès took full advantage of the unsurpassed capacity for trickery and illusion available to the filmmaker to torment an unwitting traveling businessman in a plot unchanged from the days of *Les Pilules du Diable.* The film begins with the black imp of the title, played by the director himself, leaping about the room, dramatizing its possession of its territory. Once the lodger settles in for the night, the imp begins playing with the physical space: he makes chairs vanish under his nose, tables shift position, chairs multiply around the room, all conspiring to send the bourgeois fleeing. The brief diablerie concludes with the entire room bursting into flame as the imp cavorts on the bed, grinning in his proprietorship over the ruined room. By contrast with Lumière, whose workers

2.30 Georges Méliès in typically Mephistophelean mode: *Summoning Spirits.* 1899. Star Film/Photofest.

were shown in perfect order as they departed the factory that produced the celluloid on which the film had been printed, Méliès bent the new technology toward a diabolic anarchy that was traditional, even quaintly archaic in form and genre, but at the same time wholly contemporary in its exploration of the disruptive technical possibilities of the new moving pictures. To be sure, Méliès's studio did not produce only diableries—he shot documentary footage of Paris, fabricated newsreels, stole everything his competitors made just as they stole from him—but the devil's trickery was, as it were, the framing tale of his short-lived cinematic empire, and there is no denying the verve and energy with which he satirized middle-class pomposity on the one hand while creating imaginary chaos on the other, as in the ridiculous scientists faced with the exploding Selenite imps in his most famous film, *Voyage to the Moon* (1902). Still, beyond the location of his theater on the boulevards, his state-of-the-art movie studio in the eastern suburb of Montreuil and the stockpile of tableaux and topoi, there was little of Paris about any of it. Méliès's films ranged the world and were shown around the world as well. The first vogue of the cinema may have been to show the city to its inhabitants, but the first international hits were an outer-space journey and a myth of the American West, *The Great Train Robbery.* Twentieth-century London and Paris would remain the sites of the spectacle and of the economy behind them, but they would no longer be the primary source of their imagination.

Modernist literature gave up neither the devil nor the city as subjects, but it removed the one from the other and turned both into metaphors, sometimes social, sometimes individual. In one of the classics of fin-de-siècle symbolism, Georges Rodenbach's *Bruges-la-Morte* (1892), the protagonist Hugues travels from Paris to the medieval Belgian town following the disastrous death of his wife, only to find himself in a citywide necropolis that incarnates his melancholy in its stagnant canals and empty streets. The genius of this hell is "the demon of Analogy," who haunts him with an actress that closely resembles his wife.[206] He first notices her on a playbill for *Robert le Diable*, and is quickly sucked into an infernal repetition of the tragedy for which he has damned himself. "Resemblance is the line of the horizon between habit and novelty," Hugues muses, gazing at the facades of the houses that "dwindled into infinity" along the streets.[207] The photographic illustrations incorporated into the novel recall the interplay of text and image of the city guides of the early part of the century, but like the electric light in the new metropolises, they are too real, leaving no place to hide. The city here serves the same function as the labyrinthine underworld of *Vathek* at the other end of the century, but now it is recognized as all there was to be had, embraced and rejected in the same gesture, with no Fonthill to provide a counterpoint. Wherever he goes, Hugues finds his own alienation.

The same application of the satanic to the marginal elements of urban culture was extended to the demonization of the city by romantic anticapitalists from Barbier to Spengler, who marginalized the whole of big-city culture in favor of a return to the fertility and soulful life of the village and the soil. Throughout the nineteenth century, the rootlessness of the modern city dweller had been considered a primary cause of urban disorder. London underwent particularly massive immigration during the 1830s and 1880s, the first mainly from Ireland, the second from eastern Europe; both democratic and leftist politics had staunchly urban identities, with the anarchists especially dominant at the end of the century. As the quintessential modern nomad, the Devil lent his figure well to this identity, although his power waned as the urban was made the model for the world and the individual city disappeared under the weight of metaphor. The new intellectual currency of the totalizing view from above closely reflected both the international social movements of the time and the internationalization of capital to which they were responding. A unitary theory of hell was required to counter the spreading tentacles of capital and labor. As opposed to his wild speculations about future apocalypse, Spengler's analysis of the current situation of modern capitalism, although pessimistic, is fairly persuasive and not particularly different from many others of the time. Like Marx and Engels, he argued that the money economy, by substituting abstract relations for the exchange of goods, had dissociated individuals from their traditional identities and beliefs. Just as city dwellers became interchangeable, so did the world cities themselves become indistinguishable from one another. For Spengler, the city dweller was a new version of the previllage culture of the nomad: "When . . . the mass of tenants and bed-occupiers in the sea of houses leads a vagrant existence from shelter to shelter like the hunters and pastors of the 'pre'-time, then the intellectual nomad is completely developed. This city is a world, is *the* world."[208] In this cyclical view of world history, city life had eliminated all other forms of life; the world had entered a new stage of primitive nomadism, and sterility, decline, and death were not far off.

The temptation of the great cities, Spengler maintained, was impossible to refuse: "No wretchedness, no compulsion, not even a clear vision of the madness of this development, avails to neutralize the attractive force of these daemonic creations."[209] The state of existence of modern man was that of an urban wanderer. Spengler's theoretical image belongs to a long tradition in modernist writing, from Edgar Allan Poe's Man of the Streets and Baudelaire's splenetic flâneur to the characters in Borges's story "The Library of Babel," in which Spenglerian nomads are doomed to an endless succession of identical rooms full of an infinite number of books with every possible permutation of every possible language and alphabet contained somewhere within them, and each person is doomed to wander this world seeking for the one book that contains the secret of his or her life. Like Vathek and Nouronihar wandering the labyrinths of *Vathek*'s hell, this was a satanic vision, and not merely in the metaphorical sense employed by Spengler above. A primary feature of the Devil's mythic identity is his character as a wanderer. The Dantean hell had fixed Satan at the bottom of his own infernal city, and condemned the souls around him to an endless repetition of an identical punishment. Milton's Satan already had looser bonds, and a more active relation to his urban environment in Pandaemonium easily adaptable to the looseness and anonymity of urban sociability. Moreover, his torment, like that of Spengler's urban nomad, was more internal than external, torn as he was by his exclusion, first from Heaven, and then from Eden.

In *The Political History of the Devil* (1726), Daniel Defoe had taken this nomadism a step further, arguing at great length against Milton that the Devil was not consigned to hell, but condemned to wander the earth; that, in short, hell was primarily a state of being on this earth. Defoe's description of the Devil's existence in this world fed directly into Spengler's urban nomad, and was clearly an early product of the same attitude toward urban modernity:

> In short, the true account of the Devil's circumstances, since his fall from heaven, is much more likely to be thus: That he is more of a vagrant than a prisoner; that he is a wanderer in the wild unbounded waste, where he and his legions, like the hordes of Tartary, who, in the wild countries of Karakathay, the deserts of Barkan, Kassan, and Astracan, live up and down where they find proper; so Satan and his innumerable legions rove about *hic et ubique*, pitching their camps (being beasts of prey) where they

> find the most spoil; watching over this world . . . and seeking whom they may devour, that is, whom they may deceive and delude, and so destroy, for devour they cannot.[210]

The concluding image of deceit and delusion made apparent that Defoe had primarily in mind the modern city rather than the "unbounded waste" of central Asia. Like Spengler, however, he found in the nomadic tribes of that region a fitting metaphor for the satanic activity of the urban margins.[211]

It is a measure of the distance between the early eighteenth century and the early twentieth that Defoe could still imagine a traditional division between high and low, satanic nomads and Christian city dwellers, while the modernist Spengler universalized the image to demonize the city as a whole. As the latter commented concerning the eternal character of big-city vices: "Cinema, Expressionism, Theosophy, boxing contests, nigger dances, poker, and racing one can find it all in [ancient] Rome."[212] Although material necessity had motivated the mass migrations into the modern city, there was no denying the allure of the nomadic and anonymous lifestyle for many that arrived there and for many others who had the luxury to choose it, from the bohemians and their "École du satanisme" in the Paris of Louis-Philippe to the decadents in London and the symbolists and proponents of the "modern' style" in Paris at the end of the century; to the scandalous life of the déclassée divorcée on the music-hall stage documented by Colette in her autobiographical novel *La Vagabonde* (1910); to the Dadaists in the second decade of the century and the surrealists in the '20s; to the situationists and their theory of the *dérive*, or urban drifting, in the '50s and '60s, and the flower children, swingers, hippies, and radicals of the '60s and early '70s. What changed was that the nineteenth-century city dwellers self-consciously chose the trappings of satanism, while in the absolute terms of the *entre-deux-guerres*, especially in Spengler's and Heidegger's Germany, but also in France and England, the satanic was either wholly metaphorical or absolutely historical, depending on which side one was on. In other words, the surrealists reproduced the radical terms of Spengler's critique of the urban, but simply valorized the lifestyle of nomadism rather than demonizing it. The choices had already been made: for most radical thinkers in the twentieth century, there has only ever been one way to live in the world city; one has the choice either to embrace that way or reject it.

Hell became an ever more potent image of twentieth-century life, but the devil became less and less a part of it. Defoe had already complained back in 1726 that

> Bad as he is, the Devil may be abused,
> Be falsely charged, and carelessly accused,
> When Men, unwilling to be blamed alone,
> Shift off those Crimes on Him which are their Own.[213]

The Devil's loss of his traditional power has in fact resulted in the opposite situation to what Defoe describes, for what should be blamed elsewhere is placed wholly on the head of whatever population is equated to his legacy, by virtue of their presence, whether physical or metaphorical, in his underground demesne. Meanwhile, from *Rosemary's Baby* (novel 1967; film 1968) and *The Exorcist* (novel 1971; film 1973), to satanism in rock music, to the vogue for Aleister Crowley and other esoterica that has raged unabated underground since the '60s, to satanic cults and theories of satanic possession, to "goth" fashions that hearken back to nothing so much as 1830s Paris, the devil had a resurgence in popular culture in the last decades of the twentieth century that mirrored the exploding appropriation of underground space and images of urban apocalypse. As Al Pacino's Mephistophelean Manhattan lawyer says to Keanu Reeves's Faustean neophyte in *The Devil's Advocate* (1997), his words reeking of knowing, fin-de-siècle irony: "The subway—the only way I travel."

Although it is easy to dismiss the satanic revival of the 1960s as recycled popular culture, it could just as easily be argued that popular culture was in fact what was under siege by the forces of capital during that decade. While the devil emerged full force amid the proletarianization of the third world peasantry, he emerged in a more diffuse and more commodified form in the first world, where, as Lefebvre and the Situationists argued, the sphere of everyday life was under increasing pressure from the abstract forms of capital, what Horkheimer and Adorno had labeled at the end of the Second World War as "the culture industry." The double-faced appropriation of the Devil is perhaps best exemplified by the satanic identity of the London-based rock band, the Rolling Stones, for whom the identity appears to have been simultaneously a calculated commercial move and a genuinely frightening act of rebellion. Hit singles such as "Paint It, Black" (1966) stripped bare the naive pretensions of the hippies to reveal a far angrier, perverse, and nihilistic message of subversion ("I see the girls walk by dressed in their summer clothes / I have to turn my head until my darkness goes"). That the Devil was as adept at manipulating success and capital as he was at stealing souls and wreaking chaos was a knowing part of the nihilism—there was no escape by retreating into the pastoral nostalgia of San Francisco's summer of love, importing the English pastoral to London, or safely indulging in the harmless vices of swinging London. "Sympathy for the Devil" (1968) took this stance to its logical conclusion, the transparently coy "mystery" of the first half of its chorus—"Pleased to meet you, / hope you guessed my name"—perfectly counterpointed by the true mystery of its response—"But what's puzzling you / is the nature of my game." Introduced by hypnotically driving bongo drums and staccato yelps drawn self-consciously from a stereotype of black music, the Devil's standpoint provides no answers, only a catalog of atrocities followed by an image of the world turned upside down, a request for sympathy, and a display of power. The Stones created a pop Satan at the precise moment when the world of pop was in flux, when it felt as if they might just be able to reign in hell without being co-opted by heaven. Bands like the Stones made their devil's bargain with capital the subject of the very music that would spearhead the globalization of pop culture that allows them still to perform "Sympathy for the Devil" to sold-out stadiums nearly forty years later. Disregarding the history of the Devil, or daring to change that history, their music asserted that pop could outfox itself, reaching a global audience without betraying its subversive intent. Less than ten years later, when Johnny Rotten proclaimed himself the Antichrist, there would be no pop bargain left on the table—it was all or nothing.

As the brief but violent surge of punk music made clear, the modern devil remains only in those places where the cracks in the representation of space from which he is excluded—the liberal, secular, democratic ideology of global capitalism—show through. He seldom occurred in politics during the antifascist years (the Holocaust was certainly hell, but far less frequently was Hitler himself likened to an all-powerful Satan) nor during the cold war. His most recent emergence in politics can be traced back to June 8, 1982, when Ronald Reagan delivered his "Evil Empire" speech to the House of Commons in London, adapting the Manichaean mythology of *Star Wars* to political rhetoric; that rhetoric has since returned to its Crusading roots in the Muslim-Christian invective that makes the West the "Great Shaitan" on one hand and Osama bin-Laden and his avatars the Devil incarnate on the other.[214] Where he also continues to appear is at the margins of capital, as in the devil lore of third-world Catholicism, or among the disenfranchised suburban poor of the United States for whom remembered traumas of Satanic ritual abuse raged through the 1980s. The dynamics of modern devil imagery are no simpler than in the past, as is evident in the recent documentary, *Hell House* (2001, George Ratliff), which films members of the congregation of the Trinity Church in Cedar Hill, Texas, as they plan, rehearse, and perform their tenth annual haunted house spectacle. The series of dramatic tableaux is par for the fundamentalist course: drugs, rave music, suicide, homosexuality, abortion (figure 2.31). What is fascinating is the passion and intensity with which the young actors throw themselves into their performance of these scenes of damnation, often calling on memories of past sins, as in the case of the former rave DJ who re-creates the clubbing scene he knew so well with at least as much enthusiasm as he must have done when it was for real. Playing the devil, especially when legitimated by the authority of their church, permits this congregation to let its inhibitions run wild, with sanctimony and exhilaration coupled together as it scares the bejeezus out of the paying visitors before trying to convert them. Even the damned souls writhing in pain beneath the Plexiglas floor of hell look like they're having a blast.

The devil has never really left popular culture, not only because he is thought to be safely contained there but because the spirit of subversive play he embodies continues to appeal to any person not yet or never quite properly socialized into

2.31 The devil as rave DJ. Frame enlargement from *Hell House*, directed by George Ratliff. 2001.

the middle way—the same demographic, in fact, that is most highly targeted by the producers of popular culture. In the same way, the fashions of 1830s Paris and the satanism that went with them have persisted as a mark of countercultural activity since their resurrection in the 1960s, for they constitute an outlet for adolescents either continuing to refuse or slowly making their reluctant way to assimilation into proper social attitudes. Unlike the large-scale cultural and political fissures indicated by the resurgence of devil discourse between Islam and the West—as they are conveniently and misleadingly divided through the terms of that discourse—cultural devilry these days seems fairly void of historical urgency. As it has for the past couple of centuries, such devilry does continue to testify to the insufficiency of liberal ideology and advanced capitalism to fulfill the desires of many citizens, and helps to delineate who the dissatisfied are and where they do or do not belong. Like the underworld spaces in which they tend to congregate, such groups no longer occupy the vanguard of history as they may have done in the nineteenth century, but this is all the more reason to return once again to the moment when the periphery actually occupied the center of the spatial imagination. The images that appeal to these groups remain potent and unique, and as long as the desires they represent continue to be unfulfilled, they will continue to be appropriated even as the containers appear more and more emptied of specific meaning.

3

MYSTERIES OF THE UNDERGROUND

When you're a new girl they call you a "mystery." And you're a mystery until you've been here three or four years. Then you become a "history."

C. H. Rolph, *Women of the Streets*, 1955

The principal mode in which the underground was first represented in the modern urban imagination was as a "mystery," in particular as the focal point of the genre of serialized fiction based in London and Paris that flourished during the 1840s and '50s and invented the best seller and the urban thriller as we know them. Made possible by the convergence of new automated printing technology, a rapidly changing cityscape and infrastructure, and an overcrowded and sensation-hungry populace, the fictions of urban mysteries became a prime locus for modern mythologies of Paris and London.[1] Even when their tale was ostensibly historical, the narrators of these mysteries invariably related their settings to contemporary issues of crime, poverty, and metropolitan improvement. Consequently, they set the pattern for the view from below, incorporating everyday urban life into sensationalist fiction, and grounding their promise to expose the hidden secrets of the strange new metropolis within the actual spaces of the city. This combination proved an especially potent form of the dialectic of antiquity and novelty that characterizes the representation of subterranean space in the modern city. On the one hand, the characters, plots and situations were wholly conventional, descended primarily from the gothic and barely distinguishable from one example to the next. On the other hand, the urban setting and metropolitan sights were obsessively authentic, resolutely up to date, and advertised in the title as the chief attraction for the reader: *The Mysteries of London, A Secret of the Sewers of London, The Old House of West Street*; *Les Mystères de Paris, Les Mohicans de Paris, Les Catacombes de Paris,* to name a few. The genre of the urban mysteries has proven to be resilient beyond its initial incarnation, recurring in periods of crisis and reincarnated through innovative technology: the steam press that made cheap, serial printing possible; the motion-picture technology of the feature-length film inaugurated by the movie serials at the time of the First World War; the low-key lighting and high-contrast stock of film noir at the end of the Second World War and the stubborn endurance of *neo-noir* since the 1960s; the wonders of computer-generated images (CGI) and digital video (DV) that have transformed the urban action/adventure genre over the past two decades—and in each incarnation, underground urban spaces return, simultaneously archetypal and site specific.

In this chapter, I begin by exploring the roots of the urban mysteries in medieval theater, in the gothic, and in earlier fictions of urban crime. I suggest some of the reasons the mystery has persisted as a primary mode of representation of the urban underworld. Rather than providing a chronological history or a book-by-book survey of the genre, my aim is to define the relation of the urban mysteries to underground space and modernity in both their archetypal, synchronic mechanism and in the ways they have adapted to respond to historical change and technological innovation. Consequently, when I take a more detailed look at the first explosion of the mysteries, I begin where the mechanism is most evident: in London as a sensationalistic meditation on the relation between crime, poverty, and metropolitan improvement. I compare the London mysteries to their slightly earlier Paris counterpart, which focused more on the discourse of the underground, its language, its codes of behavior, and the way it insinuated itself within the spaces of the world above. I then trace the mysteries through the second half of the nineteenth century, and analyze their appropriation into the new medium of the moving picture during the twentieth century, first in the serial dramas of the second decade of the century, then in the film noir of the '40s and '50s, and finally in the urban apocalypse of the last couple of decades. The longer the mysteries survived beyond their initial incarnation, the more clearly their structural paradox emerged, in their capacity to embody the potency of underground forces but not to give them direction or agency, to depict crisis without a viable resolution, to give a voice to oppression and suffering while precluding any revolution.

The True Mysteries of the Modern Metropolis Revealed

> —It is I who shall descend.
> —But am I not here, monsieur Jackal? said Carmagnole.
> —I know that you are a brave man, Carmagnole; nevertheless, I have thought it over: better that I descend. I do not know why, but I have a good feeling about what I will learn at the bottom of this pit.
> —Naturally! observed Carmagnole; don't they say that it is there that Truth is to be found?
>
> ALEXANDRE DUMAS ET AL., *Les Mohicans de Paris* (serialized 1854–59)

The nineteenth-century vogue for the fiction of urban mysteries was an extensive one. Inaugurated by the unprecedented success of Eugène Sue's *Mystères de Paris* (1842–43) and G. W. M. Reynolds's cross-Channel follow-up, *The Mysteries of London* (1844–48), the new genre rapidly spread over the next few decades to explore every major metropolis from Constantinople to New York, as well as Lyon, Rouen, and Marseilles in France. In Paris, we find a comprehensive survey of legendary sites, including, among others: *Les Mystères du Grand Opéra* (1843), *Les Mystères du Palais-Royal* (1845), *Les Mystères de la Salette* (1848), *Les Mystères de la nouvelle Tour de Nesle* (1858), *Les Mystères de l'Ile Saint-Louis* (1859), *Les Mystères de l'Hôtel des Ventes* (1863), *Les Mystères du Bicêtre* (1864), *Les Mystères de Vieux Paris* (1865), *Les Nouveaux Mystères de Paris* (1867), *Les Mystères du nouveau Paris* (1876), *Les Mystères de Montmartre* (1897), and the pornographic *Les Mystères nocturnes des Champs-Elysées à Paris* (1899). If we also include titles of the genre that omit the term "mysteries," the list expands beyond citability, especially about Paris, and during the 1840s.[2] In England, it was primarily variations on the *Mysteries of London* that proliferated, different versions and plagiarisms of Reynolds's long-running serial and of Paul Féval's *Les Mystères de Londres* (1842–43); we also find *The Mysteries of Old Father Thames* (1848), *The Mysteries of Bond Street* (1857), *The Mysteries of Wilton Hall* (1858), *The Mysteries of Shoreditch* (1860), *The Mysteries of the Temple* (1863), *The Mysteries of Hampton Court Palace* (1890), and numerous historical mysteries, especially concerning the Tower of London and St. Paul's. What is most striking about the extent of the list is the degree of interest in the city itself and its legends both ancient and modern. This was especially apparent on the stage, where the mysteries of London and of Paris dominated during the 1840s, along with related material such as the legend of Sweeney Todd, "demon barber of Fleet Street," whose victims were transported through a subterranean passage to be baked into Mrs. Lovett's famous meat pies in nearby Bell Yard, a story first serialized by Thomas Peckett Prest in 1846.[3]

A tongue-in-cheek article in Charles Dickens's magazine *All the Year Round* in 1860 anatomized the genre, showing how by the second half of the century the term "mystery" referred not simply to the literary genre but to a group of related but distinct elements of urban life, ranging from the most speculatively paranoid to the most concrete and mundane:

> Not mysteries of crime; no account of secret societies that exist in the heart of London—the Odd-Fellows, the Druids, the Codgers, the Foresters, the Rum Pum Pas; no revelations of unknown horrors going on in the innermost recesses of Paris; no trackings out of hidden villainies perpetrated in nooks and corners of that city—not one of these things is going just now to be made the subject of discussion. Nor are the wonderful mechanical but hidden contrivances by which the inhabitants of these two cities are supplied with gas and water, nor the secrets of the great sewers, of the Morgue, of the Dark Arches, to be treated of in this paper. The shut-up and deserted houses in Stamford-street, Blackfriars-road, London, again, it might be legitimately supposed, were likely to be included in the mysteries of London. . . . The mysteries proposed to be dealt with are of a more familiar and less alarming kind than the Stamford-street houses, but they are none the less deep and inscrutable for all that.[4]

The mysteries of metropolitan crime, the mysteries of urban technology, the mysteries of abandoned housing, and, especially, the mysteries of London and Paris, centers of the nineteenth-century urban imagination: the article anatomized not only the types of mystery mongering but also the types of underground representation. From the criminal underworld to the physical underground to the slum as a subterranean quarter: this is how the view from below represented London and Paris as a mystery.

In its modest way, "Real Mysteries of Paris and London" introduced the fundamental paradox of the view from below as an epistemological approach to the modern city. The popular imagination of the city was fixated on the underground, whether sensationalized as horror or eulogized as technology. Nevertheless, the article suggests, the most intriguing and the most fundamentally mysterious mysteries, those by which the city actually functioned, were the middle-class activities at the heart of industrial and imperial capitalism. Thus, we find posited the "commercial mystery" for which no solution is apparently possible: the importance of India to the empire, "parliamentary and pecuniary mysteries, prices of stocks, the English funds," and the enormous number of apparently unfrequented shops selling basically useless commodities: perfumers, chemists, print shops, furriers in London; jewelers and bonbon shops in Paris.[5] The bemused and jesting tone deflates the sensationalistic posturing of the view from below, but it also makes the same argument that Marx and Engels had proclaimed in the *Communist Manifesto* and Marx in the preface to *Capital*: that if one could succeed in wedding the sensational appeal to truth of the descent to the underworld with a materialist analysis of the economic and social mechanisms responsible for producing those sensations, one could potentially create a revolution.[6]

The 1830s and '40s were a period of unrest in both London and Paris, unrest focused on demands for social equality. By 1840, the main supporters of the British working-class movement for parliamentary reform known as Chartism had been either shipped off to Australia or imprisoned, and a second petition for the adoption of the People's Charter was rejected by Parliament in 1842. Nevertheless, the unsatisfied desires that had been articulated by Chartism continued to inform progressive and radical circles in Britain. In France, the signs were everywhere that the urban workers remained impoverished and discontented at the failures of the revolutions of 1789 and 1830 to live up to their promises of radical reform. Socialism was a product of industrialization in Britain and France; it spread throughout Europe during the 1840s, and 1848 would constitute the initial peak of the movement as a force for radical change. It is not accidental that the fictions of urban mysteries and their novel interest in the lives of the urban poor arose out of this context of unrest, nor that the primary innovators were highly politicized critics of the status quo: Eugène Sue participated in the revolution of 1848 and was elected Socialist deputy for the Seine region in 1850;

G. W. M. Reynolds was active in the Chartist movement during the late '40s and founded several radical newspapers with money earned from the sales of *The Mysteries of London.* Nor should it surprise us that socialists regularly borrowed the rhetoric of the view from below to lend visceral power to their scientific analyses of society, or that revolutionaries throughout the century were regularly labeled underground men. The mysteries cast the struggle for power over the emerging terrain of the modern city as a Manichaean battleground between good and evil, underground and aboveground; and whoever could control the terms of that battle was expected to emerge victorious from it.

They may have shared a political rhetoric, but we should not thereby assume that the urban mysteries constituted an undistorted transposition of socialist ideas into fictional form. Although seldom explicitly linking the villainies they reported to the agency of the devil, the plots of the mysteries continued to be driven by the conventional assumption that a metaphysically defined evil physically exists in the world. Localized within the literally and the metaphorically underground spaces of the contemporary metropolis, that same satanic evil did give material form to the contradictions that were transforming the world above, but only in the coded and confused terms of the world below. The gothic novel, which dominated popular literature and theater in the late eighteenth and early nineteenth centuries, was the first modern genre to provide a putatively secular context for the metaphysical struggle between good and evil of popular Christianity. As with the urban mysteries, the setting was a key innovation of the genre; the gothic story nearly always took place in the past and revolved around a sublime space in the country. The ruins, isolated chateaux, and monasteries provided a suitable context for the gothic novel's broad mobilization of popular anti-Catholic and antiaristocratic sentiment. The fictions of urban mysteries changed almost nothing about the gothic's lurid plotting and black-and-white moral thematics, but relocated them to an urban setting that, even when ostensibly historical, was replete with the topography and the concerns of the present-day metropolis.

Both genres are, as Eve Kosofsky Sedgwick has characterized the gothic, "pervasively conventional";[7] what makes the mystery fundamental to midcentury metropolitan culture is the way in which those conventions are shot through with the contradictions of contemporary spatial representations. The urban settings remain broadly conventional—mansions, cellars, abandoned old houses—as well as narrowly conventional from city to city—the Thames or the Seine and their respective bridges; the specific rookeries of London, the neighborhoods of Piccadilly and Soho, landmarks such as The Monument (to the Great Fire) and Newgate; the specific *îlots insalubres* in Paris; the Palais-Royal, the Champs-Élysées, the Hotel de Ville, the Bastille—but they are contemporary and specific in a way that they seldom were in the gothic novel, where it matters little if at all where Schedoni's stronghold is in *The Italian*, or that *The Monk* is set in Spain as opposed to any other Catholic country. Similarly, although the mysteries also inherited their obsessive use of underground spaces from the gothic, what had been wholly symbolic spaces equally acquired topographical and historical specificity: the Old House in West Street over the river Fleet; the sewers of London or of Paris beneath specific streets; the Catacombes of Paris and the city's different subterranean quarries.

There is no question that the urban mysteries inherited the topos of subterranean space from the gothic novel. A survey of Ann B. Tracy's index to motifs in the gothic novel shows that underground spaces appear in at least a third of the 208 novels included by her, comparable in frequency to the commonest motifs of the genre: abduction, fainting, lunacy, discovery of lost relation, storm, suicide.[8] The frequency of such spaces is if anything even more pronounced in the mystery. Moreover, subterranean spaces play a structural and thematic role above and beyond their physical prominence as a setting. Sedgwick has explained this significance in the gothic both in an ongoing fascination by readers with such spaces and through their role in the spatial dynamics of the plot. "The main streams of criticism of the Gothic novel have had a strong investment in the specialness of the underground spaces in which imprisonment and live burial take place," she argues, often linking them to the gothic dream as "privileged abodes of primal material" that hold "distinctive, otherwise unexpressed material."[9] Sedgwick refuses the traditional mythic reading of the underworld as a unique store of hidden experience, correctly noting that it is impossible to account for the importance of these motifs solely in archetypal terms unless one were to read the entire diegesis of the novel as a dream state (or the entire space of the gothic as underground). She suggests instead that the "real terror" in the gothic, and the "active violence and active magic . . . are almost always reserved for liminal moments, for the instant of moving out of or moving into the dungeon."[10] The subterranean spaces themselves, and the analogous form of the dream, are far more "a duplication of the surrounding reality" than distinct from it, and they are in fact "thrilling because supererogatory."[11] In the terms of Lefebvre's spatial triad, they are lived space rather than conceptions of space, a different, subterranean mode of representing the same space rather than a space of their own.

These two insights are usefully applied to the fiction of urban mysteries; for, indeed, it is not so much that the underground of the metropolis in itself is seen to contain or to generate secrets as that it is shown to be the catalyst for their revelation to the world above. There is after all only one London or Paris: the city of mystery (the underground) and the city where all mysteries have been revealed (the aboveground) are merely different ways of representing the same urban space. The choice of the urban mysteries to depict the city as being composed solely of lived, underground spaces has the disadvantage of militating against this insight, but it has the advantage of giving the lie to the illusion of a city composed solely of rational, conceived, aboveground spaces. The underground spaces are no less conventional in representation than those aboveground; however, in the need to maintain a connection to the world above which the reader is assumed to inhabit, they of necessity emphasize what Sedgwick terms the "liminal moments," the moments that intimate the spatial unity of the city. On the one hand, the development of physically subterranean spaces gave concrete form to the abstract divisions of the vertical city between rich and poor, virtue and crime. On the other hand, the increasing presence of physical thresholds between the underground and the world above provided firsthand evidence of the instability of those conceptual divisions.

This sense of connection is intrinsic to the rhetorical presentation of the mystery as a katabasis, a physical descent to the underworld that transports the reader from one world to another through a threshold that is physically close but leads to what conceptually is a world apart: the literal bowels of the metropolis, the depths of poverty and crime, the corrupt underbelly of the wealthy. The action of *Les Mystères de Paris* opens as the hero, Prince Rodolphe, "plunges" into the "labyrinth of dark, narrow and torturous streets that extends from the Palais de Justice to Notre-Dame. . . . Dark and putrid alleyways led to even darker and more putrid stairways, so steep that they could barely be scaled with help of a pit-rope attached to the humid sides with iron crampons."[12] The opening episode of Reynolds's *The Mysteries of London* finds the young lady Eliza (disguised as the young man Walter) losing her way during a storm "in that labyrinth of narrow and dirty streets which lies in the immediate vicinity of the north-western angle of Smithfield-market."[13] As the truth-seeking approach to deciphering the city gained popularity, the convention of the katabasis was applied not only to describe the paradox of intimacy and separation between the rich and the poor in socialist discourse but also to characterize "real-life" mysteries in popular guides to the transformed metropolis.

Rather than the satirical overview provided by *Paris; ou le livre des cent-et-un* (1831–34), the *Diable à Paris* (1845–46) and other satanic perspectives on the metropolis from above discussed in chapter 2, the factual mysteries were as resolutely humorless as their fictional counterparts. Moreover, they retained a good measure of the evangelizing tendency inherited through the word itself: whether socialist, Chartist, or conservative, and however exploitative the material might be, the mystery writer reserved for him- or herself the moral high ground. One of the earliest such works was Father North's 1844 guide through the Scylla and Charybdis of London vice, *The Mysteries of London, and Stranger's Guide to the Art of Living and Science of Enjoyment in the Great Metropolis.* Organized alphabetically, North's entries steered fairly clear of low-life territory, offering instead rather prosaic and practical advice similar to the mysteries discussed in *All the Year Round* above, telling his readers how to avoid adulterated food and beverages, and revealing the mysteries of the fraudulent behavior of the lower classes vis-à-vis the bourgeoisie—writing begging letters, kidnapping children—while exhibiting admirable credulity over the state of things in the territory of conventional mysteries such as prisons ("open to few abuses, and none of a *mysterious* kind").[14]

At the other end of the spectrum was Vidocq, the master criminal turned prison informer turned police detective in Paris, whose popular memoirs, first published in four volumes in 1828, were another formative influence on the urban mysteries. Although he maintained his innocence of any serious crimes, Vidocq's appeal lay primarily, as he himself stressed, in his firsthand experience of life both belowground and aboveground. That he gained his position in the police by volunteering to turn informer in the prison of La Force, using his celebrity as a criminal to gain the trust of his fellow inmates, never seems to have been held against him, or at least not during the 1820s. In 1844, Vidocq, following the collapse of his private investments, repackaged his memoirs as *Les Vrais Mystères de Paris par Vidocq*. He made the same assurances to his readers as Sue had done—his goal was utility not curiosity, for crime never paid; that it was permissible to use the crude argot for verisimilitude as long as it was used "chastely"—all the while guaranteeing that his readers would see the "true" lowlife of Paris. For Vidocq, as for Father North and other writers of "true" mysteries, the mystery was concerned with lower-class crime perpetrated on the middle classes, and the city they portrayed ranged from middle class to poor, but seldom extended into the physical underground of the cityscape.

By contrast, in the fictions of urban mysteries of Sue, Féval, Reynolds, Prest, and others, literally underground space played a central role, especially in positioning the lower range of characters. The plot of the *Mysteries of London* begins in the depths of the thieves' house on West Street and then takes root in a series of subterranean "cribs" elsewhere in the city, home to Anthony Tidkin, the feared Resurrection Man, or body snatcher. The upper-class mysteries in Reynolds's serial remain more metaphorical but no less subterranean, with the secret windowless spaces of the mansion a primary locus, as in the depraved Lord Holmeford's secret harem. The underworld center of the *Mystères de Paris* is the subterranean cabaret of the police informer Bras-Rouge, "Le Coeur Saignant," its cellars leading down into the sewers, and in the crib of which it is rumored that there exists "a hiding place that descends to a pit that leads to the catacombs [as the *carrières*, or subterranean quarries, were generally known]."[15] Rodolphe is later imprisoned in a *caveau* below the cabaret by the nefarious Maître d'École, and nearly drowns as the Seine floods in from below, covering him with fleeing rats (figure 3.1). Later, Rodolphe will duplicate this imprisonment as punishment for his archenemy, whom he has blinded, leaving him there with his moll, La Chouette. Haunted by images of his victims, he strangles La Chouette (figure 3.2). For Sue, the underground was both the site of crime and the site of punishment: "It is dreadful. . . . Just think! This is the vault I had tossed her down into to kill her . . . and this vault is the site of my torment. . . . Perhaps it will be my tomb. . . .

I repeat that it is dreadful."[16] Perhaps because it is consistently more ambivalent and dialectical, underground Paris has proved a more respectable topic for literature and art than its London counterpart; there is no English parallel to the investment in subterranean Paris of such nineteenth-century French cultural icons as Balzac, Hugo, Nerval, Baudelaire, de Musset, Zola, Manet, and Nadar.[17]

When a Parisian such as Féval took on London, we find a more self-contained, novelistic plot than in Reynolds's version, but an equally negative, if more exotic, underground. The center of Féval's *Les Mystères de Londres* is a complicated plot by a highly organized and aristocratic criminal organization to tunnel underneath the Bank of England and empty its safes, thereby destabilizing the entire British Empire. The so-called Great Family includes among its London members the chief of police and the head of the bank, and, we are told, in the previous decade it was headed by King Edward himself. The tunnel is being excavated by the sole efforts of Saunders "The Elephant," the celebrated Astley's Theater giant, who for the sake of secrecy is forced to remain around the clock in the half-finished tunnel. The London tunnel system is mirrored by the Family's country house, Crewe Castle, which is fissured with a complex tunnel system, including an enormous subterranean chapel, first built by Catholics at the time of the Reformation. The Family's plot is linked to and motivated by another member's scheme of revenge against England: once the empire is destabilized and attacked from all corners of the globe, Ireland will invade and take it over. While one may perhaps recognize the French authorship in the Catholic bias and anti-English sentiment, it is perhaps more interestingly evident in the scope of the paranoia.

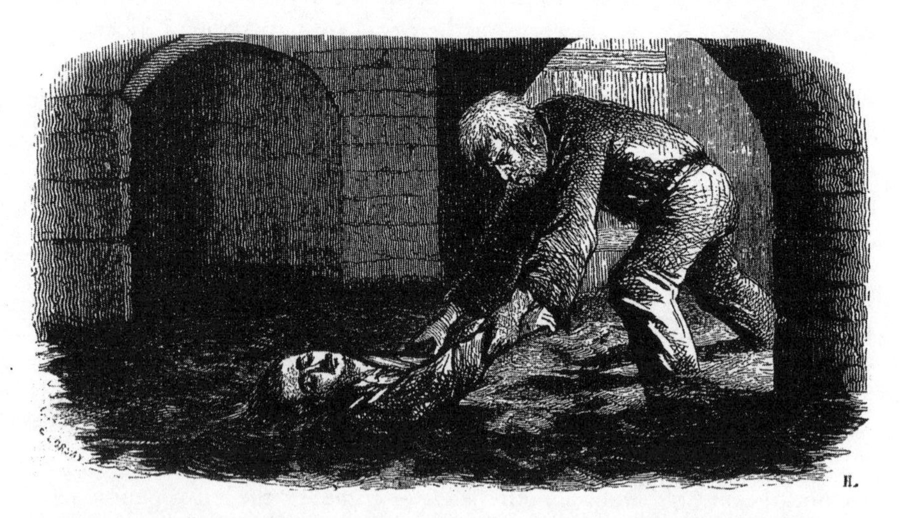

3.1 Prince Rodolphe of Gerolstein rescued from a subterranean flood. Illustration to *Les Mystères de Paris*, 4 vols. (Paris, 1843), 1:113.

3.2 The spirit of the underground: driven insane by blindness and confinement, the Maître d'École strangles his onetime accomplice, La Chouette. Illustration to *Les Mystères de Paris*, 4 vols. (Paris, 1843), 3:233.

The English mysteries such as Reynolds's invariably portrayed a scattered and fragmented city of individuals beset by other individuals. Féval's imagination is wholly paranoid: an underground organization, with a literally underground network, aiming to undermine the entire nation. Sue might have attributed superhuman abilities to his archvillain, but he never threatened more than a fractional proportion of the city or its population. Like the notary Ferrand, Sue's *Maître d'École* is exemplary of the mysteries of Paris, of the iniquities done to the poor, rather than personifying the origin and catalyst of them all.

Nevertheless, most examples of the genre do play on the feelings of powerlessness produced by the disorientating experience of the modern city, embodying those feelings in their deathless villains. To this degree, these villains remain more or less satanic figures, and if we want to look for a mythic explanation for the predominance of underground spaces in relation to these characters, it is not difficult to regard them as underworld strongholds, just as Bram Stoker's Count Dracula, at the end of the century, must sleep on his native Transylvanian soil in the darkness of the consecrated ground of a London church vault in order to preserve himself from the light of day. But such legendary traces do not in any way encompass the power or popularity of the mysteries, nor the particular moments of their vogue. The underworld offered a readily available model through which to import gothic material into the city, but once in the city it was assimilated to a new physical and moral pathology just coming into public consciousness. The Resurrection Man operates on thresholds physical, metaphysical, social, and moral as he digs up recently buried bodies, enacting along the way the grisly realities of modern burial in overcrowded cemeteries. But the power of the legendary residue he assimilates to himself, his occupation, and his house are ideological as well. That body snatching had been mostly eliminated by means of legislation early in the 1830s should remind us that, while the underground—the clogged-up sewers, the festering cemeteries, the overcrowded and poorly built cellar dwellings—was the most visible manifestation of the problems of the modern city, the solution to those problems never lay underground. The true answers to the mysteries of urban misery, as Marx reminds us, are to be found only and always in the corridors of power: "Social life is essentially *practical.* All mysteries which mislead theory into mysticism find their rational solution in human practice and in the comprehension of this practice."[18]

The satanic figures, the demonized poor, and the infernal spaces that they haunt: all of these inform us throughout these fictions of where change was desperately needed. As the historian Louis Chevalier noted about Sue's readers and his incorporation of their correspondence into future installments of the serial, for the first time they were able to see their plight plainly mirrored in a text, even if (we might add) that identification necessitated imagining themselves as troglodytes and demons. But, as Sedgwick suggests about the gothic, these imaginings merely duplicate structures of the world above, which is where we must look for the real answers. The mysteries promised and delivered a real-life journey into hell, but what the reader came back with was, as always, pure ideology, if no less powerful for being so. The resolution, like the plotting, was formulaic and ideological, a familiar set of thrilling and gratifying situations; it was the idea of a *mystery* and the urban setting that were the primary selling points at the time. As Sir Walter Scott observed in his praise of *The Mysteries of Udolpho*, the gothic novel by Ann Radcliffe that coined the term "mysteries" as a fictional title phrase, "The very name was fascinating; and the public, who rushed upon it with all the eagerness of curiosity, rose from it with unsated appetite."[19]

The word *mystery* has a long history, and until Radcliffe's coinage it had primarily been associated with the secrets of religion. The sacred and occult connotation of the term has never quite disappeared from the more secular usage, and the resulting ambiguity neatly captures the paradox of the urban mystery genre's approach to modernity. Used in the plural, the word derives from the Greek verb *múein*, "to close (the lips or eyes)," and first referred to secret religious ceremonies, such as those of Demeter at Eleusis, revealed only to initiates. In Christian Greek, *mysterium* was used synonymously with *sacramentum*, and it was in its theological senses that the word was first used in English and French: "mystically," "a religious truth known only from divine revelation; usually . . . a doctrine of the faith involving difficulties which human reason is incapable of resolving," "a religious ordinance or rite," "an incident in the life of our Lord or of the Saints regarded as an object of commemoration in the Christian church. . . . Hence, each of the fifteen divisions of the rosary corresponding to the 'mysteries of redemption.'" By analogy with these religious meanings, we find variations on the idea of "a hidden or secret thing": "the mysteries of Nature" (Junius, 1638), "un mystère d'état," "our wifes mysteryes" (Thomas More, 1529), "Mystery of Iniquity" (Edmund Burke, 1756). The location of the majority of mysteries, except those "of Nature," has always been the town: membership in the cult of Eleusis was based in Athens; we find reference to the "mysteries" of a particular trade (a common meaning in the early modern period); the Mystery play, an eighteenth-century coining for the miracle play, performed in cathedral towns, was based on the fact that they were often performed by "the mysteries or trade guilds," and derived from the late medieval French term *mystère* for the same; the biblical subject matter of the plays no doubt also contributed to the usage.

This derivation of the word was in no way unknown in the nineteenth century: witness the dual opening of Victor Hugo's novel of the fifteenth century, *Notre-Dame de Paris* (1832), which, as Richard Maxwell has argued, was fundamental in raising the urban questions to which the genre mysteries per se responded during the following decade.[20] First, a theatrical *mystère* is staged by the hapless playwright Pierre Gringoire in the Palais de Justice, against the walls of which Sue would later locate his *tapis-franc* (thieves' den). Next, Gringoire penetrates a topographical and social mystery in the modern sense, losing his way (and nearly his life) when he happens on the *cour des Miracles*, the legendarily labyrinthine underworld of Paris where, their day's work over, the crippled are once again able to walk and the blind to see. The simultaneously meta-literary, traditional, and religious opening, where the city's inhabitants gather together to join in a public rite and a royal marriage, is paired with the katabasis into the urban topography, a more dangerous, more thrilling, and, by contrast with the archaism of the mystery play, a far more resonantly contemporary encounter, notwithstanding the trappings of a 1482 setting.[21]

Hugo's etymological pairing is denser than those of the standard fictions of urban mysteries but operates on the same principle: an appeal to the sacramental nature of the theater of the city prepares the reader for and authorizes the descent into its modern mysteries as truthful and legitimate, however "*hideux*" and "*effrayants*" (Sue) or "deplorable" and "appalling" (Reynolds) they might be. Like Reynolds's discourses on the extreme contrasts of city life or Sue's commentaries on the proximity of law enforcement and crime, Hugo's re-creation was self-evidently authentic: it set the stage and framed the matter to come but revealed nothing new in itself. The Court of Miracles, like the opening episodes of Reynolds's and Sue's narratives discussed below, asserted a new form of mystery, a material reading of the religious context. The lame walk and the blind see not because of a theological but because of an economic miracle. Once safely underground, in their own space, the poor reveal themselves in their true light, not as they appear to the world above. As readers, we are initiated into a modern set of mysteries: the codes are linguistic (the argot dear to the French variation of the genre) and cultural (the different rituals, practices, and occupations of the urban underworld) while the threshold is maintained by a level of sex, violence, and crudity from which we are warned off at the onset.

Sensations of Subterranean London

> A mystery is, in a popular sense, that which cannot be easily explained; a circumstance that cannot be readily accounted for. Something is, but how or why we cannot tell. The mysteries of modern London are as the sands of the seashore. The mighty city itself is a mystery. . . . My desire is to act as guide to those who would look beneath the surface of life in the world's great capital, who would wander about its highways and byways and see with me that which lies hidden from the casual observer. If I can help my readers to see behind the veil, to peer into the dark recesses, to study out-of-the-way aspects of life as it is lived by thousands of their fellow citizens, I shall have accomplished a task which has for its object not the gratifying of a morbid curiosity, but the better understanding of things as they are in the great city which is at once the wonder and the admiration of the world.
>
> George R. Sims, *The Mysteries of Modern London* (1906)

We can obtain a better sense of the paradoxical spatial dynamics of the modern mystery by a look at the opening chapters of Reynolds's seminal bestseller, *The Mysteries of London*, initially serialized from 1844 to 1848. The episode begins conventionally enough, using a young hero, lost in a storm, to lead the reader into an already archetypal underworld of "hideous poverty and fearful crime," through a "labyrinth of narrow and dirty streets": "His common sense told him that he was in the den of lawless thieves—perhaps murderers; in a house abounding with the secret means of concealing every kind of infamy. . . . To his horror and dismay he beheld a trap-door in the floor."[22] Like the character and the situation, the description is unremarkable; the repetition of a familiar lexicon of sensational nouns and adjectives (hideous, fearful, lawless, secret; infamy, crime, murderers, den, horror, dismay) renders each underground space equivalent to the last. The only distinguishing feature is the rhetorical assertion that each space is more horrible, more labyrinthine, more lawless than its predecessor. In its meaning within the sensational plot—innocent young man lost in the wilds of urban slum—one location is no different from another, except where novelty requires a heightened intensity of the expected attributes. But the reader familiar with the city knew exactly where he or she was: the "labyrinth of narrow and dirty streets" lies "in the immediate vicinity of the north-western angle of Smithfield-market."

Once the concealed lordling has overheard the criminal details necessary for the plot, the two thieves take time off from planning a break-in to admire the space around them, the "Old House in Smithfield": "It was Jonathan Wild's favorite crib; and he was no fool at keeping things dark," recalls Bill Bolter. "No, surely," answers his accomplice Dick Flairer (whom Bill, unjustly suspecting him of treachery, will later stab to death before being taken into custody out of this very house to be hanged for beating his wife to death). "I dare say the well-staircase in the next room there, that's covered over with the trap-door, has had many a dead body flying down it into the Fleet!"[23] There is more here than the awkward exposition of topographical information, and more than the iconographic frequency with which such trapdoors into the underground Fleet River occurred in the popular culture of the time. The events are set in 1831, but the house in which the thieves have just situated the reader, once the Red Lion Tavern on West Street (previously Chick Lane), had been torn down in August 1844 amid great publicity and public interest (figure 3.3). The publication of the *Mysteries of London* in penny-weekly form began in the autumn of the same year, but opportunistic sensationalism was only part of the story as well.

The talk turns to the subject of metropolitan improvements. Times have changed, Dick observes, and the trapdoor has been nailed shut because the house is no longer in use. "I've heard it said," he continues, "that the City is going to make great alterations in this quarter." The more seasoned Bill responds, "Oh, as for alterations, I don't suppose there'll be any for the next twenty years to come. They always talk of improvement long afore they begins 'em." The conversation closes with Dick's extravagant articulation of nostalgia: "But, when they *do* commence, they won't spare this lovely old crib! It'ud go to my heart to see them pull it about. I'd much sooner take and shove a dozen stiff uns myself down the trap than see a single rafter of the place ill-treated—that I would." Rather than being restricted to a simple identification with the victim, the reader's sympathies have been neatly split between sharing Dick's fascination for the memory of this site, all the bones it hides, all the stories it can tell, and all the murders to which it will probably contribute as long as it remains standing, and the concealed youth's plot-driven and far more conventional reaction of fear: "When he thought how probable it was that his bones were doomed to whiten in the dark and hidden caverns below, along with the remains of other human beings who had been barbarously murdered in cold blood—reason appeared to forsake him. . . . There was no

3.3 *The Old House in West Street at the time of demolition*. William J. Pinks, *A History of Clerkenwell* (London: C. Herbert, 1881).

escape:—a trap-door here—a well, communicating with the ditch, there."[24] The conflict of points of view is tentatively resolved, as always, in favor of convention: the trap-door, newly pried open, is shut on the falling body of the youth as he shouts out in desperation, "—I am not what I—" in a vain attempt to reveal the mystery he is taking with him to the world below.[25]

We rediscover the youth several chapters later, now not only lost in the labyrinth of a London rookery but literally underground, beneath the trapdoor, down with the bones of past crimes, alongside the legendary lost river, then still known as the Fleet Ditch. But the view from below is not so negative as it may have appeared from above the trap; the youth has evidently assimilated some of the thieves' appreciation for the locale, as he recounts later from the comfort of his home:

> I passed my head through the aperture, and looked out over the Ditch. The stream appeared rapid, to judge by its gurgling sound; and the stench that exhaled from it was pestiferous in the extreme. Turning my head to the left I saw hundreds of lights twinkling in the small narrow windows of two lines of houses that overhung the Ditch. The storm had now completely passed away—the rain had ceased—and the night was clear and beautiful. In a few minutes I was perfectly acquainted with the geography of the place.[26]

The conventional marker of urban negativity—the pestiferous stench—is overcome by an aesthetic experience rooted in the specific perception of the individual. The disoriented wanderer is saved and the underground becomes illuminated by "hundreds of twinkling lights," when he is able to step outside of the abstract inevitability of the stock situation and acquaint himself intimately with the "geography of the place."

Finally oriented to the actual space, Walter makes his way out of the Ditch and back into the warren of alleys, where he stumbles into another stock scene, a vicious catfight between two local women, which is broken up by police, forcing the youth to take refuge in a low lodging house. He regains control of this situation also by slipping out of genre convention and into a more contingent identity, the familiar figure of the Regency swell come slumming for a tour of the rookery. Liberally scattering his money around, he is eventually able to escape "from that moral plague-house."[27] There is a complex play in these episodes between the lurid and dangerous generalities of the sensation plot—the endless litany of identical episodes of plotting and crime in endlessly identical interiors with indistinguishable low-life types, all rendered in a lexicon based on repetition—and the saving graces of the specific situation: the trapdoor over the Fleet, the precise moment after the rain, the plausible (if passé) episode of the touring swell.

The key to this contradiction lies with the preservationist thieves, for their nostalgic impulses are just as concerned with literary genres as they are with London lore. The house of Jonathan Wild, immortalized in the previous century by

John Gay and Henry Fielding, among others, and revived in popular literature during the 1820s and '30s, conceals mounds of bones with myriad stories to tell. The need to dispose of Walter sets in motion the dual machinery of the fiendishly complicated plot (prospective midcentury novelists were advised to characterize like Dickens and plot like Reynolds)[28] and of the extraordinarily detailed portrait of the metropolis. Walter's descent through the trapdoor and the inevitable escape from certain death are necessary to the plot; his discovery of the ability to orient himself and of the voice to tell his story are the fruit of that descent, and they are what distinguish the genre of Reynolds's mysteries from the Newgate tales of Wild and his criminal cohorts that had dominated the early decades of the century.[29] For very little is as it seems: even the youthful Walter turns out to have been a young woman in disguise, Eliza Sydney, who continues to assume multiple identities for many hundreds of pages in a most unusual fashion given the ostensibly strict gender roles of Victorian England.[30]

The distinction within the narrative between Walter/Eliza's point of view and that of the thieves reproduced class and gender distinctions between different ways of viewing these London sites. The distinctions emerge at the moment when the narrative shifts from stock scene to specific site. On August 6, 1844, the *Times* had reported that "the applications are becoming more numerous daily for tickets of admission to view the two strangely constructed houses . . . one of which, No. 3, is stated to have been the residence of the notorious Jonathan Wild."[31] Tickets were evidently difficult to obtain, with viewing privileges reserved for the likes of "his Royal Highness the Duke of Cambridge and a distinguished party" and "parties moving in the higher walks of literature," who "inspected the various places of concealment and contrivances for carrying on an extensive system of plunder. . . . The rooms on that occasion were lighted up by means of illumination lamps to facilitate the view of the Royal party." As the houses were further explored, numerous sliding panels, concealed chambers, and subterranean cells were discovered, including, of course, the infamous trapdoor into the Fleet, the descriptions of which Reynolds precisely reproduced in the account of Walter/Eliza's escape (figure 3.4).

Beyond demonstrating that interest in the mysteries of underground London spanned the city's demographics from highest to lowest, and that a woman would have been permitted to view them only if disguised, these reports also remind us of the varied ways in which those mysteries would have been experienced. The visit by royalty to the house at No. 3, West Street, is mirrored (and displaced) within Reynolds's text by Walter/Eliza's tour of the low lodging house, and we may judge by the use of the latter within the text that it remained a familiar, if not perhaps current, situation of the time. The majority of the population, however, could only cluster outside of the houses in the hundreds, later to read (or be read to) about the contents rather than view them firsthand, a mutation of genre that, for the *Times* at least, was patently degenerative, if not

3.4 *Secret closet in the Old House in West Street.* William J. Pinks, *A History of Clerkenwell* (London: C. Herbert, 1881).

downright dangerous: "We trust that the curiosity which these dens of infamy have excited will not be turned to account by any of those horror-mongers, who, to eke out the meagerness of their own invention, have too successfully endeavored to make heroes out of housebreakers and highway men, and to gloss over the obscene joys and miseries of vice. The attempt, if it be made, will deserve the severest reprobation." The reporter was referring in particular to the so-called Newgate novel of the previous decade and the many subsidiary forms around it: the *Newgate Calendar*, the broadsheets, the weeklies, and the theatrical pieces of which Jonathan Wild had been one of the featured stars.

In the event, three plays had been thrown together within a week and submitted to the Lord Chamberlain for licensing, but all three licenses were refused, an unusual occurrence presumably motivated by the same concern expressed in the *Times* regarding the "horror-mongering" of popular culture; for the pieces were all to be performed at popular East End or transpontine theaters: *The Thieves House; or The Murder Cellar of the Fleet Ditch*, submitted August 15 by the Albert Saloon, in Hoxton; *The Murder House; or, The Cheats of Chick Lane*, submitted the same day by the Britannia Theatre, also in Hoxton; and *The Old House of West Street*, submitted August 24 by the Surrey, on Blackfriars Road. The censorship of responses to the demolition that were aimed at the local audience mirrored the goal of the street clearance itself, based on the belief that if the fetid environment that was seen to germinate crime and immorality were eliminated, then so too would its products be. It was assumed that those displaced would move into more open, outlying areas; instead, they crowded into the nearest remaining central accommodations. As critics of the policy were quick to note at the time, conditions worsened rather than improved.[32] The popular response both romanticized and sensationalized the process of street clearance, focusing attention on the crisis within a specific urban space, while deflecting analysis underground, into the past, and into the clichés of urban crime.

That same autumn of 1844 saw the beginning of the serialization of Prest's *The Old House of West Street; or, London in the Last Century*, profusely illustrated with precise renderings of the many subterranean vaults brought to light during the demolition (figure 3.5). Unlike Reynolds's use of the recent past, Prest took full advantage of the sensational possibilities of the historical setting

3.5 The subterranean vaults. Illustration in *The Old House of West Street; or, London in the Last Century*, by Thomas Peckett Prest (London: Edward Lloyd, 1846), 185.

of the previous century. Although cleaned out and left vacant and empty by midway through the serial's extensive plot, the Old House in Prest's rendering persisted as the epicenter of a gothic London, casting its baleful influence over the subsequent underground lairs of the villains, and rendering the city at night into a vast subterranean space, to be escaped only by reaching the countryside. Where *The Mysteries of London* presented an intriguing dual perspective on metropolitan improvement, in Prest's world demolition came as a long overdue godsend:

> Every vestige of this notorious haunt of vice, which for more than two hundred years was allowed to pollute the metropolis, is now swept away, thanks to the improvements in the metropolis, which have progressed so rapidly of late, more especially in the locality in which the Old House recently reared its pestiferous head; but it will be many years ere the crimes perpetrated in that den of infamy will be forgotten.[33]

Prest's hard-line approach to metropolitan improvement made a strong division between what was worth preserving and what must be destroyed. His argument invoked the common metaphorical formulation of sanitation reform as a question of proper circulation: the house, which "polluted" the city, "is now swept away" by the "rapid progress" of improvements; crime and vice would not fester in a properly drained city. Prest took a more critical and nostalgic but equally wholesale view in *Helen Porter; or, A Wife's Tragedy and a Sister's Trials* (1845), set at the turn of the century and revolving around another subterranean space, the drainage system: "Modern improvements are destroying most of the old-fashioned, romantic, and legendary spots which once adorned our great metropolis. Ancient houses are swept away, and ancient streets are covered with houses. Churches are making way for railroads."[34] Clearly, there was a distinction for Prest between "ancient houses" and "churches" being "swept away" by railroads, and pestholes being washed out by the same. Although we should perhaps not expect ideological consistency from the "king of the penny bloods," we can certainly conclude from these passages that there was a close connection between metropolitan improvements and the new genre of the urban mysteries.

We find an even greater distaste for metropolitan improvement than that of Reynolds or Prest in the Parisian writer Féval's slightly earlier *Mystères de Londres* (1842–43). The particular target of Féval's invective was "the pitiful level" of M. Nash, who had transformed the mixed-use neighborhoods of central London, "poor, in the centre of a rich quarter . . . dark just two steps from a splendidly lit thoroughfare," into long ranks of "houses in the London style, need we say more."[35] It is difficult to determine whether Féval's stance was due to the distance from London that also caused a number of errors in his detailed topographical description, or to the stronger tradition in Paris of appreciating the positive potentialities within underworld and working-class culture.[36] On the one hand, he suggested that "the merciless Mr. Nash" had demolished the alley "with no more scruples than if it had been a hovel"; on the other, he was quite straightforward about the fact that "the place wanted none of the advantages and requisites for concealed murder." As we shall see, the depiction of Paris, including its own squalor and urban problems, was in general highly ambivalent, if not outright sympathetic, especially in contrast to the world's reaction to the slums of English cities.[37] What is somewhat unusual here is that Féval transferred that attitude to London, which in the discourse of nineteenth-century France was usually the admonitory example of what Paris was not. Indeed, much of the interplay between above- and underground in *Les Mystères de Londres* has a distinctly Parisian ring to it, as when the rookeries empty themselves out in an uprising that resonates less with any moment of London history than with the revolution of 1830: "Saint-Giles's has vomited from her cellars and miserable lodging-houses, her innumerable hosts, rushing forth like a furious inundation, which no dike can stay."[38]

Féval's attacks on John Nash and metropolitan improvement come as unexpected digressions within the diegesis of the text, pulling the narrative out of the tight sequence of events it recounts as having occurred in the space of "one week" in the 1830s, and into the present day. The two serials by Prest equally eschewed an explicit connection between the reader's fascination with the underground sites of the city and the plot formulae underpinned by them, both through their historical settings and through their lack of direct identification of the reader with the spaces they describe. Nevertheless, they did pretend to veracity in their topographical settings, and gave them pride of place in the works' titles (the running head on the pages of *Helen Porter* was *The Wife's Tragedy: A Secret of the Sewers of London*) and illustrations (figure 3.6). Reynolds's *Mysteries of London* offered a greater variety of points of view on the changing city, and its countdown plotting, which revolved around the lives of two brothers who separate in 1833, vowing to reunite and compare their fortunes twenty years later, focused the reader's attention on the dynamic process of change. For the most part, the urban background entered the text through the narrator's digressions or footnotes—Reynolds discourses on the contrasts of city life, on techniques of adulteration, on the state of prisons; Prest describes the sewers and their mudlarks—but it rarely actually merged with the traditional romance plot of aristocratic villains and victims crossing paths with the virtuous poor and criminal lowlifes. Representatives of the middle classes, which formed a large body of the readership of these serials, and were responsible for producing them, seldom appeared as such within them. When they did, it was almost always through the cityscape itself.

One of the most intriguing examples of this presence is Reynolds's introduction of the lair of Anthony Tidkin, the Resurrection Man. Although the house on West Street was the topical hook to lure the reader into the serial to begin with, it soon vanishes from sight, as Bill Bolter is rooted out of his hiding place in it and executed. In its place, we find the satanic body snatcher and a new hideout,

3.6 Subterranean illumination: a historiated initial letter in *Helen Porter; or, A Wife's Tragedy and a Sister's Trials. A Romance*, by Thomas Peckett Prest (London: E. Lloyd, [1845]), 1. Permission of the British Library.

replete with subterranean cells and secret caches of treasure, and distinguishable from the other crib only by its location much further east in Globe Town. To verify his invention, and to render it all the more immediate, Reynolds told his reader how to see it for himself, not from within the dangerous plotting of the story, but from the safe heights of a railway embankment:

> The Eastern Counties' Railway intersects Spitalfields and Bethnal Green. The traveller upon this line may catch, from the windows of the carriage in which he journeys, a hasty, but alas! too comprehensive glance of the wretchedness and squalor of that portion of London. He may actually obtain a view of the interior and domestic misery peculiar to the neighbourhood;—he may perceive, with his eyes, the secrets of those abodes of sorrow, vice, and destitution. In summer time the poor always have their windows open, and thus the hideous poverty of their rooms can be readily descried from the summit of the arches on which the railroad is built.[39]

While the gentry could safely visit the sites of "sorrow, vice, and destitution" in person, and the lower classes were constrained to experience them firsthand, the middle classes not only were beginning to read about them but were offered the spatial equivalent of that new reading experience, complete with the conventional combination of repulsion and voyeurism. To the perspective "from the summit of the arches on which the railroad is built"—this was the view from above newly adapted to the industrial reality of the embankment rather than the magic of the Asmodeus flight—was joined "a comprehensive glance of the wretchedness and squalor of that portion of London." This was the traditional view from below, not visible from a greater height. Just as the construction of the railways, the primary engine behind metropolitan improvement in the first half of the century (as Prest reminded his readers in *Helen Porter*), transformed urban topography and the possibilities of perceiving it, so did Reynolds the political radical propose that his *Mysteries* would combine the comprehensive view of the entire social fabric with the brutal details that lurked beneath. The new urban commuter was placed in the privileged position of being able both to experience the suffering of the poor and to draw structural and political conclusions from it.

The problem with this model is that most of what Reynolds shows us, the equivalent of the commuter's view from the window, was not the current state of the city, but a group of motifs that, like the house on West Street, had recently disappeared. Hence, the villainous Resurrection Man, and the gruesome set pieces of burking, disinterment, and vivisection motivated by his primary occupation, had been an endangered species since the 1832 Anatomy Act.[40] Hence, the steady procession of executions despite the sudden diminishment in death sentences and executions following the Reform Act of 1832 and subsequent reform through the decade.[41] Hence, Walter/Eliza's visit to a low lodging house, or Richard Markham's later visit to the Holy Land in Saint Giles's, drawn from the Regency tradition of the swell's exploration of the extremes of city life epitomized by Pierce Egan's mammoth success, *Life in London* (1821), rather than reflecting the growing political fervent and social consciousness of the '40s. And hence, the Chartist agitator Reynolds's continued reliance on aristocratic heroes and villains to structure the plot rather than giving some sense of "the developing working-class perception of the industrial bourgeoisie as the class enemy" characteristic of the politics of the mid-1840s, including his own.[42] Raymond Williams has suggested that we may view the continuing recourse to scandalous material about the court and the aristocracy as a reflection of the "social perspective of working-class readers because it told them that the highest people in society were, in fact, behaving scandalously," even though a more direct expression of their experience would have represented the bourgeoisie beyond their implied readership, or the workers themselves, who appeared only in a context of having fallen out of the working class and into the criminal class.[43] Now, to the extent that London was not yet industrialized and was still dominated by the aristocracy in a way that the new cities to the north were not, it could be argued that Reynolds's material remained current. There is no doubt that for a Chartist sympathizer such as Reynolds, however, the class structure he presented of the city was as anachronistic as burking or slumming. As with other conventions of plotting, character, and even types of settings—mansions and cellars—the scandalous aristocracy came directly out of gothic romance.

The use of contemporary urban setting, background, and color was less formulaic than the gothic material, but it too was derived from earlier genres: the "factual" accounts of the *Newgate Calendar*, the so-called Newgate novels, and travelogue-panorama books such as *Life in London*. These genres had had a powerful influence in determining the metropolitan improvements whose utility would be debated in the urban mysteries. As the historian Gareth Stedman Jones has observed, "The street clearance of the 1840s and 1850s included nearly all the quarters embellished with surreal horror by the literary imagination. Saffron Hill, the alleged home of Fagin, was transformed in the Farringdon Road clearances; Jacob's Island where Bill Sykes met his death was razed to the ground; West Street on Fleet Ditch, 'during two centuries the notorious haunt of felons,' was pulled down."[44] Jones attributes much of the horror inspired by the rookeries during the 1830s and '40s to the sensational fiction of Harrison Ainsworth, Bulwer-Lytton, Reynolds, and the early Dickens. Now, while it is likely that the portrayal of criminal society in *Oliver Twist* (1837–39) contributed to the decision to clear out the areas depicted in its pages (and soon afterward on the London stage), which were associated with Sykes and Fagin, or that the many narratives and stagings of the lives and exploits of Jonathan Wild, Jack Sheppard, and other legendary criminal figures of the eighteenth century were responsible for the notoriety of the house on West Street and the clearance of the surrounding area, these results were not part of the diegesis or the authorial discourse of those fictions. It is important to distinguish between the fiction of the '30s and early '40s, where the topographical was subordinated to the individual, and the fiction of urban mysteries from the mid-'40s onward, where the topographical took pride of place. What set the urban mysteries apart from the genres from which they drew so much of their themes and material, and the only direct reflection of the historical experience of the 1840s, was that for the first time the contemporary cityscape and its relationship to historical, political, and topographical change became a primary subject of the fiction rather than the extension of a particular character.

Prest entitled his narratives after the underground sites central to them; more generally, the mysteries were named according to the city or the specific urban location in which they took place. Other genres remained, of course, with their own conventions, but the way that urban place-names also insinuated themselves into popular titles outside of the specific "Mysteries of" form is equally striking. The traditional gothic appellation after the hero or heroine was invariably followed by an authentic site name: *Eliza Grimwood: A Domestic Legend of the Waterloo Road*; *The String of Pearls; or Sweeney Todd, the Demon Barber of Fleet Street*. It is a simple distinction, but a telling one. In the 1820s and '30s, the swell (including Egan's iconic Tom and Jerry) would witness "Life in London" for himself by going to Newgate Prison to visit the latest celebrated criminal as he awaited execution; the rest of the city would read or be read to about it; and a mix of all classes would attend the public execution. Similarly, the rookeries cited by Jones above were all connected to a personal figure: Fagin, Sykes, Wild. This personalization of place did not disappear completely, but the spaces themselves began to predominate rather than the characters: the sewers that Prest described as "the other city—the buried London—that lies beneath their feet";[45] the dry arches that existed under the Thames bridges and that had sprung up all over the city beneath the new railroad embankments; the Thames Tunnel, which opened in 1843; covered arcades such as the Lowther and the Burlington, both of which were featured in plays dealing with prostitution; the underground railway, which would open twenty years later. In Paris, novels and plays were written around the Catacombes; the subterranean quarries in Montmartre, Belleville, and the Left Bank quarter of Saint-Jacques; the sewers; the banks of the Seine and its bridges at night; and the slums.[46]

The urban mystery fostered a holistic view of the city rather than an individualized perception; hence not only specific, legendary houses and rookeries but all slums were to be cleared; the entire sewer system was to be flushed out and overhauled. The structure of the conventional romance narrative depends on the assumption that all events, however coincidental they may appear, are related beneath the surface; the mysteries adapted the same attitude to the modern metropolis. Even Bill Bolter and Dick Flairer are involved in the destruction of the Old House; any commuter on the Great Eastern can view the poverty described within Reynolds's text. The new forms of transport emblematized by Reynolds in the Great Eastern and the new gathering places necessitated by them intermingled the classes in public spaces to an unheard-of degree. At the same time, there was an increasing segregation of actual living quarters, especially in London. The early nineteenth century had seen the first wholesale street clearance in London, conceived by Féval's bugbear John Nash with the express purpose of dividing West from East and rich from poor.[47] *Life in London* was the first novel in which the class and spatial division between East and West was directly stated.[48] As with further clearance in London, call for improvements in Paris dated from the cholera epidemics of the early '30s, although they were not carried out until the 1850s and '60s, when Haussmann transformed the city on a grand scale under the mandate of Napoleon III, who was inspired in part by what he had seen during his London exile in the '30s and '40s.[49] Just as the urban mysteries were conflicted between nostalgia for the low-life past and horror over urban pestilence, so did they depend on and even celebrate the dense interconnectedness of urban living while deriving much of their shock effects from the fear and horror of the close proximity of wealth to poverty, and of virtue to crime.

"If the rich only knew . . ."

> The *Mysteries of Paris*! . . . first edition! . . . Engravings of the *Mysteries of Paris*! . . . The *Mysteries of Paris* serials! . . . Everywhere the same thing! . . . in the loo and in the bed! I believe my master M. Pandolphe even puts mysteries in his boots! . . . That novel has turned his head and given him ideas! . . . And, the height of tyranny, he has ordered me to read the *Mysteries of Paris* too! . . . Now that's what I call an abuse of power!
>
> MUFFE, IN EDMOND ROCHEFORT AND ARMAND D'ARTOIS, *Les Mystères de Passy* (1844)

The paradox of segregation and proximity equally underlies Eugène Sue's *Les Mystères de Paris*, which had begun the vogue of the urban mysteries a couple of years before Reynolds adapted the continental example to initiate the London mysteries. Itself begun as a Paris imitation of Egan's popular city panorama, *Life in London*, *Les Mystères de Paris* had soon escaped its roots in the panorama literature to metamorphose into the first example of the urban mystery genre, a full-fledged descent into the life of the urban poor. The new genre also pioneered a new mode of cultural production, the feuilleton, appearing serially in the *Journal des Débats* in 147 installments from June 1842 until October 1843. Where the intertextuality of Reynolds's *Mysteries* would be based on generic conventions and topographical legend, that of Sue was primarily linguistic. Both texts depicted an underground city existing metaphorically as well as physically beneath the everyday middle-class metropolis, but Sue defined his space through the language of argot as much as through the quartiers in which it was rooted. He apologizes for (and tantalizes us with) not only the horrible places we will visit and the people we will see there, but also the atrocious dialect we will hear:

> These men have their own customs, their own women, and their own language, a mysterious language, filled with dreadful images, disgusting metaphors of violence. . . . We were in a state of doubt; without the imperious exigency of narration, we would regret having set in such a terrible place the explosion of the story you are going to read. Still, we are counting a little on the sort of timorous curiosity sometimes aroused by a horrible spectacle. . . . The reader, forewarned about the excursion we are proposing to take among the natives of that infernal race which populates the prisons and penal camps, and whose blood reddens the scaffolds . . . will perhaps still want to follow us.[50]

Taking his cue from the popularity of the heavily annotated "flash" language of Egan's Tom and Jerry, Sue made underworld cant into an essential component of both the veracity and the shock value of his text. The infernal quality of the language was testament to the reality of its subject and to the perception of that subject as infernal. It was concrete evidence that this "other world" existed in the middle of Paris but remained at the same time a mystery, both of the French language and not of it, just as the underworld is of our world, reflecting it, but also not of it, incomprehensible and terrifying. As the heroine, disguised as Satan, sang of a criminal vault near the Palais-Royal in the 1844 comédie-vaudeville, *Satan ou le Diable à Paris*, the mysteries below Paris were both spatial and linguistic:

Si l'on conspire,	If we're conspiring
Dans ce caveau,	In this vault
C'est pour écrire	It's so we can write
Incognito.	Incognito.
Dans cette enceinte,	In this dungeon,
Jamais de plainte,	Never a moan
Jamais de cris	Never a cry
C'est un mystère sous Paris.[51]	It's a mystery under Paris.

The discourse of Paris enunciated the contrasts of the modern city differently than the discourse of London. Reynolds would begin his *Mysteries* with a meditation on the contrasts between wealth and poverty, "separated only by a narrow wall" from one another, and with the aforementioned set piece in the celebrated house on West Street.[52] Sue's starting point was the significantly different paradox between police surveillance and urban crime on the île de la Cité: "The Palais de Justice quarter, heavily restricted, heavily watched, nevertheless serves as asylum or rendezvous to the evildoers of Paris. Is it not strange—or, rather, fated, that an irresistible attraction causes these criminals always to gravitate around the formidable tribunal that condemns them to prison, to penal servitude, to the scaffold!"[53] Reynolds's paradoxes were physical and economic; Sue's were metaphysical and social: both, however, were rooted in the contemporary cityscape, and both relied heavily on a vertical segmentation of urban space, the one through the London discourse, the other through that of Paris.

While Sue invited the reader to find his proper place in the Paris he conjured up, Reynolds offered London as a spectacle. Sue's characters emerged from the novel larger than life; the closest Reynolds came to creating a mythical character in his own right was the Resurrection Man, but this satanic character had power only within the text, just as his moniker was more of a textual description than a mythic one. The narrative drive of *The Mysteries of London*, like most romance, works on the model of what Leslie Fiedler unabashedly termed "up and down . . . tumescence to detumescence and back."[54] The archetypal form of this structure as literalized by *The Mysteries of London* is the "buried alive" theme of peril and rescue. In *The Mysteries of London*, characters are invariably confined underground, mostly by the Resurrection Man, only to be rescued or escape once more.[55] The Resurrection Man embodies this movement, for he is left for dead in the story time and again, only miraculously to survive and return to torment the heroes once again. His occupation is not simply a gesture to the sensational news items of the previous decade; it also describes the function of the mystery as a genre: to dig up what has been buried beneath the city, whether bodies (frequently), souls (nearly as often), and treasure, or the more metaphorical secrets that materialize in sewers, vaults, and hidden chambers as the lost documents, amulets, and other heirlooms that will guarantee the restoration (or relegation) of every character to his or her proper place. Like the Devil, Tidkin could be brought back to life as many times as necessary to prolong the drama, but when the end came, if ever it did, he could just as easily be relegated to hell until next required.

Unlike *The Mysteries of London*, the *Mystères de Paris* had a bona fide hero, Prince Rodolphe of Gerolstein, who entered the novel as a properly divine opponent for the soon-to-be-chastened devil figure, the villainous "Maître d'*École*." Consequently, Sue's book and its characters rapidly took on a life of their own that long outlived the period of serialization, to such a degree that, for example, disguised chamber pots were known in the business as "mystères de Paris" (figure 3.7).[56] In *Les Mystères de Passy*, a parody first staged in March 1844 at the Théâtre des Folies-Dramatiques, and published by the same editors as Sue's own serious dramatic adaptation of the novel, a young dentist, Pandolphe (his name an amalgam of Rodolphe and Candide's master philosopher, Pangloss), obsessively identifies with the noble hero. He attempts to mold his life and acquaintances after Sue's narrative, forcing his servant to read the book as well, and inviting a trio of local drunks into his suburban house with the intention of reforming them. In a dream sequence, Pandolphe follows the novel's setup to the letter, only to find that, instead of triumphing, he has been robbed by the objects of his charity, has accidentally burned his beloved reformed prostitute to death, and has been killed by a band of counterfeiters. Having begun the play vowing that he would be the "petit-singe" of the "divin Rodolphe" and take the *Mystères de Paris* as his "guide-âme," he concludes with the proper response of a chastened bourgeois: "I wanted to play at being Rodolphe, run the garrets with him, convert beggars! . . . make them listen to moralism while paying through the nose! . . . and, finally, track down wrecked virtue . . . but fortunately, last night, I saw in a dream everything I had wanted to undertake for real . . . and here I am perfectly cured of my pitiable folly!"[57] By contrast, the only sort of imitation encouraged by Reynolds's *Mysteries of London*, outside of the de rigueur morality of the good brother Markham, would be that of the commuting reader in his railway carriage, looking down into the hovels of the poor.

The *Mystères de Paris* had a lasting effect on the image of Paris. The effect had perhaps been matched by the earlier vogue of Egan's Tom and Jerry, which had quickly seen numerous would-be swells slumming all over London, to judge from off-color guidebooks of the time such as the almost instant copycat edition, *Real Life in London* (1821), the innumerable theatrical adaptations, and racier stuff such

3.7 *Mystères de Paris* ready for use—proof that Muffe is not exaggerating when he claims his master has the book in his loo. Illustration in Henri Havard, *Dictionnaire de l'ameublement et de la decoration depuis le XIIe siècle jusqu'à nos jours*, 4 vols. (Paris: Quantin, [1887–1890]), 3:931, fig. 697.

as the 1846 *New Swell's Night Guide to the Bowers of Venus*, which gives the impression of a long tradition before it, remarking that it has avoided the "repetition of places of midnight revelry before noted by others."[58] It is harder to imagine any readers eager to seek out the evil spaces described by Reynolds or Prest. Following Reynolds's opening gambit of the house on West Street, already safely historical, the cribs were resolutely subterranean and safely viewable only from a distance, usually a literary one. In the London discourse of the view from below that was crystallizing during the 1840s, there was no middle ground between high and low.

The currency of the Paris discourse, where a romantic yearning for the bas-fonds encouraged underworld slumming long into the twentieth century, is well evident in Alfred Delvau's 1860 guide to *Les Dessous de Paris* (see figure 1.4). Delvau established that the tapis-franc immortalized in the opening pages of Sue's text had been, like Reynolds's crib in the Old House in West street, a dying institution. Unlike its London counterpart, however, plowed under by metropolitan improvements, a Disneyfied version of Sue's "Lapin Blanc" and its proprietress, the "Ogress," had in fact been preserved especially for *Mystères de Paris* tourists, who were still a fixture in the city nearly two decades after the book's initial publication. In a chapter entitled "Le Dernier Tapis-Franc," Delvau drolly registered his disappointment that the language and manners of Sue's underworld were not to be found there, although the address itself might still be accurate:

> The unhealthy alleyways of the Cité were sufficiently deserted to inspire no confidence. I thus had every right to hope that I would participate in some drama or other. . . . The father and mother of this tapis-franc on the rue aux Fèves do exist—but the tapis-franc does not. The illustrious M. Eugène Sue no doubt borrowed it from them to show it to the readers of his *Mystères de Paris*. In any case, I can certify that you will search in vain for it on the rue aux Fèves: it is nether there—nor anywhere else.[59]

Evidence either of Delvau's cultivated cynicism, of the commercialization of Second Empire Paris, or of the Londoner's inability to distinguish the ersatz from the genuine can be found in George Sala's recollection of a visit to the same bar "two days after the Coup d'Etat" in 1851, where he had found "a house almost exclusively frequented by bandits and their female companions; and the 'Ogress' who kept the establishment."[60] It may be that Sala's characteristic nostalgia for the old Paris "cut to pieces" led him to remember a more authentic experience than he had actually had; by the late '70s, he wrote, "the Paris of Eugène Sue's *Mysteries* . . . has been utterly swept away."[61]

Although Sala claimed that the "Ogress" had informed him of the imminent demise of the "Lapin Blanc" because it had "begun to smell too loudly in the nostrils of the authorities,"[62] Delvau informed his readers that it had survived for at least another decade. Rather than authentic lowlife, however, what they would find was proof of the mythical status of the personages of Sue's world. For if the tavern keepers knew Bras-Rouge, le Chourineur, and the Maître d'École only "by reputation," the walls of the cabaret du Lapin Blanc were nevertheless plastered with pictures of Sue's characters: "All around the room are *images*: there is not a corner of the wall even a handbreadth across that is not covered with them. You will see there drawings representing various scenes from the *Mystères de Paris*, portraits of popular representatives next to accusations from the newspaper *Le Diogene*, Saint Eloi, and Eugène Sue."[63] For if Sue's characters were taken as inhabitants of the real world of Paris, the author himself had equally been assimilated to the Rodolphe of his fictional world and was eventually elected as representative for a working-class district of Paris. In Delvau's account, the tourism of the bas-fonds always seeks metropolitan sites that have already been cleaned up for its delectation: "Many honest bourgeois have sought out the tapis-franc so obligingly described by M. Eugène Sue, and, as the Herculean police had long since cleaned out this Augean cabaret, the honest bourgeois have not found anything but an ordinary brandy shop."[64] The comparison is rather striking: the bourgeois become tourists to catch a glimpse of their favorites in their native habitat—and this was the vicarious thrill promised by Sue at the onset of his serial, a glimpse of the *tribus barbares* of Paris, *peaux-rouges* just around the corner[65]—while the working classes elect Sue to office on the strength of his fiction. Slumming could hardly have had as much allure to someone who had spent the majority of his or her life either permanently in or under threat of being consigned to one. Similarly, when Delvau comments that Haussmannization would soon eliminate what was left of the "filthy streets" that disgraced the Cité, including the rue aux Fèves, leaving no other choice to the Lapin Blanc "than to seek refuge in the Museum—taxidermy department,"[66] one cannot help also recalling that while metropolitan improvements may have inconvenienced the middle classes, they forcibly disrupted the poor, destroying their homes and the fabric of the local community while offering very little in return.

Where the main debate aroused by Reynolds's serial was the perceived immorality and corrosive effect of the near-pornographic descriptions of sex and violence—the scandalous depiction of the aristocracy and of the criminal class—Sue's text succeeded in crystallizing debate around the conditions of urban poverty, even if it did so primarily through an anachronistically (if enduringly) paternalistic politics, a politics attacked most notably by Marx and Engels in *The Holy Family* (1845). The plight of the poor was important to the discussion of Sue's text in a way it was not to that of Reynolds's, for where the closest to a working-class character in the *Mysteries of London* is Smithers, the hangman reformed by the moral lessons of Markham, the *Mystères de Paris* developed over the course of its serialization into a champion of the plight of working-class figures such as the much-pitied lapidary, Morel. It was Morel's character, according to the historian Louis Chevalier, who turned the trickle of letters to Sue into a flood, as working-class readers saw themselves reflected in the sufferings of the struggling family starving in its garret apartment, criticized particular elements of Sue's depiction, and advised him on what he should do with them in future numbers of the serial.[67] Chevalier persuasively documents that the *Mystères de Paris* "was a book of the people . . . because it was, to some degree written by the people and, moreover, was recognized by the people as its own book."[68] What had begun as a portrait of the "dangerous classes" was received and molded by public pressure into a portrait of the "laboring classes" of an "extraordinary authenticity," which could be demonstrated both by demographic research and by popular assent.[69] To the degree that this portrait retained "many of the physical and even moral features of the dangerous classes, the same rags, the same ugliness, the same violence," Sue's book and its reception also demonstrated the "fact of opinion" of "the truly racial character of social antagonism in the Paris of this period."[70] Sue's fiction persuaded not only through the extreme power of its manipulation of reader identification but through its faithful reflection of a perception shared by members of every class, that the city of the poor was an underground city, and that its inhabitants, "barbarians," "savages" and "nomads," were indelibly marked by this environment as troglodytes.[71]

This naturalization of the effects of poverty was the central target of Marx's polemic in *The Holy Family* against Sue's program. It is significant, however, that while he took issue with the way in which Sue essentialized the phenomenon of poverty, Marx chose to argue against him through the same metaphorical terms of mystery. He took issue not with the conceptualization of the city as a space vertically divided between the visible and the hidden, but with the definition of what was hidden and how it should be brought to light. As formulated a century later by Jean-Paul Sartre, such a Marxist argument redefines the mysterious city as the alienated city; in this model, what is hidden is not crime, horror, and abuse, but the human relations that actually constitute the urban environment:

> A city is a material and social organization which derives its reality from the ubiquity of its absence. It is present in each of its streets *insofar* as it is always elsewhere, and the myth of the capital with its *mysteries* demonstrates well that the opaqueness of direct human relations comes from the fact that they are always conditioned by all others. *The Mysteries of Paris* stem from the absolute interdependence of spots connected by their radical compartmentalization.[72]

The genre of the urban mysteries, which roots its web of plot coincidences in the metropolitan streets, arose at the very moment that those streets were being ploughed under, and that the social entwinement that had produced them was being unknotted as much and as quickly as possible.

Marx made this argument about Sue's politics as well as his geography. First, he pointed out that the basic political assertion of the mystery, "Ah! si les riches le savait," uttered most poignantly by the suffering Morel, was an anachronistic rewriting of the burghers' plea to Louis XIV, "Ah! si le roi le savait!" ("If the king only knew") and that, "In England and France, at least, this *naive* relation between rich and poor has ceased to exist."[73] Next, he argued that "for Parisians in general and even for the Paris police the hideouts of criminals are such a 'mystery' that at this very moment broad street lights are being laid out in the Cité to give the police access to them."[74] What Sue asserted as the central "mystery" of underground space, that the tapis-franc existed a stone's throw from the central police station, Marx interpreted as a statement about who actually controlled the city. Knowledge of crime was no more at issue than was knowledge of poverty. When police surveillance locates a threat, it takes immediate action; if it had not taken action it was because there was no threat to power in this tapis-franc—more likely, there was plenty of profit. As Marx argued against the young Hegelians' embrace of Sue's ideology, "Had Herr Szeliga read the records from the Paris police archives, Vidocq's memoirs, the *Livre noir* and the like, he would know that in this respect the *police* has still greater opportunity than the 'best opportunity' that servants have. . . . In Sue's novel the police spy '*Bras rouge*' plays a leading part in the story."[75]

Marx argued dialectically, consistently mobilizing primary evidence against the fictional structure of Sue's book, while simultaneously reading the *Mystères de Paris* against the grain for the empirical evidence about city life embedded within it. For Marx, as for Sartre after him, the problem was that Sue's plot structure solved the mysteries of the city by creating a false web of coincidences and interconnections within which his outdated and impractical proposals actually could appear to succeed. In other words, the problems he depicted, from the criminal underworld to the corruption of middle-class figures such as the notary Jacques Ferrand to the sufferings of the honest working poor, were genuine and contemporary, as were the milieus in which he set them.[76] What was wrong was the solution Sue proposed, and the fact that he embedded that solution so powerfully within the mechanics of identification with Rodolphe and the other figures of mythic virtue.

Consequently, a philosopher such as Szeliga, along with the large segment of the reading public parodied in figures such as Panolphe above, was alerted to a litany of social woes, but most likely led to attempt the resolution of those woes by the fantastic measures of Rodolphe's schemes of a model farm, a bank for the poor, and charity as diversion for the wealthy, measures whose practicality Marx cheerfully and thoroughly savaged in *The Holy Family*. The climax of the critique is the analysis of the plight of Fleur-de-Marie, Rodolphe's lost daughter, whom he discovers as an innocent prostitute in the Cité at the beginning of the novel, takes to the country, and teaches about morality, only to have her (after many sufferings, disappearances, and rescues) reject her inheritance at Gerolstein because she feels irredeemably sullied by her past in the gutters of Paris. As Marx reads her, Fleur-de-Marie becomes a cipher for the representation of the urban working poor, entering the novel as a basically good person who has suffered "a fate she has not deserved," but who has not yet internalized her poor social position as a reflection on herself as a person: "Her social position has only grazed the surface of her and is a mere misfortune. . . . She herself is neither good nor bad, but *human*."[77] Once made aware of her underworld existence, "Marie is *enslaved by the consciousness of sin*. In her former most unhappy situation in life she was able to develop a lovable, human individuality; in her outward debasement she was conscious that *her human essence* was *her true essence*. Now the filth of modern society, which has touched her externally, becomes her innermost being."[78] In other words, she internalizes her place in the lower depths of the modern vertical city.

Following on this argument, Peter Brooks has asserted that the prostitute constitutes the privileged means of entry for the bourgeois male into the urban underworld.[79] The specter of prostitution as the final stage of moral degradation looms over lower-class female characters in the mystery genre with obsessive regularity. Along with Walter Benjamin and others before him, Brooks persuasively argues that the prostitute, because her labor is identical with her body, raises pointedly the difficulty of distinguishing between labor and crime, between "the sold body" and "the socially aberrant body."[80] The oft-quoted words of Alexandre-Jean-Baptiste Parent-Duchâtelet, author of pioneering studies of the sewage system (1824) and of prostitution (1836) in Paris, in his introduction to the latter, directly asserted the connection: "Why should I blush to enter this other kind of cesspool (a cesspool more frightening, I admit, than all the others) in the hope of doing some good?"[81] The identification of labor with crime is consistently made through the identification of topography with the body: the prostitute is not only "sexually aberrant" but a necessary underground element in the proper drainage of the city above. And just as the prostitute could be assimilated to the infrastructure of the modern city in this way, so did she come more and more to inhabit the new urban thresholds of the nineteenth century: arcades, bridges, railway stations, boulevards. As Chevalier summarizes it, "The city had become morally pathological, too; and for the same reasons and in nearly the same way, the moral consequences of Paris's population growth coincided with the physical consequences in the same places, at the same periods, and in manifestations equally unhealthy and equally feared."[82] Compare this moral topography with one of the rare footnotes of social outrage in the earlier *Life in London*, which maintained a clear distinction between physical suffering, social oppression, and moral degradation: "The life of a prostitute is of itself a most severe *punishment*, independent of *disease* and *imprisonment*."[83]

The equation of physical pathology with moral pathology, and the projection of both onto the landscape of the city, can be traced to the cholera epidemics of the 1830s in both cities, to Edwin Chadwick's widely circulated and highly influential study of sanitary conditions in Britain, and to the growing awareness of a relation between overcrowding and mortality in the industrial cities of Britain, especially in London.[84] There was no longer a place in this new cultural map for the Regency character of Corinthian Tom, equally at home in the "highest life" of Almacks in the West and the "lowest life" of All-Max in the East, in the Golden Room at Carlton Palace and the Condemned Yard at Newgate, masked at the Grand Carnival in the Opera House and in disguise in the "back slums" of the "Holy Land" (figure 3.8). Nor was there a place for Egan's ecumenical, if dispassionate, treatment of the variety of London life, able to distinguish between "the respectable . . . the mechanical . . . [and] the tag-rag and bob-tail squad, who do not care how the *blunt* comes or how it goes," and to observe of "Lowest Life in London," where "colour or country [are] considered no obstacle" that "All was *happiness*,—everybody free and easy, and freedom of expression allowed to the very echo, the group motley indeed;—Lascars, blacks, jack tars, coal-heavers, dustmen, women of colour, old and young."[85] This is the character and attitude of which we see traces in Rodolphe at the beginning of the *Mystères de Paris*: expert at disguise, able to pass effortlessly from the tapis-franc in the Cité to a grand society ball. From the start, however, Sue's text also exudes a sense of pathology and moral propriety lacking even from Egan's aside about child prostitution being openly practiced next to honor and integrity. After all, one of Tom and Jerry's favorite pastimes was "getting the better of Charley": tormenting the policeman in his guard box, one of the most frequently reproduced illustrations from the work (figure 3.9). Rodolphe may have taken the law in his own hands, but only after lengthy rationalizing disquisitions over the propriety of the punishments he was about to mete out; in incarnations of the mysteries later in the century, officers of the Sûreté would come to play central and heroic roles, internalizing and bureaucratizing the role of divine avenger.

It is instructive to compare Sue's hero, Rodolphe, with his counterpart in the *Mysteries of London*. Rodolphe functions transparently as a divine figure, traveling high and low by virtue of his wealth and his character, dealing out vengeance and rewards as he sees fit, triumphing in the end over each and every urban evil, and finally returning to his loyal subjects in Gerolstein. As Maxwell has aptly phrased it, in Sue's world a character such as Morel "*needs* Rodolphe, not just to save him but to articulate his goodness."[86] Just as the Christian God can see beneath appearances to judge the true character of men, so Rodolphe is able to distinguish those worthy to be saved from those, like the Maître d'École, whom he will damn irredeemably. At the same time, just as original sin means life must always be lived under the necessity for redemption, so the poor must internalize the inherent degradation of their position before being saved; nor, indeed, can they ever truly be saved until the next life. So, in the same way that Morel must be driven to insanity by the plight of his family, the only blot on Rodolphe's joy is of necessity the retreat and death of Fleur-de-Marie, which reads within the economy of the novel, if not as a Christ-like sacrifice of his daughter to redeem the evil of the world, then as a fitting punishment for his one misstep in life.

Markham, by contrast, flounders in the altogether more threatening space of London. His schemes miscarry; he is captured and imprisoned; his social standing is too low for him to marry the woman he loves. But there is no solution to his woes to be found in London. The only way for him to attain the stature to which he aspires, to triumph over the dark powers of the metropolis and resolve its mysteries, is to travel to the mythical Italian principality of Castelcicala. In this fantasy world all his dreams can come true, and he is able to return to London married and raised to nobility. These are the different trade-offs made by the mysteries of London and the mysteries of Paris. There is a certain truthfulness to Reynolds's implication in this episode that grand solutions (or any permanent solutions for that matter) are obtainable only in a land of fantasy, although the corollary of that assertion is the impossibility of putting an end to the flow of mysteries both textual and material. By contrast, the power of Sue's vision lies precisely in the way it enacted its utopia within the recognizably real confines of the city of Paris. Granted, he, too, eventually had Rodolphe leave the actual and return to the mythical, but only after resolving every mystery raised by the narrative within the city.

3.8 Regency London unified as a vertical city. George Cruikshank, frontispiece to *Life in London*, by Pierce Egan (London, 1821).

3.9 *Tom Getting the best of a Charley*. I. R. and George Cruikshank. Illustration in *Life in London*, by Pierce Egan (1821).

The *Mystères de Paris* were able to be concluded in novelistic fashion and continued only in real life; the *Mysteries of London* could, and would, be extended well-nigh indefinitely: Markham's series was followed by an analogous set of characters in an analogous plot; then Reynolds (and his ghostwriters) shifted the time frame away from the present for the four further series of *The Mysteries of the Court of London* (1848–56), a sum total of some four-and-a-half million words spanning, all told, more than a decade of uninterrupted weekly installments, and brought to a close only when the genre itself had long since exhausted its initial impetus.

The Afterlife of the Urban Mysteries

> Are you in Shanghai? In Buenos Aires? In a New York "speak-easy"? Or are you in Paris?
> Without being aware of it, you have landed, simply and completely, in *gangsland*—a cynical and triumphant spectacle of neon lights in a miserable little room, where nothing is a mystery, but everything is disturbing.
>
> BLAISE CENDRARS, *Panorama de la Pègre* (1935)

The fiction of urban mysteries had receded as a popular genre by the 1850s, the underground metaphorics and gothic trappings ostensibly discarded by the naturalistic fiction and journalism of the later decades of the century. Nevertheless, the mystery proved a potent and enduring metaphor for the modern city, both linguistically and generically. London was dominated by the true mysteries genre, muckraking exposés such as William Stead's *The Maiden Tribute of Modern Babylon* and rationalizing city-surveys such as George R. Sims's *The Mysteries of Modern London* (1906). In Paris, the urban transformations wrought by Louis Napoleon and Haussmann and the growing social unrest that culminated in the Commune would inspire a new wave of urban mysteries fictions in the '60s and '70s, focused on the suburban spaces newly annexed as the outer arrondissements: the physically subterranean carrières d'Amérique, replaced during those decades by the Parc aux Buttes-Chaumont; the dives and cellars around the Canal Saint-Martin and la Villette; and the new nightlife underworld of Montmartre. And again, during the last decades of the century, while still linked to the spatial imagination of London and Paris, the mysteries underwent a revival that substituted the global imagination of a paradigmatic Great Metropolis for a detailed portrayal of individual cities per se.[87] Place-names and details remained, but they were local and anecdotal, seldom evoking the ontological force of their mid-nineteenth-century predecessors. The modern mystery novel germinated and settled most comfortably in this archetypal urban environment, from Vidocq, Poe's Dupin, or the police inspector Jackal in Dumas' *Les Mohicans de Paris*, to Sherlock Holmes in London (his deductive method an apt fictional counterpart to the factual mystery genre), Philip Marlowe, Sam Spade, and the hard-boiled detectives of the twentieth-century metropolis, including the durable Nestor Burma, protagonist of Léo Malet's postwar series *Les nouveaux mystères de Paris*, one for each of the city's twenty arrondissements, and the innumerable trench coat–clad tough guys who now populate the underworld streets of neo-noir and the postapocalyptic dark cities of cinematic, novelistic, and animated science fiction.

The turn-of-the-century mysteries featured highly organized networks of law enforcement in a Manichaean battle with supervillains and their impossibly expansive webs of power in plots that more and more spanned the world. The apogee of these new mysteries came in the celluloid serials and episodic features that adapted or copied the print mysteries, dominated silent cinema before, during, and directly after the First World War, and codified an influential model of popular film narrative as they had done with the new form of serial fiction in the 1840s. Paris and New York were the centers of these cinematic serials. Louis Feuillade's serials for Gaumont, especially *Fantômas* (1913–14) and *Les Vampires* (1915–16), were joined by Gaumont's American imports, woman-in-peril serials starring Pearl White and retitled *Les Mystères de New York* for the French market. *Fantômas*, like the earlier Zigomar and Rocambole serials, was based on literary sources. *Les Mystères de New York*, conversely, was transposed into a serial in one of Paris's biggest dailies; there was a serial novelization published as well, the first in the *Collection des Romans-Cinéma.*[88]

As with Sue's work before them, these serials attracted public acclaim, critical adulation, and critical damnation in equal measure. The well-nigh unstoppable exploits of the criminal gangs of Fantômas and the Vampires were closely associated with the daring robberies of a gang of anarchists formed by the one-time mechanic Jules Bonnot.[89] Perhaps the first criminals to employ automobiles in their schemes, the Bonnot gang terrorized the Paris establishment for some four months before April 1913, when their leader was killed and the other members arrested.[90] Such diabolical forces were shocking for their open defiance of authority, their mastery of modern technology, and their association with the modern city; they were seductive for the same reasons, and retained a following among the working classes and the avant-garde long after the material threat they represented had been removed (see figure 3.13). The belated but material relationship between mysteries and urban history persists here, but adapted to a new organization of social space in the form of a new mythology of the criminal underworld. Whether, as in Marcel Allain and Pierre Souvestre's series of novels and Feuillade's early serials, the focus was on the criminal masterminds, or, as in the Pearl White serials, on the woman in peril in the big city, the stress, even more than in the nineteenth-century mysteries, was on the omnipresence and omnipotence of urban crime as an organized activity. In the characterization of a former prefect of Police, we find these gangs engaged in a cosmic battle with the forces of good, the latter embodied by the police brigade created in response to the Bonnot gang: "They possess perfect outfits for their work, powerful automobiles, and even aeroplanes. The struggle of the Police with the bandit army, so admirably equipped, becomes every day more difficult." Nevertheless, in testimony to the innate right of the authorities despite the odds against them, "The international gangs, forever watched over and tracked by expert specialized *agents*, almost invariably end by succumbing."[91]

The anthropologist and avant-garde intellectual Roger Caillois argued in 1938 that this kind of language was characteristic of the "myth of modern Paris." The passage merits quoting at length:

> How, under these conditions, could the intimate conviction not develop within every reader that the Paris he or she knows is not the only, not the real one, but is nothing but a brilliantly lit but overly *normal* décor, whose designers will never reveal themselves, and which hides another Paris, the real Paris, a phantom, nocturnal, and ungraspable Paris, all the more powerful for being secret, and which anywhere and at any moment can mix itself up dangerously with the other one? . . . We recognized Paris in the monthly deliveries of *Fantômas.* M. Pierre Véry has brilliantly rendered their atmosphere. According to him, the typical hero is the Man-in-the-dark-glasses: "The genius of crime, the emperor of terror, the master of bizarre transformations, the man who

> can change his face at will and whose perpetually changing outfits defy description . . . the man whose tricked-out residence communicates by unimaginable elevators with the earth's core." . . . In the end, Véry's description consecrates a new stage in the mythic description of the capital: the imaginary fissure that separated the Paris of appearances from the Paris of mystery has been filled in. The two Parises that previously coexisted without becoming confused with one another have now been reduced to a whole. The myth had at first contented itself with the obvious settings of the night and the peripheral quarters, with unknown alleyways and unexplored catacombs, but it has rapidly emerged into the light of day and the heart of the city. It *occupies* the most frequented, the most official, the most reassuring edifices. Notre-Dame, the Louvre, the Prefecture [of Police] have become its favored sites. Nothing has escaped the epidemic; the mythic has contaminated the real everywhere.[92]

Brilliantly pinpointing the nature of the change in emphasis from one century to the next, Caillois was nevertheless typically modernist in his assertion of the absolute novelty of the attack on the heart of the city as of the character of the villain who led that attack. The supervillain in his subterranean lair beneath the city had his avatars in the first mysteries, as did his ability to disguise himself and move as ruler through the circles of power—the Marquis Rio-Santo, Féval's king of the Great Family, and Sue's aristocratic Maître d'École come immediately to mind; even Reynolds's Resurrection Man, although his coarse physiognomy never fails to betray his low origins, was able to insinuate himself, disguised as a faithful servant, into the highest circles of London as easily as into the lowest. The success of the urban mysteries, in the 1840s as in the period between the wars, lay in their ability to disrupt the conceptual division between center and periphery; for Sue and Reynolds, the fascination and horror of the rookeries and tapis-francs lay in the proximity of their alienness to the most familiar parts of the city, the parts supposedly most inimical to them—what else was the Great Family's tunnel beneath the Bank of London than a subterranean attack on the heart of the empire?

In his characterization of the new contamination of the real by the mythic as absolute, Caillois was likewise using the mystery form to totalize and abstract a phenomenon that was both less quantifiable and more material. First of all, the twentieth-century criminal mastermind was eminently rational, and his operations were highly rationalized, mechanized, and timed with the utmost precision. To be sure, the Great Family's plot had been calibrated to coincide with uprisings around the city and around the world, but it had originated from a mad Irishman's crazy vendetta, and it was carried out by the rather eccentric means of a whiskey-swilling theatrical giant. By the early twentieth century, however, the mysterious underground world beneath nineteenth-century Paris and London had been rationalized and excavated into a complex system of drainage pipes, underground railways, pneumatic tunnels, electrical, telephone, and telegraph wires, plumbing works, underground vaults, and private tunnel systems. As the avant-garde painter and filmmaker Fernand Léger wrote of the new urban space,

"The spectacle of modern life . . . is a vast electric and mechanical spectacle of rapidly multiplying images, conducted by an accelerating current, an expansive network within which humans move in rhythm."[93] The city was no longer primarily the stinking and filthy province of isolated toshers, counterfeiters, and body snatchers, but the realm of commuters, centralized transit authorities, assembly-line factories, and the electrically powered spectacles designed to fill the hours of leisure created by the efficient segmentation of space and time. The new mysteries' representation of the great level of organization and rationalization of the underworld as well as of law enforcement reflected this new mechanization of space and time. They equally offered a violent rejection of its premises; as the surrealists (not to mention the censorious authorities) were quick to realize, the supervillain was a mutated form of the old rebel angel, a devil figure whose supernatural powers had been recast in the form of a preternatural control of new technology. Rather than the contained and controlled tormentor, which is how the aboveground authorities wanted to portray him, this new devil was a dangerously free agent, restrained only by the view from below, which represented that agency as a criminal and demonic excess rather than a positive protest against the imposition of radical change from above.

The material sites of the modernizing city were no longer the generative spaces of the mysteries, however; they had been replaced by the concept of the "modern city" as such. Although it would continue for the most part in practice to be executed in a piecemeal fashion, the discourse of metropolitan improvement no longer focused on the elimination of particular trouble spots, which it viewed as having been eliminated. For all intents and purposes, the vertical divide that had dominated urban representation for nearly a century had now been realized in the form of horizontal segregation. Representations of London, with its west and north versus east and south and its growing population of middle-class commuters, and of Paris, similarly divided between the wealthy west and the workers of the east and the banlieues, were now invested in negating the contamination of their divisions rather than in bringing those divisions into being. Nor was either of these urban spaces any longer thought of as an unknown and unknowable quantity. Statistics and mapping enterprises such as Charles Booth's door-to-door survey of the population of London or the mapping of the persistence within central Paris of *îlots insalubres* implied two cities that thought of themselves, or wished to think of themselves, as understood, categorized, explained. At the same time, what was in fact understood about the new "giant metropolis" was simply that, as already in the 1840s, it presented serious problems of poverty, housing, and social malaise. Paris at the turn of the century had the highest population density of any city in the West; the 1911 census revealed that nearly half of the population was inadequately housed.[94] Although more spread out, the poor in London were even worse off.[95] The garden city movement in England and France, as well as rationalist urban designers such as Le Corbusier, put forth schemes to empty out the cities, scattering housing throughout the outskirts and suburbs, or to tear down the inner city and replace it with high-rises isolated in vast green zones. Characteristically, these were rationalizing schemes for wholesale change on a citywide scale. There had been such holistic schemes in the previous century as well, especially in the second half, but they had always made concessions to the values of tradition and the forces of preservation, aiming to insert change into the existing cityscape and tropes of urban representation rather than to do away with them altogether in a modernizing fervor.

The emptied city was one of the fantasies of urban planners; it was also a favorite subject of photographers and filmmakers. Eugène Atget, as Benjamin noted, specialized in shooting the streets of Paris with little or no human life on them, representing the city as if it were the scene of a crime.[96] The flip side of the paranoia of the movie serial mysteries was that the city was empty: while on the one hand vulnerable to those around you wherever you went, on the other hand you were also always alone in the city streets. Although the urban underground was a prime locus for this sensation—the subway station or train carriage in the middle of the night—the nocturnal city in general takes on this effect, and just at the time that ideologues of modernization were singing the praises of the conquest of night by the power of electricity and the nocturnal spectacle enabled by that power, especially the cinema. As Siegfried Kracauer complained of downtown Berlin, "In the main areas of night life the light is so shrill that one has to stop one's ears. . . . The glowing signs are supposed to brighten up the night, but only chase it away."[97] One of the effects of the new movie palaces and other sites of modern spectacle culture was to move the crowds indoors. The glowing signs lured them downtown, but then "chased them away," rushing them inside. The paradox, of course, was that the cinematic and literary fantasies fed to the newly interiorized crowds represented the very fears of disruption the new control of urban space was meant to dispel.

The analogous paranoia of cultural critics such as Kracauer when confronted with this new representation of the total city was to take its signs at face value, decoding their menacing message without comparing it to the uneven development of the urban landscape around them or to the conflicting messages of the mass culture itself, both of which were much further beneath their notice than they were to the metropolitan authorities. The mass culture of the new urban mysteries was no less totalizing than Kracauer or Le Corbusier were in their theorizing, but its excesses tended to undermine the new model of thoroughgoing modernity rather than to reinforce it. As Caillois implied, rather than limiting itself to the nighttime, the sensation of emptiness that had originated underground was now extended to the city in broad daylight, and, as the urban mentality strengthened its grip on the world, nowhere did it appear any longer safe from this fear. To the view from below, the completion of the transformation of the traditional dichotomy of night and day to a twenty-four hour cycle of labor and a regimented nightlife had created a new form of devil to embody the new pacts required by capital to service the metropolitan behemoths. From his stronghold in a secret interior of a public bank in Berlin, Fritz Lang's Haghi, one of the paradigmatic supervillains of 1920s cinema, could strike anyone anywhere at any moment through his powers of hypnosis and mind reading, forcing, for example, the chief detective to drive himself off an isolated cliff while sitting, supposedly a paralyzed invalid, behind his city desk (figure 3.10).

With good reason, the sociologist Georg Simmel's prescient work on changes in urban psychology has become influential in interpreting such scenarios in terms of the way in which "abstract relations were replacing the more immediate ones of physical and visual contact. . . . Urban life is ruled by such nontangible factors as money and time."[98] For Simmel, the new forms of interaction arising from mechanized public transportation in particular, no longer the novelty they had been in the mid-nineteenth century, had given rise to new modes of interacting without interacting at all, the big-city phenomenon of never looking your neighbor in the eyes. If epitomized by the subway and bus rider, it was a phenomenon that seeped into every aspect of life, as the lack of spatial isolation was compensated by the invention of other sorts:

3.10 The quintessential modern supervillain: Haghi in Fritz Lang's *Spies* (Universum-Film A.G., 1928). Frame enlargement.

> Politics, administration, and jurisdiction . . . have lost their secrecy and inaccessibility in the same measure in which the individual has gained the possibility of ever more complete withdrawal, and in the same measure in which modern life has developed, in the midst of metropolitan crowdedness, a technique for making and keeping private matters secret, such as earlier could be attained only by means of spatial isolation.[99]

Simmel used the language of middle-class culture here, and indeed his analysis applied almost wholly to the bourgeois and the capitalist culture in which he operated, for whom secrecy and inaccessibility were such important concerns.

For members of the working classes, the abstraction of space-time into twenty-four-hour units divorced from the natural cycle of night and day meant a further loss not of privacy, which had always been a bourgeois conception anyway, but of agency. As Schlör has aptly observed, the growth of modern nightlife was made possible not only by new lighting technology and a new ordering of urban space but by a marked increase in the number of nocturnal laborers. Originally limited to underground spaces of the mine, and then to the hidden spaces of the factory and the underworld of prostitution and crime, round-the-clock labor went mainstream, underpinning the new culture of nightclubs and all-night cafés. By the late nineteenth century, however, there was no conceptual place for these new nocturnal workers within the representation of night, which was composed in equal parts of the bright lights of the nightlife and the dark corners of the criminal underworld.[100] The consciousness of this division informed the left-wing rhetoric of a Marxian theoretician such as Karl Kautsky, who complained that the leisure hours of the working classes were spoiled by the postponement of any measure of enjoyment to the brief hours of nighttime, and that even the possibility of that leisure was taken from them by the very spectacle that was supposed to distract from their daily toil: "Only the spur of poverty can force people to regularly sacrifice their sleep to do night work. And without the night work of some, there is no nocturnal enjoyment for the others."[101] To be sure, Kautsky discounted the ongoing role of nighttime as the only repository for popular images that contradicted or offered any alternative to the monotony of capitalism; paradoxically, his analysis suggests one reason why there was such a powerful response to the disturbing city images put forth by the urban mysteries.

If the nineteenth-century underground city had functioned as the realm in which secrets (usually figured as proofs of inheritance and of wrongdoing) were buried and out of which they would come back to light, the early twentieth-century underground was structurally analogous but more abstract: the subway was still the site of possible exposure to the rest of the world, the transit between home and office in which the bourgeois commuter was on display, out of his or her element. The slums and haunts of the underworld were still portrayed as alien spaces to which outsiders descended at their own peril; however, as in Lang's serial-killer hit, *M* (1931), these spaces were shown to be controlled not

3.11 The shadow of the underworld duplicates the mapping control of the police: Fritz Lang's *M* (Nero-Film A.G., 1931). Frame enlargement.

only by a highly organized underworld syndicate but also by the police, who knew all the members of the underworld and every detail of its spaces (figure 3.11). The dilemma posed by the murderer Beckert, in fact, is that he belongs neither to the world above nor to the world below, but to the petit-bourgeois sphere whose members still had no conceptual place in the vertical division between authority and crime.

By all accounts, the early cinema was another such space, functioning for the first twenty years of its life not as the rationalized form of middle-class entertainment into which it was to be refined by the vertically integrated motion picture studios, but as an underground space in the traditional sense: a "cinema of attractions" rather than of self-contained narratives, exhibited in temporary spaces such as fairgrounds, variety shows, nickelodeons, and, as Giuliana Bruno has studied in Naples, covered arcades.[102] Miriam Hansen has documented the various ways in which, between 1907 and 1917, cinema was rationalized in terms of production, distribution, and exhibition as well as in terms of "a mode of narration that makes it possible to anticipate a viewer through particular textual strategies, and thus to standardize empirically diverse and to some extent unpredictable acts of reception."[103] Various signals of the context of the spectacle—the direct look at the camera, the variety of short programs, the unsegregated space of exhibition, the assumption of a varied audience—were gradually replaced by the codes of realistic narration, the feature film, the single-use, fixed-seat theater, and the assumption of a middle-class audience, or at least a middle-class point of view. The "slum tradition of the cinema" was replaced by the movie palace; in the process, an experience that itself partook of the mysteries of the city was replaced by the cinematic genre of the mysteries and its representation of a more abstract, archetypal metropolis.

According to the historian of early cinema Tom Gunning, the detective was the key figure in the urban thriller as it developed in the second decade of the century: "The city was conceived less as a kaleidoscopic space than an enigmatic labyrinth which required knowledge, perspicacity, and cunning in order to be threaded by the detective-like investigator. . . . In these narratives of danger the open bustling squares of early films, filled with constant and aleatory motion, have become the labyrinthine byways of an unfamiliar metropolis."[104] What was left to the spectator became internalized in the cinematic apparatus, represented onscreen as the ever-more-important process of surveillance. The city was empty—except, of course, for the omnipresent camera and cameraman. Gunning reads in the 1913 American feature *Traffic in Souls* a dialectic of actual problem and false solution similar in structure to what we saw in the nineteenth-century mysteries: "In its adoption of the detective genre, both the political and fictional discourse of White Slavery used mystification to obscure prostitution's actual social causes of poverty, underemployment, and sexist practices."[105] Moreover, the kidnapping of women into prostitution was less a material cause for anxiety in 1913 than was the entry of middle-class women into the workplace and the public streets in unprecedented numbers. Gunning sees a change in urban experience to a city "structured by the invisible paths of power and deceit": the forces of law and order know at every moment the movements of the white slave trade, "determining direction and circulation beyond our will or even our knowledge."[106] As in its earlier incarnations, the fiction of urban mysteries here diagnosed the problem and posited the solution correctly, but only in their appearance: prostitution was in fact an effect of the problem, total surveillance was in fact related to the solution. But they were, once again, located underground rather than aboveground. They engaged by their proximity to the problem just as by their convincingly accurate locations, but that engagement also served deceptively to resituate the actual sources of the mystery.

Although Gunning's analysis tends, as most cultural studies of the 1980s and '90s did, toward a Foucauldian mystification of the apogee of surveillance in modern society, earlier critics such as Caillois were more sanguine about the dialectic inherent in the mysteries' schematic representation of authority and deviance, arguing that the detective novel, for example, "creates a powerful phantasmagoria of anarchy versus order, its revolutionary impulses equal to the power of conservation and order to try to constrain it."[107] Similarly, the Parisian surrealists André Breton and Louis Aragon, among others, were drawn to the oneiric force of this paradox. Members of the first generation to grow up with the movies, they were enraptured by the mysteries serials: "There is nothing more realistic and, at the same time, more poetic, than the serial. . . . In *Les Mystères de New-York* and *Les Vampires*, one discovers a real sense of our century."[108] Like Caillois, Breton and Aragon were fascinated by what they saw as the modern mythology of the city embodied in this new sense of the great metropolis as a place both utterly material and wholly mysterious. As Robin Walz has argued, the ability of Fantômas and of his pursuer Juve to shift identities at will, to be anybody, anywhere, at any time, posited a vertiginous instability of space and time, just as their command of material technology and the ease with which the everyday could be instantly transformed into horrific violence created a vivid sense of the uncanny.[109] This oneiric quality of the mysteries serials in print and on film brought out an ontological truth about the urban experience as compelling as the aboveground focus on order, control, and mechanization that had consigned that truth to the underground sites of representational space. We find a similar paradox read into the architectural fiber of Paris, through Guimard's celebrated entrances to the new métro (figure 3.12): "These strange cast-iron efflorescences, like a magical contraption giving access to the subterranean world, brought an oneiric note to the city that has never been recovered since, and that successfully counterpointed the rational fantasies of [Gabriel] Davioud's furniture designs."[110] By contrast with the rationalist movement, the hallmark of which was, in schemes like those of Eugène Hénard or Le Corbusier, to reorder the city by rationalizing aboveground and especially underground space, layering streets, pedestrians, and housing, Guimard's thresholds of sinuous ironwork promised the same underworld combination of reality and poetry that the surrealists found in the cinematic mysteries, the derelict arcades, and other unforeseen remnants of the nonrational city.

So, although Walz is right in documenting the ways in which the screen adaptation of *Fantômas* toned down the violence of the serial novels, it would underestimate the visual impact of Feuillade's representation of the cityscape to assume that the decrease in luridness led necessarily to a diminishment of effect. Visual media are more archetypal in their imagery, but also more immediate in their address to the public; especially in the liminal discourse of popular cinema before its codes were fully set, there was more play for shock effects, if less for extremes of sex and violence, than in the print medium. There is still today something uncanny about the interiors and exteriors of Feuillade's serials. Both are wholly unremarkable on the surface; what distinguishes them from the analogous real-life settings of the fictions of urban mysteries is, simply, the fact that they *are* real, more so indeed than the studio settings perfected by the 1920s, an effect heightened rather than lessened by the lack of sound. As Simmel argued, interactions

3.12 The oneirism of modern Paris: one of Hector Guimard's *édicules*, at avenue Parmentier. Photograph in Jules Hervieu, *Le Chemin de fer métropolitain de France*, 2 vols. (Paris: C. Béranger, 1903–8), vol. 2, fig. 148.

based on sight were far more frequent than those of sound in the turn-of-the-century city, and this change was a major source of the uneasiness it generated: "The person who sees without hearing is far more . . . uneasy than the one who hears without seeing. Herein must reside a significant factor for the sociology of the big city. The relations of people in the big cities . . . are characterized by a marked preponderance of the activity of seeing over that of hearing."[111] Although seldom actually silent, the nontalking movies privileged vision; the mysteries serials seem especially to have capitalized on the uncanny effect of this novelty of the motion picture.[112] What could be more familiar and yet more uncanny than a photographic narrative of a silent city?

In addition to the lack of street sound and dialogue, there was in Feuillade's films none of the low-key lighting that stylized the later film noir city, nor even any of the expressionistic flourishes of Lang's *Dr. Mabuse*; and there were none of the special effects of present-day cinema or the playful tricks of Méliès's earlier theatrical diableries. These streets and buildings and bourgeois rooms are shot just as if we were in them, except that we, and no one else, are in them, and anything can happen in them at any moment. They are full of a potential that, if usually sinister, remains a transformation of reality. As art and film historian Annette Michelson has characterized the effect: "Haussmann's pre-1914 Paris, the city of massive stone structures, is suddenly revealed as everywhere dangerous, the scene and subject of secret designs. The trap-door, secret compartment, false tunnel, false bottom, false ceiling, form an architectural complex with the architectural structure of a middle-class culture."[113] Feuillade's mysteries used the uncanniness of modern urban space to represent indirectly the insecurity of a bourgeois society invested in the representation of space as solid and unchanging. Nothing is as it seems. If there is a man perched on the wall opposite the hero's apartment building, it cannot be a chance passerby; it must be one of the Vampires' spies. If a carriage is passing by on the street, it is not a fortuitous taxi to be hailed, but the kidnappers' car arriving at the scene with impossibly perfect timing. One of the rare crowds we observe out-of-doors is shown going into the rough music-hall dive near a *barrière* of the city where Irma Vep is performing; the crowd turns out to be composed entirely of the Vampires' gang, who retire after hours to a secret cellar beneath the hall to continue their revels and their scheming. The underground population is the only one to feel at home in Feuillade's city.

The thresholds of interior space are malleable and unpredictable: figures enter and exit through the fireplace; the canvas of a framed painting rolls up to reveal the Grand Vampire plotting over the sleeping body of his next victim. In a similar way, the exterior space of the city is simultaneously transparent and confusing. Day and night lose their normal meaning when early lighting technology requires that all exteriors be shot in daylight. The Grand Vampire and Irma Vep clamber down a well in a meadow only to emerge through a secret panel into the shack in the Zone outside Paris from which Guérande's mother has just escaped through the front door. In another scene, Irma Vep and her leader escape over the rooftops. For once, far below them, we glimpse street life, pedestrians crossing the Seine, a moment of everyday activity in the midst of this nightmare city. Or are they all members of the Vampires, congregating for some hidden purpose to be revealed in the next episode? There was and remains something extraordinarily seductive about this portrayal of the city; although never so closely mimicking the look of the "real" world, it reappeared in film noir in the '40s, and again in the urban thriller of the end of the twentieth century. Each time, it was predicated on a representation of what Caillois has termed the "other city," what

Lefebvre would call the representational space of the city, for it always carried a cynical, dangerous charge of disintegration and decay.

What the serial depicted as perilous and threatening, the surrealists and other avant-garde intellectuals of the time received as poetic and modern. Writing on G. K. Chesterton's celebration of the modern detective story, Caillois saw the genre as a conscious choice of modernity:

> That we are indebted above all to the detective novel for this transfiguration of modern life was already signaled by Chesterton in 1901: "Of this realization of a great city itself as something wild and obvious the detective story is certainly the 'Iliad.' No one can have failed to notice that in these stories the hero or the investigator crosses London with something of the loneliness and liberty of a prince in a tale of elfland, that in the course of that incalculable journey the casual omnibus assumes the primal colours of a fairy ship. The lights of the city begin to glow like innumerable goblin eyes." . . . If this transfiguration is really a myth, then it must like all myths be susceptible to interpretation and revelatory of destinies. . . . The election of urban life to the quality of myth immediately signifies for the more lucid among us a sharp preference for *modernity*.[114]

While the nineteenth-century mystery had rooted its perceptions in the historical substratum of the city's legendary spaces, the twentieth century embraced the modern and its new underground as mythic in and of themselves. For such inhabitants, the metro, the omnibus, and the cinema would become poetic and mysterious by dint of will, belying the fact that the city, and especially its nightlife, had indeed become highly ordered and rationalized by the time of the First World War, just as the 1920s vogue for the criminal underworld was in fact nostalgia for a nineteenth-century social phenomenon now either vanished or transformed beyond recognition.[115]

And, indeed, the most persuasive explanation for the frightening emptiness of the city, and for the "conjunction of the real and the unreal, the banal and the unexpectedly terrifying" evoked by that emptiness, is the horrifying demonstration of rationalized dehumanization taking place so near to Paris in the trenches of the First World War.[116] Total surveillance matched with absolute chaos; a labyrinthine city of underground streets, dugouts, and chambers capable of hiding thousands—even heavily sanitized for public consumption, the western front was an unbearable image of the modern city and modern urban planning gone terribly wrong. In modern warfare, death was no longer predictably located; as with the spaces of *Les Vampires*, anything could come at you from anywhere at any moment. In *L'évasion du mort* (*The Dead Man's Escape*), the fifth episode of Feuillade's film, a glamorous suburban dinner party attended by *le tout Paris* is transformed into a vision of carnage as the hosts, a disguised Grand Vampire and Irma Vep, board up the windows, seal the doors, and gas the entire contingent for a massive haul of jewelry and wallets. A lingering long shot of the drawing room interior is titled "The gas had done its work" (figure 3.13). The black-clad and hooded Vampires appear in the back of the frame, moving slowly through the dozens of bodies, stripping them of their ornaments and wealth, looking like nothing if not an urban incarnation of the cannibal deserters who were said to live between the lines of trenches and come out at night to strip and devour the war dead. In the movie version, relief finally comes when the police arrive, much too late to prevent the theft, and the Paris elite slowly revive. Before thus reassuring the audience, however, Feuillade has tormented (or delighted) it with the fantasy of the powerful warmongers struck with the same swift death and despoilment as those fighting in the trenches for them just a few miles away. In a serial punctuated by sudden and gruesome murder, with no preparation and no explanation—a severed head found in a box, an innocent commuter stabbed through the neck with a hatpin and thrown from his train, only to turn up later stuffed into a strongbox in the middle of the city—this suggestion of mass death was perfectly plausible. Instead, we are left with the fear arising from uncertainty. The Vampires escape with their loot (although they lose it shortly thereafter to their rival villain Moreno); there is no justice done, just another sequence of murder, kidnapping, theft, and a few more close calls before the next installment.

3.13 "The gas had done its work": the war seeps into a Paris drawing room. *Les vampires*, directed by Louis Feuillade, 1915–16. Frame enlargement. Gaumont Films. BFI Films: Stills, Poster, and Designs.

The serial mysteries of the second decade of the century came at an unsettled crux in the development of the film industry, of the city, and of the modern West; after the war all three settled down, at least on the surface, into rationalized, vertically integrated systems, as we shall see in more detail in chapter 4. As rationalization and vertical integration took hold in both the city and the cinematic industry in the 1920s, the metropolis became less the subject of the cinematic spectacle it had been than, as Bruno has suggested, "the subject of a number of landmark films that narrated urban space. . . . The city space becomes a genre in the German street dramas and in the Italian cinema of the street. . . . The fiction of the city dwells in the movie house."[117] An industry in flux responded to a city in flux by addressing a spectatorship in flux via outmoded yet persuasively real images of itself. Indeed, the only aspect of the urban metropolis that wholly fit the image on the screen was the cinema town itself. The camera, like the supervillain, insinuated itself into every aspect of modern life. It was the new underground railway, riding the tracks of its traveling shots in the 1920s, capturing the depths of the city streets in the stationary second decade, reproducing the Parisian locations as a preview of the studio cities it would construct between the wars. But if the cinema as mastermind was the obvious solution to the mystery, the real answer was the rationalization of which cinema was perhaps the only wholesale success story. The larger proportion of the dangerous classes and the laboring classes had been moved out of the center: in London, they were now settled in the endless and lifeless "mean" streets of the East End and the sprawling suburbs south of the Thames for which the directors of the Tube could scarcely be bothered even to construct commuting lines. The poor traveled aboveground on the trams, buses, and commuter trains, or, unable to afford them, continued to walk the ever greater distances to the center. In Paris, the poorest inhabitants settled in the Zone, the immense ring of shantytowns that sprang up, unregulated, outside the tight city limits in the space left vacant by the demolition of the old city walls, or in the isolated outer arrondissements in the east. They may have haunted the streets of the print and screen mysteries, but they certainly didn't live in them anymore. Many of their homes had been destroyed by the turn-of-the-century construction of the Paris Métro, built by cut and cover like the old London Metropolitan that had eliminated the last vestiges of the Fleet Valley slums in the 1860s. The Gaumont mysteries thus occupied the space between one act of uprooting within the city at the turn of the century, and another act of uprooting, this time of the populace into the trenches. When the surrealists and the rationalists got to the city in the '20s, this extraordinary transformation was already all in the past.

While the planners were dreaming of a gleaming white metropolis built of steel and reinforced concrete wrapped in glass, and the masses were dreaming in the cinemas of a middle-class life, the nostalgics hit the streets. Paul Morand went to London looking for the mysteries described almost a century earlier by Féval,

> that hyphen between cruel libertine novels à la *Clarissa* and the detective novel à la [Edgar] Wallace. . . . Today, the policeman's whistle has replaced the old rattle of the watchman and the electric torch the dark lantern, but the legend of that London endures. . . . It is in search of this mystery of London, so difficult to define and to situate, that one winter evening . . . we made our first nocturnal exploration to the East End . . . with the intention of hunting down a truly sinister house, which we would rent in order to set up a mysterious pied-à-terre.[118]

When it seeks the mysterious, the underground view from below is incurably nostalgic, like the Romantic satanic figure it emulates. The view from above, on the other hand, took on between the wars a polar opposite, forward-looking perspective, predicted by the Italian futurists, who wanted to raze any form of historical memory, eliminate the museums of the world, and race forward. Contrary to a dandyish yearning for the seedy underworld such as we see in Morand, mirrored by the poetic realism of 1930s French cinema and its pessimistic, existentialist view of the doomed criminal underworld figure and the popular culture that celebrated him, or a more vigorous and politicized return to the past such as we see in the surrealists or, for that matter, the Popular Front, was the dispassionate view from above, which visualized the city from top to bottom and remade it as an immaculate utopia. From Le Corbusier's radiant city and Hénard's subterranean urbanism to the science fiction utopias of Lang's *Metropolis* (1926) and *Things to Come* (1936), the futuristic city cleaned up the underground and transformed it through technology.

Henri Lefebvre has written that "in space or behind it there is no unknown substance, no mystery. And yet this transparency is deceptive, and everything is concealed: space is illusory and the secret of the illusion lies in the transparency itself."[119] The true mystery of urban space is the illusion that it is transparent, that it is what it appears to be and thus contains no secrets. Buildings are buildings, slum clearance is for the benefit of all, authority upholds the law of the city, poverty and slums are created by the immorality and slovenliness of those who inhabit them, and riches and mansions are created by the industriousness and uprightness of those who inhabit them. By placing their secrets underground, the nineteenth-century fictions of urban mysteries challenged the transparency of urban space, its legibility, and the apparent discreteness of its different parts. While it deflected attention from those truly mysterious spaces of the modern city—the corridors of power, the ministries, stock exchanges, banks, clubs, and embassies—it did challenge the epistemology behind a transparency that displaced the critical gaze underground. The early twentieth-century fiction and films of urban mysteries responded differently to a changed urban landscape, asserting the entire city as a mystery, as a subterranean space, in response both to the growing middle-class flight to the suburbs and to the growing elimination of the working class and the poor from the center altogether. If Feuillade's early serials "reveal the architectural structure of bourgeois Paris as everywhere dangerous, threatened with being undermined or subverted,"[120] it is not so much because the bourgeois structure was actually under threat, but because that structure, moved metaphorically underground, was shown not to be transparent. What was truly threatened was everything but that structure, even if it was that structure that posed the threat. And a true image of the threat was to be found in the polar opposite of Feuillade's dark vision: the white city of the modernist architects, the bright, artificial underground utopias of science fiction, in which the doctrine of transparent urban space was realized to such a degree as to extend even to the darkest, most pestiferous bowels that might once have lurked beneath the city streets.

The Urban Underworlds of Postwar America

> The hard-bitten action film finds its natural home in caves: the murky, congested theaters, looking like glorified tattoo parlors on the outside and located near bus terminals in big cities. These theaters roll action films in what, at first, seems like a nightmarish atmosphere of shabby transience, prints that seem overgrown with jungle moss, sound tracks infected with hiccups. The spectator watches two or three action films go by and leaves feeling as though he were a pirate discharged from a giant sponge. . . . At heart, the best action films are slicing journeys into the lower depths of American life: dregs, outcasts, lonely hard wanderers caught in a buzzsaw of niggardly, intricate, devious movement. . . . In the films of these hard-edged directors can be found the unheralded ripple of physical experience, the tiny morbidly life-worn detail which the visitor to a strange city finds springing out at every step.
>
> MANNY FARBER, "Underground Films" (1957)

The great paradox of twentieth-century representation was that the more the production of new subterranean space shifted away from the public cityscape into either sealed-off infrastructure or bunkers and secret complexes as far off and hidden as possible from the urban centers, or disguised those spaces as public malls, the more the representational city insisted on the iconography inaugurated by the urban mysteries in the 1840s. This process has been especially visible in the phenomenon of film noir from its inception around 1944 through its various revivals, until it now constitutes one of the stock genres of Hollywood and world filmmaking, haunting especially the marginal world of straight-to-cable movies. Film noir exhibits most of the features attributed in this chapter to the urban mysteries. It took novel advantage of new technology—the fast film stock that permitted night-for-night shooting and high-contrast interior lighting—and captured a moment of urban crisis and transformation while displacing the character of that moment into a mythic city of hard-boiled detectives, femmes fatales, underworld crime lords and everyman fall guys. Like the mysteries serials, most films noirs were produced quickly, on low budgets, and often as second features, what the '50s film critic Manny Farber approvingly dubbed "termite art."[121] And, like the serial films of the second decade of the century, they quickly found an intellectual audience to champion them: the French critics who saw the initial corpus of films in bulk postwar release in 1945 and coined the term *film noir* to refer both to their visual style and to their dark subject matter.

Even more so than the silent crime films, film noir was archetypal in its approach to urban space. The mood was existentialist, the underlying cynicism took the urban night as a metaphor for modern life, and the formulaic character triangles and crime narrative plots were gripping precisely because of their predictability. All that mattered was the style in which they were pulled off and whether the filmmakers carried through the doom-laden stories to their foregone conclusions or palliated their endings in the Hollywood manner by allowing the fleeing couple to escape to a brightly lit dreamworld of safety, usually in South America. Still, like earlier incarnations of the urban mysteries, the location shooting equally provided the pleasures of local specificity, even if the events played out were unchanging in nature: the Los Angeles of Philip Marlowe and of *The Blue Gardenia, Double Indemnity, He Walked by Night, In a Lonely Place, The Reckless Moment, Sunset Boulevard, This Gun for Hire*; the San Francisco of *Dark Passage, DOA, The Lady from Shanghai, The Maltese Falcon, Out of the Past*; the New York City of *Phantom Lady, The Naked City, The Window, The Big Combo, The Big Clock, Force of Evil, Kiss of Death, Pickup on South Street, Scarlet Street, Sweet Smell of Success, While the City Sleeps, The Woman in the Window, The Wrong Man*; the London of *Man Hunt, Ministry of Fear, Night and the City*; the Vienna of *The Third Man*. Despite these last examples, this was a phenomenon of the American city, based on the hard-boiled fiction invented in the 1930s by Raymond Chandler, James Cain, Dashiell Hammett, Cornell Woolrich, and others, although for the most part given visual form by technicians and directors recently arrived from Europe bearing the keen eye of the cosmopolitan outsider and the stylistic influence of the German expressionism of Berlin and the French poetic realism of Paris.

Many critics have linked the thematics of film noir—the powerful, morally ambivalent women; the weak, passive men; the thoroughgoing sense of entrapment and degradation—to such social phenomena as the new presence of women in the workplace during the war and a general postwar malaise. These are part of the standard discourse on film noir as it has developed since the 1950s in the United States as well as abroad; as historical explanations, they have been refuted on various levels, and cannot be seen to constitute more than minor influences on these films.[122] What remains most striking about film noir was how it developed from a series of films little remarked at the time and seldom identified as belonging to a defined genre beyond a general appellation of crime film, into perhaps the most overstudied of all Hollywood forms, celebrated for its unusually negative representation of American life and enjoyed for the mythic archetypes of sex and violence it reliably renders over and over. It has come to represent, both in the States and abroad, a particularly powerful vision of the modern city as underworld, enacted by American types in American cities. As it has expanded into a global discourse for entry into the cinematic underworld of Western cinema, film noir has marked, first, the emergence of American cities, especially Los Angeles and New York, as the centers for production of urban myth, and, second, their subsequent supersession by the world cities that have adapted those myths to their own spaces, from Latin America to East Asia.

The historical moment to which these films were first responding, as David Reid and Jayne Walker have convincingly argued, was in fact the flight of middle America from the urban centers and into suburbia:

> Just as the city-mystery registered the dreaded rise of the metropolis, *film noir* registered its decline, accomplishing a demonization and an estrangement from its landscape in advance of its actual "abandonment"—the violent reshaping of urban life sponsored by the Federal Housing Administration, the Housing Act of 1949, and in New York City the force of nature known as Robert Moses. Around the winter of 1947–48 when classic *film noir* was midway in its career, the United States reached its pitch of urbanization. In terms of both absolute numbers and percentage of the whole population, more Americans lived in central cities than ever before or since. Some 7 per cent lived in New York City alone.[123]

Film after film unobtrusively depicted the urban lifestyle of single persons just as that lifestyle was becoming more and more untenable as services were cut and downtowns were abandoned to those who had nowhere else to go. What greater contrast could exist between the bachelor routine of Walter Neff (Fred MacMurray) in Billy Wilder's *Double Indemnity* (1944)—from the garage attendant beneath his building, to the corner diner where he takes his meals, and the cinemas and bowling alleys he walks to for entertainment—and the ostentatiously rambling suburban homes to which he drives to sells insurance, the wealth and glamour of which seduce him into committing murder? Or between the idyllic small town where Jeff Markham (Robert Mitchum) has set up incognito as a gas station owner, the crime boss's mansion on Lake Tahoe, and the dark apartments in San Francisco in which he tries to escape the frame in Jacques Tourneur's *Out of the Past* (1947)? The underlying message of film noir was that the urban anomie it so accurately diagnosed, the unfulfilled desires that led ordinary men into the underworld and transformed normal women into amoral seductresses, was not to be escaped, no matter how far one fled from the city with which it had been identified for over a century. The underground men and women in these movies dream of escape—to the paradise of the small town, the countryside, Hollywood, Mexico, South America—but the tentacles of the city follow them wherever they go; in noir, the only reality was the urban underground. The stylistic tropes of film noir—the visual equivalent of the underground spaces of the earlier mysteries—always indicated what could be taken as real, because the films were hard-edged, black and white, and starkly contrasting. By contrast, the dream messages of the new representations of space being packaged by Hollywood were evoked with soft lighting, filters, and popular music to represent the accoutrements of postwar prosperity that would never fail to ring hollow as the urban past caught up with you. Film noir documented the transformation of the city from the productive center of representations of space it had previously been to an archetypal underground—the waste heap of prewar dreams, wishes, hopes, and representations, left behind as capital began its move out of the Western factories and workshops and into the third world, the service economy and the world of leisure and branding.

Materially underground spaces still appeared in film noir; however, in contrast to the metaphorical urban underworlds, they reveal characters that are so cut off from the new world above as to have lost any chance of returning. Roy Morgan (Richard Basehart) in *He Walked by Night* (1949) is a nearly catatonic underground man who murders wordlessly and without remorse, devoting himself day and night to carrying out some unspecified, unmotivated "plan" (figure 3.14). His use of the storm-drain tunnels beneath Los Angeles identifies him as a creature rather than a man—the trademark shot shows him escaping the police by slithering through a sidewalk drain opening—a creature so incomprehensible that he can only be dealt with by hunting him down and shooting him dead. In Fritz Lang's late Hollywood feature, *While the City Sleeps* (1956), a perverted serial killer is cornered by a newspaper reporter in a New York subway tunnel (figure 3.15). It is instructive to compare this scene with an analogous episode in the London Tube in the earlier Lang thriller, *Man Hunt* (1941). Made during the war, *Man Hunt* involves the pursuit by German agents of Thorndike (Walter Pidgeon), an Englishman who has failed in his attempt to assassinate Hitler. He disposes of one of them on the tracks of the Tube in similar fashion to the New York scene, but then is himself run to ground in a tiny cave in the English countryside, cornered by the master hunter, Quive-Smith (George Saunders). In the context of wartime, however, the cave turns out to be a shelter rather than a sign of animal atavism, just as the Tube tunnel had worked as Thorndike's ally against a better-armed enemy. By contrast, the alienated urban underworld was a postwar phenomenon that, in the iconic film noir that embodies the spatial myth, engulfed the objective world in its dark and deceptive logic.

Film noir was perhaps first employed as a conscious trope of the ruined city not in Hollywood but in the European films that could use the blasted landscapes

3.14 Film noir goes underground: Roy Morgan (Richard Basehart) faces off against the police in the drain tunnels of Los Angeles in *He Walked by Night* (1949). Frame enlargement. Eagle-Lion Films Inc./Photofest.

of their capitals to interrogate the legacy of the war. In *Night and the City* (1950), the first film shot abroad by Jules Dassin as he fled the Hollywood blacklist, the rubble of postwar London became both an existentialist landscape for portraying the plight of the film director caught in a web of intrigue beyond his ken and a farewell to the mythic London underworld of old. The film opens with the American small-time operator Harry Fabian (Richard Widmark) fleeing unknown pursuers through a beautifully lit night-for-night sequence of bombed-out buildings (figure 3.16). The ruins of London were aesthetic and lethal at the same time. Harry's only friends are a collection of clichés from prewar London stage and screen, an underworld out of the *Beggar's Opera*. They pale into insignificance, however, faced with the new breed of impresarios that run the gambling joints, wrestling halls, and brothels of Soho. When Harry matches wits with the latter, he is trapped, cornered by the new underworld and rejected by the old, its members now interested only in the price on his head. Run to ground along the Thames, he is last shown, back broken, his body dumped on the shore, with the crime boss Kristo (Herbert Lom) looking down from Hammersmith Bridge in the background and the sun rising, it seems, for the first time in the film. The new day, the ending implies, has left everything of

3.15 The New York City Subway as rationalized urban underworld in *While the City Sleeps*, directed by Fritz Lang (1956). Frame enlargement. RKO Radio Pictures Inc. /Photofest.

worth behind it in the past and in the night, in the mythic spaces of the underground city.

A similar use of urban space can be observed in *The Third Man* (1949), which took the ruined spaces of postwar Vienna as a similar zone of entrapment and an even more starkly observed fable of fallen man and moral ambiguity. Like Roy Morgan in *He Walked by Night*, Harry Lime (Orson Welles) uses the sewers to move freely through a cityscape divided aboveground between four occupied zones. In good urban mysteries fashion, the uncontrolled city belowground simply reproduces the hidden state of things above, the shady deals and exchanges that lubricate the complex and amoral world after the war. Only Anna (Alida Valli), the Czech theater actress who is restricted to playing comedy because her approach to life is too tragic, clings to a nostalgic past of personal loyalty and an image of Harry totally at odds with his criminal behavior in the rest of the world. Harry's friend, Holly Martins (Joseph Cotten), an American writer of pulp Westerns, undergoes an education in betrayal, finally shooting his old comrade dead as he lies wounded, trapped in the sewers he had made his own, and which he could traverse without even dirtying his gleaming shoes. The sewers are

3.16 The death throes of old London: Harry Fabian (Richard Widmark) flees at night through the ruins of the postwar city in Jules Dassin's *Night and the City* (1950). Frame enlargement. Twentieth Century Fox Film Corporation/Photofest.

a straightforward metaphor for scriptwriter Graham Greene and director Carol Reed, but employed with great subtlety and enhanced enormously by the meticulous reproductions built in the studios outside London. Like Harry Lime, they embody the allure of the dark city, intensely seductive, at least as long as mediated as spectacle by the silver screen. Atop the Prater wheel, Harry plays the Devil, restaging the Temptation on the Mount, pointing out to Holly that individual details dwindle to insignificance if one climbs high enough above them. The most brightly lit scene in the film, this episode removes *The Third Man* from the gutter of film noir, rounding it out into a worldview. Pure noir, the stuff the myth is made of, is unadulterated view from below, the power and the horror of the underworld in all of its incoherent, commonplace allure. Like many films, *The Third Man* used the tropes of noir within a broader representational framework, as the world above uses the underground to stand for all the things it cannot address directly or desires to exclude. The film ends not with the subterranean death of Harry Lime, the noir dream killed by British military efficiency, but with the refusal of either a noir or a romantic ending for Holly and Anna: he waits for her, smoking, in the pose of the deserving hero, and she walks straight past, not sparing even a glance. Neither death nor domestic bliss was to be found in the postwar city; both worlds, the film argued, belonged to the past.

Film noir gave the lie to the aboveground myths of postwar America as middle-class utopia, but it also produced a new image of America capable of seducing opponents of that myth, especially abroad. As James Naremore has observed, at the same time as they were decrying the Coca-Colization of the world, the French were singing the praises of the equally all-American export, film noir.[124] Since the 1960s, noir has become shorthand for a particular vision of the city and a particular vision of underground space, but seldom does this shorthand merge with an urban space-time particular enough to produce a potency on the order of the noir icons of the '40s. It has happened at moments—British gangster films such as *The Long Good Friday* (1980), which traced the development of the Docklands, or Louis Malle's eponymous 1980 portrayal of Atlantic City as it underwent the developers' wrecking ball; the frenetic vision of a high-rise Hong Kong sprung out of nowhere, approaching the handover to Mainland China amid triad encroachments of the film industry that underlay the operatic crime dramas of John Woo in the late '80s and early '90s; the so-called future noir inaugurated by Ridley Scott's *Blade Runner* (1982) that renovated the iconography of urban

3.17 The polyglot city of future noir, emptied of productive meaning. Ridley Scott's *Blade Runner* (1982). Frame enlargement. Warner Brothers/Photofest.

ruin at a time when noir narratives had mostly migrated into the bland territory of suburban melodrama.

Urban apocalypse was the great image of the cinematic mysteries of the last decades of the twentieth century. The futuristic twist completed the transformation from the noir city's combination of archetypal dark streets, rain-soaked alleys, and isolated streetlights, and spot-on locations or reconstructions of specific urban sites, into a truly global city with nothing of the specific left in it beyond perhaps a name or an out-of-context image. Emblematic of this transformation in *Blade Runner* were the multilingual lettering and artifacts scattered throughout twenty-first-century Los Angeles; what they signified was that the city had been entirely emptied of productive capabilities as a representation of space (figure 3.17). It was nothing but a ruin, wholly discarded and underground. As such, it became a cipher for the development of a new space—the global space of information technology for which no set of representations yet existed. The metaphorical (in neo-noir) or literal (in monster and disaster movies) destruction of the world cities that occurred either onscreen or before the action began with stunning regularity throughout the 1990s was the way the view from below registered the cataclysmic changes going on everywhere but in those cities.[125] True enough, the nerve centers might still be located in New York, Tokyo, London, Hong Kong, but not the spaces where meaning was now being actively contested and determined. These new mysteries once again diagnosed the crisis areas and showed who was to blame in an ever expanding web of universal conspiracy theories of brainwashing and terrorism. But locating the crisis areas underground was an even greater distortion of the truth about those crises than it had been back in the London and Paris of the 1840s. The only inkling of meaning beyond pure cliché was the very anonymity that exposed the vacuity of the urban image. The mysteries of the underground had expanded the view from below to such a degree that it took in global space as an image of the subterranean city. While the factual mysteries may have continued to churn out ever more horrifying but ever more cliché-bound accounts of the evils of the actual spaces of production around the world, the fiction of urban mysteries had merged with the satanic view from above; for the underground itself no longer had any contemporary meaning beyond its glorious, terrible, rebellious past.

4

THROUGH THE LOOKING GLASS

> Alice opened the door and found that it led into a small passage, not much larger than a rat-hole: she knelt down and looked along the passage into the loveliest garden you ever saw. How she longed to get out of that dark hall, and wander among those beds of bright flowers and those cool fountains.
>
> Lewis Carroll, "Down the Rabbit-Hole," *Alice's Adventures in Wonderland* (1865)

We have seen in the previous chapters how the nineteenth-century city was represented in terms of its subterranean spaces both material and metaphorical. What remains to be addressed are the means by which those spaces were imagined to communicate with the world above them: the thresholds of the modern city. The first transport revolution saw vast viaducts raised on arches and enormous cuttings opened out of the ground, imposing new forms of space onto the cityscapes of London and Paris that had, for the most part, developed slowly and in piecemeal fashion since the Middle Ages. The railroads constituted a new threshold with the outside world, importing and exporting people and goods to and from the city at a dizzying pace. As Le Corbusier put it in retrospect, "To-day the city's gates are in its *centre*. For its real gates are the railway stations."[1] Their physical presence, meanwhile, wrenched urban space out of the scale of the human form and animal locomotion; the cuttings and arches interrupted the ground-level navigation of the city, introducing instead movement either beneath or above the lived spaces of the metropolis. The cutting placed carriages and passengers below the urban observer, while the embanked viaduct placed them above the city dwellers. In addition to introducing new vantage points, both forms also physically segmented and fragmented the space through which they passed, creating divisions and barriers throughout the cityscape. Cuttings were characteristic of Paris, where bridges such as the Pont de l'Europe behind the Gare Saint-Lazare provided a novel vantage point for the flâneur to overlook a technological panorama. London was dominated by viaducts, which gave a view from the railway carriages down into the houses of the poor through whose neighborhoods the tracks had been run, but the passengers were carried over and separated from the new space of the arches beneath them. Rather than wholly subterranean, these new spaces remained partially exposed to the world above, their subordinate relationship to it newly visualized. In this chapter, I examine this new set of divisions in the metropolitan landscape, the architectural forms related to it, and later forms of threshold space that helped to visualize related later revolutions in urban space.

As Walter Benjamin famously argued, the paradigmatic threshold space of nineteenth-century Paris was the *passage*, or covered arcade, the architectural expression of a culture of the commodity based on the act of passing through, on such urban types as the gawker, the flâneur, and the detective, on the combination of business with pleasure, of the necessary transit from one place to the next with the act of window shopping, of the exterior public space with the interior private space, of the solidity of iron with the transparency of glass, of the hell of capitalism with the paradise of consumerism.[2] Rather than adapting commercial architecture and urban circulation to the scale of the railways, the *passage* reduced the new technology to the level of the pedestrian. Instead of segmenting different types of space, it condensed them at ground level, producing a rich confusion of above- and belowground that was characteristically Parisian. If nineteenth-century Paris was seen to be rich in the threshold experiences epitomized by the *passage*, the London counterpart was the omnipresent brick arch, filled in with market stalls and services, and populated with threatening phantoms, the urban underworld that sheltered beneath them. The *passage* was a basically unnecessary albeit elegant way of building shops; the arch allowed use to be made of the otherwise wasted space under the myriad London railways (figures 4.1 and 4.2). One doesn't stroll in a London arch; one either rushes through it nervously or one enters it on business and then comes back out again the same way.

Although less so in Paris than in London, the development of both arch and cutting was uneven: parts of northern and eastern Paris were for a long time wastelands bisected by the railway lines coming out of the gares Saint-Lazare, du Nord, de l'Est, d'Austerlitz, and de Lyon; arches and embankments dominate large stretches of the north, east, and south of London, but are much scarcer in the West End. Moreover, as the sociologist Charles Booth's turn-of-the-century maps of London so well documented, the embankment played a key role in determining the changing demographics of the city, cutting up its less exclusive areas into isolated enclaves and cul-de-sacs, surrounded by tracks, stations, sheds, and sidings. And while such cuts into the fabric of the city were enthusiastically documented by Parisian artists as aesthetic phenomena, especially around the gare Saint-Lazare and the Pont de l'Europe behind it, in London the arches became synonymous with the separation of the classes, as in Augustus Leopold Egg's portrait of a fallen woman isolated in an arch of the Adelphi (figures 4.3 and 4.4). If revolution in Paris was famously countered by the spatial openness of Haussmann's boulevards, class solidarity was short-circuited in London by the barriers of progress. I look in detail below at the difficulty with which two unusual construction projects, the Adelphi arches and the Thames Tunnel, fitted into the ver-

4.1 The Paris *passage. Passage Choiseul—Hôtel de Gesvres.* Photograph by Eugène Atget. 1907. Reproduced by permission from Bibliothèque Nationale de France.

tical segregation of space characteristic of London, but first I examine the threshold character of the *passage* in Paris, the ways it condensed the meanings of these new forms of verticalization, and the results of its importation to the London West End. The various tunnels through which the city communicates with the outside world suggested a different form of threshold fantasy: the risk of invasion

4.2 The London arch: workaday spaces near the site of the old Adelphi arches. Photo by the author, 1995.

by foreign bodies through its unsealed openings. Shockingly novel experiences in and of themselves, the dominant threshold experiences of the early twentieth century—the trench and the cinema—bear a largely unrecognized debt to the representations of space introduced in the previous century. In conclusion, I turn to the renovation of the arches, cuttings, and arcades of the nineteenth-century city at the turn of the following century, and address the present-day persistence of the threshold, the view from below, and the view from above as modes of conceptualizing urban environments that have, in fact, changed almost beyond recognition from those in which these modes came into being.

Et Ego in Arcadia

> The "théâtre moderne," located at the bottom of the now-demolished passage de l'Opéra. . . . Will I ever see again with these eyes the "bar" on the second floor, it too so dark, with arbors like impenetrable tunnels—a drawing room at the bottom of a lake.
>
> ANDRÉ BRETON, *Nadja* (1928)

The first of the main cluster of covered arcades between the Palais-Royal and the new leisure and entertainment center of the boulevards was the passage des

4.3 The railway creates a paradigmatic space of Paris modernity, with the Pont de l'Europe in the background. Claude Monet, *Arrival of the Normandy Train, Gare Saint-Lazare, 1877.* Oil on canvas. Mr. and Mrs. Martin A. Ryerson Collection, 1933. Reproduced by permission of the Art Institute of Chicago.

Panoramas (1800), but the classic iron-and-glass style really took off in the '20s with the passage de l'Opéra (1821), galerie Vivienne (1824–26), galerie Colbert (1826), galerie Véro-Dodat (1826), passage Choiseul (1825–27)—later extending beyond the boulevard Montmartre via the passage Jouffroy (1845–46)—and the passage Verdeau (1846), among others (figure 4.5). In a contemporary description cited by Benjamin as "the locus classicus for the presentation of the arcade," the novel building form is presented as a microcosm, a "city, a world in miniature."[3] The arcade ushered in a new and contradictory image of urban space, combining liberty from inclement nature with the novelty of natural light in an artificial interior. It was unlike its somewhat later architectural cousins in the iron-and-glass style, the railway station, the market hall, and the exhibition hall. These monumental buildings "cause[d] . . . perceptual shocks similar to those experienced by the first railway travelers," due to the "blinding" amount of light they admitted, the disorienting character of their lack of internal perspective, and the endless symmetry of their composition out of identical, small-scale components.[4] By

4.4 The arch as representational space proper to the "fallen woman." Augustus Leopold Egg, *Past and Present 3*. Oil on canvas, ca. 1857–58. Reproduced by permission of the Tate Gallery, London. © Tate, London 2006.

contrast, the arcade was backward as well as forward-looking, closely related to utopian imaginings of industrial architecture on a human scale rather than the "dream of not being *like* anything, of being nothing created," as Robert Harbison has aptly characterized the standard machine architecture of the time.[5]

Although gigantesque machine dreams have continued to resonate through the architecture of public space—the airports, parking garages, and malls since dubbed *non-lieux*, or nonplaces, by French anthropologist Marc Augé[6]—the new experiences of space promised by other nineteenth-century utopianists now appear as irredeemably quaint and archaic as the arcades they most closely resembled. In Léo Claretie's 1886 fantasy of Paris a hundred years in the future, the time traveler opens an umbrella to laughter at the onset of a storm: the city is now protected by "an enormous roof, made of plates of the purest crystal." In a new quarter of the city, he is taken to visit a subaqueous jewelry market: "We entered the underwater jewelers' hall. Never would you have believed you were so

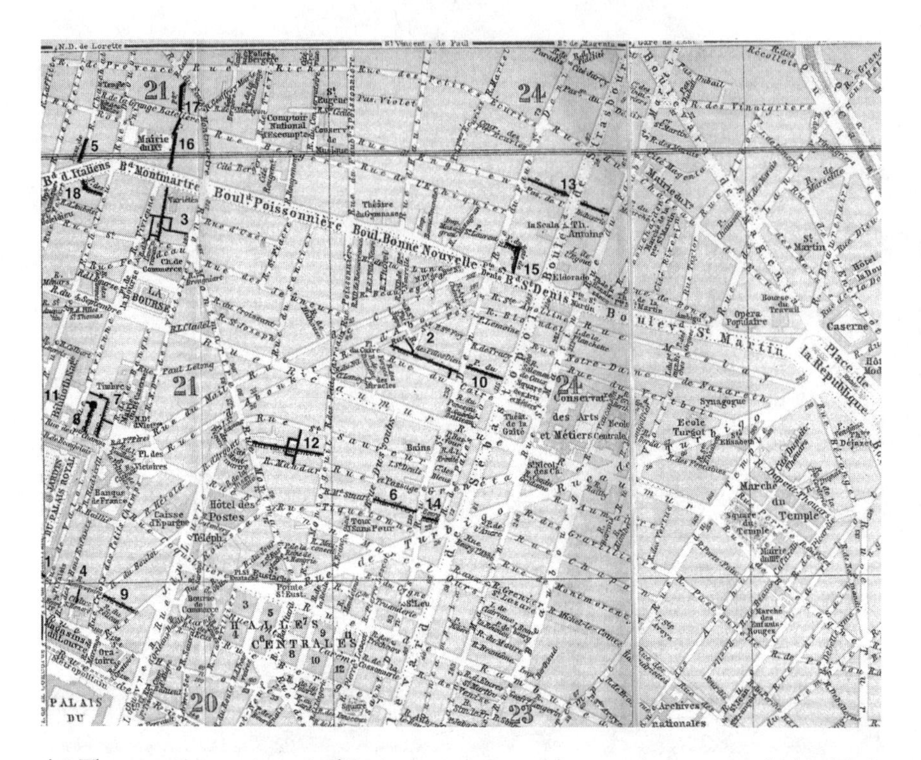

4.5 The *passage* vogue in central Paris. A 1900 map with covered *passages* marked in black and numbered: (1) Galeries de Bois, Palais Royal (1786–88, demolished 1828 and replaced by Galerie d'Orléans (1828–29, demolished 1935); (2) Passage du Caire (1798–99); (3) Passage des Panoramas (1800); (4) Passage Montesquieu (1811, demolished end of century); (5) Passage de l'Opéra (1822–25, demolished 1925); (6) Passage du Grand Cerf (1824 or 1825); (7) Galerie Vivienne (1824–26); (8) Galerie Colbert (1826); (9) Galerie Véro-Dodat (1826); (10) Passage Ponceau (1826); (11) Passage Choiseul (1825–27; off the map a block to the west); (12) Passage du Saumon (1827–30, demolished 1899, replaced by rue du Saumon, 1900); (13) Passage Brady (1828); (14) Passage Bourg l'Abbé (1828); 14) Passage Prado (orig. Passage Bois de Boulogne) (1830); (15) Passage Jouffroy (1845–46); (16) Passage Verdeau (1846); (17) Passage des Princes (1860).

far beneath dry land. An immense dome . . . covered the entire market, filled with boutiques with sparkling shop windows, brilliantly lit with electricity, full of people and life."[7] The social theorist Charles Fourier made the *rue-galeries* of his ideal city alluring by comparing them with traditional spaces of luxury. "Once a man has seen the gallery-streets of a Phalanstery," he promised, "he will look upon the most elegant civilized palace as a place of exile, a residence worthy of fools."[8] Like the arcade, Fourier's gallery-street was a fairly narrow, enclosed passageway; some were to be elevated, some underground, but all equally "sheltered, elegant, and comfortable in winter thanks to the help of heaters and ventilators."[9]

First set forth in 1822, the plan for a "palace of harmony" with not a single "outside street or open road-ways"[10] owed much to the contemporary vogue of the *passage* (and perhaps vice-versa: the first heated arcade, the passage Jouffroy, was opened in 1846). James Buckingham made the debt to the arcade explicit in his 1849 plan for the model town Victoria, proposing "a continuous covered gallery or arcade, 100 feet wide—like Burlington and Lowther Arcades in London" that would "afford the power of going from every dwelling, workshop, or store, to the remotest part of the Town, all the way under cover, completely sheltered from rain, wind, snow, dust, or sun."[11] The arrangement, in concentric squares, would both eliminate "secret and obscure haunts for the retirement of the filthy and the immoral from the public eye" and encourage business and social interaction through protection from the elements.[12]

Necessarily open on one end because of their function as transport termini, the new railway stations made far fewer concessions to the preindustrial past.[13] They were built on a machine rather than a human scale, and tended toward the inhospitably sublime rather than the quaintly domestic. Although in machine terms they functioned as an arch, allowing trains to enter and leave the protection of the shed in a businesslike fashion, they served a different purpose for the traveler, who saw them more frequently as the fantastic threshold either of a journey away from or an entry into the metropolis. Although similar in scale, the freestanding and straightforwardly neoclassical arch, such as Jean Chalgrin's Arc de Triomphe (commissioned by Napoleon in 1806 although not completed until 1836) or John Nash's Marble Arch (finished in 1827, in front of Buckingham Palace, and moved to the northeast corner of Hyde Park in 1851), had a different intent: to evoke concretely a specific military triumph. Although he ignores the reverse experience of the entrance into London via the massive shed—from behind the scenes, as it were—Harbison has nicely observed the threshold effect within the architecture of two of London's early stations, "The Euston arch and the double barrel of Kings Cross are two bold versions of the station as an Entrance to lots of other places"[14] (figure 4.6). Also in contradistinction to the commemorative arch, both the street-gallery and the railway station were designed to facilitate movement. Fourier's plan sought the closed circulation of a series of linked interiors; the railway terminals and other massive covered public spaces were conceived to be conduits and gathering places simultaneously. The arcade was contained and given the pretense of an interior like the street-gallery; in its channeling of traffic and character as a place of transit where the classes and sexes mingled, it looked forward to the monumental public-space architecture of the latter half of the century. But where the spaciousness and expanse of later iron-and-glass architecture evoked images of the city at its most populous and overwhelmingly open, joined by fantasies of escape and transformation, the *passage* was much more easily assimilated to the underground spaces of the city, and the fantasies it evoked were in a more subterranean mode.

4.6 The railway arch: *Entrance, North-Western Railway, Euston Square*. Illustration in *London*, ed. Charles Knight, 6 vols. in 3 (London, 1841–44), 6:316.

Whatever Benjamin may have claimed, however, the underground character of the arcade was no more straightforward than that of the nineteenth-century devil. There were different associations at play in its identity; those of the glamorous underworld that associated the devil so closely with nineteenth-century Paris were in particular conflict with the more literally subterranean qualities of urban squalor and the organic underground. As Alfred Delvau remarked of the passage Vérité, not every arcade lived up to the promise of its name: "Two steps from the Palais-Royal there is . . . a small, dark and twisted *passage*, adorned by a public scribe and a fruit seller. It may resemble the caves of Cacus or Trophonius, but it will never look like a *passage*—even with good will and gas light."[15] In his catalog, Kermel likewise mentioned the pseudoarcades, "or rather corridors, such as those of Saint-Roch, Désirabode, Radzivil, Henri IV, etc., etc.," adding that "it can be useful to know them, but it is dangerous to frequent them."[16] There was not enough glass in the street-width roof coverings to provide the sensational illumination of the Crystal Palace or the vast train sheds, and what glass there was appears to have been blackened in short order by the soot of the air outside and the smoke of the gas lamps inside. In addition to the latent claustrophobia of its architectural structure, the persistent identification of the space of the arcade with prostitution contributed to its underworld reputation, along with the complaints of dirt, decrepitude, and general sleaze that began to appear quite early on. As the vogue for shopping styles shifted from the arcade to the spacious department store, and the vogue for strolling moved to the new boulevards, the half-abandoned sites, which could not simply be shut down like a bankrupt shop, continued in service, shorn of the transient glitter of their heyday in the first half of the century.[17]

Part of the complexity of the *passage* as an urban space was its combination of the material underworld of its associations with prostitution and crime and the devil's demesne of glamorous commodities, gambling, and nightlife. This dual subterranean character was received in different proportions in differently located arcades, with glamour consistently identified with the west and squalor with the east. Kermel contrasted the westerly *passages*, "longtime invaded by the aristocracy of money," and those in "the regions of industry and the bourgeoisie" further east; he equally identified each category according to the different class of grisette that frequented it.[18] "By studying the physical aspect of the capital's *passages*," he maintained, "you can obtain the detailed expression of its mores. Take the galeries de l'Opéra and the passage Brady, two extreme points of the grand total, and you will arrive through deduction at a full knowledge of Paris."[19] Representative as it was, the geographical identification stuck, as is evident in a doggerel verse Léon-Paul Fargue cited in his 1939 homage to the flâneur, *Le Piéton de Paris*:

> In the passage Vivienne
> She told me: I'm from Vienna. . . .
> I ought to have found the damsel
> At passage Bonne-Nouvelle.
> But I waited in vain
> At passage Brady . . .
> So there they are, the passages of love![20]

Beginning in the heart of the central arcades, the lover's pursuit takes him inexorably east and down market, lightheartedly emphasizing his eventual failure to meet again the girl from Vienna, and hinting at the consolation of love with one of the many prostitutes that plied the eastern boulevards and the rue St. Denis in the 1930s in far greater numbers than they did those of the west.

Framing the social geography of the Paris arcades were two examples that were so extreme as to exceed the classification altogether; in the ways they occupied the conceptual center and periphery of Parisian arcade culture they bring out most clearly its paradoxical spatial practice. The "belle galerie vitrée" of the Palais-Royal, according to Kermel, was so phantasmagoric as to transcend altogether the appellation of *passage*, eliciting an "instinctive admiration" that required no analysis or specialized taste.[21] Words also could not be found to describe the passage du Caire, but for the opposite reason: it was a "profanation" of its namesake, "Cairo in this diseased caravanserai, Cairo in this damp corner . . . Silver and resplendent Cairo in this cold and ruined atmosphere, Cairo in this hallway! Profanation, triple profanation!"[22] The passage du Caire (figure 4.7) had been built in 1798 near the site of the best-known medieval *cour des Miracles* to commemorate the French entrance into the Egyptian capital, but it never really fit the classic profile. As Elie Berthet complained in 1844,

> The passageways are sad and dark, and they crisscross at every instant in a manner that is disagreeable to the eye. Neither during the day nor at night does anything about them recall the brilliant shops and the flirtatious population of the passages des Panoramas or de l'Opéra. Moreover, they seem affected by the lithography workshops and packing shops, as the neighboring street is affected by the straw-hat manufacturers. Passersby are rare, except perhaps when it rains, and people going from the place du Caire to the rue Saint-Denis willingly avoid the fetid rue des Filles-Dieu.[23]

It did serve its function as sheltered way and traffic conduit (although, according to another source, umbrellas were still needed during the rain because its galleries "in several places lacked glass covering"[24]) but with none of the glitz that otherwise made the dirt tolerable or the slumming glamorous.

Whether a hereditary sanctuary of the Paris underworld or the grimy center of its printing industry, the passage du Caire was an irrefutably down-market arcade. The association with the long-since-displaced population of the *cour des Miracles* proved stubbornly enduring. Maxime du Camp wrote of it in his monumental study of Paris in 1870: "Certain sites and certain people appear, like chemical bodies, to be endowed with elective affinities, and the subjects of the realm of argot, when the surveillance lessened or circumstances permitted, hastened to return to this court of Miracles where their ancestors had lived."[25] Places, asserted du Camp rather distressedly, have their own subterranean history; one characteristic of the threshold has always been to reveal that history more readily than a site more fixed in its spatial identity. It was typical of the Paris discourse that this history could be given a nostalgic spin as well, as in this account of the same space as center for a different type of filthy and underground activity, the printing industry:

> The printers . . . were able to appropriate, at the end of the eighteenth century, a vast area: . . . the passage du Caire and its environs. . . . But with the extension of the boundaries of Paris, printers . . . were dispersed to all parts of the city. . . . Alas! a glut of printers! Today workers corrupted by the spirit of speculation ought to remember that . . . between the rue Saint-Denis and the cour des Miracles, there still exists a long, smoke-filled gallery where their true household gods lie forgotten.[26]

One of the printers who had apparently remained true to his household gods was Lacrampe, at 2, rue Damiette, catercorner to the arcade's western entrance: "This haven for beggars and malefactors was destroyed in 1656. Today the court of Miracles is a populous, industrial quarter, at the entrance of which can be found the handsome printing works from which *Le Diable à Paris* issues every week."[27] Du Camp's 1870 focus on the material bas-fonds meets the devil's view from above in this eastern arcade, for in his version the rue Damiette was below the

4.7 *Passage du Caire (juin 1907) 33 rue d'Alexandrie*. Photograph by Eugène Atget. Reproduced by permission from Bibliothèque de Nationale de France.

surface of the city, "where the workers work in cellars, circulating through the meanders of the passage du Caire"[28]

The passage du Caire antedated the classic arcades of 1822–34. Its form, like its eastern location, was closer to the underworld than its later more famous, more fashionable, and more central neighbors between the Palais-Royal and the

Grands Boulevards. The unusual décor is especially evident on the façade of the entrance: sphinx heads placed between windows of the entrance building, hieroglyphs lining the edge of the portal, and columns marking the entrance to the *passage* itself (figure 4.8); the same iconography would later signal the Egyptian catacombs in Highgate Cemetery in London.[29] In his article in *Le Diable à Paris*, "What Is Disappearing from Paris," Balzac dryly regretted the ornamentation of the *passage* entrance as one of the greatest costs of the Egyptian campaign.[30] In another aspect as well, the passage du Caire was closer to the underworld of the necropolis than to the glittering realm of commerce; it was paved "in part with funerary stones on which the Gothic inscriptions and the emblems have not yet been effaced."[31] The archaic, exotic, and mysterious aspect of the arcade form would be downplayed by the adoption of the industrial model of unornamented iron and glass, but it persisted as a primary aspect of the spatial identity of the form.

If the passage du Caire emblematized the low-end subterranean aspect of the arcade, the late-eighteenth-century Galeries de Bois of the Palais-Royal defined them as a glamorous underworld, even down to their muckraking revolutionary pamphleteers. After all, the Galeries de Bois played "a starring role in the history of Paris; hideous and dusty constructions, . . . for forty years licentiousness, commerce, pleasure, and letters mixed together"[32] (figure 4.9). The gardens of the Palais-Royal were built in 1632 by the Cardinal Richelieu and assumed by the royal family after his death. They became notorious for the debauched *soupers* they hosted during the regency of Louis XV. Although their use varied with changes in government, the reputation for dissolution stuck: "It was a perpetual fair," wrote historian Jacques Dulaure, "the meeting place for all foreigners, the center of all manner of affairs."[33] The completion of the arcades and shops (1786–88), and the opening of brothels and gambling houses by Philippe, the fifth Duc d'Orléans, consolidated the Palais-Royal as the commercial, intellectual, and recreational center of the city.

The gardens and galleries were a revolutionary forum as well, the hotbed of pamphleteers and scene of Camille Desmoulins' speech preceding the attack on the Bastille; the interior would house Napoleon's administration, the Stock Exchange, and the Tribunal of Commerce. Renamed Palais-Egalité in 1790, and confiscated by the revolutionary government in 1793, the property was returned to the Orléans by Louis XVIII. The gardens became a favored site for duels, although the Palais-Royal did not lose its reputation for radical politics and immoral behavior. As the devil's spies reported to him on the dull state of things in 1817 France in *L'Almanach de l'Autre Monde*, "In Paris all you have left is the Palais-Royal, that is, its inhabitants, the stock market, the gambling houses, and other places that modesty does not permit me to name."[34] Rather than the literal fire and brimstone of the passage du Caire, however, the Palais-Royal was the center of the satirical view of Paris from above, as in the Asmodeus flight that

4.8 Egyptomania: *2 place du Caire (1907–08).* Photograph by Eugène Atget. Reproduced by permission from Bibliothèque de Nationale de France.

opened the urban physiognomy, *Le Livre des cent-et-un*, with the metaphor of the city as an extended *passage*: "When will you come, angel or devil, to guide us in this long gallery of modern mores, formed by two revolutions? You who see the world as it is, composed, severe, calm, and sad, do you thus believe that Asmodeus is possible in this world?"[35] The second article of the serial publication, the first five numbers of which were delivered under the title of *Le Diable boiteux à Paris, ou Paris et les moeurs comme elles sont*, was dedicated to the Palais-Royal, the only place in Paris whose counterpart could be found nowhere else in the world.[36]

Even though the fashionable hordes that thronged there frequently transformed the earthen floors of its twin arcades into so much mud,[37] the Galeries de Bois remained a center of dissolution and debauchery until 1828, when they burned down, to be replaced by the Galerie d'Orléans. Until Louis-Philippe cracked down in 1830, the Palais-Royal endured, in the words of Lavallée in *Le Diable à Paris*, as the capital of pleasure, "a sort of Paris within Paris, a center of life, of pleasure, of luxury, of intoxication of every type; all its lupanars, its gambling houses, it boutiques: no pleasure was any good, no luxury goods were worth anything, no merchandise was à la mode if it didn't come from the Palais-Royal."[38] As the confluence of an "abominable"[39] physical space and an ultra-fashionable social one, the Galeries de Bois remain premodern in character, just as the passage du Caire was archaic in its association with the cour des Miracles; however, in their identities as two types of underworld space, they are eminently Parisian.

In contrast to his easy dismissal of the passage du Caire, in the extended description Balzac gave of the Galeries de Bois during the 1820s in *Les Illusions Perdues* we find a vivid sense of the exuberant mixture of high and low, of "respectable persons and men of the greatest consequence rubb[ing] shoulders with people

4.9 The glamorous underworld of Paris: *Fig. 33—Galeries de bois (ancien camp des Tartares, au Palais-Royal (1825)*. Engraving in Fedor Hoffbauer and Edouard Fournier, *Paris à travers les ages,* 2 vols (Paris: Firmin-Didot, 1875–82), 2:187. Reproduced by permission from Bibliothèque Nationale de France.

who looked like gallows-birds," of the latest glamorous fashions with the inescapable *boue de Paris*, so typical of the previous century's descriptions, and enduring until the wooden arcades burned down. According to Balzac, a description of this "squalid bazaar" should cause any Parisian man over forty to recollect it with a pleasure "unbelievable to young folk":

> On the site of the cold, lofty, broad Orleans Gallery, a kind of hot-house void of flowers, were shanties, or more exactly wood huts, poorly roofed, small, dimly lit on the court and garden side by lights of sufferance which passed for windows but which in fact were more like the dirtiest kind of aperture found in taverns beyond the city gates. A triple range of shops formed two galleries about twelve feet high. Shops sited in the centre looked out on to the two galleries, from which they borrowed their pestilential atmosphere and whose roofing allowed only a little light to filter through invariably dirty window-panes. These bee-hive cells had acquired so high a price thanks to the crowds which came there that, in spite of the pinched proportions of some of them—scarcely six feet wide and eight to ten feet long—they commanded a rent of three thousand francs a year.[40]

Already in 1843, the new and roomy but sterile Galerie d'Orléans seemed to pale in comparison to the organic, subterranean life of the Galeries de Bois and the *galerie-vitrée* or "camp des Tartares" at their center. Balzac mobilized all of his irony for this emblematic space of Restauration Paris, where the very depth of the noise, dirt, and squalor seems to signify the height of its influence and popularity:

> The floor of the Glazed Gallery . . . like that of the Wooden Galleries, was the natural soil of Paris, reinforced by the adventitious dirt brought in on the boots and shoes of passers-by. In all seasons, one's feet stumbled against mounds and depressions of caked mud; the shopkeepers were constantly sweeping them up, but newcomers had to acquire the knack of walking across them. This sinister accumulation of refuse, these windows grimy with rain and dust, these squat huts with rags and tatters heaped around them, the filthy condition of the half-built walls, this agglomeration reminiscent of a gypsy camp or the booths on a fair-ground—the sort of temporary constructions which Paris heaps about the monuments it fails to build—this contorted physiognomy was wonderfully in keeping with the teeming variety of trades carried on beneath these brazenly indecent hutments, noisy with babble and hectic with gaiety, and where an enormous amount of business has been transacted between the two Revolutions of 1789 and 1830. For twenty years the Stock Exchange stood opposite, on the ground-floor of the Palais-Royal. There then public opinion was formed, reputations were made and unmade, political and financial affairs discussed.[41]

Along with businessmen and politicians, he tells us, there were milliners and bookmen of all sorts; the *galerie-vitrée* was filled with all manner of charlatanry and spectacle. Come evening, in a "poetry of vice," the "filles de joie" would arrive,

> from every direction . . . to "do the Palais-Royal." The Stone Galleries belonged to privileged brothels, which paid for the right to parade gaudily dressed creatures between such and such an arcade and in the garden square into which they opened; but the Wooden Galleries were a happy hunting-ground for the commoner kind: they were supereminently "The Palais," which at that time meant that they were the temple of prostitution.[42]

Architecturally, socially, and morally, the Galeries de Bois and the old Palais-Royal epitomize a Parisian conception of high and low intermingled in a great carnival, a conception enabled by the heightening of what had come to be seen as the subterranean character of the arcade as a threshold to an underworld of dirt, lowlife, and sex. "There are girls there, Courtisans, Duchesses and honest women," wrote Louis-Sebastien Mercier at the end of the eighteenth century, "and no one confuses one with the other. . . . These notions depend on easily grasped nuances: but you must study them in situ."[43] Nineteenth-century Parisians were much less sure about their ability to read the codes of public space; as the Restauration gave way to the July Monarchy and then the Second Empire, identity was more and more held to be bestowed by place rather than contingencies of dress or behavior, and, when they could not be shut down, the city's thresholds were policed.

The very filth of the old Palais-Royal was glamorous; the passage du Caire also inspired nostalgia, but for its workmanlike identification with beggars and printers. Both sites equally gave rise to condemnation. Consistent with their assemblage of all of the temptations of the devil under a single set of roofs, the Galeries de Bois polarized the public. It is here that the apparent distance between the two types of underworld represented by these spaces can be seen to have been combined within the iron-and-glass architecture of the later, classic arcade. For the moralist, of course, the spectrum from satanic high life to the infernal work of beggars and printers was all part of the corruption of urban life. Hence, responding to arguments that the Palais-Royal had declined in popularity because of the closing of its gambling houses and the exclusion of prostitutes from its grounds as of 1829, an officer of the Bureau of Morals countered that it was the new *passages* nearby that had siphoned off business. Moreover, he added, "I do not know if commerce at the Palais-Royal has really suffered from the absence of *femmes de débauche*, but what is certain is that public decency there has improved enormously."[44] Béraud contended that the "invasion" of the Palais-Royal by "a swarm of practically nude prostitutes" must have distracted the crowds from their shopping rather than have been responsible for drawing them there, and that the initial "stagnation" of the space was in fact due to the "free circulation of the *filles publiques*."[45] "Commerce," asserted Baudelaire, "is in its essence satanic";[46] in their contribution to the "free circulation" of goods and of sex, the *passages* were an essential element of the commerce of the 1820s and '30s.

Sheltering the passerby from both weather and the danger of increasingly heavy traffic, the arcade encouraged the type of loitering and hanging about that was essential not only to the streetwalker but to the business of the small boutique, with its novel shop-window displays made possible by plate-glass and gaslight. Alongside the features intrinsic to their architecture, the arcades were also during this period a center of the spectacle culture of Paris, from the titular panoramas that flanked the boulevard entrance of the passage des Panoramas to the Musée Grevin that survives to this day in the passage Jouffroy.[47] Grisettes danced in the bal d'Idalie in a basement of the passage de l'Opéra. Offenbach and Crémieux's comic opera *Orphée aux enfers* had a highly successful run at the Théâtre des Bouffes Parisiens, located in the passage Choiseul near the Palais-Royal. Such spectacles could have a lowering effect on the composition of the crowd; Du Camp complained about the incursion of beggars into what ought to have been the genteel boulevards around the passage de l'Opéra, where they "assailed . . . persons leaving the theater."[48]

Their nocturnal identity was central to the Parisian *passages.* Sleepy by day, they were at their busiest when everything else was shutting up for the night. Delvau commented of the Café Leblond, that it had "one entrance on the boulevard des Italiens until midnight, and an exit onto the passage de l'Opéra until two o'clock in the morning."[49] Julius Rodenberg wrote that "here it was never closing time, and almost never night. When Tortoni had closed, the throng made its way over to the nearby boulevards and milled around there, at its thickest around the passage de l'Opéra."[50] It was the new technology of gas lighting, perfected in the *passages,* that made nighttime strolling through them so magical: "People seem to have been fascinated by the interplay between the brilliance of the light and the wares on display, and the lively crowd. 'A labyrinth of iridescent passages, like rainbow bridges in an ocean of light. A totally magical world.' "[51] What was unique about the arcades, and what distinguished them from the soon-to-be-gaslit boulevards, is that they possessed this magical, otherworldly character by day as well as by night. Here the arcade was closer to the other iron-and-glass constructions, although the magic of the latter was of a transfigured daytime rather than a permanent twilight. This was the threshold quality of the *passage*: nocturnal in identity, it was nonetheless defined by its relation to light, be it the sunlight that filtered through its dirty glass roofs or the gaslight that illuminated it as an interior.

The *passage* was a precursor of the inorganically subterranean space dear to utopian modernity, but, unlike that space, it had not yet learned to hide the fact that its roots lay in the literally underground life that equally defines modernity. Reveries on the theme of the arcade imagine a covered city, but always with a sense of the traditional underground tinting the utopian imagination, like the underwater jewelry hall in the Claretie fantasy cited above. In *Les Passages et les rues*, a one-act vaudeville performed in 1827 at the Théâtre des Variétés on the boulevard Montmartre next to the entrance to the passage des Panoramas, we hear of a scheme to turn all of Paris into a greenhouse: "I hear they want to roof all the streets of Paris with glass. That will make for lovely hot-houses; we will live in them like melons."[52] Precisely because the Paris underground was accessible to so many positive connotations in its traditional forms, to imagine it too literally as subterranean or enclosed was seen as laughably nightmarish. The customary acceptance of or at least ambivalence toward nightlife, underworld activities, and revolution meant that the underground could be manifested as organic rather than necessitating the futuristic approach that would characterize later underground utopias.

A look at the spread of the shorter-lived *passage* vogue across the Channel shows the degree to which this nocturnal identity was integral to the architectural form. A play produced three years after the opening of the Burlington Arcade and seeking to introduce this foreign concept to the London viewer could compare it only to local spaces that were both underground and associated with crime:

> I suppose you never saw the Highgate Tunnel before it fell in, or the passage in "Brown's Hotel," from the felons' cell to the press yard; if you did, you might have some notion of an arcade; it is open at both ends, as narrow as what—a miser's heart, or an old maid's mind; a sort of horizontal funnel, which in the finest summer's day . . . conveys such a fine stream of wind, that you are as sure of catching a cold as if you were up to your neck in cold water.[53]

The Highgate Tunnel and the Archway Viaduct that replaced it were an early example of a multilevel bypass (figure 4.10), but also an infamous resort of highwaymen preying on travelers coming into London from the north. This London spoof not only compared the new arcade with two subterranean sites of crime but discounted a fundamentally positive quality traditionally associated with the underground, shelter from the elements.[54] Even the gaslight served merely to make this "devil's drawing-room" more closely resemble the underworld: "Aye, there's no occasion for candles, the gas throws such a light upon every subject, that many are enlightened subjects who are darker than Erebus."[55]

The *passage* was a properly Parisian and modern urban space that could be bent to other uses only through external force, and the accompanying representation of space was irresistibly associated with Paris, the favored resort of the devil. Still, London did import the vogue: Nash's Royal Opera Arcade opened in 1818, followed by the Burlington Arcade (1819; figure 4.11), Lowther Arcade (1830; figure 4.12), City Arcade (1830), and New Exeter 'Change (1842–43).[56] The Burlington Arcade, the only of the ventures to be a commercial success, was, along with several others in the vicinity of Piccadilly in the West End, a central location of swell London during the Regency. Like the Parisian *passage*, the London arcades combined luxury shopping with prostitution and proximity to the gambling hells of St. James's. They were a byword for high-life dissipation. In an 1822 theatrical adaptation of *Life in London*, Bob Logic takes Tom and Jerry to the Burlington Arcade:

4.10 What makes sense for traffic makes a hiding place for thieves. *Highgate Tunnel* (ca. 1830). James Pollard, engraved by George Hunt. Reproduced by permission from the Guildhall Library, © Corporation of London.

There's many a thing in London made
Surpassing comprehension;
A squeeze in Burlington Arcade,
Is worthy some attention.
The 'Façade' at the Opera-House,
Has scarce a belle to boast of;
In Burlington they pay their vows,
Where *things* are made the most of.[57]

The anonymous author of the *New Swell's Night Guide to the Bowers of Venus* singled out for attention the women of the Burlington and Lowther arcades. Of the former, which linked Piccadilly with Burlington Gardens, he wrote that after five the nobility and gentry that frequented its promenade were replaced by "the bucks in pursuit of pleasure—the high apparelled females, and no doubt of the highest class of the pavé, circumspect in conduct, here join in converse and assignation."[58] The Lowther, which ran between West Strand and Adelaide Street just north of Charing Cross, could boast of "the fondest looking females, promenading from all parts of the West End," on the lookout for "partners" to escort them to the nearby saloons.[59] The Gallicisms in each notation ("Facade," "belle," "pavé," "saloons") render the Parisian association in more or less self-conscious fashion.

The high-class identity toward which the West End arcades aspired had to be jealously guarded, for the theaters and clubs around Piccadilly drew streetwalkers, cutpurses, con artists, flower girls, and the rest of London street culture to the concentrated mass of customers and easy marks. Contrary to the common dictum that London was open for business all night, while Paris closed up early, the London arcades employed beadles at each entrance, were locked up at night, and made every effort to present themselves as self-enclosed and highly regulated shopping malls. In the one-act burletta, *The Burlington Arcade* (1838), Longstaff the Beadle is prominently posted at the Piccadilly end, interrogating any stroller that does not appear to meet the establishment's requirements of fashion and gentility.[60] Excessive loitering was discouraged: in the one-act farce, *The Lowther Arcade* (1845), the hero, Alfred Mornington, worries that he has been strolling up and down the arcade for so long that "the beadle begins to recognize me as very like the last fellow he took into custody."[61] An explicit (if characteristically joking) reference to the

4.11 London's only enduring arcade success, between Piccadilly and Burlington Gardens. *Interior of Burlington Arcade, London*, ca. 1825. Colored engraving. Collection of the author.

4.12 Center of children's toys and women of doubtful reputation. *Interior of Lowther Arcade, London*. Engraving, ca. 1850. Reproduced by permission from the Guildhall Library, © Corporation of London.

close relation between the arcades, spectacle culture, and commerce concluded the play: "Should you find anybody in doubt as to the direction, tell them that the best way to the *Lowther Arcade* is through the *Lyceum Theatre*." In a familiar state of affairs for theater of the time, the Lyceum was just down the road from the setting of its spectacle.

Matt Cook has remarked that the Burlington Arcade established a London combination of sex with shopping; it was a combination that allowed the area around Piccadilly to be consistently identified with the Continent.[62] In *Lady Audley's Secret* (1862), the eponymous heroine visits the Burlington Arcade to purchase her naughty French novels. As Jane Rendell has argued, the arcade was represented as a safe place for women to work and shop in an area traditionally the exclusive province of men; however, it appears that their primary role was nevertheless to service the male population of Bond Street, St. James's, and Pall Mall.[63] The thrill of Lady Audley's illicit purchase would probably have been heightened by the spatial association with prostitution: bribing the beadles, streetwalkers were allowed to ply the Arcade; shopgirls would sell themselves on the side in the living quarters above the shops, the windows providing an ideal preview display for their attractions. According to Mayhew, for example, prostitutes working at Hamilton's night house off the Haymarket used a room above the bonnet shop in the arcade.[64] More sensationally, there emerged from the testimony of a Burlington Arcade beadle in the 1870–71 court case of Ernest Boulton and Frederick Park (also known as Fanny and Stella) that the cross-dressing pair were wont to shop in the arcade, sometimes in full regalia, sometimes just in makeup. They had once been asked by the beadle to leave after one of the men had been observed winking at a gentleman and "turning his head in a sly manner."[65]

The London arcades could not escape their reputation. The title of another one-act farce, *The Lowther Arcade; or, Waiting for an Omnibus on a rainy day* (1854), explains how a respectable mother and daughter find themselves confined to the eponymous passage, the daughter thrilled, pleading for at least "*one* stroll up & down the Arcade" before catching the 'bus. The mother nervously insists, "Do you suppose *I* should be here if everything wasn't perfectly respectable!—for goodness sake, put that silly notion out of your head—and take care of your pockets!"[66] The beadle is still present as a comic figure—he orders another shelterer to close his umbrella—but the catalyst of the humor in the piece is the persistent threshold quality of the arcade itself. The respective reactions of suburban mother and daughter in a slightly risqué space; the difficulty in judging the class of the man who importunes them; the repeated gag of the impossibility of escaping confinement by pushing their way onto the omnibus: all contribute to a sense of middle-class discomfort over the persistently ambiguous character of the arcade. Even in the tame confines of Edith Nesbit's juvenile fantasy, *The Story of the Amulet* (1901), the site makes a cameo as the place where the "maid-of-all-works" had purchased for Anthea a "Lowther Arcade bangle . . . a sevenpenny-halfpenny trumpery thing that pretended to be silver" with which the latter is able to dazzle an Egyptian girl and her native companions.[67] Such an ambiguity of space was characteristic of the representation of nineteenth-century Paris; it was anathema to that of London. The arcades proper were soon to be assimilated to the private, regulated space of the luxury shop that the Burlington Arcade remains to this day; conversely, Regent Street, the only London thoroughfare designed with strolling in mind, was assimilated as an open-air space when the covered colonnades lining its sides were removed in 1848 after repeated complaints that their columns provided shelter and concealment for prostitutes.[68] As a writer in the *Civil Engineer and Architect's Journal* had observed on the opening of the New Exeter 'Change a few years prior, "Notwithstanding, however, that there is apparently so much in favour of such enclosed avenues of shops, they have not taken much in this country."[69]

Down by the Dark Arches

> As he spoke it the charm grew tall and broad, and he saw that Jane was just holding on to the edge of a great red arch of very curious shape. The opening of the arch was small, but Cyril saw that he could go through it. All round and beyond the arch were the faded trees and trampled grass of Regent's Park, where the little ragged children were playing Ring-o'-Roses. But through the opening of it shone a blaze of blue and yellow and red. Cyril drew a long breath and stiffened his legs so that the others should not see that his knees were trembling and almost knocking together. "Here goes!" he said, and, stepping up through the arch, disappeared.
>
> E. Nesbit, *The Story of the Amulet* (1901)

Although generally open at street level, the London railway arch was almost wholly identified with the subterranean city. This underground identity and the rigidly vertical conception of the city that went with it are especially evident in the fascinating history of two benchmark London construction projects: the Adelphi (1768) and the Thames Tunnel (1824–43). We will see how the former came to epitomize the underground image of the arch in mid- and late Victorian London, and how the latter brought out all of the contradictions between Parisian and London conceptions of the *passage* and the vertical city. The Adelphi was a riverside development of twenty-four luxurious terraced houses, built upon a complex network of arched catacombs just downriver from what is now Charing Cross station (figures 4.13 and 4.14).[70] Predating the great period of railway construction, the Adelphi offers not so much an epitome of the London arch as a singular structure that during the nineteenth century came to encapsulate the relation of the arch to the rest of the city. The Adelphi's vertical divisions concretized the class structure for its inhabitants, making visible in the center of London the social stratification expressed more abstractly in the railway viaducts, and being enacted by the swathes they cut through the north, east, and south of the city. While the *passages*, like many of the emblematic spaces of Paris, condensed fantasies of the mingling of class distinctions within a single space, those of London tended to figure increasing separation, and to express mingling wholly in terms of fear.

Although firmly embedded in the discourse of nineteenth-century London, we first find such a reading explicitly enunciated, as usual, between the two world wars, this time in the architectural historian Steen Eiler Rasmussen's analysis of the Adelphi's symbolic division of society along a vertical axis:

> The stratification of the community is plainly shown in the construction of the Adelphi itself: the fine although plain houses for the upper classes built on two dark basements containing kitchens and rooms for servants and below these again large vaulted cellars, where the poorest classes sought refuge. Bernard Shaw and H. G. Wells lived for a while in [the] Adelphi, and from this pile of human dwellings, one class over the other, Wells may have got the idea of a strange vision of the future, which he has described in a short story called *The Story of Days to Come*. In this he gives a terrible picture of what the city of the future will be if capitalism and mechanization continue as they have begun. "In the nineteenth century," he says, "the lower quarters were still beneath the sky; . . . In the twenty-second century, however, the growth of the city story above story, and the coalescence of buildings had led to a different arrangement. The prosperous people lived in a vast series of sumptuous hotels in the upper storys and halls of the city fabric; the industrial population dwelt beneath in the tremendous ground-floor and basement, so to speak, of the place." He then describes how these toilers must always live in artificial light without any chance of enjoying nature. This is the apotheosis of the Continental metropolis, the English ideal is the Garden-City.[71]

4.13 The Adelphi when completed in 1768. Benjamin Green, *The Buildings Called the Adelphi*. Engraving, 1777. Reproduced by permission from the Guildhall Library, © Corporation of London.

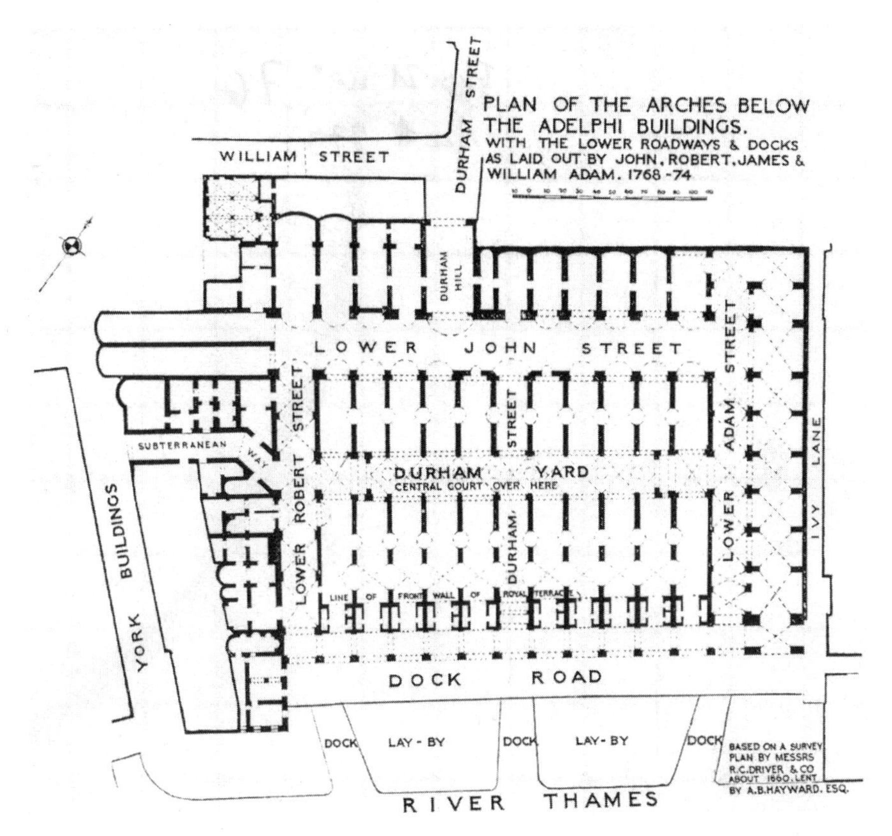

4.14 *Plan of the Arches below the Adelphi buildings*. Based on 1860 survey plan, reproduced in "The Adelphi Arches," *Country Life* 79, no. 2047 (11 April 1936): 386.

By 1934, writers such as Shaw and Wells had made available the terms for analyzing the urban environment as an expression of social symbolism; Rasmussen reads back into them the influence of the space itself on that analysis.

We find the same influence of the Adelphi as a representational space, although not consciously enunciated as such, when Dickens uses it as a structuring motif in his autobiographical novel *David Copperfield* (1849–50). When first sent to work as a child in London at Murdstone and Grinby's warehouse, David's exploration of the dry arches serves to locate his social identity as little better than an orphaned child of the streets:

> We had half-an-hour, I think, for tea. When I had money enough, I used to get half-a-pint of ready-made coffee and a slice of bread and butter. When I had none, I used to look at a venison shop in Fleet Street; or I have strolled, at such a time, as far as Covent Garden Market, and stared at the pineapples. I was fond of wandering about the Adelphi, because it was a mysterious place, with those dark arches. I see myself

> emerging one evening from some of those arches, on a little public-house close to the river [the Fox-under-the-Hill], with an open space before it, where some coal-heavers were dancing; to look at whom I sat down upon a bench. I wonder what they thought of me![72]

As part of his re-creation of the child's point of view, Dickens downplays the possible criminal elements of David's environment, choosing instead to highlight the lure of the "mysterious place" for the wandering boy.

Whenever aimed specifically at children, the underground appears, as it does here, in its more utopian and mythical aspects, sometimes with fairy-tale-level terror, but more frequently full of wonder and a space of escape from the everyday drudgery of life, as in the Regent's Park arch that leads E. Nesbit's adventuring children to Egypt in the epigraph above. As opposed to the represented space characteristic of adult life, Lefebvre writes, "lived space" has its origins in childhood, and inasmuch as it persists into adulthood, as the space where "the 'private' realm asserts itself, albeit more or less vigorously, and always in a conflictual way, against the public one."[73] When arches were conceived on an individual scale, as with the short tunnel known as the Nursery-maids' Walk that John Nash ran between the enclosed green spaces of Park Crescent and Park Square to allow safe passage under the New (now Marylebone) Road, or the "subterranean arch" connecting two parts of the Regent's Park Zoo, a likely inspiration for Nesbit's image (figure 4.15), they continued to participate in this space of fantasy.[74] The temporal gap guaranteed by the first-person narration allows Dickens to combine the potential of the underground for both reverie and terror within a London space; normally, the adult would see either the one (as pastoral fantasy) or the other (as urban reality).

The next time David mentions the Adelphi, midway through the novel, he is at the top of the world, and the new perspective he takes on his old haunt mirrors his new maturity and sense of social status: he has risen in life thanks to his aunt, Miss Betsey Trotwood. His new perspective is governed by the abstract conception of a space suitable to his new station rather than the lived perception of the child. After purchasing his apprenticeship as proctor at Doctor's Commons in Lincoln's Inn Field, David's aunt shows him a newspaper clipping, "setting forth that in Buckingham Street in the Adelphi there was to be let furnished, with a view of the river, a singularly desirable, and compact set of chambers, forming a genteel residence for a young gentleman, a member of one of the Inns of Court, or otherwise, with immediate possession."[75] To be sure, the adult narrator's ironic detachment leads him to distance himself somewhat from his youthful enthusiasm over the rooms ("the furniture was rather faded, but quite good enough for me; and, sure enough, the river was outside the window"), but he wholly retains the sense of satisfaction with which young David reflects on his changed situation: "When the coach was gone, I turned my face to the Adelphi, pondering on

4.15 The arch as a space of fantasy. F. W. Hulme, *Gardens of the Zoological Society: The Tunnel.* Engraving, ca. 1840. Reproduced by permission from the Guildhall Library, © Corporation of London.

the old days when I used to roam about its subterranean arches, and on the happy changes which had brought me to the surface."[76] This is not the first time in the novel that David has metaphorically descended to hell and returned, but it is the only time in which that descent is traced onto the physical and social topography of a specific London landmark.

The area of the Adelphi returns once more, near the end of the novel, to mark the final leave-taking of David from the acquaintances of his childhood, all ruined, if not always unsympathetically, because they chose the individual over the public. The Micawbers, with whom he lodged when he first came to London, are set to depart in search of a new and hopefully more propitious life in Australia. David goes to visit them where they are awaiting embarkment at the same public house he used to come to from beneath the arches: "The Micawber family were lodged in a little, dirty, tumbledown public-house, which in those days was close to the stairs, and whose protruding wooden rooms overhung the river. The family, as emigrants, being objects of some interest in and about Hungerford, attracted so many beholders, that we were glad to take refuge in their room. It was one of the wooden chambers upstairs, with the tide flowing underneath."[77] The Micawbers are sailing with some others of David's earliest and now ruined acquaintances, old Peggotty and his niece

Em'ly, who was seduced and left by his boyhood friend Steerforth. Em'ly's status as a fallen woman brings with it another important association with the space of the arches, the popular depiction of the suicide from above or beneath the Thames bridges. We find the same motif in a key moment in David's earlier search for the vanished Em'ly, when he followed Martha, her childhood friend and, in the novel's scheme, her double, who will also be among the party of emigrants. The search led him to a wasted stretch of riverside beneath Westminster Bridge, where he forestalled her death by drowning.[78]

Here, Dickens shades into a symbolic topography of poverty and despair; the associations of David's rise with this topography make the leave-taking a simultaneously melancholy and joyous occasion. Both the Micawbers and Em'ly are failures in terms of midcentury middle-class convention—the former in the economic and the latter in the moral sphere. Their only option if they were to remain in London would be to be assimilated to the underground environment in which David finds them here: "It was a wonderful instance to me of the gap such partings make, that although my association of them with the tumble-down public-house and the wooden stairs dated only from last night, both seemed dreary and deserted, now they were gone."[79] The same space that in his boyhood had held the promise of mystery and wandering—a promise also put forth by Micawber's financial histrionics and Steerforth's seductions—and in his youth represented a self-satisfied gentility that would have to be disciplined painfully out of him as part of his moral education—this space now "seemed dreary and deserted." David Copperfield has outgrown the social extremes of the Adelphi and will soon be settled firmly into the utopian middle way with his wife Agnes and his family around him, living happily ever after in a no-place somewhere in the genteel suburbia of North London. We see in Dickens's use of the motif what distinguished the Adelphi and the form of the arch from the solely underground spaces of Victorian London—the Thames Tunnel, the underground railway, and the sewers—of which scarcely a mention is to be found anywhere in his novels. Rather than providing one half of the puzzle, its vertical structure served as a material emblem of the stratification of the city as a whole.

It is instructive to compare the Adelphi, an eighteenth-century project that came to play a central role in the conceptualization of nineteenth-century London, with its closest Parisian counterpart, the Quai de Gesvres, a seventeenth-century development that did not survive into the nineteenth and played little role in the imagination of modern Paris. Like the Adelphi an early project of urban reclamation, the Quai de Gesvres physically bore all the features of the vertically segmented space of the bridge arches that were so important to the representation of the nineteenth-century metropolis; moreover, it constituted a prototype of the later *passage*.[80] In 1642, Louis XIII granted the Marquis de Gesvres permission to develop the right bank of the Seine between the Pont Notre-Dame and the Pont au Change (then known as the Pont aux Changeurs) with an arcaded quay covered by a pedestrian street lined with boutiques (figure 4.16).[81] The quay was regularly cited in guidebooks, which highlighted the covered gallery of the rue de Gesvres formed by the ground floor of the houses, wholly covering its extent and closed at night, and the rue du Quai de Gesvres running beneath it, houses on one side and open to the river on the other.[82] The upper street, according to Le Sage, was "full of merchants, especially of Fashion and Jewelry" as well as bookshops; its popularity was such that it soon (if briefly) was competing with the Palais-Royal.[83] The arches below were used for washing and by the slaughterhouses and tanneries that dotted the quarter of Saint-Jacques-la-Boucherie and could thereby gain access to the river for disposing of their waste.[84] These were known as "the tunnel of the Cagniards," from Parisian slang for the arches that supported the old Hôtel-Dieu on the île de la Cité; a portion of it was discovered during the construction of line 7 of the Métro, and incorporated into the tunnels of the underground railway.[85] Like the Adelphi, of which pieces of the dry arches have been preserved in the infrastructure beneath the 1936 building that replaced it, the old Quai de Gesvres was preserved for the twentieth century only in a subterranean identity.

The Adelphi development was intended to reclaim a derelict stretch of the Thames between Westminster and the City that by 1768 was "so untidy and malodorous that the neighbours repeatedly complained."[86] By contrast, although it did straighten out a bit the "inconvenience" of the narrow streets of the area, the

4.16 An early and forgotten Paris arcade. Jean-Baptiste-Louis Cazin, *Arcades Souterraine du quai de Gevres près le pont au change*. Reproduced by permission from Bibliothèque Nationale de France.

development of the Quai de Gesvres would have done nothing to improve the "mauvaise odeur" of the Grande-Boucherie and its pendant industries, which dominated the neighborhood around the Place du Châtelet.[87] Nor, apparently, was this seen as anything beyond an occupational hazard: Sauval mentions the "streets, most of them truly narrow, twisted, dark and stinking," but then goes on to note that "nevertheless, the Butchers, who are wealthy men, & married to attractive women, & clean, continue to reside there, but for the most part in bright, clean & well-furnished houses."[88] We can assume in addition that these burgher-butchers and their pretty wives were the principal customers at the luxury boutiques of the rue de Gesvres. So, where the vertical construction of the quay would have cried out in the nineteenth-century for the standard segregated representation, the earlier inhabitants appear to have taken its mixed qualities as they found them. Happy perhaps to possess clean houses distinct from the filthy industry below, they nevertheless made no symbolic distinction between these activities or their respective locations, nor did their identity appear to be any more determined by one location than by another.

What makes the Quai de Gesvres especially significant for observing changes in the way in which certain Parisian occupations and classes were assimilated to certain spatial and symbolic locations is that its particular character did not outlive the eighteenth century and appears to have taken on no later symbolic role. An edict of the king of September 1786 ruled that the pillars and arcades, as well as the shops above, should be demolished and replaced by open parapets and pavements.[89] When the Pont Notre-Dame was rebuilt in 1853, the vaults were lowered by nearly ten feet; seven years later, they were enclosed by masonry walls.[90] Rather than grow in the urban imagination as most of the subterranean spaces of Paris did in the process of being documented and modernized, or, as the *cours des Miracles*, documented and demolished, the Quai de Gesvres has remained something of an oddity. As the form of the covered gallery metamorphosed into the *passage* that underwent such a vogue in the early nineteenth century and such a revival for the surrealists, Benjamin, and others in the early twentieth, the Quai de Gesvres, a prototype of the form, and a twin of the Adelphi in its two-level design, vanished from sight and memory.

The luxury houses of the Terrace in London did not merely support wealthy local tradesmen as the Rue de Gesvres did in Paris; rather, they made the West End for the first time a fashionable address.[91] While this dual identity was a fundamental feature of Dickens's plotting of David Copperfield's social ascendancy and of Wells's later verticalized class analysis, it was the lower depths of the Adelphi that dominated the popular imagination. The fair amount of legitimate wharf activity the arches did support as a conduit between the river and the Strand prior to their enclosure by the Thames Embankment in the 1860s was overshadowed by the more sensational aspects of the underground imagery they inspired. Théodore Géricault's 1821 lithograph *Entrance to the Adelphi Wharf* depicted a coalman driving his horse through the Strand entrance down to the quay, with a low, steep arch leading into darkness (figure 4.17). Whatever labor went on below was figured as wholly distinct from the world above. In an 1850 article about the Adelphi for the *Illustrated London News*, Thomas Miller presented the same image of the coal wagon as a quintessential urban mystery, an unexplained darkness just below the feet of the average Londoner:

> Thousands who pass along the Strand never dream of the shadowy region which lies between them and the river—the black-browed arches that span right and left, before and behind, covering many a rood of ground on which the rain never beats nor the sunbeam sleeps, and at the entrance of which the wind only seems to howl and whine, as if afraid of venturing further into the darkness. Many of our readers will, no doubt, conclude that such a dreary place as this must be deserted and tenantless: such is not the case. Here many of those strong horses which the countryman who visits London looks upon with wonder and envy, are stabled—strong, broad-chested steeds, such as may be seen dragging the heavily-laden coal-waggons up those steep passages which lead into the Strand, and which seem "to the manner born."[92]

Unlike Géricault's lithograph, the rationalizing discourse of Miller's mid-Victorian writing on the underground purported to bring light into the dark recesses, describing a world that was distinct from that above, but nevertheless rational and controllable rather than excessive and dangerous.

Perhaps the best-known image of the space for modern readers, *Taking the Census in the Dark Arches of the Adelphi*, dates from a decade later; it literalizes Miller's endeavor, depicting the census taker in a vast underground space, shining a bull's-eye lantern on a collection of derelict souls, who are seated haphazardly along the walls of the cavernous arches with their worldly possessions beside them (figure 4.18).[93] *Taking the Census* shared the late-Victorian desire of the contemporary Embankment scheme to illuminate and control the lower depths while also separating them from the world above as much as possible. As befits the earlier decades' investment in a more fascinated and less proactive attitude toward the otherworld, Miller preferred to regard the arches as "a little subterranean city" (figure 4.19). The series in which the article appeared was entitled "Picturesque London"; the decorative arch had in fact been a popular Regency framing device for city views, positioning the spectators as if on a balcony (figure 4.20). Just as David Copperfield was entranced by the arches in his youth and retained a fondness long into respectable middle age for those he had then known, Miller proposed that the underground could be assimilated as a picturesque alternative, including the ground on which Lady Jane Grey walked, a collection of homeless wanderers, and even, in a moment of urban pastoral, herds of subterranean cattle, "which, rumour says, never saw any other light beyond that of the gas which gleams through their prison-bars." In both cases, by contrast with the Parisian *passage*, the Adelphi was assimilated to the cityscape in terms of its difference rather than its resemblance to the recognizable world above.

4.17 The Adelphi as descent to the underworld. Théodore Géricault, *Entrance to Adelphi Wharf*. Lithograph, 1821. Reproduced by permission from the Guildhall Library, © Corporation of London.

The dry arches under the London river bridges and railway viaduct were an important underground site both materially and culturally, a frequent setting for spectacle scenes in plays and novels, and a shelter for the down-and-out. Because of their central location, vast scale, and much greater sense of enclosure and isolation, the Adelphi arches readily stood in for what was seen generally as the illicit use of the public spaces of the city by the poor:

> As late as 1869 Daniel Joseph Kirwan came upon a dozen people who had made their home in the underground recesses of London Bridge, and were burning driftwood for their fire: he called it a "perfect gypsy encampment." The most sensational of these shelters in inner London were the Adelphi Arches off the Strand, a series of underground chambers and vaults "running here and there like the intricacies of catacombs." . . . According to one excited account . . . "no sane person would have ventured to explore them without an armed escort."[94]

It is difficult to ascertain how much credence to give such "excited accounts" as, for example, the broadside "Down by the Dark Arches near the Adelphi" (to the

4.18 The Adelphi under surveillance. *Taking the census in the dark arches of the Adelphi.* Engraving in *Illustrated Times* 12 (13 April 1861): 246.

tune of "Green Bushes"), in which a man wanders too near to the arches and is seduced by a "fair maid." She leads him to "a little back-parlour near the Adelphi," from where he is dragged, stripped, robbed, and left unconscious, to be found next morning by four policemen. The predictable moral of the song comes in the final chorus, "So all you gents, do not make so free, / Down by the dark arches near the Adelphi."[95]

The actual use of the Adelphi as a haven for criminals is at least partially testified by John Binny in the fourth volume of Mayhew's *London Labour and the London Poor,* probably one of the main sources for the later, more lurid versions. A street patterer in his late twenties tells the story of how as a boy he ran away from home and was taken in by a gang of young pickpockets who lived in an abandoned prison van in the Adelphi arches. The gang was ruled by "Larry," a Fagin-like character who sent them out to steal handkerchiefs from men passing between the Strand and the steamboat landing at the Adelphi Pier, and perhaps also at nearby Hungerford Market Pier.[96] Binny's informant apparently lived this life for some six months before being imprisoned. On his release, he moved up to the more ambitious occupations of pick pocketing, and then burglary, before retiring to the less criminal trade of street pattering.[97]

Parallel to the image of the arch as a breeding place for boy thieves and dangerously tempting locale for respectable men was its iconographic association with the Victorian cliché of the fallen woman. The topic was painted several times by George Frederick Watts around 1850, and had appeared a few years before that in Thomas Hood's well-known poem "Bridge of Sighs" ("The bleak

4.19 "A little subterranean city." by J. W. Archer. *Picturesque Sketches of London.—The Adelphi "Dry Arches"*. Engraving in *Illustrated London News* (20 April 1860): supplement.

wind of March / Made her tremble and shiver; / But not the dark arch, / Or the black flowing river"), but it was most fully realized in Augustus Leopold Egg's triptych, *Past and Present* (ca. 1857–58) (see figure 4.4).[98] Egg's three paintings depict the collapse of a Victorian home due to an overworked husband and an unfaithful wife. The right-hand wing presents the abandoned sisters in a garret looking out over the city. The same moon that is seen by the sisters shines also for the mother, as she is pictured in the left-hand wing, huddled with her illegitimate child under a gaslit arch of the Adelphi, looking out onto the Thames. As E. D. H. Johnson observes, the arches are a space overloaded with a particular lexicon of symbolic meanings: "Egg's choice of setting here calls attention to the uniformity of the tendency of Victorian artists (following perhaps Hogarth's example) to choose certain districts of London, in preference to other cities, to epitomize the moral degradation associated with urban life."[99] Lynda Nead's rigorous and sophisticated analysis distinguishes between the middle-class "fallen woman" iconography in the center panel and the coded lower-class image of the prostitute in the right-hand wing.[100] In the reviews of the painting cited by her, the association between the arches and prostitution was taken for granted, and the image was criticized for crossing a line "where the horrors that should not be painted for public and innocent sight begin."[101] The degree to which Egg's image had insinuated itself into popular iconography is evident from its use on theatrical playbills, such

4.20 The arch as framing device for an urban vista. *Four views of London sites seen through an arch.* Engraving, ca. 1820. Reproduced by permission from the Guildhall Library, © Corporation of London.

as this one for the Effingham Theatre's production of *How We Live in the World of London* (a loose dramatization of Mayhew's *London Labour*), to accompany the promised tableau of "Dark Arches under the Adelphi with View of the River Thames" (figure 4.21).[102]

As the playbill suggests, these topographical clichés of the Victorian underworld came together in the popular theater's use of the arch as a setting for sensation scenes. A fine summation of the genre was given by Percy Fitzgerald in his 1896 memoir of the arches for the *Daily Graphic*, "There are still quoted the traditions of the 'Adelphi Arches' and their horrors which used to be a standing topic in the newspapers of thirty years ago. The dramatists of the theatre close by turned these to account, transferring such horrors to the boards; the heroine decoyed into these caverns supplied a stirring head line 'Adelphi Arches by Night.' But the hero was of course at hand for the rescue."[103] The Adelphi was the mythic center for these images of liminal spaces on the banks of the Thames, arches leading into a nether world of the urban imagination. It was a crucial setting in *London by Night*

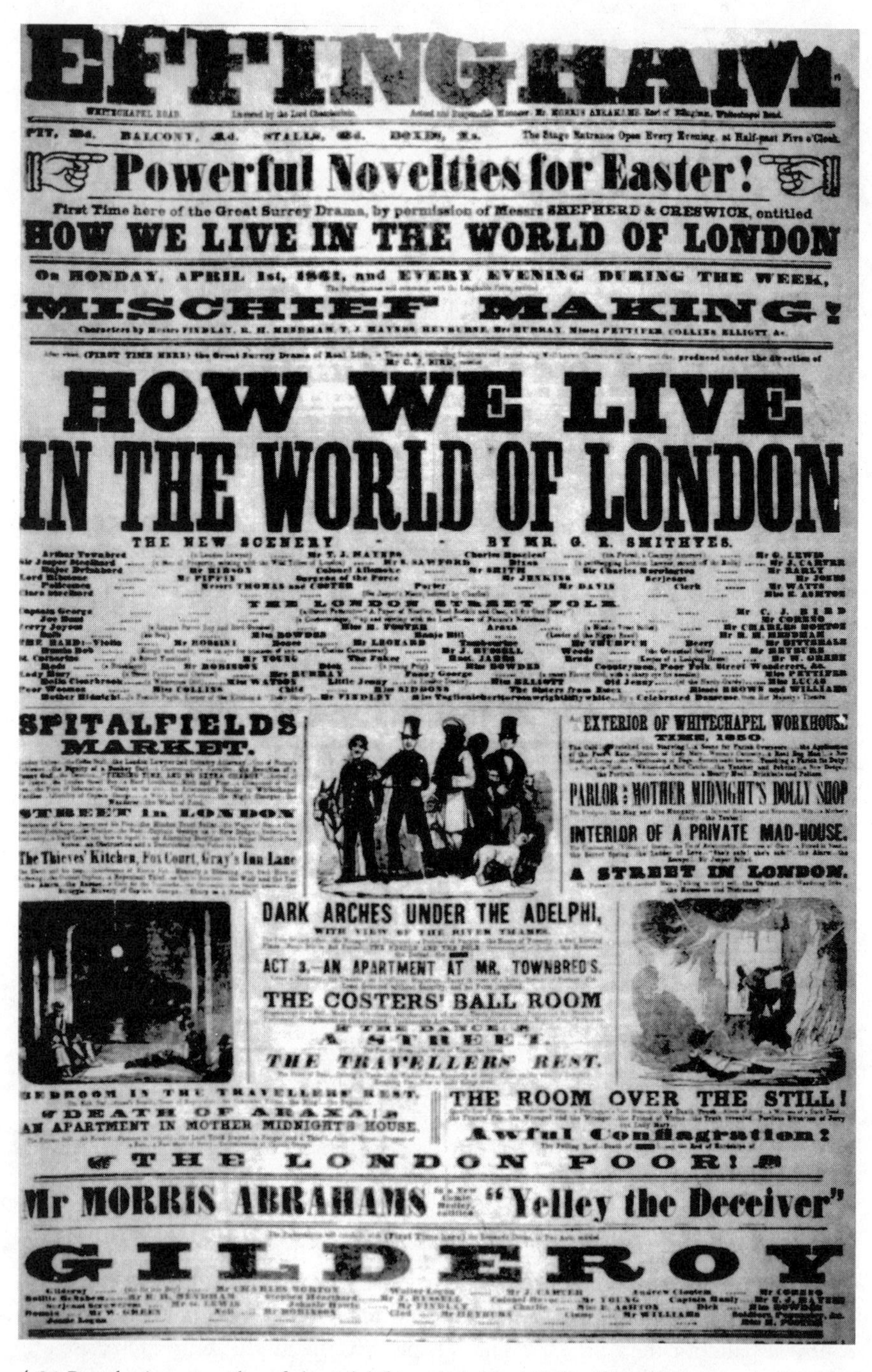

4.21 Popular iconography of the Adelphi arches. Playbill for *How We Live in the World of London*. Effingham Theatre (1 April 1861). Collection of the author.

(Strand, 1845) and *How We Live in the World of London* (Surrey, 1856), and the scene of described crimes in *The Great City* (Drury Lane, 1867) and *Black Sheep* (Olympic, 1868); a Marylebone production of the New York hit *Under the Gaslight* transposed the act 3 finale to the Adelphi Arches and nearby Waterloo Bridge. With their vertical segmentation between open roadway and covered riverside arches, the London bridges frequently served graphically to represent social stratification and the rises and falls so important to the melodramatic plot, in particular the ubiquitous suicidal plunge of the fallen woman. We find scenes set under the arches of Waterloo Bridge in *The Cross-Roads of Life* (Sadler's Wells, 1843), *Ups and Downs of Life* (Pavilion, 1843), *The Modern Bohemians; or the London Scamps* (Britannia, 1843), and *Tide and Time* (Surrey, 1867); of Blackfriars Bridge in *The Wild Tribes of London* (City of London, 1856), *After Dark* (Princess's, 1868), and *Land Rats and Water Rats* (Surrey, 1868); and of Old London Bridge in *The Stolen Heiress* (Victoria, 1855). Railway arches further afield were also reconstructed as stage spectacles, including a "sleeping apartment for millions" under the Camden arches in a Marylebone production of *How We Live* (1867) and Old Tom's doss-house in the dry arches under Victoria Street in Clerkenwell in *After Dark* (figure 4.22).

Like the cockney beneath the arches by the Thames, the clochard under the bridges of the Seine became an enduring myth of sentimental poverty in Paris during the first half of the twentieth century. As the authorities made the practice of sleeping rough more and more difficult, its imagery proliferated in a familiar combination of relief, nostalgia, and denial of the contemporary problem of the inhumane new space of the nighttime shelter.[104] During the second half of the nineteenth century, these spaces were instead identified in popular culture primarily with the earlier decades' obsession with the "dangerous classes," as in Marc Fournier's melodrama *Les Nuits de la Seine* (1852), set in 1822, and Alexandre Dumas and Xavier de Montépin's *La Tour Saint-Jacques* (1856), the entire second act of which was set under and around the Pont au Change during the fifteenth century. There were comparatively few such settings in the nineteenth-century French theater, however; more popular were the Palais-Royal and arcades during the early decades, the carrières from the *Mystères de Paris* on, and the devil and the underworld all over the city throughout the century. The imagination of London was far more heavily associated with the spectacle of the arch as threshold space, and we find more Seine arches in nineteenth-century translations of Parisian hits than in France itself. Eugène Grangé and Adolphe d'Ennery's popular play, *Les Bohémiens de Paris*, was adapted many times to London; *The Modern Bohemians* transferred one scene to the dry arches of Waterloo Bridge.[105] The suicide off a bridge into the Seine in *Life in Paris* (1822) and *The Scamps of Paris, or The Mysteries of Crime* (Effingham, 1858); Madame Chalumeau's "Marine Establishment" under the Pont Marie in *The Bohemians; or, The Thieves of Paris* (City of London, 1843); Madame Popland's Establishment at no. 2, Coal Barge, in *The Bohemians* (Adelphi, 1843); the arches of the Pont-Neuf in *The Bohemians*

The O. P. Club
Presented by
SIR EDWARD RUSSELL.

Royal Princess's Theatre

OXFORD STREET.

LICENSED BY THE LORD CHAMBERLAIN TO
MR. VINING,
Actual and Responsible Manager, Upper Montague Street, Russell Square.

DOORS OPEN AT HALF-PAST SIX
To commence at Seven.

Monday, Nov. 9th, 1868, and during the Week,
The Performances will commence at SEVEN with a Comedy, in One Act, entitled The

DAY AFTER THE WEDDING.

Colonel Freelove ... ... Mr. J. G. SHORE.
Lord Rivers ... ... Mr. TAPPING.
James ... . Mr W. D. GRESHAM.
Lady Elizabeth Freelove ... Miss EMMA BARNETT.
Mrs Davis ... ... Mrs. ADDIE.

After which, AT EIGHT O'CLOCK, a New Drama, in Four Acts, entitled

AFTER DARK;
A TALE OF LONDON LIFE!

By DION BOUCICAULT.

The subject of this work is derived from a Melodrama by Messrs. D'ENNERY & GRANGE, with their permission.

Gordon Chumley (Light Dragoons) Mr. J. G. SHORE.
Sir George Medhurst ... Mr. CHARLES HARCOURT.
(under the assumed name of Hayward)
Chandos Bellingham ... Mr. WALTER LACY.
Old Tom ... (a Boardman) ... Mr. VINING.
Dicey Morris ... Mr. DOMINICK MURRAY.
(a Keeper of a low Gaming House, near Leicester Square, and Proprietor of the Elysium Music Hall, Broadway, Westminster)
Pointer ... (A Division) ... Mr. W. D. GRESHAM.
The Bargee ... ... Mr. R. CATHCART.
Crumpets ... ... Mr. MACLEAN.
Area Jack ... (a Night Bird) ... Mr. HOLSTON.
Jem and Josey ... . Messrs. H. & J. MARSHALL.
(Kerbstone Vocalists by day, and Elysium Artists by night)
The Colonel ... ... Mr. TAPPING.
Nick ... ... Mr. CHAPMAN.
Marker ... ... Mr. TRESSIDDER.
Eliza ... ... Miss ROSE LECLERCQ.
(once a Barmaid at the Elysium, Sir George's Wife)
Rose Egerton ... Miss EMMA BARNETT.
(an Heiress, Sir George's Cousin)

PERIOD—THE SUMMER OF 1868.

ENTIRELY NEW SCENERY BY Mr. F. LLOYDS,
Mr. W. HANN, and numerous Assistants.
Music Composed and Arranged by Mons. E. AUDIBERT.

ACT I.—Scene 1.

VICTORIA STATION & GROSVENOR HOTEL.

Returning from the Derby—The Sensation Column in the Times—Fifty Pounds Reward—Dicey Morris finds a Lost Heir—The Hansom Cabman No. 8941—Old Tom the Boardman—How the Medhurst Estate was Left to the Lost Heir.

Scene 2.—No. 5½, LITTLE COMPTON MEWS.

Eliza, the Cabman's Wife, refuses to be accommodating—The Compact.

Scene 3—SILVER HELL.

Chicken Hazard—Dicey gives wrong change for a five pound note—Sir George arrives, and he renews his acquaintance with Champagne—The Proposition—The Barmaid and the Baronet

Scene 4.—No. -- RUPERT ST., HAYMARKET.

The Gambler's Wife—How Eliza proposes to Liberate her Husband.

Scene 5.—THE STRAND, NEAR TEMPLE BAR.

Old Tom's History—Fanny Dalton and Richard Knatchbull—Father and Daughter

Scene 6.—BLACKFRIARS BRIDGE ON CRUTCHES, AND THE THAMES BY NIGHT.

The Nest of the Night Birds—Bankside Hotel (Limited)—Airy Rooms—Water always laid on—The Kerbstone Drama—The Suicide.

The O. P. Club
Presented by
SIR EDWARD RUSSELL.

ACT II.

Scene 1.—DRY ARCHES under Victoria Street

Old Tom sends for his Friends and takes his Farewell to Liquor—After Dark, Light will come—How Eliza got a Situation.

Scene 2.—THE LILACS.

How the Confederates worked—Rose and Sir George—The Confession—How Eliza finds an unexpected Friend in her New Mistress.

Scene 3.—GARDEN GATE.

How Bellingham meets with his match, and Old Tom finds a clue.

Scene 4.—GREEN CHAMBER.

How Rose showed Eliza the Bracelet—The Bridegroom makes a Confession and a Happy Mistake.

ACT III.

Scene 1.—ELYSIUM MUSIC HALL, IN BROADWAY, WESTMINSTER.

The Provident Mudlarks' Benefit—How Bellingham dealt with Chumley—Old Tom objects, and how he is suppressed—A visit of the Police—All serene.

Scene 2.—WINE CELLARS.

Old Tom's Adventures in Subterranean London—A Murder in the Dark.

Scene 3.—UNDERGROUND RAILWAY.

Something on the Track—Old Tom destroys wilfully the Property of the Company—The Night Express.

ACT IV.—THE LILACS.

Bellingham's Triumph—Eliza in search of a Father—Dicey Morris throws over an old friend.

To conclude with a New Farce, by J. M. MORTON, Esq., entitled

MASTER JONES'S BIRTHDAY.

Adolphus Fitztopper ... Mr. DOMINICK MURRAY.
Major Muzzle ... ... Mr. MACLEAN.
First Boy ... ... Master TAPPING.
Second Boy ... ... Master EATON.
Mrs. Montmorency Jones Miss EMMA BARNETT.
Martha ... ... Miss POLLY MARSHALL.

Stage Manager, Mr. J. G. SHORE. Musical Director, Mons. E. AUDIBERT.
Secretary, Mr. T. ROBERTS. Treasurer, Mr. T. E. SMALE.

N.B.—Box-office Open Daily from Ten o'clock until Five, under the direction of Mr WADDS. Any person wishing to secure places, can do so by paying One Shilling for every party not exceeding six, which places will be retained the whole Evening.

Dress Circle, 5s. Boxes, 4s. Pit, 2s. Gallery, 1s. Orchestra Stalls, 6s.
Private Boxes, £2 12s. 6d. — £2 2s. and £1 11s. 6d.

of Paris; or, the Mysteries of Crime (Surrey, 1843); the Seine bridge and arches beneath in *The Thieftaker of Paris; or, Vidocq* (Britannia, 1860; it also depicted "The Rookery of Paris"!): all of these transposed the settings, situations, and verticalized society of London onto the foreign cityscape.

The explicitly vertical construction of these Thames-side thresholds set criminal activity in a physically distinct but also nearby and familiar location, as in *Land Rats and Water Rats*, which promised " 'Old Blackfriars Bridge'—Life over the Bridge" immediately followed by " 'Under the Arches'—Life under the Bridge."[106] In the latter scene, we find "a dozen wild boys and men of London discovered as they are joined by others."[107] Flitt, a mudlark (a scavenger of the riverside and sewer outlets) who will later have his conscience restored by the purity of the middle-class Rosa Mavis, comes down the steps, "Now then. Clear the way. First class h'express from the upper regions." Meanwhile, standing up on the bridge is Rosa's brother Dick Mavis, who was framed for robbery at the end of the first act. As he is meditating on his fate, his cap flies over the bridge. Unable to afford the half crown to replace it, he descends into the arches to retrieve it, commenting on the meaning of his descent as he goes: "Ugh it looks nasty down here. These grim arches seem to me like so many hungry mouths seeking what they may devour. How the water gurgles and rattles! No wonder it fills poor wretches with thoughts of drowning." As he reaches for the cap, he falls the rest of the way, and finds himself surrounded by thieves and thrown into the river. The spectacle of the underground scene locates the action in a concrete, material, and everyday setting while the spatialization of its metaphorics literalizes the ideological structure of melodrama: according to the stage directions, "scene sinks till Bridge reaches stage." Although represented with all the attributes of an underground space, the arch retained its threshold character in the ability to unite the extremes of the vertically conceived space of the city.

Mavis's fall is motivated in equal measure by physical, social, and economic factors. And the audience watches the scene from the point of view of the underworld rats. Once such a crisis has been reached, the underground is momentarily even with the world above. But it remains a passing glimpse. The sensational point of view rewards the viewers as it thrills them: once the thieves have gone, Flitt rescues Mavis, and, as reported in the *Era*'s glowing review: "By the sudden clearing away of gauzes, which, during the conclusion of the preceding scene, have represented the rising of a river fog, the roadway on the top of the bridge, is discovered, with a magnificent view of London by Night; the partially frozen river, glittering with masses of floating ice."[108] Mavis's fall and ordeal lead him

Facing page

4.22 The ubiquitous arches: scene list in a program for *After Dark: A Tale of London Life* by Dion Boucicault, Princess's Theatre, 12 August 1868. Collection of the author.

eventually to a newly clarified, almost magical view of the landscape of the city. The threat (loss of life and livelihood) must be resolved by the denouement of the play, which restabilizes the levels of the hierarchy while spectacularly eliminating the means of easy passage between them; the finale called for the bridge to be brought down altogether, a ruined mill collapsing on and killing the villains, with Mavis and his love the only survivors. Unlike wholly underground spaces such as the sewers, perfectly suited for literalizing the metaphors of criminality and poverty as dirty, diseased, and effluvial, the arches, open in varying degrees to the aboveground world, functioned as threshold spaces. Of the Paris arcades, the identification with the underworlds of poverty and crime resembles only the passage du Caire and the other "pseudo-*passages*"; they had none of the glamour of the boulevards or the Palais-Royal, and whatever lords appeared in them were perverse criminals rather than aristocrats at play. Unlike the otherworldly aura retained even by the passage du Caire, the London arches were always in the end assimilated to the subterranean pole of their identity.

A Passage under the Thames

> Où voit-on, me dit-on,
> Les monuments qui sont
> A Londres?
> Ne sachant que répondre:
> Je dis:
> Allez voir à Paris. . . .
> J'répare cet affront
> En montrant l'pont,
> Sous la Tamise,
> Un vrai chef d'oeuvre anglais,
> Imaginé . . . par un Français.
>
> JACK, the domestic, in *Le Parisien à Londres* (1829)

This same model of a threshold space being assimilated to the underground pole of its identity characterized the fate of the London arcades, as is especially evident in the example of their most extreme manifestation, the Thames Tunnel. One historian has commented on the 583–foot length of the Burlington Arcade, the longest in Britain, that it "could have been a monotonous tunnel" if not for the changes in height and building lines incorporated by its architect, Samuel Ware.[109] At over twice that length, the Thames Tunnel fought off such "monotony" for several decades by virtue of its sheer scale and the marvel of its situation deep beneath the river. Built beneath the Thames between Wapping and Rotherhithe in the East End of London from 1824 to 1843 under the direction of engineer Marc Isambard Brunel and his son, Isambard Kingdom Brunel, this was one of the most highly celebrated and visited attractions in nineteenth-century London.[110] Marketed as an underwater arcade, it brought twenty-four million persons to its far-flung location; planned as a carriage thoroughfare, it was a resounding commercial failure. Eventually sold to the East London line, it is still in use today as a tunnel for the London Underground (figures 4.23 and 4.24). Like the Parisian *passage*, the Thames Tunnel introduced cutting-edge technology before its most efficient use within capitalism had been discovered. As Benjamin wrote about the former, "Glass before its time, premature iron. . . . Around the middle of the past century, it was not yet known how to build with glass and iron."[111] In their idiosyncratic combination of the modern with the obsolete, both forms exhibited a high degree of representational space for such expensive, technologically advanced, and at least partially publicly funded works. While Joseph Paxton's Crystal Palace (1851) and Victor Baltard's covered markets at Les Halles (1852) were perfections of modernity, efficiently marrying form with function, the arcades and the Thames Tunnel quickly became outmoded commodities of the cityscape, and, as such, attracted an undue variety of reveries, dreams, and nightmares about the urban experience. And both began to recover a modicum of their early nineteenth-century glamour only at the end of the twentieth, when they were rediscovered as emblems of a new kind of Victoriana in the midst of a new underground vogue.

The West End arcades were difficult to assimilate to an aboveground model of London space, while the popularity of the principal Paris *passages* was heavily dependent on their central location; for the far-flung and underwater Thames Tunnel there was no such possibility. Unique among the obligatory sights of the city in being a practical thoroughfare employed as such almost wholly by the working classes, the Thames Tunnel was also open twenty-four hours a day. It offered the urban tourist the novel and not altogether welcome experience of emerging "in the midst of one of the most unintelligible, forlorn, and forsaken districts of London or the world," the docklands and slums of the East End.[112] The arcade was often compared to the Oriental bazaar; the Thames Tunnel grounded the metaphor in its geographical situation. The metaphor suggested that it was not only a technological wonder, but also a marvelous sight, and a triumph of civilization over the forces of nature and of the West over the East; it equally expressed the anxieties attendant on this triumph. The tension between interior and exterior, West End and East End, and daytime and nighttime identities would be condensed within the basic incompatibility of the purposes the Tunnel was meant to serve, an incompatibility perfectly commensurate with the ambivalence of a threshold.

An early account of a visit made to the Tunnel by the actress Fanny Kemble with her father Charles, manager of the Covent Garden Theatre, provides an extraordinary example of the way mythic and technological issues intertwined in

THE THAMES TUNNEL.

This day is fixed for the ceremony of opening the Thames Tunnel; and the completion of this magnificent work, alike the admiration of foreigners and the boast of our own countrymen, affords a favourable opportunity for introducing the subject to our readers.

In this age of engineering science, when invention may almost be considered to have outstripped itself, the accomplishment of all that has been looked for through so many years of anxiety and labour in the formation of a sub-aqueous communication between the shores of our noble river, cannot fail to be welcomed with universal satisfaction, and may, without fear of contradiction, be pronounced the most extraordinary performance of modern times.

The innumerable difficulties which have been successfully encountered during the progress of the work by the talent and energy of the engineer, hold out an example to posterity which must have a beneficial effect on future labourers in the same field, and assert a claim on the part of Sir Isambard Brunel to the gratitude of every Englishman.

The following brief sketch of the undertaking will be read with interest at the present moment:—

So far back as the year 1802 a project was set on foot by some enterprising gentlemen, with a view to opening an archway under the Thames between Rotherhithe and Limehouse, about a mile below the present tunnel. The engineer selected was an experienced Cornish miner named Vesey, who, having made some borings on each side of the river, reported that "he was firmly persuaded the undertaking would not cost so much as had been conceived." A company was formed under the title of the "Thames Archway Company," an Act of Parliament obtained, and the work begun. A shaft of eleven feet in diameter was sunk to the depth of forty-two feet; to avoid certain difficulties it was then contracted to eight feet, and thus continued to the depth of seventy-six feet. The horizontal excavation was there begun, in the form of a driftway, to be afterwards widened into the required dimensions for a passage, and carried to within 150 feet of the Middlesex shore, when the engineer reported that further progress was impracticable. Five or six years were thus expended, during which the talents of three different engineers had been put in requisition, and rewards offered for plans, which brought in communications from all quarters. It was under the remembrance of these discouraging circumstances that Mr. (now Sir M. I.) Brunel appeared before the public with a new proposal in 1823, which it was stated had received the sanction of many eminent persons, in particular of the Duke of Wellington and Dr. Wollaston. The novelty of Mr. Brunel's proposed mode of operation, therefore, was rightly judged of great importance. The writer of the article "Tunnel" in the "Edinburgh Encyclopedia" states

that he was informed by Mr. Brunel "that the idea upon which his new plan of tunnelling is founded was suggested to him by the operations of the teredo, a testaceous worm, covered with a cylindrical shell, which eats its way through the hardest wood, and has on this account been called by Linnæus *calamitas navium*. In the beginning of 1824 Mr. Brunel had the satisfaction to see the first and least arduous step secured, viz., the formation of a company with the

express object of carrying his designs into execution. Rotherhithe was chosen as the starting-place, and the company took the precaution of having three parallel borings made beneath the bed of the Thames in the proposed direction of the tunnel, when the report was so favourable, that the engineer went to work in a somewhat bolder way than originally intended. The soil was the great object of deliberation, for upon it depended at what level the tunnel should be commenced. The assistance of some eminent geologists was here of great moment. These informed the engineer that below a certain depth the soil would be a kind of quicksand, and therefore advised him to keep above it, and as close as possible to the stratum of clay forming the bed of the river. The preliminaries being arranged, the work commenced in March, 1825. A space being marked out 150 feet distant from the river, a cylindrical shaft, 50 feet in diameter and 150 in circumference, was raised to the height of 42 feet. This structure, destined ultimately to form the descent for foot passengers, was three feet in thickness, and strengthened in various ways by iron rods passing up the centre, &c. The excavators now commenced their work on the inside, cutting away the ground which was raised to the top of the shaft by a steam engine. It is easy to comprehend, that by clearing away the earth inside, the whole must have descended, and in this manner a structure weighing upwards of 1200 tons was sunk in a body to a depth of 65 feet, passing through a bed of gravel and sand 26 feet deep, which had caused great inconvenience on a former attempt. A well or cistern 25 feet in diameter was further made at the bottom of this shaft for draining the ground, but in sinking it a quicksand suddenly burst upon the work, at about 85 feet from the level of high water, confirming the opinion of the geologists, and guiding the engineer in the selection of his level for the horizontal cutting.

The shaft completed, the tunnel itself was commenced at a depth of 63 feet. The excavation presents a sectional surface of 850 feet; being 38 feet in width, 22½ feet high, and arranged so as to form a double arcade each 15 ft. in height, and wide enough for a single carriage-way and a foot-path. The mode in which this excavation was accomplished has been the wonder

4.23 The Thames Tunnel when it opened. "The Thames Tunnel." *Pictorial Times*, 25 March 1843. Reproduced by permission from the Guildhall Library, © Corporation of London.

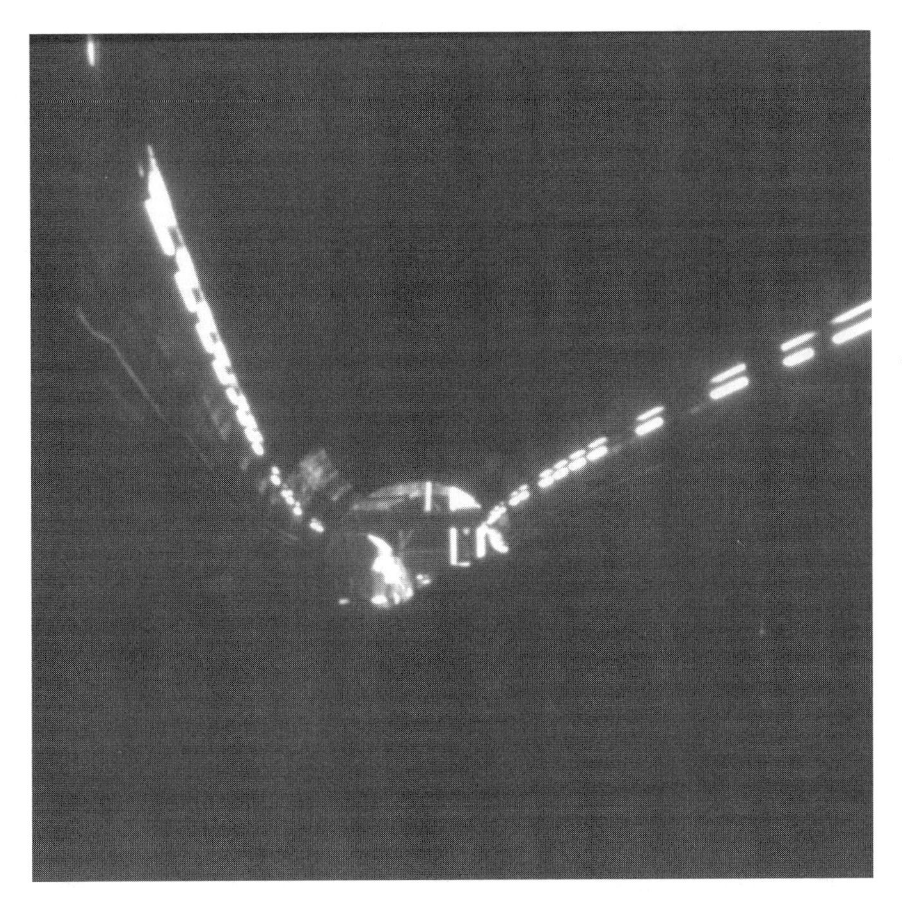

4.24 The Thames Tunnel today. Repair work on the underground tunnel on the East London line, 1995. Photograph by the author.

the threshold experience of its passageways. Kemble begins with a paean to the magical effect of this marvelous new technology:

> But I must tell you what the tunnel is like, or at least try to do so. You enter, by flights of stairs, the first door, and find yourself on a circular platform which surrounds the top of a well or shaft, of about two hundred feet in circumference and five hundred in depth. This well is an immense iron frame of cylindrical form, filled in with bricks; it was constructed on level ground, and then, by some wonderful mechanical process, sunk into the earth. In the midst of this is a steam engine, and above, or below, as far as your eye can see, huge arms are working up and down while the creaking, crashing, whirring noises, and the swift whirling of innumerable wheels all around you, make you feel for the first few minutes as if you were going distracted. I should have liked to look much longer at all these beautiful, wise, working creatures, but was obliged to

> follow the last of the party through all the machinery, down little wooden stairs and along tottering planks, to the bottom of the well. On turning round at the foot of the last flight of steps through an immense dark arch, as far as sight could reach stretched a vaulted passage, smooth earth underfoot, the white arches of the roof beyond one another lengthening on and on in prolonged vista, the whole lighted by a line of gas lamps, and as bright, almost, as if it were broad day. It was more like one of the long avenues of light that lead to the abodes of the genii in fairy tales, than anything I had ever beheld. The profound stillness of the place, which was first broken by my father's voice, to which the vaulted roof gave extraordinary and startling volume of tone, the indescribable feeling of subterranean vastness, the amazement and delight I experienced, quite overcame me, and I was obliged to turn from the friend who was explaining everything to me, to cry and ponder in silence.[113]

The 1827 Tunnel is up to this point experienced by Kemble as an industrial version of the sublime: a wholly otherworldly and alien vision of amazement that she populates with the spirits of "wise, working creatures" in the machinery and a genie, who we assume is ensconced down the passages as the personification of Brunel's celebrated shield. The vignette is strongly tinged with the atmosphere of the *Arabian Nights*, a formative influence on the Romantic sublime as well as on the popular theater of the time, the two principal contexts for Kemble's reaction here.[114]

Kemble's vision is transformed when she is faced with the material reality of what began as a perception of disembodied magic:

> Our name is always worth something to us: Mr Brunel, who was superintending some of the works, came to my father and offered to conduct us to where the workmen were employed—an unusual favour, which of course delighted us all. So we left our broad, smooth path of light, and got into dark passages, where we stumbled among coils of ropes and heaps of pipes and piles of planks, and where ground springs were welling up and flowing about in every direction . . . All this was wonderful and curious beyond measure, but the appearance of the workmen themselves, all begrimed, with their brawny arms and legs bare, some standing in black water up to their knees, others laboriously shovelling the black earth in their cages (while they sturdily sung at their task), with the red, murky light of links and lanterns flashing and flickering about them, made up the most striking picture you can conceive. As we returned I remained at the bottom of the stairs last of all, to look back at the beautiful road to Hades, wishing I might be left behind, and then we reascended, through wheels, pulleys, and engines, to the upper day.[115]

As befits her occupation of actress, Kemble takes us behind the scenes, marking the change in setting by the alteration in lighting from regular gaslight to the quite infernal image of "red, murky light of links and lanterns flashing and flickering around them." And indeed, even though she evidences a twinge of conscience, Kemble seems to regard the stagehands as an integral part of the great spectacle: "All this was wonderful and curious beyond measure." Just as the glittering underworld of the boulevard *passages* in Paris dominated the subterranean labor of the prostitutes and beggars in their representation, Kemble's view of the scene as spectacle is underlined by her assimilation of the workers to a faerie of Aladdin's Cave rather than to the gritty vision of the mines we might have expected. The language—"begrimed," "in black water up to their knees," "laboriously shovelling"—could describe either scene, but her reaction to it and the lighting of it frame the scene as an exotic and aesthetic experience. The inextricable combination of wonder and horror emerges as well in Richard Beamish's and Isambard Kingdom Brunel's descriptions of floods, where the narrowness of the escape and the loss of workers' lives are balanced by the sublimity of the spectacle. "The effect was splendid beyond description," recounted Beamish, "the water as it rose became more and more vivid from the reflected lights of the gas."[116] "The effect was—*grand*—" asserted Brunel. "I cannot compare it to anything . . . but up to that moment, as far as my senses were concerned, and distinct from the idea of the loss of six poor fellows whose death I could not foresee, [I] kept there."[117] The sense of danger and the knowledge of its costs were tightly interwoven with the "grand" and "splendid" visions created by the era of heroic engineering in early nineteenth-century Britain.

The construction of the tunnel was characterized by a constant search for funding, by periodic flooding, by horrendous and often deadly working conditions, and by the consequent strikes by the navvies: enough adversity for any properly heroic feat. After the first flood, in May 1827, the Tunnel directors staged a banquet in the completed portion of the Tunnel to convince the public of its safety, its financial viability, and its identity as an upper-class endeavor. The commemorative oil painting depicts forty or fifty "distinguished guests" transforming the dried-out tunnel into a West End fete; the band of the regiment of Coldstream Guards is in the background, the specially installed gas candelabras glow, and, we are told, formal toasts were proposed to the dukes of York, Clarence, and Wellington (figure 4.25).[118]

In the popular imagination, however, the engineers were no more in control of the river than the government was of its far-flung domains. This was the earliest major subterranean project in London, and there was even less of a shared sense of what it meant to dig beneath the city's surface than later in the century with the drainage works and the underground railway. The broadsheet poem, "The Real Devil's Walk," humorously identified the tunnel as a direct link between London and Hell, and blamed the flood on the Devil himself, exculpating the management while demonizing the works it was conducting: "Now the Devil made his entry first, / Right up thro' the Thames Tunnel; / (It was his coming made it burst, / And not the works being done ill)."[119] Others resorted to the specifically London personification of Father Thames. *The Thames Tunnell; or, Harlequin Excavator*, a summer pantomime that premiered a month after the May 1827 flood, highlighted the spectacle of destruction, advertising "three new

4.25 The respectable half of the celebrated banquet. *Banquet in the Thames Tunnel.* George Jones. ca. 1827. Oil on board. 305 mm × 253 mm. By permission of the Ironbridge Gorge Museum Trust, Elton Collection.

SCENES . . . painted expressly for the pantomime": a "Subaqueous Grotto beneath the sources of the Thames," "The Interior of the Thames Tunnell, with its curious Machinery," and the finale, "The Irruption of the RIVER. DESTRUCTION OF THE MACHINERY, and FILLING UP OF THE TUNNELL WITH WATER." Williams's 1827 caricature depicted fleeing viewers accompanied by satirical verses, "THE TUNNEL !!!

or *another* BUBBLE BURST," in which Father Thames takes issue with Brunel's disturbance of his "bed," and "destroys the great projector's fame" (figure 4.26). The moral is predictable: "Henceforth let leakages be watch'd, nor Brunel or his Neighbors / e'er count their chicks before they'r hatch'd, for fear they lose their labours." The image of the bubble equated speculation against natural forces with economic speculation, lampooning the project as a pipe dream that combined the image of an air pocket under the Thames with the memory of the Bubble of 1720 and the recent "panic of 1825." The Bubble was a notorious stock market collapse prompted by overinvestment in the nonexistent colonial assets of the South Sea Company, the panic of 1825 an apogee of speculation, in which, according to one critic of the time, nearly eighteen million pounds in private funds were fraudulently invested, including forty thousand in the Thames Tunnel.[120] Rather than a symbol of imperial ambition and engineering achievement, the Tunnel was cast by the satire as a symbol of imperial greed and unwarranted speculation.

Put forth as an icon of British technology and global empire, the Tunnel equally expressed the anxieties attendant on that dominance. The conflicted meanings surface, for example, in the way the artist chose to depict the 1827 banquet as a single rather than a double event. An earlier strike having been resolved, a representative number of one hundred and twenty miners and bricklayers also had been invited. The artist excised them, but they were seated in mirror image at separate tables in the adjoining passage; the communicating arches had been covered over with velvet drapes.[121] According to reports, the miners made their own version of a toast: "Through their chairman, [they] presented to [Marc] Isambard Brunel the pickaxe and spade as symbols of their craft."[122] The imagined reconciliation seems quite at odds with the portrait painted elsewhere of the workers, the miners in particular, who, we are told, were wont either to show up drunk or not to show up to work at all. The workers at the banquet were included in Beamish's and Law's memoirs of Brunel out of a desire to celebrate the engineer's relationship with them; they disappeared from the artist's public representation in order to produce a fundamentally uncomplicated space.

The primary theme of Tunnel promotion was to lend it the semblance of life above, or at least to maintain some semblance of connection to that life. This motif had already been evident in the concert and dinner, as well as the gas lighting; it returned with the printing of a commemorative newspaper "75 feet below high-water mark" on the day the completed tunnel opened to the public, March 25, 1843. The same motif is a consistent feature of the many illustrated pamphlets and papers produced in and around the Tunnel, such as the view of the Rotherhithe entrance, where the elegantly dressed ladies, gentlemen, and children descend winding stairways as if into the entrance hall of an enormous mansion (see figure 1.1). A writer in *The Mirror* commented that "the carriage descents will be circular; and . . . will not exceed in any part, the slope of Ludgate Hill, Waterloo

4.26 Satirizing subterranean speculation: C. Williams, "THE TUNNEL !!! or *another* BUBBLE BURST." Engraving, 1827. Reproduced by permission from the Guildhall Library, © Corporation of London.

Place, or Pall Mall. The embellished architectural character of the entrance, as shown in the print, will somewhat resemble that of the metropolitan arcades."[123] Although represented as such in the publicity and indeed related morphologically to the arcade, the Thames Tunnel did not turn out to be viable as a technically reproducible building form (although the shield design would often be employed afterward, including in the excavation of the Tube tunnels at the end of the century); it remained a unique and pioneering feat of engineering.[124] Still, its affiliation to the arcade was more than just a pipe dream of the Tunnel publicists; if anything, it embodied to a fault the paradoxical qualities that emerge from Benjamin's analysis. Already in Kemble's charmed description it is clear that the scale was all wrong. In another engraving of the period, we see again the image of the tunnel as a *passage*, but with the Thames above it almost as if superimposed, with ships afloat on the river, and a view of the rotunda-building entrance on the banks surrounded by warehouses and factories (figure 4.27). As "The Bubble Burst" suggested, the Tunnel was simply too unnatural, too ambitiously modern to be easily assimilated as an aboveground urban space, even on the ambivalent model that allowed the West End arcades and the Paris *passages* their brief heyday. A later report in the *Mirror*, basing its evaluation on the Tunnel itself rather than on its representation in drawings, saw it less as an arcade than as a somewhat freakish, underwater street: "A hundred steps conduct the visitor to the entrance of the passage or passages, for there are what may be called two streets, which pass beneath the bed of the river."[125] In its very strangeness, the

Tunnel continued to function as a threshold-space in Benjamin's terms—a hyperarcade, as it were—between the broad conceptual divisions of London.

In the representation of its day-to-day operations, the Tunnel was no less split in identity as a threshold between an underground space safely colonized by the forces of light and a criminal underworld in need of police surveillance. This was already evident from Brunel's recommendations on opening day that "tunnel men" posted to answer questions would be of greater utility than a uninformed police force, "but in regard to the public indiscriminately in the night the police would be most efficient for order."[126] By day, the Tunnel was a potent symbol of national triumph and of the proper relations between classes. During the first fourteen days, lured by the novelty, nearly two hundred thousand people passed through. The first summer it was opened, the Tunnel was blessed with an impromptu visit from Queen Victoria and Prince Albert, accompanied by various distinguished personages (figure 4.28). As one foreign visitor put it, "In truth, it may be called a glory of this country, and the name is a sufficient reward for the millions of money that have been spent."[127]

By night, the Tunnel was more difficult and less important to control than the West End arcades, and it was generally seen to revert to its local surroundings, the urban crime and dissolution that characterized the London underground as a

4.27 The Tunnel as an underwater thoroughfare. *The Thames Tunnel with a view of Rotherhithe*. Lithograph on paper, ca. 1843. By permission of the London Borough of Southwark Local History Library.

4.28 The triumph of the imperial endeavor. The tunnel lined with scarlet baize for *The Queen's Visit to the Thames Tunnel. Punch* 5 (July–December 1843): 61.

world apart. The first crime report appeared two years after the opening, the midnight robbery of a "poor man" on his way home from Rotherhithe, who was caught by the legs, thrown on his face, and dragged down the steps to the stone pavement at their foot. The article gratuitously concluded: "We are given to understand, that after a certain hour of the night the tunnel is infested with loose women. What is the committee about that it does not appoint a night police to protect the lives and property of the public?"[128] The unmotivated leap from robbery to prostitution was becoming typical of underworld reporting, linking the criminal underworld with the morally suspect world of the prostitute to imply for the aboveground reporter a general indictment of the East End as subterranean. The response of the Tunnel management followed suit: it felt compelled to deny both accusations; the next day the *Times* assured its readers that "the story of the robbery described as having taken place in that thoroughfare, is entirely destitute of foundation. We are also assured that the tunnel is not the haunt of loose women, and that it is constantly watched by a police force of its own."[129] Like the Parisian *passages*, the Piccadilly arcades had their own problematic reputation as a haven for prostitution, but as a problem within the discourse of West End respectability. The Thames Tunnel shared the double-edged quality of the *passage*, but its much sharper division between middle-class exhibition and consumption by day and underworld "thoroughfare" by night, its immense scale and its association with a segregated city magnified out of proportion what the arcade, for a time at least, had successfully negotiated.

Although most accounts of the Tunnel assume from such reports an immediate decline into disreputability, the facts (as with most underground spaces) are more equivocal. To be sure, pedestrian traffic exceeded the number of passengers previously transported by ferry only during the height of its celebrity around 1843. Still, the Tunnel continued to be a requisite part of any visit to the metropolis, appearing without fail among the illustrated sights on London souvenir. In August 1851, at the height of the Great Exhibition, 220,250 persons passed through the Tunnel, more than twice the number that visited the Crystal Palace during the same period; it drew one and a quarter million annually through the end of the 1850s.[130] The 1852 guide *Memories of the Great Metropolis: Or, London, from the Tower to Crystal Palace*, while characteristically excluding the Tunnel's location from the genteel geographical limits of its title, nevertheless asserted that "the Thames Tunnel, which is regarded as a triumph of skill rather than as a work of real utility, is yet an object of especial interest to the lovers of the marvellous."[131] As one American viewer expressed with surprise: "From the bottom the view of the arches of the Tunnel, brilliantly lighted with gas, is very fine; it has a much less heavy and gloomy appearance than I expected. . . . The air within is somewhat damp, but fresh and agreeably cool, and one can scarcely realize in walking along the light passage, that a river is rolling above his head."[132] Gaslight had made a similarly spectacular and dreamlike effect in the *passage* Colbert in Paris: "I admire the regular series of these crystal globes, from which a brightness emanates that is simultaneously sharp and soft. Couldn't they be likened to so many comets lined up in battle order, awaiting the signal to go wandering through space?"[133] In its unprecedented combination of the industrial sublime with the cozily domestic, the Thames Tunnel could be promoted and imagined as something familiar only in the backward-looking spatial conception of the arcade; even lit up, its long narrow dual corridors were a far cry from the astonishing spaciousness of the Crystal Palace.

The assertion of alienness that dogged the Thames Tunnel marks a turning point in the imagination of the city following half a century of the most ambitious planning and construction; paralleling the decline of the *passage*, the vertical trope affirmed more and more a new rigidity of spatial divisions and the resulting "deficiency of threshold spaces" that Benjamin would lament much later. Two midcentury descriptions underline the shift and suggest some reasons for it. The first is an account by Nathaniel Hawthorne of an 1855 visit, which closely follows Kemble's description in structure and degree of detail, but with all trace of sublimity, either magical or industrial, removed:

> On reaching the bottom, we saw a closed door, which we opened, and passing through it, found ourselves in the Tunnel—an arched corridor of apparently interminable length, gloomily lighted with jets of gas at regular intervals—plastered at the sides, and stone beneath the feet. It would have made an admirable prison, or series of dungeons. . . . There are people who spend their lives there, seldom or never, I presume, seeing any daylight; except perhaps a little in the morning. All along the extent of this corridor, in little alcoves, there are stalls or shops, kept principally by women, who, as you approach, are seen through the dusk offering for sale views of the Tunnel, put up, with a little magnifying glass, in cases of Derbyshire spar; also, cheap jewelry and multifarious trumpery; also cakes, candy, ginger-beer, and such small refreshment. There was one shop that must, I think, have opened into the other corridor of the Tunnel, so capacious it seemed; and here were dioramic views of various cities and scenes of the daylight-world, all shown by gas, while the Thames rolled its tide and its shipping over our head. So far as any present use is concerned, the Tunnel is an entire failure. . . . Perhaps, in coming

> ages, the approaches to the Tunnel will be obliterated, its corridors choked up with mud, its precise locality unknown, and nothing be left of it but an obscure tradition. Meantime, it is rather a pleasant idea, that I have actually passed under the Thames, and emerged into daylight on the other side.[134]

The Tunnel is again represented as a passage through the underworld, but in Hawthorne's vision this road to Hades has very little of beauty left in it. Rather than a celebration of technical marvels, he sees an urban ruin, an atavistic space inhabited by people whose lives are little better than those of troglodytes. The trademark infinite corridor is still in evidence, but what a gloomy view it has become! There does remain one curious exception, the dioramic shop, "so capacious it seemed," that it reminds him of the "daylight-world." The Tunnel persists as an infernal arcade, offering a vision of early capitalism fallen into decay, while selling a few surviving representations of a better city elsewhere. The effect of the sublime relies on its being perceived as natural; as such it should never lose its aesthetic value. Spectacle, by contrast, relies on novelty; when it ceases to be cutting edge, its effects quickly begin to appear faded and tawdry. To be sure, this is precisely what attracted later scholars writers such as Benjamin and the surrealists to the ruins of capitalism buried in the faded *passages*, but Hawthorne's reaction rings closer to the contemporary perception.

We find a similar portrayal of the Tunnel as an urban ruin in an 1860 piece in *Chambers's Journal* entitled "A Night in the Thames Tunnel."[135] The down-and-out narrator, fleeing his creditors, is trapped outside on a wintry night with only a penny to his name, not enough for even the cheapest flophouse in Deptford. Overhearing a navvy mention the Tunnel as his route home, the narrator makes his way to Rotherhithe, where, "guided by dim boards with index-hands of faded red, glimmering like those of phantom murderers in the flickering gaslight," he finds his way at last "To the Thames Tunnel." He is not detained by the remnants of attempted gentrification, "seedy works of art—damp-stained and peeling from the plaster—which decorate the walls," but hastens downward. One of the two roadways has been boarded up; the stall keepers have departed; there is no longer any music. The space has been divested of its identity as a tourist site.

Instead, his encounters in the world below constitute an inventory of the metaphorical range encompassed by the nineteenth-century imagination of underground London as a social category. First in order is a crowd of inappropriate foreigners, drunken Frenchmen who use the tunnel as an excuse for celebrating their cultural superiority: "crowing over their English *cicerone* by singing paeans, at 12 P.M., to the genius of their illustrious compatriote, 'Sir Brunel.' " 'De Tunelle,' " they asserted with much emphasis, 'vos de von only leetle ting in veech Londres bate Paris and *dat* had been made by a Frenchman.' "[136] Next come the working classes, embodied in the Lancashire navvy who inspired the narrator's descent and now appears as a creature of the underworld: "His Evelyn Street potations had evidently taken a powerful effect upon him. . . . Hideously did he howl as he staggered along. . . . I gave him a wide berth."[137] Then we come upon a mirror image of the narrator as underground man, also pacing the Tunnel's length until the hour is late enough to lie down unembarrassed to sleep, a former London curate brought low by gin, with whom the narrator shares the heat of "a piece of tarpaulin in one of the stall-recesses," and who coins the name of "Hades Hotel." Meanwhile, the narrator summons up mythic versions of the underground/underwater experience of the otherworld, imagining himself as Jonah in the whale; and from there to "river-pirates" and the reflection that "there might be corpses bobbing above my head like fish-baits." He is jolted out of an anxious dream of atavistic assimilation to this milieu—that he is "a whale compelled to swallow one of those loathsome baits"—by the final tableau, a woman, "a sort of Dutch Erinys," pursued by a policeman and a man whose watch has been stolen. The ruined Tunnel has become a waste heap of unwanted people and images from the city above; to top it off, the narrator awakens to find the space full of commuting workmen. At the same time, however, the Tunnel has lost most of its aboveground veneer as well as its physical identity as a tunnel. It has become a metaphor, and the "dim boards with index-hands of faded red" inform (and reassure) the reader that this metaphorical space, like Hawthorne's Tunnel with its approaches "obliterated by mud," was rapidly losing contact with his or her own city. The narrator hurries to the "Way Out," and secures a loan to forestall the possibility of being forced to repeat the underground experience.

The experience was not going to be repeated. Its physical connection to underground spectacle exhausted, the Tunnel would soon be incorporated for all intents and purposes into the late-Victorian technological infrastructure of subterranean London. First, there was a "bold proposal," as John Hollingshead characterized it in 1862, "to defile the Thames Tunnel, and wake up this wonder of joint-stock credulity from its long sleep of idleness," by converting it into a great sewer to carry South London waste under the river and into Middlesex, and from there out of the city altogether.[138] The Tunnel was sold instead to the East London Railway in 1865 for two hundred thousand pounds and converted into a tunnel for the Underground. This technological and transportational purpose appears to have been adequate to the Tunnel, and it is still in use today.

A similar fate happened to Peter Barlow's later passenger tunnel under the Thames between Tower Hill and Tooley Street, Southwark. Employing an improved version of Brunel's shield devised by James Henry Greathead and carried out on a much less ambitious scale, the Thames Subway was completed in 1870 in less than a year at about 2 percent of the cost of the Thames Tunnel. The descent was by lift; a single twelve-passenger carriage was pulled back and forth by cable; the crossing took less than five minutes and cost either twopence or a penny (figure 4.29). Although the managers soon dispensed with the carriage, the tunnel averaged a million pedestrian crossings a year until 1894, when it was put out of business by the construction of Tower Bridge. In its single-purpose design it was an advance in efficiency over the Thames Tunnel, and in its technology it prefigured the Tube trains of the end of the century, but it lacked the scale and the electrical traction of the later network, and after it closed down it was purchased by the London Hydraulic Power Company for use as a conduit for high-pressure water mains.[139] These conversions signal a second shift in the topography of underground London: the underground is imagined as a practical space, and thus wholly distinct from any similar activities above. This had important consequences for the metaphorical underground as well. No longer capable of functioning in any overt way as a threshold space, the Tunnel came to represent the successful separation of high and low, as in Doré's famous 1872 engraving of workers waiting for the train at Wapping; this separation also manifested itself as nostalgia for a lost underworld of illicit pleasure, or as fear of renewed contamination.

This has been the general fate of the arcades and arches that dominated the imagination of Paris and London during the first half of the nineteenth century. In London, the openings of the Adelphi arches and the Thames Tunnel to upper London were for all intents and purposes sealed off by the 1860s; similarly, the railway arches became more and more an unnoticed part of the new urban landscape, with little sense of any connection between the passengers in the railway carriages above and the business, licit or illicit, going on below. In Paris, the arcades underwent a slow decline into oblivion as the centers of commerce moved inward to the department store and nightlife moved outward to Montmartre and, later, Montparnasse. Their symbolic role was slower to fade, but from the time of Zola's *Thérèse Raquin* (1967), as we shall see below, the *passage* was becoming a modernist symbol of the city's overall identity as an alienated hell rather than the threshold it had previously constituted. The threshold identity left the arcade and the now well-regulated cityscape and migrated into later liminal spaces of modernity such as the trench, the theater, and the cinema. I will begin with a look at the underwater tunnel as a conduit for fantasies of invasion from outside, and conclude with a look at the revival of arches and arcades at the end of the twentieth century, either as subterranean or as resolutely aboveground—the threshold quality of the pre-Victorian heyday as such would never return.

Foreign Incursions

> The Tunnel which we wished to construct reminded him of the condition of the Labouring Party, low down in the social scale, weighted and put out of sight by a seat of privilege and all the weight of capital, yet,

APRIL 9, 1870 THE ILLUSTRATED LONDON NEWS 385

THE THAMES SUBWAY AT TOWER-HILL.

Several Illustrations were lately given of the works in progress for the construction of the subway or tunnel under the Thames, from Tower-hill to Tooley-street, Southwark, designed and carried through by Mr. W. H. Barlow, the engineer. It is now complete and ready for traffic. The subway consists of a narrow tunnel uniting two vertical shafts, the mouth of one being on Tower-hill and the other in Vine-street, Tooley-street. The tunnel is lined with iron tubing, bolted together in short lengths by flanges projecting on the internal surface. This tube is 7 ft. in clear internal diameter, or 6 ft. 8 in. between the flanges, and carries a railway of 2 ft. 6 in. gauge. On the railway runs an omnibus conveying twelve passengers. The tube is about a quarter of a mile in length, and sinks from both ends towards the centre with a gradient of about 1 in 30. The omnibus is of iron—light, but very strong, and runs upon eight wheels. It is connected with a rope of steel wire by means of a gripe that can be tightened or relaxed at will. At each end of the tunnel this wire runs over a drum, worked by a stationary engine. The declivity of the tunnel is such that, when once the omnibus is started, it requires only a small amount of traction, and the momentum acquired during its descent will carry it a long way up the opposite slope. It is said that the strain on the rope will never exceed 2 cwt. The omnibus is provided with brakes, so that its motion is completely under the control of the man in charge. At each end of the tunnel it is received by buffers, or catches, which are connected with very strong springs of vulcanised indiarubber.

The shafts at each end of the tunnel are 60 ft. in depth, and are lined partly with brickwork and partly with iron tubing. Within the shafts are lifts, carrying six passengers at once, and these lifts are raised and lowered by the same engines that work the drums. Each lift has a counterpoise equal to its own weight and to that of three average passengers; so that the weight of three passengers represents the maximum of work that will be demanded from the engine, either for raising or lowering. At the top of each lift is a contrivance by which a breakage of the suspending chain would close iron claws upon the lateral guiding-rails, and would bring the machine to a standstill in the course of a few feet. The ascent of these lifts is checked by springs of steel and indiarubber, which the engine employed would not be strong enough to break. The wheel over which the suspending-chain runs is also dragged, so to speak, by revolving fans; and too great rapidity of either ascent or descent seems to be rendered impossible.

The arrangements visible from above are very simple. The upper opening of each shaft is covered by a small square building, at the door of which passengers take their tickets, then enter and descend in the lift. On reaching the bottom they find a space of a few feet between the shaft and the buffers fitted up with benches, as a waiting-room. When the omnibus arrives and has discharged its load, those who are waiting step in and start off for the other end. The descent of the shaft occupies twenty-five seconds, and the omnibus journey seventy seconds; so that a passenger may descend into the shaft at Tower-hill and emerge in Vine-street in a minute and three quarters from the time of his descent. Allowing for all ordinary causes of detention—such as missing the lift at the moment of its descent, or being just too late for the omnibus — the journey from point to point cannot occupy more than five minutes. The lifts, as they only carry half as many passengers as the omnibus, will make twice as many journeys; and it is intended to give priority of ascent to first-class passengers, who pay twopence, while the second-class passengers pay one penny.

WAITING-ROOM.

ENTRANCE TO TUNNEL.

OMNIBUS CARRIAGE.

INTERIOR OF CARRIAGE.

The Preservation of Peace (Ireland) Act, which received the Royal assent on Monday, was printed on Tuesday. There are forty-one clauses in the Act, and it is to continue in force until Aug. 1 next year.

4.29 Subaqueous tunneling on a modest and remunerative scale. "The Thames Subway at Tower-Hill," *Illustrated London News*, 9 April 1860, 385.

spite the darkness, there was movement in that submarine passage. The people low down were burrowing their passage up to the surface, and would force their way up to the clear light of day, to justice and liberty!

The Channel Tunnel and Industrial Opinion. Deputation of English Workmen to Paris (1883)

There is a contemporary epilogue to the saga of the Thames Tunnel. When the Brunel Exposition Rotherhithe renovated Brunel's Engine House and installed a permanent exhibit commemorating the "Man and His Tunnel" in 1990, an important donor was Eurotunnel, which assured the press that "they will not have to wait 17 years before they can use our tunnel!"[140] Just as the Thames Tunnel mobilized anxieties and pipe dreams about a divided London, so did the Chunnel raise them about a united Europe. A Channel tunnel had first been proposed to the National Assembly in Paris by Thilorier in 1798 (figure 4.30); an equally fanciful proposal was made to Napoleon by Albert Mathieu, a French mining engineer, in 1802.[141] Although the latter was proposed during the brief spell of amity between the nations that followed the Peace of Amiens, both were doubtless related to contemporaneous revolutionary dreams of invading England to liberate its people, as in *Descente en Angleterre*, a theatrical "prophecy" staged on Christmas Eve, 1797, by two "citizens of the republic." A prison escapee hides in a Dover cellar while he prepares to bring the revolution to England. The play concludes at the port of Dover, as the gathered forces prepare to descend upon London: "In London we shall sign the general peace. . . . In London we will cement the tranquility and happiness of our peoples."[142] Still a preindustrial fantasy at this point—as the wooden props of Blanchard's caricature in Figure 4.30 demonstrate—the subaqueous tunnel was made reality only a few decades later by Brunel. Ever since, such tunnels have been the repository of fears of invasion and contamination, a passage between spaces on a scale ranging from the house to the universe. There is a dialectic at work here: when conceived as perfectly functioning and hermetically sealed infrastructure, tunnels conjure up a technological utopia; when perceived to be imperfectly sealed or open to movement, activity, and access by the organic world, they reemerge as hidden thresholds, cracks in the ideological armature.

The image of the tunnel united two popular French fantasies about their island neighbors: the liberation of the English people from the oppression of monarchy (and sometimes Protestantism as well), and the difficult traversal of the Channel. The stormy crossing was a stock piece of the many society comedies of the "Parisian in London" genre, and getting to London often occupied as much as half of the action. Conversely, Englanders never seemed preoccupied with the journey; "Londoners in Paris" plays routinely elided the transit altogether. The invasion fantasy was not limited to the Revolution, although it appears to have recurred in

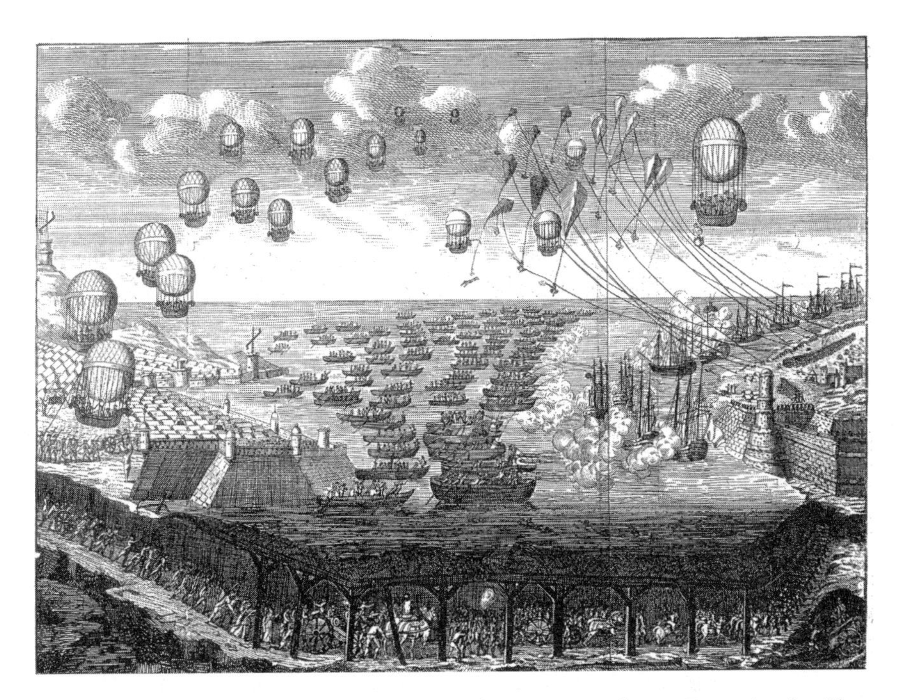

4.30 Early pipe dreams: *Divers Projets sur la descente en Angleterre.* Engraving by Blanchard, ca. 1802. In John-Grand Carteret, *Napoléon en images. Estampes Anglaises (Portraits et Caricatures) avec 130 reproductions d'après les originaux* (Paris: Firmin-Didot, 1895), 34.

times of unrest. When Paul Féval's *Mystères de Londres* was adapted for the stage in December 1848, emphasis was given to the uprising organized by the so-called Great Family. Just as *Descente en Angleterre* imagined the liberation of Scotland and Ireland before continuing to England, so Féval's Great Family was led by the mad Irishman Fergus O'Breane.[143] There was a difference, however; the successful fantasy of 1797 involved officers and good bourgeois citizens, whereas that of 1848 was a spectacular failure led by a criminal organization and supported by the denizens of Spitalfields and St. Giles's. The uprising still conjured up an underworld power, but as a natural, aquatic conflagration, the rookery of "Saint-Giles's . . . like a furious flood which no dike could possibly hold back."[144]

Féval's image of the London slums "vomiting forth" their criminal multitudes to flood the city found its material counterpart in the more important component of the Great Family's plan, a tunnel beneath the streets of the City of London through which they aimed to bring down the economy of England. The tunnel, running from the cellar of a soda-water shop to the vaults of the Bank of England, was a nightmare image of the Thames Tunnel (which was opened to the public the year the novel was first serialized), an underground arcade through which twenty-four million pounds sterling were to be invisibly siphoned out of

English pockets. In characteristic fashion for the subaqueous tunnel in the first half of the nineteenth century, the description begins with an homage to the ambition of the task: "In order truly to comprehend the enormity of the enterprise . . . it must be known that there was no question of a simple pipe through which a human being could slip through in a crouch. Milords of the Night required a Gallery, a Gallery through which you could walk and run."[145] Note the way in which Féval establishes the "enormity" of the projected "Gallery" by contrast with the utility and nonhuman scale of the "simple pipe." This was still the age of heroic engineering, and the execution needed to match the conception.

There was an added irony to the fate Féval chose for this tunnel. The grand plot is quietly foiled, although most of the culprits escape, and the tunnel entrance is bricked up by the police. Féval includes a postscript recounting that, while extending its cellars, the Bank of England discovered an "extensive subterranean passage" with puzzling fossilized remains of enormous size.[146] The Royal Society is called in, and its experts pronounce the tunnel to be the work of an ancient race of giants. The joke is that the tunnel was in fact dug by a single man, Saunders the Astley Giant, a stage performer imprisoned underground and kept going on "blue ruin" (gin). It is the product of aspirations and achievements no longer possible—there were giants in those days—either in revolution or in engineering. It is equally a comment on the ignorance of the present-day on the near miss it had run with total chaos. Not only a heroic feat of engineering, the tunnel is equally a threshold image, a reminder of how closely linked the underground is with the world above, and the ease with which the complacent world above misreads as innocent and distant antiquity what was actually a dangerously criminal recent past.

When built on the grand scale of a city street, the subterranean position of the tunnel makes spatially explicit what in the ground-level arcade or arch is only a spatial effect. In 1842, *Punch* suggested the Thames Tunnel would be "a safe and commodious harbour of refuge" for the invading forces of a foreign power.[147] In 1866, the magazine responded to a proposal (one of many in those years) by John Clarke Hawkshaw for a Channel tunnel, by recalling the Thames Tunnel, which they had sarcastically dubbed the "Great Bore": "*Vive* the new Bore de Boulong!"[148] When in 1880 plans advanced to the point that excavations proceeded some seventeen hundred meters at both ends, the Tunnel project was precipitously halted by English opposition led in Parliament by Lord Wolseley and in print by James Knowles in the journal he edited, *The Nineteenth Century*, on the grounds that the risk of invasion was too great.[149] According to the French and to the members of the "Working Men's Channel Tunnel Delegation," which visited Paris in November 1882, the opposition was a purely class-based fear of international cooperation; a later Tunnel promoter put it down to a simple case of competition between the Channel Tunnel Company and the South Eastern Railway.[150] In either case, as a number of pamphleteers fairly convincingly argued, the fear of invasion did not hold any water. Even the virulently anti-Tunnel fantasy *How John Bull Lost London; or, The Capture of the Channel Tunnel,* after imaginatively rendering the capture of London by a French strike force disguised as tourists, nevertheless went on to describe how the "manlier" citizens further north were able to repel the French and send them safely back through the Tunnel to the Continent.[151] The only casualty was the capital city itself, pillaged and nearly ruined by the unruly occupation forces.

The next concrete plans for a tunnel were submitted for authorization in 1906 after untiring efforts by the engineer of the 1880 works, Thomé de Gamond; following stiff opposition spearheaded once again by Knowles and *Nineteenth Century,* the request was withdrawn the following year. Georges Méliès's 1907 film, *Le Tunnel sous la Manche; ou, Le Cauchemar franco-anglais,* reflected popular support for the project, envisioning the promised unity between nations; the denouement reflected the equally popular taste for spectacle, as the tunnel was destroyed by a disastrous flood. The resemblance to a city street evident in the pre-1880 plans had completely disappeared by this point; Méliés's tunnel was designed for use by a locomotive (figure 4.31). Like the Thames Tunnel, the subaqueous tunnel was assimilated for the twentieth century to the less worrisome model of the underground railway. As opposed to some of the proposed designs, which imagined islands in the Channel where automobile traffic would emerge to rest, refuel, and admire the view, the Chunnel as it stands today conveys all of its traffic by rail. It is not surprising, then, that the only film so far to set a scene within this sensational setting, Brian de Palma's *Mission Impossible* (1996), used the Chunnel not for a disastrous flood as in prior centuries, but to stage a set-piece fight within and on top of a moving locomotive.

The form of the subaqueous tunnel became regularized as deep-level tube tunneling was perfected, and by the early twentieth century it had wholly shed its affinity with the arcade and lost the majority of its threshold character. Instead, its dual identity separated into streamlined inorganic pipe and filthy organic burrowing. Firmly established as a conduit, it no longer retained enough of the domestic interior or of the city street to provoke identification with either traditionally underworld nightmares or subterranean dreams.[152] Like the underground railway, it was appropriated to a new vision of the utilitarian underground, wholly separated both from the world above and from the traditional subterranean connotations of otherworldly myth and material poverty.[153] Tobinsky d'Altoff suggested that between a Channel tunnel and a Gibraltar tunnel, English goods could be freighted from Cape Town to London in a mere eighteen days; such construction would respond to the militaristic technology of the Germans with a "Channel tunnel for Peace."[154] *High Treason* (1929), Maurice Elvey's cinematic vision of London in 1940, included a fully functioning Channel tunnel, emblem of a "United Europe" pitted against "United America." A similar technological utopia was evident in the speculative thriller, *The Tunnel,* based on

VIN DU
LOUPILLON

a 1913 novel by Bernhard Kellermann, and adapted for the screen in German (1933), French (1933), and English (1935, also by Elvey) versions, most likely prompted by the most recent Channel tunnel campaign, which had been finished off by a narrow defeat in Parliament in 1930, the first such vote since 1883.[155] Designed by the heroic engineer Richard "Mack" MacAllan, already responsible for a Channel tunnel, the proposed transatlantic tunnel would join Europe and North America in a league for world peace.[156] In the continental adaptations of the novel, the European terminus was not specified; in the English version, the tunnel ran from London to New York, its entrances like enormous Tube tunnel portals. In his alternate-world novel *A Transatlantic Tunnel, Hurrah!* (1972) Harry Harrison combined the '30s films with the Thames Tunnel to come up with a subaqueous scheme to control intercontinental trade masterminded by "Sir Isambard Brassey Brunel" in the Victorian empire of 1973. Rather than Brunel's original brick-lined arches, however, Harrison's tunnel was cast in stainless steel, a gleaming conduit like those of the '30s.

And yet even the resolutely segregated and controlled space of the underground railway has always come under pressure from its appropriation by a different underworld and a different set of underground fantasies. Just as the tunnel's most time-honored identity is as the prison escape route, so it remains the most powerfully concrete image of the contemporary immigrant's desire to escape from economic or political oppression to the dreamed-of promised land of the West.[157] Similarly, the most recent furor over an underwater invasion arose from the perceived inability of the French authorities to prevent asylum seekers from sneaking into England aboard the cargo sections of Eurostar, some traveling in concealment from as far away as Italy (which is nothing, of course, in comparison with the horrific human cargo-hold smuggling undertaken by freighters from the Far East to the United States), others rushing the trains nightly from the Sangatte refugee camp in Calais. "These people should all have been detected by the French authorities but they weren't," complained a spokesman for the English freight company whose train turned out to contain eighty stowaways, thirty of whom escaped into the countryside. "We were promised proper security. Tags were attached to these wagons to say that they'd been searched."[158] Contaminated by dreams of escape and nightmares of invasion, the subaqueous tunnel remains a stubbornly fluid threshold rather than a hermetically sealed conduit.

Facing page

4.31 The early twentieth-century tunnel: for transport only. *Le Tunnel sous la Manche*, directed by Georges Méliès (1907). Star Films. Publicity still. BFI Films: Stills, Posters, and Designs.

The Arcade Entrenched

> . . . Spain is not Spain, it is an immense trench,
> it is a great cemetery red and bombarded:
> the barbarians want it this way. . . .
>
> MIGUEL HERNÁNDEZ, "Pick Up This Voice" (1937)

Consistent with the ambivalent ways in which forbidden desires manifest themselves in subterranean spaces, such feats of escape and endurance have always inspired both admiration and horror at their success, and nostalgia and relief at their temporary elimination. When the Adelphi underwent a fate similar to that of the Thames Tunnel—renovated in the 1860s, dried out and removed from the river by the Thames Embankment, converted to a storage facility, and eventually, in 1936, demolished—it was the subject of a series of nostalgic pieces bemoaning the loss of the picturesque "dark arches" of old.[159] Even more so did the same process occur with the Parisian *passages*, for which no modern identity could be found until the *entre-deux-guerres*, when, like much of the nineteenth-century underground, they were adopted imaginatively and theoretically by modernism: pilloried by Louis-Ferdinand Céline and eulogized by Benjamin, Louis Aragon, André Breton, and the other surrealists. In their very decrepitude they provided a powerful backdrop for the polemics of the first half of the twentieth century.

Already in Zola's 1867 novel, *Thérèse Raquin*, the *passage* in which the action takes place had stood in for the degenerating atmosphere of urban poverty. Rather than a "lieu de promenade," it was a place one would take a detour to avoid.[160] Its paving stones were faded and cracked, exuding "an acrid dampness"; the glass roofing was "black with filth."[161] By night, its subterranean character was absolute: "The *passage* takes on the sinister look of a veritable cutthroat. . . . One could call it a subterranean gallery vaguely lit by three funerary lamps."[162] Writing in the 1930s, Benjamin read Zola's novel allegorically, as a scientific analysis of "the death of the Paris arcades, the decay of a type of architecture. . . . The book's atmosphere is saturated with the poisons of this process: its people drop like flies."[163] These were standard tropes of German expressionist film of the previous decade, and it is quite possible that Benjamin was influenced by a viewing of Jacques Feyder's 1928 adaptation of the novel, which was filmed and released in Berlin during Benjamin's most active period as a reviewer and journalist there. According to design historian Léon Barsacq, Andrei Andrejew's sets chose the "dirty window covering the *passage*" as the primary motif, "turn[ing] it into a kind of unhealthy greenhouse whose obsessive presence symbolizes the petty bourgeois home."[164] But what Zola's choice of an arcade setting tellingly and more directly demonstrated was that the form of the *passage* had been reappropriated as representative of the Paris underground. It was no longer imagined as a threshold space, but as a cul-de-sac festering with urban pathology.

Zola's plotting makes the arcade stand in for the entire city: it is the site to which the respectable petite-bourgeoise shopkeeper Mme. Raquin chooses to return from her retirement in the country town of Vernon on the Seine, to provide a livelihood for her son Camille and his new wife, Thérèse. The indolent and sensuous Thérèse, an "indigenous woman of great beauty,"[165] born in Oran, recalls the exotic goods that the *passages* had always peddled, and the way Zola portrays her, silent and enigmatic behind the counter of the lingerie boutique, emphasizes the hothouse sexuality she incarnates. The arcade setting was the primary ingredient Zola added to the *fait divers* that was his original source, and to the short story in which he first used the material. He chose an obscure arcade, the passage du Pont-Neuf, which ran between 44, rue Mazarine, and 45, rue de Seine, in the sixth arrondissement on the Left Bank, rather than the central Right Bank cluster; he wanted the sense of Paris as a fetid backwater, and the boulevards were still glamorous in 1867.[166] Zola's language is insistently organic all the way through the novel, with words such as *trou*, *abîme*, *égout*, *souterrain*, and *tombe* repeated in a nearly obsessive fashion so that the underground qualities of the arcade seem to radiate outward to invade every corner of Paris that the characters visit: from the garret studio of Thérèse's lover, Laurent, to the *banlieue* excursion to Saint-Ouen where the lovers drown her husband, to the slab at the Paris Morgue visited daily by Laurent as he waits for Camille's body to turn up, to the heights of Belleville, where the successful plotters are supposed to celebrate their long-awaited nuptial ceremony. Nowhere can they escape the living death of Paris life.

If anything, Céline took this image of subterranean decay even further in his 1936 novel, *Mort à crédit*. Like the earlier *Voyage au bout de la nuit* (1933), *Mort à crédit* was partially autobiographical: Céline spent a few years of his turn-of-the-century childhood with his family in the passage Choiseul near the Palais-Royal (see figure 4.1). Whatever traces of glamour may have been left were totally stripped by the petit-bourgeois nightmare Céline depicted, amplifying those few years to epitomize the childhood of the narrator, Ferdinand Bardamu. In its class resentment and decades-old rot, Céline's passage Choiseul literalized the psychological and material cityscape of Baudelaire's *Fleurs du mal*. The glass-enclosed arcade, architectural and consumer glory of a hundred years before, has been retroactively transformed into city life as hell, an emblem of the degradation and asphyxiation to come in the approaching First World War:

> I have to admit that the passage was an unbelievable pesthole. It was made to kill you off, slowly but surely, what with the little mongrel's urine, the shit, the sputum, the leaky gas pipes. The stink was worse than the inside of a prison. Down under the glass roof the sun is so dim you can eclipse it with a candle. Everybody began to gasp for breath. The Passage took cognizance of its asphyxiating stench. . . . We talked of nothing but the country, hills and valleys, the wonders of nature.[167]

Down to the poison gas, Bardamu has been primed from childhood by the arcade for the trench experience: the novel was written as a prequel, some manner of explanation for the nihilism of *Voyage au bout de la nuit*, which began with the protagonist enlisting on a whim in the Great War.

Céline's grounding of the trench experience within the prewar experience of the cityscape of Paris asserted the close connection between the space of the trench and the space of the metropolis. While the wartime mysteries serials of Feuillade had imagined an empty and uncanny cityscape where death could strike at any time, modernist novelists between the wars echoed Céline's determinism with images of a world under glass, hothouse enclosures redolent of both the trenches and the arcades. Just as the First World War had united all of Europe in destruction, and modernism had fostered a pan-European set of aesthetic ideologies, so prewar urban imagery was opened out to encompass the continent as a whole, to make a spatial metaphor somehow large enough to deal with the immensity of the war. *Huguenau, or the New Objectivity* (*Huguenau, oder die Neuesachlichkeit*), the third volume of Hermann Broch's 1932 trilogy, *The Sleepwalkers*, begins with one of the mythic, undead trench deserters described in chapter 1. Tired and frightened of the war, Huguenau simply climbs out of his trench and walks away: "He knew that he might be picked off at any moment by the English, and that similar attention would be paid to him by the German outposts; but the world lay as if under a vacuum glass—Huguenau could not help thinking of a glass cover over cheese—grey, worm-eaten and completely dead in a silence that was inviolable."[168] The soundless, rotting world under glass that Broch then created for 1918 is perhaps more terrifying than the myth of the cannibal grave robbers created at the front. His Huguenau is a walking figure of a new image of the underground man, no longer the alienated and obsessive loser of the previous century, but amoral and vengeful, a destroyer of society, yet a consummate chameleon of social conventions and codes. The experience of the trench gives birth to a new social type, the embodiment of the mentality of the mine as described by Lewis Mumford during the same years. Broch expressed this postwar mind-set as *Neuesachlichkeit*, the instrumentality of the war applied to the workings of everyday society.

Thomas Mann's earlier novel, *The Magic Mountain* (1924), schematized the prewar trajectory of the tubercular Hans Castorp along the same vertical axis; it concludes by abandoning its charge in the trenches at the end of an extended interlude at the Sanatorium Berghof, a life-size version of Broch's vacuum glass, sitting high in the Swiss Alps. Mann's sanatorium narrative projected the social topography of urban segregation onto the European landscape, dissecting proleptically the cultural effects of the war through the action of "all of us up here." The brief prelude and epilogue of the novel plotted the vertical metaphorics that underpinned its body; Mann depicted the disintegration of prewar society by inverting the standard narrative of descent. The novel begins with a sudden shift in perspective: once Hans Castorp has been "carried upward into regions where he had never before drawn breath and where he knew that unusual living conditions prevailed," then home, "sea-level," must henceforth be reimagined as below, underground.[169] The lengthy novel concludes with a second shift: the same "below" that had once meant "home and regular living" has now metamorphosed irrevocably into the trenches, where a shell blows the old image to bits, raising up "a fountain high as a house, of mud, fire, iron, molten metal, scattered fragments of humanity."[170] There is no middle ground, no ambivalence remaining after the shock of the war; Castorp returns below to find nothing but a slaughterhouse. The simile of the house drives home the theme of Mann's modernist allegory: the postwar choice between above and below, between unreal heights and unbearable depths, is baldly laid out; in this new world, the only middle ground left would be occupied by the likes of Broch's Huguenau.

Mann and Broch extrapolated a totalizing vision of the world from the topography of the trench city, an abstract space of pure representation. Céline's version was rooted in the representational space of nineteenth-century underground Paris, but remained equally abstract in the way it posited the inevitability of Bardamu's enlistment. In *Voyage au bout de la nuit*, by contrast, Céline had begun with the narrator's spontaneous and unexplained decision to volunteer. Céline's unprecedented use of argot harkened back to Sue's *Mystères de Paris*; the difference was that he eschewed the controlling framework of Sue's bird's-eye perspective and redemptive plotting. There was no Rodolphe, nor was there an outside narrative perspective, as there still remained in Broch and Mann. Céline's first novel thrust the reader almost immediately into a brutally anarchic and nihilistic episode in the trenches; he continued by applying the wartime experience to the rest of the modern world: a decomposing colonial outpost in West Africa; a mechanized and dehumanized New York and Detroit; and finally back to the outskirts of Paris to discover further horror in the banality of the petit-bourgeois expanse of the *banlieues*.

Representations of the First World War, both during and afterward, have tended to reduce it to the image of the trench, and then to press the trench into the service of visualizing a fixed image, midway between the aboveground of rationalized, middle-class life and the belowground of the incomprehensible. The firsthand reports that circulated from the late years of the war onward ran the gamut from German officer Ernst Jünger's cold-blooded aesthetic appreciation of the "Storms of Steel" to Henri Barbusse's comparison of the trenches to the passages of an old city, "joined up by innumerable galleries which hook and crook themselves like ancient streets"; to Erich Maria Remarque's contrast between the everyday experience of death and the official representation of it, epitomized in the titular irony of the protagonist's death on a day marked "nichts Neues"; to Céline's imagination of the war experience as the quintessence of the senseless destruction of modernity.[171] As Mary Jane Green writes, a primary goal of this literature was to explain life in the trenches as an experience wholly distinct from both nineteenth-century war and contemporary wartime propaganda; the trench as grave symbolized the change: "Many novels abound with images of dismembered bodies, devastated landscapes, and muddy trenches filled with human excrement—a vision of war summed up in the final scene of [Barbusse's] *Le feu*, where the opposing lines of trenches are dissolved into a sea of mud filled with bloated corpses."[172] The dual desire to make understood the inexpressibility of the intensity of the experience of war and to render it tolerably familiar echoes through the representation of the trenches as a city, the closest peacetime image to offer something approaching the same duality of above- and underground.

Still, if the later literary reaction to the war experience was one of polarized absolutisms, the representational space of the trenches themselves was rather more conflicted. In the contours it took, we can recognize a phenomenon analogous to that of the earlier *passage*, resulting from the presence of a novel technology and concomitant space with no sense of what forms might best suit it. The occupants' appropriation of the space of the modern city to make sense of the trenches occurred not only on the most obvious level of the negative underground, as in Céline's reading of the trench back into the arcade form, in Max Beckmann's comment on the "strangely unreal cities" of the western front, "like lunar mountains, cities of the dead, both the newly massacred and the long-since buried, hurled into the air time and again," and in the many other renderings of the trench as simply "one huge grave," to cite the painter Paul Nash's image (figure 4.32).[173] That the trench could find itself taking the form of a positively as well as a negatively subterranean city is testimony on the one hand to the power of the representation of space fed back to civilians, and on the other to the ability of the soldiers to appropriate this space to their own needs, to render what appears to have been an entirely uninhabitable environment into a lived space. On closer examination, the trench network commonly imagined and depicted as at best a web of underground warrens of death turns out to have been a veritable trench city, multilevel, multipurpose, and multivolitional, while the trench proper more closely resembled the *passage*, a threshold space to that city, dangerously open, than it did a sealed grave.

Although seldom discussed publicly at the time, there was an entire network of deep tunneling far below the level of the trenches, used in what is now called by military historians "the underground war," a war being waged simultaneously with the better known battles above.[174] Excavated at enormous financial and human cost by skilled teams of miners and navvies, the deep-level tunnels were designed both defensively, as bona fide shelters in contrast to the exposed trenches, and offensively, as a means of burrowing beneath and undermining enemy lines. In this perspective, the trenches begin to look enough like city streets to justify reading more than just a figurative significance into the streets names given to so many of them. Weaving their way through the complex long-term networks of dugouts and entrances to the tunnels below, the trenches had both the positive and the negative characteristics of the urban thoroughfare. Open to the skies, they

4.32 Paul Nash's nihilistic vision of the war: *Void.* Oil on canvas. 1918. National Gallery of Canada, Ottawa. Transfer from the Canadian War Memorials, 1921. Photo © National Gallery of Canada.

were exposed; for the same reason, they provided the only remaining link to the normal world, a space of encounter and mingling. Like an extreme version of the experience of the city, they enforced a terrifying proximity to violent death and to suffering, and they had highly developed codes for negotiating that proximity. As Alison Booth has documented, there was no fixed boundary between life and death, living body and corpses. On the one hand, soldiers would jokingly treat the bodies around them as if they were still alive; on the other hand, the very walls and floors of the trenches were composed of decomposing bodies and body parts.[175] Still, although city living forces its inhabitants to treat people as part of the cityscape, the trench experience pushed that paradox to unheard-of extremes. The space was similarly extreme: because excavated in the earth, the trenches were closer to the situation of the arcade or the tunnel, and could never be wholly assimilated to the city street, unless it be the street during a rainstorm, or perhaps a flood such as the one that had engulfed the streets of Paris in 1910.

Newspaper depictions of the trenches in the early days of the war wavered between novel forms of everyday life and tolerable forms of the life of war. A sketch of London omnibuses pressed into duty as troop transports was titled "From the

Bank to—: The London Motor–'Bus at the Front";[176] one should read the polysemous "—" either to refer to the anonymous location of the front or as the conventional euphemism for the not-to-be-spoken name of Hell. Photographs of the French trenches advertised "Capuan Ease . . . Heating Apparatus for a Shower-Bath" and showed the "*Bains de siège* in the trenches" (figure 4.33). A sketch entitled " 'Tommy' in the 'Rabbit-Warren' " employed a familiar figure of the English countryside to assert the trench experience as a version of animal leisure (figure 4.34).[177] To "beguile" the long wait between shelling, read the accompanying text, "Some of the British troops have been able to enjoy a game of football, and in the trenches they amuse themselves with cards and dominoes, reading and writing letters. They receive newspapers, and the postal arrangements are in good working order." The normality of the scene is belied only by the location of the dominoes game five feet below the surface of the earth; the trench is placed midway between everyday life and somewhere else entirely. It is noteworthy that the artist chose a moment of leisure time and a rural image—shades of Rat and Mole in *The Wind in the Willows* (1908)—to make the space recognizable. The business of war was much more resistant to appropriation as an aboveground activity.

It is likely, however, that the artist at the front had a somewhat different conception than the writer back at the newspaper, who imparted an anodyne ideology to the image quite at odds with the soldiers' own modes of appropriation. The metaphor of a "great military rabbit-warren," which the writer borrowed from military coinage, retains (if perhaps unintentionally) some of the horror that lurks behind the enforced leisure and implied joviality. The moment a rabbit sticks its head out of its warren, it is in grave danger of losing it. There is an eerie scene in the background of the image, in much smaller scale and not signaled by the text. A second row of trenches can be identified in the distance by the flames and smoke rising from it. Between that row and the domino players lie the corpses of a man

4.33 All the comforts of home: " 'Bains de Siège' in Trenches." *Illustrated London News*, 21 November 1914, 696.

4.34 Mixed underground metaphors: *In the Trenches at the Aisne: "Tommy" in the "Rabbit-Warren"*. Drawn by Caton Woodville from a sketch by a British officer. *Illustrated London News*, 10 October 1914, 501.

and a horse. Yet an officer stands in the trench at the center of the sketch, his cap sticking unrealistically far above ground level, his back to the carnage, eyes intent on the foreground, the scene of leisure. The mirror image of the yawning domino player is the background inferno into which his trench could at any moment be transformed, the urban chaos encroaching on the subterranean pastoral.

The trench life extended to the limit the already strong contradiction in the modern city between surviving traditions of country life, modern amenities, and the randomness of urban encounters and accidents. As Stéphane Audoin-Rouzeau and Annette Becker, Paul Fussell, and others have documented, the front was far less isolated from the everyday life of the country than has usually been supposed, especially for the soldiers who often journeyed back and forth across the Channel.[178] Daily mail service assured steady contact with friends and family (some eleven million letters weekly from Britain), and surviving letters indicate that even at the front soldiers continued to concern themselves with the everyday minutiae of the harvest or their children's grades in school.[179] Many units published newspapers—four hundred in the French lines alone.[180] Leave posts further from the front offered all the culture of the city—sports, cinema, theater, music hall. In a clash between metaphorical and actual battles, the YMCA, the Salvation Army, and the Church Army set up over four thousand rest huts, or "hutments," offering a Christian alternative to such decadent urban culture: sympathy, comfort, security, and doughnuts in a "home from home."[181]

All three major armies on the western front appear to have assimilated the trenches to their respective capital city, but there were differences in the extent to which they did so and in the meanings they gave to them. Although the majority of British troops came from cities, France was still predominantly rural, and its only deeply industrialized area lay on the border with Belgium, the first territory to be occupied by the Germans. Moreover, whereas the British readily appropriated to their own spatial practices the foreign land in which they found themselves, the French were fighting at home, and were more likely to assimilate the trenches as a different, but related, space to their nearby capital than as the thing itself. The invading Germans, finally, were renowned for the elaborate and deep trench systems, fortified in concrete, some wired for electricity and even heated.[182] Their urban symbolism was equally elaborate: one archival photo of a telephone dugout near the Belgian coast records an intricately carved wooden portal emblazoned with the name of the central Berlin monument to German nationalism, the Brandenburger Tor (figure 4.35). A model biplane on one corner completes the emblematic character of what is more a microcosmic sculpture than a mirror image of the city itself. The French had their own mining teams, although, to the British clay kickers at least, they only confirmed prejudice about the disorganization of their allies and their unfamiliarity with modern techniques: "To 178 Company's engineers, the French system they had inherited seemed full of Gallic unreason. Tunnels went at varying depths and in puzzling directions a few

4.35 German trench monumentalism. *A telephone dug-out and the "Brandenburger Tor" in a trench resting on the sea just east of Lombartzyde Bad.* Archival photograph. IWM negative no. Q. 49138. Reproduced by permission of the Imperial War Museum, London.

yards towards the enemy and stopped. . . . There were suspicious signs, too, that some of the tunnels were not where the French drawings showed them."[183] Falling back on conventional discourses about national character was another way of asserting the normality of an existence based on the lack of any distinction whatsoever, whether spatial, personal, or even corporeal.

The business of war appears in sketches such as "Buried Quick and Unburied Dead" (figure 4.36) that asserted the underground character of the trenches rather than their aboveground features as another way of making sense of the experience without making it so horrible as to be hopelessly alien. Here, the distinction is between "The buried alive: Tommy in his deep shelter" and the "Unburied dead: German dead hanging in the broken wire entanglements." The trench is asserted as an underground experience much closer to the surface than the truly otherworldly horror of being dead, unburied, and German: "It is a gruesome sight, but Tommy gets used to it, and, considering the bodies are German, he is not down-hearted." Again, a mirror image is presented and denied in the dark wordplay of "the buried alive"; how can the only reassurance offered be that the English are safely buried in their trenches and the Germans dead and unburied between lines? A background line labeled "German trenches" contains the subliminal reminder that the roles could just as easily be reversed. The true fear

4.36 Upper world distinctions: *Buried Quick and Unburied Dead: A Facsimile Battlefield Sketch by Our Artist, Frederic Villiers*, in *Illustrated London News*, 31 October 1914, 602–3.

is that there is no distinction whatsoever in the space of war, that these thresholds obliterated rather than segregated above- and belowground. Indeed, it was common practice to bury the dead of all nationalities together indiscriminately in trenches between the lines.[184]

A joke reported at the end of the notes to the sketch suggests that the humor and folklore of the soldiers cut closer to this truth than the journalistic representation:

> Obstacles of every kind abound, and at night each side can hear the enemy driving in pickets for entanglements, digging *trous-de-loup*, or working forward by sapping. In some places the obstacles constructed by both sides are so close together that some wag has suggested that each should provide working parties to perform this fatiguing duty alternately, since their work is now almost indistinguishable and serves the same purpose.

While the representation of war used the trench as a threshold to attempt to unite the civilians with the soldiers and assert distinctions between different spaces, nationalities, and states of existence, the representational space expressed by those within the trenches intimated a simpler truth: like rabbits in their warrens, the soldiers were indistinguishable from one another, whether French or German, English or Belgian. To those sitting above in command, able to encompass the theater of war in a panoramic, strategic view, they were interchangeable pieces, equal in life as well as in death. As the satanic black marketeer Harry Lime (Orson Welles) put it to his old friend Holly Martins (Joseph Cotten) from atop the

Prater wheel looking down on the children playing in the rubble of post–World War II Vienna in *The Third Man* (1949): "How much is each dot worth?"

Down below, however, as one historian phrases it, "it had become a strangely intimate war where the two sides could hear each other's shouts and sometimes smell each other's cooking."[185] Similarly, as Booth has observed, it was common practice for "impromptu truces" to be arranged, either by communication or by unspoken agreement, in order for wounded men to be removed from no-man's-land.[186] The space of the trench networks resembled the experience of the modern city, replete with spatial thresholds forcing one class to mix in uncomfortable intimacy with the other just as opposing sides of the conflict would have preferred to meet only in the traditional space of the open battleground, if at all. Silence was an even more terrifying situation than in the city, for it signified imminent explosion. The ability to continue waging war under such conditions required the acceptance of this hierarchical space to at least some degree, just as it necessitated a representational space wholly at odds with the traditional codes of antagonism still assumed by those in command and at home. The humor may have recognized the ghastly truth, but of necessity it distanced it as a pleasantry. The tales of "wild men" deserters living in trenches in no-man's-land and coming out at night to prey on bodies of both sides are the most extreme of such appropriations of space from below, but they uncannily duplicate the spatial dynamics of the truces and other humane practices that existed uneasily but permanently with the ones that made the combatants inhuman. The understandable urge simply to walk away from it all could be distanced only by representation as inhuman. Like Mumford, Broch took the same image and reversed it, making the inescapable dehumanization of the survivor into a metaphor for postwar society as a whole.

The lived space of the trench itself, like that of the city, was far more variegated than the symbol. Part of this is due to the censorship of the mining operations that limited their depiction in the press, part of it to the fact that the existence of a variegated space was counterproductive either for symbolizing the normality of the experience (trenches as almost an aboveground space) or its horror (trenches as grave). We find urban humor: a carefully stenciled German signpost pointing to "Marschstrasse 4" has been chalked out and underneath it a crudely cut sign has been nailed on which, scrawled in chalk like a graffito, the name of the legendary London rookery Seven Dials signals the changing control of the space (see figure 1.15). German trenches had generally nonurban designations; the English appropriation maintained, first, that the battleground was urban, and second, that it was a lower-class slum. The majority of the street names on the trenches belonged to the properly disciplined areas of West End London, centers of the new culture of leisure. Names like Piccadilly and Regent Street, which one finds on the official Ordnance Survey maps, would have had different resonances to different soldiers, but the overall image of a familiar environment would probably have predominated. "Seven Dials," scrawled in the heat of pursuit of the

NO ROAD

4.38 *"The Strand," Ploegsteert Wood, 19th November, 1915.* Archival photograph. IWM negative no. Q. 4143. Reproduced by permission of the Imperial War Museum, London.

German retreat to the Hindenburg Line in 1917, reproduces an urban identification closer to the reality of the space, less alluring but more defiant.

We also find in photographs of the trenches evidence of a much more complex infrastructure than is usually attributed to them. In the midst of what we would normally take as a ruin of dirt and debris, a functioning set of railway tracks is laid, with a warning sign insisting on the maintenance of good order: "No articles of any description to be dumped here." The photographer's caption reads, "Preparations for the Battles of Arras, 1917. Trench railway trucks at 'Oxford Circus'" (figure 4.37). Or the opposite extreme: a high, sandbagged bank shelters an almost normal-looking wooded scene, entitled, "'The Strand', Ploegsteert Wood" (figure 4.38). Whether the humor references the London street or a shoreline is unclear; only the duck-boarded walkways betoken the likely truth that these upright soldiers and leaf-filled trees might the next instant have been transformed into a trackless,

Facing page

4.37 Trench city: *Preparations for the Battles of Arras, 1917. Trench railway tracks at "Oxford Circus" on the outskirts of Arras.* Archival photograph. IWM negative no. Q. 5093. Reproduced by permission of the Imperial War Museum, London.

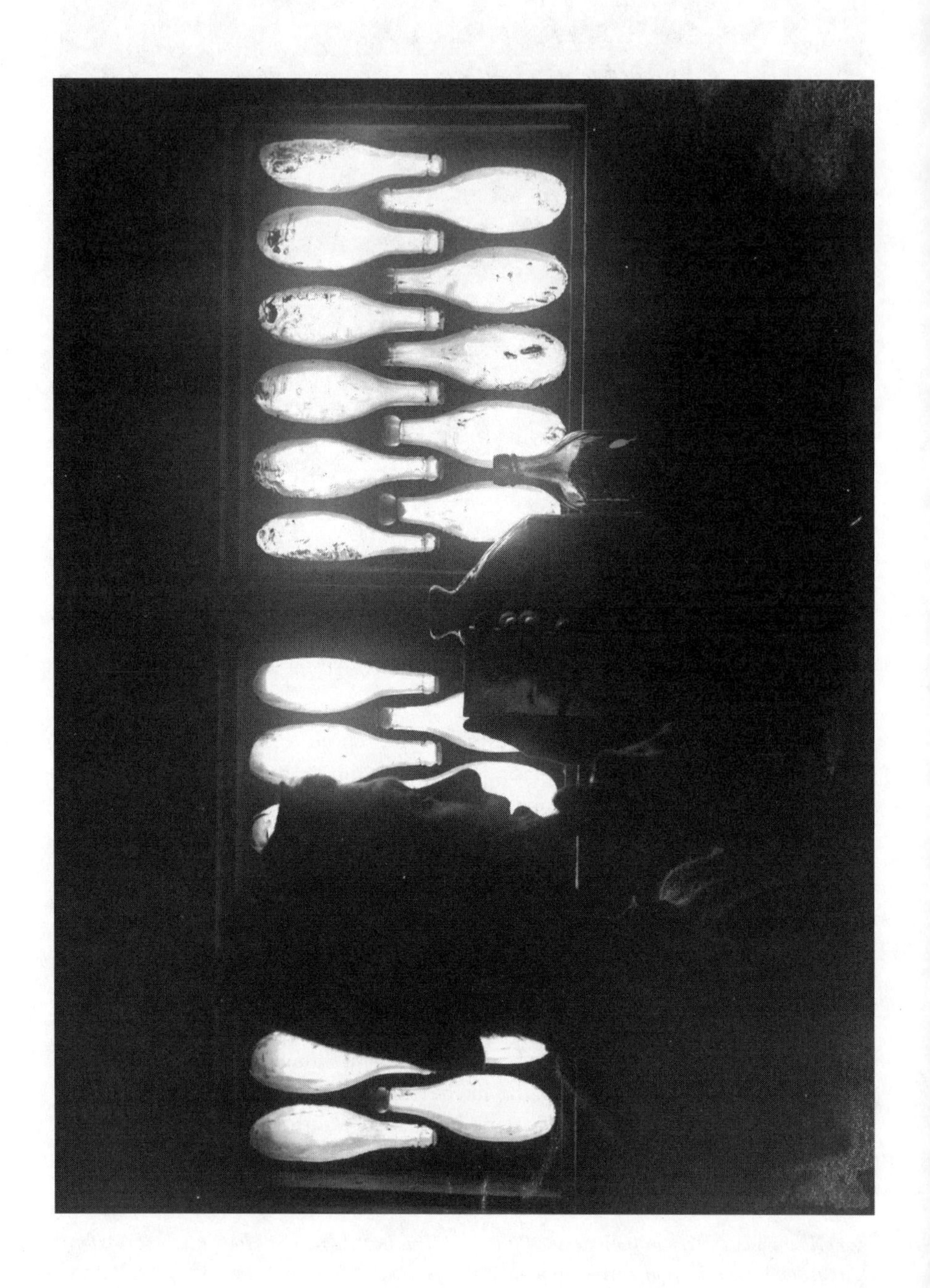

muddy wasteland. There were frontline trenches, reserve trenches, communication trenches, support trenches, and "saps," or short side routes. These were the streets of the city at war. The street network of the trenches led to dugouts, laid out in rows like houses, domestic, comfortable, and safe—in comparison, at least, with the more exposed trenches. An archival photo of a German underground dugout at Fricourt in 1916 shows the degree of domesticity achieved; it looks more like a pleasant bedroom in a normal house, with whitewashed wooden walls and ceiling, an iron-framed four-poster bed, and a framed mirror on the wall.[187] The underground may have been fragile, posing the ongoing threat of being buried alive, and it was certainly wet, muddy, and dark, but in its primary role as shelter it still nurtured a strongly positive connotation. In both aspects, it was more frequently a primordial space than a modern one, at least on the side of the Allies. At moments, it could even become a beautiful space, as in the lighting effect of the window created by rows of bottles pressed into the dugout clay (figure 4.39).

Tunnels took a number of forms. There were deep-tunnel dugouts and cut-and-cover shelters roofed over with "elephant" iron and covered with sandbags. A wide range of already existent spaces was incorporated into this underground city: the basements of ruined houses, the crypts of churches, mine craters, the lime quarries of Fresnoy, the catacombs of Comble, and the caves of the Aisne (figure 4.40). At Cambrai, vast cellars and tunnels sheltered civilians throughout the war. The most complex system was in the underground caves or *boves* of Arras, the extensive cellars characteristic of the houses of the region. In utmost secrecy, the British troops linked the *boves* with the underground sewers to form a subterranean network giving access to the middle of no-man's-land, and capable of accommodating "nearly 30,000 men, [with] lighting, ventilation, proper drainage, a power plant, administrative centers, and a hospital."[188] The positional war that locked the troops in place for years on end resulted in an urban space that exacerbated the already extreme experience of the modern city.[189] Horror at the brutality of the slaughter was countered by the extraordinary ability to maintain some semblance of the rituals of everyday life; the intensity of it all maimed and destroyed the lives of millions who did survive, but it left many others hungry for an experience unlike any other.[190]

It is easy to be cynical about the wartime ideology that installed "clean, dry, and well furnished" exhibition trenches in Kensington Gardens, or the related sensation-seeking nationalism that has made the multimedia "Trench Experience" an enduring success at London's Imperial War Museum.[191] Although both spectacles unavoidably diminish the sheer horror of the lived space of the

Facing page

4.39 Trench vernacular architecture. *An R.E. Dug-out window made of soda-water bottles and cement. Near Cambrai, 22nd February, 1918.* Archival photograph. IWM negative no. Q. 10697. Reproduced by permission of the Imperial War Museum, London.

4.40 Neotroglodytes at war: *The Cave-dwellers of the Aisne: A Subterranean Chamber Which Accommodated a Whole Squadron of British Cavalry As Well As Villagers.* Drawn by H. W. Koekkoek from sketches by British officers present at the battle of the Aisne. *Illustrated London News,* 24 October 1914, 568.

trenches, they succeed very well in familiarizing the few aspects of that space that could be made familiar for a public that still today seeks a common ground with it. One may wonder whether the submerged existence of everyday space within the trenches might not also offer a positive twist to the otherwise horrific phenomenon of trench tours that began being offered soon after the conclusion of hostilities, and have continued nearly unabated to this day. Here, again, a ghoulish voyeurism combined with a surely genuine urge for mourning to create a steady industry of leisure. Among others, Michelin had already published ten guides for such tours by 1919, combining hotel information, history, before-and-after pictures, battlefield maps, and the trademark touring directions, the aesthetically evaluative tone of which becomes positively chilling in such a context: "When coming from Ablain-St-Nazaire, the tourist, on reaching the crest of the massif of Notre-Dame-de-Lorette, sees a plateau absolutely devoid of any sign of life. The ground is a mere succession of shell-holes and mine-craters, with no *interesting* remains of the old German defences."[192] Handbooks to Paris included maps of the battlefields and information on day trips to reach them: "*Coulommiers.* (Rail, Est.) Celebrated for its cheese, and now much visited by excursionists to the battlefields of the Marne. The town was sacked by the Germans in the early days of the War, but retaken by British cavalry."[193] In 1921, the *Basel News* began offering the "unforgettable impressions" of a package tour to Verdun:

> In this small area, where more than a million men—perhaps a million and a half—bled to death, there is not a square centimeter of soil that is not exploded by grenades. . . . an unprecedentedly phenomenal panorama of horror and dread. . . . *You view* with a guide the subterranean casemates of Fort Vaux. *You visit* the Ossuaire (charnel house) of Thiaumont. . . . Wine, coffee, gratuities . . . everything included in the price.[194]

Viennese journalist and cultural critic Karl Kraus vented his indignation over "a document which transcends and seals all the shame of this age and would in itself suffice to assign the currency stew that calls itself mankind a place of honor in a cosmic carrion pit."[195] The underworld tour, long the restricted province of the wealthy, was reaching the middle classes just like so many other traditions of the leisured class.

In Elinor Glyn's 1924 novel, *Six Days*, and F. Scott Fitzgerald's *Tender Is the Night* (1939), set during the same decade, the obligatory tour became the setting for erotic awakenings and easy flirtations, just as the underground railway had done in the decades before the war. Fitzgerald used a brief episode to establish the theme of the third book of his novel, "Casualties." When Dick, Abe, and Rosemary visit a "neat restored trench" near Amiens in 1925, they play at trench warfare, argue over the significance of the Great War in military history, and parody D. H. Lawrence: " 'All my beautiful lovely safe world blew itself up here with a great gust of high explosive love,' Dick mourned persistently."[196] "The last love battle" shows love and war to be equally fickle and contradictory: Rosemary laughs and cries over the memorials just as her love for Dick "was upsetting everything, now that she was walking over the battlefield in a thrilling dream"; they meet a girl from Tennessee in tears of vexation over her inability to find her brother's grave, but a few hours later forgetting her sorrow and flirting with the two men. For Glyn, too, the threshold of the war brought together love and death, but she found in the trenches less a timely site to set off the mores of her age than the space of a mythic and transformative encounter with the underworld. When Major David Lamont of Washington Square meets up with the American heiress Laline Lester by chance in Paris, she tells him, "Why, it has been the ambition of my life to see a dug-out, and especially now I know there are almost none left, and all my friends who are coming over in the fall won't have the chance to get into one."[197] He undertakes to find her one, "safe to go down," and they set off alone in his car. He takes her to where he had fought, near the vanished village of Etticourt: "The Boche had made regular palaces! We thought ourselves darned lucky when we got in them."[198] They are chaperoned on their descent by an old priest, but the underground tour takes a classic narrative turn as a small bomb explodes, sealing them into the dugout and mortally wounding the priest, who survives just long enough to marry the young couple. They consummate their love, "happier . . . in the chilly wretched dug-out" than any bride and groom "by the Mediterranean sea,"[199] finally to be rescued a hundred pages later after five days underground, the pleasure of their life as neotroglodytes dampened only by the lack of food.

Although lighter in tone than Kraus's polemic, the Berlin humorist Arthur

Holitscher made it equally clear that the battlefield visit was not at all the exclusive province of the wealthy. In his 1925 collection of travel pieces, *Der Narrenbaedeker: Aufzeichnungen aus Paris und London* (*Baedeker Gone Mad: Sketches of Paris and London*), Holitscher narrated his experience as the only German amid a busload of Americans on a Thomas Cook tour of the trenches. He begins the piece by describing the advertising leaflets passed out on the street corners of Paris, listing a choice of five excursions ranging from the nearby Somme Battles (230 francs) to the two-day journey to "The Champagne, Argonne and Verdun Forts" (475 francs). Holitscher chooses the cut-rate visit to "Rheims and the Hindenburg Line," on which he is joined by the American national soccer team and a motley assortment of other Yankee tourists. The sketch includes descriptions of the "Kreidekrater," where "countless skeletons of all nations lie," and where nature is slowly reasserting herself in the form of scattered flowers; a visit to an underground bunker on the Hindenburg Line, where a previous visitor has left behind the graffito "Akron, Ohio, is the prettiest city of U.S.A."; and the high point of the tour, champagne tasting in the historic cellars of Mumms.[200]

Holitscher takes a tone of general cynicism about humanity, mixed with a more specific anti-Americanism, presumably tailored for his German audience. The principal irony, like Kraus's, is based on the idea of Thomas Cook operating tours to a place of slaughter. Holitscher is less concerned with the war as such than with the underground life left behind and apparently determined by it. He quotes in full the guide's wide-eyed description of the cellars, used as shelters during the war: "In these cellars, which extend for eighteen miles under the earth, thousands of citizens of Rheims, men, women, old and young, lived for four entire years. Men were born here and died here. Churches, morgues, schools, living spaces were erected in these cellars, which today are the property of the Société Vinicole, formerly Mumm Boche."[201] The tour quickly degenerates into advertising for champagne, and a discussion of the profitability of bootlegging. Degeneracy is also the keynote of the visit to the Hindenburg Line, which Holitscher can only imagine as the work of a society of cave dwellers: "We descend deep beneath the earth. Was this built by men? Or prehistoric creatures? Some contemporary of Cro-Magnon-man, or of Aurignac-man?"[202] Clearly the Great War had not only added to the stupidity of tourism, but it had hastened the decline of civilization, of which the American composition of the group, whether demographically accurate or not, was certainly symbolic. Equally noteworthy is the degree to which every aspect of the tour is subterranean. Similar to the baleful predictions of Mumford and the antiurban pessimism of Spengler, a combination of trench warfare and urban modernity was seen to have taken over and to be determining every aspect of postwar society. As Virginia Woolf's narrator muses about the shell-shocked veteran and eventual suicide in *Mrs. Dalloway*, "London has swallowed up many millions of young men called Smith; thought nothing of fantastic Christian names like Septimus with which their parents have thought to distinguish them."[203] The analogy between London and the trenches as consumers of millions of young men is simply understood.

An analogous transformation in the social space of Europe is testified to in the final volume of Proust's *A la recherche du temps perdu.* As in the case of Hans Castorp's descent from the Alps into a changed Europe in *The Magic Mountain,* the narrator in *Le temps retrouvé* returns from an extended stay at a sanatorium to a Paris transformed into a wholly underground space, dark, labyrinthine, and dangerous. The Paris sequence concludes the long process of the narrator's discovery of a second city beneath the one he had known that began in *Sodome et Gomorrhe* as a metaphor for homosexuality. For Marcel, the wartime experience literalizes the moral landscape developed in the earlier volume. In response to the air raids, the shocking consequence of the German offensive of May 1918, which had moved their big guns within range of the capital for the first time, "Others were tempted not so much by the thought of recovering their moral liberty as by the darkness which had suddenly settled upon the streets. Some of these, like the Pompeians upon whom the fire from heaven was already raining, descended into the passages of the Métro, black as catacombs."[204] The liminal space of the darkened Métro issues out to cloak the entire city in another, underworld level of meaning: Jupien affects nervousness only "so as to have a pretext, as soon as the sirens sounded, to rush into the shelters in the Métro, where he hoped for pleasure from brief contact with unseen figures."[205] For Proust, as for many others, the war signaled an unavoidable shift from conceiving the underground as a distinct space, either a hidden world of signs and metaphors or a separate physical realm, to accepting it as a dominant feature of everyday life. This was a lasting effect of trench warfare and the preexistent developments of urban modernity appropriated by it; in this the trenches functioned not only spatially but also as a temporal threshold from one subterranean era to the next—thus in the lines that form this section's epigraph the poet Miguel Hernández could use the image of the trench to sum up the horrors of the new war in Spain.

Thresholds of Stage and Screen

> As for the Roxy, it exceeds the impossible. . . . The devil has hung this disused sanctuary with red velvet; a nightmarish light falls from imitation alabaster sconces; lanterns in yellow glass, ritual chandeliers. . . . It's better than a black mass, it's a profanation of everything; of music, art, love, color. I can say that in this place I had a complete vision of the end of the world.
>
> PAUL MORAND, *New York* (1929)

In the early days of the conflict, we find another representation of the space of war as a threshold between reality and the unimaginable, the place where metaphors become realized. Entitled " 'The Theatre of War'! The Strangest Entertainment the Stage Has Seen," this newspaper piece published just three months into the war sketched the proscenium-arched stage of the Opera House of Le Mans, in the background a painted backdrop of an eighteenth-century English garden, at the foot of which were laid out several dozen soldiers draped in blankets (figure 4.41). Most of them are sleeping, but a few lean up against the wall of the stage, watching a soldier in front of a row of gaslights, declaiming to a further group of soldiers stretched out in the parterre. To the left of the sketch, a trio of officers sits in a luxurious box, enjoying and applauding the performance. "The boxes, pit, galleries, and the stage itself were used for shake-downs for the men, who seemed to be supremely comfortable and happy in their novel surroundings," asserted the caption. As the metaphor always implied, the theater is a space within which the readership could comprehend the experience of the soldiers. War takes a familiar space and transforms it. The soldier's recitation expresses the pleasure in stepping out of the role for which the space was appropriated, and into its accustomed place. Many of the other soldiers play along, especially those in the box, enjoying a privilege they were unlikely to have experienced back in England. The perspective of the sketch gives the reader the point of view of an audience, within which "theater of war" takes on another meaning. The incident is presented as an unreal spectacle. Just as it brought to-

4.41 *"The Theatre of War"! The Strangest Entertainment the Stage Has Seen.* Drawn by S. Begg from a sketch by Frederic Villiers. *Illustrated London News*, 24 October 1914, 578–79.

gether the classes in London to watch realistic spectacles of the world around it, so the theater served here to bring together the home front with the underground life of the soldiers, a novel way of making sense of the war.

The same metaphor used here in the early days of the war to assert the safely spectacularized nature of the conflict could equally be turned against the naiveté of the home front. In her analysis of Siegfried Sassoon's cynical poem "Blighters" (1917) Booth shows how the double meaning of the word "show" is used to criticize the public's blind acceptance of the war as a nationalistic spectacle: "tier beyond tier they grin / And cackle at the Show."[206] In military slang, "show" means attack, a derivation no doubt from the longstanding metaphor of the theater of war. At the same time, Sassoon's understandable bitterness belies the equally powerful (if tragically ineffectual) assertion of control contained in the appropriation of the language of spectacle to describe the suicidally nonspectacular order to attack. Not only is a familiar and relatively unthreatening threshold space—the theater—substituted for the deadly threshold of the no-man's-land of the front but the substitution places the soldiers in the role of actors rather than general's pawns or Harry Lime's dots. To be sure, the agency of the actor is barely more than that of the pawn, and a far cry from the control of all vantage points in the bivouac scene reproduced in the *Illustrated London News*. Nevertheless, the linguistic gesture demonstrates a desire for meaning, for the empty, alien space of the front to become a space replete with social relations, with an audience to appreciate the performances taking place, for a connection between the hell of the trenches and the paradise of the high, cheap stalls back in London.

The spectacular theater favored during the nineteenth century had been a formative influence on the imagination of the urban underground, both in its predominance as a subject and as a setting and in the spatial dynamics of the space itself so easily appropriated in the examples above.[207] As Wolfgang Schivelbusch has documented, the social space of the early modern auditorium was gradually superseded by isolated but more densely packed individuals in a darkened theater facing an ever more brightly lit stage.[208] The dominant proscenium arch framed the increasingly realistic and often localized spectacle scenes, opening a vista onto another world that was both escapist and close to home. By the beginning of the twentieth century, most of the spaces that had served as thresholds for so many fantasies about the new city had become familiar and domesticated, their sensations represented as ever more belonging to the past rather than the present, beneath the feet, but distant in time. The theater had by now likewise sanitized its underworld image, while the subterranean space of crime, poverty, and novel modernity had migrated to an enduring afterlife in the new popular underworld of the nickelodeon, at first one among many novelty vaudeville attractions within theaters and other exhibition spaces. In the schematic but spatially accurate words of one urban historian, "The early cinema, still violent and rudimentary, attracts the crowd, leaving to the theater the quality public."[209] In this way, as Giuliana Bruno's argument suggests, the early cinema participated in the "new spatio-visuality" of the "arcades, railways, department stores, exhibition halls, among others, [which] incarnated the new geography of modernity—all were sites of transit."[210] It is important, however, to note the century-long time span incorporated into Bruno's synchronic argument about "sites of transit" in modernity; for, far from being fixed, the threshold identity she identifies tended in fact to migrate from one space to the next as the novelty of each particular manifestation wore off. Like the nineteenth-century popular theater before it, the space of the early cinema was more readily assimilated to the underground than to the world above, while its coexistence as one among many attractions in fairgrounds, vaudeville, music halls, café concerts, and theaters kept the movies out of the dark, and within the nineteenth-century tradition of spectacles of technologically created illusion.

The Great War allowed the United States to gain a stranglehold on the industry that it would never relinquish, but already in the prior decades it had been showing signs of wresting away from London and Paris the dominant role in inventing and imagining uses for new technology those cities had enjoyed in the previous century. The penny arcade, in which rows of Edison's kinetoscopes lined a long narrow hallway as shops had lined those of the previous century, proliferated in the decade between 1895 and 1905. Each machine played a separate film loop on a separate screen for a separate spectator. The other early purpose-built exhibition space for film, the nickelodeon, began in Pittsburgh in 1905 and quickly spread through America and Europe.[211] Basically a long narrow room with a white or silver screen painted at one end, a projection booth at the other, and spectators seated on rudimentary wooden benches or seats, the nickelodeon was, as film historian Francis Lacloche notes, a transitional structure.[212] Just as the industry had yet to find the perfect narrative and technical package to replace the hodgepodge cornucopia of early film topics, so had it not yet found the best venue for projecting those packages as the underworld dream of millions.[213]

During the war years, the darkened, enclosed space of the movie theater as we know it today replaced the variety show spectacle of the early cinema. Such effects had already been experimented with in the nineteenth-century technology of the panorama and the diorama, what was called the "visual tunnel," a space lined with black cloth between the audience and the picture that created the illusion of infinity in the image and made the viewer feel as if he or she was inside the scene depicted.[214] As electrification replaced gaslight in the city from the 1880s onward, the absolutely dark interior equally became a possibility; however, it was resisted in theatrical auditoriums, which have continued to favor sufficient light for the audience at least to remain visible: "The social desire to see and be seen has survived in the theater, despite illusionism, realism and naturalism."[215] While the theater clung to its outmoded threshold identity even as its audience dwindled, the cinema's more extreme contrast between the illuminated screen and the invisible audience more closely paralleled the external divisions of the metropolis between the brightly lit wealthy areas and main streets and the darkness of the outdated technology that barely lit the poorer quarters—"a step into the side streets and you felt set back by centuries," as one journalist put it.[216] The Great War may, as Schlör observes, have temporarily darkened the capitals of Europe, but not the new space of the cinemas.[217] Left at home, Englishwomen went in droves to ever larger and more luxurious cinemas; by the '20s the new movie palace had truly come to dominate the big cities.[218] By 1914, there were 1,000 purpose-built cinemas and converted theaters in France alone; there were a further 500 by the end of the war, 2,400 in 1920, and an astonishing 4,374 in 1928, predominantly in the industrial north.[219] In retrospect, the penny arcade and the nickelodeon look like the last gasp of the nineteenth-century commodity culture described by Benjamin and rooted in the arcade; the movie palace united the pieces of that culture within a characteristically occluded modern threshold space that functioned more as a mausoleum than a space of transit: "The cinema auditorium would not be a new city agora for the living where immigrants from the whole world might gather and communicate with one another; it was much more of a cenotaph, and the essential capacity of cinema in its huge temples was to shape society by putting order into visual chaos."[220] The movie palace and the narratives it screened were the threshold spaces of the city whose streets had been emptied into the battlefields of the First World War.

The war dead continued to served as liminal figures on the border between life and death. While the trench tours promised a katabasis into the space they had actually inhabited, the memorials to the missing soldiers that greeted the visitors at each battleground suggested a more equivocal threshold between the world of the living and the realm of the dead. Eschewing any use of sculpture or other ornamentation, the arches and colonnaded arcades characteristic of memorial architecture provided, as Booth has phrased it, "the architectural boundaries of empty space."[221] Their only individual feature is the tens of thousands of names of soldiers whose bodies would never be retrieved, with the largest of these memorials, at Thiepval, Passchendaele, Arras, Loos, and Pozières, towering over the empty landscapes around them like thresholds leading nowhere. Nevertheless—and here the materialism of Booth's argument fails, I think, to capture the equivocal power of these monuments—the residual spatial promise of the arch to lead to another world precisely captures the desire of the survivors of the war to retain some manner of connection with those who were lost, even as the failure of the arches and arcades to lead anywhere in any physical sense relegated those desires to an entirely spiritual dimension, as well as giving the lie to the triumphal arches of the past that were their primary iconographic referent.

Barbusse imagined his "still-living companions . . . laid out in strange upright coffins of mud."[222] Vera Brittain similarly terms the world she saw while nursing the wounded "a kingdom of death, in which the poor ghosts of the victims had no power to help their comrades by breaking nature's laws."[223] To the convalescent soldiers under her care, however, her tired materialism is less persuasive than the anecdotes they exchange about the help they receive from the ghosts of their "mates as was knocked out on the Somme in '16."[224] One of these anecdotes rose to the status of popular legend when it was enshrined after the war in a best-selling *Image d'Epinal* (popular color illustrations that had been produced by the Imagerie of Epinal since the eighteenth century): *Debout les morts!* (*Get Up, Dead Men!*) recounted the resurrection of a dead legion of French soldiers to put the Germans to flight.[225] A frequent motif of trench writing was to resurrect the dead soldiers in consolation or recrimination, usually for either a literal or a figurative march to the capital city. Through "psychic photography," the dead were shown hovering over the cenotaph at Whitehall on Armistice Day in 1922. Roland Dorgelès, author of the influential war novel *Les croix de bois* (1919), imagined in his later novel *Le retour des morts* (1926) that the dead have risen from their graves to see whether the wrongs and injustices of the world have been righted; they besiege Paris in anger at what they find.[226] In G. W. Pabst's similarly pacifist film, *Kameradschaft* (1931), French miners buried alive on the Franco-German border are rescued by the heroic tunneling of their putative enemies, hands meeting through the subterranean rubble to seal the symbolism of the pan-European gesture (figure 4.42).[227]

Many artists and writers explicitly invoked the Christian iconography of the Apocalypse; as Winter has persuasively argued, "the period of the 1914–18 war was the apogee of spiritualism in Europe," and the religious significance of eschatology persisted into much of the putatively secular art and literature of the next two decades.[228] In his idiosyncratically Christian novel *Descent into Hell* (1937), for example, Charles Williams applied an eschatological framework to the middle-class London suburb of Battle Hill, haunted by the urban ghosts of the excluded poor and victims of the war trapped within the "anguished" history of its eponymous topography, a threshold leading straight to hell.[229] Stanley Spencer's painting *Resurrection* (1924–26) depicted the dead rising from their tombs in his beloved village of Berkshire, the Thames in the background serving as the river Styx that the souls are soon to cross (figure 4.43).[230] We find spiritualism negatively invoked in Edgar Ulmer's art-deco horror film *The Black Cat* (1934). Set in a modernist mansion built by a retired officer-architect (Boris Karloff) atop the site where he had betrayed his troops to mass slaughter, the film pitted the officer's former comrade (Bela Lugosi) against Karloff in a battle over past injustice with an innocent American couple as hapless pawns. As members of Karloff's devil-worshipping coven arrive for a black mass in the delirious climax, the narrative shatters into incoherence but the spatial metaphorics remain crystal clear. An impossibly long spiral staircase leads from the living quarters of the house to the labyrinthine catacombs wherein lie the ruins of the army fortress and the laboratory where Karloff has embalmed the body of Lu-

4.42 Enemies make peace underground in G. W. Pabst's *Kameradschaft* (1931). Frame enlargement. Nero-Film AG. BFI Films: Stills, Posters, Designs.

4.43 Great War spiritualism: the dead rise in Stanley Spencer's painting *Resurrection* (1924–26). Reproduced by permission of the Tate Gallery, London. © Tate, London 2006.

gosi's wife, whom he had apparently murdered while Lugosi was in prison. In the inevitable conclusion, the mansion and all the history it contains is demolished in a great conflagration; the only survivors are the young Americans, who find their way back to town and conclude their honeymoon in a setting less haunted by the subterranean past. To be sure, there were as many if not more artists, such as Beckmann and Nash above, who focused on the purely nihilistic aspect of apocalypse, but especially in the popular culture to which the ghost images of the cinema equally appertain, there is much evidence of a powerful imaginative link between the desolate trenches, the modern city, and the movie palace.

The most explicitly cinematic of these gestures were those of the two versions of Abel Gance's antiwar epic, *J'accuse* (figure 4.44). In the first version (1918–19), the dead march on Paris, demanding to know whether their sacrifice had been in vain; in the second version (1937), they march in order to prevent another war. The special effect of double exposure brought the ghostly souls literally out of their graves and into the dark Paris cinemas. Paul Virilio has argued, grandiosely but plausibly, that Gance was enacting the close connection between the cinema and war, that the enduring form proper to the wartime technology tried out in the trenches turned out to be the movie palace. The serials, B movies, and "quota-quickies" of the movie-palace matinee between the wars retained the spectacular content of the theater and serial novels of the nineteenth century, as well as the condensed threshold spaces of the arcades, but within a new sort of subterranean space:

> After 1914, while old Europe was being covered with cenotaphs, indestructible mausoleums and other monuments to the glory of its dead millions, the Americans, who

4.44 The dead march on Paris in Abel Gance's antiwar epic *J'accuse* (1937). Frame enlargement. BFI Films: Stills, Posters, and Designs.

> had suffered fewer losses, were building their great cinema temples—deconsecrated sanctuaries in which, as Paul Morand put it, the public sensed the end of the world in an ambience of profanation and black masses. A number of studies have recently been made of this wave of cinema palaces which spread throughout the world and finally came to an end around 1960. Their abrupt disappearance clearly shows their historical necessity in the period between the two wars which, in reality, were but one conflict interrupted by a kind of twenty-year armistice.[231]

Virilio's speculation combines the economic truth that the destruction of Europe allowed the United States to begin its dominance of the film industry—in the words of screenwriter and novelist Anita Loos, "World War One was the reason for Hollywood"—with a Mumfordian observation of the close technological relationship between the gun and the movie camera, the constant application of the cinematic apparatus to military purposes before and since, and a pessimistic cultural criticism of the power of images to mold society. The argument is encapsulated in a phrase Virilio attributes to Gance, "Abandon hope all ye who enter the hell of images."

The darkness of the movie palace brought a new literality to the otherworld identity of the theater that dated back to the hellmouth, the dominant stage set of

the medieval passion play, and the "gods" or *paradis* of the upper circles where the cheapest seats were to be had in the secular, postmedieval theater. Whereas the theater had provided an image of the afterlife, similar to the medieval otherworld visions where the kings feed off dust while the poor feast, where the low sit above the high while enjoying the same spectacle, the movie palace, along with the Hollywood narratives it projected, brought a democratic ideology to the same impossible promise of felicity for the disenfranchised. Rather than a threshold where all classes mingled and played with different identities, this was an otherworld where all were equally in the dark. Nor was it any longer a wholly threatening descent into hell; the novelty of sitting with a crowd in darkness was short lived, and the movie palace was successfully marketed as a safe, middle-class underworld, full of safe, middle-class dreams—the same for all—instead of the disordered variety of the sensation scenes of the early silent movies in the sinister nickelodeon. The lingering threat of the descent was psychic—the thrill of the plot, the power of identification—rather than physical.

The movie palace offered exotic and dreamlike décor and at least a simulacrum of luxury while the lights were up, placing the audience in a proper state of relaxed distraction for the dreams to come when the lights went down. For Virilio, the audience targeted by this new dreamworld was what was left of the urban population after soldiers had been mobilized by the war, a mobilization that for him, as for many, persisted as a state of mind throughout the interwar period:

> The cinema trance, like that of the combatant, rested upon a certain kind of social suffering, the daily grind to which life was reduced in over-populated suburbs where East met West without merging in civic fellowship. In whatever way, the target population was that "shapeless sociological conglomerate" of the military-industrial proletariat, which was calmly summoned to factory and battlefield at a time when the "Bolshevik threat" stretched from Munich to the gates of India and when the Americans expected to wake up every day with the Russians camped in Paris.[232]

We should thus regard the movie palace and the absolute reign over popular culture of the cinema between the wars as the unrecognized counterpart to the battlefield tours of the same years: the latter took the crowds out to the corpseless ruins of the trench city; the former produced displaced and sanitized versions of the trench experience within the space of the city itself, its images inculcating a dream of order and rationality just as the trenches could be seen to dictate the obedience of the troops to the commands of their superiors.

As popular architecture, the movie palace for the most part slipped under the radar of the primary debate between the proponents of the international style, which privileged new materials, whiteness, and the new transparency of structure permitted by skeletons of steel and reinforced concrete wrapped in glass, and the expressionists, mostly German, who privileged emotions, irrationally curved lines and angles, and the use of glass for its evocative qualities.[233] The international style aimed to eliminate the distinction between interior and exterior just as it aimed to eliminate any form of darkness, leaving the mire of the war and the nineteenth century far behind it. By contrast, expressionist buildings, such as war veteran Erich Mendelsohn's Einstein Tower (1920–21), were, as Booth has documented, controversial precisely because of the way their distortions of rational spaces and forms seemed to reflect the experience of the war.[234] By the end of the next war, the utopianism of the international style would have settled down into the lingua franca of urban brutalism, just as the iron-and-glass glories of the Crystal Palace and the central Paris market were adapted to the efficient functionality of the factory and warehouse. Like the murky *passages* of the nineteenth century, the often-unrealized and soon forgotten fever dreams of the expressionists were more concerned with creating thresholds than with eliminating them. The *passages* were intended to slow passersby down rather than to hasten them along; the organic visions of architects such as Hermann Finsterlin, in which Le Corbusier, for example, saw "viscous ejaculations recalling underwater horrors, or . . . viscera, or impure acts of beasts,"[235] seemed designed to counter the rationalization of space, to find some way of reproducing the dark truths of the trench experience in the space of the city. One of the showpieces of expressionism was Hans Poelzig's Grosses Schauspielhaus (1919), whose columns and arcades appear to ooze stalactites, a theater for cultured neotroglodytes, as if the German elite were meant finally to discover what it had actually been like down in the trenches. The movie palaces conjured a similarly subterranean feeling in their theaters, but the darkness in which their audiences would sit had little of the threatening irrationality so many critics found in expressionism; whatever threat was left to these thresholds was displaced and contained within the sensational narratives on the movie screens.

Notwithstanding Virilio's apocalyptic reading of the Hollywood apparatus, the movie palace presents a threshold to more underground meanings than simply an eternity of damnation to capitalism. The next generation always finds its nostalgia in the ruined dreams of the previous one, whether the anarchic imagination of early cinema or the baroque extravagance of the movie palace in today's world of multiplexes and digital technology. Benjamin found the key to the crises of Weimar Berlin in the past history of the Parisian *passage*.[236] The surrealists similarly used the derelict arcades to reveal the hidden thresholds within the modern city; André Pieyre de Mandiargue celebrated in the three-level 1843 passage de Pommeraye in Nantes, for example, the same "submarine" quality that had led his Parisian colleagues to meet for years in the Bar Certa in the passage de l'Opéra. For André Breton, the movies were not so monolithic as many histories would have us believe; during the years of movie palace domination, he found that the continuous programming of the *cinéma du quartier* still held forth the possibility of "chance encounters," glimpses of truth both on the screen and in the audience.[237] The great and unrealized dream of the surrealists, like that of Dada, was to dissolve the city until nothing remained but thresholds. The other great dream of the period between the wars, the dream from above, was to eliminate the threshold altogether. In his proposals for the "Transformation of Paris," the urbanist and inventor of the freeway Eugène Hénard found a new use for the Palais-Royal as for many of the landmarks of Paris. Emptied of history and only of interest to nostalgic tourists, he argued, the space beneath the Palais could house a central station of the Métro and the gardens themselves could be bisected by a new east-west axis of the city, the Avenue du Palais-Royal.[238] The movie palace can indeed be seen to mirror the military-industrial complex as in Virilio's argument, but faced with proposals of the extremity of Hénard's, it also can be said to have represented between the wars one of the few overt spaces remaining of the middle ground. In every aspect of urban representation, the underground had been temporally displaced from the city into the mythic past, spatially displaced into the countryside, or materially displaced until illegible as such. The London arch, entry and exit to the cinema, had replaced the Parisian passage as the quintessential urban space, giving way to an *entre-deux-guerres* that was, as Benjamin lamented, woefully lacking in threshold experiences.

The Threshold of a New Millennium

> They have begun to move. They pass in line, out of the main station, out of downtown, and begin pushing into older and more desolate parts of the city. Is this the way out? . . . No, this is not a disentanglement from, but a progressive *knotting into*—they go in under archways, secret entrances of rotted concrete that only looked like loops of an underpass . . . and it is poorer the deeper they go . . . ruinous secret cities of poor, places whose *names he has never heard* . . . the walls break down, the roofs get fewer and fewer and so do the chances for light.
>
> THOMAS PYNCHON, *Gravity's Rainbow* (1973)

The view from below dressed up current crises in the clothing of old demons, new urban settings with old gothic plotting. The view from above wrapped up novel goods and technology in the familiar trappings of a halting devil. Both stances used a representation of subterranean space to conceptualize the dizzying experience of the rapidly modernizing metropolis. The arches and arcades of London and Paris combined new technology and architectural forms with familiar domestic desires, and became the primary thresholds of a new intermingling of classes and sexes. Although the spaces that gave rise to all three modes of representing the modern metropolis have long since ceased to play the central roles they did in the imagination of Paris and London during the nineteenth century, the modes of representation themselves have persisted, and even given rise to a revival of interest in the outmoded spaces, subterranea, devils, and thresholds of the twenty-first-century city.

The thresholds of the new millennium are virtual: the gateways and portals of the information highway that promise high-speed access to everything the contemporary world has to offer without ever leaving the space of the home. Like all thresholds, however, Internet connections raise new terrors in the same gesture as they allow greater segregation. Unsolicited pop-ups leach through the wires and onto the words one is typing, warning of the very intrusion they have just performed, and promising to eliminate the means of their own livelihood. More insidious worms, parasites, and Trojans take root in your system, broadcasting its secrets to waiting information technology raiders, or sending out virus-laden e-mails bearing your own return address, blaming you for crashing the systems of your friends, colleagues, and superiors. Pornography, junk mail, and other spam overflow and crash your e-mail inbox, but so-called filter programs cannot distinguish the genuine from the bogus, and the aboveground ends up deleted as often as the underground makes it way through. Viruses are the new demons of this virtual space, let loose through the World Wide Web by a sometimes prankster, sometimes militant underground of hackers and rebels aghast at the new controls and regulations and the ever-greater appropriation of cyberspace by the forces of capital as the multinationals find the most efficient form of this new technology for the accumulation and distribution of capital. The newer and explicitly materialistic adware is equally opposed to regulation and systematization as it mines cracks in software security for the precious ore of information. Like the iron-and-glass architecture of the early arcades, the quirky and idiosyncratic utopia of the early Internet has been overtaken by a monumental architecture built of the same technology—the streamlined information technology synergy of AOL Time Warner, of Microsoft, and of that pseudoorganic alternative, the Apple Macintosh and the ubiquitous iPod—and a seedy, demonized underworld.

The mysteries of the Internet—so accessible and yet so limitless, so private and yet so open to the world, so secure and yet so vulnerable—provide a coded representation adequate to the new spaces of the twenty-first century. Global space, a conception of space with no discernible ties to the traditional nation-state or to physical geography, cannot accurately be represented through a verticalized conception of space in the way that the new urban spaces could be during the nineteenth century, or even, if in a more abstract manner, in the modernist city of the early twentieth century. The Internet's uncanny combination of plenitude, danger, and endless repetition has replicated the urban mysteries' view from below for a new middle-class audience, able safely to surf the world without ever actually stepping out into it. The myriad nooks and crannies of cyberspace conceal many truths about the actual mysteries of global space, although the answers to those mysteries always lie in the physical spaces beyond the virtual spaces where they are able to be represented. Moreover, the greatest mysteries are so well known as to constitute truisms and clichés, yet at the same time so effectively severed from their role in the new global space that even their appearance as oppression, injustice, and corruption on thousands of Web pages does nothing to reveal these connections to the world at large.

Cities still power the global thresholds of the Internet: massive urban power stations located at the densest concentrations of usage enable the transmission of countless electronic signals every second. No matter their nonexistence in spatial representations, Internet providers and virtual companies headquarter in cities, near their youthful workforces and near the vibes that will cue them into the next big thing. The factories producing the goods trafficked over the Internet are far out of sight physically as well as conceptually, tucked away in autonomous free-trade zones all over the developing world. Tax-free, fortified, and self-policed, these new spaces have all but eliminated the thresholds between their production facilities and the spaces around them; only commodities emerge. For most of the planet's inhabitants, these amplified and streamlined sweatshops are their only contact with the consumer utopia of the first world—until, that is, the desperate employees try to disguise themselves as commodities, shipping themselves into the West in cargo containers, the backs of trucks, and railway freight cars.

Beyond the utopian images of the entertainment industry, the most recognizable and widespread icon of the promise of the West—unless we give the nod to the fantasy world of Walt Disney's mouse—has long been the Golden Arches of McDonald's restaurants, nearly thirty thousand franchises worldwide, over half of them outside of the United States.[239] Like the thresholds of children's stories past and present from Alice's rabbit-hole and Nesbit's arch to the platform at King's Cross that inaugurates the world of Harry Potter, and like the train stations of old, the Golden Arches are a threshold into another world of wish fulfillment and instant gratification. And like the London arches of old, they are all business: you walk in, pay your money, consume your moment of escape, and walk back out into the real world.[240] The demonization of McDonald's and other icons of global capitalism testifies to the unsatisfactory nature of the gratification they offer, just as the proliferation of the mysteries genre in popular culture, of subterranean settings in film, of satanism and its fashions within and outside of traditional religion testifies to the unsatisfied desires of the majority of the inhabitants of the twenty-first century. But there is no longer any integral link between the vertical city and the encroachments of capital. The city is now a site of spectacle—whether it be massive antiglobalization and antiwar rallies, slumming tourism, shopping, or fodder for movie, television, and computer screens—where discarded modes are revived in search of and also to exploit the desires they contained that were never fulfilled. The initial charge is gone, however, and this is why cultural critics generally see nothing but empty images or, as Perry Anderson cynically termed the massive global peace demonstrations of February 2003, "the fixations of the fan club, the politics of the spectacle, the ethics of fright."[241]

Still, while logically incoherent, clichéd, and in itself empty, the mobilization of the oppositional imagery associated with the underground city of the past two centuries does serve as a reminder of the affective power that continues to adhere to these outmoded forms for want of a better place to go—after all, the international opening of a new McDonald's inspires not only vocal protests but mile-long queues to get in.[242] To discard everything but the most current spatial conceptions is to accept only those conceptions that most powerfully and consistently represent and thus disguise and augment the operations of capital and oppression. I would be the first to argue that the nineteenth-century obsession with all things underground, the vertical conception of space, the views from above and below, and the unified theory of urban space laid out in modernism no longer reflect the current world, and the first to be suspicious of any uncritical embrace of those concepts. At the same time, by virtue of this very obsolescence, the underground obsession and the image of the city it encapsulates remain vital tools in the analysis of current conceptions of space for which we do not yet have any viable alternative to describe outside of their own ideology. In its multiple identity as the repository of the past, as the spectacular icon of global capitalism, and as the primary destination of the world's poor, the city will continue to function as a threshold between the ostensibly disconnected constituent parts of contemporary global space. No longer a vital material component of global space, the Western metropolis nevertheless remains a vital battleground over the ways in which that space will be represented, and the degree to which the fundamental contradictions in its dominant representation will be allowed to stand. The underground city may not be anything anymore other than an image; nevertheless—and this is something the devil has long understood—the ability to control one's image has never been more imbued with power than it is today. Past battles over control of urban space may have been lost, but we have only seen the beginnings of the struggle over global space, a virtual battle that will have resolutely material consequences the world over.

Notes

Chapter 1. The Devil, the Underground, and the Vertical City

1 The literal meanings date back variously to the Middle Ages and the Renaissance: those of *underground* and *subterranean* to the sixteenth century; that of *souterrain* to the twelfth. Figurative derivations ("in secrecy or concealment"; "existing or working out of sight, in the dark, or secretly," respectively) date to the early modern period (1632; 1651), and to François Rabelais' sixteenth-century French. Definitions have been drawn from the *Oxford English Dictionary*, the *Grand Robert*, and the *Trésor de la langue française*.

2 Louis-Sebastien Mercier, "La ville souterraine," *Les entretiens du Palais-Royal de Paris* (Paris, 1786), 111–17, at 111.

3 There exist many side-by-side discussions of the two cities, especially in terms of architectural history, but there has been surprisingly little direct or in-depth comparison of representations of London and Paris. Most studies assume the model of modernity of their subject metropolis to apply equally everywhere else; where there is comparison, it tends simply to echo the polarizing discourses of the time. See Pike, *Subterranean Cities: The World beneath Paris and London, 1800–1945* (Ithaca: Cornell University Press, 2005), 313n5.

4 I deal with this issue at greater length as "modernism of reading" in *Passage through Hell: Modernist Descents, Medieval Underworlds* (Ithaca: Cornell University Press, 1997), especially in the introductory and concluding chapters.

5 Should one object to the desire for such a unitary theory in a time when such theorizing appears to have been wholly discredited, I can only echo Fredric Jameson's assertion that, as long as the "totality called late capitalism or capitalist globalization" dominates every facet of society, any nonunitary theory is unable adequately to address the current situation:

> The system has always understood that ideas and analysis, along with the intellectuals who practice them, are its enemies and has evolved various ways of dealing with the situation, most notably—in the academic world—by railing against what it likes to call grand theory or master narratives at the same time that it fosters more comfortable and local positivisms and empiricisms in the various disciplines. If you attack the concept of totality, for example, you are less likely to confront embarrassing models and analyses of that totality called late capitalism or capitalist globalization; if you promote the local and the empirical, you are less likely to have to deal with the abstraction of class or value, without which the system cannot be understood. ("The Theoretical Hesitation: Benjamin's Sociological Predecessor," *Critical Inquiry* 25 [Winter 1999]: 267–88, at 267)

Of first importance is to find a nonmodernist form for that theory, a form that would not be subject to the conceptual constraints of a disciplinary specialization in a time when such specialization no longer adequately reflects social conditions. It is in this respect, for example, that Jameson's rigorously philosophical methodology, while admirably suited for critical analysis, remains unable to formulate any way out of the aporias it uncovers.

6 Benson Bobrick, *Labyrinths of Iron: Subways in History, Myth, Art, Technology, and War* (New York: Henry Holt, 1986); Donald Reid, *Paris Sewers and Sewermen: Realities and Representations* (Cambridge: Harvard University Press, 1991). For further sources on subways, mines, and sewers, see, respectively, chapters 1, 2, and 3 of Pike, *Subterranean Cities*; on tunnels, see chapter 4 of this book.

7 Émile Gérards's durable, rational, and comprehensive *Paris Souterrain* (1908; Paris: DMI Editions, 1991) has never been equaled, nor does there exist an analogous book devoted to London. Contemporary examples of the genre include Richard Trench and Ellis Hillman's generally solid but analytically superficial *London under London: A Subterranean Guide* (1984; London: John Murray, 1993), and Patrick Saletta's visually sumptuous *A la découverte des souterrains de Paris* (Antony: SIDES, 1993).

8 Joseph Campbell, *The Hero with a Thousand Faces* (London: Fontana, 1993); more recent studies include James Hillman's Jungian interpretation, *The Dream and the Underworld* (New York: Harper and Row, 1979), and the books of the prolific Evans Lansing Smith, author of *Rape and Revelation: The Descent to the Underworld in Modernism* (Lanham, Md.: University Press of America, 1990), *The Hero Journey in Literature* (Lanham, Md.: University Press of America, 1997), *The Descent to the Underworld in Literature, Painting and Film; The Modernist Nekyia* (Lewiston, N.Y.: Edwin Mellen Press, 2001), and *The Myth of the Descent to the Underworld in Postmodern Literature* (Lewiston, N.Y.: Edwin Mellen Press, 2003).

9 Rachel Falconer, *Hell in Contemporary Literature: Western Descent Narratives since 1945* (Edinburgh: Edinburgh University Press, 2005).

10 Michael Taussig, *The Devil and Commodity Fetishism in South America* (Chapel Hill: University of North Carolina Press, 1980); see also *Walter Benjamin's Grave* (Chicago: University of Chicago Press, 2006), 69–95. I have not attempted to provide a comprehensive account of studies on the devil, but sources relevant to my argument can be found in the discussion of the devil later on in the present chapter as well as in chapter 2.

11 Rosalind Williams, *Notes on the Underground: An Essay on Technology, Society, and the Imagination* (Cambridge, Mass.: MIT Press, 1990); Wendy Lesser, *Life below the Ground* (New York: Faber and Faber, 1987); see also Joanne Gottlieb, "Darwin's City, or Life Underground: Evolution, Progress, and the Shapes of Things to Come," in *The Nature of Cities, Ecocriticism, and Urban Environments*, ed. Michael Bennett and David W. Teague (Tucson: University of Arizona Press, 1999), 233–54. Walter Kafton-Minkel's fascinating and entertaining study of hollow earth theories, *Subterranean Worlds: 100,000 Years of Dragons, Dwarfs, the Dead, Lost Races, and UFOs from Inside the Earth* (Port Townsend, Wash.: Loompanics Unlimited, 1989), constructs something like an underground synthesis in its passing references to the many influences on hollow-earth theories; however, Kafton-Minkel is content to psychologize the modern underground as an internalization of past religions and folk beliefs. Thanks to Peter Fitting for bringing Kafton-Minkel to my attention.

12 For a sophisticated if somewhat hectoring account of Lefebvre's life and its importance in understanding his writings, see chap. 1 of Edward W. Soja, *Third Space: Journeys to Los Angeles and Other Real-and-Imagined Places* (Cambridge, Mass.: Blackwell, 1996), 26–52. A more comprehensive and even-handed approach can be found in Rob Shields, *Lefebvre, Love, and Struggle: Spatial Dialectics* (New York: Routledge, 1999).

13 Henri Lefebvre, *The Production of Space*, 1974, tr. Donald Nicholson-Smith (Oxford: Blackwell, 1991), 129.

14 Soja, *Third Space*, 46.

15 Lefebvre, *Production of Space*, 174.

16 Emmanuel Le Roy Ladurie, *Montaillou: Cathars and Catholics in a French village 1294–1324*, 1978, tr. Barbara Bray (Harmondsworth: Penguin, 1980), 282.

17 Lefebvre, *Production of Space*, 33.

18 Ibid.

19 Ibid., 362.

20 Marc Augé, *Un ethnologue dans le métro* (Paris: Hachette, 1986), 17.

21 Ibid., 116.

22 Kafton-Minkel provides a summary of myths of emergence from the Earth Mother into the world above in *Subterranean Worlds*, 9–16. For an influential and typically metaphysical modernist formulation of such a conception of shelter, see Martin Heidegger, "Building, Dwelling, Thinking," 1951, in *Poetry, Language, Thought* (New York: Harper and Row, 1971), 145–61. Thanks to Jonathan Loesberg for this reference.

23 Sewage tunnels were in use in the city of Mohenjo-daro in the Indus Valley as early as 2500 BCE. Other early underground construction includes irrigation tunnels dug by the Babylonians through the plain separating the Euphrates and the Tigris rivers, rock-cut water channels in ancient Etruria, and, in 750 BCE, a 1,750–foot channel from the concealed Springs of Gihon to the city of Jerusalem to provide a steady water supply for the people of Judah if attacked by the Assyrians (Bobrick, *Labyrinths of Iron*, 26–27).

24 Kafton-Minkel provides numerous examples of the occult division of the races in global spatial terms in his chapter on "The Nazis and the Hollow Earth" in *Subterranean Worlds* (217–42). In this schema and others like it, the center of the earth is usually the secret home of the master race and the world above the abode of lesser beings.

25 There exists, especially in speculative fiction at the turn of the century, a variety of underground utopias, but they invariably either turn out by the end to be dystopic or are rendered for all intents and purposes aboveground by means of magic technology. I examine this issue in detail in *Subterranean Cities*, 75–88.

26 George Orwell, "Dickens," 1939, in *Inside the Whale and Other Essays* (London: Victor Gollancz, 1940), 7–85, at 11.

27 Peter Hall, *Cities in Civilization: Culture, Innovation, and Urban Order* (London: Weidenfeld and Nicolson, 1998), 616.

28 For a detailed discussion of the inorganic underground, see chapter 1 of *Subterranean Cities*.

29 On Greenbrier, see http://www.pbs.org/wgbh/amex/bomb/sfeature/bunker.html (March 2005). Details and photographs of Magdanz's project are available at http://www.dienststelle marienthal.de/z_frames.html (March 2005).

30 Wayne Barrar, "The Machine Room: Visualizing a Commodified Subterra," paper presented at "Going Underground: Excavating the Subterranean City," Arup, Manchester, U.K., September 2006; http://www.surf.salford.ac.uk/documents/GoingUnderground/Wayne_Barrar .pdf: accessed Sept. 29, 2006.

31 On this fraught topic, I will mention as examples of the traditional mode of attack only the Oklahoma City bombing, a groundlevel truck against the tallest building in the state, and the earlier assault on the World Trade Center, also a truck driven into the bowels of the tower. I survey some of the visual and literary fantasies that prefigured these apocalyptically intended deeds in "Urban Nightmares and Future Visions: Life beneath New York," *Wide Angle* 20, no. 4 (Oct. 1998): 8–50.

32 M. Christine Boyer, *The City of Collective Memory: Its Historical Imagery and Architectural Entertainments* (Cambridge, Mass.: MIT Press, 1994).

33 Thomas Wallace Knox, *Underground; or, Life below the Surface* (London: Sampson, Low and Co., 1873). I am grateful to Michael Taussig for first sending me in search of Knox, although his description of a thousand-page turn-of-the-century underground encyclopedia once glimpsed in an eccentric acquaintance's unkempt library in Bogotá, Colombia, did not initially inspire me with much confidence in the actual existence of the book. This was in the early stages of my research; I would soon discover that Knox's is merely the most capacious of many such works.

34 Knox, *Underground,* 3–4. English translations of Simonin's study were published in London and Glasgow in 1869. Simonin's study was also reputed to have inspired Zola's scathing novelistic portrayal of coal mining, *Germinal* (1885). I discuss both books in detail in *Subterranean Cities,* 144–55.

35 Ibid. 30.

36 Ibid., 33–34.

37 Ibid., 33.

38 Ibid., 34.

39 Lewis Mumford, *Technics and Civilization* (New York: Harcourt, Brace, 1934), 74, 157–58.

40 Ibid., 157–59.

41 Williams, *Notes,* 7–8.

42 Ibid., 1, 203.

43 Mumford, *Technics,* 86, 89.

44 Ibid., 210–11.

45 Ibid., 84–85.

46 Paul Fussell, *The Great War and Modern Memory* (New York: Oxford University Press, 1975), 123.

47 In his recent study, *Sites of Memory, Sites of Mourning: The Great War in European Cultural History* (Cambridge: Cambridge University Press, 1995), Jay Winter has demonstrated in some detail that popular responses as well as those within high culture were far more indebted to traditional aesthetic, mythic, and religious frames of reference than readings of modernism generally accept. Although Winter is correct in stressing the amount of overlap with the past, he underestimates the degree to which the *entre-deux-guerres* appropriation of older forms to work through new experience could also result in a cultural production quite distinct from that of the past. Part of what was new in the appropriation of the past was in fact the assertion of rupture that veiled that appropriation.

48 Fussell, *Great War,* 42–43.

49 Qtd. in ibid., 43.

50 Williams, *Notes,* 5.

51 On the differences between the two versions, see Hermann Willers, "*Le Diable boiteux* (Lesage)—*El Diablo cojuelo* (Guevara). Ein Beitrag zur Geschichte franko-spanisches Literaturbeziehungen," *Romanische Forschungen* (Erlangen, 1935): 215–316; and Max Milner, *Le Diable dans la littérature française de Cazotte à Baudelaire 1772–1861,* 2 vols. (Paris: José Corti, 1960), 1:73.

52 On the "Asmodeus flight" and the view from above in city guides, see Priscilla Ferguson, *Paris as Revolution: Writing the Nineteenth-Century City* (Berkeley: University of California Press, 1994); Jonathan Arac, *Commissioned Spirits: The Shaping of Social Motion in Dickens, Carlyle, Melville, and Hawthorne* (New Brunswick, N.J.: Rutgers University Press, 1979), 22, 85–86, 111–13; and Sharon Marcus, *Apartment Stories: City and Home in Nineteenth-Century Paris and London* (Berkeley: University of California Press, 1999), 10.

53 Alain René Le Sage, *Le Diable boiteux* (1726; Paris: Le Trésor des Lettres Françaises, 1968), 27.

54 J. Collin de Plancy, *Dictionnaire Infernal*, 6th ed. (Paris: Henri Plon, 1863), 152.

55 Jean de Lannel, *Nouveaux mémoires historiques de l'abbé de'Artigny*, vol. 6, p. 45, qtd. in Gérards, *Paris Souterrain*, 380–81. The words are purportedly César's own; the affair was first recounted in a pamphlet published in 1615 entitled, *Histoire espouventable de deux magiciens estranglez par le diable la semaine saincte.*

56 Joachim Schlör, *Nights in the Big City*, 1991, tr. Pierre Gottfried Imhoff and Dafydd Rees Roberts (London: Reaktion Books, 1998), 21.

57 Bryan D. Palmer, *Cultures of Darkness: Night Travels in the Histories of Transgression* (New York: Monthly Review Press, 2000), 456.

58 Lefebvre, *Introduction to Modernity*, 1962, tr. John Moore (London: New Left Books, 1995), 62, 58.

59 Ibid., 59.

60 Ibid., 61.

61 Luther Link, *The Devil: The Archfiend in Art from the Sixth to the Sixteenth Century* (New York: Abrams, 1996), 13–15.

62 Aron Gurevich, *Medieval Popular Culture: Problems of Belief and Perception*, tr. János M. Bak and Paul A. Hollingsworth (Cambridge: Cambridge University Press, 1988), 91.

63 See Arac's discussion of the attitude of realist writers such as Dickens and Nathaniel Hawthorne toward the "Asmodeus flight" as a figure for the omniscient narrator (*Commissioned Spirits*, 22, 85–86, 111–13); Marcus, who also treats the "Asmodeus flight" as a narrative trope for omniscient vision in the context of the apartment house, argues in some detail about the way in which the realist novel, while carefully distinguishing between "exterior and interior, mobile and fixed, global and local, publicly open and privately opaque" in its *content*, "blended public and private in its *form*, its narration and circulation"; she stresses "the realist narrator's tendency to simultaneously dissolve and maintain, invade and secure, the privacy of spaces and of persons" (*Apartment Stories*, 10).

64 Jameson, "Theoretical Hesitation," 271.

65 Lynda Nead, *Myths of Sexuality: Representations of Women in Victorian Britain* (Oxford: Blackwell, 1988); *Victorian Babylon: People, Streets, and Images of Nineteenth-Century London* (New Haven: Yale University Press, 2000).

66 Nead, *Myths of Sexuality*, 75.

67 T. J. Clark, *The Painting of Modern Life: Paris in the Art of Manet and His Followers*, 1984, rev. ed. (Princeton: Princeton University Press, 1999).

68 Ibid., 79–146.

69 Guy Debord, "Thèses sur la révolution culturelle," *internationale situationniste* 1 (July 1958): 20–21, at 21; rpt. in *internationale situationniste*, Édition augmentée (Paris: Fayard, 1997), 20–21.

70 Greil Marcus, *Lipstick Traces: A Secret History of the Twentieth Century* (1990; London: Picador, 1997), 308.

71 Neal Ascherson, "Reflections on International Space," *London Review of Books* (24 May 2001): 7–11, at 10–11.

72 Friedrich Nietzsche, *Der Wille zur Macht, drittes und viertes Buch*, vol. 19 of *Gesammelte Werke*, ed. Richard Oehler et al., 23 vols. (1920–29), 371; *The Will to Power*, tr. Walter Kaufmann and R. J. Hollingdale (New York: Vintage, 1968), 548.

73 Jameson, "Theoretical Hesitation," 271.

74 William Blake, *The Marriage of Heaven and Hell*, Copy F, 1794 (Pierpont Morgan Library), plate 3.

75 The descriptive language is Jameson's. On the spiral development of capitalism as a cyclical movement discontinuous in time as well as in space, see Jameson, "Culture and Finance Capital," *Critical Inquiry* 24 (Autumn 1997): 246–65, at 248. Jameson's reading in this article of Giovanni Arrighi's *The Long Twentieth Century: Money, Power, and the Origins of Our Times* (London: Verso, 1994) produces a persuasive account of capitalism as a virus with the potential to reproduce endlessly. Jameson correctly argues that an insufficiently structural reading of culture has confined Marxist literary criticism to definitions of realism, and left it unable to provide an account of cultural developments after modernism that a model such as Arrighi's could perhaps generate. In its structural and formal bias, however, Jameson's own reading of postmodernism as an ontological "deterritorialization" (259–60) results in an overly abstract and monolithic analysis of the present, unable to account for the existence of uneven development either economically or culturally.

76 Taussig, *Devil and Commodity Fetishism*, 37–38.

77 Qtd. in ibid., 174.

78 Claude Seignolle, *Les évangiles du Diable selon la croyance populaire* (1964; Paris: Laffont, 1998).

79 Carlo Ginzburg, *Night Battles: Witchcraft and Agrarian Cults in the Sixteenth and Seventeenth Centuries*, 1966, tr. John and Anne Tedeschi (Harmondsworth: Penguin, 1985).

80 Ibid., 101.

81 Ibid., 69.

82 Siegfried Giedion, *Building in France, Building in Iron, Building in Ferro-Concrete*, 1928, tr. J. Duncan Berry (Santa Monica, Calif.: Getty Center for the History of Art and the Humanities, 1995), 85.

83 Ibid., 153.

84 Karl Marx and Friedrich Engels, "Manifesto of the Communist Party," in *The Marx-Engels Reader*, ed. Robert C. Tucker, 2nd ed. (New York: Norton, 1978), 469–500, at 489.

85 Lefebvre, "Avant-propos de la 2e édition," *Critique de la vie quotidienne* (1945; Paris: L'Arche, 1958), 15.

86 Lefebvre, *Critique de la vie quotidienne: De la modernité au modernisme (Pour une métaphysique du quotidian)* (Paris: L'Arche, 1981), 31.

87 On these *lieux communs* for the critique of Lefebvre's work in the present, see Soja, *Third Space*, 181.

88 "L'aventure," *internationale situationniste* 5 (1960): 3–6, at 3; rpt. *internationale situationniste*, 149–51, at 149.

89 Boyer, *City*, 408; Rosalind Deutsche, *Evictions* (Cambridge, Mass.: MIT Press, 1996).

90 Boyer, *City*, 408.

91 T. J. Clark and Donald Nicholson-Smith, "Why Art Can't Kill the Situationist International," *October* 79 (Winter 1997): 15–31, at 29.

92 Williams, *Notes*, 90–91.

93 Jorge Luis Borges, "Avatars of the Tortoise," 1939, rpt. in *Other Inquisitions, 1937–1952*, tr. Ruth L. C. Simms (Austin: University of Texas Press, 1964), 109–15, at 115–16.

94 Ivar Ekeland, *Au hasard* (Paris: Seuil, 1991); tr. Carol Volk, *The Broken Dice and Other Mathematical Tales of Chance* (Chicago: University of Chicago Press, 1993), 37.

95 Ibid., 91.

96 Ibid., 122.

97 There are intriguing parallels between Ekeland's discussion of contingency and current theories of "emergence," or "the generation of higher-level behaviour or structures within systems made up of relatively simple components," such as a city (Adrian Woolfson, "How Did

the Slime Mould Cross the Maze?" review of Steven Johnson, *Emergence: The Connected Lives of Ants, Brains, Cities and Software* [London: Allen Lane, 2001] and Mark Taylor, *The Moment of Complexity: Emerging Network Culture* [Chicago: University of Chicago Press, 2002], *London Review of Books* 24, no. 6 [21 March 2002]: 27–28). It is possible, Woolfson, Johnson, and Taylor would argue, to imagine hypothetically that "the workings of a system as complex as a city might be computable," but what that would accomplish would be to demonstrate the degree to which the system evolved at least as much "from the ground up," from the complex networks of everyday activity, as from the top down, from the planning and from the spatial conceptions brought to bear on the problem of controlling from above a system too complex to be conceptualized without a demon in its midst. What is clear is that a vertical model of space is no longer adequate to represent this system, although it is equally clear that the tropes of the vertical model are not so easily dispensed with.

98 Lefebvre, *Éléments de rythmanalyse: Introduction à la connaissance des rythmes* (Paris: Éditions Syllepse, 1992), 15.

99 Ibid., 61.

100 Ibid., 26.

101 Steiner's metaphor was firmly grounded in German art and literature between the wars. For example, the artist Max Beckmann, who served in the trenches as a medical orderly, conceived his portfolio *Hell* (1918–19) as a collection of satirical sketches of modern society, showing how the inferno of trench warfare had infected every aspect of postwar life. Thomas Mann began his *Joseph and His Brothers* tetralogy (1933–43) with a long prelude-essay entitled *Höllenfahrt*, or "Descent into Hell."

102 On the modernist descent, see Pike, *Passage through Hell*; Falconer, *Hell*; Lesser, *Life below the Ground*; Smith, *Rape and Revelation* and *Descent to the Underworld*; Williams, *Notes*.

103 George Steiner, *In Bluebeard's Castle: Some Notes towards the Redefinition of Culture* (New Haven: Yale University Press, 1971), 24. For Williams's discussion, see *Notes*, 188–89.

104 Steiner, *Bluebeard's Castle*, 3.

105 Ibid., 55.

106 Ibid., 54. See Falconer's related argument that Steiner's claim for the immanence of hell means the realization of hell within history rather than the transference to "a private mental phobia" as its postreligious role is often characterized (*Hell*, 16–17).

107 Steiner, *Bluebeard's Castle*, 53.

108 Ginzburg, *The Cheese and the Worms*, 1976, tr. John and Anne Tedeschi (Baltimore: Johns Hopkins University Press, 1980), 47.

109 The process is analogous and not unrelated to the industrialization of leisure analyzed by Clark in *Painting of Modern Life*, in which he sees an unmooring of traditional markers of class as modes of leisure such as the country outing, the music hall, and, later, the cinema became spectacularized, addressing a putatively universal rather than class-specific audience. Clark regards this unmooring as directly related to the rise of a new class, the petite bourgeoisie, that, as it flailed around in search of an identity, obscured the conventional boundaries between working class and middle class.

110 In general, see Pike, *Subterranean Cities*, 20–75; on the Tube in particular, see Pike, "Modernist Space and the Transformation of Underground London," *Imagined Londons*, ed. Pamela Gilbert (Albany: State University of New York Press, 2002), 100–119; on the Métro, see Roger H. Guerrand, *Mémoires du Métro* (Paris: Editions du Table Ronde, 1961); on the New York Subway, see Michael Brooks, *Subway City: Riding the Trains, Reading New York* (New Brunswick, N.J.: Rutgers University Press, 1997).

111 Jorge Luis Borges, "Autobiographical Essay," in *The Aleph and Other Stories, 1933–1969. Together with Commentaries and an Autobiographical Essay*, ed. and tr. Norman Thomas di Giovanni (London: Jonathan Cape, 1971), 240.

112 Paul Thompson, *The Edwardians: The Remaking of British Society* (1975; Chicago: Academy Chicago Publishers, 1985), 39.

113 Ibid.

114 C. F. G. Masterman, *The Condition of England* (London: Methuen, 1909), 72.

115 Peter Stallybrass and Allon White, *The Politics and Poetics of Transgression* (London: Methuen, 1986), 145.

116 Mikhail Bakhtin, *Rabelais and His World*, 1965, tr. Hélène Iswolsky (1968; Bloomington: Indiana University Press, 1984), 386. Although not published until the 1950s, the book was written during the 1930s.

117 Bakhtin, "Forms of Time and of the Chronotope in the Novel: Notes towards a Historical Poetics," 1937–38, in *The Dialogic Imagination: Four Essays*, tr. Caryl Emerson and Michael Holquist (Austin: University of Texas Press, 1981), 84–258, at 157. For a lucid and insightful analysis of the chronotope of the contemporary katabasis, see Falconer, *Hell*, 41–47, and "Bouncing Down to the Underworld: Classical *Katabasis* in Rushdie's *The Ground beneath Her Feet*," *Twentieth-Century Literature* 47, no. 4 (Winter 2001): 467–509.

118 In addition to Bakhtin's theory of the chronotope, the most influential of such models on contemporary theories of space and representation have been Michel de Certeau's notion of "an other spatiality," a social practice on the level of the urban pedestrian, and Michel Foucault's concept of the heterotopia. See de Certeau, *The Practice of Everyday Life*, 1980, tr. Steven Rendall (Berkeley: University of California Press, 1984); Foucault, "Of Other Spaces," *Diacritics* 16, no. 1 (1986): 22–27. Although constituting essential formulations of the dynamics of the dominant twentieth-century conception of verticalized urban space, the solutions offered by these theories perpetuate a modernist abstraction of that space into a symbolic unity unsusceptible to any form of contradiction beyond wholesale negation.

119 On the effect of gas explosions in the experience of 1860s London, see Nead, *Victorian Babylon*, 94.

120 Charles Williams, *Descent into Hell* (1937; Grand Rapids, Mich.: Eerdman, 1977), 218.

121 Qtd. in Thompson, *Edwardians*, 267. See also Winter's discussion of depictions of apocalypse in Austrian, German, French, and English painting and literature in the first few decades of the twentieth century (*Sites of Memory*, 145–203).

122 Boyer, *City*, 14.

123 Ibid., 68.

124 Ibid., 26.

125 See Maurice Halbwachs, *Les cadres sociaux de la mémoire* (1925; Paris: Éditions Albin Michel, 1994), and *La mémoire collective*, 1950, ed. Gérard Namer (Paris: Éditions Albin Michel, 1997).

126 Boyer, *City*, 26.

127 A good example of this historicism is Boyer's analysis of Pierre-Charles L'Enfant's plan for the city of Washington, D.C. (343–64). Her reading of the ways in which L'Enfant's plan was "defaced and obscured from its very beginning" (348) is informative and persuasive, revealing that the plan was defeated both by the requirements of capital and by its incompatibility with lived space. Her critical conclusion that the return to the original plan around 1900 "became America's way of looking at public space through a mythic enactment of its dramatic foundations that eclipsed L'Enfant's rhetorical devices" (364), however, betrays an uncharacteristic embrace of monumental in contrast to representational space, and an undialectical

assumption that any set of images or rhetorical devices could actually be free from the same contamination of past and present she so decries in the late twentieth century.

128 A. R. Luria, *The Mind of a Mnemonist*, 1965, tr. Lynn Solotaroff (1968; Cambridge: Harvard University Press, 1987); Luria, *The Man with a Shattered World*, tr. Solotaroff (1972; Cambridge: Harvard University Press, 1987).

129 *Mind of a Mnemonist*, 36 (translation modified); cited in Jacques Roubaud, *L'invention du fils de Leoprepes: Poésie et mémoire* (Paris: Circé, 1993), 42.

130 Jorge Luis Borges, "Funes the Memorious," 1944, tr. James E. Irby, in *Labyrinths* (1962; New York: Modern Library, 1983), 59–66, at 66.

131 Roubaud, *L'invention*, 82.

132 "La lutte pour le contrôle des nouvelles techniques de conditionnement," *internationale situationniste* 1 (1958): 8.

133 Jacques Roubaud, "L'invention de la Mémoire," in Roubaud and Maurice Bernard, *Quel avenir pour la mémoire?* (Paris: Gallimard, 1997), 1–29, at 15.

Chapter 2. The Devil Comes to Town

1 Jacques Cazotte, *Le Diable amoureux*, 1772, tr. Judith Landry (Sawtry, England: Dedalus, 1991), 83.

2 P. J. Stahl [P.-J. Hetzel], "Prologue," *Le Diable à Paris*, ed. Hetzel, 2 vols. (Paris: Hetzel, 1845–46), 1:1–30, at 23; Thomas Wallace Knox, *Underground; or, Life below the Surface* (London: Sampson, Low and Co., 1873), 524.

3 Arsène Houssaye, "Pourquoi quitte-t-on Paris?" *Le Diable à Paris*, 1:125.

4 Jacques Albin Simon Collin de Plancy, *Dictionnaire Infernal. Répertoire Universel des êtres, des personnages, des livres, des faits et des choses qui tiennent aux esprits, aux demons, aux sorciers, au commerce de l'enfer, aux divinations, aux maléfices, à la cabale et aux autres sciences occultes, aux prodiges, aux impostures, aux superstitions diverses et aux prognostics, aux faits actuels du spiritisme, et généralement à toutes les fausses croyances merveilleuses, surprenantes, mystérieuses et surnaturelles*, 1818, 6th ed. (Paris: Henri Plon, 1863), 186.

5 Walter Benjamin, *Das Passagenwerk*, vol. 5 of *Gesammelte Schriften*, ed. Rolf Tiedemann and Hermann Schweppenhäuser, 7 vols. (1974–89; Frankfurt: Suhrkamp, 1991); *The Arcades Project*, tr. Howard Eiland and Kevin McLaughlin (Cambridge: Harvard University Press, 1999).

6 Max Milner, *Le Diable dans la littérature française de Cazotte à Baudelaire 1772–1861*, 2 vols. (Paris: José Corti, 1960), 2:484.

7 Charles Baudelaire, "De L'Essence du Rire et Généralement du Comique dans les Arts Plastiques" (July 1855), in *Oeuvres Complètes*, ed. Claude Pichois, 2 vols. (Paris: Gallimard, 1975–76), 2:525–43, at 528; tr. P. E. Charvet, "Of the Essence of Laughter, and generally of the Comic in the Plastic Arts," *Baudelaire: Selected Writings on Art and Literature* (1972; Harmondsworth: Penguin, 1992), 140–61, at 144–45.

8 In addition to the case studies in the sugar cane plantations of Colombia and the tin mines of Bolivia analyzed in detail by Michael Taussig in *The Devil and Commodity Fetishism in South America* (Chapel Hill: University of North Carolina Press, 1980), Bryan Palmer cites similar examples from Ecuador, Peru, Chile, Argentina, Panama, Puerto Rico, Cuba, Trinidad, Mexico, Guatemala, Honduras, El Salvador, Nicaragua, Costa Rica, Spain, and Greece, as well as some African and Indo-Asian societies (*Cultures of Darkness: Night Travels in the Histories of Transgression* [New York: Monthly Review Press, 2000], 257–74). Revisiting the issue in the mid-1990s, Taussig speaks simply of "the worldwide ubiquity of the story of the devil's pact." (*Walter Benjamin's Grave* [Chicago: University of Chicago Press, 2006], 71)

9 Henri Lefebvre, *Introduction to Modernity*, 1962, tr. John Moore (London: New Left Books, 1995), 57. The process was certainly aided by the Jesuits' revision of the iconography of Hell to exclude the monsters so beloved of medieval Christians, reduce punishment to the single torment of eternal fire, and eliminate Satan's agency as much as possible (Alice K. Turner, *The History of Hell* [New York: Harcourt, Brace, 1993], 173). Turner is incorrect to suggest that prior representations of the devil and hell simply vanished as a consequence, even for churchmen and women; rather, they became even less coherent and more malleable than they already had been, and more readily available for appropriation to all manner of the popular contexts for which that agency remained enthralling.

10 Qtd. in Milner, *Diable*, 2:260, 262.

11 In a posting to the discussion list VICTORIA 19th-Century British Culture & Society (27 July 2001), David Latane "jokingly" conjectured that the English preoccupation of the early 1830s with "devil deals" was a result of the Catholic emancipation of 1829. Many a truth is said in jest, and while I too doubt this was the primary reason for the preoccupation, the emancipation certainly may have helped bring back to the surface a rich and time-honored vein of invective in a new context.

12 On the Parisian *enfer* under Louis XIV, see J. A. Dulaure, *Histoire Physique, Civile et Morale de Paris*, 4 vols., 1821–22 (Paris: Au Bureau des Publications Illustrées, 1845), 3:529, 4:40. According to the *Oxford English Dictionary*, the term was anglicized from chapter 198 of Louis-Sébastien Mercier's *Tableau de Paris*, 8 vols. (Amsterdam, 1782–83). For a list of Regency hells, see *Real Life in London; or, The Rambles and Adventures of Bob Tallyho, esq. and his Cousin, the Hon. Tom Dashall, through the Metropolis; exhibiting a living picture of fashionable characters, manners, and amusements in high and low life*, by an Amateur (London: Jones & Co., 1821), 291–301.

13 The first usage of the term noted by the *OED* was in 1681. Samuel Johnson emphasized the physical likeness when he described a printer's devil as "a creature with a black face and in rags" (*OED*, "devil," 5a, 1781). Later nineteenth-century usage expanded the sense to refer to other forms of unrecompensed but skilled labor: the "Attorney-General's Devil," "a junior legal counsel who does professional work for his leader, usually without fee" (5b); an author or writer "who does work for which another receives the credit or remuneration or both" (5c).

14 G. Cruikshank, *Sunday in London* (London: Effingham Wilson, 1833); rpt. In *Unknown London: Early Modernist Visions of the Metropolis, 1815–1845*, ed. John Marriott, 6 vols. (London: Pickering and Chatto, 2000), 5:149–267, at 156. According to the editor, the text was written by John Wight; if so, then in true character as a "devil," the author did not receive credit for his work.

15 Lewis Mumford, *The Culture of Cities* (New York: Harcourt, Brace, 1938), 148.

16 Humphrey Jennings, *Pandaemonium 1660–1886: The Coming of the Machine as Seen by Contemporary Observers*, ed. Mary-Lou Jennings and Charles Madge (London: Picador, 1987), 3. The collection was compiled after Jennings's death from notes and quotations he had assembled, primarily during the 1930s.

17 For a general history of Victorian Manchester with a wealth of information on its visual and literary representation, see Gary S. Messinger, *Manchester in the Victorian Age: The Half-Known City* (Manchester: Manchester University Press, 1985). See also Steven Marcus, *Engels, Manchester, and the Working Class* (1974; New York: Norton, 1985). Rather than a comprehensive catalog, the selection of examples below is the tip of an iceberg of such conventional imagery of the industrial city; rather than enumeration, my goal is to characterize more precisely the mode of hell invoked by it.

18 *The Life and Opinions of General Sir Charles James Napier*, 4 vols. (London: J. Murray, 1857), 2:56–57.

19 Qtd. in Andrew Lees, *Cities Perceived: Urban Society in European and American Thought, 1820–1940* (Manchester: Manchester University Press, 1985), 64, 63.

20 Auguste Barbier, "La Cuve," *Iambes et poèmes* (Paris: P. Mascagna, 1840), 91–96. The verses quoted here introduce as well as conclude the poem. "La Cuve" was reprinted in the first issue of *Le Diable à Paris* in 1844 as "Paris."

21 Honoré de Balzac, *La Fille aux yeux d'or*, in *Histoire des treize*, ed. Pierre Barbéris (Paris: Livres de poche, 1983), 357–58; tr. Herbert J. Hunt, *History of the Thirteen* (Harmondsworth: Penguin, 1974), 309.

22 Ibid., 367, 318.

23 Ibid., 371, 322. Lutetia means, in Celtic, "the town in the marshes."

24 Robert Montgomery, *Satan. A Poem* (London: Samuel Maunder, 1830), 300.

25 *The Autobiography and Journal of B. R. Haydon*, ed. Tom Taylor; written around 1840–41 and published in 1847; qtd. in Jennings, *Pandaemonium*, 125.

26 Fanny Kemble, *Record of a Girlhood* (London, 1878), qtd. in Jennings, *Pandaemonium*, 169.

27 On Martin and the Thames Tunnel, see Benson Bobrick, *Labyrinths of Iron: Subways in History, Myth, Art, Technology, and War* (New York: Henry Holt, 1986), 75.

28 William Beckford, *Vathek* (1782–86), in *Three Gothic Novels*, ed. E. F. Bleiler (New York: Dover, 1966), 107–94, at 186–87.

29 Note dated 9 December 1838 appended to a letter to Louisa Pitt-Rivers, the wife of Beckford's cousin, a participant at the party and a model for Nouronihar in *Vathek*; qtd. in J. M. Oliver, *The Life of William Beckford* (London: Oxford University Press, 1932), 88–89. The German-born Loutherbourg had made his name as a painter in Paris before coming to London in 1771, where he introduced various "realistic" scenic effects to what had been a simple back canvas. Loutherbourg was also, according to Oliver, a firm believer in the occult and an intimate of Allessandro Cagliostro, the celebrated occult expert and alchemist (88). For more on Loutherbourg as a technician of spectacles, see Richard Altick, *The Shows of London* (Cambridge: Harvard University Press, 1978), 119–27.

30 Beckford himself made the connection in the letter cited above; Williams's insight is to link the two in terms of their ambivalent relationship to the artificially created environment (*Notes on the Underground: An Essay on Technology, Society, and the Imagination* [Cambridge: MIT Press, 1990], 111–12). Where I stress the spatial and social motivation of this ambivalence, Williams focuses on the psychological dimension of Beckford's "guilt and conflicts" over the homosexual components of the Fonthill celebration (112).

31 Beckford, *Vathek*, 187.

32 See, for example, *A bas les Diables, à bas les Bêtes* (1799); *Un pot sans couvercle et rien dedans* (1799); *Le Château des Démons ou le Curé amoureux* (n.d.), where the author claimed to have been forced to place his anticlericalism in a gothic framework because the public wanted nothing but stories of ghosts and *souterrains*; *Le Diable, ou aventures singulières et galante de Roch Duroc* (1801); and *Le Ménage diabolique* (1801), in which "Satan, having heard tell that there were on the earth married couples worse than demons, sends a male and female devil to challenge them, to see which can be more spiteful" (Milner, *Diable*, 1:200–201; Robert Muchembled, *Une histoire du Diable* [Paris: Seuil, 2000], 256).

33 Dolf Sternberger, *Panorama oder Ansichten vom 19. Jahrhundert* (Hamburg: Claasen Verlag, 1938); *Panorama of the Nineteenth Century*, tr. Joachim Neugroschel (New York: Mole Editions, 1977), 175.

34 Ibid.

35 *Life in London; A Play of Three Acts: Depicting the Day and Night Scenes of Tom, Jerry,*

Logic & Co. Adapted to Hodgson's Theatrical Characters and Scenes in the Same (London: Hodgson & Co., 1822), act 1, scene 3.

36 Joachim Schlör, *Nights in the Big City*, 1991, tr. Pierre Gottfried Imhoff and Dafydd Rees Roberts (London: Reaktion Books, 1998), 55; see also Louis Chevalier, *Histoires de la nuit parisienne (1940–1960)* (Paris: Fayard, 1982).

37 Byron, *Don Juan* (1819–24), book 11, canto 26.

38 Ibid., canto 28, 29.

39 Herman Melville, *Redburn, His First Voyage* (1849; Harmondsworth: Penguin, 1976), 305–6. The novel was based on Melville's 1839 journey from New York to Liverpool, from which he had made a one-night excursion by rail to London.

40 Ibid., 106–7.

41 Lynda Nead, *Victorian Babylon: People, Streets, and Images of Nineteenth-Century London* (New Haven: Yale University Press, 2000), 92–93.

42 Benjamin, *Arcades Project*, 170 (G1,1).

43 Hans Christian Andersen, *Travels*, tr. and ed. Anastazia Little; qtd. in Heather Caldwell, "Danish Modern: Hans Christian Andersen's Fairy Tales," *Bookforum* (Winter 2003): 4–7, at 5.

44 Milner, *Diable*, 1:227n48.

45 *Athenaeum* (22 April 1829); qtd. in Altick, *Shows*, 182.

46 *The Real Devil's Walk. Not by Professor Porson. Designs by Robert Cruikshank. With notes and extracts from the Devil's Diary*, 2nd ed., with additions (London: William Kidd, 1831), stanza 25, 21. The history of the conceit suggests the popularity of the devil's visit to London as a satirical frame. The original poem appeared as *The Devil's Thoughts* in the *Morning Post* of 6 September 1799, attributed to Richard Porson, although composed by Robert Southey and Samuel Taylor Coleridge. In 1812, Shelley published an imitative broadsheet, *The Devil's Walk*; Byron's *The Devil's Drive* came out the following year. In 1827, Southey spun out the original poem to fifty-seven stanzas, and between 1830 and 1831 various "more or less correct" versions were published, illustrated by Robert Cruikshank and Thomas Landseer. See Percy Bysshe Shelley, *The Devil's Walk: A Hypertext Edition*, ed. Donald H. Reiman and Neil Fraistat (2002): http://www.rc.umd.edu/editions/shelley/devil/1dwcover.html (March 2005).

47 As Muchembled put it about the Paris stage, "Satan was always a theatrical hero, in the medieval mysteries as in the baroque drama of the seventeenth century: tragedies, tragicomedies, pastorals, or ballets constituted a great quantity of diableries bereft of gravity" (*Histoire du Diable*, 253).

48 R. J. Broadbent, *A History of Pantomime* (1901; New York: Benjamin Blom, 1964), 85–86. Pamela Sheingorn has noted the great regularity of the hellmouth in the pictorial and dramatic arts of medieval England, suggesting that it was more visual and easier to stage than other possibilities such as the pit, and also imparted a sense of verticality to the basically horizontal church porches where the Mysteries were staged ("'Who can open the doors of his face?' The Iconography of Hell Mouth," in *The Iconography of Hell*, ed. Clifford Davidson and Thomas H. Seiler [Kalamazoo, Mich.: Medieval Institute Publishers, 1992], 1–19, at 5–6).

49 Turner, *History of Hell*, 115–19. On the formal importance of the interplay between contemporary folk realism and the high drama of scripture, see Erich Auerbach, "Adam and Eve," in *Mimesis: The Representation of Reality in Western Literature*, 1946, tr. Willard Trask (1953; Princeton: Princeton University Press, 1968), 143–73.

50 Turner, *History of Hell*, 150.

51 Keith Hollingsworth, *The Newgate Novel, 1830–1847: Bulwer, Ainsworth, Dickens, and Thackeray* (Detroit: Wayne State University Press, 1963), 10–11.

52 Baudelaire, "L'Essence du Rire," 539; "Essence of Laughter," 156.

53 Ibid.

54 Antoine-Jean-Baptiste Simonnin and François Llaunet, *Le Diable à Paris*, vaudeville in one act, Théâtre Beaumarchais, 31 July 1844, scene 12.1.

55 Baudelaire, "L'Essence du Rire," 528; "Essence of Laughter," 144–45.

56 Broadbent, *History of Pantomime*, 147–48.

57 "St. James's.—French Plays," *Era*, 25 July 1869.

58 John McCormick, *Popular Theatres of Nineteenth-Century France* (London: Routledge, 1993), 154. Written by Anicet Bourgeois and Laurent Franconi, *Les Pilules du Diable* was produced at the Franconis' Cirque Olympique on the Boulevard du Temple.

59 Stahl, "Coup d'oeil sur Paris. A Propos de l'enfer," *Diable à Paris*, 2:1–9, at 8.

60 Roger de Beauvoir and Lambert Thiboust, *Les Enfers de Paris*, five acts interspersed with song, Théâtre des Variétés, 16 September 1853, act 1.

61 Ibid.

62 [George Daniel], "Remarks," William Dimond, *The Lady and the Devil. A Musical Drama, in two acts. With Remarks, Biographical & Critical, by D-G*, Cumberland's British Theatre No. 375 (London: G. H. Davidson, [1849]), 5–7, at 5.

63 *The Devil on Two Sticks; or, Harlequin the Golden Tree Bird & Apple; or, The Princess and the Fairy Fancee*, pantomime, 22 December 1866.

64 William Leman Rede, *The Devil and Doctor Faustus*, drama in three acts, New Strand Theatre, 31 May 1841; Cumberland's British Theatre 45: 367 (London: G. H. Davidson, [1850?]).

65 *The Printer's Devil; or, A Type of the Old One*, burlesque burletta, Adelphi Theatre, 26 March 1832. Like so much of the language of the Devil, the term "printer's devil" was revived in the late twentieth century, as the title of "a magazine of new writing" based in southeast England, devoted to "distinctive voices, rather than adherents to cultural commonplaces and received ideas," and published complete with "The Devil's Index for future contributors," banning such topics as "Cats; Funerals; Public events and tragedies seen on TV" (Sean O'Brien and Stephen Plaice, "Editorial," *Printer's Devil* 1 [1990]: 4).

66 James Robinson Planché, *The Printer's Devil*, a farce in one act, Olympic Theatre, 8 October 1838; in Dick's Standard Plays no. 889 (London, [1887]).

67 William Blake, *The Marriage of Heaven and Hell*, copy F, 1794 (Pierpont Morgan Library), plate 24. On Johnson and radical publishing in London at the turn of the eighteenth century, see Iain McCalman, *Radical Underworld: Prophets, Revolutionaries and Pornographers in London, 1975–1840* (Oxford: Clarendon, 1988).

68 Ibid., plate 15.

69 Ibid., plate 14.

70 Ibid., plate 24, plate 3. Blake's mix of Christian theology, mythology, his own cosmology, and allegory is famously complex and unintelligible; what never disappeared from it was the materialism I have noted here, and a projection of his visions onto the actual world, especially that of London, as in *Jerusalem*.

71 [Marc-Antoine-Madeleine] Désaugiers and Marie-François-Denis-Thérésa Le Roi, baron d'Allarde, *Jocrisse aux enfers, ou l'Insurrection diabolique, vaudeville infernal en 1 acte et en prose* [Théâtre des Variétés, 6 March 1809] (Paris: Mme Cavanagh, 1809).

72 Grandville, *Un Autre Monde. Transformations, Visions, Incarnations; Ascensions, Locomotions, Explorations, Pérégrinations; Excursions, Stations; Cosmogonies, Fantasmagories, Rêveries, Folâtreries; Facéties, Lubies; Métamorphoses, Zoomorphoses, Lithomorphoses, Métempsychoses, Apothéoses et Autres Choses* (Paris: H. Fournier, 1844), 4. Taxile Delord (1815–77) was a journalist and frequent collaborator of Grandville.

73 Benjamin, "Paris, Capital of the Nineteenth Century," *Arcades*, 3–26.

74 Grandville, *Un Autre Monde*, 196–97.

75 Ibid., 209–20.

76 Ibid., 221.

77 Ibid., 222. The illustration was also published in Hetzel's prologue to the *Diable à Paris* (1:34).

78 Ibid., 224–25.

79 Ibid., 326.

80 Marriott has argued for greater attention to this phenomenon in the interplay between text, image, and theatrical adaptations in *Life in London* and other similar books of the 1830s that, he maintains, constituted a "popular literary modernism" (introduction to *Unknown London*, 1:xv–xlix, at xxxiii). The Paris version lagged slightly behind that of London, and consequently took somewhat different form, but in either case a key component of this "early modernism" was that it lacked that essential feature of full-blown modernism, the utter repudiation of the past. Rather, it occupied a peculiar threshold, looking backward and forward simultaneously.

81 Rachel Falconer, *Hell in Contemporary Literature: Western Descent Narratives since 1945* (Edinburgh: Edinburgh University Press, 2005), 205–6.

82 Planché, *Olympic Devils; or, Orpheus and Eurydice*, Covent Garden Theatre, 21 December 1831, in *The Extravaganzas of J. R. Planché, Esq, (Somerset Herald) 1825–1871*, ed. T. F. Dillon Croker and Stephen Tucker (Rouge Croix), 5 vols. (London: Samuel French, 1879), 1:61–88, at 84.

83 Planché, *Orpheus in the Haymarket*, Haymarket Theatre, 26 December 1865, in *Extravaganzas*, 5:231–76, at 246.

84 Ibid., 247.

85 Hector Crémieux and Jacques Offenbach, *Orphée aux enfers* (Paris: A la Librairie Théâtrale, [1858]), 4.

86 Planché, *Orpheus in the Haymarket*, 247–48.

87 Ibid., 248.

88 Emmanuel Le Roy Ladurie, *Montaillou: Cathars and Catholics in a French Village 1294–1324*, tr. Barbara Bray (Harmondsworth: Penguin, 1980), 343.

89 Baudelaire, "Le Joueur généreux," *Le Spleen de Paris*, in *Oeuvres*, 1:273–363; 325–28, at 327.

90 Joseph de Maistre, *Considérations sur la France* (1795); qtd. in Milner, *Diable*, 1:159.

91 Abbé Fiard, *La France trompée par les magiciens et démonolâtres du dix-huitième siècle. Fait démontré par les faits* (Paris: Grégoire and Thouvenin, 1803); qtd. in Collin de Plancy, *Le Diable peint par lui-même, ou galerie de petits romans et de contes merveilleux sur les aventures et le caractère des démons, leurs intrigues, leurs malheurs et leurs amours, et les services qu'ils ont pu rendre aux hommes, extrait et traduit des écrivains les plus respectables* (1818; Paris: à la Librairie Universelle de P. Mongie, Aîné, 1825), ix–x.

92 Milner, *Diable*, 1:169.

93 Bonaparte's supernatural authority was apparently enough to humble at least Asmodeus, who took the departed emperor on a lightly satirical and rather sentimental tour of Paris after the July Revolution, affirming that "I take a sweet pleasure in having submitted to you. We would often speak about you, while you were covering yourself in glory on the earth, and if we had not been restrained by a superior power, more than one devil would have seconded you." (Guillon, *L'Arrivée de Napoléon à Paris, sous la conduite d'Asmodée, dit le Diable Boiteux. Dialogue entre Napoléon le Grand et Asmodée* [Paris: Maldan, éditeur-libraire, passage Brady, n. 75, 1831], 2). During the early years of the Restauration, the staunch royalist Lasalle had proposed an even closer affinity between the late emperor and the Devil when he asserted that the former

was "one of his sons, whom he had vomited up in a fit of anger," and who, without his consent, "had made of France a new hell" (P. de Lasalle, *Almanach de L'Autre Monde, pour l'an du diable 1817; bluette satirique, anecdotique et morale, Contenant le Calendrier de l'autre Monde, son Conseil, son Académie, les Séances publiques d'un Revenant, la Revue de l'Ile des Fous, son Journal, son Vaudeville, les événemens memorables qui ont eu lieu aux enfers en 1816, etc.* [Paris, 1817], 88).

94 Aimé Martin, *Journal des Débats* (8 August 1826), qtd. in Milner, *Diable*, 1:170.

95 John Galt, *The Annals of the Parish* (1821; New York: Oxford University Press, 1986), 100.

96 A similar role for the countryside of France seems to have been played by the myth of the "*Montagnards*, devils who make their home in the mines under the mountains, and torment miners. They are three feet tall, with horrible faces, an ancient air, an undershirt and leather apron, like the workers whose form they often take. . . . They say there was a time when these devils were not malignant, that they even had a sense of humor, but were sensitive to insults, and rarely suffered one without taking vengeance" (Collin de Plancy, *Dictionnaire Infernal*, 473). As Collin de Plancy recounts it, duplicating the dialectic observed by Taussig among the miners of Bolivia, the subterranean demons take on the role of the overseer, wearing the form of a miner but representing oppression from above. At the same time, cast in the nostalgic form of a lost past, these demons were once merely imps, ready to joke but quick to punish an insult, figures out of a popular *féerie*. There was equally a political allegory of the Montagnard opposition, the leftist network of small towns and villages of south and central France that played an important role in the revolutions of 1789, 1830, and 1848. Typically for French attitudes toward the underground, there was more agency preserved than in the doubly losing battle of Taussig's model; what the Montagnards have lost in humanity they have gained in power and agency since the earlier days of exploitation.

97 On Dante as model, see Jean Cassou, *Quarante-Huit* (Paris, 1939), 111; qtd. in Benjamin, *Arcades*, 382 (J89a,1).

98 On the Commune, see Georges Lazonzec, *Histoire de la Commune de 1871* (Paris, 1928), 399; qtd. in Benjamin, 99 (C8a, 5):

> There wasn't one civil-service official who did not seek to expose the method of treachery then in fashion: the subterranean method [*le souterrain*]. In the prison of Saint-Lazare, they searched for the underground passage that was said to lead from the chapel to Argenteuil—that is, to cross the two branches of the Seine and some ten kilometers as the crow flies. At Saint-Sulpice, the passage supposedly abutted the château of Versailles.

99 Sénart's accusation is cited in J. M. Cayla, *Le Diable: Sa Grandeur et sa Décadence* (Paris: E. Dentu, 1864), 364. In his 1817 *Almanach du l'Autre Monde*, Lasalle did give a list of initials of "current members of the diabolical council" sent to France to topple the newly restored monarchy (94–95), but that was in the context of the Asmodean-style satire of a soldier killed in the Russian campaign returning to Paris to give séances on the other world, rather than a text invested in the truthfulness of its infernal framing device.

100 Cayla, *Le Diable*, 366.

101 Qtd. in Milner, *Diable*, 2:259.

102 Cayla, *Le Diable*, 365.

103 Ibid., 373, 379.

104 Collin de Plancy, *Dictionnaire Infernal*, 403.

105 Ibid., 336. Although no longer figuring in criminal trials, similar beliefs persisted all over the French countryside and in the environs of Paris long into the twentieth century. See the documentation assembled by folklorist Claude Seignolle in *Le folklore du Hurepoix: Traditions populaires de l'Ile-de-France, ancienne Seine et Seine-et-Oise*, with Jacques Seignolle (Paris:

G. P. Maisonneuve et Larose, 1978), and, among other works, in *Les evangiles du Diable selon la croyance populaire* (Paris: G. P. Maisonneuve et Larose, 1964).

106 Milner, *Diable*, 2:325.

107 On the legal decision, see Dulaure, *Histoire*, 3:315; on the Vatican decision, see Milner, *Diable*, 2:354–56.

108 Fred Gettings, *Dictionary of Demons: A Guide to Demons and Demonologists in Occult Lore* (London: Guild Publishing, 1988), 95.

109 Giovanni Papini, *The Devil: Notes for a Future Diabology*, 1953, tr. Adrienne Foulke (London: Eyre and Spottiswoode, 1955), 16, 14.

110 Milner, *Diable*, 1:516.

111 Ibid., 1:517.

112 Emile Levasseur, *Histoire du commerce de la France* (Paris, 1912), 2:449; qtd. in Benjamin, *Arcades*, 37 (A2,4); see also T.J. Clark, *The Painting of Modern Life: Paris in the Art of Manet and His Followers*, 1984, rev. ed. (Princeton: Princeton University Press, 1999), 55–56.

113 Stahl, "Prologue," *Diable à Paris*, 1:24–25.

114 Milner, *Diable*, 2:208.

115 In *Apartment Stories* (Berkeley: University of California Press, 1999), Sharon Marcus makes a convincing argument on the capacity of the Paris apartment house to order and hierarchize the heterogeneity of the modern city (10), linking the "Asmodeus flight" and realist narrative (37). Her focus on the apartment house as frame between indoors and outdoors, private and public, however, neglects the ways in which it also vertically organized its interior spaces, and her discussion of Asmodeus does not address the problem of agency so important for realism and taken for granted by the view from above, which allegorized it as the devil's ability to lift off rooftops and strip away façades.

116 For a history of this image, which first appeared in *L'Illustration* as an excerpt from the second volume of *Le Diable à Paris*, and the relation of the coupe to the figure of Asmodeus and representations of nineteenth-century Paris, see Diane Periton, "The 'Coupe Anatomique': Sections through the Nineteenth-Century Parisian Apartment Block," *Journal of Architecture* 9, no. 3 (Autumn 2004): 289–304.

117 As Paul M. Hohlenberg and Lynn Hollen Lees have observed, the height of housing was a major distinction between London and northern Europe, on the one hand, and Paris and the south, on the other (*The Making of Urban Europe 1000–1950* [Cambridge: Harvard University Press, 1985], 295). For a comprehensive history of the development of the Paris apartment block, see Anthony Sutcliffe, *Paris: An Architectural History* (New Haven: Yale University Press, 1993); Maurice Agulhon, ed., *La ville de l'âge industriel: Le cycle hausmannien*, vol. 4 of *Histoire de la France urbaine*, ed. Georges Duby (Paris: Seuil, 1983).

118 Alfred Delvau, *Les dessous de Paris* (Paris: Poulet-Malassis et De Broise, 1860), 9.

119 Ibid., 59–60.

120 The house in the passage Radzivil was one of the highest in Paris at the time: ten stories on the rue de Valois and nine facing the rue Neuve-des-Bons-Enfants. With a "double spiral staircase extending from the ground to the eaves," wrote the equally precise author of *Les Mystères du Palais-Royal*, "it is a quite remarkable work" (Sir Paul Robert, *Les Mystères du Palais-Royal*, 2 vols. [Paris: Le Clère, 1849], 1:33).

121 *Diable à Paris*, 1:28.

122 Théophile Lavallée, "Paris avant le Déluge," *Diable à Paris*, 1:54–67, at 58, 61.

123 Lavallée, "Géographie de Paris," 2:i–lxxx, at lxix. The piety and propriety of the Abbé Cochin were proverbial at the time; in Lasalle's *Almanach de L'Autre Monde*, Voltaire, Henri

IV, the poet Jacques Delille, and "the priest of the poor of the faubourg Saint-Jacques" were the only blessed souls identified in the Elysian Fields (31–36).

124 On the references to ragpicking in the image, see Patrice Higonnet, *Paris, Capital of the World*, tr. Arthur Goldhammer (Cambridge: Harvard University Press, 2002), 222.

125 Alain René Le Sage, *Le Diable boiteux* (1726; Paris: Le Trésor des Lettres Françaises, 1968), 36.

126 Thomas Carlyle, *The French Revolution* (1834–37), pt. 2, bk. 6, chap. 6.

127 Jonathan Arac, *Commissioned Spirits: The Shaping of Social Motion in Dickens, Carlyle, Melville, and Hawthorne* (New Brunswick: Rutgers University Press, 1979), 17.

128 Walter Benjamin, *Charles Baudelaire: A Lyric Poet in the Era of High Capitalism*, tr. Harry Zohn (London: Verso, 1983), 35–36. Louis James, *Fiction for the Working Man 1830–1850: A Study of the Literature Produced in Early Victorian Urban England* (London: Oxford University Press, 1963), 18–21.

129 Pierce Egan, *Life in London; or, The Day and Night Scenes of Jerry Hawthorn, esq. and His Elegant Friend Corinthian Tom, Accompanied by Bob Logic, the Oxonian, in Their Rambles and Sprees through the Metropolis* (London: Sherwood, Neely, and Jones, 1821), 18.

130 Jules Janin, "Asmodée," *Paris, ou le livre des cent-et-un*, 15 vols. (Brussels: Louis Hauman, 1831–34), 1:17–30. This seminal urban panorama had originally been announced under the title of *Le Diable Boiteux à Paris, ou Paris et les moeurs comme elles sont* (1:5).

131 Watts Phillips, *The Wild Tribes of London* (London: Ward and Lock, 1855), 7. Primarily a playwright, Phillips in his guidebook took in the main touchstones of low-life sensation scenes: St. Giles's, Borough, and the East End.

132 Qtd. in Arac, *Commissioned Spirits*, 112.

133 Ibid., 71.

134 Ibid., 70.

135 [P. Chaussard], *Le Nouveau Diable Boiteux, Tableau Philosophique et Morale de Paris; mémoires mis en lumière et enrichis de Notes par le Docteur* DICACULUS*, de Louvain*, 2 vols. (A Paris: chez F. Buisson, an VII de la République [1798]), 1:36.

136 Ibid., 44.

137 Ibid., 45.

138 Janin, "Asmodée," 25.

139 Ibid., 29–30.

140 Eugène de Mirécourt, *Paris la nuit*, vol. 11 of *Paris historique, picturesque et anecdotique*, 11 vols. (Paris: Gustave Havard, 1855).

141 Benjamin, *Charles Baudelaire*, 23.

142 Paul Bourget, *Essais de psychologie contemporaine: Baudelaire, M. Renan, Flaubert, M. Taine, Stendhal*, 2 vols. (1885; Paris: Plon-Nourrit, 1901), 1:7–9; qtd. in Benjamin, *Arcades*, 256 (J16,1); Maurice Barrès, *La folie de Charles Baudelaire* (Paris: Les Ecrivains réunis, 1926), 44–45; qtd. in Benjamin, *Arcades*, 251 (J13,4).

143 Benjamin, "Zentralpark," in *Gesammelte Schriften* 1:655–90; tr. Lloyd Spencer, "Central Park," *New German Critique* 34 (Winter 1985): 32–58.

144 Vincent Brunetière, qtd. Albert Thibaudet, *Intérieurs* (Paris, 1924), 16; in Benjamin, *Arcades*, 252 (J13a,5).

145 Jules Laforgue, "Notes sur Baudelaire," in *Mélanges posthumes*, vol. 3 of *Oeuvres complètes* (Paris: Mercure de France, 1902–03), 113–14; qtd. in Benjamin, *Arcades*, 243–44 (J9,4).

146 Benjamin, *Arcades*, 332–33 (57a,3); also 273 (J24a,5).

147 Laforgue, "Notes sur Baudelaire," 111–12; qtd. in Benjamin, *Arcades*, 246 (J10a,1).

148 Sternberger, *Panorama*, 19.

149 Gérard de Nerval, *Aurelia* (1855), in *Oeuvres*, ed. Henri Lemaître (Paris: Garnier, 1966), 753–824, at 824.

150 Ibid., 753.

151 Miching Mallecho, Esq., *Peter Bell the Third* (1819), in *The Complete Poetical Works of Percy Bysshe Shelley*, ed. Thomas Hutchinson (London: Oxford University Press, 1925), 342–57. Hereafter cited by line number.

152 Blake, *Marriage of Heaven and Hell*, plate 6.

153 Ibid., plate 8.

154 Benjamin, *Arcades*, 379 (J87,9).

155 Charles Leconte de Lisle, *Revue Européenne* (1 December 1861); qtd. Benjamin, *Arcades*, 311 (J45a,1).

156 Jules Barbey d'Aurevilly, *XIXe siècle Les oeuvres et les hommes*, vol. 3, *Les poètes* (Paris, 1862), 380; qtd. Benjamin, *Arcades*, 271 (J23a,2).

157 Qtd. in Henri Cordier, *Notules sur Baudelaire* (Paris, 1900), 5–7; qtd. Benjamin, *Arcades*, 241 (J8).

158 For a detailed discussion of the necropolis in the imagination of nineteenth-century Paris and London, see chap. 2 of David L. Pike, *Subterranean Cities: Subways, Cemeteries, Sewers, and the Culture of Paris and London* (Ithaca: Cornell University Press, 2005).

159 Shelley, *Peter Bell the Third*, 257–62.

160 Baudelaire, *Fleurs du mal*, 1857–61, in *Oeuvres*, 1:1–134, at 73.

161 Baudelaire, *The Flowers of Evil*, tr. Richard Howard (Boston: David R. Godine, 1982), 75.

162 Baudelaire, *Fleurs du mal*, 5.

163 Baudelaire, *Flowers of Evil*, 5.

164 Baudelaire, *Fleurs du mal*, 5.

165 Baudelaire, *Flowers of Evil*, 5.

166 Baudelaire, *Fleurs du mal*, 34–35.

167 Baudelaire, *Flowers of Evil*, 39–40.

168 Baudelaire, "L'Essence du Rire," 532; "Essence of Laughter," 148.

169 Baudelaire, *Fleurs du mal*, 86.

170 Baudelaire, *Flowers of Evil*, 91.

171 Nerval, *Petits Châteaux de Bohême, prose et poésie* (1853), in *Oeuvres*, 7–39, at 11.

172 Baudelaire, "Joueur," 325. Also published in 1866 as "Le Diable"; another working title was "Supper with Satan" (*Oeuvres*, 1:1336–37).

173 Ibid., 327.

174 Ibid.

175 Ibid., 328.

176 Baudelaire, "Assommons les pauvres!" ("Let's Beat Up the Poor!"), *Spleen de Paris*, 357–59, at 359. On the sources behind this satanic stance, its relation to the petit-bourgeois ideologies of the day, and the likelihood of its referring to the events of 1848, see T. J. Clark, *The Absolute Bourgeois: Artists and Politics in France 1848–1851* (1973; Berkeley: University of California Press, 1999), 141–77, esp. 176–77. See also Hartmut Stenzel, "Les écrivains et l'évolution idéologique de la petite bourgeoisie dans les années 1840: Le cas de Baudelaire," *Romantisme* 17–18 (1977): 79–91; Gretchen Van Slyke, "Dans l'intertexte de Baudelaire et de Proudhon: Pourquoi faut-il assommer les pauvres?" in *Romantisme* 45 (1984): 57–77.

177 Baudelaire, "Assommons les pauvres!" 359.

178 Baudelaire, "Le Mauvais Vitrier" ("The Bad Glazier"), *Spleen de Paris*, 285–87, at 286.

179 Clark, *Painting of Modern Life*, 23, 47–49, 259. I am also indebted to Clark's incisive

analysis of the emergence of the petit-bourgeois as a key context for the art of Second Empire Paris.

180 On the scandal of the *Olympia* and its relation to class, see ibid., 79–146.

181 Piero Camporesi, *Bread of Dreams: Food and Fantasy in Early Modern Europe*, 1980, tr. David Gentilcore (Chicago: University of Chicago Press, 1989), 18.

182 The last term is from Peter Hall, *Cities in Civilization: Culture, Innovation, and Urban Order* (London: Weidenfeld and Nicolson, 1998), 296, 616–17, 945. Hall periodizes the first industrial revolution from the 1780s to 1842 and the second from 1842 to 1897.

183 *The Devil upon Two Sticks: or the Town Until'd: with the Comical Humours of Don Stulto, and Siegnior Jingo: As it is Acted in Pinkeman's Booth in May-Fair* (London: J. R. near Fleet-street, 1708), 3. For a similar equation of the theater with the devil, see Samuel Foote, *The Devil upon Two Sticks*, comedy in three acts, Haymarket, 30 May 1768 (Dublin: W. Kidd, 1778), 47–48.

184 W. T. Moncrieff, *Don Giovanni in London! or The Libertine Reclaimed*, operatic extravaganza in one act, Olympic, 26 December 1817; Cumberland's British Theatre 17 (London: John Cumberland, n.d.), 1.3.17.

185 Moncrieff, *The Devil's Walk! or, Pluto in London*, Surrey, 29 September 1830.

186 Richard Brinsley Peake, *The Devil in London; or, Sketches in 1840*, a satirical drama in three acts, Adelphi, 20 April 1840; Dick's Standard Plays 718 (London, [1886]), 1.1.4.

187 Ibid., 1.2.5.

188 John Beer Johnstone, *The Devil on Town*, Surrey, 18 April 1863, 1.1.

189 Foucault, "The Eye of Power," 1977, in *Power/Knowledge*, ed. Colin Gordon (New York: Pantheon, 1980), 146–65, at 153.

190 G. W. M. Reynolds, *The Mysteries of London*, 4 vols. (London: John Dicks, [1846]), 2:239.

191 Hannes Vatter, *The Devil in English Literature*, Schweizer Anglistische Arbeiten / Swiss Studies in English 97 (Bern: Francke Verlag, 1978), 106.

192 *Edinburgh Medical Journal* 47 (1859): 1003; qtd. in Eric Trudgill, "Prostitution and Paterfamilias," in *The Victorian City: Images and Realities*, ed. H. J. Dyos and M. Wolff, 2 vols. (London: Routledge and Kegan Paul, 1973), 693–705, at 693.

193 Qtd. in J. T. Boulton, introduction to C. F. G. Masterman, *The Condition of England* (London: Methuen, 1909), ix–xxix, at xxviii. Masterman (1873–1927) was a member of the Liberal government.

194 Edouard Texier, "Paris souterrain," *Le Tableau de Paris*, 2 vols. (Paris: Impr. de Walder, 1853), 2:234–44, at 234.

195 Sue, *Adèle Verneuil*, vol. 1 of *Le Diable médecin*, 7 vols. (1855–57; Paris: Michel Lévy Frères, 1862), 3. The only other diabolical trait of the doctor was his place of abode "near the Barrière d'enfer" (18). The titular gang of Alexandre Dumas' serial *Les Mohicans de Paris* (1854–59; Paris: Gallimard, 1998) controlled an abandoned house on the rue d'Enfer in the same neighborhood; the eponymous hero-savant of A. de Gondrecourt's novel, *Un Ami diabolique*, similarly inhabited an isolated house "au diable," that is, at 17 rue d'Enfer (Paris: Alexandre Cadot, [1861], 115). In all three cases, the pun played on the venerably satanic and criminal tradition of the quarter while emphatically rationalizing the association.

196 George Gissing, *The Nether World* (1889; Oxford: Oxford University Press, 1992), 74.

197 Ibid., 345.

198 Schlör, *Nights*, 222.

199 Geo. R. Sims, *The Devil in London* (New York: Dodge Publishing, 1909).

200 Ibid., 166.

201 Barbara Wingfield-Stratford, *The Amazing Epilogue, or The Further Day and Night Scenes of Jerry Hawthorne, Esquire, and his Elegant Cousins, Thomas, Thompson, Tommy, and Tom, in their Rambles and Sprees through the Metropolis of the fourth and fifth Georges, Queen Victoria, and Edward the Seventh* (London: Lorat Dickson Limited, 1933), 198. The book is a clever pastiche of *Life in London* and Virginia Woolf 's recently published romance, *Orlando.*

202 Claude Roland and Louis Bouvet, *L'Enfer! Tout le monde descend,* two acts and five tableaux,. Théâtre-Concert La Cigale, 1904.

203 W. C. Morrow, *Bohemian Paris of To-day* (London: Chatto and Windus, 1899), 265–66.

204 Ibid., 271–72.

205 Ibid., 279–82.

206 Georges Rodenbach, *Bruges-la-Morte* (1892; Paris: Flammarion, 1998), 102.

207 Ibid., 128, 133–34.

208 Oswald Spengler, *The Decline of the West,* 2 vols. (New York: Knopf, 1926–28), 2:100.

209 Ibid., 102.

210 [Daniel Defoe], *The Political History of the Devil, as well ancient as modern* (London: T. Warner, 1726), 63.

211 The book was apparently received in this manner as well; an edition printed in Birmingham in 1772 has "prefixed, by way of appendix, Anecdotes of a scoundrel; or, Memoirs of Devil Dick: a well-known character. By an invisible spy . . ."

212 Spengler, *Decline,* 2:103.

213 Defoe, *History of the Devil,* title page.

214 For a related discussion of the concept of hell and the events on and following September 11, 2001, see Falconer, *Hell,* 224–30.

Chapter 3. Mysteries of the Underground

1 I borrow the term "urban mysteries" from Richard Maxwell's usage "novel of urban mysteries" in *The Mysteries of Paris and London* (Charlottesville: University Press of Virginia, 1992). Although Maxwell chooses to focus primarily on the relation of Hugo and Dickens to the genre rather than the more ephemeral urban mysteries per se, I am indebted to his definition of the field and the theoretical categories within which he examines it. Because I also discuss theatrical examples, and because I am less convinced about the generic status of the serialized mysteries as novels, I use the more general term "fiction of urban mysteries" or simply "urban mysteries."

2 See, for example, the catalog in Régis Messac, *Le "Detective Novel," et l'influence de la pensée scientifique,* Bibliothèque de la Revue de littérature comparée 59 (Paris, 1929).

3 Prest's serial was adapted and plagiarized throughout the century, primarily at the East End theaters. The first version was by George Dibdin Pitt for the Britannia in 1847. It was followed by new productions at the Grecian (1861), the Effingham (1862), and the Bower (1865), as well as various revivals and copied versions.

4 "Real Mysteries of Paris and London," *All the Year Round* 4, no. 79 (27 October 1860): 69–72, at 69.

5 Ibid., 70.

6 I am referring in particular to the passage from the *Communist Manifesto* used as an epigraph in chapter 1, "The bourgeoisie resembles the sorcerer, who is no longer able to control the powers of the netherworld whom he has called up by his spells," and to Marx's statement in the preface to *Capital,* "At the entrance to science, as at the entrance to hell, the demand must be posted: *Qui si convien lasciare ogni sospetto; Ogni viltà convien che qui sia morta* [Here must all hesitation be left behind; here every cowardice must meet its death]."

7 Eve Kosofsky Sedgwick, *Coherence of Gothic Conventions* (New York: Methuen, 1986), 9.

8 Ann B. Tracy, *The Gothic Novel 1790–1930: Plot Summaries and Index to Motifs* (Lexington: University Press of Kentucky, 1981). I derived this total by combining entries for "passage, subterranean," "cave," and "burial alive," while discounting duplicated titles. Including the extremely frequent and closely related motifs of "confinement (extra-legal)" and "dungeon" would have made the number even more imposing.

9 Sedgwick, *Gothic Conventions*, 21, 27.

10 Ibid., 22.

11 Ibid., 28.

12 Eugène Sue, *Les Mystères de Paris*, 1842–43, ed. Francis Lacassin (Paris: Robert Laffont, 1989), 32–33.

13 G. W. M. Reynolds, *The Mysteries of London*, 4 vols. (London: John Dicks, [1846]), 1:3.

14 Father North, *The Mysteries of London, and Stranger's Guide to the Art of Living and Science of Enjoyment in the Great Metropolis: Its Exhibitions and Amusements, Gaieties, Excursions, &c. &c.* (London: Hugh Cunningham, 1844), 77.

15 Sue, *Mystères de Paris*, 78.

16 Ibid., 886.

17 Christopher Prendergast provides a useful summary of this canonical attention in the chapter "Paris Underground" in *Paris and the Nineteenth Century* (Cambridge, Mass.: Blackwell, 1992), 74–101.

18 Karl Marx, "Theses on Feuerbach," no. 8 (written 1845, published 1888), *The Marx-Engels Reader*, ed. Robert C. Tucker, 2nd ed. (New York: Norton, 1978), 143–45, at 145.

19 Sir Walter Scott, *The Lives of the Novelists* (London: Everyman, n.d.), 216; qtd. in Victor E. Neuberg, *Popular Literature: A History and Guide from the Beginning of Printing to 1897* (Harmondsworth: Penguin, 1977), 152.

20 Maxwell's elegant and persuasive reading of *Notre-Dame* comprises chapter 2 of *Mysteries of Paris and London*; on the novel's influence, see 54–57; on the opening scenes, see 25–34.

21 On the resonance of the various *cours des Miracles* later in the nineteenth century, see chapter 4 of this book, 230. Hugo's primary source was Henri Sauval's *Histoire et Recherches des Antiquités de la Ville de Paris*, 3 vols. (Paris: Charles Moette et Jacques Chardin, 1724), 1:512–13. See also J.-A. Dulaure, *Histoire Physique, Civile et Morale de Paris*, 4 vols. (1821–22; Paris: Au Bureau des Publications Illustrées, 1845), 3:273–77. The *cour* described by Hugo and visited by Sauval had been demolished in 1688 by Nicolas de La Reynie, the first chief of police, in one of his earliest actions on assuming the position.

22 Reynolds, *Mysteries of London*, 1:3, 5.

23 Ibid., 5.

24 Ibid., 6.

25 Ibid., 7.

26 Ibid., 23.

27 Ibid., 24.

28 E. F. Bleiler, "Introduction to the Dover Edition," *Wagner the Wehr-wolf*, by G. W. M. Reynolds (New York: Dover, 1975), vii–xviii, at xvii.

29 On the fictionalized accounts of criminal lives in the early nineteenth century, see Margaret Dalziel, *Popular Fiction 100 Years Ago: An Unexplored Tract of Literary History* (London: Cohen and West, 1957); Keith Hollingsworth, *The Newgate Novel, 1830–1847: Bulwer, Ainsworth, Dickens, and Thackeray* (Detroit: Wayne State University Press, 1963); Louis James, *Fiction for the Working Man 1830–1850: A Study of the Literature Produced in Early Victorian Urban England* (London: Oxford University Press, 1963); Neuberg, *Popular Literature*.

30 Reynolds quite likely had a real-life model in mind for the cross-dressing Eliza Sydney just as he did for the house into which she blundered. Flora Tristan, illegitimate daughter of a Frenchwoman and a Peruvian man, disguised herself as a man to penetrate the upper and lower reaches of London society, reporting on her explorations in *Promenades dans Londres*, first published in 1840. In this work, Tristan mentioned the legendary houses above Fleet Ditch. There seems little doubt that a writer as conversant with French and English publishing as Reynolds was would have known about a book that had received a good bit of attention in Paris, at least from the political Left. For an example of Tristan's reception, see Louis Chevalier, *Laboring Classes and Dangerous Classes in Paris during the First Half of the Nineteenth Century*, 1958, tr. Frank Jellinek (Princeton: Princeton University Press, 1973), 133. For a reading of Tristan's critical views on London, see Deborah Epstein Nord, *Walking the Victorian Streets: Women, Representation, and the City* (Ithaca: Cornell University Press, 1995), 115–35.

31 "The Old Houses in West-street, Smithfield," *Times* (London) (Tuesday, 4 August 1844): col. e, 8. See also the articles of 9 August and 16 August; "The Charities of London," *Quarterly Review* 194 (1855): 430; and William J. Pinks, *The History of Clerkenwell* (London: J. T. Pickburn, 1865), 353–56.

32 Gareth Stedman Jones, *Outcast London: A Study in the Relationship between Classes in Victorian Society* (1971; Harmondsworth: Penguin, 1984), 179–83.

33 Thomas Peckett Prest, *The Old House of West Street; or, London in the Last Century. A Romantic Tale* (London: Edward Lloyd, 1846), iii.

34 Prest, *Helen Porter; or, A Wife's Tragedy and a Sister's Trials. A Romance* (London: E. Lloyd, [1845]), 184.

35 [Paul Féval], *Les Mystères de Londres, Semaine Littéraire du Courrier des Etats-Unis* (New York: F. Gaillardet, 1844), pt. 1, chap. 7; 35.

36 Similarly, London adaptations of Sue's *Mystères de Paris* tended to highlight the sensation-scene potential of the subterranean settings, like the "range of vaults beneath the streets of Paris," within which Rodolphe was chained in Charles Dillon's *The Mysteries of Paris!* (Royal Marylebone Theatre, 1844); Paris adaptations such as Sue's own at the Théâtre de la Porte-Saint-Martin tended to stress the social aspect of the *bas-fonds*: the plight of the Morel family, the prison scenes, the Martial family on the île des Ravageurs.

37 See, for example, the documentation in Andrew Lees, *Cities Perceived: Urban Society in European and American Thought, 1820–1940* (New York: Columbia University Press, 1985).

38 Féval, *Mystères de Londres*, pt. 4, chap. 25; 377.

39 Reynolds, *Mysteries of London*, 1:118.

40 Féval's narrative, too, was most likely set after 1832, but he also included a body snatcher, Bishop "le burkeur," although Bishop's low-life villainy is generally subordinated to that of the upper-class organization, the Great Family. The Anatomy Act replaced the purchase of bodies for dissection with the requisition of the bodies of the poor, primarily workhouse occupants, eliminating the market demand served by burking and body snatching. There were strong protests from the members of the public whose rights would be most directly affected by the new sources of supply (the poor), but to no avail. For a comprehensive and fascinating study of the circumstances surrounding the act and its effects, see Ruth Richardson, *Death, Dissection and the Destitute* (Penguin: Harmondsworth, 1989).

41 For a summary of the various laws and an analysis of the resulting changes, see Hollingsworth, *Newgate Novel*, 25.

42 Raymond Williams, "Forms of English Fiction in 1848," 1978; rpt. in *Writing in Society* (London: New Left Books, 1991), 150–65, at 154.

43 Ibid.

44 Jones, *Outcast London*, 180.

45 Prest, *Helen Porter*, 1.

46 On the arches, the Thames Tunnel, the bridges, and the arcades, see chapter 4 in this book; on the underground railway, the catacombs and quarries, and the sewers, see Pike, *Subterranean Cities.*

47 Nash's first plans for the cutting of Regent Street from Pall Mall to Portland Place at the entrance to Regent's Park and the housing to be built around it date from 1811–12; construction was completed in 1826. The eccentric route chosen for the street, Nash readily confessed, precisely demarcated the boundary between the first-class property to the west and the third-class to the east, raising the value of the area he was developing and sealing off the area he was ignoring: "If a straight line had been continued from Regent's Park to Carlton House, it would have passed through St. Giles's, leaving all the bad streets between the new street and the respectable streets at the West end of the town. . . . In forming that street, my purpose was, that the new street should cross the Eastern entrance to all the streets occupied by the higher classes, and to leave out to the East all those bad streets" (*Parliamentary Papers* 1828, vol. 4, p. 388 [1828 Report]; qtd. in J. Mordaunt Crook, "Metropolitan Improvements: John Nash and the Picturesque," in *London—World City 1800–1840*, ed. Celina Fox [New Haven: Yale University Press, 1992], 77–96, at 90).

48 Peter Keating, *The Working Classes in Victorian Fiction* (New York: Barnes and Noble, 1971), 15.

49 David H. Pinkney, *Napoleon III and the Rebuilding of Paris* (Princeton: Princeton University Press, 1958), 30–31.

50 Sue, *Mystères de Paris*, 31–32.

51 Claireville and Edouard Damarin, *Satan ou le Diable à Paris*, comedy-vaudeville in four acts, prologue and epilogue, Théâtre du Vaudeville, 23 July 1844, act 2.

52 Reynolds, *Mysteries of London*, 1:1.

53 Sue, *Mystères de Paris*, 33.

54 Leslie Fiedler, "In Quest of George Lippard," rpt. in *Cross the Border—Close the Gap* (New York: Stein and Day, 1971), 86–105, at 92. Despite its age, Fiedler's article remains perhaps the most successful attempt to read the fiction of urban mysteries critically but without condescension. His argument for the effectiveness of Reynolds's prose style is especially convincing.

55 Anne Humpherys, "The Geometry of the Modern City: G. W. M. Reynolds and *The Mysteries of London*," *Browning Institute Studies* 11 (1983): 69–80, at 72.

56 Henry Havard, *Dictionnaire de l'ameublement et de la decoration depuis le XIIe siècle jusqu'à nos jours*, 4 vols. (Paris: Quantin, [1887–1890]), 3:931.

57 *Les Mystères de Passy, parodie-vaudeville en onze tableaux, cinq actes avec prologue et épilogue*, par MM. Rochefort et Dartois, Théâtre des Folies-Dramatiques, 5 mars 1844 (Paris: C. Tresse, 1844), 40.

58 *The New Swell's Night Guide to the Bowers of Venus, Curious Account of the Cyprian Beauties and Their Little Love Affairs; the Principal Introducing Houses, West-end walks, Chanting Slums, Flashcribs, and Dossing Kens, with all the Rowdy-Dowdy and Flash Patter of Billingsgate and St. Giles'. Being a Complete Stranger's Guide to Life in London* (London: J. Paul, 1846), ii.

59 Alfred Delvau, *Les Dessous de Paris* (Paris: Poulet-Malassis et De Broise, 1860), 206–7.

60 George Augustus Sala, *Paris Herself Again in 1878–9*, 2 vols. (London: Remington and Co., 1879), 2:45–46.

61 Ibid., 44.

62 Ibid., 46.
63 Delvau, *Dessous de Paris*, 209.
64 Ibid., 211.
65 Sue, *Mystères de Paris*, 31.
66 Delvau, *Dessous de Paris*, 212.
67 Chevalier, *Laboring Classes*, 405.
68 Ibid., 407.
69 Ibid., 403.
70 Ibid., 407, 408.
71 Ibid., 408.
72 Jean-Paul Sartre, *What Is Literature?*; qtd. in Alan Trachtenberg, "Experiments in Another Country: Stephen Crane's City Sketches," *Southern Review* 10 (Spring 1974): 265–85, at 266.
73 Karl Marx and Friedrich Engels, *The Holy Family*, vol. 4 of *Collected Works* (London: Lawrence and Wishart, 1975), 5–211, at 56. The chapters on Sue are credited to Marx.
74 Ibid., 57.
75 Ibid., 73.
76 Ferrand was the exception that proved the rule; as Marx pointed out, the Paris College of Notaries exercised its influence to have the character excised from theatrical representations (*Holy Family*, 70). Similarly, the physician and medical historian J.-P. Pointe argued (not terribly convincingly) in a letter he claimed the *Journal des Débats* had refused to publish that the character of Doctor Griffon and the horrific hospital conditions depicted through his character were either "completely inexact" or "exaggerated" (*Réponse aux observations consignées par M. Eugène Sue, dans la huitième partie des Mystères de Paris, chapitre intitulé: "L'Hospice, La Visite,"* in *Loisirs Médicaux et Littéraires, recueils d'éloges historiques, relations médicales de voyages, annotations diverses, etc. Documents pour servir à l'histoire de Lyon* [Paris: J.-B. Baillère; Lyon: Ch. Savy Jeune, 1844], 555–71, at 559).
77 Marx, *Holy Family*, 169, 170.
78 Ibid., 174.
79 Peter Brooks, *Reading for the Plot: Design and Intention in Narrative* (New York: Vintage, 1985), 159. I address the role of the prostitute in the nineteenth-century underground in detail in *Subterranean Cities*, 252–69.
80 Brooks, *Reading for the Plot*, 168.
81 Alexandre-Jean-Baptiste Parent-Duchâtelet, *Essai sur les cloaques, ou Egouts de la ville de Paris* (Paris: Crevot, 1824); *De la Prostitution dans la ville de Paris, considérée sous le rapport de l'hygiène publique* (Brussels: Société Belge de Librairie, 1836), 1:6. For more on Parent and his proverbial analogy, see Jill Harsin, *Policing Prostitution in Nineteenth-Century Paris* (Princeton: Princeton University Press, 1985), 96–130; and Charles Bernheimer, *Figures of Ill Repute: Representing Prostitution in Nineteenth-Century France* (Cambridge: Harvard University Press, 1989), 8–33.
82 Chevalier, *Laboring Classes*, 46.
83 Pierce Egan, *Life in London; or, The Day and Night Scenes of Jerry Hawthorn, esq. and His Elegant Friend Corinthian Tom, Accompanied by Bob Logic, the Oxonian, in Their Rambles and Sprees through the Metropolis* (London: Sherwood, Neely, and Jones, 1821), 177n12.
84 For a summary of attitudes toward the city, especially London and Paris, in the 1830s and 1840s, see Lees, *Cities Perceived*.
85 Ibid., xiv, 286.
86 Maxwell, *Mysteries*, 198.
87 The revival was also helped in France by the Fayard publishing house's creation at the beginning of the century of a new series of cheap reissues of popular classics of the nineteenth

century, primarily old feuilletons (Robin Walz, *Pulp Surrealism: Insolent Popular Culture in Early Twentieth-Century Paris* [Berkeley: University of California Press, 2000], 45). Excellently researched, Walz's study provides a valuable history of the popular culture plundered by the surrealists; his dismissive account of the narrative limitations of the serials ("a mishmash of flat characters, stilted dialogue, and cheap thrills" [43]), while accurate enough, never confronts the excess permissible only through those trappings, the visceral charge of the view from below that made this mass culture so popular as a representation of the modern city.

88 Richard Abel, *French Cinema: The First Wave, 1915–1929* (Princeton: Princeton University Press, 1984), 71.

89 Ibid., 73–74; Richard Roud, "Louis Feuillade and the Serial," *Cinema: A Critical Dictionary*, 2 vols., ed. Roud (New York: Viking, 1980): 1:348–59, at 351.

90 On the Bande à Bonnot and its enduring myth, see Arthur Bernède, *Bonnot, Garnier, et cie* (Paris: Jules Tallandier, 1933); Alfred Morain, *The Underworld of Paris: Secrets of the Sûreté* (New York: E. P. Dutton, 1931); Ezra Brett Mell, *The Truth about the Bonnot Gang* (London: Coptic Press, 1968); Richard Parry, *The Bonnot Gang* (London: Rebel Press, 1987).

91 Morain, *Underworld*, 49–50.

92 Roger Caillois, "Paris, mythe moderne," in *Le Mythe et l'homme* (1938; Paris: Folio, 1994), 153–75, at 160–62; the description of the man in the dark glasses is quoted from Pierre Véry, *Les métamorphoses* (Paris: NRF, 1931), 178–79.

93 Fernand Léger, "Images Mobiles. Spectacle," *L'Intransigeant* (29 May 1924), 1; qtd. in Walz, *Pulp Surrealism*, 40.

94 Paul Thompson, *The Edwardians: The Remaking of British Society* (1975; Chicago: Academy Chicago Publishers, 1985), 39; Bernard Marchand, *Paris, histoire d'une ville XIXe–XXe siècle* (Paris: Seuil, 1993), 22.

95 Peter Hall, *Cities of Tomorrow: An Intellectual History of Urban Planning and Design in the Twentieth Century* (Oxford: Blackwell, 1988), 31.

96 Walter Benjamin, "The Work of Art in the Age of Mechanical Reproduction," in *Illuminations*, tr. Harry Zohn (New York: Schocken, 1969), 217–51, at 226; tr. from *Gesammelte Schriften*, ed. Rolf Tiedemann and Hermann Schweppenhäuser, 7 vols. (1974–89; Frankfurt: Suhrkamp, 1991), 1:471–508, at 485.

97 Siegfried Kracauer, "Analyse eines Stadtplans," *Frankfurter Zeitung* (1928), in *Strassen in Berlin und anderswo* (Berlin: Arsenal, 1987), 12–14, at 13; qtd. in Joachim Schlör, *Nights in the Big City*, 1991, tr. Pierre Gottfried Imhoff and Dafydd Rees Roberts (London: Reaktion Books, 1998), 278.

98 Tom Gunning, "From the Kaleidos to the X-ray: Urban Spectatorship, Poe, Benjamin, and *Traffic in Souls* (1913)," *Wide Angle* 19, no. 4 (October 1997): 25–61, at 50. See also David Frisby, *Fragments of Modernity: Theories of Modernity in the Works of Simmel, Kracauer, and Benjamin* (Cambridge: MIT Press, 1986), and "The City Interpreted: Georg Simmel's Metropolis," in *Cityscapes of Modernity* (Cambridge: Polity Press, 2001), 100–158; Fredric Jameson, "The Theoretical Hesitation: Benjamin's Sociological Predecessor," *Critical Inquiry* 25 (Winter 1999): 267–88; Maxwell, *Mysteries*, 167–69.

99 Georg Simmel, *The Sociology of Georg Simmel*, ed. and tr. Kurt H. Wolff (Glencoe, Ill.: Free Press, 1950), qtd. in Maxwell, *Mysteries*, 168.

100 Schlör, *Nights*, 102.

101 Karl Kautsky, *Vermehrung und Entwicklung in Natur und Gesellschaft* (Stuttgart: Dietz, 1910), 244; qtd. in Schlör, *Nights*, 290.

102 Giuliana Bruno, "Site-seeing: Architecture and the Moving Image," *Wide Angle* 19, no. 4 (1997): 8–24, at 9.

103 Miriam Hansen, *From Babel to Babylon: Spectatorship in American Silent Film* (Cambridge: Harvard University Press, 1991), 16.

104 Gunning, "Kaleidos," 39, 45.

105 Ibid., 45.

106 Ibid., 52–53.

107 Caillois, *Le roman policier* (Buenos Aires: Editions des lettres françaises, 1941), 72–73.

108 Qtd. in Abel, *French Cinema*, 75. The lines come from an unproduced surrealist play by Louis Aragon and André Breton which was to have featured Musidora, star of *Les Vampires* (*Le trésor des Jésuites*, 1929, in André Breton, *Oeuvres completes*, ed. Marguerite Bonnet, 3 vols. [Paris: Gallimard, 1988], 1:994–1014).

109 Walz, *Pulp Surrealism*, 61–66.

110 *Histoire de la France urbaine*, vol. 4, ed. Maurice Aguilhon (Paris: Seuil, 1983), 234.

111 Simmel, "The Sociology of the Senses," qtd. in Benjamin, *Passagenwerk*, vol. 5 of *Gesammelte Schriften*, M8a,1; *The Arcades Project*, tr. Howard Eiland and Kevin McLaughlin (Cambridge: Harvard University Press, 1999), 433.

112 On vision in modern culture, see Martin Jay, *Downcast Eyes: The Denigration of Vision in Twentieth-Century French Thought* (Berkeley: University of California Press, 1993); Lynne Cooke and Peter Wollen, ed., *Visual Display: Culture beyond Appearances* (Seattle: Bay Press, 1995); Hal Foster, ed., *Vision and Visuality* (Seattle: Bay Press, 1988).

113 Annette Michelson, qtd. in Roud, "Feuillade," 354.

114 Caillois, "Paris, mythe moderne," 162–64.

115 On the representation of the underworld during the 1920s, especially in Paris and Berlin, see Schlör, *Nights*, 136–45.

116 Abel also suggests this connection in his discussion of Feuillade (*French Cinema*, 76).

117 Bruno, "Site-seeing," 12.

118 Paul Morand, *Londres 1933*, in *Le nouveau Londres, suivi de Londres 1933*, rev. ed. (Paris: Plon, 1962), 192.

119 Henri Lefebvre, *The Production of Space*, 1974, tr. Donald Nicholson-Smith (Oxford: Blackwell, 1991), 287.

120 Abel, *French Cinema*, 75–76, referring to Michelson, in Roud, "Feuillade," 354.

121 Manny Farber, "White Elephant Art vs. Termite Art" (1962), in *Negative Space: Manny Farber on the Movies*, new ed. (New York: Da Capo, 1998), 134–44.

122 The critical literature on film noir is vast and, as befits a corpus that appeals to both academics and fans, of mixed quality. The two volumes edited by Alain Silver and James Ursini, *Film Noir Reader* (New York: Limelight, 1996), and *Film Noir Reader 2* (New York: Limelight, 1999), reproduce many of the seminal older essays that invented the noir myth from the 1940s on; the essays in *The Book of Film Noir*, ed. Ian Cameron (New York: Continuum, 1992), and *Shades of Noir*, ed. Joan Copjec (New York: Verso, 1993), provide a more revisionary approach to the subject. The best general study to date is James Naremore's *More Than Night: Film Noir in Its Contexts* (Berkeley: University of California Press, 1998).

123 David Reid and Jayne L. Walker, "Strange Pursuit: Cornell Woolrich and the Abandoned City of the Forties," in Copjec, *Shades of Noir*, 57–96, at 68–69. Although Reid and Walker's analysis of changes in urban space during the '30s and '40s is quite persuasive, they do little to apply that analysis to specific examples of film noir, and instead appear content to repeat the standard topoi about the genre.

124 Naremore, *More Than Night*, 11–27.

125 On the role of the city in what she terms the "disaster films" of the 1990s, see Despina

Kakoudaki, "Spectacles of History: Race Relations, Melodrama, and the Science Fiction/Disaster Film," *Camera Obscura* 50 (17, no. 2, 2002): 108–52.

Chapter 4. Through the Looking Glass

1 Le Corbusier, *The City of To-morrow and Its Planning,* tr. of Urbanisme *(1925),* tr. Frederick Etchells (1929; New York: Dover, 1987), 95.

2 Walter Benjamin, *Das Passagenwerk,* vol. 5 of *Gesammelte Schriften,* ed. Rold Tiedemann and Hermann Schweppenhäuser, 7 vols. (Frankfurt: Suhrkamp, 1991); *The Arcades Project,* tr. Howard Eiland and Kevin McLaughlin (Cambridge: Harvard University Press, 1999). The standard architectural history of the arcade form is Johann Friedrich Geist, *Arcades: The History of a Building Type,* 1978, based on a translation by Jane O. Newman and John H. Smith (Cambridge. MIT Press, 1983).

3 *Illustrated Guide to Paris* (Paris, 1852); qtd. in Benjamin, *Arcades,* 31 (A1,1). The sentiment dates back to the heyday of the *passage*; as Amédée Kermel asked rhetorically, "Isn't a *passage* the résumé of an entire city?" ("Les Passages de Paris," *Paris, ou le livre des cent-et-un,* 15 vols. [Brussels: Louis Hauman et Compe, 1831], 10:49–72, at 50).

4 Wolfgang Schivelbusch, *The Railway Journey: The Industrialization of Time and Space in the 19th Century* (Leamington Spa, England: Berg, 1986), 46.

5 Robert Harbison, *Eccentric Spaces* (1977; Cambridge: MIT Press, 2000), 38.

6 Marc Augé, *Non-lieux: Introduction à une anthropologie de la surmodernité* (Paris: Seuil, 1992); *Non-places: Introduction to an Anthropology of Supermodernity,* tr. John Howe (London: Verso, 1995).

7 Léo Claretie, "En 1987," *Paris depuis ses origines jusqu'en l'an 3000* (Paris: Charavay Frères, [1886]), 329–40, at 335–36.

8 Charles Fourier, *Oeuvres complètes,* 12 vols. (1841; Paris: Anthropos, 1966–68), 4:462–64; *The Utopian Vision of Charles Fourier: Selected Texts on Work, Love and Passionate Attraction,* ed. and tr. Jonathan Beecher and Richard Bienvenu (London: Jonathan Cape, 1975), 243.

9 Ibid., 244.

10 Ibid., 243.

11 James S. Buckingham, *National Evils and Practical Remedies, with The Plan of a Model Town* (London: Peter Jackson, Late Fisher, Son, & Co., 1849): 183–96 and Supplementary Sheet: 196*–99*, www.library.cornell.edu/Reps/DOCS/buckham.htm, accessed March 2007.

12 Ibid.

13 Here are some dates for the construction of the monumental stations (listed under their current names); often more makeshift platforms and buildings predated them. In London: Euston (1838), Kings Cross (1851–52), Paddington (1854), Victoria (1862), St. Pancras (shed, 1863–65; hotel, 1868–74), Charing Cross (1864). In Paris: Gare Saint-Lazare (1841–43, 1851–53, 1885–89), Gare de l'Est (1847–50), Gare de Montparnasse (1848–52), Gare du Nord (1861–66), Gare d'Austerlitz (1865–68), Gare de Lyon (1895–1902), Gare d'Orsay (1900).

14 Harbison, *Eccentric Spaces,* 40. For a general history of the railway in London, see vol. 1 of T. C. Barker and Michael Robbins, *A History of London Transport,* 2 vols., rev. ed. (London: George Allen and Unwin, 1975); the range of contemporary criticism of various stations quoted in Donald Olsen's *The Growth of Victorian London* (Harmondsworth: Penguin, 1979), 93–98, suggests a mixed reaction to a variety of strategies to make architectural sense of such novel urban spaces, although Olsen's analysis is limited to aesthetic appreciation.

15 Alfred Delvau, *Les Dessous de Paris* (Paris, 1860), 105–6.

16 Kermel, "Passages," 68.

17 On the rise of the department store in Paris and London, see Alison Adburgham, *Shops and Shopping, 1800–1914: Where, and in What Manner the Well-dressed Englishwoman Bought Her Clothes* (1964; London: Barrie and Jenkins, 1989); Michael B. Miller, *The Bon Marché: Bourgeois Culture and the Department Store, 1869–1920* (Princeton: Princeton University Press, 1981); Rosalind Williams, *Dream Worlds: Mass Consumption in Late Nineteenth-Century France* (Berkeley: University of California Press, 1991); Rachel Bowlby, *Just Looking: Consumer Culture in Dreiser, Gissing and Zola* (London: Methuen, 1985); Bill Lancaster, *The Department Store: A Social History* (London: Leicester University Press, 1995). On the transition from arcade to department store and beyond to the mall, see Anne Friedberg, *Window Shopping: Cinema and the Postmodern* (Berkeley: University of California Press, 1993).

18 Kermel, "Passages," 69–71.

19 Ibid., 72.

20 Léon-Paul Fargue, *Le piéton de Paris* (1939; Paris: Gallimard, 1993), 54. Fargue attributes the verse to "the sons of Narcisse Lebeau," a humorist and habitué of the Chat Noir cabaret. For Kermel, the passage Vivienne was "without doubt the most frequented of all the arcades in the capital" ("Passages," 58).

21 Kermel, "Passages," 62.

22 Ibid., 68.

23 Elie Berthet, "Rue et Passage du Caire," in *Les Rues de Paris: Paris ancien et moderne; Origines, histoire, monuments, costumes, moeurs, croniques et traditions*, ed. Louis Lurine, 2 vols. (Paris: Kugelmann, 1844), 1:237–52, at 250.

24 Charles Lefeuve, *Les Anciennes maisons des rues de Paris* (Paris, 1857–64), 2:233; qtd. in Benjamin, *Arcades*, 33 (A1a,7).

25 Maxime du Camp, *Paris: Ses organes, ses fonctions et sa vie jusqu'en 1870* (1870; Monaco: Rondeau, 1993), 362–63.

26 Edouard Foucaud, *Paris inventeur* (Paris, 1844), 154; qtd. in Benjamin, *Arcades*, 46 (A6,3).

27 Théophile Lavallée, "Géographie de Paris," in *Le Diable à Paris*, ed. Hetzel, 2 vols. (Paris: Hetzel, 1845–46), 2:i–lxxx, at xxxiii.

28 Du Camp, *Paris*, 363.

29 For more on the Egyptian revival in general and Highgate Cemetery in particular, see David L. Pike, *Subterranean Cities* (Ithaca: Cornell University Press, 2005), 135–36, 139–41.

30 Honoré de Balzac, "Ce qui disparaît de Paris," *Le Diable à Paris*, 2:12.

31 Joseph de Girard, *Des tombeaux ou de l'influence des institutions funèbres sur les moeurs* (Paris, 1801); qtd. in Edouard Fournier, *Chroniques et légendes des rues de Paris* (Paris, 1864), 154; qtd. in Benjamin, *Arcades*, 56 (A10,4).

32 Lavallée, "Géographie de Paris," *Le Diable à Paris*, 2:xlii.

33 J.-A. Dulaure, *Histoire Physique, Civile et Morale de Paris*, 4 vols. (1821–22; Paris: Au Bureau des Publications Illustrées, 1845), 4:56.

34 P. de Lasalle, *Almanach de l'Autre Monde* [Paris, 1817], 98.

35 Jules Janin, "Asmodeus," *Livre des cent-et-un*, 1:17–30, at 17.

36 E. Roch, "Le Palais-Royal," *Livre des cent-et-un*, 1:31–49, at 31.

37 Théodore Muret, *L'histoire par le theater, 1789-1851*, 3 vols. (Paris, 1865) 2:225–26; in Benjamin, *Arcades*, 39 (A2a,7).

38 Lavallée, "Géographie de Paris," 2:xlii.

39 Ibid.

40 Honoré de Balzac, *Les Illusions Perdues* (1837–43; Paris: Garnier, 1961), 288; tr. Herbert J. Hunt (Harmondsworth: Penguin, 1971), 260.

41 Ibid., 290, 261–62.

42 Ibid., 294, 264.

43 Louis-Sebastien Mercier, "Palais-Royal," *Tableau de Paris*, 8 vols. (Amsterdam, 1782–83), chap. 152, 2:102–4.

44 F. F. A. Béraud, *Les filles publiques de Paris et la police qui les régit*, 2 vols. (Paris: Desforges, 1839), 1:205, 207–9; qtd. in Benjamin, *Arcades*, 43 (A4,3 and 4,4). For more on the regulations, see Jill Harsin, *Policing Prostitution in Nineteenth-Century Paris* (Princeton: Princeton University Press, 1985), 41–44; Harsin also makes it clear that, following the revolution of 1830, the exclusion of prostitutes was enforced far less than Béraud would have led one to believe (127–30).

45 Ibid.

46 Charles Baudelaire, *Mon Coeur mis à nu*, in *Oeuvres Completes*, 2 vols., ed. Claude Pichois (Paris: Gallimard, 1975–76), 1:703.

47 For the Musée Grévin in the context of the spectacle culture of nineteenth-century Paris, see Vanessa Schwartz, *Spectacular Realities: Early Mass Culture in Fin-de-Siècle France* (Berkeley: University of California Press, 1998), 89–148.

48 Du Camp, *Paris*, 367.

49 Delvau, *Dessous*, 109.

50 Julius Rodenberg, *Paris bei Sonnenschein und Lampenlicht: Ein Skizzenbuch zur Weltausstellung* (Leipzig, 1867), 97.

51 Wolfgang Schivelbusch, *Disenchanted Night: The Industrialisation of Light in the Nineteenth Century*, tr. Angela Davies (Oxford: Berg, 1988), 152.

52 Gabriel Brazier and Dumersan, *Les Passages et les rues* (Paris, 1827), 19; qtd. in Benjamin, *Arcades*, 56 (A10,3).

53 *Life in London; A Play of Three Acts*, act 1, sc. 3. The Highgate Tunnel had collapsed during excavations in 1812; it was replaced by the Archway viaduct (still called Highgate Tunnel in some prints).

54 In a similar vein, a writer in *Punch* commented that the "Italian Opera House Arcade" was "suffering sadly from the want of rain. The traffic, in consequence, has been limited for the last three months, to the daily visits of the lamplighter" ("Arcadian Traffic," *Punch* 6 [January–June 1844]: 232).

55 *Life in London, A Play, in three acts: Depicting the Day and Night Scenes of Tom, Jerry, Logic & Co. Adapted to Hodgson's Theatrical Characters and Scenes in the Same* (London: Hodgson and Co., 1922), act 1, sc. 3.

56 Margaret MacKeith notes that there were more arcades opened in the new cities than in London: seven in Birmingham, five in Manchester, seven in Leeds, and nine in Cardiff, many of them with restrictions on the entrance of tradesmen (*The History and Conservation of Shopping Arcades* [London: Mansell, 1986], 20). The new cities raised problems related to the extremities of urbanization, but in general the verticalization of space and the segregation of classes were far more easily undertaken in cityscapes that were basically built from scratch in the industrial age.

57 *Life in London*, act 1, sc. 3.

58 *New Swell's Night Guide* (London: J. Paul, 1846), 27.

59 Ibid., 28.

60 *The Burlington Arcade*, one-act burletta, Olympic Theatre, licensed 17 December 1838.

61 C. Shirley Brooks, *The Lowther Arcade. A Farce in one act*, Lyceum Theatre, licensed 22 March 1845.

62 Matt Cook, *London and the Culture of Homosexuality, 1885–1914* (Cambridge: Cambridge University Press, 2003), 14.

63 Jane Rendell, " 'Industrious Females' & 'Professional Beauties,' or, Fine Articles for Sale

in the Burlington Arcade," *Strangely Familiar: Narratives of Architecture in the City*, ed. Iain Borden et al. (London: Routledge, 1996), 32–36, at 35; see also "Thresholds, Passages and Surfaces: Touching, Passing and Seeing in the Burlington Arcade," in *The Optics of Walter Benjamin*, ed. Alex Coles (London: Black Dog, 1999), 168–91. In her sustained meditation on the gender politics surrounding the Burlington Arcade, Rendell has raised key issues about women's use of space in this unusual environment; however, she has not yet unpacked the relationship between greater freedom to work and shop in the city and the more ambivalent independence of labor embodied by the prostitute in the identical space.

64 Rendell, "Industrious Females," 36; Bracebridge Hemyng, "Prostitution in London," in Henry Mayhew, *London Labour and the London Poor*, 4 vols. (1861–62; New York: Dover, 1968), 4:210–72, at 217, 222.

65 Neil Bartlett, *Who Was That Man? A Present for Oscar Wilde* (London: Serpent's Tail, 1988), 132; qtd. in Cook, *London*, 15; Morris B. Kaplan quotes in detail from the trial records and the signed depositions in *Sodom on the Thames: Sex, Love, and Scandal in Wilde Times* (Ithaca: Cornell University Press, 2005), 22–101, at 33.

66 C. W. S. Brooks, *The Lowther Arcade, or Waiting for an Omnibus on a rainy day*, one-act farce, Adelphi Theatre, licensed 24 June 1854. The theater was located a block east of the entrance to the arcade, along the same Strand bus routes.

67 E. Nesbit, *The Story of the Amulet* (London: Ernst Benn, 1906), 83. The reference was removed from later editions. In a typically Victorian contradiction, in addition to being a reputed haven for prostitution, the Lowther Arcade was also a center of toy sellers, its specialized commerce drawing, according to *Punch*, more ladies and far more children than the rival Burlington Arcade ("Arcadian Traffic," *Punch* 6 [January—June 1844]: 232).

68 Jane Rendell, "Displaying Sexuality: Gendered Identities and the Early Nineteenth-Century Street," *Images of the Street*, ed. Nicholas Fyfe (London: Routledge, 1998), 75–91, at 83–84.

69 "New Exeter 'Change," *Civil Engineer and Architect's Journal* (August 1844), qtd. in MacKeith, *Shopping Arcades*, 18.

70 Until recently, the most up-to-date comprehensive history was A. Brereton's 1907 volume, *The Literary History of the Adelphi and Its Neighbourhood*; more recent histories of the Adelphi can now be found in David G. C. Allan, *The Adelphi: Past and Present, A History and a Guide* (London: Calder Walker Associates, 2001), and David L. Pike, "Down by the Dark Arches: A Cultural History of the Adelphi," *London Journal* 26, no. 3 (Spring 2002): 19–41.

71 Steen Eiler Rasmussen, *London: The Unique City*, 1934, rev. ed. 1982 (Cambridge: MIT Press, 1988), 186–87. Wells published "A Story of the Days to Come" in 1899.

72 Charles Dickens, *David Copperfield* (1849–50; Harmondsworth: Penguin, 1966), chap. 11, 215.

73 Henri Lefebvre, *The Production of Space*, 1974, tr. Donald Nicholson-Smith (Oxford: Blackwell, 1991), 362.

74 On Nash's tunnel, see Edward Walford, "Underground London: Its Railroads, Subways, and Sewers," *Thornbury: Old and New London: A Narrative of its History, its People, and its Places*, vol. 5, *The Western and Northern Suburbs* (London: Cassell, Potter and Galpin, 1877), 229–42, at 226. According to Walford, such was the power of the wealthy local inhabitants that when the underground railway was built it was forced to be lowered "so as to carry the line under the subterranean thoroughfare, for the benefit of the nursery-maids and children of this highly-genteel neighbourhood" (226). The tunnel still exists, and the gardens are still private.

75 Dickens, *David Copperfield*, chap. 23, 413.

76 Ibid., 415.

77 Ibid., chap. 57, 874–75.

78 Ibid., chap. 47. Dickens twice used the Adelphi for such scenes. In one of the *Christmas Stories*, "Mrs. Lirriper's Lodgings" (1863), Dickens replayed the barely avoided suicide in the Adelphi Terrace; in *Little Dorrit* (1856–57), Arthur Clennam follows the villainous Rigaud to a mysterious meeting with the "fallen woman" Miss Wade, also on the Terrace in the dead of night (pt. 2, chap. 9).

79 Ibid., chap. 57, 881.

80 I borrow the idea of the Quai de Gesvres as "prototype" of the arcade from the late nineteenth-century illustrated history by Jules Cousin, "Quai de Gèvres," pt. 4 of *Paris à travers les ages*, ed. Fedor Hoffbauer, 12 pts. in 2 vols. (Paris: Firmin-Didot, 1875–82), 1:241–46, at 243. Although it fits much of Geist's definition of the arcade form ("a glass-covered passageway that connects two busy streets and is lined on both sides with shops. . . . It offers public space on private property . . . protection from the weather, and an area accessible only to pedestrians" [Arcades, 4]), Geist does not mention the Quai de Gesvres, choosing to begin with the "prototypical" Galeries de Bois of the Palais-Royal, finished in 1786 (448).

81 Henri Sauval, *Histoire et Recherches des Antiquités de la Ville de Paris*, 3 vols. (Paris: chez Charles Moette et Jacques Chardin, 1724), 1:247. The three volumes were assembled from Sauval's papers following his death in 1676.

82 Luc Vincent Thiéry, *Guide des Amateurs et des Etrangers Voyageurs à Paris* (Paris, 1787), 1:553. See also Sauval, *Histoire*, 1:247; le Sieur de Chuyes, *Le Guide de Paris* (Paris: Cardin Besongne, 1654), 125; François Colletet, *La Ville de Paris* (Paris: Antoine Raffle, 1689), 64, 158; Le Sage, *Le Geographe Parisien, ou Le Conducteur Chronologique et Historique des Rues de Paris* (Paris, 1759), 1:125–26; J-.A. Dulaure, *Nouvelle Description des Curiosités de Paris*, 2 vols. (Paris: Lejay, 1787), 2:307–8.

83 Le Sage, *Geographe*, 125–26; Cousin, "Quai de Gèvres," 243.

84 Emile de Labédollière, *Le Nouveau Paris: Histoire de ses 20 Arrondissements* (Paris: Barba, [1859], 61.

85 *Guide de Paris mystérieux*, ed. François Caradec and Jean-Robert Masson (Paris: Tchou, 1966), 231.

86 Rasmussen, *London*, 180.

87 Jacques Hillairet, *Evocation du vieux Paris*, 3 vols. (Paris: Editions de Minuit, 1952–54), 1:189. Hillairet provides a description that, although probably accurate, is couched in the full-fledged vertical rhetoric inherited from the nineteenth century: "a group of disgusting and sinister alleyways . . . the quarter of the slaughterers and flayers of the Grande-Boucherie, of which the pestilential stench emanated from pools of coagulated blood in the ditches and the refuse tossed in from all sides."

88 Sauval, *Histoire*, 1:636.

89 Dulaure, *Curiosités de Paris*, 2:307.

90 *Paris mystérieux*, 231; F. Bloch and A. Mercklein, *Les Rues de Paris: Histoire des rues, ruelles, carrefours, passages, impasses, quais, ponts et monuments de Paris* (Paris: Nadaud, 1889), 180.

91 The first and most famous tenant was the actor David Garrick, who lived in the center house of the Terrace until his death in 1779; his wife remained until 1822. His name was long connected with the place, and a room from his house was reconstructed in the Victoria and Albert Museum ("Adelphi Terrace," *London Encyclopedia*, ed. Ben Weinreb and Christopher Hibbert, 1983, rev. ed. [London: Macmillan, 1993], 7–8).

92 T[homas] Miller, "Picturesque Sketch of London, Past and Present. Chapter XXI. The Adelphi Arches and the Old Strand," *Illustrated London News*, 20 April 1850 (supplement). Miller was a poet and novelist, author of picturesque rural verse as well as volume 5 of

Reynolds's *Mysteries of London* (1849), and of *Picturesque Sketches of London Past and Present* (1852), which brought together the newspaper series that included the Adelphi piece.

93 The sketch was part of a series in the *Illustrated Times* on the 1861 census. See Michael Wolff and Celina Fox, "Pictures from the Magazines," in *The Victorian City*, ed. H. J. Dyos and Wolff, 2 vols. (London: Routledge and Kegan Paul, 1973), 2:559–82, at 573.

94 Raphael Samuel, "Comers and Goers," in Dyos and Wolff, *Victorian City*, 1:123–60, at 129–30.

95 *Down by the Dark Arches near the Adelphi.—Sunshine after Rain* (London: E. Hodges, [1860?]).

96 Adelphi Pier was on the lower end of the steamboat hierarchy, as the terminus of the halfpenny steamboat, which ran between there and London Bridge. The penny steamboats stopped only at Hungerford Market Pier; the Citizen and Iron steamboat company stopped at both Waterloo Bridge and Hungerford (Elisée Reclus, *Londres Illustré* [Paris: Hachette, 1865], 42); see also Barker and Robbins, *London Transport*, 1:42–43, 165–66). Hungerford Market was on the site now occupied by the Charing Cross railway station, for the construction of which it was demolished in 1860.

97 John Binny, "Thieves and Swindlers," in Mayhew, *London Labour*, 4:273–392, at 316–24. See also the contextualized account of this episode in Kellow Chesney, *The Victorian Underworld* (1970; Harmondsworth: Penguin, 1991), 170–79. Curiously, in the discussion of prostitution in the same volume, Hemyng asserted that the infamous Arches "are the most innocent and harmless places in London, whatever they once might have been. A policeman is on duty there at night, expressly to prevent persons who have no right or business there from descending into their recesses" ("Prostitution in London," Mayhew, *London Labour*, 239).

98 *Selected Poems of Thomas Hood*, ed. John Clubbe (Cambridge: Harvard University Press, 1970), 317–20. On Watts and Egg, see Malcolm Warner, *The Victorians: British Painting, 1837–1901*, catalog of an exhibition held at the National Gallery of Art, 16 February—11 May 1997 (Washington, D.C.: National Gallery of Art, 1997), 106–7; E. D. H. Johnson, "Victorian Artists and the Urban Milieu," in Dyos and Wolff, *Victorian City*, 2:449–74.

99 Johnson, "Victorian Artists," 458.

100 Lynda Nead, *Myths of Sexuality: Representations of Women in Victorian Britain* (Oxford: Blackwell, 1988), 71–86 and 132–34, at 75. This is by a long way the most comprehensive and insightful reading of the painting in terms of the symbolic topographies of London.

101 *Athenaeum*, 1 May 1858: 566; qtd. in Nead, *Myths of Sexuality*, 133.

102 The production was adapted from the original Surrey Theatre hit by J. B. Johnstone, *How We Live in the World of London; or, London Labour and London Poor*, licensed 24 March 1856, a "dramatization" of Mayhew's *London Labour*.

103 Percy Fitzgerald, "Where Adam Delved: A Tour through the Adelphi Arches," *Daily Graphic*, 16 December 1896.

104 On the journalistic fascination with the homeless in depictions of the "urban night," the rise of the night shelter, and the crackdown on sleeping in the open during the second half of the nineteenth century and the early twentieth century, see Joachim Schlör, *Nights in the Big City*, 1991, tr. Pierre Gottfried Imhoff and Dafydd Rees Roberts (London: Reaktion Books, 1998), 145–63.

105 Frank Rahill has discussed how the new Parisian melodrama of the 1840s, which was devoted to the urban panorama from high to low, was a consequence of the success of the *Mystères de Paris*; he identifies eight plays of the decade inspired by Sue's bestseller (*The World of Melodrama* [University Park: Pennsylvania State University Press, 1967], 85–87). Although at times bearing no resemblance to Sue's narrative, these plays seized on his new appreciation of

the vertical representation of the city, as evidenced by the easy translation to London settings. Still, preference was generally given to the literally subterranean spaces available all over Paris, and to the emblematic tapis-franc and other strongholds of the criminal classes.

106 Announcement for *Land Rats and Water Rats*, *Era*, 13 September 1868, 8.

107 Watts Phillips, *Land Rats and Water Rats*, Surrey Theatre, licensed 5 September 1868.

108 Review of *Land Rats and Water Rats*, *Era*, 13 September 1868, 14–15, at 15.

109 MacKeith, *Shopping Arcades*, 99; see also "Burlington Arcade: Stone Conduit Close," *The Parish of St James Westminster, Part Two, North of Piccadilly*, vol. 24 of *Survey of London*, gen. ed., F. H. W. Sheppard (London: Athlone Press and the University of London for the London County Council, 1963), 430–34, at 432.

110 The Thames Tunnel has received quite a bit more modern attention than the Adelphi. Much of the present discussion is drawn from my more detailed cultural history of the space, " 'The Greatest Wonder of the World': Brunel's Tunnel and the Meanings of Underground London," *Victorian Literature and Culture* 33, no. 2 (2005): 341–67. The most comprehensive study is David Lampe's straightforward history, *The Tunnel* (London: Harrap, 1963); Benson Bobrick provides a history in terms of subterranean construction in *Labyrinths of Iron: Subways in History, Myth, Art, Technology, and War* (1981; New York: Henry Holt, 1994), 49–73; Richard Trench and Ellis Hillman, *London under London: A Subterranean Guide*, 1984, new ed. (London: John Murray, 1993), place it in the context of their technological survey of subterranean London (105–15); Rosalind Williams, *Notes on the Underground: An Essay on Technology, Society, and the Imagination* (Cambridge: MIT Press, 1990), provides an excellent analysis of the tunnel in terms of the technological sublime (96–98).

111 Benjamin, *Arcades*, 150 (F1,2).

112 George Catlin, *Notes of Eight Years' Travels and Residence in Europe with His North American Indian Collection*, 2 vols. (London: published by the author, 1848), 2:112–13; qtd. in Richard Altick, *The Shows of London* (Cambridge: Harvard University Press, 1978), 373. The Thames Tunnel is an early example of a tourist attraction that was at the same time a site of labor and a transportation network. For a typology of such attractions, see Dean MacCannell, *The Tourist: A New Theory of the Leisure Class* (New York: Schocken, 1976), 51–57.

113 Frances Ann Kemble, *Record of a Girlhood* (London, 1878), qtd. in Humphrey Jennings, *Pandaemonium 1660–1886: The Coming of the Machine as Seen by Contemporary Observers*, ed. Mary-Lou Jennings and Charles Madge (London: Picador, 1987), 168–69. Williams provides an insightful analysis of this letter and its equation of the "aesthetic fantasy" with "the social fantasy of eliminating class conflict" in *Notes*, 96–98. On Kemble's Romanticism (in the context of her travel writings on America), see Christopher Mulvey, *Anglo-American Landscapes: A Study of Nineteenth-Century Anglo-American Travel Literature* (Cambridge: Cambridge University Press, 1983), 178–85.

114 For the influence of orientalism on the Romantics, see Nigel Leask, *British Romantic Writers and the East: Anxieties of Empire* (Cambridge: Cambridge University Press, 1992), and Raymond Schwab, *The Oriental Renaissance: Europe's Rediscovery of India and the East, 1680–1880* (New York: Columbia University Press, 1984); on the *Arabian Nights* in particular, see Peter Caracciolo, "Introduction: 'Such a store house of ingenious fiction and of splendid imagery,' " in *The "Arabian Nights" in English Literature: Studies in the Reception of "The Thousand and One Nights" into British Culture*, ed. Caracciolo (New York: St. Martin's, 1988), 1–80.

115 Kemble, *Record of a Girlhood*, 168–69.

116 Richard Beamish, *Memoir of the Life of Sir Marc Isambard Brunel* (London, 1862); qtd. in L. T. C. Rolt, *Isambard Kingdom Brunel* (1957; Harmondsworth: Pelican, 1970), 50.

117 The "Thames Tunnel Diary" of Isambard Kingdom Brunel, qtd. in Rolt, *Isambard Kingdom Brunel*, 60.

118 For a full account of the banquet, see Lampe, *Tunnel*, 116–18.

119 *The Real Devil's Walk. Not by Professor Porson. Designs by Robert Cruikshank. With notes and extracts from the Devil's Diary*, 2nd ed., with additions (London: William Kidd, 1831), stanza 4, 11.

120 On the South Sea bubble, see Srinivas Aravamudan, *Tropicopolitans: Colonialism and Agency, 1688–1804* (Durham: Duke University Press, 1999), 127–35. On the "memorable *panic* of 1825," when "the bubbles burst; and hundreds were hurled from a state of affluence to the most abject ruin," see George Smeeton, *Doings in London, or, Day and Night Scenes of the Frauds, Frolics, Manners, and Depravities of the Metropolis* (London: Hodgson, 1828), 372–78; rpt. as vol. 3 of *Unknown London: Early Modernist Visions of the Metropolis, 1815–1845*, ed. John Marriott, 6 vols. (London: Pickering and Chatto, 2000).

121 Henry Law, *Memoir of the Several Operations and the Construction of the Thames Tunnel by Sir Isambart Brunel, F.R.S. and Civil Engineer* (London: John Weale, [1828]), 96.

122 Beamish, *Memoir*, 258.

123 "The Thames Tunnel," *Mirror of Literature, Amusement, and Instruction* 30, no. 844 (15 July 1837).

124 Not until 1913 was a shield-constructed tunnel with a larger cross-sectional area successfully completed (Archibald Black, *The Story of Tunnels* [New York: McGraw-Hill, 1937], 27–28).

125 "Original Communications: The Thames Tunnel," *Mirror of Literature, Amusement, and Instruction* 43, no. 1188 (4 November 1843): 293–94, at 293.

126 Qtd. in Lampe, *Tunnel*, 198.

127 Najaf Koolee Meerza, *Journal of a Residence in England and of a Journey from and to Syria*, 2 vols., printed for private circulation only [1839], 2:9–10. For more on the experience of Indians traveling in London, see Antoinette Burton, *At the Heart of the Empire: Indians and the Colonial Encounter in Late-Victorian Britain* (Berkeley: University of California Press, 1998).

128 "Robbery, of a Poor Man in the Thames Tunnel," *Times* (London), 23 May 1845, 5d.

129 "Robbery of a Poor Man in the Thames Tunnel, Denied by the Tunnel Authorities," *Times*, 24 May 1845, 7f.

130 Lampe, *Tunnel*, 208. As late as 1858, we find a report in the *Builder* that, in one week in November, the still impressive number of 19,492 persons passed through the tunnel.

131 F. Saunders, *Memories of the Great Metropolis: Or, London, from the Tower to Crystal Palace* (New York: G. P. Putnam, 1852), 238.

132 Bayard Taylor, *Views A-Foot; or, Europe Seen with Knapsack and Staff* (New York: G. P. Putnam, 1880), 83.

133 Kermel, "Passages," 57.

134 Nathaniel Hawthorne, *English Notebooks*, ed. Randall Stewart (New York: Modern Language Association of America, 1941), 232–33.

135 "A Night in the Thames Tunnel," *Chambers's Journal* (1860): 203–6.

136 Ibid., 205.

137 Ibid.

138 John Hollingshead, *Underground London* (London: Groombridge and Sons, 1862), 13.

139 Trench and Hillman, *London under London*, 117.

140 "Exhibition Gets Cash Windfall," *South London Press*, 13 February 1990.

141 "Neueste Pariser Karikaturen," *London und Paris*, vol. 1 (Weimar: Verlag des Industrie-Comptoir, 1798): 87–110, at 89–92. Paul-Henry Gain, *La question du Tunnel sous la Manche* (Paris: Rousseau et cie, [1932]), has the most complete history and bibliography on the Channel

Tunnel up to 1930 (191–96); however, as with other Tunnel boosters attempting to contest the military objection, Gain declined to mention the original revolutionary fantasies of invasion.

142 Citizen Mittié, music by Citizen Rochefort, *Descente en Angleterre*, Cité-Variétés, 24 December 1797, act 2.

143 The fantasy of Irish invasion was echoed by Major-General Sir E. Hamley's objection to the 1880 tunnel project because of the "possibility of the English entrance to the Tunnel being seized upon by the Irish" (*The Channel Tunnel and Industrial Opinion. Deputation of English Workmen to Paris . . .* [London: William Bassett, 1883], 43).

144 Paul Féval, *Les Mystères de Londres; ou Les Gentilhommes de la Nuit*, drama in 5 acts, Théâtre Historique, 28 December 1848.

145 Féval, *Les Mystères de Londres*, 1842–43 (Paris: Bibliopolis, 1998), 306.

146 Ibid., 482.

147 "The Lions of London. Historical and Descriptive Sketch," *Punch, Or The London Charivari* 11 (January–June 1842): 175–83, at 178.

148 "Under the Sea! Under the Sea!" *Punch*, 14 July 1866, 15.

149 The print campaign was inaugurated by the *Times*, which would retain its animus against subaqueous tunnels for two centuries, and waged by Knowles in *The Nineteenth Century*; it was reprinted in full in a dossier attached to the February 1907 issue. For more recent studies, see Bertrand Lemoine, *Sous la Manche, le tunnel* (Paris: Gallimard, 1994), 48–55; Julian Barnes, "Froggy! Froggy! Froggy!" in *Letters from London 1990–1995* (London: Picador, 1995), 312–27; Keith Wilson, *Channel Tunnel Visions 1850—1945* (London: Hambledon, 1994). For a history of invasion fantasies related to the Channel Tunnel, see Jean-Pierre Navailles, "Le Tunnel, l'invasion de l'imaginaire," *Cahiers Victoriens et Eduardiens* 39 (1994): 153–73; Nick Hamer, "La rêve de Napoleon . . . et al!" *The Tunnel: The Channel and Beyond*, ed. Bronwen Jones (Chichester: Ellis Horwood, 1987), 245–79. On English invasion fantasies in general between 1871 and 1914, including eighteen from France, see I. F. Clarke, "Future War Fiction: The First Main Phase, 1871–1900," *Science Fiction Studies* 24, no. 3 (November 1997): http://www.depauw.edu/sfs/clarkeess.htm (March 2005); and Cecil Eby, *The Road to Armageddon: The Martial Spirit in English Popular Literature* (Durham: Duke University Press, 1987), 11.

150 For the class argument, see *The Channel Tunnel and Industrial Opinion*, 12–13, and the *Sunday Times*'s argument (16 April 1882) that the Tunnel would facilitate intercourse between continental and English "revolutionary Societies" (Gain, *Question du Tunnel*, 28n1); for the railway competition argument, see Alfred C. Tobinsky d'Altoff, *Le Tunnel sous la Manche* (Paris: H. Dunod and E. Pinat, 1919), 16. Edward Watkin, chairman of the Metropolitan Railway in London, had his own dream of extending the Underground via the South Eastern Railway, under the Thames and through to Europe (Bobrick, *Labyrinths of Iron*, 131).

151 *How John Bull Lost London; or, The Capture of the Channel Tunnel*, 4th ed. (London: Sanmpson Low, Marston, Searle and Rivington, 1882).

152 One of the earliest such utilitarian tunnel schemes can be found in a purportedly drug-induced utopian vision of 1843, published a century earlier as *Le Hachych*, in which the fédération Ibergallitale, a precursor to the European Union with a punning echo of the revolutionary slogan of 1789, has run "tunnels of several myriameters in length" to link Paris to Madrid and to Rome without passing over the Alps or the Pyrenees (F. Lallemand, *Le Hachych*, 1843, rpt. in *Révolutions politiques et sociales de 1848 prédites en 1843* [Paris: Au Comptoir des Imprimeurs-Unis, 1848], 159). My thanks to John Barberet for bringing this text to my attention.

153 I examine the underground railway in the context of the utopian city in chapter 1 of *Subterranean Cities*, and the transatlantic tunnel as it manifested itself in a newly ambitious

form in the science-fiction reveries of the *entre-deux-guerres*, accompanied by a renewed set of urban fears, in chapter 4, 282–86.

154 Tobinsky d'Altoff, *Tunnel sous la Manche*, 16, 45. Plans for the Gibraltar Tunnel dated back to 1869, and were being proposed with a new urgency in 1930, as was a tunnel under the Irish Sea between Belfast and Port Patrick in Scotland (Gain, *Question du Tunnel*, 114–15, 86).

155 On the 1924–30 project, see Gain, *Question du Tunnel*, 49–80. Kellermann's novel was published at the same time as the English campaign was being renewed by Sir Arthur Fell. As Gain argued, perhaps tendentiously, the German government feared the Tunnel for both economic and military reasons, and had actively worked against it since the 1880s (240).

156 The promotion of the Tunnel between the wars had in fact been prompted by the signing of the Kellogg-Briand Pact in 1928 (ibid., 51).

157 In addition to the harrowing tunnel-crossing scene in Gregory Nava's film *El Norte* (1983), see Lawrence Taylor and Maeve Hickey's *Tunnel Kids* (Tucson: University of Arizona Press, 2001), an account of the children living in the drainage tunnels that link Nogales, Sonora, and Nogales, Arizona.

158 Andrew Clark, "Stowaways Foil Tunnel Security: Rail Company Furious as More Than 80 Reach Kent," *Guardian* (10 April 2002): Home Pages, 7. As a result of a series of "tunnel breaches" (as one source put it) during 2001 and the first half of 2002, the Sangatte refugee camp was closed down and emptied, after much protest, by the end of 2002 ("Refugee Camp Boss Defiant," *BBC News* [28 December 2001]: http://news.bbc.co.uk/1/hi/world/europe/1730517.stm [March 2005]; "Sangatte Finally Closes Its Doors," *BBC News* [14 December 2002]: http://news.bbc.co.uk/1/hi/world/europe/2576557.stm [March 2005]).

159 See, in particular, "Adelphi Terrace. A Plea for its Preservation," 14 November 1922, report of a lecture by Mr. John Salter on "The Strand and the Adelphi: Their early history and development," Royal Society of the Arts, John Street; "The Adelphi Arches," *Country Life* 79, no. 2047 (11 April 1936): 386–87.

160 Émile Zola, *Thérèse Raquin* (1867; Paris: Gallimard, 1979), 32.

161 Ibid., 31.

162 Ibid., 33.

163 Benjamin, *Arcades*, 204 (H1,3; also a°,4).

164 Léon Barsacq, *Le décor de film* (Paris: Seghers, 1970); *Caligari's Cabinet and Other Grand Illusions: A History of Film Design*, rev. and ed. Elliott Stein (Boston: Little, Brown, 1976), 79. The film has not survived. Andrejew also designed the sets for such key expressionist films of the urban underworld as G. W. Pabst's *Pandora's Box* (1928) and *Threepenny Opera* (1931).

165 Zola, *Thérèse Raquin*, 47.

166 The passage du Pont-Neuf was built in 1823 and replaced in 1913 by the rue Jacques Callot (Geist, *Arcades*, 486).

167 Louis-Ferdinand Céline, *Death on the Installment Plan*, 1936, tr. Ralph Manheim (New York: New Directions, 1966), 70.

168 Hermann Broch, *The Sleepwalkers*, 1932, tr. Willa and Edwin Muir (1947; San Francisco: North Point, 1985), 346.

169 Thomas Mann, *The Magic Mountain*, 1924, tr. H. T. Lowe-Porter (Harmondsworth: Penguin, 1960), 4.

170 Ibid., 715.

171 Ernst Jünger, *In Stahlgewittern. Aus dem Tagebuch eines Stosstruppführers* (Berlin: Mittler, 1920); Henri Barbusse, *Le feu* (Paris: Flammarion, 1916), tr. *Under Fire* (London: J. M. Dent, 1929), 25; Erich Maria Remarque, *Im Westen nichts Neues* (Berlin: Im-Propyläen Verlag, 1929).

172 Mary Jane Green, "Death and Dissolution," in *A New History of French Literature*, ed. Denis Hollier (Cambridge: Harvard University Press, 1989), 851.

173 Max Beckmann, qtd. in Jay Winter, *Sites of Memory, Sites of Mourning: The Great War in European Cultural History* (Cambridge: Cambridge University Press, 1995), 164; see also Winter's general discussion of depictions of apocalypse in Austrian, German, French, and English painting and literature in the first few decades of the twentieth century (145–203), and Paul Fussell, *The Great War and Modern Memory* (New York: Oxford University Press, 1975). Paul Nash, qtd. in Paul Thompson, *The Edwardians: The Remaking of British Society* (1975; Chicago: Academy Chicago Publishers, 1985), 267.

174 Alexander Barrie, *War Underground: The Tunnellers of the Great War* (1961; London: Tom Donovan, 1990).

175 Alison Booth, *Postcards from the Trenches: Negotiating the Space between Modernism and the First World War* (New York: Oxford University Press, 1996), 54–55.

176 *Illustrated London News*, 21 November 1914: 697. London buses were shipped across the Channel, reoutfitted and painted khaki color for use in transporting soldiers to the front.

177 *Illustrated London News*, 10 October 1914. John Galsworthy had used a similar image in 1906 to describe the "great warren" of the underground railway in 1886 London (*The Man of Property* [Harmondsworth: Penguin, 1965], 267). See also Le Corbusier's later likening of the "great city" to a *battue*, an "infernal machine . . . where hundreds of thousands of rabbits are frightened into a series of traps formed of narrow corridors in which they get wedged and are caught" (*City of To-morrow*, 267).

178 Stéphane Audoin-Rouzeau and Annette Becker, *La Grande guerre 1914–1918* (Paris: Gallimard, 1998), 44; Fussell, *Great War*, 64–69; see also Booth, *Postcards*, 10.

179 Audoin-Rouzeau and Becker, *La Grande guerre*, 44.

180 Ibid., 130.

181 My thanks to Jeffrey Resnick at the 1998 Middle Atlantic Conference on British Studies for this reference.

182 "German Trench Architecture," *Architectural Review*, July–December 1916: 88+. Booth's analysis of this article (*Postcards*, 75–76), while insightful in its suggestion of the different attitudes of the German and English troops to the spaces they occupied and their ideological bases, ignores the degree to which the article duplicates this ideology in its assertion that the "German trench looks like the work of men who hoped, or feared, that they would be in it for years" while the British trenches were "much more of a makeshift, a sort of camping out."

183 Barrie, *War Underground*, 96.

184 Jean Norton Cru, *Du témoignage* (1930; Paris: Allia, 1989), 73.

185 Barrie, *War Underground*, 28.

186 Booth, *Postcards*, 97.

187 Imperial War Museum Photo Archive, Q.1384.

188 A. J. Peacock, "Introduction," rpt. of *Arras Lens-Douai and the Battles of Artois*, Illustrated Michelin Guides to the Battle-Fields (1914–1918) (1919; Easingwold: G. H. Smith and Son, 1994), iv.

189 At least in the East End, Londoners seem to have responded to the 1918 air raids by seeking shelter and psychological comfort in reconstructing the trenches at home as domestic architecture: "We can accommodate five hundred persons comfortably in our two arches or dug-outs, which are warmed with braziers, and have access under cover to a kitchen and other conveniences. . . . The first thing they did was to spend their Saturday afternoons digging a sloping trench so that a direct entrance might be obtained by the crypt, thus avoiding a dangerous and cramped staircase" (*Records of the Raids*, put together by the Right Rev. Henry

Luke Paget, D. D. Bishop of Stepney [London: Society for Promoting Christian Knowledge, 1918], 28–29).

190 In addition to the classic examples of the German *Fronterlebnis* (on which, see Klaus Theweleit, *Männer-Phantasien*, 2 vols. [Reibek bei Hamburg, 1980]; tr. *Male Fantasies*, Stephen Conway, 2 vols. [Minneapolis: 1987, 1989], and Jeffrey Herf, *Reactionary Modernism: Technology, Culture, and Politics in Weimar and the Third Reich* [New York, 1984]); see also Terry Castle's analysis of Vera Brittain's emotional investment in the masculine courage she saw to be required for this war and in the mythically heroic image of the courageous death of her lover ("Courage, mon amie," *London Review of Books* [4 April 2002]: 3–10).

191 On the exhibition trenches, see Fussell, *Great War*, 43; qtd. in Booth, *Postcards*, 10.

192 *Arras Lens-Douai*, 75–76, emphasis added.

193 *Handbook to Paris and its Environs. With Plan of the City, Map of the Environs, Plans of the Bois de Boulogne, Versailles, the Louvre, the English Channel, Calais, Boulogne, and a map of the battlefields*, 11th ed. (London: Ward, Lock and Co., [192?]), 211.

194 "Battlefield Round Trips by Automobile! organized by the *Basel News*," rpt. in Karl Kraus, "Reklamefahrten zur Hölle" (1921); "Promotional Trips to Hell," tr. Harry Zohn, *In These Great Times: A Karl Kraus Reader*, ed. Zohn (Manchester: Caracanet, 1984), 89–93, between 90 and 91.

195 Kraus, "Promotional Trips," 89.

196 F. Scott Fitzgerald, *Tender Is the Night* (1939; Harmondsworth: Penguin, 1974), 125. Fitzgerald began the book in 1924; it was first published ten years later, and in a revised edition in 1939.

197 Elinor Glyn, *Six Days* (London: Duckworth and Co., 1924), 115. I am grateful to David Trotter for bringing this novel to my attention and discussing it with me.

198 Ibid., 88. "Boche" was the French soldiers' name for the Germans.

199 Ibid., 135.

200 Arthur Holitscher, *Der Narrenbaedeker: Aufzeichnungen aus Paris und London* (Berlin: S. Fischer Verlag, 1925), 75, 79.

201 Ibid., 74.

202 Ibid., 78.

203 Virginia Woolf, *Mrs. Dalloway* (1925; New York: Harcourt Brace Jovanovich, 1953), 127.

204 Marcel Proust, *Le temps retrouvé*, in vol. 3 of *A la recherche du temps perdu*, 3 vols. (Paris: Gallimard, 1961), 834; *Time Regained*, in vol. 3 of *Remembrance of Things Past*, tr. C. K. Scott Moncrieff and Terence Kilmartin, with Andreas Mayor (New York: Vintage, 1982), 864.

205 Ibid., 840; 870.

206 Siegfried Sassoon, "Blighters," *The Old Huntsman and Other Poems* (London: William Heinemann, 1917); qtd. in Booth, *Postcards*, 29.

207 On the range and significance of the underground as a subject for the nineteenth-century theater, see Pike, "Underground Theater: Subterranean Spaces on the London Stage," *Nineteenth Century Studies* 13 (1999): 102–38.

208 Schivelbusch, *Disenchanted Night*, 191–212.

209 Maurice Crubellier and Maurice Aguilhon, "Les Citadins et Leur Culture," in *La ville de l'âge industriel: Le cycle haussmannien*, ed. Aguilhon, vol. 4 of *Histoire de la France urbaine*, ed. Georges Duby, rev. ed. (Paris: Seuil, 1998), 486. In fact, the theater would soon lose much of its middle-class audience as well, with attendance dropping by 90 percent between 1900 and 1920.

210 Giuliana Bruno, "Site-seeing: Architecture and the Moving Image," *Wide Angle* 19, no.

4 (1997): 8–24, at 9; also *Streetwalking on a Ruined Map* (Princeton: Princeton University Press, 1993), 35–45, where Bruno makes much of the fact that one of the major early cinemas of Naples was located in its central arcade, the 1890 Galleria Umberto I.

211 Francis Lacloche, *Architectures de cinémas* (Paris: Editions du Moniteur, 1981), 22.

212 Ibid., 25.

213 For more on the intertwined development of the cinematic apparatus and the tropes of the classical Hollywood narrative, see Miriam Hansen, *From Babel to Babylon: Spectatorship in American Silent Film* (Cambridge: Harvard University Press, 1991).

214 Schivelbusch, *Disenchanted Night*, 216–17.

215 Ibid., 209–10.

216 Bruno H. Bürgel, "Berliner Sensationen 1882," *Berliner Morgenpost* (6 July 1930), qtd. in Schlör, *Nights*, 66.

217 Schlör, *Nights*, 69.

218 Lacloche, *Architectures*, 47.

219 Crubellier and Aguilhon, "Citadins," 487.

220 Paul Virilio, *War and Cinema: The Logistics of Perception*, 1984, tr. Patrick Camiller (London: Verso, 1989), 39.

221 Booth, *Postcards*, 36. Although I disagree somewhat with her conclusions about the spatial significance of these memorials, I am indebted to Booth's insightful analysis of their role in making sense of the war in a new way (36–41).

222 Barbusse, *Under Fire*, 343.

223 Vera Brittain, *Testament of Youth: An Autobiographical Study of the Years 1900–1925* (1933; London: Virago, 1978), 416.

224 Ibid., 414–16.

225 On psychic photographs, see Winter, *Sites of Memory*, 73–76; he reports that there was widespread interest in the photos, both by the populace and by artists who appropriated them. On "Debout les morts!" see Cru, *Témoignage*, 68–72; Winter, *Sites of Memory*, 205–10.

226 Winter, *Sites of Memory*, 141.

227 The film was based on a real-life incident of 1906. The pessimistic ending, in which the military border is reestablished the moment the rescue is completed, was cut in many prints.

228 Winter, *Sites of Memory*, 76.

229 Charles Williams, *Descent into Hell* (1937; Grand Rapids, Mich.: Eerdman, 1977), 24.

230 Judith Whittet, "An Analysis of Stanley Spencer's *Resurrection*," University of Newcastle, http://www.newcastle.edu.au/discipline/fine-art/theory/analysis/judith.htm (June 2001).

231 Virilio, *War and Cinema*, 31.

232 Ibid., 39.

233 See Booth's analysis of the debate over architectural expressionism in *Postcards*, 125–57.

234 Ibid., 131–36.

235 Le Corbusier, qtd. in Charles Jencks, *Le Corbusier and the Tragic View of Architecture* (Cambridge: Harvard University Press, 1973), 60–61; qtd. in Booth, *Postcards*, 139.

236 Pike, *Passage through Hell: Modernist Descents, Medieval Underworlds* (Ithaca: Cornell University Press, 1997), 224–47.

237 André Breton, "Comme dans un bois," *L'Age du cinéma* 4–5 (August–November 1951): 26–30.

238 Eugène Hénard, "La Percée du Palais-Royal.—La Nouvelle Grande Croisée de Paris," *Etudes sur les Transformation de Paris, Fascicules 1–8* (Paris: Librairies-Impriméries Réunies, 1903–09), Fascicle 5, June 1904, 133–78.

239 Eric Schlosser, *Fast Food Nation* (New York: Perennial, 2002), 4–5, 229.

240 As James Meek has observed, both Walt Disney and Ray Kroc, the genius behind McDonald's, were in the same military camp in 1917, training to serve in the war in an ambulance unit; both, moreover, were captivated by the assembly-line operation of trench warfare, which they reproduced to construct their two global empires ("We Do Ron Ron Ron, We Do Ron Ron," review of *Fast Food Nation*, by Eric Schlosser, *London Review of Books* [24 May 2001]: 3–6, at 3)—a fascinating example of the imaginative power even of such a negative threshold as the trench.

241 Perry Anderson, "Casuistries of Peace and War," *London Review of Books*, 25, no. 5 (6 March 2003): 12–13.

242 Schlosser, *Fast Food Nation*, 230.

Index

(page numbers in italics refer to figures)

SONS *of* SINDBAD

To Bill and Mary
from your cousin,
affectionately
Will Facey
18.ii.08

Sons *of* Sindbad

An Account of Sailing with the Arabs in their Dhows, in the Red Sea, round the Coasts of Arabia, and to Zanzibar and Tanganyika; Pearling in the Persian Gulf; and the Life of the Shipmasters and the Mariners of Kuwait

By

Alan Villiers

With an Introduction by

William Facey
Yacoub Al-Hijji *and* Grace Pundyk

AP

Arabian Publishing

Sons of Sindbad
By Alan Villiers

Produced and published in 2006 by Arabian Publishing Ltd
3 Devonshire Street, London W1W 5BA
Email: arabian.publishing@arabia.uk.com

In association with
The Centre for Research and Studies on Kuwait

First published in the UK as *Sons of Sindbad* by Hodder & Stoughton Ltd, London, 1940.
First published in the USA as *Sons of Sinbad* by Charles Scribner's Sons, New York, 1940.
US edition reprinted, with a new preface by Alan Villiers and slight revisions, by Charles Scribner's Sons, New York, 1969.

A catalogue record for this book is available from the British Library

ISBN-10: 0 9544792 3 8
ISBN-13: 978 0 9544792 3 7

Typesetting and digital artwork by Jamie Crocker, Artista-Design, UK

Printed and bound in the UK by Creative Print and Design (Wales), Ebbw Vale

CONTENTS

LIST OF PHOTOGRAPHS

All the photographs in this book were taken by Alan Villiers in 1938–39, and appeared in either the first UK edition of *Sons of Sindbad* (London: Hodder & Stoughton, 1940) or the first US edition, published as *Sons of Sinbad* (New York: Scribner's, 1940). Each edition contained a selection of fifty photographs, some duplicating each other. Fifty of the best images from both editions have been selected for this reprint, by kind permission of the National Maritime Museum, Greenwich.

All the images are preserved in the Villiers Collection at the National Maritime Museum, among hundreds more of Villiers' two 1938–39 voyages. Some 160 of the previously unpublished images have been selected to appear in a new, large-format volume entitled *Sons of Sindbad: The Photographs*, co-published by the National Maritime Museum and Arabian Publishing (London, 2006).

Each image listed below is followed by its National Maritime Museum catalogue number, and can be ordered from the NMM Picture Library. For more information, tel. 020 8312 6600, or email picturelibrary@nmm.ac.uk

Between pp. 152 and 153:

9. Passengers throng the *Triumph* as she makes her way from Arabia to Africa. (PM 5260/27)

10. A Hadhrami passenger whiles away the time by playing the pipes. (PM 5387/33)

11. A Beduin baby from Hadhramaut bound for Mombasa. (PM 5358/30)

12. Kaleel the carpenter builds the small *jalboot*, *Afra*, on board the *Triumph*. (PM 5032/9)

13. Sailors repair the mainsail on deck, between Haifun and Mogadishu. (PM 5033/12)

14. Villiers was astonished at the strength and agility of the Kuwaiti sailors, who needed no footropes for their work aloft. (PM 5033/15)

15. On the halliards: hauling up the mainsail of the *Triumph of Righteousness*. (PM 5391/9)

16. Jassim, the *boom*'s cook, produced all the crew's meals with the aid of a simple firebox. (PM 5164/21)

17. The mate, Hamed bin Salim, takes a shave on board. (PM 5012/16)

18. A small *boom* from the Batina coast of Oman, like the *Triumph* unable to let its passengers go ashore at Mogadishu. (PM 5193/4)

19. A *boom* crowded with passengers, at Mogadishu. (PM 5194/7)

20. Said, from the port of Sur in eastern Oman, was one of the "smugglers" on board who kept up the age-old tradition of petty trading down the East African coast. (PM 5440/14)

21. A transom-sterned *sambuk*, from Sur in eastern Oman, leaves Mogadishu for the voyage south. (PM 5197/25)

22. The poop of the *Triumph*: a haul in the mizzen sheet. The deck is covered with sacks of goods on the voyage south. (PM 5321/31)

23. The bustling dhow port of Mombasa. (PM 5211/30)

24. The bustling dhow port of Mombasa. (PM 5207/10)

25. Zanzibar. (PM 5104/7)

26. Stem-piece of a large *sambuk*, probably at Zanzibar. (PM 5078/18)

Between pp. 280 and 281:

27. The *Triumph of Righteousness* beached for cleaning at Kwale Island. (N 83088)

28. Carrying sail, Kwale Island, with *baggala* and *boom* in the background. (N 83093)

29. Sailors sewing sail, Kwale Island. (N 83087)

30. Mubarrak, the Suri *nakhoda* who piloted the *Triumph* in the Rufiji Delta. (N 83100)

31. Hamed bin Salim, mate of the *Triumph of Righteousness*, in the Rufiji Delta. (N 83117)

32. Salale, in the Rufiji Delta. (PM 5124/9)

33. Hoisting the yard: on the voyage back from the Rufiji the sailors had to work on a deck packed with mangrove poles. (PM 5015/30)

34. Down tack! Hauling down the fore-foot of the mizzen sail. (PM 5320/29)

35. Aloft on the main lateen yard. (PM 5034/19)

36. With the *Triumph* packed to the gunwales with mangrove poles for the voyage home to the Gulf, her crew had to sleep where they could. (PM 5067/37)

37. A heavily laden Kuwaiti *boom*, possibly off the Omani coast. (PM 5175/8)

38. A fine large *boom*, perhaps off the Omani coast. (PM 5066/33)

39. Happy to be homeward bound, her sailors drum and sing the *Triumph of Righteousness* into Mutrah harbour. One of the two *serang*s or boatswains is on the left. (PM 5177/21)

40. Mutrah harbour crowded with the distinctive Omani *badan*s, with their detachable rudders, used for fishing and coastal trade. (PM 5098/9)

41. Kuwaiti and Suri: Nejdi (right) with a friend from Sur. (PM 5404/6)

42. The fine carved stern of one of the three surviving Kuwaiti *baggala*s, drawn up for overhaul on the Kuwait waterfront. (N 83090)

43. Covered *suq*, Kuwait. (PM 5230/24)

44. Decorative arch and side street, Kuwait. (PM 5230/34)

45. With the discovery of oil in 1936, these Kuwaiti boys were destined for easier livelihoods than dhow sailing and pearl diving like their fathers. (PM 5054/8)

46. His Highness Shaikh Ahmad bin Jabir Al-Sabah, ruler of Kuwait, relaxes on board his steam yacht with the British Political Agent in Kuwait, Major A. C. Galloway. (PM 5236/20)

47. On the pearl banks of the northern Gulf: a Kuwaiti pearling *sambuk* anchored with sweeps out, divers in the water, and haulers at the ready. (PM 5417/16)

48. Kuwaiti pearl divers take a breather between dives. (PM 5417/13)

49. A *tawwash*, or pearl buyer, inspects a pearl on board one of the boats on the banks. (PM 5082/5)

50. Abdullah Al-Hamad, a member of the Kuwaiti merchant house that gave Villiers so much help. (N 83225)

INTRODUCTION

While there has recently been something of a vogue for re-publishing the better-known Arabian travel writers, Alan Villiers' year at sea among the Arabs has been in danger of falling into obscurity. A celebrity cast of overland explorers has dominated the story of the West's discovery of Arabia and its peoples – a cavalcade beginning in the eighteenth century with Niebuhr, and continuing through the nineteenth with Burckhardt, Burton, Palgrave and Doughty; and with Gertrude Bell, T. E. Lawrence, Harry St John Philby, Freya Stark and Wilfred Thesiger bringing up the rear in the first half of the twentieth century. Though still revered as an authority on the twilight of commercial sail, a search for Villiers' name in anthologies of travel, or in studies of Arabian exploration, draws a blank. Villiers' right to be included among the greats of Arabian travel is only today gaining the recognition it deserves. Though he was much too modest a man to make such a claim for himself, he was, in a real sense, the Thesiger of the Arabian Sea – a claim based not just on his writings but also, like Thesiger's, on his photography.

Alan Villiers must have been born with salt in his blood. His passion for sail and the sea had already made him a name as a maritime adventurer in the 1920s and '30s because, unusually, he combined his seafaring skills with a great talent as a writer and pioneering photojournalist. In 1938, when he first came to Arabia, he had sailed the world in tall ships, survived a whaling voyage to the Antarctic, and published books and articles on his travels. He had just completed an epic two-year round-the-world voyage in his own full-rigged ship, the *Joseph Conrad*. He travelled to Arabia because he was certain that he was living through the last days of sail, and he was determined to record as much of them as he was able.

As a result of a meeting in 1938 with Harold Ingrams, the British Resident Adviser in Hadhramaut renowned as the begetter of "Ingrams' Peace",[1] Villiers chose Aden as his starting-point. Here he made contact with Captain Tom Hickinbotham, who had a dhow of his own and who was a good friend of the Al-Hamads, a Kuwaiti merchant house with offices in the main town of Crater.[2] Through them Villiers looked around for Arab dhow masters prepared to take on a lone Westerner as a crewman. He was put in touch first with the captain of a little Yemeni *zarook*, setting off for the Red Sea port of Jizan, in Saudi Arabia. Having spent two weeks on that voyage, he made his way up to Jiddah before returning to Aden by ship. Then, in December 1938, he was introduced to the captain of one of the great Kuwaiti *booms* then frequenting the port.

This Kuwaiti *nakhoda*, Ali bin Nasr el-Nejdi,[3] was making the age-old voyage from the Gulf to East Africa, coasting on the north-east monsoon winds, with a cargo of dates from Basra. The dates had been sold at Berbera, in British Somaliland, and Nejdi's *boom*, *Bayan* (which Villiers translates, rather freely, as *The Triumph of Righteousness*[4]), was continuing its voyage with cargo from Aden to pick up passengers on the Hadhramaut coast, and to sail thence to the ports of East Africa down to Zanzibar. The return voyage to Kuwait would be made in the early summer of 1939, on the first breezes of the south-west monsoon, with a full cargo of mangrove poles from the mosquito-ridden Rufiji Delta, south of Zanzibar.

From this voyage on the monsoon winds, made by Arabia's mariners from time immemorial, and regarded by Villiers himself as "my most interesting sailing experience",[5] *Sons of Sindbad* was fashioned. It was published in 1940 in Britain and the United States and was reprinted just once, in America in 1969, with a new preface and slight revisions, after Villiers had revisited Kuwait in 1967. It is the first British edition (London: Hodder & Stoughton, 1940) that is reprinted here. The book is the sole work of Arabian travel to have at its centre the seafaring Arabs. It is a great classic of the genre to rank with Thesiger's *Arabian Sands*, which it pre-dates by almost twenty years. Like Thesiger, Villiers travelled among his companions as an equal. At first critical of some of their methods, he came to defer to their superior knowledge of their business. Throughout he confesses to deep admiration of the dhow sailors' extraordinary toughness and stamina, their low material expectations, and their ability to "do without" on unbelievably slender means.

Of the hundreds of photographs Villiers took of his year among the seafaring Arabs, only a fraction were published in the British and American editions of *Sons of Sindbad*, each of which included a selection of fifty shots, some of them duplicating each other. Fifty of the best such images, chosen from both 1940 editions, are reprinted in this volume. The remainder of the collection, deposited by Villiers at the National

Maritime Museum at Greenwich, has remained a buried treasure awaiting a discoverer, and it is these pictures that are being published, concurrently with this reprint, by the National Maritime Museum as *Sons of Sindbad: The Photographs* (London, 2006). Though he hardly mentions his photography in *Sons of Sindbad*, the negatives in the archives show that he took with him both 35-mm and large-format cameras, as well as a movie camera, with which he shot footage of life on board. Though he was dismissive of his photographic skills, the images provide an unforgettably vivid record of the life and skills of Kuwait's dhow sailors, of the ports along the route, of Kuwait itself, and of the pearl divers of the Arabian Gulf.

Early Life

Alan John Villiers (1903–82) was born in Melbourne, Australia, second son in a family of four sons and two daughters. His father, a tram driver with strong socialist principles, wrote articles for working men's papers and was something of a poet. The young Alan was thus exposed from an early age to the idea of writing, and imbued with a very Australian egalitarianism and sense of fair play. This never left him, and his empathy with the common working man shines through his work, never more so than in *Sons of Sindbad*.

His parents were poor and had ambitions for their sons, but young Alan was irresistibly drawn to the docks and the ships engaged in the deep-sea bulk cargo trade to Europe. These were still the traditional steel-hulled, square-rigged tall ships, and he was rapidly infected by a yearning for sail and sea of which he was never to be cured, even by his parents' entreaties and his first wife's ultimatums. In thrall to the power of the wind in the sails, he was to devote his life to the sea and merchant sailing ships, and throughout it showed an aversion to mechanized shipping that Thesiger would have appreciated.[6] At the age of eleven he attempted to join the crew of a Norwegian barque and was only dissuaded by the mate, who warned him against romantic notions of life at sea drawn from books. But, like a previous sailor and Arabian traveller in the 1870s, John Keane of Whitby (later also an Australian), Villiers had fallen under the spell of old seafarers' tales, and all such attempts to put him off served only to deepen the enchantment.

His father's untimely death from cancer in 1918 left the family almost destitute and, in 1919, they were hit by the great influenza pandemic.

Villiers enrolled in a sail-training school, and by the age of fifteen was serving as an apprentice on the *Rothesay Bay*, an elderly barque plying the timber trade between Australia and New Zealand. The harsh reality of life at sea, so far from undermining the lad's resolve, crystallized his credo:

> The great sound of the wind in the rigging was a threat no longer but a symphony of strength and power, and I knew that in a world beset by wars and mounting daily difficulties, the sailing-ship was still a triumph of man's seafaring genius. To be one of a band of men who conducted such ships upon their voyages was to me also triumph – it was a fulfilment of life such as I had dreamed on. Here in the battered barque all men mattered: by the sure efforts of our own hands we survived.[7]

Alive to the prospect that wind ships, and the traditions of toughness and comradeship that went with them, were on the verge of extinction, Villiers began to keep a diary of sorts when he joined his next barque, the *James Craig*.[8] By now even more deeply under the spell of life afloat, he wrote:

> It seemed to me that the fo'c'sle of a happy sailing ship at sea was one of the more pleasant abodes of labouring man, where the sailors of all nations had learned through the centuries to work and live amicably together. Here there was true democracy, true international co-operation. At least all were equal in their lack of possessions, their pride in their great calling and their skill, and their spirit of service to the ship.[9]

When in 1920 the *Craig* was decommissioned, he joined a four-masted British "lime-juicer", the *Bellands*, carrying grain to Europe. A harsh voyage round the Cape of Good Hope, under officers he despised for their arrogance and superior airs, brought him in 1921 to a Britain in the grip of post-war austerity, and in London he was unable to find another ship. Crossing to France as an illegal immigrant, he tramped from Nantes to Bordeaux, living rough, before at last finding a place as able seaman aboard the *Lawhill*, an old steel-hulled, four-masted grain barque about to return from Bordeaux to Adelaide. The *Lawhill* belonged to Gustaf Erikson of Mariehamn, in the Finnish Åland Islands, the last big owner of sailing ships in the intercontinental grain trade from Australia.

Villiers found the openness and egalitarianism he so admired among the young Swedish-speaking Finns who made up the crew. He was to find this same quality of instinctive teamwork and concern for one's crewmates on board the *Triumph of Righteousness*. But, as the *Lawhill* neared Adelaide, she hit a sandbank, precipitating Villiers from the rigging to the deck in a near-fatal fall. "It seemed to me," he wrote, "in a last instant of consciousness, that the deck was surprisingly soft. It was not the deck that was soft. It was I."[10] His injuries led him to give up sailing and, after a series of odd jobs including a dispiriting spell on a cargo steamer, to begin life afresh in Tasmania. There a chance encounter with a journalist, which led him to the office of the *Hobart Mercury*, enabled him to discover his great flair for writing.

True to his instincts, he used his pen to get back to sea, persuading the *Mercury* to send him as special correspondent with an experimental Norwegian whaling fleet to the Antarctic. Here, on board the steam factory ship *Sir James Clark Ross* as a whaler's labourer at £4 a month, but with a fine new camera and a mission to report, he found his *métier*: seafaring combined with writing and photography. And on board the *Lawhill* he had already discovered a fourth talent, that of picking up a working language from scratch, which would later serve him well on an Arab vessel.

His Antarctic experiences of 1923–24 were published as articles, which he then expanded into his first book, *Whaling in the Frozen South*, published in 1925 with some success in Britain and the United States. By the time he was twenty-two, his journalistic talents had earned him promotion to senior reporter on the *Hobart Mercury*. He had also married his first wife in Hobart and was trying to settle down. But the siren-song of the sea ordained that he would use his way with a story to subsidize further sailing adventures.

In 1927, Villiers was in Melbourne on an assignment from the *Mercury* when he noticed a fine four-masted Erikson barque, the *Herzogin Cecilie*, discharging Baltic timber in the port. He went on board to find its captain, who turned out to be the very same Ålander, Ruben de Cloux, who had captained the *Lawhill* on the voyage to Adelaide. De Cloux's formidable sailing skills and perfectionism had made their mark on Villiers, who immediately set about persuading his paper to grant him six-months' leave to sail for Europe on the *Herzogin Cecilie* as an able seaman and, once there, to report home on the fruit trade in Europe. The ship was to load grain and to race another, the Swedish four-master *Beatrice*, in one of the so-called "grain races" to Britain via Cape Horn. Villiers got his permission and bought his own camera; the *Herzogin* made the 15,000-mile passage from Port Lincoln to Cornwall in 96 days and won the race, and a best-seller was born. *Falmouth for Orders* was published to acclaim in 1928 and went into several editions, creating a public appetite for Villiers' vivid accounts of the last days of the tall ships that would ensure a brisk demand for his future books.

The success of his investigations into the European fruit trade and the articles that followed made Villiers' name as a journalist, and even opened up the prospect of a political career in Australia. But, addicted to the sea as he was, he was busy contriving a saltier career for himself. His ambition now was to capture the twilight of sail on movie film before it was too late, to augment the still photographs he had already amassed. Teaming up in 1929 with a fellow journalist, Ronald Walker, he took ship as an able seaman on the ageing Finnish three-master *Grace Harwar*, the last of the full-rigged Cape Horners. She was notoriously undermanned and under-maintained, but her lack of modernization appealed to the two men as being well suited to their theme. The choice turned out to be a tragic one. Villiers' decision to go effectively put an end to his first marriage, and of this ill-starred enterprise he later wrote:

> We were lucky to arrive at all. On the voyage Walker was killed [by a falling spar], the second mate driven out of his mind, the ship sprang a serious leak, and we ran out of food. ... We were the last ship to sail and the last in the race. The whole voyage was a savage fight against the sea, in a ship which was seriously handicapped from the setting-out to the end.[11]

Another passage shows how the voyage brought out all Villiers' remarkable combination of physical stamina and creative skills:

> I was one of a handful of able seamen in a heavy ship, grievously undermanned. I steered. I pumped. I worked aloft. I often sewed sails all day on deck, and worked with them in the rigging half the night. I did what I could to help the second mate. I filmed and photographed, for that could not be given up, and I tried to make as good a job as Walker would have done. When the weather was good, I brought out my battered portable typewriter, and got on with my maritime history of Tasmania, for that had to be ready for the press when we came in.[12]

Despite the discouragements of the *Grace Harwar* experience, Villiers had managed to shoot all 6000 feet of film, and had collected material for his biggest-seller yet, *By Way of Cape Horn*. A job in Fleet Street, a lecture tour in America and a relationship with the *National Geographic Magazine* quickly followed. By 1931 he found himself with capital to spare and went in with de Cloux in the purchase of the *Parma*, a 3000-ton four-masted steel barque built in Port Glasgow. It turned out to be a shrewd investment. Villiers made two voyages on the *Parma* under de Cloux, transporting grain from Australia to Britain, in 1932 and 1933, and both turned in a very handsome profit. More best-sellers followed: *The Voyage of the Parma*, followed by *Last of the Wind Ships*, a book of some 200 photographs of the *Parma*'s voyages.

As part-owner of the *Parma*, Villiers had sailed not as an able seaman but as understudy to the masterly de Cloux.[13] With that experience behind him, he felt ready to command his own sailing vessel. He sold his share in the *Parma*, and in 1934 bought the Danish training ship *Georg Stage*, a three-master of just over 200 tons, "a tiny full-rigged ship, a veritable miniature, perfect in every detail".[14] Renaming her the *Joseph Conrad*, in homage to that great maritime man of letters, he assembled a crew of experienced hands and invited "all the young fellows who cared to come and there was room for" to make a voyage round the world, "an ambling circumnavigation by way of Good Hope and the Horn, the East Indies and the South Seas".[15] His route was inspired by the voyages of James Cook but, if Cook inspired Villiers the sailor, it was the "convincing and stirring prose of the brooding Polish-English master mariner" Conrad that helped inspire him as a writer. Villiers pondered much on the effect sailing might have on a writer's style. "The seaman", he wrote, "had time to think but not to write ... He had need to make decisions most clearly conveyed in minimal and incisive prose."[16] Villiers had literary contacts aplenty by now, and there was even some talk of T. E. Lawrence coming along on the voyage.[17] This adventure took two years, 1934–36, and took him over some 57,000 miles of ocean. It was when he was in the Pacific, after the *Conrad* had left Australia, that his first wife finally divorced him – citing the sea as co-respondent![18]

Cruise of the Conrad, yet another best-seller, was published in 1937, but the venture had exhausted Villiers' funds and, on arrival in New York in October 1936, the *Conrad* had to be sold to clear his debts. By a lucky stroke, the ship was bought by an American millionaire who happened to see her in New York harbour, and she is now preserved in the Mystic Seaport Museum, Connecticut.

While Villiers was engaged in these voyages European sail had been steadily dwindling, and by 1937 many of the ships that he had known had been sold off as hulks or for scrap. His next big idea was to turn his attention to seafaring in other, pre-industrial cultures. He opted first for the Arabian dhow world of the western Indian Ocean because it seemed to him, "having looked far and wide over a seafaring lifetime, that as pure sailing craft carrying on their unspoiled ways, only the Arab remained".[19] But this choice was part of a larger vision:

> My sailing with the Arabs was part of a programme, to occupy at least five years, by which I hoped to acquaint myself with the sailing-vessels of the world. … There were still large fleets quietly going about their share of the world's sea-borne trade in the Indian Ocean and the waters of East Asia. … A life of wandering in sailing ships appealed to me, and I proposed to make an exhaustive survey of the types of ship and the trades I came across, and to photograph and make films as records.[20]

Sons of Sindbad

On the *Joseph Conrad*, as both captain and owner of his ship, Villiers had for the first time achieved a status with which an Arab *nakhoda* would have identified. He did not ship out on Nejdi's *boom* as an ordinary crew-member, but shared the poop with Nejdi, the mate Hamed bin Salim, Nejdi's brother, the two helmsmen, and any merchants voyaging as passengers. The crew, divided into two watches under the two *serang*s or boatswains, made do as best they could on the deck among the cargo and indigent passengers. Villiers was privileged to have his space, which was more or less sacrosanct, but life on the poop was strictly *al fresco* and entailed no luxury.

Villiers did not let his status on the poop deter him from trying to join in the arduous work of the sailors. But he was very soon prevented from doing so. First, even for a hardened Cape Horner used to working aloft taking in sail in a hurricane, he found the work too hard. He was amazed at the Kuwaiti sailors' ability to climb aloft and take in sail without any need for footropes. Throughout, he pays tribute to their willingness, team spirit and sheer toughness. Second, he was felled by a serious accident early on, which not only blinded him temporarily and rendered him semi-conscious for much of the stretch between Aden and Mukalla, but handicapped him for the rest of the voyage. This was not the only occasion causing him to ponder the wisdom of his adventure. But he persevered to the end and in *Sons of Sindbad*, dashed off with his usual facility in the early weeks of the Second World War, he has given us one of the great classics of Arabian travel and, indeed, of travel writing in general.

Sons of Sindbad is the work not only of a naturally gifted sailor, writer and photographer, but also of an astute businessman. With his background in commercial journalism and nose for a business venture, Villiers was interested in the economics of the dhow and pearl trades, and the social conditions of those engaged in them. In Kuwait he was able to interview people from every walk of life, from the ruler Shaikh Ahmad Al-Sabah to ministers, merchants, captains, and homeless seamen on the waterfront. His analysis of the bonds of debt tying the sailors and divers to the *nakhoda*s, and the *nakhoda*s to the merchants, makes compelling reading. It also goes to the heart of the inequities of the old system, as it stood on the very threshold of being swept away by the wealth from oil that had just, in 1936, been discovered in commercial quantities. Until then, Kuwait had enjoyed no natural resources of its own, not even fresh water. Over the previous two centuries its rulers and people had managed, by skilful use of their geopolitical location and traditional skills, to turn their small, barren state into the foremost Arab dhow port in the Gulf. Villiers was able to use his unusual combination of talents to paint a uniquely graphic picture of the society and economy of this maritime people, not only at home but also on their far-flung voyages.

So *Sons of Sindbad* may be a rattling good sea dog's yarn but it is very much more. The wide scope of Villiers' interests lifts it out of the niche of sailing memoirs and places it squarely within the larger genres of travel writing and social study. His ambivalent position, as a Westerner connected with the imperial reach of British officials on the one hand, but, on the other, accepted as part of an Arab dhow crew, afforded him a unique vantage point. When he turns a blind eye to the smuggling ventures of his crewmates, or is amused by Nejdi's attempts to evade new-fangled, European-imposed navigation and immigration regulations, there is no doubt where his sympathies lie. Yet he could also see some benefit in modernization and administration, as when inspecting the beginnings of a new road being constructed by Ingrams from Mukalla to the Hadhramaut valley. His awareness that he was witnessing the demise of an ancient tradition of wind-borne trade in the face of irreversible mechanization lends piquancy. But he does not lull us into romantic illusions about the life of the Gulf sailors and pearlers, exploited as they were by the traditional debt system and mostly living from hand to mouth.

It is possible to fault his account in one respect only, and that is when, as he often does, he speaks of Arab navigation.[21] When Villiers was introduced to Nejdi in Aden, it was with the recommendation that the latter "was the best young nakhoda from Kuwait".[22] Nejdi was a dashing young captain of about thirty years of age, only a little younger than the thirty-five-year-old Villiers. He was a natural leader, whose crew gave him unquestioning loyalty. Confident in the enclosed little world of his ship, he could air his opinions with unchallenged authority. Nejdi was baffled by Villiers' project to write a book about the voyage and dismissed the idea with contempt, and there are other little hints in *Sons of Sindbad* that he and Villiers may at times have had a somewhat trying relationship. But in general the Kuwaiti captain humoured his eccentric guest well enough.[23] Nejdi was, after all, a *nakhoda* with a reputation to uphold. The laws of Arab hospitality were binding, and in any case Villiers was a skilled navigator and might make himself useful. This curious Westerner, friendly with but so different from the colonial officials that Nejdi usually came in contact with, was at first handicapped by the language barrier; but he soon picked up sufficient Arabic to understand the management of the *boom* and even to take part in conversations on the poop. These were dominated by Nejdi's disquisitions on everything from politics, religion, and the relative merits of Islam and the West, to the intricacies of the coastal navigation that he specialized in.

And it is here that *Sons of Sindbad* presents a slightly distorted picture. Being virtually the only first-hand English work on Arab seamanship, it has been widely accepted as the authoritative source on the subject. But Villiers' passages on navigation convey the impression that Kuwait's ship-masters had lost the art of finding their way by celestial methods across the open ocean, so well known as having been practised by Arab mariners in previous centuries.[24]

Nejdi was well aware that his predecessors had been masters of the ancient art of east–west latitude sailing by raising and lowering the Pole Star above the horizon, and of latitude-finding by means of a *kamal*. The *kamal* was a small rectangle of wood on a string, on which knots represented latitudes of particular ports. With one end of the string gripped taut between his teeth, the navigator would move the rectangle along it until it covered the gap between the horizon and the Pole Star: the nearest knot then gave him his rough latitude.[25] Nejdi and his friends knew something of sextants and quadrants without troubling themselves much with them. They expressed a certain regret at their own inability to sail direct across the ocean, while insisting that such knowledge was not really essential, as they "knew the way" well enough by using coastal landmarks and recognizing shoals and currents. For the short voyage across the open sea between southern Arabia and the Horn of Africa, Nejdi could lay a course from an old chart and his battered ship's compass, using dead reckoning to estimate the distance travelled, and that was good enough for him.[26] Villiers frequently quizzed him about the finer points of deep-sea navigation and often laments the fading of the old art, but eventually was forced to concede that Nejdi and his mate, Hamed bin Salim, were right in their way. They were supreme masters of their business, had an uncanny knack for handling the 150-ton *Triumph of Righteousness* in a tight spot and, if they could get to East Africa and India without the finer points of celestial navigation, why should they bother to learn them?

It is therefore quite true that Nejdi himself was no deep-sea navigator. However, he was far from being the most accomplished exponent of Kuwaiti navigational know-how. "The lack of proper navigational knowledge among the Arab nakhodas of today" that Villiers laments, should not be taken as fact.[27] Nejdi, perhaps averse to putting himself in their shade, might have been understandably reluctant to enlarge on the skills of his deep-sea counterparts. But he certainly knew plenty of them, such as Abdul-Wahhab Al-Kitami and Mayouf Al-Badr. Villiers too was aware of these men and himself met Abdul-Wahhab Al-Kitami at Zanzibar when he came into port on his famous large *boom*, *El-Dhow*, as well as meeting Mayouf Al-Badr in Kuwait.[28] And in both *Sons of Sindbad* and his book *Monsoon Seas*, he refers to another such master, Yusuf bin 'Isa Al-Kitami, whose *boom* they encountered in Oman:

> At Muscat and at Bahrein we met dhows in the Indian trade. There was a big beauty at Muscat called the *Samhan*, which was registered as 305 tons, with a capacity of 5,000 packages of Iraqi dates. … She carried two navigators, each with an ancient quadrant, and she had a small radio receiving set to listen to the news. … She was commanded by a man named Yusuf bin Isa, son of Isa Kitami who had compiled the Kuwait *Periplus*.[29]

> This big *boom* made longer voyages round the Indian Ocean than most dhows did. … The *Samhan*, when we saw her, was completing a voyage begun at Basra the previous September, with

> dates to Karachi, Bombay, and Mangalore: thence she had sailed with an Indian cargo directly to Mombasa, and after calling also at Malindi, had loaded mangrove poles at Lamu for the homeward journey. The previous season she had gone from India to Aden.[30]

So Yusuf Al-Kitami had taken the *Samhan* on two long deep-sea voyages in 1938 and 1939: India to Aden, and Mangalore to Mombasa. The two navigators on board were trainees, learning at his feet. Nor was he alone. Research in Kuwait has revealed at least fifty such navigators in the first half of the twentieth century.[31] Only one of these possessed a marine chronometer and so they were unable to fix their longitude exactly against noon sextant readings. They were, however, able to use quadrants and sextants to calculate their latitude, and from this they could use simple trigonometry and dead reckoning to obtain an approximate longitude position. Furthermore, there are at least thirteen surviving logbooks by Kuwaiti deep-sea captains, such as Mayouf Al-Badr, Salman Al-'Isa and 'Isa Bishara, all describing their annual crossing of the ocean between India and Oman, and between India and Africa. Ahmad Al-Khashti (1880–1964) bears the distinction of being the only Kuwaiti captain to use a sextant and chronometer to find his longitude: he was doing so from the early 1930s.[32]

That cautionary note on Arab navigation aside, *Sons of Sindbad* is a rich and heady brew of the people, ways of life, politics, governments, trade ancient and modern, cultures and human relations at the western edge of the old Indian Ocean world. At its core is Villiers' humanity. In trying to experience the realities of seafaring life at first hand, he goes to extreme lengths to identify with his companions. The book stimulates much thought on the nature of power, whether exerted by imperialism from without or by traditional merchant capitalism from within. Despite the bold brushstrokes we are never offered simplicities. The picture he presents is a complex one, a depiction as much of man's capacity for benevolence as for inhumanity to his fellows.

Why, then, has *Sons of Sindbad* been relatively neglected, and why does Alan Villiers not occupy a prominent place in the celebrity cast of Arabian travellers? Given Britain's centuries-old love affair with the sea, and its maritime hegemony in the nineteenth and early twentieth centuries, the paradox is a particularly puzzling one. The book's publication in the dark days of Second World War forms part of the answer, but there are other reasons too why it failed to make its mark as a major contribution to the literature on Arabia.

First, many of the big names of the genre, such as Gertrude Bell, T. E. Lawrence, St John Philby, Bertram Thomas and Freya Stark, were intimately linked with British political power in the Middle East, which between the wars was enjoying an unprecedented ascendancy – what Elizabeth Monroe has called "Britain's moment in the Middle East".[33] This was the case even when, like Lawrence and Philby, they felt deeply at odds with British policy. Villiers, by contrast, was an independent traveller. Though an Anglo-Saxon citizen of the British Empire, who enjoyed good relations with British officials during his voyage and would join up and fight with distinction in the Second World War, he was no agent of imperial officialdom.

That on its own, however, would not necessarily have undermined the market for his book. On the contrary, one would have thought that it might enhance it. After all, Charles Doughty had made his eccentric and alarming Arabian journey in the 1870s on his own account, and made of it an abiding classic of Arabian literature, even if *Arabia Deserta* did languish in obscurity until promoted by T. E. Lawrence in the 1920s.

Another, deeper reason is not far to seek: the sea. A sea voyage is by its very nature subversive of the stereotypical Western account of Arabian travel, the pioneering desert journey. A glance through a survey such as *The Cambridge Companion to Travel Writing* reveals the persistence of this idea. Today's theorists still appear to favour those travellers' "individual quests and their particular searches for personal redemption in the desert".[34] Helen Carr singles out Gertrude Bell for her breaking away from "an elaborate social order" to stand at the "threshold of wild travel", and Freya Stark for her sense of loss on the crossing of the desert becoming "an everyday affair".[35] Peter Hulme honours Wilfred Thesiger's "flight from materialism" through his "prolonged immersion in forms of desert life",[36] while Billie Melman identifies travel writing on Arabia as desert narratives, symbolic of redemptive pilgrimages, conquests of the void, and tales of risk. The taste for this type of adventure narrative, she argues, derives from the Victorians' fascination with what they saw as a way of life little changed from biblical times, and from their penchant for wild and barren landscapes as well as from earlier Romantic ideas of the Sublime in nature.[37]

Villiers' journey was very different from such idealized Arabian exploits. Far from bravely heading into an unmapped, potentially dangerous desert atop a camel, attended by noble Beduin tribesmen as guides and protectors, his was a rather cautious coasting voyage, certainly perilous but not especially romantic. Moreover, it was a way well travelled for centuries by myriad Arab, African, Indian and Persian sailors, following the ancient trade routes from India, along the African coast and around Arabia, and latterly picked up by the various colonial enterprises – Portuguese, Dutch, British, and most recently Italian – eager to control and cash in on the trade. Villiers had plenty of company, on board and on shore, the object being to call in at the populous ports offering business for the Kuwaiti dhow. He was able to observe colonial officials at work, and cast a humorous eye on his companions' efforts to circumvent European regulations. He had not thrown himself upon fortune in a Burtonesque quest to explore unknown lands, nor was his aim to shed light on supposed biblical ways or purge his soul in a journey of spiritual redemption.

Instead, he travelled prosaically as a Western navigator with Kuwaiti mariners steeped in their own navigation and ship-handling methods. He was on equal terms with them, but anxious to learn the tricks of their trade. Like Thesiger, he takes pains not to set himself above his companions, even when he thinks their methods could be improved, and comes to respect their superior knowledge of their own techniques. His modesty and willingness to muck in with them sits ill with that cliché of Orientalism, that Western observers must inevitably be tainted by a superior sense of detachment from and power over the Other, leading to a contemptuous appropriation of it.[38] On the contrary, Villiers was in love with the wind and his admiration for those who knew how to harness and exploit it, such as Kuwait's mariners, knew no bounds. To him it seemed a tragedy that this tradition was doomed by Western technology. Again like Thesiger, he was a modern man who was antipathetic to much of the "progress" brought by so-called civilization. But, unlike Thesiger, he was neither seeking a kind of solace in the conservatism of a traditional culture, nor was he trying to escape into it.[39] Villiers wanted to live, learn about and record the passing of a way of life that he deeply admired, but he was realistic about change.

Yet more than just co-travellers, Villiers and the Arab sailors were also collaborators. Unlike those travellers in the desert who "depended entirely on the [Beduin] tribes' protection of life and limb" for the success of their expeditions,[40] Villiers' knowledge of sailing enabled him to contribute to the workings of the ship. Likewise, Villiers respected the Arab sailors' knowledge, which, he stresses, was often greater than his own.[41]

Sons of Sindbad is one of only a handful of books that explore the Arabian Peninsula's long heritage of sail, coastal trade, and the people and lifestyles that went with it.[42] And it is by comparison with one of these, his contemporary William Makin, that Villiers' unusual empathy with his companions emerges even more starkly. In his book, *Red Sea Nights*, Makin's focus is largely on the seedy side of life – on arms smuggling and drug use, prostitution and slavery. While his adventure begins in Marseilles, it is into the sleazy "ratholes" of the city that he dives in order to sniff out "the opium gangs, the hashish smugglers, the Arabian bandits and the slavers of the Red Sea".[43] Indeed, this sets the tone for the rest of the narrative, a true "Orientalist", egocentric adventure in which "I" and "empire" are vastly superior to the exotic "queer collection of humanity", "debris", carriers of disease, and exponents of cruelty, poor hygiene and corruption, that watch the arrival of "this white man in a dhow" in the Yemeni port of Hudaidah.[44] Makin endures life on board his vessel with its innumerable "cockroaches and a veritable halitosis of smells".[45] He brags that "it still demands a brave man to venture forth" in such a craft,[46] and questions the ability of the Arab sailors "to navigate a dhow out of the Red Sea … in the teeth of a storm", which "demands a sea sense that only a few Arabs possess".[47] In similar vein, he reveres the British East India Squadron as "one of the hardest worked squadrons in the whole British navy".[48]

Villiers' narrative presents a maritime world at complete variance with Makin's. While he acknowledges that the Arabs' vessels were outmoded and "derelict by every standard of our frantic world", he also points out that the Arabs "have a delight in living we do not even know we lack".[49] And, unlike Makin, his attitude towards the people he encounters is empathetic: it shows in every telling detail, as when he describes one of his fellow passengers as "a young Beduin boy with long hair and soft gentle features" who was "a very shy and reserved youth".[50] The vainglorious Makin, in contrast, swaggers through the *suq* in Hudaidah, pushing his way "past lepers, idiots and epileptics".[51]

It is with his French counterpart Henri de Monfreid that Villiers bears most comparison. De Monfreid was capable of a similar empathy with his companions and was also a prolific writer. Unlike Villiers he spent many years sailing dhows in the Red Sea and engaging in various colourful activities, legal and otherwise. Thesiger was a keen admirer of de Monfreid, and wrote of him:

> We arrived in Jibuti next morning and there among the native craft was de Monfreid's *Altair*: he was now in France and the boat was for sale. I later went on board and met some of his crew whose names I already knew from his books, and I was half-tempted to buy the boat and see if I could make a livelihood trading and pearling in the Red Sea. De Monfreid had bridged the gap between himself and his crew, identifying himself with them to the extent of becoming one of them. He had been rewarded by their acceptance, and I envied him his achievement.[52]

While other writers on Arabia may touch on the coastal regions, towns and activities associated with the sea, they write with little first-hand knowledge of them. In doing so, they diminish and trivialize the sea's importance in the shadow of their desert quests. In *The Coast of Incense*, for instance, it is clear that Freya Stark's interests on her travels in Arabia included neither boats nor the maritime traditions that had sustained the coastal Gulf towns for centuries. On a trip to Kuwait in 1937, her cursory attention to things maritime is revealed when she writes:

> I have just been out, pottering by myself among the boats, with friendly Arabs in long gowns … I climbed up the side of an unfinished "Sambuq", built to carry water from Basra to Kuwait, and took photos of the carpenter and the old foreman. I stopped and chatted to the maker of nets … and found out that a big new boat, all carved costs 1,000 rupees. And this morning I went to lunch with the widow of the Sheikh of Muhammerah …[53]

Villiers, on the other hand, writes stirringly of the dhows at Aden, and much of opening chapter in *Sons of Sindbad* is a paean to the Arab vessels anchored at Ma'alla.[54]

To Western travel writers, readers and theorists alike, the unchanging desert in its biblical simplicity represents the polar opposite of their multifarious, multitudinous, ever-changing and over-stressed society. Thesiger and Lawrence both prized the purifying powers of the desert "which cleanse the suffering individual",[55] while the notion of authenticity – the Beduin as being of pure Arab blood (*asil*) – appealed to the English obsession with class, lineage and chivalry. But Villiers' gaze was uncontaminated by such preconceptions, and he has no truck with this romantic view of the Beduin whom, as deck passengers on board the *Triumph*, he saw as pitiable refugees from a pitiless homeland.[56]

The fabled nobility of their existence is further undermined when

Villiers alludes to social distinctions between the Beduin and the coast-dwellers: "The Kuwaiti bear no arms, for, in Kuwait, to carry arms is the mark of the Bedu; and the Bedu, according to the Kuwaiti are uncouth." Nejdi's view of Beduin pirates off the south Arabian coast was that they were just grasping opportunists, and cowards into the bargain.[57]

However open to criticism it may be, a deep-seated preference for land journeys and explorations is a hallmark of the literature on Arabia and of its readers. The desert, a measureless and mysterious Other, presented a legitimate challenge to "real" travellers, a purifying furnace, an arena for transforming experience. Such an idea would not have occurred to Villiers. The sea of course could have been represented in just the same way. But whatever parallels can be and often are drawn, as powerful literary devices, between the trackless desert and the uncharted ocean, the seas round Arabia have been regarded by devotees of Arabian travel not so much as Other, as Nowhere. Villiers' story takes place off the edge of the Western concept of Arabia. To go by sea was automatically to disqualify oneself as an authentic Arabian traveller.

To over-emphasize the desert in this way is to disregard the vital role of the sea in Arabia's history, and to overlook its coastal people and lifestyles in all the richness and diversity of their maritime contacts. The Arabian landmass has for millennia divided the peoples of the Mediterranean and the Indian Ocean, as a vast and forbidding obstacle between the two trading worlds. Without the ingenuity of its seafarers, not only would the history of Arabia have been utterly different, so also would the history of international commerce. *Sons of Sindbad* can take the credit for being the only book of Arabian travel to try to awaken a popular readership to this idea.

The Australian Eye

"Alan went on literally hundreds of journeys", recalls his widow, Nancie. "If anyone ever offered him a voyage he said 'I'll take it', and he always wrote about his experiences."[58]

Nancie Wills, a fellow Australian, was a great admirer of Villiers before she first met him in Melbourne in 1936, during the cruise of the *Conrad*. "I cut a picture of him out of a weekly magazine … and hung it over my bed," she said, alluding to his celebrity status in the 1930s.[59] Regardless of his fame and prodigious literary output, Villiers was modest about his roles as writer and seaman. In his first writing assignment, he refers to himself as the first "common man, the common seaman" to be able to go to the Antarctic as a commissioned writer. "Nobody thought that whaling, I suppose, modern whaling, was worth writing about, so I just quietly took along some paper, that's all."[60] An entry in his Arabian journal reflects the same modesty and lack of pretension. He reveals genuine surprise at the hospitality offered him by the Kuwaiti merchant, Ali Al-Hamad, in Aden: "I regret putting him to trouble and do not understand why he should so cheerfully put himself out for strangers … of neither standing nor attainment at that."[61]

Even as an established author, Villiers preferred being at sea to hobnobbing with travel-writing literati. His family describes him as a loner and showing a distinct unease with things "posh". As Nancie recalls:

> It was in 1939 and I was 24. I came to England and I was working for a publisher, John Murray, in London. I heard Alan on the radio … it was something like "In Town Tonight" and he was being interviewed. So I thought Ah! I will renew my acquaintance with Alan Villiers! We agreed to meet outside John Murray's afterwards and I thought he was going to take me to the coffee shop next door. But to my amazement he took me to a posh restaurant on the corner. Alan HATES posh restaurants! … And so I married him … [laughter]. No, we never ate at a posh restaurant again![62]

Villiers was more at ease with the Spartan conditions aboard the *Triumph*. This ability to find a "peculiar relish in discomfort"[63] fits the universal archetype of the intrepid male traveller, who revels in his physical prowess and the distinctly masculine bonds he develops with his fellow travellers.[64] And in this, one cannot help but contrast Villiers with another of his contemporaries, the British travel writer Robert Byron. In *The Road to Oxiana*, Byron's yearning for creature comforts is a conspicuous thread interwoven with his search for Islamic architecture, as when, in this entry in his travelogue, he sighs: "The King David Hotel is the only good hotel in Asia this side of Shanghai. We treasure every moment spent in it."[65]

Villiers' vocation as a Cape Horn sailor meant that he needed a self-discipline and hardihood that inevitably call to mind a certain universal stereotype of the manly adventurer. But it is also a valid question how far his Australian roots, too, played a role in shaping him. To be Australian implies a certain way of being, described by one commentator as "that intangible Australian security of being, which is not prickly about prestige and dignity".[66] This approach to life, with its scepticism of authority and dismissiveness of class and social status, ties in with the notion of "mateship", a term born out of the Anzac experience of the First World War, "a legend of free and independent [male] spirits whose discipline derived less from military formalities and customs than from the bonds of mateship and the demands of necessity".[67]

Even in today's Australia, where the Anglo-Saxon Australian of settler or convict parentage now has to share centre-stage with the country's indigenous "first peoples" and a burgeoning multi-ethnic population, this mentality has survived. The attitude also pervades the construction of Australia's national heroes. Frank Bongiorno remarks that "Australians are particularly inclined to make heroes of noble failures, such as the Eureka rebels, the suicidal Jolly Swagman in *Waltzing Matilda*, and Ned Kelly".[68] It is an inclination Villiers seems to share, especially when we consider the heroes of *Sons of Sindbad*: the smuggling, "reprobate" crew and passengers, such as Said, whom Villiers describes as "such a thorough and unscrupulous scoundrel, so absolutely without pretence, so genuinely and wholly what we call bad that I rather admired him".[69]

In Villiers' time, when white Australians still saw themselves as belonging to empire, there also existed a schism, an "us and them", felt as much in Australia as it was in Great Britain, the "mother country". This is apparent in much of Villiers' writing, especially in his journal entries that reflect the global and regional conflicts of the time. Writing at the outbreak of the Second World War, Villiers at once identifies with the collective, imperial "we" while also looking upon it with a disdainful and disconnected "I". "What are *we* up to, sinking merchantmen *we* could well use?" he asks in a journal entry dated 6 September 1939, after learning that "*we* have destroyed three German vessels which might have been converted into armed raiders".[70] The ill-feeling of the Iraqis toward the Allies is apparent when he writes: "We see many cars on the desert road, Kuwaiti and Iraqi: and at Zubair the soldiers, I soon gather, think very highly of Hitler, very little of *us*." And again, in relation to the British presence in Palestine, "Tonight I notice that the listeners only listen to Eunis Babri … (when they think I sleep) … as he rants and yells of Palestine. *We* ought not to underestimate the depth of ill-feeling against *us* on that score …"[71]

At the same time Villiers, the Australian, also identifies himself as separate from empire:

> The atmosphere of this Iraq is mightily different from that in Kuwait – different from what it seemed to be a few months ago here, too. Now one feels almost that one is in enemy territory: *they*

> [the British] put it all down to Palestine. *I* [the Australian] put it down to [political] agents – also to the silly attitude of a good many Englishmen who come to Iraq and think the Iraqis negroes.[72]

That Villiers could be at once patriotic about Britain and proud of his Australian roots is revealed in his journal entries.[73] But he did not trumpet his Australian identity because he had a truly Australian distaste for bragging, posturing and pride.[74] In this regard, a comparative reading of *Sons of Sindbad* with another of Villiers' contemporaries, Freya Stark, is telling. In *East is West*, Stark manifests a confidence in her own position and a personal pride in empire which can verge upon the smugness that occasionally mars Gertrude Bell's letters. She asserts that the British Government was responsible for "awakening the young effendi" and that the British policy "to unify and strengthen has been very great in the 'island' of Arabia."[75] Such an attitude was reassuring to her British readers, and helps to explain the success of her books on the Middle East. Villiers by contrast shows himself at once modest and distanced from attitudes of colonial superiority. When he writes, "Nejdi was welcome to his views, which gave him considerable satisfaction. I was not so sure of my own",[76] his uncertainty appears to mirror on a personal level that of a young Australian nation's sense of "unbelonging" – not quite established in its own, independent identity and therefore unsure of its position in the world. He also counters Stark's blithe and uncritical view of the boon of British administration, and reveals a true Australian's "native hostility to letter-of-the-law bureaucratic controls".[77]

From an imperial perspective, both Villiers and the Arabs could be seen as coming from colonial frontiers – Australia was a colony of the empire, and the Arabian Gulf a region where Britain ensured its influence and control through advisory, protectorate and trade arrangements. In *Sons of Sindbad*, neither Villiers nor the Arabs are colonizers, and both are travellers. In this way, the boundaries that set the traveller apart from the Other in standard Arabian travelogues are blurred. The Australian instinct for a "don't imagine you're any better" inclusiveness,[78] seems also to characterize relations among the Kuwaiti crew on board the *Triumph of Righteousness* as Villiers depicts them: "It was a free and wholly democratic life. Nejdi was king, but he had no subjects. Everybody else was king too, and Nejdi had only his natural ability to keep them in order."[79]

Alan Villiers was not only refreshingly Australian in outlook, he was ahead of his time as a travel writer. In his Arabian voyage, he exemplifies the qualities Peter Hulme ascribes to the mainstream modern, post-war travel writer – a "broad range of political interests, a lack of affectation, a robust sense of the value of the independent travelling voice, an ability to take minor hardships in [their] stride in order to report on what is happening in parts of the world which do not necessarily feature on the global news."[80]

The War and After

Having spent the summer of 1939 in Kuwait and on the pearl banks of the northern Gulf, Villiers, who had been toying with the idea of buying and restoring one of the last three surviving Kuwaiti *baggala*s, decided in September to return to England to play his part in the war effort.[81] In London, as we saw, he renewed his acquaintance with his future wife Nancie. They married in 1940, by which time Villiers had joined the Royal Naval Volunteer Reserve (RNVR). He spent most of the war on active service with Infantry Landing Craft in Italy, Normandy and the Far East, where he operated along the Arakan coast of Burma, at the landing in Rangoon and at the recovery of Singapore.[82] He reached the rank of Commander and was awarded the Distinguished Service Cross for his part in the invasion of France. After the war he became master of the training ship *Warspite*. Meanwhile Kit, Katherine and Peter had been born, and the family made their home in Oxfordshire.[83] In 1952 they moved to a house in North Oxford. Here in "Dons' Alley", as he called it, Villiers would be based for the remainder of his life.

He quickly returned to his sailing activities, but in a new guise. Commercial sail had by now completely died out in the West, and his ventures were henceforth centred on survivals of sail in other cultures, on the re-creation of historic sailing voyages, and on the preservation of the records of sail. He had been appointed a Trustee of the National Maritime Museum in 1948, and would later help found its historic photograph collection with his friend, Basil Greenhill, Director of the Museum from 1967 to 1983.[84] His own collection, of some 20,000 negatives and transparencies, constitutes an important part of the Museum's Historic Photographs archive. The Alan Villiers film collection has been on long-term loan at the National Maritime Museum since 1983, and includes footage of the 1938–39 voyage. He also served on various committees, including that of the Society for Nautical Research (of which he was successively a vice-president, chairman from 1960, and president

1970–74), the *Cutty Sark* Preservation Society, and the *Victory* Technical Advisory Committee.

He continued to travel widely until the mid-1970s in search of new adventures, from which emerged a steady stream of books, as well as of articles for the *National Geographic Magazine*. 1950 found him sailing with the Portuguese cod-fishing fleet on the Grand Banks of Newfoundland and off Greenland. True to form, he embraced the rigours of life as a common fisherman, spending days alone paying out and hauling in long-lines in a flimsy dory on a treacherous sea. Other explorations of traditional sail included voyaging on a Maldives *baggala* (1956), and a visit to the Brahmaputra (1960). His last major excursion was to the Philippines in 1975, to write an article on Magellan for the *National Geographic*. Latterly he was frequently accompanied by Nancie, who throughout was a great help with his work.

Growing fame also brought assignments of a more glamorous nature. He was called in as adviser on various films, including the Hollywood versions of the Melville classics *Billy Budd* and *Moby Dick*, in which he was master of the *Pequod*. In 1957 he commanded the *Mayflower* replica during its successful voyage to the United States, and in 1964 he recorded the Lisbon–Bermuda Tall Ships Race. He was much in demand as a broadcaster and lecturer on both sides of the Atlantic, and many still recall his idiosyncratic style. Capable of a quarter-deck delivery and endowed with a keen sense of the dramatic, he could electrify his listeners, whom he never failed to enthral.

In all he published more than forty books as well as innumerable articles, introductions and prefaces. He was one of the fortunate few authors who do not struggle with the act of creation – his first book was said to have been completed in just four days – and he also kept a regular diary, whether at sea or ashore. One of his greatest satisfactions came when his literary merits were recognized, just a few months before his death, with the award of a Doctorate of Letters by the University of Melbourne. His pre-war books had been mostly accounts of individual voyages, but he subsequently branched out into memoirs and history with books such as *The Set of the Sails* (1949) and *Monsoon Seas* (1952). A later volume of reminiscences, *Give Me a Ship to Sail* (1958), contains some of his liveliest writing. His last book, *Voyaging with the Wind*, a simple introduction to handling large square-rigged ships, returns to the essentials of his trade. It is a testament to the deep reverence for the sea and the wind, and for those who by choice or necessity had learned to harness them, that had sustained and given purpose to his life. As he once said:

> I loved the sound of the wind in the rigging, because it seemed to be challenging and – music. It was music, and it was music that struck a chord somehow in me. But I didn't know I'd pick up the chord. I did, thank God, and I stayed with it.[85]

During a life spent largely at sea, this remarkable man both lived and recorded the last days of sail. By combining his skills as seaman, writer, photographer, lecturer and adviser, he made a contribution to maritime history, research, training and public education that few others can claim to equal. In doing so, he built up a unique body of work on the world of commercial sail that vanished during the first half of the twentieth century, and amassed a huge amount of material. Its location today reflects the Anglo-Australian course of his career: his papers are held at the National Library of Australia in Canberra, the University of Melbourne holds his library of 5000 volumes, while his film and photographic archive resides at the National Maritime Museum, Greenwich.

In Kuwait he is a revered figure still and *Sons of Sindbad* is prized as a unique record of Kuwait's maritime past, despite having been written by a foreigner. Villiers kept in touch with members of the Al-Hamad family over the years and, on his 1967 visit to Kuwait, was met at the airport by a now-prosperous Nejdi. Their greeting forms a fitting valediction to the age of sail:

> "Allah is great," I said. "His winds are free."
> "Allah is great," he replied. After a while, he added as if to himself, "And sometimes I wish that I could use His winds again. For it was a good life that my sons can never know – no Kuwait sons shall know.
> "We cannot bring those ways back again."[86]

Notes

See Bibliography and Sources for full details of printed works cited. Page references to *Sons of Sindbad* (London, 1940) are to this reprint.

[1] Summarized in the *Oxford Dictionary of National Biography* entry on Ingrams (1897–1973) as "a truce ... by which the [Hadhramaut] tribes agreed to end their internecine warfare".
[2] Capt. (later Sir) Tom Hickinbotham (1903–83) began his career in the Indian Army before being seconded to the Indian Political Service. He served as an Assistant Resident in Aden in the 1930s, and was later Political Agent in Muscat (1939–41) and Kuwait (1941–43). He returned to Aden after the Second World War, first as Chairman of the Port Trust (1948–51) and then as Governor and Commander-in-Chief (1951–56).
[3] In the two 1940 editions of *Sons of Sindbad*, Villiers gives Nejdi's full name in error as "Abdul-Krim bin Mishari al-Abdul-razzaq el-Nejdi" (London edition p. 10, see below, pp. 6 and 19; New York edition p. 12). He corrected it in the 1969 edition (New York, 1969, p. 15). Both US editions use the spelling "Sinbad".
[4] The Arabic verb *bana*, from which *bayan* is derived, has as its basic meaning to become clear, plain, visible. When used of ships, the name *Bayan* means clarity or manifestation, in a commendatory sense (e.g. "Vision"): a majestic vessel that is visible on the horizon from afar. Similarly, in a literary context, the term means fineness and eloquence of expression. Villiers (p. 19 below) attributes the translation of *Bayan* as *Triumph of Righteousness* to Ali bin Abd al-Latif Al-Hamad. However, dhow names could metamorphose according to circumstance, and *Bayan* was often known simply as *boom Nejdi*, "Nejdi's boom".
[5] Dedication by A. J. Villiers in W. Facey's personal copy of *Sons of Sinbad* (New York, 1969).
[6] Summarized from Alan Villiers *The Set of the Sails* (London: Hodder & Stoughton, 1949), Villiers' early autobiography, pp. 160, 168, 174–6. See p. 194 for Villiers' first wife's ultimatum in 1929, in response to his decision to sail on the *Grace Harwar*: "I could choose the sea or her. This was a choice already made."
[7] Villiers, *The Set of the Sails*, p. 47. [8] Ibid., p. 72. [9] Ibid., p. 73. [10] Ibid., p. 123.
[11] Ibid., p. 197. [12] Ibid., p. 201. [13] Ibid., p. 216. [14] Ibid., p. 219. [15] Ibid., p. 223.
[16] Alan Villiers, *Of Ships and Men: A Personal Anthology* (London: Newnes, 1962), pp. 43–4.
[17] Villiers, *The Set of the Sails,* pp. 224–25: the connection with T. E. Lawrence was Bruce Rogers, T. E. L.'s typographer friend, who was also a devotee of sailing and a friend of Villiers. See *The Letters of T. E. Lawrence*, ed. by David Garnett, (London: Jonathan Cape, 1938), p. 843.
[18] Oswald L. Brett, "Commander Alan J. Villiers, DSC, FRGS, D.Litt.", *Sea History* 32 (Summer 1984), p. 20.
[19] Villiers, *Sons of Sindbad*, see below, p. 11.
[20] Villiers, *The Set of the Sails*, p. 231.
[21] Villiers, *Sons of Sindbad*, see below, pp. 25, 73–4, 134–5, 175–7, 239–40, 253–4, 264, 316–19.
[22] Ibid., p. 18.
[23] Ibid., pp. 19–20.

[24] Ibid., pp. 175–6. Villiers repeats the old *canard* that Vasco da Gama's pilot had been his Muslim Arab equivalent, the renowned Arabian navigator Ahmad bin Majid. That the greatest navigator of Islam, himself and in person, should have opened the door of the Indian Ocean trading world to one of Christendom's greatest maritime pioneers is an irresistible irony, and has duly taken its place in popular history books, even today. But the story is certainly untrue. The only extant Portuguese eye-witness account of the incident at Malindi in 1498 makes it very clear that the pilot in question was a "Christian" native of India (in fact most probably a Hindu Gujerati), thus not a Muslim Arab at all: Ravenstein *A Journal of the First Voyage of Vasco da Gama, 1497–1499*, (1898), p. 45 and n. 3.

[25] William Facey, *Oman: A Seafaring Nation* (Muscat: Ministry of Information and Culture, Sultanate of Oman, 1979), pp. 97–100.

[26] Villiers, *Sons of Sindbad*, see below, pp. 73–4.

[27] Ibid., p. 176.

[28] Ibid., p. 196 (Abdul-Wahhab al-Kitami at Zanzibar); p. 315 ("big Myouf al-Bedar").

[29] "The Kuwait *Periplus*": the reference is to the famous *Dalil al-mukhtar fi 'ilm al-bihar* ("A Navigational Guidebook") by 'Isa Al-Kitami (correctly Al-Qutami), to which Villiers also refers in *Sons of Sindbad.* Villiers uses the Greek term "Periplus", meaning "circumnavigation", as a nod to the *Periplous of the Erythraean Sea*, a nautical handbook to the coasts of the Indian Ocean, including southern Arabia and East Africa, by an anonymous Greek captain in the mid-1st century AD.

[30] Alan Villiers, *Monsoon Seas: The Story of the Indian Ocean* (New York: McGraw-Hill, 1952), p. 96. For Yusuf bin 'Isa al-Kitami and the *boom Samhan* at Mutrah, see also *Sons of Sindbad*, see below, p. 279.

[31] Yacoub Yusuf Al-Hijji, "On Arab Navigation: Alan Villiers and Arab Navigation", unpublished article.

[32] Yacoub Yusuf Al-Hijji, "Arab Navigational Methods after the 18th Century", unpublished article.

[33] Elizabeth Monroe, *Britain's Moment in the Middle East* (London: Chatto & Windus, 1963).

[34] Billie Melman, "The Middle East/Arabia: 'The Cradle of Islam'", in *The Cambridge Companion to Travel Writing*, ed. by Peter Hulme and Tim Youngs (Cambridge: Cambridge University Press, 2002) p. 114.

[35] Helen Carr, "Modernism and Travel (1880–1940)", in *The Cambridge Companion to Travel Writing* (see Melman, above), p. 82.

[36] Peter Hulme, "Travelling to Write (1940–2000)", in *The Cambridge Companion to Travel Writing* (see Melman, above), p. 88.

[37] Melman, "The Middle East/Arabia", p. 114.

[38] See for example Edward Said, *Orientalism* (London: Routledge, 1978), p. 157: "to be a European in the Orient always implies being a consciousness set apart from and unequal with its surroundings."

[39] Kathryn Tidrick, *Heart-beguiling Araby: The English Romance with Arabia* (Cambridge: Cambridge University Press, 1981), p. 200.

[40] Melman, "The Middle East/Arabia" p. 117.

[41] Villiers, *Sons of Sindbad*, see below, p. 39.

[42] See also William J. Makin, *Red Sea Nights* (London: Jarrolds, 1932); *Pearls, Arms and Hashish: Pages from the Life of A Red Sea Navigator, Henri de Monfreid*, collected and written down with a Foreword and Conclusion by Ida Treat (London: Victor Gollancz,

1930); and Henri de Monfreid, *Secrets of the Red Sea* (London: Faber & Faber, 1934); *Hashish*, trans. by Helen Buchanan Bell (London: Methuen, 1935); *Sea Adventures*, trans. by Helen Buchanan Bell (London: Methuen, 1937); and his numerous other works in French.

[43] William J. Makin, *Red Sea Nights*, p. 14. [44] Ibid., p. 169. [45] Ibid., p. 181.

[46] Ibid., p. 181. [47] Ibid., p. 189. [48] Ibid., p. 160.

[49] Villiers, *Sons of Sindbad*, see below, p. 20.

[50] Villiers, *Sons of Sindbad*, see below, p. 96.

[51] Makin, *Red Sea Nights*, p. 175.

[52] Wilfred Thesiger, *The Life of My Choice* (London: Collins, 1987) p. 167, writing of his visit to Ethiopia in 1934.

[53] Freya Stark, *The Coast of Incense* (London: John Murray, 1953), p. 134.

[54] Villiers, *Sons of Sindbad*, see below, p. 12.

[55] Melman, "The Middle East/Arabia", p. 115.

[56] Villiers, *Sons of Sindbad*, see below, p. 96.

[57] Ibid., p. 187; Beduin pirates: pp. 258–60.

[58] Grace Pundyk, *Sea Change: Alan Villiers and the Subversion of the Arabian Travel* Narrative (Dubai: Gulf Research Center, 2005): Nancie Villiers, personal interview, Oxford 2004.

[59] Ibid.

[60] D. Foster, *Self Portraits* (Canberra: National Library of Australia, 1993), p. 144.

[61] Alan Villiers, "Private Journal of a Voyage to Arabia", unpublished diary 1938–39, Canberra, National Library of Australia, MS6388, Papers of Alan Villiers, Sunday, 6 November, 1939.

[62] Pundyk, *Sea Change*: Nancie Villiers, personal interview, Oxford 2004.

[63] Evelyn Waugh, *Labels: A Mediterranean Journey* (London: Duckworth, 1930), p. 36.

[64] Melman, "The Middle East/Arabia", p. 117.

[65] Robert Byron, *The Road to Oxiana* (London: Macmillan, 1937), p. 15.

[66] J. Carroll, "The Blessed Country: Australia Dreaming 1901–2000", ABC Alfred Deakin Lecture, Capitol Theatre, Sydney, 12 May 2001, <http.//www.abc.net.au/rn/deakin/stories/529147> [accessed 6 January 2006].

[67] Paul Keating, Anzac Day Speech on the Entombment of the Unknown Soldier, Australian War Memorial, Canberra, Australia, 11 November 1993, audiotape (Canberra: National Archives of Australia M3983, item 959.

[68] Frank Bongiorno, "The Anzac Tradition", <http.//www.cultureandrecreation.gov.au/articles/anzac> [accessed 6 January 2006].

[69] Villiers, *Sons of Sindbad*, see below, pp. 106–7.

[70] Villiers, "Private Journal of a Voyage to Arabia", 6 September 1939.

[71] Ibid., 12 September 1939. [72] Ibid., 15 September 1939.

[73] Villiers, diary entry, 26 January 1967, Villiers papers, National Library of Australia, see n. 61 above.

[74] Carroll, "The Blessed Country".

[75] Freya Stark, *East is West* (London: John Murray, 1945), pp. xviii–xxii.

[76] Villiers, *Sons of Sinbad*, New York 1940, p. 199.

[77] Carroll, "The Blessed Country"; Villiers, *Sons of Sindbad*, see below, pp. 106–8.

[78] Carroll, "The Blessed Country".

[79] Villiers, *Sons of Sindbad*, see below, p. 78.

[80] Hulme, "Travelling to Write", p. 88.

[81] Villiers, *The Set of the Sails*, p. 233.
[82] Villiers, *Monsoon Seas*, p. vi.
[83] Born respectively in Scotland, 1943; Oxford, 1945; and Chipping Norton, 1947.
[84] Greenhill had earlier initiated the Society for Nautical Research Photographic Records Committee, of which Villiers was chairman. The photographs gathered were held at the NMM and were the basis of the collection formally established there after Greenhill became Director; K. Littlewood and B. Butler, *Of Ships and Stars: Maritime Heritage and the Founding of the National Maritime Museum, Greenwich* (London: Athlone Press, 1998), p.186.
[85] Foster, *Self Portraits*, p. 148.
[86] Villiers, *Sons of Sinbad*, (1969 ed.), p. xxi.

Bibliography and Sources

Anon., "Obituary: Capt. Alan Villiers", *The Times*, 5 May 1982

Ashton, J. Richard, "A Three Week Voyage which has Lasted My Lifetime", *Sea History* 32 (Summer 1984), p. 25

Bidwell, Robin, *Travellers in Arabia* (London: Hamlyn, 1976)

Bishara, 'Isa, *Personal Logbook* (Kuwait: Centre for Research and Studies on Kuwait, 2003)

Bongiorno, Frank, "The Anzac Tradition", <http://www.cultureandrecreation.gov.au/articles/anzac> [accessed 6 January 2006]

Brent, Peter, *Far Arabia: Explorers of the Myth* (London: Weidenfeld & Nicolson, 1977)

Brett, Oswald L., "Commander Alan John Villiers, DSC, FRGS, D.Litt.", *Sea History* 32 (Summer 1984), 14–22

Byron, Robert, *The Road to Oxiana* (London: Macmillan, 1937)

The Cambridge Companion to Travel Writing, ed. by Peter Hulme and Tim Youngs (Cambridge: Cambridge University Press)

Carr, Helen, "Modernism and Travel (1880–1940)", in *The Cambridge Companion to Travel Writing* (see above), pp. 70–86

Carroll, J., "The Blessed Country: Australian Dreaming 1901–2000", ABC Alfred Deakin Lecture, Capitol Theatre, Sydney, 12 May 2001 <http://www.abc.net.au/rn/deakin/stories/5291479> [accessed 6 January 2006]

Facey, William, *Oman: A Seafaring Nation* (Muscat: Ministry of Information and Culture, Sultanate of Oman, 1979)

Facey, William and Gillian Grant, *Saudi Arabia by the First Photographers* (London: Stacey International, 1996)

—— *Kuwait by the First Photographers* (London: I.B. Tauris/London Centre of Arab Studies, 1998)

Falconer, J., "Valediction: Alan Villiers and the Last Days of Sail", in *Sail and Steam: A Century of Seafaring Enterprise, 1840–1935: Photographs from the National Maritime Museum* (London: Viking, 1993), pp. 176–91

Foster, D., *Self Portraits* (Canberra: National Library of Australia, 1993)

Al-Hijji, Yacoub Yusuf, *The Art of Dhow-building in Kuwait* (London: London Centre of Arab Studies with Centre for Research and Studies on Kuwait, 2001)

—— "On Arab Navigation: Alan Villiers and Arab Navigation", unpublished article, copy kindly supplied by the author.

—— "Arab Navigational Methods after the 18th Century", unpublished article, copy kindly supplied by the author.

Hulme, Peter, and Youngs, Tim, *The Cambridge Companion to Travel Writing*, Cambridge University Press, 2002

Hulme, Peter, "Travelling to Write (1940–2000)", in *The Cambridge Companion to Travel Writing* (see above), pp. 87–101

A Journal of the First Voyage of Vasco da Gama, 1497–1499, trans. and ed. by E. G. Ravenstein, (London: The Hakluyt Society, 1898)

Keane, John F. T., *Six Months in the Hijaz*, with an Introduction by William Facey (Beirut: Barzan Press, forthcoming 2006)

Keating, Paul, Anzac Day Speech on the Entombment of the Unknown Soldier, Australian War Memorial, Canberra, Australia, 11 November 1993; audiotape, National Archives of Australia, Canberra, M3983, item 959. <http://www.awm.gov.au/commemoration/keating.htm>

Al-Khashti, Ahmad, *Personal Logbook* (Kuwait: Centre for Research and Studies on Kuwait, 2002)

Al-Kitami, 'Isa, *Dalil al-mukhtar fi 'ilm al-bihar – A Navigational Guidebook* (Kuwait: Kuwait Government Press, 1976)

Lawrence, T. E., *The Letters of T. E. Lawrence*, ed. by David Garnett (London: Jonathan Cape, 1938)

Littlewood, K., and B. Butler, *Of Ships and Stars: Maritime Heritage and the Founding of the National Maritime Museum, Greenwich* (London: Athlone Press, 1998)

Lloyd, Christopher, "Captain Alan J. Villiers, D.S.C., F.R.G.S.", *The Mariner's Mirror* 68 (May 1982), 99–100

Makin, William J., *Red Sea Nights* (London: Jarrolds, 1932)

Melman, Billie, "The Middle East/Arabia: 'The Cradle of Islam'", *The*

Cambridge Companion to Travel Writing (see above), pp. 105–21

Monfreid, Henri de, *Secrets of the Red Sea* (London: Faber & Faber, 1934)

—— *Hashish*, trans. by Helen Buchanan Bell (London: Methuen, 1935)

—— *Sea Adventures*, trans. by Helen Buchanan Bell (London: Methuen, 1937)

Monroe, Elizabeth, *Britain's Moment in the Middle East* (London: Chatto & Windus, 1963)

—— *Philby of Arabia* (London: Faber & Faber, 1973)

Pirenne, Jacqueline, *À la découverte de l'Arabie* (Paris: Le Livre Contemporain, 1958)

Pundyk, Grace, *Sea Change: Alan Villiers and the Subversion of the Arabian Travel Narrative* (Dubai: Gulf Research Center, 2005)

[Runciman, Leslie], "Alan Villiers, D.S.C., Litt. D. (Univ. of Melbourne)", *The Mariner's Mirror* 68 (August 1982), 237–41. Report of thanksgiving service for Villiers at the University Church of St Mary the Virgin, Oxford, 22 May 1982, including the memorial address given by Lord Runciman of Doxford.

Said, Edward, *Orientalism* (London: Routledge, 1978)

Stark, Freya, *East is West* (London: John Murray, 1945). [Published in the USA as *The Arab Island*, New York: Alfred Knopf, 1945]

—— *The Coast of Incense* (London: John Murray, 1953)

Sugg, Philip, "A Unique Vision of the Sea on Film", *Sea History* 32 (Summer 1984), 26

Thesiger, Wilfred, *Arabian Sands* (London: Longmans; New York: E. P. Dutton, 1959)

—— *The Life of My Choice* (London: Collins, 1987)

Tibbetts, Gerald R., trans. and ed., *Arab Navigation in the Indian Ocean before the Coming of the Portuguese, being a Translation of Kitab al-fawa'id fi usul al-bahr wa 'l-qawa'id of Ahmad b. Majid al-Najdi* (London: Royal Asiatic Society, 1971)

Tidrick, Kathryn, *Heart-beguiling Araby: The English Romance with Arabia* (Cambridge: Cambridge University Press, 1981)

Treat, Ida, *Pearls, Arms and Hashish: Pages from the Life of a Red Sea Navigator, Henri de Monfreid* (London: Victor Gollancz, 1930)

Trench, Richard, *Arabian Travellers*, Foreword by Wilfred Thesiger (London: Macmillan, 1986)

Villiers, Alan, *Whaling in the Frozen South: Being the Story of the 1923–24 Norwegian Whaling Expedition to the Antarctic* (London: Hurst & Blackett, 1925)

—— *Falmouth for Orders* (London: Geoffrey Bles, 1928)

—— *Voyage of the "Parma": The Great Grain Race of 1932* (London: Geoffrey Bles, 1933)

—— *Cruise of the Conrad* (London: Hodder & Stoughton, 1937)

—— *Sons of Sindbad* (London: Hodder & Stoughton, 1940). Published in the USA as *Sons of Sinbad* (New York: Scribners, 1940; new edition with a new Preface by Villiers and minor revisions, 1969)

—— *The Set of the Sails: The Story of a Cape Horn Seaman* (London: Hodder & Stoughton, 1949)

—— *Monsoon Seas: The Story of the Indian Ocean* (New York: McGraw-Hill, 1952)

—— "Passage in a Red Sea Dhow", *The Mariner's Mirror* 40 (August 1954), 171–82. Describes Villiers' voyage on the *Sheikh Mansur* from Aden to Jizan in 1938.

—— *Give Me a Ship to Sail* (London: Hodder & Stoughton, 1958)

—— *Of Ships and Men: A Personal Anthology* (London: Newnes, 1962)

—— *The Last of the Wind Ships: Photographs by Alan Villiers*, with an Introduction by Basil Greenhill (London: Harvill Press, 2000)

—— *Sons of Sindbad: The Photographs*, selected and introduced by William Facey, Yacoub Al-Hijji and Grace Pundyk (London: The National Maritime Museum, 2006)

—— Unpublished diaries, journals and notebooks in the National Library of Australia, Canberra (Papers of Alan Villiers MS6388). They include his "Private Journal of a Voyage to Arabia", unpublished diary 1938–39, series 13, box 119, folder 15. [nia.gov.au/nia.ms-ms6388]

Waugh, Evelyn, *Labels: A Mediterranean Journey* (London: Duckworth, 1930)

Sons *of* Sindbad

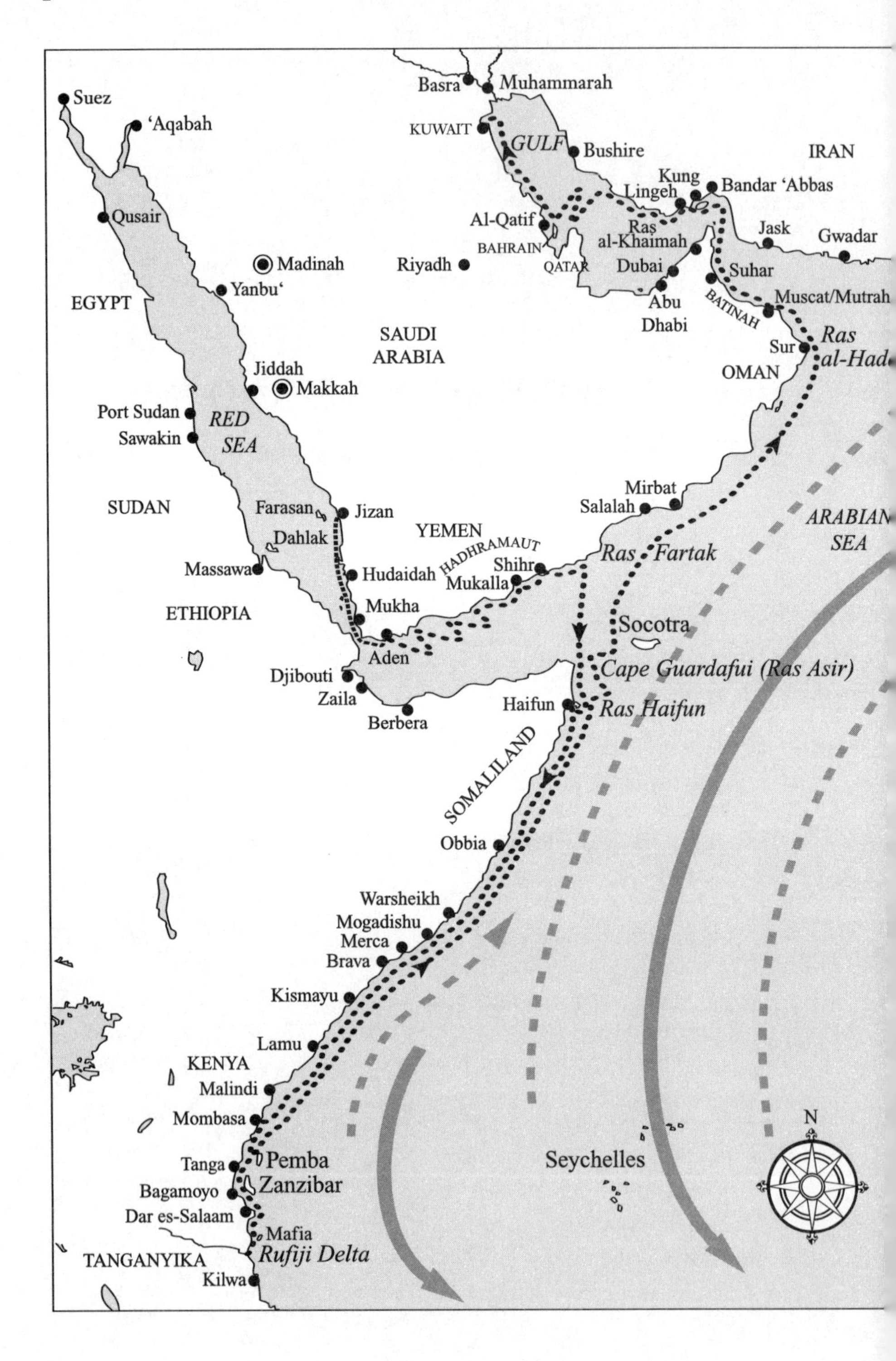
Suez
'Aqabah
Basra
Muhammarah
KUWAIT
GULF
Bushire
IRAN
Kung
Lingeh
Bandar 'Abbas
Qusair
Al-Qatif
Raṣ
al-Khaimah
Jask
Gwadar
BAHRAIN
Madinah
Riyadh
QATAR
Dubai
Suhar
Yanbu'
Abu
Dhabi
BATINAH
Muscat/Mutrah
EGYPT
SAUDI
ARABIA
Ras
al-Had
Sur
OMAN
Jiddah
Makkah
Port Sudan
RED
SEA
Sawakin
Mirbat
Salalah
SUDAN
Farasan
Jizan
YEMEN
ARABIAN
SEA
HADHRAMAUT
Ras Fartak
Dahlak
Shihr
Massawa
Hudaidah
Mukalla
Mukha
ETHIOPIA
Socotra
Aden
Cape Guardafui (Ras Asir)
Djibouti
Zaila
Haifun
Ras Haifun
Berbera
SOMALILAND
Obbia
Warsheikh
Mogadishu
Merca
Brava
Kismayu
Lamu
KENYA
Malindi
Mombasa
N
Tanga
Pemba
Seychelles
Zanzibar
Bagamoyo
Dar es-Salaam
Mafia
TANGANYIKA
Rufiji Delta
Kilwa

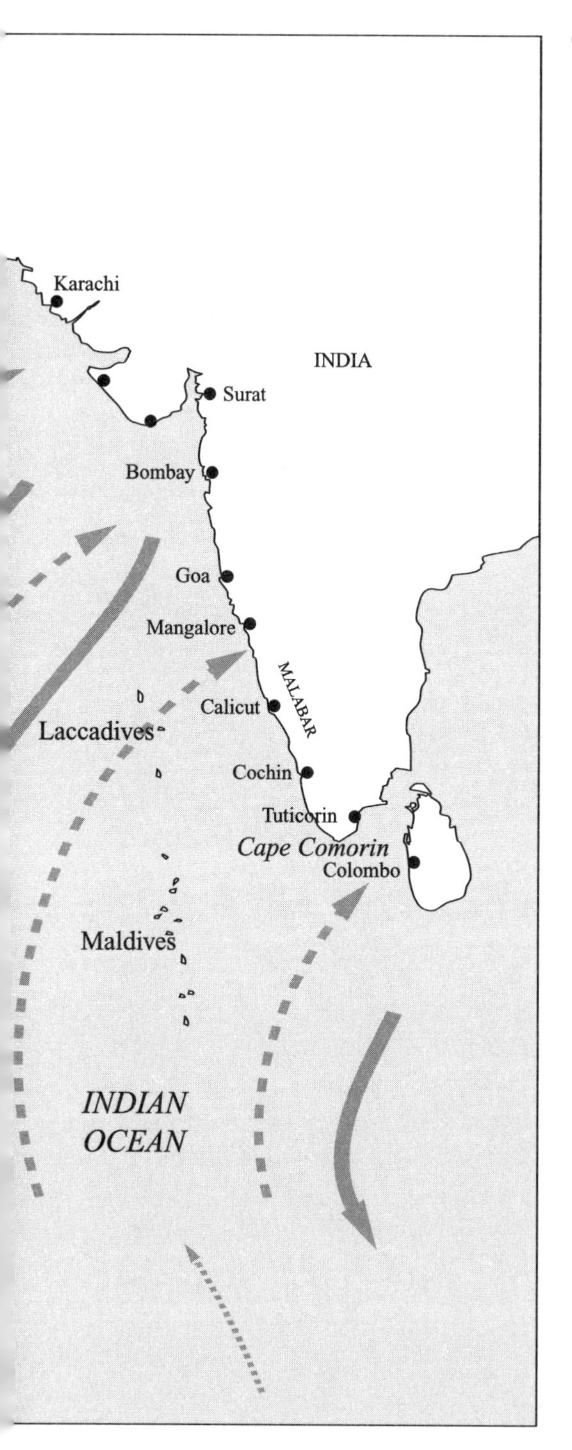

The Western Indian Ocean
showing Villiers' voyages on the *Sheikh Mansur* and the *Triumph of Righteousness* in 1938–39

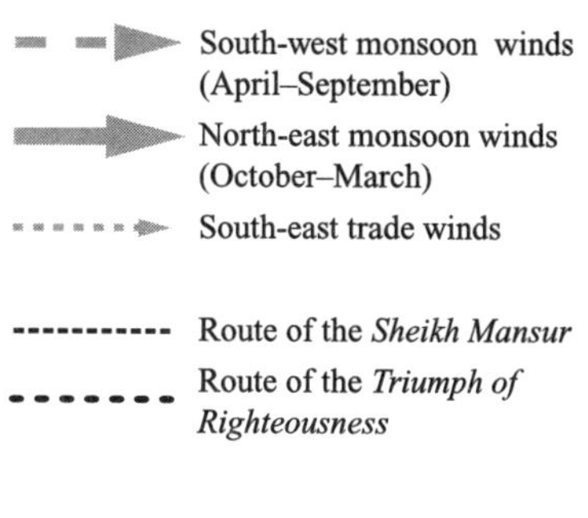

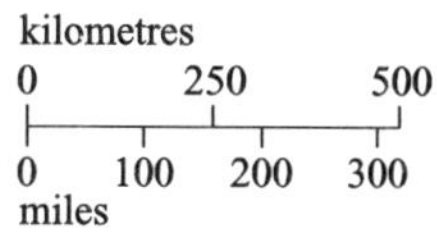

PREFACE

THE COLLECTION OF material for this book was not always easy. One cannot just go to Arabia, and expect to discover much about the Arabs and their dhows. Sailing in their ships is a hard life, and often a difficult one. The Arab, friendly and hospitable as he always is, may be forgiven if he sees little reason to welcome us, less to co-operate in the production of another book about him. But I found him helpful always, when once he felt my interest in his ships and seamen to be whole-hearted and at least tolerably intelligent; and I had the advantage of a background of experience in our own sailing-ships to help me in some appraisal of his. The Arabs treated me well, and I owe them a debt of gratitude. I found myself wondering, sometimes, what it might be like for an Arab to ship out with us, in our ships, in order to gather material for a book about them. We should look on him rather dubiously, I fear; but I hope we should treat him well. The Arabs had difficulty in understanding that a European should think it worth while to spend a year sailing with them in order merely to write a book about them, for they saw little of interest in their sailing. But if they were surprised, they were friendly, and I learned to like them well.

In making my plans and in the collection of material, I was helped by many people, and I should like to acknowledge my gratitude to them here. First, as always, there is my friend, Colonel F. C. C. Egerton, of Great Bricett, in Suffolk, whose idea the whole thing was in the first place, and who remained always its most stalwart supporter. Then to Admiral Sir William Goodenough, K.C.M.G., I owe special thanks, for it was he who laid the groundwork for the success of my plans. He introduced me to Mr. W. H. Ingrams, C.M.G., O.B.E., now Chief Secretary at Aden, then Resident Adviser in the Hadhramaut. Mr. Ingrams was another good supporter; it was he who in Aden passed me on to Captain T. Hickinbotham, who had a dhow of his own on the harbour and was the friend of the al-Hamads, of Kuwait, dhow-owners and merchants. Through his good offices, I met the al-Hamads. My worries then were at an end, at least so far as the collection of material went, for the al-Hamads had dhows going wherever dhows went, and they would cheerfully have helped me go sailing in all of them. They had chartered Ahmed the Yemenite for the voyage to Gizan; they sent me off with Nejdi, in his big *Triumph of Righteousness*, for the voyage down to Zanzibar. They, too, looked after me in Kuwait, and saw there that I met the shipmasters, the ship-owners, the pearlers, and the merchants.

To Nejdi, who put up with me for so long, I also owe a debt – to Nejdi (or to give him his full name, Abdul-krim bin Mishari bin Abdul-razzaq el Nejdi) [in fact Nejdi's full name was Ali bin Nasr el-Nedji, see pp. xii and xxxiv n.3] and his muallim, Hamed bin Salim, his serang, and all his sailors, I owe a great deal. I could not have been any use aboard their vessel and must have sometimes been in the way. They must have wondered, too, what it was all about. I always remember Nejdi's quiet comment when first I asked him if he knew of any accounts in Arabic of the sailors and their dhows. There were none, he said, for no Arab knew enough about them to write a book. Well, I know very little, too; but I did my best to gather the material for a first-hand picture of some aspects of their voyaging, and this I have presented here. Aye, to Nejdi – scornful of us, holding the views he did, feeling that one book ought to be work enough for any one man's lifetime, and that less than a lifetime of effort ought not to be offered – to Nejdi I am grateful. I liked him well, and I have tried to present a truthful and reasonably complete account of him and of his voyage – truthful, for anything else would be distasteful to the Arabs and to myself and would not have been worth going for; complete, because I may not have such a chance as this again. But it is not wholly complete. Some of the things I learned are not recorded here. I was not a government commission, inquiring into goings-on on dhows. Whatever the Arabs found it necessary to do in the successful prosecution of their voyages, my sympathies were with them. It is not an easy way to make a living, this conduct of great voyages across the face of the Indian Ocean in wind-blown dhows, wrestling a meagre life from the sea against all the competition of steam and the hindrances of European regulation. It is a hard life, and it is no part of my plan to encourage officials of any nationality to make it harder.

I owe thanks to all the al-Hamad brothers – Khalid, Ahmed, Yusuf, Ali, and Abdulla – those good merchants of Kuwait whose influence and goodwill extended everywhere I went; to the pearl merchant Mohamed bin Sheikh Abdul-latif al-Abdul-razzaq, in whose craft I went pearling in the Persian Gulf; to Kalifa al-Ganim, that wise old gentleman, who put me right on so much of the early records of Arab shipping. I am grateful too, for the hospitality I received wherever I went – from the Emir of Gizan, the Sultan of Mukalla, the Na'ib of Shihr. To His Highness the Sheikh of Kuwait, Sir Ahmed ibn Jaber al-Sabah, K.C.I.E., I owe especial thanks, for he made his interesting city-state my second home. I wish to express my gratitude, too, to the Political Agent at Kuwait, Major A. C. Galloway; to Dr L. P. Dame at Bahrein; Dr Milray [*sic*; sc. Dr C. S. G. Mylrea] at Kuwait; Miss Ailsa Nicol Smith and Captain P. R. Morgan at Zanzibar; Mr. James Hornell of Madras, and the Society for Nautical Research; Mr. J. MacDougall at Lamu, and to Forester Burrows of the Rufiji. I thank my good friends the Hansens of New York – Eleanor, Marian, and Harold – for their help with the charts.

As for my plan of campaign, it was this. First, having decided to learn what I could of dhows, I tried to discover what was already known. That meant several months of inquiries in England, and as far as first-hand material went, it yielded very little. That done, and having met Mr. Ingrams, I went off to Arabia, taking Hilgard Pannes of Long Island and Chicago with me. Pannes had been with me before, in the ship *Joseph Conrad* and the grain-racing *Parma*. He was a good shipmate. The two of us sailed in the Red Sea with Ahmed the Yemenite to Gizan, and wandered afterwards as far as Jiddah. Then followed the Zanzibar voyage with Nejdi – Pannes stayed for a short time in the Hadhramaut, and later went back to the University of Chicago – half a year of that; then Kuwait, and pearling. I wish I could have sailed three years with the Arabs, for it was all very interesting – three years with the Arabs, followed by two years on the book. But I sailed one year, and was fortunate to have that, and the book, such as it is, has been done hurriedly in time out from war.

ALAN VILLIERS

England, 1940

I

MA'ALLA BEACH

THE STERILE, pock-marked mountains of Aden stood hot and grim round Ma'alla bay, as if designed and placed there deliberately to hem in the water from the ocean's cooling winds. Across the shallow bay the sand, curiously miraged, appeared to wash against the mountains of the coastal range, as if the sea had flung it there, and then gone, abandoning for ever the fruitless task of trying to moisten or to cool the parched hard rock of that barren land. The sky was blue and hard, and the hot sun burned. The sand underfoot was dark and foul, and the beach stank. Pariah dogs ran out from the poor huts and rapidly barked themselves into a state of exhaustion. Goats bleated, their heavy udders secured in dirty calico bags against their hungry kids. Children ran crying for bakhshish, seeming to know no other word. Along the roadway towards the Crater dun-coloured camels plodded by, supercilious and deliberate, drawing little carts, or strode in empty caravan with ragged Beduin beside them dressed in indigo and rags, outward bound towards Lahej and the farther Yemen valleys. By the side of the roadway, in monotonous stone lines, stood the houses of the Somali, migrants from nearby Berbera, who now were more numerous in Steamer Point than the Arabs themselves. Overhead the drone of a bombing squadron of the Royal Air Force, twelve ancient biplanes in ragged formation, reminded one that Aden would soon celebrate its centenary of British rule. Once meeting-place of East and West and still an important world and Arab port, Aden was now an outpost of Empire marked red on the map, guarded by guns and policed by bombing aircraft. Yet it was once Eudaemon Arabia, known for its convenient anchorage and sweet water to the anonymous sea-captain who compiled the *Periplus of the Erythraean Sea* in the first century of our era, and known probably to the Arab and Indian mariners of the eastern seas for countless centuries before that. Now it was a refuelling point for ocean liners, and a post of importance for the policing of Empire trade routes.

I walked along Ma'alla beach, where in the eighth century a merchant had drawn an accurate map of the Indian Ocean in the sand and marked in it ports and routes and trade which were to remain unknown to us for almost a thousand years, and I thought of the ancient glories of this great port in the great days of eastern navigation. It was because I knew that something of those times still survived that I was there at all, for Aden is not ordinarily the kind of place in which one dallies. I knew that the Arab dhows of today were in the direct line of descent from the ancient vessels of eastern waters in which men probably first sailed; and I would have gone to hell to see them. I had to come no nearer to hell than Aden, which was close enough: but here at Ma'alla beach were the dhows, and here were the Arabs who still sailed them.

Along the beach where the hard brown earth merged into brackish, smelling mud, a dozen small dhows stood propped on stilts or leaned crazily towards the sea, while their skirted sailors carried out repairs, or, with endless chant and song, applied hot paying-stuff to their ships' undersides, using their bare hands. Here and there the shapely hulls of partly finished dhows rose above from surrounding piles of twisted wood from the Yemen and logs from the Malabar coast, out of which skilful carpenters, working only with adze and Indian drill, had hewn them. The sweetly curved bows of the new sambuks seemed to look in amazement over the odds and ends of wood which had given them birth. A gang of sailmakers, more negro than Arab, squatted on the sand, stitching the round seams of a lateen sail. Other sailors close by were laying up cable made of coconut fibre from India, or carrying out a rusted grapnel into the tidal water, to which to haul off a small dhow when next the tide served. In the bay two score small dhows swung to their moorings, or moved with jostling and chants towards the end of the stone jetty to take their turns at loading or discharging. The stench of putrid shark and fish-oil which rose from them was a deterrent against close examination. These were the small fry from the nearer coastal ports of the Yemen and southern Arabia, come to Ma'alla to load cargoes for distribution to the ports of the Hadhramaut and the Red Sea. Beyond them lay the deep-sea dhows, the big booms from Kuwait and the baggalas and ocean-going sambuks from Sur, which had brought dates from the Basra River in Iraq and were loading for their annual voyage down to Africa.

If Steamer Point is given up to liners now, and bombing aircraft drone above the Crater, Ma'alla Bay between the two is still a great port for dhows both small and large, the small dhows bringing and distributing goods for the nearer ports and the deep-sea dhows carrying such cargoes as the competition of European steam still leaves to them. They can freight dates from Basra for the local market more cheaply than any steamer can bring them; they can load bulk salt for Mombasa and deliver it there more cheaply than powered vessels. And they still can carry on their age-old trading voyages, buying and selling their own merchandise as they go – dates, salt, dried shark, cotton stuffs brought now from Japan instead of rare silks from China and dress goods from India, sesame seeds, ghee, and Arab cooking oils.

The songs of the sailors as they pulled the longboats to Ma'alla jetty were music in my ears as I walked along the hot beach, and the long-voyage dhows were a delight to see. Those big dhows were a heartening sight that hot, harsh morning, and I meant to find a berth in one of them before the day was ended. Ma'alla beach might smell, but to me it was a romantic, intensely interesting place, with its jetty where the faithful prayed facing Mecca, and its picturesque fleet of dhows. For these Arab dhows were almost the last unspoiled fleet of pure sailing vessels left in the world. The last of European sail were the square-riggers of Mariehamn in the grain trade from Australia, but of these only a handful remain. These, a few brigantines in the Mediterranean, a Portuguese Banks fisherman or two, three barques in the Peruvian guano trade, one or two Germans carrying Chilean nitrate – these were about all the engineless, unsubsidised commercial sail left in our world. The white schooners of the South Seas have long been engined and the reek of diesel oil now pollutes many an island lagoon. The junks of China are busy avoiding Japanese bombs; the deep-sea *praus* of the East Indies cannot compete with the K.P.M.; the coastal craft of India voyage under British regulation, and the steamers, have taken most of their overseas trade. Gloucester fishermen, Balinese schooners, Tasmanian timber ketches, Baltic galeasses and barquentines – all these are engined.

It seemed to me, having looked far and wide over twenty years of a seafaring lifetime, that as pure sailing craft carrying on their unspoiled ways, only the Arab remained. Only the Arab remained making his voyages as he always had, in a wind-driven vessel sailing without benefit of engines. Only the Arab still sailed his wind ships over the free sea, keeping steadfastly to the quieter ways of a kinder past. Just as the Mariehamn grain ships of Finland were the last of European sail, the Arab dhow was the proud last of the romantic East. I had sailed in most other kinds of sailing ships, from a Trobriand canoe to a four-masted barque, a Tasmanian ketch to a full-rigged ship. I had not hitherto had a chance to sail in Arab dhows. With all else gone, I was glad to turn to them, glad that they still survived. I had always been interested in Arab dhows, and always admired the Arab for the fine independence and the quiet good manners of his well-adjusted life. The Arabs had been sailing, and sailing very well, for countless centuries before we even knew the ocean existed: that they still sailed very much the same trade routes in much the same way I thought remarkable evidence both of their ability and spirit. If I could sail with them on an African voyage, to learn of their seafaring at first-hand, I should be pleased indeed.

I had already been sailing in coastal dhows in the Red Sea, in Ahmed the Yemenite's small zarook, as a kind of trial voyage. As I stopped to look over the animated waterfront I saw her swinging to her anchors out in the bay, back empty from her voyage to Gizan. The passage in her had been a good beginning; but it was the big deep-sea dhows which really attracted me, the big fellows from Kuwait and Sur and the Persian ports. These were almost pure survival from the Phoenician days, from the most ancient sailing of which we know. There they were, swinging in the sun of Ma'alla Bay, with their singing sailors rowing in longboats full of Basra dates. There they were, lying at noisy anchor off Ma'alla beach, making ready, perhaps for the thousandth or five-thousandth time, for the annual trading voyage down to Africa, as far as the monsoon blows. They were a handsome fleet of imposing vessels, with their oiled hulls shining over the blue waters of the bay, and their simple rig of two bare masts. They were a stirring fleet, as I thought of the great history and the tremendous traditions behind them. Yet now the aeroplanes roared overhead and tourists hurried, bound in their impatient motor-cars to the Tanks and Sheikh Othman, while their liners filled their tanks with oil, and no one save Arabs spared as much as a glance towards the dhows. Here at Ma'alla the deep-sea dhows were in, and from no one in the European world could I learn about them.

Well, I was about, I hoped, to learn for myself, and the prospect pleased me. I continued along the beach, slowly, for there was much to see. My destination was the office of the Kuwait dhow-owners, Khalid Abdul-latif al-Hamad and Brothers, importers of dates and owners of date plantations in Iraq, charterers and owners of dhows trading to Africa, the Yemen, Eritrea, Saudi-Arabia, Somaliland, and India. I knew that I should find there the assembled nakhodas of the Kuwaiti and Suri fleets, for it was their custom to call on the merchants in the mornings. I liked to walk, though it was so hot. The scene was too interesting to hurry by heedlessly in a car: the zigzagging road to Aden's Crater gave delightful views over harbour and sea. I did not see the macadam road or the vehicles from Detroit and Dagenham which speeded on it. I looked back over Ma'alla Bay where the dhows lay, and thought of all the great centuries of their unhurried voyaging. The idea of going out with a dhow to join in this was a pleasing prospect.

Yet I knew well that the voyage itself might not be wholly pleasing, for I had come but recently from Ahmed the Yemenite's small zarook, a mean, flea-bitten little thing that traded in the hot Red Sea. Ahmed's zarook was tough, hungry, and exceedingly primitive. In a brief month there I had lost twenty pounds' weight and had picked up a little dysentery and some malaria. Yet I had thought it worth while. The name of Ahmed's little ship was *Sheikh Mansur*, but there was nothing sheikh-like about her. She had a waterline length of less than fifty feet, two small masts raking forward, and a great thirst for the sea. She leaked as if she loved it, and the only delight of soaking more and more of the sea through her kept her afloat. She was built of odds and ends of indifferent wood scraped up on some Yemenite beach and nailed together with old iron, but her ribs and her knees were good. I had found her at Ma'alla, whence the al-Hamads were sending her with a cargo of Rangoon rice, Javanese sugar, and bales of Japanese cottons and printed stuffs for the harims, all destined for the bazaar at Gizan, by the southern borders of Asir in the Red Sea. The good *Sheikh* was nothing but an open boat with a lateen sail. Except for a small poop and a tiny working platform in the bows, she was undecked.

When I first boarded her they were hauling up clean water in goatskins from her well, bailing her constantly, though she lay then in the quiet waters of Ma'alla Bay, and they bailed almost the whole way to Gizan. Of all the dhows in port she was undoubtedly the meanest, though none of her people thought so. She was dreadfully small, horribly overloaded, and she stank frightfully. She had no accommodation of any kind, and there was never much to eat. A matting of loosely woven palm leaves, lashed above her bulwarks along both sides, served to keep out most of the sea when she rolled, but one angry sea breaking on board would have been the death of her. She was a low, rakish little thing, green-painted with a white limed mouth, where her sweet cutwater bit the sea, and a pattern of triangles in reds and blues round the railing at her sharp stern. She sat prettily in the water, and her lines were excellent. She had a graceful and fleet little hull, and her high raking mainmast grew from her gracefully. Her lateen yard was constructed from the branches of two trees, lashed together end for end, and her one sail was a loosely seamed piece of cheap Japanese cotton, roped with coir made from Indian coconut fibre. Her rudder seemed balanced precariously on one pintle, from which it threatened every moment to break adrift, and even in the quiet waters of the harbour she seemed in imminent danger of foundering.

I voyaged in that little ship 600 miles, and I enjoyed every mile of it and was sorry when the time came to leave her. Mean and incredibly poor as she was, she *was* a ship, and there was a spirit aboard her rare in these days and never found in liners. We sailed from Ma'alla along the coast of Southern Arabia towards the westwards, and through Bab-el-Mandeb and along the Yemen coast past Mocha, Hodeida, and Kamaran, and then along the inside way, within the reefs, towards Gizan. We sailed by day and anchored at night, for the way was dangerous. It was the fasting month of Ramadhan, which is an unfortunate time to be with the Arabs in their dhows, for during Ramadhan the faithful may neither eat nor drink from before dawn until after sunset. If you are with the faithful, it is mannerly to behave as they do. Our crew of eight Arabs under Ahmed the Yemenite went hungry while we sailed, and in the evenings when the sun had set and they had said their prayers, we dined on a mess of rice and fish, if there was any rice and we had caught a fish. We ate with our hands, in the Arab manner. Life was hard, but it was also simple. If no one had any possessions, no one was envious. If there were no bunks, the air was warm, and there were the stars for company. The weather was good. The little ship knew no routine, and kept no schedule. No one knew or cared what day it was, for to them days were not uniform periods to be named and numbered and regretted as they rushed by. We had a mild interest in the progress of the Ramadhan moon, for its final setting would mean the end of the long fast. I was surprised how easily I slipped into this timeless state, how pleasant it was when attained. Who cared what day it was? The sun always rose again, and set, as Allah willed, and the days were good for their own sake. It was a primitive and, at the same time, a surprisingly satisfactory existence.

Ahmed did his best with the ship and the winds Allah gave him, and did not fret when the conditions were adverse. There was a fine spirit in that happy little vessel where all men were so poor, and the master was the father of his sailors. He was in his early thirties, and most of them were grown men, but he acted as a father to them, and his leadership was benevolently patriarchal.

I was interested to see how Ahmed managed his vessel, for he knew no methods of navigation as we know them, and those seas are dangerous. He had no need of ordinary methods of navigation. The *Sheikh Mansur* was run very simply. Without any kind of windlass, and no anchor save a grapnel and a piece of stone in which a spike had been embedded; with no boat other than one small dugout canoe; with no instruments or aids to navigation beyond one decrepit, hopeless, and largely invisible boat compass dating back at least a century; without even a leadline to sound, she somehow wandered along cheerfully, and she had been sailing like that for at least thirty years in one of the most dangerous seas in the world. She had no shelter, no decks, no charts, no bell, no barometer, no clock. What need was there for shelter, when it never rained? Why have decks, when no sea broke on board? Who needed charts, when Ahmed knew every reef and every headland, every strip of beach and every rock by eye, from long and close personal association? What need was there of bells and clocks, when time was not a passing torrent to be vainly measured? Or of barometers, when the weather in the winter season was always fair? There was not even a tarpaulin to cover the cargo, which lay in the hold open to the sea; but if the sea ever came there, not only the cargo would be finished. She had not even a single pump. There was nothing to cook in save a box of sand with three stones, on which a boy kindled a brushwood fire in the evenings. The sea stores coming aboard at Aden consisted of some old palm leaves from which fibres were extracted as necessary, to be used as rope yarns or sail yarn or gaskets, or whatever else might be needed. The food for twelve people (for she also carried passengers) was kept in half a small chest on the tiny poop, from which it soon disappeared. Then there were fish. The drinking water was kept in a rusted drum exposed daylong to the intense heat of the overhead sun, and in this small squirming things flourished. There was not so much as an old hurricane lamp on board. There was no light at all. When the sun set, we lived in unrelieved blackness, though the nights were soft and the stars were clear, and the moon of Ramadhan was light enough in the evenings.

The little ship rolled and pitched abominably in anything of a sea, with a short, sharp, jerky motion. She was infested with cockroaches and all kinds of insects, and there were rats. By night hungry mosquitoes came from the little cays off which we anchored, and dined on my too well-nourished blood. Food became scarce when a shark carried away our only fishing line, and we lived three days on a handful of old dates. We washed in the sea, ate with our hands, slept on the cargo, only a foot or so above the level of the outside water. We were sunburned, hungry, tired (for the constant motion of a little ship in a short sea is very tiring). I knew little Arabic, and understood almost nothing of the gibberish those Yemenite sailors spoke.

It was a tough life, but this was a reflection which occurred to no one else on board, and I was glad enough to be there. The sailors were all good friends. Their simplicity and their direct free honesty, their utter lack of hypocrisy and all shams, the calm unworried philosophy of their simple lives, were very appealing. They fasted, prayed, washed in the sea water, did such work as was necessary, and cheerfully ate their frugal meals. It seemed to me that the very simplicity of their hard lives gave them a quality most enviable, and missing too often from our own. Their satisfactions were their own, and their delights lay in a real world round them. They were free men, though one of them was a slave. They were freer men than we are.

Day after day we wandered leisurely to the northwards, inside the reefs of the eastern side of the Red Sea. The wind blew and the ship sailed. The crew prayed, and observed the fast, and Ahmed the Yemenite knew where he was going. He knew those waters and he knew his ship; he was a good sailor. His little ship was in many ways the quietest and most peaceful in which I had ever sailed. I learned to admire Ahmed and his crew, and to like them all. Such as their little ship was, they loved her. To them she had no imperfections. In a little while, living so closely with that spirit on board, I began almost to be ashamed that I had first thought her so lowly. She was a workable little craft fit enough for the voyages she was called upon to make, though her main halliards might have been made from plaited straw. She ran well and sailed well, and she never behaved badly in the sea, though we were in a race once or twice, off Mocha and in the straits of Bab-el-Mandeb. Nothing of her cargo was ever touched, though some of it was food and we were hungry. Nothing was broached, though the crew was poor and anything from those bales would have meant wealth to them. When one day we sighted another dhow in distress, with her rudder gone, Ahmed put the helm up and ran at once to her assistance, though the wind was hard that day and we were in dangerous waters. When we spoke to small fishermen, they gave us fish and we gave them rice, if we had any.

So day followed day: beards grew, belts tightened, and the insects in the water-drum multiplied. On the evening of the eighth day we reached

Gizan, coming in through the kelp and anchoring beside a pilgrim dhow bound for Jiddah.

That had been some weeks earlier: now I looked back from the Crater Road, and the *Sheikh Mansur*, come again to Aden, was a green-painted speck far below on the busy bay. It had been a tough life, perhaps, looked at by any of our standards. I had no great desire to spend more time voyaging in the small fry of the Red Sea, for one passage in them must be very like another. I liked the Arabs, and looked forward to shipping out with the big dhows bound on a long voyage, for deep-seamen are always more interesting than coastwise craft. I continued toiling slowly up the incline of the Crater Road, and wished the day were not quite so insufferably hot.

In the cool of the al-Hamad office, a large stone building in the streets of Aden Camp, I found half a dozen nakhodas from the big dhows in the harbour. With them, seated writing at a desk with a modern filing cabinet beside it and a telephone on the table, was Ali Abdul-latif al-Hamad, second youngest of the al-Hamad brothers of Kuwait, who was at that time in charge of the Aden office. He was a tall, slightly built young man dressed in a well-made linen suit, and on his head was a sheepskin cap. The office was a plain room open to the street, with three of its sides lined with wooden benches on which carpets and cushions had been placed. The nakhodas, a bearded, silent lot, sat on the carpets. One of them had a fringe of hennaed beard that hung on his square jaw like seaweed, and a twig of the Hamdh bush was stuck in his turban to be used, I supposed, for cleaning his teeth. That this was indeed its use he proved then and there by quietly taking it out and nonchalantly scrubbing his teeth with its teased end. The other shipmasters were moustachioed men dressed in long white gowns. With the exception of one who was very negroid, they were light-complexioned Arabs and would have passed, dressed in European clothes, as swarthy Greeks or Portuguese. They were a striking assembly, as they sat swinging their amber beads and waiting to give replies to such speech as might be addressed to them.

I thanked Ali Abdul-latif for the voyage to Gizan, for it was he who had arranged it, and I asked if I could go out with one of the big deep-watermen on a voyage down to Zanzibar. Ali smiled, showing a large mouth of perfect teeth beneath his close-clipped black moustache. So I wanted to go to Africa in a big dhow, did I? I had not had enough in the *Sheikh Mansur*? Well, he went on, if I really did wish to sail in a dhow to

Zanzibar I was in luck, for the best young nakhoda from Kuwait was then on the premises, having his lunch somewhere in the mysterious chambers upstairs. Would I care to meet him? Indeed I would: and so it came about that I first met Nejdi, that hawk-nosed, keen-eyed son of the Eastern seas – Nejdi, youthful master of one of Kuwait's fastest and largest booms, pilot of great dhows down to Zanzibar and the Malabar coast, pearl-master of the Persian Gulf.

When I first saw him he was eating a sheep. Ramadhan was past, and it was again lawful to eat by day. He appeared to be making up for lost time. He was squatting on a carpet in the shade of the parapet of the al-Hamad roof where the cooling air could blow upon him, and he was nonchalantly chewing large pieces of a well-done sheep, and shovelling down handfuls of rice as fast as he could. He stopped and stood up as we came. He was a small, slight man, with a very strong face which the ravages of smallpox had not spoiled. He was handsome, in his own way, with an oval face, a close-clipped black moustache, a hawk nose, and well-defined, determined chin. He was wiry and lean, and he looked very strong. He was swarthy, darker than the other Kuwait shipmasters downstairs. He was strikingly dressed in a long flowing gown of white silk, which was gathered closely at the throat by two gold studs. On his head was a white headcloth, embroidered with needlework of pale gold, and kept in position by a black lamb's-wool aghal, the halo-like headrope of the desert Arab. His cloak of camel's hair and wire of gold was thrown on the carpet beside him, and a set of amber prayer beads peeped from one pocket. Leather sandals, embellished in red and green and looking very new, stood neatly on the roof by the edge of the carpet where he had discarded them, and a Malabar cane lay beside them. He had small, shapely hands, with long, delicate fingers. His features were strong and very good. There was about his face and all of him an air of alert ability which augured well for any ship he might command, and of complete self-assurance which boded ill for any who tried to thwart him. He had the stance of a master-mariner, of a seaman more used to the rolling poop than the dull roofs of a city house. He stood there as if he half expected the roof to roll beneath him at any moment, and as if, too, he were ready for it, if it did.

Ali introduced us, and we joined him at the sheep, not speaking again until the meal was ended. This was about five minutes later, by which time most of the sheep was ended, too. After that we washed our hands with water brought in a jar by a servant, drank three thimblefuls of very strong unsweetened coffee, wafted some incense into our noses from a burner brought by another servant, and sat silently for some time. I began to think this was all we were going to do, when Ali began at last to speak with this strange young man who had, I gathered, already been in command of deep-sea dhows trading to Africa and India for more than ten years. What they said I did not know, for they spoke in Arabic and I did not then know much of that language. But Ali had good English, and afterwards he told me that it would be all right. I could go with Nejdi in his boom. Apparently Nejdi's full name was the Sheikh Abdul-Krim bin Mishari al-Abdul-razzaq el-Nejdi [in fact Nejdi's full name was Ali bin Nasr el-Nedji, see pp. xii and xxxiv n.3]: his dhow had a name almost equally as long, which Ali translated to me as the *Triumph of Righteousness* [see p. xxxiv n.4]. This seemed a very satisfactory name for any vessel which sailed so much under the guidance of Allah as the ordinary Arab dhow, but I wondered for a moment whether the name might not be the best thing about her. I remembered the poor *Sheikh Mansur*, which also had been proudly named but turned out to be the meanest little vessel in Ma'alla Bay. I was uncertain whether, after all, Ali had not meant that Red Sea passage as a test of my calibre and the depth of my real interest in the Arabs and their dhows, and I wondered whether the high-falutin *Triumph of Righteousness* might not turn out to be the smallest, meanest, oldest Kuwait boom in the harbour. But I kept these fears to myself, for I felt Nejdi's eyes on me; and whatever she was, I would go in her.

Nejdi had little to say throughout this interview, though I gathered he did not think much of the European business of writing books. In his view, there was only one book. The Qurân was enough for him. But he knew I was a sailor and had sailed big ships on long voyages myself: perhaps I might be useful to him. As for books, he left no doubt (Ali said) that in his view there were more than enough European books about the Arabs already. Some of them were good – he mentioned Yawrens, and Stark[1] – but in many of the others the Arabs could recognise neither themselves nor their country. Ali told him that I would write only about ships and the sea – ships, and sailors, but he still looked dubious. Apparently he held the firm opinion that the sea was no fit subject for books, and he thought that the Arabs, having made their voyages unchronicled over so many centuries, might be left in enjoyment of that privilege. Nobody wanted to read about sailors, he seemed to think, and

[1] Colonel Lawrence (known to the Arabs as "Yawrens") and Miss Freya Stark.

the sailors certainly did not want to read about themselves. They would all live ashore, if they could. As for books, a list of distances and landfalls and descriptions of desirable ports would be more in their line. However, an extra navigator would be welcome in the vessel, if I would take her as I found her. I could come, if I wished. I could have six feet of the mates' bench aft, and join in the quarterdeck mess. But had I not better first see the ship?

This I thought an excellent idea, remembering the *Sheikh Mansur*. I was aboard on the Sunday. After one brief glance, I knew I need have no worries about Nejdi's boom. An upstanding, handsome thoroughbred of a ship; beside the *Sheikh Mansur* she was like a Cape Horner beside an old Thames barge. She was massive, without being heavy; strong, with no hint of sluggishness; stout, though sweetly lined. She sat the blue water of Ma'alla Bay like a handsome sea bird, and her beak-like bow added to the illusion. She was low in the bow and high aft, in the manner of deep-sea Arab dhows, though as in all Kuwait booms, her cutwater was straight and carried up into a straight sort of built-up bowsprit, which reached out twenty feet before her, more as a symbol than for use. From the low bow the lines of her hull ran in a lovely sweep to her poop, which was roomy and high. She was a vessel, I judged, of about 150 tons, though none of the Arabs I asked knew her tonnage. They did not measure their ships by tons, but by their stowage capacities for packages of Basra dates. The *Triumph of Righteousness*, they said, could stow two and a half thousand packages of dates. She was light then, for the dates had been discharged, and she towered over all the sambuks and zarooks in the bay. Her teak mainmast stood ninety feet above the sea, and her tremendous lateen yard was made of the trunks of three trees, lashed stoutly end for end with many seizings of canvas-bound rope. She stank abominably of fish-oil, as do all dhows, but I was used to that by then. In spite of the fish-oil and the other queer odours which rose from her main hatch as we climbed on board, I knew this was the kind of vessel in which I wished to sail. The atmosphere of true adventure and romance lay heavy on her graceful hull, and the very timbers of her worn decks were impregnated with the spirit of colourful wandering. What a grand ship she was! After twenty years, one learns to sense the atmosphere of ships when first putting a foot over their rails: one glance, and I knew this was a happy, well-run ship, though she reeked of fish-oil and no one on board knew where she was bound. It seemed to me that these Arabs and their ships, outmoded as they are and derelict by every standard of our frantic world, have a delight in living we do not even know we lack. I came aboard with pleasure and looked about me with pride, for this was a ship beyond a doubt, and I was glad that I should be privileged to sail with her. My six feet of the navigator's bench aft looked very good to me, under a double awning of Indian duck (which never again was bent), and the stalwart crew went about their duties alert and cheery.

As for where exactly the *Triumph of Righteousness* might be going, I must confess that I did not quite know: but that could wait. It did not matter. She was off on the old round of the argosies of Araby, and it was enough for me that such a trade and such voyaging should still survive, and I should have the chance to see it.

Nejdi, dressed in a loose linen gown and headcloth of white and gold, with a white abba thrown carelessly over his shoulders, met us at the gangway. His cloak was a handsome garment of white camel hair, with cloth-of-gold and gold-wire embellishments at lapels and cuffs, and along both arms. It was gathered across his chest by two golden tassels, loosely knotted, and his prayer beads swung in his left hand. Beside him stood his younger brother Abdulla, petty officer in the boom. Abdulla was a pleasant-faced young man whose countenance also showed the ravages of smallpox, which must be common in Kuwait. Behind these stood the muallim, or mate, who was introduced as Hamed bin Salim. Hamed was taller than the others, and had a very black chinpoint beard, so perfectly geometrical that it looked as if it had been cut out and pasted on.

There was to be a dance in our honour and the ship was spick and span. Both poop and the maindeck were shaded by large awnings, and Persian carpets in flowery reds and blues were spread about. The navigators' bench aft was especially ornate, with heavy carpets and large numbers of reclining cushions and leaning pillows, and a Beduin camel saddle or two which Nejdi was taking for sale to a curio dealer whose business was with tourists in Zanzibar. Here we reclined in easy state, the Arab guests barefoot and sucking at large hookahs made from Basra earthenware, while refreshments of bitter coffee and too-sweet tea were passed round endlessly, and the drums were warming for the dance. Sailors brought us trays of sherbet and sweetmeats, and figs and dates, all of which were very good. Nejdi, looking very dignified and very much the master of all in sight, smoked endlessly from a long hookah, while he listened courteously to the discourse of the merchant Ali and now and again softly murmured *Taiyib,* which means good, and signified his complete approval. These soft murmurings were interspersed by loud shouts for

Yusuf, an ancient sailor in a long white gown with his face half-hidden underneath a large, fierce moustache, and a fold of his headcloth over his left eye, like a visor. Yusuf seemed to act as the nakhoda's slave. Actually he was not a slave, and there were no slaves on board. His work appeared to be to replenish both the embers and the tobacco in Nejdi's hookah at frequent intervals, and to superintend the bringing of refreshments. I liked the look of Yusuf. He looked a good sailor, and a good sort.

We sat on the carpeted bench a long time, for the Arabs are never in a hurry. I looked at the animated, stirring scene all round me, with the fleet of big dhows at the crowded anchorage, among which were vessels from Kuwait, Sur, Muscat, the Trucial Coast, and the smaller ports of Persia. Nearest to us was a beautiful baggala from Kung, a port in southern Persia. The baggala was a stately galleon of a ship with a carved and quarter-galleried stern, and for the moment I regretted that I was not going out with her. Her sweet low bow sat in the water as smoothly and with as much effortless perfection as the head of a dolphin, and her windowed and galleried stern shimmered at her from its reflection in the clear waters of the bay. Several Suri sambuks, also very graceful, were moored next to the baggala, and from them came an endless chanting and stamping of bare feet while their sailors took cargo on board. I looked with pleased interest at all this and the host of lesser ships, while I examined the swarthy skirted mariners who were to be my shipmates for perhaps the next half-year. They sat in dignified, stately line along the bulwarks on the starboard side, like a group of courtiers at a sheikh's council. Behind me the long yoke of the high rudder swung quietly on its chains, and the wheel kicked very softly, just enough to add animation to the general peace of the anchored ship. Overhead, the big oiled masts leaned into the blue sky: ashore the pock-marked mountains of Aden looked better, seen from the sea, and Ma'alla Bay took on more of its proper aspect of Eudaemon Arabia, that "village by the shore," marketplace for frankincense from the Hadhramaut, and all the spices and cloths of India. No odour of incense arose from it now, and the only cloths I saw had been mass-manufactured in Japan. But the same old water lapped quietly at the stout teak planks of the same type of ship; the same swarthy mariners strode her decks and squatted on her poop, with very much the same methods and the same ideas as all their seagoing ancestors for so long before them.

The music began, as I mused, and its discord brought me back to the modern earth with a jar. We rose, and went down to the maindeck by way of the carved companion on the port side. The maindeck was also spread with carpets, and Yusuf fussed about to see that all were straight and everything was in order. The narrow, wedge-shaped main hatch, from the forepart of which the great mainmast rose, had been transformed into another reclining bench, with carpets and cushions. Here we sat while the sailors danced. The musician was a large Arab with fierce eyes and a big black moustache, who played a guitar which looked as if it might have come from Europe. (I learned later that it had been bought in Basra.) He probably played very well, according to Arab ideas of music, but unfortunately those ideas were not mine, and he made matters worse by singing endlessly in an unnatural, rasping voice. Whatever it was he sang, it seemed excellent to his listeners, but I could have done without it. Ali whispered to me that he was a famous singer from Kuwait, but even this advertisement of his fame did not make his singing any more bearable. I hoped he was not part of the permanent equipment of the vessel. They said his name was Ismael. I was glad to see the sailors and a little man who looked like a cook come along with tiny drums, which were made from cylindrical pieces of Basra pottery, across one end of which had been stretched warmed kid's skin. There were about six of these drums and also some large tambourines. The sailors took turns at beating them, with their thumbs and forefingers, which they used with an excellent sense of rhythm. I liked the drums, for they had a pleasing low note, and they helped to subdue Ismael's music.

Now and again, sailors rose to their feet and danced in couples, shuffling along the carpet side by side. It was not very interesting dancing and I'm afraid its meaning, if it had any, was lost on me. But to them it was great fun, and they all enjoyed it. They appeared to take more pleasure in it than I had ever seen at any formal European dancing, but I was unable to make head or tail out of it. I confess that, as a rule, ballet is lost on me; but I was able to understand much of the Balinese dancing, and a Fourteenth of July celebration at Tahiti, with its wonderful dance competitions, had been a treat. Even the Solomon Islanders had been able to express something reasonably intelligible in their dancing, but this Arab shuffling seemed quite meaningless. However, this it could not have been. Perhaps the boom's sailors were performing very badly. If they were, I never saw better.

Nejdi himself danced later, and the antics he performed were equally dull and unintelligible. He danced with Abdulla Kitami, youthful nakhoda of another Kuwait boom moored close by. They, too, shuffled barefoot over the carpet, ranging fore and aft, keeping time with the moustachioed ruffian's music. Though a little more graceful, their dancing differed little from the sailors'. They kept the most solemn countenances, and their silken skirts swished as they shuffled to and fro. An important part of the performance seemed to consist of cracking their fingers, which they did with a very loud noise, in time with music. They walked backwards and forwards hand in hand along the carpet, while Ismael's black fingers tortured the strings and his cracked voice wailed. Each time as they approached the musician they stopped a second or so before him, and cracked their fingers. Sometimes they agitated their bellies and their whole bodies up to the shoulders, somewhat in the manner of a Moroccan dancing girl. Then again they would shuffle off along the carpet, eyes down and brown feet slithering, their swarthy faces dull masks covering whatever emotions they might have been expressing. As the music quickened and the performance dragged on – I found myself looking out over the masts of vessels at the anchorage – they sometimes stopped and violently agitated their whole bodies. Then they would leap suddenly in the air, turn about, and walk away again. It was a curious business, and I wondered why they did it; but perhaps any other form of dancing would be unsuitable in that climate.

Sometimes the singing sailors, unable to contain themselves at some particularly moving stanza from the moaning singer, would leap up and form in formation behind the two nakhodas, while they cracked their fingers and trembled violently. With a final whoop of joy they would leap high, turn about in the air, and then go off to their places by the bulwarks again, laughing heartily. They were like a lot of merry boys. There was indeed a grand spirit of jollity about the affair which could not but be infectious, and when they all sang sea songs together, it was quite pleasant. But I felt that I should enjoy the coming voyage without either the music or the dancing.

All this time the ship's carpenter, a young man with a close-clipped black moustache, had been banging and hammering at the ribs of a new dhow in course of construction over the whole of the port side of the main deck. It was a large dhow, at least 35 feet long, and as beamy as half the deck would allow. Ali whispered that it was being built for sale in Africa. He whispered other things to me, in the brief interval of quiet, for Ali was in a communicative mood that day. Knowing the rareness of communicative moods in Arabs, I listened carefully, but all I learned was the regrettable fact that Ismael was part of the permanent crew of the vessel. At that, my heart sank: but perhaps he would put his guitar away when the ship was at sea, or I could buy a large drum.

In many ways the *Triumph of Righteousness* was an improvement on the *Sheikh Mansur*. There was a deck to walk on, which was a blessing. It was crowded with all sorts of things, from the ribs of the building dhow to the cook's firebox and the wooden water tanks, but it was roomy enough. The poop, too, was crowded, for all the sailors' chests were there – rows and rows of them, ranged round both sides, with the head of an iron capstan peering out in some bewilderment on the port side. The *Triumph* boasted a real ship's wheel, of brassbound teak, a stylish brass binnacle, and a pair of quarter davits for the cutter. In all else she was just a big dhow with sharp ends. She also had a great cabin, as became a deep-waterman. It occupied most of the poop, but any romantic notions I may have had concerning this traditional sanctum of ancient ships were quickly dispelled by one whiff from it. It was nothing but a dark, cavernous, and cockroach-filled storeroom, in which the reek of old dried fish fought a losing battle with the general stench of fish-oil and foul bilgewater. There was not even head room, and only a child could stand beneath its beams. Off the afterend of this alleged "cabin," right in the stern of the ship, were two very small enclosed rooms which were more hutches than cabins. These palatial quarters, said Ali airily, could be mine, but I doubted it. In the first place the statement was open to doubt on general principles, for I had early discovered that the Arabs are sometimes given to extravagant statements and promises more indicative of temporary good feeling than any actual intention. In the second place, they were foul places, and I preferred the open air. They were jammed to the deckhead with malodorous stores in which the predominant note seemed to be old fish. No, I thought, I shall not be down here, even when Nejdi pointed out how excellent these spots would be for the working of navigation problems and the storage of navigational instruments, for he was eager that I should bring along my chronometer and sextant. I thought differently about that, too, for it was obvious that whatever I brought in that ship would not be worth taking away again, and chronometers are sensitive and expensive instruments. Besides, if he could navigate without them, I wanted to learn how he did it. As for navigation, it did not seem to be an important matter. Nejdi said he didn't need it really, for he was only going to Zanzibar and he knew the way.

Altogether I like the *Triumph* very much, and arranged at once to ship with Nejdi in his boom. There were few formalities: I had only to be checked out through the local police station at Ma'alla. There were no articles to sign, nor anything like that. If you wished to ship with the Arabs, apparently, you just brought your sleeping-carpet on board, and your chest, and moved in, after the necessary preliminary arrangement with the nakhoda. That is, you did these things if you were an Arab yourself: without Ali Abdul-latif's help, I don't think I should have found it so easy to ship with Nejdi in his boom, for many of the older-fashioned Arabs are still suspicious of the Christian from a Europe which has never treated them very well. However, there it was: my passage was arranged, and the ship had only to sail.

We were rowed ashore in the longboat with the traditional Kuwait style, the twenty stalwart men at the long oars dressed in their best robes, and all chanting lustily. They rowed very well and their chants were better than their songs. When they were not chanting they made a queer kind of low throaty growling sound like the distant rumbling of a squadron of bombing aeroplanes. They rowed with ceremony, and the stern of the longboat was gay with carpets. It was a dashing scene, as we came slowly through the fleet of anchored dhows bound towards Ma'alla pier: I liked the ceremony and the style about it. There was obviously a dash to life in these deep-sea dhows that was missing from the *Sheikh Mansur*, and from the little I had then seen of life in the *Triumph of Righteousness*, I looked forward to the coming voyage, wherever it might take her.

She had, I gathered, completed the discharge of Basra dates at Berbera and was now on the loading berth for trade for Africa, loading goods to offer for sale at ports along the Benadir, Swahili, and Zanzibar coasts – in other words, along the coasts of Italian Somaliland, Kenya, Tanganyika, and Zanzibar. Nejdi recited a list of ports to which he vaguely announced his intention of going if the conditions were good and Allah willed – places with mellifluous and romantic names like Haifun, Obbia, Athelet, Merka, Mogadishu, Kismayu, Malindi, Mikindani, Kilwa Kisinje, and many others of which I had never heard. How many of these places she might actually visit, if indeed she went to any of them at all, no one seemed to know, for the *Triumph*, like all her kind, was bound on a trading voyage on her own account, and not on a scheduled passage with goods for merchants. What she carried was for sale, to be got rid of in the best markets. She was loading salt, rice, sugar, canned milk, some coarse Indian corn, and other foodstuffs, and they expected to be ready for sea in a few days. Then she would sail along the coast of the Hadhramaut to complete her cargo with tobacco, ghee, honey, and dried shark, and perhaps – they said – also to take aboard a few passengers for Mogadishu and Mombasa. She would certainly call at Mukalla and Shihr; and perhaps also at Hami and Seihut, farther to the eastwards. It would be as Allah willed, and Allah indeed seemed to know as much about the coming voyage as Nejdi, or anyone else on board. At any rate, she would finally arrive – Allah willing – at Zanzibar, and from there she would make her way back somehow to the Persian Gulf. Perhaps she would go on to somewhere in Madagascar or the Seychelles Islands; perhaps she would run up to Malabar and load teak for Bahrein and Basra. Her future was pleasingly indefinite: she would go where there seemed most chance of earning profits. Somehow or other, she would eventually arrive back at her home-port of Kuwait, probably in six months – perhaps more. It did not seem to matter.

If it did not matter to the Arabs, neither did it matter to me. I liked that kind of voyage. I had never been down the east coast of Africa, and this seemed a good way of seeing it. I was still a little weak from dysentery in the Red Sea, but after the *Sheikh Mansur* the big *Triumph* seemed almost to promise comfort. The wooden tanks for fresh water were at least an improvement on Ahmed's rusty drum, and though the cockroaches scampered in the great cabin, there did not appear to be any plague of insects on deck. The *Triumph* would do.

At last the day came when she was to sail. Her sailing had been announced three times before, now at last it was definite. My metal chest was on the poop among the teak chests of the sailors, and I was ready to go aboard. I joined the boom after nightfall on the eve of her sailing, going out in her cutter from the jetty at Steamer Point. In the boat were Nejdi and his fellow nakhoda and boon companion, Abdulla Kitami, who had been his partner at the dance on the Sunday. Half-way across the harbour, the pair announced that they were not going to take their ships to sea. Nejdi said quite casually, as if it were the ordinary conduct of an Arab shipmaster, that he was going with Abdulla Kitami to Mukalla in one of Mr. Besse's small motor-ships, and the muallim would sail the dhow. I thought at first that this was strange procedure, but I learned later that it was normal. Several Kuwait and Suri dhows had already sailed for Mukalla, and the only way that Nejdi and Abdulla Kitami could steal a march on them was by this unorthodox means of going there by steam. Apparently competition for cargoes and passengers from the Hadhramaut ports was keen. A nakhoda in addition to sailing his ship had to be her agent, and collect her cargo and passengers besides. Indeed the sailing of the ship on a comparatively simple passage such as the beat from Aden towards Mukalla was a minor matter which could safely be left to the mate. Mates, I gathered, were carried for that purpose. Hamed bin Salim in the *Triumph* was well able to take that noble vessel as far as Mukalla (or anywhere else), and an ex-slave of the Kitami family would have charge of Abdulla's boom.

With Nejdi and Abdulla Kitami safe aboard their steamer, whose comforts I did not envy them, the cutter pulled over to the place where the *Triumph* lay, a picture of sail-borne majesty beneath the stars. She looked picturesque and almost incredibly romantic, fleet and deep and heavy-laden, with the tracery of her darkened masts high against the stars. The beating of drums and tamtams and the stamp of dancing feet added a note of wild rhythm. There were lights aboard, as I came over the side, and I heard the sailors softly singing as they hurried at their work of bending the huge mainsail and getting ready for sea. Barefoot, their long shirts tucked about their waists and headcloths turned back, the big crew were working methodically, rapidly, going about the multifarious tasks of getting the ship ready for sea. This was different from the *Sheikh Mansur*, which was never readier for sea than Allah found her. Her preparations for departure usually took about five minutes. In this big ship there was much to do – gear to be rove off properly and set up in its place, the cutter to be hoisted to the quarter davits, and the heavy longboat to be stowed on the starboard side of the maindeck, one of the anchors to be taken up and the other hove short, the huge mainsail to be bent along the whole length of the enormous lateen yard, and then, when all else was done, the yard itself to be mastheaded with the sail secured to it lightly by stops. This job alone took an hour, despite the fact that a longboat full of sailors from the Kitami boom came to help, and there were forty men sweating at those halliards. It was heavy, brutal work. They stopped frequently to dance and sing, stamping the deck rhythmically with their great bare feet and clapping their tremendous hands so that the handclaps rang through the harbour, and the serang banged an Indian drum. This dancing was good, far better than the formless shuffling of the Sunday's performance, and it seemed to act as a tonic for them, reviving the sailors for their heavy tasks. They did nothing without a preliminary dance, and they kept up a melodic chanting all the time they worked.

On the poop stood Hamed the muallim, an upright and very dignified figure in cloak and gown, with his large head bound in the folds of his headcloth so that only the eyes and the great nose showed. I had scarcely met Hamed before this, for he was a quiet man who said nothing when Nejdi was on board: now he gave orders, very quietly, from time to time, and the work proceeded. He was a picturesque figure standing on the poop barefoot in his gold-flecked robes much, one supposes, as ten thousand Arab shipmasters might have stood upon the poops of their baggalas and booms in Eudaemon Arabia from time immemorial, setting out on voyages towards Sofala, Ophir, or Zanzibar. Hamed greeted me quietly, motioned me to a place on the bench aft, and sent Yusuf Shirazi to help me stow my gear. But I was in no mood to stow gear and Yusuf Shirazi had other employments. I wanted to watch that scene. The night had a bright moon, and the other laden booms at anchor beating their drums and playing their string instruments made the scene a stirring one. Even the harsh outlines of Aden's burned hills were softened beneath the moon, so that all the background of bay and mountain seemed a perfect setting for this departure of the deep-sea dhows for Zanzibar. The boom's high masts and great lateen yard, when it had been hoisted, seemed to reach to the lower stars. The rudder kicked softly on its pintles, and from the binnacle came the low glow of a colza-oil lamp, ready for use when the tide turned.

We came out from Ma'alla Bay with a breath of land air before three in the morning, and at daybreak were outside Aden. Behind us was the Kitami boom, and ahead a Persian baggala. The quartermaster seated cross-legged at his seat by the wheel was holding her with a spoke this way and a spoke that, and Hamed bin Salim, squatting on the bench behind him, kept watch alert and tireless.

II

IN THE *TRIUMPH OF RIGHTEOUSNESS*

IT WAS THE first week in December when we sailed from Aden, and the north-east monsoon was blowing very quietly. This was the wind which was to take us down to Africa. It would blow until the end of March or early April, by which time we should be down at Zanzibar or along the Tanganyika or Portuguese East African coasts, wherever we were bound. From there, the south-west monsoon would bring us home again. This was an excellent arrangement, with a fair wind down the African coast and another fair wind to blow us back again; but for the time being the north-east wind was ahead. It was a head wind, there in the Gulf of Aden, and we had to fight for the first five hundred miles. After that it would be all plain sailing. I did not mind the head wind or the length of the passage to our first port, for life in the big dhow soon proved most interesting and I had much to learn. I established myself on my six feet of the bench aft on the starboard side, and proceeded to learn as much as possible.

My place on the bench was a good one, at the feet of the nakhoda. The bench there was about two and a half feet wide, which was room enough, and I had a carpet to sleep on. There was only the smallest protective railing to keep us aboard as the vessel rolled, but she did not roll much. At any rate at that stage of the voyage I never fell overboard, and I slept there at night for six months. The helmsman sat cross-legged on his stool beside me and steered sitting down. I had only to look across to peer into the binnacle and see he kept a good course, and a glance aloft showed me how things were with the sails. From my vantage post I could watch all that went on board, except beneath the poop. I could watch the cook at his firebox forward and the carpenter on his dhow; I could see the fresh-water tanks, the longboat, stowed on the starboard side, the main hatch. The reclining bench was protected by an awning which gave it shade enough, though Hamed had a rooted objection to spreading the awning any more than was strictly necessary. He preferred to be in the open, for he felt the wind better that way. Unfortunately we also felt the sun.

It was not unpleasantly hot, out in the open sea. After Aden it was quite mild. I gave up those early days to learning as much as I could for, even after a month in the Red Sea, this was a strange kind of seafaring. Life went on smoothly in the big dhow and we beat slowly to windward day after day. Hamed bin Salim, Abdulla Nejdi, and the rest seemed to accept me very well, and I settled into the ship's life easily. I had little to do. There was no navigation. There was almost as complete an absence of ordinary routine as there had been on the *Sheikh Mansur*. We trailed no patent log, kept no journal, struck no bells, had no musters, did no boat drills. There were no formal reliefs of the watch on deck. There was no formal going below. How could there be when there was no 'below' to go to? All hands lived on deck, and so they were always available. Time was of even less consequence than it had been in the Red Sea, for after all, the little *Sheikh Mansur* had to make many voyages in a year. The big *Triumph*, I gathered, was satisfied with one. When a whole year did not matter, days were of no consequence whatever. I found this timeless, untroubled state very pleasant to live in, and soon I did not care what day it was, either. I kept myself busy looking after the health of the crew, and learning. I had a few medicines and some simple dressings with me, and some sailors had badly ulcerated legs.

In addition to this medical work, I learned all I could of the Arabic names of the sails and the gear, and the orders in the various manœuvres. Trying to learn Arabic in this way was not easy. I had a few books with me, but these were in Syrian and Egyptian Arabic, which did not always agree with the language used by the sailors. I had crammed all the lessons I could from a spectacled sheikh in Aden, but the most helpful expression I had learned from him was the Arabic manner of saying "What do you call that?" I followed Hamed bin Salim, Abdulla Nejdi, Yusuf Shirazi, and the quartermasters declaiming this useful phrase until they were heartily sick of both it and me, but they always gave me some answer. Unfortunately the answers often did not tally. Learning Arabic was hard, and the Arabs made it no easier, but I soon reached the stage where I could communicate with the sailors and at least learn something from them, for fortunately for me, the maritime idiom, as in most other languages, seems more simple than the speech of the land. As for the Yemenite Arabic I had acquired in Ahmed's little zarook, this was worse than useless, for I found after six months in the *Triumph* that some of the Yemenite words I had been using all that time were mistaken by the Kuwaiti for English. Expressions I had thought Arabic, they had acquired from me and used as English.

The sailors used many Swahili, Hindustani, and Persian words, all of which are simpler than Arabic, and their daily language also included some curious distortions of English. If, for instance, they wished to indicate that they were in a great hurry, they used to shout loudly, "Fullspit! Fullspit!" which I suppose meant full speed ahead, and they referred to their boom, which was alleged to be very fast, as 'fes'mail', after the fast mail liners of the Persian Gulf. Abdulla Nejdi wished to learn English and I exchanged lessons with him twice daily. I taught him English and he taught me Arabic, but both the teaching and the learning were far from easy. After a week I decided it was even more difficult to teach him English than for me to learn Arabic from him, for if I asked him, in my version of maritime Arabic, what he called this thing or that, he would give me the answer in his version of non-maritime English, and it was often several days before I realised that he had imagined he was using an English word. It was better to learn the language as a child does, in the language itself and not by translation. Nobody spoke any English. Abdulla might have had twenty words by the time I left, and he could count up to seven. Old Yusuf Shirazi could say "dammit bloodie buggah!" which he did frequently, with gusto. He said he had been called that in India.

If learning Arabic was a slow process it certainly gave me a full-time occupation. I was soon on terms of friendship with Abdulla, the carpenter and old Yusuf Shirazi, but it was some time before I knew the names of all the sailors, or could tell them apart. In those early days, at least half of them seemed to be called Mohamed and the other half Abdulla, though I learned later that really there were only five Mohameds among the twenty-seven of them, and three Abdullas. The trouble was there were so many names that sounded to my untrained ears like Mohamed – Hamed, for instance, and Ahmed, and even Hamoud and Mahmoud. Yelled along the decks the way the Arabs yelled them, these names sounded much alike. It seemed to me that when they said Mohamed they barely breathed the M, so that I thought they were saying Hamed. It was very confusing. If I wanted anyone, and old Yusuf was not about, I just shouted "Mohamed," and let it go at that. Somebody always came. Indeed, generally half a dozen did. They were usually all the Abdullas.

Life was primitive enough and very much in the raw, but after the *Sheikh Mansur* the *Triumph* was like a palace. The possibility of taking exercise by walking on her decks was a great advantage, though the Arabs never did that, and looked curiously at me when I paced up and down.

"You do not like our ship, O Nazarene?" old Hamed asked, the third time he saw me doing this.

"Indeed I do like her, O Hamed muallim," I replied (or in words as near to that as I could manage). "Why do you think I am unhappy here?"

"You pace like the lion. Your tread is of the caged beast," he answered. "If you were happy, O Nazarene, you would be still."

It was useless to argue that I walked only for exercise. Exercise? They had never heard of the word: I gave up the attempt to explain, and sat down. Sometimes I helped the sailors at the heavy work of shifting over the yard and the mainsail, or hoisting the yard when it had been lowered for some reason, but this was exercise too much in that hot sea, and their pace was killing. Sometimes there was sailmaking to do, and I helped with that, though they said I sewed the seams too well and made them too strong. They sewed them very badly themselves, with long, rambling stitches. At other times we made rope, using Indian coconut fibre.

We beat along, bound towards Mukalla. At first the ship made long tacks, over towards the coast of British Somaliland, and one day Hamed pointed me out the landmarks for Berbera. Later, as we made easting, we kept the Arab shore and ghosted along in by the land. It was better that way, according to Hamed, who should have known for this was his twenty-fifth time round those parts. Outside in the Gulf of Aden, he explained, there was still a heavy set towards the west. By keeping close inshore, he could avoid the worst of it and sometimes, if we were very lucky, pick up the advantage of a counter-set towards the east. Hamed knew all the tricks of the sailing trade. It was safe enough, close inshore, for that coast is comparatively free of dangers. We wandered along very pleasantly in the days of azure sun and gentle breezes, and if our progress was not all it might have been, nobody minded. I am sure I did not, for it was a peaceful life. One of the most striking things about the big Arab ship was the sense of peace and well-being which pervaded her.

We wore ship twice a day, usually; ate three meals, prayed the stipulated five times (at least the Arabs did), and minded our own business. We always wore round when going on the tack, instead of tacking, for the lateen sail is dangerous if taken aback. The huge mainmast was supported largely by its own strength. As in all Arab ships, there was no standard rigging. Its only supports were some movable tackles, always set up to windward and let go when the ship was being put about. The main halliards, which led aft, acted as a backstay. So we always wore her round, running off with the wind behind the sail, and swinging the huge yard when she was dead before the wind. Whenever the sailors did this I watched most carefully, for it was a complicated and difficult process. The whole sail was thrown over, the sheet and the tack changing end for end, and the manœuvre had to be done carefully when there was anything of a wind lest the sail take charge. But she was a handy ship and a very responsible one, for all the unwieldiness of the huge mainsail, and her crew certainly knew their business.

I soon discovered that I was not the only extraneous person on board, for when we were well out at sea two mysterious Arabs turned up from somewhere. Where they had been hidden I don't know, and didn't ask, for questions were not encouraged. They were most mysterious Arabs, of a tribe obviously different from the Kuwaiti. One looked like a Suri, but the other I could not place. With them was a small boy, who appeared to be the servant of one of them. They were a strange pair, but I was the only person who seemed surprised by their sudden arrival. All the rest took it as a matter of course, and I resolved early that whatever happened on board that boom, I should never show surprise. I wondered who might appear next, when this bearded, gowned pair suddenly came up on the poop the second day at sea: but no one else did. One of them was a wizened little man with a sly face and a chinstrap beard. He was a wily little devil with a shrewd, calculating expression in his slits of eyes. He carried a silver box of mascara which he applied to his eyelids twice daily, and in the folds of his pink turban was a tooth-stick with which he scrubbed his mouth everytime he prayed. His beard was dyed with henna, in spots, and I saw him also applying henna to his toenails, fingernails, and the soles of his calloused feet. He was probably about fifty years old, and all I could find out about him then was that he was a merchant. What he dealt in, I did not then know, but I was to find out later. He was a dealer in hashish and haberdashery, a venturer ready for whatever turned up, a veritable modern Sindbad setting off with his pack. His name was Said – Said the Suri, though he said he came from father up the coast of Oman and not from Sur.

The other was a very much younger man. He came marching up on the poop with imperious tread and had the look of a desert warrior in his fine eyes. He greeted Hamed, paid no attention to me, and proceeded to stow a large sword, a leather shield, and an elaborate dagger in the space behind my chest. This martial equipment intrigued me and I should have liked to ask him something about it, but I held my peace. What it was for, if anything, I should discover in due course. I was beginning to think that if I stayed in that ship long enough, I might find out lots of things. He was dressed in a yellow gown, shorter than those the Kuwaiti wore, collarless, and gathered at the neck with a touch of red embroidery. He wore a silver dagger, lashed about his waist on a gold-embellished belt which also bore a silver purse. On his head was a cream turban, very large, wrapped loosely and held in position by a light headrope of black silk. On the end of this headrope dangled his tooth-stick, and this, with his arms, seemed to comprise the whole of his luggage.

The pair settled down at once as if they had been living in the ship all their lives, and from that time onwards they were as much her fixtures as the mizzen mast. They joined in the officer's mess up on the poop, and when there were all-hands jobs such as going about, they helped with the lighter labour. They were a queer pair. The small boy with them, too, interested me. He was more communicative than they were. His name was Mohamed, and he was a cheerful youth, aged perhaps eight. He was dressed always in the same ragged shirt and even more ragged turban. He had no other clothes and no belongings, not even a tooth-stick. He worked for Said, he told me – it took about a week to get the information – for the passage to Africa, and his food. The ship gave him his food, and in return he worked for the officers and the sailors.

In the ports he worked for Said, on board he worked for the ship as nakhoda's and sailors' servant. He did not know his father's name or where he was born, but it was somewhere in the Gulf of Oman. He had been wandering in ships since he was three, for boys begin their sea careers from Sur and Oman and the Trucial Coast incredibly young. Before he was three – so far as he remembered – he had been a beachcomber. This may seem almost unbelievable, but I was assured that it was probably so. Mohamed must have been tough. He was a wiry little fellow with a huge mouth and merry big eyes, and a very cheerful disposition. He had come to Aden as one of the crew of a Suri baggala, meeting Said there (and Said being on the lookout for just such a youth). He left the baggala without the formality of asking permission, and here he was going to Africa as if he were out for an afternoon's sailing. He had been to Zanzibar before, he said: this time he hoped to stay there, for he thought it a better place than Arabia.

Mohamed had no schooling and could neither read nor write. On board, he tended Said's hookah, and ran errands fore and aft, bringing the sailors' things from their chests, and holding the water-jar for the daily meals. He slept coiled up behind a bag of rice underneath the poop, and he seemed extremely happy. What he did to help Said ashore I was to learn later.

The *Triumph of Righteousness* was altogether an extraordinary ship. The old interesting cargoes of former days in this trade have now long departed, and we carried no romantic frankincense and myrrh. Instead, we had salt, rice, sugar, coffee, cotton stuffs, and some old dates. In the smaller ports of the Hadhramaut we could complete our cargo with some ghee and dried fish, and perhaps some cooking-stones to sell in Kenya. In addition to the ship's goods, the nakhoda, Hamed, Abdulla the nakhoda's younger brother, the serang, the quartermasters, the cook, and all the crew had goods of their own. Each member of the crew, apparently, was allowed to bring along one chest of goods, and the nakhoda had to advance them sufficient rupees – ten or twenty or so – to buy their stocks at Aden. They kept their chests on the poop, ranged in two rows along both sides, and one of their principal occupations, when there was no work afoot, was to come up on the poop and admire the haberdashery in each other's chests. Some of them had clubbed together to buy large bottles of French perfumes of the less expensive kinds, and they spent many hours painstakingly blending these and pouring the blend into tiny bottles. All sorts of queer things happened there on the *Triumph*'s poop, which sometimes looked more like a store. They had turbans of all kinds and gay rags galore, and some of them had gone in for fancy things like cheap Japanese thermos flasks, flashlamps, and safety razors. Anything they could sell to the Somalis of the Benadir coast or the Swahili down Zanzibar way they had brought along: I suspected that they proposed to pay duty on none of it. Well, I wished them luck: the crew were nearly all married men, back in Kuwait, and their share in the boom's earnings would never amount to much. There cannot be any fortune in selling salt.

In addition to the ship's own goods and the crew's ventures, and the two Sindbads we had along, I gathered that we should soon have a number of passengers. How many? I asked, not expecting to be told but hoping to be able, at least, to form some rough idea. Very many, said Hamed; the number would depend upon the degree of success met with by Nejdi. Nejdi had been in Mukalla a week already by that time; perhaps, Hamed said, he had already rounded up a hundred or so. A hundred or so! I exclaimed: where on earth could they be stowed? But Hamed said he hoped to embark a whole tribe. I looked about the ship in astonishment and for the life of me could see no place where we could stow a tribe. There was no accommodation anywhere. The poop was full of chests, the maindeck filled with boats, the hold full of cargo. It was a fact that the sailors seemed to be able to sleep in surprisingly little space, the whole lot coiling themselves down somewhere round the cook's firebox and round the bole of the mainmast in space that might with difficulty have accommodated six sheep. But a whole tribe! Hamed offered no further explanation and seemed indeed to regard any discussion of the subject as quite out of place and even foolish, for the Arabs always believed in allowing the future to take care of itself. He added only that Allah was invariably merciful, leaving me to place my own interpretation on this cryptic statement. Whether he meant that Allah in His mercy would provide the tribe, or that the tribe having been provided would need all Allah's mercy to survive, I did not know. After a few days, the subject not having been raised again, I put these rumours about a tribe down to Arab exaggeration. But in that I was wrong.

All this time our carpenter had continued banging away at his new dhow. A skilful and energetic young man, he seemed to be carried only as a boatbuilder. He did little or no carpentry about the ship, which was left largely to look after herself. (Being comparatively new, she was sound and her woodwork was in order.) She was massively built and she had ribs enough – all of them great trees in their natural state – almost to keep out the sea without any planking on them. This I know to be an exaggeration, but the Arab gives his ships plenty of good ribs and puts them together solidly. It is in the fastenings that he falls short, for these are nothing but soft iron spikes. From before sunrise until after sunset every day, the carpenter banged away at his dhow. He had a large supply of natural ribs for her, some trunks of indifferent teak which he sawed lengthwise for planking, a furious energy, and very few tools. He built the dhow purely from his head. If you wanted him to build you a ship, apparently, you just told him to build you one with a capacity for so-and-so many packages of dates. He knew no other measurements. You told him the number of packages, and the type of ship you preferred – sambuk, belem, jalboot, shewe[1] – and he went ahead. All were much the same: minor hull differences marked the type. The rigging was the same. The four types differed about as much, say, as four cutters of roughly the same size, from four different builders' yards. They all had much the same sailing qualities. Jalboots had straight cutwaters, belems were double-enders, small sambuks and shewes were graceful little things, very similar except that the stempost of a sambuk differed slightly from that of a shewe. He could make any of them. He could also turn out a

[1] For description of these types, see p. 364.

small boom, if you wished, though booms were rarely made of less capacity than four or five hundred packages of dates. The dhow he was building at that time – she was a jalboot, with a straight stem – could stow perhaps 150 packages.

The tool he used most was the adze. His big bare feet were his only vice, and the adze and the Indian drill his customary tools. If he had been put in shoes he would have had to give up shipbuilding. He had also some small saws, and a kind of rough plane. He had built our cutter earlier on the voyage, on the way from Basra to Mukalla via Muscat. This also was for sale. Indeed, I gathered that all our boats were for sale. There was nothing the Arabs would not sell, if opportunity offered. Hamed said they would be glad to dispose of the *Triumph* herself at Zanzibar or anywhere else she might bring a profit, for they could then all come home in other Kuwait ships, and there would be no question of expensive repatriation. Any Kuwait ship, apparently, would always carry any sailors or even whole crews from other Kuwait ships which had been sold or lost. It was obvious to me, even in those early days, that the Kuwaiti were spared a great many of the problems which bother European masters and shipowners.

We had four boats at that stage of the voyage. According to Hamed, we should be fortunate if we returned with one.

On several days when the wind was light we drifted close to other Africa-bound dhows which had sailed from Ma'alla the same day as ourselves. The Arabs, if they can manage it, like to sail in company, particularly along their own coasts. They do this partly for company, and partly for protection. We were often in company with Abdulla Kitami's small boom, and a Persian baggala. When it was calm and there was no noise, we could hear clearly the sound of their carpenters banging away, too, busily building small dhows for sale in Africa. The business of building small dhows in big dhows, I gathered, is a very ancient one. The Kuwaiti especially have the name of being good builders, and they are able to bring new craft to places like Lamu and sell them there more cheaply than the local Arabs, Swahili, and Bajun can construct them. The price asked for our new dhow was a thousand shillings. The cutter might go for three hundred.

The carpenter was the only man on board who worked consistently through the day, but the cook also worked hard. Hamed, our acting-master, spent much of his time reclining on the bench aft, though he rarely lay on it. Most of the day he sat hunched up there, watching or reading the Qurân, and at night he squatted in his cloak with his great nose sniffing the wind. He was very good with the ship, and an excellent judge of wind. I thought I had known something about ghosting vessels along in catspaws and doldrums conditions after all those grainship voyages and coaxing the *Joseph Conrad* through the Sulu Sea; but Hamed seemed to begin where I left off. In conditions under which I could neither be sure that there was a breath of air stirring nor predict whence the next air might come, Hamed would get some progress out of the vessel. He was a past master at this sort of sailing, and he had no mercy on himself or the crew. For the slightest change or the most fleeting breath of air, he trimmed that huge lateen sail. Hamed showed himself a splendid sailorman, and though at that early stage I could not appreciate all the moves he made (and indeed wondered about some of them), later I learned to appreciate him as a very fine sailorman indeed.

So we ghosted on, sometimes with a breeze, sometimes without, treated to grand views of the South Arabian shore line and always able to watch the Kitami boom and the baggala with which we sailed in company. Life on board them went on very much as it did aboard ourselves: at least once a day we somehow managed to be close enough to one of them for a yarn, during which the masters, mates, and crews of the vessels conversed quietly across the few yards of intervening sea and now and again borrowed things from one another. We heard their muezzins, morning after morning, give the call to prayer: there used to be a kind of race between the three announcers. Ours was a sailor named Sultan, whose father had been a slave in Kuwait: every morning at the first graying of the eastern sky Sultan would mount to a high place in the vessel and, clapping his right hand to his right ear and his left forefinger to his left cheekbone (what effect this had I never discovered, but he always did exactly the same things) he would begin loudly with the call to prayer. To this pre-dawn cry he always added something about prayer being better than sleep, which I had thought the sailors might question, for they frequently had a poor night's rest. They had no proper place to sleep and no bedding: they coiled up on deck, and seemed able to drop off to sleep at will. Whenever there was nothing else to do they slept, but they followed a regular routine of work. They had none too much rest. They slept in their clothes with their headcloths round them; but at the slightest call they were up like runners at the starting gun. And how they worked. I had never seen sailors work as they did.

They began the day with prayer. First ablutions, then prayer. The dawn prayer was not communal: each man prayed as best pleased him, having first washed hands and face and feet in water hauled up from the sea. They always stood facing the direction of Mecca, threw down their sarongs or headcloths on the deck before them – they were too poor to own praying-mats – stood silent a moment or two in meditation, putting from their minds all worldly thoughts, and then fell easily and rhythmically into the exercise and words of the set prayers. It was interesting to watch the changes which came over some of their faces. The lines would soften, the flash fade from imperious eyes, and whatever there might have been of arrogance, pride, vanity, quite disappear. There was no hypocrisy in these strong faces which looked towards Mecca. It was obvious that their religion was a real and living thing. Their prayers were not simply a formula to be mouthed, but a form of real communion with a very real God. None of them prayed hurriedly: they always spent a few moments first in silent meditation, in this discard of their worldly thoughts. I watched them with some envious interest, for I did not find my own worldly thoughts so easy to dismiss. Some stood on the water tanks, some on the hatches, some even in the cutter which was carried outboard at the davits.

Jassim, the morose little cook, always prayed on the forecastle head, standing there a tiny worried figure in his sack-cloth clothes, and praying hurriedly lest the unleaven bread should burn. For if the bread burned Jassim was in trouble. Jassim was often in trouble. Hamed bin Salim always led the quartermasters and Abdulla the nakhoda's brother in prayer on the poop; Said and Abdulla, the passengers, usually joined them. Hamed was the most devout man on board and was known to be the best Muslim, a distinction which I gathered was not without importance, for it is good that a ship should have at least one devout worshipper of the first rank on board, better still that he should be in command. Not that Hamed was really in command: he was too quiet, too gentle-natured. He was only a stopgap for the turbulent Nejdi. From the few things I heard of that young man, I began to look forward to his return on board, though it was peaceful and pleasant under Hamed.

Prayers over, the morning meal was eaten. This was always the same – a piece of unleavened bread – on great occasions and feast days it might be flavoured with a little sesame – which if it were fresh from the firebox was not bad but, if it were from the previous day, was generally soggy. This bread was called *khubz*.[2] We washed it down with very sweet tea,

[2] *Khubz*: unleavened bread.

served in tiny glasses. There was never anything else. All hands ate the same food, fore and aft, but there was no special service and the mats were not brought out. A little sailor, named Kederfi, brought up the tea in a tin kettle and poured it without ceremony into the tiny glasses, which were kept in a rough box beneath the helmsman's seat; Yusuf Shirazi handed round the unleavened bread. In a minute or two it was all over. The youngest sailors poured tea for their elders. There were two young sailors about 18 years old: the average age of the crew I would judge to be about 23, but it was difficult to say, for many of them looked older than they were. Breakfast over, they did whatever work was necessary. There was always a working period of four or five hours for all hands in the early mornings. They dried the well first, if this was necessary. She leaked very little and the well required drying only once in three days. The bilge-water that came up from there was horribly foul, reeking dreadfully of bad dates and worse fish-oil and all sorts of nameless malodorous things which were most repugnant. The men stood in two lines from the well to the bulwarks, one line handing out the filled buckets and the other handing back the empty ones.

The bailing done, the sailors went on to other work. There was never any cleaning. Sometimes one or two of the younger ones helped Jassim saw firewood or pound corn for the next day's bread. Others twisted strands of coir rope from Indian roping stuff, or sewed sail. Ropemaking was their most regular employment. They sat in large groups in the shadow of the sail, yarning quietly and twisting rope. They worked so pleasantly together and always seemed to get along so well that from some months I was never able to discover who was the serang, and at first wondered whether anyone was in charge at all. There was no yelling, no bullying, no slave-driving. Those Arab sailors had long ago learned how to work together in peace for the common good, and all necessary employment went on so calmly and smoothly in that vessel that I was three months aboard before I fully realized the system of command. Then I found that there were two serangs, one for each watch. I had never previously been sure that there were watches, for how could I tell there was a watch below when there was no 'below' to go to, when all hands turned out, apparently, for every job? There was no timekeeping, and no set routine. No one in the *Triumph* ever knew what day it was, and quite a few of them did not even know what year. But they all knew very well that Ramadhan was over – a fact for which I felt no little gratitude to Allah myself, for Ramadhan in a devout Muslim country is a trial.

From the post-breakfast hour until the midday meal, all hands worked, stopping only if it became necessary to trim the sail. Usually we sailed only with the lateen main, but sometimes in a decent breeze Hamed also set the mizzen. This was much smaller than the mainsail, and it possessed so many disadvantages that I could scarcely see that it was useful at all. In really light winds, Hamed said we could set two more sails, by rigging out a light boom along the stemhead and hoisting a jib, and by rigging the longboat's mast in front of the wheel and setting the longboat main there as a sort of spanker. One day we saw that the Persian baggala had done this, and she was going along very well. Later I noticed that the Arabs and Persians could spread even a fifth sail in this lateen rig, by sending up a kind of a gossamer ringtail topsail above the main. We never did this ourselves.

Some time between 10.30 and 11 o'clock we had our morning meal. The time was never definite: it depended upon the nakhoda's whim. There was a timepiece aboard, but it was only a very old Swiss watch of the cheapest kind, large and decrepit, which was kept in a drawer in the helmsman's seat. From time to time – usually once a day – whoever was at the wheel would take out this watch, which was invariably stopped, shake it disgustedly, peer at it a long time, and announce the hour. If shaken vigorously, it would sometimes go for two or three minutes, and it had a tick like an infernal machine. Our morning meal, which was always rice boiled with some flavouring and spread with ghee, and a little fresh or dried fish boiled in some outlandish curry, was set out on the mat on the poop and eaten with proper decorum. We sat round the mat and ate with our fingers, but there was a proper style to this. It was correct only to use the tips of the fingers of the right hand, and they must not be permitted to touch the lips. One first picked up a morsel of fish, or whatever it was, and then, carefully using the finger-tips, gathered as much rice as one could manage – at least, that was what the Arabs did; I always went carefully on the rice – and then, making a neat ball of the whole, using mainly the fingers and thumb, deftly propelled the food into the mouth by a flick of the thumb. The Arabs could eat in this way without spilling any rice, without leaving any on their fingers, and without touching their lips with their hands. It took me some time to reach this stage of perfection, and I was never expert at it. But I did my best, for their mat manners were very good and I had no wish to appear a boor. They did not make fun of me when I did badly. We each ate carefully from our own places on the tray. It was, when one became accustomed to it, quite a dignified way of eating, and there was a great deal to be said for the absence of talk. It was considered most unseemly to chatter at a meal. You ate until you had done, and then rose quietly and left. Nobody spoke.

There were three messes, but all had exactly the same food and the same quantities of it. There were two messes on the maindeck, consisting of the sailors and the two serangs, and Hamed, Abdulla the nakhoda's brother (who sometimes worked as a quartermaster but often did nothing at all), the quartermasters, Kaleel the carpenter, and our two Sindbad passengers ate on the poop. The boy Mohamed held the water with which we washed our hands and rinsed our mouths. Eating was always in silence, fore and aft, as became so solemn and important an occasion, and it never wasted time. The whole meal, from the spreading of the mats until their removal, rarely took more than five minutes, and there were no dishes to clean. Our mat was spread on the poop abaft the mizzenmast, in the space between the rows of chests. The sailors' mats were spread wherever they wished to place them. If one did not have his fill, he could go from mess to mess cleaning up. There was always plenty. The only nourishment in these mounds of rice, it seemed to me, was in the ghee spread over them. This ghee was clarified goat's butter from the Hadhramaut, and though rank it probably helped to keep away the scurvy. There was very little fish.

The meal over, all hands sat about a while. Those addicted to them puffed at their hookahs, which were made simply from Basra earthenware pots pierced with a hole for the hollow smoking cane, and the tobacco was placed on a little tin of embers from Jassim's fire. The sailors seemed to draw a great deal of enjoyment from these water-pipes, but the tobacco was very coarse and the taste of the burned cane reeds was enough to put me off, if not to make me ill. Most of the sailors used these pipes but very few owned them. They were always passed round while an ember glowed, the same drawing-reed doing service for as many men as could use it. This seemed unhygienic, but it did not bother them.

With the hookahs put away, and no catspaws coming, the men would drop off to sleep on deck in the shadow of the sail. Hamed slept, if he slept at all, always with one eye open, hunched up on the bench abaft the helmsman: near him was a tell-tale, a windvane in the form of a carved wooden bird with a feathered tail. These feathers quivered in anything of an air, and moved the bird. At the slightest movement of those feathers Hamed was up. The Arabs seemed to be able to sleep soundly and lightly at the same time, and in this I envied them. They never slept for more than an hour after the morning meal. When they woke, it was time for the midday prayer – more ablutions, always performed in water drawn up from the sea, more bending towards Mecca, more mellifluous intonations of the formal prayers which, no matter how often I heard them, always sounded well. Prayers over – and they did not take long – it was usual for the sailors to work again, though they did not work so hard in the afternoons as they did in the mornings, and if there was no work requiring urgent attention, they did not look for any. Sometimes, if it was really hot or if they had to put the ship round now and again, they did not work again in the afternoon until about four o'clock, when they would work an hour or so. Sometimes if the big sail were damaged and had to be lowered, repaired, and set again, they worked hard all day. The carpenter worked hard all day always, in port and at sea. The Muslim Sabbath, Friday, was never observed at sea: there was no weekly day of rest.

Prayers began again in the mid-afternoon, announced as always by Sultan the muezzin. These prayers were individual and never led. At sunset, with the dipping of the last of the sun in the sea, there was a fourth call to prayer. This and the dawn prayers were really the main prayers of the day. The fourth prayer took about ten minutes, sometimes more: sometimes Hamed would offer up extra prayers. When this was over, we ate our evening meal, often just rice and ghee, and less often rice with dhall, a kind of fine Indian corn which was boiled with peppers or chillis. The sailors always enjoyed chillis, which were boiled, so long as we had them, with everything. The evening meal was over very quickly, before the last of the brief twilight had gone: this was the end of the day. Each sailor then came on the poop in his turn and greeted Hamed and all the others there, wishing them good evening, by name. Hamed replied to each by name, and they went down again to the maindeck. Later, those of the first two night watches might gather round the bole of the mizzenmast upon the poop, and yarn there very quietly, passing the hookah round from mouth to mouth.

So the night would find us, drifting quietly under the moon, the ship a silent ghost of peace mirrored in the silvered darkness of the placid sea while the cloaked and hooded mariners puffed at their hookahs on the poop, and the quartermaster, the folds of his headcloth wrapped about him and his bare feet tucked beneath his cloak, sat like a sphinx at the wheel, keeping the big boom to something like her course. Behind him was Hamed, silent and watchful. We showed no lights. We never had any lights, except the weak light in the binnacle. There were lights on board but they were not trimmed, and in the six months I was on board they were never shown. I wondered why this was, for sometimes laden oil-tankers coming round from Bahrein and Abadan passed very closely to us. On such occasions Hamed always waited for them to change course and never, apparently, thought of showing his own lights. The steamers, he said, always kept good lookout, and Allah was kind. Visibility was always good. Hamed seemed to think that Allah would look after Arab dhows and the steamers could take care of themselves, and really it did seem to work that way.

The days in the big boom during the beat to Mukalla passed pleasantly. I found the timelessness of things and the utter dismissal of the modern world very easy to become accustomed to. The only book on board was a copy of the Qurân, in which Hamed, Abdulla the nakhoda's brother, and the passengers often read. When he came to a good part Hamed would sometimes call a small group together and read aloud, in a very pleasant and well-modulated voice, and they would discuss whatever they read for hours. They seemed to find perfect content in this book, and never tired of reading it. Sometimes one or other of them would chant chapters from the Qurân, from memory. They were mostly a silent lot and were always quiet except when there was work afoot, when always a continuous chanting would go on. Sometimes there would not be a voice raised on those decks for hours. It was a new kind of seafaring to me, and I was most astonished at the effortless smoothness of the ship's routine, the harmony of the big crew, and the pleasant agreement with which they worked together. They were all poor. They had few clothes. Their chests held only the goods with which they were going to trade and they had no other possessions. They had nothing. After a while I began to wonder whether it was not a very good idea to have nothing.

This pleasant and most interesting life came to a sudden stop one day, when we had been about a week at sea, and I had settled down. There was an accident. What the details were I did not know then, and I do not know now. At any rate, I was in it. Something, I believe, carried away from aloft, and it must have struck me. How or why or where it carried away I have no idea and questioning later did not clear up the mystery. Questioning was not encouraged in the *Triumph of Righteousness* and cleared up no mysteries. I asked only once. Allah is generous, Hamed said. I hoped this meaning was that the accident might have been worse, and that he did not intend to convey indirect gratitude to the All-Highest for having struck down the infidel as a lesson to the faithful in their dhow. I am sure the first interpretation is the correct one, for Hamed was not a narrow-minded man or a fanatic. In any case, the accident happened. I don't remember anything about it, but it deprived me of my sight for a week and gave me a bad limp for some months. The first thing I knew was that I had bad pains in the head, and I was blind. I could not see anything; I did not know day from night. What kind of accidents have this effect I did not know, for this was my first experience of the kind: it was very unpleasant. I was lying somewhere in the interior of the ship, on some sacking with a bag for a pillow. At first, I remember, I had some difficulty in believing that I could be blind, and thought it must be the darkness of the hold. My head ached and my eyes throbbed. Over me I could hear and feel the fat rats run and cockroaches scamper, and the queer creaking noises of the rolling ship sounded almost thunderous there. But what worried me most was that the blindness might be permanent, for I knew the danger of eye infections in Arab life. Blindness and semi-blindness are common among the Arabs, and not thought of as serious disabilities, but to me either would be disability enough. If I were blind, there would be no use staying in the dhow. I could not observe what I could not see.

The pain was so great that there must have been periods of delirium and even of unconsciousness: I can only remember now long periods of ceaseless pain, followed by the most worrying nightmarish dreams. But in my more conscious moments I was more troubled by the thought that I might have to give up the voyage, than by any fear of permanent blindness. That would have been too sorry a blow from fate. Yet I wondered also whether, after all, it was reasonable to stay so long in a life where the risks one was compelled to run might be so great. I had thought myself inured to maritime hardship, merely because I'd been a whaler in the Antarctic, and had been round Cape Horn once or twice. I learned better than that.

I found that I was in the great cabin – loathsome, frightful place. The stench was abominable, even after many days. There was no air. Rats scampered, and now and again I heard their noisy fighting among themselves. Fat, greasy cockroaches dropped from the deckhead, ran on my face, made a playground of my body. It was hot, foul, and dreadful. The reek of nameless frightful things filled that fetid air, with behind all the putrid horror of decayed fish and the powerful tang of strong fish-oil, and rotten bilge-water. I lay on sacking on top of some bales, with mysterious packages all round, which chafed me as the ship slowly laboured. Occasionally I tried to move, and pain racked me. I was not used to pain and did not take kindly to an experience so unintelligible and unintelligent. There was no getting rid of that burning in my eyes. My head felt as if it had been ploughed: sometimes I wished that was all that had been done to it. My eyes felt as if they had been taken out, rolled in cinders, and then put back again. My body felt as if I had some malignant fever. Days passed. The rancid reek of the frightful place was with me endlessly. My eyes still could not see. There was no air. The heat was worse than ever.

How long I was down there I did not know: it was at least a week. I knew the date of the last entry in my journal, but I did not know the date when I recovered. No one else knew what day it was, for no one on that ship at sea named days: they merely let them pass. Hamed guessed, but his guess was wrong. I never did discover the date till I reached Mukalla. Day followed day and night followed night, and I did not know one from the other. Sometimes the sound of the crew at work as they put the ship about came to me there; distantly in seeming dreams I heard the scamper of hurrying feet close overhead, the thrash of canvas, the cries of sailors as they worked. Once I heard deep-throated chanting which went on an hour. Sometimes the sea water washed swiftly by and I could feel the ship's labour. At other times she stood upright, for there was then no movement in my couch, and beyond the hull the stilled sea gurgled. It was all quiet then, as if the crew had gone and I was left alone on board – alone with the rats and the frightful smells, the cockroaches and the other wretched things that scampered there. Sometimes it was rather bad.

But the days passed. Gradually the pain went down, even in my eyes. It was a heavenly relief at last slowly to feel my eyes trying to open, and to be able to look about the stinking loathsome den where I had lain, God knows how many days, and though I could not see properly or in true focus, I looked about me even at the smellsome casks and foul dried fish almost with affection, and wondered where it was the rats always ran. I saw the most enormous cockroaches scampering – well, not exactly scampering, for they were too sleek and fat and undisturbed to move with any such unleisurely speed. Rather they were scurvily ambling about the place, as if they owned it.

And there was old Yusuf – Yusuf Shirazi, Yusuf the old ruffian who had looked after me, Yusuf the grey-haired, tired old reprobate who seemed to combine the functions of leading-hand, storekeeper, steward, and nakhoda's personal servant. If ever by any chance I needed him, Yusuf was not there, and if I did not need him he was never absent; if I ever slept he was sure to come and yell in my ear. There he was, the well-meaning blundering old ass, in sight again at last, squatting back on his horny heels, tired, and yet alert, and plaintive. Yusuf was there, with his horny feet planted across my pillow, such as it was, looking down at me out of his own tired eyes. Yusuf had looked after me well, those days, and I regarded him now with some degree of affection. I had taken a liking to the gentle-faced old man from the start, though he did nothing to curry favour. He was a quiet old man born of a lowly Shiraz family in Kuwait, a Persian, reared in Arabia whither his parents had fled, indignant at some kingly decree against the faithful. Yusuf had obviously been bewildered when he was given the task of looking after an injured European, but he did his best. Three times a day he came down, offering me delicacies I did not want, things such as pieces of the fatty tails of long-dead Berbera sheep, and dishes of soggy dhall full of chillis and pickled lemons, and mounds of boiled rice smothered with Kuwait ghee. I wished the old chap would keep some of these things for himself, but that he would not. I talked with him sometimes, though this was difficult, for we could converse only in broken Arabic. My Arabic was very broken and far from Arabic, and Yusuf's Persian, Swahili, and Hindustani were not much help. But he was a good old chap, and it was grand to be able to see him.

"Yusuf," I murmured, "get me out of here. Get me up on deck where there's some fresh air."

"But it's good down here," said Yusuf. (I understood that all right. *Taiyib hinna, taiyib hinna*! – Good here, good here! were his words.)

It did not seem so good to me and, after a while, with the help of Yusuf, a sailor named Zaid who was a powerful negro with shoulders three feet across and a figure any young athlete would have envied, Hamed bin Salim, and Said the mascaraed old Sindbad merchant, I struggled up the vertical ladder to the sweet fresh air on deck. How sweet that first breath was. My eyes were still misty and my head swam, but the air was heavenly. Dimly above me I could sense the shape of the swelling sail, for there was some wind, and the noises of the ship on her way through the sea had in them the ecstasy of music. I could see again: I was all right. I could stay in the dhow. The littered decks looked clear and clean and beautiful, in the shadow of the sail, and the brown crew looked like gowned young gods.

It was a long time before I could walk again properly, and in those awful days cooped up in the great cabin, I had lost thirty pounds in weight. But now it was over, and I reflected that, if in the first week on board so serious an accident had overtaken me, by the law of averages that would probably be my share of mishaps for the voyage. So it proved. After that, I did not get much malaria even in the delta of the Rufiji, and my constitution thrived on water from Kenya's stagnant swamps. All hands from Hamed bin Salim down, were very good to me while I was ill. It was embarrassing to be so lamed and to have such difficulty in getting about, even after the blindness had gone, but the mariners did not seem to mind having a cripple foisted on them. They helped me always, any who were near: old Yusuf always was ready. I lay on the carpet in my place on the transom bench, and night and morning as the sailors came aft with their greetings each of them would gently add something about the mercy of Allah on my ills. These were sincere and well-meant condolences, and I felt better for them. In the sun and the air, I soon picked up again, though it was long before I had back much weight. It was a very interesting experience, when it was over, but I should hate to have to go through it again.

When I was on deck again the ship was somewhere near Ras el Kelb, close in by the Hadhramaut shore. We were drifting near some precipitous islands, one of which was topped with a deposit of guano. We were very close in, so close, indeed, that when the tide turned Hamed had to anchor, and we lay there in quiet throughout the rest of the day. No breath stirred and there was no motion: away astern of us the Kitami boom lay also with an anchor down and her big sail gathered to the yard, which like ours rested vertically against the mainmast. But the Persian baggala was out of sight. Where was she? I asked Hamed: but he only said that Allah was compassionate. I looked astern. He looked ahead. I knew where the baggala was, then. She was much more lightly loaded than we were.

Next morning with a breath of air we ghosted on, and we made the rest of the passage to Mukalla almost within stone's throw of the Hadhramaut beach. Though burned and sterile, it was not an unattractive coast, and in the dawns and sunsets sometimes it was wildly grand. Sometimes, when there was a better working breeze, we would make a short tack off the land, but we always came back in alongshore again. Sometimes, when it was calm with an unfavourable tide, we anchored for a few hours, always leaving the sail aloft. The conditions were very good, apart from the lamentable persistence of the head wind. Hamed was ghosting to wind'ard by using the favourable sets along the land. In this he was wise, for if he had made long tacks out into the Gulf of Aden we should have lost more than we gained. Out there the set was always to the west'ard with the north-east monsoon. Hamed knew the local waters, and he knew what he was doing.

Once we tacked. It was the only time I saw the big boom put about head to wind in all the time I was on board. Hamed would not have done it then had the tide not suddenly turned on him as he was standing very close to weather a low spit of land, jutting out from a place where once a river might have flowed. We were too close; and the ship was being set ashore. There was neither room nor time to wear, for if we had fallen from the wind we should certainly have gone ashore. I was glad I had back something of my sight to see Hamed tack her round. He did not get excited (though he sometimes did). He murmured an order quietly: the quartermaster at the wheel yelled it: all hands sprang to their stations. They all had their stations for wearing ship, and they were the same posts for tacking. Now down came the mizzen on the run. The quartermaster, at a nod from Hamed, who was standing up on the cutter by the davit heads, eased the helm down. She responded at once, putting her long nose into the wind. By that time we were perilously close inshore, right in the shallowing water and watching the shelving sand, just outside the breakers' line. But she came all right. She answered her helm beautifully, and the big lateen sail proved a well-balanced rig. She turned on her heel and carried round with her own way, even when the huge sail was full aback.

This was an awkward moment, for if she gathered sternway she was finished then. She did not. She kept her head and came round handsomely, though the business of handling the backed mainsail and the awkward tripping of the great lateen yard with all the pressure of the wind trying to break it were extremely difficult manœuvres. The mainsail, which like all Arab sails had no gear on it whatever, wrapped itself in huge awkward folds between the yard and the raking mast, and did its best to become entangled with all the gear – the mast tackles, the halliards, the shrouds. Out of this mood of wild recalcitrance the sweating crew had immense difficulty in getting it: they kept up a savage chanting and singing the whole time while the canvas boomed and the mast creaked and the yard swayed, and the noise of the breakers close by was ominous and unending. I feared that the lateen yard must break, for with the sail aback all the pressure of the wind was against it, and the unsupported mast could easily have come down. It was a complicated and exceedingly dangerous piece of seamanship, and nothing but sheer man-power got that great mainsail back under control. It was a piece of canvas 130 feet on the head with a luff of well over 90, and a foot 100 feet long. It was well over 6,000 square feet of canvas – an enormous sail, as it had to be when it was the main motive power of a ship of 150 tons. I was glad then that we had such a large crew, for there was work enough for all of them. Only the fighting spirit of the crew curbed and controlled that fighting, thrashing piece of canvas, and it had to be done carefully, too, lest the weak seams split, and the ship should be left in that dangerous situation with her sail unfit for use.

It was well done and I was glad I saw it, but I did not wonder that we never tacked again. I could appreciate the Arab's reluctance to go about head-to-wind, and I began to think the lateen a useful sail only in fair winds. That is the way the Arabs try to use it: with any winds other than the monsoons, lateen-rigged ships could not safely keep the seas.

The next day we were at Mukalla, coming in late in the evening. We had been, so far as I could discover, twelve days on the passage and by that time I had settled down comfortably. It was just as well, for we did not again enjoy so peaceful a passage for some months. The first thing we saw was Nejdi, waiting on the jetty and with him was a collection of the wildest-looking Arabs I had yet seen.

III

ON THE HADHRAMAUT COAST

MUKALLA AT FIRST sight is a picturesque and romantic place, and after Aden, which is British, and the Red Sea places, which are dull, it is so perfect a picture of what one expects an Arab port to be that it is difficult to accept it as real. Ashore it does not quite live up to this high promise. The principal port of the Hadhramaut, Mukalla is today as ever the place of merchants, the port from which the wandering Hadhrami set out for Java, India, and Africa, and to which they return. The Hadhrami has always been a wanderer, going out from his largely barren land to get a competence elsewhere and returning always to spend it. It was to pick up a shipload of these wanderers that we had come to the Hadhramaut port, for though in these days they usually travel to Java and the East Indies as deck passengers in steam – Dutch liners call regularly at Mukalla to take them – they still voyage to Africa and India by dhow.

Mukalla is an interesting place of white buildings struggling timorously to keep foothold between the great mountains of the Hadhramaut and the sea. Round the waterfront of the small unprotected bay, the buildings cluster stout and tall and prosperous, with the minaret of a mosque here and there. But farther back – not so far – they become dilapidated and grey in their efforts to struggle up the almost precipitous sides of Mukalla's brown mountain. It is the mountain one notices more than the town, the frowning mountain with its white tower forts which are now unused. The possibility of using mountain forts to protect the port from attack from behind probably led to its situation there. The mountains sit above the town as if wondering whether to push the whole place into the sea, which they could do with one brief shrug. Their precipitous bulk and alarming proximity are overwhelming, and in the gorges great rocks lie, waiting. Here and there one sees where a fall of rock has slipped down, with fatal consequences to any building that chanced to be in the way. If I lived at Mukalla, I should hate to see a heavy rain.

The harbour is very interesting, and quiet in the north-east season. The south-west wind would blow directly into the bay and then it would be untenable. When we came in, we were one of twenty Arab dhows at the anchorage, and there were others on the beach. In a small sheltered place east of the city there was a dhow-yard on the beach, and here men were building two large sambuks with square, picturesque sterns. The Hadhrami dhow-builder likes to decorate his craft, and the sterns of some of the sambuks on the beach and at the anchorage were elaborately carved and painted. They were usually decorated with several rows of geometrical designs, triangles, stars, and crescent moons, done in blue and red and green, and adorned with appropriate texts from the Qurân carved along the sides of the poop. Many of them had rows of dummy windows carved and painted on their quarters, one row on each side, finished off with half-drawn curtains painted in white. This was a favourite design. Other ships had a row of stern windows painted on them, in addition to those on the quarter. Many of them were covered round their whole sterns with brightly painted designs, from the water-line to the deck. The effect was sometimes striking, especially with the reflection of the pretty sterns shimmering in the clear blue sea. Their freshly limed underwater bodies gleamed and their hulls, where they were not decorated, shone with oil. They were a good-looking lot. There were also several old Aden sambuks there under the Italian flag, sailed by big crews of Somalis with many boys.

These Somali sailors had a wildness lacking in the Arabs. Even the men who pulled about the harbour in small boats, selling fruits and dates to the ships, seemed afraid to go near the Somali sambuks. The Somali sailors were very tall, with wild locks bleached and reddened: they wore white sarongs, very long, and threw folds of unsewn calico loosely over their shoulders when they went ashore. They strutted about as if they were content with life, and very well pleased with themselves.

There were other queer craft in the harbour, including some small vessels from Seihut and ports along the Mahra coast – long, low vessels with very low, raking bows, and their masts raked more than any I had seem before. Hamed said these were exceptionally fast. The largest of them did not look forty feet long, but he said they sailed to Zanzibar. There were others, manned by sullen-looking men in brown shirts and Suri shawl-turbans, which had straight sterns, ram-like low bows, and high vertical masts. These Hamed spoke of as *Bedeni*: they were very small and appeared most unseaworthy, but Hamed said they went down to Zanzibar too.

The harbour was always picturesque and interesting, but after some days I began to wonder what we had come there for. Nejdi brought out a wild gang of Beduin the first day, fierce-visaged men in black with their hands and legs and bodies covered with heavy indigo dye. This, they said, was protection against the heat and the cold, which was a comforting belief, for they appeared to have few other clothes. These men were armed with large curved daggers which they carried in silver scabbards lashed round their waists, before the pit of the stomach. The same belt which carried the dagger seemed to carry all their other possessions, and thrust in beside the dagger might be another knife – a smaller one, for finishing off the stabbed victims and for working – or a reed for music; and in pouches on the belt might be a few coins, and their tobacco. These Beduin went without head covering. They wore their hair long and smeared heavily with butter. They had no sandals. They were thin, lithe, gaunt, and wiry, and they had alert very watchful eyes. They came aboard with Nejdi, who looked curiously unlike them (though he was descended from the desert people himself, the hill desert people of Nejd), and they ran about the deck like children. They were, I saw, being shown round the ship, and they seemed as excited about her as if she had been an ocean liner. These were Nejdi's prospects, I guessed – our passengers. They included a small good-looking man who was described by Hamed as chief of a Beduin tribe from somewhere inland. It was mentioned in the most casual manner that he was considering taking his tribe to Africa, but I still refused to believe that they could come with us. He was aboard often, always scampering about peering into everything. He and the others seemed most pleased about the size of the ship, and they did not bother about appointments. Size was enough for them: to them, she was a very large ship.

I was very puzzled by the time they all spent down in the loathsome great cabin, for no matter where else they did not go, they all gazed long and earnestly into that horrible place, while old Yusuf Shirazi dilated upon its merits. Down they went, through the small hatchway on the port side aft, and after a while came out again murmuring *taiyib*, which apparently meant 'very good'. What was very good about that place? I asked old Yusuf. What did the Beduin want with it? Were they going to ship some cargo down there? But Yusuf murmured something about the compassion of Allah – a comment the appropriateness of which I did not appreciate at that time but realised later. A 'cargo' we were certainly going to have there, and all Allah's compassion would be needed to soften its hard lot. Once I got a hint from Yusuf: if I had known more Arabic I might have learned. He said something about *bints*. *Bints*? Women?

(Even in Australia, a bint is a girl). But surely Arab dhows never carried women. Migrating Arabs never took their women with them, according to the books I had been able to read. But all I could get out of Yusuf was a reiteration of his belief in the goodness of Allah, and even when the great cabin was being cleaned Hamed knew nothing. Not that that foul den was really cleaned. Some of the stuff in it was thrown into the small cabin right aft, and this was as far as the cleaning went. There might have been a clear space of eight by ten feet in the centre of the great cabin, when this re-stowage was completed.

During this time Nejdi came to the ship only for the feasts, of which there was one every second day. We just stayed at that anchorage, and nothing happened and we had feasts. It was a pleasant existence provided one had no business elsewhere, and I had none. Every day we had a sheep for the midday meal; it was made the occasion of a feast. These functions were simple. Abdulla, the nakhoda's brother, would go ashore the evening before to buy a fat Somali sheep or a skinny Hadhramaut goat, which would bleat the night away on the little forecastle head and bite the dust at the crack of dawn the next morning. Apparently all hands were expert butchers. They cut the sheep's throats with gusto and efficiency, and the poor beasts would be dragged right out of their skins into the pot. The pot was one of those big round black tubs which are traditionally represented as suitable for missionary-boiling in the wilds of Africa and the more remote South Sea Islands. Into this thing, simmering on Jassim's brushwood fire, would go the whole sheep, or lamb, or goat, with various delicacies from it scattered in smaller pots on lesser fires. On such occasions Jassim could fit five fires into his small fire-box, and really he could do wonders at turning out a feast. The principal ingredients were always the same – sheep and rice. Sometimes the rice was flavoured with raisins; sometimes there were chickens as appetisers. There was always melon to follow the main course, for melons were plentiful at Mukalla and the Arabs loved them. When everything was ready, Yusuf would bring up the Persian carpets from somewhere down below and spread them over the whole poop, placing a large eating mat of Swahili design over the centre carpet. Then the sheep and rice would be brought on by the quartermasters, and all the delicacies. By this time strangers would be coming aboard in droves.

Nejdi gave good feasts and was profligate with his hospitality. It always seemed to me that he was too profligate. Every other nakhoda in port; all the port officials; all the passenger agents and half their clients;

a group of Suri and Mahra people; a Yemeni *Sayyid* who was thinking of going to the Congo to collect some dues; customs clerks; merchants – all these piled on board, until the place was like a Rotary club, and the only way they could all get at the eating-mat together was to sit sideways, like sardines spliced into a box, each with his right shoulder in the solid phalanx of human anatomy that faced the food, and his right hand working on the feast. There was no room for anyone to sit squarely at the mat, and tear in. They could only sit sideways. The *pièce de resistance* at all these feasts was always the sheep's head, which sat on the tray of rice nearest to Nejdi. When the feast was about three parts over, Nejdi would nonchalantly reach in for the head and, using his two hands, get to work on the skull, rending out the eyes and tongue and splitting the thing on the deck to get at the brains. These he would distribute to the guests of honour. By that time Nejdi's right hand would be covered with ghee and rice, and the forearms of all and sundry would look as if they had been working in a rice mill, for at the feasts some of the decorum of our daily eating was dropped. I was always sorry for the sheep. Its head always looked so inoffensive, and its gaze was so sad. After all, it had been functioning as a the sheep only a few hours before: the thing had bleated that dawn. And here was Nejdi smashing it on the deck and plucking out its brains.

After the feast we had coffee, then sleep; after the sleep, the midday prayer followed, and after that Ismael, our musician, would play on his damned guitar. Then all peace was ended. In six months I never came to like that music. So far as I could see, there was not a thing to like about it. One can become accustomed to Scots pipes and Siamese reeds, to Balinese and Javanese gongs. Even the Swahili, banging on their drums, produce some kind of rhythmic noise, and the Beduin's reeds were not wholly unpleasant. But Ismael on his guitar was and remained an affront to the ear of mortal man. Given the slightest encouragement, he also sang, which was worse. His songs were interminable, plaintive, and most repellent, sung horribly in an unnatural and dreadfully unattractive voice. Yet everybody insisted that Ismael was a musician of note in Kuwait, and ranked among the supreme attractions of the vessel. Nejdi, I learned, had gone to great pains to induce Ismael to ship in the *Triumph* and had bought the guitar for him, as well as giving him privileges on board. I soon noticed that the musician, besides being let off work for the day, was accustomed to collecting bakhshish[1] from the more important of the

[1] Bakhshish = tips, largesse.

guests. He added lines in his songs with this in view, though the songs were mostly about love, so far as I could gather. At any rate they were full of reference to *bebes*, and ludicrously soulful looks. A bebe, I gathered, was just another bint. We heard of them only in song. That these songs were all highly moral in tone I saw reason to doubt, and there were often occasions when I regretted my lack of Arabic. Ismael must have had something to put into those songs to hold his hearers, for the melody was always atrocious and the delivery abominable. He never got any bakhshish from me for his music, though he pointed out now and again his great desire for a gold wrist-watch. Whenever possible, I gave him bakhshish to stop. This was usually wasted. It was, I suppose, inconsiderate of me to want him to stop when everybody else so enjoyed him. But he used to go on far into the night. Sometimes we had drums with the guitar, and this was better, for they helped to drown the music. Often there was dancing, but it was always the same dull shuffling, agitating, fingercracking, hopping, and jumping I had first seen in Ma'alla Bay. We never had any dancing girls: they were kept ashore.

We stayed in Mukalla for days and days. Nothing happened. The first day we had discharged some deck cargo for the Sultan. Each day some woolly Beduin came and wandered over the ship, finishing up in the great cabin from which they emerged smiling and murmuring *taiyib*. Whatever was *taiyib* about that place? What was this all about? Well, questioning would not find out for me: I could only wait and see.

Other booms from Kuwait and from Kung and Lingeh in Persia came and sailed, and still we stayed. We saw little of Nejdi apart from the feasts: apparently this gathering of the passengers was an arduous business. He came very little to the ship. Whenever he did come there was a feast, and about fifty men came with him. Our crew, who never missed a chance to trade anywhere, added to their goods here, buying large quantities of small straw fans, and basketwork which was quite attractive. They bought this in bales, cheaply. Yusuf said these baskets were much sought after by the Europeans in Mombasa and Zanzibar. The ship loaded a consignment of cooking-stones, and the pestles and mortars which the Hadhrami use for crushing corn in the preparation of the daily bread. These things, a little Hadhramaut tobacco, some ghee in kerosene tins, and some dried shark seemed all we shipped at Mukalla. The whole lot might have been five tons.

The crew also watered the ship. This they did with skins in the longboat, pulling away to a creek at the western end of the town at dawn each morning. Here they grounded the boat and marched to a pool in an oasis, about a mile from Mukalla's western gate. It took about three days to water the ship in this manner, but there was nothing else to do. The water got in this way cost nothing, and I hoped it was reasonably good. I should have to drink it. The sailors sang the morning away at this employment, and slept in the afternoon. On most days they did not bother to go ashore, for they had no money. Sometimes Ismael went off with his guitar to be a public nuisance somewhere, and on such occasions I was glad.

So the days passed. Coastal sambuks, Somali dhows, Persian booms came and went. An Indian kotia, with a cargo of tiles from Mangalore, came in; she was very similar to an Arab baggala but more heavily rigged and better built, and she had a much smaller crew. She had only eight men: an Arab of the same size would have had at least twenty. The kotia flew a large flag of dark red silk, with two narrow white horizontal bars; she moored alongside a Persian baggala named the *Hope of Compassion*. Most of the Arab dhows had these mellow religious names, but often when I went aboard and asked the name, nobody knew it, and the nakhoda would have to look it up in the certificate of registration. No names ever appeared on them. I learned later that there was good reason for this when, for example, the vessel was running a cargo of mangrove poles out of the Rufiji Delta, or skipping out of Mogadishu with a few thousand lire. The Arab does not like his ship to be too easily identified and he knows that to European eyes all dhows are alike. In their own talk, they were accustomed to speak of the vessels by the nakhoda's name; our ship was always the boom Nejdi and was rarely referred to by her own people as the *Triumph of Righteousness*. She had at least two other names, as was usual with the big dhows. The Arab hates official identification. It was the same with the others: Abdulla Kitami's small boom had two names but was always known to seafaring people as the boom Abdulla Kitami, Ganim bin Othman's big *Mercer al-Baz* was the boom Ganim bin Othman, and so on. This applied, however, only when the nakhoda was at least the nominal owner.

During this time I stayed on board, for I could not walk. It was always interesting on board, sitting up on the nakhoda's bench abaft the wheel, watching what went on. There was always plenty to watch, if not aboard our own vessel, then aboard the others by which we were surrounded. Usually four or five dhows came and left each day, bringing cargoes from Aden, Seihut, and the Mahra coast, and loading for Somaliland, the

Yemen, and Eritrea. Most of the ships lying in the harbour, like all Arab craft I have ever seen anywhere, just stayed at the anchorage and did nothing while their masters were ashore trying either to get paid for the cargoes they had delivered, or to collect fresh cargoes to take elsewhere. We did a lot of this waiting at anchor ourselves, and sometimes I found it a little exasperating. However, it was pleasant to know that we should never go anywhere without staying at least a week there, perhaps a month. One had a chance to look about and really to see the ports we visited.

Christmas came while the ship was at Mukalla. On the day I thought to be December 25th, I was at last able to go ashore. I went in the gig with Abdulla, Nejdi's young brother, and the passenger Said who was off on some mysterious errand, looking more wily and intriguing than ever. We landed at the small stone jetty and Said disappeared at once. His fellow-passenger, Abdulla, had gone the first day, so quickly that I did not see him go. Nejdi's brother and I wandered slowly along the road that leads past the dhow-yard, with its neat piles of ship's timbers and knees from the Yemen, planks from Malabar, past a new sambuk being built under a screen of date mats to protect it from the sun. This was the way to the bazaar, always the most interesting part of any Arab town. Abdulla had said that Mukalla's bazaar was good, and he was going to see if it offered any goods for sale along the Benadir coast. Before we reached the bazaar, however, my leg gave way again, and Abdulla and I sat for a time in a coffee-shop near the dhow-yard, watching the scene round us and the passing crowd while we sipped hot goat's milk flavoured with cardamoms. It was not bad, and it was not very good.

The scene was good, though, for the streets of Mukalla teemed with strange human beings dressed in all the colourful costumes of the East – Banyan merchants in their flappy diaphanous trousers and little black hats, Yemenites in sarongs and big turbans, Beduin in black and indigo, leading soft-stepping great camels laden with firewood and goods; Persian, Somali, Kuwaiti, Suri, Batini sailors and nakhodas, wandering half-castes with all the blood of the East in them, half-Malays, half-Turks, half-Africans, half-Egyptians, half-Baluchi, half-Balinese. The Hadhrami wanders far and takes his women where he finds them, bringing back the male offspring to his native land, and the blood of the whole East pulses in those busy Mukalla streets. The desert Beduin are the most striking of them all, walking always fearless and erect, gaunt and half-starved and poverty-stricken as they are, oily-haired and half-naked. Many are armed with the Hadhramaut dagger, and a few carry ancient muskets and other guns, though this practice is by no means so general as it was before the British forced peace among the warring tribes, very recently.

We sat there cheerfully in the coffee-shop, Abdulla now and again calling for fresh embers for his hookah while the crowd milled round. The coffee-shop was a rough open place more on the street than off it. It was just a shanty of three walls and a mat roofing, with the earthen floor liberally spread with benches on which squatted Arabs of all ages. The Arabs were in small groups, carrying on earnest conversation. They looked romantic as they puffed at hookahs, or tossed off tiny cups of black coffee. Now and again a Kuwaiti or a Persian nakhoda dropped in, for this was the nakhodas' coffee-shop. Coffee-shops in Arab coastal towns are sharply zoned; they are the clubs, the meeting-places, and the exchanges, where most of the business is done. I was to see a great deal of these interesting institutions before my voyage in the *Triumph of Righteousness* was over.

I was finishing my third cup of the flavoured goat's milk when Mr. Ingrams, the British Resident Adviser in the Hadhramaut, walked in. Asking why I had not been to the Residency before, he took me off at once in his car. Well, it was Christmas Day, I thought; and Christmas Day is a man's own. I was not going to intrude on the Ingrams on such a day, and that was the first time I had been ashore, the first time I could walk. I did not care to go to the Residency when I was so lame and generally helpless; but I was very glad to be taken. As a matter of fact, it was not Christmas Day, but Christmas Eve. I was one day out of my reckoning.

I was comfortably established in the Residency, a handsome white building which was once a rich Arab's town house, within an hour; and there I stayed for several days. It was pleasant at the Residency and it was good to have a meal. I had a room which once belonged to one of the former occupier's several wives, and I could look across over the Residency garden, where in the mornings the new constables were drilling, towards the palace of the Sultan, where the bands played. The harbour sounds came in through the open window, and I could hear the booms' crews singing in their longboats as they pulled in for water. I could watch them watering, carrying the quivering skins, black and wet and shaking as if they were queer headless beasts somehow alive, and I watched the west gate of Mukalla, with its constant stream of interesting life.

At that time Mr. Ingrams was pushing ahead, for the first time in history, with a comprehensive road programme for the Hadhramaut. He was constructing motor roads to Shibam and other important places. The Beduin who carried on the business of camel transport did not like it; nor did some of the tribes through whose territory the roads passed. The Beduin, accustomed to do something about the things they don't like, smashed up the roads. On such occasions Mr. Ingrams, being a wise man, did not send punitive expeditions against them. He went out himself, met the disgruntled, talked with them, and promptly enrolled them in the road protective police. These were the wild creatures who now drilled in the square every morning, and happy citizens they were.

I had a look with the Ingrams at some of the hinterland of Mukalla, along the wide beach at the town's western end. Camels plod along this beach, sedate and serious, and heavy-laden asses amble. The camel park by the west gate is always full of life; here the camels from the interior bring their burdens, sit back upon their haunches and wait for new ones. Beduin often came and spoke while we were out on these tours; often we saw the women tending the flocks and herds, and gathering brushwood for the tent fires. Much of the Hadhramaut, though I saw little of it (for my eyes turned ever towards the ships) had a wild grand beauty. We went one day along the new road over the ironstone hills, and watched the evening rest in a bowl of brown and reddened beauty among those wild rolling hills, and darken them; the stars came quickly, and the night softened all the outlines of the hard land. Beduin drivers padding by with a camel caravan sang some ageless chant of the hills, and the sea rolling in along Mukalla Bay murmured a lullaby.[2]

We dined one evening with the Sultan in his palace, in a room within sound of the sea. The service, the clothes, the dishes were all more European than Arab; the Sultan himself seemed more Indian than Arab. He was a tired-looking man in the middle fifties, looking much older; he sat in a European chair at the head of his large table, wearing a fez and a long, close-fitting Indian coat, and we sat and ate and ate. The Sultan's son, the Crown Prince of the Hadhramaut, sat happily at the other end of the table, smiling because he had that day remarried a favourite young wife whom for political reasons he had earlier been compelled to divorce. The political reasons, whatever they had been, now no longer held, apparently, and he had wasted no time in remarrying.

Late that night, Abdulla, Nejdi's brother, came to the Residency, saying

[2] The interested reader is referred to Miss Freya Stark's *The Southern Gates of Arabia* for a comprehensive and most interesting description of the Hadhramaut.

that the boom was outward bound and would be gone before morning. Would I come, or should I prefer to ride with Nejdi on a camel to the port of Shihr? Damn the camels, I said. They stink, and they make me seasick. So I went with Abdulla to the ship. I was very grateful to the Ingrams for my stay with them, and I left Mukalla with my leg strengthened, and fortified with good food enough to keep the scurvy away for six months.

I was aboard the ship at midnight, to find the poop and the maindeck so crowded with passengers that there was scarcely room to walk. Cloaked and turbaned figures sat about murmuring quietly, and everywhere I looked were forms stretched out on mats asleep. The coming of these people had changed the whole ship and she now so teemed with life that I wondered where I could sleep. But my place on the bench aft was still there for me, with my chest beneath it. There I turned in for a few hours' rest, ready to watch the ship sail out in the morning. Abdulla whispered that a few of the passengers had come on board. A few? I asked. They seemed to be about a hundred. Yes, he said, business was not good, and reports of depression down the Benadir coast and in Zanzibar and Kenya had kept many at home. No matter, his brother was going ahead to Shihr, along the coast, and we should get more there. More? Where would they fit? Abdulla smiled. I had to walk upon six Beduin, a Sayyid, and a lesser Hadhrami sheikh to reach the place where I slept, and I could not get at my chest for the recumbent forms all round it. Yet we had only shipped the first of our passengers.

I began to wonder about this voyage down to Africa. True, it is no great distance from the South Arabian shore across the Gulf of Aden and down before the monsoon to Mogadishu, in Somaliland. Abdulla said Kuwait ships had sailed from Mukalla to Zanzibar in less than eight days. But we were not bound directly towards Mogadishu, Mombasa, or Zanzibar, so far as I was aware; we were bound on a trading voyage, and Allah alone knew when we might be rid of these passengers. They snored; they took up a great deal of room; their possessions took up more. Under the light of the moon I could see that already so much baggage had come aboard that many bundles were lashed along the poop rail, outboard. We must have taken some merchant of standing, for along the port side of the poop, just forward of the toilet box, were lashed a folding-bed and four cane chairs. I went to go down into the great cabin to bring something of mine from there, but I could not, for Yusuf Shirazi was sleeping with one eye open across the hatch; he motioned to me with his open eye that my gear was all on deck, and I would find it abaft the wheel. There it was, but why this removal from the great cabin? What was the mystery of that place?

But on that subject, for the time being at least, I had to hold my peace. I should find out in due course.

We were gone from Mukalla in the first light of the morning, before the sun rose. We had a light fair wind out of the bay, and we sailed in company with the Persian baggala and Abdulla Kitami's small boom. Our position at the anchorage was a crowded one, with ships all round us and a way out only ahead, a narrow way between a ledge of rock and the small boat in which a hurricane lamp burned at night to mark the port – its only light. I was interested to see how Hamed bin Salim would get the ship out of this congested place, but he managed with surprising ease. First, as usual at anchorages, he hoisted the mainsail on its yard, fast in light stops so that a tug at the sheet would bring the canvas fluttering down. Then he unmoored, passing a line to a sambuk astern, and heaving short to one anchor. Then a puff of air came, faintly marking the surface of the bay, and, as the air struck us, he shouted an order; down fluttered the mainsail; out broke the anchor; and the sambuk astern let go our line. There we were, slipping slowly along under way. We were so close to a Bombay kotia on the one side and an Omani baggala on the other that once we had sailed from our place in the tier it was impossible to see where we had been.

Hamed handled her very well, I thought, and the sailors did their work splendidly. It was made no easier by the crowd of Beduin on deck and the gang of ancient Sindbads on the poop. When it came to manœuvring the ship, however, little attention was paid to either of these. Anyone who got in the way was simply knocked down, and the passengers learned quickly to flee to the other side of the deck as the sailors came rushing and chanting. Those sailors of ours never went at a real job of work quietly. They rushed at it, singing lustily, and fought until it was done. This was Nejdi's style, and even when Nejdi himself was not there it was continued.

So we sailed from Mukalla Bay that bright morning and the town was picturesque and beautiful as the sun rose. Later it was calm, and we were within sight of Mukalla all day. It was a hard place to leave, and the Beduin looked back at it sadly. Some of them played mournfully on their reeds; others, in spite of the calm, were already seasick. Others again jostled and crowded about on deck, stowing what little gear they had, and getting out their firepots. They brought their own food, but the merchants on the poop ate with the ship. Some of these merchants looked rather tough, and some of the Beduin were tougher. They were an unprepossessing lot, and first impressions of them were far from favourable. I wondered more about this voyage down to Africa. How long would this wild gang be on board? I asked Hamed. Not more than ten days or so, he said; and Allah was compassionate. They were going to Mogadishu, most of them; the Italians had work for them down there and in the interior. Had they permission from the Italian Consul, passports, and all that kind of thing? No, said Hamed, they had not; but this movement of the Arabs down the African coast had gone on from time immemorial, and even the foolish Europeans could not stop it. A few of the merchants, I gathered, had some sort of identity certificate, and the ship was supposed to have a passenger list. Perhaps she had. If she had, it must have been thrown overboard, for I never saw it and I know that when she arrived at Haifun, the first port of call in Somaliland, there was none on board.

The wind was quiet all that day and we made little progress; but the way from Mukalla to Shihr is short, and we came to the Sabaean port next morning with the baggala ahead of us – she ghosted beautifully – and the Kitami boom behind. We were twenty-four hours between these ports. At Shihr we found ourselves one of ten booms at anchorage. Eight were Kuwaiti, and two from Persia: we were all bound to Zanzibar. The harbour at Shihr is nothing but an open roadstead, and the ship rolled there more heavily than she ever did at sea. This made the Beduin very sick, and the maindeck was a bedlam.

Landing on the beach at Shihr was dangerous and difficult, for a high surf ran and we could not bring our longboat in. The quartermaster in charge anchored her outside the breakers; and the sailors, rolling their long shirts on to their shoulders, ran in through the surf. Zaid, the freed slave from Kuwait, carried me on his great back – Zaid had always been very good to me while I was blind and lame – but as we were almost safe a sea knocked him down and sent us both sprawling. I hurt my knee, and rose wet and cursing. I cursed the Queen of Sheba for choosing such a place for the town of Shihr (if she ever did, which I doubted). Hamed had said that here the fabled Queen built her ships of war to attack somebody or other, but I doubted that too. Now, with the pain in my knee, I only remembered that the Queen of Sheba was a woman, and womanlike had made a port of this fool place, where there was neither wood to build ships nor a place to launch them. Shihr seemed to me nothing but a walled piece of sand facing the Arabian Sea, and I wondered what excuse it had for its existence. It stretched for about a mile along the shore, but at no place was there a decent landing: the town itself was mean and poor with unmade streets and unfinished houses, a good many of them apparently going to ruin. The Sultan's palace, a huge white building, and the bastioned wall were, so far as I could see, the only buildings of importance in good repair. The bazaar was small and offered very little.

Fishing seemed the only industry, and I saw that the fishermen still used the ancient sewn boats. Some of these were small; but others, used for cargo lightering, were larger. The smaller ones had sails and the larger oars: they were built roughly of planking fastened together by a stitching of fibre, and there were no other fastenings. They were pretty boats, shapely double-enders with good lines and a handsome sheer, and they were elaborately painted in white stripes, with one black and one green triangle at bow and stern. Some were steered with paddles; others had small rudders, balanced so that they were always under water, and manipulated by a piece of cord leading to the helmsman's foot. This he held between his toes, steering the ship by a gentle movement of his foot. The small sewn boats used by the fishermen spread one square sail, and they could scud along beautifully in anything of a breeze. Fine edible fish seemed extraordinarily numerous off that coast, and all day long the fishermen were landing their heavy catches through the surf. They were very cheap, a boatload of splendid fish bringing only a few cents. Drying small fish for camel fodder was going on along almost the whole length of the beach. I saw nothing else being carried here but fish and some dates, for a Persian boom from Basrah was discharging dates at the anchorage. A poor bazaar, a few rough mosques, some tumbledown buildings, a sultan's palace, camels, donkeys, goats, chickens, some lesser merchants, a few soldiers, Beduin, a coffee shop or two, and a lot of fish – this was Shihr. Except for the poor houses, it remained largely as Nature made it, and I wondered why it had been considered worth putting a wall round. I went back aboard.

We stayed at Shihr for days and days. There was no sign of Nejdi, and nothing happened, except that the Beduin made a bedlam of the anchorage. We loaded no cargo and discharged none. Nejdi ought to have been back from his camel-ride, but he was reported to be looking for more passengers. I wondered where we could put them. Already we must have had more than fifty, though some, apparently, were coming only as far as Shihr to see their tribesmen leave.

On the third day, just at dawn, a big soldier came out in a sewn boat asking for me. What now? I thought; but it was only His Highness the Na'ib asking me to come to the palace. What exactly a Na'ib was I was not sure, but he lived in the palace and he was Mayor of the town, if nothing more. Sultans, Emirs, Na'ibs, Sheikhs – they are much the same. The only variation is in the name. At any rate, when a Na'ib asks you, you go; and I was glad to go, though my leg hurt rather badly when I moved. There was noise and confusion on board, and some of our Hadhrami had developed a horrible capacity for quarrelling. A day with the Na'ib in his great white house would not be so bad, so I went off with the soldier, expecting to be back the same evening. It was a week later before I returned.

The Na'ib himself was waiting on the beach with an ancient car, and we drove to the palace. The Na'ib of Shihr was a slight thin man with a fiery red beard. He was a very pleasant, soft-spoken gentleman, dressed strikingly in a bright green turban and a sarong with green and red stripes, surmounted by an old coat. Round his waist was a fold of cloth with a large ivory-handled dagger in a silver sheath. The ivory was adorned with gold. He wore rough sandals of coloured leather, and chewed incessantly at something which looked like snuff. Though I could not talk to him (for my few words of Arabic were purely maritime, and had been picked up from the sailors) we got along very well. He made me comfortable in his palace, which was a large handsome building overlooking the town and the sea with some picturesque ruins topping the square before it. Once in, there I stayed. We entered the palace through a gateway, where some Beduin soldiers reclined on easy guard with their rifles beside them. Other rifles and large swords hung round the walls, and a group of citizens squatted outside the doorway. These rose as we entered, with salutations. We seemed to climb a great many stairs. I was accommodated in a pleasant room furnished with a sofa, several armchairs, a table, and a large bed, with carpets on the floor, and on the white wall nothing but an Egyptian calendar three years old.

We fed very well in the palace, breakfasting always on chickens, omelets, eggs fried in ghee, unleavened bread fried in God knows what, and black coffee. At noon we ate again, very sumptuously, on roasted lamb and boiled rice, and fresh bananas and canned pineapple from the Malay States. In the evening we had fish and rice. This was the order of our meals invariably, though sometimes we had the fish at noon and the lamb at night. After every meal, the Na'ib had the ingredients for his chewing stuff brought to him. Mixing up leaves and lime and whatever else went into the concoction, he chewed loudly and methodically for some time, with frequent expectorations into a spittoon on the table. In the afternoons we drove round the town and outside it, to an oasis where a small ox, working on an inclined runway in a pit, hauled up water in a leathern bucket. We visited the Beduin camps, full of babies and yelping dogs, and saw all there was to see in Shihr. This took about ten minutes. The rest of the day I sat in the Na'ib's palace looking out, and before long, pleasant and hospitable as the old man was, I began to suspect that this was a worse occupation than sitting on the outside looking in. But, being his guest, I could not leave.

I missed the ship. I missed old Yusuf Shirazi and Zaid the freed slave, and Abdulla, Nejdi's brother, silent old Hamed bin Salim, morose little Jassim the cook, and all the rest of them. I had grown to like them all, and I wanted to know what was happening aboard the ship. I might have solved the mystery of the great cabin if I had stayed aboard. There was nothing to read in the palace, and I had brought nothing, not expecting to stay there. Indeed, I had very little to read with me on the ship, for I had not wished to have anything which might tempt me away from the fascinating observation of all that went on. I had only five books and, except for a book of poems, these were all about Arabia.

On the fourth or fifth day, when the *Triumph* had been in port perhaps about ten days – I was always hazy about times and no one else cared about them – Abdulla came up to the palace to say that Nejdi was coming back that night, and the boom would sail before morning. She was, he said, probably going to call at one or two other places along the coast before turning away for Africa: he mentioned Hami and Seihut. We wandered down to the beach in the Na'ib's wheezy old car, about four o'clock – the Na'ib, Abdulla, and I. I liked the old Na'ib, though I had never exchanged an intelligible word with him. He was very good to me, but I looked forward to returning to the ship, and to the voyage down to Africa.

When we came to the beach, we passed a large crowd of Arabs of all shapes and sizes, waiting with a vast collection of battered old tins, ancient carpet bags, and household goods done up in date matting. I did not know what these migrants were and did not look at them very closely, for I presumed they were probably for some other boom. We had our own contingent. I asked Nejdi's brother what ship they were for, but he only smiled. Out at the anchorage again, I found the ship a pandemonium of noise with all the passengers from Mukalla settled down – settled down so well there was no longer place for me on the bench aft (this, Hamed soon changed) – and there were some new faces among them. What a madhouse the ship was! It was late in the afternoon, and the sailors were getting the ship ready for sea, bending the big mainsail along the long yard with singing, chanting, and yelling, now and again stamping their feet. Half the booms at the anchorage were similarly engaged, and bursts of song, clapping of great horny hands and stamping of rhythmic feet, came from all parts of the roadstead. It was a quiet afternoon with no swell: now no one was seasick.

As the day ended and the sun set I saw a fleet of sewn boats coming out: the surf was now quiet. I watched them with mild interest and no thought beyond the reflection that possibly this was the last time I might see them in action, but after a while I saw they were coming toward us. I saw too, that all the boats were filled with human beings. They were bringing out all that great crowd of Beduin I had seen on the beach, and they were bringing them to us. Good Lord! Our decks were already so crowded, I thought, that there was no room to move, and the longboat which we had towed from Mukalla had still to be hoisted aboard. There must have been over a hundred of them. On they came, the whole wild mob, some chanting in the sewn boats, others yelling, babies crying, children screaming, Beduin looking up stolidly in their black rags.

As the sun went down and throughout the brief twilight, while the sailors prayed in the pandemonium of the poop, the embarkation of our passengers went on – on and on and on, far into the night. The poor illumination of a hurricane lamp threw a bizarre light on the scene as hordes of the wanderers scrambled up the side and clambered aboard. There was not so much as a rope ladder to assist them: nobody checked them. All who came simply clambered up the side the best way they could, threw their belongings down (if they had any), and sat where their belongings landed. In this way they made room for themselves, for first they pitched their bundle aboard, over the side before them, and then ran and placed themselves where other passengers had scrambled out of the way. If you had no baggage, you had no place, in that first scramble. Before long there was a line of them sitting along the mainyard, though Hamed and Abdulla chased them down from there, saying there was plenty of room. They filled the open space beneath the break of the poop; they piled into the carpenter's new dhow; they packed themselves between its ribs and the side of the vessel; they streamed along the forepart of the poop; they sat upon the capstan, the forecastle head, the sailors' chests. Those who were experienced among them made at once for the sheltered space beneath the poop, on the fore part of the great cabin bulkhead; while those who were making their first voyage – and they seemed the great majority – mooned about like sheep and did not know what to do with themselves. Chest after chest was passed up on the poop, bale after bale, bundle after bundle of bedding, until the sea chests stood six deep on each side, and the tins and bales and bedding were massed over them. I could not understand how the mess would ever be cleared. Old men, blind men, lame men, men in bandages, men in black, men in white, children, boys, merchants, camel-drivers still with their camel canes, a *Seyyid* with his staff, fierce-visaged men who looked ready for anything, mild-looking men, thin men, fat men – still they came, piling on board. The surge of humanity swept over the vessel and threatened to engulf her, until I felt crowded even on my six feet of the officers' bench and wondered, not for the first – or the last – time on that strange voyage, what I had really let myself in for.

But what was this? Something strange, even in this extraordinary scene, was happening. I saw that they kept on passing up queer long bundles swathed in black, one after the other, which were immediately passed with some deference into the blackness underneath the poop. Here they promptly disappeared. They were being stowed away in the great cabin. At the fifth or sixth bundle I became really interested, for the bundle moved. What *was* this? I asked old Yusuf, who was swearing and running round trying to keep order, making way for these bundles and seeing to their safe stowage. Yusuf did not hear me. I repeated the question: what were these bundles he was passing so carefully into the great cabin? Bints, Yusuf said as he rushed by, bints. Women! Great heavens! They must have passed up about fifteen of them. So that was what the great cabin was for. Poor devils! Most of them were very slight, like girls. I saw one dropped, later: she leapt to her feet and, holding the black veil before her eyes, ran lithely towards the place where a doorway led into their prison. My own recent memories of a week in that ghastly place gave me a shock, and I wondered how fifteen or twenty women or girls were going to survive a voyage cooped up in that foul and loathsome den. So that was what the Beduin had been so pleased about, always coming up out of that inferno grinning and murmuring *taiyib*; they were going to ship their women there. What was so *taiyib* about it I still did not know, if not its excellence as a place of segregation. They could scarcely have regarded the place as good accommodation. In Arabia the sexes must be segregated at all costs, though they die for it. Some of them did, aboard the *Triumph of Righteousness*, before that voyage was over.

Just before midnight, after the last of the passengers had come aboard, a headcloth which belonged to no Beduin, suddenly appeared at the rail. It was a white headcloth, touched with gold, and it was bound by headropes of black silk. One fold was wrapped about the wearer's face as he came over the rail, dropping a stick and his sandals before him, but even if only his great hawk nose had been showing all hands would have recognised him. It was Nejdi, back from his camel-ride, in from the desert; Nejdi, who had driven in all these passengers by fair means or foul, from God knows where, and now was come aboard to sail this great ship with them, again God alone knew where.

He came aboard silently. He took one look at the crowded decks and strode aft, walking on the tops of the chests for there was no other place. With him was a turbaned perfumed sheikh in silks, who remained a while squatting on the bench aft, conversing in long whisperings. At length, with a soft "Fare ye with God!" the perfumed one departed, going down silently over the side into the boat which had brought him. Nejdi still sat there aft, watching the weather, his brooding dark eyes on the wind and the sea. He looked tired, as if he had come a long way, but he was alert. The sail had been made ready before them, and all was in order for departure. Before four o'clock there was a breath of air from the land, and we sailed. Silently the ship passed out into the night, unlit and ghostlike, with her great mast seeming to rise unaided from the sea of humanity sleeping there bewildered in the shadow of the sail. The women in the great cabin were silent, and no man stirred. The mainsail fluttered down, the wheel kicked quietly; we were off.

IV

DELIVERING THE BEDUIN

WE DID NOT GO to Hami and we did not go to Seihut. Nejdi, who had scoured the countryside on his camel as far as Seihut, had decided there was nothing to be gained by visiting those ports. His must have been a great camel ride, for Seihut is more than a hundred miles from Shihr. Whether he was pleased with the results of his mission I did not know, but he did not seem to be. On general principles Nejdi rarely seemed pleased with anything. He complained that there were not enough passengers, and that the boom could have accommodated a hundred more. This I did not at first believe, but after the passengers had settled down I had to admit that it was probably so. There was room for more. The Arab passenger takes up very little room and asks nothing but a place to throw himself down. The *Triumph* had a beam of 29 feet, and her maindeck from the great cabin bulkhead to the forecastle head was nearly 70 feet long. The poop had a maximum beam of 26 feet and was 27 feet long. The main deck, then, had an available area of something like 1,900 square feet, and the poop perhaps 300. This gave actual deck space, giving each passenger 12 square feet – 6 feet by 2, which was much more than they needed – for over 180 persons, without counting the score or so who could be put into the great cabin. In addition, there were the longboat and the new dhow, and there was space beneath the forecastle head. There was no doubt that, at a pinch, the boom could carry as many as 250 Arab passengers; but I should hate to be on board among them.

The longboat and the dhow took up some deck space, but Arabs slept beneath them and all round them, in them and over them. No space was lost. Chests, bundles, everything was slept upon. The Arab slept always on his side and did not ask even for space enough in which to turn. Only the merchants on the poop had any real belongings, the merchants and two young sheikhs who were going to Lamu in Kenya for business experience. Forty of the Beduin had only one wooden box between them, and a bale of sheepdung as fuel for their tin firepot.

Exactly how many passengers we had on board at that stage of the voyage I never discovered, though I tried every day to count them. Like everything else to do with the vessel, this was a closely guarded secret.

The Arabs never volunteered any information, and though Nejdi and Hamed bin Salim sometimes asked me to identify certain of the ship's papers for them, and to examine and translate them – this was later, when I had picked up more Arabic – I rarely learned anything in this way. I never learned by questioning. There was no passenger list from Shihr; my daily totals varied by as many as twenty persons, and I could never count the women and children beneath the poop. That place was now strictly out of bounds, and no one went there but old Yusuf Shirazi. Abdulla the Suri and Said, our two passengers from Aden, were still with us, though Abdulla had gone missing in both Mukalla and Shihr. We appeared to have embarked several others of their kind, including a burly big Suri named Majid, which they pronounced "Mide," and the poop under the officers' bench on the port side was full of their merchandise. We now had some forty persons on the poop alone, and the daily prayers were a scramble, for there was not room for all to bow and kneel together.

Our passengers from Mukalla included an old blind merchant from somewhere in the interior of the Hadhramaut, a man who had long been settled down inland and now was coming out, at the age of sixty-five, to wind up the affairs of a dead brother buried somewhere in the Congo. He was a fine old man with a handsome, drawn face; he had a servant with him, and five times a day he was led upon the poop to his ablutions and his prayers, which he recited in a thin quavering voice. Hamed and Nejdi and the rest were very kind to this old gentleman, though ordinarily there was not much human consideration about them. How could there be, in all that crowd and in such a life? The old man led the prayers, standing in front of the long line of the strange congregation with his drawn tragic face sightless towards Mecca. That old face could be extraordinarily moving. When he was not praying he sank in reverie at the bole of the mizzen mast, his hands clasped together, and was lost in thought, heedless of the teeming life all round him. He was dressed always in purest white with a long white turban wound upon his high forehead, but how he succeeded in keeping himself so clean in all that mess and bedlam I could not understand. Before we had been a day at sea the maindeck was a filthy morass and it could never be cleaned, for so long as the passengers were aboard no one could get at it. How our sailors lived during this dreadful time – these conditions went on for six weeks – I never quite understood. When the last of our passengers had left the vessel, at Mombasa many weeks later, somehow and from somewhere the sailors emerged again, worn and thin and tired. As far as I could discover, they must have slept in tiers on the anchors and cables, and on top of the firebox.

On this first day of the voyage down to Africa we beat along the Hadhramaut coast, making to windward of Ras Asir. Though it was now mid-January and the north-east monsoon should have been long established, the wind was fluky and more from the east than the north-east. Nejdi made a series of short tacks along the coast, never getting far away, exactly as Hamed had done on the beat to Mukalla. If he stood too far from the land we should be caught in the set to the westwards, and lose ground; inshore the countercurrent helped us, and we came on slowly. We passed close by the picturesque village port of Hami, and the place looked so fresh and interesting I was sorry we did not stay there. Here three sambuks were anchored, but no deep-water booms. The Kitami boom and the Persian baggala had sailed before us and we were now alone. Abdulla Kitami was bound direct for Mombasa.

The Hadhramaut coast in the neighbourhood of Hami and towards Ras Sharma had great beauty, with the high, flat-topped cliffs of the *wadi* sides away in the distance, and from them, rolling down towards the sea, all the lesser hills, marked with sunlight and shade like shadowed folds in cloth. Now and then we saw a pleasant little village, picturesque and seemingly quiet.

Still Nejdi crept along the coast, determined to get to windward of all Africa along his Arab shore before falling off towards Haifun. His purpose was the sound one of getting to windward while he could, and afterwards using the east wind to run directly for Ras Asir light,[1] upon which he would have to come by dead reckoning, for he knew no navigation and I had brought no instruments. It was not far, and visibility was good. He always came that way. When an Arab shipmaster spoke of knowing the waters and the way on the sea he meant exactly what he said. He was not speaking of a theoretical ability to make a voyage with the help of astronomical observations, wind and current data, the latest Admiralty charts, headlines, patent logs, and all the rest of the long list of ordinary paraphernalia. Nejdi coaxed his ship along but his knowledge of local conditions, and the coasts of South Arabia (and the coasts of the Persian Gulf, Baluchistan, and all Western India) were an open book to him. He showed his knowledge now, and the benefits of it, though I admit I was puzzled by his short tacks. If I had been trying to get a ship out of there I should probably have made long boards, on the assumption that

[1] Our Cape Guardafui is known to the Arabs as Ras Asir.

the monsoon would be truer away from the land and would haul fair. I should have been wrong; Nejdi knew his winds and waters.

At last we drew to windward of Ras Sharma, and fell away abruptly to head towards Africa, laying a course inside the island of Socotra, to pass within ten miles or so of Ras Asir. I was interested to see Nejdi rule off this course. He did it properly, from the compass rose of a comparatively modern chart; but he had no parallel rules and he used a straight frond of date and his thumbs. Though scarcely a method likely to be approved by the Board of Trade, this was effective, but his fatalistic belief in the compass, which he always insisted in regarding as true no matter where the ship was or how much iron might be thrown round the binnacle, might have been fatal to the vessel in conditions other than those we encountered. To him the compass was always true; he had bought and paid for it. I learned more of Nejdi's navigation methods later.

A hundred of our passengers were sick, and the ship was a mess. The Beduin did not bother to go to the rail. Some of our migrants, indeed, when they sat on the rail would lean back inboard to spit, and no amount of shouting at them would change their ways. Perhaps they saw that the sea was clean and the ship dirty, and therefore spat on the ship. The more experienced travellers adopted all kinds of strange devices to keep the seasickness away. They prayed frequently and with great devotion. They sniffed at small green lemons, and stuffed wads of paper into their ears and nostrils. Some of them presented a ludicrous appearance, with large wads of newspaper protruding from each nostril, the ends of the paper attached round their necks with string. This did not save them, and many of them were very sick. They all kept eating, which was wise. The ship's motion was not bad and the weather was ideal. The sea was slight and the breeze a pleasant sailing air which, once we had got to windward, was fair, and the ship had only to fall off and run towards Ras Asir light. Conditions could not have been better. This was as well with such a welter of humanity on board.

Actual living conditions aboard the vessel during this stage of the voyage were very bad, though I doubt whether they seemed so to any of the Arabs. Right aft on the poop, we had the first-class passengers – the merchant Sindbads Said, Abdulla, and Majid; the *seyyid* from Mukalla who was going down to Africa to collect dues; the blind old sheikh, the two young sheikhs, and several others. These ate the ship's food, paying a rupee extra for that privilege for the voyage. The fare from Mukalla or Shihr to Africa – it made no difference which was the port of embarkation

– was eight rupees without food, nine with, and twelve rupees for women. Nejdi explained that he did not want women, who did not usually come – Abdulla Kitami had only three in his 150 passengers – and that was why the rate was higher for them. They had to be sheltered and segregated. It was better, he said, to have none of them, for they often made trouble. But he had to bring some that voyage. The fare was the same whether the passengers were bound to Mogadishu, Lamu, or Mombasa. It was customary that it should be paid in advance, though this was not strictly necessary. The first-class passengers, who included, apparently, several old friends of Nejdi, did not pay in advance, and indeed several of them never paid at all.

On the fore part of the poop was a group of young half-caste Hadhrami, many of whom seemed half-Malay. Some of these looked villainous, and occasionally there were fights in this section. Here also were the two young sheikhs travelling to gain business experience. The elder of these may have been 22; he was born in Sourabaya, he said, and spoke Malay as well as some Dutch, and his own Arabic. He was a fine-looking young man who prayed far more than anyone else on board. Long after all the others had finished their daily ritual he was still praying, on his knees amid that welter of humanity, praying with his hands across his chest and a rapt expression on his youthful face. When he was seasick he prayed more than ever. With him were his brother, aged perhaps 18 and by no means so ardent a Muslim, some servants, and a half-caste Malay who was one of the noisiest and most obnoxious people on board. This half-Hadhramaut-Malay had an ancient gramophone with him and some terrible records from Cairo and Damascus, and whenever there was no other noise – which was seldom – he brought these things out and raised havoc with them. Also he sang, in a voice worse even than our musician Ismael's, until that worthy was disgusted and lapsed into pained silence.

At nights other odd passengers came up on the poop and reclined dangerously along the edges of the chests and wherever else they could fit their bodies. Down on the maindeck, beneath the overhang of the poop, were some forty wanderers, who seemed to have formed themselves into small cliques. One of these cliques was made up of fellows from a village near Shibam, in the interior of the Hadhramaut, and there was another of young men from Sur. I don't know how they had managed to get to Shihr, but probably they had wandered round the coast in one of the small Suri or Mahra vessels. When an Arab begins to wander he may turn up anywhere. Our curious old Seyyid on the poop, for instance, had been an automobile worker in Detroit and had spent eight years in the stokeholds of ocean steamers. For a man who had served so long under the British flag he knew very little English, but he used frequently to address me in a queer language. It was not Arabic. I was not sure of that, but Abdulla said so, adding that it was neither Swahili, nor Persian, nor Hindustani, nor any other language known in India. It certainly had not the slightest resemblance to English or to any other European tongue that I could recognise. It took me a long time to find out that he was really speaking very bad Polish, which he had learned in Buffalo and Detroit under the impression that it was English. He had lived in Hamtranck, the Polish suburb of Detroit, and his fellow-workers must all have been Poles.

The young sheikh who prayed so much was a courageous young man. He read every day to his entourage, usually from the Qurân but sometimes from other books, and he read aloud even when he was seasick. This takes courage. He was one of the most likeable of the whole group, and I liked his brother, too.

The Beduin on the maindeck led wild lives and there was always yelling and arguing going on down there. I noticed, however, that it was never the real Beduin who began the arguments, though they often continued them. The quarrelsome ones were the half-castes, and the worst of all was a half-Somali with three children, a dreadful little boy named Abdulla, another much smaller boy who was even worse, and a little girl with her shrew face painted stupidly with black lines beneath the eyes and across her brows. This shrew-faced little girl used to go about with her big father all day and disappear into the great cabin by night. She pinched and scratched all the boys smaller than she was, when their parents were not looking, and she always shrieked if anybody touched her. She made life a hell for the small boys in that ship, but one day three little mites of about four years of age got together and gave her a hiding which she thoroughly deserved. She was perhaps seven years old: she wore long dresses and longer trousers, but her little devil of a face was covered with nothing but paint. It would have been better veiled, and the ship would have been quieter if she had been gagged, together with the rest of her family. The name of her elder brother was Abdulla, and all day long the decks resounded with yells for this youthful criminal who was loud-mouthed, noisy, quarrelsome, and bullying. Abdul-la! Abdul-la! All day that infernal half-Somali yelled, when he was not fighting the other passengers. He never had room enough for his firepot;

he never had water enough from the ship; his children were for ever in trouble. He had brought all his household possessions and was moving for good down to Mogadishu. His household goods were in a box, and he had brought two goats. These stood throughout the voyage tethered to the side of the wooden water-tank forward, and they were the best behaved and quietest members of that family.

This dreadful creature was not typical. By far the greater number of our passengers were quiet and decent people who, once they had settled down to the life on board – and this took them very little time – sat and slept and yarned and cooked their few victuals, and did their best to keep out of trouble and out of the sailors' way. The chief of the Beduin was a small, wiry man named Aura, an attractive, clean-faced Arab who had his small son of about three years old with him. I liked Aura, and the little boy, who took a constant delight in the ship and all that went on, was a great favourite with the sailors. The little child, who had a huge belly and an extraordinary coiffure – his head was shaved at the sides, and across the middle a tussock of black locks stood up like a row of palm trees on a beach – knew no greater delight than to follow the sailors at their work and pretend to haul on ropes with them and sing their songs. Sometimes he became so interested in this that he would dash about the decks for hours by himself, hauling with his baby hands on the great ropes and lustily chanting his own version of the sailors' songs. Another of his favourite sports was fishing, though I never saw him catching anything. He was a sturdy little fellow, and the dreadful shrew-faced little girl knew better than to pinch him when nobody was about. She tried once, and ran away howling with a clout on the ear. That little devil of a girl seemed born with a desire to avenge Muslim womankind on Muslim men and, though the manner of her revenge was restricted to sly hits, kicks, pinches, and scratches, and the only men she could attack were children smaller than herself, she kept to her purpose with a vixen's tenacity and ceaseless energy. Aura's little son, however, was a match for her. The little boy had a tiny black sarong perhaps four inches deep, and that was all the clothes he had. Sometimes his father put butter on his jungle of hair, or renewed his belly-band of indigo. They were a good pair.

We had a great many children. Some seemed to be travelling by themselves: I never saw anybody looking after them. Most belonged to families, and all were at least nominally in the care of an adult. I found out later that several of them had been hired by beggars to go with them down to Africa: they did the work, and the beggars begged. There was a bad-tempered blind man who had brought two boys with him, aged perhaps eight and nine. Apparently the arrangement was that they were to work for him, and he provided them with the passage to Africa and back, their clothes and food. He was not among the first-class passengers and he had to bring his own food. After a few days it became obvious that he was not feeding the children at all. He was a morose man who played mournfully on some battered reeds, nearly all day. This apparently was his manner of begging, and if I was ever near he set up a whine for alms. The children, who had not been away from Arabia before, put up with his ill-treatment for several days. Eventually the matter came to the attention of the nakhoda, when it was at once dealt with, for Nejdi was judge and jury in all disputes.

In addition to sailing the ship and seeing that the passengers were delivered to their destinations safely, Nejdi had complete charge of them: he ruled them with an iron hand. He judged in their disputes; he led them in prayer; he controlled their comings and goings; he quietened them and tamed them when necessary, and attended to all their needs, except their medicinal and surgical needs. There were no medicines on board, and no dressings.

Whenever they had anything to bring to his notice, the passengers came to the break of the poop, stuck up their wild heads, shouted "O Nejdi," and began straightaway to recount their wrongs. It was a free and wholly democratic life. Nejdi was king, but he had no subjects. Everybody else was a king too, and Nejdi had only his natural ability to keep them in order. This he did by force of character: he never shouted. He was in command because he was the natural commander, and for no other reason. Life on board the *Triumph of Righteousness* with our passengers was far from being a picnic but, without Nejdi, the ship would have been nothing more than a madhouse. As it was, if it had not been for the rigid observance of the first rule of the ship, I do not see how life would have been tolerable. The first rule was just this: that whatever happened and in all circumstances, the passenger was never right. This was an effective and thorough principle which I found pleasing. In spite of the inconveniences and the hardships of the life, the opportunity to observe the application of this sound and workable principle in regulating the conduct of passengers at sea would have made up even for a month of dysentery. In all arguments with the crew the passenger was in the way and he had to get out of it. This may seem harsh when, after all, the passenger had paid his fare; but he had paid only to be carried in the ship as she was, to be allowed to come along and take her as he found her. He had nothing to say about her running and he could not be allowed to become an inconvenience. The only way to run that ship, with her huge unhandy lateen sail – the only way to run any ship with any kind of sail, or sails, or even ships with engines – was efficiently, thoroughly, with alertness and competence. There was no opportunity for pampering passengers. The passengers could only be on the deck because there was nowhere else to go: if they were on deck they must sometimes be in the way. They were only there because the ship needed the revenue she earned from them. Being allowed to come was the beginning and end of their privileges. Once aboard they were live ballast, or worse, for the ship was deeply laden and had no need of ballast. They were a noisy and dirty inconvenience to be got rid of as soon as possible, and this fact was soon impressed on them. If they did not like it, they could go riding on camels. To them the conditions were tolerable enough.

The day the two children complained about the blind man's treatment of them was typical. Every day Nejdi was called upon to deliver Solomonic judgments in all kinds of disputes, except with regard to the women. These were shut up, locked up, and forgotten, and never allowed even a breath of fresh air on deck. This might have been hard on them, but in such a world it was unavoidable and indeed it was the best fate that could have overtaken them. As Nejdi pointed out, they would probably not be kept below for longer than two months, at the most. (He had told them two weeks.) On this day – the day of the dispute – things were much as usual: a group of Beduin were delousing their indigo-stained sarongs on the deck of the longboat; the Somali's goats bleating by the water tank, and the Somali yelling at a group of fang-toothed half-Malays by the break of the poop. The quarrelsome little girl was prowling about looking for a chance to vent her sadism on some malc baby; Aura the Beduin chief playing with his small son, Beduin and Hadhrami labourers chatting, sitting, sleeping, cooking, eating, praying, reading the Qurân, applying grease to one another's hair, pawing pieces of shark as hard and dry as basalt rocks and looking about as palatable. Suddenly this fascinating and comparatively peaceful scene was disturbed by a loud yelling, followed by fierce imprecations and a string of oaths in Arabic that would have startled a camel. Incidents like this were too commonplace to excite remark, for the half-Somali began such scenes ten times a day. The only thing strange about this one was that he had not started it.

In a moment, other noises subsided sufficiently to make it clear that the new row was originating somewhere beneath the poop overhang. In a short time a yelling and general commotion burst out on the maindeck, where firepots and trays of rice spilled in all directions, and a goat ran bleating, while the shrew-faced bint, scared for once in her life, scampered for the great cabin. The central figures in the disturbance, which was becoming more general every moment, appeared to be the blind beggar, his two small boys, a fang-toothed half-Malay, an old man in half a sarong, and a broad-shouldered Arab silversmith from Mogadishu. As far as I could make out – and it was difficult to make out anything very clearly – the blind beggar was trying to attack the two boys, who were yelling and fighting one another; the fang-toothed one and the silversmith were fighting to decide who should restrain the blind man from his attacks on the boys, while the old man had got in the way and could not get out again. More people joined in the fray, and sailors ran aft to stop them. They tried to run aft, but, even at the best of times, it was difficult to run along those decks, and now that the whole after part of the maindeck, between the stern of the longboat on the starboard side and the bow of the new dhow on the other, was a seething, yelling, milling mass of Beduin, it was impossible.

At this moment, Nejdi, who had been reclining on the bench aft reading from the Qurân to two Suri merchants, leapt to his feet faster than I had ever seen him move before, picked up a camel-driver's cane and, leaping over the low rail at the break of the poop, was down on the deck like a shot. Wielding the camel cane like a flail, the only one silent in all that mob, he cleaved a way towards the contestants, who by this time numbered at least a score, while the sailors fought through from the fore part to reach him and go to his aid. Not that Nejdi needed aid. He was doing very well alone. In almost the flash of an eye he had stopped the actual hostilities, if not the commotion – that never died down all day. He had the blind man by the scruff of his neck in one hand, the fang-faced Malay and the old man in the other, and the two boys at his feet. Then the sailors reached him, and everybody went to the poop, where a court of inquiry was constituted to deal with the case forthwith.

Nejdi was the whole court, and the only other man – apart from the contestants – who dared to open his mouth was the *Seyyid* from the Hadhramaut. Since he had the blood of the Prophet in his veins, the *Seyyid* was privileged, and he often intervened as peacemaker in the ship's disputes, though seldom to much purpose. Now all began to yell at once, together with fifty other passengers who streamed up on the poop, until Nejdi quietened them and chased them down again. It appeared, after some time, that the blind man had hired the two boys to help him on the voyage to Africa and in such other countries as he might visit. He was to clothe and feed them, and pay for their transport. But once he had got them away from Shihr, where he had posed as their father, and safely on the voyage, he had chosen to forget his bargain and refused to give them anything to eat. The two boys, disgusted – naturally enough – with this, had left his service. They declined to make his meals ready and to look after him, or even to lead him about the deck. They claimed that as the blind man did not feed them they were not obliged to work for him, and it took them all their time to ensure their survival in the crowded and hungry vessel. They had sought, then, to attach themselves to the Mogadishu silversmith, a kindly Arab named Ashuan, but Ashuan already had a family and had no place for them. Their situation was becoming desperate and, that morning, after being hungry for three days, they had mutinied and tried to raid some of their original employer's food. The blind man caught them at this – for he was very sharp in spite of his handicap – and was beating them when the silversmith intervened. Then the engagement rapidly became general.

The discovery of these few facts took half the morning. There had been several further skirmishes, though none of them was very serious, between supporters of the fang-faced Malay and others to whom, apparently, they had taken some objection. Nobody supported the blind man, because he was so obviously in the wrong. In the end Nejdi's judgment was that the blind man must keep to his bargain and feed the boys properly. He objected that they were lazy boys, good-for-nothings who had foisted themselves on him. Why, then, asked Nejdi, had he pretended to be their father? He had done this to get them aboard. It was purely out of the kindness of his heart, the beggar said. But would not the same kindness of heart send them out to beg for him on the streets of Mombasa, Dar-es-Salaam, and wherever else they might get to? The blind man admitted that it would, for he hated the idea of children being without employment. The boys, he said, had been homeless and friendless on the Shihr beach, and he had befriended them. As a reward for this great generosity they now turned on him and, refusing to work, accused him of starving them. But he *had* starved them, hadn't he? The blind man said he was short of food. The silversmith then produced the beggar's box of dried fish, and his half-sack of rice. It was clear that he had no case. Nejdi said that if he did not feed the children properly the ship would feed them, and the beggar be held aboard and not allowed to land until he had paid for all their food. The beggar whined that he was a poor man, but everybody knew that he was one of the richest men aboard. Nejdi made the boys apologise to him for their disturbance of the peace, and made them promise faithfully to serve the blind man so long as he fed them and clothed them. After some demur the children did this and the matter was ended.

By this time new trouble was brewing in the waist of the vessel, where the loud-mouthed half-Somali was yelling that somebody had milked his goats while the fight was in progress. Somebody had.

I was surprised that the starvation of the two children could have escaped attention in so crowded a vessel, and wondered that no one had bothered to look after them. I had not seen them before. The reason probably was that when all were so poor, the need of others was apt to go unobserved. They were all ready to help when the need was brought to their attention. Afterwards the silversmith saw that these children were properly fed, and Nejdi kept his eagle eye on the bad blind man.

Nejdi kept his eagle eye on many things. From the moment his great hawk nose showed above the rail until the last fold of his headcloth disappeared down the Jacob's ladder into the boat, he was in command of everything in sight. He knew all that went on, and directed most of it. He never seemed to be sound asleep. As soon as he came aboard, Hamed bin Salim ceased to have anything to do. The direction of the ship was in Nejdi's hands, and the responsibility was unshared. Hamed was not even a mate. He was a stand-by, an officer to look after the ship in port, and to sail the ship when Nejdi was not there. When Nejdi was there Hamed kept the accounts and did little else at sea. Nobody opened his mouth except to repeat what the nakhoda had said, and this often went unheard because of the continual din of the passengers about the decks and also because the sailors, whenever there was work afoot, sang and chanted with so much vigour that they could not hear the orders.

I often suggested to Nejdi that he should use a whistle to break in effectively upon the clamour, and I bought one for him once. He never used it. He said it was unseemly. He like things as they were, and was opposed to change. Sometimes this disregard of orders seemed to me as if it might be dangerous to the vessel and her gear, for when twenty stout mariners got on the end of a line and swayed away they were apt to do damage if they were not checked in time. They never watched what they were doing; they rushed at the work and waited for the orders they did not hear, and they never stopped their chants and yells so long as the work continued. At the slightest murmur of an order, they were up on their feet and singing. They sang continually; they sang as they ran along the deck to the job, scampering over and upon the boats and knocking the passengers down; they sang all the time they worked, and when the jobs were really big – such as hoisting the lateen yard – they stopped occasionally and danced.

I often wondered about the women imprisoned in the great cabin. Only once did one appear on deck, a slight small figure swathed in black who came up the first dawn at sea to pray at her husband's side. What induced her to do anything so unusual I never discovered, but she was allowed to pray briefly before being chased below. The husband, however, was warned that he must keep his women under better control. Nejdi seemed to think the episode very improper, and several times I heard him talking to the Seyyid about the worrying forwardness of females in these days, as exemplified by this and other incidents. Nejdi had very definite views about the status of women, and often gave them expression. He praised the system which maintains women in the strictest seclusion, and had nothing but scorn for our European ways.

When there was trouble on deck, or anything really interesting happened, I wondered how our women were able to curb their curiosity, for they could not see out of their prison. I discovered that they employed the shrew-faced bint and other young girls to carry reports to them, and they knew most of what went on.

By night we sailed very well upon our course to weather Ras Asir, with the moonlight bright on the swollen sail, and the ship's noises, apart from the Beduin snores, pleasant to the ear. All the passengers stretched themselves on the deck, some wrapped in sacking from the cargo, some in indigo and wretched rags, others in blankets. Some of the merchants had elaborate beds which their men spread for them each evening on six feet of the poop, beds bright with tasselled rugs and gay cushions. I lay on the starboard side of the reclining bench aft on a Turkish carpet Nejdi gave me, and though sleep was sometimes hard, I was well content. But in the greyness of the mornings, when the muezzins seemed to try to see who could make the greatest din; when the bedding and the carpets were wet with dew, and there was no prospect of breakfast other than unleavened bread; when the Beduin and the half-castes noisily sluiced themselves with sea water and the children yelled, I sometimes wondered why I had come.

Day succeeded day, and in the fascination of the voyage, I forgot little troubles like these, forgot the traces of fever that still remained from the Hadhramaut coast, and the lameness that still made walking painful. The ship wandered southward in a welter of noise and discomfort as we carried our Beduin for delivery in Africa. The monsoon blew true and our progress was steady, if not always pleasant.

V

ISMAEL SAVES A CHILD

On the morning of the fifth day after leaving Shihr, the ship coasted close in by the base of the precipitous promontory of Ras Haifun. Nejdi was cutting the corner and we were very close indeed, for the conditions were excellent. The breeze was fresh and fair, from the north-east, and there was little sea. The current here sets towards the land and it is not a place to fool with, but Nejdi knew what he was doing. The promontory's eastern end is without dangers. We were cutting the corner not to save time, which never mattered in Nejdi's existence, but in order to be able to lie up for the anchorage at the town of Haifun immediately the ship drew off the southern tip of the promontory. It was a picturesque place with great yellow cliffs towering above the ship, which slipped along quietly in the blue sea. If we did not hug it closely, we should have to beat to reach the anchorage tucked behind it.

On board everything was much as usual except that it was a little quieter, and for the moment there was no serious row in progress. The half-Somali, the father of the shrew-faced bint and the little brat Abdulla, was asleep, and this automatically reduced the noise on board by half. Our group of half-Malays, or whatever they were, lay in the shadow of the mizzen taking their ease, in spite of the noise of forty-seven Beduin sitting round them, singing. Each Beduin had a hand over one ear as he sang, and I wondered why he did not have his hands over both ears, as I had, and wads of cotton wool thrust deep in them besides. Kaleel the carpenter banged and drilled at his new dhow, now and again calmly turning over a sleeping Beduin so that he might get a fresh plank. Little Jassim, the cook, was drowning the livestock in a basket of rice with a bucket of water hauled up from the sea, while his assistants Abdul-wahhab and Mishari pounded corn for the unleavened bread. Other sailors, with Abdulla the nakhoda's brother, crouched like apes over a large basket of Iraqi dates. The dates were a congested sticky mess, and looked as if they had been trodden into that basket by a camel some years before. Abdulla and the sailors were picking out the soundest fruit, pitting it with their teeth, and re-stowing it, more or less neatly, in little paper cartons labelled 'Fresh Clean Dates, Produce of Iraq.' These dates were to be trade goods for the Somali at Haifun, who were the only people who would eat them.

On the poop the Suri were seated in a group, and Said was going through some haberdashery which he appeared to be making ready to land. Said was a smuggler, and he would soon be busy. Majid, the big villain, in a long brown shirt, examined the haberdashery with interest and offered suggestions, in a very loud voice, as to the best manner of smuggling it, while Abdulla read to himself quietly from the Qurân. Nejdi, who had been discussing subjects as diverse as the growth of Islam in Japan, the great days of science in Arabia, the property laws of the Hadhramaut, and the best way to make a passage in a dhow from Mandalay to Cutch in June, now was quiet, for the moment, puffing at his hookah. Ismael the musician had stowed away his music and was going though the contents of his chest, round which a group of Hadhramaut half-castes had gathered. He was trying to sell them some inferior ready-made Japanese coats, which they were scrutinising but not buying. Yusuf Shirazi, his eyes, which had been paining him for a long time, half-covered in a visor-fold of his white headcloth, was engaged in some mysterious occupation the nature of which I could not understand. I watched him with interest, dimly conscious of the scene all round. Children scampered along the bulwarks, playing merrily, the little son of Aura leading them.

Suddenly I heard a splash. Nejdi started. There was a scream – a child's scream. Some of the Beduin rushed to the side. "Child overboard!" they shouted, pointing. I leapt up. The child, a bawling bundle with his white gown streaming in the sea round him, was rapidly being left astern. Instantly, before I had time to collect my thoughts, there was another flash of white and one of brown. Two rescuers had leapt across the poop and were over the side before I could recognise them. In a few moments I saw that they were the musician Ismael, who went first, and Abdulla the Mysterious.

It was a brave deed. We were making about five knots, and there were sharks. The boy fell rapidly astern. We were perilously close in under the cliffs, and the wind, filling the huge lateen sail, was right behind us. The ship was not equipped for such an emergency. There were no lifebelts or lifebuoys, or any other kind of life-saving apparatus. The cutter was at the quarter davits, fortunately, but it was securely lashed there. The ship herself was in a bad position. We were so near the cliffs – we could hear the breakers and watch the backwash gurgling at the cliff-base – that to throw the ship aback would be extremely dangerous, for then she would be in grave danger of driving on the rocks. To bring her up and let her shiver by the wind on the port track, keeping the way off her, would be equally dangerous, for the set could easily put her ashore.

I wondered what Nejdi would do, for now he had to get back three people instead of one. I could not see a move open to him that would not gravely endanger the vessel. He showed himself, in those circumstances, an alert and skilful seaman. He knew what to do more quickly than I did. Without the least excitement, without as much as rising from his bench, he rapped out one curt order, so rapidly that I did not understand it. The sailors understood it. They had always worked splendidly, but in this emergency they worked like demons. In response to Nejdi's command they swung the huge mainyard mid-ships. The quartermaster slammed the helm down, and Nejdi threw the ship across the wind, aback, so that her stern was seawards and her sternway carried her from the cliffs, instead of towards them. It was smartly done, though the situation of the vessel was still critical. We must have been within fifty yards of destruction. It was a question which would affect the vessel more – her sternway – which was not much, for half the sail was now useless – or the set. Her sternway took her from the cliffs. The set put her towards them. It was a fight between them, with Nejdi, compelled to wait for his sailors and somehow get them back aboard, unable to help. But he did not seem to doubt the results, nor did the sailors. They rushed immediately to the poop and began to clear the cutter. In the *Triumph*, as in all Arab vessels, nothing was ever quite ready for use. The Arab policy was to cope with emergencies when they arose, not to prepare against them beforehand. I had been inclined to scoff at this. Now I had a lesson. Those stout fellows were as splendid throughout this whole situation as any sailors on earth could have been, and they had that boat cleared and away into the water as rapidly as any smart liner might have been getting an emergency boat overboard, starting with the boat ready. They all worked; they all chanted; they all sang – even in this predicament, with the ship five minutes away from disaster, the child drowning, and their shipmates fighting for their lives in the shark-infested seas. No one was excited. No one, except the Beduin passengers, now yelled. The sailors worked magnificently, with Nejdi and Hamed bin Salim leading them. Ismael and Abdulla by this time were far astern, specks on the blue expanse of the African sea; but we could see that Ismael had the child, and Abdulla was helping him.

Now the cutter was down and away immediately it touched the water, with Abdulla, Nejdi's brother, at the tiller and old Yusuf Shirazi and the serang at the oars. They pulled lustily, though without excitement. The cutter was only 16 feet long. It was very small in the ocean, but there was no sea. The sharks were the danger – the sharks, and the rocks. The ship was slowly, but very obviously, being set in towards the cliffs, which now seemed to tower above her masts. When she rolled we saw the cliffs above her mastheads, not the sky.

We saw the cutter reach the trio, struggling in the sea. They picked up the child. We saw them take all three aboard – the child, Ismael, and Abdulla the Mysterious. Nejdi stood by the davits on the port side of the poop, watching everything, gauging the chances for his ship, cursing the Beduin child and all the Beduin, and all the other passengers. Sometimes he signalled to the man at the wheel to give her a spoke this way or that. The cutter began to pull her back towards the ship, coming very slowly, though they were doing their best (the oars were short and bad). She seemed to come slowly because of the obvious danger in which the ship herself now lay. To make things worse, the Beduin, unable any longer to control their excitement, began to rush the poop in their anxiety to see all that went on. There was now nothing more to do than to get the cutter and its people safely aboard, and then to let the ship fall off from the wind again, but true to all the instincts of passengers the world over, the Beduin who had been helpless and useless before, now clamoured and scrambled and stormed and yelled.

"Get down off this infernal poop!" yelled Nejdi, in its Arabic version. (I assume that is what he yelled.) "Get down off this poop, you bunch of scum!"

The Beduin, as Beduin will, kept on coming; those in the front ranks being driven on by the impetus of those behind. Nejdi and Hamed bin Salim snatched up camel canes, and Majid the Suri and Said the Smuggler advanced behind them. Nejdi wasted no time, but slashed into the midst of the advancing Beduin, driving them down from the poop so that the cutter might be hoisted in safety, and the child, if he needed attention, receive it without further risk to his life. Still the mob behind came on. The cliffs of Ras Haifun gave back yell for yell from the excited passengers, and the scene aboard was pandemonium. The cutter came on; the ship drifted; the Beduin stormed the poop. They were trying to climb up by way of the stem of the longboat to leap over the rail, to jump from the carpenter's new dhow. What they hoped to do or see or to gain by this manœuvre was incomprehensible. They did not go far. Nejdi, who never wasted words in real emergencies, slashed about him with the cane, and behind him was his able lieutenant, Hamed bin Salim, also slashing. Gradually they made an impression on the hysterical Beduin, and the opinion seemed to gain some ground that it was not such a good idea to storm the poop.

All this time the sailors, who had been forward attending to the sail, were fighting to reach the poop again, but the intervening wedge of stampeding human beings prevented them. Abdulla bin Salim, the second serang, seeing that things might become desperate, ran hand over hand and foot after foot up the main halliards. Swarming from the masthead on to the yard, he ran out along the great yard and swung himself by means of the long vang out and down again on to the poop, in this way coming in over the heads of the Beduin. This would have been a good piece of climbing even for a monkey, but his example was immediately followed by the others, one behind the other. Though this was a climb, and a feat excelling most of the ordinary performances offered by highly skilled acrobats, one and all accomplished it with a speed and seeming ease that was amazing. Down they swarmed on to the poop, hand over hand, forming a living wedge behind Nejdi. In a twinkling the situation was under control, and the Beduin began to retreat before the mariners down from the poop. The situation was so bizarre and events moved so rapidly that it seemed at the time like a kaleidoscopic dream. Looking at this scene with my own eyes, my mind could only respond: this isn't happening: this *can't* be happening! The stampede of those Beduin made no sense; the rescue of the child made no sense; the bravery of the musician Ismael was of no apparent intelligence whatever, and (by me at any rate) utterly unexpected. I had so disliked his music that I had, I fear, also disliked him. After this piece of heroism, however, I tried harder to suffer his music, and I liked him a great deal. He was a good fellow, after all.

Now the cutter was alongside and the noise ceased, as suddenly and as completely as it had begun. With no excitement and no sound other than the chanting of the sailors, the boat was hauled aboard and the child taken up, and the ship fell off again, and upon her course. She had drifted within thirty yards of the backwash of the breakers at the cliff's edge. Ismael the musician and Abdulla the Mysterious were left to take care of themselves. Neither Nejdi nor Hamed nor any of the Beduin looked at them. Nejdi cuffed the child, who beyond the wetting and some fright was none the worse for the adventure, and told him that if he fell overboard again he would be left there. The child went forward, grinning, and Nejdi, who was a fierce man when roused, and a hard man always, went back bright-eyed to his bench, his hawk nose high and sniffing. He did not look at the cliffs or speak to Ismael or Abdulla. He left Hamed bin Salim to superintend the resetting of the sail. The emergency was over, and that rush of the Beduin had been very undignified. Nejdi hated things to be undignified.

So we sailed on, having narrowly escaped destruction. In the evening, when it was time for the daily salutations after the fourth prayer, Aura, the chief of the Beduin, came and said briefly, "Thank you, O Nejdi, that you saved the child." Nejdi returned the salutation with quiet dignity. The storming of the passengers upon the poop and the manner of their driving from it were not referred to, or ever mentioned again. Nor were Abdulla and Ismael thanked. When they had come aboard Ismael went on with his work, without even attending to his clothes except to ring out the bottom of his shirt, and Abdulla the Mysterious, more mysterious, more handsome, and more gaunt than ever, changed his brown shirt and returned to his Qurân reading. But after that I looked upon them both with different eyes. I liked both Ismael and Abdulla after that, and forgave Ismael his dreadful music and Abdulla all his mystery and whatever nefarious employments might have gone with it.

We hauled our wind at the south of the promontory, and headed towards Haifun, the first of our calls to Africa. We were anchored there in a few hours. The passage so far had always been most interesting, if somewhat trying, and the sailing conditions had been very pleasant. I already had some never-to-be-forgotten images from the wandering of that big boom, pictures of moonlight upon sails, the murmur of the quiet turning of the waters at the low bow, the drowsy figure of the seated helmsman aft, and the alert and bright-eyed image of Nejdi behind him, that quiet and small tornado, driver of ships and ruler of men; the softened light of the binnacle's glow falling upon the figures of the sleeping merchants, while Said the Smuggler, perhaps dreaming of some pretty slave-girl in far-off Asab or the northern borders of Baluchistan, turned in his sleep and groaned.

So we came to Haifun, which is called Dante by the Italians. By any name that place is objectionable, for it is nothing but a saltworks surrounded by sand. Once it was a famous market, and the trade of the eastern mariners down to here is very ancient. Haifun, which is a bay tucked in the farthest corner of the southern side of the gaunt promontory of Ras Haifun, was once called Opone, and under that name the anonymous chronicler of the *Periplus of the Erythraean Sea*[1] (supposedly writing in about the year A.D. 60, not long after Hippalus had stumbled upon the Arab's knowledge of the monsoon winds) has something to say about it. Exactly how much that chronicler or compiler knew about some of the places he describes on the African east coast is open to doubt, for his estimates of distances are so confusing and his descriptions of places so vague as to leave some doubt as to whether he ever saw them. In the thirteenth paragraph of his very brief *Periplus* (his Directory of the Indian Seas covers the whole of the Red Sea, the Gulf of Aden, the Gulfs of Oman, Persia, and Cutch, the Arabian Sea, the Swahili Coast, and the west coast of India, in sixty-six paragraphs, none of which is very long) the compiler says:

> "And then, after sailing four hundred stadia along a promontory, towards which place the current also draws you, there is another market-town called Opone, into which the same things are imported as those already mentioned, and in it the greatest quantity of cinnamon is produced (the *arebo* and *moto*), and slaves of the better sort, which are brought to Egypt in increasing numbers; and a great quantity of tortoise-shell, better than that found elsewhere."

The author of the *Periplus* goes on to say that –

> "the voyage to all these far-side market-towns is made from Egypt about the month of July, that is Epiphi. And ships are customarily fitted out from the places across this sea, from Ariaca and Barygaza, bringing to these far-side market-towns the products of their own places: wheat, rice, clarified butter, sesame oil, cotton-cloth (the *monache* and *sagmatogene*) and girdles, and honey from the reed called *sacchari*. Some make voyages especially to these market-towns, and others exchange their cargoes while sailing along the coast."

It is interesting that this cargo, listed in the year A.D. 60, was precisely the same as that which we carried down to Opone alias Haifun alias Dante in the year of grace 1939, and though Opone in these days is far from being the prosperous market-place it once was, and it is now difficult to sell these things, our group of Sindbads did their best. There were a few differences. Our girdles (by which I suppose is meant the

[1] I quote from Schoff's translation. (*Periplus of the Erythraean Sea*, translated and annotated by Wilfred H. Schoff, A.M.: Longmans Green and Co., 1912.)

folds of cloth the Somalis love to wrap about themselves, and not the feminine garment of the same name) were made in Japan, and our "honey from the reed called sacchari" was plain Javanese sugar from the Dutch East Indies, transhipped at Aden. Most of our ghee was in the Standard Oil Company's rejected containers. We had not made the voyage "especially to these market-towns," for the markets have long been run down: we were among the "others exchanging their cargoes while sailing along the coast". We saw nothing of cinnamon and tortoise-shell: all we got out of Haifun was some very dead shark. As for those slaves of the better sort, the only thing I learned about them was that they could scarcely have been of the same tribe as the present-day Somalis. The Somali is rarely a slave, and would never be a slave of the better class.

Our stay at Haifun was, I suppose, typical of the carryings on of the average dhow today. I had a few surprises, none of them particularly pleasant ones. When I had thought of this trading voyage before it was begun, I had visions of a succession of pleasant ports up African rivers and in romantic bays, staying in each while the ship exchanged her goods; but I had dreamt of these things without any knowledge of the Somali coast. Now we had come to our first port, and it was nothing but a semicircle of dull sand, the beach covered with sheep-dung and the entrails of fish, the centre of the scene a very modern saltworks sending out salt in steel buckets along an endless conveyor to a berth offshore. To the right of this salt plant were some Italian bungalows and the house of the Resident, with the Italian flag. To the left, a mean Somali village straggled along the hot beach, nondescript and squalid, soon giving up the hopeless attempt to find sustenance in such a place.

Out in the bay, one of a tier of three Kuwait ships and two Persians, we swung to our anchors, while the offshore wind blew the filth of the maindeck back over the poop and life aboard was hell. We stayed there two weeks, during which very little happened. For days nothing happened at all. Our first welcomers were a boarding party of two Italians, a Somali dispenser, and several soldiers. The Italians, having learnt from long experience the necessity for it, at once proceeded to draw up as comprehensive a list as they could manage of the persons on board. They tried hard to complete this day after day, but it was a farce. All the Suri and various other mysterious travellers had disappeared over the side as we came in, and the list, even after four days' hard work, was far from complete. It never was complete. The Somali dispenser, looking very depressed, went through the lot, scratching their arms with a piece of sharp steel and wiping in some smallpox antitoxin. I should not blame the Italians very much if they did not feel particularly welcoming about these visits of the Arab dhows, but, after all, they took the place, and this Arab trade is very old. The Arabs bring goods for Arab stores to sell to the Somali, and do not compete with any Italian trades: they could not if they wished, and they are not interested. I noticed then and always that our trade was with Arabs only, just as later I saw that the Indian kotias from Cutch and Bombay traded only with and for their own people.

Day after day, we swung there in Haifun Bay in a welter of filth and flying smuts, while the Beduin fished and fought and yelled, and nothing else happened. No one was allowed ashore (apart from the ship's own people), and I wondered what we had come there for. Being a European travelling with Arabs I was a suspect, though of what I did not know. I appeared to be taken for a British Agent or a subversive influence of some kind. Perhaps I was going to stir up trouble in Abyssinia, or spread a little unrest among the Somali, who never are very restful. I was inclined to laugh at all this suspicion, but it worried Nejdi seriously. It was real enough. He said if I was suspect, so also were the ship and himself, which was bad for trade. The Italians have agents themselves – or did have – in Iraq and the Yemen and elsewhere, none of whom spread the gospel of peaceful acceptance of this best of all possible worlds. Perhaps their own use of these perfidious propagandists helped to make them suspicious of me. Nejdi said they were always suspicious. He added that they refused to believe Lawrence was dead – he called him Yawrens – and that they were dreadfully suspicious of all Britishers and also of most Arabs. The idea of being mistaken for Lawrence, though highly flattering, scarcely held water, even amongst Beduin. Lawrence was a small man, short, and very fair; I was six feet high and, even after two months' sailing with the Arabs, still weighed 160 pounds. Lawrence was dead, as all the world knew: there was nothing mysterious about the manner of his passing.

However, there it was, and I certainly was a prisoner on board. My arm was scratched with the steel and the antitoxin rubbed into the wound by the Somali, and that was that. There I stayed. More booms came, more sambuks lay in idleness in their anchors, some of them seemingly deserted. This Arab trading was the most casual business. We just stayed there and nothing happened. Nothing, that is to say, with regard to the trade of the ship. Said and Majid and the other smugglers, who appeared again when the census of our passengers had been completed (in the meantime they lived aboard other ships which had already been cleared), began their smuggling without delay – Hamed bin Salim, Abdulla Nejdi, and nearly all the crew followed their example, and there was a great movement of haberdashery, gay rags, and diluted perfumes in little bottles to that dung-strewn beach. More often the Somali came out and themselves took the stuff. They came by night in dugout canoes, or slipped by in the shadow of the ship in their fishing boats, and stowed a bundle of sarongs beneath the fish as they passed. They were very smart. Other regular traders were whiskered Sindbads from the Suri ships who had no money and always asked for credit. They took a great deal, but what they did with the large stocks they were continually taking away, I was not sure. I think they often landed it elsewhere, at smaller ports along the open coast between Haifun and Mogadishu.

It was always very interesting for me on board, and the scene was always diverting. I did not mind not being allowed to land. Even in a dreadful place like Haifun, no day on board the *Triumph of Righteousness* was ever wholly like another. After some days I saw beauty in Haifun itself, for the encircling sandhills could be very beautiful in the sunsets and dawns.

I was still very lame and could scarcely walk, but I was happy enough on board. The monotony of the awful food did not really matter, and if the water was bad, I must have gained immunity by that time. If I were to catch any illness from our Beduin, it was a risk I had to take. A few of them showed the early stages of some minor form of leprosy.

I used frequently to marvel at the taciturn acceptance by the Beduin of whatever happened, whether expected or not, planned or not. When they came aboard in Shihr they had been told that the whole passage would take not more than ten days, yet they had been three weeks aboard before we even thought of leaving Haifun. They did not seem to mind. It is doubtful whether they even noticed the passing of so many days, for to them Allah's compassion was ever sufficient. They met no troubles half-way. I wondered what they did about food, but they could survive on very little, and fish were plentiful. They could usually get a piece of *khubz* from the ship, though most of them preferred to make their own. They liked theirs done in ashes, with plenty of the ashes left on.

Our days began long before dawn, and the muezzins began their calls to prayer some time before I could detect the faintest tinge of greyness in the eastern sky. The sheikh from Shihr, who had deposed our sailor Sultan from his monotonous job, insisted on making several extra calls each day, and his timing was too preposterous even for the Arabs. Though the Arab may not have very fixed ideas about the time, at least there are fairly well defined periods for the announcements of the five daily prayers – dawn, with the first lighting of the sky; morning, a little after the sun has passed its meridian; third, or afternoon, when the sun has lost its glare and its redness is whitening and the shadows are long; fourth, or evening, immediately after sunset; fifth, or night, any time between sunset and dawn, but usually, for the convenience of the ship, about two hours after sunset. Our sheikh from Shihr, who was a most scurvy creature and as un-sheikhlike as a Brooklyn longshoreman, delighted so in his muezzin calls that he used to make them three and four times in the same morning, sleeping between each and waking with a conception of time so hazy that he obviously did not know it was still the same day. He became so bad that Nejdi, who hated doing anything active about anything, had at last to rig up the ship's bell on a beam before the quartermaster's seat, and have the quartermaster strike the bell at the right time for the prayer calls. The bell, which looked more as if it should have been round a cow's neck than aboard a ship, had been bought from a junk-yard at Bombay, whence comes so much of the Arab dhows' seagoing gear. This new system worked for a few days, but then the quartermasters forgot. Things went on as before and, after a while, the bell disappeared down below again.

Prayers, breakfast, cooking, eating, sleeping, catching fish, cleaning fish, looking at what went on aboard the other vessels, fighting, yelling, picking off lice from sarongs and shirts – so the days passed for our Beduin at that hot anchorage, while the first-class passengers from the poop smuggled industriously.

One bright morning I watched the scene on deck. It was typical of what I might have observed any morning. On the port side, up on the small forecastle head – which was really only a working platform for the anchors and the fore tack – Jassim the cook and a passenger were methodically killing and skinning a Somali goat, a large beast which had stood tethered to the port cable during the night. On the other side of the forecastle head, three sailors cleaned fish caught during the night by Hassan the helmsman and Mohamed Amiri, who, having fished all night, were now snoring in the lee of the firebox while the Beduin milled all round them. This fish-cleaning was anything but a hygienic business. No time was wasted on such nonsense as stripping the scales, or washing out the fish; they were split with a blow from an axe, the backbone slit with a rusted knife, and the flesh pounded with coarse salt liberally mixed with whatever else might be blowing round on deck, stamped in by the sailors' feet. The deck was bloody and unscrubbed, the salt grubby and uncleaned. I lost all interest in fish, and firmly resolved to avoid all dishes with fish in them from that time onwards. (For that matter, any visit forward was enough to put me off the ship's food for all time.) When the fish had been opened and salted, they were threaded on a piece of light coir rope and hung in the sun.

In the meantime the goat-slaughtering was completed, and Jassim and the Beduin his mate were coiling the dead goat into the big pot. Watching them was a young Beduin boy with long hair and soft gentle features, who looked, but for the straightness of his lithe body, very like a girl. He wore a silver bracelet on his right wrist, and a dagger was thrust into the folds of his sarong. He was a gentle boy and he and the old chief Aura were the quietest persons on board. I wondered what had brought him down on this long voyage, bound towards Zanzibar. Once I asked him, but he did not know. He did not seem to know even where the ship was going. He was a very shy and reserved youth. I gathered that there was a famine in his tribe, and not enough food for the young men. He had heard the elders speak of opportunities in Africa; therefore he came. He was from the far interior of the Hadhramaut, near the borders of the Great Desert. Would he return there, I asked him. Most certainly, he said, for Allah was compassionate. He hoped he might not remain in Africa more than three or four years. I wondered where he would be allowed to land, and how he paid his fare, for even a few rupees are a fortune to such as he. He told me that he and some of the other young men of the tribe brought frankincense to Mukalla on their camels from the borders of the desert, and in Mukalla they sold both camels and cargo.

By the messy, smoky firebox, Jassim looking sadder and blacker than ever, squatted on the tiny forehatch and stirred the goat-pot with a piece of wood. The hatch itself was a dreadful sight, covered with pieces of goat's entrails and fish's scales, and littered with firewood, utensils, date stones, and scraps of *khubz*. Abdulla Nejdi and his gang, regardless of all else, continued their packing of "best" Basra dates. If these really were best Basra dates, Basra dates must be extremely bad, and I wanted none of them; but the label was libellous. They were very old dates which the Arabs wanted to sell to the Somali, who are not particular, and they disguised them in the new packages the better to make a sale. We had sixty large packages of these dates, shipped from some merchant's godown in Aden. There they had lain for years, awaiting a rising market.

Now, if they could not be sold to the Somali, they might as well be dumped in the sea, for no one else would have them.

Beneath the poop of the new dhow a tiny girl lay sleeping, a fat little mite in a long print dress with a black hood, her chubby small hands and her chubbier small face liberally decorated with lines of black and henna. From her ears hung silver ornaments, about ten to each lobe, which jingled when she walked. There were two heavy silver bangles round her ankles and she looked as if she were acting as transport for the family jewels. These little girls were seen on deck only in the daylight hours, for by night nothing female except the ship's cat was allowed outside the confines of the great cabin

Stretched along the rough planks of the dhow's bottom some of the Beduin lay asleep, their heads protected from the sun by the light fold of their black girdles, for the Beduin had no headcloths nor turbans. Others on the main deck, crouching wherever there was space, were preparing food over tiny fires, frying fish, boiling rice, frying *khubz*. Some ate. Some made coffee, in long-spouted brass pots designed to extract the maximum heat from the minimum number of embers. Some drank coffee. The poorer the coffee the more elaborate the manner of serving it, some of the Beduin handing round the thimbles' full of black mud as if it were nectar from the gods, bowing and clicking the porcelain cups against the spout, as though they were head waiters at the Ritz. Some answered the calls of nature in little pews along the ship's side; one cleaned out a pot, rather perfunctorily; two small boys fought and no one interfered with them. They were doing no harm. Elsewhere on the maindeck, Beduin oiled themselves, and buttered one another's hair. Aft on the poop, a Suri merchant wrapped a couple of new sarongs about his waist and two more above his knees before going ashore, for Aden sarongs brought good prices there, and he could sell them to the Arab stores. Near him a Hadhramaut child, not without viciousness in his coarse face, wolfed at a dish of rice as though he feared someone would take it from him. A dispute broke out, somewhere near the water tanks.

Old Yusuf Shirazi, squatting on a chest near me, was very busy at something, and did not even look up at this new outbreak of noise. I watched what he was doing. He was still at the same mysterious occupation I had observed off Ras Haifun. He was making medicine, though it looked like witches' brew to me. He had a number of tiny packages of seeds and things and some herbs tied up in corners of old turbans. Twisted pieces of weeds, odds and ends of leaves, dried and very ancient seeds, pieces of bark and lengths of something that looked like string – all these went in, and Yusuf pounded and mixed them industriously. What was it for? I asked him, but he replied only that it was medicine. He pointed to his eyes, which were running. Allah was compassionate, he said; it would be good medicine. He added that he was making a brew to drink, not a lotion. He was mixing the stuff in the lower half of a broken Basra pot, and he stirred it with the point of a Beduin dagger. I wished I could have done something for his eyes, but I could not. It was an old infection. It dated from his pearl-diving days, he said. He had been a pearl diver from Kuwait for years, and thanked God that he was finished with that life. It was hard on the eyes and on the lungs, to say nothing of the stomach. He stirred his brew methodically. It was the most extraordinary medicine I had ever seen.

I learned later that the 'medicine' was a concoction for increasing the flow of milk from the breasts of Beduin matrons. Yusuf wanted milk to bathe his eyes, because milk was good for them. The 'medicine' was a secret of the harim he had learned in Kuwait. It was to be used to induce a copious flow of milk from the breast of a Beduin lady in the great cabin, a matron of ripe years who had offered her co-operation.

In the background, fourteen sambuks, mainly from the Mahra coast and the smaller ports near Sur, lay at anchor as idly as ourselves, and the crew of a Suri drummed and danced while their water came on board. It was bad water, from a stagnant well. Perhaps the noise was to scare the jinns out of it.

The days passed at that Haifun anchorage, and the decks, which were never cleaned, grew filthier and filthier until the maindeck was a morass on which I was almost afraid to go. The sun shone, the Beduin yelled, the fish stank, and we still worked on the cargo. Nothing happened. I began to think we might have dropped in there by error. But if we were there by mistake, I wished the mistake could be rectified and we would go, for Haifun was no ideal anchorage, and to stay there on board an Arab dhow cooped up with a horde of Beduin had its less pleasant features.

While we lay there I had many opportunities to examine and to visit the lovely Persian baggala anchored near us, for the ban on my landing did not apply to visiting other vessels in the harbour. This was the same baggala which had sailed from Aden and Mukalla with us. She was called the *Hope of Compassion* (a name which, like our own, was sometimes changed); her nakhoda was a Persian named Sulieman Radhwan bin Said, exiled to Kuwait, her crew numbered thirty-three, and her capacity was

3,000 packages of dates. She was a lovely vessel of about 200 tons. I was surprised to see that, though she was larger than we were and had much roomier decks, she had no passengers. Nejdi said passengers would not go in baggalas; they preferred booms. The baggala, he said, was becoming extinct: baggalas were less seaworthy than booms, and their carved sterns, though stately and picturesque, were apt to be dangerous in a pounding sea. Perhaps the evil reputation of Sulieman bin Said had something to do with the baggala's lack of passengers, for I was told that the Persian exile had a hard name. He was a small man with very bright black eyes set closely in a parchment face, and his chinstrap beard made him appear almost devilish. Though he was Persian, he dressed always in the Kuwait fashion, in a long white gown, with a headcloth and *aghal* on his head. Other Persians wore their turbans wrapped tightly round their heads, bound in a smooth, almost geometric, manner which was quite distinctive. I gathered that Sulieman Radhwan no longer felt any pride in his nationality.

In the baggala were the nakhoda's two sons, cheerful boys about eight and twelve years old, who clamoured to be photographed whenever they saw me. They were apprentices, but what they learned was a matter left entirely to them. They appeared to have learned a great deal about skylarking.

The *Hope of Compassion* had been a week in Haifun before we arrived, and Sulieman gave a feast for us the next day. I was at this feast. It consisted of the usual goat and rice, served under an awning on the poop. It was at least better than our fish, and the baggala was most interesting. She was the largest of the surviving baggalas, and in many ways the most picturesque. To sit on the bench abaft her wheel, high in the afterpart of the steeply rising poop, and to look from there along the picturesque romantic sweep of her ancient decks, from the worn planks of the poop to the curved horn at the low bow, never failed to stir me, and though we saw that baggala many times again and I was aboard her on countless occasions, I always left her with reluctance. She was beautiful from outside, and she was beautiful on board. Her windowed stern was especially lovely. Its elliptical area of ancient teak was covered with intricate patterns of excellent carving, and her curved bow swept up from the sea as gracefully as the breast of a swan. She was big, for an Arab. Her oiled teak hull sat prettily in the water with a grace and strength and sweetness of line that sang of sea-kindliness, despite all Nejdi's comments on the vulnerability of her stern. I wondered how, if her stern were so vulnerable, she had managed to survive so long, for she dated back to the slaving days. She was very old – more than half a century. Like so many Arab vessels, every line of her flowed and blended perfectly into a harmonious and lovely whole, though she had been put together on the beach at Sur by carpenters who could not understand the most elementary plan. She was built by eye, and she was built beautifully, though she was but a heap of indifferent teak poorly fastened with weak iron, and, here and there, an ill-butted plank had warped, and all her fastenings wept with rust-stains from every pitted head, and caulking of poor cotton stuff poked from her sides. Her quarter-galleries were latticed delicately, like the narrow windows of a harim court: her five stern windows were protected by iron bars, and a teak shutter swung from the central window, richly carved in patterns of crescents and stars.

To step over her high bulwarks on to that spacious main deck was to slip back five centuries; for, aboard as overside, she was a craft of the Middle Ages. Her deck lay-out was almost exactly a counterpart of our own, even to the carpenter working on his new dhow. She had the same low forecastle head, the same heavy beams for belaying halliards and cables, the firebox with its crouching smoke-grimed cook; wooden water-tanks, one on each side; the great bole of the raking mainmast rising from the forward end of the long narrow main hatch, though her masts were higher than ours. Her main deck was made of worn old planks unfit to keep the water out, and her heavy bulwarks were made even higher by washboards raised two feet above them, fore and aft. She had a number of great ringbolts in the deck capable of lashing a liner's bower, and a big capstan, that looked as if it might have come out of Nelson's *Victory*, stood near the poop overhang. She was much more ornate and elaborate than our own new *Triumph*; and was obviously the product of a more leisured age. Wherever carving and embellishments could be added they had been, and the precincts of the poop were liberally decorated in this way. The break of the poop was low, and there was not headroom to walk under there, but the deck of the poop sheered high, and in the after part of the spacious great cabin there was seven feet of headroom. (This was the only Arab vessel I ever boarded which had good headroom in the poop.) The whole break of the poop was carved with a delicate tracery of involved patterns into which texts from the Qurân had been worked. The reclining bench for the officers aft was not a rough construction of unfinished wood as ours was, but an elaborately finished and well-joined piece of built-in furniture, protected by a carved teak railing, low enough to vault over and high enough to be of protection to the sleeping men – high enough, at any rate, to prevent them from being rolled outboard or flung inboard by a heavy roll. Aboard our *Triumph* we had no such protection. The baggala's poop was very different from our own, though like it in essentials – the small working capstan, the inevitable rows of chests, the rising mizzenmast towering above, the binnacle, the wheel, and the helmsman's chair. It differed in its air of hallowed age and its deep but indefinable attraction, its caressing song of untold romantic voyaging. It sang in every worn old plank of those ancient decks, and all its songs were stirring.

That poop and that whole ship put their arms round any sailorman who ever stepped aboard, and he had to love her, though she wept her caulking from her poor old planks and a fourth of all the sea over which she had ever sailed had leaked through her, and she reeked of fish-oil. Upon that poop I found my mind turn easily down channels that led to pirates and slaves and all those long-gone far-off things, and I could see again all the wondrous ships of my pre-maritime youth, when all the sea was wonderful and every ship an ark of grand adventure. How different had the reality been! Yet here, on board this ancient Arab dhow lying at that stifling anchorage, hundreds of miles from anywhere upon that forlorn coast, it was easy to dream again of the sea there never was, knowing so well the sea there is. Pirates and slaves, doubloons and gold, song and merriment, women and rum. The strange thing was that they *had* all been there – the pirates, the slaves (Swahili from Zanzibar and Mozambique), the pretty dancing girls and the travelling harim, the little slave virgins for the merchants of Sur and Oman and whoever else could buy them; and the song of Ismael and all his kind. In place of rum there was arrack from the Tigris dates, though Sulieman, a bigoted man, touched nothing of this kind. Aye, aye, pirates and slaves: both had walked here. For that matter, both walked there now. Down on the maindeck, after the meal, lately freed slaves chanted and danced merrily, and on the poop Sulieman Said was by way of being something of a pirate himself. For Sulieman Said was planning to steal a cargo in Haifun Bay, and he wanted – I believe – our Nejdi to help him.

VI

THE SONS OF SINDBAD

MYSTERIOUS THINGS HAPPENED on board that baggala. She was half-empty when we came in and I wondered where her cargo had been landed, for it was not sold in Haifun. It was sold somewhere in Somaliland. That at least was certain. In the nights, when there was no moon, I often noticed Somali dugouts and sewn boats moving silently over the harbour, making towards the place where Sulieman's big vessel lay. They went out deep-laden and they returned empty. What were they bringing out so mysteriously? None came to us. Their paddlers never chanted. They slipped by silently, unlit, furtive. After five nights of watching, I began to wonder what was going on. What were they taking off so furtively to the baggala? I racked my brains and thought of many things, from skins to ivory. The ancient trade round those parts in skins of leopards and of lions is now regulated and under government control: besides, it would have taken several thousand slaughtered beasts to fill all those boats with skins. But what were their cargoes? Ivory? That was still good stuff to smuggle – dangerous, though. I would put nothing beyond any Arab or Persian, wandering Africa way in a dhow. Whatever trade, legal or otherwise, might bring some rupees to his deep pockets he would try.

Night after night the canoes and the sewn boats continued to flit by. Yusuf said they were fishermen. The others pretended not to see them. Sulieman himself was often aboard our boom, usually coming in the mornings, very early, and going ashore with Nejdi.

One night the canoes stopped coming. The baggala was deep in the water then, and the sailors were bending her big lateen main. Yusuf said she was to sail in the morning, bound directly for Zanzibar. But in the morning something had very obviously gone wrong. The baggala did not sail. Instead, a boat full of Italian and Somali police came out and arrested Sulieman Said.

Even then I could learn nothing from my taciturn shipmates, who were, however, not so uninterested that they did not rush about and in five minutes effectively hide all the haberdashery and other trade goods which, after the first casual customs inspection, had been openly left in the chests and tied up in bundles all about the poop. Yusuf Shirazi disappeared hurriedly down the hatch of the great cabin. What he was doing down there I did not know, but I heard a great deal of yelling and shoving. I found out later that he was arranging the women on their mats, very carefully, so that they hid the tiny hatch leading to the secret chamber deep below, right in the bottom of the ship. What was in that chamber I did not know, but I could guess. Probably part of it was wads of Italian paper lire.

All these efforts were, however, unnecessary, for the Italians did not bother us. We saw them pull by in their boat, with Sulieman Said, looking very sorry for himself, seated in the stern sheets between two large Somalis. After the Italians had gone, Nejdi rushed ashore, taking all his henchmen with him – the muallim Hamed bin Salim, the Suri smugglers Said and Majid, the Seyyid from the Hadhramaut, and another red-bearded man who was prominent among the first-class passengers, one Abu Ali, who was generally vociferous on these occasions. Off they dashed in the longboat, with our sailors singing. We could see a Somali guard over the baggala. Yet even that morning, when our friend Sulieman had been apprehended for something obviously serious, Hamed, Said, Majid, and the others still smuggled. As they dashed over the side into the longboat, they all had sarongs, money-belts, and turbans lashed about them beneath their robes, round their waists, their thighs, and their knees, and their pockets were full as always of tiny bottles of blended perfumes.

But what was all this about? What had Sulieman been caught doing? I took my binoculars and kept them fixed on the baggala all day, determined to solve the mystery. I could find out nothing from my shipmates. Grins, shrugs, cheerful expressions of profound belief in the mercies of the All-Highest – this was all they granted me. It was useless to ask questions. So I watched, hour after hour, and before the day was out I learned that the Italians had discovered aboard the baggala a hold full of stolen salt, taken from the beach under their very eyes – two hundred tons of it. The unromantic nature of the cargo was somewhat made up for by the audaciousness of its theft. My first feeling was one of regret that Sulieman had not sailed with it, for to purloin all that salt was a fine gesture of contempt. The last canoe-load, apparently, and his own anxiety to be gone, had proved his undoing. He had gone along the beach by night to see that last boat-load go, and be finished with the business. A customs officer, chancing to be down upon the beach to take the air (or more probably with an eye upon some shapely Somali wench), saw the nakhoda, and followed him. After that, discovery was simple. The Somali were caught red-handed, and Sulieman with them. He blustered, but it was no use. Worse still, he was caught with the lire on him with which he was to pay for his cargo, and he had not got those lire from an Italian bank, as the regulations require. They were smuggled lire, bought illegally in the 'black' market at Aden. It looked as though Sulieman would come badly out of this business, for the Italians are even stricter about currency smuggling than the stealing of salt. The situation was rather bad.

We were not left very long in doubt about Sulieman's sad fate. I thought it might have been sadder. His lire were confiscated; the salt was taken back to the beach (this took three days of hard work, in five or six boats), and the baggala was fined one thousand rupees. This was stiff, for a thousand rupees is a large sum in the East. Sulieman had borrowed most of the lire from our ship, from whom I did not know. These were gone, and he had not a thousand rupees. In this emergency, an emissary was sent from the shore to appeal for our help. I was interested to see the instant response of all on board. Nejdi himself, Hamed bin Salim, Abdulla, Nejdi's brother, Said, Majid, and the others, the quartermasters, the serang, Kaleel the carpenter, even Jassim the cook, all went at once to their chests on the poop and, diving into their inmost recesses, brought forth all the rupees they had. Some had only two, others four or five. Hamed bin Salim had about 400, but these included some belonging to the ship. All were made available, and within twenty minutes we had over 600 rupees collected, thrown carelessly on to a headcloth by the capstan. I made up the balance, for they appealed to me as one of their shipmates. Then off went the emissary, looking relieved but still worried, to get Sulieman out of the jail. It was a bad jail, he said, and I can well believe it. I never saw it. Sulieman was freed that night and he sailed next morning. He went out from Haifun a sadder but no wiser man. What he proposed to do next to recoup his fortunes I did not know, but there would be something. Later – considerably later – we heard of the baggala being up to something down the Madagascar Channel.

It was a quiet day with a gentle breeze off the land when Sulieman sailed. The baggala showed no flag and her crew gave no cheers. The sailors hove her short, raised the peak of the lateen main, broke out her hook, and she turned upon her lovely heel and went. She was a picture of grace and beauty as she turned her carved and galleried stern to the sand of Haifun Bay and, though she went out without the cargo she had come to take and her nakhoda had to be considered an ignominious failure in his attempt at bare-faced stealing, she looked a ship of romance and real adventure as the land wind filled her great sail that morning. It took them a long time to masthead the sail which fluttered out golden in the morning air: her burnished hull slipped slowly through the blue water as if loth to depart from the scene of her shame.

What Nejdi had to do with the incident I should never have discovered by asking him, or indeed by seeking information directly from any Arab. But it was something. I saw him add some lovely Persian carpets to the pile with which Sulieman finally bribed himself out of the jail, and he would not have done that without a direct interest. Our Nejdi, like all the other wanderers with dhows, was ready for whatever turned up, though he was clever enough usually to keep his own hands out of the dirty work. It began to occur to me that perhaps the legitimate trade which we carried on so haphazardly was not our main source of income; but I did not know, at that stage of the voyage, what was. We had the villains for any perfidy – the Suri Said the smuggler and Majid the loud-mouthed, and Abdulla the Mysterious, who even then was skulking somewhere ashore, never seen by the eyes of European man. What *did* that fellow get up to? Whatever it was, I looked on him with favour. His prompt and able assistance of Ismael when the Beduin child fell overboard showed him to be a brave man. He could do what he liked in Somaliland, so far as I was concerned.

I suppose it was wrong of me to take that attitude: but I had grown to like the Arabs, especially this scoundrelly group of old Sindbads who dwelt on our poop. Sindbad himself, liar that he was, could not have concocted adventures such as were commonplace with them; Sindbad himself, that old Arab scoundrel, would not have been ashamed to ship out with us. I sometimes tried to imagine the old reprobate as one of these merchant-adventurers of ours. He must have been much the same kind of man. All our wanderers from the Gulf of Oman and the Persian Gulf were potential Sindbads, even the sailors, each with his chest of goods and his readiness for any sort of profitable adventure. Sindbad, for that matter, appears to have been more merchant than sailor; but the two callings go together in Arabia. Our smuggler-in-chief, the Suri Said, was a Sindbad, if ever there was one. So was Nejdi. So were Hamed bin Salim, Abdulla the Mysterious, the other Abdulla, Nejdi's brother, the Hadhrami Abu Ali, the Persian Sulieman Said.

I looked across at old Said, wily, wizened old devil, as he prepared himself for the shore, and thought of the many occasions when that older

Sindbad must similarly have prepared himself. Said was bound on a smuggling expedition. It was amusing to watch him prepare himself for this. First, he wrapped six money belts round his waist. Then he covered these with three sarongs of good quality. Then he added two of poor quality. A cape of tasselled and decorated turbans he slung over his bare back. That done, he wrapped more sarongs and turbans round his thighs, four to a thigh, and two more round his knees. When all this had been done, he pulled on a new gown. Over that he drew an old gown, the pockets of which he stuffed with small bottles of perfume. Then he carefully wrapped a new turban round his head. On top of that he placed his old one, first having wrapped a parcel of hashish in a knotted corner. He looked rather fat by this time, though he was naturally a very lean man. He added a few spare strings of prayer beads, made of artificial amber manufactured in Germany, to his pockets, and called loudly for his boy Mohamed, who was next loaded. Mohamed grinned delightedly during the performance, while he was dressed in four sarongs, eight turbans, two shirts, and three money belts. He grinned if only for the pleasure of having such finery to wear, for it was the only time the boy had it. Said his master dressed him well only when there was nefarious work afoot. Mohamed knew his part. When he had been dressed, he shuffled down into the longboat lying alongside, and took his place in the bows away from the merchants, who sat aft. It would not do if he landed with them. He was always the first ashore, hurrying off to the rendezvous with his load of haberdashery, and then, an hour or two later, wandering back aboard again to pass the morning swimming with Aura's baby son, and other cronies. Mohamed was a bright boy. He was one of the best smugglers aboard.

In the meantime Hamed bin Salim, Abdulla Nejdi, Abu Ali, and several strange Suri from a sambuk near by were similarly robing, and by the time the longboat was ready to go ashore it must have had several hundred rupees' worth of dry goods on board. The sailors did not have much, and preferred to keep their best goods for the better markets farther south. But they took enough. The only people in the ship who did not smuggle, so far as I could see, were the carpenter and the cook, both of whom were far too busy.

All this was doubtless illegal and ought thoroughly to be condemned, but it interested me. The Arabs made a game of it. They went off like a group of schoolchildren, happy and carefree: this sort of thing was their life. Said, the ringleader, was such a thorough and unscrupulous scoundrel, so absolutely without pretence, so genuinely and wholly what we call bad, that I rather admired him, if only for the complete straightforwardness of his perfidy, and I always watched with fascinated interest to see what he would be up to next. There was no nonsense about him; he did not play at being 'bad,' though he made a game of his smuggling. As for his obvious contempt for our regulation-ridden world, I confess I could not bring myself to blame him. We Europeans have never made the Arabs' life easier, and much of what we do was utterly inexplicable to them. They came down that coast to trade, and trade they did, and it would take more than the Italians to stop them. They had their belief in God, their own philosophy of life, and so long as what they did conformed with their own standard, I would not condemn them.

Said was a smuggler and, according to European standards, a bad man. Majid, by any standards, was even worse, but each day I found myself liking that cheerful old reprobate even better. If a man is 'bad,' there is some merit in being whole-hearted about it. Abdulla the Mysterious, too, was probably a public menace wherever he appeared, and the most innocent form of activity in which he would have been engaged was the collection of dues for some religious sect. This is an occupation disliked by the Italians and the British alike, for it is a drain upon African wealth to no good purpose. Abdulla was an agent of some kind; that at least was certain. But I liked him, too, though I rarely spoke to him, and he shared no thoughts not expressed by the prophet in the Qurân.

The list of our 'criminals,' I suppose, might be continued. Nejdi himself, if his iniquities were ever brought home to him, might languish for years in some Italian jail. Yet I hope he will keep out of one. Our Nejdi was a smuggler, too: he was an adventurer with a wandering dhow ready for whatever might turn up, and scrupulous about nothing except the tenets of his religion. Any enterprise which promised profit he would follow, but our own sea commerce surely developed much along those lines. Were not such qualities the envied merits of our glorious pioneers? Our own adventurers, wandering the globe in tiny ships, had opened up sea-routes and laid the foundation of empires; poor Nejdi was trying only to lay the foundation of a competence for himself, and none of the Arabs had much interest in empire. To him and to Said and all their kind, the complex and unworkable system of hide-bound regulations by which we seek to control our world and their world was a bad joke.

If the Arabs are contemptuous of our regulation-ridden world, I cannot find it in myself to blame them. According to their own lights, they are doing no wrong, and they are ready to face the consequences of any of their acts. They cry for no consul to aid them. They have no consuls. They are wandering seafarers doing their best to make a living, and they find that hard enough. They have a great contempt for all things Italian, for they complain that the Italians send propaganda among them in Arabia and yet harry them when they come to Somaliland. A people who cannot permit trade in their own colonies, they argue, ought quietly to withdraw from the field of propaganda.

I often yarned with our Sindbad Said during the long evenings in Haifun when I was cooped up on board. He had trodden on a splinter of rock somewhere ashore and had an infected foot. I treated this, and he was grateful. In this way we became friends and he talked to me about his life. It took a long time to get him started, and he soon stopped. Said was not a man much given to yarning, perhaps for fear of giving away trade secrets. He was reticent, like most of the Arabs. One night he told me of his youth, when he used to go down to Africa with his father Feisal, who was a trader in slaves. Said seemed to regret that those good days were passed, for, according to him, there was nothing wrong with the slave trade until the British came and stopped it. He frequently sighed to think that this lucrative business had come to an end. His father had run slaves from East Africa up to the Gulf of Oman, he said, generally landing them in Sur. He prospered greatly at this, for it was a good business. He had many wives, and many sons. (Said was the fourth son of the seventh wife.) Said himself had started off early, for he had no liking to stay home when the big baggalas were sailing. When he was about six years old – Said was hazy about ages and years – he went with his father to a place called Bagamoyo, on the coast of Africa opposite the island of Zanzibar. That time they went up into the Congo.

At other times they went into Abyssinia. From Asab and a place near Djibouti, but that was only to buy girls. Lovely girls, Said said with a sigh, but he had been too young to appreciate them. Eventually they drifted to other trades, finally running Baluchi girls from Baluchistan across to Oman: but fate, in the shape of the British navy, caught up at last with them, and they had to go into other fields. The father died. Said drifted about. He went here and there, buying and selling, always travelling in dhows with his cargoes. He smuggled; he ran contraband; he ran arms; but he never stole. He had, he said, done well out of the European war, from 1914 to 1918. He had been in the arms business at Muscat then: it was a good business. He ran arms up the Persian Gulf and landed them for the Beduin to carry to the Turks, to help them in their fight against the Arabs under Lawrence. I ventured to suggest that this activity was unpatriotic: were not the Arabs fighting for independence and unity? Said did not see the point. Profit was his motive, and he was not ashamed of it. If he had not run the arms, he said, somebody else would have. It was a good business. It was money from the infidel, which any of the faithful might lawfully take. Later he ran arms to Afghanistan. That was even better. He seemed to like the arms business, not only for its profits, but for its danger. Said seemed to delight in a job of smuggling or a piece of arms-running well done, and he certainly had the temperament for both occupations. But what about arms now, I said. Were there no more to be run anywhere? Well, I'm here, said Said, and I've got no arms here. I gathered that arms-running had fallen on evil days.

The old smuggler rubbed henna into his beard to redden it, while he squatted on the officers' bench of that romantic boom, and now and again shouted for the boy Mohamed to bring embers for his pipe. Astern of us Sulieman's baggala lay swinging to her anchors (for this was before she had been caught), and I thought, as I looked at her dark shape and glanced from her to the profile of old Said beside me, what a wealth of exciting adventure still exists in this seemingly dull world. There, under the African sky, at that quiet, forlorn anchorage, this smuggler talked to me of slaves and slavery as a going business – his relatives, he said, still carried it on somewhere in Oman – and I found myself liking him. According to him much of the British anti-slavery propaganda was overdone, for the conditions in slavers such as the big baggala then astern of us were, he said, no worse than those aboard our own crowded boom. It was a mistake to look at these vessels and their goings-on only through European eyes. Africans carried off to Arabia were invariably better for the change. Did I not see this, on board the boom? For she was half-manned with the descendants of these people. A third of the population of his own Oman, he said, had African blood – and a good life they led, or at any rate a satisfactory one.

When we had been ten days at Haifun it was announced that we should sail on the morrow. When we had been there twenty days, I was listening to the same announcement with less and less interest. We had watered the ship – I didn't see why we hadn't just filled our tanks from the sea, for Haifun water was so salty that I could not drink it – we sold a boat for a hundred rupees to some Somali fishermen; we tried to sell the bad dates from Aden, and failed, because the port medical officer, an Italian, would not allow them to be landed; and we exchanged a little of our rice and sugar for some very high dried fish. This was the sum total of our proceedings at Haifun, so far as the regular business of the ship was concerned. Beyond these things, and all the hashish and haberdashery and whatever else our Sindbads smuggled, we left nothing behind us at Haifun.

Nothing, that is, but the body of a girl, who died in the great cabin. She was a young girl, aged perhaps fifteen, but by Arab standards she was a woman and she was going to Zanzibar to be married. One morning Yusuf Shirazi came quietly over to me where I sat on the poop watching a small boom come in from Batina, and said in Arabic, "Come, O Nazarene; a woman has died." He said it so calmly that for the moment I did not grasp the message. What, a woman dead? From what, and how? But Yusuf did not know. It was a young woman, he said: she died. That was all he knew. She was in the great cabin now. Would I come? The faith of the Arabs in my inconsiderable medical knowledge, merely because a few clean dressings I had put on some wounds did good, was pathetic. Here was death, and they thought somehow I could cope with it.

Nejdi was ashore. So were Hamed bin Salim, and Abdulla Nejdi, Said, Majid, and the Seyyid from Mukalla. I asked Yusuf if he was sure the girl was dead. He answered that he was, in a manner that permitted no doubt. Then there was nothing I could do about it. When I heard of death and serious illness aboard that dhow I always feared epidemics and grave infections, for the conditions were such that had any bad illness come, the prospect for all of us would have been serious. Yusuf said the girl had not been sick: she just died. How? I asked him: did someone kill her? He did not know. She had taken a little *khubz* and some sweetened tea, and she fell back and died. She had not said anything. He was there at the time. He had not noticed, for he was doing some work and paying no attention to the women. One of the older women saw the girl fall back, and then they saw that she had died.

I told him to send a boat ashore for the doctor and Nejdi, for I would not go down until Nejdi came. If the girl was dead I could do nothing. Even if she had been seriously ill, I could have done nothing. But I would have tried. No one else was ill, according to Yusuf. All the occupants of the great cabin had been healthy enough, until then.

After about an hour Nejdi came with a Somali medical dresser, and we went down. The news had been kept quiet, though somehow the report of death had spread and, for once, conditions were fairly peaceful on board.

In the great cabin the scene was unforgettable. I had not been there since the women had come aboard: no man had, except Yusuf. They had now been cooped up there about a month. The place had been cleared a little, and the stores and ship's gear moved to the sides, well aft: the bulkhead across the fore part was firmly secured. It was so gloomy that, even with the hatch open, it was impossible to see when we first came in from outside, for the hatch was very small and gave little light. Through the small open port on the starboard side one ray of sunlight came, losing itself rapidly among a pile of blocks and tackles and empty ghee jars, piled in that corner. After a moment or so, I could see. I saw the women grouped about. There must have been twelve or more, sitting bundled up in black on mats and Beduin rugs. Only their eyes showed, and their eyes watched us. I felt all those eyes on me. In that dull gloom I did not at first see the place where the dead girl was. Then I saw that she was in the centre, lying on the floor. Her face was uncovered, now that she was dead. I looked at it and saw, to my surprise, that she had been lovely. It was a startling face to come upon in a place where I had not imagined anything lovely to be. Though I had been with the Arabs for some time, this was the first time I had seen the face of a marriageable young girl. I had not known they could be so beautiful.

The ship swung to her moorings and the light from the port, diffused and golden, swept across the gloom, reaching to the girl. Poor child, even in life she had never belonged down there in that dreadful place, among that crowd of older women who huddled from her suspicious, almost animal-like, watching not her but us. She ought never to have been in that frightful travelling prison, delivering her to a harim in Zanzibar, to a husband she had never seen, in an island far from home. Her skin was like ivory, her features delicate, her little profile gentle and very lovely. Her small mouth was firm and well formed. Her black hair was rich and beautiful, and her eyes were closed as if in sleep. Her dress was of black satin decorated with hand-sewn wire of gold, for someone had put her in her bridal gown. Her small hands lay folded on the half-formed breasts, which were small and delicately rounded. The light moved from her and left the place in which she lay under a dark pall of gloom, but I found myself unable to take my eyes from that dead face. The other women huddled there, silent. One old woman, veiled with the Beduin eye-slitted mask instead of the all-covering veil of the town harim, moved closer, stared at the Somali dresser, and stared at me.

"From what did she die?" she said.

Merely from being there, I should have thought: such loveliness could not survive that fetid, frightful gloom. Yet they said she had been happy. Accustomed always to hardship – she was from inland, near the desert's edge – she had not found the great cabin so bad as it seemed to me, but she must have missed fresh air. The fact that she was going far from her home to marry a man she had never seen had not troubled her, for that is woman's lot in Arabia. The stench of the place was nauseating – the fumes of the bad ghee and all the other mysterious things of the ship's stores, the ship's own aroma of foul bilgewater and fish-oil, the unpleasant odour of the cramped-up human beings. It was as much as I could do to stay down there at all, with the hatch open and the two ports, and the ship quietly moored at anchorage. Yet here this poor girl-child had lived a month. No wonder she was dead: I do not see how she could have stayed alive.

The Somali could assign no cause for her death other than heart failure.

"All hearts fail at death," Nejdi said: "do you know no more than that?"

But the Somali did not. Neither did I.

In the presence of the dead girl Nejdi seemed awed a little, and he swept a look of scorn at the other women. I discovered later that he suspected one of them of having poisoned her, for there was a woman there from the same harim, a woman sent from Zanzibar to collect this pretty virgin. Perhaps an older woman little cares to see fresh loveliness come to her lord's harim. It was all fantastic to me, like so much of what went on in that dhow. Nejdi was relieved that it was not smallpox or anything like that: a simple case of heart failure was straightforward enough. It was not his business to find out what had caused it.

In the late afternoon they buried her, taking her ashore in the sternsheets of the longboat. Nejdi had gone then. Hamed bin Salim had charge of the boat and, even in the funeral procession, he still smuggled. He was not the only one who put a few extra money-belts and sarongs about his waist and knees before he went down into the boat, for Said, Majid, and the others were also there, and the boy Mohamed, not grinning now, sat in a new gown and turban up in the bows. The slight small body was covered with a black veil and wrapped in a date-frond mat. It lay in the stern-sheets in the midst of life, for the boat was crowded, and with the Beduin singing quietly and the sailors pulling at the oars, the boat was gone. I did not go to the funeral. These were Muslims and this was their ceremony. But I was sorry for the poor girl, and wondered long about her.

The following day she was apparently forgotten. In the next port I heard Nejdi deny that there had been any deaths on board.

A few days later we left Haifun. We came out from the harbour past a German steamer loading salt, and four other Arab vessels sailed with us. The wind was light, and we passed a boom coming in which was more crowded with people than any vessel I had ever seen, even among the Arabs. She was a small vessel, very decrepit, and her teak hull looked as if it had been long without oil. Her sail was tattered, her mast spliced in two places, and her rigging festooned with Irish pennants. But she came in bravely in the morning sunlight, her white sail bellied in the easy breeze, and the white-bordered red flag of Trucial Oman fluttered at her staff aft. Her decks were so crowded that the lowered sail looked as if it must smother a hundred people, and the sailors had to run across the passengers' shoulders. That boom could not have had a waterline of sixty feet, for she was very small, yet she had at least two hundred passengers, ninety per cent of whom were large, bearded men. They were hanging over the rail and jostling one another, all dressed in long brown shirts and loosely rolled turbans. She passed close by us. Nejdi exchanged greetings with her nakhoda, an old man with a long grey beard. He said he was twenty days out from Sur, and had met nothing but light winds.

That little boom was an extraordinary sight. She was so crowded that four men sat across the nakhoda's bench, which was large enough only for him, while six more sat on the rail behind. Men sat along the mizzenyard and out on the stemhead. Men hung all along the rails on both sides, and the decks were so crowded that it must have been impossible for anyone to sleep. All round the rail outboard hung bundles and bales of belongings, very poor. Up forward the crew were banging Indian drums. How so small a ship could be cleared from any port with so many human beings on board I did not understand. Why, I asked Nejdi, did so many Arabs wish to leave their country at once, in so poor a vessel? Nejdi said there was trouble between Sharjah, the next port up the coast, and Dabai, whence the boom hailed – political trouble, bad enough to culminate in a local war. He left me to gather that perhaps these people from Dabai crowding that boom were fleeing from the war; but Hamed bin Salim said there was famine round Dabai and all the Trucial coast was so poor that anyone might gladly leave it, even in a sixty-foot boom crowded with two hundred people. Old Yusuf Shirazi said that it was just an excursion from Dabai to Zanzibar and they had all come along for the ride.

We sailed on slowly down the Somali coast, which seemed nothing but a reach of bald dull sand, and the way was so easy and the conditions so good that it was like walking down a street. All the navigating we did was to sail merrily on before the north-east wind, with Africa on our right-hand side. At first the wind was very quiet, but afterwards it began to freshen, and we made nine knots. There was no way of measuring the speed, for there was not even a chip-log on board, but I could get a good idea by noting the times when we were abeam of the different points. By day we kept close in beside the coast, which was everywhere monotonous and dull; by night we hauled out a little, though not much, for it was obvious that Nejdi feared to lose sight of the land.

When it breezed up, the Beduin were seasick again and the conditions were bad. They went about sniffing at lemons, with their noses and ears caulked with paper-wads, but it did not help: they were violently, noisily, horribly ill, and the sailors laughed. The breeze freshened on the second day until it was blowing really strong, so that we were unable to carry the big sail. The seams began to split. The *Triumph of Righteousness* could not stand much weather. The conditions, though fresh, were only those of a good trade-wind day, such as would be perfect for any grain ship or any reasonably well-kept European vessel; but the boom began to show weaknesses. The mast worked on its step and jerked with the rolling; the mizzen halliards carried away; the mainsail split its seams so badly that in mid-afternoon Nejdi ordered it lowered and unbent. The only way the area of that sail could be reduced was by changing it, by lowering the big sail, taking off a piece at both ends of the long lateen yard, and bending a smaller mainsail to the shorter yard. This the sailors now did, and it was prodigious labour. It took about two hours. With the sail down the boom rolled and pitched, though not badly. Though she had then no canvas set and presented little windage to the breeze, I was glad to see that she kept a little way and was controllable. When the new sail, which was several cloths smaller than the old and had a much shorter hoist, was being set, it blew out some seams too, and had to be lowered again and repaired. This all hands did by sitting on it and stitching away at the seam with their inadequate bent iron needles.

Afterwards, so long as the fresh wind lasted, this was a daily occupation. Yet it never occurred to Nejdi to make a better sail. I ventured to suggest a few minor improvements which would have prevented much of this work and loss of way, but he replied that Allah was compassionate. The breeze would die down: the sail was all right. Hamed bin Salim admitted, however, that they liked their sails that way, poorly sewn with the round seams, because then the sails would always give in the seams first in strong winds. Not only that, but if the sail were too strong it might carry the mast away in a puff of wind. It was better to lose an indifferent sail than a good mast. There was sense in this argument. But the constant inefficient repairing of the weak seams and the frequent hoistings of the heavy yard made a great deal of unnecessary work. This reflection, however, occurred to no one but me. According to the Arab mariners all work was unnecessary, on general principles, but that which Allah in his wisdom made unavoidable they would do.

During this stage of the voyage we often saw other vessels similarly engaged in repairing sails, and we once passed a small jalboot from Sur which had been dismasted. Once by night we even saw a dhow showing a light, which was most unusual: actually she was showing three lights, but they were all hurricane lamps on the maindeck to light the mariners at their work of repairing the sail.

Sometimes the ship laboured heavily, but even under these conditions she ran very well and did not make much water. I was surprised to see that the Arabs never made a move towards securing anything, or forestalling any emergency. Whatever was going to happen they allowed to get started before they did anything about it. For instance, the rows of sea chests and passengers' belongings on the poop, which stood there all through the voyage, were never secured, though it was apparent that the ship's motion must dislodge something. I got some lashings and secured my own chest so that it would not hurt anybody; but, even when they saw me do this, the Arabs made no move to secure their own. Perhaps Nejdi thought that, with so many human beings packed between them, the chests on the poop could not find room to move; but they did. In the middle of the night the ship, lifted by a quartering sea, took a violent roll, and all the chests on the starboard side rolled down alee. Instantly there was a wild yelling and screaming, followed by some groans. Chests rolled with a wild clamour; tins rolled with an even wilder banging; the first-class passengers pitched across the deck; Beduin yelled. There might have been a serious accident, but fortunately no one was hurt, and in a little time the barefoot sailors, chanting as they worked, had succeeded in getting the chests back again in their rightful places. Then they lashed the chests there, at last, but very badly. They lashed only those which had moved.

No sooner had they finished this, and the ship settled down again, than she took another bad roll, and the carpenter's new dhow, which also was never properly shored up or otherwise secured, fell over on twelve Beduin who were sleeping beneath it. Now there was a screaming. One of the Beduin was pinned underneath, and he, poor wretch, began to roar very loudly. The sailors moved the dhow in time, and got all the Beduin out. The one who had been pinned beneath was not even bruised, and in the morning when I looked for him I could not find him. Not that he would have accepted medical attention, for the Beduin were all scornful of that.

About this time Nejdi began to complain of a bad back. There were very severe pains in the back of his neck and below his shoulderblades, he said, which was not to be wondered at, for he always slept in the dew and insisted on removing the slight protection of the awning long before nightfall. He said the awning interfered with his view of the sail and his senses of the wind by night, and therefore it must come down. He asked me to remove the pain from his back, and I tried, using liniments; but he slept again in the dew and the pain returned worse than ever. Then he poured scorn upon all Christian remedies and called for a good Muslim from the maindeck, a Suri who lived under the break of the poop. This man went to work in great style, and I watched with interest what he did. He stripped Nejdi down to an Indian sarong and placed him in a clear space on the poop. Then he poured hot ghee on to the nakhoda's back. After that he got really down to work. He pounded, punched, smacked, twisted, pinched, and flogged Nejdi's back until even the stolid Nejdi almost shrieked. He picked up the flesh, of which there was very little to spare, in handfuls that he must have been tearing from the bones, and Nejdi started violently. He rolled handfuls of it in the hot ghee, and Nejdi squirmed; he punched and pounded up and down the nakhoda's backbone, and Nejdi had to hold himself up with his hands braced against the deck. How that Suri worked. He pounded Nejdi for a good two hours. After that, Nejdi, pronouncing himself cured, dragged on his long shirt and staggered to his bench, but I ventured to suggest that the treatment was so drastic it had made him forget the ailment. He now had to recover from the treatment as well as the ill. At this he scowled, saying that Arab medicine was vastly superior to European. In this instance he was probably right. The application of hot ghee and the very through massage of the affected parts were both good treatments, though two days later poor Nejdi was just as bad again.

At Haifun we had embarked several new mysterious passengers, all Suri, who came out from different hiding-places when the ship was at sea.

One of them was a blind man with a young son and a one-eyed servant. The one-eyed servant saw but poorly with his surviving eye, which was the only one between the two of them. They had come from Muscat and were bound down to Zanzibar to see some relatives. We also shipped an English-speaking Suri who said he had business in Mogadishu. He took his place as one of the first-class passengers, eating the ship's food, and I soon saw that his business was smuggling too. He had his merchandise with him, tied up in bundles, and joined in the daily conferences which were led by Hamed bin Salim and Said. These worthies frequently counted large sums in paper lire, which they tied up in the corners of sarongs and turbans and stowed away. They always counted the money and stowed it in full view of all hands, for they had no fear of theft.

I took a hearty dislike to this new Suri of ours, and he remained one of the few Arabs that I did not like. He spoke with a whining voice: he had enough English to be a considerable nuisance (for he knew just enough never to get anything right and to misinterpret everything, at the same time holding the opinion that he had no more to learn) and he always called me "his very dear friend." This I was not, but I had to put up with him. He said his father was a merchant of Sur, owning two baggalas which he sent trading to India. He himself – his name was Mohamed – usually commanded one baggala and his brother the other. This year, however, his father had laid up one of the ships and had sent Mohamed down the African coast to look over the prospects there. This at any rate was Mohamed's version of his voyage, but Nejdi, who also did not like him, had another. He said Mohamed, being a very bad nakhoda, had lost his baggala, and that now, having been kicked out of his home, he was making a smuggling voyage on his own. I don't know which version was correct, but my natural prejudice led me to prefer the second. Mohamed the Suri was no addition to the amenities of the vessel, and to try to follow him in English was much more wearying and considerably less effective than to cope with anyone else's Arabic, though I still had but little of that difficult tongue.

One Friday we sailed past a place called Obbia. Friday being the Muslim Sabbath, no unnecessary work was being done and no necessary work sought for, and all hands had their fill of looking at the roadstead. All we could see were a radio station, a resident's house complete with flag, and the inevitable sand. Obbia is about 350 miles from Haifun and some 260 from Mogadishu: having been then only two days at sea, we were not doing badly. Off Obbia, and all the way down this coast, we caught large numbers of fish, especially big bonita, albacore, and those bull-headed lovely fish that sailors know as dolphin. We also saw many flying-fish, and a considerable number of these fluttered over the side. The Beduin promptly pounced on them and the unfortunate ship's cat had not a chance. The cat was a poor little thing which had been sired by a Suri tom out of a stray at Berbera, and it led a miserable life on board. Its principal duty was to keep down the livestock in the great cabin, but that place was so depressing that even the cat turned up its nose at it.

We caught our fish by the simple method of trailing lines astern – seven of them, no less, trailing from the cutter, the davits, the quarters, and wherever else on the afterpart of the poop they could be attached. At first small flying-fish were used as bait, large hooks being threaded through them, but as soon as the fish began to bite the sailors used pieces of the white skin cut from the bellies of the fish. This seemed to be a better lure. Some days we caught as many as twenty or thirty large fish, when conditions were good and the ship was making the right speed: sometimes, too, a fish was roasted in the ashes. Compared with the rest of the food we had, these ash-roasted fish were grand.

We passed other Italian outposts – Athelet (otherwise Itala) and Warsheikh. These were poor places, seen from the sea. They were mainly distinguished from the sand round them by an Italian flag flying over a bungalow, though Warsheikh had an Arab house or two. We did not go into any of these places, for Nejdi said it would be a waste of time. It seemed to me he was right.

All this time the filth and dirt on the squalid maindeck had been steadily accumulating until the place was frightful and I wondered that any human beings could survive in such surroundings. I kept to my six feet of the bench aft, behind the Sindbads and the other first-class passengers, and thanked God there was a fair wind to blow the maindeck rubbish forward. During this stage of the voyage I found that the disadvantages of the life increased rather than diminished. Yet those Arabs were a good lot and, with a few exceptions, likeable. The few I actively disliked were not Arabs – the quarrelsome half-Somali; the noisy Hadhrami-Malay with his infernal gramophone; the shrill, despicable little shrew-faced bint, who still ran about the deck all day and maltreated the little boys.

If the general capacity of the Arabs to tolerate squalor far exceeded my own, and they could create hardships at sea of which I never before had dreamed, they were men. Even in the midst of noise and filth and squalor, the stately bearded Beduin from the desert maintained the little courtesies of their daily lives, the greetings, the mannerly respect towards one another, the proper decorum at the tribal eating mats, the ceremonious serving of the dreadful coffee. The constantly cramped quarters, the crowds, the wretched food, the exposure to the elements, the daylong burning sun and the nightlong heavy dews, if they continued to be disadvantages, were far offset by the interest of being there, and the voyage never became monotonous. There were occasions when I wished it would, if only for the sake of a moment's quiet; but it never did.

As we came nearer to Mogadishu our passengers, thinking they were to land there, preened themselves and got out clean clothes. As we ran on past that Somali sand, Said and Majid and Abdulla the Mysterious and the others got out their mascara and their henna, reddened their beards, and hennaed their palms and the soles of their feet, the Seyyid from Mukalla and his henchman Abu Ali leading in these arts. One of the quartermasters shaved Nejdi who, being a nakhoda, never shaved himself, and another shaved Hamed bin Salim. Said the smuggler was a lavish user of henna, and of mascara for his eyes, and when dressed to go ashore, looked rather like a nightmarish version of a chorus-boy with a beard. Doubtless he felt very good. The sailors shaved off all their hair and beards, keeping only their moustachios, as is the Kuwait and the Persian style.

In the sunset on the fifth day we picked up Mogadishu light. It was hazy and we ran on, though it was blowing fresh. It was long after nightfall when we headed towards the town, the lights of which were bright and numerous. Mogadishu seen by night from the sea looked a big place, and interesting.

VII

TROUBLE AT MOGADISHU

Mogadishu, or Mogadiscio, or Mogdishu, or Magadoxo, to give the place but a few of its many names, is a poor harbour under any of them, for it is a mere indentation in the north-eastern African coastline fronting the Indian Ocean. There is a breakwater sheltering a lighter basin for the landing of cargoes, and this is also used as an anchorage for native vessels. We came into the roads on the Saturday night, and all that night it blew hard. The sheltered basin of the dhow harbour is difficult to enter in the dark, and Nejdi fetched up off the breakwater's end, with the ship rolling and pitching in the open sea and the shelter of the breakwater close under her lee. I did not blame him for not going into so narrow and congested a place by night. It was difficult to see, and it would have been easy to put the ship on the rocks. The margin of safety for making that entrance is small: I wondered that he even thought of trying it.

All night the wind increased and the sea got up until it was breaking right over the breakwater, and our situation there in the open sea was anything but pleasant. At first we lay to two anchors, then three. Before the morning it was five. The big Arab dhows go plentifully supplied with ground tackle, for most of the harbours where they lie are foul. I had never seen a ship lie to five anchors before. She had so short a scope of cable to each of them that their number was no guarantee of her safety, and I watched apprehensively lest she should drag. I was not alone in my apprehension, for neither Nejdi nor Hamed bin Salim slept that night, and before the sunrise, when I saw that she had dragged a little and the rocks alee were perilously close, I put my few valuables in my pockets and prepared to swim for it if necessary. Those rocks under our stern were nasty things, jagged and ugly: we should have been on them in a minute if our cables had parted, and the cables were nothing but cheap ship-laid coir made out of coconuts from India.

However, they held, and we lay in safety through that wild night. Dawn showed the sea still rising, though the wind quietened a little then, and though we plunged and rolled all that long day the ship was not again in danger. By mid-afternoon we were able to take up two of the anchors and lay then to three. These anchors were let go from different places on both sides of the low forecastle-head, and being each to so short a scope of cable, and the wind being constant and strong enough throughout to overcome the force of the tide, they did not foul. The *Triumph* normally had three anchors ready at her bows and two more stowed on deck there, handy enough – though often beneath the ship's firewood and all the sleeping crew – and another large bower aft. With her sails lowered and the lateen yard stowed fore and aft, the ship presented little windage, apart from the high poop, for her masts were bare and she had very little rigging.

With daylight, in spite of the weather, a small longboat from one of the Sur dhows in port came out to us. Her nakhoda came on board. He reported the Italians were not allowing any Arab passengers to land. This was bad news, for here we were with over a hundred of them who imagined they were bound to that place. At last we had arrived only to be told they could not land. Nejdi, who never believed in meeting trouble half-way, kept this knowledge from them, and though many were now seasick again from the violence of the motion at the anchorage – it was far worse than being at sea – they continued to prepare to land. Nejdi went ashore with the Suri, though this was probably in defiance of all port regulations. Afterwards I noticed Abdulla the Mysterious had gone too, though I did not see him go. Others of the Suri were also missing, including Majid, Said the smuggler, and the blind man from Haifun. Mohamed, the small boy, always disappeared on such occasions. I saw none of these go, though I was watching.

There was no need for them to hurry, for no boarding officers came out to us. We stayed there, pitching and rolling, and life aboard that day was almost completely miserable. Sprays drove over the vessel, wetting the whole maindeck; the fresh monsoon blew cold in that exposed place, though it was almost directly under the equator; the Aden water had all gone, and there was very little left to eat. Fish which had been caught the previous day was already high, though we ate it, and the half-caste Somali from Shihr yelled and fought all day while he assembled his possessions for landing. When we anchored, the rudder was always immediately allowed to swing, and now it banged back and forth until I feared it would burst from its gudgeons. No one else was worried, but poor Jassim at the firebox spent a day of torment. The wind blew the smoke of his camel-thorn fires back over him and all the ship.

With the ship head to wind, dust and dirt and débris and filth blew everywhere. That day was pandemonium, and, before the day was out, I wondered how much more I could stand of it.

The Beduin and the others from the Hadhramaut, when they were not being seasick, chanted words of praise to Allah for their safe deliverance, though they were still by no means safe, and they had not been delivered.

Nejdi came back before nightfall, coming out in a small Diesel tug which he had hired to tow us behind the breakwater. This ought to have been a simple manœuvre, but it was a mess. By that time Hamed bin Salim had disappeared: I think he went off with some merchandise in a Somali fishing-canoe. Nejdi stayed in the tug, and only his brother Abdulla was on board. It was typical of the Arabs that though they had been expecting a tug all day they had no tow-line ready, or anything else. The tug barged and bumped into the ship heavily alongside waiting for a line. Nejdi yelled; the passengers yelled; the serang and the sailors ran and chanted. Hassan the helmsman, sent to connect the rudder chains, became so interested watching the tug bump into us that he did not do his job, and no one made him, so that we started off behind the tug with only one chain connected, and had to stop and drift until the other was made fast. Kalifa, the other helmsman at the wheel, murmured "As Allah wills" in response to every shouted order until I felt like swearing at him, for Allah was not steering the ship, but he was. He insisted on sitting in the chair at the wheel though he could not see over the passengers crowding the poop and all the deck, and when I suggested he should stand up he was grievously insulted.

"Starboard, starboard!" Nejdi would shout from the tug, waving his arms violently.

"Starboard, starboard!" repeated Abdulla, standing on the bench aft.

"As it pleaseth the Lord," Kalifa murmured piously, shoving the wheel hard over the wrong way and causing the ship to take a horrible sheer, while the water shoaled and the little tug, puffing and panting, was having hard work to hold us. The passengers kept up a constant din, and the small boys raced everywhere, while one of the Somali's goats got loose on the deck and began to eat up the halliards. A wire hawser used for heaving in the last bower, led to the capstan aft, carried away and hit the sailor Sultan across the head, laying his skull open until the blood poured into the waterways. They brought him to me and I marvelled that he was still conscious. The blow would have fractured the skull of any lesser man, and it made even Sultan depressed and thoughtful. I cleaned it up, stopped the bleeding, and bandaged it hurriedly and temporarily, hoping he was not seriously injured. He went back to his work. When the hawser carried away the capstan took charge and threw out its bars, which scattered with murderous force in all directions. How they avoided striking any of the passengers who pressed around I cannot imagine. For my own part, if they had been struck then I should not have minded. Now the anchors were away and the tug moved ahead, dragging us slowly from the rocks. Nejdi yelled again. Abdulla yelled in answer, the passengers shrieked, the Seyyid prayed, the goats bleated, and the astonished and depressed kitten scampered out of the way of galloping bare feet and hid behind a ghee-jar.

From our exposed and dangerous anchorage to the shelter of the basin behind the breakwater was only a short distance, and the Arabs aboard the other twelve or fourteen dhows already there watched us with interest that turned to apprehension as we came, for we bore down right upon them and there seemed nothing the little tug could do to keep us straight. The wind was still fresh, the *Triumph* was a large dhow, the tug very small and its handling most inexpert. Finally, as we came in close among the tiers of anchored vessels, the tug coughed and gave up the struggle. The serang threw three anchors overboard, two of which, unfortunately, were no longer connected to their cables. The tug made off, taking Nejdi with it and, in the predicament which followed this unorthodox manœuvre, the ship was in the charge of no one. She took complete charge of herself, for the single anchor could not hold her, and she drove down upon the tier of anchored vessels. First we crashed into a small ex-pearling jalboot from Bahrein, and having given her a resounding thwack midships which made all her timbers creak and groan, and carried away a considerable part of her bulwarks along the starboard side, we drove next into a Suri sambuk with a deckload of cows. The cows, fast in little stalls on top of the cargo, became frantic and tried to break out; our mizzen-boom caught in the rigging of the sambuk's main, and the protruding end of the lateen yard carried away, falling on a cow. The passengers yelled and stampeded; the serang and the sailors worked furiously to get the longboat over the side – a thing which should have been done hours earlier – to carry out moorings; and the whole of the waterfront looked on with interest.

Still we charged about that congested harbour, next side-swiping a Batina boom with fish and passengers.

It was a thoroughly bad show, and, when at last the tug brought Nejdi back he was in a frightful temper. It was not the damage done which bothered him, but the loss of prestige caused by such a public exhibition of poor seamanship.

Apart from the damage to the ex-pearler, the carrying away of part of the mizzenyard, and the breaking of Sultan's head, nothing really serious had happened. The anchors which had been thrown overboard without cables were easily recovered, for all the Kuwaiti sailors are also pearl-divers. Long before midnight the ship was moored; the cows astern of us slept soundly; and all was peace and quiet again, except for a conference of Suri, Persians, and Nejdi, which went on far into the night all round the place where I wished to sleep. What this conference was about I did not bother to learn then, for after that long day and the preceding night I was tired. It was easy enough to guess. It was about landing passengers, and restrictions on trade, and the misdemeanours of the Italian shore officials. In this conversation I heard many references to rupees and lire and many uncomplimentary remarks about the Italians. What method of overcoming the difficult restrictions of the port was being planned by those bearded, hooded conspirators I do not know, but I later learned that it was effective.

Nejdi presided over this meeting, as he was to preside over many similar ones during our stay. He had taken the *Triumph* into Mogadishu the previous year, homeward bound with cargo and passengers from the south, and he knew the ropes.

In the morning (by which time a considerable quantity of the trade goods the ship had brought but had not manifested, were already delivered to the Somali and other vessels) the boarding officials came, and after curtly shouting from their launch, without even bothering to come aboard, that no one could land, left again. This news fell upon the ears of our multitude as a sad and bitter blow. What, not land? After coming all this way? After paying their fares, and making this sea voyage of many days? The Beduin who had not travelled before appeared bewildered, and the Hadhrami and the others who were not making their first voyage were incensed. Some of them stormed up on the poop and began to shout at Nejdi who, saying it was the Italians' business and not his, went ashore. After a while most of the passengers quieted down, and they began to murmur again that Allah was compassionate, and to express the hope that the Italians would return and lift the ban on them, at least partially. Though it must have been a very serious matter to all of them – some of the Beduin had even put on clean clothes, bought carefully from long savings in the Hadhramaut for this very occasion – the resignation with which most of the Arabs accepted this bad news was admirable. Exceptions were the quarrelsome ones, particularly the half-caste Somali, who kept up a constant screaming, and a number of the Hadhrami who scowled and said that the Italians had been glad enough to impress them for labour on the Asab road and other enterprises. For the rest, *inshallah*, either a day would straighten things out at Mogadishu, or Allah would see them safely delivered somewhere else – Lamu, Mombasa, or Zanzibar. Many were beginning to run out of food, and there was no fishing at those moorings. During the day a small boom came in from Batina, the one which had been with us at Haifun, and her two hundred passengers were added to the list of the unwanted.

It might be said, on the Italians' behalf, that it is difficult for them to enter Arabia, and, except perhaps in parts of the Yemen, they are given no encouragement. It must be admitted, moreover, that one look at half our passengers would condemn them as undesirable anywhere. The Italians, pouring money desperately into their East Africa in the attempt to get some back again, and pouring still more into their new Abyssinia, look askance on wanderers from Arabia whose only aim is to take money out instead of contributing to the national wealth. They are scarcely to be blamed if they look upon the average Arab as not the best kind of immigrant. Whatever their propaganda agents may have said elsewhere, in Mogadishu they made it clear that they look upon the Arabs as a dirty, dishonest, and disunited horde, avaricious, fanatic, and quarrelsome – unskilled, covetous, lawless, and undesirable migrants from almost every point of view. They accused them of being at the bottom of every illicit trade, and of rarely producing anything other than schemes for the furtherance of various forms of intrigue and smuggling. They feared the Arabs as possible sowers of discord among the Somali and the Abyssinians. In short, except as coolie labour for such enterprises as the Asab road, the Italians had no welcome whatever for the Arabs, either as migrants, merchants, or masters of trading ships. The Arabs, in turn, heartily disliked the Italians. They had no respect for a European who possessed so many of their own faults and, so far as they could see, none of their virtues. The petty officials with whom the Arabs came in contact were too often just as noisy, irascible, avaricious, and sometimes downright dishonest, as any smuggling Suri or cunning Kuwaiti knew how to be. Some of them could be bribed, and the Arabs, knowing this, had little respect for any of them. The Somali hated them, and none of the Muslims forgave them for Abyssinia. The Arabs respected the English, who could do things they could not do, and the Germans, who were thorough and efficient. But they laughed at the Italians in Somaliland.

Mogadishu is now more an Italian than an Arab town, though it was an Arab settlement for many years and there is still a very large Arab section. The town is covered by stenciled profiles of Signor Mussolini, that 'Defender of Islam' so mistrusted by the Muslims themselves, adorning the columns and pillars and buildings everywhere, and in the centre of the town a large mosque, more ornate than usual, overlooks a café-bar on the opposite corner, and a super-cinema.

At first it seemed as if I should see all I was going to see of Mogadishu from the ship, crowded in her place in the tier of Arab vessels. The ban on landing applied equally to me, and there I stayed. It was more interesting than Haifun, and I did not mind. Each morning the official launch came alongside and sometimes officials came on board to carry out inspections, though they always did this with considerable distaste. I did not blame them, for the conditions on board were deplorable. One morning they lined up all the passengers they could find and checked them carefully. The Suri and others had disappeared, and our numbers had considerably declined. For the first time I was able to witness an accurate count of those bound to Mogadishu: there were seventy-three men, five women, and two babies. These were not all our passengers by any means, for we had another thirty for Mombasa and Zanzibar, not to mention the Suri and other merchants.

The port doctor went over all the passengers carefully, and his inspection brought to light some nasty cases of which I had not known. There was a small boy with rickets; and a tiny mite of a girl of the same family who was going blind. When I saw these, I could not help feeling a little less reliance on the compassion of Allah and a greater readiness to accept the benefits of science would save much misery in Arabia, for the causes of these two cases were obvious. Wretchedly inadequate diet was to blame for the boy's case, and some venereal infection was making the little girl blind. These two children were taken ashore, and I hope the doctor was able to do something for them.

In the end some of the passengers were allowed to land, but only those who could prove they had had previous residence in Italian Somaliland. To my great relief these included the father of the shrew-faced bint, who went ashore yelling as always, leading his family and goats and carrying all his possessions. The shrew-faced bint, horrible little thing, was dressed in a new ankle-length dress of red and yellow, with her face, hands, and feet painted red and black, and her hair more greasy than ever.

She had six silver bangles on each wrist, two more above each elbow, and round her neck a number of suitable extracts from the Qurân – if they were really suitable they should have burned her – fastened into tiny silver containers. Round each ankle she had a heavy silver ornament. She kicked the son of Aura as she went by while her father yelled from the boat. The mother, shrouded in black, and on deck for the first time, added her share of invective, and the little boy Abdulla, who had done all he could to make life a misery for everybody on board, sat back in a new sarong and clean cap and grinned from ear to ear. They were a dreadful family, and I should hate to meet them again. With them gone, the noise dropped at least fifty per cent, and the ship was almost peaceful.

Other passengers disappeared, though Nejdi was careful to see that no one who appeared on the Italians' Haifun list was allowed to leave the vessel. He allowed the Suri and the older Hadhrami to come and go as they wished. Yusuf told me that his reason for this was simply that these men, long-experienced travellers with no desire to stay in Mogadishu – or anywhere else away from their own Arabia – could be trusted to look after themselves and return to the ship in time for sailing. They would not be left behind and get the ship into trouble, whereas the others, the Beduin and the migrating Hadhrami and Shihri, wished only to land and stay. If they got ashore they would stay, and since they had all to be checked on board before the ship could sail, Nejdi took no chances. There on board they remained, cooking, praying, sleeping, yarning, as always, looking at this promised land so close and never setting foot on it.

The Suri seemed to be allowed ashore in Mogadishu more freely, probably because they could be trusted to leave – most of the Suri were bound for Zanzibar and made their headquarters there – but also because it was not possible to tell a Suri passenger from a Suri sailor, for all wore the same beards and clothes. Sailors in all ships had daylight leave, being allowed to land and go to the bazaar or to a mosque, so long as they returned to their ships before nightfall. It was easily possible for the Italians and their Somali police to distinguish our passengers from our sailors, for the Kuwaiti dress and look quite different from other Arabs. Many Kuwaiti would pass as Montenegrins, Spaniards, or Greeks if they used European clothes, but the Suri, in brown smocks alike even to the tiny embroideries at the neck, with hennaed beards, finger-nails, and toes, their heavy turbans kept on by light headcords with tooth-sticks always dangling at one end, could never look anything but what they were. They had very distinctive faces, too.

Their ships, like the men who manned them, had many features peculiar to themselves – their liking for decorations in blue and white, for example, which reminded me of the Finns and other northern mariners; and their fondness for the big square-sterned sambuk and the carved baggala. While we were there, more than five or six hundred Suri and Omani Arabs must have passed through Mogadishu. Some of the ships they came in were almost incredibly small and decrepit, though the worst were from small ports along the Mahra coast and Trucial Oman, and not from Sur. Nejdi said they were ex-pearlers from the Gulf. Pearling was a depressed industry, he said, because of the competition of cheap Japanese cultured pearls, and many vessels formerly used only for pearling now voyaged to Africa and wherever else they could find employment. There were ships in Mogadishu from Seihut, Mukalla, Sur, Kuwait, Muscat, Haifun, Massawa, Bahrein, and Persia. Some were only about thirty feet long, but they had all made long voyages. The strangest craft of all were the straight-stemmed, sheerless craft from the Mahra coast, with high upright masts and large single sails. These were always crowded, and the conditions aboard them appalling.

Though when we had passengers aboard I found life in the *Triumph* trying, I doubt very much whether I could have survived an ocean passage in one of these smaller, crowded vessels. Aboard the Suri sambuks and baggalas the crews were largely negro, descendants of slaves, and many of them still slaves themselves. They danced and chanted and clapped their horny hands all day. We often gave feasts aboard our ship, but I never attended a feast aboard any Suri. Sometimes we went calling, Nejdi and I, and then we would be entertained with black coffee, always very bad, and some dreadfully sweet stuff of which the best qualities came from Muscat and Zanzibar. For my part I wished they had stayed there, for though Nejdi praised this stuff, and said it was unrivalled for its vitalising qualities, I always felt that I could do well without it.

The days at Mogadishu went by pleasantly, and I was glad, if only because we were not at Haifun, and because the quarrelsome Somali no longer shrieked about the decks. I could now walk fairly well – not that that was much advantage when I was not allowed ashore. Italian officials, always very minor ones, were always coming to interrogate me. They seemed to suspect me of some dark purpose unknown to me. This worried Nejdi. Their questions were always the same and none of my replies seemed to satisfy them. Why did I come to Somaliland in an Arab dhow when there were steamers? When I said that I sailed with the Arabs because I liked doing things like that, and that I did not care in the least where the dhow chanced to go, they frankly disbelieved me. One day an unusually officious Italian, finding an old notebook from the voyage to Gizan in the *Sheikh Mansur*, pounced upon it. There were some rough sketches in it, one an outline of the waterfront at Gizan and the other a plan of a pilgrim sambuk. These the Italian ripped out of the book and took ashore. What he expected to find in them I don't know, but he did not bring them back. These are sad days for a European to wander about the earth, and the Arabs observed these antics with scorn. Later, I was allowed daylight leave in the city, but Nejdi swore that seven secret police watched me all the time. This was very flattering, but I doubted it. I liked Mogadishu, which was a clean and orderly place, attractive and busy.

The same official on going though the sailors' chests found a package of Japanese merchandise in Ismael the musician's. This he bore away in triumph. His triumph would have been short-lived if he had known that everyone had contributed something towards it and that it had been left there for him, in the belief that it would be as well for him to find something. The real goods were either already landed or stowed away below the great cabin, where no European would dare to go. When the searcher carried off this planted bundle of merchandise, Ismael protested loudly, so loudly and for so long that I began to think he meant it. He even carried the farce to the extent of going ashore and to the customs house to demand the return of his package because it was for Mombasa, not Mogadishu. Much to his astonishment, he actually was given back the package an hour or two before the ship sailed. But that was not until some time later.

Meanwhile we stayed and stayed in the Arab tier at Mogadishu, and if we had any reason for being there, apart from the forlorn hope of getting rid of another hundred or so passengers, I could not discover it. Said, Majid, and the others, who always turned up once the ship had been safely cleared inwards and the passengers looked over, were busy smuggling, and the conditions were good enough for them. Indeed, the conditions were excellent, for the ship lay close to the landing jetty, surrounded by other vessels, and there was communication with the shore by longboat all day long. They had to go out past Italian and Somali guards through a closely watched gate, which was the only way from the docks, but each time they went ashore, their brown gowns covered large stocks of sarongs, money-belts, perfumes, Aden cigarettes, new turbans, and all sorts of things.

As at Haifun it was amusing to watch them preparing to go ashore. A corner of a sail had been drawn across the after part of the poop, partly to keep some of the maindeck dirt from blowing back there, but really to screen the nightly conferences, and this acted also as an excellent screen for our Sindbads. Said was even more thorough here than he had been at Haifun, and always wore at least three gowns and eight sarongs, and tied more sarongs round his knees. Wherever he left the stuff ashore he kept an old gown and an old turban, and he always returned to the ship in these. He often made six trips in a day, off in the longboat loaded down with his haberdashery, with Mohamed his helper seated in the bows. They never went through the gate together, but made their ways separately to the bazaar. In a couple of hours he was back again wearing a ragged gown and an old turban. How he continued to do this without arousing suspicion I had difficulty in understanding, but Yusuf, who did his own share of the business, said it was matter of distributing the right bakhshish.

This was not the whole story, however, and Said was caught occasionally, for sometimes a suspicious gateman made him strip. Then his goods were taken from him, and he was beaten. He would return at once to the ship, worried but not contrite. In no way deterred, he would immediately load up again, for he said the Italians could not tell one Suri from another – which was true, and the Somali, having been 'fixed,' would not give him away. Sometimes he might be caught twice in one day, but if he got four cargoes through he was doing very well.

It all went to the native bazaar. Yusuf said almost every merchant there was prepared to make a deal; every stall-holder in the *suq* was prepared to buy all the smuggled goods he could get, for duties were high and the Somali very poor, and the restrictions the Italians had been compelled by their home government to impose on trade made ordinary lawful business virtually impossible.

Smuggling was carried on on a large scale at Mogadishu, not only with haberdashery. I watched our Persian carpets go ashore, and did not see them come back. Everybody aboard but the Beduin passengers, who had no funds to finance the business, and our cook and carpenter, was some sort of smuggler, and so were all the others in every other ship. It became so bad – for merchants who still had to buy duty-paid goods protested – that after a week or two the Italians insisted upon searching every Arab who went through the gates. This was not enough, for there were other ways. After we had been at Mogadishu only five days Mohamed the Suri came whining to me and said he had got all his goods ashore, being caught only twice. He seemed to think that being caught at all was a grave injustice.

The economics of this smuggling, so far as I could discover, worked out somehow like this. After a year or two of indolence and the enjoyment of his women at Sur, a wanderer like our Said makes his way towards Aden, or Muscat – Aden is the better – and there spends three or four hundred rupees, preferably on credit. A Sindbad loves credit. Because he has no banking system he regards credit as a means of making a living out of somebody else's money. He lays out this small fortune with great care upon such goods as he knows will catch the Somali and the Swahili eye, colourful sarongs, turbans, headcloths, girdles, and things like that. He prefers haberdashery because it is always appealing, and it is easy to carry and to smuggle.

Then he buys a passage, again on credit, if possible, in some such dhow as ours, though many Kuwait nakhodas will not take these merchants because they compete with the ship, frequently fail to pay their fares, and are generally no good. When he has found a nakhoda who will take him, he sets off towards Africa, perfectly content to go where the ship goes, and trade where she does. His goods are with him; he eats the ship's food; he knows his way about. He has been everywhere, and is often useful to a young nakhoda. He is not on the passenger list and never appears anywhere on the ship's papers. He has no passport. He does not wish to be identified, or identifiable, for it is easier to carry on his trade that way. He passes as a sailor in all ports: the Europeans cannot tell one Suri from another, and he has nothing to fear from his own kind. Because he visits all ports in transit, and never officially lands anywhere – never, indeed, having official existence – he never has to produce any baggage or clear himself through any customs, and in all ports he smuggles systematically and thoroughly. He knows merchants, and he knows where to sell his stuff. Indeed, he brings some on commission, and sometimes carries mail and messages surreptitiously. He is ready to undertake business of every kind, and knows how to do it. His voyage takes perhaps eight or nine months of the year, and in that time on an expenditure of four hundred rupees he will make a clear profit of a thousand. This is good; but sometimes he has to face losses. If he buys on credit, he must often sell on credit too. When he has cash he is always profligate with it. He is usually generous. In spite of the high percentage of profit it is doubtful whether he really does so well. If he did as well as he should, he ought to be able to retire ashore after a few voyages, but these modern Sindbads never do – not the Said type, at any rate. He had to extend credit himself, and he also had to take losses. I doubt whether he made very much. A great deal of his time was taken up in endeavours to collect debts owing from previous voyages. Like so much Arab business, smuggling appeared largely to be erected on a structure of debt.

Nejdi also had smuggling to do, chiefly in harim veils from India. Being a Kuwait nakhoda he never sank to actual smuggling himself, so far as the landing of goods was concerned, and always got Suri to do this work for him. Perhaps this was one reason why Suri were so prominent among the *Triumph*'s first-class passengers, if not upon her Italian passenger-lists. Every morning, after the dawn prayer and the daily *khubz*, there would be a gathering of Suri round the transom aft – always the same Suri, always for the same purpose. They talked, smoked, shouted a little, and departed laden with odd merchandise. Nearly every morning there would be a dispute over something, usually about the proceeds of the previous day's business. Many of these Suri were not sailors, but odd mates and wanderers in small jalboots and sambuks, and baggalas, and they lived by scraping up whatever they could on these annual voyages to Africa. They had no money of their own to buy trade goods, and seemed glad enough to work with the Kuwaiti on a commission basis, though old Yusuf Shirazi disliked them and said they were not to be trusted. He landed his stuff himself, as did all the sailors. Only the afterguard did not. These Suri were a dirty crowd in greasy turbans and brown gowns which looked as if they had gone unwashed since Sur was founded. Many of them had infected eyes, and partial blindness was common among them.

Among these smuggling Suri, our pock-marked Majid was prominent if not respected, and he was smuggler-in-chief to Nejdi. Nejdi had brought a large parcel of elaborate veils for the harim, which he had bought in the bazaar at Bombay on a previous voyage. They were curious-looking things in red and black. Though they did not look very attractive to me, and I could not understand how they could be worn, they were, apparently, much to the liking of Somali ladies, and brought a good price in the *suq*. Nejdi had hundreds of them. Majid's method of landing them was to stuff as many as possible inside the deep hem of his brown gown, to wrap three or four inside his turban, to fill the commodious pockets of his waistcoat with a couple of dozen more, and to lash another twenty or thirty in a sort of triple money-belt which Nejdi lent him. So loaded, Majid marched ashore every morning and through the gate. He was never stopped there. He was out like a shot and up the street, brazen and confident, and he strode through the hot sandy streets like a racer. How he could walk barefoot on the asphalt sidewalks in the heat of the equatorial sun, I do not know: but he did. I don't know where Majid went in the *suq*, and it was not my business, but he promptly got rid of the veils. Some days he would land two cargoes, but generally he was content with one, and perhaps that was why he was not caught. He was a striking man, even among the Suri, with his gaunt face, handsome and distinguished despite its pock-marks. For some reason, he always reminded me of John the Baptist, though he behaved very differently and would undoubtedly have been horrified at the idea. After once passing through the gates I am sure Majid must always have been recognised, but he knew his work, and on the third day I overheard Nejdi remark that he had never had stuff landed for him so efficiently.

On the eighth day, however, he began to wonder when he would receive the first instalment of the money for the veils. This was a detail which his friend Majid had so far overlooked. Majid landed the veils and he got them to the *suq*, but he never came back with any cash. He always had a plausible explanation for this but, in the course of time, no explanations could suffice to hide the fact that Majid would never bring that cash.

By this time all the veils were landed. That was several thousand lire gone. Then there was trouble. Abdulla, Nejdi's brother, commissioned to go to the *suq* and find out what had happened, returned with the report that the merchant who had received them had paid Majid for them. Majid, looking more like John the Baptist then ever, vociferously denied this, but there was a very great row far into the night. Nejdi had trusted him, and was not accustomed to being defrauded. Apparently, if a man was a Muslim, that was sufficient guarantee of his honesty. Majid may have been a Muslim, but he never produced the money. Towards midnight, when the dispute had reached a noisy climax, he was summarily ordered to leave the ship. He went at once, shouting in the night, but in the morning he was back again as brazen as ever. He had come back only for his belongings, a small tin trunk very old and battered, and a piece of blanket wrapped in a Swahili mat. With these things, still shouting his innocence to the assembled vessels at the anchorage, he departed in a longboat belonging to a baggala nearby in which he had found refuge.

With him went the other Suri smugglers, Said and his confederates and the boy Mohamed, and their belongings. The offence of Said and the others, who were thrown out of the vessel with him, was that when they were asked for some payment on their fares – they had then been eating the ship's food for two months and had travelled 2,000 miles with us – they pleaded poverty and refused. At this Nejdi lost all patience, and there was a general clean-up of the Suri. If the ship really lost all those fares, I could only conclude that there was something wrong with Nejdi's business methods, at any rate in his handling of the Suri. Said must have had some lire, for everyone had seen him counting them, and he still had a large store of haberdashery. Why Nejdi didn't seize some of this I don't know, or why he did not punch Said on the nose and make him pay, but to take direct action of this kind was never his way.

When I talked over the incident with Yusuf Shirazi, Yusuf said it was enough that an Arab should lose his reputation for honesty. The whole coast would know that Said and Majid had acted dishonourably, and their name would be bad. Yusuf admitted that it was bad enough before; and it seemed to me that the pair had escaped remarkably easily after what really was a piece of bare-faced fraud. Later I found that Mohamed the whiner, who always called me his very dear friend, was of the same type. He, also, landed goods for the Kuwaiti and did not bring back the cash. But he was still trusted and remained at Mogadishu to collect the money owing, on his promise to produce the money at Mombasa or Zanzibar. We saw Mohamed again, but we never saw the money.

It was a bad business, and considering the losses at Haifun, the failure to get rid of the bad dates, the enforced acceptance of Haifun fish for the Aden rice, the waste of time trying to get rid of the passengers, and the loss of so much of the Suri revenue, I could not see how the voyage thus far had been very profitable. It cost nothing, it was true, to keep the Beduin and the other deck passengers on board, but they were a nuisance. Probably, though Nejdi had lost the proceeds of the sale of his valuable veils, much of the other smuggling had been quite satisfactory.

I missed old Majid because, though he was a thorough scoundrel, he had the merit of being a picturesque one, and I had had many entertaining yarns with him about Sur. If my Arabic had been better I might have learned something of that place: as it was, I only learned about Majid. He, too, had once been a nakhoda, but his reputation for slippery dealing in business ventures had caused him to lose command of one ship after another until at last no one would give him a ship, and he was reduced to wandering up and down the coast, living by his wits. He had no money of his own, and never would have any, but he knew his way round the whole east coast of Africa and the west of India. He was a pilot for the

Rufiji River, the Comoro Islands, the Madagascar coast, and the Gulf of Cutch. He had two old quadrants, both of which were badly warped – neither of them had an eye-piece – and a general chart of the Indian Ocean corrected up to 1746. I tried to get this museum piece from him but he would not part with it, though I offered him three modern charts in exchange. The old one was decorated with Arabic script giving landmarks, distances, and other information of importance to the Arab mariner. Majid spoke Swahili, Persian, Hindustani and several Indian dialects, as well as some Somali and his own Arabic, and he could curse well in English though he did not know what the words meant. I missed old Majid, for he had been a good friend. I had cared for some cracks on his big feet, and given him pills for his chronic constipation. He neglected to return the carton in which I kept the pills, and he kept the contents too, but he probably regarded this as a gift. He frequently addressed me at great length on subjects of speculative theology, of which I understood not one word. No matter. I had only to mutter *taiyib*, very softly, whenever he paused for breath, which was not that often. At each *taiyib* Majid would smile, take breath, and begin again. We got on famously. The ship was the poorer for his going, I thought, though it is quite possible I was the only one who thought so.

Nejdi's troubles were not yet over. Some of the passengers still held him responsible for bringing them to Mogadishu and not getting them ashore there, and twice there were stormy deputations of the Hadhramaut half-castes on the poop. These incidents, however, did not matter very much. There was nothing Nejdi could do, and the situation was not of his making. He would never have accepted the passengers if he had known there would be so many difficulties in landing them and, as he said, they could land in Kenya or Zanzibar. What was the difference?

Then an utterly unprecedented thing happened. The women mutinied.

For many weeks now the unfortunate women had been imprisoned in the great cabin. It was February, and many of them had been there since December. I wondered that they had not mutinied long before. We never saw them, and day followed day with no one ever giving them a thought, unless one died. Yusuf often went down into the cavernous gloom and came up again with various stores, and sometimes I observed that he looked worried. As for the women, their fares were paid and there they were. The Italians would not have them in Mogadishu, or anywhere else, and there was nothing to do but wait and take them on to Kenya. The women were supposed to accept their fate. I don't doubt that most of them did; but one day they mutinied. Such a thing had never been heard of before.

They chose the right time for their revolt. We had a feast on board that day, for it was a holiday and we had two sheep. It was the day of the Feast of the Pilgrimage, the *Idd el Haj*, and part of the poop had been cleaned. After the feast, Nejdi, very quiet and dignified with his hawk nose in the air, sat back on some cushions placed round the bench, engaged in earnest discourse with Persian and Omani nakhodas from the other ships, and the relatives of shipowners who were guests at the feast. Ismael strummed softly – for once – on his guitar and did not sing; the water-pipe passed from mouth to mouth and everyone was well content, filled with rice and sheep. The Beduin and other passengers lay asleep over the maindeck and across the sea chests. Nejdi was appearing at his best.

Suddenly the hatchway of the great cabin burst open with a wild bang and out rushed the women. Horror of horrors, what was this? Nejdi, who could face most situations with unperturbable calm, almost started from his cushions and let the cane of his water-pipe drop from his mouth, but he quickly recovered himself and sat staring. The others looked amazed, caught off guard for a second; then they gazed on the scene with their usual dignity. First came a large Beduin lady, she who had supplied the milk for bathing Yusuf's eyes; behind her were some other women, all ancient. The large Beduin lady at once began to yell and, having begun, continued to yell. She never stopped for breath, and she never said anything pleasant. She screamed questions and paused for no answers. She stormed, she raved, she shrieked until the whole harbour was looking on and Nejdi, though he still preserved a stony silence and looked on with his usual statuesque dignity, must have been perturbed. What exactly the lady said I should hate to have to repeat, but the gist of it was obvious. She had booked a passage to Mogadishu, and this was Mogadishu. What, in the name of all this incompetent man-run world, was keeping her on board? Who, if not Nejdi? This and much more – much, much more – she shrieked, freely interspersed with appropriate vituperations. The other women stood about and, so far as one could tell from their veiled faces, looked their approval. They were all Beduin and they wore the slitted veil of the desert; their flashing eyes gleamed dangerously, and now and again three or four of them broke into a supporting chorus of the stout one's harangue.

After fifteen minutes or so the stout lady was compelled to pause for breath. Nejdi murmured *taiyib*, which I suppose signified his agreement with all that had been said. This only loosed a greater torrent, and for a while it looked to me as if one or two of those women might even think of violence. In this I wronged Arab women and underrated Arab men: there was no violence. When matters reached the stage at which any ordinary female citizen of colder climes would long have been throwing everything in sight, the clamour suddenly subsided. The women had had their say, and apparently that was all they needed. They wanted food; they wanted to know when the ship would sail; they wanted to know where they would really be landed. Nejdi replied in a quiet and thoughtful voice that they would get food; that he would sail on the morrow; and that if they were not landed at Lamu – where he thought of going next – they would certainly be landed at Mombasa. More than that, he undertook to get them there in less than two weeks.

He was so shaken by this utterly unprecedented episode that we actually did sail on the morrow, though this had not been his intention. It was extraordinary.

VIII

A CALL AT LAMU

OUR DEPARTURE FROM Mogadishu was preceded by a bad scare. The Italian boarding officers, after they had cleared us, were suddenly seen coming back to the vessel just as we had re-embarked our lire and our score of unlisted passengers from a Persian boom near by. This was serious, for if we were caught trying to smuggle Italian money out of the colony it would be bad. Nejdi watched the Somali guards and the Italian officers board the ship again in considerable alarm, though he showed no sign of it and greeted them with quiet dignity. He must have been immensely relieved to discover that they only came in search of an Arab from Brava who, apparently, had been wrongly allowed to leave. They took this Brava merchant ashore again, but it was a long time before Nejdi dared retrieve his lire from the ghee jar into which they had been hurriedly flung, and stow them away properly below the great cabin. Our unlisted passengers were cheerful, for we had not yet sailed, and they could always pretend to be visitors from other vessels. Since none of them had ever been officially entered into the country, it would obviously have been a tiresome formality to clear them out. The Arabs always sought to lessen the work of European port officials by keeping from them the knowledge of troublesome problems of this kind, and I must say that their system worked admirably. Our unlisted wanderers had not so much as one identity certificate between them, and they had been travelling about the Indian Ocean like that for years. I thought it would be a shame to stop them now.

We were away before daylight, with the last of the near full-moon setting behind the cathedral towers of Mogadishu. Outside, as the day came, it was cloudy with a high swell, though there was not much wind. Our Beduin were seasick again and miserable, but they appeared to have forgotten any disappointment they might have felt at not being allowed to land in Mogadishu. Now they looked forward to going ashore at the next place we came to, wherever that might be.

We came out from the harbour with a little sambuk so incredibly mean and poor that she merits description. She looked as if she had not been oiled since she was built, or even beached for cleaning. Her topsides were a warped and weeping mess of indifferent teak very poorly fastened, and her underside was mossy and weed-grown. Her masts were fished in several places, and her main halliards, which were made of plaited straw, were one long and very ragged splice. The sail she set was so threadbare and decrepit that it looked as if the mere act of setting it would shred it in pieces. Her few ancient blocks were battered deadeyes, and her high bulwarks looked as if they would fall back inboard at any moment. She was about sixty feet long, flush-decked, with a sort of small platform built across the after part of the poop above the wheel, and the reek of fish-oil and stinking fish from her hold was abominable. The crew were dirty-looking in their greasy gowns, and the passengers sat huddled in rags round the bole of the mizzen-mast. There were about twenty of them, and the sambuk also carried some women. The arrangements for these were exceedingly primitive. The sambuk had no cabin aft and no enclosed space anywhere, so the women were housed in a kind of makeshift shelter, if it could be called that, built round their toilet box. The box itself protruded from the side of the ship on the port quarter, and was covered with old sacking. A shelter of date matting, supplemented, here and there, by pieces of torn and threadbare tarpaulin, kept the women out of sight. The whole tent hardly covered ten square feet of that uneven deck, yet Yusuf said at least five women huddled in there. They had been there since Sur, and they were bound to Zanzibar. The only cooking arrangements on deck were a battered sandbox with a few stones, more primitive even than the 'galley' in the *Sheikh Mansur*; the longboat looked as rigid as a concertina.

I marvelled not only that such a vessel had sailed from Sur to Mogadishu, but that it had ever been allowed to set out. Later, however, I saw even worse ships. Ideal as are the sailing conditions which the Arabs ordinarily encounter in these summer runs down the African coast, yet ships can be lost there, no matter how azure and balmy the general run of the days. It had blown fresh on some of the days we lay in Mogadishu and quite a sea ran outside – sea enough, I should have thought, to trouble such craft as that decrepit sambuk from Sur. I must add, in fairness, that most of the ships I saw from Sur were sound enough, and some of them were splendid vessels.

We came on slowly down the coast, passing by the ports of Merka and Brava but not calling at them, for Nejdi had had enough of the Italians. Getting out of Mogadishu with all the lire he had – I don't know how much was on board, but it was a good deal – and the unlisted passengers, was enough. To go into any other Italian ports would be unwise, particularly as they offered no trade. We wandered pleasantly down to the south-west'ard, with the barren sand of Somaliland along the starboard beam, and the monsoon quiet. We were past Merka before noon, and had the Brava light abeam soon after sunset, with the wind fresher and a full moon to light our way.

That night was very beautiful, with the ship all quiet and the bright moon astern of us throwing graceful patterns of the masts and rigging on the sail, and the dip and roll of her rhythmic and peaceful. On the poop the children and the merchants slept, and the sailors, hooded in the longboat, kept their silent watch. Right aft, at his place on the officers' bench, Nejdi sat, muffled in his headcloth and his desert cloak, puffing at his hookah and carrying on a conversation in low earnest tones with the Seyyid from Mukalla and the merchant Abu Ali. Abdulla the Mysterious listened. He was now our only surviving Suri from the early stages of the voyage. Perhaps he had not heard of the exodus at Mogadishu until it was too late to take part in it, or perhaps he was mysterious enough not to care. The Seyyid from Mukalla had been ashore in Mogadishu, going off dressed as a Suri on the tenth day of our stay there and not returning until the ship was to be cleared.

Snatches of Nejdi's words came to me as I reclined on my carpet and dreamed pleasantly, watching the motion of the ship. It was the same old discourse – mostly about Japan, and the iniquities of Europeans. According to Nejdi, our world was about due for eclipse; his hope was in the growth of Islam in Japan. Some of Nejdi's views were disquieting, and it was interesting to listen to him expounding them. Unfortunately he spoke Arabic so well, in comparison with the sailors, that I had considerable difficulty in understanding him, and it would often be a week before a point would sink in. To acquire a knowledge of good Arabic ought to be the concentrated work of at least three years; at that time, I had had three months. Nejdi droned on to a muffled chorus of throaty *taiyib*s; the tree-mast creaked above him, and the lateen sail bellied windful in the moonlight. I wondered whether, with all our boasted progress and our scorn of his poor ship, we Europeans were really very far ahead of Nejdi. The thought disturbed me: I let him drone on, and the gurgling swish of the sea was soothing.

On the second day the wind freshened again. This day we passed a body in the sea. It was the body of an Arab man, partially wrapped in date-frond matting. It was floating face down, and there were fish. I saw it after the morning meal, at the time of the first siesta. I looked over the side, the ship foaming along, and there it was. I called no one's attention but Yusuf's. It was a buried passenger he said, dead from some crowded Batina boom. It was commonplace enough. They often died. Yusuf was not interested. He said the small boom we had seen at Haifun and again at Mogadishu would lose at least ten persons through death before she reached Zanzibar. They just died. If there were smallpox on board many would die; but smallpox was now unusual. A few years earlier there had been smallpox at Kuwait, and thousands had died.

We left the body dipping quietly in the sea among the fish; our passengers did not see it.

Yusuf told me that another small boom, one of the very old ones, had driven ashore during a day of strong monsoon somewhere north of Warsheikh, while we lay in Mogadishu. She was carrying some sixty passengers. He thought some were not drowned. In such casual manner the Arabs would announce serious and important news. Surely, I said to Yusuf, the loss of a ship full of passengers was a serious thing. Not a Batina boom, he answered. They were no good. Nobody seemed to care what happened to the little ships, and if Allah in His wisdom chose to claim one for the sea, then He had His reasons. The act seemed half-expected of Him, and I must add that this did not surprise me.

The passage from Mogadishu towards Lamu was uneventful. I was not sure that we were going to Lamu until we came off that place on the third evening and, the conditions being propitious, went in. Nejdi had not said definitely that he was going in until we got there, though the previous day I had seen him examining a chart of what he imagined to be the harbour. Unfortunately, this was Port Durnford and not Lamu Roads, and when I pointed this out to him he was not pleased, saying that charts were no good anyway, and he knew the way. South of Kismayu the character of the African coast changed a little for the better and for the first time in weeks we saw some trees along the foreshore.

There had been some calm that morning. It did not last very long, which was well, for when the wind dropped it was very hot, and the stenches from the maindeck and the well abaft the main-mast whence the bilgewater was bailed swept round the ship instead of being blown away. This was dreadful: after many months on board I never got used to that smell of bilge-water. I had served an apprenticeship I suppose, as hard as any, for I had been in whaling ships and leaky grain-carriers; but the stench of whale and the smell of sea-rotted grain were gentle fragrance compared with the bilge-water and the odour of Beduin aboard an Arab boom.

By mid-afternoon we had a light air from the north-east which grew steadily. We were able then to fall off and head towards the sand bluffs of Lamu, and we sailed in during the evening with the conditions excellent. Our entrance into the arm of the sea which leads pleasantly to the pretty township of Lamu was as ludicrous as our tow into Mogadishu. Abdulla, Nejdi's brother, was at the wheel, snatching a puff at the water-pipe at every opportunity, seated so that he could not see. The muezzins all made the sunset call to prayer with the competition among them stronger than ever, and the poop was so crowded with praying passengers that every time they rose from their knees the helmsman could see nothing at all. Rows and rows of praying upturned backs alternated with mumbling turbaned heads, and orders went unheard. So we came in through what was a difficult passage, not without dangers. At the hour of prayer the changing bearing of Mecca mattered more than the pilotage of the roads. But Nejdi knew his harbour, and we were anchored off Lamu in three fathoms of water as the moon rose above the low land.

That pilotage of Nejdi's into Lamu Roads was one of the most amusing occurrences of the whole voyage. The mixture of prayer, ceremonial ablutions, orders to helmsman, the excitement of the passengers, and the general activities of the scampering sailors preparing for arrival, was extraordinary.

The entrance into Lamu harbour, which is an arm of the sea between Lamu and Manda islands, is properly indicated by a series of leading-marks; the harbour itself is full of shoals, and a ship not expertly conned would soon be aground there. Nejdi paid no attention to the leading-marks, knowing his own. He conned by eye from personal knowledge, and I noticed that the Arabs always did this, even in a place like the Rufiji River. (There, incidentally, it is the only way.) The fact that we came to the most difficult part of the winding entrance just as the sun set was an awkward complication, but the prayers could not be delayed, no matter what happened to the ship, and the muezzins began at once with their calls to prayer. This in itself made considerable noise, but it was only the beginning. All hands began at once the noisy and thorough ablutions without which no self-respecting Arab would dream of praying, and Hamed bin Salim advanced to his post facing Mecca at the head of the assembled worshippers and, having discarded his worldly thoughts, began to intone the melodious prayers. Behind him stood the blind sheikh in the middle of a line, fifteen strong, which included mariners, quartermasters, Beduin, and the wilful Malay. Behind this was another line, filling all the space between the chests. Others stood on the chests, in the boats, on the water tanks, everywhere. Because we were at last arriving safely – so far as they knew – at a port in Kenya, the prayers of the passengers were even longer, louder, and more general than usual, and dozens who customarily prayed alone now joined in the general worship. As every worshipper had to have space in which to get down on his knees and touch his forehead to the deck, the praying took up a great deal of room.

With the ship just straightening up for the roads, Nejdi rapped out an order to his brother and turned his back before it was obeyed, for he had to climb over the reclining bench down to a little platform right aft, where his jar of washing water was kept, in order to perform his ablutions, and when he did this he could not see where the ship was going. This did not appear to trouble him. Abdulla, his brother, had been in Lamu before, though only once. I suppose he knew the way, too. (Abdulla once told me that anything he had seen once he knew for ever afterwards, which was a comforting piece of optimism, though difficult to share.) Now and again Nejdi, spluttering with the sea water on his face, thrust up his black head from which half the headcloth was thrust back – he never allowed his head to be completely uncovered – and shouted a fresh order which would go unheard. Then it would be shouted once more, and Nejdi in exasperation would climb up from his ablution platform and yell the order yet again. At last Abdulla, with the usual response 'As Allah wills,' would nonchalantly obey, and the ship, which fortunately was very responsive to her helm, would swing in the last second of time.

The chorus of worshippers, intoning loud and solemn *Amin*s to Hamed's recited prayers, rose high while the mangrove swamps loomed perilously close along the starboard side, and a sandspit showed alee, and two Suri sambuks moving in ahead echoed incantations across the waters. It was a wild and picturesque scene, and Lamu Roads was such a place as I had dreamed of when first I had thought of this African voyage. The light darkened swiftly as it does in these tropical parts, though not before the romantic hamlet of Shella showed to port, with its ruined mosques and tumble-down buildings. The importance of this once proud port has long departed. Shella, standing on the foreshore on the landward side below Lamu's bluffs, is now decayed, but it looked romantic in the day's last light with the big Arab ships sweeping past, their decks crowded with white and brown gowned figures intoning the evening prayers. It was romantic enough for anybody, though we shaved some of the corners very close, and I did not think much either of Abdulla's helmsmanship or his attitude towards the task in hand.

"Starboard! Starboard a little!" Nejdi would yell.

No answer from Abdulla.

"There is no God but God, and Mohamed is the Prophet of God," from Hamed.

*Amin*s very loudly from all and sundry.

"Starboard! Starboard!" again from Nejdi.

Still no answer from Abdulla, who bent down to get a quick whiff out of the waterpipe left there by Yusuf, while the embers still glowed. At last Abdulla, looking up again, perceived that his brother, standing in the gig at the quarter davits, was shouting something.

"As Allah wills," he replied, and put the wheel this way or that, usually the right way but sometimes not.

The ship swung; the prayers continued; the darkness deepened over the heavy green of the mangrove swamps of Manda Island low along the starboard side. The lights of Lamu showed beyond an island in the channel. But here the going was tricky, and there were awkward turns. Nejdi, busy with his prayers – for they must be said in the brief interval between the setting of the sun and the end of daylight, and there is no twilight here – looked up a moment to con the ship in and yelled at his brother to stand at the wheel instead of sitting there. Abdulla, aggrieved, obeyed. Now that we could fall off for the anchorage only a mile away, the sheet could be eased and the yard allowed to fall midships a little. The sailors chanted and ran in response to the order.

The ship was then a scurrying bedlam of running feet, praying forms, and frantically rushing passengers, for the Beduin on the maindeck must get out of the way of the sailors when they work or be knocked down. The mainsheet, eased too much, took charge and had to be got in again. Though we had only half a mile now to the anchorage – for the ship came in handsomely and the evening wind was fresh – no one had seen that the main halliards were clear or even that the hitches had been taken from the turns round the beam where the two hauling parts are crudely made fast forward. The serang, who had not had time to complete his prayers, had not yet attended to the anchors. Now the ship had way enough, and Nejdi shouted for the sail to be lowered for, as usual, we should come up to our anchor with the masts bare. The sailors rushed at the halliard-ends, sending Beduin, children, goats, and Jassim the cook flying in their path. Now while all chanted and yelled, Yusuf Shirazi, Saqr bin Hamoud, Sultan the muezzin, and half a dozen others wrestled with the hitches and turns. At the last conceivable moment of safety the halliards were let go, and the great yard came creaking down and the sail billowed out over the vessel covering the Beduin at their prayers. The ship carrying her way moved slowly to her appointed anchorage.

"Let go!" Nejdi cried, and an anchor went over to which, fortunately, a cable had been attached. Startled Beduin came out from under the sail. The worshippers on the poop finished their prayers; the sail was unbent, and the evening salutations passed quietly from man to man. The excitement which had flared up so rapidly had now subsided. Abdulla, having finished at the wheel, now puffed contentedly at the waterpipe, and his brother, hunched up behind him, called for the longboat and a fresh pipe. So night came to the now peaceful ship; we had arrived.

We stayed at Lamu a peaceful week, during which an Indian merchant once came to look at the carpenter's dhow, for which Nejdi asked a thousand shillings and was prepared to take seven hundred. The Indian found much fault and offered six hundred. Then he went away – without the dhow. We sailed some days later.

Lamu is a good place. From the harbour it appears a group of pleasant white houses, all with spacious verandahs arched beneath red roofs, and set amid trees on a gently rising slope from the sea.

On either side of the small town are Swahili huts, and stacks of mangrove poles merging into the palms. By the waterfront, mirrored in the still water, lie the small Lamu and Bajun boats, squat and fleet and able, and with them, moored in the stream, some Omani and Batina ships, booms, sambuks, and small baggalas just in from the sea.

Ashore, the town and its surroundings are even more attractive than they appear from the sea. The narrow streets of the old Arab town teem with life, and the whole place is enchanting. Lamu is the northernmost port of Kenya, a British colony on the east coast of Africa, but it is almost entirely an Arab town. The buildings, the background, much of the language, the customs, are Arab; half the little stalls in the bazaar are run by Hadhramaut Arabs. Lamu's streets are the narrowest I have seen, with hardly room for a water-laden ass to pass. The tall, flat-roofed Arab houses lean towards one another, with their upper windows open, welcoming. Many of them have beautifully carved doorways.

Here and there in Lamu one may still find some treasure of the ancient past – a piece of Chinese or Persian pottery, delicate woodwork from India, or Damascus steel. Lamu is off the beaten track, and still unspoiled. In the streets a lady of the harim sometimes hurried by, heavily shrouded in her black cloak and veil, but not so heavily that something of her charm could not seep through. The beauty of some of these Lamu girls is very striking. Many wore old American gold dollars in their ears and on their cloaks. When we were there, American gold dollars could still be bought on the beach at Lamu. American gold came there half a century ago, when American trade in sailing ships was important on that coast, and the United States was one of the first countries to send a consul to the Sultan of Zanzibar.

Outside the town I visited the dhow-yard. Swahili carpenters were rebuilding an Arab dhow. They carefully removed all the old ribs and replaced them by new. Then, having put in fresh ribs, they took off the old planking and built up new. In this way they were making a new ship with exactly the shape of the old one.

It was warm, on the yellow sand near the sea, and the shipwrights worked beneath a shelter of rough thatched palms. Near by were the hulls of all kinds of small dhows, most of them the familiar Lamu boat with its low freeboard, its fast, fleet lines, its sharp straight bow, and European transom stern. Arabs build these and Swahili sail them. They carry on most of the native coastal trade of all East Africa from Juba down to Madagascar. Lamu is the home port of most of them, the most important native dhow port of all East Africa, excepting perhaps Zanzibar.

There is a tradition that much of the European appearance of these Lamu dhows – the hull is more English than Arab, though the lateen rig remains – is due to the foresight of a local sultan of fifty years ago, who asked the captain of a visiting English frigate to show his carpenters how to improve the local shipbuilding standards. At the time of the change Lamu was famous for its ancient sewn *mtepe* boats with curious mat-like sails. These were more picturesque than useful, and were certainly not Arab. The *mtepe*s have all gone now. The last hull was rotting to pieces on the Lamu beach, with a sweet-lined dhow from Kuwait beside it, built and carried there aboard some boom. A Cutch boat from India was lying on its bilge nearby.

I watched the knee-lined double outrigger canoes come rushing in with their fish. A Bajun boat, manned by a horde of picturesque and stalwart Bajuns, went out to sea with an orchestra of string instruments playing wild, stirring music. I liked Lamu, and wished I could stay a while to learn something about it.

There were the Pyralae islands; within a stone's throw are the great ruins of Patta and Manda islands. Here live the Bajuns, a mysterious people; here a great slave-mart thrived for centuries. The Chinese came, the Arabs, Indians, Malays, Portuguese, British, each of them adding to Lamu's story and going on. Lamu is a quiet place now, thrown back upon its timber and cattle trades, and a little depressed, for few tourists come and the palmy days are gone. Shella is a ruin and Lamu's trade is declining, though it improved a little when supplies were run in from there to the northwest for the Abyssinian war. That is stopped now, and neither the Italians nor the Ethiopians buy anything they can do without.

Lamu has coconuts, shipping, beef to sell to Mombasa and points south, and the mangrove poles called *borities*, cut from the low islands. Arabia is a treeless land and any wood is at a premium there. The cheapest wood, and the strongest for many uses, has always been the mangrove pole. It can be had simply by cutting it from its swamp. Up and down the East Coast of Africa, these great swamps cluster and the mangrove thrives. There is something in the soil washed down from the interior which puts iron into the heart of these coastal trees, and long use of them in Arab building has proved their worth. The dimensions of many an Arab room are fixed on the beach at Lamu, for the ordinary Arab house, away from centres like Aden and Bahrein, is built of coral rock fastened with mud and lime, and roofed with earth-covering matting spread on mangrove poles. It is cheap, and satisfactory in a dry land.

All along the Lamu waterfront stand piles of these mangrove poles, red with their heavy gums and tan. Picturesque small dhows discharge them from upstream, and Swahili guards grade them, count them, and brand them. The ring of hammers of the Government's forestry guards is a familiar sound all day, and the stacks of *borities* grow until they tower over the Swahili huts.

Behind the waterfront, in the straight narrow streets which are parallel to the sea, are the romantic stores where dark-skinned traders deal in Turkish delight and hookahs and coffee-pots from Syria, or Persian carpets and Indian brass. Here are the sandal-makers, who provide stout shoes of an amazing cheapness, the embroiderers of Hadhrami caps, the makers of mats and weavers of cloth, the rope-makers, and the sellers of sherbet and fruits. Here, too, are the native hotels, always lively and picturesque, open to the winds, with the habitués reclining on benches in front, noisily smoking tobacco from some bubbling hookah, or passing the ceremonial coffee cup.

Sailors from the Arab and Persian deep-sea dhows walk along barefoot and erect, their weather eyes lifting for the *bebes* of whom the town offers a plentiful supply. Lamu is a place famed throughout coastal Arabia for the attractions of its women. Zaid, the ex-slave, and all our serangs and quartermasters and sailors were stepping out, their bold wild eyes searching the *harim* roofs, and little Jassim the cook, no longer morose, was bringing up the rear.

At such a place as this our Beduin stared in amazement, for this could be heavenly if they were allowed to land. They were properly counted on board and then they were allowed ashore to exercise, but not to stay. Officially, there were 104 of them, but, as usual, this number did not include them all. For the first time I was able to examine what purported to be our passenger list, and I saw that the number of women left in the great cabin was now eight. Twenty-four passengers were said to have landed in Italian ports, and twelve others had joined us. The crew list showed twenty-seven names. This gave the total number of persons officially on board, when we arrived at Lamu, as 131. Actually there may have been 150. Nejdi and all the Arabs hated these official accountings. Even if he had tried to have them correct, they would still have been wrong. He did not try, and the more wrong they were the better he was pleased. Nejdi regarded all forms of government control as unwarranted interference with the liberty of mariners and the will of Allah.

After they had been checked, our passengers were allowed to go ashore, and it was a great relief to see the decks clear of them at last, if only for the time being. Nejdi had the poop cleaned and scrubbed for the first time in my experience, but he left the filthy mess of the maindeck. It was no use cleaning it when the Beduin would soon be back aboard. The Beduin had not been ashore since Haifun, for they were not allowed to land at Mogadishu, and they wandered through Lamu's streets and round the countryside like men in a happy dream. It was the mango season, and every fruit stall was full of this luscious fruit. The Arabs are inordinately fond of them. Nejdi thought nothing of wolfing twenty or thirty large mangoes at any moment, and ate all that came on board, no matter who brought them. Lamu was indeed a good place, for fish teemed there and vegetables and meat were plentiful and cheap.

The principal occupation of our mariners and the few Sindbads we had left was smuggling, though the amount they smuggled was not very great. As in Italian Somaliland, the main items were haberdashery and the tiny bottles of cheap perfume, but here cigarettes bought cheaply in Aden were good stock in trade. At Aden, apparently, there are several manufactories which specialise in cheap cigarettes with trade names like those of well-known brands. So the unwary are misled. These sell for a few rupees a thousand in the bazaar in Aden Camp, and there is a very high duty on them in East Africa. They were ideal for smuggling, and most of our people had laid in large supplies. The only drawback to this trade was the bulk and the awkward nature of the cartons in which the cigarettes were packed; it was difficult to elude the guards with anything so conspicuous. The subterfuges which the Arabs used were sometimes amusing, but not always effective. Brazen effrontery was their main weapon. They were allowed to bring in a few of the cartoned dates which they had been packing so carefully from the large stock and, when they brought these in to sell – they were allowed only a few each – they carried them in large baskets which always contained something else. The guards, being Swahili, and well aware of most Arab tricks, always examined the baskets and found the goods. Not being hard-hearted men, they did not confiscate them but ordered them to be left in the longboat. From here it was an easy matter for the Arabs to get them ashore, for they kept coming and going continually, always with little baskets with fish and meat and fruit and vegetables. Between the baskets they brought and the baskets they took away, sooner or later those goods were landed.

Our sailors landed only the few things necessary to purchase their enjoyment in brothel and *suq*. Sometimes I sat in the shade of the commissioner's verandah, by the waterfront, and watched them. It was always an instructive, and often an amusing sight. One day I saw Zaid caught red-handed with two thousand cigarettes and, after a long harangue, he was led away. The Arabs, like most other people, considered that to be caught in wrongdoing was a most unwarranted intrusion on their liberties, and everybody was upset by the arrest of Zaid. Zaid, however, was not as badly treated as he might have been. He was kept in the prison until morning, and then brought before the local magistrate, very frightened, and tremendously relieved when his night's incarceration, together with the seizure of his cigarettes and the payment of a small fine, were deemed sufficient punishment. He returned to the ship and was cheered by his brethren.

If his arrest was meant to be exemplary it failed utterly, for that same day the tribe was ashore again smuggling more furiously than ever. I saw Abdulla, Nejdi's brother, hawking an armful of amber beads in the *suq*.

Days passed. Our Beduin still wandered wide-eyed through the shady streets, dressed in yellow and red finery and with greased hair. After five days the finery was becoming a little thin. One day on the waterfront I met Said the Seyyid from the Hadhramaut, dressed as a Swahili, and he borrowed two shillings. I wondered at this, for Seyyids need not ordinarily seek funds from Nazarenes; but Lamu was full of these descendants of the Prophet, and pickings were lean. Elsewhere on the coast, at Mombasa and the other larger towns, the Arab had become suspicious of the Seyyid's claims to near-divinity, and scornful of the absence of ambition which often accompanied them. Consequently, there had been an influx of the holy into Lamu, which is more backward and less in contact with changing ideas. This was regrettable from the point of view of Said the Seyyid, and he found himself short of ready cash. I never saw my two shillings again. I never saw the Seyyid, either, and I did not miss him. He and several of our Hadhrami merchants went missing at Lamu, where only those few who could establish Kenya Protectorate residence were officially allowed to stay. The bulk of our wanderers would have had difficulty in proving residence anywhere, for they were without official evidence that they had even been born.

Nejdi seemed worried at Lamu. It was obvious that the world depression had made business very bad, and the chances of a satisfactory profit on the voyage were dwindling. In ports Nejdi was always a harried man, and the thought occurred to me that an Arab nakhoda had a great many worries which are spared the ordinary shipmaster. Not only does he sail the ship, and navigate and pilot her, but he controls all her spending, all her people, all her papers. He buys and sells the cargo without benefit of agents; he finds the passengers and suffers them too, and rules them; settles their disputes and gets rid of them, which is not always easy. He is a business man, astute and capable, a judge of timber, of sugar and rice and ghee and frankincense and dried fish, an appraiser of dhows small and large, a master shipwright, a master sailmaker, a master maker of ropes. He knows the best places to sell things as diverse as a cargo of Malabar logs or Rufiji mangrove poles, of sesame and coconuts and Berbera goats, cotton-goods, and salt. He knows a good agent from a bad, even in Sur; a solvent Arab from an insolvent. Sometimes he errs. He has much on his mind, conducting that great ship over the face of the eastern waters, tending her people and her trade, and bringing her back safe to her home at the head of the Persian Gulf. Nejdi was a man with a man's job; and if he was sometimes, by our standards, a bit of a ruffian too, I did not blame him.

Without the passengers it was like paradise aboard the ship. Unfortunately it was a paradise that had to end, and on the seventh day Nejdi sent for his Beduin. Deep-sea dhows are allowed seven days free of port dues in Lamu Roads, but on the eighth day they must pay. So they sail on the eighth day, and this was Nejdi's intention. I do not know what mysterious emissaries went out and collected our passengers, or in what devious ways they were collected; but in the eastern world there never was a problem so complicated or so mysterious that Nejdi could not solve it immediately he wished to. Our passengers were constantly taking advantage of the freedom of movement made possible by the inability of Europeans to tell them one from another, and frequently we changed as many as twenty persons in a port, always going out, so far as the officials knew, with exactly the number we had brought in; but not always with the same persons.

If Nejdi had sent me to the *suq* to look for passengers I might, after a time, have come back with two; now Hamed bin Salim waved his hand and they came back in droves.

But they did not all come back this time, as the Arab immigration inspector unfortunately discovered. This inspector was an Arab converted to Christianity and, according to Nejdi and the rest, no longer any good. This official noticed that we were three women short. The dreadful truth burst on Nejdi that three of the women from the great cabin must have run away. I must say that, if he blamed them for that, no one else did. This was a serious thing, for we had to leave with the passengers we had brought. If the inspector had been willing to co-operate, it might not have mattered, for we could easily have covered three of the children with the women's black veils and gowns, and slipped them into the cabin. First they could have been counted as children then smuggled into the cabin to be counted again as women. Such things can be done. Unfortunately, this inspector was too conscientious, and he demanded at once that the women should be found. Nejdi said they were ashore. They certainly were, but it was sadly probable that they were half-way to Mombasa.

Arab nakhodas are brought up to cope with problems of this kind. Nejdi sent his brother ashore with instructions to bring off any three women he could find, and since there was a large supply of Swahili wenches of far from impeccable moral character, who were ready to welcome an opportunity to try the gay life of Mombasa, he had no difficulty in returning to the ship within half an hour in tow of three of these. Giggling bundles of sheathing black, they were promptly stowed away in the great cabin. Our passenger list was now complete, and we could sail. We went out to sea before dawn the following morning. The three Swahili damsels, used to a freer life than that led by their Arab sisters, raised hell down below. They had, they said, come as guests, not to be cooped up in a dungeon, and they shouted through the hatchway throughout the passage of the Kenya coast. Nejdi clamped down the hatch, locked it, and paid no attention, but the Arab women resented the character of their new companions, and there was general uproar down below.

It lasted only a day, for the wind was good and it was a short run to Mombasa. Nobody worried about the women, so long as they did not get the ship into trouble, and down below they stayed.

1. Nejdi (Ali bin Nasr al-Najdi), *nakhoda* of the Kuwait *boom* on which Villiers sailed.

2. *Booms* propped on Ma'alla beach, Aden, for overhaul, in late 1938.

3. Nejdi's *boom*, the *Triumph of Righteousness* (correctly, *Bayan*), under full sail.

4. Left: Setting up the rigging after going about.

5. Below: Hassan, one of the two helmsmen on board the *Triumph of Righteousness*, at the wheel.

6. Above: Mukalla, chief port of Hadhramaut and seat of the Qu‘aiti sultans, was flourishing in 1939.

7. Left: The palace of the *na’ib* of Shihr. Shihr, along the coast east of Mukalla, had known better days at the time of Villiers’ visit.

8. Nejdi (right) and the mate, Hamed bin Salim, check passengers from Hadhramaut crowded on board the *Triumph*.

9. Passengers throng the *Triumph* as she makes her way from Arabia to Africa.

10. A Hadhrami passenger whiles away the time by playing the pipes.

11. A Beduin baby from Hadhramaut bound for Mombasa.

12. Kaleel the carpenter builds the small *jalboot*, *Afra*, on the *Triumph*.

13. Sailors repair the mainsail on deck, between Haifun and Mogadishu.

14. Villiers was astonished at the strength and agility of the Kuwaiti sailors, who needed no footropes for their work aloft.

15. On the halliards: hauling up the mainsail of the *Triumph of Righteousness*.

16. Jassim, the *boom*'s cook, produced all the crew's meals with the aid of a simple firebox.

17. The mate, Hamed bin Salim, takes a shave on board.

18. A small *boom* from the Batina coast of Oman, like the *Triumph* unable to let its passengers go ashore at Mogadishu.

19. A *boom* crowded with passengers, at Mogadishu.

20. Above left: Said, from the port of Sur in eastern Oman, was one of the "smugglers" on board who kept up the age-old tradition of petty trading down the East African coast.

21. Above right: A transom-sterned *sambuk*, from Sur in eastern Oman, leaves Mogadishu for the voyage south.

22. Above: The poop of the *Triumph*: a haul in the mizzen sheet. The deck is covered with sacks of goods on the voyage south.

23 and 24. The bustling dhow port of Mombasa.

25. Zanzibar.

26. Stem-piece of a large *sambuk*, probably at Zanzibar.

IX

MOMBASA'S STORY

WE DRIFTED SLOWLY IN calm with Kenya's dark green coast alee pleasant in the sun, and the passengers aired their belongings on the rails. Nejdi, who missed several of his best listeners now that the Suri, Said the Seyyid, Abu Ali, and most of our other Sindbads had gone, held forth at length to the few who remained. What a man he was! I looked at him, for the five-hundredth time that voyage, as he waved at the air with the cane of his pipe and punctuated his remarks with many pious exclamations and exhortations to the All-Highest to witness that he spoke truth. Near him, forty of the Beduin sat, listening. I looked at these wanderers also for the five-hundredth time, and hoped devoutly it might be the last. They were interesting, but I felt that I had seen enough of them. Nejdi's monologue droned on and on. He was on his familiar subjects – the decadence of the western world and the coming rise of the east. On such occasions Nejdi spoke of us in Europe as if we had already ceased to matter, though we still dominated the world. He took a long view: day-by-day events neither concerned nor worried him. By his long view our day was ended: the glory of Islam would rise again soon.

It was curious to be there and listen to him, for me, a European, one of the ended. Now and again, a chorus of low *taiyib*s burst from his listeners. They paid no attention to me, for by that time I had become too much one of them.

The calm continued, and we did not sail. No matter: it did not worry Nejdi. We should come to Mombasa in good time. He was not one to fret when the conditions were adverse. He could always talk, or just sit there, on the nakhoda's bench, a brooding hunched-up silhouette in white. The calm was Allah's and, having brought it, Allah would take it away again in His own good time. The calm was Allah's and troubled no man: the satisfactions of his discourse were a man's own. So Nejdi talked, and the ship lay lifeless in the flat sea while the stench of bilge-water and the reek of the Haifun fish rose to heaven. The sailors, worn and emaciated from their past seven weeks on the hopelessly crowded deck, were repairing drums and stretching new kids' skin on tambourines, for our arrival at Mombasa would mark the end of an important section of the voyage, and it was traditional that we should be drummed in to the anchorage. Every drum in the ship was being made fit for service. I looked forward to seeing this, for we had not yet been drummed in anywhere.

When, on the second day, Nejdi suddenly said, "There is Mombasa," I scarcely believed him at first, for I saw no great port and indeed nothing to break the shoreline – nothing at all, except a few houses and a water-tower. Mombasa comes upon you suddenly, bound from the north, and for such a good harbour succeeds in tucking itself effectively away. Moreover, it seemed that we had only just left Lamu. But ports on this coast, south of the Benadir, are close and good: it *was* Mombasa. The fishtraps and the plantations along the shore were more numerous than any we had seen on our long run down and there was a prosperous settled look about the land. Now we were opening up the entrance to the harbour, and Nejdi made a wide swing to avoid the reefs at the northern point. He called me over, saying it was a bad place, and showed me how the Arabs conned their ships. The northern point was dangerous, he said: there were sets and rips there, and a nakhoda coming in had to know what he was about, for all the apparent simplicity of the place. There was a wreck in the middle of the channel, but this was marked by a buoy. As we turned and came in, we could see the remains of another wreck on the southern point. The weather was good and the breeze fair, and Mohamed the serang came scrambling over the passengers, yelling for the drums. The sailors snatched them up, and ran forward banging as they went, and singing.

The passengers, more accustomed by now to arriving at places at which they were not allowed to land, watched our entrance into Mombasa with more calmness than they had shown at Mogadishu or Lamu, but many of them ran about and were excited enough to get in the way. Now we were coming in, past the hospital on one side, and on the other a rising point with coconut palms. The ancient Portuguese fort of Jesus towered above the waterfront. We were headed for the Old Harbour, on the northern side of the town. Mombasa stands on an island in a deep bay, about 600 miles south-west of Mogadishu, and both the northern and the southern arms of the bay afford excellent harbours. The southern arm, known as Kilindini, is now reserved for steamers: the northern arm remains much as it always has been, and here the native vessels congregate – the little Lamu boats down from the north, the Swahili from Zanzibar and Dar-es-Salaam, the Persians and the Arabs from the Gulf, the Somali under the Italian flag, coasting down from Haifun and from

South Arabia, the Indians with their tiles and pottery from the Malabar coast, from Mangalore, and the Gulf of Cutch. Kilindini is a place of wharves and cranes and tugboats and regulations, like any other modern port, and as such it is a good one. But it was the native anchorage which appealed to me, this picturesque and romantic place into which we sailed that quiet Sunday evening, with all our drums beating and the sailors singing their age-old chant and, as we came in, the other Kuwaiti in the harbour breaking out their flags and cheering us to our anchorage. It was a good arrival, and I found it pleasantly moving. The green trees, the gaily coloured Arab and Indian houses, the squat strength of the old fort, the picturesque assemblage of dhows at the anchorage, the clear blue water breaking gently along the beach by the swimming club, the boats, full of ragged mariners, which flitted across the harbour with rhythmic splash of paddle and lilt of sailors' song, all these made the port interesting and colourful. We brought up to single anchor off the swimming club. It was late afternoon.

We found ourselves one of a fleet of four newly arrived vessels, one of them a Persian boom which had brought a cargo of tiles from Mangalore, the others Arabs from South Arabia. We kept our colours at the staff aft, which is how the big dhows customarily announce their arrival. Remembering our experiences at Haifun and Mogadishu, I did not think that the ship would be cleared that night, but in less than twenty minutes the port doctor, a cheerful Irishman, was aboard. He had a good look at everybody and particularly examined recent vaccination and inoculation scars, for the big dhows are much dreaded as possible carriers of smallpox. They must be watched carefully, for no Arab, Persian, Indian, or Somali nakhoda will ever admit that he has had sickness on board. I heard Nejdi deny that there had been any deaths or illness, though there is scarcely an Arab craft which brings passengers from Oman or from Hadhramaut without losing some of them. It is usually of little consequence, if they have not died from something infectious, but from a port doctor's point of view the trouble is that, when sickness does occur, the Arabs always do everything possible to conceal it. The Arabs regard all illnesses with their usual fatalism, as manifestations of the will of God, and quarantine is a hindrance wished upon them by Europeans and therefore to be avoided at all costs.

We were quickly cleared in, for we had no sickness, and I looked about me again at the picturesque harbour there in the tropic dark. Other Kuwait nakhodas were on board – Ganim bin Othman from the big boom *al-Baz*, with whom we had shared the anchorage at Haifun; Bedar bin Abdul Wahhab of the baggala *Bedri*, a sweet old vessel moored close in by the stone quay among a group of Suri; and some other Kuwaiti I had not met before. Bedar was a young man, very tall, dignified in his long white gown and brown cloak. His gown and his headcloth were of white heavily blued, as is the style of the Kuwait nakhodas on their voyages. Ganim bin Othman was dressed in the same way. Nejdi chatted with them about conditions in the port, the chances of selling cargo, and similar topics of importance. He learned that the passengers could be landed without difficulty – Ganim had already landed 150 of his own – but the market was not good. It was better at Zanzibar, Bedar said. The trouble, said Ganim, was that the Suri always undersold. If a man had a chance to make a sale, some Suri would undersell him. It was very difficult. He had been a month in Mombasa and had not sold all his cargo yet. He planned to go down to Tanga and some smaller ports and buy sesame and general cargo for the run home: he would come back to Mombasa for passengers. Bedar said he was tired of trying to sell his cargo at Mombasa, and would go on to Zanzibar on the morrow.

I liked these conferences which went on round the transom of our *Triumph* on these first nights in port, with Nejdi silent and dignified, puffing away at his pipe with Yusuf attending him, good old Yusuf who never had much chance of rest while Nejdi was aboard; and round Nejdi the other nakhodas, all equally silent and dignified, though occasionally they all became far from silent when some subject dear to heart and pocket caused a flare of interest. At times there would be as many as sixteen perched round the reclining bench, with a crowd of passengers and quartermasters and serangs from the other booms' longboats crouched on the deck at their feet. Often in the periods of silence nothing would be heard but the creaking of the ship at her anchorage, and the distant drums of the Suri sailors, and the gurgling and bubbling of the water-pipes, or the splash of passing oars. Their gowns and close-wrapped headcloths, their gold-embroidered cloaks and their black wool headropes, imparted to the Arabs a becoming air of solemnity: their faces were strong, and showed up well in the ember glow from the pipes. As always, I was struck by the air of conspiracy which seemed constantly to surround these conferences, though there was usually nothing furtive or conspiring about them. The dignified silences of these gowned men seemed fraught with threats. I well knew this impression to be erroneous, for if I sat among them myself in robe and aghal – it would not have been courteous for me to dress otherwise – I too felt a conspirator and almost equally dignified. I put this down largely to the robe and the flowing grace of headcloth and cloak, and thought how frequently man arrays himself in such garments when he wishes to create an impression of dignity. Ashore in a tropical suit, I soon felt quite ordinary.

The conference had no outcome beyond the usual crop of rumours, and I turned in on my carpet under the stars considering reports that things were good in Mombasa and we should stay there ten days; that things were bad in Mombasa and we should go on to Zanzibar the day after the morrow, probably with a cargo of bullocks (which would be better than Beduin); that after unloading we should return to Lamu to load mangrove poles for Bahrein; that we should go to the Rufiji Delta and load mangrove poles for Kuwait; that we should go down to Mikindani and ferry maize to Zanzibar. It was also suggested, during the evening, that we should beach and clean the ship at Mombasa, Zanzibar, the Rufiji, Lamu, and the Seychelles Islands. These were only a few of the rumours which drifted about that evening. I had learned by then to accept what happened and never to hope to forecast anything. This was not such a bad way to live.

I awoke in the morning to the sound of Suri drums, and saw a tiny Mahra boat warping in to her anchorage close beside us. She was one of the curious straight-bowed, double-ended, ugly little craft hailing from the Mahra coast of south-eastern Arabia, of the type known to the Arabs as Bedeni. The distinguishing features of these are an air of general unkemptness and a curious straightness of line, unusual among the Arabs. The bows, sterns, and mast are usually as near to bolt upright as the quality of their timbers will permit. The method of steering them is the most primitive of all Arab craft, a cumbersome arrangement of yoke and ropes led to a light beam. Their freeboard is invariably very low and, altogether, they are the most unprepossessing of dhows. They are without sheer and their lines are ugly, though they sail well. They have generally only one mast, stepped a little forward of midships, higher than the usual Arab mast.

Though it was before sunrise, the day was already warm and deadly still, and the poop was full of praying passengers, with Hamed bin Salim leading them in the dawn prayer. Behind him stood a line of sailors and passengers, the Beduin with their scarred cheeks, the Baluchi from Lamu in their voluminous blue trousers, and the lesser merchants already dressed in their best clothes to go ashore. Nejdi, his praying done, had requisitioned the Malay's gramophone and was grinding out some fearsome tunes. He was in a gay mood for the moment. All the passengers were milling about in their shoregoing finery and gathering up their possessions, which now seemed even fewer than they had brought on board.

The longboat from some Suri baggala drummed by, manned entirely by stalwart negroes, with a pink-turbaned mate seated in the stern, who rose to his feet and waved as he passed us. The seafaring Arab makes all his salutations standing: it is unbecoming to wave or to hail from a reclining position. The longboat was laden to the gunwales with sacks of salt. Three Suri nakhodas, in pink turbans embroidered with blue and red, and lashed on with the light headrope of Oman, were already on our nakhodas' bench even at that early hour, and Abdulla Nejdi's brother squatted there sucking at a water-pipe, 'drinking' tobacco, and making a frightful noise about it. Yusuf came up with the morning meal, a few rounds of unleavened bread washed down by cups of very sweet tea. But this morning we were in port and our arrival was celebrated by serving freshly made *khubz*, instead of the half-sodden stuff from the previous day which is more usual. Moreover the *khubz* had been sprinkled with sesame seeds for flavouring. Prepared this way and served hot, the meal, though frugal, was satisfying. The Suri joined us, for guests must always break bread. The tiny Mahra boat warping by burst suddenly into a tumult of handclapping, rhythmic and loud, though what it was for I did not know. The small craft chose to moor right beside us, and I saw, though it could not be forty feet long, there were more than sixty people on board. They stank, and the smell of the dried fish cargo blew over us horribly. Ugh! Even Nejdi could not stand this, and yelled for the serang to take the longboat and tow the Mahra dhow away. The reek of her fish was offensive and violent, making our own bilge seem like rosewater.

During the night we had moved in at high water to our place in the tier of ships, and were moored then bow and stern not thirty feet from Bedar's baggala *Bedri*, with two Suri and a Persian on the inshore side of us. Beyond them two boats from Cutch and the Lamu boats were lying in a pool of tan-stained water where their mangrove poles and firewood had been dumped on the shore. All round us were booms, Lamu boats, Indian kotias discharging fragile clay pots, Swahili cutters with their holds covered with a roof of thick hatch, Suri baggalas and sambuks. From the waterfront the sickly odour of copra came across the harbour to mingle with the hundred-odd odours competing there, a competition in which stale fish won easily. The red flag of the Sultan of Zanzibar flew over Fort Jesus. Like its sister fort in Lamu, this is now a jail; but it stands stalwart and picturesque as ever, and some of its old bronze guns still point out to sea. On the other side of the harbour, the coconuts straggled across the blue skyline, fringing the green rise beyond the beach. Outside, an oil-tanker passed distantly, bound elsewhere, and a liner moved in slowly towards Kilindini. Our passengers were moving about more eagerly than ever. It was not yet seven o'clock, but we could see the immigration officers coming out in a boat and there was great excitement.

The examination was almost perfunctory. All the Arabs produced for inspection had papers of some kind or other, but what the papers were and whether they applied to the Arabs who had them, I should not like to say. The immigration officer, a young policeman in spotless white, sat on the nakhoda's bench aft with his Swahili clerks beside him, and carefully went through the list, checking off names. Our Arabs were allowed to land freely. As the officer said to me afterwards, what else could be done? They were usually good citizens who caused little trouble. They could be trusted to take care of themselves and not to become public charges, and that, put in a nutshell, was all he had to care about. The Arabs had been accustomed to come down to Mombasa and Zanzibar from time immemorial, and though it was true that opportunities for employment grew less and less, they could scarcely be turned away. It was known that many of them had used up their last resources in coming down to the Kenya port, and perhaps they were ill-advised to do so; but if the worst came to the worst they would always get themselves away again. They never came asking to be repatriated. A few rupees brought them down, and a few rupees took them back again. If they were without money themselves, they could usually go back on the credit of some tribesman or of some tribe in South Arabia, or one of their organisations.

There they were, ships full of them, every north-east season, and they landed – blind, beggars, musicians, hawkers, porters, women, children, and all. Everybody we had was allowed to land at once, and there were whoops of joy. It was a strange scene, as Beduin after Beduin came up on the poop to have his name checked by the Swahili clerk, who seemed ready to check anybody, and stood for a moment beside the Scots constable, bewildered now that at last they were to be allowed to land. Many of them hesitated to go away, thinking that so brief an interview could surely not end so long and wearying a passage, remembering, too, other interviews in Haifun and at Mogadishu which were only preludes to further weeks on board. But this time it was real: they could land. They rushed away and dragged out their best clothes, if they had any, and there was a wild greasing of long black locks, a hasty donning of clean sarongs and cotton shirts. Boats from the shore came off and our passengers scrambled over the side, though not so quickly that Hamed bin Salim, who always watched the ship's accounts, could not keep careful check on them to see that no one left who had not paid his fare and any sums he might owe the vessel. The Shihiri from the Hadhramaut had all paid their fares in advance, but some of the passengers from Mogadishu, and the wanderers we had brought from Lamu, had not paid. Others owed a little for food, supplied by the ship after they had used up their own. Hamed watched them with an eagle eye. He was good at that kind of thing. No arguments and no promises meant anything to him; whoever had not paid his debts in full could not land, and that was final. I was amused to see the lengths to which one passenger from Mogadishu went, to impress Hamed with the vast amount of wealth which would be forthcoming from him the moment he stepped ashore. He did not step ashore, though his protestations and laments filled the harbour. He had to send for someone to bail him out of the ship before he could go. He owed about half a crown. The sailors, being paid on a share system, had a keen interest in seeing that no one left without having produced his fare, and we had already lost enough over the Suri.

I did not recognise some of our passengers as they went down the side into the shoreboats, so completely had their appearance changed. A frightful old man with one eye and the most unpleasant profile, scraggy, miserly, wizened, and almost entirely repulsive, who had never changed his gown from the evening he had boarded the dhow at Shihr until that morning – he who had called himself a sheikh, and competed crazily in the muezzin calls – now came to the rail spick and span in a new white headcloth and long flowing gown of Japanese silk, with a black camel's-wool cloak edged with gold wire on cuffs and lapels, from which hung two tassels heavy with more gold wire. The old scoundrel looked almost presentable, and, though he had long become an object of derision on board, the Beduin and the others now looked up to him. The blind piper who had quarrelled with his two boys was also there, dressed in a sarong of green and white stripes, with his pipe in his belt ready for use. The two boys with him were in clean shirts. Many of the Beduin had brought out bright sarongs of yellow and red, and some of the Hadhrami even wore coats. They had coats made of shoddy cotton, sewn in Japan and sold in the Arabian bazaars. There is scarcely a bazaar in all Arabia which does not offer these wretched garments for sale, at prices from about four annas[1] upwards. Most of the Hadhrami looked smart in clean sarongs hanging to their knees, clean singlets, money belts and coloured sashes about their waists, bands of narrow black wool about their shins, and a large and gaily coloured turban wrapped round their heads. There was very little in their money-belts and even less in their stomachs, and what was to become of them in that strange place they did not know. But they went fearlessly, in the spirit of the pioneer, determined to make their way somehow or other.

I asked the immigration officer what became of them. He said that many became lesser porters, though in recent years they had lost much of this work. The African bushboys, brought from the interior, had proved much better at it – stronger, more able, and less prone to intrigue. More than that, the bushboys kept their money in the country, and this the Arab often did not. The Arab's ambition was always to make money enough to go home again, and though he was prepared to work at anything, he rarely came prepared to make his way in the country. He was more apt to look upon it merely as a source of wealth, a place of temporary residence whose only real value was to provide him with the wherewithal to return to Arabia and live a life of ease. Many of the Arabs came and went in this way, coming down to Kenya and working hard there for a year or two, or even five years – for they had patience – but always going back to Arabia when in funds. Some went home each season. It was cheap: the journey from Mombasa to Mukalla and back might be made in any dhow for less than fifteen rupees, little more than an English pound. Life was cheap for Arabs in Mombasa, and even easier in the Hadhramaut. The wandering Arab asks no roof above his head and carries his bed with him. He can live on very little food. His total living costs do not usually exceed two or three annas a day, less than twopence half-penny. This is in the towns: in the country with his tribe, the costs would be infinitesimal. A few presents brought back from Africa and wisely distributed, a few pice spent at a coffee-shop, a little generosity with the water-pipe, a good name in the mosque – these would suffice to make him welcome indefinitely. When all his money was gone, he would return to Africa, or wander somewhere else, to Java, India, Singapore. Just as there was a large settlement of Hadhramaut Arabs in Mombasa, there was also one in Java, in all the coastal towns. I had noticed that several of our younger

[1] Four annas, a fourth of a rupee, is less than sixpence.

Sindbads brought with them newspapers published somewhere in the Dutch East Indies, printed half in Arabic and half in Dutch.

In Mombasa, I was told, the Arabs used to have practically a monopoly of stevedoring, especially in the native harbour. That also is now lost to the Africans, and the Arab must content himself with lesser burden-bearing and with the fresh-water trade, carrying and delivering water in skins and tins to the Arab homes. He finds work also as a night watchman, sleeping on a rough stretcher before a building or shop; as a coffee seller, hawing his wares through the streets with a brassbound urn and a tiny charcoal fire, clinking his porcelain cups; as a petty hawker of basketware or veils or cotton stuffs through the *suq*; or as a minor shopkeeper, though this is an envied profession. It seemed to me that most of these coastal Arabs wished to be shopkeepers. It did not matter how small the shop might be, or how few its wares; so long as there was a space to spread things and to squat on top of it and puff at the bubble-pipe, they were content. These tiny shops crowd every Arab *suq*, and the stock-in-trade of any half-dozen of them might be bought for a pound. A few mangoes, oranges, limes, and coconuts; some shallow baskets of rice, chillis, and grain; some stalks of coarse Arabian tobacco; a bright collection of trash from Japan – any of these was enough to stock a shop, according to Arab standards.

I saw some of our passengers ashore, during the *Triumph*'s stay at Mombasa. Several of them were hawking things through the *suq*, carrying small bundles of sarongs, singlets, shawls, and turbans which they offered to everyone they met. I did not see them finding many purchasers, but they looked content. Some varied their stocks with cheap imitation amber beads, in the familiar thirty-three-bead Muslim rosary, with tiny bottles of smuggled perfumes, with playing-cards bought at Aden, or violently perfumed toilet preparations. I saw others already established as helpers in tiny shops, probably the property of relatives. There is a considerable traffic in these shopkeepers between East African ports and South Arabia; one kinsman goes home for a year or two, and others come down to carry on the shop. Others were competing in the already overcrowded street coffee-selling business. They wasted no time. They were at work the day they landed.

Our beggars also wasted no time. There had not been much opportunity to beg on board, and they had not been allowed to ply their ancient trade in Mogadishu. The first afternoon I was ashore I saw our ill-tempered blind man wailing on his pipes on a pitch in the *suq* near an

Indian cinema: one of his boys was begging, and the other was gathering scraps of wood to make a fire. The blind man moaned for alms as I passed by, but I gave him none. He was one of the worst men we carried down from Arabia. Others of our passengers who were not beggars were not so well off, for porterage work was scarce, and Africans were preferred. Those who had been in East Africa before seemed to settle down quickly, for many had relatives, or tribesmen, who kept places for them. Our Beduin, who had not been away from the Hadhramaut before, did not find it so easy, for they had no relations so far from home – no relations, and no friends. I saw several of them while the ship remained in port. They were conspicuous even in the international welter of Mombasa, with their unmistakable Beduin faces, their gaunt lithe bodies, covered with indigo and clad only in short black sarongs, their wild black locks smeared in ghee. They wandered about like children who had lost their parents, staring at the strange sights as if they were unable to comprehend them. Barefoot and erect, they passed along, hungry for the sight of a camel and a swirl of sand from the desert. They did not sit in coffee-shops, for they had no money. They did not loiter in the *suq*, for its delights were not for them. They were to be found in the clear spaces, or down on a field near the Portuguese fort by the side of the harbour, with their puzzled eyes fixed on the north. They had come so far in that big ship, sailing for many days; and now what kind of fate awaited them? I hope it was a good one, for there was much that was fine in their simple characters.

One day as I wandered in a side street going back to the ship, suddenly a baby voice piped with the Arab salutation: "Peace be upon you, O Nazarene!" I looked down, in surprise. It was the baby son of Aura. He sat on the hot pavement in his tiny sarong, smiling with his limpid great eyes, a tiny mite to be alone there in Africa. He looked happy though a little tired, or perhaps hungry. He was playing with a piece of stick which he kept banging on the asphalt for the pleasure, I suppose, of hearing the noise, and he looked about him at the marvels of Mombasa. He had never been able to bang a stick on a sidewalk before. I stopped, to ask him how he fared, though his Arabic baby-chatter was beyond my depth. He was waiting for his father, he said: that much I gathered, when Aura his father silently padded into view. Aura looked tired, too, and bewildered, as if the city were too much for him, and its noisy mysteries too confusing for his clear and simple mind. Barefoot, his jet-black locks smeared with grease, his only clothing a black sarong and a cloak of black-dyed calico thrown across one shoulder, he still appeared dignified and self-possessed, in spite of his bewilderment, for a desert warrior of South Arabia was no man to be fooled by a crowd of heartless city streets.

Aura told me he could find no work, and did not know where to look for it; he and the baby were sleeping in a field. A pleasant field, he said; it had trees, and it was green. He was sure they would be all right. Allah was merciful, and they had come a long road. He asked nothing of me. The two of them were uncomplaining. Allah had brought them to Africa where they wanted to go, and that was enough. I discovered that they were hungry only when I gave the little boy some coins as a parting gift, and he gave me his man-to-man thanks and said that now they could buy a little food. Just then a camel ambled by, looking almost as much out of place as the Beduin; the little baby rose and clapped his hands, and the coins fell in the gutter.

They were a brave, grand pair, Aura and his son, hungry and alone in that Mombasa street and yet sufficient unto themselves and fearful of nothing. Their faith in the boundless mercy of Allah was in no way shaken, and their hope for the future was bright and undimmed. The pair of them, as I left, waved to me and wished me Allah's blessings, then Aura and his little son passed hand-in-hand down the road behind that camel. I liked them well; they were good companions. I wish them luck, and hope that fortune has smiled on them somewhere in Kenya. I never saw either of them again.

We were to have had a big dance the night after our passengers had left us, but Ismael the musician was missing, and the mariners, though they had not been given any money, were off hunting the local *bebes*. So we had the dance several evenings later. It was a particularly good dance, though by that time I felt I had seen all I wished to see of such celebrations. The decks were clear, for the first time since I had come aboard. The longboat and *Afra*, the carpenter's new dhow, were overside. The decks had been swept clean and even scrubbed, so that they shone with an unusual cleanliness. A sail was spread over the maindeck, from the mainyard, as an awning. Every carpet in the ship had been spread, and others borrowed from neighbouring dhows also adorned our maindeck and poop. The whole of the ship was given up for this party, the guests being received on the poop by Nejdi and Hamed bin Salim as they came up the Jacob's ladder and took off their sandals. Then they came down to the maindeck, by the poop ladder, and sat beneath the awning on carpets and leaning cushions which had been arranged along the top of the hatch. It was a dignified and pleasing sight. The sailors sat round the bulwarks in two long lines, dressed in their cleanest and best clothes. Their moustaches were carefully trimmed, and Abdulla bin Salim, the serang's mate, had his tuft of black beard in a state of geometric perfection. They squatted quietly round the side of the ship, and Nejdi and the guests sat along the main hatch in the middle. The hatch was low and comfortable. Ismael strummed his guitar and for once played some quite attractive melodies.

Some of the songs seemed to consist largely of passionate dialogue between a *bebe* and her paramour, and the listeners smacked their thighs and roared with delight.

A fiddler had been brought from a Suri baggala, whose black-bearded nakhoda sat silent by Nejdi throughout the night; and there were some tambourines, a triangle, and at least nine drums. Two of these were large Indian drums, stretched with new goatskin warmed frequently at Jassim's fire. The others were small cylindrical things, made of Basra pottery, and covered at one end with a piece of goatgut. These also required frequent warming. They were played with the hand, the sailors taking turns with them, striking them with fingers and thumb alternately. The rhythm they could keep with the tambourines and drums was very good and sometimes stirring: they all seemed to have a perfect sense of rhythm. The maindeck was lit by the soft glow of two lantern lights which I never saw used at any other time, and the red glow from Jassim's wood fire forward was reflected on the polished teak of the solid mast. The brightly coloured carpets, the stately cloaks of the men, the burnished brown of the heavy mast, and the dark canopy of the sail above made a romantic and pleasing scene. The sailors looked their best, and their singing was splendid. Along the top of the main hatch sat some twenty guests, including the nakhodas from the other Kuwait ships and the Suri, a Persian or two, and a number of Arabs from the shore.

Abdul-latif, the sailor, led our singing. That was his job. He always led the singing at the hoisting of the yard and in the boats. He was given bakhshish for that, and signed on on that understanding, just as Ismael received bakhshish for his music and old Yusuf for his excessive work. Abdul-latif sang well, but I preferred the throaty bass of the negro Zaid and his compatriots. Ismael was the worst singer of them all. His caterwauling became almost unbearable as the night wore on, until once, when no one was looking, I gave him some bakhshish to stop.

About midnight – these parties always went on all night – the Swahili immigration clerk came noisily on board in a state of considerable intoxication, and he immediately gave Ismael a large sum of bakhshish to sing again. This Swahili was a man of importance in the Arab world, but it was unfortunate that he was so drunk. He could not stand up, and insisted on singing. He sang very badly and danced worse, and he kept getting up and trying to dance, and falling into the musicians. He was the only drunkard I ever saw aboard our dhow, or aboard any dhow. Some of the Arabs drank a little, though not much. When they did drink it was in secret and very quietly, and they did not dare to get drunk. This was a condition to be avoided at all costs, for the good Muslim seen intoxicated could be a good Muslim no more. But this Swahili was frightfully drunk and careless who saw him. No one remonstrated with him or led him away: no one seemed even to notice that he was drunk. The party and the dancing went gaily on and his antics were unheeded. Next day, however, he heard about it. Drunkenness is not lightly forgiven by the devout Muslim, for the drunken man forgets his prayers.

It was the best party we ever had. Nejdi danced with several of the other Kuwaiti nakhodas, though not with the Suri. The dances consisted mainly of the usual shuffling to and fro on the carpet along the port side of the deck, with great solemnity and dignity though without much grace, keeping step with the rhythm of the drums. After about twenty minutes of this the rhythm would quicken and the pace of the dancers grow faster and faster until with a final burst of wild music from the guitar and a furious drumming, the dancers would stand before the musicians and shake their bodies violently. This part of the dance was always very exciting to the sailors, and several of them, unable to contain themselves any longer, would jump up and rush to join the dancers. There they would stand, perhaps a dozen of them, shaking their bodies. With a last flick of the guitar Ismael would bring the music to an abrupt end and the drums would thump out a last beat, at which the assembled group of dancers and sailors would jump high and turn round, yell, and go off laughing, to sit down. This was great fun and they never tired of it. I was, however, never able to follow either the rhythm or the meaning of this dance. My untrained ear could never determine when it was time to turn, or jump, or anything else. There seemed to be no order in these proceedings, and I soon gave up the attempt to look for any.

This dance was a celebration for the delivery of the passengers, and an entertainment of the friends of the ship in the town. It was also a chance to exhibit the musical skill of our friend Ismael who, apparently, was a man famed for guitar and song throughout the Persian Gulf. It was a feather in Nejdi's cap that he had been able to induce him to make this African voyage. The Suri, and Ganim bin Othman, whom Nejdi did not love, were supposed to be green with envy. Whether they were or not I do not know; but it added to Nejdi's stature among his kind. And that, to him was everything.

Far into the night and indeed all night long, our party went on. The sailors never tired. About three in the morning, the Swahili clerk fell asleep, and was promptly lowered into a boat and removed ashore, snoring. Hamed bin Salim, who never danced and who appreciated Ismael about as much as I did, betook himself to a carpet in a far corner of the poop shortly after midnight, and tried to sleep. Old Yusuf Shirazi, who also was not keen on dancing, tried to do the same, but Nejdi shouted for him so loudly and so constantly that he might as well not have tried. Yusuf, however, regarded five minutes not spent asleep as five minutes lost, and though he could take his rest only in three-minute spells, still took it. From time to time trays of red and blue sherbert and oversweet tea or bitter coffee were passed round, and dates, and figs, and the yellow sweetmeats known to the Arabs as *halwa*. This was dreadful stuff, almost sickening. It stuck to fingers and to tongue, and tasted like paste made of molasses and bad sugar flavoured with spiced honey. Nejdi could eat it by the pound and so could all the others: they were welcome to my share. As a change from these delicacies we had bowls of Italian canned fruits, bought very cheaply at Mogadishu, and Belgian biscuits made for the African trade. When I rolled my carpet on the starboard side of the nakhoda's bench aft, about five o'clock in the morning, Abdul-latif and Zaid were still leading the sailors in song. I went to sleep to the beat of drums and bursts of laughter and melody. They were singing a Persian boat song which was quite good. I woke an hour or two later to Sultan's dawn muezzin call, and I saw that the sailors were as fresh as schoolboys, though they had danced and sung all night. The Swahili came early, and apologised for his drunkenness of the evening; but he was not forgiven and the episode was not forgotten while I remained in the vessel.

Mombasa was a good place, and we all enjoyed it. I never tired of the native harbour and the native town. The heavy scent of copra at the customs steps, the singing of the sailors aboard their ships in the harbour, the picturesque and so varied ships themselves, the setting of the pretty harbour with Fort Jesus and the Arab houses in the background, the blood-red water round the Lamu wood which the matted little ships had brought, the green palm-fringed arm across the bay, the white lateen sails which always seem so piratical and picturesque, the graceful bows of the big booms and the stately sterns of the big baggalas, the crowded streets with their Indians, Baluchi, Swahili, Arabs, Punjabi, and Japanese dentists, all these were good to look upon and made Mombasa interesting. It was the sort of port I liked.

I was interested, too, to find out all I could of the trade in dhows. There is no sign of any falling-off in the dhow trade at Mombasa. While we were there, never less than thirty deep-sea dhows lay in the harbour, of which the majority were Suri and other south-eastern Arab vessels. During 1937, port statistics showed 214 foreign dhows entered the harbour. In 1938 the number was 241. In 1939 it promised to be even higher. With the setting-in of the north-east monsoon they begin to come, first the little Suri and the Bedeni from the Mahra coast, hurrying down to Zanzibar with dried fish and Mango Arabs; then the big Kuwaiti and the Persians, with general cargoes and passengers from the Hadhramaut. Then come the Indians from the Gulf of Cutch and the Malabar coast, and an odd Somali flying the Italian flag, down from Haifun. The Arabs bring passengers, and salt in bulk from Aden, where it is cheap. The Suri bring fish, which is sold in the Swahili market-place. The Arabs also bring carpets, though not many, for they are luxury articles, and the genuine product of Persia is both hard to get and hard to sell. They bring cooking stones and ghee, and other Arab products. The Indians bring tiles and earthenware pots. They do not make trading voyages as the Arabs do, but usually come on charter bringing goods for Indian merchants in the East African ports.

Compared with the expense of getting a European vessel about the ports of the world, the expenses on one of these Arab voyages are very low, and this doubtless is a main reason why their trade continues. Our stay at Mombasa cost less than four dollars – less than one English pound. The Arabs ask little in the way of port facilities. They have a bay to lie in and a stage at which to land their goods, and that is all. They lie to their own anchors and never come alongside, and they land their goods in their own boats. If they need repairs or cleaning they beach themselves, and do their own work. Pilots, tugs, dockmasters, waterside workers, watermen, stevedores – all these would starve were they dependent on Arab employment, for the Arabs do not use them. The Arabs indeed declare that they could get on quite well without any European supervision, and object to paying any dues at all, but they know very well that if Mombasa were not in European hands they might be made to pay considerably larger sums by their own countrymen. The Arab has a rooted objection to the payment of any fees or government charges, because he has a firm tradition that all fees and dues are a form of graft. He considers dues unwarranted and the upkeep of ports unnecessary, for he can find his own way where he wishes to go and choose such ports as will float him. Harbour works, breakwaters, improvements of all kinds, mean nothing to him, and he strenuously objects to being expected to pay his share of them. He has always been able to sail in those seas, he says: why should he help to make them safer for the Europeans, who do their best to drive him out of them?

One point in the harbour regulations struck me as interesting. That was the requirement, under the Native Vessel Ordinance, that "no native can be engaged as a seaman without having previously been questioned by the port officer with a view to establishing that he has contracted a free engagement." Nobody is to be shipped either as crew or passenger without supervision; both crew lists and passenger lists must be complete, and they are very important documents. These requirements, I learned, which still stand, are to prevent the Arabs from shipping extra Swahili seamen who leave for Arabia cheerfully and are then sold for slaves. I wondered that it was still necessary to take such precautions, but it appeared that it was. The Suri, Nejdi said – the poor Suri were blamed for everything – would still sell slaves, if they could: there were markets in Oman. If they could get some good stout Africans up to Sur they could still dispose of them. At Lamu I had heard of the case – well authenticated – of a sambuk from somewhere in Oman which, running through the back passage towards the open sea, had deliberately run down a fishing canoe and taken the two Africans in it to Arabia to be sold as slaves. This was recently. The Africans are still wary of the Arab in his ships, though so far as I could see, the Kuwaiti never tried to recruit any of them. Nejdi said he could not give a slave away in Kuwait, where they had only to go to the British Political Agency to be freed. Of course, if he could turn up with a cargo of bewitching virgins he might find a market anywhere; but where would he get such a cargo? He had been looking for years and had not yet found one. According to Nejdi, the Kuwaiti had never been slavers: that was a trade carried on from Muscat and Sur, from the Batina coast and Trucial Oman. It may be true that the Kuwaiti never carried African slaves, for they are comparative newcomers to the East African trade; but how much holier they really are than the greatly maligned Suri I should not like to say.

In the shipping office at the head of the ramp above the landing stage, I found one day a curious volume in which there was much recorded that gives an insight into the proceedings aboard Arab, Swahili, and Indian dhows. It was the Casualty Book, always grim reading. I read through it one morning, sitting in the customs room of the shipping office, looking through the open windows at the shipping anchored in the Old Harbour, where Suri, Kuwaiti, Indian, Hadhrami and Persian jostled one another and the small Lamu boats came and went. Now and again a Bajun came foaming in with a burst of music. They were drumming up water aboard a Suri ship at the anchorage, near our *Triumph*; and the ancient *Bedri*, which had taken herself to sea in tow of her longboat earlier that morning, lay miraged in the calm outside. There was a good breeze inside the harbour, strangely enough, and apparently no wind at all outside.

The Suri were making much noise with their triangles and drums and, every few minutes, they would all stop to clap their great hands with a thunderous noise that could be heard all over the harbour. Inshore, her crew were grounding a Muscat jalboot, at high tide, leaving her far in on the flat to be dry at low water. They, too, danced and sang, and the distant sound came pleasantly to the high windows. On the landing-stage a gang of bush coolies toiled with sacks of salt. They were a stalwart and magnificently muscular gang, so wet with sweat that they looked as if they had come up from the sea. They sang a chanting song as they worked. Everywhere was this deep-throated chanting of muscular men, forming a background to the intense toil. Overhead the sun burned and the sky was of cloudless blue. Inside, in the cool of the customs room, a group of Arab passengers were checking their baggage. Occasionally an Indian merchant would hold up these proceedings, very briefly, while a chit was signed. The customs office and the shipping place seemed smoothly run, and the Indians in charge were helpful and courteous. I saw our friend the Swahili clerk who had been drunk on board at the dance. He hurried by sheepishly when he saw me.

In this Casualty Book were accounts of strandings, dismastings, and other losses of vessels, set out in a precise handwriting as if they were entries in a merchant's ledger. The accounts seemed to have no relation to the events they narrated and, seated there even with the panorama of the ships outside, it was difficult without a conscious effort to picture the struggles, the grief, and the tragedies so prosaically listed. I was impressed by a curious similarity of many of the accidents. It was amazing how often some hard wind just "suddenly came up," or some rocks suddenly got beneath the vessel. Some of the laconic accounts of shipwreck were almost amusing. Consider, for example, the case of the Lamu dhow *Amantualla*, outward bound from Mombasa to Dar-es-Salaam. Everything was going well, according to the sworn statement of her nakhoda, when "all of a sudden a terrific gale swept over our dhow and dashed it against a rock." She was lost. She had a cargo of 250 bags of maize, and six cases of umbrellas. The crew, apparently, swam ashore each holding an umbrella, for they salved ten. Then there was the Lamu dhow *Violet* (nakhoda, Mubarak bin Khamis) which suffered a similar fate. She left Lamu with seven crew and one passenger bound south for Zanzibar, and a cargo consisting of 125 bags of beans and eighteen sacks of moong, whatever that is. The little *Violet* was going quietly along the coast somewhere off Kilifi when "suddenly our dhow was carried over and dashed against a reef, with the result that the rudder came out and two planks from the bottom were broken and the sea started coming in." She was lost, too, and they did not salve anything – not even a sack of moong.

This sudden springing up of bad weather from calms became monotonous. It is true that the neighbourhoods of Malindi and Kalifi, and outside Mombasa itself, may at certain seasons breed sudden bursts of bad weather; but these can usually be seen coming and prepared against. It seemed to me that many of these vessels had been lost in squalls. Their unwieldy lateen sails and their too close proximity to a dangerous coast, in addition to an inadequate look-out and too great a faith in Allah, had been their undoing. Not that it always took a squall to sink them. The dhow *Admiral*, for instance – another from Lamu – was quietly entering the port when "all of a sudden she struck the old shipwreck" right in the centre of the passage. That was the end of her. The shipwreck has been there a long time; surely the nakhoda knew the way past it. There is, too, the sad story of the Zanzibar dhow *Fat-el-Khair*, which was sailing from Zanzibar to Pemba in bad weather when "all of a sudden the mast came down," which would be a calamity aboard any vessel. The nakhoda, however, overcame this disability and ran for Mombasa in distress, where he duly arrived.

Some of the dhows have simply gone missing. They sailed, and never came in anywhere, and nothing of them has ever been found. Losses of the small Swahili craft are numerous, but the big Arabs seemed to be mentioned rarely in that book. The Indians had their share of woe. There is, for instance, the story of the Indian dhow *Kaalianpassa* (178 tons), which, with a cargo of 2,700 Indian mats from Pasni towards Zanzibar, sprang a leak about a month out. The sworn statement of the master, Moosa Ahmed, duly recorded in the Casualty Book goes on:

> "We could not get at the leak because of the cargo. The vessel sank quickly. We abandoned her and rowed three days and landed all safe at Malindi. I took my map of India, my map of Africa being lost."

I like the picture of Captain Moosa, his ship going down, searching for his map of Africa and, not finding it, taking the map of India instead, on the ground, I suppose, that any map was better than none. But he was a long way from India, if they had been at sea a month. He also, he adds, took two saucepans of fresh water, a compass, six pounds of flour, and the oars. It was just as well to take the oars. A sailor, Othman Bachu, confirms his captain's story, adding only that it took fifteen minutes to clear the boat, and the sea was over the decks of the dhow before they left. He admits that the boat was not stocked with provisions or water. Judging by my experience, boats never are, for the fatalistic Muslim would never dream of doing such a thing. They had not seen land, but they knew they had only to pull towards the west and they were bound to turn up somewhere in Africa. They are very prosaic about it: the three days' pull in the open boat, in bad weather and beneath a dreadful sun, seems to have inconvenienced nobody.

"We set course for the west, and got to land on the third day," Othman says, adding that they had no money. Beside his testimony is his mark, a smudged thumb-print: Captain Moosa signed his statement in the same way.

Then there is the Indian kotia *Din Ganja Pirpassa*, whose master was Mohamed Hajji Jammohamed. His kotia was of 135 tons and had a crew of ten. "On the thirteenth of January, 1939," he begins, "I with ten able crew left Mangalore for Mombasa with 60,000 flat tiles and two tins pepper pickles consigned to Mombasa Hardware Ltd. The weather was fine until the twenty-second when the wind suddenly increased in force and the sea rose and it became tempestuous." They lowered the sail and let the ship drift; this is the usual way of meeting bad weather both in Arab and Indian vessels. The kotia "laboured heavily and rolled seas on board." He thought she would founder and therefore jettisoned 12,000 of the tiles. This saved the day and the ship lived through the storm.

Afterwards the weather fined, and she sailed on to Mombasa, reaching there on the eighth of February with the rest of the cargo.

This casualty record was an interesting book. I noticed that, though accidents were frequent, loss of life was not. "They are all good swimmers," the shipping clerk said. It seemed to me that they have to be. I looked out through the window again at the animated scene down on the Old Harbour, where the longboats pulled with song and sweep of long oars among the Arab and Indian fleets, and the sound of the drum and chant and triangle mingled with the stamping of feet and the clapping of great hands. I wondered how many of those great dhows might have wallowed helplessly in the trough of the sea, sails lowered and seas on board, on the way down from Arabia, how many of the sinewy sailors chanting and working there might have rowed three days towards the west with nothing but a useless map of India to guide them.

The shipping clerk was looking out, too. He was a pleasant young Indian.

"A queer life," he said. "Don't you think?"

The diversions and these yarns of dhows were interesting, but we were rid of our passengers and had sold no salt. After five days Nejdi announced that we would sail for Zanzibar on the morrow. This, of course, we did not do; but three days later we were gone.

X

ON TO ZANZIBAR

After Mombasa, Zanzibar. That was the way of most Arab African voyages, and it was our way then. We slipped out from Mombasa before daybreak one morning, with our hold full of salt, and thirty new passengers on deck going to Zanzibar. Though with them we were still sixty persons on board, the ship seemed almost deserted, and life was heavenly. Our new passengers were Arabs from the Hadhramaut going south on business, as well as some citizens of Mombasa making an excursion, and a small group of Suri merchants who looked as if they might have been prominent in the hashish trade. The Suri clustered about the officers' bench listening to a monologue from Nejdi, and I began to wonder whether he had not shipped them simply to have an audience, for they sat at his feet most respectfully, and never were behind with their *taiyib*s.

We were passing pleasantly down the channel between Pemba – which the Arabs called the Island of Green – and the mainland long before evening. The breeze was good and the conditions perfect. We were well in mid-channel, for we were not going in anywhere in Pemba and we gave the place a good berth. As we sailed along, steadily nearing this Zanzibar which had been our goal for so long, excitement mounted in the ship. The sailors ran bright-eyed and with greater alacrity to their work and put more zest into their singing. Now that the passengers from Mukalla and Shihr were gone, there was room to dance on the maindeck again, and they danced there to every order, as if they were making up for lost time. As soon as each piece of work was done, they danced, with hand-clapping and rhythmic stamping of their horny feet; there was a greater sense of anticipation among them and an air of excitement than I had ever observed before. This place Zanzibar, this haven of the East African seas, meant a great deal to them, and not only because it marked the end of our outward voyage. From there, even if the ship continued to the southward, as she must if she were to load in the Rufiji Delta, they would be homeward bound. But I gathered that the prospect of the delights of the *bebes* of Zanzibar exceeded even the pleasurable thought of shortly being homeward bound, for these *bints* of Zanzibar, they told me, were the best in the Indian Ocean. There were enough and to spare for all comers, and they were exceedingly ready to afford delight to the virile Arab sons of the sea.

The way from Mombasa to Zanzibar is short and comparatively easy, and on the second morning we were off the northern end of Zanzibar island. The dawn was of that lovely kind which only the Indian Ocean knows, and the ship, running upright and graceful before the quiet wind, had never looked better. The mellow tones of the pre-dawn prayer were musical, and the chorused *amin*s of the sailors and the passengers ushered in the lovely day. The ship wandered onwards, quite upright in the sea for once, for the breeze was behind her and there was no sea to make her pitch or roll: she had no motion other than her own way. Flying-fish skimmed away from the side of the hull as she ran on; the wooded beaches of Tumbatu Island slipped by to leeward. Our drums were lying on the firebox ready to be warmed to drum us in to Zanzibar, for we should come in there with more noise even than we had brought to Mombasa.

The day was perfect, and the breakfast of unleavened bread tasted well that morning. On board, when the prayers were done, all was quiet and peaceful, in contrast with the conditions on the rest of the voyage. Swift little double-outrigger canoes manned by Swahili fishermen flashed rapidly by. Zanzibar is a pleasant low wooded land, with golden beaches.

I thought, as we ran down the bright fine morning, of all the great ships that had passed that way and of the sea history which had been made in those waters. The Arabs, the Persians, the Indians, the Chinese, and the Malays too, before fierce Arab rivalry had driven them to their own waters, then Vasco da Gama, the Portuguese, and after him the rest of the Europeans. We had passed in the night the reef off Pemba where Vasco da Gama had left his ship *San Rafael* during that famous passage to India at the end of the fifteenth century. The *San Rafael* touched on a reef off Pemba and was abandoned for lack of seamen to get her home. She was not badly damaged, apparently, but by that time Vasco da Gama had lost many of his men and could not get his three ships home. So the *San Rafael* was burned, and her sailors taken to the other ships.

According to Nejdi, who like most Arab nakhodas had a wide, if not very accurate, knowledge of the history of the Indian Ocean, it would have been a better world if the Portuguese had burned all his ships on a Pemba reef, and himself with them. Nejdi saw nothing remarkable in Vasco da Gama's voyage, and a great deal to be regretted. According to

Nejdi, the man was not even a sailor; and, as for the voyage, it was merely an over-publicised piece of carefully exploited good fortune. The success of the voyage, he said, had been made possible by the use of Arab pilots who were compelled to show the Portuguese the way, for they came in their well-armed ships, and forced the Arabs to pilot them. Nejdi and the others spoke about the voyage as if it were a comparatively recent event. The man they honoured was not Vasco da Gama or any other Portuguese, but the famous Arab pilot Ibn Majid who had, they said, shown him the way from Malindi to Calicut. They would have honoured Ibn Majid more if he had thrown the Portuguese fleet on the shoals of the Laccadive Islands. Ibn Majid, according to Nejdi, was an Arab from the Persian Gulf, possibly from somewhere on the Hasa coast. He had been a famous pilot, and his safe conduct of Vasco da Gama from Africa to Calicut was the only thing against him. The Portuguese, however, had made him do that. Nejdi said he was a hostage delivered by the Sheikh of Malindi, when Vasco da Gama had so harassed the town that only an offer of safe pilotage to India would induce him to leave it.

It occurred to me that Nejdi would have found it difficult to pilot his ship from Malindi to Calicut even today, for the way lies over the open sea for many hundred miles, and Nejdi did not know the way across the oceans. He knew only the way along the land. I asked him if he could make such a passage. He said, Yes, of course he could. He would hire an Indian muallim to measure the sun. This lack of proper navigational knowledge among the Arab nakhodas of today was a sore point with Nejdi, who knew well enough that in that field they compared poorly with the Arabs of old. No longer could a nakhoda of the Persian Gulf – such a man as Nejdi – take his dhow and voyage to China, Malaya, and Singapore. He could not, without employing an Indian navigator, even undertake to deliver a shipload of pilgrims from Calicut to Jiddah, and on all his African voyages he had to coast.

It had not always been so, and Nejdi knew it. In the great days of the Arab navigators, Arab dhows covered the eastern seas: now it was half a century since one had rounded the southern tip of Ceylon. Ancient methods, the old instruments, the old mathematics – in which the Arabs had so long excelled – all these were lost, and nothing had come to take their place, nothing but discarded steamship compasses bought in a junk-yard in Bombay, and uncorrected out-of-date Admiralty charts. Yet the Arabs still sailed, though they had lost much of their knowledge and some of their glory. Their voyages consisted largely of petty coastal trading and smuggling. Nejdi attributed their decline to their own softness, and the heartless and efficient exploitation of their trades by the Europeans.

All this made interesting subject for conversation that bright morning as the big dhow slipped along the island of Zanzibar. I should have listened to Nejdi with greater patience if he had not always been so sure that he was right. According to him, we Europeans were all doomed, and too stupid, to be worth bothering about. We were no longer even the 'people of the Book,' for obviously we had given up the teachings of our Book. The only advantage we had ever had had been the superiority in wealth and arms, which, for some inscrutable reason, Allah in His wisdom had allowed us. Perhaps this had only been His way of administering a lesson to the softening Arabs, and providing the Europeans with the means to destroy themselves. Yet Allah was wise and all-knowing: the day of the Europeans would soon be ended, and the Arabs come again into their own. *Taiyib*, murmured all the Suri, and Hamed bin Salim. I said nothing.

Nejdi liked to say that the Arabs had regarded the Cape as a sort of divine protection for themselves in their eastern seas. Good Hope in the south with its storms; the Red Sea with its reefs and its dangers in the north; the great bulwark of immense and unknown Africa, the deserts and the dangers athwart the path of the land caravan bound eastwards towards the Persian Gulf – these things, Nejdi said, were Allah's bulwarks against the infidels. When they fell, it was a punishment for the too great softness of the Arabs, who had held almost undisputed dominion over the whole Indian Seas from the sixth to the sixteenth centuries, and had grown fat and soft from their profits. They had spread their settlements from Zanzibar to the Philippines, from Java to Canton, from the Malabar coast to the Sudan, from Siam to Mandalay, from Mozambique to Malacca. Now the Nazarene had built far greater empires, but they, too, would fall, and again the bulwarks protecting the vast preserves of the Arabs would become effective, and only ships propelled by the lateen sail would wander over eastern waters. Allah was compassionate, and the time for the punishment of the infidels was at hand.

Thus spoke Nejdi, day after day. All his philosophy and all his arguments, all his hopes and all his views seemed grounded in fatalism and faith in the compassion of Allah. According to him, God spoke and understood only Arabic. Nejdi was welcome to his views, which gave him considerable satisfaction.

By this time it was mid-morning, and there was more work going on about the decks than I had ever seen being done in a dhow at sea before. Kaleeel and a gang were fish-oiling *Afra*, the new small jalboot, which stank horribly. *Afra* had not been sold at Lamu or Mombasa, but Nejdi hoped to sell her in Zanzibar for a satisfactory sum. She was a good-looking young vessel, with a smooth bottom, a nice run, and a saucy sheer to her. It was a pity she had to be fish-oiled and could not be decently painted. *Afra*'s price, complete with mast and sail, and one anchor, was still a thousand shillings.

Hassan, the helmsman, was cleaning the brass binnacle, for the first time since Mogadishu. The serang and the sailors, on their hands and knees, were scrubbing the poop with their bare hands: the ship had no brooms. Yusuf Shirazi was shredding tobacco for the hookah. Hamed bin Salim and Abdulla, Nejdi's brother, were asleep in the shade of the mizzen. Ismael the musician was tuning his guitar beneath the break of the poop, and Jassim the cook was boiling Haifun fish. On top of his firebox were the drums, drying in the sun. They would be warmed at the fire later.

Zanzibar Channel was a lovely place. By this time we were not far from the town itself, and we found ourselves one of a stately fleet of Arab, Swahili, and Persian vessels, big and small, sailing towards it. Round us the last double-outrigger canoes were skimming, homeward bound with fish. Once we overhauled a large Indian baggala lumbering along, rolling slightly, for she was very light. Her huge carved stern, covered with elaborate designs, was very handsome. We passed close, so that we could see through the grills in the stern windows into her great cabin, where the ghee jars hung and lots of mysterious things in raffia baskets: a silken flag with red and white bars, very large, flew over her stern. She was a Porbandar ship, Nejdi said. A good one, I ventured to remark, to which Nejdi replied that the Arabs were better, though he was surely too good a seaman to think this. He could not bear that anything Arab should ever appear at a disadvantage. True, his *Triumph* was much faster than the Indian, and we slipped past her very quickly, in spite of the fact that she was light and we were deeply laden. But I know in which ship I should prefer to face a blow.

We were in sight of the city of Zanzibar before noon. We were sailing then towards the pass in the reef not far from Livingstone's house, with our drums beating and the sailors gathered in a group on the fore deck, singing, and the red flag of Kuwait flowing out astern. We had our special flag out that day, the big one in red silk, with 'el-Kuwait' embroidered on it in Arabic characters, in white, and vertically, down the hoist, the familiar text of the Qurân which adorns all good Arab flags – "There is no God but God: and Mohamed is the Prophet of God." Nejdi always felt particularly dignified, and probably also very wise, when we flew that flag. We flew it only at Zanzibar, on this arrival day, and when we came back to Kuwait. I never saw any other Kuwait ship with a flag quite so ornate as ours. Our ordinary ensign was a piece of red linen about twelve feet by three feet, a plain flag, simply inscribed 'el-Kuwait.'

The scene was a grand one – the ship running in before the quickening breeze towards the palm-fringed beach, standing apparently right towards the land for a while, then swinging, in a wide curve, towards the anchorage: the great fleet of dhows assembled there, many of them with their colours out welcoming the Persians, the Suri, the Indian, and the Kuwaiti which were coming in together; the blue sea; and, in the background, the pleasing silhouette of Zanzibar itself, shimmering in the haze like a line of white sails. Now we straightened up on the last leg towards the dhow anchorage, which seemed so filled with dhows that I could not see where we could fit in.

The buildings of Zanzibar, which had shimmered and danced in the heat, began to take concrete form, and the great white palace of the Sultan, coming down to earth, did not bulk so huge, though it was uglier. The other houses stretching red-roofed towards the point in a long straight line ceased their miraged dance, too, and now stood in orderly array. Nearer to us were booms and dhows of all kinds high and dry on the beach, and in the brief lulls of our own sailors' lusty singing we could hear the songs of their sailors careening them, and all the tumult of the harbour – Suri drums, Omani feet-stampings, Swahili songs, Lamu fiddles, Batina triangles. Still we kept running on towards the anchorage, in which I could see no place where we could enter. It was like a war fleet assembled against us, a solid wall of oiled wooden hulls shining in the sun, with red flags flying and, here and there, the glint of burnished brass. Our own brass shone, too, and Nejdi and Hamed bin Salim were dressed in their flowing best. Nejdi wore his best aghal, the one with the half-twist in front which, I gathered, was the latest thing in Kuwaiti fashions. The passengers were standing about, also in their best clothes, all staring at the scene. Several of the Suri, in long brown gowns and embroidered turbans, were standing on the poop intently watching something. I saw that two of them had small parcels secreted in their cloaks.

Meanwhile our sailors continued to sing and there was such a banging of drums as I never had heard before. The serang was leading them, an expression of ecstasy on his negroid face. They sang and sang, banging on tambourine and drum. They sang so much that they could hear no orders, and, though they were far forward, as near to the eyes of the ship as they could get, they made so much noise that it was difficult for the helmsman to hear Nejdi's orders even when they were relayed by Hamed bin Salim in a very loud voice. Our mizzen had been made fast earlier, but the yard was still aloft: our largest mainsail was mastheaded, and the great area of that sail swelled with the freshening wind. We were coming in at eight knots. Now we were off the anchorage, our keen bow slicing through the sea.

"Port a little," from Nejdi, standing in the gig at the quarter davits.

"Port a little," louder, from Hamed bin Salim beside the wheel.

"As Allah wills!" from Abdulla, giving her a few spokes.

"Now we are coming in,
And this voyage is ending:
Thanks be to Allah,
Always the Merciful!"

Thus sang our score of mariners, to the accompaniment of loud banging on all the ship's drums, and ecstatic whoops and cheers from Mohamed the serang.

"Nejdi has brought us here,
Nejdi, good master:
Thanks be to Allah,
Always the Merciful!"

On and on and on, with never a glance at what was happening to the ship or the alarming nearness of the other vessels, the sailors sang.

"Who helped Nejdi?
Hamed good muallim:
Thanks be to Allah,
Always the Merciful!"

"Lower the mainsail!" suddenly from Nejdi.

No answer from the mariners, singing more lustily than ever, hearing nothing else.

"Lower the mainsail! Hamed bin Salim screamed, rushing to the break of the poop. "Lower the mainsail!"

Still no answer from the mariners singing away: no answer, and no obedience.

The ship was charging at the assembled moored vessels, as if she were going to break a way through them, since none seemed open by other means. There were fifty Arab ships swinging there. The wind was fresher than ever, and the short distance between the *Triumph* and the anchored fleet was becoming less with alarming speed. We could see the faces of some Persians in the nearest boom watching with mild interest. I wondered why they did not fear for their lives, for it looked as though we should be charging into them within ten seconds. I reckoned without Nejdi. He excelled at such seamanship as this.

Hamed bin Salim was still screaming orders to lower the sail, while he dashed at the halliards to let them go. As always, nothing had been prepared and nothing was ready: the two hauling parts of the halliards were still thoroughly fast with turns and half-hitches round the forward beam. It was four men's work to let them go. At last the serang saw that the sail must be lowered and, leaping up, he led half the mariners to that job while the others still sang and banged the drums. It seemed minutes before the halliards were let go, but probably it was only a few seconds. The great parrals aloft began to creak and the yard to rumble down, while the cotton sail bellied out over the lee side and engulfed the singers. Down came the yard, creaking and protesting; on rushed the ship. Still drums banged and songs came from somewhere underneath the sail.

Now we were at the outer edge of the anchored fleet, inside the buoys marking the native vessels' anchorage. It appeared to me that we must certainly collide violently with at least three vessels, sending them skittling through the rest of the fleet moored behind them. But again I reckoned without Nejdi. He knew what he was doing. He held up his hand to stop the drums, for the songs were ended, and there was now work enough for everyone. He rapped out orders while the ship raced on. I saw that he had found a place, a very narrow place, into which I did not think our boom could enter, between a large Indian dhow and two Suri moored stem and stern side by side. He was charging at that, and signalled to his brother to give her a spoke of the wheel this way or that. Meanwhile, when the sail had been gathered in and quickly cut from its stops, the sailors under Hamed bin Salim and the serang were getting lines ready. I did not know then what they were for, since we were not coming alongside. Our long oiled nose was already in the fleet: we were in the gap, bowling through. Nejdi shouted an order I did not understand, and immediately our sailors were in the water, in their clothes, swimming for dear life. They were pulling ends and bights of the mooring lines with them, and they swam rapidly to the other vessels, boarding the Indian and the outer of the two Suri. Here they quickly made fast the ends and bights of the mooring-lines, while other sailors aboard the *Triumph* gathered in the slack and checked the vessel's way.

She was coming in so quickly and she had so much way – for she was a ship of near 150 tons, and she still had more than 100 tons of cargo – that the sudden checking of her way made the Indian and the two moored Suri strain violently at their own anchors, and they ranged a little so that they brushed other ships. But they brushed them only lightly and did no harm. Nejdi, using these checks brilliantly, and very rapidly, eased his big vessel through the gap and alongside the Indian, bringing her there so quickly that the manœuvre was accomplished almost as soon as I could perceive its aim.

At first I could not understand how he would take up his moorings, or even find any, in that crowded place, yet there he was, the ship in a good position, safe, and brought there without so much as rubbing against another vessel. The brilliant use of the two checks, and the fine watermanship of the sailors, alone made it possible. I was to observe later that feats of seamanship of this kind were common at the Zanzibar anchorage, where the native craft were herded together in a buoyed-off area not large enough to hold them, and certainly not large enough to give them elbow room.

The Arabs did not seem to mind this. They would probably have herded together anyway, for they loved that. They made use of the confusion which naturally surrounded such an arrival to evade the most irksome of the European regulations. No amount of strict inspection could possibly oversee all that went on when a ship came driving into a fleet like that; when she had, perforce, to take up her moorings cheek by jowl with half a dozen other dhows. It was a severe offence for a dhow to anchor beyond the limits of the dhow anchorage, and a motor-boat from the port office would soon bring out officials to shout at her and shift her. No matter. The moment we came charging into that fleet, I saw our Suri hop over the side, on the side farthest from the town. One swam to a small boat astern of a sambuk, and this he quickly rowed back to us. The other jumped into it and they rowed away at once. Within a minute they had disappeared, and where they had gone into that fleet I did not know – though I had been watching closely. With them went the mysterious parcels they had been carrying.

At the same time, some of the passengers disappeared. It was too easy. Only those remained on board, I suppose, who possessed the necessary official papers, and were entered on the proper list. The Suri grinned like happy schoolboys as they rowed away, and seemed to regard everything as a joke. What was in those parcels they so carefully landed? I asked Abdulla, not expecting to be told anything and knowing that I should have to disbelieve anything I might be told. Abdulla grinned. Hashish? I ventured, having heard that this was likely. Abdulla grinned again. After some time, he remarked that the Suri were no good, and grinned still more.

Later, ashore in Zanzibar, I was talking to a medical man. It was a strange thing, he said, that as soon as the north-east monsoon set in and the Arabs and the Indians began to come down, none of his patients asked for opium, until the dhows had gone again. Perhaps, he said, the Indians brought some down.

Perhaps they did, I said.

Our arrival at Zanzibar marked the end of an important stage of the voyage. From there on we were homeward-bound, though we still had to go farther to the South, down to a place called Simba Uranga at the mouth of the Rufiji River. Our salt was sold and the rest of our cargo disposed of, except the bad dates, which by this time were fermenting horribly. With their sickly stench, and the frightful odour of the Suri fish all round the harbour, the anchorage was a foul place. Half the assembled fleet there seemed to be Suri, all laden with stinking fish. Fortunately, we lay on the outside of the fleet, and the wind blew from us toward the land. Our anchorage was across from the entrance to Funguni Creek, where the smaller ships were taken in and beached for cleaning.

When we came in, Abdulla Kitami's boom was on the beach, propped up on stilts. One of our first visitors was Abdulla Kitami himself. He came aboard all smiles. He had, he said, already been at Zanzibar a month. He had been fourteen days sailing from Shihr to Mombasa direct, and had had no trouble landing his 150 passengers, none of whom had died. The bulk of his cargo had been sold at Mombasa where he had stayed ten days. Abdulla Kitami had then come on to Zanzibar, while we sweltered in Mogadishu and Lamu. He had now sold the remainder of his cargo. He was waiting until the north-east monsoon quieted, and it was time to go up to Lamu to load mangrove poles for home. It was not yet the end of February, and he had still some time to wait.

Abdulla Kitami seemed pleased with himself, but some of his sailors who pulled him out in the boom's longboat talked with our sailors, and were not so pleased. They liked Zanzibar, but two months there was too much. It was, they said, an expensive place, with far too many distractions. If they spent all the money there, they would have nothing left when they got home. Why, they murmured, had their nakhoda not gone elsewhere? Why had he not found it possible, as the Suri and many of the Persians did, to get a freight locally from some port to the south'ard, and earn a little with that instead of lying there on the beach earning nothing? A ship, they said, made her voyage to earn money. She earned nothing sitting on the Zanzibar beach. She could have gone tramping down to the Rufiji, to bring a cargo of poles from there for sale at Zanzibar, and then have gone northwards to Lamu for her second cargo. She could have gone for corn from Mikindani, as Sulieman Said was reported to have done with his big baggala. She could have found something to carry from Zanzibar, or to bring to Zanzibar, if only the nakhoda had bestirred himself and tried. The sailors had a direct interest in seeing that the voyage was properly conducted since they shared in its receipts. If Abdulla Kitami himself, they pointed out, wished to stay in Zanzibar and waste his money, he could do so. Saud the slave could take the ship. Saud was every bit as good a sailor and navigator. He had taken the small boom from Aden to Mukalla and Shihr, just as Hamed bin Salim had brought us. He was to have a boom himself the following year. Saud was a good man, not over interested in the flesh pots, and not one to leave his ship rotting in the sun two months on the Zanzibar beach.

I listened to all this with interest, for it was only about that time that I really was beginning to learn the sailors' ideas about what went on. I mentioned the subject to Abdulla Kitami later, and asked him why he had not tried to earn some freights with his ship instead of waiting. Nearly all the other vessels were earning something. He said the Suri took such low freights that he could not compete with them; he could not, he said, possibly make any money hauling corn from Lindi or Mikindani or from Kilwa at half a shilling a bag, and the Suri accepted freights at less than that. He blamed it on the Suri; but I am not sure whether he was justified. He would not have lost money. At least he would have earned expenses, which was better than nothing. The sailors had to pay for all the food eaten in idleness at Zanzibar. He could have bought his own cargo in the Rufiji, if he had cared to. The cash could have been advanced by merchants in Zanzibar if he had none himself.

Nejdi made no mystery, for once, about his intentions. The *Triumph* was not going to be laid up, or even hauled into Funguni Creek and cleaned. She was going on to the southward as soon as her cargo was discharged. If there were time, she would make two trips there, the first back with a cargo for sale at Zanzibar, and the second to load for the Gulf. Nejdi would not take her. Hamed bin Salim would do that. The Rufiji, according to Nejdi, who had never been there, was a frightful place, quite the worst place any Arab ship went to. It was a gloomy swamp of ooze and mud covered with mangrove poles and jungle, in which the mosquitoes bit like dogs. It rained every day and the place was full of fever. The river teamed with crocodiles and other beasts, which overturned boats; the jungle was alive with snakes and chattering monkeys. Surely, Nejdi suggested, I did not want to go to a place like that? The ship might be there three weeks, or even a month: she would have to find her own cargo. It would be better, he went on, if I stayed with him; he had a place in Zanzibar, and we could go to Dar-es-Salaam and Bagamoyo, and up to Pemba.

I admit that this was an enticing prospect, and the idea of six weeks in Zanzibar and the surrounding ports was tempting. However, I decided that I would stay with the ship. I would go where she went, with or without Nejdi. He seemed to have some reason for not wishing me to go to the Rufiji; I must look into that. It was hardly likely that I should ever make such a voyage again, and I wanted to learn all I could. I should not learn much about ships with Nejdi in Zanzibar.

In the *Triumph*, it was impossible to foretell when something interesting might happen. One had to be there all the time, and enter wholly into the ship's life. It was no use being an onlooker. It was no use, either, to stay at Zanzibar, or to run across to Bagamoyo or any other place, for I should lose the thread of things in the ship. At that time, after being three months on board, I was only just beginning to find out what was really going on, for the Arabs, though not deliberately secretive, were expert at covering both their deeds and their thoughts. It was only by watching the proceedings of every day, watching and observing them carefully, and deciding for myself what really had been happening, that I came slowly to know what was going on. The obvious facts of the voyage stood out plainly – the wind and the weather, and where the ship was. But the more interesting things – the social and economic life of the sailors, the business structure of the ship and her voyage, the human side of things, the questionable activities of ship and crew – had to be dug out patiently, waited for, pounced upon, inveigled out of friends, discovered somehow in spite of the attempt to hide them. I do not believe that there was any deliberate attempt to keep things from me, but secretiveness is deep in the Arab character.

It helped a little if I photographed the sailors, for many of them were very vain – vain enough to take great delight in contemplating their own photographs. But the standard of excellence expected of me in this field was embarrassing. It was difficult to make satisfactory photographs of those dark faces, handsome as some of them were. Often my subjects did not recognise themselves when they were handed the finished results, and the lamentations were loud and long. They had a great conceit of themselves, and very firm ideas as to how they should appear. Any falling short of their standard they declared at once to be my fault. It was useless to explain that I could only photograph them as they were, not as they imagined themselves to be.

I found their importunities in this respect sometimes hard to bear, but when I saw the childish delight with which they bought themselves cheap picture frames in the *suq* at Zanzibar, and watched them going to the unheard-of length of employing public letter-writers to write letters home in which to enclose these things, I forgave them and tried to photograph my failures again. The photographs were handed round among all the Kuwaiti in the harbour – more than two hundred men, for there were seven Kuwait ships there at one time during our stay, and their average crew was nearly thirty – to be admired, and I soon found sailors from the other ships hailing me in the street and coming out to the ship to be photographed. This, however, was an honour I declined.

I would stay with the ship, wherever she might go, and indeed looked forward to visiting the Rufiji. It was a place usually inaccessible. It was the place, too, where the destroyed German cruiser *Königsberg* still lay, and I wanted to see her. In the meantime, Zanzibar was very pleasant. The harbour was always interesting, with its great fleet of dhows, and ashore the town was attractive and the hinterland more so. Zanzibar is still the centre of Arab life in East Africa, though the influence of the Arabs has declined. The Arab Sultan of Zanzibar, descendant of the famous Seyyid Said of Oman, still nominally rules the island and its neighbour Pemba. His white-painted steamers, very smart, lie in the harbour; his uniformed band plays on the square before the English Club, and once weekly by the beach. His new white palace is a pleasant sight on the waterfront, and almost any day one may see him come out of it in a large Rolls-Royce with a red flag on the radiator, a bearded and benign old gentleman in a turban, going for a ride. Beside his palace stands the great House of

Wonders which a former sultan built and then lost because it was too expensive to keep up: this is now the government offices, and the old harim quarters have been made into a girls' school.

Not long ago Zanzibar was the headquarters of the Arab slave trade, and here stood one of the last public slave-markets in the world. Where the market was, there is now a cathedral. In these days Indians appear to own most of the businesses of any size in Zanzibar, as well as most of the coconut and clove plantations. Africans do the porterage and the stevedoring; the British do the governing. But the Arabs still crowd in their dhows with the coming of every north-east monsoon, and the Suri, brown-shirted and erect, still strut in the streets of the *suq*. They are allowed to carry arms, and hardly one Omani Arab is seen abroad who does not sport at least a curved dagger, silver-mounted in an ornate silvered sheath, lashed about his waist. The Kuwaiti bear no arms, for, in Kuwait, to carry arms is the mark of the Beduin; and the Beduin, according to the Kuwaiti, are uncouth. The *suq* of Zanzibar is considered satisfactory even by the Kuwait sailors, who regard nothing as approaching the standard of excellence set by their own town.

Once away from the stench of the near-putrid fish by the harbour, I found Zanzibar a good place. In the *suq* were all kinds of tropic fruits, and fish and meats and vegetables. The confection called *halwa*, melons, mangoes, sickly sweet cakes, and other Arab delicacies were there in abundance, and the confectionary-makers had the reputation of being second only to those of Muscat. There were arms shops in the *suq*, too, where one could buy an Omani dagger, though I saw none that was first-class.

I gathered from our mariners that Zanzibar was also the finest place on the whole coast for *bebes* and *bints* of all kinds, and for them the delights of Zanzibar's nights were boundless. In that port we had not even a dance on board, for the sailors were never there at night. Nejdi was away ashore, and often did not come near the ship for days. Everybody else was ashore except Hamed bin Salim, who went only on business, and old Yusuf Shirazi, who went to the *suq* to do the ship's buying by day, and landed for only two other reasons – to sell the last of the goods from his private chest, and to buy presents for his wife and children in Kuwait. Often, Hamed bin Salim, old Yusuf, and I were the only ones on board, after the day's work was done; and I was not there much. I liked the harbour, but I also liked the town. Yusuf hawked Hadhramaut baskets in the shops, where he offered them for ninepence each, and they sold them for two shillings. Yusuf had several sacks full of Mukalla baskets and fans which he had been selling to shops at all our ports: he sold the last of them in Zanzibar. Ismael was much in demand as a musician, and was engaged to play at parties and in the Arab night clubs. This pleased him and it pleased me. It pleased him because it meant cash, and it pleased me because it meant a quiet ship.

There was not much a sailor could not do in Zanzibar. To the Arabs and the other Asiatics, it was a wide open town and both the night life and the day life of the place were free enough for anybody. Our sailors usually worked all day, except for the siesta after the mid-morning meal which they took aboard, and they did not go ashore until the late afternoon. The routine was always the same. First they sold something – their stocks never seemed to give out – and then they spent the proceeds on the *bebes*. Any time between midnight and the dawn prayer, they came aboard again. Night after night it was the same: they were never satiated. Old Yusuf once confided in me that he did not think much of the goings-on at Zanzibar where, he said, the women were too free. He would hate, he said, to take a wife from that place. By the age of twelve the women had acquired a taste for variety which made them poor spouses for any man, most of all a sailor.

When they were short of money the sailors had not necessarily to go short of women, for I gathered that a lusty man of the sea was much sought after and, if his money was done, all a sailor need do was to go for a short walk out of town, across the plantations or towards some watering-place, preferably at the time of the midday siesta when the men should be asleep. On such occasions he was sure to find some *bebe* on the lookout for adventure. The women must have been sad when the fleets sailed away, but some of the sailors always remained behind. The sparkle had gone from the eyes of those Arabs who had been there too long, and they had obviously become soft. An Arab who had been five years in Zanzibar, Yusuf said, was no good in Arabia again. He had better stay in the island.

When the Arab was away from home, according to Yusuf, his story was always the same. First he traded; then he settled. Then he went to ruin. Women, drink, easy-living – that was the way of it. Forgetfulness of the word of the Prophet, disregard of the daily prayers, non-observance of the severe fasts, an overpowering sensuality which found full play for its every wanton urge – so he went down the primrose path, and rarely fought his way back again. Less than half a century before, the Arab had been master in Zanzibar and of all that coast: now the Goanese sewed his pantaloons and made his coats; the Hindu had his business and half his plantations; the Indian took his thalers, his rupees, his pounds. The British told him how to manage his ship and where he might anchor her. The customs made him register his vessel, and compelled the nakhoda to have a certificate of competence. Every move of his ship was controlled and approved according to the Act.

The supervision of Arab dhows was far-reaching and at least nominally effective. It was enacted that all dhows must be properly surveyed and in possession of current registration papers. Crew lists must be complete and strictly correct. Crews must be engaged voluntarily, and not be in excess of the number of sailors reasonably required for the working of the ship. (This to prevent slave-running.) The number of passengers a vessel might carry was limited – ten for her first ten register tons, and seven for every succeeding ten tons. This would have restricted our *Triumph* to 94, since she was registered there as 130 tons, which seemed to me a reasonable allowance. Vessels must be seaworthy; crew lists must be checked on entering and leaving – they were not; no one might be signed on without supervision; all passengers must be in possession of proper identity papers, and entered on the passenger list; dhows must sail when cleared, and have no further communication with the shore; no dhow might sail at night except with special permission. It was all very nicely laid down in the local Act. Dhows must carry proper navigation lights, including anchorage lanthorns; they must fly their colours, entering and leaving; they must not dump rubbish in the harbour; nakhodas, if otherwise unlicensed, must pass an examination before the port officer for certificates of competency. The port officer, or his substitutes, must be satisfied as to the competency, sobriety, experience, ability, and general good conduct of the applicant, whose certificate when granted was subject to cancellation or suspension for reasonable cause.

And so on, almost ad infinitum. The lives of the Arab seafarers seemed well defined and circumscribed by legal regulation – not that it mattered a great deal, for the regulations had come into existence to correct flagrant abuses rather than to control the Arab's every act. No one bothered the dhows, so long as they stayed in their own anchorage and did not smuggle too flagrantly. As for the certificates of competency, though these were undoubtedly a step in the right direction, and the Arabs were proud of them when gained – they were accustomed to frame them and stow them carefully away in their chests – passing the examination was not unduly difficult. In theory, a satisfactory knowledge of the Rule of the Road, so far as it applied to them and to possible collisions with steamships, a thorough grasp of seamanship and of the intricacies of African coastal pilotage, and some elementary ability to cope with ordinary maritime accidents, were demanded of the Arab applicants. When it was discovered that the nakhoda of a deep-water dhow from Arabia had no certificate, he was duly paraded before the port officer and 'examined.' The examination is by no means severe. As the port officers themselves point out, if a man has sailed his dhow from Arabia, it is reasonable to assume that he may be trusted to take her back again. The deep-water dhows are rarely in trouble: it is the small fry, the loosely built Swahili and the ancient craft brought from Arabia and sailed by local mariners, which figure far more in the casualty returns.

One day I was with the port officer, a pleasant young Scot who had been a ship's officer in steam, when one of the Arab nakhodas presented himself for examination. It was Abdul-razzaq, a cross-eyed Suri. I knew him well: we had seen a lot of him. His baggala, a pretty little vessel of about 70 tons, was moored next to ours. Like most of the Suri craft, she had an afterguard of five or six old men. With these, and nominally over them, was the youthful Abdul-razzaq. He was a bombastic young man of about nineteen, over six feet tall, and very thin. Nejdi said his father owned the baggala and several more like her, and that was how the young man had become a nakhoda.

The examination of Abdul-razzaq was perfunctory and very soon over. The port officer, looking bored, first asked him through an interpreter if he knew the rule of the road. Abdul-razzaq certainly did not know it and never would, but the answer was 'Yes.' What lights should a dhow carry under way? None whatever, said Abdul-razzaq. To carry lights was a waste of good money and good oil, an embarrassment to the crew, a disturbance of the slumbers of the afterguard, and a temptation to swordfish to ram the vessel. This seemed to me, even as it was passed on by the interpreter, a fatally incorrect answer; but at that moment the Indian master of the Sultan's Pemba steamer happened to come in. He usually conducted the examinations because he had a good command of Arabic and a better knowledge of nakhodas. With a gesture of resignation, the port officer turned my friend Abdul-razzaq, who was still holding forth on the foolishness of carrying lights at sea, over to him. He implored the Indian captain to overhaul the Suri's unsound views about ship's lights, and the pair of them went into another room. The Indian took some small models to illustrate points in the rule of the road, and a chart of Zanzibar. A few moments later, they were back again. It was announced that Abdul-razzaq had passed. I saw a dubious look flit over the port officer's face, but he said nothing, and a certificate was made out. If masters' licences could be handed out like that in Zanzibar, I felt inclined to sit for one myself, for it was about time I had one. So I sat, and passed, too, and was duly certified as fit to act as nakhoda of deep-sea dhows. The fee for this service was fifteen shillings.

In celebration of this event I decided to take Nejdi to the cinema. He had often expressed the wish to go, and there was a good cinema in Zanzibar. I inquired for him at the office of the agent, which was in a confectionary shop in the heart of the *suq*. It had a large verandah given up to the nakhodas of the more important vessels, and an inner sanctum in which the agent, a Seyyid of devout mien and very few scruples, conducted his business. There were many mysterious chambers upstairs. In one of these, on the third floor, I found Nejdi. He was sitting with Abdulla Kitami, and the pair of them were casting sheep's eyes at a room full of girls behind an iron grill across the courtyard, while a Swahili squatted on the floor entertaining them with a violin. Lunch was being put on a mat, though it was late, and they asked me to join them. We had a good meal of roasted chickens, fish, rice, chilli sauce, and fruit, mainly pineapples and bananas, washed down with curdled milk. When the meal had been consumed, in surprisingly little time, though Nejdi ate three chickens and eight fish, we washed our hands in water brought by a servant, and went to sleep. By the time I woke, about an hour later, a group of Suri were squatting on the floor. We refreshed ourselves with tea and sweetmeats freshly made in the shop downstairs. I then had to sit listening to the Suri for another two hours, and, at the end of that time, Nejdi thought of playing the gramophone which stood in one corner. This was too much for me, though he assured me that Egypt's greatest singer performed on most records. I left them, and strolled to the water-front.

In the early evening I met Nejdi and we went to the cinema, an Indian cinema not far from the *suq*. We took a rickshaw which hurried precariously through the narrow streets, with a negro panting in the shafts and another pushing behind. Nejdi was pessimistic, and confided to me that things were not good in Zanzibar. Soon, he said, he would be pulling a rickshaw himself. There was no price for the salt, and the merchants had no money. The Suri would not pay for services performed, and he could not sell the small dhow. Nejdi was full of woes. The clove crop, he said, on which the prosperity of the island largely depended, had not been good, and in consequence money was scarce. Copra, the only other product exported on a large scale, was almost unsaleable. He did not understand it. The previous year things had been very good, with a large clove crop and good prices: the Arabs had plenty of money, and trade was thriving. Nejdi, like most of the Arabs I knew, found it difficult to adjust himself to sudden changes, indeed to any change at all. If things had been good last year, he argued, why were they not good this year? It must be somebody's fault. If it were not, then it was his own great misfortune. In either case, it was most lamentable. But life was difficult in these days, Nejdi went on, as the rickshaw swung round a corner too violently and came into collision with a large Banyan seated on the step of his shop. It was the Europeans' fault. All the troubles of the world were due to them, because of the unnatural, unstable life they led, unprincipled, avaricious, violently jealous of all other peoples and of one another. They had made a mess of a good world. They should believe in God, and keep their women in order – these were the prime necessities, said Nejdi. These were the fundamentals – belief in God, and the ability to control women. By denying these two truths, the whole European race had lost its balance and was dragging the rest of the world with it.

I did not pay much attention. Nejdi often spoke like that, and I was watching our progress with interest, for the Zanzibar bazaar was a striking place. It was very cosmopolitan. Greek, Goanese, Hindu, Punjabi, Sikh, Cingalese, Omani, Hadhrami, Yemenite, Persian, Iraqi, Kuwaiti, Kurd, Swahili, Baluchi, and Africans of all kinds jostled in the streets, or crowded to one side of the narrow way, making room for our progress, while Nejdi ranted on and I raised no arguments against him. What was the use? He was always so sure that he was right: and in this case, I did not know quite how to answer him. We dashed on through the streets, now at full speed, seeming bound to collide with a melon shop, spilling the colourful contents in all directions, now slowed down to a walk on a rising slope, now passing by a group of merry children, little Arab girls in European frocks with red ribbons in their hair, or an old Banyan walking with his young wife in the street.

It was an unfortunate mood in which to take Nejdi to the cinema. It was also an unfortunate film. It was an American production, typical of Hollywood – a competent piece of showmanship, so far as it went, but uninspired. Usually I should have attached no importance to it, and indeed I should have found it dull, but seen through Nejdi's clear eyes, it assumed a significance that was almost frightening. Before we got out of that cinema I began to wonder very seriously whether, after all, a great many of my Arab friend's views were not nearer right than some of my own. The film dealt with a New York stenographer and her efforts to escape, at least temporarily, from the monotony of her life and her work by spending a holiday in an American vacation camp – a noisy, commercialised, completely vulgar and largely insane place which, apparently, was patronised mainly by large numbers of over-sexed and repressed young women, and a few inane men.

If the film was intended to be a satire on these places, it was without mercy upon them; but I do not think it was meant as a satire. It was just a film, made from a Broadway play, which had run long enough to catch the attention of the Hollywood producers, and it was no more than that. It was not intended, I am sure, as any sort of social documentary. It was intended to make profits, and nothing else. Nejdi read into it a very great deal indeed, and insisted on regarding it as a damning indictment of the white race. He thought it incredibly foolish. If he had had his way, the heroine would have been covered in black and kept within the four walls of a harim. She did not conform to Arab standards of beauty in women, for she had neither breasts nor buttocks worth mentioning, and her bearing was deplorable. She was like a limp rod. She had a very large mouth, somewhat loose, and this was her greatest sin in Nejdi's eyes. With a large mouth no woman could be good, according to him. Why the amorous adventures of this uninspiring young woman, tame and dreadful as they were, should have been made into a motion picture he could not understand. Not that he looked upon it as a motion picture: to him it was a piece of European life. The craziness, the hollow shams, the inane futilities that paraded through that Hollywood production jarred upon him and disgusted him, until he got up, at the fourth clinch, and we went out. I was glad, for the evening was not successful.

He asked me again and again, when we were outside, what did it all mean? The behaviour of the curious people who thronged that American vacation camp was utterly beyond his comprehension, and my description of them as New York Beduin failed to satisfy him, though he thought very little of Beduin. The standard of intelligence of those people should have caused their confinement. How, he asked, could sane people live that way? At the first opportunity the heroine was in the hero's arms. There was nothing wrong in that from the man's point of view, according to

Nejdi, who was never against a little clean lechery. But why film it? Why picture such things as part of our lives? As for the girl, well, at her age, perhaps poor Miss Stenographer had to offer herself rather freely, as she obviously did. But why had she not been married, asked Nejdi? She had been pretty, once. Properly fed, she might have developed a normal appearance, though her mouth would always be against her. But had she no father? What about her family? She should have been taken care of, and married when young.

The picture of life which was given in that film was both sick and sickening. With Nejdi beside me making caustic comments and asking awkward questions, its real significance came home to me. It was a poor show: it *was* a damaging mirror held up to us all. And it was a very poor commentary to be shown there to an audience of Indians and Arabs, most of whom were as bewildered as Nejdi.

Our visit to the cinema was not a success. Nejdi never forgot it, and its destructive picture of ourselves. Throughout the rest of the voyage, and months afterwards when we were in Kuwait, he kept referring to it and preaching to me on the iniquitous stupidity of European life.

I left Nejdi at the gateway of the house where he was staying, and went back on board. The anchorage was quiet and the stars were mirrored in the black water: there was no moon. Ashore, somewhere in the distance I could hear some Swahili singing, and once there came a low sound of song from a Persian longboat pulling back to a Kung boom. When that died away I heard the ring of laughter from a house ashore. All was quiet and peaceful on board and the ghost-like apparition of Yusuf Shirazi rose to meet me at the gangway head. I looked about me at the silent anchorage and above at the raked masts of the boom, silhouetted against the stars, and I thought how satisfying it was to be there, a wanderer with those vagrants of the sea – satisfying, vaguely adventurous, pleasingly picturesque, a man's life in a man's world, which is hard to find anywhere in these days.

Was it not possible that these seafarers from Arabia knew more of living than we did, for all our boasted superiority? Certainly they seemed to know more about contentment, and the acceptance of each day for its own worth and the pleasure of its own living. They were not for ever wanting to be somewhere else, doing something else. They had no desire to be much wealthier than they were, to acquire vast possessions. They had not to be forever switching on radios lest their minds should think, to accept the thoughts handed out to them ready made by the morning's press, to fight and to crowd and to carry on the heartless, meaningless, pitiless enmity of city life. No! They lived and were sufficient unto themselves. Now they were ashore with their *bebes*, and I thought none the less of them for that. Perhaps there are worse things than plain lechery. It seemed to me that some of them were portrayed in that film, and many of them had become mixed up in what passes for our life.

XI

AT KWALE ISLAND

WE STAYED TWO WEEKS at Zanzibar, though all the cargo was out after the first two days. After we had been there a week our departure was announced daily for the morrow. No one paid the least attention to these announcements. They were not even regarded as pious hopes. Tomorrow simply meant some time in the indefinite future. They might have said next week, or next month. The real cause of the delay, I discovered, was the difficulty in collecting payment for the cargo. It was easy to sell it, but collecting payment was a different matter. We had to have silver shillings to pay for our mangrove poles from the Rufiji Delta, and it was no use to leave Zanzibar until we had a chest of shillings on board. In the Rufiji nothing was done on credit. Once we had the shillings, we sailed quickly enough.

In the meantime, a very large boom came in from Kuwait *via* the usual ports, and took up her moorings close to us. Our sailors named her *el-Dhow*, and this was the only time I heard the word 'dhow' used by Arabs. Though she could stow 4,000 packages of dates in her big hold, *el-Dhow* was not an ungainly vessel. She had, they said, been built to carry 5,000 packages and had been cut down, for her original size was too big. She had a crew of forty-five, and there was a new dhow on her maindeck, built on the way down the coast, which was forty feet long. Her nakhoda was the famous Abdul-wahhab-al-Kitami, a stern-looking Arab with a mild voice and blue eyes. *El-Dhow* was kept up in style. She had a gangway, slung from the break of the poop, and the jackstaff at her stemhead bore an excellent model of an Imperial Airways flying-boat. This was a popular form of adornment among the Kuwaiti, who said that their port had recently been made a stopping place for the English aeroplanes. The big boom also had a small model of a biplane mounted as a wind-vane on a movable staff aft, where the helmsman could see it. Our sailors were very proud of the big *Dhow* whose own crew, I noticed, always swaggered through the *suq* with a special roll of their own. She was full of salt and rice, and general cargo. Abdul-wahhab announced his intention of beaching at Zanzibar when this was out of her, and then going up to Lamu to load. She could load over a thousand score poles.

We finally got away from Zanzibar on a Friday. Usually we did not sail on Fridays, for that day is the Muslim Sabbath, when the sailors, if the ship was in port, liked to go to the public prayers in the mosques ashore. It was not a day of rest, and necessary work was always done. The ship's routine, such as it was, was not much affected. But it was a day for visiting, for calling on the other ships from Kuwait which were in the harbour, for drinking coffee and smoking the hookah. When we sailed on a Friday it was always late in the day, for, according to the Arabs, the day ended with the sunset. By their reckoning, sunset on Friday evening ushered in Saturday, when it was proper to sail. We were ready long before that pleasant hour, with the yard mastheaded and the sail in stops ready to be sheeted home, and *Afra* and the longboat on towlines astern. The weather would be quiet for the short run to the Rufiji Delta, little more than a hundred miles south of Zanzibar, and we could tow our boats. We would take *Afra*, since she had not been sold, for she would be handy to ferry mangrove poles from the jungle to the ship.

Our anchors were aweigh, and we lay through the afternoon by a single line to Abdul-wahhab's *el-Dhow*, on the outside of the fleet. Hamed bin Salim was ashore collecting the last sack of shillings. Most of the crew, returned from the noon prayer in the waterfront mosque, were asleep in such shade as they could find. The anchorage was quiet and no one sang, for there was no work going on. Nothing was being floated into or out of Funguni Creek, or on to or off the beach, and the few boats which pulled across the roadsteads were bringing mates and quartermasters to their ships.

We were very high out of the water, for only the bad dates from Aden remained in the hold: these were to be our ballast down to the delta. Being so light, two sections were taken from the mainyard and our smallest sail was bent, for the ship, beamy as she was, could easily be blown over. Abdul-wahhab's crew helped us to masthead the yard, after the third prayer, and sixty men danced on our decks until the planks groaned. That sixty strong men should find hard work in hoisting the single yard of a 150-ton ship may seem unbelievable, but it was so. It is certainly an indication of the inefficiency of the gear. It took them little less than half an hour, though about a third of this time was taken up with dancing and singing. They stopped twice, once when the yard was two-thirds of the way aloft, and again just before it was mastheaded. How they worked, and how they danced and sang! Those Kuwaiti sailors never did things by halves. The whole of the deck was taken up by the hauling, sweating men.

There is a regular ritual about this yard-hoisting which was always religiously observed. As soon as the order to hoist the yard was given, the sailors at once began to sing. There was a special leader for this song – Abdul-latif the sailor, in our case, and he led off in a high-pitched voice. The rest, before the actual hauling was begun, answered with a chorus of the deep throaty growls which seem peculiar to the Kuwaiti. How they could get such a volume of thunderous and almost frightening growling out of their throats I do not know, but the sound always seemed to come from deep inside them. None of the other sailors ever made this noise, not the Suri, or the Persians, or any crews from South Arabia, or Oman, or the Red Sea. It was a deep, powerful, thrilling sound which the Kuwaiti seemed able to keep up almost indefinitely. I do not know what the origin of this habit was, but I should not be surprised if it were very ancient, and had its origin in primitive attempts to scare off bad *jinns*. The sailors I asked did not know why they did it. It was the style, they said, and they liked doing it. It had always been done. They would not think of hoisting up the yard without beginning that way, or of setting off in the boats, or of bringing a pearler to new moorings.

When all hands had answered Abdul-latif's verses, always about Allah and the ship, the wind and the sea, with a sufficient volume of menacing growls, the soloist, striking a yet higher note, suddenly quickened his pace and all hands fell at once upon the halliards. The deep growling stopped and the sailors took up the song while they hauled away on the two parts of the halliard. They hauled like athletes in a mighty tug-o'-war. They did not just work: they *fought* the halliard down and the yard up. They attacked those inanimate ropes as if they were living things to be subdued. The sweat poured from them; the song swelled; the taut yellow line, eightfold in its huge blocks, stood rigid as steel as those great muscled arms brought it down, down. The blocks creaked, protestingly; the loosened parrals groaned; the yard trembled and quivered along its length.

Up, up it went! The blazing sun beat down and there was no shade; the very sea burned with the sun's fierce light, and the sweat ran in streams. This was brutal work. It was difficult to keep foothold as they stamped and stamped again their great calloused feet on the wooden decks and hauled and sang. Up, up! The pace of the song quickened.

"Oh, Allah! help us with our work:
Fill this great sail with wind.
Allah helper, Allah helper

Give strength to our arms
And all of us.
Allah helper, Allah helper,
Breathe Thy winds bravely
On all this Sea.
Allah helper, Allah helper,
And let us go.
Oh, Allah, let our good ship go."

So they sang, all of them, and the effort of the singing was enough for any ordinary strong men, in that fierce climate. Muscles strained and sweat ran unheeded on the deck. The sun blazed until the white beach hurt the eyes, and the glare from the white buildings was impossible to face. They sang with the deep power of virile masculinity. They sang lustily, with power issuing from their throats, sufficient itself to hoist that yard, had it better gear. But the blocks were inefficient and unoiled: the coir halliards were sticky, and full of friction; the parrals were unwieldy, and the yard huge. The leaning angle of the mast made the work heavier. But they worked on, worked and sang. When inefficiency can be redeemed by brute force, the Arab will never trouble about efficiency.

Their breath was not laboured, though they worked so hard. They were all lean and sinewy men, in splendid condition, despite the flesh-pots of Zanzibar. They threw off their long gowns and stood barechested, with only their sarongs. Their headcloths had long since slipped to the deck. Their great bare feet stamped, stamped, stamped, into the deck: Yusuf Shirazi and Jassim the cook worked furiously, getting the slack over the belaying beam for'ard. The muscles rippled on those brown backs like heads of ripe corn in a clean field, swept by a wayward wind. Up, up! The great yard came, slowly, slowly. The song swelled.

The yard was half-way. Mohamed the serang saw this. As one man, they stopped, Yusuf and Jassim holding the ends fast by turns round the beam. Now they danced, three or four on the hatch, with Mohamed the serang and the others round them. They still sang, though with a different rhythm; they stamped their feet, and clapped their great scarred hands in time with the song, hands like great drums. *Allah-si-i-idi*! *Allah-si-i-idi*! they sang; and stamp, stamp, stamp went their bare feet until the whole ship shook. They sang and danced for some moments, with an air of complete abandon, keeping the rhythm sometimes with their whole bodies, sometimes only with feet and hands. Occasionally one would dash on to the hatch and execute some special step with wild yelling and whoops and shrieks. Mohamed the serang was a good leader.

Refreshed by the dance, the sailors rushed upon the halliards again with throaty growls, followed at once by Abdul-latif's song. If they had worked furiously before, now they were like madmen. Hassan the helmsman, Abdulla bin Salim, Ebrahim bin Sulieman, Nasir the pearler, leaped at the halliards on the forepart of the knighthead, swarmed aloft, and attacked them at the block, hauling and fighting that taut yellow line, forcing the unwilling block to descend and the yard to rise. Every muscle of their great bodies whipped and played.

The song of Abdul-latif was even faster, broken into by warrior roars and shrieks from Saud and some of the sailors from the big dhow.

"Rise up, you yard:
Think not that you can rest.
Swell out, great sail,
And gather to your breast
God's wind,
For we are bound for home."

So Abdul-latif sang, his face contorted as his broad back strained to the work, for he hauled upon his share of the halliards as well as leading in song. The time was faster, faster, as the block descended. More sailors leaped aloft, running up the halliards like apes, hand over hand with the rope between their toes, old Yusuf again, and Mohamed, Kalifa the helmsman, Sultan the prayer-caller. Up they ran, and fought the halliard down, dropping, sweat-covered, yelling figures, into the crowd on deck by the knighthead, stamping, yelling, singing, straining. Round the knighthead, at the upper block, were knots of them, and two packed lines strung out along each side of the maindeck along its length from the break of the poop to the belaying beam forward. They danced again, and back to the work. So the yard went up. Now it was time to belay; but they sang so much and made so much noise they did not hear the orders, and threatened to pull the yard right out of the ship. But they heard in time, and the job was done.

Well done, I thought. It never failed to stir me. Sometimes I joined them at this work, but the pace was usually too much for me. A quarter of an hour of it was as much as I could stand, and I could never master either the throaty growling, or the thunderclap with the hands. Banging the deck with my bare feet hurt. My feet had been bare aboard that ship for months, and my soles were tough enough to walk on flints, but to jump on that uneven deck was more than they could do.

The yard aloft, the sailors went to carry out further orders for the setting up of the parral tackles and the rigging, and the trimming of the gear. They turned to these new tasks like warriors who, having just repelled a great assault, hear of some minor breach in the walls elsewhere. Their song was different, but there was no pause. It was a quieter song, as they ran and gathered in well-trained groups. The work all done, they scooped a hasty drink of lukewarm water from Jassim's tank.

Abdul-wahhab's men left us, when the yard was aloft, and returned to their ship. Just before sunset Hamed bin Salim came aboard, with a sack of shillings. With the sunset there was prayer, and then, very quietly, the mainsail was broken from its stops, the line to *el-Dhow* let go, and we were off. It was a beautiful evening with a quiet sailing air from the north, and we went out from Zanzibar with a Persian boom, a small sambuk, and two jalboots from Sur. We stood past the point with the sunset behind us: the breeze held, and by midnight we were abeam of the light at Dar-es-Salaam.

Daylight found us off Ras Kimbiji, and the breeze which had been fresh all night was then quieter. Rain clouds hung heavily over the coast of Tanganyika, and before long some heavy showers passed over us. They left brief calms, after which the north wind came in again, and we sailed on. Throughout the morning the *Triumph* sailed quietly down the Tanganyika coast, steadily approaching the mouths of the Rufiji. We stood close by the shore and sometimes had very little water, though the boom was not drawing five feet. These were the most dangerous waters we had yet been in. Reefs and low islands abounded to windward, out to seaward of us, and often patches of the sandy bottom rose until they seemed almost to be touching our keel. No matter, we had with us Mubarrak the Suri, pilot for those parts, who had been put aboard by Nejdi on the recommendation of the mysterious agent, the Seyyid in the *suq*. Neither Hamed bin Salim nor Abdulla the nakhoda's brother nor anyone else on board had been to the Rufiji before, for the Kuwait ships are newcomers in that region. The inside passage down called for accurate local knowledge. No other kind of navigation could get a ship through there. The actual navigation of the Rufiji itself, they told me, would be worse. Meanwhile our sailors were overhauling the bad dates from Aden, bringing them on deck out of the hold until I began to think the ship would capsize. They threw overboard all the fermented packages, which stank abominably. Any that were not actually bad they kept, and stowed away again. There were perhaps sixty packages left when they had overhauled the lot, but even the 'good' dates remaining were exceedingly bad. I tried one, at Hamed's suggestion: it tasted like fermented molasses flavoured with engine oil, and I wondered why we kept them.

When we had almost reached the northern end of the Rufiji Delta, we passed close by a spit of beach running out from a low island. Suddenly, at an order from Mubarrak the Suri, the ship hauled her wind and stood inside this spit. The sail was run down, and we anchored. On the inshore end of the spit two big baggalas were beached for cleaning. Hamed said this was Kwale Island, and we too would beach there for cleaning.

I had not known we were to visit Kwale Island. I had never, indeed, heard of the place until that moment. No one had mentioned it, and it was too small to be on our small-scale chart. Kwale is a low island close to the Tanganyika coast, by the northern end of the Rufiji Delta. Though I had never heard of it, it is a place much frequented by Arabs bound to the south. The Germans used it when Tanganyika was German East Africa before 1914, and their stone Customs House still stands. It is a port of entry for dhows bound to Salale, Kilwa, and Lindi. A Swahili customs clerk enters the ships inwards, collects their small dues, and watches that they do not smuggle too much. This gentleman, a Mr. Timothy Anton, was soon aboard, pulling out in a boat from the beach, but even before he appeared our sailors had begun to make the ship ready for hauling out. I was interested to watch this operation. I had seen the big dhows hauled out before, at Aden, in Mombasa, and in Zanzibar, but this was the first time that the *Triumph* had been beached while I was on board. Our boom was a deep vessel with considerable deadrise, so that she would not stand on the beach unaided. She could not stand up like a Thames barge. Like all Arab craft, she would have to be propped on stilts. Even so, it would be dangerous to leave the heavy mainmast aloft, for she might easily topple over with the weight of that, in anything of a breeze.

It is the custom of the Arabs to clean their ships' bottoms and to effect any repairs which may be necessary by hauling them in to a shelving beach where there is a big rise and fall of tide. They float them in, dismasted and empty of all cargo, on a high tide, and get them in stern-to the beach as far as they can be induced to float. The falling tide grounds them, and they hold them up with a series of stout spars, eight or ten of them, ranged along each side. Each returning tide floats the ship again and often knocks down some of these props, so that tending the grounded ship is an important, and sometimes also an anxious, business. The ship is held securely in position with anchors carried out ahead and astern, one over each bow and one from each quarter. The flood floats her and the ebb grounds her again.

The ship usually remains on the beach only two or three days – longer, if repairs are necessary. A comparatively new ship like the *Triumph* had no bad planks and did not need repairs. On the first day, the old paying-stuff is scraped off. On the second day, the new is applied, with a great deal of work and much singing. On the third day, the ship is floated off again, and re-rigged, and the job is done. Only the ship's people join in this work, and she carries her paying-stuffs with her. Ours were camel-tallow kept in old paraffin tins, and coarse lime.

The first thing was to get the mainmast down. Ours was seventy-eight feet high from the deck, with a girth at the deck of almost six feet, a very solid and heavy piece of teak. I wondered how the Arabs would go about the difficult task of unshipping so heavy a spar, but they had worked out a system, perhaps centuries or even thousands of years old, which made this a simple operation. First they got rid of the two long yards, main and mizzen, and all the other spars lying about the deck, by throwing them bodily over the side, where they were lashed together and floated ashore in tow of *Afra* and the longboat. They were moored to some bushes on the beach, and remained there until it was time to go. Then, the mast-lashings and the wedges were unshipped. The mainmast in our boom, and in all Arab dhows, was stepped in the forepart of the trough-like main hatch, which forms a sort of bed in which the mast lies back. When aloft, it rests against the fore end of the hatch: when down, it lies back in the trough. It is raised and lowered easily by its own rigging. To get it down, all that was necessary was to cast off the lashings where the bole of the mast rested against the stout beam at the forepart of the hatch, and then to heave the mast upright and cant it a little sternwards with the main halliards, then carefully lower it backwards, steadying it down with its gear. There was no standing rigging to send down. All the rigging consisted of purchases suited admirably to this manœuvre. The mast lay back along the trough of the main hatch with its weight on a beam across the break of the poop, and the masthead projecting over the stern. Our mizzen was not unstepped, because it was a light spar stepped only in the deck, and we could take the ground safely with it up. If it were to be unstepped, as it always was at Kuwait, it was lifted out bodily by means of a simple tackle from the mainmasthead, the mainmast being held steadied by its tackles on its way down long enough to use it as a derrick to lift out the mizzen.

It was a simple method, and it worked well. Our spars were overside and beached, the mast down and along the deck, and the ship ready for beaching three hours after the sailors began. Baggalas, being sharper and deeper than booms, had not only to send both masts down but to get them off the decks before they dared trust themselves to be propped up on the beach. Ahmed Radhwan's big *Hope of Compassion* had once capsized on the Ma'alla beach through neglecting this precaution, and had lain there until the spring tides floated her off. The two baggalas on the beach at Kwale had their masts overside. One of these baggalas was Bedar bin Abdul-wahhab's stately *Bedri*: the other was the Suri Abdul-razzaq's, he who had taken his master's licence so recently at Zanzibar. We were to see a good deal of this cross-eyed young man both there and in the Delta, for he was bound down to the Rufiji. So was Bedar.

With our spars floated away and our mainmast down and resting along the length of the ship, we were ready to be kedged in to the beach as the tide made. Our wheel had been unshipped and hung over one quarter, and the binnacle stowed away, in the great cabin. On deck the ship looked rather a mess. Beaching her was a simple but extremely laborious business of kedging in at high water and being left aground by the receding tide. It took all night to do it, for the low beach ran out for miles, and the ship had to be kedged a long way. Again and again the longboat shifted the kedges farther ahead, until at last they were secured to trees along the point. The singing sailors danced and sang and hauled all night. When they hauled on the kedging lines they always went through the same ritual. The port side of the deck was clear, and they danced along this in a rough elliptical formation, half of them always hauling on the line, and the other half dancing back again to the forepart to take their turn. They kept up a continuous movement, round and round, each man hauling his section of the rope aft and then dancing and hand-clapping his way back to the front as he reached the break of the poop, ready to take up the burden again. This dancing, which they could keep up for hours under conditions such as these, seemed to refresh them, and they never dreamed of doing any heavy work without it.

I marvelled at the lung-power which could keep them going, to say nothing of the strength of arm which sent the ship along at a good rate to her two kedge anchors. It was all done in high good humour, though they sweated heavily even at night. It was full moon, and the work went on and on. We had to get in with that tide. As we came nearer to the beach we saw it would be a tricky business to thread the ship between the *Bedri* and the Suri baggala, for there was barely room for her to fit. Once there, however, she could not be in a better place. Hamed managed her well, and coaxed her into the berth, but the day was breaking over Kwale Island before the last of our supporting props was lashed in position alongside and the last line hauled taut to the anchors ahead and astern. Examination of our bottom showed it to be in first-rate order, though the paying-stuff was sadly in need of replacement. She had been cleaned and paid at Berbera four months before, but though the Arab method of paying with lime and tallow might be effective, it certainly was not lasting.

In spite of the fact that they had been up all night the sailors at once began to scrape the bottom, singing their old song for jobs of this kind:

"A little at a time.
Allah helper, Allah helper.
A little at a time;
Soon all is done."

They sang the same verse for hours, but sometimes phrases more appropriate to the work in hand were introduced or little sallies about some incident or someone on board, in the manner of the old English sea chanteys. Scraping the bottom continued until it was finished, while others scraped away on *Afra* and the longboat, also grounded and propped up near by. By the time the scraping was done the tide was coming in again. Then we had rice and fish, and after that all hands coiled up in the shadow of the trees on the Swahili village green ashore, and slept.

Kwale was a good place, and I was glad I had stayed with the ship. It was pleasant to bathe in the early mornings from the long spit which ran out so far towards Tanganyika. It was pleasant, too, to stroll in the Kwale woods with Abdulla and Kaleel the carpenter and Said the carpenter from the *Bedri*, who was busy all day repairing the old baggala's rudder in the shade of a sail spread from a tree across the beach. Kaleel helped him at this work, and I liked to watch them. They were good shipwrights. They had built booms together, back in Kuwait, and were old friends. We used to stroll in the early evenings, between the third and the fourth prayers, through the Swahili village and across the island. The two carpenters were keen students of botany and took a delight in examining the trees and shrubs. They also looked with expert eyes at the Swahili girls we passed at the wells and in the fields and gardens: but the girls were far from comely, and we never dallied there.

Kwale seemed to consist mainly of uneven coral, surrounded by mangroves. It is low and the soil is very thin, but water is plentiful. There are some sheep and cattle. The village is of mud huts, rudely thatched. A few small dhows are owned in the village, and the majority of the 200 Swahili inhabitants support themselves by fishing. Fish are plentiful in the waters around Kwale, and the big shark and the dugong are dried. The dugong is a favourite with the people of the mainland, and brings a good price. There is one Indian store in the village.

Strolling along the beach one day, I came upon some interesting vessels lying on their sides in a flat behind some gnarled old mangrove trees. One was a Muscat jalboot about fifty feet long, and the other a small Cutch boat, from India. They had come a long way to rest their old bones. I should like to know what their records had been, before they had been brought, no longer seaworthy, to rot out their derelict years on that Kwale beach. They were both registered in Dar-es-Salaam. It seemed an appropriate place to bury them, in that silent corner of the white beach, with trees all round and nothing but the sighing of the wind in the forest to sing their dirge. Across in full view was the mainland of Africa, with some fishing dhows skimming over the blue water. Overhead, flying high, a great aeroplane passed. It was a British Imperial Airways machine, recognisable even at that height, flying the mails from Durban to London. The Swahili with me did not look up. The air mail was a commonplace down there and he was more interested in ships.

Outside the customs compound I saw part of the rudder of a deep-sea boom, slightly worm-eaten, which Mr. Anton said had been washed ashore recently from some wreck. Which wreck, he did not know. There were wrecks fairly often, he said. In a squall only a few days earlier a Swahili dhow had foundered not far from the island, and four men were drowned. The salvaged cargo of copra was piled on the beach close to the *Triumph*.

What I liked best about Kwale was the village green. This was a fine green patch near to the point where the beached ships lay, at the north-western end of the island. The customs house stood on one side of it, and a path led across it to the village. In the trunk of a large tree shading the nearer part of this green was carved "Football Ground, 1933," but Mr. Anton said that little football was played now. It had led to too many injuries and too many fights, and the villagers had given it up. Beneath this sporting legend something else had been cut into the tree, but this was now difficult to decipher. All that could be made out was H.M.S. Something, and a date, which may have been 1889, or even 1839. Under this was an anchor. This may have been a relic from some slave-chasing frigate of the old days, for many of the slavers passed this way, coming up from Kilwa. According to local accounts, and the Arabs corroborated them, the slave-dhows, when the British were looking for them, were accustomed to sail up inside the reefs of Mafia, hiding in the mouths of the Rufiji if small boats came in search of them. Then they came up between Kwale and the mainland, and dashing through that channel by night, ran for the open sea and carried on from there, far outside, towards Arabia.

There are records of sharp encounters between armed boats from Her Majesty's ships and Arab slavers off this Kwale Island. Many slaves, freed by British sailors, first tasted their freedom on the beach where we now were grounded. The Arabs knew the Rufiji very well, and apparently found it an excellent hiding-place. Not only was navigation difficult on that reef-strewn, bad coast, but it was notoriously unhealthy. Kwale, now quiet, had known other stirring days, not only with slave-runners. It had bee an outpost for the German cruiser *Königsberg*, when, in September 1914, after her attack on Zanzibar, she fled for shelter to the Rufiji. For the *Königsberg*, too, the Rufiji was an excellent hiding-place, too good, perhaps, for she still lies there.

I liked to sit in the shade of the old tree on the village green, and watch our sailors, and the sailors from the *Bedri*, repairing their sails. Our sails were carried up and spread on the green, where they were pegged down and repaired. The green made an excellent sail loft. It was a good life, and I was glad that I had not stayed behind in Zanzibar. With my monkey Yimid for company – he was bought from a local Swahili for a shilling – and my good friend Mr. Anton to yarn with, I could stay there for hours. It was a grand spot. In the background, on the beach, were the big ships, Bedar's baggala very picturesque, like a galleon of Spain, with her carved and galleried stern towering over the trees and her low, sweet bow pointing out to sea. Every line of her was beautiful, except where she was hogged, and the stempost was a little out of true. The flowing grace of her lovely bow was as beautiful as anything I had ever seen. Every line of her blended sweetly towards that low, keen bow, and the flowing grace of her cutwater, rising from the comparatively short keel in a long, soft line until it became a carved stemhead, high before her, was a sight to delight the eye of a sailor.

She was a much prettier model than our big boom, which looked plain and almost ugly beside the *Bedri*. The boom's straight stem and straight sternpost, her sharp ends, the long stempost carried far out before the bows, the huge rudder, the lack of carving or embellishment – these things were products of a later day, more utilitarian, even among Arabs. The *Bedri* was more than half a century old. What if she were hogged a little, and her fastenings wept a staining rust? What if the planks of her ancient decks were worn and old? What if her rudder was a little worm-eaten, and had to be patched before she could go on? She was a good old ship, beautiful to look upon; and when the day came that she floated off, I saw that she rode in the water with the grace of a gull. She was a ship, a real ship, in her own way just as lovely and as completely seaworthy (at her best) as any clipper. No one could say that she was wholly seaworthy now. Her day was done. So would the day of any iron-fastened wooden ship be, after half a century. Throughout her long life she had been in hard trades, bringing up logs from Malabar, carrying heavy dates to the Yemen, running down to Africa. She had not been much to Africa. She had been mainly in the trade between Kuwait, Basra, and the Malabar coast, the hardest which the Arab knows.

As I looked at that sweet old ship – I could hear her sailors singing as they paid her undersides – I thought I should like to get hold of such a vessel, and save her type from complete extinction in this humdrum world. There she was, one of the last carved-stern galleon-baggalas of Kuwait. There was only one other like her, for the Persian Sulieman Said's did not properly count. She was built in Sur, owned by a Persian, and registered in Kuwait only as a convenience. It seemed to me that someone ought to get hold of one of these old galleons and see that she remained in the world, with proper care. Someone? Why not me? I should be a good one for such a job as that, and the more I thought of it the more I liked the idea. The Arabs would never keep a baggala for historical reasons. Sentiment for ships meant nothing to them. They were fast changing to booms, and the carved stern would soon be extinct. To preserve a baggala would be of historical interest, for not only was the hull of the baggala directly descended from the best and fastest of Arab ships, but her galleried and lavishly decorated stern, I believe, was a survival from the Portuguese.

I sat beneath the tree and looked at the old *Bedri*, and at Abdul-razzaq's smaller galleon which was then being floated off. There was a terrific banging of drums and, every now and then, a tremendous burst of hand-clapping – more noise than work, by the look of things. It would be very difficult to preserve a baggala. You could not keep her in eastern seas. She would go to pieces. There was, moreover, little point in keeping her there when the people who would be most interested in her would be on the other side of the world. She would have to be sailed either to England or to the United States. I thought about this and the possibilities of making such a voyage. With a well-found dhow it seemed feasible. One could go into the Red Sea with the south wind, about December, and with luck get half-way, before running into the belt of calms which cushion the north wind between Perim and Suez. From then on it would be a dour beat to Suez, a beat of five or six hundred miles, for the Red Sea is long. But it could be done. Then would come Suez – the longboat could tow her through – and the Mediterranean, and after that, Gibraltar, probably another dour beat through the straits, for they can be very unkind to the westbound sailing-ship. Then, however, the worst would be over, for the northerly airs off the Portuguese coast soon bring a sailer down to the trade winds and she has only to drift before them towards the West Indies, as Columbus did.

There were no great hazards to this voyage, it seemed to me, as I lolled on the village green at Kwale. Even the *Bedri* was as well-found as the *Nina*. If Columbus could do it, the Arabs and I could do it too. It could be done. The Mediterranean might not be so easy; the lateen rig is a hard rig to beat with, and there might be a lot of windward work on such a voyage. Still, it seemed to me that it might be worth trying – not, unfortunately, with the *Bedri*, which was obviously unfit for such an undertaking. But perhaps the other surviving baggala from Kuwait might be better. I resolved to keep my weather eye lifting for her.

It was a pleasing subject to play with, beneath that African tree, with the sound of the surf and the sailors' cries in my ears. Whether I ever could 'save' a baggala or not, it was pleasant food for thought. One of the many difficulties I could foresee was that of holding an Arab crew. If I were to sail an Arab ship on this Transatlantic voyage, I must have an Arab crew. My Arabs, good fellows as they were, might take holding if they ever landed, say, among the *bebes* of Brooklyn, or even down in Florida.

I looked across at our sailors, sewing sail in the sun, and wondered what they would think of such a voyage. They were like merry boys. Sewing sail was the one job at which they did not sing, and at which they allowed themselves to sit down. They sat on the pegged-out sail and sewed rough round seams, with Hamed bin Salim and Abdulla Nejdi overseeing them. The sailors did not think much of Kwale Island, picturesque spot as it was. To them, it meant much work, with more to come, for the collection of our mangrove poles in the grim Rufiji would not be fun. What was good about Kwale? Abdulla asked when I ventured to suggest it was a pleasant place. There was no *suq*, he said, and there were no *bebes*. There was not even fruit. But I liked Kwale, for all that; and most of all I liked that shaded village green.

We paid the bottom, sunny side first, on the third day, beginning as soon as the sunny side was dry. The tallow was heated at a brushwood fire on the beach and mixed with lime under the expert eye of the serang, and the sailors slapped it on with their bare hands. They worked in the mud and slime, and some of the stuff got in their eyes. Before the work was done they were covered with lime and tallow, and mud, and sweat; but still they sang. The bottom finished, they carried the anchors ahead far out over the flat to kedge her off, when the tide came in; and in the late afternoon we were afloat. She came off easily, and we kedged her into the bay.

In the morning she was rigged again, and we sailed towards this mysterious place, Simba Uranga, in the delta of the Rufiji.

XII

DELTA OF MISERY

THE RUFIJI IS AN impetuous African river flowing from the heights of Tanganyika eastwards towards the Indian Ocean, which for countless years has been bringing down soil from the hills and depositing it along a hundred miles of coast. The sea outside is littered with banks, shoals, and coral reefs, which the mud swept down from the river makes it impossible to see. The entrances to the Rufiji are a rain-swept, wretched maze, as though designed by Nature to make the passage of vessels as difficult as possible. Bars, banks, shoals, tide rips, eddies, unpredictable sets, rapidly changing channels, combine to propound a conundrum of navigational difficulties which would cause a nightmare to any mariner.

Over all the vast area of the delta the water is only three parts water; the fourth part is mud. The soil of the islands and the banks is three parts mud and one part water. Miasmic vapours, steaming swamps, rotting jungles, and pestilences of all kinds abound. The river is never stable, never sure even of its own channels from one day to the next, changing them with bewildering rapidity and without reason. The forces of the tide and the river's current change swiftly and beyond the range of human forecast, so that even the direction of the stream in any of the arms is unpredictable. Over the whole watery, wretched maze of the muddy, dreadful delta, the arms of the Rufiji constantly send out new feelers connecting and changing the charted streams. A mariner who knows the delta one year may return the next and not know it at all. It has defied all attempts at control. A whirlpool today may be an island tomorrow; a sandbank today may have been swept away by the morning. The whole river seems possessed of a spirit wilful, petulant, and destructive. Forever changing, it is never still. Always deceptive, it is never safe. The whole delta is gloomy, morose, and depressing almost beyond endurance. It rains almost daily, in heavy squalls which beat down like punishment, and leave clouds of steam in an atmosphere like a Turkish bath. When it is not raining the hot sun burns fiercely, and the fetid steam rising from the jungle-swamps is fever-laden. It is hot, uncomfortable, and wretched without relief. The mangrove swamps and all the trees are a dark dank green; the banks are muddy, so that one sinks to the thighs in them at every landing; the whole place is tormented by the most savage, fearless, and horrible mosquitoes in the world.

In all this world, if there is a worse place than the Rufiji Delta, I hope I may never find it. The list of its enormities is not yet complete, for the murderous crocodile and the clumsy hippopotamus lurk in the stream, ready to capsize a frail canoe and make short work of the occupants. In the jungle monkeys chatter and scream, and kingfishers and herons, a splash of gay colour, fly by the water's edge. In the high trees eagles perch, watching; and in the jungle there are snakes – boa-constrictors, and small venomous things. The poisonous mud of the mangrove swamps abounds in leeches and ticks, ready to attach themselves to the foot: creepers beset the way, and thorns tear at the legs. Here only jungle beasts live, and there is no food. There are no gardens, for there is hardly a piece of dry land fit to put a hut upon, away from Salale and the few other villages. The banks are low, barely lifted from the swift waters when the delta is in flood: at high tide many of the islands are awash. The swift sets in the river pull at the moorings of ships with dangerous strengths, and bring down great tree trunks from inland to hurl upon them. Pilotage in such a place is a nightmare: the whole delta is a bad dream. There is nothing to eat, and all food must be brought there.

The mosquitoes were worse than I had been led to believe, and I had frequently been reminded of their evil habits. They were unbelievably savage, and fell upon each Arab crew as the dhows came in with the ferocity of small flying tigers. It seemed to me that probably, never having tasted human blood before, the sweetness of it drove them mad. They bit and bit, and returned always to the attack no matter how many of them one destroyed. Walking through the swamps one would brush one's forearm to leave it a solid mess of black and blood, the black the squashed bodies of a hundred mosquitoes, and the blood theirs, too, but not their own. The only defence was to cover oneself up, and it was too insufferably hot for that. Nothing else kept the mosquitoes back, but one could not go entirely covered. When there was wind and the ship was moored midstream they were not so bad, for they could not fly far in the wind; but when it was calm they were upon the ships like a locust plague in a rich field. Bees came, too – great stinging beasts, attracted by a strong smell from our spoiled dates; and when they came we had to forget the dates, for we could not go near them. The bees hummed and fought and stung all day long, and the nights brought the mosquitoes. The rain was penetrating; the river angry; the Swahili surly, silent, and morose; our crew took fever; some from a Suri sambuk died.

In this awful place, this gloomy, wretched delta of the swift Rufiji, we spent a month. It was the worst month of the voyage.

I did not know what was in store for us when we came bowling into the grey Simba Uranga mouth of the great river early one March evening, with the ship cleaned after her beaching and so light and high out of the water that we dared not set the mainsail, but had the lightest mizzen aloft on the mainmast instead. Any greater press of sail might have capsized her, for there was nothing in the hold. We came out of a rain squall, with the tide at the flood and the wind fair, and Mubarrak our pilot watched carefully as we swept wide round a point with casuarina trees and stood on past a coconut plantation on our starboard hand. Away before us a great reach of the river stretched towards the west, but Mubarrak said that this was the most dangerous of all the Rufiji's many mouths and was not negotiable even by the Arabs in their dhows. We stood close by the bank on the port side of the Simba Uranga, which was the name of the mouth we entered, and swept round a bend almost at a right angle, so close that the branches swept the peak of our sail. We hauled our wind then, and stood across to the other bank for, though this was a broad reach, Mubarrak said there were dangerous banks in it. There was also the half-covered wreck of a large cargo steamer, lying athwart the channel at the southern end. Something of the bridge, two masts, and two samson posts showed above the stream. This, said Mubarrak, proud of his knowledge, was a German warship sunk by the British in the world war. Hamed bin Salim looked impressed, and so did I, for they could believe that if they liked. But unfortunately it was nothing of the kind. It was the wreck of the British collier *Newbridge*, which had been sunk there in an attempt to bottle up the German cruiser *Königsberg* when she was hiding at Salale early in 1915. The *Newbridge* had been brought from Zanzibar, and run in past the entrance through which we sailed: at that time the place was fortified by the Germans, and the *Newbridge* had a hot reception. Men had died in that swift stream, bringing the *Newbridge* in: and there she lay, an ugly blot on the grey scene, and the river had gouged a fresh channel beside her.

We ran close by the *Newbridge*, keeping well clear of her submerged bow – to touch that would have ripped us to pieces – and shortly afterwards followed another bend in the river inland. Herons watched us pass, standing in the mud by the river-banks; monkeys chattered in the trees, and once we saw a family of them swinging through the forest. My

Yimid from Kwale was wildly excited and chattered loudly. We twisted and turned round bend after bend, and at the turn of the tide fetched up at a place about six miles from the mouth we had entered, which Mubarrak said was Salale. All I could see were coconut palms, one house, and a tumble-down jetty. Off the jetty were two small Swahili dhows, and Abdul-razzaq's Suri baggala lay moored farther up. We let go two anchors and the stream swept by, muddy and ill-natured. Then the mosquitoes found us, and it was hell. It remained hell for the rest of that month.

We spent most of that time moored in an arm of the delta, miles inland from Salale, near the place where the gutted hull of the *Königsberg* lay broken-backed in the stream, not far from the village of Kikale.

Like the useless hulk of a dead hippopotamus the hull of the former proud cruiser lay fore and aft in the Kikunya mouth of the Rufiji, close by the landing-place for the village of Kikale. Our sailors ferrying the mangrove poles passed her daily, coming and going. To them she was just another finished "ma-nowar Hitrar," as was every other wreck in the delta. She lay on her side with little more showing than a part of a splintered deck, a little of the hull, and some davits. Her back was broken, and the hull was split in two somewhere abaft the bridge, as if she had been blown up when the British monitors finally found her range. A dull, desolate sight in the midst of the swirling water, against a background of swamp and rainy sky, she lies in deep water at a place where the stream makes a wide curve. Eagles watch from the baobab trees and the white-winged herons fly by, and the Swahili, paddling past in their canoes, never give the battered hulk a second look. She is too familiar a sight in the Rufiji now, for she has been there a quarter of a century.

At another bend of the river, in the Kiomboni mouth, about a mile or two north of the village of Salale, lies another twisted wreck battered to pieces by British shells in 1914. This is the cargo steamer *Somali*, once a coaster for the German East Africa line, and later tender and storeship for the *Königsberg*. Now she lies a red, twisted wreck upon a yellow sandbank, her mainmast and funnel askew, her foremast lying overside like a crumpled tube, her back broken, and her hull virtually in two pieces, with the jungle on the other side showing through.

From this jungle, and the swamps near the *Königsberg*, we cut our cargo. But that took time. In the meantime, we waited.

The method of loading in the Rufiji was for the Arabs to come, with their cash, and enter their ships and their requirements at Salale, where there was a British forestry officer. He sent them on to the part of the delta he thought would most quickly provide them with their poles, for though the whole place abounded with these poles, they had been cut heavily from the more accessible places nearer the sea. Now the ships were far back, for it was best to get a cargo as close as possible to the banks of the stream. Cutting the trees down and trimming them took comparatively little time; it was carrying them to some landing-place where they could be inspected, graded, and marked, and from which they could be ferried to the dhow, that took the time. Therefore the ships liked to be in new places, alone, where the mangroves grew thick by the water's edge. (There were, I discovered later, other reasons why they liked to be alone.)

A dhow having been entered and assigned her place, moved upstream and recruited labour, which was sometimes difficult, for the district was not populous. It had no attractions to offer and the Swahili had no liking for the back-breaking, wretched work. For this no one could blame them. Sometimes it took two weeks to recruit a gang of cutters, for the dhows were all in together and the demand was considerable. When we arrived we were one of twelve dhows. The Swahili lived aboard, at the ship's expense, and they cut the poles by day. It took a long time to cut a cargo, though we soon had eighty Swahili living on board. Many of these were tribesmen, children, helpers; and some of them just ate. If you recruited a few Swahili to work, before long a whole tribe moved in to eat. They slept aboard, wherever they could lie down, and they ate the ship's food. Hamed tried the bad dates on them, but they would not eat them, and before long we were borrowing dates from the other Kuwait ships in the delta. The appetites of our Swahili were tremendous, and several times they ate so much that there was no supper left for the crew. The sailors suffered without complaint, because they knew that though their hunger might not be necessary, they must do nothing to displease the Swahili. Without them, we should never be gone from that miserable place. And they had to be fed.

The Tanganyika Government controls cutting rights in the forests of the Rufiji Delta, but it is the practice to let them out to a private company on a royalty basis. The Arabs buy from the company, and the Government's forester superintends them. No cargoes are ready, and each ship must cut her own. The poles cannot be cut and stored for the ships to come and load them, for not only would this cause much unnecessary work, but it would lead to loss, because the banks of the river are nowhere stable enough to support a dump for long. Poles dumped today may be washed away tomorrow. The Swahili dump them a few score at a time, and the forest guards, under the forester's supervision, inspect them, see that they are graded properly, and brand them with the government mark. No pole may be loaded without this brand. Tallies are kept, and when the ship is full she pays cash for what she has taken, and the labour is paid on a piece-work basis. The Arab crews ferry and load their own poles. They may take dead wood from the forests for firewood, and water from the river to drink. Nothing else is free.

The Arabs have been accustomed to come to the Rufiji Delta for mangrove poles from time immemorial, and the trade is a very ancient one. Though, as a matter of policy, they appear, at least on the surface, to conform with the temporary regulations of what they regard as interloping governments, they see no reason why they should pay a European company for the right to take these poles. If they pay the Swahili, whose country the delta really is, they think that should be sufficient. It is a matter of great difficulty and some danger to bring a big dhow from the Persian Gulf to the Rufiji and load her with mangrove poles, and it is only in comparatively recent years that the business has been more or less organised. It did not take me long to discover that the Arabs continue an effective campaign to ensure that, so far as possible, the organisation has no more than the appearance of smooth working.

We bought some poles, certainly, and so did all the other Arabs in the delta. We had a forest guard on board, and so had all the other dhows in the delta. We were frequently visited by the energetic forester, a man from the Forest of Dean, with keen blue eyes and no intention of having dust blown into them; and so were all the other dhows in the delta. Our poles were inspected, graded, and duly marked with the official axe. Our Swahili headmen seemed docile, law-abiding, anxious to please. We loaded, and paid for, 150 score poles. Yet we had loaded another 150 score before we left that place, though we were 2,000 miles away before I could be sure of that, in spite of the fact that I had been there the whole time.

Every Arab ship in that delta, and probably the Persians, too, stole half her cargo in spite of every effort to check them. There existed, and I did not learn this until months afterwards, a widespread and very effective system for cutting and loading poles, unseen by the official eye. The headmen, the forest guards, the labourers, the Arab nakhodas and crews were all in it. It was a close-knit thing. No European could hope to break through the childlike front of these people: they acted in the whole affair like a group of schoolchildren organising something against teacher, a teacher who was not so clever as he thought himself. How could one man control that vast area, and check these things? The Arabs loaded over an area little short of a hundred square miles, along a river-front of more than a hundred miles. Even to visit each of them was the work of a week. In all that area, there was only one officer, and it seemed to me that he had in his department no native he could really trust. To pay guards to watch the Arab vessels, alone in their lonely reaches, was a waste of money. The guards, if honest, were largely powerless, for they dared not stand against a machine as effective as that pole-stealing organisation. It was like a racket in America, as well run and as unscrupulous. So far as I could gather, the local Swahili headmen were the arch-conspirators, the leading racketeers. It was with them, and through them, that the Arabs received their unchecked cargoes. Great dumps of poles would be cut in secluded places, away from the river banks, for it was known that the forester had no time to prowl through the dreadful swamps and would probably have died of fever if he had tried. His predecessor had been carried away from Salale. Besides, he trusted his guards and looked after them well. The headmen cowed the guards and cowed the labourers. Not only did they take the Arabs' money for the stolen poles, but, in the tradition of the true racketeer, they withheld much of the labourer's share besides. There was one amongst those headmen who was a powerful man indeed, as powerful in his own way as any gangster in the United States, and even more unscrupulous. This man controlled the whole northern end of the delta, rigidly, with an iron hand. No labour could be employed, no guard enter service, no poles be cut without his command: and he profited very handsomely by his power. This man, I discovered, looked after us, and Mubarrak our pilot was the go-between.

He was a mysterious Arab, this Mubarrak the Suri. A short, stout man of middle age, grey-bearded with bushy whiskers in the Suri style, he was an old Rufiji trader. He was always barefoot, and he wore the long brown shirt of Sur, with a red sarong under it. He generally carried a silver dagger, and his eyelids were darkened with mascara. He had a low, soft voice which could rise to a whine when he was excited; and he affected an air of great humility. He had a dhow of his own, back in Zanzibar, it was said: I wondered, if that were so, why he agreed to be a pilot for us. The truth was, of course, that though competent to act as a pilot, that was not his main function. He knew the ropes. He was a 'fixer.' He seemed to look, not only after us, but after every other Arab dhow in our part of the delta. He was very seldom on board. He came and went mysteriously, and was the friend of most of the Swahili. He spoke Swahili fluently: it is a tongue easily managed by the Arabs.

Unfortunately for Mubarrak, however, his own dhow arrived in the river from Zanzibar for a second cargo, not long after we had come in, and though her name had been changed and Mubarrak was no longer the nakhoda, the forester recognised her as a dhow wanted for pole-stealing. Earlier in the year, with Mubarrak in command, she had come in, asked for a ridiculous number of poles, and then sailed so deep-loaded that the forester's suspicions had been aroused. Unknown to Mubarrak, he had the cargo carefully counted by the authorities at Zanzibar, when it was discharged there for sale to a local merchant. There was more than twice the number of poles Mubarrak had ordered. Here was Mubarrak, back again, our 'pilot.' Usually the Arab can rely on his general likeness to his kind – at least to inexperienced European eyes – as disguise enough. But Mubarrak foolishly admitted his identity, and admitted – not suspecting anything – that he was also nakhoda of the wanted dhow. That was enough, and Mubarrak was arrested. One of the Swahili headmen was implicated with him, having supplied the extra poles to his dhow, and the pair were taken for trial up-river to Utete.

Not that this inconvenienced us. Mubarrak's work was too well done for that, by that time, and the organisation too smooth. We had our fill of poles, and did not pay for half of them. So, very likely, did every other Arab in the delta.

For this dishonesty the Arabs, it seems to me, are not too greatly to be blamed. "If we complied with every regulation," Hamed bin Salim said, "we could not come. It is known," he went on, "that no ship here takes only that cargo she has officially paid for. If she cannot take the unofficial balance, then she cannot afford to pay for the other, and the trade stops. The present system works smoothly. Nobody loses. Why interfere? The Europeans do not own the mangroves, for Allah put them there and they are for all men. There is timber enough in Africa; but we in Arabia are very badly off for wood, or we would not make so long and hard a voyage to get these poles."

So argued Hamed, who was seldom given to speech. (This was long afterwards. He said nothing while the ship was in the delta.) He pointed out, further, that the Arab dhows had slight encouragement to visit the Rufiji, for the loading delays were very bad, labour difficult to get, the river exceedingly dangerous, and not only had cash to be paid on the spot, but nakhodas were required to carry the cash with them over a dangerous and exhausting trek from the northern part of the delta to Dima, in the south, where the company's agent waited to collect it. So far as they could see, the company's agent existed to take their cash, and for no other reason. They made it a point of honour to see that he got as little of it as possible. If the trade were properly organised and poles waiting to be loaded, Hamed said, there would be no need to receive them from the Swahili. As it was, he did not think the *Triumph* would come to the Rufiji again. This was her first visit, and it would be her last. In future she would go to Lamu.

It was certainly true that loading was a slow, difficult, and labourious business. We lay ten days in our arm of the river without loading anything at all, while the Swahili ate. We had, we were told, to wait until they had got together a number of poles large enough for the guards to mark them. This they did, eventually; but in the meantime they had also collected a larger dump at a secluded spot not far from the wrecked *Königsberg*, whence they would be removed by night when the time came. As soon as the first of our cargo had been marked and officially released, we could load this dump. It was more than a hundred score, and the lot was put in in two nights. Neither the company nor the Government, apparently, had any idea of the capacities of the Arab dhows. When we asked for 150 score it was presumed that that was our capacity, though if he had any suspicion, the forester could compel vessels to unload and check their cargoes at Salale or anywhere else he thought fit. But he was a forester, not a shipping clerk and he had much to do.

When the loading began we were busy. The poles were ferried off at high tide in *Afra* and the longboat, both of which were rigged with sails to make the work easier: two cargoes came by day, and two by night. I was sorry for the sailors, for the conditions were appalling. Throughout that wretched Rufiji month they led a life of incessant and excessive hardship, never dry; sleeping without shelter from the heavy rains; working all day and half the night wet with mud, water, sweat; bitten by the fever mosquito; their hands torn by the jagged, splintered wood and their feet by the tangled undergrowth and thorns, and the wounds of both infected; their only food a little rice and fish twice daily – sometimes only once. They worked steadily, never seeking rest when there was work to be done; and they sang while they worked. They did not sing at night, when they ferried the stolen poles. These came down the river in the rain, in silence, and were hurriedly stowed on board.

The days were either windless, heavy, and exceedingly hot, or it was raining. There was no recreation and no place even to walk – it was not safe to swim. The ship was covered with mud, though everyone tried to wash the clinging stuff off before returning on board. A thatched roof was built over the after end of the poop, above the nakhoda's reclining bench, but this did not keep out the rain. Nothing could keep the mosquitoes down. They laughed at mosquito nets and seemed to delight in crawling inside them: one mosquito inside a net is worse than a hundred outside it. The sailors had no nets. They accepted the mosquitoes as they came. At first they tried to fight them off, but after a while they gave up the unequal struggle and let them bite, on the principle, I suppose, that if they were filled they would go away. If they fought them off they would only come back again, with others of their kind even hungrier. Better a comparatively few well-fed mosquitoes than thousands of hungry ones. I could never put this philosophy to the test. The mosquitoes bit so savagely that one's hands and arms swelled up.

Ashore there were sandflies and other pests, as a change from the mosquitoes. I was kept busy with my medical work and often wished that I had some real skill at it. There were many ills I had not seen before – tropical infections, bad skin diseases, outbreaks of discharging sores on the head, and fevers. Those who had been pearl divers in the Persian Gulf suffered terribly, for many of them had a skin disease which broke out here. It was a kind of rash of blind pimples, and they always had some signs of it, usually on their legs. As long as the pimples were not discharging it was not so bad, but in this wretched delta they were torn by thorns and splinters and jagged creepers. Every pimple that was open became infected, either from the heavy tannin in the mangrove bark or from the poisonous river mud. I could do no more than try to keep the wounds clean, stop the bleeding and prevent infection. Sometimes it was hard, and I ran short of medical supplies. I never had very many, and the demand was great. The sailors, too, contracted boils, as if they had not already ills enough. Some had small worms embedded in their knees and leg muscles, from which they had to be gouged.

The Arabs were good patients and, not for the first time, I had reason to be thankful for their immense powers of recuperation. But by the time we had been three weeks in the delta they were obviously wearing down. They were thin and wan by that time, even the most stalwart of them; and I saw that many who were much less than thirty were now quite grey. It was a hard life; yet even here, old Yusuf Shirazi said one day that, bad as the Rufiji was, it was better than pearling. He thanked God, he said, that he would never have to do *that* again. I began to wonder about this pearling.

If it was hard for our sailors, it was also hard for the Swahili, whose moroseness I forgave when I saw the conditions under which they worked. Up to their knees in mud, cutting down mangroves with a small axe – those mangroves were iron-hard – stripping them, dragging them through the jungle to some creek or backwater where their dugouts were moored. Their small dugouts would hold only five or six poles. When they were full, the poles would have to be taken to the central dump, graded, and stowed. In places where the mangroves were plentiful, it was bad enough, but where other cutters had thinned them out it was exceedingly hard work. Early in the morning, immediately after the dawn prayer, which they always recited sonorously together, they left the boom, pulling in their dugouts upstream against the race. They pulled close inshore, keeping watch for the savage crocodile, which could easily upset their small canoes and drown them, before taking the bodies off to its lair to rot into a fit state for eating. They used the branches overhead to help them on their way. When bound downstream, they drifted in the middle of the river. That was easy. All day long they worked, with only a handful of inferior dates for food. Rain or sun made no difference to them.

They were picturesque, in spite of their surly looks. Most of them had tribal scars on the cheeks, two on each side. They were all dressed in Arab rags, mostly in very old Suri shirts which hung on their great backs by threads. They were devout Muslims, at any rate while the Arabs were in port, and they recited their prayers with gusto. Indeed, those who worked the least prayed the most, sometimes keeping the sailors awake half the night with their sonorous mumbo-jumbo, and it is not fitting that the faithful should rebuke the convert for saying his prayers. So they prayed on and on, until I often felt like rebuking them myself. The only excuse I could see for this exceedingly great devotion was that it was to make up for the rest of the year, when the Arabs were not there. Indeed, the Swahili confided to me privately that they did not pray much after the Arabs had gone.

If life was bad in the Rufiji for our sailors and the Swahili labourers alike, it must have been a nightmare for poor Hamed bin Salim. He had never been there before, and there he was, in command of a large and somewhat unwieldy boom, far up an uncharted arm of the impetuous

Rufiji, charged not only with her safe navigation to and from Zanzibar, but responsible also that her cargo was secured in the least possible time, and half of it not paid for. He had eighty Swahili labourers in his care, to pacify, feed, and make work; he had the ship to tend and that was job enough, in that swirling headstrong reach – and the boats to look after; and he had our crew to care for. During that grim month in the Rufiji I grew to appreciate Hamed bin Salim. I had liked him well enough before, but I had had little chance to get to know him on the run from Ma'alla to the Hadhramaut, and after that he was always overshadowed by Nejdi.

Hamed was an unusual Arab in some ways. He was 36 years old, and not yet a nakhoda. He was the muallim, the small nakhoda of Nejdi's boom, and it was very likely that he would never attain a command. He was a biggish man, for an Arab seafarer, with a close-clipped beard, high forehead, and a very large, straight nose. His father was from Nejd, and he had left there to settle in Kuwait. His strong face was marked by a great number of heavy creases, and bad teeth, very prominent, spoiled his mouth. He wore his iron-grey hair very short, shaving it off frequently. He usually wore a jawpoint beard, cropped very close and becoming. He was a big-limbed man, with brawny arms and powerful hands. He had a strong voice which could get excited at times. His voice was very sonorous in prayer, which he often led, for he was the ship's most devout Muslim. There was no question of this devotion, which was quite genuine. He was a high-principled man, scrupulously honest in all matters apart from such things as receiving Rufiji mangrove poles, and smuggling, and the like, all of which, in his view, were thoroughly proper; reserved, and very quiet, as became the second nakhoda of any ship Nejdi might command. He was a capable seaman and a good pilot. His visits ashore were concerned only with business, and he left women alone even in Zanzibar. He had been nineteen years at sea, beginning as ship's boy and rising to be quartermaster. From quartermaster to second nakhoda was a big step, and he may have owed his promotion to the fact that he had married one of Nejdi's sisters. Be that as it may, he was a good man and deserved the advancement, which was probably all he would ever get.

Hamed might have got a great deal farther if it had not been for his somewhat unfortunate personality. He had no knowledge of those little graces and ways and means by which men such as Nejdi commanded other men easily, and got them to follow him. No one could say that Hamed was born to command. Nejdi, from the moment his nose appeared above the rail until the last of his headcloth disappeared down the Jacob's ladder, was in undisputed command of everything in sight. Hamed was not; Hamed merely carried on in his absence. Hamed was capable, competent, energetic, and trustworthy. But he did not know how to command. He was not popular with the sailors, who preferred the fault-finding, dashing Nejdi. Perhaps it was the old feeling against officers promoted from the ranks, for Hamed had been a working sailor with some of them, in other ships. But I think it was simply that Hamed lacked the personality to command. His ambition was to get money enough to buy a small plantation by the Basra river in Iraq, and there settle down and sleep while the dates grew. As things were, he had no idea when he might achieve this ambition, if ever. Plantations were expensive, and money was difficult to get. It was as much as he could do to keep his home going with the money he received as his share of the *Triumph*'s earnings, and the little he made from his ventures. He was a married man, with one wife and four children.

I grew to like Hamed on those long Rufiji nights while the rain beat down on the thatch above the nakhodas' bench, and we huddled up together out of it. Old Yusuf Shirazi squatted by the wheel, pulling at his bubbly-pipe, and little Mohamed Kederfi, now and then, brought up a round of coffee or tea. Hamed and I yarned at such times, though usually he did not talk much. We yarned about all kinds of things, principally about dhows, and Kuwait. After a while he began to tell me things about the economic side of the voyage – what the voyage cost, for instance, and how much the ship could earn. She had, he said, been able to pay the sailors over 160 rupees a share the previous year, but he doubted whether she would be able to pay even one hundred on this. Difficulties in Mogadishu, poor price for the cargo in Zanzibar, low rates on the passengers, and then all the extra time they had spent on board, the high cost of Rufiji mangroves – he said nothing about those received from the Swahili – and the probable difficulty of selling them in the Persian Gulf, these things made it difficult to earn profits. It would be better, Hamed said, to carry merchants' freights, but the merchants preferred that the nakhodas should take the risks. If the merchant sent his own cargo, he had to pay the ship, and support the investment of the cargo. If the ship carried her own goods, the merchants got them anyway, more often at their own prices than not, for no nakhoda could afford to wait long for a sale, or give indefinite warehousing to his cargoes. So the merchants received their goods without having to pay freight or run the risks of the voyage. It was an iniquitous system, Hamed said; but it was the way the

Arabs worked. What could he do about it? Then he asked me about steamers, and how they were run, for Hamed was a man with ideas.

Throughout that bitter month Hamed worked dreadfully. Three times we shifted ship, carefully watching the tides, now farther in towards the *Königsberg*, now out again towards another part of the river, for the boom by that time was beginning to draw a lot of water. We were loading her to the rails, and before she left the Rufiji we were drawing nearly thirteen feet of water. If we were caught in a far arm with a draft like that during a period of low tides, we might stay in the delta two months instead of one. Two months! The prospect was too dreadful to think about, though we knew that the Kuwaiti Abdul-wahhab bin Kalifa had already been in the river over forty days, with his big boom *Tai-seer*.

Shifting ship down those swift streams was a dangerous manœuvre, and often in some tide rip we would swing right across the narrow channel and ground both bow and stern. At such times the sailors had to work extremely hard, even for them, carrying out lines to trees to straighten the ship again. Not even the greatest care would prevent such accidents. They did no harm, for we moved only with the rising tide, and all the banks were mud. But it was difficult, worrying, back-breaking work. Meanwhile day succeeded day, and often no poles were brought at all, while the Swahili steadily ate all the provisions in the ship. Hamed knew that, whatever he did, Nejdi, sitting all this time at ease among the fleshpots of Zanzibar, would disapprove, or at least give the impression that things would have gone much better if he had been there. But if he were envious of Nejdi he never said anything, or showed his feelings. Hamed looked after the ship, and did his best always for the ship and crew, and led the prayers. He overcame difficulties as they arose, and went on to look for more. He asked for no favours, and gave none. The sailors, when Nejdi was aboard, always came on the poop night and morning to offer their salutations. With Hamed, in the Rufiji, no one came. That was the difference between them.

When at last our cargo was on board, and the deeply laden ship lay at anchor off Salale again, with her maindeck below the level of the water, the tired, thin crew looked to the rigging and bent the sail. Hamed had to set off on the trek to Dima to give the company its shillings. It took him two days to get there, for Salale is in the north of the delta and Dima in the south. It was the fourth day before he returned, looking thinner and more worn than ever. Much of the way had been by dugout canoe, and twice they were overturned, once by a hippo and once by a log which they feared for a moment was a crocodile. When they were not paddling along the moody river they forced their way across swamps, and through jungle. Hamed, who was barefoot, returned with his feet lacerated, and his legs torn by thorns. They had seen snakes, he said: once they passed a boa-constrictor asleep after a meal. At Dima there was nothing to eat, and no rest, and he was worried about the ship. She was drawing a great deal of water by that time, and he wanted to get her out with the spring tide. So he stumbled back again, the shillings paid and the official receipt given, and the return was worse than the going, for it rained almost the whole journey. Sheets of rain alternated with torrid, humid heat; the mosquitoes were thick and fierce; sandflies tormented him, flying in his face. He floundered on up to the knees in the slimy ooze which was full of stabbing snags; foothold was impossible: the bush was full of thorns, insects, snakes. Crocodiles waited by the river, and bad-tempered hippos, to overturn canoes. Wet through, muddy, bloody, torn, hungry, with nothing to eat and only river water to drink, Hamed struggled on. When at last he returned to the ship, and I ventured to say that it was not right the Arabs should face such difficulties to take a company its money, he said only that Allah was compassionate, and he did not complain. But he was very tired, and the spring tides had gone. A flood whirled in the river from heavy rains upstream, and débris of all kinds littered the broad stream, while logs, bushes, and tree-trunks thundered into us. The stream was running a good six knots, and the deep-laden boom strained at her anchors. Mubarrak was gone, led away for his trial upriver, and we were without a pilot. It was stormy outside, and the rain squalls over the river were frequent and depressing, and sometimes whipped up savage winds. But we had our cargo now, the company was paid, and the Swahili were gone. We could sail. Praise be to Allah! We could sail.

Hamed called all hands to special prayer, and in the morning we were gone.

It was the end of March when we sailed at last from Salale. We touched once, going down, but she came off easily, for we moved down with a fresh wind against the flood. The rising water floated her as she grounded, but we went carefully. Mubarrak was in Utete jail, and there was no one else who knew the river. It rained that morning, and the dark and mournful river was a place of gloom. Our decks were full to the rail with wet and muddy poles, so that the ship floated sluggishly with her maindeck below the level of the water, and she drew thirteen feet. The sailors, worn and thin, had no shelter and nowhere to go, for not only the space beneath the break of the poop, but the whole great cabin had been filled with poles. The bulkhead of the great cabin was unshipped, and the main deck packed with poles to the rails. The top of the cargo was rough and full of unevennesses, splinters, and projecting ends which stubbed the sailors' toes as they ran. Everyone had suffered, more or less severely, from the Rufiji stay. Abdul-latif and Ebrahim the helmsman were laid up badly with the fever. The others had heavy colds. Jassim the cook was worn almost to a shadow. Poor old Yusuf Shirazi was now completely grey, and so thin that his long gown hung on him like a bag and, where it was open at neck and chest, his ribs showed like a skeleton's. All hands were in much the same condition. Even Abdulla, the nakhoda's brother, who did the least work of anyone on board, showed signs of wear, and poor Hamed bin Salim was like a pessimistic ghost.

It rained all the way down-stream. We swept on past mudbanks and weeping trees, through rain and past mud, past always more and more arms, rivulets, backwashes, channels, and creeks of the swift-flowing turgid stream, past a clearing here that was the landing-place for Kiomboni, now again in sight of the sunken *Newbridge*, and the banks of the Simba Uranga mouth, where the Germans had their trenches and small guns. The wind dropped as we came towards the mouth, but the tide had begun to ebb then and we continued. As we came out the rain cleared, stopping suddenly as we emerged from the gloomy river-mouth, as though, having done its worst, it was saying to itself: "Now, damn you, you can go!" The rain was like the spirit of that sad place and, having emerged from it, we thanked God and did not look back. Inside it still rained – rained and rained and rained. Ahead of us was comparatively open sea – not really open yet, for we had still the tortuous reef and bank-filled passage to Zanzibar to negotiate, and a call to make at Kwale to clear the ship. But the wretched Rufiji was behind us and the sailors smiled. Until they smiled, I had not observed how rare pleasure had come to be upon their faces. Hamed bin Salim did not smile.

We were not yet out of danger, and our troubles were not over. We drew a great deal of water – more than any other craft which sailed out that day, and we were one of seven. Shallows, reefs, sandbanks, sudden squalls abounded; it was the changeable period between the north-east and the south-west monsoons, when anything may happen. If we took the ground in our heavy-laden condition, we could do the ship serious damage. Any cargo we might have to jettison would be our loss, for it was all bought with the ship's money, or secured by her people's sacrifice. Simba Uranga mangrove poles sink; they are too heavy to float.

For that matter, we were not yet away from the delta, though we were outside the land. We were still in the narrow channel between the mudbanks beyond the Simba Uranga mouth when the breeze came again, from ahead, and we could lay our course only with difficulty. Ahead of us, almost hull-down, we could see the sails of six other Arab vessels which had sailed that morning. Hamed was conning us quietly along when suddenly Abdulla, the nakhoda's brother, who had never been noted either for his abilities or his ambition at any other stage of the voyage, decided he would take charge. He began to give the helmsman orders conflicting with those given by Hamed. Seeing the ships ahead, he maintained that we could fall off and follow them. We could not, Hamed said, for there was a sandbank in the way. We could, said Abdulla, and ordered the helmsman to let the ship fall off.

"Keep her up!" said Hamed.

"Fall off!" said Abdulla.

"There cannot be two masters," Hamed said. "Let go the anchors!"

And he sat down.

In this brief interchange, fraught with some peril to the ship, Hamed bin Salim was so obviously in the right that the helmsman paid no attention to Abdulla's orders. It is a poor pilot who can only follow ships ahead, and a poor officer who seeks command when the worst is over. Hamed was in charge of the ship, and Abdulla wronged him both by upsetting his orders and his command. Abdulla, being Nejdi's brother, was in a privileged position, and knew it. Hamed, being only Nejdi's brother-in-law, was in an unprivileged position, and he knew that, too. His duty was to take the *Triumph* to the Rufiji, fill her with poles, and bring her back to Zanzibar. He had to put up with Abdulla. Nominally no more than one of the helmsmen, Abdulla's position was not clearly defined on board, but everybody knew he was Nejdi's brother. Everybody knew, too, that he would probably get a ship for himself when the *Triumph* came home, if she made any money. Hamed would not; Hamed would not get a ship of his own, no matter how long he faithfully served both Nejdi and Abdulla, no matter how many weary voyages he made or how many bitter months he might tend their ships in the terrible Rufiji. The only way Hamed would ever get a ship of his own would be by accumulating enough money to buy one, and that he would ever be able to do that, try as he might, was most unlikely. He was a poor man with a large family. Abdulla was a young man with no family but a wife; he was a younger brother, and his home was provided for him. He lived with Nejdi, and they both lived with their father. His three children had died.

So Hamed sat down. Then he washed himself, and prayed, for it was the time for the noon prayer. He said nothing about the incident. Abdulla appealed to me. I said he was wrong, and that if Nejdi trusted Hamed to have command of the ship, then it was not Abdulla's place to make his command impossible. But, said Abdulla, Hamed was going a wrong way. There was no pilot. He knew as much as Hamed did. He could see the other ships. Well, I said, they drew less water than we did, and they were much farther out. They could fall safely off and stand towards the north when we could not. At that Abdulla appealed to one or two of the helmsmen, who said nothing. Then he, too, sat down. The breeze by this time had hauled a little fair again. We had been lying anchored with the mainsail aloft, gathered loosely to the yard which had been hauled in against the mast. From this condition it was easy to get under weigh again. Noticing the fair wind, Hamed weighed anchor and we went on. Abdulla took no further part in the pilotage of the vessel, and we got an offing beyond the banks, and then fell off towards the northwards.

After that the sailors, who had not greeted him throughout our stay in the Rufiji, came aft on the poop to greet Hamed night and morning. I was pleased at that. They had thought Hamed right, and this was their way of showing their sympathy. I had never known them to show much sympathy over anything or anybody; it was not a conspicuous virtue among them. But their quiet greetings night and morning to Hamed after this were very pleasing. If he noticed, Hamed gave no sign; but I think he was pleased. For my own part, I knew the sailors better and liked Hamed bin Salim more, for that hard month in the Rufiji. I was glad I had gone with the ship, and I felt that I had learned a great deal more in that way, and had got to know all hands better. It pleased Hamed and the crew, I think, that I had chosen to come with them to that dreadful place, when I could as easily have stayed with Nejdi at Zanzibar. We were good friends before that Rufiji loading; after it we were shipmates.

Now we stood up towards Kwale, and the sun shone, and the sailors brought out their poor rags to air them, and try to get a little dryness into clothes which had not been dry for a month. My monkey Yimid, which had been hiding beneath the forecastle head for the past two weeks, came out again and chattered cheerfully, running up and down and jumping on Jassim's legs. Bizz the cat, which had found the combination of discomforts in the delta beyond even her capacity for endurance – Bizz was used to a hard life – also came out again, looking woefully thin. I gave her some milk, which she lapped gratefully. Bizz looked round for mosquitoes, which had made her life a plague in the preceding month and, seeing none, almost smiled. Poor Bizz, there was not much joy in her life, and she must often have regretted leaving her native Berbera. She was very scared of Yimid, and never went near his end of the ship. Bizz lived aft, and Yimid for'ard; they never met if Bizz could help it.

Throughout the afternoon we looked back at the gloomy depression of the great delta where the rain lay heavy over all the Rufiji's mouths and our crew again gave thanks to Allah. In the evening it rained again, and we fetched the anchorage off Kwale in a rain squall after dark – a ticklish pilotage, for there was not too much water and nothing could be seen. Hamed looked a queer sight piloting the ship in the dusk, with his skirts tucked up out of the wet and a Bombay umbrella overhead to keep off the rain. The sailors scampered about wet through. It rained that night more than it had at any time during our stay in the Rufiji. It came down almost like a cloudburst, so heavy and so continually that the rainwater filled the cutter hoisted at the quarter davits, and the cutter became so heavy that it wrenched the forward davit adrift from its iron fastenings and tipped into the sea. *Afra* and the longboat, lying astern, were filled until they were waterlogged. More serious than this was the fact that the rainwater, pouring out of the sky, poured into the hold and came very near to foundering the ship at anchorage off Kwale, with the voyage back to Arabia not begun. With the maindeck under water, there was no way of draining any rain or any sea that might come aboard. It went into the hold. The ship was just a catchment area, drawing all the rain it could into its own hold, and the only way to get it out from there was to bail. During the cloudburst, bailing was sadly ineffectual; the water came in faster than it could be bailed out. Bailing was a laborious and difficult process. A well had been left, as always, abaft the mainmast, and most of the rain eventually drained into this. As in all Arab craft, there was no real attempt to make the deck watertight. Indeed, it had holes left in it for the express purpose of allowing water to drain into the hold. All the water that came aboard, even on the forecastle head, went into the hold.

Seeing the ship settle so perilously close to the borderline of safety in that shower of rain, I began to wonder whether she really would be seaworthy enough to make the coming voyage back to Arabia. We might get rain enough, in the south-west season, before we were away from the

African coast. She was very deeply laden. What would be the position, I wondered, if she shipped a few seas? It would take very few to finish her, for you cannot bail out the sea. Her rails, though they were built up with washboards and matting, were very close to the level of the water. The mangrove poles were a heavy, dead cargo. They were not even secured, for it was not the Arab style to secure anything. The ship was full of poles and there they lay, and it seemed to me that we should need some help from Allah if we were to reach Arabia. This reflection, however, did not seem to occur to anyone else on board, or perhaps it was with them always. They were not worried. I asked Hamed what would happen if a sea came aboard, but his only reply was that Allah was compassionate. After some time he added that the longboat would float off, as if he had been turning the matter over. I admit, however, that not for the first time I wondered just how foolhardy it was to stay in the ship knowing the chances she really was taking. I wondered, too, how good an insurance risk I might be supposed to be. Not that that mattered, for I had no insurance and wanted none; but I am a poor swimmer, and I did not wish to lose my photographs. At Mukalla, after the blindness; again at Shihr when our horde of Beduin came on board; and again at Kwale, when I watched the ship settle until she almost foundered in a shower of rain, I wondered whether I was wise in staying to see the voyage through. But I could not give up; if the Arabs stayed I would. Perhaps Allah would give a hand to me also. As Hamed said, if the worst came to the worst, the longboat would probably float off.

We went on from Kwale in the morning, with a little better weather. My friend, Mr. Anton, was not aboard, for there were many ships to clear. We went in with the bailed-out cutter and got our papers, and sailed without further formality. Again it was raining heavily, but there were partial clearings, and we went on easily under the jib, so that she could be brought up quickly if danger showed. We passed near the upturned wreck of what looked like a Bedeni, which must have gone down in a squall. The wind was light from the south'ard, and in the afternoon it cleared. We set the mainsail then. The horizon was still very black all round, but occasional brief clearings showed us the picturesque sails of our sailing companions, the other dhows. Cross-eyed Abdul-razzaq was still with us, and the dignified old *Bedri*, as well as three sambuks from Sur and two Bedeni. During the afternoon, with a little spasmodic sun, we sailed pleasantly to the north, for we were now past the worst dangers. In the evening we had Ras Kimbiji light, and it was good to see a welcoming navigation light again after that month of mud-bound wet hell.

The next day we were back in Zanzibar. Having taken so long to load the first cargo, there could be no thought of going back to the Rufiji for a second. It was now April and the south-west wind had come. It was time to be on our way.

We came in by moonlight to the crowded dhow anchorage at Zanzibar, and I thought Hamed did a good job of taking up a berth in the congestion, though Abdulla criticised him loudly. We moored astern of Sulieman Said's big *Hope of Compassion*, which we had not see since Haifun. As soon as we were in, and before our anchor was down, Mosa her muallim was aboard giving us the news. There had, it seemed, been a minor uprising at home in Kuwait, and there was a big fight between the Suri and the Somali in the *suq* at Zanzibar. Our sailors gathered excitedly on the poop to hear this news, and Abdulla dashed ashore to look for Nejdi.

XIII

HOMEWARD BOUND

THE TROUBLE IN KUWAIT had apparently come to a head while we were in the Rufiji, loading our mangrove poles, during March, when the sailors gathered nightly to tell me what a beautiful and peaceful place their homeport really was. Now they gathered excitedly to discuss the latest news of the riot or whatever it had been, and there were soon as many versions current on board as there were sailors. According to Hamed bin Salim, there was only one trouble with Kuwait. It was, he said, too close to Iraq, though what he meant by that remark he did not explain. According to old Yusuf, there was nothing the matter with Kuwait; by their very nature the Arabs could not face a peaceful life, without intrigue. They had to intrigue about something, against somebody. Sometimes their intrigues got them into trouble. That, he judged, must have been the case on this occasion.

In the course of time I gradually came to understand something of what had been going on in this great dhow port which then I had never seen. Old Yusuf's version was nearest to the truth. But, having disclosed his views, he never mentioned the subject again. Abdulla, Nejdi's brother, was my best informant, and certain Arab gentlemen in the *suq*. Some of these gentlemen seemed surprisingly well informed on happenings in the Persian Gulf and elsewhere in the Arabian peninsula, even so far away as Palestine, and were in touch with political events throughout the world. As far as I could gather, trouble had been simmering in Kuwait for some time. There was no Arab town, principality, sheikhdom, village, or even Beduin tent where some form of intrigue was not going on either openly or under cover, and the rumours and the gossip and the general condition of talkative unrest in the city had, apparently, bothered no one very much. But it seemed that there had been some real basis for discontent.

The Kuwaiti, alongside the headstrong and somewhat self-satisfied new country of Iraq, decided that they had too little to do with their own government. They wanted more, and gradually acquired the habit of saying so. There was nothing wrong in this, and in the course of time, their Sheikh, His Highness Sir Ahmed ibn Jaber al-Sabah, had agreed to the appointment of an elected council. The council had been duly elected.

Then it fought the Sheikh, desiring more and more control of administration and expenditure – especially of expenditure. The Sheikh, who liked things as they were and thought that Kuwait had been going on comfortably, fought back. The council tried to raise the people. The people were apathetic, being largely of Persian, Beduin, or recently freed slave stock. They loved intrigue as much as the next man, but they were in no mood to be shot for it, particularly not at the bidding of businessmen whose motives seemed suspiciously in their own interests. The greater part of the best men of Kuwait were at sea.

Trouble dragged on and on. If the situation in Kuwait showed signs of settling down in the lethargy natural to any well-run Gulf town, some mysterious person in a privately-controlled radio station in Baghdad hurriedly heaped coals on the fire. If there was no fire, he started one. He was indefatigable: for him there could be no peace in Kuwait. He did not want peace. Who he was and what business it was of his, I did not know nor did the Arabs; but he did much harm. Trouble which might otherwise have died down continued to simmer. Conspirators lurked in coffee-shops, round merchants' courtyards, in the inner sanctums of lesser sheikhs. One day a local firebrand overstepped the mark and, with his eloquence, raised the rabble to a mild show of interest in what was going on. They began to demand their 'rights.' They badgered the Sheikh, more for the fun of the thing than any real animosity.

The Sheikh had to put up with a good deal of badgering. The Sheikh was at heart a quiet and peaceful man who desired nothing better than to live at peace with his subjects. But the firebrand would not let him. In the end the firebrand became unbearable. He was arrested, beaten, and led off through the *suq* to the jail. As he was being led through the *suq* some of his friends tried to raise a riot to free him. The ringleaders were Yusuf Murzook, a shipowner, and Mohamed Kitami, a nakhoda who had been given a shore job by the elected council of state and was now showing his gratitude. The Sheikh's guards, as they took the prisoner through the *suq*, repeatedly warned Murzook and the others not to interfere, but since neither of them paid any attention, they at last opened fire. They shot Murzook in the foot and killed Kitami. This was unintentional, they had no desire to kill him. They fired as a warning, and he jumped in front of a bullet. Shot in the abdomen, he fell mortally wounded. The mob then ran, and for a moment or two nothing could be seen but the dust of their flying feet. Afterwards a vast number of sandals, cloaks, and headcloths remained in the covered street of the *suq* – sandals, cloaks, headcloths, and the dead body of Mohamed Kitami. But the citizens had fled.

That was the story of the 'riot' in Kuwait, in 1939. Doubtless the intrigues continued, for many of the ringleaders had escaped to Iraq; but the citizens – the Persians, the coolies, the descendants of the Africans and the Beduin – had fled. They did not return that day to reclaim their sandals.

"It was," Hamed bin Salim said, "no place for a self-respecting seafaring man." He was glad that he had been at sea. Who wielded the power in Kuwait was, he went on, of no interest or importance to him, for his life would always be at sea, making money for the merchants. If any chose to be shot down in the dust of the Kuwait *suq*, that was their business. But he and the others were sorry that if anyone had to die, it was Mohamed Kitami. For Mohamed was the brother of our friend Abdulla Kitami, and he was well known to them all.

When Nejdi came back he was full of gloom at the news, for Mohamed Kitami had been a friend. He was more gloomy at the sad fate which had overtaken Mubarrak the Suri, our 'pilot' for the Rufiji. Mubarrak had been fined one thousand shillings by the court at Utete, and Nejdi had had to help pay it. What sort of intrigue had gone on behind all this I was not told, but it was easy to guess. It had seemed to me that Mubarrak had been lucky to escape with a fine. He had been given his sambuk back, and was then on his way to Zanzibar from Salale, a sadder, wiser, but not a reformed man. Nejdi, in addition to this feeling of deep gloom and a great capacity for finding fault with all that had been done with the vessel, brought back from Dar-es-Salaam some washed-out, characterless photographs of himself which he exhibited to me as masterpieces of the photographer's art which I should do well to study. If the reason for his stay in Zanzibar had been to collect passengers for our return voyage to Arabia, he had wasted his time, for he had only secured three Swahili school-teachers. These he had undertaken to carry for nothing, as a favour to Seyyid Sulieman.

What interested me more than the politics of distant Kuwait and the fate of pole-stealing Mubarrak the Suri was the dispute going on ashore in Zanzibar between two or three baggalas of Suri and five sambuks of Somali. This at one time showed promise of being an excellent engagement: that it came to comparatively little was not the fault of the Suri, for they wanted the Somali to come outside in their sambuks and have a battle royal on the sea. For two or three exciting days it seemed that this encounter might really be staged, but in the end it petered out in a minor riot behind the fish market. It was too bad. I should have liked to see a clean fight on the sea.

This dispute with the Somali had begun over a slight misunderstanding about money. In this case, Italian money, a parcel of paper lire, which the Suri had collected in Haifun but could not smuggle out because they were too closely watched. For a consideration, the Somali in a nearby sambuk had undertaken to do the smuggling. The Suri showed them how to go about it. They had to put the wads of notes in hollow pieces of bamboo, then put the cane into ghee jars and fill the jars with ghee. The Suri delivered the notes to the Somali, together with the bamboo and the ghee jars, and then sailed away in their baggala. After some time, they met the Somali in Zanzibar. The Somali were very rich. They explained, with apologies, that they were unable to hand over the lire because the bamboo which the Suri had given them had disintegrated in the ghee. So, apparently, had the lire. It was an accident profoundly to be deplored.

Perhaps it was, but the Somali had more reason to deplore having thought of it, for the Suri fell upon them in the crowded Zanzibar *suq*, and beat them up in the most thorough fashion. They would have made an end of them had not the Swahili constables foolishly intervened. The constables, however, were in duty bound to intervene, for it looked as though a major riot might rapidly develop if they did not. The rival factions of Somali and Suri were led to their longboats by the water-front, and told that if they came ashore again to continue their brawling they would be imprisoned. This did not deter the Suri, who thought highly of the Zanzibar jail; and it did not bother the Somali. What did bother them was the reflection that there were a great many more Suri than there were Somali in Zanzibar, and if they came ashore again there might be a massacre. So they retired to the outer edge of the native anchorage, in their mean sambuk, and waited until the rest of the Somali fleet were loaded and ready to join them.

That was the state of hostilities when our *Triumph* had come back from Salale. There were the Somali, glowering in a corner of the anchorage. And there were the Suri sambuks and baggalas massing round them, imploring them to come outside and fight where no constabulary could interfere. I watched with interest for several days to see if the Somali would accept this sporting challenge, while the whole anchorage looked on and a police launch patrolled to see that war did not break out in the harbour. Six Somali sambuks were at length assembled, their tall, lean sailors as noisy, impetuous, and impertinent as ever. They had very large crews, but their crews included many boys. So did the Suri. They were fairly evenly matched. Day after day the Suri baggalas, loaded and ready for the voyage home to Sur, moved through the fleet and fetched up to their sailing moorings alongside the Somali. There were five of them – five Suri, six Somali. It should have been a fair contest. Morning, noon, and night the anchorage resounded to the threats and imprecations of the warlike Suri imploring the Somali to come outside and fight. Day after day the Somali stayed, and would not go. Days passed. A week passed. Still the Somali stayed grimly at their anchors. Ship after ship of the Arab, Persian, and Indian homeward-bound fleets had been obliged to sail with the issue still undecided, giving up their chance of seeing the fun. Two of the Suri baggalas sailed at length, on the tenth morning, to see if the lessened numbers would tempt the Somali out. But the Somali knew that those Suri were probably only waiting outside, somewhere in the narrow waters of the Zanzibar channel. They stayed at their anchors.

Meanwhile the south-west season settled in with more and more determination. Sometimes strong winds and rain drove across the native anchorage. It became obvious that neither the Arabs nor the Somali could wait much longer. The Suri outside must have been driven away by that time, in the fresh squalls, if they were not lurking in Pemba, and the authorities would have something to say if they tried that. At last the Somali made a dash for it in a squall one rainy, blowy night, running for their lives out of the harbour when the remaining Suri were too busy tending their anchors to observe their departure. In the morning there was a great wailing from the Suri and, though they immediately gave chase, they had slight chance then of bringing the Somali to action. They dared not follow them into an Italian port, and with the strong south-wester blowing, they could not hope to overtake them earlier. It was too bad.

On this second visit to Zanzibar we stayed two weeks, during which very little happened. We sold some twenty score light rafters from the top of our cargo, being offered a satisfactory price for them by a local Indian, and we tried again to sell *Afra* which, somewhat battered from her hard work in the Rufiji, was beached and cleaned. But no buyers came, and eventually we had to sail and leave her on the beach, in charge of the ship's agent. Our crew were given a few shillings each and refreshed themselves in the time-honoured manner, though now that most of their smuggling was done and they could raise funds in no other way, they were very careful of their shillings. Not many of them went to the local ladies. Instead, the sailors bought cheap manufactured things, most of which came from Japan, as presents for their families at home. Babies' rattles and simple toys were favourites, as well as safety razors for themselves, cheap pocket torches, and cigarette lighters. Dishes and small cups were also popular, and flavouring for sherbet was much sought after.

In the Rufiji and at Zanzibar the sailors had been busy in their spare time bottling lemon juice, which they squeezed with wooden pegs out of the juicy lemons which were everywhere available, preserving the juice with a pinch of salt. We had hundreds of these bottles of lemon juice stowed everywhere it could be stowed. This was the crew's own venture, and the custom of the dhows made it necessary to find space for them. Throughout our stay in the Rufiji, ragged Swahili had brought canoe-load after canoe-load of lemons, and at Zanzibar they were plentiful and cheap. A canoe-load could be bought for a shilling or two. All hands joined in the work. Empty bottles, corks, and even packing-cases had been brought from Aden. The bottles were cleaned out roughly in the river water. The sailors, now and again, sucked a lemon with some salt on it, as fruit. I tried one of these salted lemons and it tasted abominably to me and was not in the least like fruit, but the sailors enjoyed them. Lemon juice would bring three or four annas a bottle in the bazaar at Kuwait, where it would be diluted and used in the making of sherbet. It was a good business.

Zanzibar harbour during this second visit was a very busy place, with the native fleet assembling for the voyage home – Somalis bound back to Haifun and Berbera and Eritrea; Suri loading for the Mahra coast and Sur; Persians loading for anywhere; Indians coming up from Madagascar and elsewhere, putting in for water before beginning the long run to Bombay or Goa, or the Gulf of Cutch; Kuwaiti homeward bound from the Rufiji to the Persian Gulf and the Gulf of Oman; little double-ended things from the Hadhramaut and round Seihut way, which looked as if they were hardly fit for river sailing. One morning I counted seventy-two dhows, of one sort and another, at the anchorage, not counting Swahili and Lamu boats. At least half these seventy-two ships had waterlines less than fifty feet long, and they were all very deeply laden. However, they would probably arrive.

When we had been in Zanzibar ten days and the sailors were beginning to feel restive about the delay in setting off for home, we took on board a cargo of coconuts and stowed it among the mangrove poles. We loaded also some bags of cloves, a few boxes of soap, several drums of coconut oil, and a hundred cases of vermicelli. With all this on board and the longboat stowed on top, we sailed from Zanzibar in the early evening of Friday, April 14, bound, as far as I could gather, towards Muscat direct, for orders. Bedar's baggala *Bedri*, next to us in the anchorage, was to sail with us, and they were getting the sail on her as we came by. We carried a hurricane lamp at the flagstaff aft to show the *Bedri* where we were, and ran through the English pass with a fair wind from the south. We had taken aboard the three Swahili school-teachers, and the Seyyid Sulieman had kissed them good-bye. He also kissed Nejdi, who appeared much affected. Abdulla had been sent in a baggala to Lamu, to make his way back to the Persian Gulf by way of Mogadishu to collect the money that was owing to us. Going out of Zanzibar we were thirty souls all told, and I hoped we should arrive in Arabia.

In the morning we were off the northern end of Pemba, with that island in sight on our starboard hand and the coast of Tanganyika to port. There was no sign of the *Bedri*, and we did not see her again throughout the passage to Arabia. The breeze was fresh from the south-west, and we bowled along handsomely towards the north, in spite of our heavy cargo. The sailors spent a busy morning restowing the coconuts from Zanzibar and flaking the cables down on top of them, along the cargo on the maindeck, to keep them in position, and stowing the cases of vermicelli and other things in nooks and crannies among the poles in the space beneath the poop. Our vermicelli was an odd lot bought by Nejdi at a bargain price through a friend of the Seyyid Sulieman's, and he hoped to sell it at a good profit in Muscat or Kuwait. It was part of an overstock, laid in at Zanzibar for sale to the Swahili during Ramadhan. Our other odds and ends – the mottled soap, some cheap and highly perfumed soap, the drums of coconut oil, the lemon juice, the bags of cloves – would, I was assured, all find ready market. Indeed, we began to use one sack of the cloves at once, and from that time onwards our coffee was always flavoured with cloves. I did not care for this, but the Arabs seemed to like it.

We still had our Rufiji thatching over the bench aft. It had been put on well and it served to keep off the rain so long as the south-west wind was with us. The sailors made themselves a rough shelter by night by throwing the clew of a sail across the lowered mizzen-yard, and there they lay between the longboat and the cutter, on top of the cables. The cables were of tough coir and could not have made satisfactory mattresses, but the men slept soundly and were content. When we set the mizzen they had no shelter, but we did not set that sail until the rainy weather had ended.

At first the wind blew fresh, and we bowled along, making perhaps eight knots. Nejdi said it was ten, but I doubted that, and there was no way of measuring. Nineteen hours out of Zanzibar we were abeam of Mombasa, which was not bad going, but I found it difficult to accept Nejdi's optimistic forecast of sixteen days to Muscat. I was surprised to notice that he made no attempt to lay off a course for the Gulf of Oman direct, and make for the place as I should have done had I been in command of a ship on that voyage. Instead, we hugged the coast, exactly as we had done on the passage down. We had come down from Arabia with Africa on our right. Now we went back with Africa on our left; and that was the only difference in our 'navigation.' From Zanzibar to the Gulf of Oman direct is perhaps 2,200 miles; by coasting up we should add at least 300 to that total. Nejdi said that he certainly would coast the whole way. That was the way to go, he said, as if it were a road: he knew no nonsense about going direct. He knew the way, he said. If he wandered off into the Indian Ocean, who knew what might happen to the ship? All the Arabs coasted on that voyage. They coasted down from Arabia, and coasted back again. It was not merely a matter of navigation (for he was not able to discover his ship's position by any means other than visual); he knew the winds and the currents along the coast, he said, and they were more important than saving a few hundred miles. What did these few miles matter?

I had to confess that there was something in this argument. Indeed, there might have been a great deal. By coasting up, Nejdi certainly played for safety. His big boom, with the heavy cargo she was carrying, could easily founder any time a few seas came over her rail. If she did that, it was as well to be able to pull the longboat in to the land. Nejdi said we should sail as far as Ras Asir and then run on towards the coast of South Arabia, passing inside Socotra, as we had on the way down, and then coast along the Hadhramaut, the Mahra, and the Oman coasts to Ras al-Hadd. I expressed my surprise that, after all their centuries of ocean wandering, an Arab nakhoda like Nejdi should have no knowledge of astronomical navigation, though he had spent his life making long voyages. Well, he said, he coasted to India as well as to Africa; it was all coasting. But he regretted the decline in the Arab art of navigation and confessed as much that night. He blamed it on the bad influence of the

Europeans who, with their cut-throat competition, had left the Arabs only coasting trades.

We very nearly foundered the second night out from Zanzibar, and I was glad then that we were near the coast. The first night we had a touch of what might be in store for us, when the ship passed through a few rain squalls in the confused seas off Malindi. We began to roll heavily, and to slop the tops of a few seas aboard over either rail as she rolled – nothing heavy, but enough to keep the sailors busy at the well every hour. Sprays broke over the poop when a cross sea got up and smashed at the vessel, but there was no weight in them. It was a confused sea but not a dangerous one. Once in a fresh squall, a sea lifted the cutter in its falls and threatened to tear it away; it was hurriedly taken in board and stowed on top of the cargo. With the ship's heavy rolling, the chests on the poop took charge, and careered about like a lot of unsecured guns. "*Allah karim*," said Nejdi, smiling, but the three Zanzibar school-teachers were plainly scared, and Hamed bin Salim looked anxious. Our bailing system was working at full pressure for three hours while the tops of seas came aboard, but the wind gradually subsided and we worked through the area of confused seas. It was a meeting-place of the currents, and the sea is always bad at such places. The ship rolled and pitched violently under these conditions, and the mast worked horribly on its step – so much, indeed, that in the heavier squalls the mainyard was half lowered to ease the strain on sail and mast. But the ship behaved very well, all things considered. She was all right. Her vulnerability, then as always, was owing to her overload and the lack of elementary precautions on the part of her builders, master, and crew. The gear stood and we suffered no damage that night, beyond the wetting of several of the chests.

I wondered in the morning how the old *Bedri* had fared and, when we did not see her, feared that she might have gone down. She was even more heavily laden than we were, and she had been carrying heavy cargoes half a century before the *Triumph* was thought of. The trouble with these big dhows, as I saw it, was that they could not stand up to anything like a heavy sea, and it seemed to me that they would quickly disintegrate in anything like weather – in anything like, say, the conditions of the Roaring Forties, the North Atlantic, or the great storms of far southern seas with which European square-rigged ships had always to contend. Their one huge sail, though a glorious puller in ideal conditions of continuous trade wind without squalls, is a definite source of danger under any other conditions. It is a poor sort of ship which dares keep the seas only with an assured continuance of azure conditions.

The very next night, somewhere off Kismayu, we ran again into the same bad conditions of a cross sea with rain and heavy squalls. Again the squalls were not really heavy for a well-found and wholly seaworthy ship. I could have carried the topgallants in the *Joseph Conrad* through all of them. They were bad-tempered squalls, with lightning and much noise, and the cross sea ran eerily, throwing up soapy crests which caught queer lights from the flashes of lightning. It was worse than the previous experience. In a heavier squall than usual, about midnight, the wind shifted suddenly to the north-west with vicious rain. The thunder boomed and the lightning lit the decks, and the tops of the seas breaking over the rail – they were only sprays – threw up a greenish light. The wind had been in the south-west, working to the west'ard and freshening. We knew for once where the ship was, for we had seen the lights of Kismayu shortly after sunset, forty-eight hours out of Zanzibar. The westerly wind brought rain, and in one of these rain squalls the wind jumped twelve points. It was a freak squall, and a really nasty one for the moment. As in all lateen-rigged craft the tack of the sail had to be to windward, and this sudden shift made it necessary to dip the yard. This was always a work of difficulty, even under good conditions. The conditions now were anything but good. To dip the yard, the great sail bent to it had to be allowed practically to get out of control, for the yard had to be brought in vertically to the mast and swung across to the other side, while the whole of the sail took a turn in itself over the yard, the mainsheet going over – or, more properly, right round – to the other side, at the same time as the tack was dipped across. This was a manœuvre comparable to trying to turn over the tarpaulin of a huge haystack in a heavy gale, with rain or, if such a thing were possible, to swinging the wings of a big monoplane end-for-end in flight. It was like turning a very large circus tent inside out, in a minor hurricane, with very few ropes on the canvas to control it.

The manœuvre on this occasion was further complicated by the rolling and pitching of the vessel, by the obvious danger she was in of sailing straight under, by the absence of light other than the spasmodic and frightening lightning flashes, and by the constant and extremely loud singing of the crew who made so much noise, even in that predicament, that they could hear no orders. The wind howled and the rain lashed and the tops of sprays dashed aboard. The chests on the poop took charge again, for their extremely temporary lashings during the previous evening's blow off Malindi had been cast off. The longboat and the cutter rolled precariously on top of the cargo. Loose coconuts and long mangrove poles careered about, and there was scarcely a secure place to work on board. The binnacle lamps blew out, as they invariably do on such occasions (not only in Arab vessels); the sail took charge, which was understandable when both its sheet and tack had to be let go, and it had no other gear. The mast creaked and groaned with its working; the canvas thundered and roared with its wild flappings, and Nejdi roared even louder. Through all this the scampering sailors still sang, their singing punctuated now and again by the shrieks of some poor victim who had been struck by a loose mangrove pole, or the curses of a mariner who had slipped on a coconut. Yimid, my monkey, had got loose and scampered to the top of the lateen yard, where he hung chattering madly.

To make things worse, the mainsheet carried away and the whole area of the great mainsail now flapped round mast and yard so that, while it roared and crashed and cannonaded and tore itself into pieces, the yard could not be lowered or the sail got down. The ship rolled and pitched, and the sea got up so viciously that I was sure she must be overwhelmed, but the *Triumph* seemed to fight back at that sea as if she knew she was in peril and was fighting for her life. As the foaming great sea dashed at her on one side she raised herself towards it to shoulder it off, so that instead of a fatal wall of water thundering aboard nothing but spray dashed harmlessly over, though the spray reached half-way up the mainmast. Again, as she dug her long nose deep into a trough and another sea came up to take her on the quarter, she rose to that, avoiding it – always avoiding the worst weight of the seas like a real thoroughbred, never permitting them to overwhelm her or even to get a part of their real weight aboard. God help us if they did!

Still the rain hissed across the contorted face of the waters and the sail flapped and thundered, but that, indeed, may have been our saving. For the sail, blowing itself out, let go its fatal hold of mast and yard and we could at last get the yard lowered, right down to the top of the cargo, and the remnants of the sail unbent. With the sail lowered we did not bend another, but lay like that through the night. The sudden freak change in the wind which had put us in danger did not last long, and it went round quickly to the west'ard, and blew more quietly. This was all right, for we could then lie and drift off the land. About four o'clock in the morning, when the sky was beginning to grey with the dawn's first light, Nejdi grew worried lest we should drift out of sight of land, and he gave her back the smallest mainsail. We set that, and sailed on, for the weight was gone from the wind then and there were no more squalls. We had gone, too, from the cross seas, and the sea ran true from west-south-west though still a little lumpy. The ship settled to a steady lilt and dip and roll, and we wandered quietly along while the sailors spread the remnants of the blown-out main across the decks to dry, and Yimid, who had remained there all night, chattered merrily at the masthead.

After that we had no more bad weather, and we never again lay hove-to without canvas. I was interested to see the ship's behaviour under those conditions. It was the nearest approach to bad weather we ever had. She lay-to very well, with the helm eased down and no canvas showing. Her high poop kept her shoulder to the wind, and she behaved quite well in the sea. She no longer even wet her decks, and though she was without canvas she was not out of control. She drifted surprisingly little – perhaps five or six miles to leeward through the night. I feared that with the canvas taken from her she might just wallow in the trough, as more than one Cape Horner of my acquaintance would have done, deep-loaded as she was and in relatively the same conditions. But she kept out of the trough, head to sea, and lay very quietly, as a ship hove-to should. I thought the more of her and of her builders, after that night's experience. Though she was in effect nothing but a pile of iron-fastened teak put together on the beach at Kuwait by a group of shipwright carpenters who could not read a plan, I knew that these men could build good ships. While they can build them so well as that, I hope no one will give them plans.

Nejdi was cautious the next night, lowering the lateen main and going through the night under only the jib, the tack of which was shifted to the heel of the stemhead. Under this light piece of canvas we rolled on quietly, with the stars out and the black sea all gone down, and we yarned of ships and storms, round the chests on the poop. The sunset prayer that night was made a special occasion. Nejdi summoned the sailors to the poop to stand in a line beside him, while Hamed bin Salim led the prayers in front. Beside Nejdi on the one hand stood Ismael the musician, and on the other the helmsman Ebrahim. They offered up extra prayers that evening, and Hamed remained seated on the deck facing Mecca long after all the others had done. From that time onwards, we had communal prayer on the poop night and morning, though our Swahili school-teachers were very irregular in their attendance. This habit of praying was of great importance to the Arabs, and none of them would have thought of missing a prayer, or of coming to the prayers not properly cleaned, but they did not always rid themselves of all worldly thoughts during their numerous devotions. Occasionally one of them would crack a brief joke while Hamed intoned a melodious verse, or the serang would sneak a quick puff at the nakhoda's hookah while the gang were prostrate in one of the attitudes of prayer. These were unusual occurrences; prayer was generally solemn. It must be a difficult thing to rid one's mind of all worldly thoughts at the muezzin's call five times a day, seven days a week.

We talked that night of a host of things, as we always did, Nejdi's quick mind flitting from subject to subject and dealing deeply with none of them, except politics, in which I was not interested. Talking with Nejdi at any time was apt to degenerate into listening to a monologue punctuated by loud suckings at the hookah; on politics, and all allied topics, his talk became a sermon. His views may have been sound and, since I had none of my own, I did not dispute them. On some other subjects he was a strangely ignorant man. He denied, for instance, that the world was round, and he had no conception of geography away from the seas he knew. He had never heard of America or New York, though he had heard of Paris (which he called Baris) having, as a child, seen pearl-buyers from there. He knew London by name, and most of the countries of Europe, and a surprising amount about their politics. He had very little knowledge of the stars, and almost none of natural phenomena. One evening we were chatting as usual, and the subject turned on the powers and properties of lightning. Lightning, I said, in response to his question, was nothing but stored-up electricity freed from clouds in the sky. At this Nejdi laughed uproariously. Electricity! he laughed. He called it 'trick,' as did the sailors. That comes in torches made in Germany and Japan; the lightning is God's. Ha ha ha! Such a good joke as that he could not keep to himself, and my remarks on the mysteries of 'trick' were bawled across the Indian Ocean to every Arab ship we spoke. And that, by the time we had been drifting off Ras Haifun for a week, was quite a number.

We lost the south-west monsoon somewhere north of Warsheikh, on the Benadir coast, and after that had nothing but light airs and calms. Daily we saw anything between ten and twenty Arab craft, all bound to the northwards, and sometimes Persians and Indians. We were one of a great armada sailing homewards from Zanzibar, and often we were treated to glorious views of the big dhows. When we saw one from Kuwait we showed our colours, and sailed across to hail her, unless the nakhoda was not a friend of Nejdi's. To my surprise, the *Triumph* overhauled every ship we saw, including both Indians and Persians, though some of the Indians were showing a lot of kites, and I had never before thought our boom particularly speedy. Perhaps the cleaning at Kwale had helped her, or perhaps she was at her best deeploaded in these light airs. By that time we had every sail aloft that we could set, which was only three – the largest mainsail, set from the extended mainyard; the largest mizzen; and a jib set on a boom lashed along the stemhead. One day we stepped the mast of the longboat just for'ard of the wheel – there was a step in the deck for it – and set the longboat's mainsail there, but this was more trouble than it was worth. The mast carried away, and we did not set the sail again. We saw several Persians carrying a third mast of this kind, with the longboat's sail. Hamed said it was an old custom but it did not really help much. It helped the balance of the canvas, and consequently the steering, when the ship was carrying the big jib. Many of the Indians and a few of the Persians sported flying kites of lateen tops'ls above their mainyards, but I never saw a Kuwait ship which set this sail. Nejdi preferred to put his faith in larger and larger mainsails and did not bother with kites. They only made work, he said, annoyed the crew and disturbed the nakhoda's rest. Give him a few sails and big: not a number of sails, small. That was all very well in the Indian Ocean, running before the north-east monsoon or before the first of the south-west, before its strength has come.

At this stage of the voyage Nejdi took things more easily than he had ever done before, and kept watch only by day. Hamed the muallim kept watch at night while Nejdi slept. The bad weather was over, and most dangers were past. We had only to sail to the north in sight of the coast, keeping always to the north-east, and in the course of time we should come to Ras al-Hadd and the Gulf of Oman. If there we swung to the left, still following the coast, Muscat was a little way up-gulf. Visibility was good, and the weather perfect. It was neither hot nor cold, and the nights were ideal for sleeping. We took down the thatch over the bench aft and stored it for sale in Kuwait, and after that slept in the open beneath the stars. With the end of the rains our mangroves began to dry out and the ship rode lighter, and sailed better. Kaleel the carpenter, with *Afra* left in Zanzibar and the longboat repaired after its strenuous work in the Rufiji, took his ease for the first time on the voyage, and the sailors did nothing but make rope out of coir shipped at Zanzibar, and the necessary tending of the sails. Kaleel could do little round the decks when they were beneath six feet of mangrove poles, and in any case the ship was in good order. We still had some spare ribs ands balks of wood for boatbuilding, left over from *Afra*, and before long it occurred to Nejdi that he would like a small boat for Hussein, his son. Hussein was his eldest son, eight years old. It was time he knew something of the sea. So the chests were cleared from the starboard side of the poop, and Kaleel began to build a small shewe, a fleet-lined, pretty cutter, about 16 feet long, out of *Afra*'s spare ribs. Hussein and Nejdi's other sons, of whom there seemed a very large number, would have the use of the small boat during the summer months, and when the boom went out again she would take it down to Lamu or Zanzibar for sale. She would take Hussein too, for it was considered time that he was getting on with his seamanship.

Kaleel went about his boatbuilding in a business-like way, first putting down the keel on a bed of small blocks raised slightly from the deck, and then attaching a stempost and the stern. His next move was to add two bottom planks on each side, forcing them into shape with wedges and lashings to the deck. Then he put in the ribs – half of them first and the other half when the planking was finished. But first he had to saw the planks out of a log of Indian wood. So far as I saw, he made no measurements and never planned anything: he simply went ahead and built the boat by eye. His tools were an adze, which was used most, an Indian saw or two, an Indian bow-type drill, a hammer, and a primitive plane. All day long, from immediately after the dawn prayer until time for sunset prayer, he worked on that boat, with Nejdi watching and criticising, and a small sailor to help. All through that voyage Kaleel worked harder than anyone else on board, but I gathered that he was considered not so much one of the crew as Nejdi's personal boatbuilder. His reward included not only his share in the ship's earnings, but an agreed proportion of the proceeds of the sale of his boats. Alone among the crew, too, he kept no night watch. He rolled himself in his sleeping carpet about nine o'clock every evening, and slept there soundly until Sultan announced the dawn prayer. He turned out for important all-hands jobs, such as getting in the sail that night off Malindi and again in the blows off Kismayu.

We wandered on pleasantly towards the north, going more slowly the more northerly we came, for it was too early for the south-west wind to have reached up there. No matter: when it came it was apt to set in blustery and to blow really hard, with bad conditions of squalls and bad visibility. Our aim was to reach the Gulf ahead of the monsoon, and so avoid bad weather. We caught a few dolphins, which were a pleasant addition to the morning meal: at sunset we always had rice and the Indian corn called dhall. Made with a stew of chillis and other things not so easily recognised, this was not bad. I was never hungry. Nejdi had bought a sack of onions in Zanzibar, and we had onions with the dhall. Sometimes he got old Yusuf to make an onion soup, flavoured with chillis and dhall; and the fish was roasted in the ashes of the wooden fires. We fared well. With no passengers other than our three school-teachers, there was no congestion and life was very pleasant on board. Day succeeded day in a pleasing routine of sunshine and easy labour, while I worked on a dwindling number of patients, studied Arabic out of books which never agreed with the spoken word, yarned with Nejdi, watched Kaleel at his work, and learnt all I could while the coast of Africa slipped lazily by and our lateen-rigged armada sailed leisurely up that sunlit sea.

It was a good life, and this was the best part of the voyage. We still had several bad fever cases from the Rufiji, and these lay in their cloaks on some sacking in the shade of the longboat. I gave them quinine, and the bad ones atebrin: they recovered, in due course, probably none the more rapidly for my treatment. But they were grateful for the medicines. There were still many, particularly among the pearl-divers, with bad ulcers and other skin wounds, and one or two with bad heads. I was busy at my amateur doctoring and, not for the first time, wished I really knew something of that art.

One morning, when we were somewhere south of Ras Haifun, meandering slowly north-eastwards with a quiet air, we picked up Abdulla Kitami's small boom. It was hazy that dawn, with the Somaliland coastline perhaps ten miles away. We were one of a fleet of eight Arab ships drifting along very quietly, the bigger fellows without much way, and the small ones, such as the Hadhramaut double-enders and a Bedeni or two closer inshore, ghosting along very nicely. By mid-morning we were one among ten, and Nejdi declared the sail of a boom ahead to be Abdulla Kitami's, though it must have been eight miles away, and nothing could be seen except the upper part of the sail. I knew Nejdi made no mistakes in his identification of Arab ships, especially from Kuwait; though how he could tell one boom from another at that distance I do not know: the differences between the vessels were extremely slight. I had to see any two booms close together before I could detect differences: Nejdi and his crew knew every boom in Kuwait five miles away. I suppose it was a matter of being reared with them, and knowing nothing else. I could do the same with square-rigged ships. So could Captain de Cloux, or any other grain-ship master, or mate. To Nejdi all other ships were confusingly alike, but he knew his dhows. The differences between one Kuwait boom and another were so slight, a little variation in the cut of the sail, a minute difference in the angle of the stempost or the sternpost, different lashings on the lateen yards, that only an experienced Arab sailor could detect them.

But Nejdi could only recognise three kinds of steamer. They were *markobs gaz*, *markobs strick*, and *fastmail*. A *markob gaz* was an oil-tanker to Nejdi, any vessel with engines aft; a *markob strick*, so named from the Strick Line steamers, which trade to Basra, was any cargo vessel; all passenger steamers were *fastmails*. He was familiar with oil-tankers because the road from Abadan leads past Kuwait and he had seen them all his life. *Fastmails* were the Bombay-Persian Gulf traders of the British India company.

The wind came in from the east, a pleasant sailing breeze, and we began rapidly to overhaul the Kitami boom. Nejdi set a course straight for her and looked carefully to the trim of all his sails. He was a past-master at the trimming of sails, which is half the sailing-ship master's art. In that ancient calling, he was, in his own way, as good as de Cloux. I could give him no higher rating. De Cloux in the Cape Horners *Herzogin Cecilie* or *Parma*, Nejdi in a dhow, were at the top of their profession. Now he watched the trim of main and mizzen and set a larger jib, and as the breeze freshened we dashed on. By noon we had Abdulla's boom close ahead and shortly afterwards were abeam. Nejdi spoke to her from the poop, and the sailors from the forecastle head. He was eight days from Lamu, Abdulla Kitami said: the sailors said they were ten. Actually they were fourteen. They were bound towards Muscat for orders, as we were, and had nothing but calms and head winds. They had seen nothing of the *Bedri*, about which we felt some anxiety, fearing that those dirty nights off Malindi and Kismayu might have finished her. That day we were only seven days from Zanzibar ourselves so that we were certainly making a better passage than they were.

The small boom looked very well as we sailed by, plunging along in the blue sea under her two great sails, her lateen yards waving like willows in the wind and her canvas of pure white swelled out beautifully. Now and then, as she pitched into the crest of a sea, a roll of foam turned back from her low bow or swept along her wet sides, and her wake stretched away straight and smooth. We saw a dozen Suri passengers on her deck-cargo, and eight fishing lines trailed astern. We sailed on ahead, and then Nejdi eased the sheets, and put the cutter over to pull back and visit his friend. At sunset, with us close by the Kitami boom for company, he sent the cutter back asking for his photographs, of which he was inordinately proud, and the date, which no one in the other ship knew. They did not, indeed, even know the month, having a vague idea that it had lately changed. In the day's last light, after the sun had set, the crews of the two ships prayed together, each aboard their own craft, and afterwards Ismael regaled them with music. Some time before midnight our boat came back with Nejdi and Abdulla Kitami, and it was announced that the two ships would sail together to Muscat. The two nakhodas yarned away most of the night, while Hamed looked after the *Triumph*, and the ex-slave Saud sailed Abdulla's boom.

In the morning we were well ahead of our sailing companion and had to take the mizzen and the jib off to give her a chance to catch up. Nejdi said disparaging things about Abdulla's boom which were returned in kind, but we still kept company. We had a big Persian boom in sight hull-down ahead and a Bombay kotia alee; we might have passed both these if our comrade had not delayed us. We spent a considerable part of the day dodging about the Indian Ocean with eased sheets in order not to leave his ship too far astern, much to the disgust of Hamed, who said, very quietly, that Allah's good wind should not be wasted. I ventured to suggest to Abdulla that his boom was somewhat slow, but he replied that she sailed very well indeed. Perhaps she was not doing her best just then because he was not aboard, and the sails were badly set.

Indeed, I said; what about the other fourteen days coming from Lamu? The sails were set and drawing very well: to suggest otherwise was a libel on poor Saud, who was as good a muallim as sails from Kuwait.

Well, said Abdulla, cornered on that, and grinning, the sails were too small and he had no money to buy larger. He swore also that his boom did not leak, but, unfortunately, just at that moment his sailors began to bail out water and kept at it for the next half-hour. They hauled up skin after skin all that time. Abdulla said it must be rain. It had not rained for a week. Then he said the buckets were half-full. It is a good sailor who sees no fault in his own ship; and I did not blame Abdulla. He lied about the performance of his vessel cheerfully, as a good sailor should, and refused to believe that she had any faults or even that our *Triumph* was faster. At that we sailed two rings round him, though he stood on the poop and shouted to his little boom 'Come on! Come on!' Having sailed the rings round him, we took him back to his slowcoach in our cutter and left him aboard, promising to carry any letters he might like to send to Muscat. He grinned, and we parted friends. By the following morning his little boom was out of sight astern. So much for our keeping company.

Poor Abdulla Kitami! Throughout our visit, which had been a wholly pleasant interlude, there had been no mention of the shooting of his brother in the riot at Kuwait. He did not know about it and we did not tell him. He was greatly attached to his brother, and we did not wish to be bearers of bad news. He would find out, poor fellow, in good time, when he brought in his ship from the sea.

XIV

THE PROPHET'S LANTHORN

FOR A WEEK WE DRIFTED about somewhere between Ras Haifun and Ras Asir, with variable winds and calms. Sometimes we lost sight of the land, but never for long; Nejdi soon put about and stood in again until we picked up the African coast. He did not like to be out of sight of land. This stage of the voyage, from the time we lost the boisterous squalls of the south-west monsoon until we reached Mutrah Bay in the Gulf of Oman fifteen days later, was the most pleasant of all. The ship wandered along upright and placid as a Balinese girl, with no motion other than her forward speed. If this was three knots or perhaps four, it worried nobody. The sea was flat and a glorious blue. The breaths of wind we had were from the east, anywhere from east-south-east to north-east, cooling the deck by day and making the nights restful. It was a good life. No voice was raised about our decks. There was no sound other than the sounds of toil – the carpenter's adze, Hamed's clink of Austrian thalers and Indian rupees as he cast up the accounts, the lilt of happy laughter from the boyish sailors forward, the noise of the rudder tackles and the slow, easy creaking of the masts. They were good days, each very like the last, but none of them monotonous. Our food was good. We caught many fish, and we still had oranges and bananas from Zanzibar. We caught a shark one day, and ate that. I did not care for it, and I noticed that Yusuf Shirazi and Kaleel the carpenter, both of whom were Muslims of a different sect from the others, ate none of it. It was pig of the sea, Kaleel said, and this view I shared. Nejdi and the rest ate it cheerfully, made into a kind of mince-meat with rice and smothered with hot ghee.

It was pleasant to be on board under conditions such as these, and though I wanted to see Kuwait, I found myself not looking forward to the end of the voyage, for I did not know when I might make another one. I often turned over in my mind the project, half-born at Kwale, of saving an old baggala and sailing her over the North Atlantic to America, but after that Malindi night it seemed to me that it would be asking a lot of God to expect to accomplish such a voyage. Anyone who wished to sail an Arab baggala, rigged and handled as the Arabs sailed her, over the North Atlantic or anywhere else away from her own Indian Ocean would need more help from God than any sailor has a right to expect. We sometimes talked for an hour or two in the early evenings about long voyages and the prospects of making an Atlantic voyage in a baggala, for Nejdi and all the sailors were very interested. At first inclined to be scornful, they soon became enthusiasts for the idea. Before long they were demanding that I should do it, Nejdi offering to come as pilot for Arabian waters, Hamed as salesman for a cargo of Persian carpets, Arab brassware and swords, and Kuwait carved chests he proposed to bring, and the sailors fired by the adventure and eager to try the lures of the harim material in America.

It was a good topic for a moonlight yarn, in the pole-laden boom with the quietness of the Indian Ocean all round. The moonlight seemed to give the decks an ordered and romantic beauty they lacked by the light of day, and the serang with his watch gathered round the bole of the mizzenmast, wrapped in their cloaks, assumed the grace of a noble painting. They yarned very quietly, about Kuwait, and ships, and Zanzibar nights, and they talked to me about the outside world. The helmsman sat in the steersman's chair like Buddha; the halliards and the tackled rigging gently creaked, and the peak of the great mainsail – old Oud, our largest – seemed very high. There was no light but the moon's, for we had no lamps; the silvered water parted before the raking bow silently as the ship sailed on, and for all her breadth of beam she trod the sea quietly, and left little wake astern.

As in all sailing-ships, each day could be trusted to provide its own diversion. Sometimes we went ship-visiting, whenever one of Nejdi's friends showed above the horizon. Sometimes there were minor accidents, as on the day that five of the sailors fell overboard. Falling overboard was not at all unusual, though this was the only occasion that so many went at once. There was a slight change of wind, and we could set the mizzen and make it draw. The sail was set, and the five sailors were hauling the parral tackle tight, down to windward, when the tackle suddenly carried away and they fell over the side. They were standing on the chests on the poop, and there was nothing to prevent them from falling when the tackle carried away. There was no railing. So away they went – Sultan the prayer-announcer, Mohamed with the bad head, the thin Yusuf, Nasir the pearl-diver, and Jassim the cook, who had come along for exercise while his rice boiled. They had no chance: when the tackle went, they went. She was close by the wind at the time and Hassan, at the wheel, had been shaking her while they got a purchase on the tackle. This was well, for the ship in consequence had little way and did not sail on to leave our five behind. All five of them, laughing heartily, swam like fish alongside.

"Down helm!" Nejdi roared, and Hassan spun the wheel down until the sails were almost aback and the ship stood in her stride, while every spare end on the poop was thrown overboard. Inside half a minute the five had climbed aboard again, spluttering and laughing, none the worse for their dip. They did not trouble to change their clothes but went straight on with their work. This incident over, Nejdi went back to his bench aft and called for his 'pickchure,' the wash-out one taken by an Indian in Dar-es-Salaam, the contemplation of which never ceased to give him great satisfaction. Hamed bin Salim had slept through this minor incident, and the only member of the crew who showed any excitement was Yimid the monkey.

One of the ships we visited was the small boom of Mosa Abdul-aziz, of Dabai on the Trucial Coast. Mosa was a friend of Nejdi, and we had seen him in several ports. His boom was coming up from Dima, in the south of the Rufiji Delta, bound in the first instance towards Mukalla in the Hadhramaut. She was a poor, old little ship, not more than forty tons, but she made a brave show, with her great white mainsail full of the morning wind, and the long lateen yards curved gracefully. She was a lofty little thing, with very sweet, fast lines, low in the water, with a keen bow, and a sheer that promised great seaworthiness, if only her hull could be trusted to remain in one piece. They spread a carpet for us above the cargo on the poop, and Mosa, welcoming us, offered refreshments of confectionery, clove-flavoured coffee, sweet tea, and pieces of a Zanzibar orange, very green. We talked for half an hour or so, while our two ships drifted together. She had a very ancient compass in a huge binnacle which looked as though it had come from some old East Indiaman of two centuries ago. Perhaps it had. It was from a junkshop in Bombay, Mosa told me. He did not know how old it was. A hundred years? Very likely – perhaps even more than that. He had bought it with the ship, and the ship was forty years old. He had heard that it had been in at least two other Kuwait ships before that. I often noticed very old pieces of maritime equipment of this kind in the poorer Arab dhows. I noticed also that the wheel, which was a handsome brass-bound piece of ship's furniture, bore the name of one of Her Majesty's Indian shipbuilding establishments of long ago. Mosa had neither sextant nor charts, and this old compass was his only aid to navigation – that, an Australian insurance company's map of the world, and a well-thumbed copy of Isa Kitami's Arab directory of the eastern seas. I was interested in this book and turned its pages: we had no copy. Nejdi said it was no use to him, for all its information was available in better form on the charts, but it seemed from that hurried inspection that the book contained some good descriptions of landmarks, if nothing else. I liked Mosa, and liked his little ship. He was a plain man, and neat. He spoke very affectionately of his ship, and his crew seemed to like him, for they all squatted about very pleased while we were aboard. The little ship was spotlessly clean, and there was peace in all the lines of Mosa's open countenance. They told me afterwards he was one of the best smugglers in Dabai.

Ten days out from Zanzibar we found ourselves off Ras Asir, the eastern extremity of the African coast. The wind was light from the south-east that day, which was fair, and we ran on towards Arabia. At sunset we came in sight of the picturesque islets of Abd-el-Kuri, to the west of Socotra. It was a beautiful red sunset such as only the Indian Ocean can show, and the rocks of Abd-el-Kuri were most alluring. The moon was very bright that night, and we sailed on upright and slowly with the wind quiet, and the mizzen and jib both furled. We were bound then on our only real open-water crossing of the voyage. I was interested to watch how Nejdi laid off his course for the Arab coast: he could not very well miss it, so long as we went ahead. He took a rough bearing of Ras Asir – a thing I had not seen him do before – and transferred it, using his thumbs as parallel rules, to the chart. Then he looked at the point, said it was thirty-five miles away, and ruled off that distance, also with his thumbs. Next he looked over the side; announced, after a brief inspection, that the current was in our favour – though how he knew that I don't know – and that we were making four knots. This I thought a gross over-estimate. He added that we should see Abd-el-Kuri right ahead, in two and a half hours. We did: I put it down to an Act of God.

We were only out of sight of land one day. The African coast round Ras Asir is high, the islands of Socotra and Abd-el-Kuri are high, and so is the coast of South Arabia. We had picked up the Hadhramaut coast, somewhere about Ras Sharma, by the second evening after leaving Africa, and we remained in sight of land until we reached our destination.

We were welcomed back to Arabia by an eclipse of the moon. This simple phenomenon was predicted in my pocket diary but, imagining it to be as commonplace to the Arabs as it is to us, I had made no mention of it. It scared our sailors greatly, and during the whole of the time that the moon was obscured, they prayed, chanted, and beat on Indian drums in a state of superstitious alarm. It was the night of the full moon in May, 1939. Shortly after the sunset prayer, with the group of us assembled round the bole of the mizzenmast for the nightly yarn – Nejdi, moaning with a bad toothache, tossed on his carpet aft – it became obvious that something was wrong. Instead of the bright clear light of the moon, the light on the sea was sickly and green. A silence fell on the sailors. One after another of them stared at the heavens, watching with alarmed astonishment while the shadow of the earth fell across the moon's face. Sultan, our muezzin, noticing this, leapt up and dashed away to his high place for'ard, where he began at once to call the faithful to instant prayer, very loudly. His call to prayer was the only sound then, for the night was quiet and the murmur of the ocean stilled. When Sultan called, the sailors rose and hurriedly performed their ablutions, quickly forming up in a line behind Hamed bin Salim on the poop. Nejdi, rousing himself with a groan from his carpet, hurried to join them, though the application of cold sea water to his neuralgic face must have been extremely painful.

When they were all lined up, facing Mecca, Hamed began to pray, and he prayed steadily for as long as the eclipse lasted. There was no fear about Hamed: his faith was in Allah and the shadow on the moon did not alarm him. But most of the others were exceedingly alarmed, and it was a strange experience for me, though I knew well enough what was happening and had been looking forward to seeing the eclipse all that day, to notice how the feeling of superstitious fear rapidly communicated itself to all hands. I had to fight against it myself, though I knew it was foolish. Several of the sailors, having offered up their prayers, dashed away forward and began to beat on the Indian drums. The Swahili school-teachers, who also professed indifference to the proceedings and knew well enough the natural explanation of what was going on, prayed as fervently as the rest, though I believe that they prayed because they did not dare not to pray. They dared not to be abstainers in that display of religious fervour, though they knew it to be based on fallacy. They had prayed very little on the way up the African coast, but now that we were off Arabia they remembered they were Muslims. The nearer we came to Muscat, the more frequent and devout did their prayers become.

The eclipse lasted only a few moments, but it was a long time before the sailors settled down. A sigh of relief went up as the shadow finally moved from the face of the moon, and they offered up a new prayer in gratitude. Afterwards, the watch gathered round the mizzenmast, to discuss in awed voices the phenomenon they had just seen. The moon, according to them, was the light of the Prophet in the heavens. The shadow upon the Prophet's lamp was a threat to the Prophet, and through him to them; that was why they prayed. They asked me what I thought about it, and I told them that what they had seen was nothing but a plain eclipse of the moon, a predictable and very ordinary astronomical phenomenon to be explained by any schoolboy. But they were not impressed, though they asked for details. It was not an easy matter to explain an eclipse to those simple superstitious men, with their background of belief in *jinn*s and the superstitious basis of so much of their religion.

They laughed uproariously at my ignorance, Nejdi with them. This was almost as good a yarn as my explanation of the 'trick,' which was stored in clouds. They laughed and laughed, so much that they gradually forgot their superstitious dread. The moon, they said, was the Prophet's lamp in the heavens; every little Beduin child knew that. The shadows were caused by some enormous *jinn* attacking the Prophet's lamp. It was a sign, a test of them to see that they observed it and answered with fervent prayer. They prayed to drive off the *jinn*. The slowly moving line of shadow across the moon's face was the advancing and retreating mouth of the *jinn*; others said it was the drying saliva where the *jinn* had vomited the lanthorn forth. The three Swahili were scornful of these curious beliefs. Yet they, too, had prayed as fervently as the rest, and had done their share of banging on the drums. The feeling of alarm which had gripped all hands was eerie and moving. I was glad when the eclipse was ended.

They never accepted my explanation. I should, they said, be telling them next that the moon was made of 'trick,' which was stored in clouds.

Day after day we slipped slowly along the coast of South Arabia, bound towards Ras al-Hadd and the Gulf of Oman. Nejdi's toothache grew worse and worse. It might have had a chance of improvement if he had left his mouth alone for half an hour, but he would not. He kept poking at it, like a small boy, as if he hoped that somehow he could torment it back into its normal condition. In Zanzibar a Japanese tooth-torturer had fitted him with a bridge (of sorts) of three gold teeth. The gold was not gold and the teeth were not teeth, but the gold looked like gold and Nejdi was happy. At least, when we left Zanzibar he was happy. But the poor workmanship of this unsatisfactory bridge soon caused an abscess beneath it; the gold teeth pressed terribly on the afflicted part and made it ten times worse. Nejdi could neither sleep nor eat, and life must have been purgatory for the poor fellow. He scorned the simple remedies I suggested, such as hammering off those gold teeth with anything that came to hand; he poked at his mouth, filled it with hot ghee, smoked incessantly, and moaned. He did not fear any dental operation, but he could not bring himself to part with the golden teeth. They were a too greatly prized possession. Meanwhile his mouth grew worse and worse. His face was swollen, and his spirits grew lower and lower. One day he told me how he had suffered from toothache in a pearler in the Persian Gulf as a child and, after putting up with the pain for a few days, his father pulled the tooth out with a nail and a pair of pliers. Six men held his head, he said; the operation took two hours. He suggested that I should repeat it there and then, but the tooth he pointed out to me was a sound one and I was sure its removal, even if accomplished, would gain nothing. Those gold false teeth would have to be scrapped. Moreover, I had no instruments. Nejdi admitted that, after the experience as a child in the Gulf, he had had to spend two weeks in hospital with an infected jaw. I admired his courage, but I tried to impress on him the fact that an infected jaw was worse than any toothache, and we must remove the golden rubbish. No, he said; and continued to moan.

After some days more, however, he weakened. All right, he said, the gold teeth should go. But he must chisel them off himself. He did so, using the carpenter's chisel and the head of a small adze. It took two days – two days which must have caused him excruciating agony. But he got the teeth off, though he declared at once that it was a grievous error and made no difference to his state of pain. But his mouth cleared up at once, and within a day the worst of the pain had gone.

Nejdi made Yusuf stow the gold teeth carefully in his chest, and announced that he would have them put back properly in Basra or Bahrein.

By that time we were off Kuria Muria, an old sign-post on the slave-ships' road from Zanzibar. The islands of Kuria Muria are beautiful in their own way. We sailed through them, passing near a mountain of rock whose worn strata were shadowed in the overhead sun so that it looked like a designed pattern, and at sea level was half an acre of yellow sand flung at the cliff's edge, burning in the sun. Away on our port hand lay the high coast of south-east Arabia, hazy all day and defined only at sunset and sunrise. All round in the water sea life teemed, and far out to windward a Persian baggala sailed in company, homeward bound light from Hodeida in the Yemen towards Kung.

Nejdi, recovered from his toothache, kept a particularly alert eye open while we crossed Kuria Muria Bay, for he said that the wind played dirty tricks there, and the Beduin of the coast could play worse ones. He went on to tell a story of a Kuwait boom, outward bound from Basra towards Berbera, which had got into difficulties there the previous year, and had been cut out by the Beduin. They gutted her of everything, and stole the dates. It was easy for a ship to get into difficulties there, and once she did so the Beduin had no mercy. They were a hungry tribe, for their coast was a poor one, and they regarded date-laden wrecks as gifts from Allah. Piracy, I gathered, is still a real risk of the sea to the Arab dhows. Nejdi, who usually did not dilate on his own adventures, told me of a narrow escape he had had himself in that neighbourhood a few years earlier, when making his first African voyage. He was bringing a small boom, the predecessor of the *Triumph of Righteousness*, on the old road from Basra towards Mukalla, for orders, by way of Muscat, with a cargo of 1,200 packages of Iraq dates. It was early in the season, and the north-east monsoon had not set in. The only way to make a passage to the westwards at that time of the year was by standing along close inshore, taking advantage of every favouring eddy of the counter-current there, and coaxing the ship along with the land airs. Outside in the open sea all the conditions were against her, for there was still more than enough south-westerly wind, and the set was strong from that direction. It was difficult to sail close inshore, for that section of the coast bristled with dangers. Moreover, the Beduin there were treacherous and unfriendly. It was necessary to anchor frequently, for it was dangerous to stand close inshore by night. A dhow anchoring in those parts often found it necessary to keep careful watch, lest her cables should be cut and she should drift ashore to become a gutted wreck. The cargoes of Basra dates were a great temptation to the Beduin.

One night, Nejdi said, he came to anchor in a small cove near Ras Sherbetat, not far from the place where the *Triumph* was then sailing. He knew that the reputation of the local tribe of Beduin was a particularly bad one, but he did not worry. He had succeeded in making friends with worse Beduin, and he had been giving dates away generously to all the Beduin camps the ship had met. Nejdi knew that news of such generosity travels swiftly in Arabia, and he thought that the good tidings sent before him would be sufficient to assure him of safe anchorage, and at least keep his cables whole. That day he had seen no Beduin. He did not land, for he was very tired and he planned to sail again before the morning. So he showed no lights, and all hands, save one watchman, rolled in their cloaks and slept. The watchman, as the night wore on, must have slept, too. Some time after midnight Nejdi found himself rudely awakened, to stare into the bearded faces of half a dozen hungry Beduin who had heard nothing of the young master's generosity, and obviously wanted nothing less than his ship's whole cargo. The Beduin were armed with ancient muskets and swords, and had the familiar Oman curved dagger at their waists.

"O Sheikh," Nejdi said (so he told me), addressing the leader of the Beduin robber band, "to what do I owe the pleasure of this midnight call?"

The dirty Beduin gave a greasy laugh.

"Dates, dates! That's what we want, young nakhoda: dates. Every package on board."

"But I have given dates all along this coast," Nejdi said, while the elderly muallim of the dhow, who had always been against these proceedings, openly sneered. "I will give you dates. You have no need to take them. Only do no harm to my good ship."

"We want more than dates, oh nakhoda!" the greasy one replied. "Hand over the keys of your chest. Come on, now. The ship's money will also be welcome to us poor men here. You can get more."

"Are you not Muslims?" Nejdi implored, knowing how strongly the Prophet expressed his abhorrence of theft. The Beduin were unimpressed. If they did not steal, they did not eat. That was the usual way of their lives: to them theft was allowable, and life was cheap.

The situation looked desperate. It did not take Nejdi long to realise that his crew had been rounded up and were being kept prisoners under the break of the poop. He could see the mastheads of two small sambuks alongside. There were, he thought, at least forty Beduin on board. It looked hopeless. Some of the Beduin were already passing down packages of dates from the hold into their sambuks. Muslims or not, those Beduin were not going to be content with less than everything in sight. Very probably, when they had finished with the cargo, they would burn the ship and seize the crew as slaves. Nejdi's quick mind worked desperately, trying to find some way out of this bad situation. Suddenly an idea came to him. They wanted his chest.

He began to talk again to the old Beduin, trying to amuse him, to throw him off his guard. Nejdi affected to look on the whole thing as a joke, as an expression of Allah's great compassion for the poor Beduin. He said he would open his chest. There was no money in it; it would do no harm for the Beduin to peer in and look. They were welcome to the few clothes it contained. But there was something else in that chest, something that Nejdi hoped he could find, before the Beduin did so. He joked on. His crew, hearing the conversation, looked at him amazed.

Nejdi's arms had to be free while he opened his chest, and when he treated the whole affair so light-heartedly, the old Beduin did not think of taking precautions against him. The keys of the chest, as is usually the case on board the big dhows, were fastened with a thong round Nejdi's waist. In order to open the chest, he had to kneel over it, and bring the end of the thong to the padlock. He knelt down, calling out some pleasantry to the Beduin chief and telling him to be sure to keep the best dates for himself. He knelt down, not seeming greatly interested in the proceedings. Slowly he brought the key to the lock, fumbled a little. The Beduin crowded round, gloating in anticipation of the treasures the chest contained. Nejdi turned the lock, very slowly. The Beduin craned over. Some of them were so interested they had put down their arms.

Suddenly Nejdi pulled up the lid, reached in rapidly, and drew out a big Turkish revolver.

"Now, desert scum! May the Prophet burn you all in hell! Out of my ship!" he roared, suddenly leaping to his feet. "On, sailors! Drive these pigs to the sea!"

To his own great surprise, and to the considerable astonishment of the crew, who were finding his behaviour extremely difficult to understand, the horde of Beduin took to their heels and flung themselves over the side, not waiting to cut the painters of their sambuks, and throwing down their muskets as they went. The sailors set up a terrific shouting and the cove re-echoed to the noise, while the Beduin splashed out for the shore.

Nejdi picked up the muskets. They were not loaded. They were so old that it would have been extremely dangerous to fire most of them. Then he looked, very thoughtfully, and thanking Allah, at his own revolver. It was not loaded, either.

Remembering these things Nejdi gave that place a wide berth. He said that the Beduin, too, would remember that night, and they would not fail a second time. He had been lucky. Other Kuwait nakhodas had not done so well, and the bones of many of their ships littered that hard coast – their ships, and themselves.

In the nights we wandered on through a queerly phosphorescent sea, with the breaking crests of the black swells looking as though they were floodlit in green from below. At moonrise black clouds piled swiftly over the western sky, with a little lightning and some rumble of distant thunder, while Nejdi, scared and still weak from his toothache, ran down the sails and let the ship drift, lest there should be a sudden shift of the wind. But no wind came, and towards midnight, with the stars clear, we sailed again.

We were now close to Ras al-Hadd, the turning-point of the Arab coastline, and the Swahili school-teachers, who had been wearing trousers throughout the rest of the voyage, changed to long Arab gowns. They were a strange trio. Keeping very much to themselves, they lived on the port side of the officers' bench aft, crowding out Hamed bin Salim. They talked together all day long in the mellow Swahili tongue, as if they were engaged in a deep conspiracy. Nejdi, who understood the language, said they were discussing the politics of Zanzibar. He upbraided them for their trousers, which he thought unseemly, and for their poor performance of the daily prayers which, he said, gave a bad example to the sailors. But the school-teachers took little notice of Nejdi's upbraidings: they continued their earnest talks in the strange Swahili tongue.

When I saw them for the first time, I thought they were three negroes, for they were more negroid in appearance than any of the sailors. But they said they were two Baluchi, brothers, and one Arab, a distant relation of a prince of Zanzibar. They all spoke English well. They had been boy scouts, and were proud of it. Now they were setting out to see the world. The Baluchi were the progeny of an ivory-trading Baluchi and a woman from the Congo, and had been born somewhere in the interior of Africa. The Arab, who was a quarter negro, was born at Zanzibar. They were fine, upstanding youths, aged between 18 and 20. What was behind their sudden desertion of Zanzibar I do not know, but they had left without proper passports. According to their own story they were rebels against parental authority and against the traditional upbringing of Muslim youth. They had been educated, and the old ideas would not do, they said. The life at Zanzibar was too cramping; besides, there were too many Indians there, and the Indians had too much to say. They wished to see the world, and as a beginning, the Seyyid Sulieman had arranged this passage to Muscat with Nejdi. Nejdi, after the first flush of enthusiasm, did not seem very keen about them, and, apart from his daily criticisms of their trousers and their backwardness in prayer, left them alone. He was not being paid for carrying them, and he seemed to regret the thoughtless generosity which had caused him to promise the Seyyid Sulieman to see them safely to Muscat.

I talked to them sometimes in English, which was a pleasant change from the constant grappling with Arabic. They liked the life at Zanzibar, they said, but it was too narrow. They wanted to see the world, and they felt that the time for that was when they were young. They would have been glad to enlist in the British Navy at Zanzibar, if there had been any way of doing so, but now there was not. So they were going to the Gulf in the hope of finding a steamer somewhere there in which they could sign on. They had relatives in Muscat.

"Our parents, sir," they told me, "do not approve of this."

Apparently their parents wanted them to marry and settle down, but they had other ideas. I wished them luck. They were cheerful lads, very likeable, but they seemed strangely ineffectual.

We rounded Ras al-Hadd three weeks from Zanzibar, in company with five sambuks bound to Sur, for the Suri never pass their home port homeward bound. The cargo they have not sold then they put on the beach and wait until it is time to go up the Gulf for the Basra dates. Homeward bound with mangroves from the Rufiji or Lamu, they sell them along the coast of the Hadhramaut if they can, or in their own Sur. If they cannot sell them they discharge them, store them and, after the summer's lay-up, reload them and hawk them up the Gulf of Oman and the Persian Gulf, to Bahrein, Qatar, Kuwait, Basra, and the ports along the Persian side. This, I believe, was largely our reason for not returning to the Hadhramaut. We left that market to the Suri, knowing we could beat them to the better one in the more populous ports of the Persian Gulf.

We saw nothing of Sur but the mountains behind it. I was sorry not to go into that picturesque place, the home of Majid and Said the smuggler, Abdulla the Mysterious, Mubarrak our delta pilot, those colourful characters. But we could sell nothing there and so sailed by, though Nejdi said he might go in the longboat if it was calm. He had old debts there, he said, and would like to collect them. He might as well forget them, Hamed said; to go in after debts in Sur would be only to delay the ship. So we went on, with a quiet southerly wind, and stood on up the Gulf of Oman, while our three Swahili-Baluchi-Arabs, or whatever they were, changed to gowns and began to take more interest in their prayers, and the sailors at the evening yarns spoke more and more of Kuwait. Kuwait, Kuwait, Kuwait – that was all I heard; the place, according to them, was a paradise on earth. We should, they said, go into Muscat only to pick up mail. Nejdi's father would write to him there, telling him where to take our cargo for prompt and profitable sale. After that, we should romp home to Kuwait. They seemed to take it for granted that this would be the best place to sell the cargo.

But past Sur it was calm again, and we lay silent and still in the Gulf of Oman with the ship upright and mirrored in the blue sea as if she were standing there to behold her own reflection, and, liking the sight, would not sail over it. Away to port, all along our beam, stood the high burned hills of Oman, brown and sterile. Ahead we could see the white buildings of Muscat, seeming from there to be perched on cliffs. We seized the opportunity of the calm to send the sailors overside, stripped naked, to scrape the sea growth from the ship's bottom. Though I knew them to be pearl-divers, I was amazed at the length of time those sailors could stay under water. They swam slowly beneath the keel, from side to side, scraping as they went, and paid no attention to two large sharks which swam lazily astern. On his bench aft, Nejdi crooned to himself in the morning sun, his toothache gone and himself very happy, and Mohamed the serang warmed the drums at Jassim's fire, and Bizz's new kittens, on deck for the first time, rolled and played.

We drummed her in to Mutrah Bay that afternoon, twenty-three days from Zanzibar, with our Kuwait flags fore and aft, a new airplane model at the stemhead, and the decks full of drums and song. It was a stirring entry, and we came to anchor among a fleet of Kuwaiti up from Zanzibar and India with their flags out to welcome us. A group of Persians, Omani, and Indians filled the inner waters of the small bay. Abdul-wahhab Kalifa, who had sailed his big boom from the Rufiji two weeks before us, was aboard; there was no word of the *Bedri*, and Abdulla Kitami was not expected for some days. We had the best passage up thus far in the season and, though hasty reports from the other nakhodas did not indicate much chance of selling the cargo there or in Muscat, Nejdi was all smiles. Everything was quiet again in Kuwait, and a letter from his father had announced the birth to his favourite wife of another strapping son.

XV

MUTRAH FOR ORDERS

As we came into Mutrah Bay from Zanzibar, I wondered again about Nejdi's navigation. When I had first heard that we should coast home, after having coasted the whole way down from Zanzibar, I was inclined to feel some contempt for Arab navigation. Now I knew I was wrong. As Nejdi said, he had come by the right road. He had often said that he was not a navigator; he knew the way. I had to admit that he did, and that he had made a good passage. If I had been bringing a ship on that passage I should have tried to lay a course direct, and I could not doubt, looking back with the *Triumph*'s passage safely accomplished, that mine would have been a worse way. We had always had some wind, except for a few brief and not unpleasant intervals of calm: the wind we had was nearly always usable, and helped us on our way. Nejdi had done very well. I had often been a little envious of the storehouse of maritime knowledge that must repose in his head; now I admired him. It might be true that he had no use for anything he did not know, but it was equally true that his knowledge was his own, complete and personal to him, and he did not need to look up things in books. If, as he said to himself, he could make a long passage like this with comparative ease, why all this fuss about navigation? Yet I knew he would like to master that art, if he had a chance. Old Abdul-wahhab Kalifa was always after me to instruct him in the mysteries of sextant, chronometer, and tables, and often expressed his regret that there was not a school of navigation in Kuwait. He thought that the ancient art should be preserved even if there was not much need of it on the ordinary African voyage. The Arabs, he said, ought to preserve the art of navigation as well as the art of sailing, for their day would surely come again.

I liked the way all these nakhodas were friends. In Mutrah Bay, as in all other ports we had visited, groups of them assembled on our officers' bench aft as soon as we came in, and there they sat all night and talked and talked, while the bubbling pipe went round continually. They stopped talking only for prayers and the evening meal. In the evening prayer they joined our sailors, the nakhodas with Nejdi in the centre of the line behind the leader Hamed, and our sailors and their own on either flank from end to end of the vessel, all facing Mecca and intoning the mellow prayers while the light died. The boat songs of the Persians as they ferried logs from their baggalas, were stilled then, and peace came to the anchorage. By night they slept with us, and later there were feasts, with Ismael, though he was still weak from the Rufiji fever, playing his guitar. The friendship of these nakhodas from the same home port was a very real thing and they formed a united band. They were prepared at any time to assist another's vessel in any circumstances, to perform risky feats of salvage without payment, to lend one another a carpenter, a dozen seamen, a cook, or a bale of carpets, or anything else that might be needed. In case of distress they were prepared to carry another crew for thousands of miles. They carried one another's junior officers, sent here and there to collect long due debts; and for none of these things did they accept payment. No Arab nakhoda looked on his brother shipmasters as a possible prey. Theirs was a real brotherhood of the sea, and I respected and liked them for it. Maritime accidents were far from unknown to them, for they sailed on dangerous coasts; but they rarely lost a sailor's life. Sometimes their ships opened up and foundered under them, and it was not unknown for one to sail down in a shower of rain, coming up too deeply laden from Africa or the Malabar coast; but the crews rarely went missing. They were a good lot, those Kuwait nakhodas. I had learned to know them well, in the long months with Nejdi's boom. Those who sat round our transom in Mutrah Bay were all old friends.

We learned from them now that things were not good in Muscat or in Mutrah Bay and, though the merchants wanted our poles, they had, they said, no rupees to pay for them. In these circumstances, we did not delay. We landed our three Swahilis, sold a few coconuts, took in fresh water from a mosque well, sold half the vermicelli to a boom from Dabai into which it was transhipped by night, bought some of the famous Muscat sweetmeats, and departed. We were in Mutrah Bay three days, the shortest stay we had ever made anywhere. Perhaps Nejdi was eager to see his new son.

I saw what I could of Mutrah and Muscat during this short stay, but I did not care greatly for either place. Mutrah was the dirtiest place we were ever in, and the stench of the beach was frightful. Mutrah is on a small bay, a mile or two to the north of Muscat, set in brown mountains, on two of which stand Portuguese forts now falling into decay. Along the beach in front of the little town are the homes of the merchants and brokers of the better class with, here and there, the minaret of a mosque.

At one end of the beach is a junk yard of old ships, and here two derelict *dhangis* lay half submerged in the water. The customs landing is at the other end. The beach itself is used as road, park, junk yard, market, fish shed, landing-stage, dog-house and public lavatory by all Oman and half Baluchistan. The place is full of scabby dogs, more dead than alive. Dogs, Baluchi, fish, goats, and human filth fill the Mutrah beach, so that one hesitates to walk along it. Armed Omani Beduin strut in brown shirts, barefoot in spite of all the beach's putrid filth, with belts of brass-bound cartridges about their waists and silver-handled daggers slung conveniently. Many carry fearsome guns, elaborately worked with silver filigree, or bound with brass and silver bands. Not all the guns are ancient; most of them look fit for use.

Once Muscat and Mutrah Bay were centres of the arms trade for the Middle East, and from here many a cargo was run across the Gulf to Afghanistan, or up to Hasa, Persia, Iraq, Kuwait. There was, perhaps, some smuggling to Iran, but now the arms trade is regulated and there are no fortunes to be made in it, not in Oman at least. Dabai and Sharjah are more conveniently placed for smuggling into Persia. With the loss of the arms business, Muscat's importance has declined, and now it is among the lesser ports of Arabia, used by the Arabs chiefly for orders. Life is still cheap there; it is not proper, even now, for a man of self-respect to be seen unarmed. In the bazaar are many arms shops offering the Beduins' guns and the townsman's sword. The well-dressed Omani does not walk, even on Mutrah beach, without his dagger at his waist.

Along the beach lie all kinds of fish, from hammerhead shark to giant ray: the nearer waters of the Gulf of Oman teem with fish, and much is shipped from here to Europe as fertiliser. Occasionally, an ancient motor-car, shaken by the pot-holed Muscat road, wanders along the beach among the children and dogs. Behind the front of better houses is the labyrinth of the *suq*, a place of narrow winding streets sheltered by rough overhead matting, and crowded with tiny shops offering the trash of Japan. Yet Mutrah is picturesque, and it really does not smell as badly as it might do.

The Kuwait nakhodas patronised a favourite coffee-shop facing the beach near the fish market, where their longboats landed. Here I used to sit with them, when I was ashore, drinking from time to time – with intervals as frequent and as long as possible – tiny cups of clove and cardamom flavoured coffee, or tiny glasses of sweet boiled tea. From this coffee-shop one could look along the beach, or watch what was going on in the harbour. It was a good coffee-shop for shipmasters. The beach was always crowded with people, Baluchi – thousands of them – Omani, Arabs, Persians, Indians and Kuwaiti from the ships, Beduin armed to the teeth; women in trousers and horrid masks, who shrieked shrilly at their dreadful children, stoning dogs; children with faces painted with mascara till they looked like little clowns in their tinselled fezzes and purple coats; Baluchi in voluminous trousers which had enough material in a leg to make a small tent; little girls in trousers, little boys in nothing, annoying the mangy pariah dogs. Over all, the high fortresses frowned from their burned hills, and the road to Muscat wound round the rocks away to the south.

In the nakhodas' coffee-shop Nejdi called loudly for a boy to relight his pipe, and Abdul-wahhab bin Kalifa al-Ganim, sipping a tiny cup of cardamom-coffee, kept an eye on the mangrove poles being landed from his longboat in the surf. Two Indians were arriving at the anchorage, kotias from Bombay by the look of them, flying big silken flags with red and white horizontal stripes. Hamed bin Salim came in, bound to the money-changers with a sack of Austrian thalers to be changed to rupees. They were dated 1786, but had been coined at the Royal Mint in London the previous year; Hamed brought them from Zanzibar. The Omani Beduin still love the large round coins with the fat face of Maria Theresa, and they bring a good price in Mutrah *suq*. We could buy them in Zanzibar for 80 rupees a hundred, and sell them for 90 at Mutrah.

Yusuf came in, on a buying excursion to get sweetmeats for Nejdi's harim; he sought instructions as to the best kinds. Mates, quartermasters, nakhodas' younger brothers, from all the ships in the bay, drifted into this thatched coffee-shop where business is always brisk; but only the nakhodas sat on the benches – the nakhodas and the agents and brokers whose business was with ships, and merchants who wished to buy from the ships' cargoes. These coffee-shops are like exchanges and clubs, and most of the sea business is done in them. The nakhodas never pay for what they have when they order it. They are known to the proprietor, and pay generously when they leave. A deep-sea nakhoda of Arab dhows sets considerable store by his reputation in these coffee-shops, and runs accounts in them from Jiddah to Zanzibar, Ashar to Berbera, Mogadishu to Mutrah Bay.

As a change from the coffee-shop, a few of us sometimes wandered through the congested *suq*. It is a big *suq*, though according to our mariners nothing compared with that of Kuwait. They seemed glad enough to buy lengths of red and yellow cloth in it, for they told me that these were good, and they all bought small baskets of sweetmeats as presents for their homes. The sweetmeat shops of Muscat and Mutrah are famous for the quality of their wares, but they would wait a long time for custom if they depended on me. The sickly-sweet taste of those cloying confections remained too much for me, after six months. The *suq*, however, was interesting to walk in for a while, with its teeming life – men shaving, men writing, men turning tiny sandstones grinding knives, men and boys beating iron in a wayside foundry; shops full of tinsel, calicoes, camels' hair cloth; arms shops, money-changers, hardware shops with a selection of small padlocks – for the Arab locks everything he can – and simple, cheap tools. The streets of the *suq* are of hard-trodden sand, and if it ever rained the place would be a quagmire.

Compared with the teeming life of Mutrah, Muscat itself was not so interesting, for it was a quiet place when we were there, apparently much run down. I did not go there often and the sailors did not go at all. It was reached by car ride in an ancient taxicab, over a well-made pass. It looked picturesque as one came over the pass, and there were some good buildings: the Sultan's palace – the ruling Sultan was a young man whose father, a descendant of the great Seyyid Said, had abdicated and lived in Japan – the British Residency, and the homes of a few leading merchants. Across the bay on the southern side were the remains of a large Portuguese fort, now used as a jail.

The prison was in the charge of a venerable Baluchi, who showed his prisoners with the air of a proprietor. There were perhaps a score of them, all leg-ironed. One was there for stealing a camel; he had been in a year, he said, and did not know how much longer he might stay there. There were four ancient sheikhs, from somewhere in the Batina, in for the suspected burning of a garden in some local feud. They were dressed in long gowns and turbans, and grinned expressively when asked for an account of their sins. To judge from their grins, they did not object overmuch to their incarceration. In the course of time, no doubt, Allah would be generous and they would be free again. In the meantime they were fed. More interesting than the prisoners were the drawings of square-rigged ships scratched on the walls of the entrance chamber of this curious jail. I wondered that such vessels should be depicted there in that ancient stronghold of the dhow. Nejdi said he had seen no such ships. They were good drawings, technically correct. They showed frigates and other men-o'-war of the previous century.

Lying in the sand by the side of the British Residency was a topmast from one of these frigates which had been maintained by Seyyid Said in the great days of Muscat and Oman, when Zanzibar and half the east coast of Africa were under the dominion of the Sultan. Seyyid Said had bought old frigates from the English and from India, for the better maintenance of his power and for his periodic visits to his African dominions. The Seyyid, apparently, had had a partiality for old frigates and ships of the line. He had, indeed, once sent one, a sloop named the *Sultana*, on a mission to America, but the churlish New Englanders of Salem had pulled the Arabs' beards and laughed at them, and the mission came to naught.

The tradition of old British sailing men-o'-war is still strong in the Persian Gulf, and I noticed later in Kuwait that a shipmasters' directory of the Eastern Seas given me by Kalifa al-Ganim, father of the nakhoda Abdul-wahhab, was illustrated with drawings of frigates and not of dhows. It was, he said, a Muscat production, and had been brought to Kuwait when the Kuwaiti were first starting as deep-water sailors. I thought I detected, too, a resemblance between some of the terms used by the Arab sailors and those in use in the old Navy – *jalboot*, for instance, from the naval jolly-boat; *bowrah* for anchor, from the English bower; *kittah* for cutter; *lanch* for the naval launch.

The guns in the Portuguese fort faced the Sultan's palace. There was a mixed battery of ancient muzzle-loaders which included iron guns from India and from Yorkshire, and two beautifully carved old Portuguese guns. Their carriages were rotten and the platform on which they stood looked hardly strong enough to walk on.

Muscat had fallen on evil days; there was no shipbuilding, and not much trade beyond a mean local trade from Mutrah across the Gulf to Baluchistan, or coastwise to Sur and Batina. Very few deep-sea dhows are now owned there, most of the long-voyage carrying of Oman being in the hands of the Suri and the ancient ships from Batina and the Trucial Coast. Beggars abound in the Mutrah *suq*, and there seem more Baluchi there than Omani. The only big ship sailing out of Mutrah at the time of our visit was a former Persian boom transferred there for the greater freedom of the Oman flag, the boom of Mohamed Kunji whom we had met in Zanzibar at the mysterious establishment of the Seyyid Sulieman bin Said.

Abdulla Kitami came in two days after our arrival. It was now considered time to tell him of the death of his brother and, as soon as he had moored, all the Kuwait nakhodas in the harbour, seven of them, went aboard very solemnly and told him the news. They told it as gently as they could, but it went hard with Abdulla. Afterwards they left, very quietly, when they had expressed their sympathy and their willingness to help the young nakhoda; only Nejdi stayed. Nejdi stayed with his friend until we sailed, for Abdulla had had much fever after parting company with us, and this news was a great blow. Mohamed had been a favourite brother. Abdulla had not heard of the riot; the death of his brother was a profound and terrible shock, for such tragedies are rare in Kuwait. A man of the sea does not often give his life for political foolishness, which is more properly the concern of shore-dwellers, and Abdulla found the tragedy difficult to believe. The death of his brother, he was convinced, must have been an accident. In a *suq* riot, anyone who has the misfortune to be near may suffer. He wished that his brother had not stayed ashore.

On the day of Abdulla Kitami's arrival the anchorage was full of Persians. Five of their booms arrived, having come up from Africa in company. The bay resounded with their haunting boat songs as their longboats pulled for the beach, the nakhodas standing and waving as they passed their countrymen's ships. After sunset, the creak of their great halliards getting the sails aloft ready for sea again came very clearly in the intervals of dancing and the tramp of hard bare feet. Mutrah Bay, that night, was very beautiful under the bright stars. There was no moon, but the stars gave light as the Persians made ready for sea. One of them was an enormous baggala with a capacity of 5,000 packages of dates, a lovely thing with a coppered underbody. She was the last baggala of Qishm, they said, and seventy years old. She had come in from the Malabar coast, laden with teak logs and a cargo of roping stuffs and coils of coir, with thirty dugout canoes stowed on deck, and Indian furniture hanging round the poop rail. A Kuwait baggala came in the same night, nineteen days from Lamu. The wind came from the north-west before midnight, gusty, burning with the heat of all the surrounding stone and the desert beyond, hot so that it scorched the face like a furnace blast, and even aboard ship out in the bay it was impossible to sleep.

I lay awake, and was thankful that I did so when, in the early hours of the morning, the great *el-Dhow* of Abdul-wahhab al-Kitami came ramping into a berth like a great black ghost, her blocks creaking as the yard came down, and her sailors calling quietly in order not to disturb the rest of the anchorage. It was stirring to see that heavy-laden great boom take up her moorings in the blackness of the night, for she came in in a gust and it was tricky work. It would have been tricky by day, when Abdul-wahhab could see the ships all round him. None of them showed anchor lights, and I do not know how he threaded a way through them at speed in that great ship and came to anchor beside the small boom of his nephew Abdulla Kitami. It would have been fine seamanship by day; by night, it was little short of miraculous. To judge distance the way Abdul-wahhab did that night, and come into a berth in an unlit and crowded anchorage with grace and style, shows the consummate seaman. These booms have always to be brought to anchorage without sail, which makes the judgment of the nakhoda all-important. If he makes a mistake at such a time he cannot rectify it either by setting sail, or backing it. He must come in with way or his vessel will not steer. The smallest error of judgment, and he must collide with probably two or three vessels at least. Yet this skilful ship-handling of a great vessel like the *Dhow* was taken as a matter of course.

Old Yusuf Shirazi, looking at the *Dhow* later in the dawn, murmured that she was back where she belonged; she had taken many a cargo of arms from the bay, and he had sailed with her. He sailed with her once when the British intercepted her and took her into their naval base near Ormuz. The *Dhow* was a vessel with history.

We sailed the following morning, going out as one of a fleet of eight, which included Abdulla Kitami's small boom, now under the command of Saud the freed slave. Abdulla Kitami, broken up and sick with fever, had gone to his uncle Abdul-wahhab in the *Dhow*. Also sailing with us that sunny morning were the big boom *Samhan*, commanded by the well-known Kuwait nakhoda Yusuf bin Isa, the big baggala from Qishm, an old Kuwait boom homeward bound with fish-oil from the Mahra coast, and three Persians from Africa. It was a beautiful morning, and the ships going out in company were glorious to see with their great white sails above the small hulls set in the blue sea, against the background of bold mountain. We had very light airs all day, barely enough to give us way, but if we dallied nobody cared. The conditions were ideal, and we enjoyed lovely views of the other vessels. We dropped most of them quickly, but we could not sail by the big *Samhan*. The two of us sailed in company through the day, not a stone's throw apart, and her sailors sat in the shadow of their sail and watched ours, who sat in the shadow of our sail and watched them. She was from Lamu, with 1,200 score mangrove poles. She was a very big ship, larger even than *el-Dhow* (now that the *Dhow* had been cut down), but she sailed beautifully through the water with a straight clean wake, and she kept steerage way with only the flap of her sails. At sunset I looked back at the Arab-Persian fleet, sailing up the Gulf of Oman, strung out astern of us with their gilded sails against the blue-grey of the evening sky. It was a peaceful and very pleasant sight, in this world of wars. By day and night we sailed in company, and the big *Samhan* under the stars was very lovely.

We wandered pleasantly up the Gulf of Oman towards Ras Musandam and the Persian Gulf for the next five days. The wind was quiet and we could sail only slowly. Nejdi, eager to see his new son, showed a little impatience, and the sailors looked forward to their homecoming. Where we were next bound I did not know, nor did anyone else on board, for it would depend largely upon conditions. It was scarcely likely that she would take a full cargo of building materials direct to Kuwait without first trying to sell some of it elsewhere. We had left Zanzibar officially cleared for Kuwait by way of Muscat, Bahrein, and a place called Jubail in Saudi-Arabia. Now Nejdi talked of Basra, and even of the Persian side; he never mentioned Jubail. I should not have known we were supposedly bound there, if he had not given me the ship's papers. They were in English and he could not understand them; he wanted the manifest for Jubail. Jubail is a small pearling place on the Hasa coast roughly a hundred miles south of Kuwait Bay. I don't know why we had papers for it, for we certainly never went there and, so far as I could discover, never had any intention of doing so. Perhaps in certain circumstances a spare set of papers might have been desirable, and Nejdi like to be prepared.

We drifted and dribbled along, now with a catspaw and now with none, now for a few hours with a good sailing breeze, and now becalmed. Allah would bring us to Kuwait in His own good time, and meanwhile it was good that He did not send the north wind. Nobody wanted the north wind, which would be right in our teeth and could blow hard for forty days. I shared the general hope that Allah would hold back this wind until we were well up the Gulf; but Nejdi, worried, said it always followed calm. In the meantime we had many visits with Yusuf bin Isa, who pulled across in his small cutter. He was a big, bluff, hearty man, six feet tall and built in proportion, who always laughed uproariously at his own jokes. He came in a long white gown and well-blued headcloth, with a Japanese umbrella to keep off the sun. He would visit us one day, and yarn the afternoon away with Nejdi and Hamed bin Salim, and we would return his visit the next day. I liked Yusuf bin Isa, and it was a pleasure to visit his big clean boom. He had a little cabin in the poop, with electric light and radio, neither of which worked. When we went to his boom, his sailors came to the poop and greeted Nejdi. When Yusuf came to us, our sailors who had been with him came up and greeted him, shaking him warmly by the hand. The discipline in the Kuwait booms was excellent and they were well run; yet the sailors and the officers knew how to behave properly towards one another without hypocrisy, without obsequiousness, and without familiarity. An officer was an officer among the Arabs, because he deserved to be. He was a natural leader, and was given the respect such a man deserves.

In the afternoons, Hamed and Hassan the helmsman worked at the accounts, Hamed for the ship and Hassan as the crew's representative, for with our homecoming there would be the pay-off, and the casting up of shares. This was an intricate and involved business and the two of them worked steadily, while Yusuf bin Isa shook his merry sides on Nejdi's carpet at his own mysterious jokes and kept his eye on his vessel, and Nejdi looked out with those keen eyes of his, dreading the north wind. There was little work at this stage of the voyage, beyond the necessary sailing of the vessel. Kaleel and his helpers continued to work on the new boat and, in the mornings, Mohamed the serang led the sailors in the laying of a new cable. We now had four sailors ill with fever, and Ismael, who had played his guitar merrily in Mutrah Bay, complained of rheumatism and piles.

Nejdi, when not entertaining Yusuf or aboard Yusuf's boom, sat on a carpet on the bench aft singing verses from the Qurân, nursing a bare brown leg while he watched the sails, the sea, and the other ships, and perhaps mused on his newest son and his brother's luck with the ship's debts at Mogadishu. Now and again, he would begin a dissertation upon politics, or ask me for the hundredth time how any conception of Christian ethics could be converted into a basis for sane living, and when I was going to say my prayers.

We were many days reaching Ras Musandam, coming slowly along the Batina coast almost under the mountains, or standing towards the Persian side. The Batina mountains looked very old, very hot, and very bad-tempered, as if they were tired of having to stand for ever under the burning rays of the hot sun. Dun and sterile, their abrupt faces pock-marked, fluted, scarred, they add no welcoming note to the Omani seascape; they stand solid at the sea's edge unassailable and sheer, a frowning bar to the mariner going by, fit coastline for Arabia the backward and the land of the robber barons. As I looked at them day after day I thought of the Portuguese who had passed this way, and of all the ancient vessels which had sailed this road – caravels, galleons, frigates, East Indiamen, junks from China bringing silks and precious goods to the great market-places of the Persian Gulf. Now came our old boom, last of that great line of Eastern mariners, wandering northwards with a cargo of mangrove poles cut from a jungle in Africa. The wealth of the Indies had flowed here: here slaves, pirates, admirals had sailed and fought, and discoverers and pioneers ventured. Now an oil-tanker from Abadan hurried by us, pushing half the Gulf before her stodgy bow and pulling the other half behind as she hurried on with petrol for motor-cars in Chelsea and Golders Green. Nejdi, looking at the steamship, murmured, "They come: they go. So it has been always, here." He looked after the smoke of the departing steamer a long time; and then washed himself and prayed.

In the sunset we had a little breeze and the mountains stood softened, dark, and grand against the long line of the dying light of the sun. Away to the east coast of Persia was a long blue haze; the mountains of Batina in that light were very beautiful. I said so to Nejdi, but he did not share my enthusiasm.

"What is beautiful about those hills?" Nejdi said; "they grow nothing. They give no life."

I answered that they are of the kingdom of Allah and He has made them beautiful. He was silent then, but he was not impressed. The idea that mountains can be beautiful did not appeal to him. If I wished to see beauty, he said, I should wait until we reached Kuwait.

Though we were in the neighbourhood of Ras Musandam where the Gulf of Oman enters the Persian Gulf and all the tankships from Abadan and Bahrein converge, and the date tramps from Basra and Bushire come and go, we showed no lights. I asked Nejdi if he did not think it wise to show at least a hurricane light on such occasions, but he answered that the camel knew its way without lights on the sand. Why then, he asked, should an Arab ship go lit at sea? A camel, I ventured to suggest, could avoid collision more easily than a ship at sea. He was not interested. Our lights stayed down below. Nejdi, with his ship again becalmed, retired to his sleeping mat after the night prayer, and I wandered along to yarn the first night watch away with the sailors of the serang's watch, in the sternsheets of the longboat, on top of our cargo. The yarns that night were of Kuwait, as they nearly always were then. Above us the great mainsail made wonderful patterns as it rolled gently under the stars; aft the snores of Nejdi smote the peaceful air, and Hamed bin Salim, wrapped in his cloak and gown, kept drowsy watch. Ebrahim the helmsman was silhouetted in the binnacle's glow, seated at the wheel. The water gurgled lazily along the smooth sides and at the low bow, and the blocks aloft creaked as she slowly rolled.

When we entered the Persian Gulf there was a sudden end to these conditions. The calms disappeared at once and the north wind came instead, quietly at first, but soon freshening. Nejdi was worried, but we bent our smallest mainsail and beat on. Before the day was out the wind howled in the rigging and the sea got up, so that we made little progress. Afterwards day after day remained the same, and we beat and beat. Now we stood along the Persian coast, hoping for a windshift there; and now in desperation made a board across towards the Trucial Coast, down towards Sharjah and Dabai. One after another we had slowly passed the ports which sent their fleets down to Africa – Muscat, the Batina places, Sharjah and Dabai, Kung, Lingeh, Qishm. Still we beat, day after day, for our home port was at the head of the Gulf and we had a long way to go. We stood close in along many Persian beaches and passed within hail of several ports and towns. We passed close by Hanjam, which had been a British naval post and now seemed deserted. Here a Persian in a small boat boarded us, wanting to buy coconut oil, piece goods, sugar, tea and tobacco from Muscat. We passed Ruvvan, Charak, and Chiru. We beat three days between Charak and the island of Kais and another day between Chiru and Hindarabi.

The wind was quiet for a while in the Kais passage, and we dawdled through with time to look at that interesting island. There were a number of small pearling boats at work on banks inshore, but Nejdi said that they were poor, and that the pearls on the Persian side were not good. The good pearls, he said, were on the Arabian side of the Gulf. The best of all were on the banks off Bahrein. We saw, too, the three towns of Kais, which seemed to be largely in ruins though there were substantial buildings in them. It seemed to me that the island had fallen on evil days. Hassan the helmsman, who had maintained until then that he was a Kuwaiti, now disclosed that he came from Kais, and he confirmed that things were not good there. He had, he said, left Kais ten years earlier, with his family, and gone to Kuwait. It used to be a good place, rich in pearling; now it was neither good nor rich. He would say no more about the place, and seemed to regret that he had been born there.

We saw several more half-abandoned towns as we stood along the Persian coast close beneath the coloured hills, some of which looked like great dumps of coloured slag and seemed as if they had been put there by man. Near a town known to Nejdi and the Persians as Kalat, we saw a large castle-like fort on the crest of a hill. A sambuk lay at anchor off the town, which appeared a large one, but we saw no sign of life although we passed close by, very slowly. The people of Kalat, Hassan said, had gone, migrating in a body to a town on the Batina Coast which he called Khor Fakkan. If he had had little to say about the island of Kais, Hassan was communicative about this place Kalat. It appeared that he had gone there first, from Kais, and had finally reached Kuwait in a most roundabout way. He told me a long story of how it all happened. First, life at Kais had become impossible, principally, according to Hassan, because of the tyranny of the local sheikh, who was a sort of local robber baron, so far as I could make out. Then, Hassan and his family – he was a boy at the time – had gone up the coast a little way to this place Kalat. At that time, Kalat was prosperous, and life was good there. But there was an undercurrent of trouble, largely on account of the innovations of the new Shah who, apparently, had taken a violent dislike to things as they were and was in a great hurry to change them. Rumours and reports began to trickle in to Kalat of the most astounding things going on in the kingdom of Persia. According to some, the Shah was making a monstrous attack on the precepts of Islam; according to others, he was ruining the country. It was said that he had demanded elsewhere that the old customs should be dropped. Women must no longer go veiled, or be enclosed in the harim. Men must no longer wear the flowing cloak and graceful turban; instead they must free their women, and wear hats.

This was sacrilege. Even then, Hassan seemed to have difficulty in believing that any Persian would put forward such proposals. But the Shah had done so. More than that, he began to see that they were carried out. The corner of Persia where Kais and Kalat are situated was remote from authority, and reforms reached there slowly. But one day the dreaded edicts arrived. An emissary came from the court of the Shah to tell the people of Kalat that they must no longer carry on in the ways of their fathers. They must abandon ancient ideas, emancipate their women and themselves, as the Turks had done. Much else he said, chiefly about new taxes and the collection of customs duties, not to mention the suppression of the ancient business of smuggling. The citizens of Kalat, Hassan said, listened to the emissary in astonished silence. Then he went away. When he had gone, they paid no attention to the new decrees, for they were violently opposed to such sudden changes. They liked things as they were, and it would take more than a distant Shah with big ideas to change them.

In the course of time, the Shah heard of this disobedience. He sent, then, soldiers to Kalat to enforce his decrees. The soldiers were the best equipped the people of Kalat had seen, and they were most impressive. But doubtless they liked their arrack and anything else alcoholic as well as other military men. The townsmen of Kalat gave them a feast, to welcome them and cement the bonds which united them with the rest of new Persia. They plied them heartily with arrack, and other drink. They had, they explained, to offer this excellent entertainment in the town jail, for there was no other building large enough. They had decorated the jail very handsomely. However, there was more in this design than at first appeared, for, no sooner were the soldiers thoroughly intoxicated and helpless, than the citizens, who had drunk water instead of the potent arrack, locked them all in the jail, and departed. Hassan said it was a great joke. He helped to lock the soldiers up, himself. That done, the townspeople knew they could not remain in Kalat, for sooner or later a greater force would be sent to punish them. But they had made their plans. They could not stay in a Persia where the women would walk the streets unveiled and the men wear hats. So man, woman, and child, they went down to the harbour, and sailed away in the soldiers' ships. It was the first time Hassan had been at sea – apart from the brief crossing from Kais – and though he was seasick, it was a grand adventure. They took everything they could carry and sailed away, and none of them ever returned. From that day to this, Kalat has been a deserted town.

Hassan said his family went to a place called Khor Fakkan, in Oman, first, and later he migrated to Kuwait by way of Bahrein. Whether Hassan's account was correct or not, Kalat was dead when we passed by. The town might have been dead, but it was not so dead that Nejdi dared anchor there, though conditions were against us and we should have done well to anchor. He had a great dread of the modern Persians and all their works. The Persians are suspicious of the Kuwait booms, and accuse them of being inveterate smugglers. Nejdi scoffed at this and said big deep-water dhows did not smuggle; that was work for small fry. Any fool, he said, ought to know that small ships from Sharjah, Dabai, Bahrein, and Khor Fakkan ran cargoes into Persia now. It was sense to use small ships which could run small cargoes by night, instead of large ones which took longer to unload and ran greater risks. Small craft could slip in anywhere, and be beached and burned if danger threatened; large craft were at a disadvantage. Smuggle? Not he. But, he added in a whispered aside, did I not know any spot of earth where a poor Arab ship-master might run in cargoes.

From all I could gather, a considerable amount of smuggling goes on along that Persian coast, and I doubt very much whether the Kuwaiti are entirely innocent of it. Smuggling in the big dhows running down to Africa is mostly a minor business carried on by a few wandering Sindbads and the crews; but the profit from running a cargo of tea or soft-goods in to a Persian beach was a different proposition. Yarning in the longboat by night, after we had seen a camel caravan going down in the sunset to a low point off which a small Dabai boom was anchored, old Yusuf spoke of smuggling voyages from the Trucial Coast over to Kalat and elsewhere in those parts. Often, he said, they took back deckloads of Persians to lonely beaches on Bahrein where they landed them by night and left them to seek work as coolies on the oil-fields. What the Bahrein Government would have had to say about this I do not know and Yusuf did not care, but it would not have been pleased, for indigent Persians have long been a problem in that island.

Yusuf also told a story about a ship he was in which was caught once landing a cargo to a camel team by night. Three Persian soldiers were put aboard to take the ship to Bushire, but on the way the crew overpowered them and carried them off, later throwing them ashore somewhere on the Hasa coast across the Gulf. What became of them then? I asked. Yusuf said he did not know, and shrugged his shoulders. This smuggling business along the Gulf must be a thorn in the side of the Shah of Persia, with his trade declining, and his more independent subjects, rebellious at his strange idea of sex-equality and the emancipation of women, disappearing into Oman. I was told that there were large numbers of Persian exiles in Bahrein and Kuwait, as well as in the ports of the Trucial Coast.

At this time we had five of the crew sick – Ismael, Abdul-latif the singer, Jassim the cook, Nasir the pearl-diver, and Ebrahim the helmsman. Nejdi said one look at Kuwait would make them all well again, but I doubted it. Nasir the pearl-diver, who had been diving since he was thirteen, looked far gone in tuberculosis, and his days were numbered; he was twenty-five. The constant hardships of the sea life, with its wholly inadequate food, its broken rest often in wet and always insufficient clothes, its exposures to fevers and all sorts of tropical ills – these things must take their toll. Every sailor in that ship, except one sixteen-year-old boy, was grey; most of them iron-grey. Many looked old, but there were no old men. Salim the toothless who looked sixty was not yet forty. Yusuf Shirazi who looked seventy, sometimes, was at least five years on the right side of fifty. He had three nails torn out by the roots from hands and feet: this sort of mishap was too commonplace to receive attention. According to Nejdi, who scorned all remedies save the burning iron, and the bandage of good Qurân texts, none of his sailors was really ill. In Arabia, he said, the weak died young; anybody old enough to be a sailor was strong. One look at Kuwait, he repeated, and they would all recover. I hoped so.

In the meantime we drew no nearer to this place of beauty which could heal the sick and in which all joy abounded, for the wind was still ahead. It was still from the north, blowing at times with force, and we began to split our sails. In the short, steep sea of the almost entirely closed Persian Gulf, the *Triumph* jumped and tossed and made little progress. Her motion was violent and continuous, and Nejdi began to grow pessimistic. "None of my wives wants me," he moaned after the eleventh day of steadily adverse conditions, and admitted for the first time that perhaps a new mainmast might be an improvement to his vessel. He had always maintained that the *Triumph* was the height of perfection, in spite of the obvious flaws in her mainmast which worked violently with every roll. What really depressed him was that the big *Samhan* had sailed out of sight. He grew more pessimistic at the thought of trying to sell our mangroves with that great dump of 1,200 score from the *Samhan* sold ahead. They would flood the market.

"None of my wives loves me; the *Samhan* will spoil the market; we have only the north wind," he moaned, believing none of these things except the obviously true last, but worried by them all.

"Why not go to Bahrein?" I suggested.

I had been looking at my charts. It seemed a good idea to have a look at the market for mangrove poles in Bahrein, and surely it would not delay us any more than the north wind was already doing. Also, it would be much more comfortable. Then, too, we were far enough up the Gulf by that time, almost to reach Bahrein by going about and standing across the Gulf on the other tack.

Nejdi looked at me. For once in his life he agreed, though he did not want to go to Bahrein. There was only one place he wanted to go to, and that was Kuwait.

"As Allah wills," he said. "If we cannot go elsewhere, we shall go to Bahrein."

What really appealed to him, I think, was the possibility of stealing a march on the big *Samhan*. While she beat on up the Gulf to the markets of Kuwait and Basra, he would slip into Bahrein and possibly sell his cargo without competition there. The more he thought of the idea, the better he liked it, for his father had said there was much building in Bahrein, as a result of the oil company's rapid expansion and the Government's increased revenues.

Towards midnight, with the wind howling from the north and the *Triumph* pitching and rolling in a confused sea somewhere off Ras Nayband, we went about with the usual yelling and splitting of seams. Once safely round, we stood on a long board towards Bahrein. We went about at midnight, so that the ships in company, if there were any, would not see us go; it was important to go alone and to find an unimpeded market in Bahrein, or our visit there might be in vain.

27. The *Triumph of Righteousness* beached for cleaning at Kwale Island.

28. Carrying sail, Kwale Island, with *baggala* and *boom* in the background.

29. Sailors sewing sail, Kwale Island.

30. Left: Mubarrak, the Suri *nakhoda* who piloted the *Triumph* in the Rufiji Delta.

31. Right: Hamed bin Salim, mate of the *Triumph of Righteousness*, in the Rufiji Delta.

32. Salale, in the Rufiji Delta.

33. Hoisting the yard: on the voyage back from the Rufiji the sailors had to work on a deck packed with mangrove poles.

34. Down tack! Hauling down the fore-foot of the mizzen sail.

35. Aloft on the main lateen yard.

36. With the *Triumph* packed to the gunwales with mangrove poles for the voyage home to the Gulf, her crew had to sleep where they could.

37. A heavily laden Kuwaiti *boom*, possibly off the Omani coast.

38. A fine large *boom*, perhaps off the Omani coast.

39. Happy to be homeward bound, her sailors drum and sing the *Triumph of Righteousness* into Mutrah harbour. One of the two *serang*s or boatswains is on the left.

40. Mutrah harbour crowded with the distinctive Omani *badan*s, with their detachable rudders, used for fishing and coastal trade.

41. Kuwaiti and Suri: Nejdi (right) with a friend from Sur.

42. The fine carved stern of one of the three surviving Kuwaiti *baggalas*, drawn up for overhaul on the Kuwait waterfront.

43. Covered *suq*, Kuwait.

44. Decorative arch and side street, Kuwait.

45. With the discovery of oil in 1936, these Kuwaiti boys were destined for easier livelihoods than dhow sailing and pearl diving like their fathers.

46. His Highness Shaikh Ahmad bin Jabir Al-Sabah, ruler of Kuwait, relaxes on board his steam yacht with the British Political Agent in Kuwait, Major A. C. Galloway.

47. Top left: On the pearl banks of the northern Gulf: a Kuwaiti pearling *sambuk* anchored with sweeps out, divers in the water, and haulers at the ready.

48. Bottom left: Kuwaiti pearl divers take a breather between dives.

49. Above: A *tawwash*, or pearl buyer, inspects a pearl on board one of the boats on the banks.

50. Abdullah Al-Hamad, a member of the Kuwaiti merchant house that gave Villiers so much help.

XVI

IBN SAUD BUYS A CARGO

TWO DAYS LATER WE anchored in the shallow harbour of Manama Roads, at the island of Bahrein, and the first thing we saw was Yusuf bin Isa's *Samhan* with her Kuwait flag flying to welcome us. Inshore was Hamed Yusuf's Persian boom from Dima, and out to sea, astern of us, the morning sun showed the big boom of Abdul-wahhab Kalifa, also full of mangrove poles, coming in. During the next few days half the homeward-bound Kuwait fleet arrived, both from Africa and India, including Abdul-wahhab bin Abdul-aziz with the big *el-Dhow*, Sulieman Radhwan with his baggala, Nasir bin Isa with his baggala *Cat* – which was not known to him by that name – and his brother Hamoud with a cargo of teak and roping stuffs from Malabar, and three or four Persians besides.

Nejdi looked gloomy when we came in to find the anchorage so crowded, and immediately announced his intention of going about and standing to sea again to beat on up the Gulf and race them to Basra. The north wind had brought them in, as it had brought us. But, as things turned out, we were in luck for once, for we had sold our full cargo within a few hours of our arrival. All the ships in harbour found their cargoes easy to dispose of, for Abdul-aziz Ibn Saud, King of Saudi Arabia, had recently been in town and left orders with an agent to buy the next twenty cargoes of building timber that arrived. The great king, enriched by oil royalties from the American fields on the mainland, was beginning a building programme in Riyadh and other towns of his kingdom. Bahrein was the logical place to buy supplies. We were in luck. Allah, with His north wind, had been kind. Ibn Saud's price was a good one – better than we should have got elsewhere – for the Saudi king has always been generous. We sold our whole cargo through a Persian intermediary at twenty rupees the score. The highest price for the heaviest poles in the Rufiji was less than ten rupees, so we had a good freight, after all, and the voyage which, until then, had not promised well, turned out much better than had been expected.

It was not easy to reach Bahrein, and we had to beat to get there. The set down the Gulf, as we stood across, forced us off our course, and instead of fetching Bahrein we found ourselves instead off Qatar, a low peninsula of sand jutting into the south-west corner of the Persian Gulf, round which the sea is a green shallow and reefs abound. These were dangerous waters; we saw the sand glare of the distant desert before we picked up the low land, and some pearlers scudding for safety behind a reef. It was a day of fresh wind, with the sea running white caps, short and steep and breaking. These were conditions unsuited to our short, beamy ship, and she pitched and jumped and flung her masts about without making much way. We were close enough on Qatar to make out a ruined town before we went about. Nejdi named it as Zubara, and said it had been an important place once; many Kuwaiti came from there, and so had many of the people now in Bahrein. It did not look much of a place now, and I was glad when we went about and stood away from Qatar. There was much trouble there, Nejdi said. He put the blame for the trouble on bad sheikhs. There must, at some time or other, have been many bad sheikhs round the Persian Gulf.

When we went about and stood once more towards the Persian side, we sighted two booms, hull-down ahead. Nejdi immediately recognised one as a vessel which had sailed from Zanzibar a month before we did, which pleased him. The other was from Batina, bound north with firewood. We overhauled them steadily, with the wind hot like a blast from a furnace, hazy, and full of desert sand, and the sea short and steep and angry. We rolled and pitched violently and the sailors bailed out frequently. Spray clouds drove over us, wetting Yimid the monkey, who had come out to watch the sailors doing something and was drenched by the sea for his pains. He looked round bitterly to see who had done that to him, and chattered at the sea excitedly, as if he were telling it something. After that he crept, very wet, inside the lee of the firebox, looking malevolently aft. Bizz the cat, with more sense than Yimid, had long removed herself and her offspring to a place of safety.

In the last light of that day, still with the same tumultuous sea, we passed close by the two other booms. They were both standing along under their smallest mainsails, making good weather in spite of the sea. The pair made an unforgettable sight as they slogged along in the first of the windy night, showing the handsome lines of the Kuwait boom at its best as they alternately lifted low bow and high stern and rolled to the rounds of their bilges, lurching to windward down the side of a sea. We hailed them, and wished them good-night. They looked brave little ships. It struck me then as it had before – on Kwale beach, looking at the old

Bedri; the night off Malindi, and again off Kismayu – what a pity it is that the Kuwaiti, building such good ships, do not build them a little better, just that little which would make them seaworthy at all times; and rig them a little more sturdily, in the Indian style. Better attention to fastenings, better selection of wood, properly watertight decks and seamanlike precautions for the shedding of water – it would take little to bring these improvements to the Kuwait ships. With them, they could go anywhere. Personally, I should prefer to rig one as a ketch, if I had to take her anywhere away from the Indian Ocean.

The wind hauled fair towards midnight, and we wore round again to stand towards Bahrein. This time we made it. We came in with the daybreak on our eleventh day from Mutrah Bay, having sailed through the night. This was a creditable feat on Nejdi's part, spoiled only by his frequent assertions that no other nakhoda would do it, for Bahrein stands in a reef-filled corner of the Persian Gulf which mariners rightly dread. Its waters are shallow and the pearl banks bite perilously close at the surface here and there, ready to bite holes in any ships which try to pass over them. Most of the other nakhodas would only have dared sail in towards Bahrein with daylight, which was prudent. It was a memorable sight to see Nejdi, very pleased, unconcernedly singing behind the helmsman through the night as his ship came in. The night was moonless but bright with stars; our wake was a milky stream shot through by the phosphorescence of the indrawn lead as the sailors took soundings from time to time, the sails swollen black shapes against the stars, the helmsman hunched over the spokes of his wheel, and the sailors off duty stretched asleep on the chests.

We came bowling in at the rate of knots. It was well done and Nejdi was very pleased with himself, but his pleasure left him when the rising sun disclosed the other big dhows in the harbour. Even the fact that the best of them had cleared from the Rufiji or from Lamu at least two weeks before we left Zanzibar did not cheer him. Within five minutes of our arrival Yusuf bin Isa was aboard, laughing as merrily as usual and recounting the news of Ibn Saud's generous buying. Sure enough, our next visitor was the King's agent, out to buy cargo. This he did on the spot and after the most cursory examination, for Ibn Saud is not a man to quibble about his bargains. The agent was a Bahrein Persian in white mushla and pale silk pantaloons beneath a cotton gown, an optimistic and energetic man who had the whole of our cargo bought within five minutes. For this his commission was the half of one per cent. We sold him 300 score, though down in the Rufiji we had paid for less than 150. How, in spite of all the difficulties and the supervision, we had succeeded in loading twice the official cargo I did not know, but I could guess who had managed it. It was Mubarrak our 'pilot,' who had been carried off to the Utete jail.

It was deadly hot in Bahrein, which seemed even less an Arab port than Aden is. Manama was a busy and animated place, but it was not Arabic. It was full of Indians, Persians, and Americans, with Arabs pearl-diving and Persians doing the labour. Manama was too hot and too humid a place for any undue display of energy in unravelling its story; it seemed to me mainly a market-place for the distribution of inferior goods to Hasa, nearer Nejd, and Persia, without undue interference from the customs authorities of those places, and for the accumulation of any stray wealth the infidels of oil might have to scatter. This, in spite of American efficiency, appeared from Arab accounts to be considerable. Sleek automobiles prowl and purr through the Manama *suq*, not all owned by the oil men, and the sailors, padding barefoot, nowadays find most of the prices beyond them.

When our cargo was sold so readily, Nejdi announced that we should be at Manama only three days, for he was anxious to be home. The sailors shared his eagerness to be gone, but it was three days before we began to discharge our cargo. When once a start had been made, it was landed rapidly. It was ferried ashore by the sailors, using the longboat and some boats hired from the shore, and flung on the waterfront road. Before we had been in a week the waterfront road was almost covered with Rufiji and Lamu poles bought for Ibn Saud; and Nejdi, who at first had been very pleased at the rapid sale of his cargo, fretted that he had come to Bahrein, for it delayed his homecoming. He seemed almost to regret the speed and ease with which our cargo was disposed of, for this is not the Arab way of doing things: I believe he took a delight in haggling over sales for days. There we had come in, the agent had come aboard, and the cargo was sold. There was no thrill in it at all – no finesse. Nejdi loved some finesse in his business ventures; it was half the fun of living.

Nevertheless, it seemed to me that he allowed himself to have a tolerable time in Manama. I went ashore with him several times, and visited other ships. The nearer they came to home the better the life these nakhodas of the big ships lived. We used to go in the longboat in the cool of the morning – to walk about in Manama after 10 a.m. was a sweat-bathed purgatory – and land at the head of a long quay of coral stones.

The quay was being extended, and the fleet of harbour boats skimming across the water with their high lateen sails and their little hulls full of stone looked like a regatta. All round the inner waters of the harbour men stood in the sea, naked, breaking up coral and hauling up the broken pieces to be loaded into these boats, which carried them to the quay. On our way in we always pulled close by the other Kuwait ships and brought in any nakhodas who wished to come, which was usually all of them, though sometimes the longboat of a big ship would be waiting by its gangway for us to come by, when they would leave and we would race. How we raced! Crews singing, great paddles splashing, nakhodas exhorting their own crews and reviling the others, serangs shouting, quartermasters lively at the helm, and all the harbour looking on. We always made a great race of it with *el-Dhow*'s people. Their longboat was a lovely thing, thirty-seven feet long, rowed by forty great men with Abdul-wahhab himself at the helm. The evening races were the best. All the longboats would be at the quay waiting for their nakhodas, to take them off to their ships for the evening prayer. The nakhodas, seven or eight of them, always came down together, strolling along from the coffee-shop swinging their beads. At the pier-head they were into their boats like a shot and we would be away. How those sailors pulled, and how the harbour resounded to their songs. It was about half a mile out to where the bigger vessels were anchored – a long pull in that climate. But the sailors made a joke of it and, day after day, night after night, we raced. Honours were about even between our men and *el-Dhow*'s. Their boat was long and powerful and sleek. Nejdi vowed he would have a better one the next voyage.

The intervals between these morning and evening races were given up to strolling in the *suq*, dawdling in the coffee-shops, dining in the homes of merchants and sleeping on their carpets in the comparative cool of a shaded room. The *suq* itself, spacious and covered, had all sorts of desirable things for sale, from handsome Arab cloaks to American underwear, and from Paris perfumes to evening dress ties. One could buy almost anything in Manama, and the prosperity of the place was obvious. It was a very recent prosperity, due mainly to oil, for in the past few years Bahrein has moved from nothing to the twelfth largest oil-field of the world. Formerly pearling had been the island's greatest industry, but that had long been in decline, largely owing to world depression and the competition of the Japanese cultured pearl. Agriculture, once also important, was now generally neglected. The wealth of the place was in its oil. I found myself wondering, as Nejdi and I wandered in the *suq* past the well-stocked shops, whether this temporary influx of wealth was altogether good for a place. I did not, however, meet anyone who objected to it.

"Kuwait," Nejdi said, "will be like this soon."

"God forbid!" I said. "Is it not a town of the Arabs?"

He looked at me. "But there is oil," he said, and then, after a while, added: "Perhaps you are right. This is not Arab." Then he said no more.

Wandering about the suq with Nejdi was an interesting experience, watching him greet relatives, merchants, friends. We called on a leading merchant, who was a distant relative. He was a tight-lipped gentleman of haughty demeanour, dressed in sumptuous clothes. When we called on him in his office in the *suq*, he was very busy, telling a number of Banyan moneychangers, in few and not at all gentle words, exactly why their business propositions did not appeal to him. Here, as everywhere, we were regaled with sweetmeats, sherbet, and the too-bitter coffee, too-sweet tea. The merchant asked us to his home for a meal, but we did not go.

"Merchants," said Nejdi, "are tough. To them all is money."

"And nakhodas?" I asked.

"Nakhodas have the sea," he said. "To them money is only for their ships."

We delayed a little at that merchant's place, but passed along the narrow alleys of the back part of the *suq*, where the porters' asses hurried by laden with bales of goods, and the porters ran along behind them shouting "Make way! Make way!" We dropped into other offices not so imposing, where grave, dignified Arabs sat at their desks doing nothing and long lines of hangers-on stared at them from seats on the benches, also doing nothing. They were bare places, those offices, and what business was supposed to be conducted in them I did not discover. They were brokers, Nejdi said. It seems, in Arabia, that every merchant who is nothing else can always be a broker.

In the offices, where we apparently called merely as a matter of courtesy, the talk was always of merchandise, and Nejdi took no part in it. Out in the *suq* and along the waterfront, however, we frequently ran into groups of the other nakhodas. With them the talk was of ships and Nejdi had always much to say. He cut a small figure in the big merchant's place, but he was a man when there was talk of ships – or action in ships. I had never noticed how small he was until I saw him hunched up meekly in the merchant's chair, and even the fact that he had on his best silk gown and his most elaborately embroidered cloak could not give him his proper self-confidence. He was always dressed in his best on these shore excursions, in silks and gold-embroidered gown with headcloth of white and gold held in position by a headrope of black Persian wool, with his hand-sewn sandals decorated in green and red, and his best amber beads in his hand.

When we met the nakhodas it was never long before we adjourned to a coffee-shop, always the same one. It was a big one in the Hilal building by the waterfront, where a large black sheep wandered in and out as a pet and queer pictures lined the walls, and the hookah and yarns of the sea were the order of the day. The pictures on the walls were of Sheikhs and voluptuous Egyptian beauties with brazen eyes, interspersed with advertisements showing girls smoking American cigarettes, and comic sections cut from some Chicago Sunday newspaper. The central picture was a horrible coloured print showing a group of non-Aryans mutilating the prophet Isa. Above this was a lurid lithograph of the Shah of Persia, beneath which a group of indigent Persians lounged in the corner complaining about the Government. In another corner a gramophone brayed, and Arabs reclined on the benches sipping tea and smoking. Nejdi kicked off his sandals and got down to the business in hand – some yarn about the voyage – in earnest. Here we whiled away the hours, for time in coffee-shops meant nothing to customers or proprietor. You may sleep if you wish, or spend all day playing a curious game of draughts.

Later we used to eat at an Arab place across the road, where they served good meals of meat and fish and vegetables washed down with curdled milk. After that, it was usual to return to the coffee-shop for a final smoke, before pulling off to the big *el-Dhow* for a sleep. There we slept the hot hours away, and in mid-afternoon a breeze crept pleasantly to the anchorage to awaken us to tea and prayer. Again the talk was of ships and adventures at sea, with much swinging of the amber beads and bubbling at the water-pipe and gesturing of graceful hands. Nejdi, no longer quiet or in any way subdued, held forth to his cronies upon the performances of his boom and the happenings of the voyage, and narrated great maritime events which never happened at all. Sometimes we yarned and slept aboard this vessel, sometimes that. It made no difference. The nakhodas took it in turns to entertain the group. It was all very cheerful, very pleasant, and completely unaffected. Once having got aboard a boom, we never knew when we should leave it again; it might not be until the following morning, or even the day after that.

I must admit that this abundant and acceptable hospitality can be readily offered by the Arab mariner, for he has no bed to make up for his guests and no extra chairs to draw up to the table. For a bed, there is the deck, and for covering the stars. You have your cloak and your forearm for a pillow. As for eating, there are no utensils to be provided; there are rice and meat enough on the big dish, and room for half a dozen extra hands. Yet I could not help thinking sometimes that these good men could show us something of real hospitality; I could not help comparing their ways with our own, and the comparison was not to our advantage.

The end of May found us still moored off Manama, our cargo discharged and the boom empty, but there were no signs of leaving. No one was upset by that. Each day was good in itself, and the morrow would bring its own blessings. Some were anxious to be gone, for several of the sailors proposed to buy themselves brides in Kuwait, and the quartermaster, Kalifa, met a man ashore who spoke to him of his new baby, a bright little lad now six months old, whom Kalifa had never seen. He smiled at the prospect of seeing this new baby, and went about his work with double energy, but day succeeded day and still we lay at anchor. There was plenty of news of Kuwait in the *suq*. According to all accounts things were quiet there now, and business was good. The hotheads behind the riot languished in the Sheikh's dungeons, from which there was slight chance of their emerging. The oil business, though still in its early stages, promised well. Ibn Saud had lifted the old ban on his Beduin and now allowed them to trade freely in and with Kuwait. Most of the Arab news was word of mouth, but it was surprising how quickly it travelled, and often, too, how accurate it was.

If Nejdi ever worried about the possible fate of his friend Bedar in the baggala *Bedri*, of whom nothing had been heard since Zanzibar, he gave no sign of it. That day – the last of May – I went off early to find him aboard the boom of Hamoud bin Abdul-latif, lately come from India, where he was seated on a carpet aft pulling at the hookah with a dish of sweetmeats before him, and a negro sailor seated on the capstan entertaining him with the guitar. Hamoud's boom was laden with ropes, teak and timber in general, bamboos, chests, and chairs, with half a dozen small dugout canoes on top of the lot. She had been fifty-two days from Malabar to Muscat, which is far from fast, but as she was twenty days from Muscat to Manama I concluded that either she sails very poorly or was sailed badly, for these are poor passages. With Nejdi and Hamoud was Hamoud's brother Nasir, master of the baggala *Cat*. Nasir was a little man with a big moustache, who laughed uproariously at his own jokes and everybody else's, even more than big Yusuf did. He was a merry little tub of a man, not five feet high, fit master for his little *Cat*. Not that she was little to him, or cat-like either. It was supposed to be a great joke to call his baggala the *Cat*, though I could see nothing funny in it, and it was the one joke Nasir himself could never see. According to him, the name of his craft was *Lord of the Waters*, or something equally flowery: she was no cat. However, *Cat* she was to all the other nakhodas and all the crews. The *Cat*, otherwise *Lord of the Waters*, was a lovely little baggala with a capacity of about 1,800 packages of Basra dates. She had a beautifully carved stern, and, though over fifty years old, seemed sound and staunch. She was the best of the three surviving Kuwait baggalas, and I looked at her with interest. I still toyed with the idea of perhaps saving a baggala by a transatlantic voyage; the *Cat* looked ideal for the purpose. But I said nothing about it: there would be time enough to examine her thoroughly in Kuwait, for she would be on the beach there with us three months.

Sometimes, instead of pulling back to some ship for the midday rest, we slept in the apartment of the young Kuwait merchant Bedar al-Saar, in the Hilal building. His apartment looked over the waterfront and a section of the *suq*, and it was always interesting up there. Five minutes after we were in, the group of nakhodas – the two Abdul-wahhabs, Nejdi, Hamoud, Nasir, Abdulla Kitami, and a sixty-six-year-old Persian just arrived with an enormous boom from Lamu – would be stretched on the carpets asleep, each with his head covered with his headcloth and resting on his hairy arm, and their snores shook the room. The hot afternoons passed pleasantly while we slept. With the worst heat gone from the sun, life came to the waterfront and *suq* again. Flocks of fat Kuwait sheep were driven along the quay from a small boom, to be converted into Bahrein's meat; little asses with jingling bells hurried along laden with bales of skins, bags of rice, or packages of dates. A noisy group of Persians in trousers and dreadful Russian caps argued at the customs gate about the admission of a number of bundles of indifferent carpets; and all the gramophones in the *suq* started up. So life came again to Manama, with the afternoon regatta of the pretty harbour boats skimming over the nearer waters carrying coral to extend the quay, and, in the distance, the pearlers coming in from the sea and the sambuks and jalboots from Hasa.

In the streets the cosmopolitan eastern crowd assembled – Persians, many dressed in their country's idea of European clothes, others in gowns and carefully wrapped turbans, Banyans, Punjabi, Baluchi (not many of these), Arabs from Oman, the Trucial Coast, Hasa, Nejd, Kuwait, Qatar; negroid sailors of Kuwait, stalwart and sturdy, swinging their rosaries and rolling along like men, long-haired Beduin from the desert, prisoners marching along shackled down the road with a guard behind them, a Somali or two, long and lean and vociferously independent as usual. One of these, claiming to be a poet, called on me, at Bedar's place, and read some of his poetry, which was listened to with interest. Apparently it was about the stand of the Ethiopians against the Italians in Abyssinia, and there were many throaty *taiyib*s from the assembly. Unfortunately the poetry was beyond me; the complications of Arabic prose and the spoken word were difficult enough. It may have been good poetry for all I know, but the poet did not look to me much like a good Somali. However, with some bakhshish he went on his way, in his golden waistcoat and mantle of calico, and we strolled across the square to the Persian baths behind the house, by the fruit garden. These baths were big enough to swim in, and we all plunged in and swam for an hour. Old Abdul-wahhab bin Kalifa, who was stout and large, swam like a seal, though I expected him to flounder about like a whale. The pool was often full of nakhodas, splashing about and playing like boys. It was a good place, with the scent from the flowers and the fruit blossoms blowing over it and the cooling breeze from the sea. Outside it was humid, and even to stand still was to find oneself bathed stickily in a heavy sweat. Our deep-water shipmasters managed to have, all in all, a pretty fair time.

With these pleasant interludes the time at Manama passed happily, and I by no means looked forward to the approaching end of the voyage. Bahrein was our last stop. After this came Kuwait, and though the north wind called *shemaal* still blew with strength, its forty days must soon be over. Sometimes, Nejdi said, it blew only for twenty; then it stopped for ten, and came again stronger than ever for forty days. He wanted to slip out and run up to Kuwait some day when the *shemaal* was off duty, because, he said, two days of good sailing would bring us home if we went direct, over the reefs. Though he spent his days pleasantly in idleness there, he watched the weather like a hawk, and was ready to sail at five minutes' notice. But we could not sail too hurriedly, wind or no wind, for we had not yet been paid for our poles.

However, there was no reason to worry about that; we should get our silver in good time. There was not a better payer in all Arabia.

We went once to the dhow yard, a small place at the end of the town where the shipwrights and their apprentices were making more money by building models for sale to the oil-men from America than by building booms for Arab mariners. They had once made these small models very well, but the influx of indiscriminate buyers and the rush of orders were having their inevitable effect. The models I saw were poor things, though the little booms unfinished on the stocks were sweet. Some of them had lain there unfinished for four or five years, for things were not good with the seafarers. The distributing trade to Hasa and smuggling to Persia might all be very well, but pearling, the real backbone of the place, had been cut by more than half. For other diversion, we visited the Portuguese ruins. We dined sumptuously with a Persian in Muharraq, eating a great meal of meat and chicken and fish and fruit spread on carpets on his roof top, under the moon. We watched the water booms piping up fresh water from the springs under the sea. We gave feasts, and attended them; we yarned, and listened to yarns; we wandered in the *suq*, and looked at the life of Bahrein. While our sailors worked we had, indeed, a very good time.

We went to the oil-fields, a piece of Texas set in Bahrein with the climate of hell, and though the Americans had air-conditioned their bungalow homes, no one could cool the works. To walk into a bungalow there was to come from desert to Chicago by the mere process of opening a door, and the sudden unexpected transition was almost frightening. The oil-field was a huge place, very well run, but to us from the sea it was a frightening array of tremendous retorts and great cauldrons and all sorts of weird pipes, presided over by men who, for all they had in common with the Arabs round them, might have come from Mars. We saw everything but oil, though there was enough of that – scores of thousands of barrels a day, they told us. We saw no barrels either, for that matter; but we saw the oil-tankers carting the stuff away. The oil-field belonged geographically to Bahrein, and its royalties enriched the island; but really it might have been in Mexico or Venezuela. It was barb-wired off from the rest of the island, but it stood sufficiently alone without barricade.

From the heights on a clear evening one could see the oil-field of Saudi Arabia, on the mainland perhaps twenty miles away, where another air-conditioned town was springing up and the oil-men from Texas and Southern California were pumping liquid gold from the earth. King Ibn Saud himself had recently visited this field, on the occasion of the first bulk shipment of a cargo of oil from his new port of Ras Tanurah. He had come across to Bahrein at the invitation of the Sheikh, His Highness Sir

Hamed bin Isa al-Kalifa. This had happened a few days before we arrived. I was sorry we had missed the Saudi king who was held in veneration by the Kuwaiti and all the Arabs. He had, they told me, come with three hundred motor-trucks and two thousand Beduin troops, who had almost eaten the Americans out of house and home. It was said that each Beduin had eaten half-a-dozen sheep, and drunk two cases of pineapple juice.

When we were at Bahrein the oil was bringing nearly five million rupees a year to the island, of which a third went to the ruling family. We saw the sons of the Sheikh roaring around the place in the latest model American cars, with police sirens which wailed continually. Whether this marked the limit of their cultural advancement I do not know. There were those who said it did. Nejdi scowled at the young Sheikhs rushing about in siren-wailing motor-cars.

"Noise, noise!" he said. "It is not good, for the emptiest drum sounds the loudest." Bahrein, he went on, had changed out of all recognition in the past ten years, though he admitted that many of the changes had been for the better. But the oil-field, the great towers of the wells, the rushing motor-cars, bewildered and worried him, and he complained that he had not seen a man in the *suq* who did not wear at least one article of European clothing. Even the women wore stockings and shoes. What was wrong with the Arabs? Did they want to ape Europeans? The women would soon be going unveiled, and the men forgetting their prayers. I feared that Nejdi would begin a theological diatribe at any moment, and dropped behind with old Abdul-wahhab, who took things as they came, looked at them quietly with his old eyes, and made no comment.

On a hot day in the first week of June, Hamed and our agent came out with a sack of six thousand rupees, payment for the poles. We sailed the same evening, for the *shemaal* was quiet and there was no time to lose. Our ballast was some coral rock from the floor of the harbour, broken out by the sailors and ferried in our longboat. While the nakhodas had taken their ease in Manama, there had been plenty of work for the sailors. We still had a few coconuts and five bags of cloves. Everything else had been sold.

Nejdi came out with a group of nakhodas in the cool of the evening and we sailed at once, with infinite work and too little preparation, the sailors alternately bathed in their sweat and wet with the sea as they plunged overboard to work the anchor out of the coral or to clean the cable, and then climbed aboard again to hoist the sail. We took up our boats as we sailed, and the men of *el-Dhow* helped us at the halliards. Then they left in their longboat, and they and the other Kuwait ships cheered us as we passed. The wind was fair but very light, and we gathered way slowly. Two other booms sailed with us, Hamoud's and the Persian Mansur's, and Nasir's little baggala *Cat*.

We headed out slowly across the shoals, bound the direct way to Kuwait, for Nejdi was anxious to be home. The way from Bahrein to Kuwait direct is littered with shoals and reefs and dangerous banks, and in the ordinary way, I suppose, we should have given these dangerous spots a good berth. But now Nejdi had heard that his favourite wife was very ill, from some trouble after childbirth, and he was desperately anxious to drive his ship home.

The evening breeze freshened. We stood on, and all our tired sailors smiled. After many months we were now bound for home. We had six thousand silver rupees in the nakhoda's chest, and the wind was fair.

XVII

NEJDI'S RACE HOME

OUR DASH HOMEWARDS across the reefs from Bahrein to Kuwait was the most dramatic episode of the voyage. Daylight the morning after sailing showed that the other vessels were out of sight, and we sailed over a shallow sea through a fleet of pearlers – tiny vessels full of men who, as we sailed by, were squatting round their decks opening oysters. These were the fleet of al-Qatif and Darin, Nejdi said, and they were greatly thinned out by the depression. We hailed a few of them asking what luck they were having, but they replied only that Allah was compassionate. Nejdi asked them also if they had seen any other Kuwait deepwatermen, but they said they had not. Three of four had sailed several days before we did, but Nejdi said none of these would dare to try this dash across the reefs. The western side of the Persian Gulf from Bahrein almost to Kuwait is littered with destruction, for coral reefs and banks and shifting sands abound for 200 miles. Most of the area, being of no interest to steamships, has never been properly charted, but Nejdi had been pearling there since he was a child.

Every man in the ship knew those waters: there was none among them who had not been sailing there at least ten years. Nejdi knew every bank, every overflow, every low sanded point. We sounded frequently as we ran on, always with the lead armed, though it had never been armed before. Some camel-fat was poked into a rough hole in the bottom of the lead, and Nejdi examined with care the grit and shells and sand brought up on this. He seemed able to follow our way in this manner, as though he were reading signs on a city street. Sometimes we heaved about leaving a wake behind us like the twistings of a snake, though I could see no safe passage or distinguish the places where there were two fathoms of water from those where there was only one.

We saw little of the land, for the Hasa coast is low, but Nejdi seemed to know every inch of the water, every tiny craft we saw, every minute variation of the gulf-bed. This was native pilotage at its best, and I watched him with envious interest. I could not have done this, not after ten years of pearling and sailing there, not with all the sextants and tables and chronometers and slide rules in the world. This was pilotage by eye and personal knowledge, almost by instinct. To navigate in this way a man must never clutter his mind with book learning; perhaps Nejdi was right, after all, in his scorn of our methods. Nejdi said that, in this kind of work, he was helped even by the colour of the sky, for he professed to detect a change in it over the shallowest places. What I found most amazing, however, was his apparent ability to always detect which way the sets were running and the tides, and to predict them. He had no tables and he did not even know the date. The moon, he said, was enough; the moon, the stars, and the behaviour of the sea.

We ran on, that morning, with the wind light and Nejdi impatient; for the first time in the voyage he was excited and craved speed. We had gone out with the second mainsail, not wishing to spread great Oud with the ship so lightly ballasted. A capful of wind in Oud could capsize her, with less than thirty tons of coral rock in the hold. But with our speed dropped to five knots Nejdi gave the order to lower the *sifdera*, as the second mainsail was called, and bend old Oud instead. This the sailors did with a will, and Oud was aloft again faster than he had ever been before. No sooner was the great sail set than the wind freshened and we bowled along at ten knots in a welter of foam with the lee rail not far from the water. Let her go! Nejdi, crouching anxiously aft, watched her like an old sea-eagle, and though she lurched now and again till it seemed that she must blow over, there was no sea, and she ran on. She lay with a heavy list and the sea skimming past the lee side within inches of the rail, and the sailors laughed. Let her go! We gave her the mizzen and added the biggest jib, set on a spar lashed along the raked stemhead, and the breeze hummed in the rigging. The spray drove away before the bows and her wake ran behind for miles. The sea birds welcomed us, and the pearling fleet from Jubail looked up in astonishment as we raced by.

We ran on through tide rips and across reefs where the bottom rose up alarmingly to bite at us; but Nejdi said there was water enough. We avoided the worst places. The quartermasters not on wheel duty sounded continually with a handlead on each side, and their chanting of the depths sounded sweetly in the wind.

We saw nothing of the land but the Gulf bottom, and of that we saw enough. Once we saw the low spit of the point of Abu Ali, which was nothing but sand. All the Hasa coast, beyond this brief glimpse of yellow sand, was hidden in haze. All day we foamed and raced along, and in the evening still kept all sail, though we were then in one of the most dangerous quarters of the whole Gulf. During the day the sailors had scrubbed the maindeck and the poop and cleaned their chests, and all the brasswork. We raced onwards beneath the moon, a spotless ship with white sails bathed in beauty and moonlit decks cleaner than they had ever been before. The sailors gathered round the bole of the mizzenmast wrapped in their cloaks and grinned happily and talked about Kuwait. Kuwait, Kuwait! That was all I heard. Kuwait, Kuwait! At last this paradise on earth was just below the horizon's rim and on the morrow would rise. Kuwait, Kuwait, where every ship was a sturdy clipper and every girl was beautiful; where the houses of the Sheikh and the merchants were mansions full of the wealth of the Indies; where the water was sweet and the fruit glorious, and the melons lying upon the earth were flavoured with myrrh and honey. What a place this Kuwait must be, more fruitful than Zanzibar, more blessed than Beirut, more healthy than the Indian hills.

So the sailors raved, and Nejdi, squatting on his bench watching the driving ship, for once said nothing. Well, I should soon see. The patriotism of the Kuwaiti was not to be questioned, but I wondered what sort of town it could really be, from which so many men had to sail out in great ships most of the year, wresting a poor living from the sea. Though I wondered, I said nothing, for the enthusiasm of the group was infectious. Gone were all ills, even Ebrahim's fever, and little Jassim the cook hopped and skipped while Ismael, who a few days before had been suffering agonies of rheumatism, played merrily on his guitar. Sultan and the dying pearl-diver Nasir spoke cheerfully of the girls they would marry the day after we came in, and Kalifa the helmsman smiled about his new baby. He had the best girl in all Kuwait, Sultan boasted. No, *he* had, said Zaid; and Saud, the little surly seaman, said neither of them could have, for he had already married them all. Hassan the helmsman, coming forward after his trick at the wheel, spoke of his two wives waiting for him, both with child, one aged about twenty and the other, new last year, aged sixteen. He found he needed two, he said, in his brief summer at home after nine months at sea; one was not enough. Now he was looking forward to acquiring a third, for the two he had got along splendidly and were a delight in his life. With three it would be paradise. Two wives, he said – apart from the initial expense – cost no more than one; three would cost little more. The two he had were the best of friends and kept his little home spotless and pleasant always. He slept with one in the noon siesta, the other at night, in strict rotation, he said; there was no jealousy.

"If you will listen to an old man," Yusuf said when Hassan had ended, "you will consider long before you take a third wife. If you are so doubly blessed as to have found two women who will get along together and keep peace in your home, leave well alone, my son. For there are no three women on earth who can share one man; and the third may be a virago."

"Oh moaner, thy wife is thirty!" Hassan rejoined, and they all laughed at this joke. To say that a man had a wife aged thirty was to condemn him to the society of the ancient. But old Yusuf, though his wife might have been thirty, looked forward to seeing her and his home again no less than the others. Poor old fellow, his feet were in a dreadful state from the constant hardships of the voyage, lacerated on the jagged knots of the Rufiji poles, torn on the coral rocks of Manama roads, bruised and battered by the heavy work. His feet, like those of all sailors, were tough and tremendously hard; their soles were of calloused skin a quarter of an inch thick. Yet the coral and the pronged wood had broken through even this armour, and now his feet bled whenever he ran. I looked at them for him, though he did not ask. There was little I could do except bathe them in boracic lotion and wrap them in adhesive tape, but my adhesive tape was all gone. No matter, Yusuf said, his wife would fix them up when he reached home. She could do this very well; she always fixed him up between voyages. I had a vision of old Yusuf in his little home in some back street of Kuwait, his little home with his three children, his herd of goats with their kids, and his chickens (for he had told me of these things) and being made ready for another voyage by the tender ministrations of his wife, bathing his feet and anointing his eyes. Only the strength of his body could keep that little home going, and the pace in the Kuwait ships is hard; no man receives favours. No man, that is, unless he is a musician of the standing of Ismael, who could bargain with nakhodas anxious to exhibit his talents down the African coast.

The pace in the Kuwait ships is dreadfully hard, and the style killing. It must be especially severe on a man who has previously been pearl-diving. All jobs are rushed at; all orders obeyed on the run day and night; all sailors live on the sufferance of the nakhoda who, if he be impatient and overbearing, must still be put up with. Consideration for others is not a noticeable quality in the nakhoda class; life goes hard, I fear, with the old sailors. One who cannot stand the life drops out of it, I suppose; but usually he drops out in harness. There comes a day when he dies. The pace in Kuwait ships is hard, foolishly hard, for there is no need for all this rush.

"It is our manner," Nejdi said, not excusing or explaining it, but surprised that I should ask. The sailors themselves take pride in this rushing at all jobs, though some of them are often knocked down in the rush. It is a matter of pride to be first, to be the highest aloft, to pull the longest oar, to stow the heaviest poles. The Suri did not do it, or the Yemenites, or the Hadhrami, or the sailors from the Trucial Coast and from Batina, or the Indians, or the Persians. It is the style of the Kuwait ships alone – smart, efficient, and very impressive; but, I fear, also sometimes killing. I wondered how long old Yusuf would stand up to the rigours of his life, and what would become of his little home when he was ended. He spoke to me of a younger brother who had died in a boom at Karachi the previous year; it seemed to me that he would need the three-month rest in Kuwait between voyages. Not many sailors died ashore. Old Yusuf said it was the pearling that killed them, mostly, and he thanked God that he had to do that no more. His own small debt had been worked off, for it was five years since he had been diving, and in all that time he had paid twenty rupees a year from his deep-sea earnings. With his debt gone, he was free. Compared with pearling, he said, even a month in the Rufiji, loading mangrove poles, was a holiday.

Next morning we still foamed on, for Nejdi had driven his ship without sleep or food through the night, squatting on his bench abaft the helmsman watching, watching, examining in the binnacle's light the sand and the shingle brought to him from the arming of the lead, sniffing at the wind. Sometimes we would fall off and change our course, this way or that, though I could see no reason. Nejdi said there were reefs, many of them. I knew that; it was how he knew where they were and how he found a channel between them that baffled me. But he did. By mid-morning of the next day, storming past headland after headland, we were abeam of Ras Zor, which marks the southern border of the city state of Kuwait. The breeze freshened, and Nejdi pointed to the land, murmuring, "Kuwait, Kuwait!" as if he could hardly believe that at last, after all these months, his homeland was again in sight. He called to me.

"Kuwait, Kuwait!" he said, pointing. "There, there is a land of beauty for you to see! Do you not see that that is beautiful?"

"What, that piece of sand?" I asked, pretending to be unimpressed.

Nejdi looked horrified, though the coast-line of Arabia in the neighbourhood of Ras Zor is, in fact, far from impressive, and none but the Kuwaiti would see much beauty in it.

"Sand! Piece of sand!" Nejdi almost shouted. "Look at it, Nazarene!

Here are no rough mountains, but the soft, low land, gentle as the swelling of a virgin's breasts. Are you not ashamed that you said the mountains of Oman were beautiful, those useless hills? Look now at this Kuwait." And he looked himself, very long, and kept on looking, no longer caring whether I was impressed or not.

It looked very much like any other piece of sand, and about as impressive as the Benadir coast south of Ras Haifun. But I did not say so, for I could see the emotion of Nejdi's dark face and the tears in his tired eyes. He had said during the night why he so drove his ship, with her lee rail skimming the sea and the seams of great Oud splitting in the fresh south wind. He had heard at Manama that his favourite wife was in danger, and might die.

Now we foamed by the islet of al-Kubbar, where the birds rose in cloud-like flocks as we ran by, with the ship making perhaps twelve knots. We overhauled and sailed by the slow mail British India steamer which had left Bahrein when we did, carrying Nejdi's letter announcing his homecoming. We foamed by, and Nejdi showed the flag of Kuwait while the sailors laughed. The drums were warming at Jassim's fire, for the distance from al-Kubbar to Kuwait is less than twenty miles and we might be there in two hours. The sailors, in great excitement, rushed about getting out their best gowns and their most heavily blued headcloths, trimming their moustaches, cleaning their teeth. Some of them were too excited to do anything. Nejdi, with all dangers safely passed, and only Kuwait before him – for al-Kubbar marked the end of the worst waters – made Hassan shave him and scrub him down, bathing him with water from the sea. After that, Yusuf perfumed him, and rubbed some Paris scent into his forehead and behind his ears, and searched through his chest to put the gold ornaments for his wives on top, handy for landing. Even the monkey Yimid joined in the excitement, hopping about and looking at the shoreline of Kuwait, while Bizz the Somali cat led her offspring Fahad, Farid, and Fatima, in a raid on the fire-box when Jassim was not looking. The sea was very green there, and there was a white sand-glare over the land (abeam and ahead), for we were close to the head of the Persian Gulf.

But then the wind dropped, steadily, and we sailed on slowly, taking the whole afternoon to make the twenty miles between al-Kubbar and Ras al-Ardh. The slow mail steamer passed us again, and this time we did not look. We picked up the low island of Failachah to the east'ard of Kuwait Bay. It was the last landfall. The voyage was done. It remained only to turn the corner, and anchor in Kuwait Bay. We saw the houses of Failachah and some sambuks on the beach, the water booms and the firewood booms, and the little belems coming down from Basra between Failachah and the mainland. We saw the tiny date-frond boats of the fishermen fishing in the sea off Ras al-Ardh, the fishermen sitting more in the water than out of it, for their boats are but bundles of water-logged reeds afloat, not water-tight or meant to be. We rounded the triangular beacon on Ras al-Ardh and saw the lights there flashing, as we stood in for Kuwait Bay – slowly now, very slowly, with the breeze dying away and the tide against us.

With the last of the light we came in sight of the town of Kuwait, with all our drums going and the decks full of song. We came on slowly past the Sheikh's house. The night shut off the view of the town as we came to it, and we came to our anchor in darkness while the drum-banging and the singing went on and on. We were forty-eight hours from Bahrein – 'fastmail' time, Nejdi said (though the slow mail beat us), and though he had driven his ship so splendidly home and brought his long and difficult voyage to a successful conclusion, he was consumed with disappointment because we had arrived by night and he was robbed of his triumph. If we came by day the town would see us, and boats full of his friends would come out to cheer and welcome, and all the waterfront would know that Nejdi was back again, up from Africa by way of Bahrein with a 'fastmail' passage – Nejdi the driver of ships and men, Nejdi with the *Triumph of Righteousness*, triumphant over the seas again. It was a blow to him to have no welcome, for we were unexpected and his letter announcing our coming would not be delivered until the morning.

The sailors still drummed and sang, but the sense of achievement was ended, temporarily, for Nejdi. The sails were lowered and unbent for the last time this voyage, the sailors singing all the time, singing praises to Allah and praise of Nejdi – singing, singing, first as we came in under the shade of old Oud with his fifty-nine cloths, and then at the anchorage under the stars.

We hailed some big Persian booms anchored near by, and learned from them that ships which were known to have sailed from Bahrein several days before us had not arrived. At this news Nejdi was pleased, but he continued to sit lethargic on his bench, very tired, with half the spirit gone from him now that the day was ended and the voyage done. He advised the Persians to return to Bahrein and sell their cargoes there. This was a good tip, and they set to work at once to get under way, for the best price of mangroves in Kuwait was eight or nine rupees a score. His voice as he answered "Boom Nejdi," to the Persians' hail of "What ship?" had a ring of pride in it; but he was bitterly disappointed that it was not day. But the voyage was done. It remained only to go ashore; and yet, after driving the ship and himself so hard to reach her, he seemed to dread landing to meet his wife.

With the sailors' songs of praise still echoing over the harbour, the longboat was swung out, and everybody went ashore – Nejdi, and Hamed, the serang, the quartermasters, Yusuf, everybody, leaving only three of us aboard – Ismael, who was an orphan and had neither wife nor home, old Salim from the desert, and myself. All the others had gone, making the longboat fly across the water, still singing their songs. I heard the echoes of their song until they landed; and there the boom was anchored in Kuwait Bay, with her cargoes all discharged and her voyage ended. I sat alone on the transom to think about the voyage, while Ismael and old Salim slept.

What a voyage it had been! Ten thousand miles, and nine months of hard life and hard sailing, from mid-August of one year to mid-June of the next – to Basra first, after the summer's lay-up at Kuwait, to load a cargo of dates for Mukalla for orders; then down the Persian Gulf and the Gulf of Oman, standing out into the Arabian Sea before the last of the south-west monsoon had gone, with a call at Muscat for water on the way. Water may well be needed for the long beat along the South Arabian coast from Ras al-Hadd, where the Beduin still may turn pirates and pilotage is difficult, where conditions are adverse, and the coast harbourless and dangerous along much of its length. Then Mukalla, and orders for Berbera across the Gulf of Aden: to Berbera, and the dates discharged for sale there, in Somaliland and Abyssinia, the sailors working painfully in the heat landing the heavy packages through the surf, and afterwards beaching the ship. Then Aden, the traditional turn-round port for African voyages, a hot oven with the cheapness of the trash in the bazaar its only attraction. From Aden beating again, eastbound towards Mukalla and the ports of the Hadhramaut, to complete the cargo and load Beduin for Africa. Then away for Africa, with Haifun, that hellish dump of salt and sand; Mogadishu, where business was impossible and Abdulla was still trying to collect debts; Lamu, the first pleasant port of the voyage, but not much better for business than Mogadishu had been, for we had found Lamu depressed. Then Mombasa, the sunny island, where our passengers were landed and the decks could be cleaned; and so to Zanzibar, isle of delight. Then the Rufiji, after the call at Kwale – the terrible swamp of the Rufiji where all hands grew thin and half of them caught fever while they worked under conditions almost intolerable. From the Rufiji to Zanzibar again, where the soft arms of the houris and the caresses of the local bints drive away dull care: and then the long haul from Zanzibar along East Africa and up the Arab coast to the Gulf of Oman again, homeward bound. Muscat, the beat up the Gulf, Bahrein; and now the last run home.

What a round it had been! Ten thousand miles, down with one monsoon and back with the other, and not by any means so easy as that might indicate, for there were many adverse conditions, and many perilous places to be negotiated. Yet it had been done, and well done, without accident and without fuss; done as one of a fleet of a hundred Arab ships making much the same voyage; done by a group of skirted mariners illiterate and fanatic, but seamen to the backbone – men who knew no fancy knots or tricks of the sea, many of whom did not even know the points of the compass, men who spend most of their sea lives without storms, without even seeing rain. Yet they could do a day's work alongside any man, and they suffered hardships enough. They could handle sails and masts and yards cumbrous and awkward often far beyond the danger-point.

I thought of the life these men lived and of Nejdi and his muallim, Hamed bin Salim, who led them. Nejdi had his faults, and I have not spared them. Headstrong, often inconsiderate, no ascetic when a pretty bint was in sight, satisfied with his own knowledge, and secure in his expectation of a paradise where God speaks only Arabic, he was a sailor of outstanding qualities, an able leader, a pilot and ship-handler of supreme merit, and a shrewd man, able to stand up to merchants and brokers ashore. Nejdi was a man and I liked him. All our crew swore by him, and the sailors in the other ships respected him, though they did not always respect other nakhodas. Even the sailors of the big *el-Dhow*, swaggering through the Zanzibar bazaar, looked round when Nejdi passed. For three years in succession he had paid his sailors higher shares than any other nakhoda on the African voyage from Kuwait, and that was a fine reputation. He had sailed his *Triumph* well all that time, though he had only recently come from the Indian trade. He had always kept her free from accidents. And he had always been a good friend to me, a friend from whom I learned much.

Hamed bin Salim, who took command when Nejdi was not there, was a real man, too. Aboard that ship Nejdi was God and Hamed never more than a very minor prophet. Nejdi commanded, and Hamed never really took his place. He did no more than deputise temporarily in his absence. But what he did, he did well. Quiet, intensely reserved, profoundly religious, he was at first hard to know. But I liked him, too, from the first, and he improved on acquaintance. Hamed had stayed with the ship throughout the hard nine months of the long voyage and had never had a rest. Hamed was always there, awake when Nejdi was asleep, in charge of the ship in the Rufiji, solving the awkward problems which followed Mubarrak's arrest. Hamed was more considerate of the sailors than was Nejdi, because he had been a sailor himself. That Nejdi had never been; he had always belonged to the nakhoda class, and Hamed had only married into it. I hoped that, by the next season, he would have a ship of his own. He hoped so, too; but he did not permit himself to hope for it too fervently. Certainly he deserved one.

The crew were good fellows, without pretence and without any nonsense. They knew their work, and did it well, and no sort of hardship deterred them. They lived a life of toil and extreme hardship. They had not even six feet of the deck to call their own. They were paid no wages apart from a share in the earnings of the ship. They ate nothing for which they had not paid, for in the computation of the ship's earnings the cost of the sailors' food was always first deducted. They knew nothing of workmen's compensation, and insurance was against the rules of their religion. They had neither adequate clothing nor a bed to lie upon. They seldom had a night of unbroken rest, and life in the ports was no less trying than life at sea. Yet they extracted a great deal of joy from their daily life, and there was none among them who did not feel a strong affection for the ship and the sea. They were true seamen, a true band of brothers. There may be port officials and customs officers in half the ports of the East who would like nothing better than to see them under lock and key, for they are inveterate smugglers; there may be irate tanker captains who would wish all unlit dhows driven from the sea, for they are a menace to powered navigation; there may be harassed port officials in Mogadishu, Mombasa, Zanzibar, and the ports of Western India who pray every night that they may never see an Arab or his dhow again. Yet these mariners of ours were fine men, and if Kuwait, of which I had heard so much, could produce ship after ship of them, it must be a good place.

I looked at the stars, and at the darkness which was Kuwait. There was nothing to see, for it was midnight. I thought of Yusuf, whose wife was then, perhaps, bathing his feet, of Kalifa with his little son, of Hassan with his two good wives, and of Nejdi. I hoped they had found things well at home, all of them; for they were good men and deserved a good homecoming.

So I fell asleep, and slept late into the morning, for there was no prayer-call, and no one to bake the morning *khubz* or boil the tea. But the longboat was out early, with the serang and all the sailors and Hamed bin Salim. They at once set about the work of rigging down the masts and getting the ship ready for beaching. She was to be rigged down and all her gear taken ashore, and then she would be floated in at high tide to a safe berth behind the small breakwaters of coral stone which stood along the waterfront. Here, covered with a roof of date fronds and mats to protect her from the too strong rays of the sun, and with more mats hung round to protect the undersides, she would wait until the new season's dates were ready along the Basra River.

The sailors fell upon this work with a will. Arrival in the home port, though it might mean the end of the voyage, did not mean the end of the work, for the sailors had not finished until the ship was shored up in her safe berth and all her gear was landed. They showed me Nejdi's house, on the waterfront road, in front of which they said the boom would rest through the summer. I thought it a good arrangement that a nakhoda should have his ship berthed opposite his front door. All along the waterfront I could see these shored-up booms, and the nakhodas' houses beyond them.

It was three days' work, Yusuf said, to get the ship ready and beach her. After that, they would have to oil her, inside and out. Then they would have finished, and could consider themselves free. They would not be paid until Abdulla returned, for the outstanding debts in Mogadishu had to be collected before the shares were computed. It might be a month or two. In the meantime, he said, they could get any money they needed in advance from Nejdi. What with advances at the setting-out and the payments in Aden and Zanzibar, some of the crew had very little coming to them. No matter, Yusuf said, they could draw against the next voyage enough to see them through the summer, if they wished. I gathered that they usually wished. A sailor's life in Kuwait seemed to be financed almost exclusively by this system of advances, so that most of them were always in debt, and they were considered bound to the nakhodas to whom they were indebted.

Nejdi was out before noon, with four of his sons who stood and stared wide-eyed at everything. His wife, he said, was not so ill as he had feared, and he had much to be thankful for. But he still regretted missing the triumph of a daylight entry after that great run from Bahrein. We were the first of the African traders home to lie up. The ships already beached were back from voyages to India, or pearlers waiting for their season, due to start almost any day.

With Nejdi came merchants, brokers, other nakhodas, among whom was a pearling nakhoda looking for his crew. Our sailors were nearly all pearlers of one sort or another, divers or tenders. Once a pearler, always a pearler; and those who owed money to nakhodas still in the trade had to go out to the banks with them. If the nakhodas went, they must go. They must do one thing or another – go pearling, or repay the advances. For a few years, the depression had saved them, but now, apparently, the nakhodas were going to try their luck again. I saw melancholy looks on the faces of many of the sailors, for pearling had been so depressed for years that many nakhodas had not gone, and debts had been in abeyance. It was no use going when they could not hope to make money. This year, however, more than a hundred ships were fitting out, and pearl-divers were needed. I saw the terrible disappointment on Sultan's face when a merchant approached him, for Sultan had saved his poor share to get himself a bride. Now the merchant was requiring that he should either pay or go pearling. *Allah karim*! Sultan said, though the sentiment seemed inappropriate. Perhaps it was a prayer. The small Mohamed, who had saved his share to make the pilgrimage to Mecca, was also cornered. *Allah karim*! Seven or eight others were in the same position.

Poor fellows, here they were back from their long voyage, with one foot on the beach, and they were being impressed for pearling. They had no alternative. If they had once accepted a pearl nakhoda's advance they were done for: somehow or other these advances never seemed to be earned. There was no crying, not even grumbling, when the first shock had passed. It was the custom of the port. They had known it from infancy. There was always a chance. Fortunes had been made at it. It was not all hardship and poverty. The sailors, like most of their kind, were inveterate gamblers. Before long, those who had been impressed had recovered their spirits and were joking with the others about the huge pearls they were going to find in the coming season, and the wealth that would be theirs. That day, however, there was little mirth in their joking.

I was glad no nakhoda had impressed old Yusuf, for he needed rest. It was several years, he had told me, since he had been pearling. He ought to be safe now. He had worked out his debts and would be careful to contract no new ones. He had had enough pearling to last him a lifetime. I looked along the decks to see my old friend, always a leader in the heaviest work. There he was, singing and working.

But what was this? A pearl merchant approaching him, taking him by the sleeve, beginning a long harangue? He could have no business with Yusuf, for Yusuf's debts were paid.

I was wrong. Business with old Yusuf he had, though he was not Yusuf's own nakhoda. He was, I learned afterwards, nakhoda of the belem in which Yusuf's brother had served. Yusuf had succeeded to his dead brother's debts, and he must go pearling again. This was a hard blow. It seemed that the Islamic law, as interpreted by pearl merchants, required a man to work out a dead brother's debts. It was the practice of the port, old Yusuf said. Debts must be paid. If his dead brother's nakhoda wanted him, he must go. He must give up the idea of spending the summer at home. The brother had owed 400 rupees, marked up against him over twenty years of pearling. It was not a large sum; there were divers who 'owed' thousands. But it was a sum far beyond the capacity of Yusuf ever to repay. It was doubtful if his whole earnings in any year, from long voyages and from short, ever exceeded 200 rupees, and he had a home to support. The cost of living even for an Arab sailor in Kuwait, with a tiny home, is the best part of a rupee a day – twelve annas, at least, if his family is not to starve.

It seemed to me iniquitous that poor Yusuf, just in from the sea, should be compelled to go out again and to be a pearl-diver, hardest of all sea professions. Even he, accustomed to a life of hardship as he was, admitted that pearling was nothing but continuous heavy toil under conditions of severe discomfort, and the prospects of coming through a season without becoming more in the nakhoda's debt were slight. God is compassionate, said old Yusuf, and even smiled as he bent to his work with redoubled effort, raising his voice in the praise of Allah.

I decided that if old Yusuf was to go pearling, I would go with him. They would not go for a week or two, he said. In the meantime I could look round Kuwait, which seemed to become more interesting. Far from being the heavenly paradise it was made out to be, it produced no fruits and little else except fish and sheep, and it had not even fresh water. The drinking water for the town was brought from the mouth of the Basra River in small booms, which came and went throughout the day. The beautiful sand which so delighted Nejdi that it appeared soft and warm as a woman's breast, blew about the harbour and got in my eyes. It was gritty and thoroughly uncomfortable, and the glare from it was painful to the eyes. There was old Yusuf, singing, and the four sons of Nejdi staring about them wide-eyed. The pearl-merchants, after claiming their divers, clambered down into their small boats and departed.

XVIII

EL-KUWAIT – PORT OF BOOMS

THE WALLED CITY OF Kuwait does not appear at its best, seen from the anchorage, but it has one of the most interesting waterfronts in the world. There are more than two miles of it, and the place is one great shipyard of Arab dhows. All along the waterfront, running east and west along the shore of the shallow bay, from the British Residency in the east to the American hospital in the west, almost from wall to wall of the town, the big ships and the little ships jostle one another. On the beach, on the tidal flats, and in the sea they lie cheek by jowl. Long lines of them stand behind stone breakwaters facing the sea, six or eight in a row, square on their long keels with their bows pointing to the sea, their rudders unshipped, their sides skirted and their decks protected with mats. The big ships stand on the tidal flats, and the small ships high and dry on the beach.

Though it was only mid-June when we came in and many booms had still to return from their long voyages, there were already a hundred deepwatermen snugged down at their summer berths, their hulls propped up with Lamu or Rufiji poles and the trunks of Indian trees, and all their gear ashore. Other ships were being floated in, or rigged down at the anchorage in readiness for grounding with the next tide. Longboats full of singing sailors were towing in their booms, carrying out lines to the breakwaters and to anchors embedded in the sand, to bring them to their berths. Big booms, small booms, old booms, new booms, there they were, and their sailors hurried along the busy waterfront in a ceaseless stream. Sailors staggered up the beach bearing the long rolls of canvas which were the mainsails, the jibs, and the mizzens of their ships. Sailors danced and sang as they hauled up longboats and tucked them away in their summer coverings of frond mats; sailors sweated at capstans, heaving in their ships; sailors chanted and danced as they floated in heavy masts and long slender spars, and made neatly lashed parcels of them fore-and-aft on the beach among the litter of capstans, longboats, cutters, gigs, Malabar teak, anchors, rudders, washboards, water-tanks, fore-boxes, and all the kinds of other maritime paraphernalia with which the whole length of the place was littered.

Persians passed in the dusty street carrying the burdens of the town. Persians seemed to do the porterage, the water deliveries, and most of the coolie work of the port, as well as the labour in the dockyards. There were thousands of them. They were sawing planks out of huge Malabar logs, frightful work in that hot climate; they were unloading the water-booms, driving their asses into the sea to take their dripping loads of water-skins; they carried the firewood, the bags of rice, the packages of dates, and everything else which was being taken to the warehouses of the merchants. Persians and pack-horses were doing the work of the town; the Kuwaiti were doing the work of the sea. I stopped with Nejdi to watch some Persians getting a boom ready for launching from a shipyard where five partially completed dhows stood in a row behind a mud and coral wall. The coolies were knocking down the wall in front of a completed boom, and carrying out a large bower anchor into the shallow water. It would take only an hour or two to build the wall up again, Nejdi said; they would heave the ship out and haul her on to the flats at low tide, and the next flood would float her off.

"But why bother to build up the wall again," I asked, "if it has to be knocked down every time a new boom is launched?" There were at least a dozen of these graceful vessels being built in such enclosures, and half a dozen more on the open beach where they towered over the other vessels.

"It is good that the boom should be protected while it is being built," he said.

"But why?" I asked again.

"The wall keeps out *jinns*."

"But what of the booms in the open, along the beach?" I asked then. "Aren't they just as subject to *jinns*?"

"Well," he admitted, "some owners and some nakhodas don't bother much about *jinns* nowadays; but there is one thing they will always watch most carefully. That is, to see that no woman jumps across the freshly laid keel of a new boom."

"Whatever for?" I asked. "Why should a woman want to jump over the keel of a boom? And if she does, why shouldn't she?"

Nejdi looked at me with amusement as if I ought, having sailed with him for more than six months, and with Ahmed the Yemenite before that, to know something of these things. "Anybody," he said, "knows that a barren woman will conceive, if she can only jump over the keel of a new boom."

This was news to me, but it was a serious thing for a wife to be barren in Kuwait, where the principal business of women seemed to be the bearing of children. I had not heard of this strange custom of leaping over the keel of a boom in course of construction, but, I asked, if to be barren was so much dreaded, and sons were so welcome, why not encourage the girls to jump over the keels of all booms?

"Ah, my friend," said Nejdi, "a life for a life: do you not know that? It is so, with the *jinns*. If a woman leaps across the keel of a boom and afterwards conceives and bears a child, the life of the nakhoda of that new boom is forfeit. A life for a life. If not the nakhoda, then one of the carpenters will die before the boom is launched. It is very bad."

We walked along, and I imagined that I saw crowds of barren women, beating their laundry on the hard rocks by the beach, looking enviously at the keels of the booms. Nejdi went on to tell me that, day and night, twenty men watched the keel of his *Triumph* when she was under construction, for he had no intention that his life should pay for the satisfaction of any child-desiring woman. I noticed, too, that the shipwrights, when the keel was laid, worked furiously until they had built up planks enough on either side to prevent a woman from jumping. If she wished to jump over the keel she would have to be quick, and come down on the first day of the keel's laying.

The women we saw along the waterfront that morning were mostly negroes and Persians, all swathed in black. The women washing clothes in the sea had their faces covered with heavy black veils, though they were often immersed in the water, and every curve of their bodies showed against the clinging calico of their gowns. Most of them were old and haggish, but there were some who were not. Nejdi did not look at them, for it is not fitting that a man should notice the activities of these women washing in the sea. They were mostly the wives of coolies, and I saw very few who needed to leap over the keel of a new boom; the great majority had large numbers of pretty children with them, pretty little bright-eyed girls and boys who romped in the sea while their mothers worked.

I trudged on in silence beside Nejdi while he greeted the many long benches of nakhodas sitting in the shade of the walls before their homes. The walker, he said to me – for it was time I learned something of the etiquette of the nakhodas' home life – must always salute the sitter; and the rider the walker. The returned shipmaster and the stranger arriving in the city must greet all the sheikhs. As half the nakhodas in the place were sitting down, and the town seemed well populated with sheikhs, it seemed to me that we were in for a busy time. But we ourselves often sat, and sipped sherbet or coffee, or both, with groups of nakhodas and merchants. Then all the sailors and the townsmen passing by saluted us. "Peace be upon you," ran their mellow greeting. "And upon you peace," we would answer; and then, "God grant you good morning" from them, and a similar response from us. Often nakhodas kissed Nejdi, and he kissed relatives and friends, on both cheeks. Those who did not kiss grasped his right hand and right forearm, looked affectionately into his eyes, and asked repeatedly after his health.

Apparently it was the custom in Kuwait to ask after a man's health, at this first greeting, all the time he was within earshot. People asked so frequently and with such insistence that it seemed to me they never heard the reply. Not that a reply was given or needed, for they all were obviously in excellent health.

We were going along the shore road towards the palace of the Sheikh of Kuwait, His Highness Sir Ahmed ibn Jaber al-Sabah, to pay our respects, for the nakhoda newly come in from the sea and the stranger in town must do that. When we were half-way to the Sheikh's palace we met him, coming round a bend in the road in an American car which was preceded and followed by large trucks of armed Beduin troops. After the troubles His Highness deemed it unwise to go through the town without a guard. The car stopped, and we salaamed. I took an instant liking to the Sheikh of Kuwait. He was a handsome man, stoutly built, with a black moustache and beard, and large, flashing eyes. He was dressed in the picturesque robes of an Arab sheikh, a long white gown covered with a cloak of camel's hair embroidered with gold wire, like Nejdi's, but much more elaborate. On his head was a flowered headcloth through the fine material of which could be seen his crocheted skullcap in floral designs. His aghal was of gold wire, solid, with the ropes arranged so that they lay upon the headcloth more squarely than round, in the manner of an Arab chieftain's. His complexion was dark olive and his countenance very open. Here was nothing of the tyrant, obviously, and I began to wonder more about the riot when Mohamed Kitami died.

We made our salaams, and His Highness welcomed me to Kuwait, asking me to be his guest in his town palace, which was a large house built round a courtyard along the east wall of the town. I thanked him for his courtesy, but said that, if he did not mind, I should like to stay with my friends, at any rate for the time being. I had only one purpose in coming to Kuwait and that was to learn all I could about its ships. I feared I should not learn much in a sheikh's palace. His Highness said he hoped I should make Kuwait my second home, and drove on with a smile. Later in the day we had coffee with His Highness at his waterside palace, the one in the heart of the city where his grandfather, the Lion Mubarak, had decorated the bedrooms with ceilings filled with the lithographs of actresses and queens. This palace was now unused, except for the daily court which any citizen might attend, and no one is doomed to toss upon a sleepless bed gazing at the hard eyes of painted actresses and queens. In a room of this strange palace, I noticed a photograph of Lord Kitchener on horseback, autographed by the great soldier.

We also paid our respects to Sheikh Ali Kalifa, the right-hand man of the Sheikh of Kuwait. We found him smoking in the shade of the portico of his stockade, looking out over the large square at the southern side of the town, not far from the main gates. The square was almost empty when we came, for it was mid-morning and the day's life died down as the sun waxed. In a large space by the sandy roadway leading to the gates, a herd of camels rested knee-haltered in their desert harness, while their Beduin owners shopped and gossiped in the town, their arms left at the guardhouse by the gate and their bright eyes wide open at the marvels in the *suq*. Kuwait's *suq* is famed among the Beduin of all north Arabia as far as the borders of Syria and Transjordan. A shepherd came in slowly with a flock of black sheep, strolling behind them in the robes of an apostle, but with a cheap Japanese umbrella held up to shield him from the sun. Camels moved with dignified tread from the gate towards the square. Some Persian women veiled in black but with their long trousers showing frills at their bare ankles came from a merchant's house, though it was late for women to be buying in the *suq*.

Sheikh Ali Kalifa, a bearded handsome man in the early fifties, was surrounded by a wild-looking gathering of Beduin troops armed with modern and very business-like rifles. He rose as we came, and coffee and sherbet were brought. I liked Sheikh Ali Kalifa. Besides being an able and far-famed generalissimo, he was something of a humorist. As I had chosen to come to Kuwait in a dhow, he said, when the time came to leave I must go on a camel. I said I should be happy enough to leave in a dhow.

We greeted many sheikhs that day, Sheikh Abdulla Jaber, who presided over the pearling court – we found him ordering a ragged Beduin to go at once to sea with his nakhoda – Abdulla bin Salim, who was president of the town's *Majlis* or council; Fahad, nephew of Sheikh Ali Kalifa, who had been to Beirut University and talked a great deal; Sheikh Sabah, who was admiral of the pearling fleet – we found him in the pearlers' coffee shop, opposite the mosque of the *suq* – odd sons and relatives of the Sheikh who were managing police posts, armouries, and offices. There seemed to be dozens of them. We found the Sheikh Abdulla bin Salim holding court above the dungeons where the political prisoners languished in irons after the recent trouble, with a group of long-gowned dignitaries seated round. He was a large florid man, with smouldering, thoughtful eyes. Most of the sheikhs, except Sabah who was pearling admiral, deemed it wise to have slaves and Beduin guarding them, though how much of this was for show and how much really necessary I did not know. The Sheikh of Kuwait himself – Sheikh Ahmed Jaber – as his subjects invariably called him – never moved without a considerable bodyguard, some of whom were armed with Bren guns.

From the houses and the stockades of the sheikhs we returned to the waterfront to Nejdi's house, with its blind wall facing the sea and its harim windows latticed against the prying onlooker. Nejdi's house was a large one, not far from the old British Residency, near the basins where the small pearlers were docked. It was two-storied, built of coral laced with a rough cement of sun-dried mud, like most of the other 8,000 houses in that city of 70,000 inhabitants.[1] The walls were irregular and the building squat, but it was not without beauty. The carvings on the teak gateway were well done. From the roof-top a large number of long spouts extended over the roadway. These were a feature of all the Kuwait streets, and it struck me as odd that in a place where water was so scarce, such thorough arrangements should be made for wasting any little rain that might fall. Nejdi said that in winter there might often be a heavy shower, and the flat roofs of the coral and mud houses could not stand a heavy rain. So they were fitted with spouts, most of which were the halves of hollowed date palms, to carry off the water. In a heavy rain a year or two before, he said, 2,000 houses in Kuwait had collapsed. He went on to explain that the circumstances of that shower were peculiar and such a heavy house mortality was not usual. There had been a soft penetrating rain first, for two days or so, which wore down the houses. After that a sudden heavy shower had mown down the weaker houses, for all their lacing mud had been washed away by the earlier rain. The noise of

[1] These figures were supplied to me through the Kuwait Town Council. The houses in town have now been numbered, but no vital statistics are kept.

collapsing houses was like that of a battle, he said, and several people lost their lives. Thousands were homeless for months. So far as I could see this disaster had not brought about any improvement in the style of building. Houses were still without foundations, still only walls of coral stones. Here and there I saw new houses laced with Japanese cement, and some of these looked a little better. The habit of using cement was on the increase, he said; but he doubted its value, for the local builders put too much sand in the cement.

In the street near his home we passed a little boy, naked and freshly circumcised, crying against a wall. He was about six years old. The street barber had been round that morning, Nejdi told me. A little farther on we passed two more, also bawling. They would get over it, Nejdi said, and shouted to them to desist from their unmanly noise. They paid no attention, but went on bawling. A merchant passed us leading his son, also freshly operated upon, with his gown tucked above his waist, and a daub of black ointment on him. He was walking as though he were lame, but he was not crying. "There goes a man," Nejdi said, looking after the child in admiration.

We entered his home, where a group of relatives and other nakhodas and some merchants and pearl-buyers had assembled for the mid-morning meal. We ate in silence in the shadow of the verandah before the main living-room, facing the courtyard. The verandah was supported by carved posts from Malabar, and the roofing was Iraq date mats on lattices of bamboo resting on Lamu mangrove poles placed closely together, the mats being covered with mud and rubble. Beneath this roof two large Persian carpets had been spread, and upon these was the food, on white cloths. There were two sheep, roasted with stuffing of dried fruits and herbs and hard-boiled eggs; chickens roasted so that they shredded easily at the touch of the hand; large dishes of the delectable fat flounders for which Kuwait Bay is famous, and other fish; mounds and mounds of rice, boiled with raisins and other things I could not recognise, and smothered with ghee; and tremendous dishes of watermelons from the plantations along the Shatt-el-Arab in Iraq. It was a good spread and, after washing our hands, we fell to without ado. There was no idle chatter until all present – there were about forty men there – had had their fill. Nejdi's father was there, eating heartily though he was over seventy years old. He was a little man with an enormous paunch and bright, piercing eyes. He was much fairer than most of the others, though many of the guests could have passed for Spaniards and Portuguese if they had worn European clothes. Some of them had blue eyes. Others were almost pure negro, though I was told they were Arab. The negroes were the sons of merchants or big nakhodas and their slave concubines.

Though I was a stranger to most of these people, their natural good manners forbade them to display any curiosity about me. I liked these feasts ashore. There was elbow room, for one thing, which there rarely was aboard the dhows. The food was excellent, and the idea of spreading everything out at once and tucking in was a good one. So was the absence of chatter. It is bad to talk at meals, Nejdi said; it upsets the nerves of the stomach. So we ate. And how we ate! The sheep were especially good, and so were the chickens. Each man had a chicken or two as an appetiser, then a few pounds of rice shovelled down in handfuls; then anything from three to seven pounds of lamb, with a few fish. I sat between Nejdi's father and a leading merchant who was at work on a trough of rice and sheep like a steam-shovel. From time to time one or other of them would tear off a few pounds of steaming mutton, or skilfully split away the starboard half of a fowl, and fling the delicacy to me. I was expert at doing my own rending by this time, but in the matter of capacity I lagged far behind. It was not fitting to pick at one's food on such occasions; the proper enjoyment of a proper quantity – anything up to half a sheep, and five or six chickens – was required by the rules of courtesy. I was hungry, being just in from the sea; but the south wind blew that day and it was hot and humid. I have never liked rice.

Though I ate what I should have considered supplies for a month even in a Cape Horn ship, I was rebuked for my sparrow's appetite as we all fell away from the carpet, washed our hands again, belched, drank the clove-flavoured coffee, and sat heavily about on the carpet in the verandah's shade.

I looked across at the long pearling sweeps piled in a corner of the yard and the masts of the booms outside, and Nejdi's father began to question me, this being the proper moment when we were all well filled with food. How many sons had I? Where was my harim? Had his son treated me well? What happened at Zanzibar? Big Myouf al-Bedar whispered to me that Seyyid Sulieman, who had kissed Nejdi a fond farewell, had written to his father reporting his son's scandalous behaviour in the African island. I knew nothing of Zanzibar. I had no sons, I was sorry to admit; no sons, no harim. What, no harim? No, no harim; I preferred ships. What, ships to women? This raised a laugh as if it were a great joke. I should have no sons from ships, the old man said, seriously. In the Europe

I knew, I wanted no sons, I said. Ah, there I had spoken wisely, said the old man. But why not stay there with them? In Kuwait there were many desirable maidens. It would be easy to settle there.

This suggestion seemed to appeal to the assembled merchants and mariners, and there were many murmurs of approval. Perhaps there was something to be said for it. Indeed, the life of these Kuwait nakhodas seemed from many points of view one to be envied. I liked their homes along the Kuwait shore road, and the endless panorama of the busy ships before them. I liked these fleet stately vessels which they sailed to Zanzibar and the Malabar coast, to Somaliland and the Yemen; I liked their generosity, their fine open-handed hospitality, their utter lack of cant and hypocrisy. I had a momentary vision of useful work, there along the Kuwait waterfront, learning what I could of Arab maritime history, doing what I could to improve the breed of ships – a little better building, a little care of waterways and shedding the sea, a little better method of stepping the masts, sewing the sails, and perhaps a navigation school too. There were requests enough for it. The older men did not like the way that knowledge of real navigation was slipping from the young ones, for there were few among them who really knew the way on the sea. They were content with the way along the coasts. Nejdi's father had a grand idea. If some delectable dark-eyed damsels might serve me in that sea paradise, it could be paradise indeed.

But these pleasant illusions were pipe dreams – pipe dreams without the pipe. The idea was good; but in these days we do not find escape from ourselves, or from the mess we have created, so easily as that.

With our bellies full, we slept, and a cooling air stole under the verandah's shade from the punkahs agitated by the slaves. This was the life. What, Nejdi asked, had America and England to offer that was better than this? What indeed? Why then should I trouble to go back? It was only my first day in Kuwait. We should see.

We awoke to tea and little cakes from the Persian bakery round the corner; then the guests trooped off to prayer, and the family prayed on the verandah. It was early in the afternoon, and again the sounds of toil and dance and song began to echo along the waterfront as the sailors returned to their work. We walked slowly past the grounded pearlers, many of which had not been to sea for years, towards the abandoned palace of the Sheikh of Muhammerah, and the wall in the east end of the town. The palace of the Sheikh of Muhammerah, with the base of his harim near by, is a prominent landmark between the British Residency and the Sheikh of

Kuwait's town house. They are large buildings standing alone in an open space, looking rather as if they were sorry for themselves in all the long years they have waited for the return of their master. In one of them, the more dilapidated, there still lives one of the Sheikh's widows, the youngest one, a girl-bride he married on his last visit to Kuwait. He fell ill and died before the marriage could be consummated. There she still lives, no longer young, this strange virgin widow. I never saw her, or indeed any sign that either palace was now lived in. But her wedding-chest, a great Arab chest of teak with beaten brass designs, stands in the drawing room of the British Agency at Kuwait, and the Political Agent assured me that a widow still lives in the palace.

Down by the waterfront were the fishtraps, and some of the Sheikh's Beduin troops shooting birds. We passed a large house which was abandoned and growing derelict. Nejdi said it had been a pearl merchant's. The pearl merchant, he said, still had sacks full of pearls but there was no market. He had bought the pearls before the slump and could never sell them; he had held them and held them, and still held them though he had lost his home, his ships, his business, everything. He had only the pearls, and they were worth a fraction of the money he had invested in them. He could not bring himself to part with his beloved jewels at so low a price, and now they were all that remained to him.

Out in the harbour, two large booms were coming in, light after discharging their Indian cargoes. They came swooping in like great swans under their clouds of white canvas, and the crews filling their decks sent the music of song and the rhythm of their beating drums across the bay. Nejdi looked at them enviously. "We should have come in like that," he said, "but we had to come by night." He still felt it keenly.

We strolled back, past the maze of windowless side streets running from the shore road with mud walls and long spouts from the roof-tops, and here and there a group of sailors or of nakhodas sitting in the shade. Once we joined a group discussing a bad passage back from the Malabar coast, and a bearded nakhoda was tracing his route with a Zanzibar stick in the sand. Here was India, here Arabia, here the Persian Gulf. He showed how he left Calicut, together with two other ships, bound to Muscat for orders. The north-east wind came very light down the Arabian Sea and the set was towards the south-west. The wind, he said, never gave them a chance; the three ships drifted slowly across the Indian Ocean headed towards Socotra, and made painfully slow progress. They tried to regain the

Indian side, but the current was against them and they could not. So they stood on. Weeks passed. The conditions grew no better. They saw no ships, no land. They sailed alone. They did not know where they were, for there were only two among them who understood the sextant well enough to get a noon sight and work up the latitude. These two were in the same ship, but the three sailed in company. They kept together. Two months passed. One ship was short of water. The others gave her some. Seventy days passed. Two ships were short of water and the third was running very low. Still there was no rain, no improvement in the sailing conditions. They were far from the steamer lanes. On the seventy-fifth day they had no water between the three of them. They all came together in a calm and prayed fervently to Allah to send them rain. And there was rain! A great black squall rose within the hour, with the wind fair for the first time that voyage, and the life-giving rain. Truly Allah was compassionate, the nakhoda said.

Truly it was a piece of excellent good luck, I thought, and asked how it had been possible to take so many days on a comparatively short passage. Nejdi said that in midsummer there was often little wind, and the ships made long passages between the Malabar coast and Muscat. If they were driven or drifted out of their course, they could not get back again; they had water for seventy days. It was very unusual to be longer. He himself had had to go in to Socotra for water on such a voyage. It was the way of the sea, under the will of Allah. So be it. *Allah karim*! I said this might be a comforting philosophy, but a better knowledge of navigation would surely be an advantage. Yes, it was so, said Nejdi; but what could they do? There was no school in the town, no school in Arabia. And no knowledge of navigation would have any effect on the wind. It was Allah's will, and seamen must bow to it.

It was Allah's will too, I suppose, which caused the loss of the big boom *Light of the Oceans*, of which I heard many conflicting stories that day. There seemed no general agreement even about the vessel's name, though I talked with her nakhoda and several men who had sailed on her fatal voyage. Some said she was the *Light of the Sea*, others the *Light of the Sea and the Land*, others again *Inspiration of the Oceans*. She was a famous boom of some 500 tons built by the Kuwaiti on the Malabar coast about twenty years ago – there was vagueness about this too – and lost on her first voyage. She was built on the Malabar coast to save the freight on the timber to Kuwait. Instead of bringing the timber, the Kuwait shipwrights went where the timber was. This was not the good idea it may have appeared, for the quality of the local labour was indifferent, and the ship took six months to build, costing 120,000 rupees. The Bahrein merchant Abdul-rehman Za-ahni financed it; the nakhoda was a Kuwaiti; the supervising shipwrights were the famous Kuwait builders Salim bin Rashid and Mohamed Thwaini. The crew for the maiden voyage were thirty-seven Kuwaiti, forty men of Calicut experienced in the ways of the sea, and three boys. The boom had a capacity of 7,500 packages of Basra dates; her main halliards were of 19-stranded coir; a man could climb through the sheaves at her mainmast-head, according to the tailor Saud, who had sailed in her. She loaded all the cargo in Calicut, went out to sea to the banging of drums and songs, and with flags all over her, sailed cheerfully all day, struck a squall of rain in the night, filled in the rain, and foundered. Her coir swelled, and she burst and just sailed on down. Saud said he swam a night and a day to reach the shore; he still had scars from the exploding timbers.

I met the nakhoda that same day. He was then an old man with a grey beard, still taking booms to sea. When I met him, with Nejdi, he was talking cheerfully in the *suq*. The loss of the big boom was an act of God, he said. It was Allah's will. I still thought it strange that a great ship which could not survive a shower of rain had more than a little ungodly wrong with her; why had he not protected the cargo? This, he said, was not done. He did not expect rain. Allah sent it. It was clearly Allah's will that the great ship should not make her voyage. Since then, Kuwait shipwrights had built their ships at home and there had been no more expensive ventures to the Malabar coast.

So we wandered in this amazing place Kuwait, which never ceased to interest me. I was there four months, not all that time in the city, for I made a pearling voyage and wandered here and there – down the Hasa coast, to Iraq, and to the Gulf islands. But all that time was tremendously interesting. Every day, every walk along the waterfront, taught me something new, yet in the end I left knowing how much I still had to learn. I lived at first with my friends the al-Hamads at their country place at Dimner, outside Kuwait, in a walled house by the beach of Kuwait Bay. Here we lived the life of the well-to-do Arab, and lunched on succulent fish and dined on sheep day after day. We bathed in the dawns and the sunsets, and slept through the hot noon hours. Sometimes nakhodas came to visit us, and we yarned of the sea. At other times pearl merchants came, and wanderers from so far away as Syria, Singapore, Harar, and Zanzibar. The al-Hamads were among the leading merchants of Kuwait.

They were shipowners, plantation owners, and business men, with establishments in Kuwait, Basra, and Aden, and branches up and down the Red Sea. They were five brothers, the sons of the venerable Abdul-latif al-Hamad who had then been dead some years. The brothers were Khalid, Ahmed, Yusuf, Ali, and Abdulla. Khalid ran the Aden establishment, Ahmed the house in Basra, Yusuf the business in Kuwait. Ali was resting and Abdulla travelled to India. He had recently returned from Berbera to help in the date season, before going to Calcutta or wherever else his brothers might decide to send him. Abdulla was prepared to go anywhere at five minutes' notice, and rather hoped to be sent to America.

With the three younger brothers and their families, I lived at Dimner. We slept in a sand lot protected by a low cement wall to keep out the snakes; the sand lot was outside the house, beyond the walls. It was near the sea and we slept nightly with the murmur of the quiet surf in our ears, and the stars overhead for covering, and awoke in the dawns to bathe. It was a good life. Here the men gathered before sleep and the talk was of ships and ships' business. Many of the nakhodas who visited us carried the al-Hamad's cargoes, and they were all good friends of the family. When their ships came in, they all wandered out to Dimner. One of the most interesting of these nakhodas – and they were all good – was the sturdy Myouf al-Bedar, son of one of the Bedar merchants and an Abyssinian. Myouf sailed the boom *Fat-el-rehman* for the al-Hamads, and had taken Basra dates that season to Gizan, returning with a load of soap from Aden to Basra. Myouf was a famous nakhoda, a wiry, handsome, virile man, who usually arrived in the early mornings shortly after the dawn prayer. He had walked from Kuwait, and began the day by eating all the children's butter from the breakfast mat. He ate all the butter he saw whenever he saw it. I liked Myouf. He was a downright, forceful man. He knew what he wanted and took it if he could. He padded about in his sandals with his cloak over his head to protect him from the sun, and the gold tassels hanging down. Myouf's yarns of the sea were amazing and possibly sometimes truthful. It was unusual for a Kuwait ship to go so far into the Red Sea as Gizan, Hodeida in the Yemen usually marked the limit of their voyages up that coast, and not many passed Aden. Myouf was proud that he had sailed his big ship along the reef-filled way to Gizan, but not so proud of having taken sixty-five days to beat back again, empty, from Gizan to Aden.

Myouf, Saud the maker of cloaks, Abdulla the youngest of the al-Hamads, Nejdi, Ali Abdul-latif – these were my friends, and the days at

Dimner and Kuwait slipped by very pleasantly in their company. It was dreadfully hot, but life was organised for that. The north winds brought stinging sand across the bay, and the south winds and the calms caused humidity. It was always better at Dimner than in Kuwait itself, because we had the cooling air of the sea, and the worst of the desert sand did not blow there. We used to go into the *suq* in Kuwait each morning – no Arab would spend a whole day out of the *suq* if he could avoid it – arriving there about 6.30, and then spend the morning visiting and being visited, drinking coffee, chatting, calling on this merchant and that, and greeting sheikhs and wise men, sitting on carpets outside shops or inside shops, looking on at the teeming life all round. So passed our mornings until about 11, when we returned to Dimner for the morning meal. That eaten, we slept; then rose and bathed, drank tea, yarned, and went off to the waterfront and the *suq* again in the cool of the afternoon for more salaams, more visiting and being visited, more sitting in the coffee-shops listening to good yarns and bad gramophones. In this manner the merchants passed their days, while their businesses prospered, and the nakhodas grew fat from good feeding and indolent from the enjoyment of their women.

"Pray, eat, and enjoy our women. That's all we do at home," Myouf said one day. "It is good; but it is also good to return to the sea."

If the merchants and nakhodas had this good life the sailors had not, and after a few days the familiar countenances of the *Triumph*'s mariners disappeared from the *suq*. Many of them had gone pearling. The pearlers begin their season when the big ships come in, and end it when it is time for the big ships to go out again. To a considerable extent the same sailors work both, and life is hard for them. For a few days the sailors in from the long-voyage booms swagger in the *suq*, dressed in their best clothes, swinging their canes and their rosaries, sitting in the coffee-shops, drinking from the hookahs, visiting and exchanging stories. Some have no homes, but this is no inconvenience, for they may sleep on the beach or in the streets. By night the beach along the waterfront in the summer months resounds with their snores, where they lie asleep wrapped in their cloaks beneath the stars. A sailor, if he is young and single, needs little to keep him going; his food may be bought for a few annas a day. Without money, he will not starve. There is always an eating-mat he may join. His clothing is made up of gown and cloak, headcloth and aghal; all he owns he can carry, and he has no bed. His chest is left for the laying-up season in his nakhoda's shed. If he goes pearling he will not need it. It is for the carrying of his trade goods and not his clothes. No sailor could fill a chest with his own clothes. If he could he would sell them. The youthful unmarried men sleep on the beach in the shadow of the ships they serve so faithfully – careless happy men, superbly fit and in good condition. When the pearling is over it is different. Pearling is hard.

Days passed. Weeks passed. Old Yusuf had gone pearling, to dive in his dead brother's place. Abdulla Kitami had come in, and his boom rested on the beach before the Kitami house, by the waterfront. The two Abdulwahhabs, Radhwan with his baggala, Ganim bin Othman's big boom, Yusuf bin Isa, Nasir with his little *Cat*, Mahmoud with the *Glory of the Morning*, Mosa, Isa, Hamoud, Ismael, Saqr, Mohamed, Said bin Ali – all these were in, and the nakhodas swelled the crowd sitting in the shade by the waterfront or wandering in the *suq*. Still there was no news of Bedar's *Bedri*.

When we had been back a month, however, she turned up at Muscat, after a long passage from Zanzibar, and had gone to some place in Qatar to discharge. She had had a bad time that night off Malindi, and again off Kismayu. Abdulla, Nejdi's brother, was not yet back, but there was news of him. He was coming up slowly from Mogadishu with the Suri, changing from ship to ship as he came along the South Arabian coast. He ought to be home within a month. The crew of the *Triumph* had not yet been paid and the shares had not been cast up, but Nejdi gave them money as they needed it. Indeed, many of them would have very little coming when the shares were cast up, for the system of advances and debts more than swallowed up their earnings. It was hard for a sailor not to be in debt and, so far as I could see, none of them tried very much not to be. Debt was an accepted thing, and to spend a lifetime owing money was apparently usual. The sailors owed money to the nakhodas, the nakhodas to the merchants, the merchants to other merchants, or the Sheikh. Working without any banking system, with insurance, usury, and even interest forbidden – at any rate in theory – by the Islamic law, the economic side of the port of Kuwait was a dark maze. It was obvious, however, that the whole industry rested on a structure of debt. It was equally obvious that the nakhodas, though they imagined themselves to be the owners of their booms, were not the real owners at all. The merchants owned them. It suited the merchants, apparently, to finance the nakhodas rather than to run the ships themselves, and for this there were many excellent reasons. The nakhodas, perhaps, paid more for the financing they received than the ships could be expected to earn. In other words, money advanced to nakhodas to run ships for themselves brought larger dividends than the same money would have done if the merchants had invested it directly in the ships. The merchants did very well out of it, and the nakhodas made a good living too. But it appeared to me that, by this system, the merchants really owned the nakhodas as well as the ships, for the nakhodas could scarcely expect ever to be free of debt. Indeed, so far as I could see, they made little active effort in that direction. They were satisfied. They led good lives. If a man bestirred himself and had a chance to start level, he could rise to be a merchant himself. Very few merchants, however, had ever been nakhodas.

In their turn, the nakhodas owned the sailors, for the sailors were considered bound to any nakhoda to whom they owed advances. Most of them owed the balance of some advance. The nakhodas were tied to the merchants, and the sailors to the nakhodas, though they were not slaves. There was little slavery in Kuwait. There was little need of it. Slavery had become uneconomic. It was better to own a man's work than to own and support the man himself. To own his work, you had not to support him.

I should have gone pearling with old Yusuf, as I had intended, but for one reason. I could not find room in his ship. He went off in a little sambuk about two weeks after the *Triumph* came in, and though the sambuk was only forty-six feet long she carried a crew of more than sixty men. I could not understand how they could all sleep on board, unless they slept in tiers. But they went off with song, old Yusuf singing as lustily as any of them and lending a hand at the sweeps. It was a hot, breathless morning when the pearlers went. Fifty-seven of them went out that day, all gaily decorated with flags and with their sailors singing and banging drums. The admiral's sambuk – the pretty sambuk of Sheikh Sabah – led the procession, and they looked like a fleet of galleys going out from Tyre two thousand years ago, as their sweeps flashed in the sun and their freshly-oiled hulls gleamed on the bay. It was a stirring sight, but I was sorry for poor Yusuf. He was to be gone a hundred days, he said, while the sea was warm. He would be back, probably, just in time to join the *Triumph* for her new voyage. He looked thoughtful, and I saw that his feet were far from healed. Along the waterfront road, I saw a tiny figure wrapped in black waving to him as his sambuk sailed, and the tiny figure looked after that fleet of departing ships a long, long time.

XIX

THE GULF PEARLERS

If I could not go with Yusuf, I was determined to get to the pearling banks somehow. It was easy to see something of the industry from Kuwait. During my four-months stay, small pearling vessels were coming and going from the nearer banks, for water and food. Many of the small vessels did not go more than thirty or forty miles from the bay, and fleets of them were accustomed to anchor each evening under the shelter of nearby places such as Shi'aiba, villages along the coast of Kuwait which were connected with the city by bus service. From time to time buyers went to these anchorages to meet the nakhodas on the beach, or to be present at a dawn opening of the oysters and see how things were going. This was helpful to them in gauging the probable 'take' for the season, and the consequent state of the new market. The smaller ships, many of which were boats less than thirty feet long, opened the season earlier than the larger ones. As the big booms came in from their long voyages, many of them sent out their longboats, rigged up and temporarily decked, to try their luck at pearling, manned by a quartermaster or a younger brother of the nakhoda, with some of the sailors as his crew.

In 1939, one hundred and fifty craft of all kinds went pearling from Kuwait. Forty years ago, the number would have been six hundred, at least. The fleet which went out the summer I was in Kuwait was the largest since the slump. Many of the merchants who had been most badly hit by the slump had gone out of the business entirely, leaving new ones to come and try their luck. In the meantime, the competition of the Japanese cultured pearl had come to mean less and less. The cultured pearl, when it was comparatively rare, was a worse competitor, I was told, than it is today, when it is commonplace. When it first came on the market it sold at something like one-third of the price of a real pearl; now it brings more like a thirtieth, and it competes more with the better-made artificial pearls than with the real. This may be so, but the effect has been to cheapen all pearls, whether real, cultured, or the product of laboratories. The better cultured pearls defy detection even by the Arab expert, and there was not one merchant in Kuwait who, in spite of a lifetime in the business, could distinguish a cultured pearl from a real pearl without the most exhaustive examination, and often destructive tests. By the time he knew whether the pearl was real or cultured, it was spoiled. If the expert could be so inconvenienced, the layman had no chance. The result had been a general falling-off in the demand for real pearls, for milady scorns to wear gems which will be regarded as cheap. Pearls have been cheapened. Since men buy pearls to please women, and women are not pleased when men give them something which cannot immediately be recognised as both genuine and expensive, it follows that the pearl market has suffered a very severe decline. Real pearls do not bring a tenth of what they did in Kuwait or Bahrein fifteen years ago.

In such circumstances, it has hardly been worth while to dive for them, and the Kuwait beach is littered to this day with the hulls of hundreds of pearlers which have lain neglected for so long that they are fit for nothing but firewood. This in spite of the fact that many of the larger vessels, and nearly all the booms and sambuks, have been bought by Persians, by the people of Batina and the Trucial Coast and Mahra, and converted for use as passenger-carrying cargo vessels. Hundreds of ships have left Kuwait registry in the last ten years, but many still remain. There is a basin, not far from the American hospital, where the pearlers lie almost as thick as the discarded shells of empty oysters on a pearling beach – big ships and little ships, jalboots, sambuks, belems, shewes. The shapely timbers of the little craft throw long shadows under the moon and beautify the beach, but they are warped and rotted now and they can sail the seas no more.

Kuwait has long been a pearling port of great importance, second only to Bahrein in the whole Persian Gulf. This position it still holds, but the decline of the industry has been steep and probably also permanent. From some points of view, I should hardly say that it is to be regretted. The pearl season – known locally as the *ghaus* – must have been dreaded by the divers, for it was accompanied by hardships almost intolerable, by risk to health and life and limb, and its rewards were scanty, often distributed most unfairly, and sometimes withheld from their rightful owners altogether.

All through history, the Persian Gulf has been famous for its pearls, and pearl-diving there is an industry of great antiquity. The pearl-oyster has always thrived on the great banks which cover so much of the Arabian side of the Gulf. The formation of the Gulf, its shallowness, the intense heat of the summer sun – the pearl-oyster seems to like warm water – together, probably, with the proximity to the great and wealthy market of

India, which to this day buys most of its pearls, made the waters of the Gulf the most famous and prolific pearling ground of the world. At the turn of the century there were probably between seventy and eighty thousand men engaged in Persian Gulf pearling. Shortly after the end of the European War, in 1919, the number was not much less. It is doubtful now if there are many more than ten thousand pearling from Bahrein, el-Qatif, the Trucial ports, and Kuwait. Compared with five thousand craft forty years ago, perhaps there are now a thousand. Bahrein, for instance, sent out six hundred ships and more, even as recently as ten years ago. When we were there in the *Triumph of Righteousness*, less than half this number had been licensed for the current season. If oil had not been found, it is probable that Bahrein would have been close to bankruptcy, for the island had no other industry. If Kuwait could not so readily have changed to the deep-sea carrying trade it, too, would have suffered badly.

As it is, the worst effects of the decline of the pearl market have now passed. As the merchants of Kuwait were saying when we came in, that season they might as well try their luck again, for the market could not very well get any worse. If they could afford to fit out a few ships on the expectation of prices no worse and no better than those then prevailing, it was probable that in the course of time the industry might get back some of its old importance, on a much sounder footing. It was always something of a gamble. The meanest ship might take the most valuable pearls. Mere size did not mean anything. To this day, the ways of the pearl oyster and the success of the season remain unpredictable. In some seasons, pearls are numerous but not of high quality. In other seasons, they are both plentiful and valuable. This was the case in 1939, but the outbreak of war in Europe ruined any market there might have been. At other times, the pearls are neither plentiful nor valuable. Sometimes one bank will give good pearls, and all others in the Gulf give nothing but indifferent ones. The best banks have always been recognised as those closest to Bahrein, north and east of the island, but there are others near Kuwait. Sometimes, for several years in succession, a bank will yield scarcely anything, and then, for no apparent reason, it suddenly begins to produce oysters loaded with rare pearls. There is no rhyme or reason in it. Each nakhoda on the banks has only his own knowledge and his luck to guide him. The banks are not charted; there is nothing scientific about it. The ancient methods are still used, without variation. Diving is without costume, without gear. All the banks are free, though usually those nearer inshore are left to the fleets from the nearest port; out in the Gulf, the larger vessels fish together. I have seen more than a hundred on one bank, most of them from Kuwait.

Though the banks are free, there is a homicidal prejudice against the introduction of new methods. The Persian Gulf, the home of pearl-diving, is no place for divers, and the only diving gear in the Gulf belongs to the lighthouse tender *Nearchus* and the Royal Navy. The Arabs dive with a peg on the nose, and no other gear. Most of the diving is on banks with from five to twelve fathoms of water. Big ships stay in the open waters of the Gulf, but smaller ones usually run into neighbouring anchorages by night. There are two seasons, first a sort of free-for-all, not closely organised, in which the smaller craft go out and test the nearer banks and more accessible places as soon as the summer sun has made the water warm enough for shallow diving. About a month later the main season begins, when all the ships go out, and this last season lasts so long as the summer sun warms the water. That is usually about four months – most of June, July, August, September, and a little of October. During these months the climate of the Persian Gulf is more like that of an inferno than of a habitable region, but the intense and continuous heat is necessary to warm the water so that the naked divers can bear the almost constant immersion. They lie in the water beside their boats, or grope on the sea-bed half the day, and dive to sixty and seventy feet of water. For any human being to stand this – even the tough, magnificent Arab or the huge muscular slave – over a period of months with little food, the water must be warm. Immediately the water begins to cool, the diving must stop and the boats return to port. The principal duty of the admiral of the fleet is to fix and announce this quitting day, before which it is not considered proper for a large ship to return. What the small craft do is largely their own business, for they never have sufficient pearls to affect the market.

When pearling was at its height and as many as twenty thousand men took part in the season from Kuwait, Beduin, Persians, slaves, and anyone else who could be induced or compelled to go, went with the fleet to the banks. There were many more pearlers than sailors. Now there are more sailors than pearlers. Sailing on long voyages was formerly a change from pearling; now pearling is a change from sailing in the cargo-ships. When I was in Kuwait, probably about three thousand men were engaged in the pearling industry. While many were deep-water sailors, others were not, particularly the divers. I saw many among these who were obviously Beduin, with long hair; but I never saw a long-haired Kuwait or Saudi-Arabian Beduin in a deep-water Kuwait ship. The explanation was that these Beduin had inherited the obligation to dive. They were young men who had inherited their parents' debts. This passing on of debts from father to son has stopped now, in Kuwait, and has been abandoned in Bahrein for the past ten years. But if a man went diving to pay off his father's debt and then incurred a debt of his own, as he invariably did, he must go out to pay off his own debt, even after the inherited debt had been annulled.

The whole economic structure of the industry, even more than in ship-owning, was based on debt. Everybody was in debt – the divers to the nakhoda, the nakhoda to the merchant who financed him, the merchant to some other merchant bigger than himself, the bigger merchant to the Sheikh. Even the broker who came out to buy the pearls was probably heavily in debt to some moneylender who financed him. The whole business was based on debts – debts which were rarely paid because the paying of them was impossible. If money in Islam could not earn interest in banks, and there was no banking system, it certainly found a way of more than making up for the disability. The man who advanced money usually saw that there was a big return, though it was never called interest. The return was disguised in all sorts of ways, but it was always there. The divers paid interest on their advances by open and barefaced robbery and chicanery of every kind. They were an optimistic, gambling, irresponsible class who often died young. The nakhodas paid their interest by all sorts of subterfuges in the selling of pearls. I heard of one financier who had a rule that all ships financed by him should give him their pearls at four-fifths of their value, a barefaced rate of interest of twenty per cent over four months. This would not be the only profit. Having got the pearls at four-fifths of the Kuwait value, he would pocket the difference and sell them in Bombay for anything up to five or six times the sum he had invested in them. Moreover, if the ship's earnings, as calculated by himself, did not come to the amount he had advanced, the difference remained owing, and until it had been repaid that nakhoda must go out and pearl for him, under the same conditions. The nakhodas were tied no less than their men, and the merchants were tied no less securely to larger merchants. Though large profits could be made, large losses could be incurred. There was a considerable element of gambling all through the industry, and many of the leading Kuwait merchants would have nothing to do with it, not even as a personal favour to their own nakhodas. Pearling, in their opinion, was a business best left alone. The more I learned of it, the more I shared this view.

In Bahrein the worst abuses have long disappeared, though it was difficult to bring about reforms. In Kuwait, things are much better than they were. The Bahrein Government, which appears to have received little thanks for its pains, has effected far-reaching and permanent reforms, which cannot but make themselves felt throughout the Gulf. Formerly no accounts were kept – the divers keep none now, in the Kuwait ships – but the Bahrein Government insists that all divers shall be given clearly made-out account books, properly kept, and sends round inspectors to see that it is done. Not only are the divers' interests looked after, but the nakhodas also are protected. Formerly there was much trouble and a great deal of sharp practice over the amounts of the advances to be made to the divers and the tenders at the beginning of each season. It was realised that, unless advances were controlled, the debt system could never be. The Government now calls a meeting of the merchants and other interested parties before the season begins, and the amount of the advances is agreed upon and proclaimed. So much and no less – and no more – may be paid. This innovation met with organised opposition, especially from the divers themselves, for they were misled by cunning propaganda into imagining the restriction of advances to be a curb upon them. It was difficult to convince an ignorant and improvident man, told that he could have an advance of thirty rupees instead of sixty, that the cut was in his own interest, since, if he earned sixty rupees, the Government would see that he got them, and, if he did not, they would not be added to his debt. The divers only knew they had less money in their pockets. They did not mind increasing their debts, for that was a condition to which they were well accustomed. There were riots, which grew serious enough to involve shootings and loss of life. But the innovations stood.

At the same time, Bahrein abolished the practice of hereditary debts; a diver's debts died with him. The pearl merchants' court was abolished, and merchants and nakhodas were no longer allowed to compel divers to work for them in their gardens in the off-season. The pearl merchants' court, in former days, settled all questions of law between divers and nakhodas, but since only the nakhodas and the merchants were represented, its decisions could hardly be expected to be fair. There is still a pearlers' court in Kuwait, but it is fairer there. There are keen-sighted enthusiasts to keep an eye on it, to see that its decisions are not too grossly unfair, but at the same time it is recognised that changes in an industry so loosely knit and so ancient ought to come gradually if their effect is to be permanent. Kuwait is already a long way along the road first opened by Bahrein.

Along the Hasa coast also, pearling has suffered a severe decline, and the ports of el-Qatif, Darin, and Jubail send few ships to the *ghaus*. Many of the divers now work instead for the Standard Oil Company of California, which has the valuable oil concessions there. They pay a proportion of their wages to the nakhodas to whom they are in debt, and the nakhodas, since they can sit back and enjoy these sums regularly, have not much desire to go pearling. The market is bad, and the life is hard. It is better to sit on the beach at el-Qatif and enjoy the fruits of the oil-men. The pearlers of el-Khobar and el-Qatif now stand rotting on their beaches. At el-Khobar I saw the last of the famous *betil*s, those curiously decorated craft which once were the galleys of the pearling admirals of the Gulf. The admiral of el-Khobar now works for the oil company, though his task is not arduous and his income from his debtors is probably much greater than his earnings.

From all this it may be seen that pearling, as it is practised on the banks of the Persian Gulf, is an arduous, difficult, and complicated business. I looked forward to finding out what I could about it and, though the prospect of spending the season in a sambuk really alarmed me, I was determined to go out some way or other. Having survived six months in Nejdi's boom, I thought I could stand anything. However, I had imagined wrongly. I thought, too, that I had graduated in hardship and crowding aboard Arab dhows, but, when I saw the pearlers, I knew I was looking at really overcrowded vessels for the first time. The maindeck of a Kuwait pearler going to sea was like a platform of the subway at Times Square in New York at the rush hour with no trains coming in. Compared with the pearlers, the *Triumph* had been an ocean liner. If she stowed human beings like cattle for the run from the Hadhramaut to Africa, with frequent calls at ports, the pearlers packed them in like sardines in a double-layer tin, and called at no ports at all. If life in the *Triumph* had sometimes been hard, existence in the pearlers must always be a nightmare. I quailed at the thought of going in them. I had to confess that the degree of hardship involved in a pearling voyage over the Persian Gulf banks, working with the crew for a hundred days in that frightful climate and under the dreadful conditions prevailing, was more than I could hope to stand. I could not, by myself, alleviate the conditions. I suppose I could, had I so wished, have financed my own ship; but in that way I should have learned little of the real conditions and probably only succeeded in deluding myself. No, if I went at all it must be properly. So I compromised, having first looked over the banks, on a trip with the Political Agent in his comfortable launch, by arranging to ship for a buying voyage with Sheikh Mohamed Abdul-razzaq. Mohamed Abdul-razzaq was a buyer of good pearls for the Bombay market, where his father sold them. He had a jalboot, a large retinue, a bundle of mysterious equipment tied up in a large red rag, a clerk, and a lifetime knowledge of the industry. Moreover, he was a good fellow and I liked him. I shipped with him for a buying voyage from Kuwait across the banks and the whole of the way down the Hasa coast to Bahrein. It would, he said, take at least a month. It took two months and we never reached Bahrein. But it was extraordinarily interesting, and I learned a great deal.

We sailed from Kuwait one fine morning in early August, three weeks after our sailing had first been announced. Sheikh Mohamed's – he was a sheikh by courtesy – jalboot was about thirty-six feet long, a beamy little thing with one high mast. She was loaded to the waterline with seven sheep, half a ton of rice, fresh water in drums, camel-thorn fuel, a firepot, four dozen bottles of sherbet, six trunks and three chests, several hundredweight of sheep-feed (grass from the Shatt-el-Arab), two hookahs, a large quantity of sweetmeats, sugar and other stores for two months, twelve human beings, and a chest of rupees in a dark space underneath the poop. We had our sleeping-mats with us, a small carpet each and a cloak, and there were leaning pillows round the poop. We could, the sheikh said, go into some quiet cove along the beach and sleep on the sand each night. It seemed to me that we should have to, for there was not room to sleep on board. We would eat the sheep, change the rupees for pearls as opportunity offered, and go where the wind took us.

It appeared to promise a good programme. So we set off, out of Kuwait Bay, hours after the hour announced, twenty days later than the announced day. We saw very little either of pearlers or pearls the first day, and fetched up for the evening at a walled place called Shi'aiba. Here we ate a sheep and then stretched ourselves to sleep on the sand. It was a good place, but there were no pearlers there; the fleet had gone on to the south. We sailed again in the morning after the dawn prayer; and for a month after that we dodged about the nearer waters of the northern Gulf, now coming in to some lonely beach to sleep, now anchored for days in the rolling sea behind a reef with the fleet of pearlers jostling round us, now spending a day or two with the Beduin of the sheikh's acquaintance, living on camel's milk and the flesh of sheep. We went where the pearlers were and sometimes spent a week round one reef, while Sheikh Sabah's big sambuk led the Kuwait fleet combing the bank. It was often stirring to watch these fleets of pearlers on the banks, with their sweeps out and the divers near-naked in the sea, their crews chanting and dancing while they shifted the sambuk to a new berth. Sometimes we were one of a fleet of sixty Kuwait pearlers; at others, one of six. The big fellows kept the sea and only the smaller craft came in by night to the beaches. At dawn they opened the oysters taken the previous day. Then we hovered about, listening for news, waiting for the cheers that would greet the finding of a really good pearl.

I soon discovered that Sheikh Mohamed was after not good pearls cheap, but first-rate pearls for next to nothing. That is, if he could get them. Very often he could not, for the nakhodas were alert and not anxious to sell to brokers visiting the fleet in launches, so long as they had hope of a rising market in Bombay or Bahrein. Some of them had to sell, to buy more dates or rice or water.

What the buyer really loved to see was a big pearl whose value was unrecognised by nakhoda and crew. Such pearls were rare, but they did exist. The sheikh told me that a pearl of seemingly little value, if operated on properly by an expert, could sometimes be made into a gem of rare beauty. He excelled at this art and was constantly on the look-out for gems on which to practise. We did not find many. Blister pearls, which he could skilfully remove from the shell, large discoloured pearls which he could carefully peel, misshapen pearls which he would whittle down in the hope that only the outer skin was blemished and out of shape – these we purchased. They were cheap. He usually paid about five rupees for them, and the 'operations' took days. As a rule, after he had 'operated' on them, they were not worth even one rupee. The blister pearls proved to be excrescences covered with a thin layer of pearl tissue; the misshapen ones remained misshapen, the discoloured ones retained their unprofitable idiosyncrasies through all their skins. No matter: it was a gamble. The whole business was a gamble. *Allah karim*! One day would come the pearl bought for five rupees, worth five hundred – even five thousand. It was a risk worth taking; performing the 'operations' was interesting, and served to pass the time. We had a great deal of spare time.

I do not mean that the Sheikh Mohamed ever doctored a pearl. That was impossible. He simply tried to detach blisters from their shells in the hope that there might be a good pearl inside, or peeled a skin from a big coarse pearl in the hope that there might be a perfect gem under it. Such were his 'operations.' He did not adulterate anything; he loved his pearls too much for that. Everyone in the Persian Gulf pearling business knew that the only way he could retain a market was by the strictest and most thorough honesty. It would, apparently, be easy to introduce a parcel of Japanese cultured pearls into a group of real gems, since their detection is so difficult. But in fact it would be almost impossible to do this; the supervision of the catch is too strict. Anyone found doing such a thing would run the risk of instant execution. Justice in Arabia is summary, and often final. Even the importing of cultured pearls to any of the Arab market-places is a most serious offence, punished by penal servitude at least. Penal servitude there means languishing indefinitely in a dungeon.

For diversion, we sometimes went hunting with falcons with a Beduin sheikh on Ras Zor. The smaller pearlers came to the beach to rest their crews one day in every ten, and when they came we came with them to visit their ships and see what sort of catch they had. Usually they had very few pearls, and only of a poor quality, and we did not often buy from them. But we had some good visits with the Beduin who wandered along the coast with their flocks, coming in to the water-holes for summer and going to the desert again for winter and spring. They all kept falcons, which are favourite hunters in Kuwait. The falcons were better fed than some of the children. They also had large numbers of hungry dogs which came running to the tents every time they heard the smacking of lips. When we were not engaged in falconry or watching the flocks, we lolled against the camel saddles in the tents, a partition of coarse matting separating us from the harim. It was a free, untrammelled life and I wondered why any of the Beduin troubled to go pearling. Our friends of Ras Zor certainly had no intention of doing so.

Though the intervals ashore were pleasant, I liked best to be out on the banks with the pearling fleets, learning the methods of working, getting some knowledge of the secrets of the trade. Being with the Sheikh Mohamed was an ideal way to study pearling, for in that way I could watch everything – the dive, the manœuvring, life in all kinds of vessels, buying, selling, 'operating.' I learned how the brokers competed with each other, each always anxious to hear of a great pearl before any of the others knew of it, so that he might dash off and buy it before competing bids forced up the price and before the nakhoda discovered its real value. We distributed largesse right and left to make friends amongst the nakhodas in order to hear these tips – a sheep here, a tin of sweetmeats there, a piece of camel meat to one friend, a pound of tobacco to another. All news was given by word of mouth, and most of it was unreliable. Several times we dashed after reported great pearls, but we never found any. The brokers, I noticed, brought nothing but bad news. Our visits to the pearlers were always introduced after the proper salutations, by sad accounts of the dullness of the market – true enough, unfortunately – designed to decrease the nakhoda's expectations for his pearls. Then, after some time – we were never in a hurry once we had got aboard a vessel – the nakhoda, after discussing every other subject on earth, would dive into a mysterious recess beneath his tiny poop and drag out a chest. It was often a dilapidated chest tied up with string, but usually it was locked in some way or other, and the keys were tied to a short thong round the nakhoda's waist, beneath his gown. The divers always watched as the pearls were brought out. The chest would be opened slowly, as became the receptacle of so many hopes, and as we watched, various small bundles tied up in scraps of red bunting or bits of black cloth would be extracted. Often in the smaller vessels each bundle was identified, usually by the manner of tying its knots, as the property of such and such a diver; in the larger vessels the take was pooled, but there was always a division of the pearls. They were not graded, for no nakhoda on the bank bothered to grade or to value his pearls until the season was over. They were kept in separate parcels according to the banks on which they were taken. Most of the pearls were useless. The red bunting contained mostly tiny seed pearls, and discoloured or misshapen lumps. But there always were some perfect gems.

Usually the nakhoda would uncover one small parcel and hand it round to us for examination. No one watched the individual pearls, though all hands, except those actually diving and tending, watched the performance. There was obviously scrupulous honesty on board. If there was sharp practice in the industry, it was not between the men and their nakhoda on the banks. No man kept his own pearls. The nakhoda had them all. Often, when a parcel was produced for our examination, Sheikh Mohamed, pretending to despise it, would give it only a cursory glance before tying it up and throwing it back. He often did that with ten or a dozen little parcels before we got down to business in earnest, and it was sometimes hours before his clerk, his brother Mosa, produced the sieves and the scales and all the rest of the buying apparatus.

We used to board these ships by small boat from our jalboot, and our cargo was invariably the same, a sack of jingling silver rupees, Sheikh

Mohamed's red bundle, some sweetmeats and some Arab cigarettes as gifts. The Sheikh's red bundle contained magnifying glasses, a small neat balance to be held in the hand, two sets of agate weights and some tiny weights of very light metal, a book in Hindustani on the grading and value of pearls, another book with the sheikh's secret information of the prices ruling in the markets at Bombay and Bahrein, a set of small brass sieves with carefully graduated holes for grading pearls, and a piece of red cloth to keep the wind from the scales. The scales were held by hand and hardly accurate, but the sheikh was very skilful at getting an idea of the weight of a take with them. I noticed that he never overweighed them. He piled all the small pearls together, and deducted ten per cent for stray bits of oyster adhering to the pearls. (We often weighed them and examined them almost fresh from the fish.) When the pearls had been thoroughly examined, despite the appearance of casualness, there would be another interval of pious discourse. Then at last would come the query, how much? The nakhodas were generally most reluctant to name a price, and the sheikh was always reluctant to pay anything. The nakhodas had a good idea of the value of their pearls. The dialogue might go something like this:

The nakhoda, reluctantly, after a long pause, fingering the red bundle: "Four hundred rupees."

Sheikh Mohamed bursts into ironical laughter. He gets up to leave. He comes back again. He bundles his apparatus.

The nakhoda: "Four hundred rupees is little enough."

Sheikh Mohamed: "There is no market for pearls. You know that. Anything I spend now I may lose. If you can get four hundred rupees for that, I will give six hundred."

The nakhoda: "Four hundred."

Sheikh Mohamed: "I offer two hundred and fifty. And that's final. There is no market for pearls. There is not a good pearl in the bundle. It is only our old friendship which prompts me to make this generous offer. Hold them, if you wish; see if you are offered any more than I offer now. By the grace of Allah, I am generous."

The nakhoda: "Four hundred. See how many poor men must share in this. We have dived for these gems two months – two hard months. They are worth four hundred rupees."

Sheikh Mohamed: "*Allah karim*! I cannot help the bad market. I will give their worth. You know me. But I cannot give more than their worth. It is bad. All the markets are bad. Bad, bad, bad." And then follow many pious exclamations, which impress the crew.

The nakhoda, also exclaiming piously, and now sadder than ever: "Four hundred rupees."

An hour later, the pious exclamations rumbling on and on and the red cloth having been opened and tied up again three or four times, while the gaunt divers warming themselves at the tiny firebox stand and look on, Sheikh Mohamed suddenly seizes his brother's hand, takes it by the fingers, and slips a red cloth over them so that the onlookers may not see what is being done. This is his way of finding out what his brother thinks the pearls are worth. He will not ask him straight out. This is a brokers' consultation. I see the fingers working: he touches a nail of this finger, takes hold of the third joint of that, shifts rapidly to the second joint of a third. His brother responds just as rapidly. The mathematics of this finger-juggling, time-honoured method of pearl-buying in the Gulf, are simple to grasp; but the practice itself takes years to learn. Each finger, each joint in every finger, each degree of pressure, has an exact mathematical value.

I was told, by the sailors, that brokers and merchants communicating in this way could even fix the amount of bakhshish to be divided between them, and the practice could be used dishonestly. With Sheikh Mohamed, it was always merely a part of the proceedings: it was not the whole. The price was agreed upon orally and not by this covered touch system. He used that only to communicate with his brother during the driving of bargains, for his brother also was a shrewd judge of pearls, and had better eyes.

After a long time, we buy the parcel at two hundred and sixty rupees. Then the sack of silver coins is opened, the agreed price counted out, the pearls transferred to the sheikh's pocket and, after a round of coffee, we return in the small boat to our launch. It was amazing, after a day's buying had been done, to see how the value of the pearls increased once we had bought them. Sheikh Mohamed would bring them out, gloat over them, weigh, grade, and value them properly, instead of just haphazard as he did when buying, and tie them all up in a large parcel with the others he had bought. He did not keep them separately, or try to grade them until his buying was finished. On the banks, we kept all pearls in one big piece of bunting, locked in a chest. He had them out of that chest ten and twenty times a day, when buying was not in progress, and he and his brother gloated over them. The transfer of a parcel of pearls from the nakhoda's piece of bunting to their own seemed to double the pearls' value. Probably it trebled it.

While we were anchored off the beach at a place called Ras Misha‘ab, a small pearler came in to bury one of her divers who had died. He looked to me as if he had died of scurvy, which was not at all surprising, for the diet on the banks was very poor. All there was to eat was rice and fish. The rice itself might have been nutritious, and with a liberal covering of real Arab ghee might have sufficed to keep scurvy at bay for a few months. But, recently, the nakhodas had taken to the purchase of artificial ghee, made in Europe and imported by the merchants to Bahrein and Kuwait. It looked all right, and it was cheap. It was nothing but a low-grade cooking oil, and it had practically no value as nutriment. So the divers were getting scurvy again and the nakhodas were surprised.

The burial of the poor diver was a simple ceremony. It was over in a few minutes. They carried him up the beach and put him in the sand. The poor, worn-out old body seemed pitifully easy to carry. I looked to see that it was not my old friend Yusuf, for I feared it could easily have been. It was not; it was a man from Hasa. I had seen this artificial ghee aboard the ships, in tins; and I asked Sheikh Mohamed if he could not induce the nakhodas to stop purchasing such stuff. But he could not, he said; it was cheap, and they were ignorant men. They used it liberally, not knowing it was useless. The real ghee of Kuwait was expensive, he said; the nakhodas were poor men.

So they were burying the diver in the sand. How many divers died like that? I asked. Death was rare, the sheikh said. Some drowned. Some just died. But we were never aboard a ship on all those banks which had not at least one sick diver lying wrapped in his desert cloak on the bare boards aft. Most of them looked like scurvy cases.

Some miles south of Ras Misha‘ab we came upon the main Kuwait fleet, sixty ships on one large bank, and others grouped about lesser banks. There were more than a hundred craft in sight altogether, but most of them were small vessels. The sight was a stirring one – the burned brown hulls of the pearling ships with their long sweeps out looking like ancient galleys, the flags flying from the admiral’s sambuk, the beating of drums and the chant of lusty voices as here and there a jalboot or a big belem moved with slow grace towards a new berth with melodic swing and splash of the great sweeps, the deep chesty grunting of her two-score sailors as a large pearler took up her berth and the oarsmen bent together for the final burst of sound. Occasionally, a small vessel would bend a great genoa jib and skim over the water for a mile or so. All the vessels used these manœuvring sails on the banks and rarely set their big lateens except for leaving and making the anchorages night and morning. Usually they were shifted during the day only by their sweeps.

A fleet of vessels would take up positions on a bank, each anchoring on the outer edge in such a way that by veering out cable they would drift across the bank, and then slowly work their way across with divers out on each side, veering out cable until the farther edge of the bank was reached. Then they would weigh and stand back to the other side, under the sweeps, with song and chanting. Everything was done with a set style. They would anchor again a little farther from their old position, and once more slowly scour a section of the bank with divers out on either side.

This method of cleaning up a bank was thorough, and after a day or so the bank would have been dealt with almost as efficiently as a ploughed field. The different craft, crossing and recrossing the beds of oysters with their divers out on either side of them, were like harrowers going across a field; they missed very little. Each time the vessel lay to her anchor the divers scoured the bottom until they could not see an oyster left. Then the ship slacked away again until a new place was reached. Each ship had her own track, her own section of the bank, and it was not considered proper for others to anchor anywhere in her path. Occasionally, some of the smaller vessels, apparently despairing of getting their due share of oysters from a bank so thoroughly combed, would weigh anchor, set their big jibs, and be off somewhere to a bank of their own.

The skill of the nakhodas was in their knowledge of the banks and their efficiency in cleaning them, for, with fifty or sixty vessels on the one bank, it was a shrewd and determined man who knew always how to keep his vessel anchored in virgin water and his divers bringing up oysters by the basketful. Sometimes we would board a vessel where the divers, try as they would, never brought up more than two or three oysters apiece, yet near them the divers of another sambuk might be bringing up baskets filled with big shells. It was not luck. It was intuitive skill, you had it or you didn't have it. Sheikh Mohamed used to point out to me the nakhodas who did have it, and usually, though not always, these had the larger ships. One of them was blind. He was quite blind, but according to my merchant friend, he had retained his skill. We saw many nakhodas who dived themselves, though they did not stand their regular turns. They made the first dives to test the beds.

In the evenings, while we were with the main fleet, we anchored behind a reef far out in the Gulf, out of sight of land. It was about midway between Kuwait and Bahrein, in that part of the Gulf which is most dangerous to ocean vessels. It was not dangerous to us, for all these nakhodas knew the banks as if they were garden beds. The small craft used to come hurrying in of an evening like a crowd of yachts returning from a regatta, though the odour that came from them was not that of a regatta, and the lithe brown sailors pulling at the sweeps chanted haunting songs. Aft the divers were always huddled, seeming only half-alive, bent and shivering.

The big ships and the main fleet had been working down-gulf like that for two months; they worked down until they met the Bahrein fleet working up, and afterwards smaller ships came behind them to take the leavings. Little pearlers worked close inshore, using different methods. Sometimes we saw these with all their crews swimming about looking very queer with their heads in boxes, pushing the boxes along. The box had a piece of glass in its underside, in the water, and through this glass the swimmers could see the bottom clearly. When they saw oysters they let go the box and dived down for them. They swam about for hour after hour and seemed never to tire, or to suffer any inconvenience.

In this way the banks of the Gulf, or at least the shallower of them, must be scoured of their oysters efficiently, in spite of the persistence of ancient methods and the sharp decline in the number of ships and men in the business.

We stayed in this reef anchorage while the fleet was on the adjacent bank, and Sheikh Mohamed bought many parcels of good pearls. In the evenings, in the brief interval between light and darkness, we ate our meal, and then visited the other ships or were visited, yarned with nakhodas and other merchants, admired their pearls, and gloated over our own. With the setting of the sun came the muezzin's call, and then the evening prayer. After that a drum might beat aboard a Beduin craft from the Kuwait coast, or there might be a brief flare of camel-thorn as a late comer warmed some coffee. After that, silence, for the night is given to sleep. The little ships rolled and pitched at their anchorage and jostled and bumped together, but the pearlmen, packed like sardines, slept the heavy sleep of the exhausted until daybreak. Then they were up again, opening their oysters: the previous day's catch always stood in its sacks overnight for the oysters to die. They were more easily opened when they were dead. While they were being opened the sun gained strength to light the divers at their undersea work. It was no use to dive before the sun was strong. It was no use to dive, either, on days when the fierce north wind filled the Gulf with stinging sand, and visibility was so impaired that the divers could not see one fathom down; or when the sea ran white-capped and the little ships plunged and bucked so much that diving was dangerous. There were many of these off-days, but for the most part the weather during the diving season was settled.

One of these days at the reef anchorage, we found old Yusuf. It was evening when he came – a very beautiful, calm evening, with the sunset colours soft and grand, and the songs of the pearlers coming in by sail and sweeps, giving the scene a romantic atmosphere which was far from real. The lovely lateen sails were mirrored in the deep blue. He came in with his sambuk, which had moved to the bank that day from some mysterious bank in mid-gulf which apparently was that nakhoda's own. I was horrified at the change in his appearance. His face was strained and gaunt; his grey hair was greyer and more scanty than ever; his cheeks were sunken until they seemed only skin stretched over shrunken bone; his feet and hands were lacerated, though he had leather tips on his nails to protect them from the jagged rocks and coral spikes. His stomach was hollow, as though there were nothing in it and had been nothing for weeks. He could not stand upright; his body had bent over his empty stomach. His legs were thin, worn almost to the bone. His feet and hands were water-worn and shrivelled. The skin on his thin legs was covered with a rash of what appeared to be small pimples, many of which had come to a head and broken.

Many of the divers in his sambuk – and others – had this disease on their legs, and some also on the arms. It must have been very painful. I had noticed it before in the *Triumph*; it never responded to any treatment, though if the sailors could be kept out of salt water for a time it appeared to show some improvement. Poor Yusuf was a sorry sight. He had aged twenty years, and he seemed more dead than alive. He greeted me cheerfully, however; there was nothing wrong with his spirit. If he accepted his fate with resignation, there was nothing stolid or apathetic about him. It was a courageous kind of resignation.

He told us their take of pearls was bad. They had found many, but none of the first quality and very few of the second. It was amazing to notice how rare first-quality pearls were. In the two months I was on the banks, seeing pearls by the bagful every day, I don't think I saw more than a dozen which were really large, flawless gems. Sheikh Mohamed said the Gulf fisheries yielded no more than two first-rate necklaces in any year.

In the morning I went out with Yusuf's craft to spend the day on board watching the diving. The old man would accept nothing from me except a few cigarettes and a handful of dates. The divers, he said, could not eat. It was better not to eat. A few dates in the morning and some coffee, a bite at night when the day's work was through – that was all. They could not dive on full stomachs, or they would die. He had only another six or seven weeks to go. He could stand it; he had stood it for twenty years before. At first it had been hard, after having, by the grace of Allah, been away from the banks five years; but now he was used to the hardships. Only six more weeks. It would have seemed an eternity to me.

We were out on the banks when the sun had been an hour risen, and the water was limpid and clear. The seven sacks of oysters from the previous day, opened at dawn immediately the prayer was ended, had yielded only a teaspoonful of pearls, none of them of the best quality. Truly the luck was bad, for other craft at the anchorage had taken good pearls and the admiral's sambuk had 10,000 rupees' worth already. *Allah karim*! The Lord was merciful. Their luck would change. I hoped so, as I watched old Yusuf make ready for the dive.

The sambuk was an old one which had been on the beach four years, but it was larger than most, and in good order. It had eight sweeps a side. It was decked, and without bulwarks, like all the pearlers. When the sambuk was anchored, the sweeps lay athwart the ship, lashed to the thole-pins and standing out over the sea at right angles to the ship. The sweeps were always left like that out on the banks, for they were of importance to the diving. To each sweep there were two divers, and one tender. The divers' lines passed over their sweeps to prevent any possibility of becoming entangled. Over each sweep – and they were worn by the constant passing and repassing of the lines – hung a piece of coir line about fifteen fathoms long, to which a stone was attached. The divers went down with this stone, which was hauled up again as soon as they had reached the bottom. They took down with them another line to which was fastened a light basket made of roping stuff on a neck of twisted cane. This they held, and it was their life-line as well as their oyster basket. If they lost hold of this, they were done. They dived in tiny black shorts, and wore no other garments.

Yusuf had a piece of string round his neck with a nose-clip attached to it. His nose-clip was made form a piece of ram's horn, but some of the other divers' were of wood. Before each dive he carefully adjusted this clip; it was all the protection he had. I asked him why all the divers wore something black, and he said that the big fish, the sharks, did not like black. So long as they wore black they were safe. This was a comforting belief, but I wondered how well-founded it was. If there were giant rays about, he said, they would wear a wisp of white also. There were no rays that day, and they all wore only these black shorts. Each diver seemed to possess two pairs of black shorts and one sarong. As they came up shivering after their turn of ten dives and were hauled on board again, they changed their shorts, hung the wet ones to dry, and stood round the camel-thorn fire until it was time to go down again.

There were two shifts of divers, one to a sweep on each side, each doing ten dives and then resting ten. Yusuf said he dived about 120 times a day, more in shallow water. Each dive averaged about a minute; anything from forty seconds to ninety seemed the rule. Thus he spent two hours a day on the bottom of the Gulf, without air. Two hours a day! It seemed a great deal to me. But there were spells, he said: they rested one day in ten, though sometimes, if they were on a good bank in diving weather, they worked eighteen days and rested two. They went in to a beach for rest, because the ship needed fresh water and fuel. The sailors, who did the tending of the divers, went in search of fuel and water while the divers had a meal, and slept.

Now old Yusuf, hanging to his rope, was in the water by the aftermost sweep on the starboard side. That was his place. It was the place of the head diver who was always expected to bring up the most oysters. He hung there a moment, treading water and adjusting his nose-clip. The tally of ten bones rove on a date frond on a stanchion aft showed that no dives had yet been made. As a dive was made, the aftermost hauler moved one bone along the frond; when all ten were moved he shouted, and the divers came back aboard to be relieved by their mates. There were thirty-two divers, twenty tenders, a nakhoda, a clerk, a cook, and five boys. So far as I could see, all the boys did was to keep the hookahs filled, to fetch water to wash the sailors' hands at meal times, and to stand in a group about the nakhoda every time the anchorage was shifted, ready to pass on his orders with a shrill yelling that could be heard above the din of song from the sixty men. One of the boys was Yusuf's son, aged six.

"I see him, when he is here," the old man said. "But I will see he incurs no debts."

Yusuf was ready to dive. He took his basket, holding it by the rim. He took a twist of one leg about the rope with the stone, with his foot on the stone. He looked up at his tender. The tender let go; down he went, down, down. I could watch him drop three, four fathoms. I saw the tide take him and sweep him astern, a brown blur in the blue water. Then he was gone. A few seconds and, feeling it loose as it took the ground, his tender hauled up the stone, caught it with a slippery hitch about the sweep, and then took Yusuf's basket-line and carefully tended that, slacking out and feeling for the slight tug which would indicate that Yusuf's lungs could stand no more, and his dive was done. How long he was down! It seemed a long time waiting there. I did not count the seconds, at first. They seemed like minutes. All the divers were down now. There was silence aboard as the tenders, erect and alert, held the lines. Still the divers were down. The lines were taut, all leading aft, each separated from the others by the round arm of the sweeps. It was obvious that there must be a considerable set running there; Yusuf, the aftermost diver, must have been thirty yards astern of the ship. Still he was down. A minute had passed. It seemed like five minutes to me. Now! A slight tug, barely perceptible, and the tender was hauling in fast, hand over hand, long pulls and strong. He hauled and hauled, but it was a long time before I saw any sign of Yusuf. Now I could see a faint brown smudge deep below, at an angle of forty-five degrees from the vessel. Quickly the smudge grew; it became the blurred outline of a man; it was the head and shoulders of a man, the close-cropped grey head of a man. It was old Yusuf. Here he came, breaking water at last. His oyster basket first, well-filled with oysters, then his old head with an arm thrown up to shield his water-tired eyes from the glare of the sun, and his shoulders streaming water like a seal. He blew once, like a whale, slipped off his clip, drew in the air, trod water at his sweep by the ship's side. The tender hauled the coir basket aboard.

Now all the divers had come to the surface; Yusuf was the last. The tenders took their baskets. Some were half-filled, some were quarter-filled, some had as few as two or three oysters in them. Each tender held his basket aloft, turning inboard. Then, '*Allah karim*!' was the shout, followed by a deep-toned '*Y'Allah*!', as the contents of the baskets were thrown on the deck, making a clatter as they fell. 'God is merciful!' 'Oh God!'

By this time the divers were sufficiently rested. They dived one minute, rested two; then took their baskets again and their stones, adjusted their nose-clips, and were down. Again the long, almost alarming, pause before the grey heads broke surface again, and the muddy oysters came up in their bags. Again the shout '*Allah karim*!' '*Y'Allah*!'; again the clatter of oysters on the wet deck, the shifting of the tally bone, the blowing of the divers.

Ten times they dived, while their reliefs sat aft, dispassionate, stolid, seemingly disinterested. Ten times they dived, and then were hauled in again. Their mates slipped into the water to take up the work, while Yusuf and his shift shivered and shook round the cook's poor fire, where nothing was cooking. A scrap of sail had been spread there to give them shelter; the day was young and they felt cold. To me the day was almost unbearably hot, for the early morning shade temperature was over a hundred. Yet the divers, bent and haggard, stood and shivered in their sarongs.

As the strength of the sun increased, awnings of cheap Japanese material were spread fore-and-aft, for the sun beat down all day on the hard-working tenders. If the divers ate nothing they went without food; if the divers could not eat, no meal was cooked. There was no midday meal on the banks. Many of the divers were Beduin, many of the tenders Persian, and others negroes, ex-slaves. By this time, twenty dives had been made in the one place and all the oysters had been scoured from there. The cable was veered and the ship dropped back thirty yards, in the tide. Again Yusuf slipped to the side and into the sea; again came the ten dives, the number of oysters in his basket decreasing each time. I asked him how he worked. How could he stay down, without weights. It was an eight-fathom bank. He said he crawled along the bottom with his eyes open; he had to fight his way, clutching coral spikes and rocks. When he saw oysters, he forced them from the rock and put them in his basket. He had to be quick. He went as far from the ship as he could. Each man kept to his own part of the bottom, going back with the set from his sweep, and immediately his stone was on the bottom, setting off as directly at right angles to the ship as he could. In this way they covered the bottom thoroughly, missing little.

Again ten dives, ten rests; ten dives, ten rests; more cable veered. Half a sackful of oysters had been taken. The oysters were kept in sacks by the bole of the mizzenmast. The decks were wet and the whole ship was nothing but a wet, congested working platform. The tenders sweated and the divers shivered; the tenders were fat and the divers painfully lean; the tenders knew no rest and the divers no warmth. Gaunt, hollow-cheeked men, they squatted by the fire until it was their turn to dive. The tenders wore red and blue sarongs, the nakhoda a white shirt, the divers only their black. The wet and crowded decks had only space for the men; by the fire were some bundles of camel-thorn, and empty water-skins. The fresh water was in wooden tanks in the hold. Aft lay the inevitable sick diver –

there were two in this sambuk. Forward were some fish-traps made of coir weighted with oyster-shells; underneath the poop, by the nakhoda's bench, was the chest of pearls. There was only one chest on the poop, the nakhoda's; there was only one rough sleeping-place. Above the poop and all round were tied the little bundles of the crew's possessions, each in his own small bag – a rag of clothing, prayer beads, a leaf or two of coarse Persian tobacco, a tooth-stick. Nothing else – no bedding, no medicine, no comforts.

Still they dived, broke surface, blew, and rested. The cable veered; the boys piped their loud 'Belay!' The decks were a mess of sea slime and crawling things from the newly caught oysters. The sun climbed high, and its heat shimmered over the broiling sea. It was a day of dead calm. Away from us on either beam across the banks were the other ships, scores of them, now with the splash of sweeps glinting in the sun and the chant of the toiling crew, now silent for the dive, the farther ones miraged so that they seemed immense, and the genoa jib of a Beduin shewe looking like a flaccid balloon. As the day advanced, the heat grew until, though I thought myself acclimatised, it was nearly unbearable. Still the work continued. These were ideal conditions for diving.

With the cable veered to the end it was hauled in again, the divers huddled by the fire not sharing in this work unless they wished to stamp some circulation back into their bones, the sailors dancing and chanting. The sailors did the tending and the ship's work; the divers only dived. They were too weak to work; every ounce of energy they had went into the dive.

Now the sailors dance along the deck in two endless lines, round and round, clapping their great hands and singing as the taut cable comes in, fathom after fathom, dripping wet. Now the anchor – it is a piece of stone with a spike in it – is up-and-down; it is broken out. "Man the sweeps!" Two men to a sweep and three at the stroke, the sailors dip lustily into the sea and strain at the huge sweeps. Each of the sweeps is eighteen feet long. I begin to understand what life in the old galleys must have been like, and to see, too, why big craft can never be moved at speed with only one tier of sweeps. It is slow, heavy, painful work, all done with chant and rhythm. I think I see now how much of the Kuwait deep-water style has come from the banks. They are the same songs, the same chants, the same hand-clappings. the same deep grunting, the same powerful deck stampings, the same steps in the brief intervals of dancing.

The long sweeps flash through the air with perfect rhythm, bite deep into the sea; the straining sailors, wet with sweat, walk their inboard ends along the deck, their muscles bulging, their throats vibrant with song. The nakhoda, hawk-eyed old man, watches. He must know these waters better than most of their own fish, though how he gains such knowledge is a mystery. How he tells one bank from another, I do not know, for they are out of sight of land here. Yet he knows; he knows exactly where his ship is to go, and sees that she goes there. His clerk is at the tiller; he nods to him to steer this way or that. The boys stand ready by the mizzenmast to echo his orders. The drums are beating forward to mark the rhythm of the sweeps. Now and again comes a burst of laboured breathing from a sailor at the sweeps, but always they sing – praises to Allah, prayers for great pearls. The sambuk crawls across the burnished sea in a din of song. Now, now it is enough! A nod from the nakhoda, a shrill shriek from the boys – belay, belay! Way enough! The stone anchor goes down; the sweeps are secured outboard, the stones and the basket-lines are thrown across them.

Before the dive starts at this new place, the sailors gather round the mainmast. Hands over their ears or on their jawbones, their bodies bent, they give out that great chesty growl of Kuwait, that long-drawn noise of rumbling that comes only from the extraordinary vocal chords of the Gulf sailors. It sounds like a pack of subdued lions hungry for a meal, like a pit of heavy bears growling for a bone, like the rumbling of a deep volcano. It is an extraordinary noise, and I could never make it, try as I would. The amazing growls continue a long time. Why? I ask old Yusuf. Is it to scare off sharks, stingrays, *jinns*? But he does not know. Nobody knows. It is the Gulf style. Perhaps is it the survival of an ancient ritual for scaring off bad *jinns*, calling up good ones, or intimidating the oysters far beneath the keel. There are many survivals in these Kuwait ships. Why is there always the strange black end to the long stemheads, themselves perhaps survivals from phallic worship? Why the sacrifice of the kid at launchings? This is done to this day at Ma'alla, and elsewhere. Why now this curious noise-making on the pearling banks?

Now there has been grunting enough. Suddenly, at a nod from the nakhoda, the boys shrill forth again. The noise stops. The divers shuffle to the side; the dive begins again. Ten dives down, ten rests; basket after basket of slimy oysters flung down on deck: '*Allah karim*! *Y'Allah*!'; the cable veered; ten dives again, ten rests; the grey heads breaking the blue water, the tired arms flung across weary eyes, great chests bursting into a sob of breath as the nose-clips are removed. Ten dives again, ten rests; and the cable veered. Ten dives again, and ten rests; and the cable veered.

The sun is high now, the heat dreadful. The weak shade of the awnings serves only to darken the decks and not to shade them. Still the haggard divers shiver and crowd by the brushwood fire. Some pray. It is the midday prayer. There is no siesta on the banks. Ten dives again, ten rests. And the cable veered. No food. The air is breathless and deadly hot. A boy hauls in a fish-trap forward: no catch. Ten dives again, ten rests. Poor Yusuf! This life must be the death of many good men.

I know that hardship recorded from a writer's notes may often be more harrowing than the actual experience. The stories of some Cape Horn roundings are painful. But the capacity of the human frame to endure punishment can be well-nigh unbelievable. Yet, judged by any standard I know, compared with any form of maritime hardship I have experienced, or seen, or read about, pearling in the Persian Gulf can be terrible indeed. I came away from Kuwait favourably impressed by most aspects of its life, keenly enthusiastic about its ships, and an admirer of its seamen. But the infernal *ghaus*, the hellish diving, is another matter. If there must be pearls, let them be dredged.

I left poor Yusuf there, making his ten dives, shivering through his ten rests, as fervent a believer in the mercy of Allah as any of them. God has been merciful to him if only in the granting of that comforting belief, a belief without which his life would be unbearable.

A month later I was back in Kuwait. The smallest ship I had seen was a little thing fourteen feet long with a crew of one old man and four boys, aged between twelve and seventeen; the largest was the sambuk of the admiral, Sheikh Sabah. I had seen quite enough of pearling and found nothing to admire in that romantic industry, except the courage and the fortitude of the crews.

XX

NEJDI'S OTHER WIFE

BACK IN KUWAIT all was activity. It was not yet the end of August, but many of the ships were being got ready for their new voyages, and the two miles of the waterfront hummed with the activities of the fitting-out. During the latter part of August and throughout September, ship after ship was floated out of her laying-up berth and taken into the bay to be rigged and ballasted for the passage to Basra, where the dates had ripened and the export of the new season's crop was in progress.

At each high tide from ten to twenty of the larger ships were floated off, and the smaller ones were towed out with every flood. The basins along the length of the town resounded all day long with the chanting of the sailors, and the shore road was full of hurrying nakhodas and seamen joining their ships. Wherever there was an open space, sailors squatted sewing sails. Carpenters worked feverishly to complete the new booms in time for the season. Here one was being hauled out on the mud at low water; there, another was being pushed broadside into the bay at the top of springs, for it had been built in a restricted place on high ground and could only be launched broadside. It went in with a splash, rolled once or twice, with its flags flying, and then steadied, its sea career begun. The sailors who had helped launch it leapt at once into the water and swam out to the new ship, in their clothes, to begin the work of rigging. The booms are launched as stripped-down hulls and rigged out in the bay. It does not take long. A few days suffices to see the masts stepped and the lateen yards rigged up, the wheel shipped, and the compass placed in its binnacle.

Ships, ships, ships, all along the sea. Sailors, quartermasters, carpenters, nakhodas, all along the shore road – what a place this Kuwait was. The ring of caulking irons, the throaty songs of sailors stepping the masts, the thump of Indian drums and the slapping of great hands as the undersides of the deep-watermen were paid with tallow and lime, the clank clank of ancient capstans warping in a pearler to the beach, the shouts of the sailors hauling out her yards to a newly floated boom, the ring of the marine blacksmith's irons as he beat out ironwork for the ships, the ripping of the Persian saws through the logs of Malabar teak high on the cutting stage, the thud of drums and the burst of joyful song from a pearling sambuk coming in from the *ghaus* – these were the sounds of the waterfront all day and every day, with respite only for prayer.

The weather was milder as September passed, and sometimes there were tolerable days, for the worst of the dreadful heat of the sun was gone and the Beduin were moving out of town. As the big ships went out the Beduin went, and the pearlers came in. The Beduin went out to the desert, the sailors to the sea. If activity had increased along the waterfront so it had also in the bazaar, for the Beduin made haste to complete their purchases, and the business men and the money-changers had their hands full. Sailors were buying their scanty needs, and a venture or two to take with them; the coffee-shops were crowded nightly, and the pearling coffee-shop was busy all day with the pearl men come in from the sea to sell their pearls. The deep-sea nakhodas cast critical eyes at the Persian carpets dragged in the dust, seeking bargains to take to Mogadishu and Zanzibar. The nakhodas' coffee-shop was deserted in the daylight hours and the crowds came only in the evenings, for the nakhodas were busy buying their ships and fixing freights, collecting advances on their freights, and giving advances to their crews. From merchants' office to merchants' coffee-shop the nakhodas hurried, fat after the summer at home but not so fat that they could not hurry when there was business to be done.

This year there was much business, for during the long summer evenings on the waterfront there had been much discussion, and many decisions had been made. The nakhodas of the deep-sea ships demanded that every vessel on a long voyage should carry a muallim as well as a nakhoda, for it is not right that one man only should know the way. They demanded, too, that the merchants should pay demurrage when they fixed the freights from the Shatt-el-Arab and then kept the booms waiting for weeks before the dates were delivered – an old grievance, this, and one difficult to avoid. One thing more they wanted, an end to the practice of holding a nakhoda always responsible for his ship's debts, and all advances of freight and so forth, even after his ship is lost. This is another old practice, and not a very honest one, for the nakhodas, though they nominally own their ships, are rarely the real owners. It is unfair, the nakhodas argued, that if they lose a ship which never really belonged to them, they should still be responsible for its debts. In other words, the existing system of nominal ownership was not good enough: by permitting the nakhodas to finance the ships themselves, the merchants transferred what rightly should be their own risk to the nakhodas. If a ship were lost, the nakhodas argued, that should be loss enough; the loss of the freight should fall on the merchant. But the merchants argued that they lost the dates, and that was loss enough. The ships belonged to the nakhodas, and the debts to the merchants. Debts must be paid. I heard a great deal of argument about all this and it seemed to me that right was on the nakhodas' side, but the merchants granted only that a muallim should be carried. If the nakhodas could make new rules, they said, so could they, and they were in a better position to enforce them than the nakhodas were. The nakhodas had decided to stand together, but they did not. Here and there one went over to a better merchant. Soon their points were lost, and they went out again without demurrage, still responsible for finance as well as freights, still as heavily indebted to the merchants.

It did not pay the merchants to own and run ships themselves, for the liking of the Arab for private trade and bargain-driving was too ingrained. If the nakhodas ran the merchants' ships, they were too prone to run them only for their own benefit. It was better, then, that the merchants should finance the nakhodas to run the ships, and use them only for such freights as they needed. The advances were well secured. There was no insurance to pay; the unfortunate nakhodas, it seemed to me, were the insurance. When they lost their ships, they lost their livelihood and the merchants' money besides, but they had to repay the merchants' money. Interest was not charged. It was forbidden by the Prophet. They were merely required to pay back more than they had borrowed.

The nakhodas' worries, however, were the nakhodas' own, and not the sailors': the sailors held no meetings and drew up no rules. They went out again in the ships to which they were bound.

Days passed, and ship after ship moved out to the north, many of them going lightly rigged, for the passage up to the Shatt-el-Arab is very short. The muallims, many of them newly appointed, often took the ships to the Shatt-el-Arab to wait for the dates, while the nakhodas adjusted financial matters in Kuwait, or stayed as long as possible to enjoy the delights of their harims. The scene along the waterfront remained busy and most interesting. By the al-Kalifa mosque a gang of sailmakers worked in the shade, sewing a mainsail a hundred and sixty feet long. Wooden water tanks were being fish-oiled, anchors freshly tarred carried out to their vessels, parrals of the lateen yards adjusted, sails carried along rolled up like circus tents, longboats taken from their summer coverings of matting and floated into the sea. Small boys played about with model booms which they sailed and scampered after in the shallow water, singing the sailors' songs as they played. Nakhodas interviewed muallims – generally their own relatives – along the shady stone benches on the west side of their homes. Ships were being built, paid, caulked, repaired, launched, floated off, rigged, danced to, and sung about. The little reed huts of the *khubz* makers, and the wayside stands of the sherbet sellers, did good business.

In one of the basins near the middle of the town, Nasir's little *Cat* stood silent, the last deep-waterman left behind her breaker, and little Nasir himself sat on his bench waiting for the pearlers to return. Nasir was a poor man, and the *Cat* was old. He could not afford big advances, and his little *Cat* could not earn much. Nasir, then, must take such seamen as he could find; and so he waited for the pearlers to return. The poor pearlers, more penniless than ever, after their dreadful season, were in a better mood to accept the little he could offer. The *Cat* would wait. There would be dates enough for her.

For the hundredth time I walked across the flats to look at the lovely lines of the ancient *Cat*, which had never seemed cat-like to me. She was a sweet-lined and beautiful old vessel, but I had long noticed with regret that her hull was strained, after half a century of timber carrying. Her decks were warped and sunken by her mainmast; she wept a fastening now and then, and I picked them up, poor rusted spikes of indifferent iron, in the mud all round her. No, it would not do. It would be foolhardy to take such a ship on a long voyage in the Atlantic Ocean, without hoping for – and urgently needing – more good fortune from the weather and from God than the mariner has a right to expect. The poor *Cat* must stay in Kuwait: I could not save her. She might be bought for 5,000 rupees; little Nasir, who knew my interest, always sang her praises – not that he wished to be rid of his sweet baggala, for he loved her. Yet he knew her days were done. If I took her, it was better than the Suri. He could buy a boom with the money.

But I could not take the *Cat*, much as I should have liked to: it was September now and there were more serious things afoot in Europe than the saving of the lovely *Cat*. So I left Nasir, waiting for his pearlers. He had sailed the *Cat* twenty-three years, I knew, with a year off once for the Hajj. I knew, too, that I was unlikely to find a sweeter old baggala in these days, or ever again, for she belonged to the days when Kuwait ships were built by craftsmen who added each plank with loving care, after the most painstaking deliberation. Her carpenter was a man who so loved the ships he built that he left instructions that his body must be buried where ships would be built over it; he wished to be near the ships he loved, even in death.

One day I met our carpenter from the *Triumph*, the youthful Kaleel. He was shipbuilding again, and I found him helping with the laying of the keel of a new boom. He was working hard, and all the carpenters were rushing at their work almost as hard as the sailors do at theirs. "What is the hurry?" I asked.

"We always hurry like this now," he said. "It is not good – rush, rush, rush! That is not the way to build ships. Here, you will see that we build three planks a day – three planks a day on both sides."

He went on to tell me of the days when the *Cat* was built, and the big *Samhan*, and all the best of the Kuwait ships. They were the days, he said. None but bearded carpenters touched the planks of new ships then, and the proper rate of progress was one plank a day. Work was leisurely, painstaking, and thorough. Nothing mattered but that it should be well done. Only old skilled men, shipwrights with beards, were permitted to do the actual placing of a vessel's timbers, and all others, even carpenters of ten years' experience, sawed planks and drilled holes. A plank a day was the proper rate of progress, for everything had to be first-class and no other condition was tolerated. Discipline over apprentices and labourers was strict, and apprenticeship long and arduous. Every man, when a ship was launched, felt a sense of personal pride in the achievement, and the old greybeards went from ship to ship along the waterfront criticising, commending, improving. There was time for embellishment and good carving in those days, and old carpenters asked to be buried in the shipyards, beneath the keels of ships. Those were the days, Kaleel said. He was not an old man; he was only twenty-four. He scarcely remembered the conditions he depicted. He had heard of them from his father, a carpenter before him, and regretted their passing. Now all was rush and bustle, he concluded, with as little care in the workmanship as in the selection of the timbers. A great ship, instead of taking eight or nine months to build, was turned out in two; and in less than fifteen years she was fit for nothing but scrap. Fifty years was a great age now for an Arab ship: it used to be a hundred.

I listened to much the same kind of talk in the evening walks round the waterfront. I always stopped at the home of Kalifa al-Ganim, head of the clan of the Abdul-wahhabs, those fine nakhodas. Kalifa al-Ganim was a man over seventy, a dignified bearded man with a soft gentle voice and a great knowledge of the history of Kuwait, and the ways of the sea. I often sat and chatted with him, sometimes in his private room in the house overlooking the waterfront, with its yard before it where his sons' booms were built; sometimes I talked with him and the other wise men, in their evening meeting. For these they always sat in a long row, seated on carpets and leaning against cushions, with their aghals thrown off and their sandals on the street before them, and their backs against a wall. They were a dignified, stately line of elderly gentlemen, and I was honoured to be received among them.

We used generally to talk of the early days of Kuwait, and how shipbuilding had grown there. Kuwait, they said, was perhaps the youngest port of the whole Persian Gulf. Kalifa al-Ganim said that, as a city, it was probably not much more than two centuries old. It had always been a seafaring place, first because the Beduin had to fish to live; secondly because Bahreini and Hasa pearlers moved up there, for it was a better base for the northern banks; and thirdly, when the Persians over-running Basra seriously affected the carrying and distributing trade of that port, much of it went to Kuwait. Kuwait was well situated geographically as a port of distribution for northern Nejd. Remaining independent, it was, moreover, an excellent port for the infiltration of goods over a wide area of Iraq and Iran. Its merchants were good merchants and its shipbuilders, brought in from Muscat and Bahrein and from the Persian ports of Qishm and Lingeh, made a name for themselves throughout the eastern seas.

More and more settlers came, people from Zubara in Qatar, who had gone there originally from Nejd; people from Zubair on the Iraq frontier; people coming directly from Nejd; and later, many Persians. Kuwait had a tradition of good government, old Kalifa said; this tradition it has kept. Its merchants, too, had a name for fair dealing. Its nakhodas were good men and its sailors, even a hundred years ago, had a name for being the best from Arabia. A hundred years ago, Kalifa said, Kuwait could send two hundred ships to sea, not counting pearlers. Most of them were small, but he spoke of a baggala of over 400 tons which his grandfather remembered. Perhaps twenty were vessels of more than 100 tons. Their trade was to India, in the Gulf, round the coasts of Arabia, and to Red Sea ports of Africa. They did not then sail much to East Africa. That was a trade jealously guarded by the Omani. The town was prosperous enough to satisfy its hard-living inhabitants, and not rich enough to tempt the marauder – not at any rate, when Basra was so near.

Kuwait came to the forefront of Arab ports under the great Sheikh Mubarak, who murdered his way to sheikhdom shortly before the turn of the last century. Kalifa pointed out to me the house where the murders were done. Mubarak's usurpation was a good thing for Kuwait, he said, though the Kuwaiti did not at first approve of it. Mubarak was an ambitious and despotic man, but he governed the city state with an able patriarchal hand, and it prospered. The decline of other ports farther down the Gulf; the slipshod methods of the easy-going Turks who succeeded the Persians in Basra; troubles in Bahrein and in Persia; the decline of Muscat after Seyyid Said – all these things helped Kuwait. Its pearling prospered; its ships continued to make good voyages. Now the port could muster upwards of a thousand ships of all shapes and sizes – 150 large deepwater booms, 200 smaller Gulf traders, 200 pearlers, with 300 more on the beach, if there were trade for them, 200 fishermen.

The Kuwaiti, with their background of desert hardship and of troubles elsewhere, appreciated the comparative quietness of Kuwait, and I found in them all a great love for the city state. Sometimes the intelligentsia, dropping in at these evening talks, were more apologetic than they needed to be, and spoke of the democracy of Iraq as an ideal to strive for. Youths coming back in silk trousers from Iraq affected a great discontent with their own Arabian Kuwait; but it seemed to me an honest, straightforward, and satisfying place, despite the backwardness which they alleged. The silk-clad youths could leave again, if they did not like it; Kuwait was for the real Arabs. I should hate to see its women suddenly unveiled and all its citizens in trousers and the curious Italian headgear affected in Iraq. I should hate to see Diesel engines put into its fine booms, the Sheikh in a sun-helmet, the stalwart habitués of the coffee-shops trooping into the cinemas. Kuwait is all right as it is, and its citizens can effect the necessary improvements gradually – good schools, paved streets, a proper water system, hospitals, control of public health. Kuwait has had a municipal council for seven years; it has taken these things in hand. The coming of oil, still in the experimental stage when I left, will provide the revenue.

Late one afternoon I met Nejdi, in front of the divers' shop in the *suq*. The divers' shop is not far from the women's market, where elderly women squat in the street and try to sell junk from four o'clock onwards every afternoon. It is on a side street, among the old clothes stalls, next to one that sells old Finnish uniforms. Its wares are nose-clips, black shorts, white diving shirts (to frighten off the rays), cane rings for the oyster baskets, lengths of rough-laid coir, lead weights – I did not see these used – and black diving suits to be used, I suppose, in waters where sharks were particularly bad. Here I met Nejdi, not looking at anything in the divers' shop; he was merely passing by. He told me that Abdulla, his brother, had a new boom which the family had just bought, and that he would be sending both Abdulla's boom and his own to Basra within a few days. Would I like to come down to the dancing when they were paid? It would be good. But I had my fill of dancing along the waterfront every morning, for all the booms in Kuwait were being paid, and the ceremony had become commonplace. He had, he told me, managed to pay off his sailors with 135 rupees a share – poor, he knew, for the previous year it had been 165. But his was the best rate paid in Kuwait that season. Radhwan had paid only 95, Abdul-wahhab 125, big Abdul-wahhab 120. It was a bad year.

I could see there was something on Nejdi's mind and, taking me into a quiet corner in a coffee-shop, he confided in me. He was in trouble, he said. It was over the virgin Ayesha. Virgin! She had not been virgin since she was nine. The story of the ex-virgin Ayesha, it seemed, had to do with a car-ride Nejdi had taken her in a hired vehicle over the sands one night, beyond the walls. Her servant was with her, for no member of the harim would dare go out from a house alone. It seemed that the servant would herself have welcomed the attentions of our handsome Nejdi and did not hesitate to make this clear. But Nejdi had the ill-grace to be unresponsive; the wench was far from comely and the fair Ayesha was a much more satisfactory object for his affections. Then the maid went home and told. This was serious, for Ayesha was the daughter of a prominent man. Worse still, not only Ayesha was involved, but her sisters Miriam and Fatima, it was discovered, had been equally indiscreet. What could a poor sailor do, Nejdi asked plaintively, when he came in from the sea to find his wives ill? There were so many fair damsels in the town. If a sailor did not care for them, who would? He appeared to look upon himself as something of a public benefactor. He had, I found, Ayeshas and Miriams and Fatimas in almost every street. When his ship was laid up, and his sailors pearling, he lived the life of a Casanova.

I had long noticed that, whenever I walked in a back street with Nejdi, there was a constant rustle of black silk behind almost every doorway.

Fair hands emerged from latticed windows in the rooms overhead, and notes fluttered down which Nejdi picked up and thrust in his pockets. Often old Swahili women, slaves, would run after him and pass him a hurried message as they slipped by. He always had his eyes on the roof and upper parts of the houses. I soon discovered why he did this. Members of the harim often showed there. If a pretty girl showed herself on a rooftop, Nejdi said, she was ready for adventure. He took note of all we saw and marked the streets. Afterwards, he had some way of getting in touch with brokers, go-betweens, who would arrange a meeting with the damsel. They would take his notes, bring hers. Black slave-women, little boys, younger brothers in the poorer classes – these were his brokers, and the town was full of them. I was amazed: I should never have known these things had it not been for the confidence of Nejdi and his boon companions. I was surprised to see how beautiful some of these girls were.

Now fate had caught up with him and he was aggrieved. The fair Ayesha had been immured in her home, and there she would stay for three months until it was known definitely whether she was pregnant. If she was, the chances of her getting out of that room, I gathered, were slight; but Nejdi was not worried about that. She knew enough, he said, not to be pregnant. What bothered him was the accusation that he had 'ruined' her. In all his amorous adventures Nejdi had one strict rule, and that was never to touch a virgin. The Prophet, he said, had enjoined all men against tampering with virgins, for a man who spoiled a virgin was responsible for her whole subsequent history. A non-virgin could not marry; and if she did, she would be driven from her deceived bridegroom's house in public disgrace.

The matter was sufficiently serious to force Nejdi, at least temporarily, to a new way of life. His two wives, I gathered, were again with child. The father of Ayesha and her sisters had been to the mosque about him. It had been decided that he must take a new wife, outside Kuwait. He was going to marry a maiden of Zubair: would I like to come? Would I be a guest at his wedding? He was leaving for Zubair in the morning, Nejdi said, stooping to pick up a scented note that had just fluttered from an open latticed window. He read it out: it was a warning that some husband was watching him. We left in the morning, and I went to Nejdi's wedding at Zubair. He said he did not wish his two wives in Kuwait to know about it, explaining that what they did not know would not hurt them. But, I asked, why the secrecy if you are not afraid of them? He had preached to me always that a man may have four wives. It was so, Nejdi said, but sometimes women do not understand. If a man can satisfy his women and they bear him sons, that is sufficient. But alas! women have tongues.

We went quietly to Zubair, and it was a very quiet wedding. Zubair is about a hundred miles north of Kuwait, close across the Iraq border. Though it is within twenty miles of the modernised city of Basra, where the women walk unveiled in the streets and you may buy all the intoxicants you want, it remains strictly a town of Nejd. Nejdi, I gathered, had chosen it for this reason. Not for him any of these modern ideas; he was against them, even for men. So he had chosen a maiden of Zubair, where he had relatives who could keep an eye on her while he was at sea, and he knew she would not be contaminated.

We came to Zubair by night, and went to the courtyard behind the wall of the maiden's house. It was very quiet and no more solemn than any ordinary evening visiting. The bride's father and an uncle were there, some of Nejdi's people, and I. When we had drunk three rounds of coffee – it was proper always to drink three rounds – an elderly *imam* arrived from the mosque. Without even bothering to drink coffee, he went to work. He took Nejdi's hand in his right, and the bride's father's in his left. Then he mumbled a few words, and the ceremony was over before I knew it had begun. This was the ceremony; but it was scarcely the wedding. We went away, after more coffee, and slept in a courtyard at Zubair. It was the next evening, at the third hour after sunset, when Nejdi came to his bride. He had never seen her and knew nothing of her except that she was of good family, aged fifteen, could cook and sew and manage a household, and was recommended by his clanswomen, who had seen her. Apparently this clan recommendation was enough: he had to take a chance on her looks. But, he said, few girls of fifteen could be wholly undesirable, and he had urged his clanswomen to pick him a pretty bride.

We came down the narrow street of Zubair again to the place where his bride's people lived, and a small room had been built for him on a secluded part of the rooftop. Nejdi was in his best clothes, scented, and his short-clipped moustache well trimmed. His bright hawk's eyes shone with anticipation, even with some excitement, for a man did not marry a virgin every evening. At the doorway of the bride's home stood a group of Zubair women, swathed in black, waiting to see and hear the fun. We strode past them quickly, and one of them shouted, "What kind of a wedding is this? You come up the dark street without lights and without music? Which of you is the groom?" But Nejdi gave no answer: he wanted this kept quiet, though I saw that it hurt him that the thing was not done in style. He whispered that his other weddings had been better done than this. Six hundred men followed him to the home of his other brides. Now we were six.

We came to the stairs, and went up. Nejdi's little home was a comfortably furnished room made gay with candles and tinsel. It contained a table, a large Indian wardrobe, and a double bed. The floor was covered with two beautiful Persian carpets, smuggled from Kuwait. We filed in. The bride's father was there. We salaamed, sat a while, drank coffee and tea, and ate sweetmeats and little cakes. Nejdi could scarcely contain himself: I had never seen him so excited. Now, he whispered to me, I shall soon see her.

We sat about ten minutes; then, taking leave of Nejdi and wishing him luck, solemnly filed out and down the stairs again. We passed through the considerable crowd of women who waited there. So we were gone, and I returned to Kuwait in the morning. I never saw the bride, but when next I saw Nejdi, he smacked his lips and said she was a good wife. What Ayesha, languishing in her room, thought about it all I do not know. Nejdi himself was at sea within a month. His other wives did not know.

There was a noticeable lessening in the numbers at the sailors' coffee-shops, and even in the nakhodas'. By night along the waterfront, the voices of the old men were raised again. The young men were gone, and the greybeards came into their own again as the booms departed. Most of the pearlers were in, for it was the end of September, and the gaunt Beduin went off to their flocks when the sailors, thin and worn, returned to their ships. There was war in Europe, and the pearl market, which had been bad before, was almost non-existent. They were bad days, bewildering days, to the Arabs, who asked me what it was all about. But I was as bewildered as they were, and I had to go.

It was time to leave Kuwait and my friends the Arab sailors. I paid my final respects to His Highness the Sheikh, and went the round of the other dignitaries. His Highness was seated at his morning court on the upper verandah of Mubarak's palace, and I looked for the last time at the faded beauties adorning the rooms there, all with ornaments of large pearls, and out across the bay where some of the great ships were making ready at anchor. Mubarak had been gone for many years, but the beauties still looked down on those unused rooms, and Mubarak's grandson held his court on the verandah overlooking the sea. I thanked His Highness for the pleasure of my stay in Kuwait, drank some coffee with him, and chatted a little. A Beduin with a Bren gun stood behind His Highness, and other Beduin squatted about with loaded rifles in their hands, but this martial appearance was belied by the orderly peacefulness of the proceedings. He hoped, His Highness said, that Kuwait had been my home and that it would be so again. It had indeed; and I wish I could have shared his hope for the future.

I went then to Sheikh Ali Kalifa's, at his stockade. Two pearl thieves from Hasa hung on the cross in front of it. Where was my camel? asked old Ali Kalifa. There was war, I said, I had to hurry. "You will haste enough to this war on a camel," the good Sheikh said. I salaamed, and went away. They were taking the thieves down from the cross to lead them, disgraced, through the *suq* to the jail. I paid my respects to the admiral of the pearling fleet, Sheikh Sabah; to the president of the pearling court, Sheikh Abdulla bin Jaber; to Sheikh Abdulla bin Salim, the president of the Council of State; to my friends the old nakhodas, the wise men, the merchants. It took me some time to make my last round, for it had been easy to make good friends in Kuwait. It was in the heat of the noonday sun that I left at last, going out through the south gate with a Beduin wedding party dancing their way out arm-in-arm, and a flock of sheep and camels coming in. Asses ambled in water-laden from the wells beyond the walls, and the Beduin were striking their tents.

So I went from Kuwait, bound across the desert road to Basra and Europe, and I was sad at leaving the good city behind me. Troubles it has had, though less than most Arab towns of comparable size; difficulties it must surmount, too. But it has overcome its difficulties and solved its problems until now, and there is no reason why it should not continue to do so. Its ships and sailors are favourably known throughout the eastern seas; the lustre of its pearls is famous in Paris and New York; its merchants are respected from Syria to Singapore, from Cairo to Calicut. It is a pleasant place where the citizens live at peace, where the rich merchants – as is required of them by the Islamic law – take care of the poor, and the Sheikh is father to them all.

As I left in the sunshine, with the camel-trains coming in laden with brushwood and camel-thorn from the desert and a crowd of donkey-boys hurried singing on their tiny asses bound to the city's wells for garden water, I felt that I should have liked to stay there, to buy a baggala, to sit with the wise men another season, and learn more of the ways of the eastern seas. The sun shone brightly in a clear sky, but it was not hot. It was mild and pleasant and peaceful, and I thought that the red ensign of Kuwait, flying from the stockade and all the ships in the bay, was a standard I should like to sail and live under once again. Adieu, Kuwait! You build good ships, and your sailors can sail them.

EPILOGUE

In the shimmering waves of sickly heat that hung low over the Basra River, the hulls and masts of a hundred dhows were miraged strangely, so that the nearer vessels seemed to dance and tremble like leaves in a passing wind, and the dhows farthest away were separated from the water by a clearly defined but non-existent band of intervening air. It was October, but the port of Fao at the entrance to the Basra River was still insufferably hot. The day was windless, sultry, and humid almost beyond bearing. The green palms along the Iraq side stood with their roots in water and their mop-like heads in hell, and the ripe yellow dates clustered thick among the fronds. Away to the north, the smoke-wrack of Abadan, that mighty port of Persian oil, smeared ten miles of the inoffensive sky. The yellow waters of the wide river flowed swiftly out to sea, bearing laden dhows outward bound with dates. Dhows sailed, and dhows came in. All kinds of dhows lay off Fao, or moved slowly on the water – sweet-lined great booms from nearby Kuwait, shapely baggalas and sturdy sambuks from Sur, kotias from Bombay and the Gulf of Cutch, Persians, Omani, Hadhrami, dhows from the Mahra coast and the Trucial coast, and from Batina. Dates brought them all; they were the forerunners of the season's date fleet, to distribute the produce of Iraq over the eastern seas.

It was an animated and interesting scene, and might have been a pleasant one, had the day been not quite so hot and Fao not so excessively humid. At the small landing-stage in the heart of the port, longboats were coming and going, bringing in nakhodas, muallims, and quartermasters from the dhows. Stately Persians in white gowns and carefully rolled turbans; bearded and hennaed Suri in brown shirts and embroidered waistcoats; lithe Kuwaiti in gowns and headcloths of well-blued white, Hadhrami in knee-long sarongs and wisps of black worn below the knee; Indians in folds of flapping, diaphanous cotton-stuffs and silk shirts worn as coats – these came and went along the landing-place, bound on errands for their dhows. Far outside, beyond the bar at the river's mouth, the lovely triangles of lateen sails blurred upon the hot horizon showed where a trio of date dhows had sailed that morning, and now fretted in the calm outside waiting for the wind. As I watched, the big *el-Dhow* came slowly in from Kuwait, bound upstream to take her cargo from the landing-stage of a riverside plantation. Her skirted sailors hung round her rails feasting their green-hungry eyes upon the gardens as their ship sailed by. This green and this fresh water made up the Kuwaiti's Paradise. This was Hamed bin Salim's Paradise – this land where the water flowed and all things grew, and all a good Arab need do was to sleep and take his ease while the dates ripened and the fruits of the earth came to his table.

Yet for Hamed bin Salim and all his kind, their eyes gave them their only share of this favoured spot; for Hamed bin Salim and all the muallims and nakhodas were outward bound again to sea. Amongst those hundred dhows were Nejdi's boom and his brother Abdulla's newly acquired dhow, and Hamed bin Salim, having faithfully brought the *Triumph* to the river, and loaded her with dates, was to go out as muallim of Abdulla's dhow. The two dhows were ready; only Nejdi was not there. I had come down with the merchants who had provided the freights, and had come now to clear the dhows out to sea. To them nothing mattered but the prompt despatch of their laden dhows, for there was war again in Europe and, with steamship traffic dislocated, for the first time in years there was real urgency in sending off the new dates to market. If the steamers took no dates to Aden, the dhows must race to the market, and the first in would earn good profits.

So the merchants had come down to see that their dhows made all haste to sea, and I came with them to see the dhows go. Nejdi was coming that day; he had been summoned from Zubair, and told his dhow was ready. While we waited I saw an old bus come down the Fao Road. It passed us, and we saw Nejdi. The bus stopped. Out of it, climbing down slowly like stiff and travel-weary men, came Nejdi, followed by Ismael the musician, and Yusuf Shirazi.

"Peace be upon you," Nejdi said.

"And upon you peace," the merchants returned. Then almost at once, "Sail! Sail! There will be wind tonight and your dhows are laden. Sail! Sail! Hasten to Aden. May Allah send you good winds!"

Nejdi stood barefoot in the Fao Road with his gown stained from his long ride, and a fold of his headcloth about his jaw to keep some of the desert from his mouth. He was dusty and tired, and sad at leaving his Zubair bride. He plucked at his close moustache and gently murmured '*Taiyib*, *taiyib*.' "Sail! Sail!" the merchants said, for that was all they knew. "Sail! Sail! Make haste to sea!"

I thought of that hawk-eyed man standing there and of the long, hard voyage before him – out again along the nine-month, ten thousand-mile road that leads from the Basra River round half Arabia, along the Hadhramaut, and past the east coast of Africa, down to Zanzibar, and Tanganyika. Sail! Sail! That was all the merchants could say. And Nejdi gently murmured '*Taiyib*.'

Only Ismael, fat from four months of guitar-playing in the *suq* at Kuwait, seemed the better for his stay on shore, but he too was sad, and he turned tired eyes towards the river. Poor Yusuf Shirazi stood silent, a grey, gaunt wraith of a man shrivelled in his long white gown. He had just come from the pearling banks, his only reward for the summer's pearling a new debt of his own to add to the inheritance of his dead brother's. Poor Yusuf! Off again now for nine months of hardship and work which, in spite even of the grim Rufiji, would be a holiday after the *ghaus*. Yusuf smiled in farewell as the three men turned and padded barefoot down the Fao Road, bound for the sea.

THE END

APPENDIX 1

The following is a list of the various types of Arab dhows as I saw and knew them, together with the distinguishing features of each. The differences are in nearly all cases hull differences only. The Arab differentiates between types by variations in the shape of the hull, and the rigging in all is essentially the same.

Here is the list:

BAGGALA – The baggala is the traditional deep-sea dhow of the Persian Gulf and the Gulf of Oman. Its distinguishing features are the five-windowed stern, which is often elaborately carved in the manner of an ancient Portuguese caravel. Baggalas have quarter galleries, and their curved stems are surmounted by a horned figure-head. Baggalas are built now only at the port of Sur, in Oman, and are practically extinct at Kuwait. There are probably less than fifty in existence.

BOOM – The boom has taken the place of the baggala as the general sea-going Arab dhow, particularly from the Persian Gulf. Booms are double-ended, have their straight stemposts built out into a sort of planked bowsprit, and are further distinguished by their yoke steering. The port of Kuwait uses booms almost exclusively for its deep-sea trade, and the Persians also prefer this type of vessel.

BELEM – Usually small craft trading from the Basra River in the nearer waters of the Persian Gulf. They have often only one mast, and are pretty little double-ended craft with curved bows, lacking the projecting stempost of the boom and the built-up horn of the sambuk and baggala. Belems are much used in the Kuwait pearling fleet.

BETIL – Now practically extinct. I saw only one, laid up on the al-Khobar beach, not far from Bahrein. Betils were double-enders and were marked by their elaborately decorated bows and sterns, both the stempost and sternpost being carried up in a series of distinctive designs. Betils were formerly much used in Persian Gulf pearling and were favoured by the pearling admirals. Their embellishments, though picturesque, served no useful purpose, and they have now been discarded.

BEDENI – The common craft of the smaller ports of Oman and Mahra coasts. Their distinguishing features are their straight lines, their flat, sheerless hulls, their upright masts, and the curious ancient method of steering by means of an intricate system of ropes and beams. The sternpost is carried up very high, and when anchored, or in port, the rudder is usually partly unshipped and secured to either quarter. Bedeni are usually small craft and often have one mast only, though two-masters are common in the trade to East Africa.

JALBOOT – Distinguished by its bolt-upright bow and transom stern, reminiscent of the old English naval jolly-boat from which its name is probably derived. Used considerably on the Gulf pearling banks, particularly from Kuwait and Bahrein, and also by the Suri and Omani in general in their deep-sea trades. Jalboots never approach the size of the larger booms and baggalas, and are generally from 20 to 50 tons.

MASHUA – A general term for a longboat, usually propelled by oars but also rigged on occasion. Longboats may have either straight or curved stems and usually have transom sterns.

SAMBUK – Perhaps the most common of all Arab types. Indeed, it is so common that the term sambuk is often used as applying to all vessels, as the European uses the term dhow. Sambuks proper have low, curved stems and high, built-up sterns, which are square and often decorated but without quarter-galleries or the traditional stern windows. The stern is often pierced – usually in four places – to ventilate the space below the poop, but there is an entire absence of the beautiful carved embellishments which so distinguish the baggala. Sambuks are common in the Red Sea, along the southern coast of Arabia, and in Sur, where they are replacing the baggala as that ancient port's most favoured type. The lines of the sambuk are usually very beautiful. Like all dhows, it is a smart sailer. The big sambuks from Sur are decked, but the smaller Red Sea craft are usually undecked.

SHEWE – Small boats common in Kuwait. They are very like sambuks, except that they are much smaller (rarely exceeding 15 tons) and there is a slight difference in the manner in which the timbers of the stempost are carried up into a pillar above the bow. Shewes are much used as pearlers from Kuwait.

ZAROOK – A sort of double-ended sambuk, small and very fast, commonly used from the Yemenite ports of the Red Sea. They are undecked, and rarely exceed 50 tons. The ordinary zarook has much the lines of a first-class English lifeboat.

Note – The Indian kotia is very like the Arab baggala, as also is the other common Indian type known as the ghunja or ganja. Today the Arabs very rarely buy Indian vessels. Suri and Persians often buy from Kuwait; but Sur and most of the other ports usually build their own vessels.

There are minor variations in type in the smaller Red Sea and Hadhramaut ports, but these craft are very small. The deep-sea dhows are usually booms, baggalas, or sambuks, with a sprinkling of jalboots and bedeni.

APPENDIX 2

ECONOMICS OF A DEEP-SEA DHOW

The average cost of constructing a large boom at the port of Kuwait in normal times – my figures are all gathered from the years 1937 to 1939 – works out at from six to seven rupees[1] per package of Basra dates. Since the capacities and the tonnage of the ships are reckoned always in terms of stowage of these 180-lb. packages of Basra dates, it is reasonable to keep that unit for arriving at the costs. A boom of 1,000-package capacity could be built for 6,000 rupees. The *Triumph of Righteousness*, which could carry some 2,300 packages, cost, as nearly as I could discover, between 12,000 and 13,000 rupees, though the reason for this comparatively low cost was partly due to her nakhoda-owner's great care in buying her timbers and equipment, and partly because he contented himself with comparatively indifferent masts. She was worth 14,000 rupees – about £1,050. A pure sailing-ship, ketch or schooner-rigged, of the same dimensions, would cost at least twice that sum, built of softwood in Finland or Estonia, two and a half times as much built of oak and elm in Denmark or South Sweden, and probably three times as much built of good Tasmanian hardwoods in the shipyards of Tasmania, but any of these vessels would be far more seaworthy and, with the possible exception of the softwood craft, much longer-lived than the Kuwait dhow.

A nakhoda intending to build himself a new boom often brings his own timber from the Malabar coast, selecting it with an eye chiefly to its cheapness. As a result, the timbers used for planking are frequently indifferent. The ribs and knees are natural-grown timbers, imported from Persia, Iraq, and India. The masts, an expensive item, are Malabar teak trunks. If the nakhoda is in a hurry, and has not imported his own timber, he buys from the timber-yards in Kuwait. Having bought the timber, he contracts with a master-shipwright for the finished hull. The shipwright, in his turn, engages the necessary carpenters, apprentices, and coolies. Carpenters may be paid two and a half rupees a day, working from dawn to dusk, and the coolies are doing well if they receive one rupee. An exceptionally good carpenter may receive three rupees a day. Their meals must be provided for them.

In the case of the *Triumph of Righteousness*, the cost of wood imported for her from Malabar was some 6,000 rupees. A contract was made for her building with a master-carpenter for 2,800 rupees, for the bare hull and rudder. Masts

[1] Indian rupees, worth normally about one shilling and sixpence each.

were bought separately for another 1,000 rupees. A suit of sails cost 2,000 rupees. The work was done by the sailors, who were not paid for it, this counting as part of the necessary fitting-out of the vessel and the labour going into the general effort necessary in the earning of their shares. If the sailors wanted jobs in the new ship, they must sew her sails. They were given small advances, in the usual Arab style, in order to keep their homes going during the fitting-out. The rule is that when a sailor has once accepted a nakhoda's advance he is bound to that nakhoda's ship.

The sailors also rig the ship, so that this operation (which would be quite expensive in Tasmania, or Denmark, or on the New England coast) also costs nothing. The sailors sew the sails, rig the ship, pay her bottom, and float her away from the dockyard. The carpenters are responsible only for the building of the hull, and caulking. The sailors ship the rudder, the wheel, the binnacle, the capstan, and any other fittings that may be carried. Usually these, in addition to the items listed, are limited to a longboat, a gig for the nakhoda (which may be an old dug-out canoe), a firebox, some old anchors, and a couple of wooden water tanks. The nakhoda buys all these things as cheaply as he can, and also the caulking and paying stuffs, the fish-oil, the fastenings, the deadeyes, and the few blocks with which the vessel may be fitted. He also buys roping stuff, and his sailors, when they have been engaged and in the intervals when they are not sewing sails or rigging the ship or otherwise helping to fit her out, lay her cables and all the ropes for her halliards, tacks, sheets, falls, and such adjustable standing-rigging as it is proposed to provide. The cost of the rigging is reduced to the cost of this roping stuff, which, since it is cheap coconut fibre from India, is very little. The cost of the sails is reduced to the cost of the cotton-stuff necessary to put into them, which, being a produce of India or cheap mill-ends from Japan is comparatively inexpensive. Roping is of coir, stitches are indifferent, seams are round and very rough. Refinements such as a little Stockholm tar to add life to the yarn are unknown. The cost of the masts is reduced to the bare purchase price of the wood. Anchors, wheels, compasses, binnacles, are usually extremely second-hand, having, perhaps, been originally acquired from a junk yard in Bombay many years before and used in at least two other vessels. Longboats are built on the beach under a shade of mats while the boom is building. A large longboat is expensive at 8 rupees a foot. The average cost of a longboat thirty feet long is between 200 and 300 rupees, but one may be had much more cheaply. This cost includes her mast and one sail, as well as a small anchor.

The building costs of the boom *Triumph of Righteousness*, then, may roughly be set out in this manner:

	Rupees
Cost of the timber	6,000
Carpenters' contract price for labour	2,800
Sails	2,000

Masts	1,000
Longboat	200
Gear, including capstan, compass, binnacle, water tanks, firebox, four anchors, and necessary roping stuffs and blocks	340
Caulking and paying stuffs, including fish-oil for outside and inside coats	100
Gig	60
	Total: Rs. 12,500

The proper number of sails with which a new boom is provided would be seven, including three mainsails (in varying sizes, the largest of all – known as *Oud* – having nearly twice the size of the smallest, which is meant for use only in strong winds), two mizzens, and two jibs or headsails. Often, however, a boom is sent out on her first voyage with by no means this full complement.

A baggala of similar capacity would cost at least 2,000 rupees more, because of the considerably larger amount of timber she would need with her square, built-up stern, and because of the extra labour involved. The carving alone, if well done, would cost at least a thousand rupees. No baggala has been built at Kuwait for over a quarter of a century, and the baggalas now built at Sur are often without any decoration.

Fastenings are always of poor iron, beaten out by hand at a waterfront forge. The iron is not treated in any way before being driven into the ship.

Finance is always provided by a merchant – usually a merchant with an interest in date plantations on the Basra River, or some sort of interest in the date business of Iraq, who wishes to use the new vessel for carrying his dates, but does not want the bother of owning her. Therefore nakhodas are financed and permitted to be the nominal owners. No nakhoda ever has sufficient ready cash to finance the building of a ship himself: if he had, he would be a merchant.

There is no insurance: the method of financing makes the merchant's investment really the nakhoda's responsibility. If the ship is lost, the nakhoda is still held responsible for the debt. Depreciation on a well-built ship is practically non-existent for the first five years. Indeed, such a ship as the *Triumph of Righteousness*, which was built by a first-class carpenter at an exceptionally low cost, actually appreciates considerably in value during this period, when her reputation as a fast sailer and a first-class sea-boat is established. After the first five years, average depreciation on a large ship of this tonnage is about 1,000 rupees a year, from the fifth year to the tenth. Thereafter, until the fifteenth year, her value should remain fairly constant. After the fifteenth year it may show a sharp decline, particularly if the vessel has been allowed to run down.

Stores are bought as cheaply as possible. Kuwait is a free port. Roping stuffs, sail-cloth, lime and tallow for paying, cotton for caulking, anchors and other marine paraphernalia, dug-out canoes from the Malabar coast, paddles made of Lamu and Rufiji rafters with a square or circular blade lashed to one end – all of these are cheap. The ship's longboat is her tug, invariably; her crew are her stevedores and dock workers; her carpenter is her shipwright; her nakhoda is her surveyor, the designer of her sails, her pilot on all occasions. Charts and other aids to navigation are kept at a minimum, and though if she be intended for the Indian trade she must carry sidelights, these are trimmed but never lit and are a source of no expense beyond their original purchase price. There are no lifebelts or lifebuoys, or flares or rockets, or anything of that kind.

As for the earnings of an average voyage in such a ship as this, perhaps some sort of approximate balance-sheet – which I fear is all I can offer, for these details are jealously kept and guarded – may give some idea of the manner in which the ordinary trading voyage of a deep-sea Arab dhow is carried on. Consider then, the business side of the *Triumph of Righteousness* during her 1938–39 voyage. First, she carried dates from the Basra River to Mukalla for orders, and then discharged them at Berbera, in British Somaliland. From Berbera – except for a sack or two of frankincense carried over to Aden as a favour for a Kuwait merchant – she brought nothing to Aden. At Aden, using the money earned as freight for the dates, she bought salt, rice, sugar, canned milk, Indian corn, and a few other odds and ends, all these goods being intended for sale in the ports of Italian Somaliland, Kenya, and Zanzibar. In the ports of Mukalla and Shihr, in the Hadhramaut, she loaded a little tobacco and Hadhramaut honey (which is much relished by the Arabs on the African coast and is supposed to have strong invigorating qualities), some ghee, and some Arab cooking-stones. She also embarked 130 passengers, of whom the men paid eight rupees for the passage to Africa, and the women twelve. At Haifun, finding normal trade impossible because of Italian restrictions on the export of currency, the ship had to content herself with exchanging some rice and sugar for the local dried fish, and more salt. Here an old boat was sold for 100 rupees. At Mogadishu, normal trade was again impossible, but a few passengers were picked up for Mombasa and Zanzibar, and ways were found to dispose of most of the ghee and the cooking-stones, as well as various other goods. At Lamu, the ship earned nothing, but a few passengers were shipped for Mombasa and Zanzibar. At Mombasa, some ghee was sold, as well as a little of the rice, and more passengers were shipped, this time for Zanzibar only. At Zanzibar, the whole of the outward cargo was cleared, and all the remaining passengers landed. With some of the money earned in this way, the ship went on to the Rufiji Delta, and there bought and otherwise secured a full cargo of mangrove poles. Returning to Zanzibar, she sold a few of the lighter poles, took on board cloves, coconuts, vermicelli, and some odd lots of soap – all of which were intended for sale in Muscat and the Persian Gulf ports – and returned to Arabia.

The proceeds from the sale of these goods, as well as the income from passengers and the total selling-price of the mangrove poles, were all regarded as profit, and the business side of the voyage worked out something like this:

Item		*Rupees earned*
Freight on 2,300 packages dates, Basra River to Berbera, at 1½ rupees a package	Rs. 3,450	
Purchase price of salt, rice, sugar, canned milk, etc., at Aden	Rs. 3,000	
Balance		**450**
Mukalla and Shihr: embarked passengers: fares collected for 103 men at 8 rupees per head, 15 women at 12 rupees per head		1,000
Haifun: sold a boat		100
Also exchanged rice, etc., for dried fish and salt: Profit on this transaction when fish and salt sold later at Zanzibar		500
Mogadishu: fares of various passengers for Lamu; including odd earnings (sale of ghee, stones, etc.)		250
Lamu: fares for odd passengers to Mombasa and Zanzibar		100
Mombasa: fares for odd passengers to Zanzibar		100
Zanzibar: Gross profit on sale of cargo (not including result of Haifun barter)		800
Rufiji Delta: total cost of mangrove cargo (including various unofficial fees, etc.)	Rs. 1,700	
Selling price of same, Bahrein	Rs. 6,000	
Balance (profit on poles)		**4,300**
Homeward voyage: profit on soap, cloves, vermicelli, coconuts, etc. (Approx.)		1,000
Earnings, source and manner not recorded but crew entitled to share. (Approx.)		1,000
Total gross earnings		**Rs. 9,600**

From this total of 9,600 rupees, which was 3,000 rupees less than the ship had earned the previous voyage, the cost of food was deducted when the balance sheet was finally made up at Kuwait two months after the end of the voyage. All hands shared in the cost of the food, which in accordance with tradition is always deducted from the gross earnings. The cost of the food, at the rate of 3 annas a day for 30 men over a period of 270 days, was some 1,500 rupees. This, when deducted from the gross of 9,600 rupees, leaves 8,100. By the Kuwait method of arriving at the shares this sum was then halved. Of it, 4,050 rupees went to the ship, and 4,050 were divided among the crew. Out of the ship's share, the boom had to be kept up and the regular voyage expenses met. As far as I could gather, the actual sharing of the sum of 4,050 rupees was worked out practically on a basis of equal shares, except that sailors who had responsibility received extra half or quarter shares. The system of dividing the shares in the *Triumph of Righteousness* was as follows:

	Shares
Nakhoda	5
Muallim	3
Quartermasters: three, at 1½ shares each	4½
Serang	1½
Serang's Mate	1¼
Cook	1½
Storekeeper-Steward (Yusuf Shirazi)	1¼
Sailors: 18 at one share each	18
Total	**36**

Of these, the nakhoda's four, and the muallim's two, extra shares come from the ship's half, not from the crew's, so that the crew's 4,050 rupees is divided equally into 30 shares, making 135 rupees a share. Of these shares, the sailors take one each, and the others – the petty officers – take their single shares, and fractions. The carpenter is paid by the nakhoda personally, and does not share in the crew's proceeds. His income comes from the sale of the boats he has built during the voyage, whether sold or unsold.

In addition to the extra portions accruing to the petty officers, such men as the solo singer, our Abdul-latif, Ismael, the ship's musician, and the sailor whose duty it was to serve coffee to the officers, are invariably given bakhshish by the nakhoda, either from his own share as nakhoda or from the ship's half of the gross earnings. The general principle of this bakhshish is to keep everybody happy. Sailors who have worked particularly well, or who have done extra work of any kind, or who distinguish themselves by especial alacrity or unusual capabilities, also receive bakhshish. In addition to his shares, such a man as Yusuf Shirazi would receive some bakhshish to recompense him for his extra work in attending to the nakhoda.

In addition to their share of the ship's legitimate earnings, nearly everyone on board has some other source of income, whether from minor smuggling or by the lawful sale of trade goods. Each sailor may bring one chest and one chest only, and by tradition he can fill it with such goods as he thinks he can best sell. The nakhoda, too, has his private ventures, which often include half the great cabin full of Persian carpets, and a few old carved chests. Money-changing, the carriage of messages and small parcels, the importation and sale of texts from the Qurân and sacred amulets, talismans, and such things – all these bring such grist to the mill as may be ground from them. But it is improbable that the average earnings of the ordinary sailor from his ventures and the sale of his goods, both outwards and homewards, exceed fifteen or twenty rupees over the whole voyage. A nakhoda, however, may make a thousand, if conditions are good and he restrains his profligacy. A muallim may easily make several hundred rupees. The musician often does very well – so well that he can afford to pay off his pearling debts. He may make so much from his music that his pearling-nakhoda prefers a share of the income from this source rather than the doubtful proceeds of the musician's enforced work on board his vessel. Our Ismael was usually given bakhshish by leading merchants and other prominent men who were entertained at our feasts. He was provided with his instrument by the nakhoda, who also gave him suitable bakhshish at the end of the voyage. He was an important man, for his music helped to make a success of the nakhoda's feasts, and by increasing his prestige, made business the easier. The solo singer received his bakhshish because his efforts helped to make the ship happy, and to lighten the work. He would receive perhaps fifteen rupees for the voyage.

When boys are carried, they are not paid regular shares, but receive bakhshish from the nakhoda and crew.

Here is a list of food consumed during the nine-months voyage of the *Triumph*, as nearly as I was able to compute it. It should be borne in mind that the collection of statistics from Arabs is no easy matter, and only the most dogged persistence and a thorough examination of every item of expense as it was incurred (as far as this was possible) gained me any knowledge at all. Nothing ever seems to be done in a thoroughly straightforward manner. The figures are not presented as completely accurate, but may serve as a reasonably correct guide.

Our consumption, as closely as I could discover or estimate it, was, then, as follows:

	Rupees
Dates, at Rs.3 per package: 40 packages	120
Rice, at Rs.8 to 10 per bag: 53 bags	500
Flour, at Rs.6 per bag: 12 bags	72
Sugar, at Rs.12 per bag: 7 bags	84
Dried fish (only bought when fresh not available: price varying, but never high)	40
Dhall (Indian corn), at Rs.15 to 16 per bag: 6 bags	90
Salt, at Rs.2 per bag: 3 bags	6
Tea (a great deal consumed, but very poor quality)	Say 50
Coffee (a great deal consumed, but very poor quality)	Say 30
Ghee (some first-class, from Kuwait, at Rs.20 a tin: other inferior)	120
Saleet (oil)	50
Pickled stuffs (very mysterious: for use in stews, at feasts, etc.)	50
Chillis (a great favourite: always bought fresh)	10
Onions (used in stews and feasts)	50
Potatoes (very little used)	30

Cloves (for the coffee) 5
Ginger (for the coffee – an abominable habit) 5
Tomato essence (used very sparingly, for flavouring goat-entrail stews, etc., at the feasts. This was bought at Aden in very small tins: half a case for the voyage) 15
Canned milk (also used very sparingly) 20
Sesame seeds (for the unleavened bread: used rarely, as a treat) 5
Ladies' fingers and peppers (almost as popular as chillis, bought fresh in the *suqs*) 5
White radishes (at Aden) 5
Lemons 5
Other fresh vegetables 15
10 live sheep, bought at Berbera at Rs.4 per head 40
15 live sheep and goats, over rest of voyage, at Rs.5 to 6 per head 80
Total **Rs. 1,502**

I believe this is a generous estimate, for a well-run and well-found ship. Sometimes a few fresh chickens are bought for a feast, but if this is done, the nakhoda usually pays for them. In ports, merchants sometimes send on board gifts of a goat, a sheep, or a few chickens, or some fruit. Fish are caught plentifully almost throughout the voyage.

The average cost of feeding a sailor in a Kuwait ship works out at about three annas a day – something less than threepence halfpenny, or seven American cents. In making this average, the cost of feeding the first-class passengers, and the Swahili pole-cutters in the Rufiji, is included, as well as most of the cost of the ship's feasts, of which there was at least one in every port, except Salale.

I was informed, but could not verify, that sailors in the Sur ships are fed at an average cost of two annas a day, and are fortunate if their round-voyage earnings bring them sixty rupees.

APPENDIX 3

LIST OF ARABIC WORDS USED IN THE TEXT

The following is a brief list of Arabic words used in the text, together with their English equivalents:

Abba	Arab cloak.
Abu	Father.
Aghal	Headrope to hold headcloth in position.
Allah	God.
Allah karim	God is merciful.
Baggala	Ship (see list of ship types).
Bakhshish	Tip, graft.
Bebe	Girl.
Bint	Girl.
Beduin	Nomad, Arab.
Bin (also Ibn)	Son of.
Ghaus	Pearling.
Ghee	Clarified butter.
Emir	A ruling chieftain.
Hadhramaut	District of Southern Arabia.
Hadhrami	Arab from Hadhramaut.
Hajj	The pilgrimage.
Hajji	One who has made the pilgrimage.
Halwa	Sweetmeat.
Hookah	Water-pipe.
Inshallah	If God pleases.
Khubz	Unleavened bread.
Kuwaiti	Arab of Kuwait.
Muallim	Mate (of a ship).
Muezzin	Prayer announcer.
Nakhoda	Captain.
Nejd	Interior plateau of Saudi Arabia.
Nejdi	An Arab of Nejd.

Oud	Large.
Omani	Arab of Oman, in South-east Arabia.
Qurân (often Koran)	The book of the Prophet Mohammed.
Ras	Cape.
Swahili	Natives of the East Coast of Africa.
Suq (sometimes spelled Souk)	Bazaar; marketplace.
Sheikh	A ruler; also used widely as courtesy title.
Suri	Arab from the port of Sur, in Oman.
Seyyid (sometimes Sayyid)	Descendant of the Prophet.
Serang (an Indian word)	Boatswain.
Taiyib (sometimes Ta'ib)	Good.

INDEX

INDEX

Villiers' renderings of Arabic names have been retained without alteration except in clear cases of typographical error. And, *Ibn*, *bin*, *el-* and *al-* are ignored in alphabetization.

Abbreviation: *ToR* = *Triumph of Righteousness*